MEDIUM ÆVUM MONOGRAPHS

EDITORIAL COMMITTEE
K.P. Clarke, A.J. Lappin, S. Mossman,
N.F. Palmer, P. Russell, C. Saunders

EDITOR FOR THIS VOLUME
A. J. Lappin

MEDIUM ÆVUM MONOGRAPHS XXXVIII

SUMMA CONTRA HERETICOS

AD PETRUM MARTYREM ATTRIBUTA

curavit

Donald S. Prudlo

THE SOCIETY FOR THE STUDY OF MODERN LANGUAGES AND LITERATURE

OXFORD · MMXX

THE SOCIETY FOR THE STUDY OF MEDIEVAL LANGUAGES AND LITERATURE

OXFORD, 2020

© 2020 Donald S. Prudlo

ISBN:
978-0-907570-77-6 (pb)
978-0-907570-81-3 (hb)
978-0-907570-82-0 (pdf)

British Library Cataloguing in Publication Data
A catalogue record for this book is available from the British Library

fratribus ordinis
fratrum prędicatorum

TABLE OF CONTENTS

Abbreviations viii

Acknowledgements ix

Introduction xi

    Manuscript witnesses xii

    Contents and organization xiii

    Authorship xv

    Conclusion and textual notes xix

Summa contra hereticos 1

    Elenchus titulorum 3

    Liber I 17

    Liber II 256

    Liber III 289

Index biblicum 361

ABBREVIATIONS

AFP	*Archivum Fratrum Praedicatorum*
Burci	Ilarino da Milano, "Il 'Liber supra Stella' del piacentino Salvo Burci," *Aevum* 16 (1942): 272–319; 17 (1943): 9–146; 19 (1945): 218–341.
Dondaine, *Hierarchie*	Antoine Dondaine, "La hierarchie Cathare en Italie," *AFP* 19 (1949): 280–312.
Douais	Celestin Douais, *La somme des autorités à l'usage des prédicateurs méridionaux au XIIIe siècle* (Paris: Picard, 1896).
F	Florence, Biblioteca Nazionale, Conventi Soppressi, ms. A. IX. 1738.
Georgius	Georgius, "Disputatio inter catholicum et paterinum hereticum," ed. E. Martène and U. Durand, in *Thesaurus novum anecdotorum* (Paris, 1717), V. Recently edited in Carola Hoecker, *Disputatio inter catholicum et paterinum hereticum: die Auseinandersetzung der katholischen Kirche mit den italienischen Katharern im Spiegel einer kontroverstheologischen Streitschrift des 13. Jahrhunderts* (Florence: SISMEL Edizioni del Galluzzo, 2001).
Käppeli	Thomas Käppeli, "Une somme contre les hérétiques de saint Pierre Martyr (?)," *AFP* 17 (1947): 29–335.
Lambert	Malcolm Lambert, *Medieval Heresy* (Oxford: Blackwell, 1992).
Moneta	Moneta of Cremona, *Adversus catharos et valdenses libri quinque*, ed. Thomas Ricchini (Rome: 1743).
P	Perugia, Biblioteca Comunale Augusta, ms. 1065.
Sacconi	Franjo Sanjek, "Raynerius Sacconi, O. P. *Summa de catharis*," *AFP* 44 (1974): 31-60.
Summa Theologiae	Thomas Aquinas, *Opera omnia*. (Rome: Typographia Polyglotta S. C. de Propaganda Fide, 1882—).
Vacarius	Vacarius, *L'eresia di Ugo Speroni nella confutazione del Maestro Vacario: testo inedito del secolo XII con studio storico e dottrinale*, ed. Ilarino da Milano (Città del Vaticano: Biblioteca Apostolica Vaticana, 1945).
Wakefield, *Heresies*	*Heresies of the High Middle Ages*, ed. and trans. by Walter L. Wakefield and Austin P. Evans (New York: Columbia University Press, 1991).

ACKNOWLEDGEMENTS

When finishing this work my editor sent me a cartoon that depicted "manuscript study" to one side and "manuscript study under quarantine" on the other. Both sides showed the same picture of a solitary monk at a scriptorium. While there is certainly some truth to the loneliness of manuscript work, one is never really alone. In such study you not only enter dialogue with a "cloud of witnesses" from the Christian world and beyond, but also penetrate deeply into the thoughts of another in the most intentional textual way possible, from individual writer to individual reader. Such community endures into the contemporary world. I am exceptionally fortunate to know my editor and his family personally. They have been my close friends and advisors for many years. Anthony Lappin and Barbara Crostini are models for me in my textual and academic work, and without them much would have been left undone, and I personally would have been much worse off. I extend them my profound thanks. In addition Barbara painstakingly proofread the whole of the work, saving me from many errors.

This project took 13 years. I remember sitting at a farm table in Tuscany in 2007 copying down the scattered few snippets that had been previously edited thinking, "ah, only two manuscripts, this won't be so bad. " A decade and over 1000 pages of text and translation later I can only marvel at the patience of my family, particularly my wife Therese, without whom I could do nothing at all.

I am beholden to all my academic friends as well, particularly the staff at the Biblioteca Comunale Augusta in Perugia and the Biblioteca Nazionale in Florence who both hosted me through many a quiet and pleasant hour. I thank my former colleagues at Jacksonville State University, in particular the patient and longsuffering Russ Lemmons. Andrew Beer read over my translation and offered many comments on difficult passages, for which I am much in his debt. However, all the mistakes of this "magnum opus et arduum" are entirely my own. I offer gratitude to Simon Tugwell and Otfried Krafft for their particular encouragement on this project. Finally thanks are due to the fine scholars, many long since passed, of the Dominican order for their erudite and monumental studies. It is to that present order that I dedicate this edition of a work written by one of their first members.

INTRODUCTION

In the hagiography of St. Thomas Aquinas there lies an odd story. Once while supping with St. Louis IX of France and his nobles, the eminent Dominican professor seemed lost in thought. Ignoring the sparkling conversation around him, Thomas sat subdued and seemingly inert. All at once he dropped his huge fist, shaking the entire table. "That finishes the Manichees!" he belted out. The room was shocked into silence, but Louis IX — a paragon of courtesy — gave a response only a fellow saint could have come up with. "By all means get the friar some paper, so that he does not lose his thought."[1] The vignette itself should be odd to anyone familiar with the vast corpus of Thomas' work, for in that copious collection there is no specific text against the Manichees, only tangential references among diverse philosophical subjects. This is not surprising, as Thomas was the direct beneficiary of a generation of scholarship from his own order and beyond, which had already done that heavy lifting for him. His colleagues had been engaged against the "Manichees" or the medieval Cathars from the very foundation of the Order of Preachers. Indeed the Cathars had been handled so completely that Thomas really had no need to engage in controversial theology with them, and he was free to develop his thought in relative peace from the threat of Christian heterodoxy.

While Thomas may have been immune from the need to address heresy, contemporary scholarship has certainly rekindled its interest in the subject. There has been an efflorescence of study over the previous eighty years on the subject of medieval heterodoxies. Herbert Grundmann's pioneering work *Religiöse Bewegungen im Mittelalter* began the modern reappraisal, which continued with the post-war efforts of scholars such as Borst, Dondaine, and Manselli.[2] This study matured in the 1970s and 1980s with numerous assessments of the various contexts and settings of medieval heresy. In recent years it has increasingly turned to microhistory, cultural and social history, and finally to a radically nominalist approach that denies the very existence of systematic medieval heterodoxy.[3] Similarly inquisition studies and

---

[1] The story is reported by all of Thomas's early biographers (William of Tocco, Peter Calo, and Bernard Gui), although modern authors have cast doubts on it, see: René Antoine Gauthier, *Saint Thomas d'Aquin: Somme contre les gentils. Introduction* (Paris: Editions universitaires, 1993), pp. 17, 23-25. Simon Tugwell seems to agree with Gauthier, *Albert & Thomas: Selected Writings* (New York: Paulist Press, 1988), p. 341 n583. I think the story may perhaps compress several episodes, but does have a ring of truth, see my: *Thomas Aquinas: a Historical, Theological, and Environmental portrait* (New York: Paulist Press, 2020), 280. I think Tocco, not himself a theologian, is collapsing enemies and episodes into a convenient placeholder.

[2] Herbert Grundmann, *Religious Movements in the Middle Ages*, trans. Steven Rowan (Notre Dame: University of Notre Dame Press, 1995; 1st German edn, 1935). The literature on the Cathars is extensive: see for example, Antoine Dondaine, "La hierarchie Cathare en Italie." *AFP* 19 (1949): 280–312; and, idem, "Le Manuel de l'Inquisiteur," *AFP* 27 (1947): 85–194; Arno Borst, *Die Katharer* (Stuttgart: Hiersemann, 1953); Raoul Manselli, *Studi sulle eresie del secolo XII* (Rome: Istituto storico per il Medio evo, 1953); Walter L. Wakefield, *Heresy, Crusade, and Inquisition in Southern France, 1100-1250* (Berkeley: University of California Press, 1974); and the essays in *The Concept of Heresy in the Middle Ages (11th–13th c.)* (Louvain: Louvain University Press, 1976); more recently see; Malcolm Lambert, *The Cathars* (Oxford: Blackwells, 1998); and Gerhard Rottenwöhrer, *Der Katharismus*, 4 vols. in 6. (Bad Honnef: 1982).

[3] Mark Pegg has repeatedly argued that characterizations of Cathar belief are largely idealized and intellectualized. See his "On Cathars, Albigenses and Good Men," *Journal of Medieval History* 27.2 (2001): 181–95; in this he follows the outlines developed by R. I. Moore and reaffirmed in Moore's *War on Heresy: Faith and Power in Medieval Europe* (London: Profile Books, 2014). This view is too extreme; Catharism was far more than a clerical invention. It may not have been as systematic as many churchmen thought. Nonetheless, it really existed. People on both sides of the debate argued, struggled, persecuted, and died for their beliefs.

works on the religious orders which persecuted medieval heretics have also proliferated. These included editions and translations of some of the major anti-heretical works produced by the churchmen of the twelfth to fourteenth centuries. Most recently new attention has been drawn to this genre by the general history of anti-heretical texts by Lucy Sackville, in her *Heresy and Heretics in the Thirteenth Century*.[4] It is in the context of such efforts that the present study finds its relevance.

In the thirteenth century, particularly among the mendicants, and especially the Dominicans, a certain type of literature arose which strove to make systematic, sustained arguments from scripture, tradition, and reason against the various heterodoxies of the day. These generally went by titles like *Summae contra Hereticos*. Such texts attempted to lay out the belief systems of the various groups and to provide substantive critiques and arguments against them from the Catholic position. The most famous of these were Moneta of Cremona's *Adversus Catharos et Valdenses* and Rainerio Sacconi's *Summa de Catharis et Pauperibus de Lugduno*.[5] There were many other efforts both before and after them, but these two set the standard, Moneta's for scholastic rigor, and Rainerio's for his brief, intense, personal recollections from having been a member of the heretical groups himself.

In light of the foregoing, the present work under consideration has flown under the radar. This is for several reasons. The most notable is that — being written in the mid 1230s — it became quickly overshadowed by the massive, magisterial work of Moneta. The present work lacks the scholastic rigor and elaboration of that massive compilation. In addition, this *Summa* is unfinished, lacking its fourth part, which was to have been an examination of heretical practices, an aspect that would have made it of exceptional interest to historians of the lived experience of medieval heretics. Because of these reasons the manuscript exists in only two copies, each of which seem to be transcriptions of a common model, but which do not show any evidence of influence on each other.

Manuscript Witnesses

P: Perugia, Biblioteca Comunale Augusta, ms. 1065.

Parchment, probably written at the end of the thirteenth century. 150 folios. 2 columns. 309x219mm. Paginated throughout, with pagination probably made soon after the production of the manuscript.

Incipit: De uno principio solo deo creatore et factore omnium ac domino universorum. In nomine domini nostri Ihesu Christi et beatissime uirginis Marie genitricis eius et sancti Dominici confessoris dei. probatur per multas rationes naturales quod unus est solus deus principium omnium et solus omnipotens. Omne compositum habet suum compositorem … (fol. 3ra)

Explicit: … et fatuos esse ostenditis. (fol. 150va)

Wooden boards.

---

[4] Lucy Sackville, *Heresy and Heretics in the Thirteenth Century: The Textual Representations* (Woodbridge, UK: York Medieval Press, 2011).

[5] Moneta of Cremona, *Adversus catharos et valdenses libri quinque*, ed. Thomas Ricchini (Rome: 1743); Franjo Sanjek, "Raynerius Sacconi, O.P. *Summa de catharis*," *AFP* 44 (1974): 31-60. Translated in: *Heresies of the High Middle Ages*, ed. and trans. by Walter L. Wakefield and Austin P. Evans (New York: Columbia University Press, 1991).

Title and attribution: On back inside of wooden cover, from the late fourteenth century "…. hereticos pata… p…. ". On 124ᵛ, in another hand to that of main text, probably fourteenth century:

> beatus petrus martir qui a parentibus hereticis fuerat missus bononiam pro defensione perfidie. cognita veritate scripturarum. factus est pugil christi. Ipse egregius predicator. thi. I. b: fidelis sermo. . . Quidam puer valde pertinax apud urbem veterem. cum non posset converti ad fidem. ad istam rationem a fratre alberto reductus est ad fidem.

There is a late sixteenth-century title: "Contra Patarenos Petri Martiris".

Provenance: On fol. 3ʳ on the left top, "Liber conventus sancti dominici de perusio". To the right, partially cut by the binder "fr… acquisivit ordini, servato sibi uso". On the bottom of 3ʳ from the sixteenth century, A sinistris in Decimonono banco". On the back cover from the late thirteenth century is a list of some names of Dominicans of the Roman province. On 19ʳ, "In dominica palmarum satisfactum est huic scriptori de sermone hoc in totum et pro hoc opere accepit xx s."

F: **Florence, Biblioteca Nazionale, Conventi Soppressi, ms. A. IX. 1738.**

Parchment, probably end of thirteenth or beginning of fourteenth century. 121 folios in a single column. 154x105mm Blue and red rubrics throughout books 1 and 2, but missing from 3. Some marginalia, added in another hand.

Incipit: (fol. 1ʳ) De uno principio solo deo creatore et factore omnium ac domino universorum. In nomine domini nostri Ihesu christi.

Explicit: (fol. 121ᵛ) et fatuos esse ostenditis.

Followed by a brief colophon, today effaced, but reported in an eighteenth-century Dominican bibliography, where one could read the name of Fr. Ruggiero Calcagni, O. P., the inquisitor at Florence at the time of Peter of Verona's visit.

Provenance: The Servite convent of Santissima Annunziata in Florence, ms. 197: on fol. 1ʳ, "Magistri Elisei Maxxonii florentini Servitae".

Contents and Organization

The work lacks a contemporary title, but it is clear from the contents it is meant to be an antiheretical *Summa*. It is divided into three unequal parts, with the fourth book missing from both manuscripts, but referenced several times in the text. The first and longest portion of the text is concerned with a refutation of the Cathar (called here "Patarene") heresy in its various forms, and this occupies nearly three-quarters of the surviving text. The second book discusses Waldensianism and other very minor heresies, some of which are only known from this work. This makes up less than ten percent of the whole effort. The final book discusses errors which are common to all heresies, particularly regarding the veracity of the Catholic Church and the validity of secular authority. This section, which appears incomplete as well, occupies just under twenty percent of the text.

The work is well-organized, and divided and rubricated into sections and subsections. It generally follows the plan of the Apostles' Creed, a system adopted by other authors.[6] The

---

[6] This system can be found in the anonymous antiheretical *Summa* in Vat. Lat. 4255. Moneta of Cremona also uses it to organize part of his work.

author proceeds in a generally scholastic format. In the main, the author commences with a truth of the Catholic faith that the heretics deny. He then usually continues by making arguments from reason or nature, before proceeding to scriptural defenses, which are numerous and occasionally devolve into proof-texting. In some cases the heretic responds with the beliefs of the heresy in question. The *Summa* is quite useful because usually the author or the interlocutor explain that there are various sects of Cathars who hold distinct positions. However, maddeningly, he never names the particular sects in question, making it necessary to refer to other works like Moneta and Rainerio to ascertain the sects to which he is referring. At the same time the document is valuable corroboration for the existence of such divisions among the heterodox.

Most interestingly, the author uses the conceit of a debate as the form in which to write the work. The Catholic speaks, and the heretic responds. While the Catholic comes off best, and while the heretic is usually left speechless (or goes immediately to the next point), it makes for lively reading. This is not a dispassionate scholastic production. Rather the interlocutors seem to be locked in active combat, on the ground. Invectives fly back and forth, and genuine heat can be discerned in the text. At several points one can almost hear a real conversation in the background. It is for this reason (in addition to the arguments that I make in the authorship section) that I contend this text was not meant as a formal academic work, or as a disinterested preaching manual. I argue that this book was meant to be a vademecum for debating with heretics on the ground, a manual by an experienced debater who recorded and refashioned many disputations into a usable whole. The model for this was not to be formal inquisitorial interrogation of the kind which can be found in the later thirteenth century, but rather was patterned on the open public debates that we see recorded in the lives of Dominic and Peter of Verona. These exchanges were common in the period before the systematization of the medieval inquisitions. Sparks fly in this text, the Catholic interlocutor is a master of imprecation and debate. What we seem to have here is a stylized series of arguments, written down from long experience of public disputation with heretics, of a man who is at the same time intimately familiar with heretics and heretical beliefs on the ground, zealous for their conversion, and angered, sometimes beyond measure, with their obduracy and hard headedness, particularly on issues which he cares about (such as the goodness of the Old Testament and devotion to Mary). Deep theological discussion and citation of authorities lie close beside polemics and insult, making this one of the most engaging of antiheretical tracts of the Middle Ages.

The work reads in places as if it is meant to be a memory aid in active disputation. This is clearly evident in the piling up of scriptural proof-texts to illustrate a debate point. However the deployment of scripture is at the same time both traditional and innovative. While the author clearly defers to the traditional glosses and patristic interpretations, he is not afraid to use scripture in new ways to meet new challenges. He also has a predilection for the plain sense of scripture, and is often irritated at aggressive anti-material allegorizations by his heretical interlocutor: "one ought not to read otherwise than literally, especially in the New Testament, or to construe otherwise than what the passage seems to say, unless one can prove it from the text … for if it were left to the liberty of each reader to explain differently than what the literal text implies, it would reduce it to meaninglessness."

That said, while his command of external literature is extensive, he does not always demonstrate particular depth. While the author clearly understands the arguments, some of his external sources behave as proof-texts as well, or as commonplaces from the philosophical tradition, perhaps coming from *Florilegia*. Yet in spite of that the citations are impressive. He is clearly well read in St. Augustine, quoting him in excess of a dozen times. There are few other Christian authors cited however, with only St. Gregory, Cyprian, the pseudo-Clementine literature (cited twice), and Boethius and Cassiodorus, though the last two are cited as philosophical authorities. Aristotle is very much in evidence, surprisingly so given the early date (ca. 1235) and its Dominican provenance.[7] He is clearly familiar with some of Aristotle's metaphysical and scientific literature, and he cites Proclus' *Liber de causis* as being Aristotelian, as was common before William of Moerbeke and Thomas Aquinas.[8] One finds short quotations from other authors and citations to their commonplaces, including Plato, Socrates, Cicero, Sallust, Seneca, Virgil, Lucan, Hippocrates, Macrobius, and the Latin Quran, though these are little more than snippets or mere references to the source. One gets the impression of a man of wide — but not necessarily deep — education in the Arts, but who is exceptionally well-versed in controversial theology and immersed in the scriptures.

The text has never before been edited or translated in its entirety, which is the justification for the present effort. Thomas Käppeli, O. P., drew attention to the *Summa* in 1948 in an article in *Archivum Fratrum Praedicatorum*.[9] He described the manuscripts, and discussed the contents and interlocutors briefly, particularly in light of Antoine Dondaine's efforts in reconstructing the Cathar hierarchy. As such his aims were bounded by his context, for Dondaine's elaborate efforts have been challenged recently by scholars such as Gabriele Zanella and Mark Pegg (though I think that their critiques go too far).[10] This text shows that disputations over heretical ideals were not simply academic exercises, but involved personal and sometimes bitter exchanges. Käppeli edited some short sections dealing with divisions within heterodox groups, totalling less than 1% of the work. A small portion of this, dealing with the five minor heresies, was translated by Wakefield and Evans for their *Heresies of the High Middle Ages*.[11] Scholars seem content to have used these short excerpts, though Sackville has actually consulted the manuscripts herself. This is why I thought it useful to produce an edition from the two existing manuscripts and to provide a translation.

Authorship

The authorship of this work is in dispute. It has, with high probability, been assigned to St. Peter of Verona. Käppeli has established this possibility, and I shall add some further circumstantial data. It is clear that the work is of Italian provenance. The author is more focused on the cisalpine branches of Waldensianism, which he would have known first-hand, rather than those of the transalpine areas. He uses several vernacular words, particularly those taken from Lombard dialects, and is familiar with the customs and government of the northern Italian

---

[7] For the educational curriculum of the Dominicans see: M. Michèle Mulchahey, *'First the Bow Is Bent in Study ... ': Dominican Education Before 1350* (Toronto: Pontifical Institute for Medieval Studies, 2000). Also see Leonard Boyle, "Notes on the Education of the Fratres Communities in the Dominican Order in the Thirteenth Century," *Xenia medii aevi... oblata Thomae Kaeppeli*, 2 vols (Rome: 1978), I, 249-267.

[8] See the introduction to: Thomas Aquinas, *Commentary on the 'Book of Causes,'* eds. Vincent A. Guagliardo, Charles R. Hess, and Richard C. Taylor. Thomas Aquinas in Translation, 1. (Washington (D.C.): The Catholic University of America Press, 1996).

[9] Thomas Käppeli, "Une somme contre les hérétiques de saint Pierre Martyr (?)," *AFP* 17 (1947): 295-335.

[10] Gabriele Zanella, "Malessere ereticale *in valle padana* (1260–1308)," in her *Hereticalia: temi e discussioni* (Spoleto: Centro di Studi sull'Alto Medioevo, 1995).

[11] Wakefield, *Heresies*, 274-278.

city-states. In addition it is clear that the author conducted some disputations at Bergamo, and has a passing familiarity with Venice, not to mention knowledge of local heresies at Piacenza, leading one to conclude that he was active in northern Italy, particularly Lombardy. The approximate date for the work is between 1235 and 1238, since the author speaks of around sixty years having elapsed since Waldo founded his group in Lyon sometime between 1173 and 1178. However one can allow more precision if we accept the data given by the contemporary *Liber supra stella* of Salvo Burci, who fixes that date in 1175, which would result in 1235 as the general date of composition.[12] It is plain that the author is a friar of the Dominican order, since his interlocutor addresses the author as "you religious," and on several occasions attacks the Friars Preachers in particular. Our author invokes St. Dominic on the first page (further specifying the *terminus post quem* to 1234, the date of the founder's canonization). Because of the foregoing it is plain that the Dominican author was of the province of Lombardy, which was centered on the great city of Milan.

While the author does not aver directly to his having been a heretic (unlike Ranierio), he is intimately aware of the beliefs and practices of the various sects of the Cathars, so much so that he gives personal details of contact with them and claims knowledge of some of their secrets. He declares that he has made many converts from among them. He has engaged in physical as well as spiritual struggle with the heterodox: "But tell me, you hypocritical heretics, do you not oppress those wishing to convert to us, and you violently cast us out with many reproaches and blows, which has happened many times." Indeed on two occasions the author clarifies that he acted in the office of inquisitor, and has released heretics to the secular arm: "I handed them over for bodily punishments to the secular power," and "I do this, I only say the word, and they are killed. For instance I say, I release these heretics to secular judgment, and they are immediately burned." The author's knowledge seems quite immediate and his emotional investment is greater than nearly any other antiheretical writer. Here was a man committed to combat, on the ground.

How then did such a work come to be attributed to Peter of Verona? We can see that the manuscript of Perugia had a fourteenth-century title, "Contra Pata... P", which was later expanded in the sixteenth century to "Contra Patarenos Petri Martiris." Later in the manuscript fourteenth-century marginalium gives an account of Peter's being sent to Bologna for study, before his conversion. A Dominican bibliography of the seventeenth century by A. Rovetta has a list of friars who wrote *Summae* in the early 1200s in the Lombard province.[13] He lists Albert of Piacenza, Bartholomew of Trent, Bartholomew of Vicenza, Rudolph of Piacenza, Bonvisus of Piacenza, Guido da Sesto, Peter of Verona, and Roland of Cremona. With regard to the present treatise, Käppeli dismisses Roland of Cremona, who might fit the biographical details, due to his having a totally different style ("diffuse and disorganized"); further, Roland's habit of citing his own works and experiences make it almost impossible that he could have been the author. Bartholomew of Vicenza is perhaps a likely candidate, especially since he is recorded as debating the heretic Peter Gallus, who is cited three times in the present *Summa*. However, Bartholomew's style was mystical, focusing on the Dionysian tradition and the school of St. Victor: Käppeli likewise eliminates him. Neither do the others fit the bill, as their works are known or their biographies would not conduce to the authorship of this work. One other

---

12) Ilarino da Milano, "Il 'Liber supra Stella' del piacentino Salvo Burci," *Aevum* 16 (1942): 272-319; 17 (1943): 90-146; 19 (1945): 218-341.
13) Andreas Rovetta, *Bibliotheca chronologica illustrium virorum provinciae lombardicae* (Bologna: 1691), 11-12.

possibility is that the author could be Ruggiero Calcagni, the Dominican inquisitor at Florence in the mid 1240s, especially since the Florentine manuscript perhaps once contained his name in a colophon at the end of the work, which has since been effaced. This would be the most likely explanation besides Peter, were it not for a few problems. First, he is not mentioned by Rovetta as having authored a *Summa*, second he was of the Roman province, not the Lombard (being active in Florence, Orvieto, and, later, Castro in the Maremma), and third he began to be active about a decade later than Peter.

One can point to strong circumstantial evidence that the anonymous work, having been cleared of relations to other possible known authors, may indeed be a work of Peter of Verona. Besides the late evidence of the title, one can look at the circumstances of Peter's own life.[14] Unique among medieval saints, Peter was born a heretic, associated with the absolute dualists of Verona. Gradually Peter removed himself from heterodox influence, went to study at the University of Bologna, and fell under the spell of St. Dominic. Peter was one of the first generation of Dominicans, ordained in the late 1220s and well educated and successful enough to earn a later appointment as a Preacher General, a title with significant influence and freedom of movement. He was active from 1233 around the city of Milan, assisting in the insertion of anti-heretical statutes in the city laws. While his relation to the revivalistic Alleluia movement of 1233 is obscure, he is clearly at one with them in his style of preaching, which was charismatic, incendiary, and anti-heretical. In any case, he was engaged with anti-heretical preaching his whole life. In 1234 he made a visit to Venice. Between 1235 and 1238 he was resident at the convent of Como, a useful central location in Lombardy for preaching, and for access to the Alpine valleys where the Waldensian heresy found strength. During this time he had not yet been given a position of governance in the order, he was not yet Preacher General (not until the early 1240s), and he would not formally be appointed Inquisitor until 1251. In other words, Peter had more leisure at this point of his life than at any other. After the beginning of the 1240s he was constantly on the move, being given positions of responsibility, and burdened with the necessities of the active, public life.

It was for this reason, I propose, that the *Summa* was never finished (an unfortunate fact since the final part was to deal with the practices and morals of the heretics, something with which the author would have been very familiar). Peter was simply called away to do important work for the Church. The incompleteness of the work, and the fact that Moneta wrote his definitive *Summa* in the early 1240s, probably indicates why it never received any significant popularity or distribution. Peter himself may have simply left it behind. Such information corresponds with the internal evidence cited above.

But we may be able to push further. Peter was a polemicist, an active debater against the heretics, often in very bitter confrontation with them, given the details of his hagiography. In addition he was highly successful in converting them. These two facts led to the creation of a conspiracy to kill him. Such high stakes are present on every page of the document. Peter is engaged in a life or death struggle to convert the heretics from the errors that he himself left. More than that, the eternal salvation of souls was at stake, evincing the traditional *zelus animarum* of the Dominicans, and the fervent belief in the necessity of his mission. If the work is indeed a vademecum, it was a book that just such a person as Peter, as a travelling preacher and debater, would have found useful during the nascent period of the inquisition (one may

---

[14] For Peter, see my *The Martyred Inquisitor: The Life and Cult of Peter of Verona (†1252)* (Aldershot: Ashgate, 2008).

even call it the age of the "Charismatic Inquisition") as it existed before Peter's murder and the promulgation of *Ad extirpanda* in 1252. While inquisitors had some legal powers, the institution was in flux, and Peter's career seems closer to the preaching and disputing of Dominic in Provence rather than to the later, more formal, thirteenth-century inquisitions.

One can also point to the significance of the Apostles' Creed in Peter's life. It had been its simple profession that turned Peter as a boy against his family. His life was formed by the creed, particularly by the confession of the unity of God and the goodness of creation in its first few lines. As he lay mortally wounded in the forest of Barlassina, north of Milan, Peter once again turned to the creed, "Credo in Deum" as the assassin struck his skull. Perhaps it is no mistake that the author chose the organizational principle of the Apostles' Creed for his great work against heresy. We also possess one authentic writing by Peter himself, a letter to the prioress of a monastery he had founded in Milan.[15] While the text is very short, it is a precious remnant of his writing, and a testimony to his interior life. Several points may be noted. In the first place, Peter pines for the nun's life of contemplation, and complains that his whole career has been taken up by the active life, indicating the difficulty of any sustained intellectual or written work by the late 1240s when the letter was written. Further, he uses strong language, even when writing to a nun, "to the inflexible be rigid. Imitate John to the incestuous, and Phineas to the apostate fornicators, Peter to the liars, Paul to the blasphemers, and Christ to the sellers of holy things." Such stark and combative language, while at the same time being deep in scripture, comports with what is found in the *Summa*. Indeed it is reminiscent of Dante's description of Dominic, "kind to his own and ruthless to his foes."[16] Further, most of the scriptural quotations contained in the letter also figure prominently in the *Summa*, but they are not simply mere commonplaces. Where we do not find a correspondence between the two texts in their scriptural quotations is in the specific case of several which laud the contemplative life, which was not a topic in the *Summa*. One more point may be mentioned, though it is tenuous. Twice in the same sentence, and occurring very nearly together, Peter uses the word *benignus*: "Exhibere te maioribus devotam, minoribus blandam, equalibus *benignam*, rigidam superbis, *benignam* humilibus, penitentibus misericordem, obstinatis inflexibilem" (italics mine). While certainly a stylistic infelicity, it may be a telling one. Though it is a common adjective, the word is repeated dozens of times in the *Summa* as well: it is one of the author's favorite adjectives. For it to occur twice within the short space of a sentence may betray the authorship of the *Summa*. As another interesting tidbit, Bartholomew of Trent called Peter *benignus* while the saint was still alive.[17] Taken separately, these are admittedly weak indications, but when put together, they seem to add up to something more. The author of the letter to the prioress and the *Summa* surely had much in common.

The objection can be raised that the *Summa* is not mentioned by the contemporary biographers of Peter; one searches in vain through Gerard of Frachet (1256-1259), the Golden Legend (1260-1266), or the official biography by Thomas Agni of Lentino (1260-1267). This is not particularly remarkable. The *Summa* in many ways was *juvenilia*, probably forgotten when Peter became a famous preacher. It had been wholly superseded by Moneta's, and to a lesser

---

[15] The text is edited in Antoine Dondaine, O. P., "Saint Pierre Martyr," *AFP* 23 (1953): 67–150, and translated in Prudlo, *Martyred Inquisitor*, 184–185. I have corrected his edition from the original Prague manuscript.

[16] Dante, *Paradiso*, XII. 56–57.

[17] Bartholomeus Tridentinus, *Epilogus in Gesta Sanctorum*. Bologna: Biblioteca Universitaria MS 1794. fols. 80^{rb-vb} (written 1245–1251). The most recent edition of the text is Bartholomew of Trent, *Liber epilogorum in gesta sanctorum*, ed. Emore Paoli (Florence: SISMEL Edizioni del Galluzzo, 2001).

extent by Rainerio Sacconi's, works. In any case, Thomas Agni was based in Naples, far removed from Peter's geographical home (a fact testified to by his hazy chronology of Peter's preaching tours) and Jacobus of Voragine was certainly not interested in making intellectual catalogues. Nonetheless the biographers do agree on some relevant points. All attest to his excellent education, starting in Bologna, and continuing in the order. While at Bologna he would have been in the Arts courses, which would have given him a familiarity with the philosophical tradition. In fact, I would propose that the author's facility with Aristotle would have been somewhat rare among the Friars in 1235, unless he had an education in the Arts before entering the order, as Peter did. Both Thomas Agni and Jacobus testify that he was always reading and had intimate knowledge of the scriptures (on bravado display in the *Summa*). They report he had "a steadfast memory for loyally protecting the deposit of faith and a learned tongue for dispensing that same deposit. His heart was made a repository for the Sacred Law and the holy armor of the scriptures." Agni also adds the tantalizing detail that in Peter's efforts against heresy "in his words *or his studies* he gave off the sweet aroma of the truth of the faith. "

Final clues can be gleaned from the remaining manuscripts themselves. One was kept at the convent of San Domenico in Perugia. This is the exact place where Peter was canonized in March of 1253 by Pope Innocent IV. It is possible that the manuscript is descended from documents gathered by the *inquisitio in partibus* that was convened to examine his cause for the papal curia, then resident in Perugia. The second manuscript comes from the great Servite convent of Santissima Annunziata in Florence. Peter was materially involved in the regularization of the Servants of Mary in the mid 1240s. He had befriended the founders, involved them in the struggle against heresy, and helped to regularize their position in the Church. The Servites remained exceptionally devoted to Peter's cult after his canonization. Käppeli proposed that Peter had brought his vademecum with him on his journey to Florence in 1243, and left a copy with the inquisitor Ruggiero Calcagni, who donated it to the Servites in memory of Peter when he left to become the Bishop of Castro. This would also explain the appearance of the Roman Dominican's name at the end of the work.

In the absence of anything short of a contemporary attribution, this is indeed the closest we can get. The work was written around 1235 by a Lombard Dominican, who had debated and served as inquisitor against the heretics. The data fit Peter better than any known Dominican, both from internal and external evidence. If the author was not Peter of Verona then most likely it was another early thirteenth-century Lombard Dominican inquisitor of the same name. Many medieval texts receive attribution with less evidence than this. In all likelihood, we have here a work by the martyred Dominican himself.

Conclusion and Textual notes

Independent of authorship however, in the end, the work itself is a significant monument to the struggle against heresy, taken as a snapshot of the situation in the mid 1230s, by a person who is involved in the conflict on the ground. Far from being a staid, scholastic document, the text is lively and in places even bears a touch of humor. It is instructive and offers to the reader a clear example of the conditions of Dominican life in the early order, one of preaching, disputation, education, and above all, the unending struggle for souls in medieval Europe.

In editing these texts I have striven to reproduce as faithfully as possible the structure and orthography of the manuscripts themselves. The capitalization has been reproduced as well as the paragraph and section structures. Very often there are spelling mistakes which are common in medieval Latin, and these have been left in the text. I have noted where there are divergent readings, though both of the manuscripts are indeed very close to one another. I have not noted a particular priority, sometimes Florence has a better reading, sometimes Perugia. The Florence manuscript is the one that usually makes additions, most commonly a fuller transcription of a scriptural quotation. I have left the spelling of the words as close as possible to the manuscript, which means sometimes a word like "justicia" sometimes begins with *i* and sometimes with a long-*i* (represented in the edited text as "j"); similarly sometimes words will use *z* and sometimes ç. The Latin has not been normalized in any way. I have left the punctuation as I have found it in the text; when there is a divergence I have usually found that *F* makes more sense. I have noted where words have been corrected and expunged, but I have generally not noted reduplications or eyeskips, which were quite common especially in the Perugia text. I have thought it expedient, since there are only two manuscripts, to provide an apparatus that allows reference to the original pagination for each. On a few occasions I have supplied or replaced a word in the manuscripts for one that makes more sense. In that case I leave the original word in the Latin, with a note in the apparatus, and a correction in the translation. Though by-and-large these manuscripts were very good and quite clear, there are a few instances where unfortunately both were effaced to such an extent that I had to make a guess, although there are only a handful of such *cruces*.

In terms of the translation, I tried to make it literal, with a smoothing of the sometimes choppy scholastic prose. On occasion I have rendered passive or subjunctive sentences more vividly. The advantage of a side-by-side translation is that the reader is able to see the Latin and supply an alternate translation if they wish. In a smattering of passages the sense is not clear, and these are marked in the notes. Sometimes the copyists themselves seem not to have understood the sense. I have tried to supply an explanatory apparatus that points out obscure concepts or points to some relevant works. As a means of achieving greater clarity in the translation, I have employed reverential capitalization, since it makes it much easier to get the gist when multiple pronouns are used. In terms of biblical quotations, I have generally used the Douay-Rheims version as it is translated directly from the Vulgate, but if there is a discrepancy, I translate directly from the manuscript. I note where a reading differs from the Vulgate in the apparatus. In the manuscripts the citations end with "etcet." but I have not translated these. In the transation I put the references inline, with full citation first, and then only chapter and verse later. In Latin I have relegated the citations to the apparatus for the sake of legibility. Usually the speakers are labelled in the manuscripts, but when they are not I bracket them, i.e. [Cath:]. On a few occasions the speaker is not clear, and I have made a speculation. One element I have sought is to convey the vividness and emotional power of the *Summa*, which was far from a dry scholastic treatise. If I can recapture what must have been a tense, exciting, and dangerous time during a medieval clash of ideas and worldviews, I will not have totally failed.

SUMMA CONTRA HERETICOS

AD PETRUM MARTYREM ATTRIBUTA

THE SUMMA AGAINST THE HERETICS

ATTRIBUTED TO PETER MARTYR

ELENCHUS TITULORUM LIST OF HEADINGS

LIBER I BOOK I

I

I.1	De uno principio solo deo creatore et factore omnium ac domino uniuersorum	17	On the one principle, the one God, creator and maker of all things and Lord of the whole world
I.2	De omnipotentia dei per rationes naturales	19	On the omnipotence of God from natural proofs
I.3	Quod unus est solus deus et omnipotens	21	That God alone is one and omnipotent
I.4	Quod unius deus creauit et fecit omnia	21	That one God created and made all things
I.5	De diabolo spiritualiter quod deus creauit eum	22	On the devil, that God created him spiritually
I.6	Quod simpliciter dicitur deus	22	That He is simply called God
I.7	Quod dicitur solus deus	22	That He alone is called God
I.8	Quod ponitur omnium creator et factor deus	23	That God is proposed to be the creator and maker of all things.
I.9	Quod terra et secula inuisibilia sunt creata et diffinita a deo	26	That the earth and the invisible world are created and ordained by God
I.10	Quod solis ortus et plurima cibi corporales et omnis habundantia terra temporalium sunt a deo	26	That the sunrise and many corporeal foods and all the plenty of the temporal world are from God
I.11	Quod quadrupedia et serpentes sunt a deo	27	That quadrupeds and serpents are from God
I.12	Quod infernus est a deo	27	That hell is from God
I.13	Quod omnes pene temporales et eterne et potestas puniendi sunt a deo et peccata fiunt non nisi deo permittente	27	That all temporal and eternal punishments, and the power of punishing are from God, and that sins cannot exist unless they be permitted by God
I.14	Spiritualiter de potestate puniendi quod a deo sit et de permissione peccandi	29	That it speaks spiritually regarding the power of punishing, which is from God, and of the permission for sinning
I.15	Quod dampnati homines sunt a deo	29	That damned men are from God
I.16	Quod diabolus est a deo	30	That the devil is from God
I.17	Quod corpora humana sunt a deo	30	That human bodies are from God.
I.18	Quod angeli et mundus et anima non sunt eterna nisi deus tantum	32	That angels, the world, and souls are not eternal, but only God.
I.19	De omnipotentia dei	32	On the omnipotence of God

II

II.1	Quod diabolus est deus et creator et factor omnium uisibilium et quorumdam spirituum uel secundum quosdam quod est tantum factor uel secundum alios quod omnia sunt eterna in sui natura et quod ipse est omnipotens in regno suo	33	That the devil is the creator and fashioner of all visible things, and of certain spirits, or, according to some, that he is only the fashioner, or, according to others, that all things are eternal by their nature and that he is all powerful in his kingdom
II.2	Probatio per rationes naturales	33	Proof by natural arguments
II.3	Probatio per scripturas	36	Proof from the scriptures

---

[1] A list of contents is found in an early-modern hand at the beginnning of *P*; here, for the reader's convenience, I have provided a list of the rubrics with their page-references, drawn directly from the edited text.

ELENCHVS TITVLORVM SVMMAE

II.4	Quod diabolus est eternus	37	That the devil is eternal
II.5	De diuinitate diaboli	39	On the divinity of the devil
II.6	De creatione et factione diaboli	41	On the creation and fashioning of the devil
II.7	Duobus modis dicitur ueteris homo	49	On the two ways that a man is called "old"
II.8	Quinque modus dicitur mundus	51	Five ways in which the world is spoken of
II.9	Pro illis qui dicunt quod omnia sunt eterna in sui materia	52	For those who say that everything is eternal in its material
II.10	De dominio et omnipotentia diaboli regni sui	52	On the lordship and almighty power of the devil in his kingdom
II.11	Duplex principatus id est diaboli	53	The double principate, that is, of the devil
II.12	Tria sunt in mundo	53	Three things are in the world
II.13	Triplex principium	54	The threefold principle

III

III.1	De summa et indiuidua trinitate diuinarum personarum. patris et filii et spiritus sancti	55	On the highest and unique Trinity of divine persons, of the Father and of the Son and of the Holy Spirit
III.2	Probatio de trinitate in semetipsa per rationes naturales	56	Proof of the Trinity in itself through natural arguments
III.3	De Spiritu sancto	57	On the Holy Spirit
III.4	Probatio de trinitate per rationes naturales ex creaturis	58	Proof of the Trinity by natural arguments from creatures
III.5	Probatio de trinitate per scripturas ueteris testamenti	59	Proof of the Trinity from the scriptures of the Old Testament
III.6	Probatio de trinitate per scripturas noui testamenti	60	Proof of the Trinity from the scriptures of the New Testament
III.7	Auctoritates phylosophorum de trinitate	61	Philosophical authorities on the Trinity
III.8	Quod non est in deo nisi una persona	61	That there is not in God anything save one person
III.9	Probatio per scripturas contra trinitatem	63	Proofs against the Trinity from the scriptures

IV

IV.1	De diuinitate filii dei	64	On the Divinity of the Son of God
IV.2	Probatio quod christus duas habuit naturas per auctoritates ueteris testamentum	64	Proof that Christ had two natures by the authorities of the Old Testament
IV.3	probatio de duabus naturis christi per auctoritates novi testamenti	65	Proof of the two natures of Christ from the authorities of the New Testament
IV.4	Auctoritates noui testamenti de una natura christi scilicet de diuina	67	The authorities of the New Testament of the one nature of Christ, namely, the Divine nature
IV.5	Quod christus est idem substantia cum deo patre et illi equalis in persona	70	That Christ is identical in substance with God the Father and is equal to Him in personhood
IV.6	Quod christus non est deus nec equalis patri in persona nec idem in substantia	71	That Christ is not God, neither is He equal to the Father in personhood, nor identical in substance
IV.7	Quod Christus est angelus	75	That Christ is an angel

V

V.1	Quod spiritus sanctus est deus et quod ipse est tamen unus essentialiter	76	That the Holy Spirit is God and that He is one only essentially
V.2	Probatio per naturales rationes quod spiritus sanctus est deus et equalis patri et filio et in substantia idem	77	Proofs from natural arguments that the Holy Spirit is God, and equal to the Father and the Son, and identical in substance.
V.3	Probatio per naturales rationes quod spiritus sanctus est unus tantum essentialiter	78	Proof from natural arguments that the Holy Spirit is one only by essence
V.4	Probatio per diuinam scripturam quod spiritus sanctus est deus	78	Proof from the Holy Scriptures that the Holy Spirit is God
V.5	Probatio per scripturas quod unus est tantum spiritus sanctus	80	Proof from the scriptures that there is only one Holy Spirit
V.6	Quod spiritus sanctus non est deus et quod sunt plures spiritus sancti	80	That the Holy Spirit is not God and that there are many Holy Spirits
V.7	Ratio naturalis quod spiritus sanctus non sit deus	80	Natural arguments that the Holy Spirit is not God
V.8	Probatio per scripturas quod spiritus sanctus non est deus	81	Proof from the scriptures that the Holy Spirit is not God.
V.9	Quod tot sunt spiritus sancti quot sunt boni homines	81	That there are as many Holy Spirits as there are good men
V.10	Quod tres sunt spiritus sancti	81	That there are three Holy Spirits
V.11	Quod septem sunt spiritus sancti	82	That there are seven Holy Spirits

VI

VI.1	Quod deus ueteris testamentis fuit bonus deus	82	That the God of the Old Testament was the good God.
VI.2	Quod deus ueteris testamentis non fuit bonus deus	86	That the God of the Old Testament was not the good God

VII

VII.1	De ueteri testamenti quod fuit bonum	95	That the Old Testament was good.
VII.2	Decem in quibus concordat utrumque testamentum	97	Ten things in which both testaments agree
VII.3	Duodecim rationes quibus commendatur uetus testamentum in nouo. de bonitate prima	98	Twelve arguments in which the Old Testament is commended by the New. First of goodness
VII.4	Quod patres et patriarche et multi alii qui fuerunt ante legem moysi sunt salui	102	That the Fathers and Patriarchs and many others who lived before the Law of Moses are saved
VII.5	De enoch	102	On Enoch
VII.6	De noe	102	On Noah
VII.7	De Melchisedech	103	On Melchizedek
VII.8	De loth	103	On Lot
VII.9	De Iob	103	On Job
VII.10	De abraham ysaac et iacob	103	On Abraham, Isaac, and Jacob
VII.11	De sarra et aliis sanctis mulieribus que fuerunt in ueteri testamento	104	On Sarah and other holy women who were in the Old Testament

VII.12	De moyse et aliis sanctis qui fuerunt sub lege	104	On Moses and other holy people who lived under the law
VII.13	De aaron	105	On Aaron
VII.14	De iosue et sociis suis	105	On Joshua and his associates
VII.15	De Gedeon barach et samson iepte et de consimilibus	106	On Gideon, Barak, and Samson, and Jephthah, and of others like them
VII.16	De samuele	106	On Samuel
VII.17	De dauid	106	On David
VII.18	De helia et heliseo	107	On Elijah and Elisha
VII.19	De prophetis in genere	107	On the Prophets in general
VII.20	Quod omnes fuerunt salui qui seruauerunt uetus testamentum	108	That all were saved who observed the Old Testament
VII.21	Quod uetus testmentum non fuit bonum	109	That the Old Testament was not good
VII.22	De malitia ueteris testamenti	110	On the wickedness of the Old Testament
VII.23	Quarta ratio	117	The fourth reason
VII.24	Quod qui fuerit sub ueteri testamento non sunt salui	117	That those who were under the Old Testament were not saved
VII.25	De Abel. quod patres et prophete ueteris testamenti non sunt salui	119	On Abel, that the fathers and prophets of the Old Testament were not saved
VII.26	De enoc	119	On Enoch
VII.27	De noe	119	On Noah
VII.28	De melchisedech	119	On Melchizedek
VII.29	De loth	119	On Lot
VII.30	De Job	119	On Job
VII.31	De abraham et moyses et samuel et dauid	120	On Abraham and Moses and Samuel and David
VII.32	De iacob	120	On Jacob
VII.33	De heliseo	120	On Elisha

VIII

VIII.1	De beata uirgine Maria quod fuerit mulier	120	That the Blessed Virgin Mary was woman
VIII.2	Quod beata uirgo maria non fuit mulier	122	That the Blessed Virgin Mary was not a woman

IX

IX.1	De beato Iohanne baptista quod fuerit bonus et saluus et quod fuerit angelus bonus annunciator eius	123	On Blessed John the Baptist, that he was good and saved, and that the angel that announced his birth was good
IX.2	Quod beatus iohannes fuit bonus et sanctus	124	That Blessed John was good and holy
IX.3	Quod beatus iohannes fuerit homo	127	That blessed John was a man
IX.4	Quod angelus annuntiatio eius fuerit bonus	127	That the angel of his annunciation was good
IX.5	Quod iohannes baptista non sit saluus et quod fuerit angelus uel spiritus helie et quod angelus annuntiaior eius non fuit bonus	127	That John the Baptist was not saved and that he was an angel or the spirit of Elijah and that the angel of his annunciation was not good
IX.6	Quod iohannes fuerit angelus	130	That John was an angel
IX.7	Quod iohannes fuit helias	130	That John was Elijah

X

X.1	De Christi humanitate	130	On the humanity of Christ
X.2	Probatio per rationes naturales de humanitate christi. et quod christus fuit homo	131	Proof by natural arguments of the humanity of Christ, and that Christ was a man
X.3	Probatio per scripturas de humanitate christi	132	Proof from the Scriptures regarding the humanity of Christ
X.4	de anima christi	133	On the Soul of Christ
X.5	Quod christus habuit carnem humanam passibilem de massa protoplausti deriuatam ade	134	That Christ had passible human flesh taken from the stock of Adam, the first man.
X.6	Quod christus habuit carnem suam de carne beate marie uirginis	136	That Christ took his flesh from the flesh of the Blessed Virgin Mary
X.7	De esurie et siti ihesu Christi	137	On the hunger and thirst of Jesus Christ
X.8	De esu et potu christi	137	On the eating and drinking of Christ
X.9	Quod christus comedit carnes	137	That Christ ate meat
X.10	De comestionem et potu christi post resurrectionem eius	138	On Christ's eating and drinking after His resurrection
X.11	De vestibus et calciamentis christi	139	On the shoes and garments of Christ
X.12	Quod christus usus est domibus	139	That Christ made use of houses
X.13	De laxione et labore christi	139	On the leisure and labor of Christ
X.14	De dormitione et requie christi	139	On the sleep and rest of Christ
X.15	De passione et crucifixione et morte et sepultura et resurrectione ihesu christi	139	On the passion and crucifixion and death and burial and resurrection of Jesus Christ
X.16	Quod christus semel tantum passus est	141	That Christ suffered only once
X.17	De descensu christi ad inferos	142	On the descent of Christ into hell
X.18	De ascensu christi in celum	142	On the ascent of Christ into heaven
X.19	De aduentu christi in fine mundi ad iudicium	142	On the coming of Christ at the end of the world for judgment
X.20	Quod christus non fuit uerus homo	143	That Christ was not truly a man
X.21	Quod christus non habuit carnem uel saltem nostre conditionis	144	That Christ did not have flesh or at least [a body] subject to our conditions
X.22	Quod christus non comedit temporaliter	148	That Christ did not eat in time
X.23	Quod christus non fuit uere passus	148	That Christ did not truly suffer
X.24	Quod christus pluries quam singulo passus est	149	That Christ suffered many times, rather than once

XI

XI.1	Quod lucifer de aliquo loco non ascendit in celum. et quod angeli qui ceciderunt sunt eternaliter dampnati	150	aThat Lucifer did not ascend from someplace to heaven and that the angels who fell are eternally damned
XI.2	Probatio per rationem quod diabolus non adscendit in celum de terrestri habitatione ad decipiendum angelos dei	152	Proof from reason that the devil did not ascend into heaven from a terrestrial habitation for the purpose of deceiving the angels of God
XI.3	Probatio per rationes de dampnatione eterna cadentium angelorum	152	Proof from reason about the eternal damnation of the fallen angels
XI.4	Probatio per scripturam quod lucifer non ascendit in celum neque aliqui angeli eius	153	Proof by the scriptures that Lucifer did not ascend into heaven, neither did any of the other angels

XI.5	Probatio per scripturam quod eternaliter sunt dampnati angeli de celo cadentes	154	Proof from scripture that the angels who have fallen from heaven are eternally damned
XI.6	Quod lucifer de terrestri habitatione ascendit in celum cum angelis suis et quod angeli qui ceciderunt de celo saluabuntur uel per incorporationem de ascensu luciferi	158	That Lucifer ascended from an earthly habitation into heaven with his angels and that the angels who fell from heaven shall be saved or through assuming a body by the ascent of Lucifer
XI.7	De prelatione luciferi super angelos	158	On the rule of Lucifer over the angels
XI.8	De prelio quod dicunt in celo fuisse	160	On the battle that they say was in heaven
XI.9	Probatio per scripturam quod angeli qui ceciderunt debeant saluari per corpora	161	Proof from scripture that the angels who fell ought to be saved through bodies

XII

XII.1	Quod spiritus humani cotidie de nouo creantur neque ueniunt ex traduce neque transeunt de corpore in corpus et quod sancti homines finita uita corporis ascendunt in celum cotidie	165	That the spirits of humans are daily created from nothing, neither do they come from traducianism, neither do they cross from body to body, and that holy people at the end of bodily life ascend into heaven daily
XII.2	Quod spiritus humani cotidie de nouo creantur probatur rationibus similibus	166	That human spirits are daily created from nothing is proven by similar reasons
XII.3	Quod spiritus non ueniuntur ex traduce probatur naturaliter	167	That spirits do not come from traducianism is proven by natural reason
XII.4	Quod anime non transeant de corpore in corpus probatio rationabiliter	167	That souls do not cross over from one body to another, by rational arguments
XII.5	Quod sanctorum anime cotidie ascendunt in celum	168	That the souls of holy people daily ascend into heaven
XII.6	probatio quod deus creat cotidie nouos spiritus	168	Proof that God daily creates new spirits
XII.7	Probatio per scripturas quod spiritus scilicet non ueniunt ex traduce sed ex nichilo creatur a deo	169	Proof from the scriptures that spirits, namely, do not come from traducianism but are created 'ex nihilo' by God
XII.8	Probatio per scripturam quod spiritus non transeunt de corpore in corpus	170	Proof from scripture that spirits do not cross from body to body
XII.9	Probatio per scripturam quod sanctorum anime cotidie ascendunt in celum	171	Proof from scripture that the souls of holy people daily ascend into heaven
XII.10	Quod spiritus humani fuerunt simul creati ab initio mundi. uel quod ueniant ex traduce secundum alios et quod uadunt per diuersa corpora et quod anime sanctorum non ascendunt in celum usque ad finem mundi	172	That human spirits were all created together at the beginning of the world, or that they came by means of traducianism, according to others, and that they go through different bodies and that the souls of the saints do not ascend into heaven until the end of the world
XII.11	quod omnis spiritus fuerint simul creati ab initio mundi	172	That all spirits were created together at the beginning of the world.
XII.12	Quod spiritus ex spiritu fit sicut caro de carne	174	That spirits are made from spirit, as flesh from flesh
XII.13	Quod spiritus transeunt de corpore in corpus	174	That the spirits cross from body to body
XII.14	Quod nulle anime sanctorum ascendunt modo in celum	176	That no souls of holy people ascend in any way into heaven

XIII

XIII.1	De resurrectione corporum mortuorum	176	On the resurrection of dead bodies
XIII.2	Probatio per rationes naturales de resurrectione corporum	177	Proofs from natural reasons for the resurrection of the body
XIII.3	Probatio de resurrectione corporum per uetus testamentum	178	Proof of the resurrection of bodies from the Old Testament
XIII.4	Probatio de resurrectione corporum per nouum testamentum	178	Proof of the resurrection of bodies from the New Testament
XIII.5	Quod corpora ista uisibilia non debeant resurgere probatio per rationes contra resurrectionem	181	That these visible bodies ought not to be resurrected, proven by arguments against the resurrection
XIII.6	Probatio per scripturas contra resurrectionem	182	Proof from the scriptures against resurrection

XIV

XIV.1	Quod erit iudicium uniuersale et quod mundus destruetur secundum formam exteriorem et non secundum essentiam suam et quod infernus est et erit alibi quam in mundo isto	184	In what the universal judgment shall consist, and that the world shall be destroyed according to its external form and not according to its essence and that hell exists and shall exist in that other world
XIV.2	De iudicio uniuersali	185	On the universal judgment
XIV.3	De singulari iudicio	186	On the particular judgment
XIV.4	Quod infernus est et alibi quam in mundo isto	186	That hell exists and is in another place than this world
XIV.5	Quod mundus destruetur secundam formam exteriorem et non secundum materiam elementorum	187	That the world shall be destroyed according to its external form but not according to its material constitution
XIV.6	Quod non erit iudicium uniuersale nec etiam singulare secundum aliquos et quod mundus destruetur totaliter uel quod conburetur in sempiternum et erit ibi infernus et non alibi	187	That there will not be either a universal or particular judgment according to some and that the world will be totally destroyed or that it shall burn forever and that hell will be here and not elsewhere
XIV.7	Contra iudicium uniuersale	187	Against the universal judgment
XIV.8	Contra utrumque iudicium generale et singulare	188	Against both the universal and particular judgment
XIV.9	Quod Mundus semper comburetur et infernus ibi erit et non alibi	188	That the world shall always be burned and that Hell is here and not elsewhere
XIV.10	Quod mundus totaliter destruetur	189	That the world shall be utterly destroyed

XV

XV.1	Quod peccata et supplicia et merita non sunt equalia	189	That sins and sufferings and merits are not equal
XV.2	Quod peccata et supplicia non sunt equalia	189	That sins and sufferings are not equal
XV.3	Quod merita et premia non sunt equalia	190	That merits and rewards are not equal
XV.4	Quod peccata et supplicia et premia et merita sunt equalia	191	That sins and sufferings and rewards and merits are equal

XVI

XVI.1	De septem ecclesie sacramentis. quomodo et qualiter spiritus sanctus datur	193	On the Seven Sacraments of the Church, how and in what manner the Holy Spirit is given
XVI.2	Probatio per rationes naturales quod spiritus sanctus non datur substantialiter	193	Proof that the Holy Spirit is not given substantially from natural arguments
XVI.3	Probatio per rationes naturales quod sanctus spiritus non datur ab homine sed a deo solo	194	Proof from natural reasons that the Holy Spirit is not given by man but by God alone
XVI.4	Probatio per scripturas quod spiritus sanctus non datur substantialiter sed per carismata	195	Proof from the scriptures that the Holy Spirit is not given substantially, but by grace
XVI.5	Probatio per scripturas quod spiritus sanctus datur a solo deo	195	Proof from the scriptures that the Holy Spirit is given by God alone
XVI.6	Quod gratiam spiritus sancti sepius potest dari et perdi et recuperari	197	That the grace of the Holy Spirit can be given and lost and recovered several times
XVI.7	Quod spiritus sanctus datur substantialiter et ab homine et quod semel datus non potest recuperari uel secundum quosdam uel secundum alios semel datus non potest amplius perdi	198	That the Holy Spirit is given substantially and by man and that, once given, cannot be recovered or — according to those or others — once given is not able any more to be lost
XVI.8	Quod spiritus sanctus datur ab homine	199	That the Holy Spirit is given by man
XVI.9	Quod spiritus sanctus semel datus et perditus non potest amplius recuperari	200	That the Holy Spirit, once given and lost, is not ever able to be recovered again
XVI.10	Quod spiritus sanctus semel datus non potest perdi amplius	201	That the Holy Spirit, once given, cannot be lost any more

XVII

XVII.1	De baptismo aque. quod sine eo non est salus et quod in eo debite celebrato datur spiritus sanctus et quod paruuli saluantur per eum	202	On the baptism of water, that without it there is no salvation and that in its appropriate celebration the Holy Spirit is given, and that little children are saved through it
XVII.2	Quod sine baptismo aque non est salus et quod in eo debite celebrato datur spiritus sanctus	202	That without the baptism of water there is no salvation and that in its appropriate celebration the Holy Spirit is given
XVII.3	Quod pueri paruuli baptizati saluantur	205	That baptized little children are saved
XVII.4	Quod baptismus aque nullius est utilitatis nec quo ad remissionem peccatorum nec quo ad acceptionem spiritus sancti et maxime baptismus paruulorum	206	That the baptism of water is of no use, neither for the remission of sins nor for the reception of the Holy Spirit and especially the baptism of children
XVII.5	Quod pueri paruuli non saluantur per baptismum neque per aliquid	209	That little children are not saved by baptism nor in any other way

XVIII

XVIII.1	De manus impositione	210	On the imposition of hands (Confirmation)
XVIII.2	Quod sine manus impositione potest esse saluus	211	That one can be saved without the imposition of hands

XVIII.3	Quod spiritus sanctus non datur in manus impositione ad remissionem peccatorum sed tantum ad confirmationem et robur recepte gratie baptismalis	213	That the Holy Spirit is not given in the imposition of hands for the remission of sins but only for the confirmation and strengthening of the grace received in baptism
XVIII.4	Quod manus impositio que dicitur confirmatio non potest fieri nisi per episcopos	213	That the imposition of hands which is called Confirmation cannot be conferred but by bishops
XVIII.5	Quod sine manus impositione non potest esse saluus et quod per solam manus impositionem datur spiritus sanctus et quod ipsa potest fieri etiam per non episcopos	214	That without laying of hands one cannot be saved and that only through the laying of hands is the Holy Spirit granted and that it can be done also by those who are not bishops
XVIII.6	Quod manus impositioni tota potest fieri per non episcopos	215	That the imposition of hands can be entirely accomplished by those who are not bishops

XIX

XIX.1	De sacramento penitentie	216	On the Sacrament of Penance
XIX.2	Quod oportet hominem contritionem habere et penitentiam facere de omnibus peccatis que fecit in hac uita et non de aliquibus celestibus que numquam fuerunt	217	That it is fitting that a man should have contrition and do penance for all of the sins he committed in this life, and not about those what never happened in another heavenly place
XIX.3	Quod homo non habet nisi unum spiritum qui et anima dicitur	219	That man has but one spirit, which is called the soul
XIX.4	Quod non potest aliquis saluari nisi resistuat male ablata si potest	219	That one cannot be saved unless one makes restitution concerning illgotten goods, if one can
XIX.5	Quod usuria est mortale peccatum	221	That usury is a mortal sin
XIX.6	Quod non est penitentia habenda uel facienda nisi de peccatis in celo commissis et quod homo habet duos spiritus quorum unus spiritus uocatur et altera anima et quod non tenetur aliquis aliena et quod usura non est mortale peccatum	222	That one ought not to have penitence or to do penance save for sins committed in heaven and that man has two spirits, of which one is called spirit and the other soul, and that one ought not to retain any ill-gotten goods and that usury is not a mortal sin
XIX.7	Quod non est habenda penitentia uel facienda nisi de peccatis in celo commissis	222	That one ought not to have penitence or to do penance save for sins committed in heaven
XIX.8	Quod homo habet duos spiritus. quorum unus spiritus uocatur et altera anima	222	That man has two spirits, of which one is called the spirit and the other the soul
XIX.9	Quod non tenetur quis restituere aliena	223	That one is not obliged to return other people's stolen goods
XIX.10	Quod usura non est mortale peccatum	224	That usury is not a mortal sin

XX

XX.1	De sacris ordinibus	226	On Holy Orders
XX.2	Quod in ecclesia dei non sunt nisi duo sacri ordines scilicet presbiteratus et diaconatus	226	That in the Church of God there are only two sacred orders, namely, priesthood and diaconate

XXI

XXI.1	Quod in sacramento eucharistie debite celebrato panis in corpus christi et uinum in sanguine eius transubstantiatur probatio per rationes naturales	226	Proof by natural reason that in the appropriate celebration of the Eucharist the bread is changed into the body of Christ and the wine into His blood
XXI.2	Probatio per scripturas	227	Proof from the scriptures
XXI.3	Quod panis non transubstantiatur in corpus christi. neque uinum in sanguinem eius	230	That the bread is not transubstantiated into the body of Christ, nor is the wine changed into His blood
XXI.4	Probatio per rationes naturales	230	Proof from natural reasons
XXI.5	Probatio per scripturas	231	Proof from the scriptures

XXII

XXII.1	De sacramento matrimonii	234	On the sacrament of marriage
XXII.2	Probatio per rationales naturales	234	Proof from natural reasons
XXII.3	De matrimonio	234	On Marriage
XXII.4	De matrimonio	234	On Marriage
XXII.5	Probatio quod matrimonium est bonum et sanctum	237	Proof that marriage is good and holy.
XXII.6	Probatio quod matrimonium est bonum	238	Proof that marriage is good
XXII.7	De illo qui habet uxorem infidelem	238	On that one who has an unfaithful wife
XXII.8	De matrimonio	239	On Marriage
XXII.9	De matrimonio	239	On Marriage
XXII.10	De matrimonio	239	On Marriage
XXII.11	De matrimonio	239	On Marriage
XXII.12	De matrimonio	240	On Marriage
XXII.13	Probatio quod matrimonium est bonum	240	Proof that marriage is good
XXII.14	De Matrimonio	241	On Marriage
XXII.15	Quod matrimonium carnale sit dampnatum secundum patarenos	242	That marriage according to the flesh is condemned according to the Patarenes
XXII.16	Probatio per rationes naturales	242	Proof from natural reasons

XXIII

XXIII.1	De sacramento extreme unctionis	248	On the sacrament of Extreme Unction
XXIII.2	Contra unctionem extremam	249	Against Extreme Unction

XXIV

XXIV.1	De quorumdam ciborum esu. scilicet carnium. ouorum et casei et huiusmodi in quibus patareni errant	249	On the eating of certain foods, namely of meat, eggs, cheese, and the like, in which the Patarenes err
XXIV.2	Quod sit peccatum predicta comedere. patarenus tribus rationibus uult probare	252	That it be a sin to eat the aforesaid things, the Patarene wishes to prove by three reasons

LIBER II / BOOK II

XXV

XXV.1	De quinque aliarum heresim propriis naufragiis scilicet predestinationum. circumscisorum. speronistarum. pauperum leonistarum ac rebapticatorum	256	Regarding five other heresies who make their own shipwrecks, namely, of the Predestinarians, of the Circumcisers, of the Speronists, of the Poor of Lyons, and of the Rebaptizers
XXV.2	De libero arbitrio	257	On Free Will
XXV.3	Quod omnes homines saluari uel dampnati possunt secundum sua opera	258	That all men are able to be saved or damned according to their works
XXV.4	Contra errorem illorum qui dicunt omnia inferiora regi secundum motum et cursum corporum superiorum	260	Against the error of those who say that inferior bodies are ruled by the motion and course of superior ones
XXV.5	De anima	260	On the soul
XXV.6	Item de eodem.	260	Further on the same subject
XXV.7	Dicta patarenorum	261	The sayings of the Patarenes
XXV.8	Error patarenorum	261	Error of the Patarenes
XXV.9	De illis qui oppinantur omnia tam mala quam bona preordinata esse a deo	262	On those who imagine that all things, both good and evil, are preordained by God
XXV.10	Contra illos qui hoc nomen predestinatorum occuparunt	263	Against those who claim this name of Predestinarian
XXV.11	De Anima	263	On the soul
XXV.12	Quod anima est immortale	263	That the soul is immortal
XXV.13	De immortalitate	264	On Immortality
XXV.14	De illis qui non possunt inducere aliquam rationem seu auctoritate alicuius philosophi dicentis quod mundus sit eternus	264	On those who are not able to adduce any argument or give the authority of any philosopher saying that the world is eternal
XXV.15	Quod secundum patarenum omnia sunt ordinata a deo et a diabolo	264	That according to the Patarenes everything is ordained by God or by the devil.
XXV.16	Quod mundus est eternus	270	That the world is eternal
XXV.17	Quod omnia bona et mala sint preordinata a deo	272	That all good and bad things are preordained by God
XXV.18	De illi qui dicunt non esse angelos et qui dicunt animam finiri cum corpore	273	On those who say that angels do not exist and who claim the soul's existence ends with that of the body
XXV.19	Probatio secundum patarenum quod anima moritur cum corpore	273	Proof according to the Patarenes that the soul dies with the body
XXV.20	Item de eodem	274	More on the same
XXV.21	Probatio quod paradisus est et infernus	276	Proof that paradise exists, and also hell

XXVI

XXVI.1	De propriis erroribus circumcisorum. qui grauius errare uidentur quam alii heretici	277	Concerning the particular errors of the Circumcisers, who seem to err more grievously than other heretics
XXVI.2	Quod christus seruauit circumcisionem	278	That Christ observed circumcision

XXVII

XXVII.1	De erroribus speronistarum. quorum proprii sunt tres	280	Concerning the errors of the Speronists, of which three are particular to them

ELENCHVS TITVLORVM SVMMAE XXVII.2 – XXX.20

XXVII.2	De baptisma	281	On Baptism
XXVII.3	Ante aduentum chrisi nullus ascendit in celum	282	Before Christ's coming no one ascended to heaven
XXVII.4	Probatio quod homines non portant peccatum ade	282	Proof that men do not carry the sin of Adam

XXVIII

XXVIII.1	De pauperibus leonistis. quorum sunt iiii^{or} errores proprii	284	On the Poor of Lyons, whose particular errors are four
XXVIII.2	Quod solus sacerdos tractare ecclesiastica sacramenta	285	That only a priest may celebrate the sacraments of the Church
XXVIII.3	Quod eleemosyna de superhabundantia mundat a peccatis	285	That alms from one's excess wealth cleanses from sin

XXIX

XXIX.1	De rebapticatis. quorum proprius est error bis baptizare	288	On the Rebaptizers, whose particular error is to baptize twice
XXIX.2	De errore illorum qui dicunt baptismum posse reiterare	289	On the error of those who say that baptism can be repeated

LIBER III — BOOK III

XXX

XXX.1	De communibus erroribus in quibus hereses omnes uel plures errare uidentur	289	On the common errors in which all heresies, or many of them, seem to err
XXX.2	Secundus articulus	290	Second article
XXX.3	[Tertius]	290	[Third]
XXX.4	[Quartus]	290	[Fourth]
XXX.5	[Quintus]	290	[Fifth]
XXX.6	[Sextus]	290	[Sixth]
XXX.7	VII^a	295	Seventh
XXX.8	[Octauus]	296	[Eighth]
XXX.9	[Nonus]	296	[Ninth]
XXX.10	[Decimus]	296	[Tenth]
XXX.11	[Undecimus]	297	[Eleventh]
XXX.12	[Duodecimus]	297	[Twelfth]
XXX.13	[Tertius decimus]	298	[Thirteenth]
XXX.14	xiiii^a	299	Fourteenth
XXX.15	xv^a	299	Fifteenth
XXX.16	xvi^a	300	Sixteenth
XXX.17	xvii^a	301	Seventeenth
XXX.18	[Octauus decimus]	302	[Eighteenth]
XXX.19	xix	302	Nineteenth
XXX.20	xx	302	[Twentieth]
XXX.21	[Vicesimus primus]	302	[Twenty-First]

XXX.22	xxii[a]	303	Twenty-Second

XXXI

XXXI.1	Omnis potestas est a deo	303	All power is from God
XXXI.2	De dignitatibus	304	On ranks

XXXII

XXXII.1	Quod secundum patarenum ecclesia romana dicitur babillonia siue meretrix	306	That according to the Patarenes the Roman Church is called 'Babylon' or 'Whore'
XXXII.2	Hec sunt dicta falsorum hereticorum	310	These are the sayings of the false heretics
XXXII.3	Item idem in eodem	311	Also regarding the same topic
XXXII.4	De ecclesia militante	314	On the Church Militant

XXXIII

XXXIII.1	Quod malus prelatus seu sacerdos uel predicator potest fungi suo officio	317	That an evil prelate, priest, or preacher can exercise his office
XXXIII.2	Quod malus homo non potest esse sacerdos uel prelatus seu predicator	320	That an evil man cannot be a priest or prelate or preacher

XXXIV

XXXIV.1	De iuramento	325	On oath taking
XXXIV.2	De iuramento	325	On oath taking
XXXIV.3	Item de eodem	325	More on the same
XXXIV.4	De iuramento	326	About swearing
XXXIV.5	De eodem	326	On the same topic
XXXIV.6	De Juramento	326	About swearing
XXXIV.7	De iuramento	326	About swearing
XXXIV.8	Quod iurare sit peccatum. secundam patarenum	329	That to swear is a sin, according to the Patarenes

XXXV

XXXV.1	Quod iustitia temporalis sit bona et a deo ordinata	334	That earthly justice is good and ordained by God
XXXV.2	Quod nullum iudicium seculare possit exerceri in corpus humanum	346	That no earthly justice is to be executed on the human body
XXXV.3	De eodem	351	On the same

XXXVI

XXXVI.1	Quod confessio debet fieri sacerdotibus	356	That confession ought to be made to priests
XXXVI.2	Idem de eodem	356	Also regarding the same

XXXVII

XXXVII.1	De purgatorio	358	On Purgatory
XXXVIII.2	Quod purgatorium sit iterum probatur	358	That Purgatory exists again be proven
XXXVIII.3	Item de purgatorio	360	Also on Purgatory

De uno principio solo deo creatore et factore omnium ac domino uniuersorum I

In nomine domini nostri ihesu christi et beatissime uirginis marie genitricis eius. et sancti dominici confessoris dei. probatur per multas rationes naturales quod unus est solus deus principium omnium et solus omnipotens. Omne compositum habet suum compositorem. Sed cum sint composita quecumque uisu corporeo uel intellectu capere possumus. restat aliquid esse quod composuit. quod non sit compositum quod uisu uel intellectu capere non possimus. sed omnia corporalia et spiritualia scilicet angelos et animas et demones et huiusmodi intuemur et eorum materias et formas uel uisu corporis uel intellectu animi possumus comprehendere ergo prima essentia que est indiuisibilis inuisibilis et intelligibilis atque incomprehensibilis est solus deus et omnium causa. item omne quod mouetur. motorem habet et non est inuenire aliquid quod non habet motionem. et si dicas quod res ista habet istum motorem et iste mouens illam cum sit mobile quid motorem habet. Sed cum non sit uia infinitatis. patet quod est aliquid mouens alia et ipsum non mouetur qui est unus deus. Item nulla creatura est perfecte bona et nulla perfecte pulcra. ergo omnis creatura est imperfecta. Sed cum priuatio semper relinquat habitum quia non dicitur aliquid imperfectum nisi ratione alterius quod perfectum est. constat aliquid esse perfectum scilicet solum deum. Et istis tribus rationibus cognouerunt philosophi unum deum esse. et omnium causam. quarum prima est per compositionem. secunda per mobilem. tertia per imperfectum duplex scilicet bonitatis et pulcritudinis. primam tangit apostolus ad colosenses primo. in ipso inquit condita sunt uniuersa. Secundam tangit idem in actibus xvii. In ipso enim uiuimus et mouemus et sumus sicut et quidam nostrorum poetarum dixerint. ipsius enim et genus sumus etcet. et tertius tangit de in lucam xviii. Nemo bonus nisi solus deus. Quod ita intelliget nemo bonus scilicet perfecte nisi solus deus.

Patarenus: Per ista tua phylosophyca argumenta non habes quod unum solum sit principium omnium rerum. sed tantum ut omnia principium habeant a causa incomposita immobili et perfecta. quam dico duplicem scilicet deum et diabolum. et alterum dico principium esse suarum creaturarum. alterum uero suarum. ut supra me credere inseruisti in prologo tuo. et sic dico diabolum esse incompositum. immobilem et perfectum perfectione mala.

On the one principle, the one God, creator and maker of all things and Lord of the whole world

In the name of our Lord Jesus Christ and of the most blessed Virgin Mary, His mother, and of Saint Dominic the confessor of God. That there is one sole God, principle of all things and alone omnipotent is established by many proofs from nature. Every composite thing has its maker. But since whatever things we are able to understand by bodily sight or the intellect are composite, it remains that there is some being that has composed [other things] and that is not composed, that we are not able to understand by sight and intellect. But we consider all corporeal and spiritual things, namely angels and souls and demons and the like, and we are able to comprehend their form and matter either by bodily sight or by the understanding of the soul. Therefore the first essence that is indivisible, invisible, and intelligible, as well as incomprehensible, is God alone, and the cause of all things. Further, everything which is moved has a mover and nothing is found that does not have motion. And if you should say that this thing has this mover, and this which moves that thing, since it is moveable, has a mover, but since this cannot proceed in that manner to infinity, the Father is something which moves other things, yet is Himself unmoved, who is the one God. Further no creature is perfectly good, and none is perfectly beautiful, therefore all creatures are imperfect. But with privation a habit should always remain, since nothing is called imperfect except by means of another thing which is perfect, and it is obvious something is perfect, namely God alone. And by these three reasons the philosophers knew that one God, the cause of all things, existed. The first is by composition, the second by motion, and the third from imperfection, considered in two ways, namely goodness and beauty. The Apostle touches upon the first in 1 Colossians (1:16) "For in him" he says "were all things created." He touches upon the second in Acts 17 (17:28) "For in him we live, and move, and have our being, as some also of your own poets said, 'For we are also his offspring.'" And the third is touched upon in Luke 18 (18:19) "no one is good but God alone." This is so that one understands that no one is good — that is, perfect — save God alone.

Pat: By these your philosophical arguments you do not establish that there is one single principle of all things, but only that all things have a principle from an uncomposed, immobile, and perfect cause, which I say is double — that is, God and the devil — and one I say is the principle of all His own creatures, the other yet of his own proper creatures, as above you observed me to believe in your prologue.[1] And so I say the devil is uncomposed, immobile, and perfect by the perfection of evil.

I.1.33 in... 34 uniuersa] Col. 1:16.   35 In... 37 sumus] Act. 17:28.   38 Nemo...deus] Luc. 18:19.

I.1.9 restat] rextat *P*   11 uel] et *P*   15 ergo] igitur *F*   18 quod] om. *P*   29 philosophi] phylosophy *P*   30 quarum] quia *P*   31 mobilem] mobile *P* | imperfectum] imperfectione *P*   33 inquit] inquid *P*   38 xviii] xix *F*   44 et²] om. *F*

I.1.1 fol. 3ra|De uno *P*; fol. 1r | De uno *F*   23 deus|fol. 3rb *P*   45 uero|fol. 3va *P*

---

1) It is possible this refers to a prologue omitted in both mss.

Catholicus: Hanc tuam responsionem nullam esse pluribus rationibus inprobare possum. Prima quia dicis diabolum esse simplicem et inmobilem sicut deus est. quod falsissimum esse probo sic. Credis quod diabolus sit penitus contrarius deo? sed deus est summe simplex et penitus immobilius. ergo diabolum te credere oportet compositum et mobilem et per consequentiam creaturam. Item deus aut est compositus aut simplex et scio quod credis eum simplicem esse. et si non credis probo quod credere debeas et hic tribus rationibus

Prima est quia quicquid est compositum constat ex partibus scilicet materia et forma sed partes naturaliter sunt prius suo integrali et sic esset deus prius seipso quod est impossibile.

Secunda est quia si esset compositus. aut se eduxisset de partibus compositionis ad compositionem quod esse non poterat. ut seipsum quis educat aut alius eduxisset et tunc ille esset prius eo. et sic deus non esset eternus.

Tertia est quia si esset compositus esset diuisibilius quia omne quod ex partibus constat diuisibile est et sic corruptibile. Igitur propter predictas inconuenientias. necesse est te credere quod deus est summe simplex. quod si est ergo speciem incircumscriptus et ita est ubique ergo est in diabolo et in omni re. per essentiam id est dans suum esse ei et omni creature tamquam creator. Item si deus est ubique diabolus aut nusquam est aut est in deo sicut creaturam in creatore. creatura autem in creatore est. sicut effectus in causa et sic patet quod diabolus est creatura. igitur compositus et mobilis quia omnis creatura composita est ex materia et forma. et mobilis est ut probatum est superius. ad hoc est quo legitur in apocalypsis xii. et proiectus est draco in terra ille magnus serpens antiquus qui uocatur diabolus et sathanas etcet. ergo est mobilis et localis et ita creatura. et sic etiam compositus. Igitur uera sunt argumenta mea phylosophica que ideo blasfemas. quia ipsa intelligere non uales. est enim uestra consuetudo o heretici. ut que de rationibus naturalibus uel de scripturis capere non potestis uel non uultis. illa tamquam mala aut nullius utilitatis blasfematis. sicut beatus petrus in sua epistola ii scripsit dicens hii uero ueluð in irrationabilia pecora naturaliter in captionem. et in perniciem. in his que ignorant blasfemantes in corruptione sua peribunt etcet. Item manifestum est quod omnes homines appetunt vitam. qui habet in actu et in habitu infinita bona. Item manifestum est quod omnes homines appetunt uitam eternam et utrumque diligunt deum et omnes amant bonum quod faciunt etiam dampnati unde in luca xvi. pater abraham miserere mei etcet. et infra. ibi. ut qui uolunt

---

81 et...83 sathanas] Apoc. 12:9.   90 hii...93 etcet] 2 Pet. 2:12.   98 pater...99 mei] Luc. 16:24.   99 ut...100 trasmeare] Luc. 16:26.

49 responsionem] reprehensionem F   50 pluribus...52 esse] om. F   53 deo] interrog. om. F   56 aut¹] om. F   60 naturaliter] similiter P   63 si] sit P   75 diabolus] dyabolus P   76 creatore] creatione P   77 creatore] creatione P   82 in terra] om. F   90 scripsit] scribit F   93 Item...95 bona] om. P   98 faciunt etiam] transp. F

68 diuisibilius|fol. fol. 3vb P   69 partibus|fol. 1v F   89 blasfematis|fol. 4ra P

transire ad uos non possint neque inde huc trasmeare etcet. Quod faciunt etiam demones. Vnde matt. viii: clamabant dicentes. quid nobis et tibi ihesu fili dei uenisti huc ante tempus torquere nos etcet. et infra: si eicis nos hinc mitte nos in gregem porcorum etcet. sed ad hoc non mouet malos et demones gratia. quia non habent eam. ergo natura bona qui in eis est mouet eos a desiderandus uel diligendus bonum. ergo natura illorum a domino est a quo est omne bonum. alias enim si natura bona non esset in eis numquam diligerent aut uellent bonum. Et si a diabolo essent secundum naturam numquam diligere aut uelle possent nisi malum. quia omne esse ad suam causam tendit. et omne generatum suum generans requirit. unde omnis aqua tendit ad mare unde habet originem. serpens magis ad serpentem quam ad agnum. et talpa potius ad tenebras quam ad lucem currit. Et quod aliqui mala diligunt et bona non currant. hoc ex uitio accidentis procedit non ex natura instituta.

Item in omnibus creaturis uisibilibus est aliquam utilitatem et delectationem et gaudium et quietem inuenire. et etiam sunt adminicula ad benefaciendum. sed hic in eis apponere non potuit nisi qui in se habuit huiusmodi in actu uel in habitu. Sed diabolus non habet hoc sibi in actu. quod communiter credunt omnes. nec etiam in habitu. quod patet. quia potius sibi huiusmodi posuisset quam rebus aliis. si potuisset. igitur a deo sunt omnia qui habet in actu et in habitu infinita bona.

De omnipotentia dei per rationes naturales

Regnum dei aut est infinitum et item diabolus nichil habet ex se et sic est deus omnipotens ubique aut uero est terminatum. quod si est. iterum aut alius determinatum et sic est ille maior eo. que est abusio. aut sibi ipse determinauit. et tunc si infinitum non acceptat stultus fuit. quod stultissimum est credere. Igitur solus deus est omnipotens.

Patarenus: Dico quod non potuit accipere plus quam fecit.
Catholicus: Aut enim alius constrixit quia non potuit. item ille fuit longe potentios eo. aut ipse se constrinxit. et sic fuit iterum stultus. ergo sane de deo loquendo restat ut ipse dicatur et credatur. omnipotens solus. item aut diabolus est omnipotens in regno suo. aut non. si non ergo deus est omnipotens ubique. si uero dicis quia diabolus est omnipotens in regno suo. ergo potest perimere animas sanctorum quando sunt in regno suo. quod falsum est. quia libenter faceret si posset. ergo non est omnipotens in regno suo. ergo deus solus ubique est omnipotens. preterea anime

who would pass from here to you, cannot, nor from there come here." This even the demons do, whence in Matthew 8 (8:29) "they cried out, saying, 'What have we to do with you, Jesus Son of God? Have you come here to torment us before the time?'" And later (8:31) "if you cast us out from here, send us into the herd of swine." But by this He does not move evil men and demons by grace, since they do not have it, therefore He moves them by the goodness of nature which is in them by desiring or loving the good, therefore their natures are from the Lord, from whom is every good thing. And if they were from the devil according to nature, they would never be able to love or wish anything but evil, since all beings tend towards their cause and all generated things seek their origin, just as all water seeks the sea whence it has its origin, just as the serpent has its origin more from the serpent than from the lamb or the mole, and hastens more towards the darkness than the light. And that some evil things love and do not hasten to good things, this pro-ceeds from the accidents of sin and are not fixed in nature.

Further it is possible to find in all visible creatures some utility and enjoyment and joy and rest and there exist also some aids for doing good, but none could have put these things in them but He who had in Himself things of this kind in act or in habit. But the devil does not have this for himself in act, which everyone commonly believes, nor even in habit, which is clear since he would have put such things in himself rather than in other things, if he had been able. Therefore all things are from God, who has infinite goodness both in act and in habit.

On the omnipotence of God from natural proofs

Either the kingdom of God is infinite and likewise the devil has nothing from himself, and so God is omnipotent everywhere, or yet it is bounded, because if it is, again either He is determined by another, and so that one is greater than He — which is improper — or He determined Himself and then if He did not accept His infinity, He was foolish, which is most stupid to believe. Therefore God alone is omnipotent.

Pat: I say that He was not able to accept more than He did.
Cath: For either He was constrained by another since He was unable, also that one would be far more powerful than He, or He constrained Himself, and so again He was foolish. Therefore indeed in speaking of God it remains as it is said and believed, He alone is omnipotent. Also either the devil is omnipotent in his kingdom, or not. If not, therefore God is omnipotent everywhere. If you still say that the devil is omnipotent in his kingdom, therefore he can kill the souls of the saints when they are in his kingdom, which is false since he would immediately do it if he were able. Therefore he is not omnipotent in his kingdom, therefore God alone is omnipotent everywhere. Further the souls of

---

102 clamabant...103 nos] Matt. 8:29. 103 si...104 porcorum] Matt. 8:31.

104 sed] om. *F* 118 instituta] add. u^a *P* rubricated. 119 omnibus...uisibilibus] omnes creature uisibiles *P* | omnibus...est] om. *F* creaturis...est] om. *F* | est] etiam *P* 126 huiusmodi] huius *F* I.2.2 aut] om. *P* 3 uero] om., ante corr. non *F* 6 ipse] om. *F* 7 est] om. *P* 11 Catholicus] om. *P* 14 solus] om. *P*

110 secundum|fol. 4rb *P* 127 in¹|fol. 2r *F* I.2.3 est|fol. 4va *P*

sanctorum sunt in corporibus que dicis de regno diaboli esse. sed deus est omnipotentes in suo regno et ille anime sunt de suo regno. ergo est omnipotens in illis. sed non potest potentiam suam omnimodam exercere in illis nisi perforet corpora que sunt de regno diaboli. ergo deus est omnipotens etiam in regno diaboli.

Patarenus: Non sequitur propter hoc quod deus sit omnipotens etiam in regno diaboli sed sequitur quod aliquid possit in eo. quod fateor de plano quod ideo est quia ipse illum deuicit.

Catholicus: Ista potentia quam habet deus super diabolum et regnum eius aut secundum plus et minus aut equaliter. primum uero non est dicente beato iacobo in epistola sua i. de deo apud quem non est transmutatio nec uicissitudinis obumbratio etcet. si secundum est. ergo mentitus es dicens quod potentiam habet in regno illius. quia ex tempore uicerit illum. quia ab eterno equalem potentiam habet. deus. et sicut potest unum potest et reliquium. quia equaliter potest apud eum non sit transmutatio etcet. Igitur equaliter potest omnia

Catholicus: Item regnum dei et diaboli aut sunt coniuncta aut disiuncta. primum non est. dicente apostolo ii ad corinthios vi. que enim participatio iustitie cum iniquitate aut societas luci ad tenebras que autem conuentio Christi ad Belial etcet. si uero sunt disiuncta. ergo per aliquod medium cuius medii aut aliquis illorum dominus est et tunc iterum sunt coniuncta regna ipsorum aut nullius est dominus illius medii et tunc est illud medium tertium sed principium quod est absurdum dicere. ergo unum est regnum solius dei omnipotentis.

Patarenus: Dicam aliter scilicet quod regnum dei et diaboli sunt spiritualia. et ideo nichil est quod de conuinctionem illorum opposuisti. et est regnum dei omne bonum et regnum diaboli omne malum.

Catholicus: Ergo diabolus potest omne malum. igitur potest perimere sanctos quod est magnum malum. et etiam ipsum deum quod est summum malum. quod falsum est quia non potest. quia si posset hodie non differeret in crastinum. preterea deus potest omne bonum ergo potest destrueret omne malum. quod uerum est ergo est omnipotens deus bonus.

Item patet quod deus punit diabolum et demones et malos homines. et quod ipse facit omnes penas temporales. et eternas et quod peccatam fiunt non nisi deo permittente. et quod diabolus et demones et mali homines et infernus obediunt et seruiunt deo. sicut in isto tractatu in spirituali rubricella continebunt hic

the saints are in bodies, which you say belong to the kingdom of the devil, but God is omnipotent in His kingdom, and those souls are of His kingdom, therefore He is omnipotent over them, but He cannot exercise His power in them, unless He pierces through the bodies which are of the kingdom of the devil, therefore God is also omnipotent in the kingdom of the devil.

Pat: It does not follow that on account of this God is omnipotent also in the kingdom of the devil but it does follow that He can do something in it, since I plainly affirm that He is powerful since He has defeated him [the devil].

Cath: This power which God has over the devil and his kingdom is either more or less or equal. Yet it is not the first, according to the saying of Blessed James regarding God (1:17) "in whom there is no change, nor shadow of alteration." If it is the second then you lie, saying that He has power in that one's kingdom, for how could He have conquered him from that time, since from eternity God had equal power, and just as if he can do one thing, he can do the rest, so he can do equally with Him "in whom there is no change." Therefore he is equally able to do all things.

Cath: Further the kingdom of God and of the devil either are conjoined or not. The first is not true, the Apostle having spoken in 2 Corinthians 6 (6:14-15) "For what participation does justice have with injustice? Or what fellowship does light have with darkness? And what concord does Christ have with Belial?" Yet if they are not joined, then there exists some intermediate space of which area either one of them is lord and then, again, their kingdoms are conjoined, or else there is no lord of that intermediate space, and then that space is a third thing but also a principle/primary element, which is absurd to say. Therefore there is only the kingdom of the single omnipotent God.

Pat: I might say, namely, that the kingdom of God and the devil are spiritual and so there is nothing to your contention which you assert regarding them, and so the kingdom of God is all good, and the kingdom of the devil is all evil.

Cath: Therefore the devil can do all evil, so he can kill the saints, since it is a great evil, and also God Himself because he is the highest evil. That is false, since he cannot do such a thing, since he could do it today it would not differ from tomorrow, further God can do all good things, therefore He can destroy all evil things. Since this is true, then God is good and omnipotent.

Also it is clear that God punishes the devil and the demons and evil men, and that He causes all temporal punishments as well as eternal ones, and that sins do not happen unless permitted by God, and that the devil, the demons, and evil men, and lower things obey and serve God just as is contained in this treatise, in the part about spiritual things,

---

I.2.35 de…36 obumbratio] Iac. 1:17. 45 que…47 Belial] 2 Cor. 6:14-15.

29 etiam] om. *F* 30 aliquid] aliquis *F* 32 Catholicus] om. *P* 33 eius] om. *F* but add. *al. man. marg. dex.* | secundum] om. *P* 43 Catholicus] om. *F* 51 sed] om. *F* 54 Patarenus] om. *F* add. in marg. sin. *P* 58 potest] om. *F* | omne] om. *P* 62 deus] om. *F*

25 potentiam|fol. 4vb *P* 50 coniuncta|fol. 5ra *P* 67 temporales|fol. 2v *F*

omnia. ergo diabolo non est omnipotens est in regno suo. si regnum habet immo nichil in eo potest nisi per deum. Igitur solus deus est omnipotens.

Visis rationibus naturalibus ad probationem propositi sequitur de auctoritatibus diuine scripture. primo de quibusdam ueteris testamenti quas isti canes non audent in publicum lacerere.

Quod unus est solus deus et omnipotens

In cantico Moysi uidete quod ego sim solus et non est alius deus preter me etcet. Item Ysayas xliii: Ego dominus et ab initio ego ipse. et non est qui de manu mea eruat etcet. Et xliiii: ego primus et ego nouissimus etcet. et xlv Ego dominus et non est amplius extra me non est deus etcet. Et infra. absque me non est deus ego dominus et non est alter. et infra michi curuabuntur omnia genua etcet. Item Baruch iiii. hic est deus noster non extimabitur alius aduersus eum etcet.

Quod unius deus creauit et fecit omnia

Dauid in principio tu domine terram fundasti et opera manuum tuarum sunt celi etcet. Item Ysayas xlii haec dicit dominus deus creans celos et extendens eos firmans terram et que germinant ex ea dans flatum populo qui est super eam et spiritum calcantibus eam. Et xliiii: ego dominus faciens omnia extendens celos solus. stabiliens terram et nullus mecum. irrita faciens signa diuinorum et ariolos in furorem uertens. etcetera. Et xlv: formans lucem et creans tenebras faciens pacem et creans malum ego dominus faciens omnia haec etcetera. Et item: ue qui contradicit factori suo testa di sammis tere etcetera et infra: Ego feci terram et hominem super eam creaui manus mee tetenderunt celos et omni militie eorum ego mandaui etcetera. Et xlviii: manus mea fundauit terram et dextera mea mensa est celos etcetera. Item Ieremias x: dominus autem deus uerus est ipse deus uiuens et rex sempiternus ab indignatione eius commouebitur terra et non sustinebunt gentes conminationem eius etcetera. et infra: qui facit terram in fortitudine sua preparat orbem in sapientia sua et prudentia sua extendit celos. ad uocem suam dat multitudinem aquarum in celo et eleuat nebulas ab extremitatibus terre fulgura in pluuiam facit et educit uentum de thesauris suis etcetera. et infra: qui enim formauit omnia ipse est deus etcetera. Et xxvii: ego feci terram et homines et iumenta qui sunt super faciem terre. et xxxi: haec dicit dominus qui dat solem in lumine diei ordinem lune et

therefore the devil is not omnipotent in his kingdom. Indeed even if he had a kingdom he could do nothing except through God. Therefore God alone is omnipotent.

The natural proofs having been established now we proceed to the authorities of the divine scriptures. The first of these are in the Old Testament, which these dogs do not dare to impugn in public.

That God alone is one and omnipotent

In the canticle of Moses (Dt 32:39) "See that I alone am, and there is no other God besides me." Also Isaiah 43 (43:12–13) "I am the Lord and from the beginning I am the same, and there is none who can deliver out of my hand." And 44 (44:6) "I am the first, and I am the last," and 45 (45:5) "I am the Lord, and there is no other, there is no God, besides me." And also (45:6) "There is none besides me. I am the Lord, and there is none else." And later (45:23) "For every knee shall be bowed to me." Also Baruch 3 (3:36) "This is our God, and there no other will be accounted of in comparison of him."

That one God created and made all things

David (Ps 101:26) "In the beginning, O Lord, you established the earth, and the heavens are the works of your hands." Also Isaiah 42 (42:5) "Thus says the Lord God who created the heavens, and stretched them out, who established the earth, and the things that spring out of it, who gives breath to the people upon it, and spirit to those who tread thereon." And 44 (44:24–25) "I am the Lord, who makes all things, who alone stretch out the heavens, who establishes the earth, and there is none with me. I am he who makes void the tokens of diviners, and makes the soothsayers mad." And 45 (45:7) "I form the light and create darkness, I make peace and create evil, I the Lord that do all these things." And also (45:9) "Woe to him who contradicts his maker, a shard of earthen pots," and later (45:12) "I made the earth and I created man upon it, my hand stretched forth the heavens, and I have commanded all their hosts." And 48 (48:13) "My hand also has established the earth, and my right hand has measured the heavens." Also Jeremiah 10 (10:10) "But the Lord is the true God, he is the living God, and the everlasting king, at his wrath the earth shall tremble, and the nations shall not be able to abide his menacing," and later (10:12–13) "He who makes the earth by his power, who prepares the world by his wisdom, and stretches out the heavens by his knowledge. At his voice he gives a multitude of waters in the heavens, and lifts up the clouds from the ends of the earth, he makes lightning for rain, and brings forth the wind out of his treasures." And later (10:16) "for it is God who formed all things." And 27 (27:5) "I made the earth, and the men, and the beasts that

---

I.3.2 uidete...3 me] Deut. 32:39.   3 Ego...5 eruat] Is. 43:12-13.   5 ego¹...nouissimus] Is. 44:6.   7 absque...8 alter] Is. 45:6.
8 michi...9 genua] Is. 45:23.   9 hic...10 eum] Bar. 3:36.   I.4.2 in...3 celi] Ps. 101:26.   3 haec...6 eam²] Is. 42:5 (5 firmans] formans
Vulg.)   7 ego...9 uertens] Is. 44:24-25.   12 ue...13 tere] Is. 45:9 (factori] fictori *Vulg.*)   13 Ego...15 mandaui] Is. 45:12.
16 manus...17 celos] Is. 48:13.   17 dominus...20 eius] Ier. 10:10.   21 qui...25 suis] Ier. 10:12-13.   26 qui...27 deus] Ier. 10:16.
27 ego...28 terre] Ier. 27:5.   28 haec...31 eius] Ier. 31:35.

---

72 immo] in uno *F*   I.3.2 sim] sum *F*   9 Baruch] baruth *P*

74 naturalibus|fol. 5rb *P*   I.4.10 creans|fol. 5va *P*

stellarum in lumine noctis qui turbat mare et sonta fluctus eius etcetera.

De diabolo spiritualiter quod deus creauit eum

Iob penultima. Ecce Becmoth quem feci tecum etcet. et infra. ipse est principium uiarum dei etcet. et infra: qui fecit eum aplicabit gladium eius etcet. Item Dauid: draco iste quem formasti ad illudendum ei. Item Ysayas liiii: ego creaui fabrum sufflantem in igne prunas et proferentem uas in opus suum et ego creaui interfectorem ad disperdendum etcet.

Per auctoritates noui testamenti probabimus hoc modo et hic ordine. prius enim ponemus et inducemus testimonia de nouo testamento ad hoc quod simpliciter et indeterminate dicitur deus. Quare intelligendus est quod ipse solus sit deus secundum naturam. secundo quia dicitur solus deus. tertio quia scribitur unus deus. Quarto quia ponitur omnium creator deus. Quinto quia legitur omnipotens id est omnia potens deus.

Quod simpliciter dicitur deus

Iohannes primo. deum nemo uidit unquam etcetera. Et Paulus ad romanos i: reuelatur enim ira dei de celo etcet. et ad hoc sunt multe alie auctoritates quas non curaui inserere proper operis prolixitatem.

Quod dicitur solus deus

Lucam xvi. nemo bonus nisi solus deus etcet. Item Iohannes vi. gloriam a solo deo est non queritis etcet. et xiiii. hec est uita eterna ut cognoscat te solum uerum deum etcet. Item Paulus i ad tymotheum i. regi seculorum immortali inuisibili soli deo etcet. item: iude ii. soli deo saluatori nostro etcet. Marcum viii: quid me dicis bonum nemo bonus nisi unus deus. idem x: bene in ueritate magister dixisti quia unus est deus et non est alius preter eum etcet. quod Christus confirmat unde sequitur. Ihesus autem uidens quod sapienter respondisset dixit illi non es longe a regno dei etcet. ergo praue et tortuose delirant patareni duos esse deos. et ex his longe sunt a regno dei. item ad romanos iii. quem quidem unus deus qui iustificat circumcisionem et fide et preputium per fidem etcet. item x: idem dominus omnium etcet. idem ad corinthios i vii. nullus deus nisi unus. idem ad galatas iii: deus autem unus est. idem ad ephesios iiii. unus dominus una fides. unum baptisma unus deus et pater omnium etcet. idem ad Tymotheum i ii: unus est deus unus et

On the devil, that God created him spiritually

In the penultimate chapter of Job (40:10) "Behold behemoth whom I made with you." And later (40:14) "He is the beginning of the ways of God," and also (40:14) "who made him, he will apply his sword." Also David (Ps 103:26) "This dragon which you have formed to play therein." And Isaiah 54 (54:16) "Behold, I have created the smith who blows the coals in the fire, and brings forth an instrument for his work, and I have created the killer to destroy." By the authorities of the New Testament, we will prove in this way and in this order, for before all we shall propose and adduce testimonies from the New Testament to the fact that God is spoken of simply and indeterminately. Whereby it is understood that He alone is God according to nature. Second why it is said that God is alone. Third, why one God is written of. Fourth why He is proposed as God, creator of all things. Fifth that God is read as omnipotent, that is, powerful in all things.

That He is simply called God

1 John (4:12) "no one has ever seen God." And Paul in Romans 1 (1:18) "For the wrath of God is revealed from heaven." And the fact is that there are many other authorities which I do not care to insert since otherwise the work might become overly lengthy.

That He alone is called God

Luke 16 (18:19) "No one is good except God." Also John 6 (5:44) "and the glory which is from God alone, you do not seek?" and 13 (17:3) "Now this is eternal life, that they may know you, the only true God." Also Paul in 1 Timothy 1 (1:17) "Now to the king of ages, immortal, invisible, the only God." Also in Jude 2 (1:25) "to the only God our Savior." Mark 8 (10:18) "why do you call me good, there is none good save the one God." The same in 10 (12:32) "Well, Master, you have said in truth, that there is one God, and there is no other besides him." And Christ confirmed it, since it continues (12:34) "And Jesus seeing that he had answered wisely, said to him, 'You are not far from the kingdom of God.'" Therefore the Patarenes rave perversely and tortuously that there are two Gods, and these then are far from the kingdom of God. Also Romans 3 (3:30) "For it is one God, who justifies circumcision by faith, and uncircumcision through faith." Also 10 (10:12) "Lord over all." The same in 1 Corinthians 7 (8:4) "there is no God but one." The same in Galatians 3 (3:20) "But God is one." The same in Ephesians 4 (4:5) "One Lord,

---

I.5.2 Ecce...tecum] Iob 40:10. 3 ipse...dei] Iob 40:14. 4 qui...eius] Iob 40:14. 5 draco...illudendum] Ps. 103:26. 6 ego...8 disperdendum] Is. 54:16. I.6.2 deum...unquam] Ioh. 4:12. 3 reuelatur...5 prolixitatem] Rom. 1:18. I.7.2 nemo...deus] Luc. 18:19. 3 gloriam...queritis] Ioh. 5:44. 4 hec...5 deum] Ioh. 17:3. 5 regi...6 deo] 1 Tim. 1:17. 7 soli...nostro] Iud. 1:25. 8 quid...deus] Mar. 10:18. 9 bene...10 eum] Mar. 12:32. 11 Ihesus...12 dei] Mar. 12:34. 15 quem...16 fidem] Rom. 3:30 (16 et] ex *Vulg.*) 16 idem...17 omnium] Rom. 10:12. 18 nullus...unus] 1 Cor. 8:4. | deus²...19 est] Gal. 3:20. 19 unus²...20 omnium] Eph. 4:5. 21 unus¹...22 Ihesus] 1 Tim. 2:5.

I.5.8 est] *no paragraph division* PF 9 probabimus] probabimus probamus F 12 Quare] quia P

I.5.2 quem|fol. 5vb P 8 ad|fol. 3r F I.7.3 etcet|fol. 6ra P

mediator dei et hominum homo Christus Ihesus etcet. Ex hiis patet manifeste quod unus tantum deus est.

Patarenus: Respondeo ad illa tua per que uoluisti probare unum tantum deum esse quia dicitur simpliciter deus et solus et unus unico uerbo quia subauditur scilicet bonus. sicut legitur in Mattheum xix. unus est bonus deus.
Catholicus: Huic responsioni reseruo confutationem facere infra in tuis allegationibus cum hanc auctoritatem allegabis ad probandum quod diabolus sit deus.

Quod ponitur omnium creator et factor deus

Iohannes i. omnia per ipsum facta sunt etcet. cum dicit omnia nichil infectum ab eo relinquitur cum sit signum uniuersale sic et paulus argumentur ad hebreos ii: dicens in eo enim quod omnia ei subiecit nichil dimisit non subiectum ei etcet. idem ad romanos i. inuisibilia enim ipsius per ea quae facta sunt intellecta conspiciuntur etcet. ergo que facta sunt bona sunt si per ea deus conspicitur. inuisibilia ergo a deo sunt et non a diabolo. Et xi. quoniam ex ipso et per ipsum et in ipso sunt omnia. idem ad corinthios. i. iii. omnia enim uestra sunt siue paulus siue apollo siue cephas siue mundus siue uita siue mors siue presentia siue absentia. audias o cathare quod si mundus et uita et mors et presentia et absentia et huiusmodi sunt filiorum dei ergo sunt opera dei et non diaboli. item ex hoc patet quod diabolus nichil habet a se. idem viii unus deus pater ex quo omnia et nos in illo etcet. idem ad corinthios ii v omnia autem ex deo etcet. idem ad ephesios iii in deo qui omnia creauit etcet. et infra ad patrem domini nostri ihesu christi ex quo omnis paternitas in celis et in terra nominatur etcet. idem ad heb ii. decebat eum propter quem omnia etcet. idem iii. omnis namque domus fabricatur ab aliquo qui autem omnia creauit deus est etcet. item actus xiiii ad deum uiuum qui fecit celum et terram mare et omnia que in eis sunt etcet. item apocalypsis iiii quia tu creasti omnia et propter uoluntatem tuam erant et creata sunt etcet. idem .v. omnem creaturam que in celo est et super terram et super terram et que sunt in mari omnes audiui dicentes sedenti in throno et agno etcet. ergo sunt dei opera si ei dant benedicentem et honorem et huiusmodi. item x. per uiuentem in secula qui creauit celum et ea que in illo sunt et mare et que in eo sunt etcet. idem xiiii adorate eum qui fecit celum et terram mare et omnia que in eis sunt et fontes aquarum etcet.

one faith, one baptism, one God and Father of all." The same in 1 Timothy 2 (2:5) "For there is one God, and one mediator between God and men, the man Christ Jesus." From these it is plainly clear that God alone is one.
Pat: I reply to your reasons through which you wanted to prove there to be only one God that it is simply said, God and alone and one, by the only word that is understood, namely 'good,' as is read in Matthew 19 (19:17) "One is good, God."
Cath: To this reply I reserve making the refutation below, in your claims using this authority you will try to prove that the devil is God.

That God is proposed to be the creator and maker of all things

John 1 (1:3) "all things were made through him." When he says all things, nothing was left undone by Him, since it was a universal sign, thus Paul argues in Hebrews 2 (2:8) saying "For in that he has subjected all things to himself, he left nothing not subject to him." The same in Romans 1 (1:20) "For the invisible things of him are clearly seen, being understood by the things that are made." Therefore those which are made are good, if through them God might be known. Therefore invisible things are from God and not from the devil. And also, (Rm 11:36) "For of him, and by him, and in him, all things are." Also 1 Corinthians 3 (3:22) "For all things are yours, whether it be Paul, or Apollo, or Cephas, or the world, or life, or death, or things present, or things absent." You hear, O Cathar, that if the world and life and death and presence and absence and the like are of the sons of God, then they are the works of God and not of the devil. Also from this it is clear that the devil has nothing of himself. In the same place 8 (8:6) "one God, the Father, and we in him." The same in 2 Corinthians 5 (5:18) "but all things are from God." The same in Ephesians 3 (3:10) "in God who created all things," and later (3:15) "to the Father of our Lord Jesus Christ, by whom all fatherhood is named in heaven and on earth." The same in Hebrews 2 (2:10) "For it was fitting for him, for whom are all things." The same in 3 (3:4) "For every house is built by some man, but he that created all things, is God." Also Acts 14 (14:14) "to the living God, who made the heavens, and the earth, and the sea, and all things that are in them." Also Apocalypse 4 (4:11) "because you have created all things, and for your will they were, and have been created." And the same in 5 (5:13) "every creature, which is in heaven, and on the earth, and under the earth, and such as are in the sea, and all that are in them, I heard all saying, 'To him who sits on the throne, and to the Lamb.'" Therefore they are the works of God, if they give Him blessing and honor and the like. Also 10 (10:6) "by him who lives forever and ever, who created

---

28 unus…deus] Matt. 19:17. I.8.2 omnia…sunt] Ioh. 1:3. 5 dicens…6 ei] Heb. 2:8. 7 inuisibilia…8 conspiciuntur] Rom. 1:20. 10 quoniam…11 omnia¹] Rom. 11:36. 11 omnia²…14 ab-sentia] 1 Cor. 3:22. 17 unus…18 illo] 1 Cor. 8:6. 19 omnia…deo] 2 Cor. 5:18. 20 in…creauit] Eph. 3:10. | ad…22 nominatur] Eph 5:15. 22 dece-bat…23 omnia] Heb. 2:10. 23 omnis…25 est] Heb. 3:4. 25 ad…26 sunt] Act. 14:14. 27 quia…28 sunt] Apoc. 4:11. 29 omnem…31 agno] Apoc. 5:13. 33 per…34 sunt²] Apoc. 10.6 (secula add. saeculorum *Vulg.*) 35 adorate…36 aquarum] Apoc. 14:7.

I.7.24 tua] tria *P* 25 quia] scilicet *P* I.8.4 hebreos] ebreos *P*

24 Patarenus|fol. 6rb *P* I.8.15 presentia et|fol. 6va *P* 21 christi|fol. 3v *F*

ergo patet expresse quod deus creauit et fecit omnia. igitur diabolus nichil creauit et fecit omnia.

Patarenus: Respondeo quia dico quod deus creauit et fecit omnia bona et sic intelliguntur auctoritates quas induxisti. que intelligo esse tantum ea que sunt inuisibilia oculis corporeis. alia uero creauit et fecit diabolus uel secundum illos qui dicunt quod unum est principium in creatione. dicam quod ubicumque dicitur. deus fecit. ponitur improprie fecit. id est creauit. scilicet in materia prima et confusa.

Catholicus: Probo quod fatuus et reprobus est tuus intellectus. quia cum dicam omnia nichil relinquitur non creatum et non factum a deo. igitur diabolus non fecit nec creauit aliquid. presertim cum in nulla scriptura legatur de ipso quia quicquid creauit aut fecerit. Item aperuit que sunt creata a deo scilicet celum et terram mare fontes aquarum et multa alia dicta superius et dicenda inferius que non est reperire in inuisibilibus per singula. Item legit ad colosenses i quia in ipso scilicet dei filio condita sunt uniuersa in celo et in terra uisibilia et inuisibilia. etcet. ergo deus pater creauit omnia atque fecit per filium suum uisibilia et inuisibilia.

ad illud quod dicis quia deus creauit mundum sed diabolus fecerit et quia non ualeat tibi expositio falsa fecit id est creauit. respondet apostolus ii. ad corinthios. iiii. dicens. deus qui dixit de tenebris lucem splendescere etcet. ergo deus machinam prius confusam dilucidadauit per opera diuisionis et huiusmodi et ad hebreos etiam dicit xi fide intelligimus aptata esse secula uerbo dei ut ex in uisibilis uisibilia fierent etcet. ergo per uerbum dei ex informi materia facta et aptata sunt secula. non ergo per luciferum. item multotiens dicit scriptura creauit et fecit. ergo aliud est creare et aliud est facere presertim cum dicat fecit omnia que in terra sunt et in mari et huiusmodi que non sunt creata sed facta. creare est enim de nichilo aliquid facere. sed facere est de preiacenti materia. aliquid in lucem et compositionem producem.

Catholicus: Mattheum xiii simile factum est regnum celorum homini qui seminauit bonum semen in agro suo etcet. et infra colligent de regno eius omnia scandala etcet. et postea exponit dei filius quid homo

heaven, and the things which are therein, and the earth, and the things which are in it, and the sea, and the things which are therein." Also 14 (14:7) "adore him, who made heaven and earth, the sea, and the fountains of waters." Therefore it is plainly clear that God created and made all things, therefore the devil did not create and make all things.

Pat: I reply that I say that God created and made all good things, and that is how the authorities you adduce are to be understood, since I interpret them to be only those things which are invisible to the bodily eye, otherwise the devil created and made them or, according to those who say that there is one principle in creation, I might say that wheresoever it says 'God made' one should understand 'He made' is used loosely, that is, He created, namely, 'in prime and indefinite matter.'

Cath: I am proving that your understanding is foolish and reprobate, since when I say 'all things' nothing is left that is not created or made by God. Therefore the devil neither made nor created anything, particularly since it is never read in scripture about him creating or making anything. Also it is plain that those things which were created by God — namely heaven and earth and the sources of water, and many other things spoken about above, and to be spoken of below — it is not possible to find these numbered among invisible things in each point. So one reads in Colossians 1 (1:16) "For in him" — namely, in the Son of God — "were all things created in heaven and on earth, visible and invisible." Therefore God the Father created all things and made them through his Son, all things visible and invisible.

Regarding your claim that God created the world, but the devil made it, such a claim does not benefit your false position, for 'made' means 'created' as the Apostle replies in 2 Corinthians 4 (4:6) saying "God, who commanded the light to shine out of darkness," therefore God separated the works, previously unformed, through the work of division and the like, and also Hebrews says in chapter 11 (11:3) "By faith we understand that the world was framed by the word of God, that from invisible things visible things might be made." Therefore material things were made from formless things by the word of God, and the world was framed. Not therefore by Lucifer. Also many times Scripture says 'created and made.' therefore it is one thing to create and another to make, certainly when it says He made all things which are on earth or in the sea and the like, which are not created, but made, for to create is to make something from nothing, but to make is to take some preexisting material and bring it to light and give it form.

Cath: Matthew 13 (13:24) "The kingdom of heaven is like a man who sowed good seed in his field." And later (13:41) "and they shall gather out of his kingdom all scandals," and after the Son of God explained that the man who

---

55 quia…57 inuisibilia] Col. 1:16. 63 dicens…64 splendescere] 2 Cor. 4:6. 66 fide…67 fierent] Heb. 11:3. 76 simile…78 suo] Matt. 13:24. 78 colligent…79 scandala] Matt. 13:41.

44 dicam] dico *F* 45 id est] sciliet *P* 47 est] add. et *P* 49 factum] statum *P* 61 expositio] ex ipso *F* 76 Catholicus] om. *F* add. Quod deus decit mundum istum visibilem.

38 omnia] fol. 6vb *P* 59 inuisibilia] fol. 7ra *P*

qui seminauit est filius hominis et quod ager est mundus ergo a deo bono est mundus iste etcet.
Patarenus: Respondeo loquitur de mundo celesti.
Catholicus: Ergo in illo mundo sunt zizania quod falsum est. Item igitur per hoc euangelium non habes quod mali non sint eradicandi de mundo uisibili sicut ex isto euangelio argumentantis contra me in tractatu de iudicio et potestate seculari. Item idem xx. simile est regnum celorum homini paterfamilias qui exiit primo mane conducere operarios in uineam suam etcet. sed haec uinea autem est mundum et sic mundus a deo est aut ecclesia dei etsi conuincitur de alio errore quo negatis in ecclesia dei esse bonos et malos.

Patarenus: Dico quod hic uinea celum empireum est.
Catholicus: Mentiri te probat testo euangelii qui de murmure et labore loquitur. quia ibi non est labor neque murmur. item iohannem i In mundo erat et mundus per ipsum factus est etcet. ergo filius dei fecit mundum
Patarenus: Sic intelligo istud. mundus per ipsum factus est id est contra ipsum.
Catholicus: Ista expositio stulta est et falsa quia nusquam in grammatica uel in aliqua scriptura ponitur per deum factum est hoc uel illud id est contra deum.
Catholicus: item ad heb i. et tu in principio domine terram fundasti et opera manuum tuarum sunt celi etcet. ergo deus creauit terram pariter cum celo

Patarenus: Per terram intelliguntur credentes nostri et per celum significantur perfecti nostri quod dicuntur consolati.
Catholicus: Sed audi quod sequitur. ipsi peribunt etcet. ergo consolati uestri peribunt. item ii petri iii celi autem qui nunc sunt et terra. eodem uerbo repositi sunt etcet. ergo a deo sunt.
Et si uis istam exponere. sicut modo aliam exposuisti. audi quod sequitur igni reseruati in die iudicii et perditionis impiorum hominum etcet. Item actus xvii inueni aram in qua scriptum erat ignoto deo etcet. et postea deus qui fecit hunc mundum etcet. et dicit hunc quia est demonstrantium ad oculum et intellectum qualiter de mundo uisibilium necesse est illud intelligere

Patarenus: respondeo in nostris libris non est hunc. nec etiam in omnibus uestris.
Catholicus: Esto pro eodem est quia non est alius mundus nisi iste uisibilis. quia nusquam reperies in ueteri uel nouo testamento. quod alius dicatur mundus. item apocalypsis xi factum est regnum huius mundi domini nostri etcet. ergo est suus quia alienum non usurparet. preterea omnes sapientes scripserit quod

sowed was the Son of Man, and that the field was the world, therefore the world is from the good God.
Pat: I reply that He is speaking of the heavenly world.
Cath: Therefore there are tares in that world, which is false. Also therefore from this gospel you do not have it that the evil might not be eradicated from the visible world, just as you have used this gospel passage against me in the section on judgment and secular power. Also in the same gospel in chapter 20 (20:1) "The kingdom of heaven is like a householder, who went out early in the morning to hire laborers into his vineyard." But this vineyard is the world, and so the world is from God, or the Church of God, even if one be convinced by a different error in which you deny that in the Church of God there are good and evil men.
Pat: I say that this vineyard is the heavenly Empyreum.
Cath: One can prove by the witness of the Gospels that you lie, those which speak of murmuring and toil, since there no toil or murmur exist, also John 1 (1:10) "he was in the world, and the world was made by him," therefore the Son of God made the world.
Pat: So I understand this "world was made by him," that is, 'against him.'
Cath: This interpretation is foolish and false, since never in grammar or in any scripture is it proposed that for this or that to be made by God means 'against God.'
Cath: Also in Hebrews 1 (1:10) "You in the beginning, O Lord, founded the earth, and the works of your hands are the heavens." Therefore God created the earth, together with the heavens.
Pat: By 'earth' our believers are to be understood, and by 'heaven' our perfects are interpreted, since they are said to be consoled.
Cath: But hear what follows (1:11) "they shall perish." Therefore your consoled shall perish, further 2 Peter 3 (3:7) "But the heavens and the earth which are now, by the same word are kept in store." Therefore they are from God.
And if you wish to explain this just as you recently explained another, hear what follows, "reserved in fire against the day of judgment and perdition of the ungodly men." Also Acts 17 (17:23) "I found an altar also, on which was written, 'To the unknown God,'" and later "God, who made this world." And he says 'this' because it is [one] of the things that demonstrate to eye and intellect how it is necessary to understand that from connection with the world of visible things
Pat: I reply that in our books [the word] 'this' [is not found] nor in all of yours.
Cath: All the same, since there is no other world save this visible one, for you will find nowhere any other world spoken of in the Old or New Testaments. Also Apocalypse 11 (11:15) "The kingdom of this world has become our Lord's." Therefore it is His, since He would not usurp another's. Further all wise men wrote that this world was

---

87 simile...89 suam] Matt. 20:1. 96 In...97 est] Ioh. 1:10. 104 et...105 celi] Heb. 1:10. 110 ipsi peribunt] Heb. 1:11. 111 celi...113 sunt¹] 2 Pet. 3:7. 117 inueni...118 mundum] Act. 17:23. 127 factum...128 nostri] Apoc. 11:15.

83 Catholicus] om. P 87 de iudicio] om. F 91 alio] alieno P 93 Patarenus] om. P 107 nostri] vestri F (either provides a plausible reading) 124 Catholicus] om. P

82 celesti|fol. 7rb P. 4r F 106 etcet|fol. 7va P 129 usurparet|fol. 7vb P

mundus iste creatus et factus est a deo ut puta philosopha inter gentes. plato. socrates. arystoteles. et seneca et huiusmodi prophetes inter hebreos et apostolis et doctores inter christianos. quare patet dilucide quod mundus iste uisibilis creatus est et factus a deo.

Quod terra et secula inuisibilia sunt creata et diffinita a deo

ad hebreos i per quem fecit secula etcet. secula enim mutabilia sunt temporalia. Item idem xi de intelligimus aptata esse secula uerbo etcet. item actus xvii definiens statuta tempora et terminos habitationis etcet. item marcum ii sabbatum propter hominem factus est etcet. sed diabolus non fecisset sabbatum propter homines. sed potius destruxisset si potuisset igitur deus fecit diem. ergo deus fecit tempora et secula mutabilia.

Quod solis ortus et plurima cibi corporales et omnis habundantia terra temporalium sunt a deo

Mattheum v qui solem suum oriri facit super bones et malos. et pluit super iustos et iniustos et ii ad corinthios viiii potens est autem deus omnem gratiam habundare et facere in uobis. ut in omnibus semper omnem sufficentiam habentes etcet. et in eodem Qui autem aministrat semen seminanti et panem ad manducandum ministrabit et multiplicabit semen uestrum et augebit incremata frugum iustitie uestre etcet. Et prima ad tymotheos iiii. spiritus manifeste dicit etcet. ibi abstinere a cibis quod deus creauit. etcet. et actus xiiii. de celo dans pluuias et tempora fructifera. implens cibo et letitia corda uestra etcet.

Catholicus: mattheum vi. nonne enim anima plus est quam esca et corpus plusquam uestimentum. Respice uolantilia celi quoniam non serunt nec metunt nec congregant in horrea et pater uester celestis pascit illa. etcet. scilicet et infra considerate lilia agri etcet. et ibi. si enim fenum agri quod hodie est et in clibanum mittitur deus sic uestit etcet. Et postea scit enim pater uester quod hiis omnibus indigetis etcet. et ibi primum querite regnum dei et iustitia eius et hic omnia adicientur uobis etcet. et eadem uerba sunt luce. xii. Ex hiis patet manifeste quod uolatilia et flores sunt a deo et quod deus dat cibum anime et corporis. alias enim si essent opera diaboli nunquam pater celestis pasceret et nutrit illam. Cum potius miserit filium suum de celis ad destruxionem operum illius. Vnde id est iohannes iii hoc apparuit filius dei ut disoluat opera diaboli etcet

created and made by God, for example the philosophers among the gentiles; Plato, Socrates, Aristotle, and Seneca and the like; the prophets among the Hebrews; and the Apostles and Doctors among the Christians, hence it is plainly clear that this visible world is created and made by God.

9 That the earth and the invisible world are created and ordained by God

Hebrews 1 (1:2) "by whom he made the world." For the mutable things of the world are in time. Also in the same 11 (11:3) "we understand that the world was framed by the word of God." Also Acts 17 (17:26) "determining appointed times, and the limits of their habitation. Also Mark 2 (2:27) "The Sabbath was made for man." But the devil did not make the Sabbath for men, but rather would destroy it if he could, therefore God made the day, therefore God made time and the mutable world.

10 That the sunrise and many corporeal foods and all the plenty of the temporal world are from God

Matthew 5 (5:45) "who makes his sun rise upon the good and bad, and rain upon the just and the unjust." And 2 Corinthians 9 (9:8) "And God is able to make all grace abound in you, so that you may always have enough of everything." And in the same (9:10) "And he who ministers seed to the sower, will both give you bread to eat, and will multiply your seed, and increase the growth of the fruits of your justice."

And 1 Timothy 4 (4:1) "Now the Spirit clearly says," here (4:3) "to abstain from foods which God has created."
And Acts 14 (14:16) "from heaven, giving rains and fruitful seasons, filling your hearts with food and gladness."

Cath: Matthew 6 (6:25–26) "Is not life more than food, and the body more than the clothing? Consider the birds of the air, they neither sow, nor do they reap, nor do they gather into barns, and your heavenly Father feeds them." Further later, (6:28) "consider the lilies of the field," and then (6:30) "if the grass of the field, which is today, and tomorrow is cast into the oven. God does so clothe." And later (6:32) "For your Father knows that you have need of all these things." And there (6:33) "Seek therefore first the kingdom of God, and his justice, and all these things shall be added unto you." And the same words are found in Luke 12. From these it is plainly clear that the birds and flowers are from God and that God gives food to souls and bodies. For otherwise if they were the works of the devil the heavenly Father never would have fed and preserved them. Rather He might have sent His Son from heaven for the destruction of those works, whence it is in John 3 (1 Jn

---

I.9.3 per...secula¹] Heb. 1:2.   4 de...5 uerbo] Heb. 11:3.   6 definiens...habitationis] Act. 17:26.   7 sabbatum...8 est] Mar. 2:27.
I.10.4 qui...5 iniustos] Matt. 5:45.   6 potens...8 habentes] 2 Cor. 9:8.   8 Qui...11 uestre] 2 Cor. 9:10.   12 spiritus...dicit] 1 Tim. 4:1.   13 abstinere...creauit] 1 Tim. 4:3.   14 de...15 uestra] Act. 14:16.   16 nonne...19 illa] Matt. 6:25-26.   20 considerate...agri] Matt. 6:28. | et²...22 uestit] Matt. 6:30.   22 scit...23 indigetis] Matt. 6:32.   23 primum...25 uobis] Matt. 6:33.   31 hoc...diaboli] 1 Ioh. 3:8.

I.10.7 uobis] nobis P   21 si] sic P   30 ad] a P | destruxionem] destruen P

I.10.7 habundare|fol. 8ra P | ut|fol. 4v F   26 deo|fol. 8rb P

Patarenus: Loquitur de uolatilibus et liliis celestibus id est de sanctis angelis qui in celo sunt.
Catholicus: Sed audi quod ibi dicit dominus de illis uolantibus quanto magis pluris estis illius etcet. ergo appellati erant maioris meriti quam angeli quod est contra tuam sectam. qui dicis quod santi sunt eiusdem meriti.
Item quoniam stabit quod dicit de liliis.
Si enim fenum quia hodie etcet. Ergo hodie angelis sunt et cras in clibanum mitterentur. et de cibis et de uestibus corporalibus. Vide qualiter expressim loquitur dicens. Nonne enim anima plus est quam esca et corpus plusquam uestimentum etcet. Et postea. scit enim pater uester quod hiis omnibus indigetis etcet. et omnia adicientur uobis etcet. Tace ergo indiscreta belua.

Quod quadrupedia et serpentes sunt a deo

Ad romanos i et mutauerunt gloriam incorruptibilis dei in similitudinem ymaginis corruptibilis hominis et uolucrum et quadrupedum et serpentium etcet. et postea et seruierunt creature potius quam creatori. qui est benedictus in secula etcet.
Catholicus: uituperat enim paulus illos quod relicto creatore benedicto. seruierunt potius creaturis eius inter quas conuenerat quadrupedia et serpentes et huiusmodi ergo ista sunt dei opera.
Patarenus: loquitur de creaturis diaboli.
Catholicus: Cum creator et creatura sint relatiua. et nulla fiat mentio hic nisi de creatore bono. et simpliciter de creatura addatur nec alius creator nominetur. reliquitur necessario quod de creatura nominati creatoris intelligatur. qui est deus benedictus.

Quod infernus est a deo

matt xxv discedite a me maledicti in ignem eternum qui paratus est diabolo et angelis eius etcet. si est preparatus diabolo et demonibus ignis eternus ergo ab aliquo sed autem a se aut a deo a se non est credendum ergo a deo.

uod omnes pene temporales et eterne et potestas puniendi sunt a deo et peccata fiunt non nisi deo permittente

matt iii paleas autem comburet igni inextinguibilem etcet. et xvi tunc reddit unicuique secundum opera sua etcet. item luca primo. Ego sum Gabriel qui asto ante deum et missus sum loqui ad et et hec tibi euangelizare

3:8) "For this purpose the Son of God appeared, that he might destroy the works of the devil."
Pat: He is speaking of birds and lilies in the heavens, that is, of the holy angels who are in heaven.

Cath: But hear what the Lord says about those birds (Mt 6:26) "Are not you of much more value than they?" Therefor those people had been called greater in merit than the angels, which is against your sect, who you say are holy by the same merit.
Also what He says of the lilies remained valid. (6:30) "If the grass of the field, which is today." Therefore the angels are today and tomorrow they will be cast into the oven, and of foods and of bodily clothing, see how plainly He speaks, saying (6:25) "Is not life more than food, and the body more than the clothing?" And later (6:32) "For your Father knows that you have need of all these things," and "all things shall be added unto you." Therefore be silent you indiscriminate beast.

That quadrupeds and serpents are from God

Romans 1 (1:23) "And they changed the glory of the incorruptible God into the likeness of the image of a corruptible man, and of birds, and of four-footed beasts, and of serpents," and later (1:25) "and served the creature rather than the Creator, who is blessed forever."
Cath: For Paul reproaches them since, having left the blessed creator, they rather worshipped His creation, among which were assembled quadrupeds and serpents and the like, therefore these are works of God.
Pat: He is speaking of the creations of the devil.
Cath: Since creator and creature are related terms, and no mention is made here except of the good creator, and of 'the creature' is simply added, neither is any other creator named, it necessarily remains that concerning 'the creature' it is understood of the creator, who has been named the blessed God.

That hell is from God

Matthew 25 (25:41) "Depart from me, you cursed, into everlasting fire which was prepared for the devil and his angels." If eternal fire is prepared for the devil and his demons, therefore it was prepared by someone, but either it is prepared by himself or by God, yet it is unbelievable that he prepared it himself, therefore it was prepared by God.

That all temporal and eternal punishments, and the power of punishing are from God, and that sins cannot exist unless they be permitted by God

Matthew 3 (3:12) "but the chaff he will burn with unquenchable fire." And 16 (16:27) "and then will he render to every man according to his works." Also Luke 1 (1:19–20) "I am Gabriel, who stands before God, and I am sent to speak to you, and to bring you these good tidings.

---

35 quanto…illius] Matt. 6:26. 40 Si…hodie¹] Matt. 6:30. 43 Nonne…44 uestimentum] Matt. 6:25. 44 scit…46 uobis] Matt. 6:32. I.11.2 et…4 serpentium] Rom. 1:23. 5 et…6 etcet] Rom. 1:25. I.12.2 discedite…3 eius] Matt. 25:41. I.13.4 paleas… inextinguibilem] Matt. 3:12. 5 tunc…sua] Matt. 16:27. 6 Ego…8 loqui] Luc. 1:19-20.

33 sanctis] santis P 37 eiusdem] eiusde P 41 mitterentur] micterentur P I.11.8 seruierunt] seruietur F

I.11.2 gloriam|fol. 8va P I.13.2 et|fol. 5r F 5 reddit|fol. 8vb P

et ecce eris tacens et non poteris loqui etcet. et xii ne terreamini ab hiis qui occidunt corpus et post hec non habent amplius quid faciant. ostendam autem uobis quem timeatis. timete eum qui postquam occiderit habet potestatem mittere in gehennam. etcet.

Et xvi deus autem non faciet uindictam electorum suorum clamantium ad se die ac nocte et patientiam habebit in illis. dico uobis quia cito faciet uindictam illorum etcet. et xvii quid faciet illis dominus uinee ueniet et perdet colonos istos etcet. Et in eodem uerumptamen inimicos meos illos qui noluerunt me regnare super se. adducite et interficite ante me etcet. et xviii quia dies ultionis hii sunt etcet.

Item Johannes viiii respondit ihesus neque hic peccatum neque parentes eius sed ut manifesentur opera dei in illo. etcet. Ergo deus fecit eum nasci cecum. Non enim deus fecissent ut manifestarentur opera dei. Simile dicit infirmitate et morte laçari.

Unde dominus dicit. x. infirmitas hec non est ad mortem. sed pro gloria dei ut glorificetur filius dei per eam etcet. Item ad romanos primo. Reuelatur enim ira dei de celo super omnem impietatem et iniustitiam etcet. Et in eodem propter quod tradidit illos deus in passiones ignominie etcet. et infra tradidit illos deus in reprobum sensum etcet. et .ii°. scimus enim quoniam iudicium dei est secundum ueritatem in eos qui talia agunt etcet. et infra thesauriças ubi iram in die irae justi judicii dei. quod reddit unicuique iusta opera ejus etcet. Et ibi his autem qui sunt ex contentione etcet. Ibi. ira et indignatio. tribulatio et angustia. inomnem animam operantis malum etcet. et xi uide ergo bonitatem et seueritatem dei etcet. et xii mihi uindicta et ego retribuam. Item ad corinthios x neque tentemus christum sicut quidam eorum tentauerunt. et a serpentibus perierunt etcet. Item ad galatas. penultimo qui autem sunt christi carnes suam crucifixerunt cum uitiis et concupiscentiis. etcet. Item iia ad thesalonicenses. i .in reuelatione domini nostri ihesu christi de celo cum angelis uirtutis ejus inflamma ignis dantis uindictam. his qui non nouerunt deum etcet. item ad hebreos xii quem enim diligit deus castigat etcet. Item i petri ii qui redent rationem ei qui paratus est iudicare uiuos et mortuos etcet. item iiª. v. si enim deus angelis peccantibus non pepercit usque ibi per totum hii iia etcet. Item uide iude comonere autem uos uolo etcet. item actus xii confestim autem percussit eum angelus domini etcet.

And behold, you will be dumb, and will not be able to speak." And 12 (12:4–5) "Do not be afraid of those who kill the body, and after that have no more that they can do. But I will show you whom you should fear. Fear him, who after he has killed, has power to cast into hell."

And 16 (18:7–8) "And will not God avenge his elect who cry to him day and night, and will he have patience in their regard? I say to you, that he will quickly avenge them." And 18 (20:15–16) "What therefore will the lord of the vineyard do to them? He will come, and will destroy these tenants." (19:27) "But as for those my enemies who would not have me reign over them, bring them here, and kill them before me." And 18 (21:22) "For these are the days of vengeance."

Also in John 9 (9:3) "Jesus answered, 'Neither has this man sinned, nor his parents, but that the works of God should be made manifest in him.'" So God made him to be born blind, for did not God do this that the works of God might be made plain? Similarly He speaks of sickness and of the death of Lazarus.

Whence the Lord says in 10 (11:4) "This sickness is not unto death, but for the glory of God, that the Son of God may be glorified by it." Also Romans 1 (1:18) "For the wrath of God is revealed from heaven against all ungodliness and injustice." And in the same (1:24) "Wherefore God gave them up to the desires of their heart, unto uncleanness," and later (1:28) "God delivered them up to a reprobate sense." And in 2 (2:2) "For we know that the judgment of God is according to truth, against those who do such things," and later (2:5–6) "You treasure up for yourself wrath, against the day of wrath, and revelation of the just judgment of God, who will render to every man according to his works." And there (2:8) "But to those who are contentious," there (2:8–9) "Tribulation and anguish upon every soul of a man who does evil." And 11 (11:22) "See then the goodness and the severity of God," and 12 (12:19) "Revenge is mine, I will repay." Also 1 Corinthians 10 (10:9) "Neither let us tempt Christ, as some of them tempted, and perished by the serpents." Also in the penultimate chapter of Galatians (5:24) "And those who are Christ's have crucified their flesh, with the vices and desires." Also 2 Thessalonians 1 (1:7–8) "the Lord Jesus shall be revealed from heaven, with the angels of his power, in a flame of fire, giving vengeance to those who do not know God." Also Hebrews 12 (12:6) "for he whom the Lord loves, he chastises." Also 1 Peter 2 (4:5) "Who shall render account to him, who is ready to judge the living and the dead." Also 2 Peter 5 (2:4) "For if God did not spare the angels that sinned," through the whole of the rest of the second chapter. Also see Jude (1:5) "I will therefore

---

8 ne...12 gehennam] Luc. 12:4-5 (hiis) his *Vulg.*) 13 deus...16 illorum] Luc. 18:7-8. 16 quid...17 istos] Luc. 20:15-16. 17 Et...19 me] Luc. 19:27. 20 quia...sunt] Luc. 21:22 (hii) hi *Vulg.*) 21 respondit...23 illo] Ioh. 9:3. 26 infirmitas...28 eam] Ioh. 11:4. 28 Reuelatur...29 iniustitiam] Rom. 1:18. 30 propter...31 ignominie] Rom. 1:24. 31 tradidit...32 sensum] Rom. 1:28. 32 scimus...34 agunt] Rom. 2:2. 34 thesauriças...35 ejus] Rom. 2:5-6 (ubi) tibi; iusta] add. secundum *Vulg.*) 36 his...contentione] Rom. 2:8 (his) iis *Vulg.*) 37 ira...38 malum] Rom. 2:8-9. 38 uide...39 dei] Rom. 11:22. 39 mihi...40 retribuam] Rom. 12:19. 40 neque...42 perierunt] 1 Cor. 10:9. 42 qui...44 concupiscentiis] Gal. 5:24 (carnes) carnem *Vulg.*) 44 in...47 deum] 1 Thes. 1:7-8 (his) iis *Vulg.*) 48 quem...castigat] Heb. 12:6. | qui...50 mortuos] 1 Pet. 4:5. 50 si...51 pepercit] 2 Pet. 2:4. 52 comonere...uolo] Iud. 1:5. 53 confestim...54 domini] Act. 12:23.

25 laçari]fol. 9ra P 46 inflamma]fol. 9rb P

Spiritualiter de potestate puniendi quod a deo sit et de permissione peccandi

Mattheus viii dixerunt demones si eicis nos hinc mitte nos in gregem porcorum. etcet. ergo non habuerunt potestatem intrandi in grege porcorum. nisi per licentiam et potestatem domini ihesu. item apocalypsis i habeo claues mortis et inferni. et iii hec dicit sanctus et uerus qui habet clauem dauid. qui aperit et et nemo claudit. claudit et nemo aperit. etcet. ergo nullo habet potestatem nisi per deum. item ix. et uidi stellam de caelo in terram cecidisse et data est illi clauis putei abissi etcet. ergo diabolo non habet a se clauem a potestatem male faciendi nisi detur ei. Sed si datur et data est non nisi a deo. Item romanos ultimo deus autem pacis conterat satanam sub pedibus uestris etcet. Item johannes xv. Non haberes potestatem aduersus me ullam. nisi tibi datum esset tibi desuper. Item Jacobi ultima. elias erat similis nobis passibilis et oratione orauit ut non plueret super terram et non pluit annos tres et menses vi. etcet. quod quidem non nisi a dei habuit. Cum in exemplum iusti orantis. introducat eum beatus jacobus. Item apocalypsis. xi hii habent potestatem claudendi ne pluat celum in diebus prophetie ipsorum. et potestatem habent super aquas multas conuertendi eas in sanguinem et percutere terram ab omni plaga quotienscumque uoluerint etcet. et infra. Et munera mittent inuicem quoniam hii duo prophete cruciauerunt eos etcet. Item actus xiii Et nunc ecce manus domini super te et eris cecus etcet.

Quod dampnati homines sunt a deo

Mattheus xii. Cum autem immundus spiritus exierit ab homine etcet. Ergo diabolus aliquando exit de homine in quem postea redit dampnosius. Sed cum exit aut naturali potestate quod esse non potest. aut potestate quem habet in homine ratione peccati. et sic aliquo tempore est homo sine peccato in quo diabolus postea intrans manet finaliter. ergo non fuit creatura diaboli sed dei. Si potuit esse sine peccato. Idem xviii ideo asimilatum est regnum celorum homini regi. qui uoluit rationem ponere cum seruis suis etcet. ibi oblatus est unicus etcet. de quo dicitur qui dominus tradidit eum tortoribus. et sic seruus dei dampnatus est quod non potest dici seruus dei nisi rationi creatoris.

14 That it speaks spiritually regarding the power of punishing, which is from God, and of the permission for sinning

Matthew 8 (8:31) "the devils spoke, saying, 'If you cast us out from here, send us into the herd of swine.'" Therefore they did not have the power of going into the herd of swine, save by the license and power of the Lord Jesus. Also Apocalypse 1 (1:18) "I have the keys of death and hell." And 3 (3:7) "Thus says the holy and true one, he who has the key of David, he who opens, and no man shuts, who shuts, and no man opens." Therefore no one has power, except by God. Also 9 (9:1) "and I saw a star fall from heaven upon the earth, and there was given to him the key of the bottomless pit." Therefore the devil does not have the key of the power of doing evil from himself, unless it were given to him. But if it is given — and it was given — it was not save but by God. Also Romans at the end (16:20) "And the God of peace crush Satan under your feet." Also John 15 (19:11) "You would have no power over me at all, were it not given to you from above." Also James (5:17) "Elijah was a man able to suffer like us, and with prayer he prayed that it might not rain upon the earth, and it did not rain for three years and six months." For he had nothing, except that it came from God, as in the example of the just man praying, when Blessed James introduces him. Also Apocalypse 11 (11:6) "These have power to shut heaven, so that it does not rain during the days of their prophecy, and they have power over waters to turn them into blood, and to strike the earth with all plagues as often as they wish," and earlier (11:10) "and they shall send gifts one to another, because these two prophets tormented them." Also Acts 13 (13:11) "And now behold, the hand of the Lord is upon you, and you will be blinded."

15 That damned men are from God

Matthew 12 (12:43) "And when an unclean spirit has gone out of a man." Therefore the devil sometimes goes out from men to whom he later returns more harmfully. But since when he goes out, it is either by natural power, which he cannot do, or by the power which he has over men by reason of sin, and so at some time man is without sin, in whom the devil, later going in, remains to the end. Therefore he was not a creature of the devil, but of God, if he was able to be without sin [at some time]. Also 18 (18:23) "Therefore is the kingdom of heaven like a king, who would take an account of his servants." And there, "one was brought to him." Regarding whom it is said that the lord handed him over to the torturers, and so the servant of God is damned, since he would not be able to

---

I.14.3 dixerunt...4 porcorum] Matt. 8:31.   7 habeo...inferni] Apoc. 1:18. | hec...9 aperit] Apoc. 3:7.   10 et...12 abissi] Apoc. 9:1.   14 deus...15 uestris] Rom. 16:20.   16 Non...17 desuper] Ioh. 19:11.   18 elias...20 vi] Iac. 5:17.   22 hii...26 uoluerint] Apoc. 11:6 (multas) om. *Vulg.*)   27 Et...28 eos] Apoc. 11:10.   28 Et...29 cecus] Apoc. 13:11.   I.15.2 Cum...3 homine] Matt. 12:43.   10 ideo...11 suis] Matt. 18:23.

I.14.3 mitte] micte *P*   27 mittent] mictent *P*   I.15.1 Quod...deo] Quod dampnati homines sunt a deo *F* | homines sunt] transp. *P*   4 dampnosius] dapnosius *P*   5 esse] esset *P*   13 dampnatus] dapnatus *P*

I.14.11 data|fol. 5v *F*   14 romanos|fol. 9va *P*   I.15.7 peccato|fol. 9vb *P*

Idem xxi homo erat paterfamilias qui plantauit uineam etcet. ubi loquitur de agricola domini qui fuerunt dampnati. idem xxv homo peregre proficiscens etcet. ubi loquitur de seruis domini quorum unus dampnatus est. Item lucam xiii arborem fici etcet. ad idem xviiii uocatis autem etcet. ibi de ore tuo te iudico serue nequam. Idem xii beatus ille seruus etcet. ibi ueniet dominus serui illius die qua non sperat et hora qua nescit et diuidet eum partemque eius cum infidelibus ponet etcet. ad idem item idem xvi de diuite qui uocauit abraham patrem etcet. ad idem item iohannem i sui eum non receperunt etcet. qui non erant sui per gratiam quia recepissent eum. igitur per naturam. addidit idem xv omnem palmitem non ferentem fructum tollet eum pater etcet. ad idem item ad romanos xi si enim deus naturalibus ramis non pepercit etcet. ad idem.

Quod diabolus est a deo

Lucam x. ait illis. uidebam sathanam sicut fulgur de celo cadentem etcet. ergo ante superbiam eius sunt erectus. quod non nisi secundum bonam naturam esse potuit et illa non potuit esse nisi a deo. Item iohannes ix in ueritate non stetit. quia sonat in ueritate non permansit. ergo. fuit in ea aliquando. igitur fuit a deo. quia omnis ueritas a deo est.

Quod corpora humana sunt a deo

Mattheus xviiii num legistis quod que fecit ab initio masculum et feminam fecit eos etcet. Et marcus x ab initio autem creatione masculum et feminam fecit eius deus. Item lucam iii. loquens adam dicit qui fuit dei etcet. Idem xii nunc uos pharisei quod deforis est calicis et catini mundatis. quod autem intus est uestrum plenum est rapina et iniquitate. Stulti nonne qui fecit quod deforis est etiam id quod intus est fecit etcet. idem xii quis autem uestrum potest addicere ad staturam suam cubitum unum etcet. item ad romanos vi sed neque exibeatis membra uestra arma iniquitatis peccato. sed exibete uos deo tanquam ex mortuis uiuentes et membra uestra arma iustitie deo etcet. Et infra sicut enim exibuistis membra uestra seruire imunditie et iniquitati ad iniquitatem ita nunc exhibete etcet. et viiii numquid dicit figmentum ei qui se finxit. quid me fecisti. an non habet potestatem figulus luti ex eadem massa facere aliud quidem uas in

be called the servant of God, except by reason of being a creature. The same in 21 (21:33) "There was a householder who planted a vineyard." Here it speaks of the farmer of the Lord, who was damned. Also 25 (25:14) "For even as a man going into a far country," where it speaks of the servants of the Lord, of whom one was damned. Also Luke 13 (13:6) "a fig tree" and the same (19:13) "and calling." Here (19:22) "out of your own mouth, I judge you, wicked servant." Also 12 (12:43, 46) "blessed is the servant," and there "The lord of that servant will come in the day that he does not expect, and at the hour that he does not know, and shall separate him, and shall appoint him his portion with unbelievers." Also the same in 16 (16:23) of the rich man who called upon father Abraham. Also John 1 (1:11) "and his own did not receive him." Which ones were not by his grace, since they received him, therefore by nature. Also 15 adds (15:2) "Every branch in me, that does not bear fruit, the Father will take away." It is the same in Romans 11 (11:21) "For if God has not spared the natural branches."

That the devil is from God

Luke 10 (10:18) "And he said to them, 'I saw Satan like lightning falling from heaven.'" Therefore in view of their pride they were raised up, and this would not be possible except in relation to a good nature, and this was not able to be given except by God. Also John 9 (8:44) "he did not stand in truth." Since this denotes that he did not remain in the truth, therefore it was in him at some point, therefore he was from God, since all truth is from God.

That human bodies are from God

Matthew 19 (19:4) "have you not read that from the beginning he made them male and female." And Mark 10 (10:6) "yet from the beginning of creation God made them male and female." Also Luke 3 (3:38) saying "Adam who was from God." Also 12 (11:39–40) "Now you Pharisees clean the outside of the cup and of the platter, but inside you are full of rapine and iniquity. Fools! Did not he who made what is outside, also make what is within?" The same 12 (12:25) "Yet which of you is able to add a single cubit to your height." Also Romans 6 (6:13) "Neither yield your members as instruments of iniquity for sin, but present yourselves to God, like those who are alive from the dead, and your members as instruments of justice to God." And later (6:19) "For as you have yielded your members to serve uncleanness and iniquity, for iniquity, so now yield." And 9 (9:20–21) "Will the thing formed say to he who formed it, 'why did you make me thus?' Or does the potter not have power over the clay, of the same lump, to make one vessel unto honor, and another unto dishonor?" Also 1

---

15 homo...uineam] Matt. 21:33.   17 homo...proficiscens] Matt. 25:14.   19 arborem fici] Luc. 13:6.   20 uocatis autem] Ioh. 19:13.   de...21 nequam] Ioh. 19:22.   21 beatus...seruus] Ioh. 12:43. | ueniet...24 ponet] Ioh. 12:46.   24 de...25 patrem] Ioh. 16:23.   26 sui¹...receperunt] Ioh. 1:11.   28 omnem...29 pater] Ioh. 15:2.   29 si...30 pepercit] Rom. 11:21.   I.16.2 ait...3 cadentem] Luc. 10:18.   6 in¹...stetit] Ioh. 8:44.   I.17.2 num...3 eos] Matt. 19:4.   3 ab...5 deus] Mar. 10:6.   5 loquens...dei] Luc. 3:38.   6 nunc... 9 fecit²] Luc. 11:39-40.   10 quis...11 unum] Luc. 12:25.   12 sed...14 deo] Rom. 6:13.   15 sicut...17 exhibete] Rom. 6:19.   17 numquid...20 contumeliam] Rom. 9:20-21.

16 agricola] add. qui F   18 dampna-tus...19 est] dampnatur F   I.16.4 secundum] om. P, but add. al man. sin.   I.17.14 iustitie deo] iustitie F but effaced.

28 fructum|fol. 10ra P   I.17.6 deforis|fol. 6r F   11 romanos...12 vi|fol. 10rb P

honorem aliud uero in contumeliam etcet. Item prima ad corinthios iii Nescitis quia templum dei estis uos. et spiritus dei habitat in uobis etcet. et vi corpus autem non fornicationi sed domino etcet. Et in eodem nescitis quoniam corpora uestra membra sunt christi. tollens ergo membra christi fatiam membra meretricis. absit. etcet. Et infra. Omne enim peccatum quodcumque fecerit homo extra corpus est. qui autem fornicatur in corpus suum peccat etcet. et infra. An nescitis quia corpora uestra templum est spiritus sancti quem habetis a deo et non estis uestri etcet. Empti enim estis pretio magno. glorificate et portate deum in corpore uestro etcet. idem xi. uir quidem non debet uelare caput suum quoniam ymago et gloria Dei est etcet. et infra nam sicut mulier de uiro. ita uir per mulierem. omnia ex deo etcet. et infra. decet mulierem non uelatam orare deum. Nec ipsa natura docet uos etcet. Et xii multo magis que uidentur membra infirmiora esse corporis. necessariora sunt et que putamus ignobiliora esse membra his honorem habundantiorem circumdamus. Et que inhonesta sunt nostra habundantiorem honestatem habent. etcet. Et infra sed deus temperauit corpus. ei cui deerat habundantiorem tribuendo. honestatem. ut non sit sisma in corpore. sed in idipsum pro inuicem sollicita etcet. item actus xvii fecitque ex uno omne genus hominum habitare super uniuersam faciem terre etcet.

Ex istis auctoritatibus probatur vii modis quod deus fecit corpora humana. primus est quia ponitur quod deus fecit masculum et feminam. quod non nisi ratione corporis potest intelligi. secundus est quia dicitur quod nullus potest addere ad staturam corporis quicumquam nisi ille qui uestit lilia. qui legitur ibi pater celestis. tertius quia traditur quod corpora que primus exibuimus peccato debemus et possimus exibere deo. in sanctificatione bonorum operum. Quartus legitur quod spiritus sanctus habitat in corporibus nostris quod numquam esset si essent opera diaboli. propter hoc quod probatum est supra in rationibus naturalibus quod nulla est coniunctuo regni dei ad regnum diaboli. et quia dominus dicit mattheus viii neque mittunt uinum nouum in utres ueteres etcet. Quintus quia inuenitur quod corpora quedam sint bona quedam mala. et dicitur quod idem fecit hic et illa. sed diabolus non posset facere bona. ergo deus fecit utraque. et nota quod dico mala esse corpora quorumdam non ex natura creationis. sed ex accidenti

Corinthians 3 (3:16) "Do you not know that you are the temple of God and that the Spirit of God lives in you?" And 6 (6:13) "but the body is not for fornication, but for the Lord." And in the same (6:15) "Do you not know that your bodies are the members of Christ? Shall I then take the members of Christ, and make them the members of a harlot? God forbid." And later (6:18) "For every sin that a man does, is without the body, but he who commits fornication, sins against his own body." And later (6:19) "Or do you not know, that your bodies are the temple of the Holy Spirit, who is in you, whom you have from God, and you are not your own?" (6:20) "For you are bought with a great price. Glorify and bear God in your body." The same in 11 (11:7) "The man indeed should not cover his head, because he is the image and glory of God." And later (11:12) "For as the woman is of the man, so also is the man by the woman, but all things of God." And later (11:13–14) "Is it proper for a woman to pray to God uncovered? Does not even nature itself teach you." And 12 (12:22–23) "Yes, much more those that seem to be the more feeble members of the body, are more necessary, and those we think to be the less honorable members of the body, about these we put more abundant honor, and those that are our shameful parts, have more abundant dignity." And later (12:24–25) "but God has assembled the body together, giving to that which wanted the more abundant honor, that there might be no schism in the body, but the members might be mutually careful for one another." Also Acts 17 (17:26) "And he has made of one, all mankind, to dwell upon the whole face of the earth."

From these authorities one can prove in seven ways that God made the human body. The first is that it is proposed that God made male and female. This cannot be understood except in relation to the body. The second is that it is said that no one can add anything to the stature of his body, except He who clothes the lilies, who is read there to be the heavenly Father. The third since it is handed down that the bodies which we first present for sin, we ought, and are able to, hand them over to God for the sanctification of good works. Fourthly, it is read that the Holy Spirit dwells in our bodies, which would never be possible were they the work of the devil, on account of what was proven above by natural arguments that there is no joining of the kingdom of God with the kingdom of the devil, and that the Lord says in Matthew 8 (9:17) "neither put new wine in old skins." Fifthly, it is found that certain bodies are good, certain ones evil, and it is said that the same one does this and that. But the devil cannot do good, therefore God made them both, and mark that I call certain bodies evil, not on account of the nature of [their] creation, but on account of the accidents of sin. The

---

21 Nescitis…22 uobis] 1 Cor. 3:16.   22 corpus…23 domino] 1 Cor. 6:13.   24 nescitis…26 absit] 1 Cor. 6:15 (fatiam] faciam *Vulg.*)   26 Omne…28 peccat] 1 Cor. 6:18.   28 An…30 uestri] 1 Cor. 6:19 (quia corpora] quoniam membra | est] sunt *Vulg.*)   30 Empti…32 uestro] 1 Cor. 6:20.   32 uir…33 est] 1 Cor. 11:7.   34 nam…35 deo] 1 Cor. 11:12.   35 decet…36 uos] 1 Cor. 11:13-14.   37 multo…41 habent] 1 Cor. 12:22-23.   41 sed…44 sollicita] 1 Cor. 12:24-25 (honestatem] honorem *Vulg.*)   45 fecitque…46 terre] Act. 17:26 (habitare] inhabitare *Vulg.*)   61 neque…ueteres] Matt. 9:17.

47 vii] vi F   51 addere] adicere F | staturam] statura P   57 essent] esset P   61 mittunt] mictunt P

32 non|fol. 10va P   54 exi-bere|fol. 10vb P

peccati. Sextus quia inuenitur quod uir et mulier secundum modum et formam corporis. secundum quod unus est dignior alio. et secundum quod datur secundum apostolo preceptum dicit uelando mulieri et de non uelando uiro sunt a deo. Septimus est et expressissimus quia legitur quod deus temparauit corpus secundum uarietatem membrorum.
Patarenus: Respondeo loquuntur predictam auctoritates dicit corporibus que sunt in celo prostrata.
Catholicus: Sed apostolus dicit supra de istius corporibus de quibus loquitur ita nunc exibete etcet. Illa namque non possunt exiberi nunc ad opera bona. Si sunt aliqua corpora ibi quod falsum est. ergo de istis loquitur que hic gestamus. Item dicit de illis quia sunt nunc templum spiritus sancti. igitur de istius loquitur.

Quod angeli et mundus et anima non sunt eterna nisi deus tantum

iohannes xiiii clarifica me pater apud temetipsum claritate quam habui priusquam mundus esset etcet. et infra. quia dilexisti me ante constitutionem mundi etcet. Ergo mundus non est eternus. Item ad romanos ultimo secundum preceptum eterni dei etcet. ergo solus unus deus est eternus et omnia alia sunt temporalia ad idem est quod legitur apostolo i ad corinthios iii loquimur dei sapientiam in misterio que predestinauit deus ante secula etcet. Et ad ephesios i sicut elegit nos in ipso ante mundi constitutionem etcet. Item ad titum i quam promisit qui non mentitur deus ante tempora secularia etcet. Item prima petri i ihesu christi precogniti quidem ante constitutionem mundi etcet. Ecce quam aperte habemus in istis quod mundus non est eternus. De angelis uero quod non eternum et de omnibus aliis rebus. nisi solus deus. dicit apostolus ad colosenses. i quoniam in ipso condita sunt uniuersa in celis et in terra. uisibilia et inuisibilia siue thronum. siue dominationes. siue principatus siue potestates omnia per ipsum et in ipso creata sunt et ipse est ante omnes et omnia in ipso exstant etcet. Et infra qui est principium etcet. Item ad romanos ultimo secundum preceptum eterni dei etcet. ergo solus deus est eternus et creator omnium.

De omnipotentia dei

mattheus xi omnia mihi tradita sunt a patre meo etcet. Idem xxviii apud deum omnia possibilia sunt etcet. Idem xxiii. data est mihi omnis potestas in celo et in terra etcet. Item marcum iii dicit forti quod alligauit forte etcet. et xiii. abba pater omnia possibilia tibi sunt

sixth is that it is found that there are men and women according to type and form of the body, but one is more dignified than the other, and according to the command given by the Apostle, he says that women are to be veiled, and that men are not to be veiled is a precept from the Lord. The seventh is most clear, that it is read that God assembled the body according to the variety of members.
Pat: I reply that the foregoing authorities speak of bodies which are prostrate in heaven.
Cath: But the Apostle speaks above regarding these bodies, of which he says "so now yield." For those are not able to be given over now to good works. If there are other bodies there, that is false. Therefore he is speaking of those which we bear here. Also he says of them that they are now the temples of the Holy Spirit, therefore he is speaking of these here.

That angels, the world, and souls are not eternal, but only God

John 14 (17:5) "glorify me, O Father, with yourself, with the glory which I had before the world was." Later (17:24) "because you have loved me before the creation of the world." Therefore the world is not eternal. Also at the end of Romans (16:26) "according to the command of the eternal God." Therefore the one God alone is eternal, and all other things are temporal, the same is read in the Apostle, in 1 Corinthians 3 (2:7) "but we speak the wisdom of God in a mystery, which God ordained before the world." And to the Ephesians 1 (1:4) "As he chose us in him before the foundation of the world." Also Titus 1 (1:2) "which God, who does not lie, has promised before the ages of the world." Also 1 Peter 1 (1:20) "Jesus Christ, foreknown indeed before the foundation of the world." See how plainly we have it in these passages that the world is not eternal. Also that the angels are not eternal, along with all other things, except God alone. The Apostle says in Colossians 1 (1:16–17) "For in him all things were created in heaven and on earth, visible and invisible, whether thrones, or dominations, or principalities, or powers, all things were created by him and in him, and he is before all, and by him all things exist." And later (1:18) "who is the beginning." Also Romans, at the end (16:26) "according to the command of the eternal God." Therefore God alone is eternal and the creator of all things.

On the omnipotence of God

Matthew 11 (11:27) "All things are delivered to me by the Father." The same in 19 (19:26) "With God all things are possible." The same in 28 (28:18) "All power on heaven and on earth is given to me." Also Mark 3 (3:27 paraphrase) He says "unless he first bind the strong man,"

etcet. item ad romanos x nam idem dominus omnium etcet. et xiiii scriptum est enim uiuo ego dicit dominus quoniam mihi flectetur omne genu et omnis lingua confitebitur deo etcet. Item ad philipenses iii. in finem secundum operationem qua potest etiam subicere sibi omnia. etcet. Item ad ephesios iiii unus deus etcet. Item i ad timotheos i Regi autem seculorum etcet. Et ultimo beatus et solus potens rex regum etcet. Item apocalypsis xviiii quoniam regnauit dominus deus noster omnipotens etcet. Et infra calcat torcular uini furoris dei omnipotentis etcet. Et xx. apprehendit draconem. Igitur deus est omnipotens etiam super diabolum. Mentimini ergo uos patareni quod dicitis quod ipse non potest omnia. de quibus prouidit beatus petrus dicens ii^a ii dominationem contemnunt etcet. et iudas i dominatio nem autem spernunt etcet. Constat enim quod vos estis soli inter omnes homines dicit mundo. Qui negatis deum omnipotentem esse et eum facitis medipotentem. dantes et attribuentes ex magne parte damnationem suam diabolo. Non recordantes scripture sancte dicentes quod heresiarcha uester diabolus eiectus est de celo in tartarum eternum cruciandus. eo quod deo omnipotenti partem demonii auferre curauit. cui non minus estis similes quam angeli facti demones qui in hoc ille sceleri consenserunt.

and 13 (14:36) "Abba, Father, all things are possible to you." Also Romans 10 (10:12) "for the same is Lord of all." And 14 (14:11) "For it is written, 'As I live, says the Lord, every knee shall bow to me, and every tongue shall confess to God.'" Also Philippians, at the end (3:21) "according to the work by which also he is able to subdue all things unto himself." Also Ephesians 4 (4:6) "one God." Also 1 Timothy 1 (1:17) "Now to the king of ages," and at the end (6:15) "the blessed and only mighty, the King of kings, and Lord of lords." Also Apocalypse 19 (19:6) "for the Lord our God the Almighty has reigned." And later (19:15) "and he treads the winepress of the fierceness of the wrath of Almighty God." And 20 (20:2) "and he laid hold of the dragon." Therefore God is omnipotent, even over the devil. You Patarenes lie then when you say that He is not able to do all things, of which Blessed Peter foresaw, saying in his second epistle (2:10) "they despise government," and Jude 1 (1:8) "they despise dominion." For it is obvious that you are alone — among all men in the world — who deny God to be omnipotent, and made Him only half-powerful, giving and attributing the greater part of His damnation to the devil, not remembering Holy Scripture saying that your heresiarch the devil was cast out of heaven into the depths, in order that he might suffer eternally, because he caused part of the demons to be cut off from almighty God, to whom you are made similar like angels turned demonic, since they consented to this crime.

Quod diabolus est deus et creator et factor omnium uisibilium et quorumdam spirituum uel secundum quosdam quod est tantum factor uel secundum alios quod omnia sunt eterna in sui natura et quod ipse est omnipotens in regno suo

Intendit patarenus probare per naturales rationes et per scripturas quod duo sint principia et primo per rationes naturales.

Probatio per rationes naturales

Qualis est causa talis est effectus et econtrario. sed deus bonus est inuariabilis incorumptibilis pulcherimus et huiusmodi. temporalia que sunt uariabilia et corruptibilia et plerumque ualde turpia et deforma non sunt ab eo. igitur ab alio qui est diabolus. ergo sunt duo principia. unum bonorum et aliud malorum.

II. That the devil is the creator and fashioner of all visible things, and of certain spirits,[1] or, according to some, that he is only the fashioner,[2] or, according to others, that all things are eternal by their nature and that he is all powerful in his kingdom

The Patarene intends to prove by natural reasons and by the scriptures that there are two principles, and he will proceed firstly by natural arguments.

2. Proof by natural arguments

As is the cause, such is the effect, and vice versa. But the Good God is invariable, incorruptible, and most beautiful, and the like. Those temporal things are variable and corruptible, and all are greatly full of baseness and deformity, and are not from Him. Therefore they are from

---

7 nam…omnium] Rom. 10:12.   8 scriptum…10 deo] Rom. 14:11.   11 secundum…12 omnia] Php. 3:21 (potest) possit *Vulg.*)
12 unus deus] Eph. 4:6.   13 Regi…seculorum] 1 Tim. 1:17.   14 beatus…regum] 1 Tim. 6:15.   15 quoniam…16 omnipotens] Apoc. 19:6.   16 calcat…17 omnipotentis] Apoc. 19:15.   17 apprehendit…18 draconem] Apoc. 20:2.   21 dominationem contemnunt] 2 Pet. 2:10.   22 dominatio…spernunt] Iud. 1:8.

---

10 philipenses] ephesios *F*   23 vos] om. *P* | soli] add. vos. *P* | inter] om. *F* with space left for word.   27 dicentes] dicentis *P*
30 facti…31 demones] om. *P*   II.2.4 que] om. *F*   7 unum…malorum] transp. *F*

I.19.18 draconem|fol. 11va *P*   30 angeli|fol. 7r *F*   II.2.3 inuariabilis|fol. 11vb *P*

---

1) The absolute dualism preached by the Albanenses, see Moneta, 3; Sacconi, c. 16–17. | 2) Mitigated dualism attributed to the Concorezzans or the Garatenses, see Moneta, 5, 109; Sacconi, c. 24–25.

Catholicus: Respondeo. Regula illa locum habet in causis necessariis et que sunt coniuncte suis effectibus ut in igne et calore. Ignis enim calidus est et calor qui est eius effectus habet calefacere. Et de huiusmodi inuenit in exempla multa. sed secus est in causis uoluntariis que non sunt coniuncte suis effectibus. ut in creatore et creaturis. Item locum haberet regula illa in hac parte si temporalia essent de substantia dei. Quia quicquid de deo est. deus est. Sed nullla creature est de deo sed a deo. quod aliud est. uerbi gratia. domus ista tota est de ligno. tunc sine dubio. quicquid de domo est lignum est. sed non sequitur quod quicquid a domo est uel procedit lignum sit. immo potest esse ferrum lapis fumus a huiusmodi. Sed nunc responde mihi de tua phylosophya angeli qui cediderunt sunt uariati et corrupti. ergo non sunt a deo. quod est contra tua secta. Item sancti uiri uariantur et corrumpuntur per multas passiones. ergo non sunt a deo. preterea termpoalia transeunt sed cum effectus sic talis sicut causa prout phylosophyzas et ista sint a diabolo. secundum tuum errorem. ergo diabolus transibit et desinet esse. quid tibi uidetur.

Patarenus: Item contrariorum contraria sunt principia sed mundus est contrarius uiris sanctis. Sicut dicit domunus in iohanne xiiii si mundus uos odit etcet. et illi sunt a deo. ergo mundus est a contrario principio quod est diabolus. ad hoc facit quod dicit jacobus iii Numquid fons de eodem foramine emanat dulcem et amaram aquam.

Catholicus: Respondeo quia falsa est illa regula. qui bona et mala sunt contraria tamen procedunt ex eodem corde. Nec obstat illud Jacobi numquid fons etcet. Quia sicut intelligitur numquid fons emanat etcet. id ist inconueniens est ut lingua quam fontem appellat dicat bona et mala. sed licet sit inconueniens est tamen. Vnde subdit in ipsa benedicimus deum et patrem et in ipsa maledicimus etcet.

Item uita et mors sunt contraria. et tamen ab uno principio procedunt id est a deo. a quo procedere omnia probatum est. efficaciter superius.

Vel forte locum habet regula illa in naturis causatis et eorum effectibus. quia si effectus sunt contrarii et eorum cause sunt contrarie. Sicut dulce et amarum et hiis similia. Sed modo responde mihi de tua obiectio-

another who is the devil. Therefore there are two principles, one for good things and another for evil things.
Cath: I respond. That rule holds in necessary causes which are conjoined to their effects, as in fire and heat. For fire is hot and heat, which is its effect has [the power of] making warm. And one finds similar things in many examples. But it is otherwise in voluntary causes which are not joined to their effects, as in creator and creature. Further this rule holds in this part: if temporal things might be of the substance of God, for whatever is of God, is God. But no creature is of God, but rather from God, which is another thing. For example, this house is wholly made of wood, then without a doubt whatever is of the house is wood, but it does not follow that whatsoever is from a house or comes out of it, should be wood. It might yet be iron, or stone, smoke or the like. But now tell me about your philosophy. The angels who fell are changed and corrupted. Therefore they are not from God, which is contrary to your sect. Further, holy men change and become corrupted by many passions, so they are not from God. Further temporal things pass away, but since the effect is thus like the cause, as you philosophize, and so they are from the devil according to your error, therefore the devil shall pass away and cease to be. What do you think?

Pat: The principles of contrary things are contrary,[1] but the world is contrary to holy men, as the Lord says in John 14 (15:18) "if the world hates you," and these are of God, therefore the world is from another principle, which is the devil. This is established when James says in chapter 3 (3:11) "Does a fountain send forth sweet and bitter water out of the same hole?"

Cath: I reply that this standard is false, that good and evil are opposites, yet proceed from the same heart. Neither does that passage in James oppose this (3:11) "Does a fountain." For one should interpret "Does a fountain send forth," that is, it is unsuitable that the tongue, which is called "fountain," might say good and evil, but although it may be incongruous, yet it is true nevertheless, whence he adds (3:9) "By it we bless God and the Father and by it we curse men."

Also life and death are opposites and yet they come forth from one principle, that is, from God, from whom it is proven effectively from the foregoing arguments that all things come forth.

Or perhaps that rule holds in the natures of the causes and of their effects, since if their effects are contrary, their causes are contrary, for example sweet and bitter and the like. But how will you respond to me regarding your

---

II.2.32 si…odit] Ioh. 15:8.   35 Numquid…36 aquam] Iac. 3:11.   39 numquid fons] Iac. 3:11.   43 in…44 maledicimus] Iac. 3:9.

12 inuenit] sunt *F*   22 angeli] singuli *F*   38 contraria] om. *P*   40 fons] om. *F*   48 naturis causatis] om. *F*. add. veteris creaturis   50 sunt contrarie] transp. *F*

21 nunc|fol. 12ra *P*   42 inconueniens|fol. 12rb *P*

---

1) Aristotle, also cited in Moneta, 23. Also cited by St. Albert, and St. Thomas in his commentary on the *Physics*, 1.10. Moneta says the Cathars used this as a philosophical defense of dualism.

ne. Si tua regula uera est. Cum infinita sint contraria infinita sunt principia. quodam fatuissimum est dicere.

Item in eadem re duo contraria simul et semel esse non possunt. Sed cum peccatum sit in malo homine natura qua est non est contraria peccato. igitur mala est et sic a malo principio.
Catholicus: Respondeo quod peccatum non est directe contrarium nature. quia non per se pugnat sed per ipsam naturam.
Illa regula locum habet in hiis que per se pugnant ad inuicem. Vel dicam quod peccatum non est aliquid substantiale et illa regula locum habet in contrariis substantiis.
Sed modo responde mihi. angeli qui ceciderunt fuerunt creature dei peccauerunt. ergo fuerint in eis simul et semel duo contraria esse contra tuam positionem.

Patarenus: Item peccatum est sed non potest esse a deo uel a bona creatura neque a creatura mala quia eodem modo illa creatura mala processit ab alia re. mala et cum in infinitum non possit procedi. patet quod processit ab eterno principio mali qui est diabolus.
Catholicus: Respondeo quod peccatum processit a libero arbitrio angelorum et hominum et ex defectu gratie.
Patarenus: Ergo malum fuit angelis et hominibus liberum arbitrium si per eum peccauerunt. et mali etiam fuerunt in sui creatione si caruerunt gratiam per quam possent mereri et bene facere.
Catholicus: Dico quod liberum arbitrium fuit angelis et hominibus bonum quia per eum poterunt stare in statu innocentie et per eum cum gratia qua custodisset illos deus poterant mereri. Nec dicuntur mali propter hoc quod non habuissent gratiam merendi sed potius boni quia ipsi habebant naturalia bona. Exemplum de pulcro equo qui non potest duci conuenienter sine sella et freno et tamen non est propter hoc turpis in sui natura.

Patarenus: Sed quare non creauit eos deus ita ut non peccare potuissent.
Catholicus: Respondeo propter tria. unum fuit ut lucerent in angelis et hominibus uie deitatis que sunt iustitia et misericordia. iuxta illud Dauid uniuerse uie domini misericordia et ueritas. Nam in opere magister relucet. iustitia enim dei non poterat apparere si ex coactione necesse fuisset deo seruire. misericordia uero dei in illis apparet quando dat eis de primo ultra condignum. Secundum fuit quia deus non uult coacta seruitia quod esset nisi habuisset liberum arbitrium. Deus enim est summe bonus et maior est bonitas

objection, if your standard is true. Since the principles are infinite, there are contrary infinities, something which is most foolish to claim.
Further there are two contraries in the same thing, together at the same time, which is not possible. But since sin is in a bad man, which is by nature, the contrary of sin does not exist, therefore he is evil and so from an evil principle.
Cath: I reply that sin is not directly contrary to nature, for it does not struggle against itself, but through its nature.

That rule holds for those things which struggle against themselves towards each other. Or I might say that sin is not a substance, and that rule holds in contrary substances.

But how will you reply concerning the angels who fell? They were creatures of God and sinned. Therefore there were in them two contraries at the same time, which is against your position.
Pat: Also sin exists but cannot be either from God or from a good creature, nor from an evil creature since in the same way an evil creature would proceed from another evil thing, and since one cannot regress to infinity it is clear that it processes from an eternal evil principle, which is the devil.
Cath: I reply that sin proceeds from the free will of angels and men, and on account of an absence of grace.

Pat: Then the free will of the angels and men was evil, if through it they sinned, and they were evil in their creation if they lacked grace through which they would be able to merit and to do good.
Cath: I say that the free will of the angels and men was good, since through it they were able to remain in their condition of innocence, and through which, with the grace by which God kept them, they were able to gain merit. Nor are they called 'evil' on account of this, since they might not have had the grace for meriting, but rather 'good' since they had natural goodness. For example, of a fine horse which cannot be easily led without a bridle and saddle, and yet it is not, on that account, ignoble in its nature.
Pat: But why did not God create them so they could not sin?
Cath: I reply in three ways. One was that the ways of God might shine before angels and men, which are justice and mercy, according to David (Ps 24:10) "All the ways of the Lord are mercy and truth." For in works the master is reflected. The justice of God cannot be revealed if it was necessary to force them to serve God. For the mercy of God is revealed in them when He first gave them beyond what was proper. The second is that God does not want coerced slaves, which one would be unless one had free will. For God is good in the highest degree and it is a

---

93 uniuerse...94 ueritas] Ps. 24:10.

58 Catholicus] om. *F* 60 ipsam] ipsa *P* 67 contra] om. *P* 71 possit] om. *P* add. *al. man. marg. dex.* 86 pulcro] pultro *P* (probably from vernacular for 'foal', *puledro*) 89 Patarenus] om. *P* 90 potuissent] possent *F* 96 coactione] necessitate *F* | fuisset] fui esset *P* 98 condignum] quam dignum *F*

59 pugnat|fol. 7v *F* 64 substantiis|fol. 12va *P* 87 turpis|fol. 12vb *P*

uoluntarie uelle seruire et amari quam coacte. Tertium est quia non fuissent ita elegantes si essent serui et non liberi. quid esset si liberum arbitrium non habuisset.

Patarenus: Sed cur fecisset eos deus si sciuisset eos peccatores et dampnandos. Non uidetur uerisimile. Cum ipse sit summe bonus et misericors. qui non letatur in perditione impiorum. Sed omnes uult saluos fieri et ad agnitionem ueritatis uenire sicut dicit apostolus prima ad timotheum ii[a].

Catholicus: Respondeo propter tres rationes. prima est propter semetipsum id est propter suam bonitatem propter quam uoluit illos facere uero participare illa si uellent. Quod et facere potuissent nisi per eos remansissent. Queris enim heretice stulte quare deus non dimisit bonitatem suam propter timorem illorum quod futuros esse malos preuidit. bonitas enim dei est et gloriam suam cum suis creaturis participare. quod esse non poterat nisi prius essent creature. et bonos et malos equali potentia. et equali conditione creata et equali natura capaces sunt ad gloriam dei participandam et quod mali non participant illa. non est ex defectu creationis diuine sed ex illorum nequitia stulta. Eadem est ergo bonitas dei in creatione malorum que et in creatione bonorum est. Secunda ratio est propter illos ut haberent bonum eternum quidam habere potuerent si uoluerunt. per id quod deus dederat eis et dare uolebat si ab eo uoluntarie non recesissent. Tertia est quia prosunt bonis et etiam in eis puniendis laudatur deus. propter iustitiam eius que apparet in peccatis iudicandis illorum. nec propter hic uidetur deus malus. uel imisericors. quia prescit peccatores quos aliquando creata. quia illa scientia non importat necessitatem peccati et dampnationis sicut scientia medici non infert necessitatem moriendi infirmis. propter hoc quod ex peritia artis uideat eos morituros. Quantum enim in se est deus saluat omnes et equali bonitate. licet plurimi non saluentur quia nolunt.

Probatio per scripturas

Propositum suum intendit patarenus probare hoc modo. primo inducit scripturas que uidentur dicere de diaboli eternitate. Secundo de ipsius diuinitate. tertio de illius creatione uel factione. quarto inducat illas que uidentur sonare quod ipse sit dominus uel omnipotens in regno suo. ut ecce.

greater goodness to wish to serve and love voluntarily, [which is] something bitter when coerced. The third is that they would not have been so refined if they had been slaves and not free men, which is what they would have been had they not had free will.

Pat: But why did God make them if He knew they would be sinners and damned? It does not seem likely, since He is good in the highest degree and merciful, who does not rejoice in the loss of the wicked. But (1 Tim. 2:4) "he wishes all to be saved and to come to the knowledge of the truth," as the Apostle says to Timothy

Cath: I respond with three arguments. The first is on account of He Himself, that is, on account of His goodness by which He wished to make them truly partake in it [His goodness], if they wished, which also they could have done unless they had remained [good] by their own power. For you ask, O foolish heretic, why God did not abandon His goodness on account of the fear of those that He foresaw would be evil in the future. For the goodness of God is to share His glory with His creatures, which could not have been unless creatures had first existed and had an equal power for both good and evil, and in equality of created condition, and natural equality of capacity for participation in the glory of God. That evil men do not participate in it is not on account of a defect in divine creation, but on account of their own foolish iniquity. The goodness of God then is the same in the creation of evil men as in the creation of the good. The second argument is on account of those that they might have eternal good, which they could have if they wished it, through that which God gave to them and wished to give if they had not voluntarily withdrawn from it. The third is that they benefit the good, for also by their punishments God is praised on account of His justice, which is manifested in seeing their sins judged. Nor on account of this does it seem that God is evil or unmerciful, for He preknew sinners which He had created at some point, since that knowledge does not impose necessity to sin and damnation, just as the knowledge of physicians does not impel the necessity for the death of the sick, but on account of their skill in the art they simply see them on the edge of death. For as much as God in Himself might save all men, and in equality of goodness, yet many are not saved, since they refuse to be.

Proof from the scriptures

The Patarene intends to prove his supposition in this way, first he will adduce scriptures which seem to speak of the eternity of the devil. Secondly, those that imply his divinity. Thirdly, those which imply his creation or making of things. Fourthly he will adduce those which seem to say that he is Lord or all powerful in his kingdom. To wit.

---

107 omnes... 108 uenire] 1 Tim. 2:4.

118 essent] esset *P* 131 prescit] presit *F* 137 plurimi non saluentur quia nolunt] plurimi saluentur quia volunt *F*

108 agnitionem|fol. 13ra *P* 123 in|fol. 8r *F* 127 recesissent|fol. 13rb *P*

Quod diabolus est eternus

Ezechiel xxxv hec dicit dominus deus. ecce ego ad te mons seyr. ibi eo quod fueris inimicus sempiternus. sed per seyr intelligitur diabolus qui est sempiternus quod sonat semper eternus ergo est eternus. Simile ad romanos i sempiterna quoque eius uirtus et diuinitas etcet.

Catholicus: Respondeo non est uerum quod seyr sit diabolus. immo erat quidam mons ubi erant milite gentes ydumeorum et semper male fuerant cum filiis israel. et in suis angustiis male tractauerant illos et ideo deus minatur illius dextructionem in uindictam. Vnde subdit ibi. urbes tuas demoliar etcet. Et postea faciam iuxta iram tuam et secundum zelum tuum quem fecisti odio habens eos etcet. preterea esto quod seyr sit diabolus per hoc enim quod dicitur inimicus sempiternus. non habes ut ipse sit eternus. immo ut incidas in foueam quam parasti habes potius contrarium. quia ibi sonat hec dicto semper qui est aduerbium temporis. sonat ergo de in uerbi sempiternus id est temporaliter eternus quod etiam per diuinam scripturam habetur ysayas xxiiii dissipauerunt fedus sempiternum. etcet. et xxv precipitabit mortem in sempiternum etcet. et xxxiiii Nocte et die non extinguetur in sempiternum. etcet. et lxiii ut faceret sibi nomen sempiternum etcet. Item ecclesiasticus xlvii. et parare sanctitatem in sempiternum. et xvliii consolatus est lugentes syon usque in sempiternum etcet. Ecce quomodo sempiternum significat tempus. Nec obstat illud ad romanos. sempiterna quoque uirtus eius etcet. quia ibi improprie ponitur sempiterna id est eterna. Quod habetur exin illius uerbi quod sequitur scilicet diuinitas quia diuinitas non potest esse in tempore.

Catholicus: Sed responde tu michi ex auctoritate ezechiel quam allegasti ibi enim dicit dominus contra seyr. Cum te iudicauero etcet. ergo diabolus non est principium eternum. cum dominus sit eum iudicaturus.

Item iohannes viiii. ille homicida erat ab initio et in ueritate non stetit etcet. quod sic putamus. Ille homicida erat ab initio. et sic intelligimus. ab initio id est ab eterno sicut uos romani exponitis illud. in principio erat uerbum. et illud ego sum alpha et omega. principium et finis et similiter exponimus illud. quod dicit iohanne prima iii quoniam ab initio diabolus peccat etcet.

That the devil is eternal

Ezekiel 35 (35:3, 5) "Thus says the Lord God, 'Behold I come against you, mount Seir'" and there "because you have been an everlasting enemy.'" But 'Seir' is interpreted as the devil, who is everlasting, since everlasting denotes that which is 'always eternal,' therefore he is eternal. Similarly in Romans 1 (1:20), "his eternal power also, and divinity."

Cath: I reply that it is not true that 'Seir' is the devil. In fact, there was a certain mountain where the gentile army of Idumeans were, and they were always doing evil against the children of Israel, and treated them shamefully in their sufferings, and so God threatened their destruction in revenge. For he adds there (35:4) "I will destroy your cities," and later (35:11) "I will do according to your wrath, and according to your envy, which you have exercised in hatred towards them." Further suppose that 'Seir' might be the devil, for by this since it says 'everlasting enemy,' you do not have it that he is eternal, yet lest you fall into the pit which you have prepared, rather it is to the contrary, because this saying there denotes 'always' which is an adverb of time. It denotes therefore in the word 'everlasting,' that is, 'temporally eternal' which also one has through the divine scriptures in Isaiah 24 (24:5) "they have broken the everlasting covenant." And 25 (25:8) "He shall cast death down forever." And 34 (34:10) "night and day, it shall not be quenched forever." And 63 (63:12) "to make himself an everlasting name." Also Ecclesiasticus 47 (47:15) "and prepare a sanctuary for ever." And 48 (48:27) "and comforted the mourners in Zion forever." See by what manner 'everlasting' means 'in time.' Neither does Romans 1 oppose this (1:20) "his eternal power also," since there 'eternal' is used loosely, since one has immediately following those words, namely, 'divinity,' since divinity cannot be in time.

Cath: But answer me by the authority of Ezekiel which you adduce there: "says the Lord against Seir." (35:11) "When I shall have judged you." Therefore the devil is no eternal principle, since the Lord shall judge him.

Also John 8 (8:33) "he was a murderer from the beginning, not standing in the truth." For we consider it thusly "he was a murderer from the beginning," and so we understand "from the beginning," that is, to be from eternity, just as you Romans explain that passage (Jn 1:1) "in the beginning was the word," and that (Apoc 1:8) "I am the alpha and the omega, the beginning and end," so similarly do we explain it. For it says in 1 John 3 (3:8) "for the devil sinned from the beginning."

II.4.2 hec...3 sempiternus] Ezech. 35:3, 5.   6 sempiterna...diuinitas] Rom. 1:20.   13 urbes...demoliar] Ezech. 35:4. | faciam...15 eos] Ezech. 35:11.   22 dissipauerunt...23 sempiternum] Is. 24:5.   23 precipitabit...24 sempiternum] Is. 25:8.   24 Nocte...25 sempiternum] Is. 34:10.   25 ut...26 sempiternum] Is. 63:12.   27 et¹...sempiternum] Ecclesiastic. 47:15 (parare) pararet *Vulg.*)   28 consolatus...sempiternum] Ecclesiastic. 48:27.   30 sempiterna...31 eius] Rom. 1:20.   37 Cum...iudicauero] Ezech. 35:11.   40 ille...41 stetit] Ioh. 8:44.   43 in...44 uerbum] Ioh. 1:1.   44 ego...45 finis] Apoc. 1:8.   46 quoniam...47 peccat] 1 Ioh. 3:8.

II.4.3 ibi...4 seyr] om. *P*   5 Simile] Symile *P*   17 ut²] non *F*   35 Catholicus] om. *F*   41 putamus] puctamus *P*   42 ab initio¹] a principio *F*

II.4.6 quoque|fol. 13va *P*   26 sempiternum|fol. 13vb *P*   43 eterno|fol. 8v *F*   47 etcet|fol. 14ra *P*

Preterea dicit christus de illo in ueritate non stetit. quod sonat in ueritate non finit quod sicut ergo non fuit a deo quia omnis creatura dei bona est. igitur fuit eternum principium malum.

Catholicus: Respondeo propter istas auctoritates habeo expressim quod diabolus non est eternus quia dicitur ab initio esse. quod sonat post initium ex vi istius prepositionibus ab. que proponitur huic dictioni initio. Vnde abstrahit atque diminuit de vi illius uerbi initio et primum est ac si diceret in tempore homicida fuit et punctatur sic. ille homicida. fuit ab initio. scilicet hominis id est post initium creationis hominis statim lucifer occidit eum spiritualiter et quod ab initio significe temporis patet. Mattheus xviiii. qui fecit ab initio masculum et feminam etcet. et marcus x. ab initio autem creature masculum et feminam fecit eos deus etcet. et prima iohannes i non mandatum nouum scribo uobis. sed mandatum uetus. quod habuistis ab initio etcet. et ecclesiastius xxxviiii bona bonis creata sunt ab initio etcet. nec obstat illud in ueritate non stetit quia non intelligitur sicut falso exposuisti. Sed dicit natura uerbi proprie exponitur non stetit scilicet nulla permansit. ac si diceret ille in ueritate fuit sed in ea non perseuerauit et quod ita debeat intelligi patet. Genesis xviiii ubi dixit angelis loth. noli respicere post tergum nec stes in omni circa regione etcet. scilicet non ibi moraberis sed statim fugies. simile. josue iii. Cum ingressi fueritis partem aque iordanis state in ea etcet. Quod ita necesse est intelligere state id est per manente. Item mattheus ii lege de stella usque dum ueniens staret supra domum ubi erat puer etcet. scilicet permanseret et xx. quid hic statis tota die otiosi scilicet permansetis Et marcus iii si sathanas insurrexerit in semetipsum dispertitus est et non poterit stare scilicet non poterit perdurare. Vnde subdit sed finem habet etcet. Item prima ad corinthios xvi uigilate et state in fide etcet. scilicet perseuerate. et quod iste scilicet non stetit in ueritate. ita intelligatur sicut probatum est. Dominus ihesus ipsemet in eodem loco cum subdit. quia non est ueritas in eo etcet. Non dixit non fuit ueritas in eo sed dixit non est. ac si diceret in ueritate fuit sed in non permansit quod patet quia in eo non est ueritas in eo quia postquam a statu ueritatis decidit per superbiam semper est mendax.

Patarenus: Item ad hebreos viii sine patre sine matre. sine genealogia. neque initium dierum neque finem

uite habens etcet. hoc legit apostolus de melchisedec qui fuit diabolus. numquam enim hec de homine aliquo potest intelligi. ergo diabolus est eternus et per consequentiam deus.

Catholicus: Respondeo loquitur de homine puro qui uocabitur melchisedec qui dictus sine patre. sine matre. sine genealogia et sine initio dierum et sine fine uite propterea quia apud homines penitus ignorabatur eius pater et mater et parentela et quando natus est et etiam nescitum est quando mortuus est. sit et hic innuit apostolus cum subdit cuius autem generatio non annuntiatur in eis etcet. Sed responde tu mihi blasfemator sanctorum. quomodo potest hic esse diabolus. de qui dicit supra precursor pro nobis introiuit ihesus secundum ordinem melchisedec etcet. numquid presumere audes quod dominus ihesus pontifex sit ordinatur secundum ordinem diaboli. Item dicitur ibi. hic est melchisedec rex salem sacerdos dei summi etcet. quando est diabolus sacerdos dei summus. Item sequitur de melchisedec qui interpretatur primum rex iustitie deinde rex pacis. numquid diabolus est rex iustitie et rex pacis. Item subditur de illo assimilatus autem filio dei manet sacerdos in perpetuum etcet. et hic dici tibi uidetur quod diabolus sit similis dei filio. preterea sequitur de illo quod ipse benedixit abram et subdit apostolus sine autem ulla contraditione quod minus a meliore benedicitur dic quo sensu tibi uidetur quod diabolus melior abraham. obmutesce ergo scelerate canis.

De diuinitate diaboli

Dauid non erit in te deus recens neque adorabit deum alienum etcet. ergo est deus recens alienus qui est diabolus.

Respondeo loquitur de idolo quod ab aliis nationibus colebatur ut deus de quo dicit dominus in ysaya xliiii quis formauit deum et scultile conflauit ad nichil utile. Sed modo responde mihi de auctoritate super quem uideris fidem tuam fundare. dicit enim non erit in te deus recens neque adorabis deum alienum etcet. hic autem de diabolo dictum esse deliras. ergo diabolus est deus recens. igitur non est eternus et sic non est deus naturaliter. preterea ipse dicitur secundum tuum intellectum deus alienus. Sed nulli homines dicunt et credunt eum esse deum nisi uos patareni. ergo uero deus tantum est diabolus. tenete autem et habete illum absque conditione.

Patarenus: Item idem omnes dii gentium demonia etcet. ergo plures sunt dii.

Catholicus: Respondeo plures sunt dii nuncupatiui. dii sunt ydola gentium que dicebantur ad eis dii. In

days nor end of life." This the Apostle gathers about Melchizedek who was the devil, for it was never possible to say this about any man, therefore the devil is eternal and, consequently, God.

Cath: I respond, that it speaks of the pure man who was called Melchizedek, who was called "without father, without mother, without genealogy, having neither beginning of days nor end of life" on account of the fact that his father and mother and relations, and also his birth and death, are thoroughly unknown to men. And this the Apostle intimates when he adds (7:6) "But he, whose pedigree is not numbered among them." But answer me, you blasphemer of the saints, by what reason can he here be the devil of whom was said earlier (6:20) "the forerunner Jesus is entered for us ... according to the order of Melchizedek." Do you dare presume it possible that the Lord Jesus, the high priest, might have been ordained according to the order of the devil? Further it says there (7:1) "this Melchizedek was king of Salem, priest of the most high God." Further it follows with Melchizedek (7:2) "who first indeed by interpretation is king of justice, and then also king of Salem, that is, king of peace." Is it possible that the devil is the king of justice and peace? Further it adds (7:3) "but like the Son of God, remains a priest forever." And I say this to you, does it seem that the devil might be similar to the Son of God? Further it follows about him that he blessed Abram and the Apostle adds (7:7) "And without any contradiction, that which is less is blessed by the better." Say by what sense it seems to you that the devil is better than Abraham? Be silent then you accursed dog!

On the divinity of the devil

David (Ps 80:10): "there shall be no new god among you, neither will you adore a strange god." Therefore there is a new god, a stranger who is the devil.

I respond that he is speaking of idols which were worshiped by other nations, so that god of which the Lord speaks in Isaiah 44 (44:10) "Who has formed a god, and made a graven thing that is profitable for nothing?" But how will you reply to me of the above authority which you seem to root your faith in? For he said (Ps 80:10) "there shall be no new god among you, neither will you adore a strange god." Yet to say here he is speaking of the devil, you are mad! So the devil is a new god, therefore he is not eternal, and so is not god by nature. Further he is called — according to your understanding — a strange god, but no men call or believe him to be god except you Patarenes, therefore your god is certainly the devil. Take hold of him then and hold to him unconditionally.

Pat: Further in the same (Ps 95:5) "For all the gods of the Gentiles are devils," therefore there are many gods.

Cath: I reply that many are called gods, these are the idols of the gentiles who are called among them 'gods.' Through

quibus demonia dabant responsa. que ydola facta erant in quibusdam partibus ad honorem hominum mortuorum. quos gentes deos esse putabant. sicut in oriente de bel et de astaroth et de berit traditur et in quibusdam. sicut in gretia et in ytalia fiebant ad honorem planetarum. de quibus dicit apostolus prima ad corinthios viii. etsi sunt qui dicantur dii etcet. Nota quod non dicit qui sunt sed qui dicantur scilicet a gentibus et sequitur ibi siue in celo. ut planete scilicet saturnus iupiter et ceteri siue in terra ut bel et astaroth et berith et huiusmodi. si quidem sunt dii multi uidelicet gentium oppinione. nobis autem scilicet qui habemus oppinionem ueritatis. unus deus pater etcet. unde dixerat superius. scimus quia nichil est ydolum in mundo id est non est quod putant homines scilicet deus unus subinfert nullus deus nisi unus etcet. hinc et beatus stephanus dicit in actibus vii suscepistis tabernaculum moloch et sydus dei uestri rephan etcet. et postea subdit figuras quas fecistis adorare eas etcet. ad hoc est quod ieremias ii si mutauit gens deos suos et certe ipsi non sunt dii. et. apostolus ad galathas iiii tunc quidem ignorantes deum hiis qui natura non sunt dii seruiebatis etcet. Et nota quod isti dii nuncupanti quandoque dicitur opera manuum hominum secundum materia ydola. Vnde Dauid symulacra gentium argentum et aurum opera manuum hominum etcet. quandoque uero dicitur nichil esse quia non sunt sicut putabant gentiles scilicet dii et sic intelligitur quod dicit apostolus ad corinthios nichil est ydolum etcet. quandoque vero dicuntur demonia quia demonia loquebantur ydolis et decipiebant uariis in omnis ydolatras et sic intelligitur istud dauiticum. omnes dii gentium demonia etcet. et quod dicit apostolus i^a ad corinthios x que imolant gentes demoniis imolant etcet.

Patarenus: Item malachias ii transgressus iudas etcet. ibi et habuit filiam dei alieni etcet. sed deus alienus dicitur diabolus ergo ipse deus.

Catholicus: Respondeo ut supra quia deus alienus dicitur ydolum. ibi appelat namque uxorem alieni propter cultum quia colebat ydolum.

Patarenus: Item mattheus xviiii. unus est bonus deus ergo etcet. ergo alius est malus deus qui est bonus deus.

Catholicus: Respondeo non dicitur unus bonus deus ratione alterius mali. quia nulla mentio facta erat de duobus diis. licet de uno. sed tantum de bono. quia dixerat domino quidam magister bone et hic loque-

these the demons gave replies, by which the idols were made in which places were erected to the honor of dead men, whom the gentiles considered to be Gods. Just as the east was handed over to Bel and to Astaroth and to Berit, and the like, and just as in Greece and in Italy they paid honor to the planets, of which the Apostle says in 1 Corinthians 8 (8:5) "For although there be those that are called gods." Note that he did not say 'who are' but 'that are called,' namely, by the gentiles, and it follows here 'either in heaven,' like the planets, for example Saturn, Jupiter, and the like, 'or on earth' like Bel, Astaroth, and Berit and the like, if there are many gods evidently in the opinion of the gentiles, yet to us, namely, we who have the true opinion (8:6) "one God and Father." Whence he said above, (8:4) "we know that an idol is nothing in the world." that is, it is not what men think, namely what he adds "that there is no God but one." And this is what Blessed Stephen says in Acts 7 (7:43) "And you took unto you the tabernacle of Moloch, and the star of your god Rempham," and later adds "figures which you made to adore them." On this point is Jeremiah 2 (2:11) "If a nation has changed their gods, and indeed they are not gods." And the Apostle to the Galatians 4 (4:8) "But then indeed, not knowing God, you served them, who by nature are not gods." And note that those called gods, wherever they may be, are said to the works of men's hands according to the material of idolatry. Whence David (Ps 113:12) "The idols of the gentiles are silver and gold, the works of the hands of men." Everywhere they are said to be nothing, since they are not what the gentiles considered them to be, and so it is to be understood what the Apostle says to the Corinthians (1 Cor 8:4) "an idol is nothing." Sometimes they are yet called demons, since demons are said to be idols and they deceived various people into all idolatry, and thus is to be understood that saying of David (Ps 95:5) "For all the gods of the Gentiles are devils," and what the Apostle says in 1 Corinthians 10 (10:20) "the things which the gentiles sacrifice, they sacrifice to devils."

Pat: Also Malachi 2 (2:11) "Judah has transgressed," there and "has married the daughter of a strange God." But a strange god is called the devil, therefore the same one is god.

Cath: I reply as above that the strange god is called "idol," there being termed "foreign wife" on account of the cult which worships idols.

Pat: Also Matthew 19 (19:17) "one is good, God," therefore the evil god is different from he who is the good God.

Cath: I reply that it does not say "one is good, God" by reason of another evil one, since no mention was made of two gods, but only one. But only of the good God since he spoke to the Lord as a 'good master,' and here He was

---

28 etsi...dii] 1 Cor. 8:5.   34 unus...pater] 1 Cor. 8:6.   35 scimus...36 mundo] 1 Cor. 8:4.   38 suscepistis...39 rephan] Act. 7:43.   41 si...42 dii] Ier. 2:11.   43 tunc...44 seruiebatis] Gal. 4:8.   46 symulacra...47 hominum] Ps. 113:12.   50 nichil...ydolum] 1 Cor. 8:4.   53 omnes...54 demonia] Ps. 95:5.   55 que...imolant^2] 1 Cor. 10:20.   57 transgressus...58 alieni] Mal. 2:11 (transgressus] add. est *Vulg.*)   63 unus...64 ergo^1] Matt. 19:17.

31 iupiter] iupitter *F*   42 sunt] stant *P*   53 dauiticum] 13th-century term for the Psalter, see Hugh of St. Cher, *Postilla, seu Divina expositio in Daviticum psalterium* (Paris, 1539).   61 alieni] alienigenam *F*   63 Patarenus] om. *F*

23 hominum|fol. 15rb *P*   43 quidem|fol. 15va *P*   58 alienus|fol. 9v *F*   63 est|fol. 15vb *P*

batur de eo tamquam de homine puro et dominus respondit quod nullus est bonus scilicet pure licet perfecte nisi unus deus. et est sensus unus est bonus deus id est unus est bonus qui deus est et ita est in luca et in marcho. ubi est ista materia nemo bonus nisi unus deus etcet.

Patarenus: Item ii^a ad corinthios iiii. in quibus deus huius seculi excecauit mentes infidelium etcet. sed hoc non de bono deo potest intelligi. quia ille non excecat mentes homini sed illuminat. ergo de diabolo intelligitur.

Catholicus: Respondeo quod de bono deo intelligitur quod excecauit infideles et obstinatos duobus modis scilicet lucem glorie sue non dando illi. et illos errare permittendo quod est excecare. unde dominus dicit in iohannes ix in iudicium in hunc mundum ego ueni ut qui non uident uideant et qui uident ceci fiant etcet. Et. xii excecauit oculos eorum et indurauit cor eorum ut non uideant oculis et intelligant corde et conuertantur et sanem eos etcet. Item ad romanos i propter quod tradidit illos deus in reprobum sensum etcet. et ix deus cui uult miseretur miseretur et quem uult indurat etcet. Et xi conclusit enim deus omnia in incredulitate ut omnium misereatur etcet. Ad thesalonecenses ii° ideo mittet illis deus operationem erroris etcet. Item actus ultimo incrassatum est enim cor populi huius et est hic uerior lettura et secundum hoc sic debet punctari hec littera pauli. deus huius seculi excecauit mentes infidelium etcet. Et construitur sic. deus excecauit mentes infidelium huius seculi. Et sic legit beatus augustinus uel secundum hunc intellectum potest intelligi plane. Sic deus huius seculi id est deus bonus qui est deus non solum seculi eterni sed etiam seculi temporalis uel potest intelligi ut quidam uolunt mihi non placet de diabolo et sic si bene aduertas in ista sola auctoritate uocatur diabolus deus. Et secundum hoc dicitur deus in lectione. quia illicit homines ad seculares illecebras. Vel dicitur deus electione. quia mundani homines ipsum ut deum elegerunt et maxime uos patareni qui ipsum deum eligitis dum illum deum creditis et uocatis et predicatis et eius adimpletis uoluntatem.

Nec propter hoc quod dicatur deus huius seculi. Sequitur ut ipse sit deus naturalis ab eterno et seculi creator. uel deus huius seculi appelatur secularitas que dicitur deus huius seculi id est secularum hominum nuncupante sicut uenter dicitur deus gulosorum. Vt

speaking of Him just as of a man simply considered,[1] and the Lord responded that none was good, namely, pure or perfect, save the one God, and this is the meaning of "one is good, God," that is, "one is good, who is God," and the same in Luke and in Mark, where this is (Mk 10:18) "None is good but one, that is God."

Pat: Also 2 Corinthians 4 (4:4) "In whom the god of this world has blinded the minds of unbelievers." But this cannot be understood of the good God, since He does not blind the minds of men, but rather illuminates them, therefore it must be interpreted as the devil.

Cath: I reply that it is to be understood of the good God because He blinds the unbelievers and obstinate in two ways, namely, by not giving to them the light of glory, and by permitting them to err, which is called 'blinding.' Whence the Lord speaks in John 9 (9:39) "For judgment I have come into this world, that they who see not, may see, and they who see, may become blind." And 12 (12:40) "He has blinded their eyes, and hardened their heart, that they should not see with their eyes, nor understand with their heart, and be converted, and I should heal them." Also Romans 1 (1:24) "God gave them over," (1:28) "to a reprobate sense." And 9 (9:18) "he has mercy on whom he will, and hardens whom he will." And 11 (11:32) "For God has confined all in unbelief, that he may have mercy on all." In 2 Thessalonians 2 (2:11) "Therefore God shall send them the working of error." Also Acts at the end (28:27) "For the heart of this people has grown fat." Here is the truer reading, and according to this one ought to punctuate this reading of Paul (2 Cor 4:4) "the god of this world has blinded the minds of unbelievers," and is to be construed thusly, "God blinded the minds of the unbelievers of this world." And this is the way that Blessed Augustine reads it, or at least he can plainly be understood according to this sense. Thus the "god of this world" is the good God who is God not only of eternity but also of the temporal world, or it can be understood, as some wish to, [but] I don't like it, concerning the devil, and thus if you should pay close attention, by this authority alone God is called the devil. And in this sense god is spoken of in the passage, that he entices men to secular allurements. Or he is called god in terms of election, since worldly men choose him, that he might be god, and especially you Patarenes who have chosen him god, since you believe him to be god, and call him such and preach him and fulfill his will. Nor on this account might he be called the God of this world. It follows that He is the God of nature from eternity and the creator of the world, or that the 'God of this world' be called 'worldliness,' as termed by secular men, as the stomach is called the god of gluttons. As in

---

73 ubi...74 deus] Mar. 10:18. 75 in...76 infidelium] 2 Cor. 4:4. 84 in¹...85 fiant] Ioh. 9:39. 86 excecauit...88 eos] Ioh. 12:40. 88 propter...89 sensum] Rom. 1:24, 28). 89 deus²...90 indurat] Rom. 9:18 (deus cui] ergo cuius *Vulg.*) 91 conclusit...92 misereatur] Rom. 11:32. 93 ideo...erroris] 2 Thes. 2:11. 94 incrassatum...huius] Act. 28:27. 96 deus...97 infidelium] 2 Cor. 4:4. 98 beatus...99 augustinus] Citing Ordinary Gloss on 2 Cor. 4:4. Augustine, *Contra Faustum*, 21.9.

77 excecat] excecauit F   97 construitur] constitutur F   102 mihi] michi P   111 Nec] ne P | dicatur] om. F   113 uel] ut F

84 ut|fol. 16ra P   104 deus|fol. 16rb P

---

1) That is, according to His human nature.

phylipenses iii quorum deus uenter est etcet. et tamen uenter non est naturaliter. uenter gulosorum. et nota quod tribus in modis dicitur deus. primo per naturam scilicet deus omnium ut probatum est superius nostra parte huius tractatus. secunda per adoptionem unde psalmus Ego dii estis et filii excelsi omnes etcet. tertio per nuncupationem et hic quinque modis scilicet prelatione exodus vii constitui te deum pharaonis id est prelatum sacerdotis dignitate. unde in eodem xxii diis non detrahes id est a sacerdotibus. Errore non dii gentium de quibus diximus modo paulo ante super illa oppinione de dauid omnes dii gentium etcet. in sollicitudine et amore ut uenter gulosorum uel secularitas et uanitas mundi mundanorum que ut deum diligat in lectione et electione ut diabolus malorum.

De creatione et factione diaboli

Job vii O custos hominum quare posuisti me contrarium tibi etcet. ergo natura corporis uel anime Job mala erat cum esset contrarius deo et sic erat a malo principio.
Catholicus: Respondeo Job dicitur contrarius deo secundam naturam corporis secundum quem mortalis est. omnis homo propter peccatum primum parentis ad romanos v corpus propter peccatum mortuum est etcet. deus enim mori non potest et secundum hoc contrarius est homo deo. Sed modo respondeas mihi job loquebatur deo bono cui contrarium se dicebat. et deus bonus loquebatur ei. et comendabat eum de santitate ergo deus bonus locutus est patribus et job sanctus homo fuit quarum utrumque mendacitur inficiaris.
Patarenus: Item dauid. Ecce enim in iniquitatibus conceptus sunt etcet. ergo mala natura sua erat igitur a malo principio.
Catholicus: Respondeo non dicit quod de iniquitatibus sit conceptus. sed in iniquitatibus id est in peccato originali quod ad prothoplaustis deriuatum est et ideo mala est illatio tua. quod patet per instantiam lapis iste inuentus est in aqua. igitur de aqua est et non sequitur. preterea ipsemet subdit. asperges me domine ysopo et mundabor etcet. ergo exiit bona natura sua si poterat a peccato mundari.
Patarenus: Item ecclesiates i. uidi que fiunt cuncta sub sole et ecce uniuersa uanitas et afflictio spiritus etcet. ergo non sunt de creatione dei non sunt bona ista

Philippians 3 (3:19) "those whose god is their stomach." And nevertheless the stomach is not by nature the stomach of gluttons. And note the three ways in which God is called. First through nature, namely, God of all things, as was proven above in the first part of our work. The second by adoption, whence the Psalm (81:6) "I have said, 'You are gods and all of you the sons of the most High.'" The third by declaration and this in five ways, namely, by appointment as a prelate in Exodus 7 (7:1) "I have appointed you the God of Pharaoh," that is, by the prelatial dignity of the priesthood, whence in the same book, chapter 22 (22:28) "You shall not speak ill of the gods," that is, of the priests, not in the error of the gods of the gentiles, of which we said in the manner of Paul, regarding that opinion of David (Ps 95:5) "all the gods of the Gentiles." By solicitude and love, as the belly for dainty things or worldliness and worldly vanity for worldly things, in order to love them as God in the choice [of them] as the devil [in his love] of wicked things.

On the creation and fashioning of the devil

Job 7 (7:20) "O keeper of men, why have you set me opposite to you." Therefore there was evil in the body or soul of Job by nature, since he was contrary to God, and so he was from the evil principle.
Cath: I respond that Job was called contrary to God according to his bodily nature whereby he was mortal, as are all men on account of the sin of the first parents. Romans 5 (8:10) "the body is indeed dead because of sin." For God cannot die and by reason of this, man is contrary to God. But how might you reply to me? Job was speaking of the good God, to whom he was saying was contrary to himself, and the good God was speaking to him and commended him for holiness, therefore the good God spoke to the fathers and Job was a holy man, and in denying it you lie.
Pat: Further, David (Ps 50:7) "for behold in sin was I conceived," therefore his was an evil nature, so then from the evil principle.
Cath: I reply that he did not say that of sins one might be conceived, but in sins, that is, in original sin which was derived from the first man, and so your suggestion is evil, as is clear by the instance of a rock found in water, therefore it is of water, and this does not follow, since he immediately adds (50:9) "wash me with hyssop Lord, and I shall be clean," therefore he came forth from a good nature if he was able to be cleansed from sin.
Pat: Ecclesiastes 1 (1:14) "I have seen all things that are done under the sun, and behold all is vanity, and vexation of spirit." Therefore these visible things are not of the crea-

---

116 quorum...est] Php. 3:19.   121 Ego...omnes] Ps. 81:6.   123 constitui...pharaonis] Ex. 7:1.   124 diis...125 detrahes] Ex. 22:28.   127 omnes...gentium] Ps. 95:5.   II.6.2 O...3 tibi] Iob 7:20.   9 corpus...est] Rom. 8:10.   17 Ecce...18 sunt] Ps. 50:7.   26 asperges...mundabor] Ps. 50:9, and in sprinkling rite of Mass.   28 uidi...29 spiritus] Eccl. 1:14.

---

120 huius] om. P   125 non²] om. P   127 dauid] dauit P | in] item P   130 et electione] uel elector P   II.6.6 Respondeo] om. F   8 omnis homo] om. F   10 hoc] add. esset F   14 santitate] sanitate F   15 utrumque] utrum F   18 erat] erant F   22 prothoplaustis] phylosophantis F   27 exiit] exiit erat F   28 Patarenus] om. F   29 afflictio] aflictio P   30 non²...32 diaboli] non sunt uanitas ergo sunt de creatione diaboli. P

126 illa|fol. 16va P   127 oppinione|fol. 10r F   II.6.21 sed|fol. 16vb P

uisibilia. quia que sunt de creatione dei non sunt uanitas ergo de creatione diaboli.
Catholicus: Respondeo non loquitur de creaturis mundi. sed de laboribus et operibus hominum unde dicit que fiunt et appellat ea uanitatem propter afflictionem que in eis est. Vnde dicit et afflictio spiritus etcet. Vel dicitur uanitas propter mutabilitatem sui.

Patarenus: Item Sapientia xii. nequam est natio eorum et naturalis malitia ipsorum quoniam non poterat mutari cogitatio illorum in perpetuum semen enim erat maledictum ab initio etcet. ecce quomodo habetur aperte ex hiis uerbis quod quorumdam natura mala est. et quod nullo modo potest bene facere. igitur est a malo principio.

Catholicus: Respondeo loquitur de vii gentibus quos expulit deus de terra chanaan ante filios israel. Vnde dicit superius misisti antecesores exercitus tui uespas ut illos paulatim exterminarent etcet. quod nunquam de terra uite eterne potest intelligi. quia ibi non sunt uespe. sunt ergo uerba predicta sic intelligenda. nequam est natio eorum. id est de nequis et malis parentibus nati sunt qui etiam docebant illos nequitiam ydolatrie et a aliorum malorum. sequitur et naturalis malitia ipsorum id est perseuerans. sicut dicitur naturalia bona. quia perseuerant uel naturaliter id est a natura id est a primis parentibus deriuata nascendo. unde ad romanos v. per unum hominem peccatum intrauit in hunc mundum et per peccatum mors. ita et in omnes homines mors transiit etcet. Similiter ad ephesios ii. eramus natura filii ire etcet. Ad illud quod sequitur non poterat mutari etcet. subintelligitur scilicet sine magna difficultate. similiter mattheus xii qui dixerit contra spiritum sanctum non remittetur ei neque in hoc seculo neque in futuro. quod intelligitur sine magna difficultate. ad idem est illud iacobi iii linguam autem nullus hominum domare potuit. scilicet de facili. et tamen quandoque domatur licet difficile sit. Vnde dicit quis in uerbo non offendit hic perfectus est uir etcet.

uel aliter potest exponi. non poterat mutari. scilicet a seipsis. Vnde dauid spiritus uadens scilicet in peccatum et non rediens scilicet per se. Vnde et dominus dicit johannes xv sine me nichil potestis facere etcet. quod autem sequitur. semen erat maledictum ab initio id est in presencia dei. de quam dicit job xxxiiii Conteret multos et inumerabiles et stare faciet alios per eis. Nouit enim opera eorum etcet. uel ab initio id est postquam esse ceperunt infuit eis causa maledictionis id est peccatum originale id est ab adam contractum ab initio id est a suo progenitore scilicet acham filio noe a

tion of the good God, for the things of the creation of God are no vanities, therefore they are creations of the devil.
Cath: I respond that it is not speaking of creations in the world, but of the labors and works of men, whence it speaks of things done and calls them vanities on account of the affliction that is in them, whence it speaks of the "vexation of spirit." Or otherwise they are called vanities on account of their changeable nature.

Pat: Also Wisdom 12 (12:10–11) "they were a wicked generation, and their malice natural, and that their thought could never be changed for it was a cursed seed from the beginning." See how one has it plainly from these words that speak about some wicked nature, and that in no way can it do good, therefore it is from an evil principle.

Cath: I reply that it is speaking of the seven tribes which God expelled from the land of Canaan before the people of Israel, whence it speaks above (12:8) "and you sent wasps, forerunners of your host, to destroy them by little and little." It is impossible to interpret it as speaking of the land of eternal life, since there are no wasps there. Therefore the foregoing words "they were a wicked generation," are to be understood thusly, that is, they were wicked since they were born of evil parents, who also were teaching them the wickedness of idolatry and other sins. And it continues "and their malice natural," that is, continuing, as if to say innate good, which they continue to possess, or naturally, that is, by nature, which means that by birth they have derived it from the first parents. Whence Romans 5 (5:12) "Since as by one man sin entered into this world, and by sin death, and so death passed upon all men." Similar is Ephesians 2 (2:3) "we were by nature children of wrath." To that is what follows (Wisdom 12:10) "could never be changed," by which one is to understand "without great difficulty." Similar is Matthew 12 (12:10) "who speaks against the Holy Spirit, it will not be forgiven him neither in this age nor in the next," which is interpreted "without great difficulty." The same is that is in James 3 (3:8) "But the tongue no man can tame," namely easily, and yet sometimes one may tame it, though it be difficult. Whence he says (3:2) "If any man does not offend by word, he is a perfect man."

Or another way one can construe "could never be changed," namely, 'by themselves,' for David (Ps 77:39) "a wind that goes," namely, by sin, "and does not return," namely, through one's own power. Whence the Lord says in John 15 (15:5) "without me you can do nothing," yet it continues (Wis 12:11) "it was a cursed seed from the beginning," that is, before the presence of God, of which Job 34 speaks (34:24–25) "He will break into pieces many and innumerable, and will make others to stand in their stead, for he knows their works." Or from the beginning, that is, after they began to be involved in the cause of their

---

38 nequam...41 initio] Sap. 12:10-11. 47 misisti...48 exterminarent] Sap. 12:8. 57 per...59 transiit] Rom. 5:12. 59 eramus...60 ire] Eph. 2:3. 60 non...61 mutari] Sap. 12:10. 62 qui...64 futuro] Matt. 12:10. 65 linguam...66 potuit] Iac. 3:8 (potuit) potest *Vulg.*) 68 quis...uir] Iac. 3:2. 70 spiritus uadens] Ps. 77:39. 72 sine...facere] Ioh. 15:5. 73 semen...initio] Sap. 12:11. 74 Conteret...76 eorum] Iob 34:24-25.

36 afflictio] aflicio P 38 natio] ratio P 49 ibi] om. F 62 similiter...65 difficultate] om. F 67 difficile] dificile P | dicit] om. P

43 potest|fol. 17ra P 65 difficultate|fol. 17rb P 69 poterat|fol. 10v F

quo descenderat ille gentes que semper fuerunt sine cultu et reuerentia dei. acham citra. Sed responde nunc tu mihi fera bellua ibidem enim dicitur dans scilicet deus tempus et locum per quem possint mutari. a malitia et supra. uindicans dabas locum penitencie et iterum et his tamquam hominibus pepercisti etcet. ergo natura illorum non erat mala. si penitentiam poterant facere et dei misericordia consequi. igitur de illis vii gentibus loquitur ut dixi.

Patarenus: Item ecclesiasticus xlii omnia duplitia unum contra unum etcet. ergo sunt duo creatores et due curie et due creationes.

Catholicus: Respondeo loquitur de operibus unius dei. sicut ipsemet exponit xxxiii contra malum bonum. contra mortem uita. contra uirum iustum peccator et sic intuere omnia opera altissimi duo contra duo unum contra unum etcet. Et xi bona et mala uita et mors paupertas et honestas a deo sunt. Non dixit a diis tamquam a pluribus sed a deo tamquam ab uno. Nec de malo deo possunt intelligi. quia ab eo non possunt esse bona. Sed nunc responde mihi tu de hac auctoritate. omnia duplitia etcet. Si uniuersaliter intelligis hec uerba sicut uidetis. ergo sicut in mundo que dicis esse de creatione diaboli ita et in celo quod est de creatione dei. sunt asini et equi serpentes et bufones. pueri et senes. coitus carnales et bella. et huiusmodi quod cogitare derisione dignum est.

Patarenus: Item ieremias xiii sicut ethiops non potest mutare pellem suam etcet. ergo natura eorum mala erat.

Catholicus: Respondeo ista impossibilitas non erat a natura. sed a praua consuetudine et a disciplina erroris. que maxime indurant uos hereticos. Vnde dicit ibi. cum uos didiceritis malefacere etcet. quod enim quis didicit non est nature. sed doctrine et consuetudinis. sed responde tu ita enim dicit. sicut adheret lumbare ad lumbos uiri. sic adglutinaui mihi domum israel. et omnem domum iuda dicit dominus ut esset in populum mihi etcet. ergo non erant de mala creatione.

[Patarenus:] Item idem xvii peccatum iuda scriptum est stilo ferreo etcet. ad idem

Catholicus: Respondeo ut supra proximo. Et quod iudas de quo loquitur sit de bona creatione patet per id quod ibidem dicit audite uerbum domini reges iuda et omnis iuda cunctique habitatores ierusalem et nolite

curse, which is original sin which they contracted from Adam in the beginning, through their progenitor, Ham the son of Noah, from whom all those peoples descended who were always without worship or reverence for God, who are on the side of Ham. But answer me now, you wild beast, for there it says (Wis 12:20) God "giving them time and place in which they might be changed from their wickedness," and above (12:10) "judging, giving a place of penitence," and again (12:8) "even those you spared as men." Therefore they were not evil in their natures, if they were able to do penance, following upon the mercy of God. Therefore it was speaking of these seven tribes, as I said.

Pat: Also Ecclesiasticus 42 (42:25) "All things are double, one against another." Therefore there are two creators and two heavenly courts and two creations.

Cath: I respond that it is speaking of the works of the one God, as it itself explains in 33 (33:35) "Good is set against evil, and life against death, so also is the sinner against a just man. And so look upon all the works of the most High. Two and two, and one against another." And 11 (11:14) "Good things and evil, life and death, poverty and riches, are from God." He did not say "from gods" as if they were from many, but he said "from God" as if they were from one. Nor is one able to interpret it as being the evil god since from him good things are unable to come. But now answer me this regarding the passage "all things are double." If you understand these words all together, as you seem to, therefore, just as in the world, which you say exists by the devil's creation, so also in heaven, which exists by God's creation, there are asses and horses, snakes and toads, boys and old men, carnal intercourse and wars, and things of this kind. To think this is worthy of derision.

Pat: Also Jeremiah 13 (13:23) "As if the Ethiopian can change his skin," therefore their nature is evil.

Cath: I respond this is impossible, since it is not by nature, but by wicked custom and by the habit of error, in which you heretics are especially hardened. Whence he says there "when you had learned of evildoing," for since he was taught it was not by nature, but by teaching and custom, but answer, for so he says (13:11) "For as the girdle sticks close to the loins of a man, so have I brought close to me all of the house of Israel, and all the house of Judah, says the Lord, that they might be my people." Therefore they were not of an evil creation.

[Pat:] Also the same in 17 (17:1) "The sin of Judah is written with a pen of iron," to the same.

Cath: I respond as I recently did above, and that it is Judah of which he speaks, that they are of the good creation is clear by that there when he says (17:20) "Hear the word of the Lord, kings of Judah, and all Judah, and all the

---

83 deus...84 malitia] Sap. 12:20. 84 locum penitencie] Sap. 12:10 (uindicans] iudicans *Vulg.*) 85 et...pepercisti] Sap. 12:8. 89 omnia...90 unum²] Ecclesiatic. 42:25. 93 contra...96 unum] Ecclesiastic. 33:15. 96 bona...97 sunt] Ecclesiastic. 11:14. 107 sicut...108 suam] Ier. 13:32. 115 sicut...118 mihi] Ier. 13:11. 119 peccatum...120 ferreo] Ier. 17:1. 123 audite...124 ierusalem] Ier. 17:20. 124 nolite...126 sabbati] Ier. 17:22 (exercere] ejicere *Vulg.*)

82 mihi] michi *P* 89 Patarenus] om. *F* 106 cogitare] agitare *F* 110 impossibilitas] imposibilitas *P* 112 uos] add. et *P* 115 ita] ibi *P* 116 mihi] michi *P* 120 ad idem] ad diem *F* 122 iudas] iudeis *P*

86 natura]fol. 17va *P* 106 derisione]fol. 17vb *P*

125 honera de domibus uestris exercere. et omne opus non faciatis sanctificate diem sabbati. etcet. et infra promittit eis multa bona si obediunt.

Patarenus: Item mattheus vii non potest arbor mala fructus bonos facere etcet. ergo sunt due. una bona et 130 alia mala.

Catholicus: Respondeo arbor dicitur intentio bona et mala uel bona doctrina et peruersa. alias enim de homine non posset stare. quia petrus et paulus et maria magdalene et huiusmodi fuerit quandoque mali. et 135 tamen fecerunt bonos fructus penitentie.

[**Patarenus:**] Et idem xv omnis plantatio quam non plantauit pater meus celestis eradicabitur etcet. ergo aliquam sunt que non sunt creata a deo. igitur a diabolo.

140 **Catholicus:** Respondeo de doctrina phariseorum loquitur qui non erat ex deo et ideo eradicanda erat. simile actus v si est ex hominibus consilium hoc autem opus dissolueret etcet. preterea falsa est argumentatio tua. quod per istantiam probo paulus plantauit 145 corinthios sicut ipse dicit ia iii ego plantaui etcet. ergo creauit eos non sequitur. Sed responde mihi. christus hoc dicit quod omnis plantatio quam non plantauit pater eius eradicabitur. ergo omnes creature diaboli eradicabuntur.

150 **Patarenus:** Item iohannes i quod factum est in ipso uita erat etcet. ergo animalia que moriuntur non sunt facta ab ipso.

Catholicus: Respondeo male punctas. debes enim sic punctare. quod factum est in ipso uita erat id est uitale. 155 quasi dicat sicut omnia per ipsum facta sunt. ita omnia ab ipso uita habent. Vel secundum tuam punctationem sic intelligitur quod factum est in ipso id est obprobria et passio et mors et huiusmodi uita erat scilicet nostra unde apostolus prima ad corinthios i quod infirmius 160 est dei fortius est hominibus etcet

Patarenus: Item idem in eodem dedit potestatem filios dei fieri his qui credunt in nomine eius qui non ex sanguinibus etcet. ergo homo exterior qui est natus ex sanguinibus et ex uoluntate carnis non est natus ex deo 165 ergo a diabolo.

Catholicus: Respondeo quod due sunt. natiuitates una nature que sit per carnis propagationem et altera gratie que sit per fidem in baptismo et penitentia. Vnde dominus infra iii. quod natum est ex carne caro est et 170 quod natum est ex spiritu. spiritus est etcet. et loquebatur ibi de spiritu sancto. Sicut patet ex littera illam etiam duplicem natiuitatem insinuat cum dicit oportet uos nasci denuo etcet. quasi dicat qui nati estis natiuitate nature oportet ut nascamini natiuitate gratie.

inhabitants of Jerusalem," and (17:22) "And do not bring burdens out of your houses on the Sabbath day, neither do any work. Sanctify the Sabbath day." and later promised much good to them if they obeyed.

Pat: Also Matthew 7 (7:18) "An evil tree is not able to bear good fruit," so there are two trees, one good and one evil.

Cath: I respond that the tree stands for good and evil intentions or good doctrine and perverse teaching, for otherwise some men would not be able to stand, since Peter and Paul and Mary Magdalene were at some point evil, and yet they bore the good fruits of penitence.

[**Pat:**] And also 15 (15:13) "every plant which was not planted by my heavenly Father will be rooted up," therefore there are some who are not created by God and therefore, they originate from the devil.

Cath: I reply that he is speaking of the teaching of the Pharisees which was not from God, and so was to be rooted up. It is similar in Acts 5 (5:38) "for if this council or this work be of men, it will come to nothing." Further your argumentation is false, which for instance I prove that Paul planted the Corinthians as he himself said in 1 Corinthians 3 (3:6) "I planted." Yet it does not follow that he created them. But tell me this, Christ said that all plants not planted by His Father would be rooted up, therefore all the creatures of the devil shall be rooted up.

Pat: Also John 1 (1:4) "that was made in him was life," therefore the animals who die are not made by Him.

Cath: I respond that you do not think clearly, for you ought to think thusly, "that was made, in him was life," that is, life-giving, as if to say just as all things were made by Him, so all things have life from Him. Or according to your punctuation, it is to be understood that what was made in Him, that is, scandal, and suffering, and death and the like, was life, namely, ours, whereas the Apostle says in 1 Corinthians 1 (1:25) "the weakness of God is stronger than men."

Pat: Also in the same He taught (Jn 1:12-13) "he gave them power to become sons of God, to those who believe in his name, who are not born of blood." Therefore the exterior man, who is born of blood and of the will of the flesh, is not born of God but rather of the devil.

Cath: I respond that there are two births, one by nature which is through carnal propagation, and the other through grace which is by faith through baptism and penitence. Whence the Lord has it later (Jn 3:6) "what is born of flesh is flesh, and what is born of the spirit is spirit," and He was speaking there of the Holy Spirit. This is clear from that passage also when the double births are suggested when He says (3:7) "you must be born anew," as if to say he who is born according to nature must be

---

128 non...**129** facere] Matt. 7:18 (mala] malos *Vulg.*) **136** omnis...**137** eradicabitur] Matt. 15:13. **142** si...**143** dissolueret] Act. 5:38. **145** ego plantaui] 1 Cor. 3:6. **150** quod...**151** erat] Ioh. 1:4. **159** quod...**160** hominibus] 1 Cor. 1:25. **161** dedit...163 sanguinibus] Ioh. 1:12-13. **169** quod...**170** est²] Ioh. 3:6. **173** oportet...denuo] Ioh. 3:7.

128 Patarenus] om. *F* **134** magdalene] magdalena *P* **141** et ideo] om. *F* **142** simile] symile *P* | consilium] conscilium *P* **144** istantiam] istam *F* **146** mihi] michi *P* **173** denuo] de uno *F* **174** oportet] opportet *P*

126 facitis|fol. 18ra *P* **133** paulus|fol. 11r *F* **145** ego|fol. 18rb *P* **167** nature|fol. 18va *P*

si uultus in regnum celorum intrare. nec per hoc habetur quod naturas carnis sit mala sed quia non sufficit sola id est. sine spirituali que sit per fidem. unde hic dicitur dedit eis potestatem filios dei fieri. Sed quibus his qui credunt in nomine eius id est qui credit. unde i johannes v. omnis qui credit quoniam ihesus est christus ex deo natus est. Item ad galathas iii omnes enim filii estis per fidem que est in christo ihesu etcet. quod autem sequitur qui non ex sanguinibus etcet. Sic intelligitur quia quod sint filii dei. non habent ex prima natiuitate que est ex duobus sanguinibus. sed ex deo id est eius gratia ex fidem ipsius. sed responde tu mihi. dicitur hic quod illi qui non sunt nati ex sanguinibus haberent potestatem filios dei fieri. alii uero non. sed uos heretici ex sanguinibus nati estis secundum corpus sicut et nos. ergo non potestis fieri filii dei sed secundum uero animam nec uos nec nos nati sumus ex sanguinibus sed ex nichilo creati. ergo nos possimus fieri filii dei. presertim quod credimus in nomine eius uos autem non potestis quia non creditis sicut iohannis dixerat scilicet quia uerbum deus sit et homo.

Patarenus: Item idem viii uos deorsum estis ego de supernis sum etcet. et infra uos de hoc mundo estis ego non sunt de hoc mundo etcet. ergo due sunt creationes.
Catholicus: Respondeo de mundo dicuntur per amorem illicitum non per creatorem malam. alioquin quomodo dixisset eis. sine crediditis quia ego sum moriemini in peccato uestro etcet. ergo poterant credere et uiuere et sic erant de bona creatione.
Patarenus: Item idem in eodem uos ex patre diabolo estis etcet. ergo creauit illos.
Catholicus: respondeo diabolus dicitur pater malorum per imitationem. unde subdit et opera eius facitis et quod. id est. quia opera eius facitis. simile in petri iii cuius. scilicet sayre estis filie benefacientes etcet.
Patarenus: Item idem xv Si mundus uos odit etcet. ergo non est dei creatura. si odit filios eius igitur diaboli.
Catholicus: Respondeo mundus hic ponitur pro mundialibus hominibus et secularibus principibus. Non enim o stulta bestia machina mundialis odit uel diligit. quia nullum affectum habet. cum sit res inanimata sit.
Patarenus: Item ad romanos vii. scio quod non inhabitat in me. hoc est in carne mea bonum etcet. ergo mala est natura carnis.

reborn according to the birth of grace, if you wish to enter into the kingdom of heaven. Nor by this does one have it that the nature of flesh is evil, but that it alone does not suffice without the spiritual birth which is through faith. Whence it says here (1:12) "He gave them power to become sons of God." But to those who believe in His name, that is, he who believes. Whence 1 John 5 (1 Jn 5:1) "Whoever believes that Jesus is the Christ, is born of God." Also Galatians 3 (3:26) "For you are all the children of God by faith, in Christ Jesus." But then it continues "who are not born of blood," this is to be understood as those who might be sons of God, who do not have from the first born which is from two bloods, but are of God, that is, by his grace from faith in Him. But tell me this, it says here that those who are not born of blood shall have the power to become sons of God, or otherwise not. But you heretics are born of blood according to the body, just like us, therefore you are not able to become sons of God, yet according to the soul neither you nor we were born of blood, but were created from nothing. Therefore we are not able to become sons of God, particularly since we believe in His name, you though are unable since you do not believe, as John taught, namely that the Word of God was a man.

Pat: Also in the same chapter 8 (8:23) "You are from below, I am from above." And later (17:16) "They are not of the world, as I also am not of the world." Therefore there are two creations.
Cath: I respond that 'the world' is spoken of through illicit loves and not as though it had an evil creator. Otherwise how could He have said to them, (8:24) "For if you do not believe that I am he, you shall die in your sin." Therefore they were able to believe and to live, and so they were of the good creation.
Pat: Also in the same (8:44) "You are of your father the devil," therefore he created them.
Cath: I reply that the devil is called father of evils by imitation whence it adds "you do his works" that is, because you do his works. Similar in 1 Peter 3 (3:6) "whose (Sarah's) daughters you are, doing good."
Pat: Also in the same 15 (Jn 15:18) "If the world hates you." Therefore it is not a creature of God if it hates His sons, therefore it is of the devil.
Cath: I reply that the world is here mentioned in place of worldly men and secular princes. For it is not, you stupid pest, that the world system hates or loves, since it has no affections at all, for it is an inanimate thing.

Pat: Also Romans 7 (7:18) "For I know that there does not dwell in me, that is to say, in my flesh, that which is good." Therefore the nature of flesh is evil.

---

178 dedit…fieri] Ioh. 1:12. **180** omnis…**181** est] 1 Ioh. 5:1. **181** omnes…**182** ihesu] Gal. 3:26 (filii] add. dei *Vulg.*) **196** uos…**197** sum] Ioh. 8:23. **197** uos…**198** mundo] Ioh. 17:16. **202** sine…**203** uestro] Ioh. 8:24 (sine creditis] si enim non credideritis *Vulg.*) **205** uos…**206** estis] Ioh. 8:44. **210** estis…benefacientes] 1 Pet. 3:6. **211** Si…odit] Ioh. 15:18 **219** scio…**220** bonum] Rom. 7:18.

186 ex fidem] et fide *F* **187** mihi] michi *P* **190** et] om. *P* **209** quod] add. id est *F* **210** sayre] saire *F*. leg. 'Sarah': perhaps evidence of transcription from a debate. **211** Patarenus] om. *F* **214** pro] quod *F* **217** sit] om. *P* **219** Patarenus] om. *F*

186 eius|fol. 18vb *P* **205** patre|fol. 19ra *P*. New hand. **206** etcet|fol. 11v *F*

Catholicus: Respondo loquitur de stimulo fomitis scilicet carnis pruntis et appetitus. qui malus est. tamen carnis substantia non est mala. de isto dicit ibi postea uideo aliam legem repugnantem in membris meis etcet. unde ueniunt hic fomes qui dicitur peccatum. dicit apostolus superius v per unum hominem peccatum intrauit in mundum.

Patarenus: Item idem in eodem. infelix ego homo quis me liberabit de corpore mortis huius etcet. et dauid educ de carcere animam meam etcet. ergo mala est natura carnis.

Catholicus: Respondeo non dicit apostolus simplici de corpore. sed de corpore mortis huius id est in quantum est mortale. et sic intelligitur illud dauid quia sermo quod corpus est mortale et corruptibile carcer est. Sapientia ix. Corpus quod corrumpitur aggrauat animam etcet. numquam enim simpliciter apostolus uolebat expoliari a corpore. sicut dicit ii ad corinthios v. nos qui sumus in hoc tabernaculo ingemiscimus grauati eo quod nolumus expoliari sed superuestri ut adsorbeatur quod mortale est ad uitam etcet.

Item idem viiii non qui filii carnis hii sunt dei etcet. ergo natura carnis non est a bono principio.

Catholicus: Respondeo ut supra iohannes i non ex sanguinibus etcet. licet filii carnis dicitur iudei qui ex abraam sunt secundum carnem. unde ad romanos iiii. Quid ergo dicemus inuenisse abraam patrem nostrum secundum carnem etcet. filii autem promissionis dicitur gentiles id est filii dei. est ergo sensus. non qui filii carnis scilicet tantum et quod ita sit. patet ad romanos iii. an iudeorum deus tantum immo gentium etcet. notandum est quod tribus modis dicuntur filii. uno per creationem et hoc modo omnes filii dei sunt tam boni quam mali. lucam xv homo quidam habet duos filios etcet. secundo per inmitatiom tam boni quam mali. mali autem sunt filii diaboli per imitationem uel filii seculi. uel filii ydoli et huiusmodi. iohannes viii uos ex patre diaboli estis etcet. et lucam xv filii huius seculi etcet. et deteronomium xiii egressi sunt filii Belial etcet. boni uero dicuntur filii lucis uel filii dei uel filii sanctorum et huiusmodi. Vt lucam xv. et filiis lucis etcet. ephesios iiii estote imitatores dei sicut filii carissimi etcet. et tobit viii filii sanctorum quippe sumus etcet. tertio modi dicitur filii carnis ut hic.

Cath: I reply that he is speaking of the stimulation of the 'fomes'[1] as evil, namely to the enkindling of the flesh and the appetites. Yet the substance of the flesh is not evil, of this he says there after (7:23) "But I see another opposite law in my members," whence comes this 'fomes' which is called sin, as the Apostle says above in 5 (5:12) "through one man sin came into the world."

Pat: Also in the same place (7:23) "Unhappy man that I am, who will deliver me from the body of this death?" and David (Ps 141:8) "Bring my soul out of prison." Therefore the nature of flesh is evil.

Cath: I reply that the Apostle was not speaking simply of the body, but of "the body of this death," that is, insofar as it is mortal. And thus one can interpret David's phrase that the body, mortal and corruptible, is a prison. Wisdom 9 (9:15) "For the corruptible body is a load upon the soul." For never did the Apostle want to be sundered from the body, just as he says in 2 Corinthians 5 (5:4) "For we also who are in this tabernacle, do groan, being burdened because we would not be unclothed, but clothed upon, that that which is mortal may be swallowed up by life."

Also the same in 9 (Rm 9:8) "they that are not the children of the flesh, are the children of God." Therefore the nature of the flesh is not from the good principle.

Cath: I reply as above, John 1 (1:13) "not from blood," although the sons of flesh are called the Jews, who are from Abraham according to the flesh. Whence Romans 4 (4:1) "What shall we say then that Abraham was found to be our father according to the flesh." Yet the sons of the promise are called the gentiles, that is, the sons of God, and this is the sense, they who are not sons of the flesh only, this is so, as is clear in Romans 3 (3:29) "Is he the God of the Jews only? Or yet the Gentiles also." It should be noted that they are called sons in three ways; one by creation, and in this way all are sons of God, be they good or evil. Luke 15 (15:11) "A man had two sons;" the second by imitation, in the good just as in the evil, yet the evil are sons of the devil by imitation or sons of the world or sons of idols and the like. John 8 (8:44) "you are of your father the devil," and Luke 15 (16:8) "the sons of this world," and Deuteronomy 13 (13:13) "The children of Belial are gone," the good are called sons of light, or sons of God, or sons of the saints and the like, as in Luke 15 (16:8) "and sons of the light," Ephesians 4 (5:1) "Be imitators of God just as most dear sons." And Tobit 8 (8:5) "for we are the children of

---

225 uideo...226 meis] Rom. 7:23 (repugnantem] om. *Vulg.*)   227 per...228 mundum] Rom. 5:12.   229 infelix...230 huius] Rom. 7:24.   231 educ...meam] Ps. 141:8 (carcere] add. custodia *Vulg.*)   237 Corpus...238 animam] Sap. 9:15.   240 nos...242 uitam] 2 Cor. 5:4 (nos] om. add. nam; ad uitam] a uita *Vulg.*)   243 non...dei] Rom. 9:8 (hii] hi *Vulg.*)   245 non...246 sanguinibus] Ioh. 1:13.   248 Quid...249 carnem] Rom. 4:1.   252 an...gentium] Rom. 3:29.   255 homo...256 filios] Luc. 15:11.   259 uos...estis] Ioh. 8:44. | filii...260 seculi] Luc. 16:8.   260 egressi...261 Belial] Deut. 13:13.   262 et²...263 lucis] Luc. 16:8.   263 estote...264 carissimi] Eph. 5:1.   264 filii...265 sumus] Tob. 8:5.

---

223 pruntis] pluntus *F* | est...224 isto] om. *F*   229 Patarenus] add. *al. man. marg. sin. P* | om. *F*   233 Catholicus] om. *P*   234 de] om. *P*   235 et] om. *F*   237 ix] viiii *P*   248 abraham] abraam *P*   251 ita] ista *F*   254 sunt] om. *F*   256 quam...257 mali¹] om. *F*   264 tobit] thobit *P*

231 etcet|fol. 19rb *P*   261 Belial|fol. 19va *P*

---

[1] Thomas, *Summa Theologiae* I. q. 91. a. 6.

Patarenus: Item idem in eodem uasa ire apta in interitum etcet. ergo si non poterant saluari erant de mala creatione.
Catholicus: Respondeo non dicit quod non possent saluari. sed cum essent mali. dicit quod sunt uasa apta in interitum. Nec dicit quod sunt posita in interitum sed quod sunt apta. ut non excluderet dei misericordiam sed penitere uellent et quod poterant saluari. et sic erant de bona creatione. ostendit in sustinuit in multa patientia uasa ire etcet. ergo poterant saluari si deus patienter expectauit illos ad penitentiam. preterea quale est hoc argumentum tuum. Hec sunt uasa ire id est diaboli. siquidem concederem quod ira pro diaboli poneretur licet quod non est uerum. immo pro uindicta eterne dampna-tionis ponitur ibi et si sunt uasa diaboli. ergo diabolus creauit illa. non sequitur. unum instancia. uxor est uas uiri sicut dicit petrus prima iii. uiri similiter cohabitantes secundum scienciam quasi infirmiori uasculo mulebri. ergo uir creauit uxorem suam. non sequitur.

Patarenus: Item ii ad corinthios iiii. Que uidentur temporalia sunt. ergo non sunt creata a bono deo. quia opus dei manent in eternum ut dicit ecclesiasticus ibi xlii.
Catholicus: Respondeo temporalia sunt quantum ad formam exteriorem sed quantum ad materiam elementorum manent in eternum. ecclesiastes i° terra autem in aeternum stat. Nec est bona tua conclusio. instancia de angelis qui ceciderunt. quia transierunt quantum ad primam formam per peccatum et penam et tamen a deo sunt creati.
Patarenus: item in eadem xii datus est mihi stimulis carnis mee angelis sathane etcet. ergo natura carnis mala est.
Catholicus: Respondeo loquitur de temptatione diaboli cum qua carnem stimulat intus et extra.
Patarenus: Item ad galatas i° ut eriperet nos de presenti seculo nequam etcet. ergo est a malo principio.
Catholicus: Respodeo quia dicitur hic secundum secularitas.

saints." The third way is when they are termed sons of the flesh, as here.
Pat: Also in the same (Rm 9:22) "vessels of wrath, fitted for destruction." Therefore if they are not able to be saved, they are from the evil creation.
Cath: I respond that he does not say they are unable to be saved, but since they are evil he says that they are "vessels of wrath, fitted for destruction." Neither did he say that they are situated in destruction, but that they are fitted [for it], so the mercy of God might not be excluded, but that they would wish to do penance and that they would be able to be saved, and so they are of the good creation. (9:22) "And to make His power known, He endured with much patience vessels of wrath," therefore they were able to be saved if God awaited penance from them. Further what kind of argument do you have? These are the vessels of wrath, that is, of the devil. If I might have conceded that wrath stands for the devil there — though that is not true — yet he is put there for the vengeance of eternal damnation even if they are the vessels of the devil. So it does not follow that the devil created them. One example, the wife is the vessel of the husband just as Peter says in 1 Peter 3 (3:7) "husbands, likewise dwelling with them according to knowledge, giving honor to the female as to the weaker vessel." However it does not follow that the man created his wife.
Pat: 2 Corinthians 4 (4:18) "For the things which are seen are temporal." Therefore they are not created by the good God, since the world of God remains forever, as Ecclesiasticus says in chapter 42.
Cath: I respond that they are temporal according to their external form, but as to their elemental matter they remain forever. Ecclesiastes 1 (1:4) "yet the earth remains forever." Nor is your conclusion valid in the case of the angels who fell since they passed over according to the first form by sin and punishment, and yet they were created by God.

Pat: In the same (2 Cor 12:7) "there was given to me a sting in my flesh, an angel of Satan," therefore the nature of the flesh is evil.
Cath: I reply that he is speaking of the temptation of the devil, since by it the flesh is stung both inside and out.
Pat: Also Galatians (1:4) "that he might deliver us from this present wicked world," therefore it is from the evil principle.
Cath: I reply that this is speaking according to worldliness.

---

266 uasa...267 interitum] Rom. 9:22.   274 ostendit...275 ire] Rom. 9:22.   283 uiri...284 mulebri] 1 Pet. 3:7.   286 Que...287 sunt¹] 2 Cor. 4:18.   292 terra...293 stat] Eccl. 1:4.   297 datus...298 sathane] 2 Cor. 12:7.   302 ut...303 nequam] Gal. 1:4.

271 sunt] sint *F*   274 sustinuit] substinuit *P*   276 patienter] om. *P*   278 concederem] concedere *F*   279 licet] om. *P*   285 suam] add. etcet *F*   286 Patarenus] om. *F*   289 xlii] om. *P*   292 elementorum] elementorum helementorum *F* | manent] manent manet *F* ecclesiastes...293 stat] om. *P*   297 Patarenus] om. *F*   299 est] om. *F*   302 Patarenus] om. *F*   304 secundum] seculi *P*   305 secularitas] sic *PF* leg. secularitatem

272 excluderet]fol. 12r *F*   288 ecclesiasticus]fol. 19vb *P*

[Patarenus:] Item in eadem v caro concupiscit aduersus spiritum etcet. ergo mala est natura carnis et a malo deo.

Catholicus: Respondeo caro pro habitatione carnis ibi sumitur id est pro fomite sicut supra diximus. ad romanos vii scio etcet.

[Patarenus:] Item ad ephesios ii natura eramus filii ire etcet. ergo secundum naturam aliqui sint filii ire id est diaboli.

Catholicus: Respondeo ut supra. Sapientiam xii. nequam est natio eorum etcet. notatum inueniens. Sed responde tu mihi. apostolus dicit hoc de se et de aliis uiris de peccato conuersis. natura eramus filii ire etcet. ergo secundum tuam expositionem paulus et alii uiri sancti erant creatura diaboli. Nec potes exponere de creatione carnis quia dicit eramus et non dicit sumus. ad huc enim eandem carnem habebant quam prius.

[Patarenus:] Item in eadem iiii deponite uos secundum pristinam conuersationem ueterem hominem qui corrumpitur secundum desideria erroris. renouamini autem spiritu mentis uestre et induite nouum hominem qui secundum deum creatus est etcet. ergo uetus homo id est corpus non est a deo.

Catholicus: Respondeo uetus homo dicitur hec congeries peccatorum. cuius membra sunt singula peccata de quibus habes in colosenses iii. mortificate ergo membra uestra que sunt super terra fornicationem inmunditiam etcet. et de isto ueteri homine dicit ibi. exuite ueterem hominem cum actibus suis et secundum hec nouus homo dicitur congeries bonorum operum. unde ad ephesios ii ipsius enim sumus factura creati in christo ihesu in operibus bonis.

duobus modis dicitur ueteris homo

Item uel uetus homo dicitur adam cuius similitudem debemus exuere. nouus uero dicitur christus. cuius similitudinem debemus induere ad romanos xv sicut portauimus ymaginem terreni sic portemus ymaginem celestis. Sed modo attendas parum. dicis enim quod uetus homo est natura carnis. ergo nos adimplemus preceptum apostoli quia deponimus corpora natura per ignem. sed tamen uos non induimini nouum homine sed in exitu corpore remanetis nudi. in infernali igne cruciandi.

[Patarenus:] Item prima ad tymotheum iiii. omnis creatura dei bona etcet. sed uirus serpentum et ira

[Pat:] Also in the same 5 (5:17) "the flesh lusts against the spirit," therefore the nature of flesh is evil and from the bad God.

Cath: I reply that by the flesh is here meant the habitation of the flesh, that is, for [the tinder of] 'fomes,' as we said above to Romans 7 (7:18) "I know."

[Pat:] also Ephesians 2 (2:3) "we were by nature sons of wrath," therefore some are sons of wrath according to their nature, that is, of the devil.

Cath: I respond as you find noted above (Wis 12:10) "they were a wicked generation." But answer me this. The Apostle says this of himself and of other men converted from sin, "we were by nature sons of wrath," therefore, according to your explanation, Paul and other holy saints were creatures of the devil. Nor are you able to explain it as creations of flesh, since he says "we were" and not "we are." For until now they had the same flesh as before.

[Pat:] Also in the same place in chapter 4 (Eph 4:22-24) "To put off, according to former conversation, the old man who is corrupted according to the desire of error. And be renewed in the spirit of your mind and put on the new man, who is created according to God." Therefore the old man — that is, the body — is not from God.

Cath: I reply that the old man spoken of here is the mass of sins whose members are single sins, of which you have in Colossians 3 (3:5) "Mortify therefore your members which are upon the earth: fornication, uncleanness." And of this old man, he speaks there (3:9) "stripping off the old man with his deeds," and according to this, the new man is called the mass of good works, whence Ephesians 2 (2:10) "For we are his workmanship, created in Christ Jesus in good works."

On the two ways that a man is called "old"

Also the old man might be said to be Adam, whose likeness we ought to strip off, yet the new man is called Christ, whose likeness we ought to put on, as Romans 15 has it (1 Cor 15:49) "Therefore as we have borne the image of the earthly, let us bear also the image of the heavenly." But you pay too little attention when you say that the old man is fleshly nature. Therefore we fulfill the command of the Apostle because we destroy natural bodies by fire,[1] but still you have not put on the new man, but in your exit from the body you remain naked, tortured in eternal fire.

[Pat:] Also 1 Timothy 4 (4:4) "every creature of God is good," but the venom of snakes and the anger of beasts

---

306 caro...307 spiritum] Gal. 5:17.   311 scio] Rom. 7:18.   312 natura...ire] Eph. 2:3.   316 nequam...eorum] Sap. 12:10.   324 secundum...327 est] Eph 4:22-24 (deponite] deponere *Vulg.*)   331 mortificate...333 inmunditiam] Col. 3:5.   334 exuite...suis] Col. 3:9 (exuite] expoliantes vos *Vulg.*)   336 ipsius...337 bonis] Eph. 2:10.   II.7.4 sicut...6 celestis] 1 Cor. 15:49.   12 omnis...13 bona] 1 Tim. 4:4.

312 ii] iii *F*   315 Sapientiam xii] om. *P*   316 Sed] et *P*   322 enim] om. *P*   II.7.1 duobus...homo] om. *F*   2 Item] om. *F* | cuius] eius *P*   3 cuius] alius *P*   4 romanos] sic *PF* leg. Corinthians   6 attendas] adtendas *P*   7 natura carnis] transp. *F*   13 uirus] uirtus *F*

321 sumus|fol. 20ra *P*   II.7.12 tymotheum iiii|fol. 12v *F*

---

1) Peter was an inquisitor, the inquisition would release relapsed heretics to the secular arm for execution by burning. See also below, XXIV.2,167 and XXIV.2,200-202, below.

bestiarum et huiusmodi sunt mala. ergo sunt de mala creatione.

Catholicus: Respondeo bona sunt in quantum creatura creauit enim illa deus ad refrenandam superbiam hominum atque puniendam. ecclesiasticus xxix Spiritus sunt qui ad uindictam creati sunt etcet. Et infra ignis grando fames et mors omnia hec ad uindictam creata sunt bestiarum dentes et scorpii et serpentes et romphea uindicans in exterminium impiorum. etcet. Et xl ad hec mors sanguis contentio et romphea et oppressiones fames et contentio et flagellum super iniquos creata sunt etcet.

Patarenus: Item jacobi iii non est enim ista sapientia desursum sed terrena animalis diabolica etcet. ergo mala sapientia a diabolo est.

Catholicus: Respondeo uerum est in quantum mala est.

Patarenus: Item prima petri vi fideli creatori etcet. ergo est alius creator qui non est fidelis.

Catholicus: Respondeo ad maiorem comendationem dei ponitur ibi fideli id est creatori qui est fidelis simile ad romanos vi ut probetis que sit uoluntas dei bona etcet. non est enim uoluntas dei nisi bona.

Patarenus: Item ii petri ii hi uelud etcet. ibi naturaliter in pernitiem etcet. ergo natura illorum erant mala.

Catholicus: Respondeo exponitur de fomite uel de praue consuetudine uel exponitur naturaliter id est naturali appetitu cibi tenent incorumptionem.

[Patarenus:] Item prima iohannes ii. nolite diligere mundum neque ea que in mundo sunt quia omne quod est in mundo est concupiscencia carnis etcet. ergo mundus et ea que in mundo sunt mala sunt. si prohibentur diligi et si sunt concupiscentia carnis et huius.

Catholicus: Respondeo quia loquitur de illa dilectione. de qua dicit mattheus x si quis diligat agrum aut uineam plusquam me etcet. uel appelat mundum uanitatem mundi licet hominem mundanum qui non debet diligi in quantum talis est. sed responde mihi si de machina mundiali intelligis ergo non debemus diligere homines qui in ea sunt et sic facerent contra de preceptum. diliges proximum tuum etcet. Item non debemus diligere panem et uinum et huiusmodi necessaria. et illa essent omnia peccatum. quia in mundo sunt. Et nota quod mundus ponitur multus modis.

and the like are evil. Therefore they are of the evil creation.

Cath: I reply that they are good insofar as they are creatures, for God created them for checking the pride of man and punishing it. Ecclesiasticus 39 (39:33) "There are spirits that are created for vengeance," and later (39:35–36) "Fire, hail, famine, and death, all these were created for vengeance. The teeth of beasts, and scorpions, and serpents, and the sword taking vengeance upon the ungodly unto destruction." And 40 (40:9–10) "Moreover, death, and bloodshed, strife, and sword, oppressions, famines and afflictions, and scourges, all these things were created for the wicked."

Pat: Also James 3 (3:15) "For this is not wisdom descending from above, but earthly, sensual, diabolical" Therefore evil wisdom is from the devil.

Cath: I reply that is true, insofar as bad things exist.

Pat: Also 1 Peter 6 (4:19) "the faithful creator," therefore there is another creator who is unfaithful.

Cath: I reply that 'faithful' is placed there for the greater commendation of God, that is, in the creator who is faithful, similar to Romans 6 (12:2) "that you may prove what is the good will of God," for there is no will of God that is not good.

Pat: Also 2 Peter 2 (2:12) "and those. . . naturally tending to destruction," therefore their natures were evil.

Cath: I reply that this is to be attributed to 'fomes,' or to evil custom, or is to be explained naturally, that is, by their natural appetite for food they maintain their incorruptibility.

[Pat:] Also 1 John 2 (2:15, 16) "Do not love the world, nor things which are in the world . . . For all that is in the world is the concupiscence of the flesh." Therefore the world and those things in the world are evil, if to love them is forbidden and if they are the concupiscence of the flesh and the like.

Cath: I reply that he is speaking of that love of which Matthew speaks in chapter 10 (10:37) "if one loves field or vineyard more than me." Or it is naming the world, the vanity of the world, or the worldly man who ought to love insofar as he is able. But answer me this, if you interpret it as the world system, therefore we ought not to love men who are in it, and thus they act contrary to the precept, "love your neighbor." Also we ought not to love bread and wine and similar necessary things and so they are all of them sins, since they are in the world. And note that 'the world' is used in many different ways.

---

19 Spiritus...sunt²] Ecclesiastic. 39:33.   20 ignis...23 impiorum] Ecclesiastic. 39:35-36 (impiorum] impios *Vulg.*)   23 ad...25 sunt] Ecclesiastic. 40:9-10 (flagellum] flagella *Vulg.*)   26 non...27 diabolica] Iac. 3:15.   31 fideli creatori] 1 Pet. 4:19.   35 ut...bona] Rom. 12:2.   37 hi uelud] 2 Pet. 2:12.   42 nolite...44 carnis] 1 Ioh. 2:15, 16.   49 si...50 me] paraphrase Matt. 10:37.

19 xxix] xxviiii *P* | Spiritus sunt] transp. *F*   20 Et infra] om. *F*   31 Patarenus] Catholicus *P* exp | *al. man. marg. sin.* add. patarenus *P*   37 ibi...38 etcet] om. *F*   39 exponitur] deponitur *F*   54 facerent] faceremus *F*   58 sunt] est *F*

14 bestiarum|fol. 20rb *P*   45 et|fol. 20va *P*

Quinque modus dicitur mundus

Quandoque ponitur pro machina mundiali. iohannes i mundus per ipsum factus est etcet. quandoque pro mundi habitatione ut id est in mundo erat etcet. quandoque pro mundiali uarietate uel pro mundi superfluitate ut hic. quandoque pro mundi principibus et mundanis hominibus iohannes xv si mundus uos odit etcet. Quandoque uero ponitur pro predestinatis iohannes iii in hoc cognouimus caritatem dei quia ille unigenitum filium dedit pro mundo etcet.

[Patarenus:] Item in eadem iii omnis qui facit peccatum ex diabolo est. ergo est creator malorum.

Catholicus: Respondeo qui facit peccatum ex diabolo est per imitationem. sapientia iii inuidia diaboli etcet. et infra imitatur autem illum qui sunt ex parte eius etcet.

[Patarenus:] Item idem in eodem. omnis qui natus est ex deo peccatum non facit quoniam semen ipsius in eo manet et non potest peccare etcet. ad idem.

Catholicus: Respondeo loquitur de natiuitate gratie. et de natis per imitationem. Vnde caute posuit qui natus est ex deo et non dixit qui natus est a deo uel creatus est a deo quod autem dicit. peccatum non facit uel non potest peccare. intelligitur quamdiu manet in natiuitate tali. quia quamdiu est filius per gloriam peccare non potest. Vnde dicit infra iiii qui diligit ex deo natus est etcet. et iohannes ultimo in fine omnis qui natus est ex deo non peccat sed generatio dei conseruat eum etcet. uel loquitur de predestinatis et quod dicit non potest peccare intelligitur scilicet finaliter. Sed responde mihi. si loquitur de natis per creatorem. ergo petrus et paulus et angeli qui ceciderunt non fuerunt creati a deo quia ipsi peccauerunt quandoque.

Patarenus: Item in eodem sicut eam qui ex maligno erat quia ergo erat a diabolo creatus.

Catholicus: Respondeo erat ex maligno per imitationem. unde subdit et occidit fratrem suum propter quid occidit eum quoniam opera eius maligna erant etcet. quasi dicat ex maligno erat quia maligna opera fecit.

Patarenus: Item quare clamat sacerdos super puerorum exi ab eo spiritum immundus nisi sit in eo per creationem.

Catholicus: Respondeo quia diabolus est in puero ante baptismum tamquam impeditor gratie uel tamquam ligator. Est in eo non substantialiter sed per quadam potestate. Et nota quod in nulla de istis auctoritatibus uel rationibus quas allegasti uel in aliqui alia dicitur aut ostenditur quod diabolus creauerit uel plasmauerit aut fecerit aliquid.

Five ways in which the world is spoken of

Sometimes it refers to the world system, John 1 (1:10) "the world was made through him." Sometimes it refers to the worldly habitation as in "he was in the world." Sometimes it refers to the variety of worlds, or the superfluity of the world, sometimes it stands for the princes of the world and worldly men, John 15 (15:18) "if the world hates you." Other times it is used instead for the predestined as in 1 John 3 (3:16) "In this we have known the charity of God, by which he gave his only Son for the world."

[Pat.] Also in the same place in chapter 3 (8:34) "all those who do sins" are of the devil, therefore he is the creator of evildoers.

Cath: I reply that those who do sins are from the devil by reason of imitation, Wisdom 3 (2:24) "the envy of the devil," and later (2:25) "And they who follow him are of his side."

[Pat.] Also in the same (1 Jn 3:9) "Whoever is born of God does not commit sin, for his seed abides in him, and he cannot sin."

Cath: I reply that it is speaking of the birth by grace and of the birth by imitation. Whence beware, he posits he who is 'born from God,' and He did not say he who is born of God or is created by God, since yet he says he does not sin or he cannot sin. This is to be understood of one who remains for a long time in such a birth, since such a one is a son by the glory for a long time is not able to sin. Whence he says later in chapter 4 (1 Jn 4:17) "And every one who loves, is born of God," and at the end (1 Jn 5:18) "whoever is born of God, does not sin, but the generation of God preserves him." Or he is speaking of the predestined one, and that he says he cannot sin is to be understood as saying that he will persevere to the end. But answer me this. If he is speaking of birth by the creator, therefore Peter and Paul and the angels who fell were not created by God since they sinned sometimes.

Pat: Also in the same (1 Jn 3:12) "who was of the wicked one," therefore he was created by the devil.

Cath: I reply (1 Jn 3:12) "he was evil," by imitation, whence he adds "and he killed his brother, and why did he kill him? Because his own works were wicked," as if to say that he was evil since he did evil works.

Pat: Also why does the priest say [Rite of Baptism] over the children "go out from him unclean spirit," unless it be in him by virtue of creation?

Cath: I reply that the devil is in the child before baptism as an impediment to grace or like one who binds. So he is not in him substantially, but by a certain power. And note that in none of these authorities or arguments which you adduced or in any other is it said or demonstrated that the devil created or molded or made anything.

II.8.3 mundus...est] Ioh. 1:10.   7 si...8 odit] Ioh. 15:18.   9 in...10 mundo] 1 Ioh. 3:16.   11 omnis...12 peccatum] Ioh. 8:34.   14 inuidia diaboli] Sap. 2:24.   15 imitatur...eius] Sap 2:25 (eius *illius Vulg.*)   17 omnis...19 peccare] 1 Ioh. 3:9.   26 qui...27 est] 1 Ioh. 4:7.   27 omnis...29 eum] 1 Ioh. 5:18.   36 erat...38 erant] 1 Ioh. 3:12.   41 exi...immundus] Ritus baptismalis.

II.8.1 Quinque...mundus] om. *F*   2 ponitur] om. *P*   5 mundiali] add. habitationem *P* exp.   6 ut] ait *F*   22 dixit] om. *P*   34 Patarenus] om. *F* | add. *al. man. marg. dex. P*

II.8.15 illum|fol. 20vb *P*   25 natiuitate|fol. 13r *F*   44 tamquam²|fol. 21ra *P*

Pro illis qui dicunt quod omnia sunt eterna in sui materia

[**Patarenus:**] Ecclesiastes prima nichil sub sole nouum. etcet.

Catholicus: hunc oppositioni reseruo infra responsionem. libro secundo titulo de predestinatis.

De dominio et omnipotentia diaboli regni sui

[**Patarenus:**] Mattheus vi nemo potest duobus dominus seruire etcet. sed unus est deus et alter est mamona qui est diabolus. ergo est dominus in regno suo.

Catholicus: Respondeo non loquitur de diabolo quicquid. sed de diuitiis huius seculi. mamona est diuitie interpretatur est enim uerbum siriacum. quod ebraice dicitur mamon. latine uero sonat diuitie cum quibus non possumus seruire deo. si illas diligimus sicut deum. et quod non loquatur de diabolo patet per id quod dicit idem facite uobis amicos de mamona iniquitatis etcet. numquid enim de diabolo potest quis facere amicum. uel si de diabolo uis intelligere. dico quod est dominus malorum per ipsorum electionem per mala opera que faciunt eligunt dominium ipsius. unde sapientiam primo Deus mortem non fecit etcet. et postea impii autem manibus et uerbis accessierunt illam et estimantes illam amicam defluxerunt et sponsiones posuerunt ad illam. quoniam morte digni sunt. qui sint ex parte illius etcet. Item propter hoc quod diceretur diabolus dominus aliquorum. non sequeretur quod esset dominus naturaliter et omnipotens quia de multis dominis mentionem facit scriptura.

Patarenus: Item idem xxv qui paratus est diabolo et angelis eius etcet. ergo diabolus habet angelos in sua curia et est omnipotens in eis.

Catholicus: Respondeo quia demones dicuntur angeli diaboli propter prelationem eius quam elegerunt quando adheserunt ei per peccatum superbie contempto deo. Nec enim dicit quod sint de regno diaboli uel quod sit omnipotens in illius

Patarenus: Item lucam primo regni eius non erit finis etcet. sed mundus transibit ergo non est regno filii dei igitur diaboli.

Catholicus: Respondeo loquitur. Sed mundus debebat regnare per gratiam christus. et hoc est quod exponens dixerit angelus ibi et regnabit in domo iacob in eternum etcet. uel loquitur de regno ubi regnabit cum sanctis suis in eternum. hic enim non regnat cum illis in eternum. quia de mundo isto recedit per mortem.

For those who say that everything is eternal in its matter

[**Pat:**] Ecclesiastes 1 (1:10) "There is nothing new under the sun."

Cath: My opposition to this I will reserve until my responses in the second book, under the title 'on the Predestinarians.'

On the lordship and almighty power of the devil in his kingdom

[**Pat:**] Matthew 6 (6:24) "no one is able to serve two masters," but one is God and the other is Mammon, who is the devil. Therefore he is lord in his kingdom.

Cath: I reply that He is not speaking about the devil at all, but about the riches of this world. Mammon is riches, for it is interpreted as a Syriac word which in Hebrew is called 'Mammon,' (Ordinary Gloss) yet in Latin it means riches, by which we cannot serve God if we love them as much as the Lord. And that He is not speaking of the devil is clear from what He says there (Lk 16:9) "you make yourselves friends of the Mammon of iniquity." For no one can befriend the devil, or if you do wish to interpret the devil in this passage, I say that he is the lord of evildoers who, through their own choice [and] through the evil works that they do, elect to be under his dominion. Whence in Wisdom 1 (1:13) "God did not make death," and later (1:16) "But the wicked with works and words have called it to them, and esteeming it a friend have fallen away, and have made a covenant with it because they are worthy of death, who might be from its part." Also on account of this that just because the devil is called 'lord' by some, it does not follow that he is lord by nature, nor that he is omnipotent since scripture makes mention of many lords.

Pat: Also in the same book (Mt 25:41) "which is prepared for the devil and his angels." Therefore the devil has angels in his court and is omnipotent among them.

Cath: I reply that the demons are called angels of the devil on account of his preeminence, to which they raised him when they joined with him in the sin of pride in contempt of God. For neither does He say that he might be of the kingdom of the devil, nor that he might be omnipotent in it.

Pat: Also Luke 1 (1:33) "Of his kingdom there will be no end." But the world will pass away so it is not the kingdom of the Son of God, therefore it is of the devil.

Cath: I respond by saying that the world ought to be ruled by the grace of Christ. And this explanation was offered by the angel here (1:32) "and he shall reign over the house of Jacob forever." Or it speaks of the kingdom where He shall reign with His saints forever, for He will not reign with them eternally here, since this world passes away unto

---

II.9.3 nichil...nouum] Eccl. 1:10.   II.10.2 nemo...3 seruire] Matt. 6:24.   6 mamona...7 siriacum] Ordinary Gloss to Matt. 6:24.
11 facite...12 iniquitatis] Luc. 16:9.   16 Deus...fecit] Sap. 1:13.   17 impii...20 illius] Sap. 1:16.   24 qui...25 eius] Matt. 25:41.
32 regni...finis] Luc. 1:33.   37 et...eter-num] Luc. 1:32.

II.9.5 hunc] om. *F* | infra] om. *F*   II.10.7 ebraice] arabice *P*   9 si] si sed *F*   10 per id] om. *P*   14 per...electionem] om. *P*
15 eligunt] diligunt *F*   17 manibus] add. quibus *F*   19 quoniam] add. morte *F*   21 non] nisi *P*   22 dominus] om. *P*   23 mentionem] rationem *P*   24 Patarenus] om. *F*   32 Patarenus] om. *F*   33 sed...35 loquitur] om. *F*   36 christus] *sic PF* leg. Christi | hoc est] om. *P*
38 loquitur] om. *P*

II.10.20 illius|fol. 21rb *P*

nec propter hoc sequitur ergo hic non sunt de regno eius. uel mundus non est de regno eius. Nec etiam mundus transibit quantum ad materiam elementorum. sed tantum secundum formam exteriorem ipsa in melius mutata.

[Patarenus:] Item idem iiii ubi diabolus ostendit christo omnia regna mundi et gloriam eorum et dixit tibi dabo potestatem hanc mundi et gloria eorum. quia mihi tradita est etcet. ergo diabolus est dominum omnium uisibilium.

Catholicus: Respondeo mentitus est sicut solet quia ipse est mendax sicut dicit ueritas. Vnde propter hoc habeo potius contrarium. quod etiam patet. quia ea que dixit dei filius uera esse non demonstrauit. preterea ut ex uerbum domini tui te confundam quibus inniteris audi quid dicit quod tradita sunt ei. ergo non est naturalis deus. sed ille qui tradidit. erubesce igitur miserabile fantasia qui confidis in uerbis mendacii et crede ueritati dicenti omnia mihi tradita sunt a patre meo etcet.

Patarenus: Item iohannes xiiii uenit enim princeps mundi huius etcet. ad ephesios ii aliquando ambulastis secundum seculum mundi huius secundum principem aeris huius huius spiritus etcet. ergo diabolus est dominus mundi et omnipotens.

Catholicus: Respodeo diabolus dicitur princeps id est rectorum malorum. ecclesiasticus x secundum iudicem populi et sic ministri eius et qualis est rector ciuitatis et tales et habitantes in ea etcet.

Duplex principatus id est diaboli

Vel est princeps mundi id est mundialitatis et peccatis et quia est princeps malorum uel uanitatis suggerende. et deducende per corda hominum. hoc habet ex permissione. usque ad tempus apocalypsis xii. sciens quod modicum tempus habet etcet. unde demonia clamabant ihesu filii dei qui uenisti ante tempus torquere nos etcet.

Tria sunt in mundo

Vel aliter dico quod in mundo tria sunt scilicet essentia eius. usus licitus et abusus. primum est solius dei ut probatum est supra pro parte de nostra tractatus huius. Secundum est hominis omnia subeicisti sub pedibus eius oues et boues etcet. Tertium uero est diaboli apocalypsis viii cecidit de celo stella magna ardens tamquam facula et cecidit in tertiam partem fluminum etcet. et istud tertium dicitur mundus cuius diabolus

death, nor on account of this does it follow therefore that this place is not of His kingdom, or the world is not of His kingdom, nor that the world shall pass away according to its material elements, but it shall only be changed for the better in its exterior form.

[Pat:] Also the same in 4 where (Mt 4:8–9) "Again the devil. . . showed him all the kingdoms of the world, and their glory, and said to him, 'All these will I give you (Luke 4:6) power over this world and its glory, which was handed over to me,'" so the devil is the Lord of all visible things.

Cath: I reply that he is contradicted, as usual, for he is himself a liar, as the Truth says. Whence regarding this I hold rather the contrary, which is also clear since by that which the Son of God says he did not show to be true. Further as from the word of your lord you are confounded in what you support. Listen to those things he says are handed over to him. Therefore he is not god according to nature, but rather He who handed it over [is God over nature], blush therefore in your miserable fantasy, who trust in the words of a liar and believe in the truth spoken (Lk 10:22) "all things are handed over to me by my Father."

Pat: Also John 14 (14:30) "For the prince of this world comes." Ephesians 2 (2:2) "In time past you walked according to the course of this world, according to the prince of the power of this air." Therefore the devil is the lord of the world and all powerful.

Cath: I reply that the devil is called prince, that is, of the leadership of the evildoers. Ecclesiasticus 10 (10:2) "As the judge of the people is himself, so also are his ministers, and what kind of man the ruler of a city is, such also are those who dwell there."

The double principate, that is, of the devil

Either he is the prince of the world, that is, of mundane things and sins and so he is the prince of evildoers, or of vanity, by suggesting and leading through the hearts of men, this he has in virtue of permission until the end of time. Apocalypse 12 (12:12) "knowing that he has but a short time," whence the demons clamor (Mt 8:29) "Jesus son of God, you have come before your time to torment us."

Three things are in the world

Or otherwise I say that in the world there are three things, namely His essence, legitimate use, and abuse. The first pertains only to God, as is proven above in our work. The second pertains to men (Ps 8:8) "you have subjected all things under his feet, all sheep and oxen, moreover the beasts also of the fields." Yet the third pertains to the devil. Apocalypse 8 (8:10) "and a great star fell from heaven, burning as it were a torch, and it fell on the third part of

---

46 diabolus... 48 dabo] Matt. 4:8-9. 48 potestatem... 49 est¹] Luc. 4:6 (mundi) uniuersam *Vulg.*) 59 omnia... 60 meo] Luc. 10:22. 61 uenit... 62 huius] Ioh. 14:30. 62 aliquando... 64 spiritus] Eph. 2:2 (principem) add. potestatis *Vulg.*) 67 secundum... 69 ea] Ecclesiastic. 10:2. **II.11.**5 sciens... 6 habet] Apoc. 12:12. 7 ihesu... 8 nos] Matt. 8:29. **II.12.**5 omnia... 6 boues] Ps. 8:8. 7 cecidit... 8 fluminum] Apoc. 8:10.

42 mundus] om. *P* | non... 43 mundus] om. *P* 49 dominum] om. *F* 54 uera] †† nesu *F*. Corrupt text. 61 Patarenus] om. *F* | add. al. man. marg. sin. *P* 62 ad] om. *F* **II.11.**1 Duplex... diaboli] om. *F* 8 etcet] add. uel aliter *P* **II.12.**1 Tria... mundo] om. *F* 2 Vel aliter] om. *P*

42 mundus|fol. 13v *F* 55 ex|fol. 21va *P* **II.12.**8 partem|fol. 21vb *P*

princeps est. Sed responde tu si de machina mundiali intelligis et christus in ea fuit sicut dicit iohannes primo. in mundo erat etcet. ergo diabolus poterat eum eicere tantum si mundus est regnum suum et si in eo est omnipotens quod falsum est. quia de porcis tantum non habuit potestatem nisi per christum. Item dicit dominus in iohanne xv nunc princeps mundi huius eicietur foras etcet. ergo eiectus est de mundo ergo nichil in eo habet ulla potestas.

Triplex principium

[**Patarenus:**] Item idem xviii regnum meum non est de hoc mundo etcet. ergo diabolus est in eo rex.
Catholicus: respondeo regnum hoc de quo loquitur est illud de quo dicitur ad romanos xiiii regnum dei non est esca et potus sed iustitia et pax et gaudium in spiritu sancto et tale regnum non est de hoc mundo. et si de regno id est de potestate sua intelligere uis. ita est sensus. regnum dei non est de hoc mundo id est a mundanis hominibus sed a mea propria uirtute qui deus sum. unde eleganter adiecit regnum meum non est hinc etcet. non dixit non est hic quia ubique est eius potestas et imperium. uel regnum dei dicuntur sancti in quibus deus regnat. apoc v. fecisti nos deo nostro regnum etcet.

Patarenus: Item prima iohannes v totus mundus in maligno positus est etcet. ergo totus est de regno diaboli.
Catholicus: Respondeo totus mundus in maligno positus est id est in malo igne. unde dominus dicit iohanne xvi. in mundo pressuram habeatis etcet. totus mundus id est omnis mundialitas in quantum peccatum est. licet totus mundus id est homo mundanus qui positus est totus in diabolo. sed quo ad animam per prauum desiderium. et quo ad corpus per prauam operationem. sed responde tu mihi. si de machina mundiali intelligis. ergo christus qui erat in mundo erat in diabolo positus. quia si domus est in ciuitate et homo est in domo. ergo homo est in ciuitate quod falsum est quod christus in diaboli fuerit quia ipse dicit in iohanne xiiii. uenit princeps mundi huius et in me non habet quicquam etcet.

Patarenus: Item apocalypsis xiiii dedit illi draco uirtutem suam et potestatem magnam etcet. ergo habet primam potestatem in suo regno et omnimodam.
Catholicus: respondeo sine dubio potestatem magnam. sed illam habet a deo. Vnde dicit similiter. ix et data est illi clauis putei abyssi et hoc capitulo dicitiur et

the rivers." And this third is said to be the world of which the devil is prince. But answer me, if by this you mean the machine of the world, and Christ was in it, as John 1 (1:10) "he was in the world," therefore the devil was able to expel Him only if the world was his kingdom and if in it he was omnipotent, but this is false, for he did not even have power over the pigs, except through Christ. Also the Lord says in John 15 (12:31) "Now will the prince of this world be cast out." Therefore he is cast out of the world, and so there is nothing in him at all that has power.

The threefold principle

[**Pat:**] Also in the same 18 (18:36) "my kingdom is not of this world," so the devil is king in that world.
Cath: I reply that this kingdom of which he speaks is that which is spoken of in Romans 14 (14:17) "For the kingdom of God is not meat and drink, but justice, and peace, and joy in the Holy Spirit." And such a kingdom is not of this world, and if you are willing to understand it of His reign, that is, of His power, this is the [correct] sense. And the kingdom of God is not of this world, that is, of worldly men, but is of my own proper power, who am God, whence He properly adds (18:36) "my kingdom is not from hence," He did not say 'it is not here' since His kingdom is everywhere in power and lordship, or the kingdom of God is said to be the saints through which God reigns. Apocalypse 5 (5:10) "And you have made us to our God a kingdom."

Pat: Also 1 John 5 (5:19) "and the whole world is seated in wickedness." Therefore it is wholly the kingdom of the devil.
Cath: I reply that the whole world has been placed in the evil one, that is, in the evil fire, whence the Lord says in John 16 (16:33) "In the world you shall have distress." The whole world, that is, all worldly things insofar as they are sinful. That means all the world. That is worldly man, who has been placed totally in the power of the devil: as to the soul through a wicked desire, as regards the body through wicked deeds. But answer me this, if you understand the machine of the world, you think that Christ, who was in the world, was in the devil, since if a house is in a city and a man is in the house, therefore the man is in the city. It is false that Christ was in the devil since He Himself says in John 14 (14:30) "For the prince of this world comes, and in me he does not have anything."

Pat: Also Apocalypse 14 (13:2) "And the dragon gave him his own strength, and great power." Therefore he has the first power in his kingdom and of every sort.
Cath: I reply that without doubt it is a great power, but he has it from God. Whence it says similarly in 9 (9:1) "and there was given to him the key of the bottomless pit," and

datum est illi scilicet draconi ut daret spiritum ymagnii bestie etcet. ergo non habet potestate a se nisi detur ab alio qui est deus. Nec obstat quod dicit hic uirtutem suam etcet. quia uirtus dicitur sua postquam data est ei. sicut regnum celorum dicitur esse sanctorum postquam datum est eis a deo. lucam v. Beati pauperes spiritu quia uestrum est regnum dei etcet. uel dicitur sua id est ad suam dampnationem. similiter lucam xxi hec est hora uestra et potestas tenebrarum etcet. et nota quod in omnibus allegatio-nibus tuis non induxisti nec inducere posses aliquam occasionem uel scripturam uolentem quod diabolus sit omnipotens in aliquo regno uel in aliqua re. Ex superioribus allegationibus tam nostris quam aduer-sariorum probatum est quod unus solus est deus creator et factor omnium atque omnipotens et quod diabolus est creatura. et quod nichil creauit aut fecit. et quod nichil potest nisi per deum et quod ipsi pertinacium inficiantur.

this chapter (13:15) "And it was given him," namely, to the dragon, "to give life to the image of the beast." Therefore he has no power of himself unless it might have been given by another, who is God. Neither does it matter that he says here (13:2) "his own strength" since the power is said to be his only after it is given to him, just as the kingdom of heaven is said to belong to the saints after it is given to them by God. Luke 5 (Mt 5:3) "blessed are the poor in spirit, for yours is the kingdom of God." Or it is called "his" that is, to his damnation. Similarly Luke 21 (22:53) "this is the hour and the power of darkness," and note that in all your assertions you have not adduced anything, nor are you able to adduce any occasion or scripture wishing that the devil might be all powerful in any kingdom or in anything. From the foregoing passages — as much mine as those of the adversary — it is proved that God is one alone, creator and fashioner of all things, also omnipotent, and that the devil is a creature and that he neither created nor fashioned anything. And that he can do nothing except by the permission of God, and that these heretics are infected by stubbornness.

De summa et indiuidua trinitate diuinarum personarum. patris et filii et spiritus sancti

Dictum est supra et probatum contra errores patarenorum quod unus solus est deus. nunc autem probandus est illis quod deus est trinus et unus pater et filius et spiritus sanctus. tres personem unus deus habentes hunc errorem in se ab arrio deriuatum qui asserit filium et spiritum sanctum non esse diuinitatis personas. nec domino patri equales. ac illi consubstantiales. Dicebat enim quod filius et spiritus sanctus erant pure creature. unde et de filio ait. non inuideo deo filio dei. quia possum et ego fieri filius dei sicut et ipse. Vnde et diuino iudicio crepuit medius. ut sicut diuinam essentiam separabat sic ille separatus est insemetipso diffusis in triam uisceribus. nos autem catholice sentientes probare uolumus et possumus euidenter quod pater et filius et spiritus sanctus sunt tres persone coequales ac consubstantiales. ad quod hoc ordinem perueniemus. primo per rationes naturales. secundo per scripturas. per rationes autem naturales dupliciter scilicet per illas que directe insemetipsis probant trinitatem et per eas que nobis ex creaturis inducunt communione. per scripturas uero tamen ueteris testamentum quam noua et per quasdam philosophorum auctoritates tres tenetur personis unam esse diuinitatis essentiam ostendemus.

III On the highest and unique Trinity of divine persons, of the Father and of the Son and of the Holy Spirit

It was spoken of and proven above against the errors of the Patarenes that there is one God alone, yet now it remains to be proven to them that God is three and one. The Father, the Son, and the Holy Spirit are three persons, one God. Having derived this error among them from Arius, who asserted the Son and the Holy Spirit were not divine persons, neither equal to the Father nor consubstantial with Him. For they were saying that the Son and the Holy Spirit were simply creations, whence of the Son he said there cannot be in one God a Son of God, since I can and I will become the son of God like Him. Whence according to the judgment of God he was split down the middle, just like he was separating the Divine essence, so was he separated himself being divided into three piles of flesh.[1] But we Catholics desiring to prove it, we wish and are able to establish evidently that the Father and the Son and the Holy Spirit are three persons, coequal and consubstantial, and to this we shall arrive in due order, first by natural arguments, second through the scriptures. By rational or natural arguments in a twofold way, namely, through those which from the created [world[lead us to infer the communion [of the Trinity]. We shall demonstrate through scriptures, as much from the Old Testament as from the New, and through certain philosophical authorities, three persons in one divine essence.

---

44 Beati…45 dei] Luc. 6:20, but actually quoting Matt. 5:3.   47 hec…tenebrarum] Luc. 22:53.

41 alio] aliquo F   42 sua] om. F   44 eis] ei F   46 dampnationem] donationem F   48 allegatio-nibus] allegoribus P   49 nec] ubi F
III.1.14 diffusis] difusus P   22 inducunt] inducit P | communione] connicionemur P (unclear word)   25 tenetur] om. F

50 omnipotens|fol. 22rb P   III.1.22 inducunt|fol. 22va P

---

[1] Arius died the day before he was to be readmitted to communion with the Church. According to medieval tradition he suffered a horrible death, being reduced into three parts in memory of his denial of the Trinity. This is extrapolated from the Greek legend that he died of internal hemorrhage while on the toilet.

Probatio de trinitate in semetipsa per rationes naturales

Constat sine contradicione ut deo fuisse summum et perfectum bonum ab eterno et omni delectationem plenum. sed maius bonum est in societate quantum in singularitate. igitur societas fuit in deo ab eterno. sed cum naturalior et honestior et delectabilior omnibus aliis societas patris et filii. ergo deus filium habuit cum quo delectatur eternaliter mediante summi amplectente amore utriusque qui est spiritus sanctus. sed maior est delectatio in eodem quam indiuerso et insimili omnimode quam indissimile ergo filius et spiritus sanctus sunt due persone patri equales ac consubstantiales eidem.

Patarenus: eodem modo posses argumentari quod in diuinitatis essentia plures essent filli ac plures spiritus sancti.

Catholicus: Non possem nec possum quia non potest esse quod in diuinitatis essentia sint plures filii ac plures spiritus sancti. quia in diuinitate nichil dissonum nichil diuisum nichil denique quod a concorde discepat simphonia esse potest. Cum ergo pater et filius mutua se relatione respiciant et pater et filius cum spiritu sancto. et spiritus sanctus cum patre et filio. quia pater et filius respiciunt generationis relatione et pater et filius respiciunt spiritum sanctum et spiritus sanctus patrem et filium. relationem spirationis. sic est in diuinitatis essentia omnimoda et concors simphonia. sed si essent in diuinitate plures filii aut plures spiritus sancti. illi filii aut illi spiritus sancti mutua relatione carentes ad inuicem discreparent. et ideo est impossibile in diuinitatis essentia. nisi tres esse personas patris et filii et spiritus sancti.

Item aut pater ab eterno uoluit generare filium coequalem sibi et potuit. aut potuit et non uoluit. aut neque potuit nec voluit. et si potuit et noluit inuidus fuit. Si uoluit et non potuit impotens fuit. Si autem potuit et uoluit et per consequentiam sciuit. quia omnia sciuit que potest et uult. sequitur quod deus ab eterno generauit filium ab eterno coequalem sibi. quod autem pater uoluit generare filium equalem sibi probatur sic. ad summam auaritiam pertinet nichil de bonis suis uelle comunicare. igitur ad summam bonitatem et libertatem pertinet omnia comunicare uelle. Sed cum pater sit ab eternum summe liberale. ergo ab eterno totum suum esse alteri comunicauit. quod est generare filium equalem sibi ab eterno. et hic est quod dicit filius in euangelio Iohannes capitulo xvi. Omnia quecumque habet pater mea sunt etcet. et xvii omnia mea tua sunt et tua mea sunt etcet. quod autem

Proof of the Trinity in itself through natural arguments

It is obvious, without contradiction, that in God is the highest and perfect good, from eternity and full of every delight. Yet it is a greater good to be in a community rather than in isolation. Therefore there is a community in God from eternity. But since the relation of Father and Son are more natural and more worthy and more delightful than any other, therefore God had a Son in whom He is delighted eternally by means of a supreme being embracing the love of both, who is the Holy Spirit. But it is an even greater delight in it, rather than being indivisible and similar in every way than being dissimilar. Therefore the Son and the Holy Spirit are two persons, equal with the Father and consubstantial with Him.

Pat: In the same way you can argue that in the divine essence there are many Sons and many Holy Spirits.

Cath: I could not and I cannot since there cannot be anything in the divine essence that might be many Sons or many Holy Spirits, since in the divinity there is no dissonance or division, nor indeed is anything which could disrupt the existing symphony of concord. Since therefore the Father and the Son together mutually consider one another in their relation, and the Father and the Son with the Holy Spirit, and the Holy Spirit with the Father and the Son, because Father and Son are in regards to the relation of generation, and the Father and the Son in regards to the Holy Spirit, and the Holy Spirit in regards to the relation of spiration in the Father and the Son. Thus there is in the divine essence a harmonious symphony in every way. If, however, there were many Sons and many Holy Spirits in the divinity, these Sons and Holy Spirits would be lacking the mutual relations between themselves and so would be in disagreement and disharmony, and such a thing is impossible in the divine essence, except that there be three persons: Father, Son, and Holy Spirit.

Also either the Father wished to generate a coequal Son from all eternity for Himself, and He was able, or He was able and He did not wish it, or He was neither willing nor able. If He was able and did not wish it He was hateful. If He wished to but was unable, He was impotent. If yet He was able and He willed it, and as a consequence knew, since he knew all things and was able and willing, it follows that God generated the Son from all eternity, coequal with Himself. But that the Father wished to generate a Son equal to Himself is proven thusly. Nothing of His goodness that He wishes to share pertains to the highest avarice, therefore it corresponds to the highest goodness and liberality that He wishes to share everything. But since the Father is the most liberal from all eternity, therefore from eternity He shared His whole being with another, that is, to generate a coequal Son to Himself from eternity. This is what the Son says in the gospel of John chapter 16 (16:15) "everything which the Father has is mine," and 17 (17:10)

III.2.49 Omnia...sunt] Ioh. 16:15.   50 omnia...sunt²] Ioh. 17:10.

III.2.3 ut] in F   9 eternaliter] naturaliter F   12 insimili] inconsimili P   19 essentia] constantia F   22 simphonia] add. et P   23 respiciant] reformaretur Pr   37 impotens] add. et invidus F   44 comunicare...45 uelle] transp. F

III.2.2 naturales|fol. 14v F   29 si|fol. 22vb P

deus potuit generare filium sibi coequalem probatur hoc modo. infirmus homo potest hic scilicet generare filium equalem sibi. et hic est in eo laudabile et perfectionis naturalis signum. ergo multo fortius omnipotens ab eterno potuit generare filium coequalem sibi.

De Spiritu sancto

De Spiritu sancto probatur sic. Sicut enim emanatio quam aliquid emanat ab alio per modum generationis perfectissima. ita emanatio quam aliquid emanat ab alio per modum benignitats uel liberalitatis gratissima et iocundissima est. et sicut oportet ex necessitate ut a summo fonte bonitatis sit emanatio perfectissima que est generatio ut predictum est. ita necesse est ut a proprio fonte qui est primus et summus fons et omnis uere iocunditatis et beatudinis plenissimus sit emanatio gratissima et iocundissima et ita emanatio que est per modum benignitatis summa liberalitatis donum est et donatio. nichil enim uero proprio donum nisi illud quod mera libertate procedit. ergo quod ex summa liberalitate procedit. est summum bonum. sed quod primo procedit tamquam primum donum a benignitate est amor. amor enim est donum in quo omnia alia dona dantur. qui enim dat uere alicui amorem suum omnia facit ei communia. et quod datur non ex amore non proprie datur. Sed quod ex amore datur proprie donum est. Quod ergo a summo fonte bonitatis procedit primo sed modum benignitatis est amor summus et summum donum. Sed amor est donum intrinsecum. quod est in ipso dante in quo datur dona extrinseca. amor igitur qui procedit ex deo est in eo a quo procedit. sed quicquid est in deo deus est et quicquid est in deo eternum est. ergo amor qui procedit ex deo deus est. et fuit ab eterno. Istud autem amorem vocamus spiritum sanctum. quod etiam ille amor fuerit ab eterno probabitur infra tractatu de spiritu sancto et sic patet quod tres persone sunt in una diuinitatis essentia.

Item in summo bono ab eterno fuit summa beatitudo. ergo ibi fuit summa iocunditas. Sed nichil est gratiosius et iocundius quam mutua caritas. quia nullius rei sine consortio iocunda est possessio. ergo mutua caritas ab eterno fuit in summo bono. sed mutua caritas non potest esse nisi inter plures personas. ergo ab eterno fuerunt plures persone in summo bono. Sed in diuinitate oportebat quod igitur esset mutua caritas et summa propter summam beatitudinem. summa autem caritas et mutua probat equalitatem personarum. quia si summa persona summe diligebat aliam. ergo alia persona erat summe diligenda. aliter enim non esset defecta dilectio. sed si alia persona est summa diligenda. ergo ipse est deus. fuit summum

"and all my things are yours, and yours are mine." That God was also able to generate a coequal Son to Himself is proven in this way. A weak man here can generate a son equal to himself, and here it is praiseworthy in him and a sign of natural perfection, therefore how much more the is the omnipotent one able to generate a coequal Son to Himself from all eternity.

On the Holy Spirit

Regarding the Holy Spirit, one can prove Him thusly. For just as an emanation which emanates from another in the manner of generation is most perfect, so an emanation which emanates from another in the manner of benevolence and liberality is the happiest. And just as it is fitting that by necessity from the highest source of goodness there be the most perfect emanation, which is by generation, as was said already; so is it necessary that from the same source, which is the first and highest, of all true delight and fulness of blessedness there might be an emanation most agreeable and delightful and so the emanation which is in the manner of goodness and the height of liberality is a gift and a donation. For what indeed is properly a gift unless it proceeds from pure freedom? Therefore that which proceeds from the highest freedom is the highest good. But what proceeds first, such as a first gift from benevolence, is love. For love is a gift in which all other gifts are given, for he who gives his love to another gives him all gifts together in common. And what is not given from love is not, properly speaking, given at all, yet that which is given from love is properly speaking a gift. Therefore that which proceeds first from the highest font of goodness, but in the manner of goodness, is the highest love and the highest gift. But love is an intrinsic gift, that is given in itself into whom it is given as an extrinsic gift. Therefore the love which proceeds from God is in Him from whom He came forth, but whatever is in God is God, and whatever is in God is eternal. Therefore the love which comes forth from God is God, and was from eternity. Yet this love we call the Holy Spirit, and also that this love was from eternity shall be proven in the section on the Holy Spirit, and so it is clear that there are three persons in one divine nature.

Also in the highest good from eternity there was supreme blessedness, therefore there was also supreme delight, but nothing is more pleasing and delightful than mutual love, because nothing delightful is possessed without companionship, therefore mutual love was present from eternity in the highest good. Yet mutual love cannot exist unless between several persons, therefore from eternity there were multiple persons in the highest good. But it is fitting that there be mutual charity of the highest level in the divinity, on account of supreme blessedness, and moreover the highest love proves the mutual equality of persons, since if the highest person loved another person in the highest manner, therefore the other person would be the highest thing to be loved. For otherwise there would be no defect in love. unless another person would be the highest thing

---

54 ergo] om. *P* **III.3.1** De...sancto] om. *F* **3** alio] aliquo *F* **11** que] quam *P* **13** donatio] donatio donatis *F* | proprio] add. dicitur *F* **14** ergo...**15** procedit] om. *F* **28** Istud...**30** eterno] om. *P* **33** bono] om. *P* **40** oportebat] opportebat *P* **45** defecta] defecta difecta *F* **46** ipse] ipsa *F* | fuit] sunt *F*

III.3.2 emanatio|fol. 23ra *P* **11** que|fol. 15r *F* **28** fuit|fol. 23rb *P*

bonum. et ita sequitur quod uterque erat equalis alteri. summa etiam caritas et mutua probat trinitatem personarum. Si enim erat summa caritas inter duas personas necesse erat ut utraque tertiam inquireret cui communicaret delitias sue bonitatis. aliter enim esset illabilis dilectio. si altera illarum personarum ab ea que diligi summe uellet. uellet aliam equaliter diligi. In tribus ergo personis potuit esse totius maiestatis communicatio. et ita ab eterno fuerunt tres persone in diuinitate.

Patarenus: Sed eadem ratione mutua caritas trium personarum exigebat quartam personam esse cui communicaret delitias suas.

Catholicus: Respondeo non sequitur beatitudo enim consistit in cogitatione et dilectione. et cognitio dei potuit esse inimica persona. sed mutua caritas non potuit esse ad minus nisi inter duas personas. ille autem persone due habentes in se mutuam caritatem non essent summe liberales nisi communicassent delitias suas mutue caritatis perfectam cognitione. et per hoc oportuit triam esse persona in trinitate que esset deus. aliter non esse ibi perfectam cognitione et ita patet quod in tribus personis est summa beatitudo et perfecta communicatio summe beatitudinis. et ideo non oportuit esse quartam. Et nota quod ista est eadem quasi ratio cum prima licet in processu argumentationis diuersificet.

Probatio de trinitate per rationes naturales ex creaturis

Constat quod in opere relucet magister. sed in qualem creatura tria sunt scilicet origo species et ordo. et hec tria una res sunt. sic et in creatore est pater origo. filius species. spiritus sanctus ordo et hec tres persone una diuina essentia sunt. Item aliter in qualibet creatura sunt materia forma et connexus et hec tria sunt una res. sic et in creatore pater est uelud materia quia est principium filii et spiritus sancti. filius est sicut forma et spiritus sanctus est amor qui est amborum scilicet patris et filii connexus. item in mente humana tria sunt scilicet memoria intellectus et uoluntas et hec tria una mens sunt. et hec tria sunt equalia. quia equaliter unum capit aliud. Memoria enim cum capit intelligentia et uoluntatem. et intelligentia capit memoriam et uoluntatem. et uoluntas autem capit memoriam et intelligentiam et sic in deo sunt tres persone coequales que sunt una diuina essentia.

Item aliter in anima tria sunt scilicet mens et notitia eius et amor. et hec tria una sunt alia. sic et in deo tres sunt persone qui sunt una substantia. Item in sole tria sunt scilicet sphera sole. splendor et calor et sic in

to be loved. Therefore He is God. He was the highest good and so it follows that both were equal to the other, and so the highest mutual love proves the Trinity of Persons. For if there existed the highest love between two persons it would be necessary that each should seek a third to whom He might communicate the delight of his goodness. Otherwise the loving would be unfailing, if the other of those Persons by which He wishes to be loved wholly, wishes the other equally to be loved. Therefore in three persons there can be a communion of the full majesty, and so from eternity there were three persons in the Godhead.

Pat: By that reasoning the mutual love of three persons might have demanded a fourth person to exist, to whom their delight might be communicated.

Cath: I reply that it does not follow, for blessedness consists in knowing and loving, and the knowledge of God could be harmful to a person, but mutual love cannot exist unless it is between at least two persons. But those two persons having in themselves mutual love could not achieve the height of liberality unless they communicate their delight in mutual love by perfect knowing, and by this reason it is fitting that there be three persons in the Trinity which is God. Otherwise it would not be perfect knowledge and so it is clear that in the three persons is the height of blessedness and perfect communication of the highest blessedness. And so it is not fitting that there be a fourth. And note that this is nearly the same rationale as in the first, although there is a difference in the manner of argument.

Proof of the Trinity by natural arguments from creatures

It is clear that the master is reflected in his works, but in creatures there are three things, namely, origin, likeness, and right order, and these three are one thing. Thus in the creator the Father is the origin, the Son is the likeness. and the Holy Spirit is the right order, and these three persons are one divine nature. Also otherwise in all creatures there is matter, form, and its connection, and these three are one thing. So in the Creator the Father is like the matter, which is the principle of the Son and the Holy Spirit. The Son is like the form, and the Holy Spirit is the love which is of both, namely the connection between Father and Son. Also in the human mind there are three things, namely memory, intelligence, and will, and these three are one mind. and these three are equal, since they equally understand one another. For memory understands the intelligence and will, and intelligence understands memory and will, and will also understands memory and intelligence, and so in God there are three coequal persons in one divine essence.

Also in another manner, in the soul there are three things, namely, (Augustine, *On the Trinity*, 9.4.4) mind and selfconsciousness and love, and these three are in one another, so also in God there are three persons who are one substance. Also in the sun there are three things, namely,

---

III.4.20 mens...21 alia] Augustine, *De Trinitate*, 9.4.4.

47 uterque] utraque *F* 50 inquireret] inquiret *F* 60 Respondeo] om. *F* III.4.3 relucet] reducet *F* 15 enim] om. *F* | cum capit] cepit *P*

57 caritas|fol. 23va *P* III.4.2 creaturis|fol. 15v *F* 14 sunt¹|fol. 23vb *P*

diuinitate pater est sphera. filius splendor et spiritus sanctus calor et hec tres persone unus deus sunt.

Item in panno possunt esse plures plictere et tamen est unus pannus. sic et in diuina essentia sunt plures distincte persone scilicet pater et filius et spiritus sanctus. et caueas lector ne intelligas creaturas aliquas diuine trinitati omnimode fileres esse. Vnde per creaturas non sunt proprie probationes de trinitate diuina. sed tantum cogitationes. sicut et unitas diuine essentie per creaturas non potest probari sed tantum per illas de ipsius cognitionem cognitiones haberi.

Probatio de trinitate per scripturas ueteris testamenti

Genesis prima In principio creauit deus etcet. ubi nos habemus deus hebraica ueritas habet eloyim. quod sonat dii uel iudices. quod est numeri plurale et ponitur ibi hec uerbum creauit quod est numeri singularis ergo in una diuina essentia sunt plures persone quod non latuit diabolum serpentem antiquum. unde ad protoplaustos nostros dixit. eritis sicut dii etcet. id est sicut diuine persone

Item in eodem in principio creauit deus celum et terram etcet. et infra spiritus dei ferebatur super aquas etcet. in principio id est in filio. deus id est pater. spiritus domini id est spiritus sanctus etcet. Ecce tres persone et postea sequitur. dixit quoniam deus fiat lux etcet. ecce unitas diuine essentie. Item idem xviii. cum eleuasset oculos. scilicet abraam. apparuerunt ei tres uiri stantes prope eum. quos cum uidisset cucurrit in occursum eorum de hostio tabernaculi sui et adorauit in terra et dixit domine si inueni gratiam in oculis tuis etcet. et postea cum comedissent dixerunt ad eum etcet. et infra cui dixit reuertens ueniam ad te tempore isto etcet. ecce habemus hic quod in plurali fit mentio de illis angelis tamquam de tribus. et in singulari tamquam de uno. et isti figurabant trinitatem diuinam. eius denique essentie unitatem. et ille unus dicitur ibi deus. quare habes quod tres sunt persone diuine unus deus.

Et idem in eodem. Et uidit deus quod esset bonum et ait faciamus hominem ad ymaginem et similitudinem nostram etcet. cum dicit faciamus quod est numere plurale personarum pluralitatem denumerauit. inde cum autem adierit ymaginem et similitudinem qui sunt numere singularis imitatione significauit. uel alter per ymaginem et similitudinem pluralitas personarum

the solar sphere, brilliance, and heat, and so in the Godhead, the Father is the sphere, the Son is the brilliance, and the Holy Spirit is the heat, and these three persons are one God.

Also in a garment there can be many folds and yet it remains one garment, so also in the divine essence there are several distinct persons, namely the Father, the Son, and the Holy Spirit. And beware O Reader, lest you understand certain creatures in some way to be threads of the divine trinity. Whence by means of creatures there are not proper proofs of the divine Trinity, but only reflections, just as the unity of the divine essence cannot be proven by creatures, but only through them can one have recognition of that knowledge.

Proof of the Trinity from the scriptures of the Old Testament

Genesis 1 (1:1) "in the beginning God created." Where we have it that the true God of the Hebrews is termed Elohim, which has the sense of 'gods' or 'judges,' that is, plural in number and it posits here with this word 'created' which is singular in number, therefore in one divine essence there are several persons which was not hidden from the devil, that old serpent, whence he said to our first parents (Gen 3:5) "you shall be as gods," that is, like divine persons.

Also in the same (1:1) "in the beginning God created heaven and earth." And later (1:2) "the spirit of God brooded over the waters." "In the beginning", that is, in the Son; "God", that is, the Father; "the spirit of the Lord" that is, the Holy Spirit. See three persons, and later it continues, God said, (1:3) "let there be light," behold the unity of the divine essence. Also in the same book in 18 (18:2-3) "And when he had lifted up his eyes," namely, Abram, "there appeared to him three men standing near him. As soon as he saw them he ran to meet them from the door of his tent, and adored down to the ground, and said, 'Lord, if I have found favor in your eyes.'" And later (18:9) "and when they had eaten they said to him," and later (18:10) "And he said to him, 'I will return and come to you at this time.'" See we have here that in the plural it makes mention of these angels just as of three and in the singular just as of one, and these are a figure of this divine Trinity, and in the end the unity of nature, and that one was said there 'God,' whence you have it that there are three divine persons, and one God.

And in the same (1:25–26) "And God saw that it was good, and he said 'Let us make man in our image and likeness.'" When He said "let us make" that is, in the plural, He denoted plurality. So then when He adds "image and likeness" which are singular He means 'in imitation,' or otherwise by "image and likeness" is signified the plurality of persons, since no one is the image of themselves.

III.5.3 In...deus] Gen. 1:1. 9 eritis...10 dii] Gen. 3:5. 11 in²...12 terram] Gen. 1:1. 12 spiritus...aquas] Gen. 1:2. 15 dixit...lux] Gen. 1:3. 16 cum...20 tuis] Gen. 18:2-3 (terra) terram *Vulg.*) 21 cum...eum] Gen. 18:9. 22 cui...23 isto] Gen. 18:10. 29 Et²...31 nostram] Gen. 1:25-26.

26 plictere] plicature F 30 fileres] PF. **leg. fila** III.5.27 sunt] om. P 32 inde] om. F 33 cum] om. P | qui...35 similitudinem] om. F

III.5.8 persone|fol. 24ra P 31 est|fol. 16r F 33 ymaginem|fol. 24rb P significatur. quia nulla est ymago sui ipsius. unde in hiis uerbis plures diuine persone denotantur. cum uero addit nostram quod significet comfortii identitatem elegantur designat diuine essentie unitatem. Item exodi xx. ego enim sum dominus deus tuus etcet. cum dicit ego sum in singulari signat unitatem essente diuine. cum autem subicit dominus quod ad patrem refertur et deus quod ad filium. tuus quo ad spiritus sanctum diuinarum personarum pluralitatem designat.

Item dauid uerbo domini celi firmati sunt et spiritu oris eius omnis uirtus eorum etcet. cum dicit uerbo designat filio qui est uerbum patris. cum dicit domini notat patrem. cum dicit spiritu oris eius intelligit spiritum sanctum. ecce tres persone et postea subdit in singulari congregans etcet. cum uero dicit congregans etcet. ponit unitatem diuine essentie.

Item idem. Benedicat nos deus deus noster. benedicat nos deus dicit ter deus. scilicet deus pater deus filius deus spiritus sanctus. ecce tres persone et postea subdit in singulari. metuant eum etcet. ecce unitas diuine essentie.

Item Ysaias vi Sanctus sanctus sanctus dominus deus etcet. cum dicit ter sanctus tres persona diuinas significauit. cum uero addit in singulari dominus deus etcet. unitate diuine essentie designat.

Probatio de trinitate per scripturas noui testamenti

Mattheus ultimo docete omnes gentes baptizantes eos in nomine patris et filii et spiritus sancti etcet. In nomine itaque ait et non in nominibus. ut unitas essentie ostendatur per nomina tria que sit proposuit. tres esse personas declarauit.

Item iohannes xv cum uenerit paraclitus quem a patre procedit etcet. In hiis uerbis ostendit aperte tres esse diuinitas personas scilicet patrem et filium et spiritum sanctum. Item ad romanos prima inuisibilia enim ipsius a creatura mundi per ea que facta sunt intellecta conspiciuntur. sempiterna quoque uirtus eius et diuinitas etcet. cum dicit ipsius signat patrem cum ponit sempiterna quoque uirtus eius notat filium. cum uero addit diuinitas significat spiritum sanctum.

Item in eadem xi. ex ipso et per ipsum et in ipso sunt omnia etcet. Ex ipso scilicet patrem. per ipsum scilicet filium. et in ipso scilicet spiritus sanctus. et postea subdit in singulari. ipsi gloria etcet. ecce unitas essentie diuine. Item ii ad corinthios. in finem gratia domini nostri ihesu christi et caritas dei et communicatio san-

Whence in these plural words it denotes the several divine persons, since yet it adds "our," which signifies strong identity, elegantly designates the unity of the divine essence. See Exodus 20 (20:2) "For I am the Lord, your God." When He says 'I am' in the singular it means the unity of the divine essence, but when placed under 'Lord' which refers to the Father, and 'God' to the Son, and 'your' to the Holy Spirit, it designates the several of the divine persons.

Also David (Ps 32:6) "By the word of the Lord the heavens were established, and all the power of them by the spirit of his mouth." When he says 'word' he means the Son who is the word of the Father, when he says 'Lord' he indicates the Father, when he says 'the Spirit of His mouth,' one interprets that as the Holy Spirit. Behold, three persons, and later he adds (32:7) "Gathering together," so when he says 'gathering' he proposes the unity of the Divine essence.

Also in the same (Ps 66:7–8) "May God, our God bless us, may God bless us." He says God three times, namely God the Father, God the Son, and God the Holy Spirit, see three persons and then he adds in the singular (66:8) "they fear him," see the unity of the Divine nature.

Also Isaiah 6 (6:3) "Holy, holy, holy, Lord God," see he says "Holy" three times, signifying the three divine persons, and yet he adds in the singular, 'Lord God' designating the unity of the divine essence.

6 Proof of the Trinity from the scriptures of the New Testament

Matthew at the end (28:19) "Teach all nations, baptizing them in the name of the Father, and of the Son, and of the Holy Spirit." Accordingly He says 'In the name,' and not 'in the names,' so that the divine unity is shown forth through the three names which He proposes, He declared them to be three persons.

Also John 15 (15:26) "when the Paraclete shall come, who proceeds from the Father," in these words He clearly shows the three to be divine persons, namely the Father and the Son and the Holy Spirit. Also Romans 1 (1:12) "For the invisible things of him, from the creation of the world, are clearly seen, being understood by the things that are made, his eternal power also and divinity." When he says 'his' he means the Father, when he posits 'his eternal power also,' it denotes the Son, and when he yet adds 'divinity' he signifies the Holy Spirit.

Also in the same 11 (11:36) "of him, and by him, and in him, are all things." And 'him' is the Father, 'by him' is the Son, and 'in him' is the Holy Spirit, and then he adds in the singular, "to him be glory," and so the unity of the Divine nature. Also 2 Corinthians at the end (13:13) "The

---

40 ego…tuus] Ex. 20:2.   45 uerbo…46 eorum] Ps. 32:6.   49 in…50 congregans²] Ps. 32:7.   52 Benedicat…53 deus¹] Ps. 66:7-8.   55 metuant eum] Ps. 66:8.   57 Sanctus…deus] Is. 6:3.   III.6.3 docete…4 sancti] Matt. 28:19.   8 cum…9 procedit] Ioh. 15:26.   11 inuisibilia…14 diuini-tas] Rom. 1:20.   17 ex…18 omnia] Rom. 11:36.   21 gratia…23 spiritus] 2 Cor. 13:13.

37 hiis] om. P   38 identitatem] ydepnitatem P   47 cum] sum P   50 etcet] om. P | cum…51 etcet] om. F   III.6.5 itaque] utique F   6 tria] tua F | proposuit] posuit F   9 aperte] om. P   14 signat] signi[fi]cat F   15 eius] add. et divinitas F   18 Ex] Et P   21 Item…24 significat] om. F

III.6.4 In|fol. 24va P

cti spiritus etcet. ecce trinitas personarum. cum uero subdit postea sit etcet. unitatem essentie significat.

25 Item prima iohannes v. tres sunt qui testimonium dant in celo pater uerbum et spiritus sanctus et hii tres unum sunt etcet. ecce quam manifeste ponit tres esse diuinas personas in una essentia.

Auctoritates phylosophorum de trinitate

Aristoteles in libro physicorum in tractatus de causa rerum naturalium. ibi. quidam enim eorum scilicet phylosophorum amorem et uictoriam dicunt. et 5 dicunt quidam eorum intellectum etcet. amor est spiritus sanctus. uictoria pater et intellectus filius. ecce trinitas personarum diuinarum et postea subdit de unitate diuine essentie. ibi. plurimam facit uenire deus gloriosus et sublimis. Item idem in libro celi et mundi. 10 totum et res terminantur tribus dimensionibus. fine et medio et principio et hic quidem est numerus omnis rei et significat trinitatem rerum. Nos uero non extraximus hunc numerum nisi ex natura. et retinuimus ipsum similem legi earum. et per hunc quidem 15 numerum adhibuimus nos ipsos magnificare deum unum creatorem eminentem proprietatibus eorum que sunt creata. Item seneca in libro epistolarum ad lucilium neronem. Miraris homines ad deos ire? Deus ad homines uenit immo plus in homines uenit etcet. 20 cum dicit deos personarum pluralitatem denotat. cum dicit deus ydemtitatem essente significat.

Catholicus: Item Macrobius monas monadem genuit et in seipsum reflectit ardorem etcet. hoc est deum. unus unum genuit id est pater genuit filium. ardorem 25 intelligit spiritum sanctum. et sic euidentur personarum diuinarum trinitatem designauit.

Quod non est in deo nisi una persona

[Patarenus:] Dicitis o romani quod pater genuit filium de sua substantia ab eterno et quod pater et filius spirant spiritum sanctum. sed contra pater est deus et 5 dicitis similiter quod filius est deus. quod idem de spiritu sancto asseritis. ergo deus genuit deum et deus deum spirauit. sed aut deus genuit se deum. aut alium deum. Similiter aut deus spirauit se deum aut alium deum. si autem seipsum deum genuit. aut se ipsum 10 spirauit. ergo aliquam res se ipsam potest generare uel spirare quod falsum est. si autem alium genuit deum uel spirauit ergo sunt plures dii substantialiter quod uos non consentitis et sic ex hac inconuenientia sequitur cum non sit nisi una persona diuina sicuti est 15 una substantia.

grace of our Lord Jesus Christ, and the Love of God, and the communion of the Holy Spirit."
Also 1 John 5 (5:7) "there are three who give testimony in heaven, the Father, the Word, and the Holy Spirit, and these three are one." See how clearly he posits there to be three divine persons in one nature.

Philosophical authorities on the Trinity

Aristotle in the Physics in the section on the causes of natural things, where some of them, namely of the philosophers, speak of love and victory, and others speak regarding the intellect. Love is the Holy Spirit, Victory is the Father, and the Intellect is the Son, behold the Trinity of divine persons, and later he speaks of the unity of the divine essence in the passage, (Aristotle, Meteorology 1) "God causes to come most glorious and sublime." Also in the book On the Heavens and Earth (De Caelo et Mundo, 1) "everything is bounded by three dimensions, end, and middle, and beginning, and this is the number of all things," and signifies the triple nature of things. Yet we have not drawn this number except from nature, and we have kept it because it is similar to their laws, and by this number indeed we have employed ourselves to magnify the one God as eminent creator, by the characteristics of those things which have been created. Also Seneca in the book of epistles to Lucilius Nero (ep. 73) "do you marvel that men go to the Gods? God comes to men, yet what is more, he comes into men." When he says 'gods' he denotes the plurality of persons, when he says 'God' he signifies identity of essence.

Cath: Also Macrobius (Hermes Trismegistus) "monad begat monad, and in itself reflected the heat." This is God, one generates another, that is, the Father begets the Son, by 'heat' is understood the Holy Spirit, and so evidently he designated the Trinity of divine persons.

That there is not in God anything save one person

[Pat:] You say, O Roman, that the Father begat the Son from His substance from eternity and that the Father and the Son spirate the Holy Spirit, but against this, the Father is God, and you speak similarly that the Son is God, and that in the same way you [make a] claim regarding the Holy Spirit. Therefore God begat God, and God spirated God, but either God generates Himself as God, or another God. Similarly either God spirated himself as God or another God, if He yet generates himself as God, or He spirates Himself. Therefore something can generate or spirate itself, which is impossible. If yet another generates or spirates God, therefore there are several Gods substantially, which you do not confess, and thus from this difficulty it follows that there is not but one divine person, just like there is only one substance.

---

25 tres...27 sunt] 1 Ioh. 5:7 (Johannine comma)   III.7.8 deus...9 sublimis] Aristotle, *Meteorology*, 1, medieval interpolation.   10 totum...17 creata] Aristotle, *De Caelo et Mundo*, 1.   18 Miraris...19 uenit²] Seneca, *Ad Lucil. Ep. Mor.*, ep. 73.16.   22 monas...23 ardorem] Hermes Trismegistus, common medieval citation, see Thomas, *Summa Theologiae* I.32.1.

25 prima] in *F*   III.7.5 quidam] om. *P*   16 eorum] om. *P*   22 Catholicus] om. *F* | Macrobius] Marthobius *F*   III.8.4 spiritum] spiritus *F*   13 hac] hanc *F*

III.7.8 plurimam|fol. 24vb *P*   15 adhibuimus|fol. 16v *F*   III.8.9 autem|fol. 25ra *P*

Catholicus: Respondeo quod prima pars propositionis tue uera est. secunda uero falsa. uerum est enim quod deus genuit deum et quod deus spirauit deum. sed falsum est quod deus seipsum genuerit uel spirauerit uel alium deum. uel dicam quod hic est uera scilicet deus alium deum genuit uel spirauit si terminus iste alius adiectem ponatur et est sensus. deus genuit uel spirauit alium deum id est aliam personam que est deus sin autem ponatur substantem tunc falsa est.

[**Patarenus:**] Item conceditis uos ecclesie romane cultores quod deus pater genuit deum. Sed aut deus pater genuit deum qui est deus pater. aut deum qui non est deus pater. si genuit deum qui non est deus pater. ergo deus est qui non est deus pater. non ergo unus tantum deus est substantialiter. si uero genuit deum. qui est deus pater ergo genuit seipsum quod est impossibile. quam oppositionem facio similiter. de processione spiritus sancti ex patre et filio procedente prout dicitis.

Catholicus: Respondeo determinando illam propositionem quam sic propositis. Si deus pater genuit deum. aut deum qui est deus pater. aut deum qui non est deus pater. hic enim sane et praue intelligi potest. ideo respondendi est ita. deus pater genuit deum. qui est ipse pater. sed dicamus esse falsum. concedimus alteram scilicet genuit deum qui non est deus pater. nec tamen genuit alterum deum. nec ille qui genitus est alius deus est quam pater. sed unus deus cum patre. si uero additur genuit deum qui non est deus pater. hic distinguimus quia dupliciter potest intelligi. genuit deum qui non est deus pater sed deum filium. qui filius non est pater qui deus est. hoc sensus uerus est. Si uero intelligatur sic. genuit deum qui non est deus pater id est qui non est deus qui est pater. hoc sensus falsus est. unus est et idem deus est pater et filius et spiritus sanctus. est unus deus.

Patarenus: Item pater genuit filium. uel necessitate uel uoluntate. si necessitate ergo miserabilis fuit si necessitati subiectus fuit. si uoluntate ergo uoluntas generationem filii processit et sic non est filius eternus. quod idem de processione spiritus sancti oppono.

Catholicus: Respondeo quod deus pater genuit filium non necessitate nec uoluntate sed natura sed tu respondas mihi utrum deus pater uolens ac nolens sit deus.

Patarenus: dico quod uolens.

Catholicus: ergo deus pater uoluntate sua deus est. non natura quod falsum est.

Patarenus: Dicamus ergo quod necessitate.

Catholicus: Ergo deus pater miserabile est. si necessitati subiectus est. et sic sequitur quod deus pater est deus non necessitate nec uoluntate sed natura et eodem modo genuit filium et eodem pater et filius spirauit spiritum sanctum.

Cath: I reply that the first part of your proposition is true, but the second is false. For it is true that God begets God, and that God spirates God, but it is false that God might have begotten or spirated Himself or another God, or I might say that this is true in this sense, God generates or spirates another God, if something else is added to the sense of the term: God begat or spirated another God, that is, another person who is God, but if one should posit that it is another substance, then it is false.

[**Pat:**] Also you concede, O supporters of the Roman Church, that God the Father begat God. But either God the Father begat God who is God the Father or a God who is not God the Father. If he begat God who is not God the Father, then God is He who is not God the Father. Therefore there is not only one god substantially. If He yet begat God, who is God the Father, therefore He begat Himself, which is impossible. Similarly, I make the same argument concerning the procession of the Holy Spirit, proceeding from the Father and the Son, just as you say.

Cath: I reply by determining that proposition which you have thus proposed. If God the Father begat God, either it was God who is God the Father, or it was God who is not God the Father, then this is reasonably and easily able to be understood. Therefore one can reply thusly, God the Father begat God, who is the Father Himself. But we declare this to be false, but let us concede another, namely, He begat God who is not God the Father, neither yet did He beget another God, nor is He who is begotten another God than the Father, but one God with the Father. If one adds He begat God who is not God the Father, here we distinguish that it can be understood in two senses. He begat God who is not God the Father, but God the Son, who is God, and this is the true sense. If yet one understands it thus, he begat God who is not God the Father, that is, who is not God, who is the Father [alone], this is a false sense. God is one and the same. The Father, the Son, and the Holy Spirit are one God.

Pat: Also the Father begat the Son either by necessity or in freedom, if by necessity therefore He was wretched if he was subject to necessity. If in freedom, therefore, He willed the generation of the Son, He proceeded and so the Son is not eternal, and I can also propose the same against the procession of the Holy Spirit.

Cath: I reply that God the Father begat the Son neither by necessity or by free will, but by nature. But answer me this, whether God the Father is God willingly or unwillingly.

Pat: I would say willingly.

Cath: Therefore God the Father is God by His willingness to be God, and not by nature, which is false.

Pat: Then let us say by necessity.

Cath: Therefore God the Father is wretched, if He is subject to necessity, and so it follows that God the Father is God neither by necessity or by free will, but by nature, and in the same way He begat the Son and the same Father and Son spirated the Holy Spirit.

---

17 vero falsa] transp. *P* **21** deum] om. *P* **22** et] om. *P* **37** aut²...**38** pater] om. *F* **38** praue] *sic PF* leg. **pure** **40** sed] hoc *P* **46** sed] scilicet *F* **47** qui...**49** pater²] om. *P* **59** ac] an *P* **63** Dicamus] Dicam *F* **64** Catholicus] Patarenus *P* **68** spiritum sanctum] transp. *P*

36 genuit|fol. 25rb *P* **54** ergo|fol. 17r *F* **68** spirauit|fol. 25va *P*

Patarenus: Item ego uideo quod tres persone tres substantias supponunt. uerbi gratia. petrus et iohanes et iacobus sunt tres persone sunt et tres substantie. eodem modo pater et filius et spiritus sanctus. cum sint tres persone sunt et substantie tres.

Catholicus: Respondeo quod malum exemplum mihi posuisti. posuisti namque tres personas in tribus substantiis. sed secus est in diuinis personis quia ille sunt in una eademque substantia.

Patarenus: nonne persona substantiam significat.

Catholicus: Dico quod quandoque sic. quandoque non. persona enim uera est quod per se sonans et materia per se sonat et forma per se sonat et conexus materie et forme per se sonat et tamen sint una substantia. item substantia per se sonat et qualitas per se sonat. et tamen substantia et qualitas sunt una res.

[Patarenus:] Item nullo modo possum uidere quomodo pater et filius et spiritus sanctus sunt tres et unus quia unus non est tres. nec tres sunt unus.

Catholicus: Non uides. quia non credis. crede autem et uidebis. ait enim ueritas. Omnia sunt possibilia credenti etcet. hic namque archanum trinitatis non nisi humiliter credenti reuelatur.

Probatio per scripturas contra trinitatem

[Patarenus:] Deuteronomium vi. audi dominus deus tuus unus est etcet. et mattheus xix. unus est bonus deus. etcet. ecce habes in istis duabis actoritatibus et multis aliis ueteris et noui testamenti quod unus solus est deus maxime bonus. ergo filius et spiritus sanctus non sunt dii. uel sunt dii non boni. quomodo ergo dicis quod pater est deus et filius est deus et spiritus sanctus est deus. et sic essent tres dii.

Catholicus: Respondeo non dico quod pater et filius et spiritus sanctus sunt tres dii substantiales. sed sunt tres persone et unus deus. quia sunt una essentia. quod si sunt una essentia sunt utique unus deus. unde cum dico pater est deus filius est deus et spiritus sanctus est deus. ergo pater et filius et spiritus sanctus sunt unus deus. uerus est sillogismus. patet ex superioribus allegationis nostris. non obstantibus aduersariorem obiectionibus quod pater et filius et spiritus sanctus sunt tres persone unus deus et nota quod duo subse-quentes tractatus sunt de materia huius in sententiis.

III.8.89 Omnia...90 credenti] Mar. 9:22.   III.9.2 audi...3 est¹] Deut. 6:4.   3 unus²...4 deus] Matt. 19:17.

69 ego...70 substantias] ego quidam tres personem tres naturas *P*   70 supponunt] supponit *F*   72 cum...73 tres²] om. *F*   75 personas] add. mihi *P*   79 Catholicus] om. *P*   80 uera] idem *F*   82 se] add. format *P* exp. | et tamen] et tamen cum *P*   III.9.3 xix] xviii *P*   4 duabis] duobus *P*   8 dicis] dicitis *F*   9 et] om. *F* | sic] add. enim *F*   11 sunt¹] sint *P*   12 sunt] sint *P*   13 utique] add. et *F*   16 sillogismus] silogismus *P*   18 et filius] om. *P*

III.9.6 ergo|fol. 25vb *P*

---

1) *Per se sonans*, used similarly in Boethius and Lombard.

De diuinitate filii dei

Dicto superius de sancta et indiuidua trinitate prosequamur specialiter de filio et spiritu sancto et primo de filio in hoc tractatu. in sequenti uero de spiritu sancto declarabimus in quibus probabamus euidenter filium dei deum esse per naturam equalem patri in persona. idemque in substantia secum. et quod spiritus sanctus est similiter naturaliter deus equalis patri et filio personaliter. eiusdemque substantie cum illis. de patre autem non est necessarium probare quod sit deus. quia hic non negat patarenus. nec alias hereticos. De filio autem pertractantes ad presens. primo uidendum est quid de ipso sentiant patareni oberrantes. Vbi sciendum est quod communiter credunt et affirmant quod non habuerit nisi unam naturam.

Item communiter blasphemant quod non fuerit idem in substantia cum patre et spiritu sancto nec illis equaliter personaliter. Sed quid fuerit in natura sua dissentiunt. quia quidam illorum autumant quod fuerit simpliciter angelus in hoc ipso dissintientes. quia quidam eorum ipsum dicunt de minoribus angelis fuisse. quidam uero de maioribus. Item alii de illis garriunt quod ipse non fuit angelus neque deus. sed dei filius. Quidam autem uocant eum deum. sed non patri equalem. Item alii asserunt eum non eternum esse. alii uero eternum ipsum esse fatentur. eius diuinitatem tamen abnegantes. contra quorum errores. hoc ordine incedemus. quia primo ponemus testimonia scripturarum ueteris et noui testamenti. quod ipse duas habuit naturas diuinam scilicet et humanam. secundo scripturas noui testamenti apponemus. in quibus specialiter probatur deus. tertio subiungemus illas in quibus de ipsius equalitate cum patre. ac essentie identitate declaratur.

Probatio quod christus duas habuit naturas per auctoritates ueteris testamentum

Dauid. homo natus est in ea. ecce humanitas christi. et ipse fundauit eam altissimus. ecce diuinitas eius. et idem ante luciferum genui te. ecce diuinitas eius. et idem. quia si ante luciferum fuit genitus. ante quod nulla creata fuit ergo fuit eternus. et sic deus. et infra de torrente in uia bibit. ecce alia natura ipsius. Item ysaias vii. ecce uirgo concipet et pariet filium. etcet. ista est humanitas. et puer uocabitur nomen eius emanuel quod interpretat nobiscum deus. ecce diuinitas et humanitas eius. item viiii. paruulus enim natus est nobis etcet. ecce humanitas et postea

IV On the Divinity of the Son of God

I spoke above of the Holy and Undivided Trinity, let us proceed more specifically to the Son and the Holy Spirit, and first to the Son in this section, and in the following one we shall speak of the Holy Spirit. Here we shall prove clearly that the Son of God is God and by nature equal to the Father in personhood and in substance, and with it that the Holy Spirit is similarly by nature God, equal to Father and Son in His personality and of the same substance with them. Regarding the Father it is not necessary to prove that He is God, since the Patarene does not deny this, neither do other heretics. Regardinthe Son, treating this presently, it first is seen that in regarding Him the Patarenes err in different ways. Whence it is known that together they believe and assert that He had only one nature.

Also they all blaspheme that He was not identical in substance with the Father and the Holy Spirit, nor equal to them in personhood. But they disagree as to what He was in His nature, since certain of them assert that He was simply an angel. In this they disagree, others say that He was one of the lesser angels, others however [say He was] of the greater angels.[1] Also still others prattle that He was neither angel nor God, but the son of God. Yet some call him God,[2] but not equal to the Father. Also others claim He is not eternal,[3] still others admit Him to be eternal, while denying His divinity. Against these errors we shall proceed in order, since first we will posit the testimonies of the scriptures of the Old and New Testaments that He had two natures, namely divine and human. In the second we shall present the scriptures of the New Testament, in which He is especially shown to be God. We shall add in the third place those in which His equality with the Father is established, and which proclaim their identity in essence.

2 Proof that Christ had two natures by the authorities of the Old Testament

David (Ps 86:5) "that man is born in her," behold, the humanity of Christ, "and the highest himself has founded her," behold, the divinity of Christ. And in the same (109:3) "before the daystar I have begotten you," behold His divinity, and the same, because if He was begotten before the daystar there was nothing created before Him, therefore He is eternal, and thus God. And later (109:7) "he will drink of the torrent in the way," behold, another of His natures. Also Isaiah 7 (7:14) "behold a virgin shall conceive and bear a son," this is humanity, "and the child will be called Emmanuel, which means, 'God with us,'"

IV.2.3 homo...ea] Ps. 86:5. | et...4 altissimus] Ps. 86:5.   5 ante...te] Ps. 109:3.   8 de...bibit] Ps. 109:7 (bibit) bibet *Vulg.*)   9 ecce...filium] Is. 7:14.   12 paruulus...14 deus] Is. 9:6.

IV.1.7 idemque] idem *P*   9 eiusdemque] add. quam *P*   11 alias] aliquis *P*   15 affirmant] animant *P*   16 communiter] om. *P*   18 equaliter personaliter] *sic PF,* corrected to equalis persona.   25 eternum...26 esse¹] transp. *F*   28 ponemus] ponebimus *P*   34 identitate] idemptitate *F*   IV.2.5 eius...6 idem] om. *P*   12 viiii] xi *F*

IV.1.14 credunt|fol. 26ra *P*   16 Item|fol. 17v *F*   IV.2.7 fuit¹|fol. 26rb *P*

---

[1] Burci, 313, 321, 327; Moneta, 239. | [2] Mitigated Dualists, Moneta, 6, 112. | [3] Moneta, 238.

uocabitur nomen eius admirabilis consiliarius deus etcet. ecce diuinitas ipsius. item xlii ego ipse qui loquebar scilicet in ueteri testamento. ecce diuinitas. sequitur ecce adsum. ecce humanitas. item baruc iiii. hic est deus noster non estimabitur alius aduersus eum hic aduenit omnem uiam discipline etcet. ecce diuinitas et postea et post hec in terris uisus est etcet. ecce diuinitas et humanitas. item michea v tu betleem effrata paruulus es in millibus iuda. ex te enim egredietur dux etcet. sequitur qui sit dominator in israel. et egressus eius a diebus eternitatis. ecce diuinitas item ecclesiasticus xxiiii. uero loquitur sapiencia dei id est filius dei. igitur ego ex ore altissimi prodiui primogenita ante omnem creaturam ego feci in celis ut orietur lumen indeficiens etcet. usque ibi et dixit mihi etcet. ecce diuinitas et infra qui creauit me et requieuit in tabernaculo meo etcet. ecce humanitas.

probatio de duabus naturis christi per auctoritates novi testamenti

Mattheus prima liber generationis ihesu christi filii dei etcet. ecce humanitas filii dei et postea christi autem generatio sic erat etcet. ecce natura diuinitatis secundum quam erat ab eterno genitus a patre de qua dicit ysaias liiiº generationem eius quis enarrabit etcet. item viiii Mattheus ut sciatis autem quia filius hominis habet potestatem in terra dimittendi peccata etcet. et marcum ii quis potest dimittere peccata nisi solus deus et postea ut sciatis autem etcet. ecce ergo quoniam christus filius hominis et deus dicitur. ubi utraque eius natura declaratur. item mattheus xii dominus est filius hominis et sabbati etcet. et hic utraque eius natura exprimatur. idem xiii simile factum est regnum celorum homini etcet. et postea qui seminat bonum semen est filius hominis etcet. et dixit quod seminauit in agro suo. ubi notatur eius natura humana et diuinum ipsius nature diuine. Item idem xvi filius hominis uenturus est in gloria patris sui etcet. ad idem item lucam primam. ut ueniat mater domini mei ad me cum dicit mater notatur quod fuit filius mulieris et sic exprimatur natura humana eius. cum autem ponit domini mei designatur diuina. ex qua dominus erat. item idem ii. nesciebatis quia in hiis que patris mei sunt oportet me esse et infra. et erat subditus illis etcet. ex quibus uerbis utraque ipsius natura insinuatur. item iohannes primo. omnia per ipsum facta sunt ecce diuinitas quia solius dei est creare et facere. et postea

behold His divinity and His humanity. Also 9 (9:6) "for a child is born to us," behold humanity, and later "his name will be called wonderful counselor, God," behold divinity. Also 52 (52:6) "for I myself spoke," namely, in the Old Testament, behold the divinity, for it follows "I am here," behold humanity. Also Baruch 4 (3:36–37) "This is our God, and no other will be taken account of in comparison to him. He found out all the way of knowledge," behold the divinity, and later "Afterwards he was seen upon earth," behold the divinity and the humanity. Also Micah 5 (5:2) "you Bethlehem of Ephrata are little among the thousands of Judah, out of you he will come forth," and it follows "who is to be the ruler in Israel and his going forth is from the beginning, from the days of eternity." Also Ecclesiasticus 24, which speaks of the wisdom of God, that is, the Son of God, therefore (24:5–6) "I came out of the mouth of the most High, the firstborn before all creatures, I made it that in the heavens there should rise light that never fails," up to (24:13) "he said to me," behold the divinity, and later "and he who made me, rested in my tabernacle," behold the humanity.

Proof of the two natures of Christ from the authorities of the New Testament

At the beginning of Matthew (1:1) "the book of the generations of Jesus Christ, the Son of God," behold the humanity of the Son of God, and later (1:18) "Now the birth of Christ occurred in this way," behold the divine nature, according to which He was begotten from eternity by the Father, of which Isaiah says in 54 (53:8) "who shall declare his generation?" Also in the same book of Matthew (9:6) "that you might know that the Son of Man has power on earth to forgive sins." And Mark 2 (2:7) "who is able to forgive sins except God," and later "that they might know," behold therefore how Christ is called Son of Man and God, where both of His natures might be made plain. Also Matthew 12 (12:8) "The Son of Man is Lord of the Sabbath," and here both of His natures are clear. Also 13 (13:24) "the kingdom of Heaven is like a man," and later (13:37) "he who sowed good seed is the Son of Man," and He said that He sowed it in his field, where it makes note of His human nature and also of His divine nature. Also the same in 16 (16:27) "For the Son of man will come in the glory of his Father." And to the same point is Luke 1 (1:43) "that the mother of my Lord should come to me," when she said "mother" note that He was the son of the woman, and so expressed His human nature, but when she spoke "of my Lord," she designated divinity, by which He was Lord. Also the same in 2 (2:49) "did you not know that I must be about my father's business?" And later, "and he was subject to them," from these words both of His natures are suggested. Also 1 John (1:3) "all things were made through him," behold the divinity, since it pertains only to

---

15 ego…17 adsum] Is. 52:6. 18 hic…20 est] Bar. 3:36-37. 21 tu…24 eternitatis] Mic. 5:2. 26 ego…28 indeficiens] Ecclesiatic. 24:5-6. 28 et…30 meo] Ecclesiastic. 24:13. IV.3.3 liber…dei] Matt. 1:1. 4 christi…5 erat] Matt. 1:18. 7 generationem…enarrabit] Is. 53:8. 8 ut…9 peccata] Matt. 9:6. 10 quis…11 autem] Mar. 2:7. 13 dominus…14 sabbati] Matt. 12:8. 15 simile…16 homini] Matt. 13:24. 16 qui…18 suo] Matt. 13:37. 19 filius…20 sui] Matt. 16:27. 21 ut…22 me] Luc. 1:43. 25 nesciebatis…26 illis] Luc. 2:49. 28 omnia…sunt] Ioh. 1:3.

---

26 dei] om. F IV.3.1 per…2 testamenti] om. P 11 sciatis] sciant P | ecce] om. F 24 qua] om. F

IV.3.1 christi|fol. 26va P 12 christus|fol. 18r F

uerbum caro factum est etcet. ecce humanitas eius. idem iii. nemo ascendit in celum nisi qui de celo descendit. filius hominis qui est in celo. etcet. hic apertissime demonstrat dominus ihesus quod duas naturas habuit. cum enim dicit filius hominis. ostendit humanitatem secundum quam cum hic dixit non erat in celo cum enim dixit. ascendit et descendit est in celo. manifestat diuinitatem secundum quam est in celo et in terra. et ubique. idem viii me scitis etcet. et infra neque me scitis neque patrem meum scitis etcet. in istis uerbis clare demonstrat dominus duas naturas se habere scilicet unam secundum quam cognoscebant eum qui erat diuina. uos autem patarenum in duplo erratis quid iudei quia negastis utramque naturam christi. item ad romanos primo de filio dei qui factus ei ex semina dauid secundum carnem etcet. ad idem item idem viiii quorum patres ex quibus est christus. qui est super omnia benedictus deus. etcet. ergo est christus homo et deus. item prima ad corinthios nos autem predicamus christum crucifixum iudeis quidem scandalum gentibus autem stultitiam. ipsis autem uocatis iudeis atque grecis christum deum uirtutem et dei sapientiam etcet. cum uero dicit crucifixum demonstrant humanitate christi cum autem subdit christum dei uirtutem et dei sapientiam eius diuinam eternam naturam insinuat nisi forte uelis dicere insaniendo quod deus fuerit aliquando sine uirtute et sapientia. item ad titum ii^a apparuit enim gratia saluatoris nostri dei etcet. sed post apparuit in humanitate pater enim non apparuit et christus debet uenire ad iudicium et ipse dicitur deus et magnus deus. ergo ipse est homo et deus. Item ii^a petri ii. Fuerunt uero pseudoprophete in populo sicut et in uobis erunt magistri mendaces qui introducent sectas perditionis et eum qui emit eos deum uel dominum negat. etcet. Sed christus emit nos sanguine corporis sui sicut idem dicit prima primo scientes quod non corruptibilibus auro uel argento redempti estis de uana uestra conuersatione paterne traditionis sed pretioso sanguine quasi agni imaculati et incontaminati ihesu christi. etcet. et hec dicit deus uel dominus a petro et sic utraquam naturam christi declarat. quam utraquam uos soli magistri mendaces negatis. item prima iohannis iii°. in hoc cognouimus karitatem dei quoniam ille pro nobis animam suam posuit etcet. Sed hic fuit christus qui mortuus est pro nobis. Ergo deus et homo est. Item actus xx. attendite uobis et uniuerso gregi in qui spiritus posuit uos episcopos regere ecclesiam dei quam acquisiuit sanguine suo. ergo christus uere deus et homo fuit. item apoc. ego sum primus et nouissimus id est deus et homo. deus enim primus est. quia eternus et homo fuit

God to create and fashion, and later (1:18) "the Word was made flesh," behold His humanity. Also 3 (3:13) "no one ascends to heaven except he who descended from heaven, the son of Man who is in heaven," this most clearly proves that the Lord Jesus had two natures, for since He says "Son of Man" He shows humanity according to which He said He was not in heaven, for then when He said "ascend and descend," it is in heaven. He shows the divinity according to that by which He is in heaven and on earth, and everywhere. Also in the same gospel in chapter 8 (8:19) "you know," and later "you neither know me or my Father," and it these words the Lord plainly shows Himself to have two natures, namely, one according to which they knew Him who was divine. You Patarenes then err twice as much as the Jews, since you deny both the natures of Christ. Also Romans 1 (1:3) "Of the Son of God who was made to him from the seed of David according to the flesh," and regarding the same topic 9 (9:5) "of whose fathers, and of whom is Christ according to the flesh, who is over all things, God blessed forever." Therefore Christ is God and Man. Also 1 Corinthians (1:23-24) "yet we preach Christ crucified, a scandal to the Jews, and foolishness to the gentiles, but to those who are called, both Jews and Greeks, Christ the power of God, and the wisdom of God." Yet when he says 'crucified' he shows the humanity of Christ, but when he added "Christ the power of God, and the wisdom of God," he implied His eternal divine nature, unless you wish to madly claim that at some time God was without power and wisdom. Also Titus 2 (2:11) "For the grace of God our savior has appeared," but after He appeared in His humanity, for the Father did not appear, and Christ ought to come for justice, and He Himself it is said, is (Tit. 2:13 paraphrase) God and the Great God. Therefore He is man and God. Also 2 Peter 2 (2:1) "There were also false prophets among the people, just as there will be among you lying teachers, who will bring in sects of perdition, and deny the Lord who bought them." But Christ bought us by the blood of His body, just as the same Apostle says in 1 Peter 1 (1:18-19) "Knowing that you were not redeemed with corruptible things as gold or silver, from your vain conversation of the tradition of your fathers, but with the precious blood of Christ, as of a lamb unspotted and undefiled." And thus the Lord speaks, or the Lord by Peter, and so he declares both natures of Christ, both of which only your lying teachers deny. Further, 1 John 3 (3:16) "In this we have known the charity of God, because he has laid down his life for us." But this was Christ who has died for us. Therefore He is God and man. Also Acts 20 (20:28) "Take heed for the whole flock, in which the Holy Spirit placed you bishops to rule the church of God, which he has purchased with his own blood." Therefore Christ was true God and true man. Also Apocalypse (22:13) "I am the first and the last,"

---

30 uerbum...est] Ioh. 1:18.   31 nemo...32 celo] Ioh. 3:13.   39 neque¹...scitis²] Ioh. 8:19.   44 de...45 carnem] Rom. 1:3.   46 quorum...47 deus] Rom. 9:5.   48 nos...52 sapientiam] 1 Cor. 1:23-24.   57 apparuit...58 dei] Tit. 2:11.   60 deus¹...deus²] Tit. 2:13 (paraphrase).   61 Fuerunt...64 negat] 2 Pet. 2:1.   66 scientes...69 christi] 1 Pet. 1:18-19.   72 in...74 posuit] 1 Ioh. 3:16.   75 attendite...78 suo] Act. 20:28 (spiritus) add. sanctus Vulg.)   79 ego...nouissimus] Apoc. 22:13.

42 duplo] dupplo P

30 caro|fol. 26vb P   57 titum|fol. 27ra P   75 deus|fol. 18v F

ultima creata mundi. item idem v. dignus es domini deus accipere librum et soluere vii signacula eius. quoniam occisus es et redemisti nos dei scilicet patri in sanguine suo etcet. ergo christi est deus et homo.

Auctoritates noui testamenti de una natura christi scilicet de diuina

Mattheus viii et respondens centurio ait ibi ego homo sub potestate constitutus etcet. ac si diceret ego qui sum homo purus et impero et obeditur mihi ne dum tu qui est deus sub nullius potestate constitutus. quod et dominus confirmauit cum dixit sequentibus uerbis amen dico uobis non inueni tantam fidem in israel. etcet. ergo christus est deus. item idem iiii. accedens temptator dixit et si filius dei es. dic ut lapides isti panes fiant. etcet. ecce quod ipse diabolus omnipotentiam attribuerat dei filio. unde uos patareni peiores estis ipso in hac parte. quia christum dei filium negastis omnipotentem. et diabolo attribuistis diuinum. quod ipse se habere tacite inficiatur. Item viii imperauit uenti et mari etcet. Ex hoc et aliis locis diuine scripture in quibus legitur quod christus non in alterius nomine sed in propria potestate imparabat. patet ipsam naturalem deum et dominum esse. item xii. ihesus autem sciens cogitationes eorum etcet. Et Iohannes xvi nunc scimus quia tu scis omnia. ex hiis patet quidam christus est deus quia legitur quod ipse scit secreta cordium et quod scit omnia. quod solius diuinitatis est. ad hec est quidem legitur iohannes ii°. ipse enim sciebat quid esset in homine etcet. item idem mattheus ultimo et adorauerunt eum. etcet. et apocalypsis v et xxiiii seniores ceciderunt coram agno et ad hebreos. i. et adorent eum omnes angeli eius etcet. ergo ipse est deus. cum solus deus debeat adorari. unde in mattheus et in marcum et in lucam ubi diabolus dixerat ei. si cadens adoraueris me etcet. ipse respondit scriptum est dominum deum tuum adorabis etcet. et apocalypsis xiiii. legitur quidam angelis uolans per medium celum clamabat adorate deum qui fecit celum et terram etcet. unde in eodem xviii scribit beatus iohannes quidam cum cecidissem ante pedes angeli adorare eum quod dixit ei angelis uide ne feceris conseruus tuus sum. etcet. et postea. deum adora etcet. et maxime de angelis nusquam inuenitur. quod adorauerunt nisi deum. item iohannes iii. qui de celo uenit super omnes est. ergo est deus. si est super omnes. item idem xvii. ut cognoscant te solum deum et quem misisti ihesum christum etcet. ergo filius est

that is, God and man, for God is the first, since He is eternal, and man was the last thing created in the world. Also in the same book in chapter 5 (5:11) "You are worthy, O Lord, to take the book, and to open its seven seals, since you were slain, and have redeemed us to God," namely, to the Father in his blood. Therefore Christ is God and man.

The authorities of the New Testament of the one nature of Christ, namely, the Divine nature

Matthew 8 (8:8–9) "and the centurion responding, said. . .'I also am a man subject to authority,'" as if he might have said 'I am he who is only a man, and I command, and am obeyed, though you who are God are not subject to any power whatsoever,' which the Lord confirmed when He said in the following words (8:10) "Amen, I say to you, I have not found such faith in Israel." Therefore Christ is God. Also in the same book, chapter 4 (4:3) "the tempter coming to him said, 'and if you are the Son of God, command that these stones become bread.'" See that this devil had attributed omnipotence to the Son of God, whence you Patarenes are worse than him on this matter, since you have denied that Christ, the Son of God, is omnipotent, and have attributed divinity to the Devil which he himself tacitly denies having. Also 8 (8:26) "he commands the winds and the sea," from these and other passages of Divine Scripture in which it is read that Christ has not commanded in any other name, but rather in His own power, it is clear that He is God and Lord by nature. Also 12 (12:25) "Yet Jesus, knowing their thoughts," and John 16 (21:17) "now we know that you know all things," from these words it is clear that Christ is God since it is read that He knew the secrets of hearts and that He knew all things, which pertains solely to divinity. To this point is that which is read in John 2 (2:25) "for he knew what was in man." Also at the end of Matthew (28:9) "and they adored him," and Apocalypse 5 and 24 (5:8) "the elders threw themselves down in the presence of the lamb," and Hebrews 1 (1:6) "and let all the angels of God adore him," therefore He is God, since only God alone is to be adored. Whence in Matthew, Mark, and Luke, where the devil said to Him (Mt 4:9) "if, falling down, you adore me," He replied "it is written, you will adore the Lord your God," and Apocalypse 14, where it is read of a certain angel flying through the midst of heaven, crying out (14:7) "adore God who made heaven and earth." Whence in the same, chapter 18, Blessed John wrote of a certain one when (22:8) "I fell down to adore before the feet of the angel," and the angel said to him, "do not do this, I am your fellow servant," and later "adore God." And this is especially found among the angels, who never adore anyone else but God. Also John 3 (3:31) "he who comes from heaven is over all," therefore He is God, if He is over

---

81 dignus...84 suo] Apoc. 5:9 (suo] tuo *Vulg.*)   IV.4.3 et...4 constitutus] Matt. 8:8-9.   8 amen...israel] Matt. 8:10.   9 accedens...11 fiant] Matt. 4:3.   15 impera-uit...16 mari] Matt. 8:26 (venti] ventis *Vulg.*)   20 ihesus...eorum] Matt. 12:25.   21 nunc...omnia] Ioh. 22:17.   25 ipse...homine] Ioh. 2:25.   26 et¹...eum] Matt. 28:9.   27 seniores...agno] Apoc. 5:8.   28 et²...eius] Heb. 1:6.   31 si...me] Matt. 4:9.   34 adorate...35 terram] Apoc. 14:7.   36 cecidissem...38 sum] Apoc. 22:8.   40 qui...41 est¹] Ioh. 3:31.   42 ut...43 christum] Ioh. 17:3.

84 etcet...christi] om. P   IV.4.1 Auctoritates] auctoritas F   12 attribuerat] actribuerat P | patareni] pactareni P   14 attribuistis] actribuistis P

84 homo]fol. 27rb P   IV.4.29 ergo]fol. 27va P

deus. item in eodem. clarifica me pater claritate quam habui apud te priusquam mundus esset etcet. ergo eternus est et sic deus. item idem ultimo. dicit ei thomas. dominus meus et deus meus etcet. item ad romanos xiiii omnes enim stabimus ante tribunal christi. scriptum est enim. uiuo ego dicit dominus. quoniam mihi flecteretur omne genu etcet. et omnis lingua confiteatur deo. itaque unusquisque numerum per se rationem reddet deo etcet. ad phylippenses ii. ut in nomine ihesu omne genu flectatur celestium et terrestrium et infernorum. etcet. Ecce ex istis duabus auctoribus manifeste patet quod christus est uerus deus et omnipotens in celo et in terra. Item prima ad corinthios ii. si enim cognouissent numquam dominum glorie crucifixissent. item ad idem. item ad phylippenses ii. saluatorem expectamus dominum ihesum christum. etcet. id est secundum operationem qua possit enim subicere omnia. etcet. ecce quomodo dicit christum omnipotentem esse. ergo est deus. item ad colossenses. i qui est imago dei inuisibilis primogenitus omnis creature quia in ipso condita sunt uniuersa in celis et in terra uisibilia et inuisibilia etcet. ecce quam dilucide narrat quod dominus ihesus christus est creator et conditor omnium et principium. igitur deus. item in eadem ii. quia in ipso inhabitat omnis plenitudo diuinitatis corporaliter etcet. ergo est deus. item ad hebreos prima. ad filium autem thronus tuus deus in seculum seculi etcet. ecce quod ipse pater celestis perhibet testimonium de christo quod ipse est deus. item in eodem qui cum sit splendor glorie etcet. sed quandocumque gloria patris fuit splendor. sed illa fuit eterna. ergo filius est eternus. et sic deus. item in eodem. cui enim dixit aliquando angelorum filius meus es tu ego hodie genui te etcet. ergo ab eterno est genitus. cum non determinet diem in qua sit genitus et sic deus est. idem ii. non enim angelis subiecit deus orbem terre etcet. ergo christus non fuit angelus sed deus. presertim cum in eodem dicat. nusquam enim angelos apprehendit id est angelicam naturam. item in eodem. decebat enim eum propter quem omnia etcet. ergo est deus. si omnia per ipsum sunt. idem iii. quapropter sicut dicit spiritus sanctus hodie etcet. et infra. quibus sicut iuraui in ira mea si introibunt in requiem meam. et postea uidete fratres ne forte sit in alique uestrum cor malum incredulitatis discedendi a deo uiuo etcet. Et infra nam si eis ihesus requiem prestetisset etcet. item primo iohannes ultimo ut cognoscamus deum uerum et simus in uero filio eius. hic est uerus deus et uita eterna etcet. ad idem item.

all. Also in the same, in chapter 17 (17:3) "That they may know you, the only true God, and Jesus Christ, whom you have sent." Therefore He is the Son of God. Also in the same chapter (17:5) "And now glorify me, O Father, with yourself, with the glory which I had with you before the world was made." Therefore He is eternal, and so, God. Also at the end of the same Gospel (21:20) "Thomas said to Him, 'My Lord and my God.'" Also Romans 14 (14:10–11) "For we shall all stand before the judgment seat of Christ. For it is written, as I live, says the Lord." (Php 2:10–11) "every knee will bow to me, and every tongue shall confess to God." (Rm 14:12) "Therefore every one of us will render account to God for himself." Philippians 2 (Php 2:10) "so that in the name of Jesus every knee shall bend in heaven, and on earth, and under the earth." See from these two authorities it is plainly clear that Christ is true God and omnipotent in heaven and on earth. Further 1 Corinthians 2 (2:8) "for if they had known it, they would never have crucified the Lord of glory." Also in the same. Also Philippians 2 (3:21) "the Savior, our Lord Jesus Christ." That is, "according to the operation by which also he is able to subdue all things to himself." See how he says Christ is omnipotent, therefore He is God. Also Colossians 1 (1:15–16) "Who is the image of the invisible God, the firstborn of every creature. For in him all things were created in heaven and on earth, visible and invisible." See how clearly he recounts that the Lord Jesus Christ is the creator and maker and beginning of all things, therefore he is God. In the same book in 2 (2:9) "Since in him bodily the fulness of divinity was pleased to inhabit," therefore He is God. Also Hebrews (1:8) "But to the Son, your throne, O God, is forever and ever." See that the heavenly Father bears witness to Christ that He is God. Also in the same book (1:3) "who being the splendor of his glory." But wherever there was the glory of the Father, there was splendor, but He is eternal, therefore the Son is eternal, and so, God. Also in the same (1:5) "For to which of the angels has he said at any time, you are my Son, today I have I begotten you." Therefore He is begotten from eternity, since the day is not limited in which He might be begotten, and so He is God. Also in the same book in chapter 2 (2:5) "For God has not subjected the world to come to angels, of which we speak." Therefore Christ was no angel, but God, especially since in the same place it might say, (2:16) "for no where does he take hold of the angels," that is, angelic nature. Also in the same (2:10) "For it became him, for whom are all things." Therefore He is God, if all things were for Him. Also 3 (3:7) "So as the Holy Spirit says: Today." And later (3:11) "As I have sworn in my wrath, if they will enter into my rest." And later (3:12) "See, brethren, lest perhaps there be in any of

---

44 clarifica...45 esset] Ioh. 17:5.   46 dicit...47 meus²] Ioh. 21:20.   48 omnes...50 genu] Rom. 14:10-11.   50 et...51 deo] Php. 2:11.   51 itaque...52 deo] Rom. 14:12.   52 ut...54 infernorum] Php. 2:10.   57 si...58 crucifixissent] 1 Cor. 2:8.   59 saluatorem...60 christum] Php. 3:20-21.   63 qui...65 inuisibilia] Col. 1:15-16.   68 quia...69 corporaliter] Col. 2:9.   70 ad²...71 seculi] Heb. 1:8.   73 qui...glorie] Heb. 1:3.   76 cui...77 te] Heb. 1:5.   79 non...80 terre] Heb. 2:5.   81 nusquam...82 apprehendit] Heb. 2:16.   83 decebat...omnia] Heb. 2:10.   85 quapropter...hodie] Heb. 3:7.   86 quibus...87 meam] Heb. 3:11.   87 uidete...89 uiuo] Heb. 3:12.   89 nam...90 prestetisset] Heb. 4:8.   90 ut...92 eterna] Heb. 5:20.

80 orbem] add. eterne exp. P   83 decebat] dicebat P

51 lingua|fol. 19r F   59 saluatorem|fol. 27vb P   87 forte|fol. 28ra P

iude primo. subintroierunt quidam homines igitur et solum dominatorem ihesum christum negantes. etcet. et ibi quoniam ihesus etcet. et igitur in iudicium magni diei etcet. ergo ihesus est deus. qua in illi christiani neganti nisi uos patareni et sic estis illi de quibus dicit iudas. subintroierunt etcet. item actus viiii. adnuntians pacem per ihesum christum hic est omnium dominus etcet. ergo est omnipotens et sic deus. idem xxvi uidi regem de celo etcet. ad idem item apocalypsis. princeps regem terre etcet. et xviiii et habet in uestimento et in femore suo scriptum rex regum et dominus dominantium etcet. ad idem. idem in eodem ab eo qui erat et qui est et qui uenturus est omnipotens etcet. sed filius est uenturus. ergo est omnipotens et fuit absque principio. igitur est deus uerus. idem in eodem. ego sum alpha et omega. principium et finis etcet. et in euangelio iohannes viii. ego principium qui et loquor uobis etcet. ergo est eternus. et sic deus. et sic probatum est expresse quod christus dominus est uerus deus.

Patarenus: responsio dico quidam christus est deus per adoptionem siue per gratiam. sicut alii sancti licet forte magis.
Catholicus: sed probo quod mentiris quia per gratiam dicuntur et sunt dii. sunt creature. sed ipse est eternus. ut probatum est. item quicquid soli deo conuenit filius habet. sicut omnipotentia. omnis scientia. creatio et factio rerum omnium propria curanis reddere unicuique mercedem suam. et huiusmodi. sicut supra diligenter probata sunt. ergo deus est naturaliter. item ipse dicitur filius dei simpliciter. igitur alter est filius quam sancti. ergo per naturam. preterea dicitur unigenitus dei. iohannes iii. quia non credit in nomine unigeniti filii dei etcet. ergo est genitus hoc modo quo nullus alius. ergo per naturam. igitur non est filius adoptionis.

Patarenus: Dicam ergo quod ipse est deus eternus. sed tamen non est idem in substantia cum patre.
Catholicus: ostendo tibi quod nichil dicis. quia probatum est supra in primo tractatu quod non est nisi unus deus maxime bonus. igitur si christus est deus. licet ipse non est bonus deus. quia falsum est. uel ipse est idem in sui substantia cum patre quod uerum est.
Patarenus: quid tibi uideretur si ego dicerem quod ipse esset idem in substantia cum patre tamen minor patre.

you an evil heart of unbelief, to depart from the living God." And later (4:8) "For if Jesus had given them rest." Also 1 John at the end (5:20) "we may know the true God, and may be in his true Son. This is the true God and life eternal." Also on the same, Jude 1 (1:4) "For certain men have secretly entered in … and denying the only sovereign Ruler, and our Lord Jesus Christ." And there (1:5) "that Christ," and therefore (1:6) "unto the judgment of the great day," therefore Jesus is God, and no Christians deny this except you Patarenes, and you are those of whom Jude said "have secretly entered in." Also Acts 9 (10:36) "preaching peace by Jesus Christ, he is Lord of all." Therefore He is all powerful, and so, God. Also 26 (26:13) "I saw, O king, from heaven." To the same point is Apocalypse (1:5) "prince of the kings of the earth." And 19 (19:16) "And he has on his garment, and on his thigh written, King of Kings, and Lord of Lords." Also in the same (1:4) "from him that is, and that was, and that is to come," is omnipotent. But the Son is to come, therefore He is omnipotent and was without beginning, therefore He is true God. Also in the same (1:8) "I am the Alpha and the Omega, the beginning and end," and in the gospel of John 8 (8:25) "The beginning, who also speaks to you." Therefore He is eternal and God, and so it is thus proven clearly that Christ the Lord is true God.

Pat: As a reply, I say for certain that Christ is God by adoption or by grace, just like other saints, though more strongly.
Cath: But I prove that you lie, for they are called and are 'gods' through grace. They are creatures. But He is eternal, as was proven. Also whatsoever is appropriate to God alone, the Son has, like omnipotence, knowledge of all creation, and the fashioning of all things by their proper offices, and rendering to each according to his merit and the like, as were carefully proven above. Therefore He is God by nature. Also He is called the Son of God simply, therefore there is another Son besides the saints, therefore [there is] one by nature. Further He is called the only begotten of God. John 3 (3:18) "since they do not believe in the only-begotten son of God," therefore he was begotten in this way in which no other (was begotten), so by nature, therefore He is not a son by adoption.
Pat: I might say therefore that He is the eternal God, but still not identical in substance with the Father.
Cath: I am showing that you are speaking nonsense, since it was proven above in the first section that there is no other save one God, the highest good. Therefore if Christ is God, then He is not a good God, which is false, or He is the same in his substance as the Father, which is true.
Pat: What would it seem to you if I should say that He might be of the same substance with the Father, yet lesser than the Father.

---

93 subintroierunt...94 negantes] Iud. 1:4.   95 quoniam ihesus] Iud. 1:5. | in...96 diei] Iud. 1:6.   99 adnuntians...100 dominus] Act. 10:36.   101 uidi...celo] Act. 26:13 (regem) rex *Vulg.*)   102 princeps...terre] Apoc. 1:5. | et² ...104 dominantium] Apoc. 19:16.   105 ab...106 omnipotens] Apoc. 1:4 (omnipotens) om. *Vulg.*)   108 ego...109 finis] Apoc. 1:8.   110 ego...uobis] Ioh. 8:25.   125 quia...126 dei] Ioh. 3:18.

120 curanis] primatus *F* unclear.   121 sicut] add. hic *P*   130 dicis] dicitis *F*   132 igitur] ergo *F*   133 ipse¹] spiritus *P*   134 sui] om. *F*

116 mentiris|fol. 19v *F* | per|fol. 28rb *P*

Catholicus: michi uideretur quod si hoc dicens tu blasphemares maiestatem dei. quia hic esset dicere quod deus esset minor seipso. quod esset blasphemum et erroneum pessimum. et quod sit idem in substantia cum patre et equalis in persona. ostendam tibi per scripturas diuinas inferius.

Quod christus est idem substantia cum deo patre et illi equalis in persona

Mattheus xiii. nemo nouit patrem nisi filius etcet. sed hoc non potest intelligi nisi de omnimoda cognitione. alias enim multi angeli et sancti cognoscunt eum secundum quid. ergo filius est equalis patri. item. iohanne primo in principio erat uerbum. et uerbum erat apud deum et deus erat uerbum. cum audis heretice uerbum dei esse in principio intelligere te oportet ipsum eternum esse. cum uero sequitur uerbum erat apud deum. recognosce ipsum esse in equalitate patris. cum autem subiungitur et deus erat uerbum. ostendit beatus iohannes dei filium idem semper fuisse cum patre in substantie manifeste. idem. v. Pater meus usque modo operatus est et infra. Propterea ergo magis querebant eum iudei interficere. quia non solum soluebat sabbatum sed et patrem suum dicebat equalem se faciens deo. Sed iohannes ponit quod iudei uolebant ipsum occidere. quia faciebat se equalem deo. ergo ita erat. huic sentencie concordat paulus ad phylippenses ii° dicens qui cum in forma dei esset non rapinam arbitratus est esse se equalem deo etcet. item idem v ubi dicit ihesus de se et de patre suo quecumque enim ille fecerit hec et filius similiter facit etcet. et xvi pater omnia mea tua sunt et omnia mea tua sunt mea. etcet. ergo idem est cum patre et equalis illi. idem viiii. Et non cognouerunt quia patrem eius dicebat deum. ad idem. idem x. in me est pater et quo in patre etcet. et xiiii Si cognouissetis me et patrem meum utique cognouissetis. et amodo cognoscetis eum etcet. et postea dicit ei phylippus. ostende nobis patrem et sufficit nobis. Dicit ei ihesus. tanto tempore uobiscum sum. et non cognouistis me. phylippe: qui uidet me uidet et patrem meum. quomodo tu dicis ostende nobis patrem. Non creditis quia ego in patre. et pater in me est ex hiis uerbis patet aperte quod dominus ihesus christus est equalis patri in persona et idem in substantia.

Patarenus: Responsio. dico quod pater est in filio per gratiam et filius est in patre per fruitionem paterne glorie. et sic intelliguntur auctoritates quas contra me allegasti. que dicunt quod pater est in filio et filius est

Cath: It would seem to me that if you were saying this, you would be blaspheming the majesty of God since this is to say that God would be lesser than Himself, which is blasphemy and the worst sort of error, and that He is identical in substance with the Father, and equal in personhood, I will show you by divine scriptures below.

That Christ is identical in substance with God the Father and is equal to Him in personhood

Matthew 13 (11:27) "no one knows the Father except the Son." But God cannot be understood except through comprehensive knowledge. For otherwise many angels and saints would know Him absolutely. Therefore the Son is equal to the Father. Also in John 1 (1:1) "In the beginning was the Word, and the Word was with God, and the Word was God." When you hear, O heretic, of the true God being in the beginning, you ought to understand Him to be eternal, yet when it adds "the Word was with God," you should recognize Him to be in equality with the Father, and yet when it adds "and the word was God," Blessed John clearly shows that the Son of God is always identical with the Father in substance. Also 5 (5:17) "My Father works up to now," and later (5:18) "therefore the Jews sought all the more to kill him, because he did not only break the Sabbath, but also said God was his Father, making himself equal to God." But John posits that the Jews wished to kill him because He was making himself equal to God, therefore He was so. Paul agrees with this meaning in Philippians 2 saying (2:6) "he who was in the form of God did not consider equality with God something to be grasped." Also in chapter 5 where Jesus speaks of Himself and His Father (Jn 5:19) "for whatever he does, these the Son also does likewise." And 16 (16:15) "Father, all I have is yours, and all things of yours are mine," therefore He is identical with the Father and equal to Him. Also 9 (8:27) "and they did not understand that he called God his Father." Also on the same topic in 10 (10:38) "that the Father is in me, and I in the Father." And 14 (14:7) "If you had known me, you would without doubt have known my Father also, and from henceforth you will know him." And later Philip says to Him (14:8–10) "'Lord, show us the Father, and it is enough for us.' Jesus said to him, 'Have I been so long with you and you have not known me? Philip, he who sees me sees the Father also. How can you say, Show us the Father? Do you not believe that I am in the Father, and the Father is in me?'" From these words it is plainly apparent that the Lord Jesus Christ is equal to the Father in personhood and is identical in substance.

Pat: In reply I say that the Father is in the Son through grace and the Son is in the Father by the realization of His paternal glory, and thusly the authorities which you adduced against me are to be understood which say that

---

IV.5.3 nemo...filius] Matt. 11:27.　7 in...8 uerbum] Ioh. 1:1.　15 Pater...est] Ioh. 5:17.　16 Propterea...18 deo] Ioh. 5:18 (dicebat) add. deum *Vulg.*)　21 qui...22 deo] Php. 2:6.　24 quecumque...facit] Ioh. 5:19.　25 pater...26 mea] Ioh. 16:15 (paraphrase). 27 Et...28 deum] Ioh. 8:27.　28 in...29 patre] Ioh. 10:38.　29 Si...30 eum] Ioh. 14:7.　31 ostende...36 est] Ioh. 14:8-10.

138 quod] quia P　139 blasphemares] blasphemans P　140 blasphemum] blasfemum P　IV.5.2 et...persona] om. P　5 sancti] si non P　11 recognosce] add. te F

IV.5.4 omnimoda|fol. 28va P　34 meum|fol. 28vb P

in patre. nec obstat auctoritas apostoli ad phylippenses quia sic intelligitur. qui cum in forma dei esset id est quamuis esset tam magnus filius dei forma non rapinam arbitratus est scilicet hanc esse se equalem deo id est non attentauit facere se deo equalem.

Catholicus: Fatuum esse tuum intellectum probat ipse dei filius qui dicit in iohannes x. ego pater unum sumus etcet. dic mihi heretice quomodo pater et filius unum sunt. numquid unum sunt in gratia. ut pater det gratiam suam filio et filius det gratiam suam suam patri. uel numquid idem sunt in participatione glorie. ut sicut participat filius gloria paterna. ita pater participat gloria filii. cum filius sit creatura secundum tuam dementiam loquor. oportet igitur te ita intelligere uerbum christi. Ego et pater unum sumus id est ego et pater sumus una diuina essentia. et per consequentiam in personis equales. nec obstat expositio quam fecisti in auctoritate pauli. quoniam falsa est. non enim dicit. non rapinam arbitratus est dicens uel faciens se equalem deo etcet. nichil enim est ibi de dicto uel facto. sed dicit eternum etcet. Quod enim impossibile est quod non sit. et est hic sententia illorum uerborum. Qui cum in forma dei esset id est in essentia dei. non rapinam arbitratus est. id est alienum non rapuit. esse se equalem deo id est cum fuit equalis patri deo in persona qui habuit quod suum erat. sed responde tu mihi quid dices ad illa uerba. pater omnia mea tua sunt et omnia tua mea sunt. ergo pater et filius sunt equales in personis sunt. sed quicquid est patris est filii et econtrario. et idem in substantia. item quid dices ad illa qui uidet me uidet et patrem meum etcet. ergo pater est in filio substantialiter. siquidem uidendo filium uidemus et patrem. et attende heretice quod probatum est tibi. per testimonia dei et prophetarum et appostolorum et etiam per dicta patris tui diaboli. et fratrum tuorum demonium quod christus est deus eternus equalis patri in persona et idem in substantia cum illo. ergo stipulatio eterni incendii desine blasfphemare dei maiestatem. et da honorem ihesu christo benedicto. qui cum patre et spiritu sancto uiuit et regnat deus excelsus et sublimis in eternitate sine fine.

Quod christus non est deus nec equalis patri in persona nec idem in substantia

[**Patarenus:**] Ecclesiasticus xxiiii ab initio et ante secula creata sum etcet. sed hic dicit sapientia legitur id est de filio dei. ergo est creatura et sic non est deus.

---

the Father is in the Son and the Son is in the Father. Neither does the passage in Philippians from Paul contradict my position, "who was in the form of God," that is, although He was so great in the form of the Son of God, He did not consider it something to be grasped, namely, that by this He was Himself equal to God, that is He did not attempt to make Himself equal to God.

Cath: The Lord Himself proves your interpretation to be idiotic, who says in John 10 (10:30) "I and the Father are one." Tell me, O heretic, how the Father and Son are one, surely they are one in grace, as the Father gives His grace to the Son, and the Son gives His grace to His Father, or surely they are the same in their sharing in glory, just as the Son shares in the glory of the Father, so the Father shares in the glory of the Son. Since the Son is a creature — I am speaking according to your insane babbling — it is fitting therefore for you thus to understand the word of Christ, "I and the Father are one," that is, 'I and the Father are one Divine essence and, as a consequence, equal in personhood.' Nor does the explanation which you made about the saying of Paul contradict this because it is false, for he did not say, 'He did not consider it something to be grasped, saying or making Himself equal to God.' For there is nothing there of saying or doing, but he said, 'eternal.' For it is impossible that it not be, and this is the meaning of these words, "who, though he was in the form of God," that is, in the essence of God, "he did not consider it something to be grasped," that is, He did not grasp something different "being equal to God," that is, since He was equal to God the Father in personhood, who had what was His. But answer me this, what do you say to that passage "Father, all I have is yours, and all things of yours are mine." Therefore the Father and the Son are equal in personhood, but whatever belongs to the Father belongs to the Son, and vice versa. It is the same as regards substance. Further what do you say to that passage "he who has seen me has seen the Father." Therefore the Father is in the Son substantially, so accordingly, by seeing the Son we see the Father as well. And pay attention, O Heretic, what was proven to you by the witness of God and of the prophets and Apostles and even by the teachings of your father the devil, and your brothers the demons: that Christ is eternal God, equal to the Father in personhood, and identical with Him in substance. Therefore by the promise of eternal fire, cease to blaspheme the majesty of God, and give honor to Jesus Christ, the Blessed one, who, with the Father and Holy Spirit, lives and reigns, exalted and on high in eternity without end.

That Christ is not God, neither is He equal to the Father in personhood, nor identical in substance

[**Pat:**] Ecclesiasticus 24 (24:14) "From the beginning, and before the world, was I created." But this speaks of wisdom, and is read in reference to the Son of God, therefore He is a creature, and so is not God.

---

49 ego…50 sumus] Ioh. 10:30.   IV.6.3 ab…4 sum] Ecclesiastic. 24:14.

47 attentauit] attentatum P   57 id…58 sumus] om. F   63 enim] est P   71 sed] si F   76 attende] actende P   80 in substantia] transp. F | stipulatio] stipula F

43 nec|fol. 20r F   63 facto|fol. 29ra P

Catholicus: Respondeo quod illud uerbum creata improprie ponitur id est genita ut patet supra. in eodem ubi dixerat. ex ore altissimi prodiui primogenita ante omnem creaturam etcet. sed responde tu mihi. dicit quod est creata ante secula. sed autem secula nulla creatura est uel esse potest. ergo est eterna. item dicit ista sapientia ibi supra prouidui primogenita ante omnem creaturam etcet. ergo est ab eterno quia si est creatura esset. tunc esse ante se ipsam quod est impossibile ut aliqua res sit ante se secundum idem.

Patarenus: Item Marcum xiii de die autem illo uel hora nemo scit neque angeli in celo neque filius nisi pater etcet. ergo in filio cadit diuini consilii ignorantia et sic non est deus.

Catholicus: Respondeo loquitur quod filius nescit inquantum est minor patre id est in quantum est homo. hoc est de humanitatis. scit autem de uirtute diuinitatis secundum quam est equalis patri et hoc est quod dicit. nisi solus pater id est nisi ex uirtute ex quam pater scit id est ex diuina. uel dicitur filius nescire quia in hoc ad modum nescieritis se humiliauit quia neminem fecit istud scire. simile mattheus xxv amen dico uobis nescio uos etcet. id est ad modum nescientis se habebit ad illas. quinque. uirgines fatuas. Et quia filius dei sciat de die iudicii sibi probatur multas rationibus. prima quia legitur in mattheus xi. nemo nouit patrem nisi filius etcet. si enim nouit patrem quam nemo alius nouit. multo fortius credibile est quod noscat de die iudicii. quam noscere multo minus est absque ulla comparatione. secunda quia dicitur in iohanne xiii. sciens quia omnia dedit ei pater in manus etcet. et xvi omnia quecumque habet pater mea sunt etcet. et xvii mea omnia tua sunt et tua mea sunt etcet. si enim pater dedit ei omnia in manus. ergo item si omnia sunt sua que sunt patris ergo et istud. tertia ratio est quia probatum est supra. quod ipse est equalis patri et sic oportet quod hic sciat cum patre sciat illud.

[Patarenus:] item idem penultimo. Deus deus meus ut quid dereliquisti me etcet. et dauid in Psalmis in persona eius. clamabo per diem et non exaudies etcet. ergo non fuit deus. si fuit relictus a deo.

Catholicus: Respondeo ideo non fuit exauditus in passione sed sensualitatem quod est humanitatis indicium. quod est insuper martyrum confortatio. et ideo ualde utile fuit dominum sic orare et eum minime

Cath: I reply that the word 'created' is used loosely, that is, 'begotten,' as was shown above, in the same place where it said (Sir 24:4) "From the mouth of the most High I came forth before all creatures." But answer me this. It says that He is created before the world, but yet that the world is no creation, or can be, therefore it is eternal. Also it speaks of that wisdom there, "I came out the firstborn before all creatures," therefore He is from eternity since if He had been a creature, then He would be before Himself, which is impossible, as a thing would be before itself in the same respect.

Pat: Also Mark 13 (13:32) "But of that day or hour no man knows, neither the angels in heaven, nor the Son, but the Father." Therefore an ignorance of Divine decisions was in the Son and so He is not God.

Cath: I respond by saying that the Son did not know insofar as He was less than the Father, that is, insofar as He was human, yet He knew according to divine power according to which He was equal to the Father and this is what He says, "but only the Father," that is, except by the power through which the Father knew, that is, by divine power. Or it means that the Son did not know for the reason that He might not know so that He could humble Himself, because He made it so that no one should know that. Similar is Matthew 25 (25:12) "Amen, I say to you, I do not know you," that is, in the way that He might not know them Himself, as He will have it with regard to those five foolish virgins. And that the Son of God would know the day of judgment Himself is proven by many arguments. The first is read in Matthew 11 (11:27) "no one knows the Father except the Son." For if He knows the Father, whom no one else knows, how much more believable it is that He should not know the day of judgment, than to know a much lesser thing which is devoid of any comparison. According to what is said John 13 (13:3) "Knowing that the Father had given him all things into his hands," and 16 (16:15) "all things whatsoever the Father has are mine," and 17 (17:10) "everything I have is yours, and everything of yours is mine," for if the Father gave all things into His hands, also if all things are His which are the Father's, and so the third argument is this which was proven above, that He is equal to the Father, and so it is appropriate that He should know this, since the Father knows this.

[Pat:] Also in the penultimate [chapter] (Mt 27:46) "My God, my God why have you forsaken me," and David in the Psalms (Ps 21:3) in His person, "I have called all day and you did not hear," therefore He was not God, if He was abandoned by God.

Cath: I reply therefore that He was not heeded in the passion, but it was in sensuality, which is a sign of His humanity, and which furthermore is also a consolation to the martyrs. And so it was highly appropriate the Lord was

---

8 ex...9 creaturam] Ecclesiastic. 24:5.   16 de...18 pater] Mar. 13:32.   28 amen...uos] Matt. 25:12.   32 nemo...filius] Matt. 11:27.   36 sciens...37 manus] Ioh. 13:3.   37 omnia...38 sunt¹] Ioh. 16:15.   38 mea²...39 sunt] Ioh. 17:10.   44 Deus...45 me] Matt. 27:46.   46 clamabo...exaudies] Ps. 21:3.

IV.6.6 creata] creatura F 9 etcet...13 etcet] om. P 16 Marcum] Mattheum P 22 scit...23 diuinitatis] om. P 33 nemo] add. P 50 indicium] inditium P

IV.6.8 ore|fol. 29rb P 32 nemo|fol. 20v F 41 tertia|fol. 29va P

exaudiri et hoc ipsum volebat secundum rationem. unde ipse dixerat supra in capitulo proximo. Non quod ego uolo secundum quid tu etcet. sed modo respondeas mihi. dicis quod christus non fuit deus. quia legitur quod inquantum fuit homo relictus est a deo in tribulatione passionis. eodem ergo modo dices quod non fuit amicus dei quia scriptum est in psalmis non derelinquit deus sperantes in se etcet. Obmutesce itaque scelerate canis.

Patarenus: Item iohannes x dixerunt iudei ad christum tu homo cum sis facis teipsum deum. quibus ipse respondit. non ne scriptum est in lege uestra. Ego dixi dii estis etcet. Ecce qualiter cum esset reprehensus a iudeis. quia se deum faciebat probauit se deum per auctoritatem de diis adoptionis loquentem ergo non fuit deus naturaliter.

Catholicus: Respondeo quia ex ista auctoritate sequitur contrarium tue conclusionis. propter id quod subdit postea. Si illos dixit dii estis a quo sermo dei factus est et non potest solui scriptura quem pater sanctificauit et misit in mundum et uos dicitis quia blasfemo. quia dixi filius dei sum. Si non facio opera patris mei nolite credere mihi. Si autem facio etsi mihi non uultis credere operibus credite ut cognoscatis et credatis quia pater in me est et ego in patre etcet. Ecce quoniam probat quod potest se dicere dei filium per naturam quod est deum esse naturaliter et sic intelligebant etiam iudei. probat autem sic. ego scilicet filius dei dixi id est constitui quod sancti essent dii eo quod de mea bonitate participant. Et quia dixi eos deos nos uocatis id est uocare debetis illos deos. quia scriptura dicit hoc. que solui non potest multo fortius ego debeo uocari deus qui feci eos deos. qui facio opera diuinitatis qui sum idem cum patre. ut patet quia pater in me est et ego in patre.

Patarenus: Item idem xiiii pater maior me est etcet. ergo non est equalis patri et sic nec deus.

Catholicus: respondeo uerum est quod pater qui est deus. maior est christo inquantum ipse est homo. immo homo ipse seipso maior est. inquantum est anima et corpus. quia anima dignior est corpore. et quod de ista comparatione scilicet diuinitatis patris ad humanitatem suam loquitur. patet ex uerbis que dicit ibi. Non turbetur cor uestrum neque formidet. audistis quia ego dixi uobis uado et uenio ad uos si diligeritis me gauderitis utique quia uado ad patrem quia pater maior me est etcet. ac si diceret. nolite turbari si ego recedo a uobis ad horam per mortem quia ego morior de uoluntate patris. de quo debitis gaudere. quia

---

to pray thusly, and for Him not to be heard, and this He did wish according to reason, whence He said above in the next chapter. (Mt 26:39) "Nevertheless not as I will, but as you will." But how will you reply to me? You say that Christ was not God, it was read that insofar as He was man He was abandoned by God in the tribulation of His passion, therefore in the same way since you say that He was not a friend of God, since it was written in Psalms (*i.e.,* Judith 13:17 combined with Ps 36:28, 33) "God does not abandon those who hope in him." Be silent then, you wicked dog.

Pat: Also John 10 (10:33–34) "The Jews answered Christ, 'you, being a man, make yourself God.' 'Is it not written in your law, I said you are gods?'" See how He — when he was upbraided by the Jews because He was claiming to be God — proved Himself to be God through the authority which speaks of gods by adoption, therefore He was not God by nature.

Cath: I reply that from this passage it goes on against your conclusions, on account of what comes later (10:35–38) "If he called them gods, to whom the word of God was spoken, and the scripture cannot be broken. Do you say of him whom the Father has sanctified and sent into the world, you blaspheme, because I said, I am the Son of God? If I do not the works of my Father, do not believe in me. But if I do, though you will not believe me, believe the works that you may know and believe that the Father is in me, and I in the Father." See how He proves that He was able to call Himself Son of God by nature, since He is God naturally and so the Jews also understood Him. Yet He proves it so 'I' namely, the Son of God, said, that is, "I decree, that the saints are gods by the fact that they participate in My goodness and I said that those are called gods because you ought to call them gods, since the scripture says this, 'and the scripture cannot be broken.' How much more ought I to be called God, who made them gods, who do the works of God, who am identical with the Father. It is clear that the Father is in me and I am in the Father."

Pat: Also in the same in 14 (14:28) "the Father is greater than I." Therefore He is not equal to the Father, neither is He God.

Cath: I respond that it is true that the Father — who is God — is greater than Christ insofar as He is man, just as man himself is greater insofar as he is soul and body, since the soul has more dignity than the body, and that is the comparison, namely, of the divinity of the Father to His humanity of which He speaks. It is clear from the words that He says there (14:27–28) "Do not let your heart be troubled, nor let it be afraid. You have heard that I said to you, I go away, and I come to you. If you loved me, you would indeed be glad, because I go to the Father, for the Father is greater than I," as if to say, 'do not be troubled if I go away from you for a while through death, since I will

---

53 Non...54 tu] Matt. 26:39.   59 non...se] Conflation of Judith 13:17, Ps. 36:28, 33.   61 dixerunt...64 estis] Ioh. 10:33-34 (dixerunt iudei ad christum] om. et add. responderunt ei iudei *Vulg.*)   70 Si...76 patre] Ioh. 10:35-38 (a quo] ad quos *Vulg.*) 87 pater...est] Ioh. 14:28.   94 Non...98 est] Ioh. 14:27-28.

56 relictus] delictus *F*   57 tribulatione] tribulacione *P*   61 Patarenus] om. *F*   77 se dicere] transp. *P*   81 dixi] dixii *P*   87 Patarenus] om. *P*   91 homo] om. *F*

70 Si|fol. 29vb *P*   93 humani-tatem|fol. 30ra *P*   96 ad|fol. 21r *F*

obedio patri. qui maior me. scilicet homine est. secundum enim diuinitatem suam non dicitur christus ire et redire. nec secundum illam potuit mori. nec in illa. aut in angelorum natura si illam habuit quod non est uerum. quicumque accidit aut accidere potuit unde turbati et formidare deberent apostoli.

[Patarenus:] Item idem xv sicut dilexit me pater etcet. sed omnis pater prius est filio. ergo primus fuit deus pater quam christus qui est eius filius. ergo non est deus per naturam.

Catholicus: Respondeo quia falsa est tua positio et ideo nulla est tua conclusio. quia pater et filius sunt relatiua. unde quicumque fuit pater fuit filius et quod pater est eternus utique filius eternus est.

Patarenus: Item idem xvii. ut sint unum sicut et nos sumus. ego in eis et tu in me etcet. sed apostoli nunquam fuerunt unum in essentia cum ei ad inuicem. ergo nec filius est idem cum patre in essentia.

Catholicus: Respondeo illud sicut tale est. quale est illud. lucam vi. estote ergo misericordes sicut et pater uester misericors est etcet. et illud mattheus v. estote ergo uos perfecti sicut et pater uester celestis perfectus est.

[Patarenus:] Item idem xx. sicut misit me pater etcet. sed alius est qui mittit et alius est qui mittitur. ergo alius est pater et alius est filius. et sic sequitur quia filius non est deus. uel si est deus non tamen una substantia cum patrem.

Catholicus: respondeo hoc oppositia locum habent in diuersis substantiis. ut cum timotheus mittitur a paulo. sed secus in personis diuinis que sunt una eademque indiuisa substantia. simile aliquando et in creaturis reperitur. Nam alius est splendor solis quam rota solis procedit et alia est rota solis et tamen idem est sol. preterea possum concedere et uerum est quod alius est pater et alius est filius. si iste terminus alius adiectiue ponatur id est alia est persona patris et alia est persona filii.

Patarenus: Item prima ad corinthios xv deinde finis eandem tradiderit regnum deo et patri etcet. ergo non est deus si desinet esse rex.

Catholicus: Respondeo non dicit quod tradat ita regnum patri quia ipse desinat esse rex. presertim cum subiungat. cum euacuerit omnem principatum etcet. ergo postquam regnum tradidit patri euacuabit omnem principatum et potestatem scilicet euacuare omnem principatum regni est. ergo regabit filius. post-

die by the will of the Father, on account of which you ought to rejoice, since [I am doing it] in obedience to the Father, who is greater than I, namely, as man.' For according to His divinity Christ did not say 'I go away and I come,' nor according to His divinity was He able to die, neither in that or in the nature of the angels — if He had that, which is not true — whatever happens or can happen, whence the Apostles ought to be troubled or to fear.

[Pat] Also the same in 15 (15:9) "as the Father loved me," but every father is prior to a son, therefore God the Father was before Christ who is His Son, therefore He is not God by nature.

Cath: I reply that your position is false and so there is nothing to your conclusion, for the Father and the Son are relative [to one another], whence whatsoever was proper to the Father was proper to the Son and since the Father is eternal, just so is the Son likewise eternal.

Pat: Also the same in 17 (17:22–23) "that they may be one as we are one, I in them and you in me," but the Apostles were never one in essence with Him among themselves, therefore neither is the Son identical with the Father in essence.

Cath: I reply that it is the same as in Luke 6 (6:36) "be merciful therefore just as your Father is merciful," and that in Matthew 5 (5:48) "be therefore perfect as your heavenly Father is perfect."

[Pat] The same in 20 (Jn 20:21) "as the Father has sent me," But there is one who sends, and another who is sent, therefore the Father is one, and the Son is another, and so it follows that the Son is not God, or if He is God, still He is not consubstantial with the Father.

Cath: I reply that your objection holds when considering different substances, as when Timothy was sent by Paul, but it is different with Divine persons who are one and the same indivisible substance, something which likewise are sometimes found in creatures. For the splendor of the Sun is one thing, proceeding from the sphere of the Sun, and another thing is the sphere of the sun, yet it is the same sun, further I am able to admit and it is true, that the Father is one and the Son is another, if to that term another word is added, that is, the Father is one person, and the Son is another.

Pat: Also 1 Corinthians 15 (15:23) "Afterwards the end, when he will have delivered up the kingdom to God and the Father." Therefore he is not God if He ceases to be king.

Cath: I reply that he did not say that He handed thus the kingdom to the Father because He had ceased to be king, particularly because it continues, "when he will have brought to nothing all principality." Therefore after He hands over the kingdom to the Father, He will bring all principality and power to nothing, namely, to make empty

---

107 sicut...pater] Ioh. 15:9.   115 ut...116 me] Ioh. 17:22-23.   120 estote...121 est] Luc. 6:36.   121 estote...123 est] Matt 5:48.   124 sicut...pater] Ioh. 20:21.   139 deinde...140 patri] 1 Cor. 15:24 (eandem) add. cum *Vulg.*)

115 Patarenus] om. *F* | nos] add. unum *F*   117 cum ei] om. *F*   125 est²] om. *F*   132 indiuisa] in diversa *F*   136 est] om. *F*   147 filius] deus *P*

121 estote|fol. 30rb *P*

quam redidit regnum patri. sunt ergo uerba pauli sane intelligenda sic. cum tradidit regnum deo et patri etcet. id est cum christus ostendet deum patrem una secum regnare in omnibus et cum euacuarent omnem principatum id est cum demonstrabit solum deum principem esse omnium. simile id est iohanne xx. ubi christus dixit marie magdalene. Noli me tangere nondum enim ascendi ad patrem meum etcet. et postea parum stetit et permisit illam una cum alia maria. tangere et tenere pedes suos. Quare necesse est ut illud sic intelligatur. Nondum enim ascendi ad patrem meum scilicet in corde tuo. quia nondum credis me esse equalem patri. Sed responde tu mihi. dicis enim quod dei filius desinit esse rex. quid est ergo quod dicit angelis lucam primo regni eius non erit finis. et intellige ergo ydiota hanc pauli auctoritatem iuxta sanctorum intellectum. pro quo facit quod legitur apocalypsis xi factum est regnum huius mundi domini nostri ihesu christi et regnabit in secula seculorum amen. etcet. potest etiam alio modo intelligi scilicet dei regno electorum quod tradet christus deo patri. quando ecclesiam electorum deo presentabit non habentem maculam neque rugam in quibus nunc regnat per fidem et opera sancta.

[**Patarenus:**] Item ad colosenses primo qui est ymago dei inuisibilis etcet. sed quod est ymago alterius non est idem. ergo filius non est eadem substantia cum patre.

Catholicus: Respondeo hoc oppositio locum habet in creaturis. secus est in diuinis personis. uel dicitur filius ymago patris secundum humanitatem. et sic est ymago totius trinitatis et unitatis diuine essentie qui dicitur spiritualiter ymago dei secundum humanitatem. quia ymago dei relucet in eo inter omnes creaturas. uel concedam conclusionem tuam. si procedis secundum istum terminum alius supradicto modo et non aliud quia filius est ymago patris et est alius a patre. id est alia persona.

Quod Christus est angelus

[**Patarenus:**] Malachias iii statim ueniet ad templum sanctum suum dominator dominum quem uos queritis et angelus testamenti quem uos uultis etcet. Sed ille angelus christus. ergo christus est angelus. ad idem est

all principality for the kingdom, therefore the Son will reign after He hands over the kingdom to the Father, therefore the words of Paul are properly read thusly, "when he will have delivered up the kingdom to God and the Father," that is, when He shall show that God alone is the principle of all things, similar to John 20 (20:17) where Christ said to Mary Magdalene "do not touch me I have not yet ascended to my Father." And later (12:3) he lingered a bit and permitted her, together with the other Mary,[1] to touch and to hold His feet. Therefore is it necessary to interpret it thusly, for I have not yet ascended to my Father, that is, in your heart, since you have not yet believed me to be equal to the Father. But answer me this, for you say that God the Son will cease to be king, what is that which the angel speaks about in Luke 1 (1:33) "of his kingdom there will be no end." And understand therefore, fool, this passage of Paul together with the understanding of the saints, for whom he offers what one reads in Apocalypse 11 (11:15) "The kingdom of this world has become our Lord's and his Christ's, and he will reign forever and ever. Amen." It can also be understood differently, namely, that Christ will hand over the kingdom of the elect of God to God the Father, when He shall present the Church of the elect to God, not having in it any spot or wrinkle, in which He now reigns by faith and holy works.

[**Pat:**] Also Colossians 1 (1:15) "who is the image of the invisible God," but what is an image of another is not identical, therefore the Son is not of the same substance with the Father.

Cath: I reply that your argument holds in creatures, but it is different with divine persons. Or it is said that the Son is the image of the Father according to humanity, and so is the image of the whole Trinity and unity of the divine essence, which is spiritually called the image of God according to humanity, since the image of God shines out in it among all other creatures, or I might concede your conclusion, if you proceed according to that other term in the manner spoken above, since the Son is the image of the Father and is different from the Father, that is, [He is] another person.

That Christ is an angel

[**Pat:**] Malachi 3 (3:1) "And presently the Lord, whom you seek, and the angel of the testament, whom you desire, shall come to his temple." But that angel is Christ, so

---

153 ubi…155 meum] Ioh. 20:17 (enim) om. *Vulg.*) 156 cum…157 tenere] Refers to Ioh. 12:3. 162 regni…163 finis] Luc. 1:33. 165 factum…167 amen] Apoc. 11:15 (domini nostri ihesu christi) om. add. domini nostri et christi eius *Vulg.*) 172 qui…173 inuisibilis] Col. 1:15. IV.7.2 statim…4 uultis] Mal. 3:1 (sanctum) om. | dominum] om. *Vulg.*)

152 demonstrabit] †† Unclear word. *FP* 160 esse] om. *P* 161 est] om. *P* 163 ydiota] idiota *P* 179 et unitatis] om. *F* 183 istum terminum] transp. *F* | alius…non] om. *P* | non] add. secundum istum terminum *F* IV.7.1 Quod…angelus] om. *F* 4 Sed…7 etcet] om. *F*

154 christus|fol. 30va *P* 163 hanc|fol. 21v *F* IV.7.1 Christus|fol. 30vb *P*

---

1) Clearly "Mary" in *P*, however may be an error for "Martha." By this time Gregory I's conflation of the Marys in the Gospels was well established. It is unlikely that the author was distinguishing Mary of Bethany from Mary Magdalene.

in ysaia vii et uocabitur nomen eius magni consilii angelus etcet.
Catholicus: Respondeo quod auctoritas malachi loquitur de angelo ueteris testamenti et est sensus dominator ueniet ad templum sanctum suum. qui est christus et angelus testamenti ueniet cum eo. quia cum multitudo angelorum semper sequeretur dei filium. maxime ille magnus angelus debuit eum sequi ad misteria noui testamenti. qui in ueteri figuram eius tenuit. quod atque dicis de uerbo ysaie. dico quod non ita iacet in littera hebraice ueritatis. quam nos imitamur. sed est ibi emanuel quod est interpretatum nobiscum deus.
Patarenus: Item apocalypsis x. et uidi alium angelum fortem descendentem de celo etcet. sed ille angelus fuit christus ergo christus est angelus.
Catholicus: Respondeo non est uerum quod ille angelus fuerit christus. quia christus non descendit de celo eo modo quo dicitur de angelo illo. uel dicam quod christus dicitur angelus non natura sed officio. angelus enim interpretatur missus et ipse fuit missus a deo patre pro nostra salute. hoc enim modo pastorem se dicit et hostium et huiusmodi et patrem uocat agricolam. sed dicite mihi filii perditionis. quare filium dei tam impudente inhonoratis auferendo ei diuinitatis honorem? et cur diabolum deum esse eternum tam pertinaciter predicatis. cum natura et scriptura concordet dei filium deum uerum esse et diabolum honorare tota pertumescat uere uobis maledictionem eterna dampnationis predictis ysaias v cum dicit ue qui dicitis bonum id est christum qui est bonus id est pura bonitas. quia deus eternus est. dicitis eum inquit malum id est creaturam qui dicitur mala id est temporalis et mutabilis et malum id est diabolum qui in sui natura est malis id est mutabilis et est malus per accidens peccatam. dicitis enim eum bonum id est deum eternum. et quia hoc dicitis ue uobis id est dampnatio eterna.

Christ is an angel. The same is in Isaiah 7 (9:6) "And his name will be called the angel of great counsel."
Cath: I reply that the passage in Malachi is speaking of the angel of the Old Testament and that is the sense of the "Lord shall come to the holy temple," who is Christ, and the angel of the testament shall come with Him, for, since a multitude of angels always attended the Son of God, that great angel especially ought to have attended Him for the mysteries of the New Testament, [the angel] who prefigured Him [held His figure] in the Old. What you also claim about the word of Isaiah, I say that it does not read that way in the true literal Hebrew, which we follow, but is there 'Emmanuel' which is interpreted "God with us."
Pat: Also Apocalypse 10 (10:1) "and I saw another mighty angel come down from heaven." But that angel was Christ, therefore Christ is an angel.
Cath: I reply that it is not true that the angel was Christ, since Christ did not descend from heaven in that way which was said of that angel. Or I might say that Christ was called an angel, not by nature, but by office, for angel is interpreted as 'sent' and He was sent from God the Father for our salvation, for in this way He called himself 'shepherd' and 'victim' and the like and calls the Father 'husbandman.' But tell me you son of perdition, why do you still dishonor the Son of God by so impudently denying to Him the honor of divinity? And why do you so obstinately preach the devil to be an eternal God, when both nature and scripture agree that the Son of God is the true God and to honor the devil is to be completely swelled up with pride? Truly for you is the curse of eternal damnation, as in the preceding quotation of Isaiah 5 (5:20) "Woe to you that call evil good," that is, Christ who is good, that is, goodness simply considered, since God is eternal. You call Him evil, that is, a creature which is called evil, that is, temporal and changeable and evil, that is the devil, who in his nature is evil, that is, changeable and is evil [only] accidentally (per accidens) because of sin. For you call him good, that is, eternal God, and because you say this, "woe to you," that is, eternal damnation.

Quod spiritus sanctus est deus et quod ipse est tamen unus essentialiter

Sequitur de spiritu sancto. circa quem duobus modis errant patareni. Vno quia non credunt eum esse deum equalem patri et filio eiusdemque substantie cum illis. autumant enim illum esse creaturam. sicut de filio credunt. tamen ipsum asserunt esse non minorem non solum patre. sed etiam filio. alio modo errant de spiritu sancto quia non credunt eum unum esse substantialiter. sed plures exceptis quibusdam illorum

V That the Holy Spirit is God and that He is one only essentially

Now it remains to treat of the Holy Spirit, regarding whom the Patarenes err in two ways. One, since they do not believe Him to be God equal to the Father and the Son, of one and the same substance with them, for they assert Him to be a creature, just as they believe about the Son, yet they claim Him to be created, just as they believe about the Son, yet they claim not only that He is less than

---

6 et...7 angelus] Is. 9:6. using the Septuagint version of Ο Μεγάλης Βουλής Άγγελος.   19 et...20 celo] Apoc. 10:1.   35 cum...36 bonum] Is. 5:20 (dicitis) add. malum *Vulg.*)

12 semper] om. *P*   14 misteria] *FP* unclear word.   26 missus²] om. *P*   27 salute] salite *P*   37 inquit] inquid *P*   38 id est¹] a *P*   V.1.1 sanctus] santus *P* | et...2 essentialiter] om. *P*   6 sicut] add. et *F*   7 esse] add. non *P* exp.

29 perditionis|fol. 31ra *P*

qui ipsum unum esse predicant. Quidam autem illorum aiunt quod tot sunt spiritus sancti quot sunt boni homines. dicentes quod cum fit manus impositio alicui. quod expellitur quidam malus spiritus qui est in eo et datur ei quidam nouus quem dicunt spiritum sanctum uocari. alii uero garriunt quod sunt tres spiritus sancti. quorum unus proprie dicitur spiritus sanctus. secundus uero paraclitus. tertius autem nuncupatur spiritus principalis. Primum dicunt accipere bonos homines ad remissionem peccatorum et gratie infusionem. secundus datur ad consolationem. unde dicitur paraclitus id est consolator. tertius autem datur ad confirmationem. et hunc spiritum principalem uocant et hunc dicunt semper in celis stetisset. Primum uero dicunt se dare hominibus per manus impositionem. secundum dicunt dari a deo sibi cum sunt in tribulationibus ad consolationem. tertium autem expectant in celis ad confirmationem ut amplius peccare non possint. Primum dicunt dedisse Christum apostolis post suam resurrectionem. secundum misisse in pentecosten. tertium autem dabit pater in glorificatione. nos autem catholici reiectis huiusmodi dampnatis erroribus dicimus et credimus spiritus sanctum unum deum esse patri et filio coequalem idemque unum essentialiter esse. ueneramur. que rationibus et scripturis probamus aperte.

Probatio per naturales rationes quod spiritus sanctus est deus et equalis patri et filio et in substantia idem

Spiritus sanctus est spiratio sancta dei. sed ista spiratio aut est alia substantia a deo. aut eadem. si est alia. aut temporalis aut eterna. Temporalis non est. quia sic fuisset deus quandoque sine spiratione et esset nunc aliud in deo quem fuisset aliquando. quod non potest esse. quia nulla mutatio est apud deum. et sic patet quod est eterna. quod si est. aut est alia substantia a deo et tunc sunt plures dii naturales et eterni. quod falsum est secundum omnes. aut est eadem substantia cum deo et sic est spiritus sanctus deus eternus et eiusdem substantie cum spirante deo. sed constat quod pater spirat eum et filius etiam spirat eum. ergo est eadem substantia cum patre et filio. preterea in deo nulla inequalitatas est. ergo spiritus sanctus est in persona patri et filio coequalis.

Item donum amoris prius est quam aliquid donum extrinsecus. ergo donum amoris primus fuit in deo ad creaturas antequam ipse conferret creaturis suum esse

the Father, but also less than the Son.[1] Another way they err regarding the Holy Spirit is that they do not believe Him to be one substantially, but many, excepting certain ones among them who preach that He is one. Yet certain of them say that there are as many Holy Spirits as there are good men, saying that when one makes imposition of hands on anyone that a certain evil spirit is expelled which is in them, and a new one is given to him, which they say is called the Holy Spirit. Others yet prattle that there are three Holy Spirits,[2] of which one is properly called the Holy Spirit, the second the Paraclete, and still the third termed the principal Spirit. The first they say accepts good men by the remission of sins and the infusion of grace. The second is given unto consolation, whence he is called the Paraclete, that is, the consoler, yet the third is given for confirmation, and this they call the principal Spirit and this one they say always remains in heaven. Yet the first they say gives himself to men through the imposition of hands, the second they say is given by God to them when they are in tribulation for consolation, the third yet they expect in heaven for confirmation, so that they might not able to sin any more. The first they say Christ gave to the Apostles after His resurrection, the second was sent on Pentecost, yet the third the Father will give in glorification. But we Catholics, by rejecting damnable errors of this sort, say and believe that the Holy Spirit is one God, coequal to the Father and the Son, and identical with them in essence, we venerate that which by arguments and scripture we prove plainly.

Proofs from natural arguments that the Holy Spirit is God, and equal to the Father and the Son, and identical in substance

The Holy Spirit is the holy spiration of God, but this spiration is either a different substance from God or is the same. If it is a different substance either [it is] in time or eternal. It is not in time since God was never without spiration and there would be now something other in God than there was before which is impossible, since there is no change in God, and so it is clear it is eternal. If it is, either it is another substance from God, and then there are two natural and eternal gods, which is false according to everyone, or He is the same substance with God, and thus the Holy Spirit is eternal God of the same substance as God since He was spirated from God. But it happens that the Father spirates Him, and the Son also spirates Him, therefore He is the same substance with the Father and the Son. Further in God there is no inequality, therefore the Holy Spirit is coequal in personhood to the Father and the Son.

Also the gift of love is prior to an extrinsic gift, therefore the gift of love was first in God towards creatures, after which He conferred it on His creatures to be their external

---

18 tertius] tercius *P*   22 tertius] tercium *P*   23 confirmationem] consolationem *P*   24 stetisset] fuisset *F*   27 tertium] tercium *P*
V.2.1 quod...3 idem] om. *F*   5 aut² ...alia²] om. *P*   19 Item] ante corr. Patarenus *P*   21 antequam] quam *P*

V.1.11 predicant|fol. 22r *F*   16 sanctum|fol. 31rb *P*   V.2.10 eterna|fol. 31va *P*

---

1) Moneta, 4, 6, 112, 264, 269. The mitigated dualists accepted the divinity of the Holy Spirit. The absolute dualists considered Him to be a creature like Christ. | 2) This was a doctrine found among the Absolute Dualists, see Moneta, 4, 269; also Célestin Douais, *La somme des autorités à l'usage des prédicateurs méridionaux au XIIIe siècle* (Paris: Picard, 1896), 120.

exterius uel aliquam bonitatem. ergo fuit ante omnem creaturam. sed nihil ante nisi deus ergo ipse est deus.

Patarenus: Respondeo dico quod fuit ante omnem creaturam et tamen ipse fuit creatura.

Catholicus: Aut donum amoris erat in deo accidentaliter. aut essentialiter. primum non potest dici. quia deo nichil accidit quia si accideret ei aut aliunde accideret aut a se. si aliunde. ergo indigeret adminiculo alterius ad habendum amorem suum. et sic non esset perfectus et esset maior eo qui daret et perficeret. si a se accideret ergo esset mutabilis quod est impossibile. et sic patet quod ante omnem creaturam donum amoris erat in deo naturaliter. et hoc est spiritus sanctus. ergo spiritus sanctus est deus.

Probatio per naturales rationes quod spiritus sanctus est unus tantum essentialiter

Constat quod diuine essentie beatitudo potuit esse in trinitate personarum scilicet patris et filii et spiritus sancti ut probatum est supra in capitulo de summa et indiuidua trinitate. ergo alius spiritus sanctus superflueret. Sed nichil est in deo superfluum. ergo non est nisi unus spiritus sanctus.

Item si essent in deo plures spiritus sancti non esset in eis mutua relatio sed inter patrem et filium et spiritum sanctum mutua est relatio. ergo in deo esset diuersitas quod esse non potest. igitur non est nisi unus spiritus sanctus.

Patarenus: Respondeo quod iste rationes locum haberent si spiritus sanctus esset deus. sed ego dico quod spiritus sanctus est creatura pura.

Catholicus: Et ego dico quod si tu dicis spiritum sanctum esse creatura quod tu pessime dicis. quia ego tibi probaui per rationes naturales quod ipse est deus et hoc tibi etiam probabo per diuinam scripturam.

Probatio per diuinam scripturam quod spiritus sanctus est deus

Mattheus xii. omne peccatum et blasfemia remittetur et quicumque contra filium hominis uerbum dixerit remittetur ei. qui autem dixerit contra spiritum sanctum uerbum non remittetur ei neque in hoc seculo neque in futuro. ergo peccatum in spiritum sanctum. excedit omnia peccata quod fiunt in patrem aut in filium ergo spiritus sanctus non est minor patre et filio. ergo deus est.

Patarenus: Per hoc poteris argumentari quod spiritus sanctus sit maior patre. cum peccatum quod sit in patre remittatur et peccatum quod sit in spiritum sanctum sit inremissibile.

Catholicus: Dico quod ideo dicit grauius esse spiritum sanctum offendere. quam patrem uel filium propter id

end or some good. Therefore He was before all creatures, but there was nothing before God, therefore He is God.

Pat: I reply that though He was before every creature, yet He was still a creature.

Cath: Either the gift of love was in God accidentally or essentially. The first cannot be said, since in God nothing happens, for if something might happen to Him it happens either by another or by Himself. If by another, He would be in want of the other's support to have His own love, and so He would not be perfect, and it would be greater for Him for the reason that He would give and complete. If [something] happened [to Him] from Himself, then He would be mutable, which is impossible, and so it is clear that, before all creatures, the gift of love was in God naturally, and this is the Holy Spirit, therefore the Holy Spirit is God.

Proof from natural arguments that the Holy Spirit is one only by essence

It is clear that in the blessed divine essence there can be in a Trinity of Persons, namely, of the Father, and of the Son, and of the Holy Spirit, as was proven above in the chapter on the supreme and undivided Trinity, therefore another Holy Spirit is superfluous, but there is nothing superfluous in God, therefore there is not but one Holy Spirit.

Also if there were many Holy Spirits in God, there would not be mutual relations between them, but between the Father and the Son and Holy Spirit there is a mutual relation, therefore in God there would be diversity which cannot exist, so there cannot be but one Holy Spirit.

Pat: I reply that these arguments hold water if the Holy Spirit is God, but I say that the Holy Spirit is a creature simply considered.

Cath: And I say that if you claim the Holy Spirit is a creature, you speak wickedly, because I proved against you by natural arguments that He is God and now I will prove it by the Holy Scriptures.

Proof from the Holy Scriptures that the Holy Spirit is God

Matthew 12 (12:31) "whosoever shall speak a word against the Son of man, it will be forgiven him, but he who will speak against the Holy Spirit, it will not be forgiven him, neither in this world, nor in the world to come." Therefore the sin against the Holy Spirit exceeds every other sin which is done against the Father or the Son, therefore the Holy Spirit is not less than the Father and the Son, therefore He is God.

Pat: By this you are able to argue that the Holy Spirit is greater than the Father, since the sin against the Father is forgiven and the sin which is against the Holy Spirit is unforgivable.

Cath: I say then that He explains that it is more grievous to offend the Holy Spirit than the Father or the Son on

---

V.4.3 omne...7 futuro] Matt. 12:31.

V.3.1 Probatio...2 essentialiter] om. *F*   5 capitulo] titulo *F*   9 in deo] om. *P*   15 sed] si *F*   20 probabo] probo *F*   V.4.8 fiunt] sunt *F*   10 deus est] transp. *F*   11 poteris] add. ergo *F*   14 inremissibile] inremiscibile *F*

V.3.5 sancti|fol. 31vb *P*   15 deus|fol. 22v *F*   V.4.15 Catholicus|fol. 32ra *P*

quod ei attribuitur id est propter bonitatem quem offendere grauius est. quam potentiam que patri attribuitur uel quam sapientiam que attribuitur filio. Item ioannes iii. Spiritus ubi uult spirat etcet. ergo est absolute uoluntatis. igitur est deus. quia nichil est absolute uoluntatis nisi deus. ad hoc prima ad corinthios xii. hec autem omnia operantur unus idem atque diuidens singulis prout uult. etcet. Item idem iiii. Spiritus est deus. etcet. quod sic intelligitur uno modo. Spiritus sanctus est deus.

Item ad romanos i. in euangelio quod ante promiserat deus etcet. et ad hebreos primo olim loquens deus patribus in prophetis etcet. et actibus. iii. deus autem que prenuntiauit per os omnium prophetarum pati christum suum etcet. sed qui locutus est in prophetis fuit spiritus sanctus sicut dicit secunda ad corinthios. iiii. habentes autem eumdem spiritum fidei sicut scriptum est. credidi propter quod locutus sum. etcet. et secunda petri. primo. non enim uoluntate humana allata est aliquando propheta sed spiritum sancto inspirati locuti sunt sancti dei homines. etcet. ergo spiritus sanctus est deus.

Patarenus: Dico quod illud ad romanos. et ad hebreos intelligitur de patre et non de spiritum sanctum. quia ibi expressim dicit de filio suo etcet.

Catholicus: Respondeo quod pater dicitur loqui cum spiritus sanctus loquitur. quia spiritus suus est. sed tu dic mihi de quo spiritum credis quod loquatur petrus cum dicit quod prophete locuti sunt spiritu sancto inspirante. numquam enim potes de spiritu sancto non potest nisi intelligere qui deus est. quia secundum tuam sectam prophete non habuerunt aliquid spiritum sanctum. si dicis quod de uoluntate dei loquabatur quandoque. sed ille deus dicitur a beato petro. spiritus sanctus ergo spiritus sanctus est deus. Item in eadem et in eodem. testis enim mihi est deus etcet. Et hec sepe dicit. secundum infra ix. dicit testimonium perhibente consciencia mea in spiritu sancto etcet. ergo spiritus sanctus qui testatur in bona consciencia. est deus.

Catholicus: Item ad corinthios iii. nescitis quia templum dei estis etcet. et postea vi. dicit nescitis quia membra uestra templum spiritus sanctus qui in uobis est etcet. ergo spiritus sanctus est deus.

Catholicus: item prima iohanne iiii. deus karitas est. etcet. sed karitas est amor patris. qui est spiritus sanctus. unde supra. quoniam karitas ex deo est. ergo spiritus sanctus est deus.

---

account of that which is attributed to Him, that is, on account of goodness, which it is more grievous to offend against than power which is attributed to the Father or than wisdom which is attributed to the Son. Also John 3 (3:8) "The spirit blows where he will," therefore He is absolute will, and therefore is God, because nothing is absolute will except God. On this topic is 1 Corinthians 12 (12:11) "But all these things one and the same Spirit works, apportioning to each one according as he will." Also in the same, in chapter 4 (Jn 4:24) "the Spirit is God," which can only be understood in one way: the Holy Spirit is God.

Also Romans 1 (Rm 1, paraphrase) "in the gospel which God had promised from of old," and Hebrews 1 (1:1) "God spoke in times past to the fathers by the prophets." And in Acts 3 (3:18) "But those things which God before had announced by the mouth of all the prophets, that his Christ would suffer." But (Nicene Creed) "He who spoke through the prophets," was the Holy Spirit just as he said in 2 Corinthians 4 (4:13) "But having the same spirit of faith, as it is written, 'I believed, for which cause I have spoken,'" and 2 Peter 1 (1:21) "For prophecy came not by the will of man at any time, but the holy men of God spoke, inspired by the Holy Spirit."

Pat: Regarding that which Romans and Hebrews say, I say it is to be understood of the Father and not the Holy Spirit, since He explicitly speaks there of His Son.

Cath: I reply that the Father is said to speak, while the Holy Spirit is speaking, since it is His Spirit. But tell me by what Spirit you believe that might speak to Peter when he says that the Prophets were speaking by the inspiration of the Holy Spirit, for you are never able to understand anything of the Spirit except that He is God, since according to your sect the prophets did not have any of the Holy Spirit, if you say that they ever spoke by the will of God. But that God spoke to blessed Peter, by the Holy Spirit, therefore the Holy Spirit is God. Further in the same place (Rm 1:9) "For God is my witness," and he says this often, like in 9 (9:10) "my conscience bearing me witness in the Holy Spirit," so the Holy Spirit who bears witness in good conscience is God.

Cath: Also Corinthians 3 (3:16) "Do you not know that you are the temple of God," and later in 6 (6:19) "do you not know that your members are the temples of the Holy Spirit who is in you," therefore the Holy Spirit is God.

Cath: Also 1 John 4 (4:8) "God is Love," but Love is the Love of the Father, who is the Holy Spirit, as above, because love is from God, therefore the Holy Spirit is God.

---

20 Spiritus...spirat] Ioh. 3:8.   23 hec...24 uult] 1 Cor. 12:11 (atque) add. spiritus *Vulg.*)   25 Spiritus...deus] Ioh. 4:24.   27 in...28 deus¹] Rom. 1 (paraphrase).   28 olim...29 prophetis] Heb. 1:1.   29 deus...31 suum] Act. 3:18   31 qui...prophetis] Nicene Creed.   33 habentes...34 sum] 2 Cor. 4:13.   35 non...37 homines] 1 Pet. 1:21 (spiritum) spiritu *Vulg.*)   52 testis...deus] Rom. 1:9.   53 dicit²...54 sancto] Rom. 9:1.   56 nescitis...57 estis] 1 Cor. 3:16.   57 dicit...59 est¹] 1 Cor. 6:19 (paraphrase; quia) quoniam *Vulg.*)   60 deus...est] 1 Ioh. 4:8.

---

19 attribuitur¹] actribuitur *P* | attribuitur²] actribuitur *P*   **21** quia nichil] ergo *P*   **27** romanos] corinthios *P*   **46** potes] om. *P*   **49** quod] om. *F*   **51** sanctus²...deus] om. *F*   **53** ix] ix viiii *P*   **56** Catholicus] om. *F*   **62** est] add. etcet *F*

46 enim|fol. 32rb *P*

Probatio per scripturas quod unus est tantum spiritus sanctus

Prima ad corinthios xii. diuisiones uero gratiarum sunt idem autem spiritus etcet. Et infra hec autem omnia operantur unus atque idem spiritus diuidens singulis prout uult etcet. et infra et enim in uno spiritu omnes nos in unum corpus baptizati sumus etcet. et infra omnes in uno spiritu potati sumus etcet. et ad ephesios ii. quoniam propter ipsum habemus accessum ambo in uno spiritu ad patrem. etcet. et. solliciti seruare unitatem sancti spiritus in uinculo pacis unum corpus et unus spiritus etcet. ex hiis patet aperte quod non est nisi unus spiritus sanctus. et attende quod in omnibus locis diuine scripture. ubi de spiritu sancto tractatus fit sermo de illo singulariter. et non dicitur unus de spiritibus sanctis. sed simpliciter spiritus sanctus. quare unum tantum debemus credere spiritum sanctum esse. preterea et numquam legimus quod sic nobis datur uel operetur nisi spiritus patris et filii. ergo non est nisi unus diuinus spiritus sanctus.

Quod spiritus sanctus non est deus et quod sunt plures spiritus sancti

[**Patarenus:**] Procedit hereticus in hoc tractatu sic. Primo inducit quamdam rationem naturalem et quasam auctoritates diuine scripture. secundo allegat quasdam scripturas diuine pagine ad arguendum quod plures sunt spiritus sancti.

Ratio naturalis quod spiritus sanctus non sit deus

Quicquid potest et uult pater potest et uult spiritus sanctus. sed pater potest et uult spirare spiritum sanctum. ergo spiritus sanctus potest et uult spirare sanctum spiritum et sic erit in deo quaternitas quid tu inficiaris. et eadem est argumentatio de filio et sic per istam abusionem sequitur quod spiritus sanctus non est deus. nec etiam filius sed solus pater.

Catholicus: Respondeo in argumentatione tua est fallatia scilicet figure dictionis. mutatur enim quod inequale cum enim dicis. quicquid potest pater et uult. supponis quid id est omnium ita rem quid potest et uult pater potest et uult spiritus sanctus. sicut est creare facere. saluare et huiusmodi. et hec omnia potest et uult spiritus sanctus. Tamen autem dicis. sed pater potest et uult spirare spiritum sanctum. transfer te ad relationes scilicet paternitatis et spirationis que non supponunt diuinam substantiam. sed sunt quasi sicut qualitates circa diuinam essentiam. Simile cum dicitur carnes quas emisti heri comedisti hodie. sed tu emisti heri carnes crudas. ergo comedisti hodie carnes crudas.

Proof from the scriptures that there is only one Holy Spirit

1 Corinthians 12 (12:4) "Now there are varieties of graces, but the same Spirit," and later (12:11) "But all these things one and the same Spirit works, apportioning to every one according as he wills." And later (12:13) "For in one Spirit were we all baptized into one body." And Ephesians 2 (2:18) "For by him we have access both in one Spirit to the Father." And (4:3–4) "Careful to keep the unity of the Spirit in the bond of peace, one body and one Spirit." From these it is plainly apparent that there is but one Holy Spirit, and see that in every place in divine scripture that treats of the Holy Spirit uses only the singular, and it is not saying "one of the Holy Spirits," but simply "the Holy Spirit." Hence we ought to believe there to be only one Holy Spirit. Further we never read that thus it is given or worked in us unless by the Spirit of the Father and the Son, therefore there is only one divine Holy Spirit.

That the Holy Spirit is not God and that there are many Holy Spirits

[**Pat:**] The heretic proceeds in this tract thusly, first he adduces certain natural arguments and certain passages of divine scripture. Secondly he alleges certain divine scriptures for arguing that there are several Holy Spirits.

Natural arguments that the Holy Spirit is not God

Whatsoever the Father can do and wills, the Holy Spirit wills, but the Father is able and wills to spirate the Holy Spirit, therefore the Holy Spirit is able and wills to spirate the Holy Spirit and so there will be a quaternity in God, which you deny. And it is the same argument regarding the Son, and so by this error it follows that the Holy Spirit is not God, also neither is the Son, but only the Father.

Cath: I reply that there is a fallacy in your argument, namely, in a figure of speech, for one substitutes what is unequal, for when you say the Father is able and willing to do anything, you suppose that it is so among all the things which the Father is willing and able to do, the Holy Spirit willing and able to do, just as in creation and fashioning things, salvation and the like, and the Holy Spirit is willing and able to do all these things, but nevertheless you say, but the Father is willing and able to spirate the Holy Spirit. Cross over to relations, namely, paternity and spiration which do not suppose the divine substance, but they are like qualities of the Divine essence. It is similar when one speaks of meat which you bought yesterday, but you ate today. But to say that you bought raw meat yesterday, and

---

V.5.3 diuisiones...4 spiritus] 1 Cor. 12:4.   4 hec...6 uult] 1 Cor. 12:11.   6 et²...7 sumus] 1 Cor. 12:13.   9 quoniam...10 patrem] Eph. 2:18 (propter) per *Vulg.*)   10 solliciti...12 spiritus] Eph. 4:3-4 (sancti) om. *Vulg.*)

V.5.12 aperte] om. *F*   13 attende] actende *P*   16 quare] quia *P*   18 et...19 spiritus] om. *F*   V.6.1 Quod...6.2 sunt] om. *F*   2 sancti] santus *P*   7 sancti] sanctus *P*   V.7.5 ergo...6 spiritum] om. *F*   6 quaternitas] paternitas *P*   8 non] om. *P*   11 mutatur] mittatur *P*   12 inequale] †† in quale *F* | cum enim] †† crimen *F*   13 ita] om. *F*   16 Tamen] cum *F*

V.5.5 diuidens|fol. 23r *F*   14 tractatus|fol. 32va *P*   V.7.20 qualitates|fol. 32vb *P*

non sequitur. est enim ibi fallatia predictam. uel aliter cum dicis quicquid potest et uult pater. potest et uult spiritus sanctus. debes addere et quod non potest pater nec vult. non potest nec vult spiritus sanctus. cum ergo procedis et dicis. pater potest et uult spirare spiritum sanctum id est debes supplere scilicet istum et non alium et sic male argumentaris. ergo spiritus sanctus potest et uult spirare spiritum sanctum id est aliam personam. quia pater non potest nec uult illam quartam personam spirare. unde falsus est sillogismus tuus.

Probatio per scripturas quod spiritus sanctus non est deus

Patarenus: Matthaeus ultimo. in nomine patris et filii et spiritus sancti. etcet. sed ibi posponitur spiritus sanctus patri et filio. ergo est minor patre et filio. itaque nec deus.

Catholicus: Respondeo et alii posponitur pater filio ut ibi ego et pater unum sumus. tamen pater non est minor filio. scriptura enim diuina quandoque anteponit pater quandoque filium. quandoque uero spiritum sanctum. ut una persona non credatur maior alia.

[**Patarenus:**] Item spiritus sanctus datur ab homine ut infra probabo in rubrica de datione spiritus sancti.

Catholicus: Respondeo cum infra probabit infra respondebo.

Quod tot sunt spiritus sancti quot sunt boni homines

[**Patarenus:**] Prima iohannes iiii. Nolite omni spiritui credere sed probate spiritus si ex deo sint etcet. ergo sunt tot spiritus sancti. quot sunt boni homines.

Catholicus: Respondeo quod loquitur de spiritibus humanis. quos appellerat non esse ex deo uel extra eam fidem christi non habent. uel habent et de hic dicit illos esse probandos et hoc est quod sequitur ibi. quoniam multi pseudoprophete exierunt in mundum in hoc cognoscitur spiritus dei omnis qui confitetur ihesum christum in carne uenisse ex deo est et omnis spiritus qui soluit ihesum christum ex deo est. etcet.

Quod tres sunt spiritus sancti

[**Patarenus:**] Iohannes xiiii. ego rogabo patrem et alium paraclitum dabit uobis etcet. et dixit ei accipite spiritum sanctum etcet. et spiritu principali confirma cor meum deus. etcet. ergo sunt tres spiritus sancti.

Catholicus: Respondeo unus enim idem spiritus est qui diuersis nominibus appellatur propter diuersos

Proof from the scriptures that the Holy Spirit is not God.

Pat: At the end of Matthew (28:19) "in the name of the Father and of the Son and of the Holy Spirit," but there the Holy Spirit is placed after the Father and the Son, so he is less than the Father and the Son, and so not God.

Cath: I reply that in other passages the Father is placed after Son, as there, "I and the Father are one," yet the Father is not less than the Son. For Divine Scripture sometimes puts the Father first, sometimes the Son, sometimes the Holy Spirit, so that one person might not be believed in more than another.

[**Pat:**] Further the Holy Spirit is given by men, as I will prove later in the section on the granting of the Holy Spirit.

Cath: I reply that later he will argue, and later I will respond.

That there are as many Holy Spirits as there are good men

[**Pat:**] 1 Jn 4 (4:1) "Do not believe every spirit, but test the spirits if they be of God." Therefore there are as many Holy Spirits as there are good men.

Cath: I reply that he is speaking of human spirits, which are said not to be of God or those outside [of the Church] not having the faith of Christ, or they have it and of this He speaks of those as 'proven,' and this is what follows there, (1 Jn 4:1–2) "because many false prophets have gone out into the world, by this is the spirit of God known, every spirit which confesses that Jesus Christ is come in the flesh, is of God."

That there are three Holy Spirits

[**Pat:**] John 14 (14:16) "I will pray the Father that he might give to you another Paraclete." (20:22) "And he said to them, 'Receive the Holy Spirit,'" and (Feria 6, Lauds antiphon), "strengthen my heart with a perfect spirit, O God." Therefore there are three Holy Spirits.

Cath: I reply that it is the one and the same Spirit who is called by different names on account of the diverse effects

---

V.8.3 in...4 sancti] Matt. 28:19. V.9.3 Nolite...4 sint] 1 Ioh. 4:1. 10 quoniam...13 est] 1 Ioh. 4:1-2 (omnis) add. spiritus | ex deo] add. non *Vulg.*) V.10.2 ego...3 uobis] Ioh. 14:16. 3 et...4 sanctum] Ioh. 20:22. 4 sanctum...5 deus] Conflation of Ps. 50:14 and 56:8, most likely taken from Friday Lauds antiphon.

25 debes...26 sanctus] om. *P* 28 debes...30 sanctum] om. *P* V.8.1 Probatio...8.2 deus] om. *P* 16 respondebo] reprobabo *P* V.9.7 extra eam] esse cum *F* | eam] add. cum *F*

V.9.5 sunt¹|fol. 23v *F* 9 sequitur|fol. 33ra *P*

effectos quos in nobis operatur. de quibus habes sapientiam vii spiritus enim intelligentie etcet. prima ad corinthios xii. diuisiones uero gratiarum sunt etcet. et dominus in euangelio iohannes iohannis xv. manifeste ostendit cum autem uenerit paraclitus etcet. ecce de primo nomine et postea. quem ego mittam uobis a patre spiritum ueritatis etcet. ecce secundum nomen scilicet spiritus sanctus. idem enim est spiritus sanctus quod spiritus ueritatis. quia ueritas est qui sanctificat. et in xvi dicit cum autem uenerit ille arguet mundum de peccato et de iustitia et de iudicio. etcet. ecce tertium nomen scilicet spiritus principalis quod igitur dicit de principatu eius in mundo. igitur unus tantum est spiritus sanctus. substantialiter sicut deus declarat.

He works in us, of which you have Wisdom 7 (7:22) "the spirit of understanding," and 1 Corinthians 12 (12:4) "now there are varieties of grace," and the Lord in the Gospel of John 15 plainly shows (15:26) "but when the Paraclete shall come," see of the first name and later, "whom I will send to you from the Father, the Spirit of Truth." See the second name, that is, Holy Spirit. For the same Holy Spirit is the Spirit of Truth, since truth is He who sanctifies, and in chapter 16 He says (16:8) "And when he has come, he will convict the world of sin, and of justice, and of judgment." See the third name, that is, the Perfect Spirit which therefore He speaks of His reign in the world, therefore there is only one Holy Spirit, just as God reveals.

Quod septem sunt spiritus sancti

[Patarenus:] Apocalypsos primo et a vii spiritibus etcet. ergo sunt septem spiritus sancti.
Catholicus: Respondeo spiritus sanctus qui est unus essentialiter dicitur septem propter vii karismatum dona. que ab eo procedunt. de quibus habes ysaias vii. et requiescet super eum spiritus domini. spiritus sapientie et intellectus. spiritus consilii et fortitudinis spiritus scientie et pietatis et replebit eum spiritus timoris domini etcet. ecce quomodo primo nominat spiritum sanctum in singulari numero. quia est unus essentialiter et postea nominat eum in plurali. per diuisiones donorum eius. ostendendo vii. esse eius karismata. sunt ergo vii spiritus id est septem dona spiritus sancti. qui etiam dicitur vii. oculi filii dei. qua per illa dona que a suo spiritum procedunt illuminat fideles suos. unde subdit in v. apocalypsis. in medio seniorum agnum stantem tamquam occisum habentem cornua vii et oculos vii qui sunt vii spiritus dei missi in omnem terram. etcet.

That there are seven Holy Spirits

[Pat:] Apocalypse 1 (1:4) "from the seven spirits," therefore there are seven Holy Spirits.
Cath: I reply that the Holy Spirit is He who is one essentiality, [He] is called seven on account of the seven spiritual gifts, which proceed from Him, of which you have Isaiah 7 (11:2–3) "And the spirit of the Lord will rest upon him, the spirit of wisdom, and of understanding, the spirit of counsel, and of fortitude, the spirit of knowledge, and of piety, and he shall be filled with the spirit of the fear of the Lord." See how he first names the Holy Spirit in the singular, since He is one essentially, and later names Him in the plural, on account of the varieties of His gifts, by showing His spiritual endowments to be sevenfold, there are therefore seven spirits, that is, the seven gifts of the Holy Spirit, which also are called the seven eyes of the son of God, because through those gifts which proceed from His Spirit He illuminates his faithful. Whence it adds in Apocalypse 5 (5:6) "In the midst of the ancients, a Lamb standing as it were slain, having seven horns and seven eyes, which are the seven Spirits of God, sent forth into all the earth."

Quod deus ueteris testamentis fuit bonus deus

Dictum est supra de uno deo et trino qui est pater et filius et spiritus sanctus super omnia benedictus dominus. nunc autem sequitur uidere utrum ipse benedictus deus ueteris testamenti fuerit conditor. quod per auctores noui testamenti contra falsarios patarenos hoc denegantes. quattuor modis probamus euidenter.
Primus modus.
Primus est quia simpliciter in nouo testamento nominatur deus. quare bonus deus intelligendus est

That the God of the Old Testament was the good God

The One and Triune God, who is Father, and Son, and Holy Spirit, the blessed Lord of all things, has been dealt with above. Yet now it remains to see whether that blessed God might have been the creator of the Old Testament, which shall be evidently proven in four ways, through the authors of the New Testament against the Patarene forgers, who deny this.
The first way.
The first is that He is simply called God in the New Testament. Hence He was understood to be the good God,

---

9 spiritus...intelligentie] Sap. 7:22.   10 diuisiones...sunt] 1 Cor. 12:4.   12 cum...paraclitus] Ioh. 15:26.   17 cum...18 iudicio] Ioh. 16:8.   V.11.2 et...spiritibus] Apoc. 1:4.   7 et...10 domini] Is. 11:2-3.   17 in² ...20 terram] Apoc. 5:6.

V.10.11 et] om. F   V.11.13 ostendendo] ostendo F   16 dona] om. P   VI.1.8 euidenter] om. F   9 Primus modus] P makes this a rubric, F does not.   10 quia] qui F   11 intelligendus est] iintelligere dominus est F

V.11.6 quibus|fol. 33rb P

maxime cum in bonis nominetur exemplis. ut ecce. Mattheus xii quomodo intrabit in domum dei. etcet. et xv quare et uos transgredimini mandata dei. propter traditionem uestram. nam deus dixit. honora patrem et matrem etcet. quod et in multis locis noui testamenti reperies. etcet.

Secundus est quia nominatur per huiusmodi uerba qui bonitatem diuinam insinuant. ut ecce. Mattheus xviiii num legistis quia qui fecit homines ab initio masculum et feminam fecit eos etcet. et postea quod ergo deus coniunxit homo non separet. etcet. ergo ille deus de quo dicit moyses in uetero testamento quod fecit homines et ordinauit matrimonium est ille de quo precipit christus in nouo quod eius coniuctionem nemo separet. igitur bonus deus est. alias enim dixisset quos deus non bonus coniunxit homo separaret. item iohannes viii est pater meus qui glorificat me quem uos dicitis quia deus uester est etcet. ergo bonus fuit deus iudeorum. si fuit pater domini nostri ihesu christi. item ad romanos primo in principio segregatus in euangelium dei quod ante promisserat per prophetas suos in scripturis sanctis de filio suo etcet. igitur bonus deus qui locutus est in ueteri testamento. Malus enim deus non est pater domini nostri ihesu christi. nec scripture sue dicerentur sancte. sed prophane item. idem secundo. qui in lege gloriaris. per preuaricationem legis deum inhonoras etcet. reprehendit apostolus iudeum qui inhonorabat deum legis mosayce non seruando illam. igitur bonus deus fuit. alias enim commendasset eum si diaboli uoluntatem obseruasset. Item idem viiii. numquid iniquitas apud deum. absit. moysi enim dicit etcet. ergo deus apud quem non est iniquitas. locutus est moysi ergo bonus deus fuit.

Item actus iii. Deus abraam. deus ysaac et deus iacob. deus patrum nostrorum glorificauit filium suum ihesum etcet. ergo fuit optimus deus patrum ueteris testamenti quia fuit pater domini nostri ihesu christi. Item idem vii. uiri fratres et patres audite. deus glorie apparuit patri nostro abraam cum esset in mesopotamia etcet. usque ibi. audientes autem hec etcet. igitur bonus fuit deus ueteris testamenti. si fuit deus glorie et si dedit legem moysi per angelos. ut ibi legitur.

Item idem xiiii surgens autem paulus et manu silentium indicens ait ibi deus plebis israel elegit patres nostros etcet. et infra. inueni dauid filium iesse secundum cor meum qui faciet omnes uoluntates meas. cuius deus ex semine secundum promissionem eduxit

especially when He was named in many good analogies, is as follows. Matthew 12 (12:4) "How he entered into the house of God," and 15 (15:3–4) "Why do you also transgress the commandment of God for your tradition? For God said, 'Honor your father and mother.'" And you discover that in many places of the New Testament.

The second is that He is named through some words which imply He who is divine goodness, as here Matthew 19 (19:4) "Have you not read, that he who made man from the beginning, made them male and female?" and later (19:6) "what then God has joined, let no man separate," therefore that God — of whom Moses speaks in the Old Testament that made men and ordained marriage — is He about whom Christ commanded in the New that one might never separate what He has joined. Therefore He is the good God. For otherwise He might have said that God was not good, who permitted man to separate. Also John 8 (8:54) "It is my Father who glorifies me, of whom you say that he is your God." Therefore the good God was the God of the Jews, if He was the Father of our Lord Jesus Christ. Also Romans 1 (1:1–3) "Set apart for the gospel of God, which he had promised before, by his prophets, in the holy scriptures, concerning his Son." Therefore it was the good God who spoke in the Old Testament, for an evil God is not the Father of our Lord Jesus Christ, neither were his scriptures called holy, but profane. Also in the second chapter (2:23) "You who make your boast in the Law, by transgression of the law, dishonor God." The Apostle upbraids the Jews who dishonored God by not serving Him in the Law of Moses, therefore He was the good God, for otherwise would He have commended Him if He observed the will of the devil? Also in the same in chapter 9 (9:14–15) "What shall we say then? Is there injustice with God? God forbid. For he spoke to Moses." Therefore God, before whom there is no iniquity, spoke to Moses, therefore He was the good God.

Also Acts 3 (3:13) "The God of Abraham, and the God of Isaac, and the God of Jacob, the God of our fathers, has glorified his Son Jesus." Therefore He was the most High God, the Father of the Old Testament, since He was the Father of our Lord Jesus Christ. Also in the same book (7:2) "You men, brethren, and fathers, hear. The God of glory appeared to our father Abraham, when he was in Mesopotamia," up to there (7:54) "now hearing these things," therefore the good God was the God of the Old Testament, if He was the God of history and if He gave the Law to Moses by means of the angels, as it is read there.

In the same in 13 (13:16–17) "Then Paul rising up, and with his hand asking for silence, said, 'Men of Israel, the God of the people of Israel chose our fathers.'" And later (13:22–24) "I have found David, the son of Jesse, a man according to my own heart, who will accomplish all my

---

VI.1.13 quomodo...dei] Matt. 12:4. **14** quare...16 matrem] Matt. 15:3-4 (mandata) mandatum *Vulg.*) **20** legistis...21 eos] Matt. 19:4 (num) non *Vulg.*) **21** quod...22 separet] Matt. 19:6. **28** est...29 est] Ioh. 8:54. **31** in¹...33 suo] Rom. 1:1-3. **37** qui...38 inhonoras] Rom. 2:23. **42** numquid...43 dicit] Rom. 9:14-15. **45** Deus...47 ihesum] Act. 3:13. **49** uiri...51 mesopo-tamia] Act. 7:2 (abraam) abrahae *Vulg.*) **51** audientes...hec] Act. 7:54. **54** surgens...56 nostros] Act. 13:16-17. **56** inueni...59 iohanne] Act. 13:22-24 (iesse) add. uirum | cuius] huius | nostram] om. *Vulg.*)

17 etcet] om. *F* **24** matrimonium] add. naturam *F* **36** sed] uel *F*

VI.1.19 ecce|fol. 33va P **20** homines|fol. 24r F **47** deus|fol. 33vb P

israel saluatorem nostram ihesum predicante iohanne etcet. per totum quasi uersum ad finem huius capituli. ex quibus uerbis patet expresse quod deus in ueteris testamenti fuit bonus deus. quia fuit ille qui eduxit dominum ihesum christum ad salutem mundi.

Tertius modus est quia legitur in nouo testamento. quod ueteris et noui testamenti fuit idem deus. ut ecce. mattheus xxi homo erat paterfamilias qui plantauit uineam. etcet. et ibi aiunt illi. malos male perdet et scilicet uineam suam locabit aliis agricolis etcet. ecce habes quod idem dominus unam eademque vineam locauit iudeis et christianis. igitur unus est deus ueteris et noui testamenti. itaque bonus fuit deus ueteris testamenti. quia fuit deus noui. item prima ad corinthios x. nolo enim uos ignorare fratres quoniam patres nostri omnes sub nube fuerunt etcet. ibi bibebant autem de spiritali consequente eos petra. petra autem erat christus etcet. ergo christus fuit dux eorum. ergo bonus deus fuit. deus ueteris testamenti quia fuit deus noui qui est christus. quod apertius declaratur ex inferioribus infra neque temptemus christum sicut quidam eorum temptauerunt et a serpentibus perierunt. etcet. ergo christus fuit temptatus a filius israel in deserto. sed legitur quod ipsi temptauerunt deum ad hebreos iii. quapropter sicut dicit spiritus sanctus. hodie si uocem eius scilicet dei. audieritis. etcet. ergo christus fuit deus ueteris testamenti. qui fuit et noui testamenti deus. item ad galatas. iiii. abraam duos filios habuit etcet. igitur que sunt per allegoriam dictam hec enim sunt duo testamenta. etcet. ergo uetus et nouum testamentum processunt a eodem patre. Sed nouum processit a christo ergo et uetus. item ad hebreos quarta nam si illis ihesus requiem prestitisset etcet. ergo dominus ihesus fuit deus ueteris testamenti. item idem viii ecce dies ueniunt dicit dominus et consumabo super domum israel. et super domum iuda testamentum nouum non secundum testamentum quod dedi patribus eorum ut educerem illos de terra egypti quoniam ipsi non permanserunt in testamento meo et ego neglexi eos dicit dominus etcet. ecce quam manifeste introducet quod unus fuit deus ueteris et noui testamenti. item secunda petre ii. si enim deus angelis peccantibus non pepercit etcet. usque ad finem capituli. ergo bonus deus fuit ille qui induxit diluuium et subuertit pentapolim. quia ille est qui dampnauit angelos apostatantes et qui eripuit pios de temptationibus et iste est deus noui testamenti. igitur utriusque testamenti unus est deus.

designs. Of this man's seed God according to his promise, has raised up to Israel our savior, Jesus, John first preaching." And through all the rest up to the conclusion of this chapter. From these words it is clearly plain that the God of the Old Testament was the good God, since it was He who raised up the Lord Jesus Christ for the salvation of the world.

The third way is what is read in the New Testament, that the Old and New Testaments were from the same God, as for example in Matthew 21 (21:33) "There was a man who was a householder, who planted a vineyard," and there they say to him (21:41) "He will bring those evil men to an evil end, and will let out his vineyard to other tenants." See you have it that the Lord was one and the same who let it out to Jews and to Christians, therefore the God of the Old and New Testaments was one, thus the God of the Old Testament was the good God, since He was the God of the New Testament. Also 1 Corinthians 10 (10:1) "For I would not have you ignorant, brethren, that our fathers were all under the cloud." There (10:4) "and they drank of the spiritual rock that followed them, and the rock was Christ." Therefore Christ was their leader, so the good God was the God of the Old Testament, since He was the God of the New, who is Christ, since it is openly proclaimed later below, (10:9) "neither let us tempt Christ, like some of them tempted, and perished by the serpents." Therefore Christ was tempted by the sons of Israel in the desert, but it is read that these tempted God in Hebrews 3 (3:7) "So, as the Holy Spirit says, 'If today you hear his'" — namely God's — "'voice.'" Therefore Christ was the God of the Old Testament, who was also the God of the New Testament. Also Galatians 4 (4:22) "Abraham had two sons," therefore "these things are said by an allegory, for these are the two testaments." Therefore the Old and New Testaments came from the same Father, but the New comes forth from Christ, and so also the Old. Also Hebrews 4 (4:8) "For if Jesus had given them rest," so the Lord Jesus was the God of the Old Testament. Also in the same book in chapter 8 (8:8-9) "Behold, the days will come, says the Lord, and I will bring to perfection the house of Israel, and to the house of Judah, a new testament, not according to the testament which I gave to their fathers, that I might lead them out of the land of Egypt, because they did not continue in my testament, and I despised them, says the Lord." See how plainly it is presented that there is one God of the Old and New Testament. Also 2 Peter 2 (2:4) "For if God did not spare the angels that sinned," up to the end of the chapter. Therefore the good God was He who brought forth the flood and overthrew the Pentapolis, since it was He who condemned the apostate angels and He who delivered the pious from temptations, and He is the God of the New Testament. Therefore in both testaments God is one.

---

66 homo...67 uineam] Matt. 21:33.   67 malos...68 agricolis] Matt. 21:41.   73 nolo...74 fuerunt] 1 Cor. 10:1.   74 bibebant...76 christus¹] 1 Cor. 10:4.   79 neque...80 perierunt] 1 Cor. 10:9.   83 quapropter...84 audieritis] Heb. 3:7.   86 abraam...habuit] Gal. 4:22.   87 que...88 testamenta] Gal. 4:24.   91 nam...prestitisset] Heb. 4:8 (illis] eius *Vulg.*)   93 ecce...98 dominus] Heb. 8:8-9 (dedi] feci | eorum] add. in die qua apprehendi manum eorum *Vulg.*)   100 si...101 pepercit] 2 Pet. 2:4.

69 uineam] om. *P*   88 sunt] fuit *P* exp.   89 testamentum] om. *F*   102 deus] om. *P*   103 est] om. *P*

73 quoniam|fol. 34ra *P*   85 fuit¹|fol. 24v *F*   101 angelis|fol. 34rb *P*

Item iude primo comonere autem uos uolo. scientes semel omnia quoniam ihesus populum de terra egypta saluans. secundo eos qui non crediderunt perdidit. angelos uero etcet. ergo dominus ihesus christus fuit ille qui eduxit populum israel de egypto. nec potes hec intelligere de ihesu naue. quia ille non eduxit filios israel de egypto aliquo modo. sed moyses ministerio. christus uero eduxit illos uirtute et gloria. nec potest etiam hoc intelligi de ihesu summo sacerdote. uel de ihesu syrac quia illi temporis non erant in rerum natura.

Item apocalypsis ultimo. dominus deus spirituum prophetarum misit angelum suum etcet. qui misit angelum istum fuit deus noui testamenti. ergo utriusque testamenti unus est deus. quartus modus est. quia precipitur et suadetur nobis in nouo testamento ut eius precepta seruemus. qua bonus esse comprobatur. ut ecce. mattheus xiii. ait illis ideo omnis scriba doctus in regno celorum similis est homini patrifamilias qui profert de thesauro suo noua et uetera. etcet. et xviiii. si autem uis ad uitam ingredi serua mandata. dicit ille. que? ihesus autem dixit. non homicidium facies. non adulterabis. etcet. illud autem est notandum quod lex quattuor modis dicitur. uno moralia mandata. ut mattheus v. non soluere legem sed adimplere etcet. et secundum hoc preceptum est seruare eam semper et sic intelligitur illud serua mandata etcet. secundo modo legalia sive cerimonalia. ut mattheus xi. omnes enim prophete et lex usque iohannem prophetauerunt etcet. et sermo hoc transiuit eius obseruantia a passione christi antea. postquam dixit in cruce consumatum est. quia postquam uenit signatum. cessare debuit figura. unde apostolus dicit. ad hebreos. x umbram enim habens lex futurorum bonorum non ipsam ymaginem rerum etcet. et infra. ideo ingrediens mundum dicit. hostiam et oblationem noluisti. corpus autem aptasti mihi. holocautomata pro peccato non tibi placuerunt. etcet. Et fuit data lex cerimonium iudeis usque ad christi passionem. duris infra flagellum rudibus in pedagogum et perfectis in signum. de primo dicitur ad galatas iii. lex propter transgressiones posita est etcet. secundo in eodem. lex pedagogus fuit noster in christo de iii. ii° dicitur ad hebreos ix. hoc significante spiritu sancto nondum prolatam esse sanctorum uiam etcet. tertio modo dicitur lex. v. libro moysi. apostolus in actus xxiiii. credens omnibus que in lege et prophetis scripta sunt etcet. et

Also Jude 1 (1:5–6) "I will therefore admonish you, though you once knew all things, that Jesus, having saved the people out of the land of Egypt, afterwards destroyed those who did not believe, and the angels." So the Lord Jesus Christ was He who led the people of Israel out of Egypt, nor are you able to interpret this of Jesus [Joshua, son of Nun],[1] since He did not lead the children of Israel out of Egypt in just any manner, but by the ministry of Moses, Christ yet led them in power and glory. Nor can this be understood of Jesus the high priest, or of the Jesus in Sirach who at that time did not exist.

Also at the end of Apocalypse (22:6) "And the Lord God of the spirits of the prophets sent his angel." He who sent this angel was the God of the New Testament, therefore there is one God of both Testaments. The fourth way is this, because it is commanded and advised for us in the New Testament that we might observe His commandments, which are proven to be good, as follows. Matthew 13 (13:52) "He said to them, 'Therefore every scribe instructed in the kingdom of heaven is like a man who is a householder, who brings forth out of his treasure new things and old.'" And 19 (19:17–18) "'But if you would enter into life, keep the commandments.' He said to him: 'Which?' And Jesus said, 'Do not murder, Do not commit adultery.'" Yet it is to be noted that that law is spoken of in four ways. One, of the moral commandments, as in Matthew 5 (5:17) "I have come not to abolish the law but to fulfil it." And according to this command, one is to observe them always, and thus is "keep the commandments" to be interpreted. The second way is about legal things or ceremonies, as in Matthew 11 (11:13) "For all the prophets and the law prophesied until John," and this saying carried over to its observance up to the passion of Christ. After He said "It is finished," on the cross, since after the thing represented arrives, it ought to cease being a figure, whence the Apostle says in Hebrews 10 (10:1) "For the law having a shadow of the good things to come, not the very image of the things." And later (10:5) "So when he comes into the world, he says, 'You do not want sacrifice and oblation, but you have made a body for me, holocausts for sin did not please you.'" And the ceremonial law of the Jews was given up to the passion of Christ, the hard whip sent to teach the uneducated and made perfect in representation, of the first as is said in Galatians 3 (3:19) "the law was given for our transgressions," the second in the same in chapter 3 (3:24) "So the law was our teacher in Christ." The second was spoken of in Hebrews 9 (9:8) "The Holy Spirit signifies this, that the way into the sanctuary was not yet made plain." The third way of speaking of the law is

---

107 comonere...110 uero] Iud. 1:5-6. 118 dominus...119 suum] Apoc. 22:6. 124 ait...126 uetera] Matt. 13:52. 127 si...129 adulterabis] Matt. 19:17-18 (ille] illi *Vulg.*) 131 non...132 adimplere] Matt. 5:17 (non] add. veni *Vulg.*) 135 omnes...136 prophetauerunt] Matt. 11:13. 140 umbram...141 rerum] Heb. 10:1. 142 ideo...144 placuerunt] Heb. 10:5-6. 147 lex...148 est] Gal. 3:19. 148 lex...149 christo] Gal. 3:24. 150 hoc...151 uiam] Heb. 9:8 (prolatum] propalatam *Vulg.*) 152 credens...153 sunt] Act. 24:14.

137 obseruantia] add. eius *P* exp. 138 uenit] novit *P* 150 ix] viiii *P*

129 non|fol. 34va *P* 150 significante|fol. 25r *F*

---

1) See Augustine, *De. civ. Dei*, XVI, c. 43 for this usage of 'Jesus nave'.

secundum hunc modum debemus seruare eam sic. quia debemus eam uenerari et credere. quod omnia que in ea scripta sunt. doctrinam scripta sunt. sicut innuit ibi paulus cum dicit. credens omnibus etcet. ad romanos xv. quecumque enim scripta sunt ad nostram doctrinam scripta sunt. Quarto uero modo dicitur lex. quicumque in ueteris testamento continetur. iohannes x. nonne scriptum est in lege uestra. quia ego dixi dii estis etcet. constat enim quod illa auctoritas est in psalterio et secundum hunc modum debemus ei seruare. sicut secundum tertium.

quod deus ueteris testamentis non fuit bonus deus

[Patarenus:] Quod deus ueteris testamenti non fuit bonus deus sed malus. probari potest tribus rationibus. prima quarum hec est. quia deus noui testamenti contrarius est. ut ecce. Genesi primo. In principio creauit deus celum et terram terra autem erat inanis et uacua et tenebre erant super faciem abyssi etcet. ecce quod ille incepit opera sua a tenebris. sed deus noui testamenti incepit a luce. unde prima iohanne primo. deus lux est et tenebre in eo non sunt ulle.

Catholicus: respondeo quod ipse fuit deus noui testamenti. de quo dicit secunda ad corinthios iiii. deus qui dixit de tenebris lucem splendescere illuxit in cordibus nostris etcet. nec obstat auctoritas. iohannes. quia sic intelligitur. deus lux est. in lucidus illuminans et tenebre non sunt in eo ulle id est peccata et quod peccata dicuntur tenebre. habes petri primo. ut uirtutes annuntietis eius qui de tenebris uos uocauit in admirabile lumen suum etcet. et intellige stulte quod tenebre non fuerit aliquod opus dei nec hoc inuenies. sed est sensus illorum moysi. tenebre erant super faciem id est absentia lucis id est non erat lux ibi. sed modo respondeas mihi de tua ratione. nonne deus bonus fecit suam lucem.

Patarenus: utique.

Catholicus: ergo prius non erat. et sic oportet te confiteri deum bonum incepisse a tenebris opus suum. ubi temetipsi te contrarium inuenies. aut nostram expositionem humiliter et fideliter recipies.

[Patarenus:] Item in eodem. benedixitque illius deus et ait. crescite et multiplicamini et replete terram etcet. ecce quod ille ortatur homines ad coitum carnalem et benedicit illos qui carnaliter coniungitur. unde est contrarius deo noui testamenti qui dehortatur ab illo. et benedicit eis qui caste uiuunt. sicut infra titulum contra matrimonium demonstrabo.

the five books of Moses, the Apostle in Acts 24 (24:14) "believing all things which are written in the law and the prophets," and according to this way we ought to observe them thus. For we ought to venerate and believe them, since all which is written in them is written for teaching, just as Paul intimates when he said "believing all things." And Romans 15 (15:4) "For whatever things were written, were written for our learning." The fourth way of speaking of the law is whatever is contained in the Old Testament. John 10 (10:34) "Is it not written in your law that I said you are gods?" For it remains that this authority is in the psalter, and according to this understanding we ought to observe it, just as according to the other three.

That the God of the Old Testament was not the good God

[Pat:] That the God of the Old Testament was not the good God but an evil one can be proven by three arguments. The first of these is that he is opposed to the God of the New Testament, as for example in Genesis 1 (1:1–2) "In the beginning God created heaven and earth, and the earth was void and empty, and darkness was upon the face of the deep." See how he begins his work with darkness, but the God of the New Testament begins with light, whence in 1 John 1 (1:5) "That God is light, and in him there is no darkness."

Cath: I reply that He was the God of the New Testament, of which he speaks in 2 Corinthians 4 (4:6) "For God, who commanded the light to shine out of darkness, has shined in our hearts." Neither does the authority of John oppose this, since it is to be interpreted thusly, "God is light" in luminous brilliance "and in him there was no darkness," that is sin, since that which is called sin is darkness, you have in 1 Peter (2:9) "that you may declare his virtues, who has called you out of darkness into his marvelous light," and understand, O Fool, that darkness was not any work of God, neither do you find this, but this is the sense of Moses, "darkness was over the face," that is, the absence of light, which is to say there was no light there. But how might you respond to me regarding your argument, did not the good God make the light?

Pat: Certainly.

Cath: Therefore it did not exist prior to that, and so it is fitting for you to confess the good God to have begun His work in darkness, so you find you contradict yourself, rather humbly and faithfully accept our explanation.

[Pat:] Also in the same (1:28) "and God blessed them and said, 'Be fruitful and multiply, fill the earth.'" See that this urges men to carnal intercourse and he blesses those who join together carnally, which is contrary to the God of the New Testament who counsels against it and blesses those who live chastely, as I will demonstrate below in the section against marriage.

---

158 quecumque…159 sunt] Rom. 15:4. 161 nonne…162 estis] Ioh. 10:34. VI.2.6 In…8 abyssi] Gen. 1:1-2. 11 deus…ulle] 1 Ioh. 1:5. 13 deus…15 nostris] 2 Cor. 4:6 (splendescere] add. ipse *Vulg.*) 18 ut…20 suum] 1 Pet. 2:9. 31 benedixitque…32 terram] Gen. 1:22.

163 hunc] om. *P* VI.2.34 benedicit] add. qui *P* 35 dehortatur] deortatur *P*

155 credere|fol. 34vb *P* VI.2.22 illorum|fol. 35ra *P*

Catholicus: et ego ibi tibi respondebo et ostendam quod deus noui testamenti ordinauit matrimonium carnale et benedicit ac saluat uiuentes in illo.
[Patarenus:] Item in eodem idem. replete terram et subicite terram etcet. ecce quod ille ortatur suos ad magnitudinem dominii. deus autem noui testamenti ortatur suos ab humilitatem seruitutis. unde dicit lucam. xviiii. reges gentium dominatur eorum etcet. ibi. sed qui maior est in uobis fiat sicut minor et qui precessor est sicut ministrator etcet.
Catholicus: Respondeo loquitur in Genesis de dominio super bruta animalia. unde statim subdit. ibi et dominamini piscibus maris et uolatilibus celi et uniuersis animantibus que mouentur super terram etcet. de hoc dominio habes in mattheus xvii. uade ad mare et mitte amum et ipsum piscem qui primo ascenderit tolle etcet. et iohannes ultimo mitte in dexteram nauigii rete etcet.
Patarenus: Item idem tertio inimicitias ponam inter te et mulierem et semen tuum et semen illius etcet. ecce quod deus ille posuit discordiam. igitur. contrarius fuit deo noui testamenti. quia in iohanne xiii pacem uobis etcet.
Catholicus: Respondeo iste inimicitie bone erant. quas christus posuit finaliter. unde dicit in mattheus. x. non ueni pacem mittere in terram sed gladium. etcet. nec obstat iohanne. pacem relinquo uobis etcet. quia de pace hominum cum dei et hominum inter se. loquitur quod est inimicitiam cum serpente ponere.
[Patarenus:] Item in eodem. maledicam terra in opere tuo etcet. ecce quod ille maledicit terram suam et maledicit hominem etiam unde infra. iiii nunc igitur maledictus eris super terram etcet. deus uero noui testamenti benedicit terram suam et seruos suos. unde dicit. benedixisti de terram tuam etcet. et mattheus xxi. uenite benedicti patris mei etcet.
Catholicus: Respondeo quod deus ueteris testamenti maledixit terram maledictione pene id est sterilitatis. unde subdit. ibi. spinas et tribulos germinabit tibi. etcet. cuius arborem deus noui testamenti maledixit eadem maledictione. mattheus xxi. et ait illi. numquam ex te fructus nascatur in sempiternum et arefacta est continuo ficulnea etcet. et maledicit etiam malos homines. ut mattheus xxv. Discedite a me maledicti in ignem eternum etcet.
[Patarenus:] Item in eodem. nunc ergo ne forte mittat manum suam et sumat etiam de ligno uite deus autem noui testamenti dicit. apocalypsis secundo uincenti dabo edere de ligno uitae etcet.

Cath: And I will reply to you there and will show that the God of the New Testament ordained carnal marriage and blesses and saves those who are in that state.
[Pat:] Also in the same (1:28) "fill the earth and subdue the earth," see that He exhorts them to the greatness of lordship, yet the God of the New Testament counsels them to humble service, whence He says in Luke 19 (22:25–26) "the kings of the Gentiles lord it over them," and there "but he who is greater among you, let him become as the lesser, and he who is the leader, as one who serves."
Cath: I respond that Genesis speaks of dominion over the brute animals, whence it follows immediately there (Gn 1:28) "and rule over the fishes of the sea, and the birds of the air, and all living creatures that move upon the earth." Regarding this dominion you have Matthew 17 (17:26) "go to the sea, and cast in a hook and take the first fish to come up." And in the last chapter of John (21:6) "Cast your net to the right side of the ship."
Pat: Also in the third chapter of the same (Gn 3:15) "I will put enmity between you and the woman, between your seed and hers." See how that god brings discord? Therefore he is opposed to the God of the New Testament, as in John 13 (14:27) "Peace be with you."
Cath: I reply that these enmities were good, which Christ shall finally bring, whence He says in Matthew 10 (10:34) "I come not to bring peace but a sword on the earth," neither does John stand against this (Jn 14:27) "my peace I leave to you," which is the peace of men with God and of men between themselves, Matthew is speaking of that enmity brought by the serpent.
[Pat:] Also in the same (Gn 3:17) "cursed is the earth in your work." See that he curses his earth and curses men also later in 4 (4:11) "Now, therefore, cursed will you be upon the earth." Yet the God of the New Testament blesses His earth and His servants, whence He says (Ps 84:2) "Lord you have blessed the earth," and Matthew 21 (25:34) "come, you blessed of my Father."
Cath: I reply that the God of the Old Testament cursed the earth with a curse of punishment, that is, of sterility, whence He adds there (3:17) "it will bring forth thorns and thistles for you," whose tree the God of the New Testament reviled with the same curse, Matthew 21 (21:19) "and he said to it, 'May no fruit grow on you forever.' And immediately the fig tree withered away," and so He also curses men, as in Matthew 25 (25:41) "Depart from me, you cursed ones, into the eternal fire."
[Pat:] Also in the same (Gn 3:22) "therefore, lest perhaps he put forth his hand, and take also from the tree of life," yet the God of the New Testament says in Apocalypse 2 (2:7) "I will give to eat of the tree of life."

---

41 replete...42 terram] Gen. 1:28.   45 reges...eorum] Luc. 22:25-26.   50 et¹...51 terram] Gen. 1:28.   52 uade...54 tolle] Matt. 17:26.   54 mitte...55 rete] Ioh. 21:6.   56 inimicitias...57 illius] Gen. 3:15.   59 pacem uobis] Ioh. 14:27.   62 non...63 gladium] Matt. 10:34.   64 pacem...uobis] Ioh. 14:27.   67 maledicam...68 tuo] Gen. 3:17.   69 nunc...70 terram] Gen. 4:11.   72 benedixisti...tuam] Ps. 84:2.   73 uenite...mei] Matt. 25:34.   76 spinas...tibi] Gen. 3:18.   78 et...80 ficulnea] Matt. 21:19.   81 Discedite...82 eternum] Matt. 25:41.   83 nunc...84 deus] Gen. 3:22.   85 uincenti...86 uitae] Apoc. 2:7.

---

53 amum] hamum F   69 hominem etiam] transp. F

50 dominamini|fol. 35rb P   53 ipsum|fol. 25v F   80 arefacta|fol. 35va P

Catholicus: Respondeo prohibuit deus ade sumere de ligno uite. quia uictus erat. et ideo indignus erat. in apocalypsis uero promittit uincenti et per consequentiam negatur uicto. simile habes mattheus viii. Nolite dare sanctum canibus etcet.

[**Patarenus:**] Item idem xvii. masculus cuius caro preputii circumcisa non fuerit delebitur anima illa de populo suo etcet. sed deus noui testamenti prohibet circumcisionem. ad Galatas. v. si circumcidamini christus uobis nichil prodest. etcet.

Catholicus: De hac materia tibi satisfaciam infra in secundo libro. titulo de circumcisis.

[**Patarenus:**] Item ille constituit principes carnales in mirabilibus ambulantes ut puta reges et centuriones et huiusmodi prout habes in multis locis ueteris testamenti. deus autem noui ordinauit apostolos et alios prelatos spirituales et temporales humiliter seruientes.

Catholicus: Respondeo quod deus ueteris testamenti constituit principes spirituales et temporales sicut habes in pentateucum. et in regem et in multis aliis locis testamentum ueteris et deus noui testamenti similiter ordinauit omnem potestatem tam temporalem quam spiritualem. prout habes ad romanos xiii. non est enim potestas nisi a deo etcet.

Patarenus: Item ille iussit bella fieri et ordinauit deus uero noui testamenti iussit non resistere alicui etiam iniurianti. Mattheus v. audistis quia dictum est antiquis oculum pro oculo. dentem pro dente. ego autem dico uobis non resistere malo etcet.

Catholicus: Respondeo quod ille qui iussit fieri bella et ordinauit in ueteri testamento. fuit deus glorie et qui eduxit dominum ihesum saluatorem mundi. ut legitur actus vii. deus glorie apparuit etcet. per totum et xiii. deus plebis israel etcet. igitur fuit deus noui testamenti. nec obstat illud. mattheus prout respondebimus. infra terti libro titulus de iudicio et potestate seculari. in oppositione illius auctoritatis contra iudicium seculare etcet.

Patarenus: Item ille occidit et iussit occidi quasi infinitos homines. non enim sunt tot homines super terram quanto ille occidit et occidi fecit et gloriatur etiam de hoc in cantico moyses dicens. ego occidam etcet. sed deus noui testamenti noluit occidere sed absoluit. johannes vii. de muliere deprahensa in adulterio. cum dixit. nec ego te condemnabo etcet.

Catholicus: Respondeo quod deus noui testamenti hoc facit et faciet. Vt probatum est supra titulo primo. in rubricella quod pene omnes sunt a deo. et gloriatur etiam ipse de hoc. unde dicit apocalypsis primo et habeo claues mortis et inferni etcet. ad illud autem

---

Cath: I reply that God prohibited Adam from eating of the tree of life since he was alive, and so he was unworthy, yet in Apocalypse He promises it to those who conquer and, consequently, it is denied to the conquered. Similarly you have Matthew 8 (7:6) "do not give that which is holy to the dogs."

[**Pat:**] Also in the same (Gn 17:14) "The male who will not be circumcised in the flesh of his foreskin, his soul will be blotted out of his people," but the God of the New Testament prohibits circumcision. Galatians 5 (5:2) "that if you be circumcised, Christ will be of no profit to you."

Cath: I will discuss this material later in the second book in the section on Circumcisers.

[**Pat:**] Also he appointed carnal leaders and surrounded them with miracles, as for example, kings and captains and the like, just as you have in many places in the Old Testament. Yet the God of the New Testament commanded Apostles and other spiritual and temporal leaders to serve in humility.

Cath: I reply that the God of the Old Testament appointed spiritual and temporal leaders as you see in the Pentateuch and in Kings and in many other places in the Old Testament, and that the God of the New Testament similarly ordained every power, be it temporal or spiritual, just as you have it in Romans 1 (13:1) "there is no power except from God."

Pat: Also he commanded war to be waged, and the God of the New Testament commanded that resistance not be offered to any, even for injuries. Matthew 5 (5:38–39) "You have heard it said of old, an eye for an eye, a tooth for a tooth. Yet I say to you, do not resist evil."

Cath: I respond that He who commanded that war should be waged in the Old Testament is the God of glory from whom came forth the Lord Jesus, the savior of the world, as is read in Acts 7 (7:2) "The God of glory appeared," and all the way through the entire chapter and 13 (13:17) "God of the people of Israel," therefore He was the God of the New Testament. Nor does what Matthew say contradict that, just as we shall reply in the third book in the section on judgment and secular power, in opposition to that passage against secular judgment.

Pat: Also he kills and orders to be killed nearly an infinite number of men, for there are not so many men on the earth as those he killed and ordered to be killed and gloried also in it, as the Canticle of Moses says (Dt 32:39) "I shall kill." But the God of the New Testament does not wish to kill but to forgive. John 7 (8:11) of the woman taken in adultery, when he said "neither do I condemn you."

Cath: I reply that the God of the New Testament did this and does do this, as was proven above in the first section in the subsection that all punishment is from God, and He also boasts of this, when he says in Apocalypse 1 (1:18) "I have the keys of death and hell." But to that which you

---

91 Nolite...canibus] Matt. 7:6.   92 masculus...94 suo] Gen. 17:14.   95 si...96 prodest] Gal. 5:2 (prodest) proderit *Vulg.*)
111 non...deo] Rom. 13:1.   114 quia...116 malo] Matt. 5:38-39 (antiquis om. *Vulg.*)   120 deus...apparuit] Act. 7:2.   121 deus¹... israel] Act. 13:17.   129 ego occidam] Deut. 32:29.   131 de...132 adulterio] Ioh. 8:11.   136 et...137 inferni] Apoc. 1:18.

88 uictus] uirtus *F*   90 habes] om. *F*   112 Patarenus] om. *F*   137 ad] sed *F*

109 ordinauit|fol. 35vb *P*   130 deus|fol. 26r *F*   135 omnes|fol. 36ra *P*

quod dixisti quod deus ueteris testamenti occidit plures quam super terram sint uiui. Dico quod deus noui testamenti occidit longe plures. qui occidit omnes qui mouentur. ut inuenitur in auctoritate predictam de apocalypsis. nec obstat illud. iohannes ultimo. de muliere deprehensa in adulterio. ut infra tibi respondebo titulus de iudicio et potestate seculari.

[**Patarenus:**] Item ille dedit multi precepta. que deus noui testamenti remouit. ergo fuerit contrarii.

Catholicus: Respondeo quod christus remouit precepta cerimonalia quia impleta erant et hic de ista materia plenius infra de circumcisis.

[**Patarenus:**] Secunda ratione est. uarietas et mutabilitas dei ueteris testamenti. que probabitur sic. Genesis v penituit eum quod hominum fecisset in terra. ecce quod deus ueteris testamenti fuit uariabilis et mutabilis quia penituit eum de hoc quod fecerat. et doluit uehementer de creatione hominis cum magno tripudio composuerat dicens. faciamus hominem ad imaginem et similitudinem nostram etcet. de deo uero noui testamenti dicit iacobum primo. apud quem non est transmutatio nec uicissitudinis obumbratio etcet.

Catholicus: Respondeo quod in illis uerbis scilicet penitet me et tactus cordis dolore intrinsecus est antropos id est humana propassio. deus enim numquam penitet in se neque tristatur. uel aliter possunt uerba hec exponi secundum beatum augustinum ut sit sensus. penitet me fecisse hominem id est pena me tenebit quia feci eum et tunc tangar eum dolore cordis intrinsecus sicut legitur. mattheus. xxvi. factum ubi dominus dicit. tristis anima mea usque ad mortem etcet. sed responde tu mihi heretice de ista auctoritate quod contra me pro magno trepudio allegasti. ibi enim dicitur uidens autem deus quod malitia hominum esset in terra et cuncta cogitatio hominis intenta esset ad malum omni tempore. pentituit eum quod hominem fecisset etcet. ergo bonus deus fuit. numquam diabolum penituisset nec doluisset ipse de malitia humana.

[**Patarenus:**] Preterea multe alie mutationes inuenitur in deo ueteris testamenti. quas hic esset inserere longum. ergo fuit mutabilis.

Catholicus: Respondeo quod nulla mutatio inuenitur umquam in deo ueteris testamenti. quantum in se. sed tantum in effectum in nobis operato et idem reperies de deo noui testamenti. sed talis mutatio ex parte nostram est. non ex deo.

[**Patarenus:**] Tertia ratio est. quia inuenimus de ipso multa scripta in ueteris testamento. qui defectum et malitiam eius exprimunt. ut ecce. Genesis secundo de

said that the God of the Old Testament killed more than lived on the earth, I say that the God of the New Testament kills far more, since He kills all things that move, as is found in the preceding passage from Apocalypse. Nor does the last passage of John oppose this, regarding the woman taken in adultery, which I will address later in the section on judgment and secular power.

[Pat:] Also he gave many commands that the God of the New Testament removed. So they are opposed.

Cath: I reply that Christ removed the precepts of the ceremonial law since He had fulfilled them, there will be plenty of material on this in the section on Circumcisers.

[Pat:] The second reason is the variety and changeable nature of the God of the Old Testament, which is proven thusly. Genesis 5 (6:6) "He repented that he had made man on the earth." See that the God of the Old Testament was variable and changeable since he repented that he had done this, and he sorrowed strongly regarding the creation of man, which he had done with such care, saying (1:26) "let us make man in our own image and likeness." Yet regarding the God of the New Testament it says in James 1 (1:17) "in whom there is no change, nor shadow of alteration."

Cath: I reply that in these words, namely "he repented and being touched inwardly with sorrow of heart," is human, that is, a human emotion. For God never repents nor is saddened within Himself, or otherwise the words are able to be truly explained according to Blessed Augustine (*City of God*, 15.25) that the sense, "He repented because he had made a man," that is, it will bind me to the penalty since I made him, and then I may touch him with inner sorrow of heart, as is read in Matthew 26 (26:38) where the Lord said "My soul is sorrowful even unto death." But answer me this, O heretic, by this authority that you have adduced against me with great solemnity, for there it says (Gn 6:5) "And God seeing that the wickedness of men was great on the earth, and that all the thoughts of men's hearts were bent upon evil at all times, He repented that he had made man." Therefore He was the Good God, for the devil never repented nor sorrowed himself over the wickedness of men.

[Pat:] Further many other changes are to be found in the God of the Old Testament, which would be too numerous to mention here, therefore he was changeable.

Cath: I reply that no change was ever found in the God of the Old Testament, insofar as He Himself was concerned, but only in the effects wrought in us, and you also discover this of the God of the New Testament, but such changes are only on our part, not on God's.

[Pat:] The third reason is that we find [a god] in many passages of the Old Testament, who is portrayed in his defects and his malice, as in Genesis 2 (2:17) "Of the tree of the

---

152 penituit...153 terra] Gen. 6:6.   **156** faciamus...157 nostram] Gen. 1:26.   **158** apud...159 obumbratio] Apoc. 1:17.   **165** penitet...167 intrinsecus] Augustine, *City of God*, 15.25 (paraphrase).   **168** factum...169 mortem] Matt. 26:38 (tristis) add. est *Vulg.*)   **171** uidens...174 fecisset] Gen. 6:5-6 (quod) add. multa | hominis] add. cordis *Vulg.*)   **187** de...188 comedas] Gen. 2:17.

155 cum] quantum *P*   **161** tactus...dolore] est dolore cordis *F*   **162** antropos] antropatos *F*   **168** dominus] Christus *F*   **182** reperies] repperies *F*

161 penitet|fol. 36rb *P*

ligno scientie boni et mali ne comedas etcet. qualis deus fuit iste qui prohibebat comedere bonum.

Catholicus: Respondeo non dicitur quod prohibuisset eum simplicem comedere bonum. sed de ligno scientie boni et mali eo quod eius comestio contra dei preceptum faciebat scire bonum et malum per experientia quia ex hoc incurrebant penam mortalitatis. Unde ex experto cognoscebant prothoplausti malum et per consequentiam bonum. quia contrario probato aliud melius innotescit.

[**Patarenus:**] Item idem tertia ecce adam factus est quasi unus ex nobis etcet. sed adam peccauerat. ergo et deus suus peccator erat. si filius ei factus est.

Catholicus: Respondeo ironice et derisorie loquitur ibi deus. simile habes de deo. mattheus xxi. forsitan uerebuntur filium meum etcet. et apostolus eodem modo loquitur prima de corinthios. iiii. sine nobis regnetis etcet. uel dic quod in genere est uox compassionis illa.

[**Patarenus:**] Item ipse fuit mendax. promiserat ei tempore diluuii cxx annos ad penitentia hominibus et tempore subtractis. xx. annis induxit diluuium ut hoc conituntur in genesis v et vii. item promisit abrahe quod daret ei et semini eius terram chanaan totam ut legitur. genesis xvii. daboque tibi et semini tuo post te terram peregrinationis tue omnem terram chanaan in possessionem sempiternam etcet. et tamen non dedit de illa passum pedis abrahe. ut dicit beatus stephanus in actibus. vii. et non dedit illi hereditatem in ea nec passum pedis etcet. nec semen abrahe possedit illam uniuersam unquam. item in xxxii. dixit ad iacob. nequaquam iacob appellabitur nomen tuum sed israel etcet. et tamen postea non solum homines sed etiam ille deus uocauit nomen illius iacob. sicut ipse dicit multos. ego sum deus abraam et deus ysaac et deus iacob etcet.

[**Catholicus:**] Respondeo ad primum dico. quia ideo subtraxit. xx. annos illis. quia malitia illorum processerat ad omnimoda in correctionem unde ipsa fuit temporis supplementum. sic etiam faciet deus noui testamenti in fine mundi. mattheus xxiiii. nisi breuiati fuissent dies illi. etcet. uel dico quod illud tempus. cxx. annorum intelligitur de cursu uite humane post diluuium. ad secundum dico quod deus dedit terram chanaan ex parte abrahe. ysaac et iacob et semini abrahe debuit dare totam si fuissent obediens ei. nec obstat dictum beati stephani quia sic intelligitur non dedit abrahe nec passum pedis in ea scilicet numquam permanenti. sed tantum tamquam peregrino. quod idem fuit de ysaac et iacob. sicut paulus ad hebreos xi. fide demoratus est in terra repromissionis

knowledge of good and evil, you shall not eat," what kind of God was he who prohibited them to eat good things?

Cath: I reply that He did not say that it was prohibited for them simply to eat good things, but that the eating from the tree of the knowledge of good and evil was against the command of God. He caused the knowledge of good and evil by experience since on account of it they incurred the penalty of mortality. Whence from experience the first people knew evil and, as a consequence, the good, since once a contrary is proven, the other becomes better known.

[**Pat.**] Also the same in 3 (Gn 3:22) "Behold Adam has become like one of us," but Adam sinned, therefore his god was a sinner, if he was made son to him.

Cath: I reply that God is speaking ironically and in a mocking tone there, as is similar of God in Matthew 21 perhaps (21:37) "They will respect my son." And the Apostle speaks in the same manner in 1 Corinthians 4 (4:8) "you reign without us," or say in general that it is the voice of His compassion.

[**Pat.**] Also he was a liar, for he promised to them in the time of the flood they would have 120 years for the penance of men, and 20 years was taken away when he unleashed the flood as is put forth in Genesis 5 through 7. Also he promised to Abraham that he would give to him and his seed the whole land of Canaan, as is read in Genesis 17 (17:8) "And I will give to you and your seed the land of your sojourn, all the land of Canaan for a perpetual possession." And yet he did not give Abraham even a foot of it, as Blessed Stephen says in Acts 7 (7:5) "And he gave him no inheritance in it, no, not the space of a foot." Neither did the seed of Abraham ever possess it wholly. Also in 32 (32:28) he spoke to Jacob, "Your name shall not be called Jacob, but Israel," and yet after that not only men but also God called his name Jacob, as he himself said many times "I am the God of Abraham, and the God of Isaac, and the God of Jacob,"

[**Cath:**] I reply to the first saying that the reason He took away 20 of their years was because their wickedness of every kind had gone before them, whence as a correction there was a supplementary time [subtracted]. For the God of the New Testament will do likewise at the end of the world. Matthew 24 (24:22) "And unless those days had been shortened," or I say that that time of 120 years is to be understood as the course of human life after the flood. To the second I say that God gave the land of Canaan on behalf of Abraham, Isaac, and Jacob, and to the seed of Abraham, He ought to have given it completely had they obeyed Him. Nor does what Blessed Stephen says detract from that, since this is to be interpreted "not the space of a foot in it," namely, never permanently, but only like a pilgrim as the same was of Isaac and Jacob, as Paul says in

---

198 ecce...199 nobis] Gen. 3:22. 203 uerebuntur...meum] Matt. 21:37. 204 sine...205 regnetis] 1 Cor. 4:8. 212 daboque...214 sempiternam] Gen. 17:8 (sempiternam] aeternam *Vulg.*) 216 et...217 pedis] Act. 7:5. 218 dixit...219 israel] Gen. 32:28. 228 nisi...229 illi] Matt. 24:22. 238 fide...240 coheredibus] Heb. 11:9.

192 eo] om. P 213 chanaan] chanahan F 226 correctionem] add. in fine P exp. 227 etiam] enim P 232 chanaan] chanahan F 235 num-quam] tamquam F

189 prohibebat|fol. 36va P 200 peccator|fol. 26v F 217 nec|fol. 36vb P

tamquam in aliena in casulis habitando cum ysaac et iacob coheredibus etcet. uel intelligitur quod illa promissio facta erant abrahe complenda in semine suo. qui est christus. ut dicit apostolus ad galatas. iii. et semini tuo qui est christus etcet. in quo complete sunt omnis promissiones sancte tam abrahe quam alius pluribus patribus ut dicit ad hebreos. iº. ad tertium uero dicimus quod sic intelligitur nequaquam quam uocabitur nomen tuum iacob scilicet prope sed testamentum erit nomen tuum proprium de cetero. uel aliter nequaquam quam uocabitur nomen tuum iacob scilicet tantum secundum testimonium. simile dicit in iohannes primo. tu uocaberis cephas id est et cephas.

[**Patarenus:**] Item. ille apparuit in flamma rubi moyses. ut legitur exodus iii. et rapuit heliam in curro igneo ut habetur iiii regnum ii. unde non uidetur bonus deus qui apparuit in igne et cuius opera fuerunt per igne.

Catholicus: Respondeo quod ipse fuit ille deus de quo beatus petrus in actibus ii. qui dixit per iohelem prophetam. dabo prodigia in celo sursum et signa in terra deorsum sanguinem et ignem et uaporem fumi. quem tu non inficiaris deum uerum esse. Hic fuit deus apostolorum qui super ipsis ignitis linguis apparuit. unde legitur in actibus. in eodem hic est deus de quo dixit apostolus ad hebreos xiii deus noster ignis consumens est etcet.

[**Patarenus:**] Item ipse docuit filios israel expoliare egyptos ut legitur in exodo xii. et sic docuit furtum. unde malus deus fuit.

Catholicus: Respondeo quod docuit filios israel remunerationem habere laborem suorum. preterea deus est et poterat auferre quibus uolebat. presertim cum illi essent indigni habere et filii israel essent digno. propter remunerationem laborem suorum. sed responde tu mihi. nonne christus priuauit dominos porcorum etiam per demones. lege. mattheus. viii. numquid dices quod christus fecit rapinam.

[**Patarenus:**] Item ipse fuit deceptor ut patet in israel qui pugnauit contra benjamin. quia iudicando scelere maximo qui bis de consilio eius pugnantes terga uerterunt occisis ex eis circa. xl milia uirorum ut hec leguntur in iudices xx. et sic patet quod ipse decepit populum suum atque perdidit et sic fuit malus deus uel ignorauit euntum belli et sic non fuit deus.

Catholicus: Respondeo quod in prima uice absque consilio dei pugneretur. numquam enim legit quod in prima uice petierunt consilium a deo de certamine sed tantum quis esset quorum princeps. de quo ipse optime consuluit scilicet de tribu iuda. in secunda uice accesserunt contra deum. licet uerbotenus peterent

Hebrews 11 (11:9) "By faith he remained in the land like an alien, dwelling in cottages, with Isaac and Jacob, the co-heirs." Or it can be understood that the promise was made complete to Abraham in his seed, who is Christ, as the Apostle says in Galatians 3 (3:16) "And to your seed, which is Christ." In whom all of the promises were fulfilled not only to Abraham but to all the many fathers, as is said in Hebrews 1. To the third yet we say that it is to be understood in this manner (Gn 32:28) "Your name shall not be called Jacob, but Israel" will be your proper name from now on, or otherwise "Your name shall not be called Jacob, but Israel," namely, only according to the covenant. He speaks similarly in John 1 (1:42) "You will be called Cephas," that is "and also Cephas."

[**Pat:**] Also He appears in the burning bush to Moses, as is read in Exodus 3 (3:2), and He took Elijah up to heaven in a fiery chariot as one has it in 4 Kings 2 (4 Kn 2:11), whence it does not seem right that a good God would appear in fire and who accomplished his works by fire.

Cath: I reply that he was that God of which Blessed Peter speaks in Acts 2 (2:19, after Joel 2:30) who speaks through Joel the Prophet, "And I will show wonders in the heaven above, and signs on the earth beneath, blood and fire, and vapor of smoke," which you do not deny to be the true God. This was the God of the Apostles who appeared to them as in tongues of fire. Whence it is read in Acts, He is the same God of whom the Apostle spoke in Hebrews 13 (12:29) "For our God is a consuming fire."

[**Pat:**] Likewise he taught the sons of Israel to despoil the Egyptians, as is read in Exodus 12, and so he taught theft, so he is the evil God.

Cath: I reply that He taught the sons of Israel to take recompense for their labors, further God is and can take what He wishes, especially since they were unworthy to have them, and the sons of Israel were worthy, on account of the recompense for their labors, but answer me this, did not Christ deprive the owners of the pigs also through the demons, read Matthew 8 (8:30), or do you say that Christ stole them?

[**Pat:**] Also he was a deceiver as is clear in Israel who fought against Benjamin, since by judging a most wicked crime, who twice by the advice of the fighters turned their backs, killing around 40,000 men, and this is read in Judges 20 (20:2) and so it is clear that he deceived and destroyed his people and so was an evil God, or he was ignorant of going to war and so was not God.

Cath: I reply that the first time they sought to fight was without the counsel of God, for it is never read that the first time they sought counsel from God regarding the battle but only from he who was their leader, of which he rightly decided, namely, of the tribe of Judah. The second time they moved against God, for example they sought the

---

242 et...243 christus] Gal. 3:16.   246 nequaquam...247 iacob] Gen. 32:28 (uocabitur] appellabitur *Vulg.*)   251 tu...cephas¹] Ioh. 1:42.   258 dabo...259 fumi] Act. 2:19, citing Ioel 2:30.   263 deus...264 est] Heb. 12:29.   280 et...281 perdidit] Iudic. 20:2.

247 scilicet] sed *P*   248 testamentum] add. Israel *F*   255 cuius] eius *F* | fuerunt] om. *P*   260 deum uerum] transp. *F*   269 preterea... 272 suorum] om. *P*   272 sed] set *P*   274 etiam] om. *F*   277 quia] quod *F*   281 deus] om. *P*   283 quod...284 legit] om. *P*   288 peterent] penetrent *P* exp.

243 sunt|fol. 37ra *P*   262 quo|fol. 27r *F*   277 pugnauit|fol. 37rb *P*

consilium a deo quia confidentes de uiribus suis et in maxima superbia processerunt ad bellum. unde dicitur ibi. rursumque israel et fortitudine et numero confidentes etcet. et ideo male contigit eis sicut debuit. quia deus superbia resistit et solis humilibus autem dat gratiam. sic enim intelligitur. omnis spes boni data a deo scilicet si humiliter incesserint quibus dat illam. preterea illam licentiam non habuerunt de beneplacito dei. sed habuerunt eam extortam. unde non sequebantur gratiam dei. sicut cum habuerunt regem saulem per licentiam dei uiolentam. ideo male contigit eis de illo. item numquam legitur quod deus promiserit uictoriam eis. nec aliquid boni. sed quia ipsi alias ibant ad certamen sicut ibi dicitur in eodem loco in quo prius certauerant aciem direxerunt etcet. eis uerbotenus querentibus ab eo consilium dixit simpliciter. ascendite etcet. id est priusquam uultis ascendere ascendatis. sed nichil promisit eis boni et erat consuetudo quod quando aliqui consilium petebant a deo. super aliquo negotio et ipse non respondebat eis prosperitatem quid eis male contingebat et hoc ipso malum futurum significauit illis. attamen tertia uice petierunt consilium a deo flentes et humiliter incedentes. respondit eis de uictoria dicens ascendite cras enim tradam eos in manus uestras etcet. et contigit eis sicut dominus dixit.

[Patarenus:] Item ipse est inmisericors. ut habes in primo regum xv porro triumphator in israel non parcet et penitudine non flectetur etcet.

Catholicus: Respondeo quod ideo deus non miserebatur sauli quia peccauerat in spiritum sanctum. quod peccatum nec deus noui testamenti remittit. quid intelligitur scilicet de facili et ideo non remittebatur illud peccatum sauli. quia non erat grauiter contritus. uel melius. non flectitur deus ad penitentiam que non est de bono corde. quam saul non habebat. petebat enim ueniam ne uerecundia coram populo de repulsa pateretur. unde dicitur ibi at ille ait peccaui sed nunc honora me coram senioribus populi mei et coram israel etcet. uel aliter. non flectitur deus ad ueniam quin puniat temporaliter. sicut puniuit dauid de peccato bersabee. licet propter penitentiam translatum esset peccatum eius quantum ad culpam et penam eternam. quod facit et deus noui testamenti. unde dicit. puniuit enim deus saule temporali pena id est priuatione regni quam meruerat ex graui delicto.

[Patarenus:] Item ille fuit iniustus quia occidit innocentes et peccantem non puniuit ut habes in secundo regum ultimo ubi legitur quod pro peccato

counsel of God yet, trusting in their men and in the greatest arrogance, they went forth to battle, whence it says there (Jgs 20:22) "Again Israel trusting in their strength and their number," and so it went ill for them, just as it ought to have. For God resists the proud and gives grace to the humble alone. For it is to be interpreted thus, that all hope for good is given by God, that is, if they to whom He gives it approach humbly. Further, they did not have that freedom from God's good pleasure, but had extorted it; therefore they were not following God's grace, just as when they caught the violent King Saul by the permission of God, therefore bad things happened to them on his account. Also it is never read that God promised victory to them, nor anything good, but since others went to the battle, as is said there (Jgs 20:22) "they set their army in array in the same place where they had fought before" with them for example seeking counsel from Him, he said simply (20:23) "Go up," that is, before you wish to climb, go up. But He never promised good to them, and it was customary that when they sought any counsel from God regarding any business, and He did not reply with prosperous tidings to them, it went poorly with them and this evil outcome was signified to them. They nevertheless sought counsel from God the third time, weeping and humbly approaching, He responded to them [promising] victory saying (20:28) "Go up, for tomorrow I will deliver them into your hands." And it happened to them just as the Lord said.

[Pat:] Also he is unmerciful, as you have it in 1 Kings 15 (1 Kgs 15:29) "But the conqueror in Israel will not spare, and will not be moved to repentance."

Cath: I reply that God was not merciful to Saul since he had sinned against the Holy Spirit, which sin not even the God of the New Testament forgives. Which is interreted, namely, [not forgiven] easily, and so that sin of Saul's was not forgiven, since he was not deeply contrite, or better, he did not kneel before God in penance, which does not come except from a good heart, which Saul did not have. For he sought a pardon, lest he suffer shame in the sight of the people from whom he suffered a defeat, whence it says there (15:30) "Then he said, 'I have sinned, yet honor me now before the elders of my people, and before Israel.'" Or otherwise, he did not bow to God for forgiveness since He punishes in time, as He punished David for his sin with Bathsheba (2 Kgs 24). Although on account of the penance, his sin was carried over, as far as guilt and eternal punishment, that was also accomplished by the God of the New Testament, when it says, for God punished Saul with temporal pains, that is, the deprivation of the kingdom which he had merited by grave sin.

[Pat:] Also he was unjust since he killed innocents and did not punish sinners, as you have it in 2 Kings at the end, where it is read that he killed 70,000 of the murmuring

dauid murmuratione populi occidit. lxx. milia uirorum et dauid nichil pene intulit et quod populus fuerit innocens et dauid solus peccauerit. habes ex dicto dauid dixit enim ego sum qui peccaui ego inique egi. isti qui ciues sunt quid fecerunt.

Catholicus: respondeo quod iuste et sancte iudicauit dominus. quia populum malum et obstinatum puniuit de multis quorum nequitus per illam uindicam peccauerat enim in multis populus israel et dignus erat plaga illa et longe maiori. unde legitur in principio capituli et addidit furor domini irasci contra israel etcet. et puniuit dominus dauid de peccato suo in populo in quo enim deliquit punitus est. peccauerat enim in uana gloria de multitudine populi et punitus est in tristitia de diminutione eius. nec obstat quod dauid illos excusat et se inculpat quia quantam ad illud peccatum forte ipse solus erat culpabilis. et ipsi erant inculpabiles uel minus inculpa. peccauerant autem illi in grauioribus in quibus dauid non derelinquit. et ideo maiori pena digni fuerunt.

Patarenus: Item ille fuit nequam. quia malum habuit spiritum ut legitur. primo regum xviii. inuasit spiritus dei malus saul etcet.

Catholicus: respondeo quia loquitur de spiritu malo creato id est de demone qui est domini per creationem.

[Patarenus:] Item ille mittebat demonem ad decipiendum ut legitur in tertio. regum ultimo. ait deus quid decipiet achab ut ostendit et cadat in ramoth galath etcet. et infra. egressus est autem spiritus et stetit coram domino et ait ego decipiam illum cui locutus est dominus in quo ille ait egrediar et ero spiritus mendax in ore omnium prophetarum eius etcet. ecce quomodo ille deus decepit achab per demonem. ergo malus deus fuit.

Catholicus: Respondeo tradidit deus spiritum mendaci potestatem decipiendi achab. non enim uoluerat credere spiritum ueritatis. et ideo dignum fuit ut per spiritum fallacem deciperetur. simile facit deus noui testamenti secunda ad thesalonicenses secundo. ideo mittet illis deus operationem erroris ut credant mendacio ut iudicentur omnes qui non crediderunt ueritati etcet.

[Patarenus:] Item ille irascebatur sicut multotiens legitur in ueteri testamento. sed ira est peccatum. ergo malus deus fuit.

Catholicus: Respondeo. et deus noui testamenti irascitur ut habes matheus xviii. et iratus dominus eius etcet. et marcus iii. circumspiciens eos cum ira contristatus super cecitate cordis eorum etcet. et ad romanos

people on account of the sin of David, and David suffered nearly nothing, and that the people were innocent, and that David alone sinned, you have it from the saying of David, for he said (24:17) "I am he who has sinned, I have done wickedly, these that are the citizens, what have they done?"

Cath: I reply that the Lord judged in a just and holy manner, since He punished the evil and obstinate people for many of their wicked deeds through that vengeance. For they sinned against many of the people of Israel and it was right that they suffer that wound, and a much greater one. Whence it is read at the beginning of the chapter (24:1) "And the anger of the Lord was again kindled against Israel," and the Lord punished David for his sin among the people whom he failed to punish. For he sinned in vainglory of the multitude of the people and was punished in sadness by their diminution. Nor does it matter that David excused them and blamed himself, insofar as he alone was greatly guilty of that sin, and these were not guilty, or less guilty, and yet they sinned against Him in graver things that David left behind, and so were worthy of a greater punishment.

Pat: Also he was wicked, since he had an evil spirit, as it is read in 1 Kings 18 (18:10) "the evil spirit from God came upon Saul."

Cath: I respond that it is speaking of a created evil spirit, that is, of a demon who is from the Lord through creation.

[Pat:] Also he sent a demon for deception as is read in the third book of Kings at the end (3 Kn 22:20) "And the Lord said, 'Who will deceive Ahab, king of Israel, that he may show up and fall at Ramoth Galaad?'" (22: 21–22) "and a spirit came forth and stood before the Lord, and said 'I will deceive him.' And the Lord said to him, 'By what means?' And he said, 'I will go forth, and be a lying spirit in the mouth of all his prophets.'" See how that god deceives Ahab by a demon, therefore he is the evil god.

Cath: I reply that God handed him over to a lying spirit that had the power to deceive Ahab, for he did not wish to believe the spirit of truth, and so it was fitting that he would be deceived by a false spirit. God acts similarly in the New Testament in 2 Thessalonians 2 (2:11–12) "Therefore God will send them the operation of error, to believe lying, that all may be judged who have not believed the truth."

[Pat:] Also he was angered as is read many times in the Old Testament, but anger is a sin, therefore he is the evil god.

Cath: I reply, the God of the New Testament is also angered, as you have it in Matthew 18 (18:34) "and his lord was angered," and Mark 3 (3:5) "And looking around them with anger, being grieved for the blindness of their

---

341 ego¹...342 fecerunt] 2 Reg. 24:17 (cives) oves *Vulg.*)   348 et...israel] 2 Reg. 24:1.   359 inuasit...360 saul] 1 Reg. 18:10.   364 ait...365 galath] 3 Reg. 22:20 (quid) quis | ostendit] ascendat *Vulg.*)   377 ideo...379 ueritati] 2 Thes. 2:11-12.   384 et...eius] Matt. 18:34.   385 circumspiciens...386 eorum] Mar. 3:5.

339 dauid] dauid dicende *F*   342 ciues] canes (!) *F*   343 iudicauit] add. quia *P* exp.   344 malum] om. *P*   345 uindicam] domibus *F*   353 quia...355 inculpabiles] om. *P*   356 derelinquit] derelinquid *P*   357 pena] postea *P*   366 et¹...367 domino] om. *P*   373 mendaci] mandati *P* | achab] acab *F*   375 facit deus] raimundus *P* (it is not clear what *P* might mean or intend here)

363 decipien-dum|fol. 38ra *P*

primo. reuelatur enim ira dei de celo. intellige stulte quod cum dicitur in ueteri testamento uel in nouo quod deus irascitur. humana propassio est. quia admodum irascentis se habet cum penam pro peccatis infligit.

[Patarenus:] Item ille facit omnia mala ciuitatis ut dicitur in amos iii. si erit malum in ciuitate quod dominus non fecerit etcet.

Catholicus: Respondeo quod deus noui testamenti facit omnia mala mundi. ad romanos xi. conclusit enim deus omnia in incredulitate. dico autem quod deus facit omnia mala scilicet permissiue. licet facit omnia mala id est omnes penas et hic de ista materia ut supra titulum primo. rubricella quod pene omnis sunt a dei.

[Patarenus:] Item dicit apostolus prima ad corinthios. christo neque murmuraueritis sicut quidam eorum murmurauerunt et perierunt ab exterminatore etcet. sed ille exterminator percussit egyptum et occidit hebreos in deserto. sed legitur in ueteri testamento quod deus fecit hoc. ergo deus ueteris testamenti fuit angelis abyssi. igitur malus. ut legitur apocalypsis. ix. et habebant super se regem angelum abyssi etcet. igitur habens nomen exterminans. ergo deus ueteris testamenti fuit angelis abyssi igitur malus.

Catholicus: Respondeo quod deus percussit egyptios et filios israel auctoritate et potestate et angelis exterminator percussit eos ministerio et actualiter et fuit ille malus angelis per quam percussit et puniuit illos deus qui dicitur exterminator. uel forte fuit bonus. licet uocetur eodem nomine quo malus angelis sicut et deus noui testamenti uocatur quandoque eodem nomine cum diabolo. quia uocatur leo.

Item. apocalypsis v. ecce uicit leo de tribu iuda etcet. et diabolus etiam dicitur leo prima petri. ultimo. aduersarius uester diabolus tamquam leo etcet. nota quod deus quandoque punit malos per malos angelos. Psalmos misit in eos iram indignationis sue. immissiones per angelos malos etcet. et quandoque per bonos. ut secunda ad thesolonicenses. primo. in reuelatione domini ihesu de celo cum angelis uirtutis eius in flamma ignis dantis uindictam etcet. et actus xii. confestim autem percussit eum angelus domini etcet.

[Patarenus:] Preterea ille deus fuit ualde rusticus qui turpissima uerba dixit de colla et de colliba in ezechiele et multa similia in aliis locis ueteris testamenti. ergo non fuit bonus deus.

hearts," and Romans 1 (1:18) "For the wrath of God is revealed from heaven." Understand, O Fool, that when it speaks in the Old Testament or the New that God was angered, that is a human emotion, for He is like an exceedingly angry person, when He inflicts punishment for sins.

[**Pat**:] Also he does all evil things in cities as is said in Amos 3 (3:6) "Shall there be evil in a city, which the Lord has not done?"

Cath: I reply that the God of the New Testament causes all evils in the world. Romans 11 (11:32) "For God has consigned all men to disbelief." Yet I say that God causes all evil, namely, by permission. Although He causes all evil, that is, all punishments — and this matter is taken up above in the first book, in the subsection that all punishments are from God.

[**Pat**:] Also the Apostle says in 1 Corinthians (10:10) in Christ "Neither do you murmur as some of them murmured, and were destroyed by the destroyer" But this destroyer struck the Egyptians and killed the Hebrews in the desert. But it is read in the Old Testament that God did this, therefore the God of the Old Testament was a destroyer. Therefore the God of the Old Testament was of the angels of the abyss, and so was evil, as is read in Apocalypse 9 (9:11) "they had over them a king, the angel of the bottomless pit," therefore having the name 'destroying,' so the God of the Old Testament was an angel of the bottomless pit, and so evil.

Cath: I reply that God struck the Egyptians and the sons of Israel with authority and power, and the destroyer angel struck them by his ministry, and actually it was that evil angel through whom God struck and punished them, who is called the 'destroyer' or perhaps he was good, though called by the same name which is the evil angel, just as the God of the New Testament is called by the same name as the devil, who is called 'lion.'

Also Apocalypse 5 (5:5) "behold the lion of the tribe of Judah conquers," and the devil is also called "lion," in 1 Peter at the end (5:8) "your adversary, the devil, like a lion." Note that God sometimes punishes evildoers by means of the evil angels. Psalms (77:49) "And he sent upon them the wrath of his indignation ... which he sent by evil angels." and sometimes by means of good angels, as 2 Thessalonians 1 (1:7–8) "the Lord Jesus shall be revealed from heaven with the angels of his power in a flame of fire, giving vengeance." And Acts 12 (12:23) "And immediately an angel of the Lord struck him."

[**Pat**:] Further that God was terribly backward who, with disgraceful words, spoke of Colla and Colliba in Ezekiel (23:4) and many similar things in other places of the Old Testament, therefore he was not the good God.

---

387 reuelatur...celo] Rom. 1:18.   393 si...394 fecerit] Amos 3:6.   396 conclusit...397 incredulitate] Rom. 11:32.   403 christo...404 exterminatore] 1 Cor. 10:10.   408 et...409 abyssi] Apoc. 9:11.   420 ecce...iuda] Apoc. 5:5.   421 aduer-sarius...422 leo] Apoc. 5:8.   424 misit...425 malos] Ps. 77:49.   426 in...428 uindictam] 2 Thes. 1:7-8.   429 confestim...domini] Act. 12:23.   431 ezechiele] Ez. 23:4, Oola and Ooliba.

398 scilicet...399 mala] om. F   408 igitur malus] om. F | ix] viiii P   412 egyptios] gyptios F   416 fuit] om. P

392 mala]fol. 28r F   395 Catholicus]fol. 38rb P   424 indignationis]fol. 38va P

Catholicus: Respondo quia turpissimam loquitur deus noui testamenti in paulo ad romanos primo. quem deus ueteris testamenti fuerit locutus in ezechiele. uel alibi disce autem turpissime leccator. quia non est turpe corrigenti. dicere peccata ad delinquetium reprehensionem.

Cath: I reply that the God of the New Testament speaks most shamefully — in Paul in Romans 1 — than the God of the Old Testament ever spoke in Ezekiel, or anywhere else. Listen, you repulsive lecher, it is not shameful for the person who corrects to name sins in order to correct the sinner.

De ueteri testamenti quod fuit bonum

Dictum est supra de deo ueteris testamenti. Nunc autem de ipso testamento discutiamus. Vbi primo sciendum est quid sub nomine ueteris testamenti comprehendatur. Dicitur autem uetus testamentum tribus modis. Primo ut contineat omnia sacra eloquia a principio mundi scripta usque ad nouum testamentum. mattheus xiii. ideo omnis scriba doctus in regno celorum similis est paterfamilias qui profert de thesauro suo noua et uetera etcet. secundo ut ibi legem Moysi comprehendat. Galathas iiii. hec enim sunt duo testamenta. unum quidam in monte synai in seruitutem generans etcet. ad hebreos viii. non secundum testamentum quod feci patribus eorum in die qua apprehendi manum illorum ut educerem eos de terra egypti etcet. tertio uero modo appelatione ueteris testamenti tantum cerimonialia continentur. ad hebreos viii. Dicendo autem nouum ueterauit prius. quod autem antiquatur et senescit prope interitum est. etcet. Et secundum hunc omnem triplicem intellectum dicunt patareni semper malum fuisse uetus testamentum. Verumtamen super hoc diuersi diuersa sentiunt sicut et in ceteris capitulis fidei faciunt. Aiunt enim quidam ex eis de ueteri testamento et lege Moysi quod bonus deus fecit quoddam testamentum in celo et quamdam legem. quam dedit cuidam Moysi celesti. ad cuius contrarium diabolus transfiguratus in angelum lucis fecit quoddam aliud testamentum et aliam legem in monte Synai terrestri et dedit Moysi terreno. qui dicunt quod diabolus admiscuit quedam bona malis ut facilius decipere posset. De primis dicunt loqui scripturas noui testamenti. que uetus testamentum commendant et legem Moysi. de aliis dicunt loqui scripturas ueteris testamenti et legem Moysi et scripturas noui testamenti que de illorum uituperatione fatentur. Alii uero contrario dicunt non nisi unum testamentum esse et unam legem Moysi et dicunt illa a diabolo fuisse et dicunt quod diabolus in illis quedam bona inseruit que audiuerat a bono deo in primis

VII That the Old Testament was good

We spoke about the God of the Old Testament above, but now we shall discuss the same testament. First it is known that it is comprised under the name of the Old Testament. But the Old Testament is spoken of in three ways. First that it might contain all the holy sayings from the beginning of the world up to the New Testament. Matthew 13 (13:52) "Therefore every scribe instructed in the kingdom of heaven is like a man who is a householder, who brings forth out of his treasure new things and old." The second as that which contains the Law of Moses. Galatians 4 (4:24) "For these are the two testaments. The one from mount Sinai, engendering unto bondage." Hebrews 8 (8:9) "Not according to the testament which I made with their fathers, on the day when I took them by the hand to lead them out of the land of Egypt." The third way of speaking about the Old Testament is what is only contained in the ceremonial law. Hebrews 8 (8:13) "Now in speaking anew, he has made the former old. And that which decays and grows old, is near its end." And according to all three of these understandings the Patarenes say that the Old Testament was always evil. Nevertheless in the same group, different people think different things, just as they all do in other things as well. For certain of them say that the good God did certain things in the Old Testament and the Law of Moses, making a testament in heaven and He gave certain laws to a certain heavenly Moses,[1] to whose contrary the devil — transformed into an angel of light — made a certain other testament and other laws on the earthly Mount Sinai, and gave to the earthly Moses, and these say that the Devil mixed certain good things with evil ones, that he might be able to deceive more easily. Regarding the first group, they say that they are speaking about the scriptures of the New Testament which commend the Old Testament and the Law of Moses, of others they say that they claim to speak of the scriptures of the Old Testament and the law of Moses and writings of the New Testament which acknowledge their blameworthiness. Yet others speak to the contrary, that there is but one Testament and one law

---

VII.1.8 ideo…10 uetera] Matt. 13:52.   11 hec…13 generans] Gal. 4:24.   13 non…16 egypti] Heb. 8:9 (illorum] eorum *Vulg.*) 18 Dicendo…19 est] Heb. 8:13.

VII.1.1 fuit] fuerit *P*   13 non…17 continentur] om. *F*   29 Synai] synay *F* | qui] et *F*   31 De…dicunt] om. add. de primo. di. primus dicunt *P*

VII.1.16 de|fol. 38vb *P*   28 aliud|fol. 28v *F*

---

1) The doctrine of those called Albanenses. Burci, 323-324; Sacconi, c. 17, 22; Moneta, 179, 208.

tabulis posita. quas Moyses per iracundiam confregit. Sunt et alii inter eos autumnantes quod in primis et secundis tabulis bonus deus dederit legem bonam. sed Moyses et Aaron et Iosue et ceteri principes ueteris testamenti addiderunt et miscuerunt quedam mala. sicut de sacrificiis et iudiciis et huiusmodi. quas dicunt non dei. sed ordinationes hominum fuisse. De patribus autem et patriarchis et prophetis et de omnibus qui in ueteri testamento commendantur blasphemant eos omnes esse dampnatos et dicunt quod nouum testamentum non loquitur de illis. sed de quibusdam aliis celestibus qui habuerunt talia nomina. Alii uero subtiliantes telam araneam retexentes distinguunt inter eos. dicentes quod illi de quibus legitur quod occiderint uel homicidiis consenserint sint dampnati sicut Abraam Ysaac et Iacob et Moyses et Aaron et Iosue et Samuel et Dauid et Helias et huiusmodi. illi uero qui non consenserunt homicidiis sint salui quod dicunt fuisse maxime quattuor prophetas maiores. uidelicet Ysaiam Ieremiam Ezechielem et Danielem et duodecim prophetas minores. Et quod diximus illos credere hos saluos esse. intelligas non in illis corporibus in quibus prophetauerunt sed in aliis que dicunt eos recipisse post aduentum Christi. Quorum scripturas quidam ex eis recipiunt omnes. quidam uero dicunt quod triplici spiritu fuerint locuti scilicet diuino humano et diabolico et sic que uolunt recipere dicunt esse a spiritu dei. que autem uolunt spernare aiunt a spiritu malo et diabolico esse. Nos autem reiectis ambagibus suis dicimus quod uetus testamentum una cum lege moysi et prophetis semper bonum extitit atque sanctum et omnis que in eodem comendantur fuerunt boni et saluatione digni. que omnia per scripturas sacras noui testamenti comprobamus quinque modis. primus modus est. quia legimus ista a bono fonte procesisse id est a bono deo prout probatum est in proxima superiori rubrica. secundus est quia christus et apostolis et discipuli noui testamenti rationes suas firmauertur per scripta veteris testamenti et sanctorum eius. prout in multis locis novi testamenti reperies. ut mattheus iiii. qui respondens ait non in solo pane uiuit homo etcet. et infra scriptum est. non temptabis dominum deum tuum etcet. et infra scriptum est. dominum deum tuum adorabis etcet. que tria testimonia sunt in lege moysis. primum est in deuteronomium viii. secundum in eodem vi tertium in eodem. v. item

of Moses, and they say that it was of the devil,[1] and they say that the devil inserted certain good laws which were accepted by the good God and placed in the first Table, which Moses then broke in anger. And there are others among them who assert that in the first and second tables the good God gave a good law but that Moses and Aaron and Joshua and certain leaders of the Old Testament added and mingled in certain evil laws, like those of sacrifice and judgments and the like, which they say are not of God, but the ordinances of men. Yet of the Fathers and Patriarchs and Prophets and all who were commended in the Old Testament, they blaspheme against these saying all are damned, and they say that the New Testament does not speak of them, but of certain other celestial figures that had such names.[2] Yet others weave clever arguments distinguishing between those, saying that about those things which one reads that they killed or that they consented to homicide, and are damned, like Abraham, Isaac, and Jacob, and Moses and Aaron and Joshua and Samuel and David, and Elijah and the like, yet to those who did not consent to homicide, these are saved, and they speak mainly of the four greater prophets, namely Isaiah, Jeremiah, Ezekiel, and Daniel, and the twelve minor prophets. And that we agree, believing those to be saved, [yet] you understand [that they are not saved in those bodies in which they prophesied, but in others which they say they received after the coming of Christ, of these certain of them receive all the scriptures.[3] Yet certain others say that it is speaking of a triple spirit, namely divine, human, and diabolical,[4] and thus those they wished to receive, they say are from the spirit of God, yet those who they wish to reject, they say that the evil spirit is from the devil. Yet we reject their tortured interpretations, saying that the Old Testament together with the law of Moses and the prophets are always good and holy, and all those who are commended in it were good and worthy of salvation. This we will prove by all of the Holy Scriptures of the New Testament in five ways. The first way is that we read that it comes forth from a good source, that is, from the good God just as was proven in the last section above. The second is that Christ and the apostles and the disciples underscored their arguments by the writings of the Old Testament and its saints, just as you will find in many places in the New Testament, as in Matthew 4 (4:4) "who replying said, 'Man does not live on bread alone.'" And later it is written (4:7) "you shall not tempt the Lord your God," and later it is written (4:10) "you shall adore the Lord your God." And these three witnesses are from the Law of Moses. The first in Deuteronomy 8 (8:3). The second in Deuteronomy 6 (6:16). The third in

---

80 qui...81 homo] Matt. 4:4 (ait) dixit *Vulg.*) 81 non...82 tuum] Matt. 4:7. 82 do-minum...83 adorabis] Matt. 4:10.

46 sed] set *P* | ordinationes hominum] transp. *F* 51 sub-tiliantes] subtilizantes *F* 62 prophetauerunt] prophetarum *P* 77 rationes... 79 testamenti] om. *P*

42 bonam|fol. 39ra *P* 70 extitit|fol. 39rb *P*

---

1) The mitigated dualists, or Concorezzenses. Sacconi, c. 24; Burci, 314; Moneta, 5, 112. Similar statements can be found in the early work by the Milanese convert Bonacursus written around 1180, see Wakefield, *Heresies*, 172. | 2) A doctrine of John of Lugio and of the Cathars in general. Sacconi, c. 21; Burci, 324; Moneta, 75ff, 179, 208. | 3) On the Cathar rejection of the Old Testament, see Sacconi, c. 17, 23; Moneta, 3, 5-6, 218. | 4) Mitigated dualists. Moneta, 6, 218.

idem mattheus xii. at ille dixit eis non legistis quod dictum est a deo. dicite uobis. ego sum deus abraam. deus ysaac. et deus iacob. etcet. hoc est ex deo. tertio item ad romanos x. an nescitis in helia quid dicit scriptura quemadmodum interpellat deum aduersum israel etcet. hoc est in tertio. responsum xviiii. item ad galathas iiii. scriptum est enim abraam duos filios habuit etcet. hoc in genesios xxi. item ad hebreos iii. dixit enim in quodam loco de die septima etcet. Hoc est in genesios ii.

Mattheus primo. hoc autem totum factum est ut adimpleretur quod dictum est a deo per prophetam. ecce uirgo concipiet etcet. hoc est in ysaias vii. item secundo. sicut scriptum est per prophetam. et tu betleem etcet. hoc est in Michaea v. item in eodem. tunc adimpletum est quod dictum est per ieremiam dicentem. uox in rama etcet. hoc est in prophetia sua. xxxii. item in eodem. quoniam nazarenus uocabitur etcet. In michaia. idem iii. hoc est. etcet. in ysaias. xl. idem. iiii. ut adimpleretur etcet. ysaias viiii. idem viii. ut adimpletur etcet. et ysaia liii. idem xii. etcet. ysaias xlii. idem xiii. ut adimpleretur etcet. ysaias primo. idem xxi. ut adimpleretur etcet. zacharias viiii. et in eodem scriptum est. etcet. ysaias xvi. idem in eodem numquam legistis in scripturis etcet. psalmis. confitemini. idem xxii. quomodo ergo dauid in spiritu etcet. psalmis dixit deus etcet. idem xxiiii cum ergo uideritis etcet. danielis x. item in eodem. hoc autem totum factum est ut adimpleretur scripture prophetarum. item marco primo sicut scriptum est in ysaia. ysaias xl. item primo iohannes secundus quia scriptum est. etcet. psalmis. saluum me fac etcet. item quinto est scriptum in prophetis etcet. erunt omnes docibiles dei. item actus secundo. hoc est quod dictum est. etcet. Ioel. iii idem vii. sicut scriptum est in libro prophetarum. idem xiii. quod dicum est in prophetis idem xiii. quod dictum est in prophetis. uidete contemptores etcet.

Decem in quibus concordat utrumque testamentum

Tertius modus est quia concordant uetus testamentum et nouum. concordant autem in decem. primum est quia utrumque ostendit peccata et detestatur et illa fieri prohibus et qui in utrius scripturis diffuse sunt ordinata. secundo quia utrumque punit delinquentes. de ueteri dicit paulus i^a ad timotheum primo. sciens hoc quia lex iusto non est lex posita sed iniustus etcet. de nouo dicit. idem ad Romanos. ii. thezauriças tibi iram in die ire etcet. tertio quia ambo docent bona et

Deuteronomy 5 (5:9). Also in Matthew 12 (12:3 & 22:31) "have you not read that which was spoken by God, saying to you, 'I am the God of Abraham, and the God of Isaac, and the God of Jacob,'" and this is from God. The third also Romans 10 (11:2) "Do you not know what the scripture says of Elijah; how he calls on God against Israel." And this is in the third, response 19. Also Galatians 4 (4:22) "for it is written Abraham had two sons." This in Genesis 21. Also Hebrews 3 (4:4) "For in a certain place he spoke of the seventh day." This is in Genesis 2.

Matthew 1 (1:22–23) "Now all this was done that it might be fulfilled which the Lord spoke by the prophet, saying, 'Behold a virgin shall be with child.'" This is in Isaiah 7. Also in the second, just as is written in the prophet (Micah 5:13) "and you Bethlehem," this is in Micah 5. Also in the same (Mt 2:17–18) "Then was fulfilled that which was spoken by Jeremiah the prophet, saying, 'A voice in Rama was heard.'" This is in his prophecy, chapter 32. Also in the same (Mt 2:23) "That he shall be called a Nazarene." In Micah 3, "this is". In Isaiah 40, also 4, "that it might be fulfilled," Isaiah 9, the same in 8 "that it might be fulfilled," and Isaiah 53, and 12. Isaiah 42, also 13 "that it might be fulfilled." In Isaiah 1, also 21, "that it might be fulfilled." Zechariah 9 "and in the same it is written." Isaiah 16 also in the same (Mt 21:42) "have you never read in the scriptures," Psalms "Give glory." Also 22. (22:43) "How then does David in Spirit." Psalm (49:16) "God said." Also Matthew 24 "when therefore you will see." Daniel 10, also in the same (Mt 26:56) "Now all this was done, that the scriptures of the prophets might be fulfilled." Also in Mark 1 (Mk 1:2) "as was written in Isaiah," Isaiah 40. Also in 1 John 2 (2:17) "for it was written" Psalms "Save me," Also in 5 (6:45) "this is what was spoken, and they shall all be taught of God." Acts 2 (2:16) But this is that which was spoken of by Joel" (in Joel 3) and 7 (Acts 7:42), "just as was written in the book of the Prophets." Also 13, "what was spoken in the prophets." Also 13 (Acts 13:40–41) "which is spoken in the prophets, 'Behold, you despisers.'"

Ten things in which both testaments agree

The third way is that the Old Testament and the New agree. Moreover they agree in ten ways. The first is that both make sin plain, and it is deplored, and that it is to be prohibited, and this is ordained in both scriptures in many places. In the second way, that they both punish sinners. Of the old testament, Paul says in 1 Timothy (1 Tm 1:9) "Knowing this, that the law is not made for the just man, but for the unjust." And of the new, Romans 2 (2:5) "you treasure up for yourself wrath, in the day of wrath." The

---

86 at...88 iacob] Matt. 12:3 conflated with 22:31.   89 an...91 israel] Rom. 11:2.   92 scriptum...93 habuit] Gal. 4:22.   94 dixit...septima] Heb. 4:4.   96 hoc...98 concipiet] Matt. 1:22-23.   99 et...100 betleem] Mic. 5:13.   101 tunc...102 rama] Matt. 2:17-18.   103 quoniam...104 etcet¹] Matt. 2:23.   110 numquam...scripturis] Matt. 21:42.   111 quomodo...spiritu] Matt. 22:43.   112 dixit deus] Ps. 49:16. | cum...uideritis] Matt. 24:15.   113 hoc...114 prophetarum] Matt. 26:56.   115 sicut...ysaia] Mar. 1:2.   116 quia...est] Ioh. 2:17.   117 est...118 prophetis] Ioh. 6:45.   119 hoc...est²] Act. 2:16.   120 sicut...prophetarum] Act. 7:42.   121 quod²... 122 contemptores] Act. 13:40-41.   VII.2.8 sciens...9 iniustus] 1 Tim. 1:9.   10 thezauriças... 11 ire] Rom. 2:5.

93 hoc...94 etcet] om. F   119 Ioel] Iohel F   VII.2.8 timotheum] titum P | sciens] scientes F   9 quia] quod F | lex iusto] iustis F

89 romanos x|fol. 29r F   106 adimpletur|fol. 39va P

hortantur ad nos ad illa. prout patet in utroque testamento diffuse. iiii°. quia ambo promittunt uitam eternam benefacientibus de nouo planum est. de ueteri habes. iohannes. v[a]. ubi dixit deus iudeis. scrutamini scripturas quia uos putatis in ipsis habere uitam eternam. v°. ambo procedunt ab uno fonte id est ab uno deo. ut supra probatum est. vi. quia ambo sunt spiritualia. de nouo non est questio. de ueteri dicit apostolus ad Romanos vii. scimus enim quia lex spiritualis est etcet. vii. quia sicut nec nouum. ita nec uetus testamentum. aduersatur promissis dei. nec ad inuicem contrariatur ad Galathas iii. lex ergo aduersus promissa dei. absit. etcet. ad romanos iii. legem ergo destruimus per fidem. absit. sed legem statuit. etcet. viii°. quia ambo dedicantur per sanguine. ad hebreos. viii. unde nec primum quidem sine sanguine dedicatum est. ix. quia utriusque sacrificia emundat ad inquinamentis. ad hebreos ix. si enim sanguis hircorum et taurorum et cinis uitule aspersus inquinatos sanctificat etcet. decimo quia uetus prohibetur contempni sicut et nouum et redarguuntur eius contemptores in nouo testamento sicut et contemptores noui. unde dominus dicit. iohannes. v. est qui accusat uos Moyses etcet. et vii. nonne moyses dedit uobis legem et nemo ex uobis facit legem etcet. ad thesolonicenses ultimo. Spiritum nolite extinguere prophetias nolite spernare

Duodecim rationes quibus commendatur uetus testamentum in nouo. de bonitate prima

Quartus modus est quia uetus testamentum et lex moysis. et prophete commendantur in nouo testamento de bonitate et utilitate xii rationibus. prima quia dicuntur sanctam. ad romanos vii. lex quidem sancta. et mandatum sanctum et iustum et bonum etcet. et in eodem. omnia qui nolo illud facio constituo legi quoniam bona est etcet. secundo quia dicuntur lex dei et testamentum dei. et mandata dei et mandata uite. mattheus xv. ipse autem respondens ait illis. quare et uos transgredimini mandatum dei propter traditionem uestram nam deus dixit etcet. et mattheus x. magister bone quid boni faciam ut uitam eternam possideam etcet. Ihesus autem dixit ei. ibi precepta nosti etcet. et in mattheus xviiii dicit. si autem uis ad uitam ingredi serua mandata etcet. et in lucam. ii. postquam impleti sunt dies purgationis eius secundum legem moysi tulerunt illum in ierusalem ut sisterent eum domino. sicut scriptum est in lege domini etcet.

third because both teach the good and exhort us towards it, just as is clear throughout both testaments. The fourth, since both promise eternal life to those who do good is clear from the New, of the Old you have John 5 where God speaks to the Jews (5:39) "Search the scriptures, for you think in them to have life everlasting." The fifth, both proceed from one source, that is, from the one God, as was proven above. The sixth that both are spiritual, that of the New is not in question, of the Old the Apostle says in Romans 7 (7:14) "For we know that the law is spiritual." The seventh is that neither the New nor the Old testament set themselves against the promises of God, nor are they contrary to one another. Galatians 3 (3:21) "Was the law then against the promises of God? God forbid." Romans 3 (3:31) "Do we, then, destroy the law through faith? God forbid! But we establish the law." The eighth, both are consecrated through blood. Hebrews 8 (9:18) "Whereupon neither was the first indeed dedicated without blood." The ninth, is that both of their sacrifices cleansed from uncleanness. Hebrews 9 (9:13) "For if the blood of goats and of oxen, and the ashes of a heifer being sprinkled, sanctify." The tenth is that the Old prohibited despising just like the new, and its despisers are condemned in the New Testament just like those who despise the New Law, whence the Lord says in John 5 (5:45) "It is Moses who accuses you," and 7 (7:19) "Did Moses not give you the law, and yet none of you keep the law?" Thessalonians at the end (1 Thes 5:19–20) "Do not extinguish the spirit, do not despise prophecies."

Twelve arguments in which the Old Testament is commended by the New. First of goodness

The fourth way is that the Old Testament and the Law of Moses and the prophets are recommended in the New Testament for goodness and usefulness by twelve arguments. The first because they are called holy. Romans 7 (7:12) "Wherefore the law indeed is holy, and the commandment holy, and just, and good." And in the same (Rm 7:16) "If then I do that which I do not will, I consent to the law, that it is good." The second is that it is called the law of the God and the Testament of God, and the commandments of God and the commandments of life. Matthew 15 (15:3) "But he answering, said to them, 'Why do you also transgress the commandment of God for your tradition?'" And Matthew 10 (19:16) "Good master, what good shall I do that I may have eternal life?" And Jesus said to him (Mk 10:19) "you know the commandments." And in Matthew 19 He says (19:17) "if you wish to enter life, keep the commandments," and in Luke 2 (2:22–23) "And after the days of her purification were completed, according to the law of Moses, they carried him to Jerusalem, to present him to the Lord, as it is written in

---

15 scrutamini...17 eternam] Ioh. 5:39.   20 scimus...21 est] Rom. 7:14.   23 lex...24 absit] Gal. 3:21.   24 legem...25 statuit] Rom. 3:31 (statuit) statuimus *Vulg.*)   27 unde...28 est] Heb. 9:18.   29 si...30 sanctificat] Heb. 9:13.   34 est...Moyses] Ioh. 5:45. 35 nonne...36 legem] Ioh. 7:19.   36 Spiritum...37 spernare] 1 Thes. 5:19-20.   VII.3.6 lex...7 bonum] Rom. 7:12.   8 omnia...9 est] Rom. 7:16 (constituo) consentio *Vulg.*)   11 ipse...13 dixit] Matt. 15:3.   14 magister...15 possideam] Matt. 19:16 (possideam) habeam *Vulg.*)   15 precepta...16 nosti] Mar. 10:19.   16 si...17 mandata] Matt. 19:17.   18 postquam...20 domini] Luc. 2:22-23.

12 patet] paritus *P*   28 ix] viiii *P*   36 etcet] add. 1[a] *F* | Spiritum...37 spernare] om. *P*   VII.3.1 Duodecim...3.2 prima] om. *F*   5 xii] tribus *P*

VII.2.16 uos|fol. 39vb *P*   31 sicut|fol. 29v *F*   VII.3.7 sanctum|fol. 40ra *P*

ad romanos vii. delector enim legi dei etcet. prima ad timotheus primo. scimus autem quia bona est lex etcet. tertia ratio est quia dicuntur sacre scripture et sante littere et eloquia dei. ad romanos primo. quod ante promiserat deus in scripturis sanctis. et iii. secundum quidem quia credita sunt illis eloquia dei etcet. et ii° ad timotheus iii°. quia ab infantia sacras scripturas nosti etcet. quarta quia a spiritu sancto dicuntur esse. ad hebreos ix. tabernaculum enim factum est primum etcet. ibi. hoc significante spiritu sancto etcet. et prima petro primo. de qua salute exquisierunt atque scripta sunt prophete qui de futura uobis gratia prophetauerunt scriptantes in quod uel in quale tempus significaret in eis spiritus christi. et secunda primo. non enim uoluntate humana allata est aliquando prophetia. sed spiritu sancto inspirati locuti sunt etcet. et secunda ad timotheum iii°. omnis scriptura diuinitus inspirata etcet. hic clauditur os uestrum patareni quid dicitis quod prophete spiritu dei. quandoque spiritum dei. quandoque spiritum humano. quandoque spiritum diabolico sunt locuti. quia dicunt apostoli petrus et paulus quia omnis prophetia est per spiritum sanctum promulgata. ad hoc est actus primo oportet impleri scripturam quam predixit spiritus sanctus per os dauid etcet. et iiii°. qui spiritu sancto per os patris nostri dauid etcet. unde est quia dicuntur non esse peccatum. ad romanos. vii°. quid ergo dicemus. lex peccatum est. absit. etcet. sexta quia adiuuare ad benefacendi dicuntur. ad romanos vii. inuenio igitur legem uolenti mihi facere bonum etcet. vii^a dicuntur nos ducere ad christum ad Galathas iii°. itaque lex pedagogus noster fuit in christo ihesu. etcet. viii^a. quia inuenitur ibi quod per illa uitari poterat eterna dampnatio. lucam xvi. habent moysen et prophetas etcet. ix^a. quia dicitur quod credenda sunt omnia qui leguntur. lucam ultimo. o stulti et tardi corde ad credendum in omnibus que locuti sunt prophete. et iohannes v°. si enim crederetis forsitan moysi et mihi. de me enim ille scripsit etcet. et paulus in actibus xxiiii. sic deseruio patri et deo meo credens omnibus qui in lege et prophetis scripta sunt. decima quia dicitur quod precipiat que bona sunt scilicet iudicium et misericordiam et fidem. mattheus xxiii. reliquistis que grauiora sunt legis iudicium et misericoriam et fidem. quia ea que ibi sint dicta et scripta et factam et gesta recitantur et autenticantur in nouo testamento. uerbi gratia de creatione et forma-

the law of the Lord." Romans 7 (7:22) "For I am delighted with the law of God." 1 Timothy 1 (1:8) "Yet we know that the law is good." The third argument is that they are called the Sacred Scriptures, the Holy Books, and the Word of God. Romans 1 (1:2) "Which he had promised before. . .in the holy scriptures." And 3 (3:2) "First indeed, because the words of God were committed to them." 2 Timothy 3 (3:15) "And because from your infancy you have known the holy scriptures." The fourth is that it is said to be from the Holy Spirit. Hebrews 9 (9:2) "For there was a tabernacle made first." (9:8) "By this the Holy Spirit indicates." And 1 Peter 1 (1:10) "Receiving the end of your faith, even the salvation of your souls, of which salvation the prophets have inquired and diligently searched, who prophesied of the grace to come in us. Searching what or what manner of time the Spirit of Christ did signify in them." And 2 Peter 1 (1:21) "For prophecy did not come by the will of man at any time, but the holy men of God spoke, inspired by the Holy Spirit." And 2 Timothy 3 (3:16) "All scripture is inspired by God." This shuts your mouth, you Patarenes, who say that the prophets of the Spirit of God sometimes speak in the spirit of God, sometimes in the spirit of man, sometimes by a diabolical spirit, since the Apostles Peter and Paul say that all prophecy is brought about by the Holy Spirit, to this is Acts 1 (1:16) "the scripture must be fulfilled, which the Holy Spirit spoke before by the mouth of David." And 4 (4:25) "Who, by the Holy Spirit, by the mouth of our father David." Whence it is because they speak of it not being a sin. Romans 7 (7:7) "What then shall we say? The law is sin? God forbid!" And the sixth is that it is called an aid to doing good. Romans 7 (7:21) "I find then a law, when I have a will to do good." The seventh is that it is said to lead us to Christ. Galatians 3 (3:24) "Wherefore the law was our pedagogue in Christ Jesus." The eighth is that it is found there those things by which one can avoid eternal punishment. Luke 16 (16:29) "They have Moses and the prophets." The ninth since it is said that all things which are read in it are to be believed. In the last chapter of Luke (24:25) "O foolish, and slow of heart to believe in all things which the prophets have spoken." And John 5 (5:46) "For if you did believe Moses, you would perhaps believe me also, for he wrote about me." And Paul in Acts 24 (24:14) "so do I serve the Father and my God, believing all things which are written in the law and the prophets." The tenth is that it is said that it commands things that are good, namely (Mt 23:23) "judgment, and mercy, and faith." Matthew 23 (23:23) "you have left the weightier things of the law; judgment, and mercy, and faith." Since in it they are spoken, and written, and done, and deeds

---

21 enim...dei] Rom. 7:22 (delector] condelector *Vulg.*)   22 scimus...lex] 1 Tim. 1:8.   24 quod...25 sanctis] Rom. 1:2 (promiserat] add. per prophetos suos *Vulg.*)   25 secundum...26 dei] Rom. 3:2 (secundum] primum *Vulg.*)   27 quia...28 quarta] 2 Tim. 3:15 (scripturas] litteras *Vulg.*)   29 tabernaculum...primum] Heb. 9:2.   30 hoc...sancto] Heb. 9:8.   31 de...34 christi] 1 Pet. 1:9-11 (scripta] sructati; scriptantes] scrutantes *Vulg.*)   35 non...36 sunt] 2 Pet. 1:21.   37 omnis...38 inspirata] 2 Tim. 3:16.   44 oportet... 45 dauid] Act. 1:16.   45 qui...46 dauid] Act. 4:25.   47 quid...48 absit] Rom. 7:7.   50 inuenio...bonum] Rom. 7:21.   52 itaque... ihesu] Gal. 3:24 (ihesu] om. *Vulg.*)   54 habent...55 prophetas] Luc. 16:29.   56 o...58 prophete] Luc. 24:25.   58 si...59 scripsit] Ioh. 5:46.   60 sic...61 sunt] Act. 24:14.   63 iudicium...fidem] Matt. 23:23.

---

23 sante...24 littere] transp. *F*   26 quidem] add. est *P* exp.   53 quod per] transp. *P*   55 ix^a] viiii° *P*   56 leguntur] add. in eis *F*   61 decima...65 fidem] om. *F*   67 uerbi gratia] ubi ergo *F*

36 locuti|fol. 40rb *P*   62 scilicet|fol. 30r *F*   66 recitantur|fol. 40va *P*

tione omnium rerum. ut supra. titulum primo. notatum est. de requie diei sabbati. a deo. ad hebreos. iiii°. dixit enim in quodam loco de die septimo sic et requieuit die. vii ab omnibus operibus suis etcet. de hystoria deceptionis ade et eue factam per serpentem et de peccato eorum romanos. v. regnauit mors ab adam usque ad moysen etiam in eos qui non peccauerunt in similtudinem preuaticationis ade. ii^a ad corinthios. ix. timeo ne sicut serpens deceptor eua. et primo ad timotheus ii°. adam non est seductus scilicet a serpente. mulier etcet. de istoria cain et abel. de translatione enoc et de noe et diluuio et de sacrificio quod melchisedech. cum abraam fecit et de pugna abrahe et de loth et subuersionem pentapolim et de tribulatione iob et de abraam. ysaac et iacob et de hiis que circa illos acciderunt. Dic ut in rubricella de patribus qui ante legem moysi fuerunt notabuntur. de introitu israel in egyptum et exitu eius. et de lege data et de pugnis eorum et huius actibus. vii. qui ait sanctus stephanus. uiri fratres et patres audite etcet. usque ibi dure ceruice etcet. et xiii. surgens autem paulus usque ibi exeuntibus etcet. ad hebreos. xi. fide transierunt mare rubrum etcet. de circumcisionem. ad romanos iii°. Quid ergo amplius est iudeo aut que utilitas circumcisionis? multum quidem per omnem modum etcet. et in multis aliis locis noui testamenti legitur de illa. de sacerdotio et sacrificiis et oblationibus et pascha et aliis festiuitatibus legitur mattheus xiii. uade ostende te sacerdoti et offer munus quod precepit moyses in testamonium israel illis etcet. lucam ii°. secundum consuetudinem diei festi etcet. et ultimo magister dicit ubi pascam ubi est diuersorium cum discipulis meis manducem etcet. et xi. erat autem dies festus azimorum in quo necesse erat pascha. et iohannes ii°. erat autem proximum pasca dies festus iudeorum scenofegia etcet. et ad hebreos viiii. Si enim sanguis hyrcorum et taurorum etcet. de prohibitione inmundorum ii^a ad corinthios vi. propter quod exite de medio eorum et separamini dicit dominus et immundum ne tetigeritis etcet. de tabernaculo sancto sub moyse ad hebreos ix. tabernaculum enim factum est primum. de exaltatione serpentis in deserto. iohannes. iii°. sicut moyses exaltauit serpentem in deserto etcet. de factis sub iosue ad hebreos xi. fide muri et ierico circuitu dierum septem. etcet. fide raab meretrix non periit cum incredules. etcet. et actus xii.

recounted and authenticated in the New Testament, for example, of the creation and formation of all things, as was made clear above in the first section. As regards rest on the Sabbath day by God, Hebrews 4 (4:4) "For in a certain place he spoke of the seventh day thus, 'And God rested the seventh day from all his works.'" Regarding the story of the deception effected by the serpent on Adam and Eve and of their sin, Romans 5 (5:14) "But death reigned from Adam to Moses, even over those also who have not sinned in the manner of the transgression of Adam." 2 Corinthians 9 (11:3) "But I fear lest, as the serpent seduced Eve." And 1 Timothy 2 (2:14) "And Adam was not seduced," namely by the serpent, "but the woman." Regarding the story of Cain and Abel, of the taking up of Enoch, and of Noah and the flood, and of the sacrifice that Melchizedek offered with Abraham, of the fight between Abraham and Lot, of the overthrowing of the Pentapolis, and of the tribulations of Job, and of Abraham, Isaac, and Jacob and about what happened to them, it is spoken of in the subsection about the Fathers who lived before the law of Moses was make known. Regarding the going in of Israel to Egypt and of their exodus, and of the giving of the law and of their wars and the like is in Acts 7 (7:2) it is Saint Stephen who says "You men, brethren, and fathers, hear" up to (7:51) "you stiff-necked." And 13 (13:16) "Then Paul rising up," to (13:42) "as they went out." Hebrews 11 (11:29) "by faith they crossed the Red Sea." Regarding circumcision, Romans 3 (3:1-2) "What advantage then does the Jew have, or what is the profit of circumcision? Much every way." And in many other places in the New Testament one reads about the priesthood and sacrifices and oblations and the Pasch and other festivals. In Matthew 13 one reads (8:4) "Go, show yourself to the priest, and offer the gift which Moses commanded for a testimony of Israel to them." Luke 2 (2:24) "according to the custom of the feast," and at the end (22:11) "The master says to you, 'Where is the guest chamber, where I may eat the pasch with my disciples?'" And 11 (paraphrase of 22:1) "it was the day of the Feast of Unleavened Bread in which a Pasch was necessary," and John 2 (6:4) "It was near the day of the Paschal Feast, the Scenofegia of the Jews," and Hebrews 9 (9:13) "For if the blood of goats and bulls." Regarding the prohibition of uncleanness, 2 Corinthians 6 (6:17) "Wherefore, go out from among them, and be separate, says the Lord, and do not touch the unclean thing." Regarding the holy tabernacle under Moses, Hebrews 9 (9:2) "For the Tabernacle was made first." Regarding the raising up of the serpent in the desert, John 3 (3:14) "And as Moses lifted up the serpent in the desert." Regarding the deeds done by Joshua, Hebrews 11

---

70 dixit...**71** suis] Heb. 4:4 (septimo) septima *Vulg.*) **73** regnauit...**75** ade] Rom. 5:14. **76** timeo...eua] 2 Cor. 11:3. **77** adam...**78** mulier] 1 Tim. 2:14. **86** qui...**87** audite] Act. 7:2. **88** dure ceruice] Act. 7:51. | surgens...paulus] Act. 13:16. **89** exeuntibus] Act. 13:42. | fide...**90** circumcisionem] Heb. 11:29. **91** Quid...**92** modum] Rom. 3:1-2. **95** uade...**97** illis] Matt. 8:4 (israel) om. *Vulg.*) **97** secundum...**98** festi] Luc. 2:42. **98** magister...**100** manducem] Luc. 22:11. **100** erat...**101** pascha] Luc. 22:1 paraphrase. **102** erat...**103** scenofegia] Ioh. 6:4 (scenofegia om. *Vulg.* but common in medieval bibles, eg. Hugh of St. Cher, where it means "Feast of Tabernacles") **103** Si...**104** taurorum] Heb. 9:13. **105** propter...**107** tetigeritis] 2 Cor. 6:17. **108** tabernaculum...**109** deserto] Heb. 9:2. **110** sicut...**111** deserto] Ioh. 3:14. **111** fide...**112** septem] Heb. 11:30-31.

69 diei] die *P* **73** eorum] add. ad *F* **81** abrahe] add. pro loth *F* **82** tribulatione] add. et de *P* | abraam] abraham *F* | ysaac] ysac *P* de hiis] illis *P* **101** ii°] vii *F* **108** ix] viiii *P*

93 de|fol. 40vb *P*

suscipientes patres nostri cum ihesu in possessionem gentium quas repulit deus a facie patrum nostrorum etcet. de datione iudicium et regum et de factis sub eis. actus xii. post hoc dedit iudices usque ad samuelem prophetam et exinde postulauerunt regem et dedit illis deus saul filium etcet. cis uirum de tribu beniamin annis xl et anmoto illo suscitauit illis dauid regem etcet. de templo domini. actus vii. Salomon autem hedificauit illi domum etcet. de sanctis helye et helysei. lucam iiiᵒ. et ad nullam illarum missus est helyas nisi in sarepta sydonie etcet. et in eodem et multi leprosi erant in israel sub helyseo propheta etcet. et ut breuiter transeamus de hac materia omnia que in ueteri testamento leguntur uel quasi omnia in nouo testamenta recitantur et sua recitatione redduntur autentica. xiiᵃ. ratio est quia leguntur uetera in nouo fuisse bona. quia legitur illa figurasse noua. prima ad corinthios x. hec autem omnia in figura contingebant illis etcet.

quintus modus est quia christus et apostoli eius impleuerunt illa et seruauerunt que in ueteri testamento mandata erant ut patet ex multis scripturis noui testamenti. ut ecce. primo. de circumcisionem. lucam iiᵒ. postquam consummati sunt dies octo ut circumcideretur puer etcet. et ad romanos xv. dico enim ihesum ministrum fuisse circumcisionis etcet. item de representatione in templum cum oblatione hostiarum. lucam iiᵒ. postquam impleti sunt dies purgationis eius. item ascensu in ierusalem secundum consuetudinem diei festi. in eodem. cum factus esset ihesus annorum xii. etcet. et quid plura. in omnibus christus seruauit legem et impleuit. sicut ipse. mattheus v. nolite putare quoniam ueni soluere legem. non ueni soluere sed adimplere. apostoli uero seruauerunt legem in omnibus usque ad passionem christi. post passionem autem eius seruauerunt quidam legalia quandoque et etiam circumcisionem aliquando prout notabimus infra. libro secundo titulo de circumcisis. preterea seruauit. dominus non solum legem sed etiam gesta patrum. quia cum illis fuit peregrinus in egypto et tamen rursus rediit in terram patrum legitur mattheus iiᵒ. et recessit in egypton etcet. et iiiᵒ. defunto autem herode etcet.

(11:30–31) "By faith the walls of Jericho fell down, by going round them seven days. By faith Rahab the harlot did not perish with the unbelievers." And Acts 12 (7:45) "Which also our fathers receiving, brought in with Joshua, into the possession of the Gentiles, whom God drove out before the face of our fathers." Regarding the giving of the Judges and kings and of their deeds, Acts 12 (13:20–22) "and after these things, he gave them judges, until Samuel the prophet, and after that they desired a king, and God gave them Saul the son of Cis, a man of the tribe of Benjamin, forty years. And when he had removed him, he raised them up David to be king." Regarding the temple of the Lord, Acts 7 (7:47) "But Solomon built him a house." Regarding saints Elijah and Elisha, Luke 4 (4:26) "And to none of them was Elijah sent, but to Sarepta of Sidon." And in the same (4:27) "And there were many lepers in Israel in the time of Elisha the prophet." So that we might cover briefly all this material which is read in the Old Testament or is repeated in nearly all the New Testament, and that its recollection is authentic. The twelfth argument is that the Old is read in the New, it was good, since it is read that it prefigured the New. 1 Corinthians 10 (10:11) "Now all these things happened to them in prefigurement."

The fifth way is that Christ and His Apostles fulfilled it and observed those things which had been commanded in the Old Testament, as is clear from many passages of the New Testament, for instance, in the first place, circumcision. Luke 2 (2:21) "After the eighth day had come that the boy might be circumcised." And Romans 15 (15:8) "For I say that Christ Jesus was minister of the circumcision." Also of the presentation in the temple with the offering of victims, Luke 2 (2:22) "And after the days of her purification." Also the going up to Jerusalem according to the custom of the festival days. In the same (2:42) "when Jesus was twelve years old." And there are many others in which Christ observed the law in all things, and fulfilled it himself. Matthew 5 (5:17) "Do not think that I have come to abolish the law, I have not come to abolish but to fulfill." The Apostles also observed the law in all things up to the Passion of Christ. Yet after His Passion they observed certain laws sometimes, and also circumcision sometimes just as we note in the second book in the section on the circumcisers. Further the Lord did not only observe the law but also the deeds of the fathers since like them He was a pilgrim in Egypt and also returned back to the land of the Fathers, as is read in Matthew 2 (2:14) "he fled into Egypt," and (2:19) "But when Herod was dead."

---

114 suscipientes...**115** nostrorum] Act. 7:45 (repulit] expulit *Vulg.*) **117** post...**120** regem] Act. 13:20-22. **121** Salomon...**122** helysei] Act. 7:47. **123** et...**124** sydonie] Luc. 4:26. **124** et²...**125** propheta] Luc. 4:27. **131** hec...**132** illis] 1 Cor. 10:11. **137** postquam...**138** puer] Luc. 2:21. **138** dico...**139** circumcisionis] Rom. 15:8 (enim] add. Christum *Vulg.*) **141** postquam...**143** festi] Luc. 2:22. **143** cum...**144** xii] Luc. 2:42. **146** nolite...**147** adimplere] Matt. 5:17. **155** et...**egypto**] Matt. 2:14 (recessit] secessit *Vulg.*) **156** defunto...herode] Matt. 2:19.

---

127 omnia] om. *P* **129** quia] quare *F* **133** quintus] quartus *P* **134** impleuerunt] impleuertur *F* | seruauerunt] seruauertur *F* | que] qui *F* **137** octo] viii *F*

120 anmoto|fol. 41ra *P* **127** uel|fol. 30v *F* **148** seruauerunt|fol. 41rb *P*

Quod patres et patriarche et multi alii qui fuerunt ante legem moysi sunt salui

Mattheus xxiii. ut ueniat super uos omnis sanguis iustus qui effusus est super terram a sanguine abel iusti etcet. ad hebreos. xi. fide plurimam hostiam optulit cayn quam abel etcet. prima iohannis iii°. audistis ab initio ut diligatis alterutrum non sicut cain qui ex maligno erat et occidit fratrem suum. et propter quod occidit eum. quia opera eius maligna erant. fratris autem eius iusta. etcet. ecce quale fuit abel. nec potest intelligere hoc hereticus de quodam abel celesti quam fingit. quia iohannes dicit quod cain qui ex maligno erat fuit frater eius. quia secundum hoc fuit abel ex maligno similiter. quia dicit quod opera eius erant iusta. igitur loquitur de illo abel de quo scripsit moyses. nec potest etiam dicere quod abel commendetur apud homines et non apud deum. quia apostolus dicit quod ipse obtulit hostiam domino per fidem. nec etiam potest fugere ut dicat abel fuisse iustum secundum statum noui testamenti per nouam incorporationem et non secundum statum in quo primitus erat. quia christus comprehendit eum in hac figura. qui dicit ut ueniat super uos omnis sanguis iustus qui effusus est super terram a sanguine abel iusti etcet. ergo iustus erat a tempore quando sanguis eius effusus est.

De enoch

ad hebreos xi. fide enoc translatus est ne uideret morte et non inueniebatur quia transtulit illum ante translationem eius testimonium habuit placuisse deo etcet. et hoc numquam de celesti enoc potest intelligi. quia propter hoc quod placuisset deo translatus esset de celo in alium locum. de quo subdit scribit beatus iudas in sua canonica. ii°. prophetauit de his ab adam enoc dicens etcet.

De noe

Ad hebreos xi. Fide noe responso accepto de hiis que adhuc uidebantur metuens ad optauit archam in salutem domus sue. per quam dampnauit mundum et iustitie qui per fidem est. heres est institutus etcet. et prima petri. iii°. in quo his qui in carcere erant conclusi spiritibus ueniens predicauit qui increduli fuerant aliquando exspectabant dei patientiam in diebus noe cum fabricaretur archa in qua paucia octo anime salue facte sunt per aquam et in iiiª. ii°. et originali mundo non pepercit. sed octauum noe iusticie preconem custodiuit. diluuium mundo impiorum inducens etcet. ergo saluus est noe una cum

That the Fathers and Patriarchs and many others who lived before the Law of Moses are saved

Matthew 13 (23:35) "That upon you may come all the just blood that has been shed upon the earth, from the blood of Abel the just." Hebrews 11 (11:4) "By faith Abel offered to God a sacrifice exceeding that of Cain." 1 John 3 (3:11-12) "You have heard from the beginning, that you should love one another, not as Cain, who was of the wicked one, and killed his brother. And why did he kill him? Because his own works were wicked, and his brother's just." See how Abel was described. Nor is one able to understand this in a heretical manner as a Celestial Abel whom John imagined, saying that Cain — who was of the wicked one — was his brother, since according to this Abel was similarly of the wicked one, yet since he says that his works were just therefore he is speaking of that Abel of whom Moses wrote. Nor also is one able to say that Abel is to be commended before men but not before God, since the Apostle says that he offered a victim to the Lord by faith, nor also is one able to flee by saying Abel was just according to the condition of the New Testament, by incorporation in the New, and not according to the state in which he existed at first since Christ included him in that figure when He said (Mt 23:35) "That upon you may come all the just blood that has been shed upon the earth, from the blood of Abel the just." Therefore he was just at the time when his blood was spilled.

On Enoch

Hebrews 11 (11:5) "By faith Enoch was translated, that he should not see death, and he was not found, because God had translated him for before his translation he had testimony that he pleased God." And one is never able to understand a Celestial Enoch by this, since it was on account of his pleasing God that he was translated to heaven from another place, of which one adds what Blessed Jude wrote in his canonical epistle 2 (1:14) "Now of these Enoch also, the seventh from Adam, prophesied, saying."

On Noah

Hebrews 11 (11:7) "By faith Noah, having received an answer concerning those things which as yet were not seen, moved with fear, framed the ark for the saving of his house, by which he condemned the world, and was instituted heir of the justice which is by faith." And 1 Peter 3 (3:19-20) "In which also coming he preached to those spirits that were in prison, which had been some time incredulous, when they waited for the patience of God in the days of Noah, when the ark was built, wherein a few, that is, eight souls, were saved by water." And in the second book, chapter 3 (2 Pt 2:5) "And he did not spare the original world, but preserved Noah, the eighth person, the

---

VII.4.3 ut…4 iusti] Matt. 23:35.   5 fide…6 abel] Heb. 11:4.   6 audistis…10 iusta] 1 Ioh. 3:11-12.   23 ut…24 iusti] Matt. 23:35.
VII.5.2 fide…4 deo] Heb. 11:5 (morte) mortem *Vulg.*)   8 prophetauit…9 dicens] Iud. 1:14.   VII.6.2 Fide…5 institutus] Heb. 11:7 (optauit) aptauit *Vulg.*)   6 in¹…10 aquam] Heb. 3:19-20 (conclusi om. *Vulg.*)   10 et²…13 inducens] 2 Pet. 2:5.

VII.4.1 qui] add. de abel *F*   2 salui] add. ab ea *P*   3 xxiii] xiii *P*   7 cain] cayn *P*   12 cain] cayn *P*   19 fidem] add. igitur deo iustus fuit per fidem. *F* | dicat] dicit *F*   25 a] eo *F*   VII.5.1 De enoch] om. *P*   7 scribit] subdit *PF*, but exp. *P*   VII.6.6 his] hiis *F* | carcere] carne *F*   7 spiritibus] spiritu *F*   9 paucia] pautia *P* | octo] viii *F*   13 saluus] salus *P*

VII.4.20 nouam|fol. 41va *P*   VII.5.8 adam|fol. 31r *F*

domo sua. nec de celesti noe potest hoc intelligi. quia secundum hoc fuisset diluuium in celo et appellaretur celum mundus impiorum et si nisi. viiii. spiritus fuisse in celo salui.

De Melchisedech

ad hebreos. vii. hic enim melchisedech sacerdos dei summi qui obuiauit abrahe regresso a cede regum etcet. et adde hic de commendatione melchisedech. ut supra. titulus primo. in parte hereticorum notatum inuenies.

De loth

secunda. petri. ii°. iustum loth oppressum a nefandorum iniuria et luxuriosa conuersatione eripuit aspectu enim et auditu iustus erat habitans apud eos qui de die in diem animam iustam iniquis operibus cruciabant. nouit dominus pios de temptatione eripere etcet. ergo bonus et sanctus fuit loth. nec potes dicere quod beatus petrus loquatur de loth aliquo celesti quia secundum hoc appellaretur celum sodoma et fuisset ibi luxuriosa conuersatio et huiusmodi de quo fuisset loth eductus a domino in alium meliorem locum quid non est inuenire quod diceret scelus est.

De Iob

Iacobus ultimo. sufferentiam iob audistis et finem domini uidistis. quoniam misericors est dominus et miserator ergo bonus fuit iob. si fuerit sufferens et si dei misericordiam consecutus est.

De abraham ysaac et iacob

Mattheus xiii. dico autem uobis quod multi ab oriente et occidente uenient et recumbent cum abraham ysaac et iacob in regno celorum. Ecce quales sunt patriarche predictam si sunt in regno dei. Item lucam xiii. cum uidistis abraam ysaac et iacob et omnes prophetas in regno dei etcet. item iohannem vii. scio quia filii abrahae estis etcet. sed queritis me interficere etcet. et infra. si filii abrahe estis. opera abrahe facite etcet. ergo abraham pater iudeorum bonus fuit. si christus confortat homines ut eius opera faciant. et si ipse non quesiuit christum interficere ut ibi. dicit idem in eodem. abraham pater exultauit ut uideret diem meum et uidit et gauisus est. etcet. ergo bonus fuit abraham pater iudeorum si exultauit uidere diem incarnationis dominice. et si in spiritu uidit illum. nec potest intelligere hereticus hoc de deo patre dictum. quia

preacher of justice, bringing in the flood upon the world of the ungodly." Therefore Noah was saved together with his house, nor is one able to interpret this as a Celestial Noah, since according to this the flood was in heaven, and heaven would be called the world of the ungodly and if so, none save eight spirits would be saved in heaven.

On Melchizedek

Hebrews 7 (7:1) "For this Melchizedek was king of Salem, priest of the most high God, who met Abraham returning from the slaughter of the kings." And this adds here a commendation of Melchizedek, as above, in the first book, you will find noted in the part of the heretics.

On Lot

2 Peter 2 (2:7–9) "And delivered just Lot, oppressed by the injustice and lewd conversation of the wicked. For in sight and hearing he was just, dwelling among them, who from day to day vexed the just soul with unjust works. The Lord knows how to deliver the godly from temptation." Therefore Lot was good and holy, nor are you able to say that Blessed Peter spoke of some Celestial Lot since according to this, heaven would be called Sodom and there would be lewd conversation and the like there from which Lot was led by the Lord to another better place, which is not found since it was called wicked.

On Job

At the end of James (5:11) "You have heard of the patience of Job, and you have seen the end of the Lord, that the Lord is merciful and compassionate." So Job was good, if he was patient and if God followed him with mercy.

On Abraham, Isaac, and Jacob

Matthew 13 (8:11) "And I say to you that many shall come from the east and the west, and shall sit down with Abraham, and Isaac, and Jacob in the kingdom of heaven." See of what quality were the aforesaid patriarchs if they are in the kingdom of heaven. Also Luke 13 (13:28) "when you shall see Abraham, and Isaac, and Jacob and all the prophets in the Kingdom of God." Also John 7 (8:37) "If you be the children of Abraham. . .But now you seek to kill me." And later (8:39) "If you be the children of Abraham, do the works of Abraham." Therefore Abraham, Father of the Jews, was good, if Christ encourages men that they ought to do his works, and he himself would not demand to kill Christ as those there. He says the same (8:56) "Abraham your father rejoiced that he might see my day, he saw it, and was glad." Therefore if Abraham, father of the Jews, was good if he rejoiced to see the day of the Incarnation of the Lord, and if in spirit he saw Him, nor is

---

VII.7.2 hic...3 regum] Heb. 7:1.   VII.8.2 iustum...6 eripere] 2 Pet. 2:7-9.   VII.9.2 sufferentiam...4 miserator] Iac. 5:11.
VII.10.2 dico...4 celorum] Matt. 8:1.   6 uidistis...7 dei] Luc. 13:28 (uidistis) uideritis *Vulg.*)   7 scio...8 interficere] Ioh. 8:37.
9 si...facite] Ioh. 8:39.   13 abraham...14 est] Ioh. 8:56 (pater) add. uester *Vulg.*)

14 sua] suo F   16 si] non F   VII.7.3 a cede] ad cedem F | cede] cedem F   4 ut] ait F   5 primo] prima P   VII.8.1 De loth] om. P
4 habitans] habitant F   12 inuenire] numerare F   VII.9.4 miserator] add. etcet. F   VII.10.1 abraham] abraam P   2 xiii] viii F
3 abraham] abraam P   5 Item...7 etcet.] om. F   7 scio quia] dico quod P   8 queritis] nunc uultis P   9 filii] om. P   13 abraham]
abraam P   15 iudeorum] add. ergo bonus fuit pater abraam P exp.   16 illum] illam F; add. etcet. P | nec] neque P

VII.6.14 noe|fol. 41vb P   VII.10.3 occidente|fol. 42ra P

subdit ibi dominus. antequam abraam fieret ego sum etcet. nec etiam potest exponere de abraam celesti. quia dicit abraam pater uester etcet. ergo de abraam patre iudeorum loquitur. ad hec etiam sunt ad romanos iiii°. Quid ergo dicemus inuenisse abraam patrem nostrum secundum carnem. et infra. quid enim scriptura dicit. credidit abraam deo et reputatum est ei ad iustitia. etcet. item ad Galatas iii°. abraam credidit deo et reputatum est etcet. et infra. abraham dicte sunt promissiones et semini eius etcet. et in eodem. abrahe autem per repromissionem donauit deus etcet. item ad hebreos. xi. fide qui uocatur abraam obediuit in locum exire etcet. et in eodem. fide moratus est in terra repromissionis in casulis habitando cum ysaac et iacob coheredibus repromissionis eiusdem etcet. et infra. fide optulit abraam ysaac cum tentaretur et unigenitum offerebat etcet. et postea. fide et de futuris benedixit ysaac et iacob fide iacob moriens singulos filiorum ioseph benedixit etcet. item. iacobum ii°. abraam pater noster nonne ex operibus iustificatus est. etcet. et infra. credidit abraam deo et reputatum est illi ad iustitiam et amicus dei appellatus est. etcet. ex hiis patet quod sanctissimi fuerunt abraam ysaac et iacob.

De sarra et aliis sanctis mulieribus que fuerunt in ueteri testamento

Ab hebreos xi. fide et ipsa sarra sterilis uirtutem in conceptionis seminis accept et preter tempus etatis quoniam fidelem credidit esse eum qui promiserat etcet. et prima petri iii°. sic enim et aliquando et sancte mulieres sperantes in deo. ornabant se subjecte propriis uiris sicut sarra obediebat abrahe dominum eum uocans etcet. ex superioribus ergo testimoniis noue testamenti demonstratum est quod superiores patres cum pluribus sanctis feminis sunt salui et quod eorum scripta et gesta sunt autentica.

De moyse et aliis sanctis qui fuerunt sub lege

Ad hebreos. xi. fide moyses occultatus est mensibus tribus a parentibus suis eo quod uidissent infantem et regis non timuerunt edictum etcet. et Actus vii°. Eodem tempore natus est moyses et fuit gratus deo etcet. item ad hebreos. in eodem fide moyses grandis factus negauit se esse filium filie pharaonis magis eligens affligi cum populo dei quam temporalis peccati habere iocunditatem. maiores diuitias existimans

the heretic able to understand this of God the Father, since it adds there, (8:58) "before Abraham was, I am." Nor also is he able to explain it as referring to a heavenly Abraham, since he says (8:56) "Abraham, your father." Therefore he is speaking of Abraham the Father of the Jews. To this point also is Romans 4 (4:1) "What shall we say then that Abraham has found, who is our father according to our flesh," and later for what the scripture says (4:22) "Abraham believed and it was reckoned to him as righteousness." Also Galatians 3 (3:6) "Abraham believed God, and it was reputed to him as justice." And later (3:16) "To Abraham were the promises made and to his seed." And in the same (3:18) "But God gave it to Abraham by promise." Also Hebrews 11 (11:8) "By faith he who is called Abraham, obeyed to go out into a place," and in the same (11:9) "By faith he remained in the land, dwelling in cottages, with Isaac and Jacob, the co-heirs of the same promise," and later (11:17) "By faith Abraham, when he was tried... offered up his only begotten son," and after (11:20) "By faith also of things to come, Isaac blessed Jacob, and in faith Jacob dying, blessed each of the sons of Joseph." Also James 2 (2:21) "Was not Abraham our Father justified by works?," and later (2:23) "Abraham believed in God and it was reckoned to him as righteousness and he was called friend of God." From these it is clear that Abraham and Isaac and Jacob were most holy.

On Sarah and other holy women who were in the Old Testament

Hebrews 11 (11:11) "By faith also Sarah herself, being barren, received strength to conceive seed, even past the time of age, because she believed that he was faithful who had promised." And 1 Peter 3 (3:5–6) "For after this manner the holy women also, who trusted in God, adorned themselves, being in subjection to their own husbands as Sarah obeyed Abraham, calling him lord." From the foregoing testimonies of the New Testament therefore it has been demonstrated that the foregoing fathers, along with many holy women, are saved and that their writings and works are authentic.

On Moses and other holy people who lived under the law

Hebrews 11 (11:23) "By faith Moses, when he was born, was hid three months by his parents because they saw he was a comely baby, and they did not fear the king's edict." And Acts 7 (7:20) "At the same time Moses was born, and he was acceptable to God." In the same (Heb 11:24–26) "By faith Moses, when he was grown up, denied himself to be the son of Pharaoh's daughter, choosing rather to be afflicted with the people of God, than to have the pleasure

---

18 antequam...sum] Ioh. 8:58.   20 abraam¹...uester] Ioh. 8:56.   22 Quid...23 carnem] Rom. 4:1 (nostram) om. *Vulg.*) 24 credidit...25 iustitia] Rom. 4:22 (ei) illi *Vulg.*)   25 abraam...26 est] Gal. 3:6.   26 abraham...27 eius] Gal. 3:16.   28 abrahe...29 deus] Gal. 3:18.   29 fide...30 exire] Heb. 11:8.   30 fide...33 eius-dem] Heb. 11:9 (moratus) demoratus *Vulg.*)   33 fide...34 offerebat] Heb. 11:17.   34 fide...36 benedixit] Heb. 11:20 (Iacob) add. et Esau *Vulg.*)   37 abraam...38 est] Iac. 2:21.   38 credidit...39 est²] Iac. 2:23.   VII.11.3 fide...5 promiserat] Heb. 11:11 (conceptionis) conceptionem *Vulg.*)   6 sic...9 uocans] 1 Pet. 3:5-6.   VII.12.2 fide... 4 edictum] Heb. 11:23 (uidissent) add. elegantem *Vulg.*)   5 Eodem...deo] Act. 7:20.   6 fide...10 christi] Heb. 11:24-26 (existimans) aestimans *Vulg.*)

---

23 carnem] add. nostram P   36 iacobum] iacobus F   VII.11.5 eum] etati P

22 abraam]fol. 31v F   28 repromissionem]fol. 42rb P   VII.12.2 mensibus]fol. 42va P

thesauro egyptiorum improperium christi etcet. item actus vii. et cum uidisset quemdam iniuriam patientem uindicauit illum etcet. et ad hebreos. in cathalago fide reliquit egyptum non ueritas animositatem regis et inuisibilem enim tamquam uidens substinuit etcet. cui concordat beatus stephanus. actus. vii. sequenti uero die apparuit illis ligantibus et reconciliabat eos in pace etcet. et in eodem. et factus est aduena in terra madian ubi generauit duos filios et completis annis. xl. apparuit illi in deserto montis synai angelis in igne flamme rubi. moyses autem uidens admiratus est uisum etcet. et infra. ad eum uox domini dicens etcet. et infra. hic est qui fuit cum ecclesia in solitudine cum angelo qui loquebatur et in monte synai et cum patribus nostris etcet. item ad hebreos xi. fide celebrauit pasca et sanguinis effusionem ne qui uastabat primogenita tangeret eos etcet. item actus vii. hic eduxit illos faciens signa et prodigia in terra egypti et in rubro mari et in deserto annis. xl. etcet. et ad hebreos. xi. fide transierunt mare rubrum tamquam per aridam terram quod experti egypti deuorati sunt etcet. item ad hebreos iiio. et moyses quidem fidelis erat in tota domo eius tamquam famulus in testimonium eorum que dicenda erant. christus uero tamquam filius in domo sue etcet. de quo uero moyses loquitur ostendit infra in eodem cum dicit. sed non uniuersi qui profecti sunt ex egypto per moysen etcet. item iohannes. v. si enim crederetis moysi crederetis forsitan et mihi. de me enim ille scripsit etcet. illud maxime quod est actus. vii. hic est moyses. qui dixit filius israel. prophetam suscitabit uobis deus de fratribus uestris tamquam me ipsum audietis etcet. ex hiis patet quod sanctissimus fuit moyses.

De aaron

Ad hebreos. v°. nec quisquam sumit sibi honorem sed qui uocatur a deo tamquam aaron etcet. ergo bonus fuit aaron si uocatus fuit a domino ad honorem sacerdotii.

De iosue et sociis suis

actus vii. suscipientes patres nostri cum ihesu in possessionem gentium etcet. bonus ergo fuit iosue cum sociis suis. se deus pugnabat pro illo.

of sin for a time, esteeming the reproach of Christ greater riches than the treasure of the Egyptians." Also Acts 7 (7:24) "And when he had seen one of them suffer wrong, he defended him." And Hebrews in the catalog (11:27) "By faith he left Egypt, not fearing the animosity of the king, for he was sustained by seeing him that is invisible." To which Blessed Stephen concurs, Acts 7 (7:26) "And the day following, he showed himself to them when they were fighting, and would have reconciled them in peace." And in the same (7:29–31) "and was a stranger in the land of Madian, where he begot two sons, and when forty years were completed, there appeared to him in the desert of mount Sinai, an angel in a flame of fire in a bush, and Moses seeing it wondered at the sight." And later "the voice of the Lord speaking to him," and later (7:38) "This is he that was in the church in the wilderness, with the angel who spoke to him on mount Sinai, and with our fathers." Also Hebrews 11 (11:28) "By faith he celebrated the pasch, and the shedding of the blood, so that he who destroyed the firstborn might not touch them." Also Acts 7 (7:36) "He brought them out, doing wonders and signs in the land of Egypt, and in the Red Sea, and in the desert forty years." And Hebrews 11 (11:29) "By faith they passed through the Red Sea, as if it were dry land, which the Egyptians, attempting, were swallowed up." Also Hebrews 3 (3:5–6) "And Moses indeed was faithful in all His house as a servant, for a testimony to those things which were to be said [later], but Christ [was faithful] as a Son over His own house." About which Moses is speaking is shown below in the same passage when it says (3:16) "but not all that came out of Egypt through Moses." Also John 5 (5:46) "For if you did believe Moses, you would perhaps believe me also, for he wrote of me." And that especially in Acts 7 (7:37) "This is that Moses who said to the children of Israel, 'God shall raise up a prophet to you of your own brethren, as myself, him shall you hear.'" From these it is most plain that Moses was most holy.

On Aaron

Hebrews 5 (5:4) "Neither does any man take the honor to himself, but he who is called by God, as Aaron was." Therefore Aaron was good, if he was called by God to the honor of the priesthood.

On Joshua and his associates

Acts 7 (7:45) "Which also our fathers receiving brought in with Joshua into the possession of the Gentiles." So Joshua was good, along with his allies, if God fought for him.

---

11 et...12 illum] Act. 7:24.   13 fide...14 substinuit] Heb. 11:27 (ueritas) veritus *Vulg.*)   15 sequenti...16 pace] Act. 7:26.   17 et²...21 dicens] Act. 7:29-31 (completis) expletis *Vulg.*)   22 hic...24 etcet] Act. 7:38.   24 fide...26 eos] Heb. 11:28 (primogenita) primitiua *Vulg.*)   26 hic...28 xl] Act. 7:36.   29 fide...30 sunt] Heb. 11:29.   31 et...34 sue] Heb. 3:5-6.   35 sed...36 moysen] Heb. 3:16.   37 si...38 scripsit] Ioh. 5:46.   39 hic...41 audietis] Act. 7:37.   VII.13.2 nec...3 aaron] Heb. 5:4.   VII.14.2 suscipientes...3 gentium] Act. 7:45.

VII.12.15 actus] in actibus *F*

27 faciens|fol. 32r *F* | et²|fol. 42vb *P*

De Gedeon barach et samson iepte et de consimilibus

Ad hebreos xi. et quid adhuc dicam. deficiet enim me tempus narrare de gedeon. barach. samson. iepte. etcet.

De samuele

Item in eodem samuel etcet. et actus iii°. et omnis prophete a samuel etcet. et xiii°. (13:20) usque ad samuelem prophetam. etcet.

De dauid

ad hebreos xi. et quid adhuc dicam? etcet. ibi dauid etcet. et actus primo. oportet impleri scripturam quam dixit spiritus sanctus per os dauid etcet. ergo bonus erat dauid. si sanctus erat. et si spiritus sanctus loquebatur per os eius. sicut patet in predictis duabus auctoritatibus. Nec potes obiecere hoc intelligere de aliquo dauid uel celesti. propter id quod de eo dicit beatus petrus. actus. ii°. Dauid enim dicit ipsos prouidebam dominum etcet. et postea uiri fratres liceat ad uos audenter dicere ad uos de patriarcha dauid. quoniam defunctus est et sepultus et sepulchrum eius est apud nos usque in hodiernum diem. propheta igitur cum esset et sciret quia pure iureiurando iurasset illi deus. de fructu lumbi eius sedere super sedem eius. prouidens locutus est. quia neque etcet. ergo de dauid propheta et rege loquitur qui mortuus est et sepultus est cum hominibus et cuius sepulchrum est in terra iudeos. nec potes etiam dicere quod scriptura commendat dauid secundum laudem humanam et non secundum diuinam. quia dicit beatus petrus de ipso in actibus. iiii°. qui spiritu sancto per os patris nostri pueri tui dixisti. Quare fremuerunt gentes. etcet. ergo sanctus et bonus fuit. si fuit puer dei. ad hoc est quod dicit beatus stephanus in eodem vii°. usque in diebus Dauid. qui inuenit gratiam ante deum etcet. et paulus. xiii. et amoto illo scilicet saule suscitauit illis regem dauid cui testimonium perhibens dicens inueni dauid filium iesse uirum secundum cor meum qui faciet omnes uoluntates meas. cuius deus ex semine secundum promissionem eduxit israel saluatorem nostrum. Ergo dauid propheta et rex ex cuius semine secundum carnem ortus est christus. qui mortuus est et sepultus fuit amicus dei. ergo bonus et sanctus.

15 On Gideon, Barak, and Samson, and Jephthah, and others like them

Hebrews 11 (11:32) "And what shall I yet say? For the time would fail me to tell of Gideon, Barak, Samson, Jephthah."

16 On Samuel

Also in the same "Samuel," and Acts 3 (3:24) "And all the prophets, from Samuel." And 13 (13:20) "until Samuel the prophet."

17 On David

Hebrews 11 (11:32) "And what shall I yet say?" and there "David." And Acts 1 (1:16) "Men, brethren, the scripture must be fulfilled, which the Holy Spirit spoke before by the mouth of David." Therefore David was good if he was holy and if the Holy Spirit was speaking through his mouth, just as is plain from the foregoing two passages. Nor are you able to object that one can understand some celestial David, because of that which Blessed Peter says of him in Acts 2 (2:25) "For David said concerning him, 'I foresaw the Lord.'" And later (2:29–31) "Men, brethren, let me freely speak to you of the patriarch David, that he died, and was buried, and his tomb is with us to this present day. Whereas therefore he was a prophet, and knew that God had sworn to him by an oath, that of the fruit of his loins one should sit upon his throne. Foreseeing this, he spoke of the resurrection of Christ. For neither. . ." Therefore he was speaking of David the prophet and king, who died and was buried with men and whose tomb is in the land of the Jews. Nor are you also able to say that the scriptures commend David according to human praise and not according to divine approval, since Blessed Peter says of him in Acts 4 (4:25) "Who, by the Holy Spirit, by the mouth of our father David, your son, has said, 'Why did the Gentiles rage.'" Therefore he was holy and good, if he was a child of God, and to this is related what Blessed Stephen says in the same chapter 7 (7:45–46) "unto the days of David, who found grace before God," And Paul in 13 (13:2223) "And when he had removed him," namely Saul, "he raised up for them David to be king, to whom giving testimony, saying, 'I have found David, the son of Jesse, a man according to my own heart, who shall do all my will.' Of this man's seed God according to His promise, has raised up to Israel our Savior." Therefore David, prophet and king, from whose seed was the origin of Christ according to the flesh, who died and was buried, was a friend of God, therefore good and holy.

VII.15.3 et...4 iepte] Heb. 11:32 (narrare) ennarantem *Vulg.*) VII.16.2 et²...3 samuel] Act. 3:24. 3 usque...4 prophetam] Act. 13:20 (samuelem) samuel *Vulg.*) VII.17.2 et...dicam] Heb. 11:32. 3 oportet...4 dauid] Act. 1:16 (dixit) praedixit *Vulg.*) 9 Dauid... 10 dominum] Act. 2:25 (ipsos) in eum *Vulg.*) 10 uiri...16 neque] Act. 2:29-31. 22 qui...23 gentes] Act. 4:25 (nostri) add. David *Vulg.*) 25 usque...26 deum] Act. 7:45-46. 27 et...32 nostrum] Act. 13:22-23 (illis) add. David; dicens] dixit; cuius] huius; nostrum] om. add. Iesum *Vulg.*)

VII.17.7 intelligere] om. *P* 8 celesti] add. intelligere *P* 14 iureiurando iurasset] uerando iurasset *P* 17 est] om. *P*

VII.16.2 et²|fol. 43ra *P* VII.17.28 regem|fol. 43rb *P*

De helia et heliseo

Mattheus. xvii. et apparuerunt illis moyses et helias etcet. et in eodem. subdit. heliseo propheta etcet. et iacobus. ultimo. multum enim ualet deprecatio iusti assidua. helias homo erat similis nobis passibilis et oratione orauit etcet. ergo helias et heliseus fuerunt boni et maxime habes de helia quod fuerit homo sanctus.

De prophetis in genere

Mattheus xxv. ut ueniat super uos omnis sanguis iustus qui effusus est a sanguine Abel iusti usque ad sanguinem zacharie etcet. et infra. ierusalem ierusalem que occidis prophetas et lapidas eos qui a te missi sunt. etcet. et lucam. primo. sicut locutum est per os sanctorum qui a seculo sunt prophetarum eius. etcet. xiii. cum uideritis abraam. et ysaac. et iacob et omnes prophetas in regno dei etcet. item. iohannes.v. et qui metet mercedem accipiet et congregat fructum in uitam eternam ut et qui seminat simul gaudeat et qui metit etcet. et appellat seminantes prophetas. apostolos atque metentes. unde subdit. alii laborauerunt et uos in labores eorum introistis etcet. et ad romanos primo. per prophetas suos etcet. ad hebreos. vi. in hac scilicet fide testimonium consecuti sunt senes etcet. et in eodem et alius prophetis etcet. et iacobus v. exemplum accipite fratres exitus longanimitatis et laboris et patientia prophetarum etcet. et ii^a petri. primo. habemus firmiorem sermonem propheticum cui benefacitis attendentes etcet. item in eodem. spiritu sancto inspirati locuti sunt sancti dei homines etcet. item actus iii^o. deus autem prenuntiauit per os omnium prophetarum etcet. et infra. et omnes prophete a samuele deinceps qui locuti sunt annuntiauerunt dies istos etcet. et ibi uos estis filii prophetarum etcet. item apocalypsis. x. sicut euangelizauit per seruos suos prophetas etcet. et xi^o. et reddere mercedem seruis tuis prophetis et sanctis. et xvi^o. justus es qui et qui eras sanctus qui hec judicasti quia sanguinem prophetarum et sanctorum effuderunt etcet. et xviii^o. qui in ea sanguis prophetarum et sanctorum inuentus est. ergo prophete qui commendantur in ueteri testamento sunt salui et sancti.

On Elijah and Elisha

Matthew 17 (17:3) "And there appeared to them Moses and Elijah." And in the same it goes on (Lk 4:27) "Elijah the prophet." And in the end of James (5:16) "For the continual prayer of a just man avails for much. Elijah was a mortal man like us, and with prayer he prayed." So Elijah and Elisha were good and that especially you have it regarding Elijah that he was a holy man.

On the Prophets in general

Matthew 25 (23:35) "That upon you may come all the just blood that has been shed upon the earth, from the blood of Abel the just, even to the blood of Zachariah." And later (23:37) "Jerusalem, Jerusalem, you who kill the prophets, and stone those who are sent to you." And Luke 1 (1:70) "As he spoke by the mouth of his holy prophets, who are from the beginning. 13 (13:28) "When you shall see Abraham, Isaac, and Jacob and all the prophets in the kingdom of God." Also John 5 (4:36) "And he who reaps receives wages, and gathers fruit unto life everlasting, so that both he who sows, and he who reaps, may rejoice together." And He calls the sowers prophets, and the Apostles the reapers, whence He adds (4:38) "others have labored, and you have entered into their labors." And Romans 1 (1:2) "through his prophets." Hebrews 6 (11:2) "For by this," namely by faith, "the ancients obtained a testimony." And in the same and others [they are called] "prophets." And James 5 (5:10) "Take, my brethren, for an example of suffering evil, of labor and patience, the prophets." And 2 Peter 1 (1:19) "And we have the more firm prophetical word, to which you do well to attend." Also in the same (2 Pt 1:21) "but the holy men of God spoke inspired by the Holy Spirit." Also Acts 3 (3:18) "But those things which God before had showed by the mouth of all the prophets," and later (3:24) "And all the prophets, from Samuel and afterwards, who have spoken, have told of these days," and there (3:25) "You are the children of the prophets." Also Apocalypse 10 (10:7) "as he has declared by his servants the prophets," and 11 (11:18) "and that you should render reward to your servants the prophets and the saints," and 16 (16:5–6) "You are just, O Lord, who are, and who were, the Holy One, because you have judged these things, for they have shed the blood of saints and prophets," and 18 (18:24) "And in her was found the blood of prophets and of saints." Therefore the prophets who are commended in the Old Testament are saved and holy.

VII.18.2 et^1...helias] Matt. 17:3.   3 heliseo...4 iacobus] Luc. 4:27.   4 multum...6 orauit] Iac. 5:16.   **VII.19.**2 ut...4 zacharie] Matt. 23:35 (est) add. super terram *Vulg.*)   4 ierusalem^1...5 sunt] Matt. 23:37.   6 sicut...7 eius] Luc. 1:70.   8 cum...9 dei] Luc. 13:28.   9 et...12 metit] Ioh. 4:36 (metet) metit | accipiet] accepit *Vulg.*)   13 alii...14 introistis] Ioh. 4:38.   15 per...suos] Rom. 1:2. | in...16 senes] Heb. 11:2.   17 exemplum...19 prophetarum] Iac. 5:10 (longanimitatis) om. add. mali | patientia] patientiae *Vulg.*)   20 habemus...21 attendentes] 2 Pet. 1:19.   21 spiritu...22 homines] 2 Pet. 1:21.   23 deus...24 prophetarum] Act. 3:18 (autem) add. qui *Vulg.*)   24 et^2...26 istos] Act. 3:24.   26 uos...prophetarum] Act. 3:25.   27 sicut...28 prophetas] Apoc. 10:7.   28 et^2...29 sanctis] Act. 11:18.   29 justus...31 effuderunt] Act. 16:5-6.   31 qui...32 est] Act. 18:24.

VII.18.1 helia] helya *F* | heliseo] helyseo *F*   2 helias] helyas *F*   3 heliseo] helyseo *F*   5 helias] helyas *F*   6 helias] helyas *F* | heliseus] helyseus *P*   7 helia] helya *F*

VII.18.5 homo|fol. 32v *F*   **VII.19.**17 alius|fol. 43va *P*

Patarenus: Dico quod omnis scripture per allegate loquitur de prophetis celestibus qui fecerunt prophetias suas in celo.

Catholicus: Sed lege quod dicit beatus lucas in actibus. xiii°. hunc ignorantes et uoces prophetarum que per omnem sabbatum leguntur etcet. ergo scripture loquntur de prophetis quorum scripture legebantur in synagogis iudeorum in diebus sabbatinis. alias enim prophetias non legebant.

Patarenus: Dicam ergo aliter quod prophete commendantur secundum humanam laudem et non diuinam.

Catholicus: sed ipsi commendatur si bene intellexisti in diuina scriptura de fide et sanctitate atque constantia et quod sunt in regno celorum. nam intelligis hanc esse diuinam commendationem.

Patarenus: Dicam ergo quod ipsi sunt salui secundum statum noui testamenti in quo corporati gratiam christi receperunt et non secundum statum ueteris testamenti in quo prophetantur.

Catholicus: Sed attende quid dicit beatus petrus in actibus. xv. nunc ergo quid tentatis deum imponere iugum ceruices discipulorum quod neque patres nostri neque nos portare potuimus sed per gratiam domini nostri ihesu christi credimus saluari quemadmodum et illi etcet. ergo salui fuerunt illi secundum statum ueteris testamenti.

Quod omnes fuerunt salui qui seruauerunt uetus testamentum

Mattheus xiii. amen quippe dico uobis quia multi prophete et iusti cupierunt uidere que uos uidetis etcet. item ad romanos. xi. quod si delibatio sancta est et massa et si radix sancta et rami etcet. item prima ad corinthios x. nolo uos ignorare fratres etcet. ibi omnes eandem escam spiritalem manducauerunt etcet. et infra. consequente eos petra. petra autem erat christus etcet. Item in eodem. sed non in pluribus eorum beneplacitum est etcet. item ii\u1d43. ad corinthos. iii°. nos uero reuelata facie gloria domini speculantes in eamdem ymaginem transformamur a claritate in claritatem. item ad hebreos iii°. quidam enim audientes exacerbauerunt sed non uniuersi qui profecti sunt ab egypto per moysen etcet. idem xi. sancti per fidem uicerunt regna operati sunt iustitiam adepti sunt repromissiones etcet. Quas autem repromissiones sint adepto subdit cum dicit. hii omnis testimonio fidei probati non acceperunt promissiones domino pro nobis aliquid melius prouidente. ut ne sine nobis

Pat: I say that all these passages are speaking through an allegory of celestial prophets, who made their prophecies in heaven.

Cath: But read what Blessed Luke says in Acts 13 (13:27) "not knowing him, nor the voices of the prophets, which are read every Sabbath." Therefore the scriptures speak of the prophets of whose writings are read in the synagogues of the Jews on the Sabbath day, for other prophecies are not read.

Pat: Therefore I might say otherwise that the prophets are commended according to human praise and not divine approval.

Cath: But they are commended if you understood the divine scriptures by faith and holiness and constancy, and that they are in the kingdom of heaven, for you understand this to be divine approval.

Pat: So I might say that they are saved according to the condition of the New Testament whereby they are incorporated, receiving the grace of Christ and not according to the condition of the Old Testament whereby they prophesied.

Cath: But pay attention to what Blessed Peter says in Acts 15 (15:10) "Now therefore, why do you tempt God to put a yoke upon the necks of the disciples, which neither our fathers nor we have been able to bear? But by the grace of the Lord Jesus Christ, we believe to be saved, in like manner as they were also." Therefore they were saved according to their status in the Old Testament.

20 That all were saved who observed the Old Testament

Matthew 13 (13:17) "For, amen, I say to you, many prophets and just men have desired to see the things that you see." Also Romans 11 (11:16) "For if the first fruits be holy, so is the lump also, and if the root be holy, so are the branches." Also 1 Corinthians 10 (10:1,3) "For I would not have you ignorant, brethren. . .And did all eat the same spiritual food." And later (10:4) "the rock that followed them, and the rock was Christ." Also in the same (10:5) "But with most of them God was not well pleased." 2 Corinthians 3 (3:18) "But we, all beholding the glory of the Lord with open face, are transformed into the same image from glory to glory." Also Hebrews 3 (3:16) "For some who heard did provoke, but not all that came out of Egypt by Moses." Also 11 (11:33) "The Saints by faith conquered kingdoms, wrought justice, obtained promises." Yet which promises were obtained he continues when he says (11:39–40) "And all these, being approved by the testimony of faith, did not receive the promise, by God

---

39 hunc...40 leguntur] Act. 13:27 (omnem) omne *Vulg.*) 55 nunc...59 illi¹] Act. 15:10-11 (patres nostri) om. *Vulg.*) VII.20.3 amen...4 uidetis] Matt. 13:17. 5 quod...6 rami] Rom. 11:16. 7 nolo...fratres] 1 Cor. 10:1, 3. 9 consequente...christus] 1 Cor. 10:4. 10 sed...11 est] 1 Cor. 10:5. 11 nos...14 clari-tatem] 2 Cor 3:18 (vero) add. omnes *Vulg.*) 14 quidam...16 moysen] Heb. 3:16. 16 sancti...18 repromissiones¹] Heb. 11:33 (sancti) om. add. qui *Vulg.*) 19 hii...22 consummarentur] Heb. 11:39-40 (hii)hi *Vulg.*)

VII.19.35 allegate] *sic PF*, **leg. allegoriam.** 40 loqun-tur] locuntur P 42 synagogis] sinagogis P 43 non] ubi F 48 nam] num F 51 corporati...53 quo] om. F 54 attende] actende P VII.20.1 seruauerunt] fuerunt P 20 acceperunt] receperunt P

47 diuina|fol. 43vb P VII.20.4 uos|fol. 33r F 15 uniuersi|fol. 44ra P

consummarentur etcet. ergo promissiones quas acceperunt fuerunt ille quas nos recipimus que sunt premia
eterna. ergo sunt salui. Ex hiis ergo declaratum est
euidenter quod uetus testamentus fuit bonum. et quod
patres ac patriarche et prophete et alii omnes qui
seruauerunt eum fuerunt sancti et salui.

Quod uetus testmentum non fuit bonum

[Patarenus:] Vetus testamentum dicimus non fuisse
bonum quattuor. de causis. prima est quia in eo
promissa est uilis hereditas scilicet terra chananeorum
et tam longe quod superueniente meliori testamento
scilicet christi in quo nullus datur hereditas celi ut
merito repudiata hereditate uili et tabule illius ueteris
testamenti in quibus illa uilis hereditas promittebatur
debeant esse in contemptum et derisum.

Catholicus: Respondeo quod temporalium rerum
promissio ad litteram erat in ueteri testamento facta
iudeis. et ideo dicitur uetus testamentum. sed
temporale illa promissio erat figura promissionis uite
eterne. unde apostolus dicit. prima. ad corinthios. x.
hec autem in figura sunt etcet. et in eodem hec autem
omnia in figura contingebant illis. scripta sunt autem
ad correptionem nostram. in quos fines seculi
deuenerunt etcet. audi heretice. si scripta sunt propter
nos. ergo a nobis legenda sunt. intelligenda credenda.
ueneranda et spiritualiter obseruanda. sed quia dicit in
figuram non est nobis spes ponenda. in cortice illarum.
cum iam nucleum figurate promissionis gustauerimus.
sed audi miser quid dominus dicit in euangelio. omnis
scriba doctus in regno celorum similis est homini
patrifamilias qui profert de thesauro suo noua et uetera
etcet. sed uos non estis docti in scriptura sancta et ideo
non profertis uetera immo nec noua. quia illa prophano corde peruertitis et profertis eis quasdam uestras
abusiones more phariseorum que sunt quidam blas-
femie diabolice. quas secreta uestra nuncupatis.

[Patarenus:] Secunda est quia in illo maledicitur pati
nostro christo. scriptum est enim in deuteronomos xxi.
maledictus a deo est qui pendet in ligno etcet. ideo
malum est testamentum uetus.

Catholicus: Respondeo quod non est illa maledictio
sed prophetia de maledictione pene quam per spiritum
sanctum predicebat moyses et si appellas illam maledictionem reprobationis eodem modo reprobabis
nouum testamentum. ubi filius maledictio est. ait enim
apostolus de christo ad Galathas. iiiº. factus pro nobis
maledictum etcet. et quod maledictione pene intellexit
moyses. ipse apostolus exponit cum post quam de
maledictione pene christi dixerat probat illam testimo-

That the Old Testament was not good

[Pat:] The Old Testament we say was not good for four
reasons. The first is that it promised a worthless
inheritance, namely, the land of the Canaanites and that it
was so far surpassed by a better covenant, namely that of
Christ. In which [covenant] there was given no inheritance
of heaven, so that merited repudiation of that worthless
inheritance, and the tablets of that Old Testament in
which that worthless inheritance was promised ought to be
held in contempt and derision.

Cath: I reply that the promise of temporal things was
made to the Jews in the Old Testament in a literal way, and
therefore it is called the Old Testament. But that earthly
promise was an image of the promise of eternal life,
whence the Apostle says in 1 Corinthians 10 (10:6) "Now
these things were done in an allegory," and in the same
(10:11) "Now all these things happened to them in
allegory, and they are written for our correction, upon
whom the ends of the age are come." Listen, O Heretic, if
these were written for us, they are to be read by us,
believed by us, venerated by us, and spiritually observed by
us, but about that which it says in allegory, we are not to
put hope in its husk, because we are already about to taste
the core of the prefigured promised. But listen, O Wretch,
to what the Lord says in the Gospel (Mt 13:52) "Therefore
every scribe instructed in the kingdom of heaven is like a
man that is a householder, who brings forth out of his
treasure new things and old." But you are not educated in
holy scripture and so you cannot bring forth old things,
nor indeed new ones, because in that profane heart you
pervert and bring forth from them in the manner of the
Pharisees improper terms which are certain diabolical
blasphemies, which you call upon in your secrets.

[Pat:] The second is that in it the suffering of our Christ is
cursed, for it is written in Deuteronomy 21 (21:23) "for he
who hangs on a tree is accursed of God." So the Old
Testament is evil.

Cath: I reply that was not a curse but a prophecy of the
curse of punishment, since Moses predicted it by the Holy
Spirit, — and if you call that rejection accursed you reject
in a similar way the New Testament — where there are the
accursed sons (cf. 2 Pt 2:14), for the Apostle says of Christ
to the Galatians (3:13) "he was made a curse for us." And
that curse of punishment was understood by Moses. The
Apostle himself explains that when, after he spoke of the
curse of the punishment of Christ, he proved that
testimony of Moses, saying (3:13) "for it is written, 'cursed

nio moysi dicens. quia scriptum est maledictus omnis qui pendet in ligno etcet. Sed incongo te. si credis quod christus fuerit passus in cruce. cui sic uideris compati ypocrita mendax. et ideo sic indignaris moysi tamquam ipsius passionis blasfemator. quare non indignaris tue incredulitati et perfidie qui de corde pessimo et ore prophano blasfemas et irrides christi passionem.

Patarenus: Tertia est quia inuenitur in nouo testamento uetus et legem mosaicam continere malitiam ac stultitiam et importabilitatem aut defectum uel finem.

De malitia ueteris testamenti

[**Patarenus:**] De primo ezechiele. xx. dedi eis precepta non bona et iudicia in quibus non uiuent et pollui eos in muneribus suis etcet. ergo malitiam continebat uetus testamentum.

Catholicus: Respondeo quod deus appellerat precepta ueteris testamenti esse mala iudeis eo quod per illorum preuaricationem et ingratitudinem incurrerunt dampnationem. que tamen in se essent precepta uite. unde dicit supra. in preceptis meis non ambulauerunt et iudicia mea non custodierunt ut facerent ea. que cum facerent homo uiuet in eis etcet. et propter illorum trangressionem quia incurrerunt in penam dampnationiis. dicit deus ergo et ego dedi eis precepta non bona etcet. similiter in euangelio iohanne. xv. si non uenissem et locutus non fuissem peccatum non habuisset etcet. uel dicantur precepta non bona quantum ad immolationes animalium et huiusmodi cerimonialium eo quod non de beneplacito dei fuerunt data. sed conditionaliter ne ipsi imolassent ydolis. unde in ysaias. ultimo. legitur que nolui elegerunt etcet. sicut fuit de datione regem saule tamen faciendo cerimonialia ex fide uel obediendo saulo propter deum merebantur. uel dicitur legalia precepta non bona id est non meritoria quantum ad opera operata.

[**Patarenus:**] Mattheus xv. quare uos transgredimini mandata dei propter traditionem uestram etcet. uocat enim dominus legem moysi. et totum uetus testamentum doctrinas et mandata hominum exceptis mandatis moralibus et in hiis que de ipso dicantur. quia omnia alia fuerit iustificationes hominum uel traditiones diaboli contra dei uoluntate. ideo malitiam continent.

is every one who hangs on a tree.'" But I accuse you if you believe that Christ had suffered death on the cross, a belief with which you seem to sympathize, being a lying hypocrite, and so this Moses you regard with indignation just as a blasphemer of His passion, why do you not regard your own belief with indignation and perfidy by which you blaspheme the Passion of Christ with the wickedest heart and profane mouth.

Pat: The third is that it is discovered in the New Testament that the Old, and Law of Moses, contains malice and stupidity, interpolations, and failure or limit.

On the wickedness of the Old Testament

[**Pat:**] Regarding the first, Ezekiel 20 (20:25–26) "I also gave them statutes that were not good, and judgments, in which they shall not live, and I polluted them in their own gifts," therefore the Old Testament contains wickedness.

Cath: I reply that God named the commandments of the Old Testament as evil for the Jews, for the fact that through their lying and ingratitude they incurred damnation, while nevertheless in themselves they were the commands of life, as it says above (20:21) "they did not walk in my commandments, nor observe my judgments to do them: which if a man do, he shall live in them," and on account of those transgressions by which they incurred the penalty of damnation. God says therefore "I also gave them statutes that were not good." Similarly in the gospel of John 15 (15:22) "If I had not come, and spoken to them, they would not have sin." Or they speak of precepts that are not good such as the immolation of animals and similar ceremonial laws that were not given out of the beneficence of God, but conditionally lest they might sacrifice to idols, whence at the end of Isaiah it is read (66:4) "and have chosen the things that displease me," just as was the giving of the kingship to Saul, yet following the ceremonial law by faith or by obedience to Saul they earned merit from God, or it speaks of the legal precepts which were not good, that is, not meritorious according to the work worked.[1]

[**Pat:**] Matthew 15 (15:3) "Why do you also transgress the commandment of God for your tradition?" For the Lord calls the Law of Moses, and all of the Old Testament, the doctrines and commands of men, with the exception of the moral commandments and in these which He is speaking, since everything else was justified by men or traditions of

---

44 quia...45 ligno] Gal. 3:13 citing Deut. 21:23. **VII.22.2** dedi...4 suis] Ez. 20:25-26. 10 in...12 eis] Ex. 20:21 (facerent) fecerit *Vulg.*) 15 si...16 habuisset] Ioh. 15:22 (habuisset) haberent *Vulg.*) 21 que...elegerunt] Is. 66:4. 26 quare...27 uestram] Matt. 15:2 (mandata) mandatum *Vulg.*)

---

45 incongo] Clear in both mss.; the meaning is unclear. It is a vernacular word; cp. *Statuti di Sarzana dell'anno MCCLXIX* (Modena, 1893), year, 1269, p. 41. "utrum habeat uel consueuerit tenere ab incongante uel alia persona cum qua incongans causam habuit." 46 fuerit] fuit *F* 47 compati] conniti *P* 53 ac...54 stultitiam] om. *F* **VII.22.15** similiter] similis *F* 16 locutus] add. eis *F* 20 ne] ne ut *P* 25 ad...operata] om. *F* 30 dicantur] loquuntur *F*

VII.22.8 ingratitudinem|fol. 44vb *P*

---

1) The Catholic principle for the manner of operation for the sacraments of the New Law, which give grace 'ex opere operato' that is, through the work itself, as opposed to the sacraments of the Old Law, or the sacramentals, which give grace 'ex opere operantis' or according to the disposition of the recipient.

Catholicus: Respondeo quod non reprehendit dominus aliquo modo scribas et phariseos de obseruatione legis moysi et ueteris testamenti immo redarguit eos de transgressione eius. Manifestum est enim quod illud mandatum scilicet honora patrem tuum etcet. in lege moysi est et de transgressionem eius uituperat illos. sed redarguit eos de quibusdam suis preceptionibus superstitionibus quas inuenerant et proponebant eas legi moysi et doctrine ueteris testamenti. lectio quorum uos patareni estis qui uestras traditiones quas appellatis secta uestra que non sunt nisi ad inuentiones diabolice proponere multis non solum legi moysi et ueteri testamento etiam legi euangelice et testamento nouo.

[**Patarenus:**] Mattheus. v. audistis quia dictum est diliges proximum tuum et odio habebis inimicum tuum. ego autem dico uobis diligite inimicos uestros etcet. ecce quod uetus testamentum continet odium et nouum continet dliectionem. quare malum est uetus. testamentum quia malum doctrinam id est odium. quia contrarium est nouo.

Catholicus: Respondeo quod de doctrina phariseorum fuit illa additio scilicet odio habebis inimicum tuum etcet. nec usquam in ueteri testamento reperitur. nec dominus dixit quod in eo contineretur. sed potius continetur in eo de dilectione inimicitium propter illud uniuersale scilicet diliges proximum tuum etcet. tum propter illud speciale ut mandatum est de oratione babyloniorum quos constat. inimicus iudeorum fore ut legitur. ieremiam xxix. querite pacem ciuitatis ad quam transmigrare feci uos et orate pro ea ad dominum etcet. uel dici post quod in ueteri testamento habetur de odio exteriori habendo ad inimicos scilicet de pena que uidetur effectos odii. sed per hoc iudei intelligebant quod liceret eis odio cordis odire illos maxime quia sic a scribis et phariseis docti fuerant. ideo dominus exponendo dicit. diligite inimicos uestros etcet. quasi dicat sic debetis eos exterius corrigere interius diligatis illos et de tali odio dicebat Psalmis perfecto odio oderam illos etcet.

[**Patarenus:**] Item iohannes primo. lex per moysen data est. gratia atque et ueritas per ihesum christum facta est etcet. ergo mala est lex moysi si gratia et ueritate caret.

Catholicus: Respondeo quod loquitur de effectum gratie et ueritatis per ihesum christum fuit scilicet de redemptione animarum per solutionem pretii eius sanguinis et apertione porte celestis per baptismum. hec enim effectus non erat in lege. nec per legem. non

the devil contrary to the will of God, so it contained wickedness.

Cath: I reply that the Lord did not blame the scribes and Pharisees in any way for the observation of the Law of Moses and the Old Testament, yet He convicted them for their transgressions. For it is plain that the command, namely "honor your father," is in the Law of Moses and he blames them for their transgressions but upbraids them about those superstitious commands which they invented and put forward into the Law of Moses and the teaching of the Old Testament, the proper reading of which is that it is you Patarenes who are those who appeal to the traditions of your sect which are nothing other than diabolic inventions proposed to many, not only about the Law of Moses and the Old Testament but also in the Law of the Gospel and the New Testament.

[**Pat:**] Matthew 5 (5:43–44) "You have heard that it has been said, 'You shall love your neighbor, and hate your enemy,' but I say to you, 'Love your enemies.'" See that the Old Testament contains hate, while the New contains love, hence the Old Testament has an evil doctrine, that is, hatred, which is contrary to the New.

Cath: I reply that the teaching of the Pharisees was an addition, namely "you shall hate your enemy." Nor is that to be found in the Old Testament at all, nor did the Lord say that it was contained in it, but rather what is contained in it is the love of enemies on account of that universal command, namely, "love your neighbor," rather than on account of that specific command in the prayer of the Babylonians who it happens would be the enemies of the Jews as it is read in Jeremiah 29 (29:7) "And seek the peace of the city, to which I have caused you to be carried away as captives, and pray to the Lord for it." Or I say after that in the Old Testament one has exterior hatred towards enemies, namely, of the penalty which seems the effects of hatred, but by this the Jews understood that it was permitted to them to have hatred of heart, to hate those especially since the scribes and Pharisees were teaching thusly, for so the Lord explaining says "love your enemies," as if to say one ought to correct externally those whom you love internally, and of such hatred in the Psalms it says (138:22) "with a perfect hatred, I hated them."

[**Pat:**] Also John 1 (1:17) "For the law was given by Moses, grace and truth came by Jesus Christ." Therefore the Law of Moses was an evil, if it lacked grace and truth.

Cath: I respond that it is speaking of the effect of grace and truth that was through Jesus Christ, namely, of the redemption of souls through the payment of the price of His blood and by the opening of the gates of heaven through baptism. For this effect was not in the law, nor

---

46 audistis...48 uestros] Matt. 5:43-44. 61 querite...63 dominum] Ier. 29:7. 71 perfecto...illos] Ps. 138:22. 72 lex...74 est¹] Ioh. 1:17.

37 honora] honorum *P* 39 preceptionibus] om. *F* 41 lectio] †† unclear word *PF*, loco? 45 testamento¹] add. vestram *P* 51 testamentum...odium] om. *P* 58 uniuersale] add. speciale. ut mandatatm scriptum *F* 60 babyloniorum] babilloniorum *P* inimicus] om. *F* but space left for word. 61 ut] ubi *F* 66 quod] quam *P*

33 domi-nus|fol. 45ra *P* 52 quia|fol. 34r *F* 59 de|fol. 45rb *P*

tamen sequitur propter hoc quod fuerit mala quia poterat habere et habuit alia bona ut supra notauimus in parte nostra tractatus huius. insuper do instantiam contra argumentationem tuam. petrus non predicat quod facit iohannes. ergo petrus nullum bonum facit. ideo non sequitur. preterea esto quod per legem dicam nullam gratiam dari id est per mandata cerimonialia secundum per christum tamen id est per eam fidem que erat in christum implicite. nobis autem est explicite. non sequitur propter hoc quod mala sit lex mandatorum. quia si dico predicatio pauli ab ipso audita est. secundum gratia predicationis a solo deo est. non sequitur propter hoc quid mala sit pauli predicatio.

Patarenus: Item ad romanos iii°. per legem enim cognitio peccati etcet. ergo mala est si per eam cognoscitur peccatum.

Catholicus: Respondeo sic intelligitur per legem cognitio peccati scilicet maior quam si non esset lex talis est de domino ihesu christo. unde dixit. si non uenissem peccatum non habuissent etcet. item per legem est cognitio peccati id est lex facit cognoscere peccatum a deo non esse inpunitum. uel per legem est peccati cognitio subaudi tantum. secus est per euangelium. quia per eum est non solum cognitio peccati. sed et consumptio eius per iustitia qui est ex fide christi. nec sequitur propter hoc quod mala sit lex.

[Patarenus:] Item idem iiii°. lex enim iram operatur etcet. ergo est mala.

Catholicus: Respondeo ut infra. vii°. nunc autem soluti etcet. Item idem v°. peccatum autem non imputabatur id est non cognoscebatur uel non credebatur quod deberet puniri non tamen sequitur quod ex hoc sit mala ut supra.

[Patarenus:] Item in eodem. lex autem subintrauit ut habundaret delictum. ergo mala est. si fecit habundare delictum.

Catholicus: Respondeo quod sic intelligitur lex subintrauit ut habundaret delictum id est habundantius appereret id est cognoscentur.

[Patarenus:] Item idem vii°. nunc autem soluti a lege mortis in quo detinebamur etcet. ergo pessima fuit si fuit lex mortis.

Catholicus: respondeo quod tribus modis dicitur lex moyses. lex mortis et dapnationis. primo occasionaliter contempnentibus eam sicut est apostolus cum aliis predicatoribus qui in uia iustitie contempnuntur. unde ipse dicit secunda ad corinthios. ii°. aliis quidem odor mortis in mortem etcet. secundo quia non liberabat a morte. quia dimittebat homines in ea nec ducebat eos

through the law, yet it does not follow on account of this that it was evil, since one was able to have, and had, other goods that we remarked upon earlier in our section of this work. On top of that I give another objection against your argument. Peter did not preach what John does, therefore Peter does no good. That does not follow. Further, let it be that I say that through the law no grace is given, that is, through the ceremonial commands according to Christ alone, that is, through that faith in Christ which was for them implicit, yet for us is explicit. It does not follow on account of this that the law of commandments was evil, because if I say that the preaching of Paul was heard by him, according to the grace of preaching which is from God alone, it does not follow on account of this that the preaching of Paul is evil.

Pat: Also Romans 3 (3:20) "For by the law is the knowledge of sin." Therefore the law is evil, if by it one comes to know sin.

Cath: I reply that "by the law is the knowledge of sin" is to be understood in this manner, greater than if there had not been the excellent law of the Lord Jesus Christ, whence He says (Jn 15:22) "If I had not come ... they would not have sin." Also "by the law is the knowledge of sin." That is, the Law makes it known that sin is not unpunished by God, or "by the law is the knowledge of sin" one should only add, alongside the Gospel, or through the law comes only the knowledge of sin, but of its wearing away through justice which is by the faith of Christ, nor does it follow on account of this that the Law is evil.

[Pat:] In the same in chapter 4 (Rm 4:15) "For the law works wrath." Therefore it is evil.

Cath: I reply as it goes on below (7:6) "But now we are loosed," and 5 (5:13) "but sin was not imputed," that is, it was not known or it was not believed that one ought to be punished, nevertheless it does not follow that this was evil as above.

[Pat:] Also in the same (5:20) "Now the law entered in, that sin might abound." Therefore it was evil if it caused sin to abound.

Cath: I reply that it is to be understood that the law entered in so that sin might abound, that is, that it might appear to abound more, that is, that it might be known.

[Pat:] Also the same in 7 (Rm 7:6) "But now we are loosed from the law of death, in which we were detained." Therefore it was most wicked if it was the law of death.

Cath: I reply that the law of Moses can be called the law of damnation and death in three ways: first, occasionally for those who disdain it, just as the Apostle is with other preachers who were spurning it in light of the way of justice, whence he says in 2 Corinthians 2 (2:16) "To the one indeed the odor of death unto death." The second because it does not deliver from death, since it was abandoning men in it, neither was it leading them to

in eternam uitam. uel dicitur tertio modo lex non mortis et dampnationis quia mortem et dampnationem temporalem statuit contra delinquentes et secundum duos primos modos etiam lex euangelica potest dici lex mortis et dampnationis.

[**Patarenus:**] Item in eodem peccatum occasione accepta per mandatum seduxit me et per illud occidit etcet. ergo mala fuit.

[**Catholicus:**] Respondeo contrarium in sanctus paulus apostolus ibi dicens. itaque lex sancta et mandatum sanctum et iustum et bonum. dicimus quod tribus modis lex operata est peccatum siue concupiscencia scilicet. augmentando ut supra. v. lex autem subintrauit ut habundaret delictum etcet. secundo per cognitionem ut supra in hoc capitulo. peccatum enim non cognoui nisi per legem etcet. tertio uero occasionaliter. unde propter hoc occasionaliter sequitur bona sit lex et non mala. unde illatio pauli uera est. tua uero falsa. uera si augmentet peccata per prohibitionem bona est quia si mala esset non esset peccatum facere contra prohibitionem eius. item quia facit cognoscere peccatum bonam est. si enim mala esset potius occultaret illud. item quia occasionaliter fomes uel diabolus per eam operatus nobis peccatum. bona est. quia numquam dicitur nisi ratione boni. sicut ratione spirituale unguenti super caput saluatoris. iudas inuidie liuorem incurrit et hiis etiam modis. lex euangelica peccatum operatur.

[**Patarenus:**] Item ii^a ad corinthios iii°. quod si ministratio mortis litteris deformata in lapidibus etcet. et infra. nam si ministratio dampnationis etcet. ergo mala est. si est litteris deformata et si est ministratio dampnationis. mortis et dampnationis.

Catholicus: Respondeo quod ideo dicitur deformata litteris in lapidibus tabulis quia in tabulis lapideis fuit scripta. ubi pulchra et formata littera non apparet. uel dicitur deformata in bona parte id est bene formata. ad aliud uero responsum est supra ad romanos vii. nunc autem soluti a lege mortis etcet.

[**Patarenus:**] Item ad Galatas ii°. si enim que destruxi hec iterum hedifico preuaricatorem me constituo. ego enim per legem legi mortuus sum etcet. ergo mala fuit lex moysi. si sanctus paulus eam destruxit et si ab ea separatus est per legem christi.

Catholicus: Responsio. destruxit ei eam quantum ad cerimonialia ueniente gratia christi per illam figurata.

eternal life. Or one can say in a third way the law is not of death and damnation since it commands death and temporal damnation against criminals and according to the first two ways also the Law of the Gospel can be called the law of death and damnation.

[**Pat:**] Also in the same (Rm 7:11) "For sin, taking occasion by the commandment, seduced me, and by it killed me." Therefore it was evil.

[**Cath:**] I reply that Saint Paul the Apostle is saying the contrary here (7:12) "So the law indeed is holy, and the commandment holy, and just, and good." We say then that there are three ways the Law works sin, or concupiscence, namely, by enlarging it as above in 5 (5:20) "Now the law entered in, that sin might abound." The second by knowledge as above in this chapter (7:7) "I do not know sin, except by the law." However the third occasionally, whence on account of this it follows that the Law is good and not evil. So Paul's assumption is true, yours is false. True if one increases sin through the prohibition of good since if it were evil, it would not be a sin to act against its prohibitions. Also since it makes the knowledge of sin to be good, for otherwise evil would be more hidden. Also occasionally regarding the tinder [*fomes*],[1] or the devil, having through it worked sin in us, still it is good, since it is never mentioned except by reason of good, just as by reason of the spiritual anointing over the head of the Savior, Judas becomes envious with spite, and also in these ways the Law of the gospel works sin.

[**Pat:**] Also 2 Corinthians 3 (3:7) "Now if the administration of death, graven with letters upon stones," and later (3:9) "For if the ministration of condemnation." Therefore it is evil if it is graven letters and if it is an administration of condemnation, of death and damnation.

Cath: I reply that it speaks of "graven with letters upon stone," because they were written on stone tablets, where one cannot have beautiful, wellformed letters, or it is said to be graven in the good part, that is, well formed, to the other the response is above in Romans 7 (7:6) "But now we are loosed from the law of death."

[**Pat:**] Also Galatians 2 (2:18–19) "For if I build up again the things which I have destroyed, I make myself a liar. For I, through the law, am dead to the law." Therefore the Law of Moses was evil if Saint Paul destroyed it and if from it he was separated for the Law of Christ.

Cath: Response. He destroyed it insofar as the ceremonial law, with the coming of the grace of Christ that it prefigured.

---

136 peccatum...137 occidit] Rom. 7:11. 140 itaque...141 bonum] Rom. 7:12. 143 lex...144 delictum] Rom. 5:20. 145 peccatum...146 legem] Rom. 7:7. 159 quod...160 lapidibus] 2 Cor. 3:7. 161 nam...dampnationis] 2 Cor. 3:9. 168 nunc...169 mortis] Rom. 7:6. 170 si...172 sum] Gal. 2:18-19.

---

151 contra] om. *P* 156 spirituale] sparsionis *F* 158 euangelica] om. *P* 175 destruxit...180 Responsio] om. *P*

147 unde|fol. 46ra *P* 173 moysi|fol. 46rb *P*

---

1) The "law of sin", see Thomas, *Summa Theologiae* I. q. 91. a. 6.

[Patarenus:] Idem in eodem. si enim per legem iustitia etcet. ergo non fuit bona si per ea non potuit esse iustitia.

Catholicus: Responsio. non fuit iustitia per legem id est per sacramenta eius ex ui sacramentorum illorum. sed tantum ex ui fidei licet non fuit per legem iustitia scilicet perficiens. sed per gratiam qui est lex noua euangelium.

[Patarenus:] Idem iii°. si enim data esset lex que posset uiuificare uere ex lege esset iustitia sed conclusit omnia sub scriptura omnia sub peccato etcet. ergo mala fuit si non potuit uiuificare et si fuerunt omnia sub peccato sub ea.

Catholicus: Respondeo non potuit uiuificare id est ad uitam eternam conducere. et ideo omnia erant sub peccato id est sub pena peccati donec ueniret redemptor.

[Patarenus:] Item ad hebreos. viii. nam si illud a culpa uacasset si utique secundi locus inquireretur. ergo malum fuit uetus testamentum si fuit culpabile.

Catholicus: Respondeo quod dicitur ideo uacasse a culpa. quia ueritas fidei sine qua culpa est non fuit in eo manifestata sicut fuit in nouo. unde subdit quia hoc testamentum quod disponam domui israel post dies illos dicit dominus dabo leges meas in mentem eorum etcet. uel dicitur non uacasse a culpa quia non liberabat ab eius effectum id est a pena culpe.

Patarenus: Item cum datum est uetus testamentum fuit ibi motus terre et obscuritas tremor et pauor. ergo fuit malum.

Catholicus: Respondeo quia et cum nouum testamentum fuit traditum et confirmatum in passione christi. fuit ibi terremotus et obscuritas et tremor longe maior quam fuerit in datione ueteris testamenti.

[Patarenus:] preterea ab adam usque ad christum legimus diuersos fuisse cultus et ritus in sacrificiis et huius. quare malum inde fuisset uetus testamentum

Catholicus: respondeo quod in nouo testamento hoc idem reperies. primo enim dixit christus apostolis suis ne irent in unum gentium et postea precepit illis ut irent per uniuersum mundum. predicare euangelium omni creature. item. indulsit eis ut ieiunarent donec cum illis esset in carne et poste ieiunanerunt ex eius precepto. iterum tradidit illis formam baptizandi. in nomine patris et filii et spiritus sancti. et dispensauit cum eis cum spiritum sanctum. ut baptiçarent in nomine ihesu christi Preterea uos heretici non seruatis tenorem Christi et apostolorum eius in uestris obseruantiis. immo inuenistis et mutastis multas. de quibus in quarto libro dicemus. ergo mala est uestra doctrina.

[Pat.] Also in the same (2:21) "For if justice be by the law," therefore it was not good if by it there was unable to be justice.

Cath: Response: there was no justice by the law, that is, by its sacraments or by the power of its sacraments, but only by the power of faith, even though there was not justice by the law, namely, completed justice, but through the grace which is in the new Law of the Gospel.

[Pat.] Also 3 (3:21–22) "For if there had been a law given which could give life, truly justice should have been by the law. But the scripture has consigned all under sin." Therefore it was evil if it was unable to give life and if all were under sin who lived under it.

Cath: I reply that it cannot give life, that is, to lead to eternal life, and so "all" was "under sin," that is, under the penalty of sin until a redeemer might come.

[Pat.] Also Hebrews 8 (8:7) "For if that former had been faultless, there should not indeed have been a place sought for a second." Therefore the Old Testament was evil if it was culpable.

Cath: I reply that it says "it was faultless," since the truth of faith, without which there is no guilt, was not made plain in it, just as was in the New. Whence it adds (8:10) "For this is the testament which I will make to the house of Israel after those days, says the Lord, I will give my laws into their mind." Or it says that it is not faultless since it was not delivered from its effect, that is, from the penalty of guilt.

Pat: Also when the Old Testament was given there was at that time an earthquake, darkness, and panic, therefore it was evil.

Cath: I reply that when the New Testament was handed on and confirmed in the Passion of Christ there was then earthquake, and darkness, and long tremors greater than in the giving of the Old Testament.

[Pat.] Further from Adam up to Christ we read that there were diverse observances and sacrificial rites and of the like. Hence the Old Testament was in that time evil.

Cath: I reply that in the New Testament you find the same thing. For first Christ said to His Apostles that they should go to one people, and later He commanded them that they might go throughout the whole world to preach the Gospel to all creatures. Also He indulged them that they should not fast while He was with them in the flesh and later they fasted by His command. Further He handed on to them the form of baptizing, in the name of the Father, and of the Son, and of the Holy Spirit, and He dispensed them by the Holy Spirit, that they might baptize in the name of Christ. Further you heretics do not observe the path of Christ and His Apostles in your observances, you

---

177 si…iustitia] Gal. 2:21. 185 si…187 peccato] Gal. 3:21-22. 194 nam…195 inquireretur] Heb. 8:7 (a) add. prius | si] add. non *Vulg.*) 199 quia…201 eorum] Heb. 8:10 (dabo] dando *Vulg.*)

180 id…182 iustitia] om. *P* 181 illorum] add. moyses *F* 188 omnia] om. *F* 191 erant] enim *P* 195 uacasset] uocasset *F* 196 fuit¹] om. *P* 197 dicitur ideo] transp. *F* 198 sine] sanctum *P* 202 non²] si *P* 204 datum] dictum *F* 208 passione] possessione *F* 213 quare] quod *P* 214 quod] quia *P* 218 ut] ne *F*

178 potuit]fol. 35r *F* 208 confirmatum]fol. 46va *P*

[Patarenus:] Secunda causa est quare uetus testamentum malum dicitur. quia inuenitur in nouo. quod illud stultitias continebat. unde ad titum. ultimo. Stultas autem questiones et genealogias et contentiones et pugnas legis deuita sunt enim inutiles et uane etcet. ergo mala est lex illa que stultitias et uanitates continet.
Catholicus: Respondeo quia loquitur de questionibus cerimonialium que sunt stulte et inutiles et uane post gloriam noue legis ad inducendum ut illos seruent.

[Patarenus:] Tertia causa est quia legitur in nouo quod illud continent importabilitatem. unde ad hebreos. xii. non enim portabant quod dicebatur etcet. et actus. xv. quod neque patres nostri neque nos portare potuimus etcet. ergo malum fuit uetus testamentum si habuit impossibilia precepta.
Catholicus: Respondeo impossibilia non erant. sed propter superbiam filiorum israel. deus in tanta multitudine dederat illis dicebant namque de se presumentes quod deus non posset tot precepta facere illis quot ipsi seruarent. ut ergo ipsorum iactantiam iusto iudicio domaret. tradidit eis deus omnipotens multitudinem preceptorum. que sine magna difficultate adimplere non poterant et alia enim ratione fecit scilicet ut oppressi sub honere cerimonialium multorum clamarent ad cellarationem mediatoris uenturi cum suauitate glorie salutaris.

[Patarenus:] Quarta causa est quia nouum dicit uetus uarios habuisse defectus. ut ad romanos iii°. ex operibus legis non iustificabitur omnis caro etcet. et in eodem exclusa est gloriatio tua per quam legem factorum non etcet. item ad Galatas. ii°. non iustificatur homo ex operibus legis etcet. et iii°. nam si ex lege hereditas. iam non ex promissione etcet. et iiii. misit deus filium scilicet ex muliere factum sub lege ut eos qui sub lege erant reduceret. Item ad hebreos vi. non rursum iacientes fundamentum penitentie ab operibus mortuis etcet. et vii. reprobatio quidem fit precedentis mandati. nichil enim ad perfectum duxit lex. etcet. et in eodem. in tantum melioris testamenti etcet. et infra. lex enim homines constituit sacerdotes infirmitatem habentes. etcet. et x. Vmbram enim habens lex futurorum bonorum non ipsam imaginem rerum et infra. impossibile enim est sanguine taurorum

always invent and change things, of which I will speak in the fourth book.[1] Therefore your teaching is evil.
[Pat:] The second reason why the Old Testament is called evil is because in the New one finds that it contained foolishness. Whence at the end of Titus (3:9) "But avoid foolish questions, and genealogies, and contentions, and strivings about the law. For they are unprofitable and vain." Therefore that Law is evil which contains foolish questions and vanities.
Cath: I reply that he is speaking of questions of the ceremonial law which are foolish and useless and vain, persuading that they be observed, after the glory of the New Law [was revealed].
[Pat:] The third cause is that it is read in the New that it contains unbearable things, Whence Hebrews 12 (12:20) "For they did not endure that which was said." And Acts 15 (15:10) "which neither our fathers nor we have been able to bear?" Therefore the Old Testament is evil since it imposes impossible commands.
Cath: I reply that they were not impossible, but [that it was] on account of the pride of the children of Israel that God had given such a multitude of laws to them; in fact they were speaking of themselves presuming that God could not make as many commands for them that they might observe. So that therefore He might subdue their boasting with a just judgment, Almighty God gave them a multitude of precepts which they were not able to fulfill except with great difficulty. He did it for another reason, namely, that being oppressed under the weight of many ceremonial laws they might shout out more quickly for a Savior to come with the sweetness of saving glory.
[Pat:] The fourth cause is that the New says that the Old suffered various defects, as in Romans 3 (3:20) "Because by the works of the law no flesh shall be justified," and in the same (3:27) "Where is then your boasting? It is excluded. By what law? Of works? No." Also Galatians 2 (2:16) "man is not justified by the works of the law," and 3 (3:18) "For if the inheritance be of the law, it is no more of promise," and 4 (4:4-5) "God sent his Son, born of a woman, born under the law, that he might redeem those who were under the law." Also Hebrews 6 (6:1) "not laying again the foundation of penance from dead works." And 7 (7:18, 19) "There is indeed a setting aside of the former commandment ... the law brought nothing to perfection." And in the same (7:22) "By so much of a better testament," and later (7:28) "For the law makes men priests, who have weaknesses." And 10 (10:1) "For the law having a shadow of the good things to come, not the very image of the things," and later (10:4) "For it is impossible that

---

230 Stultas...231 uane] Tit. 3:9. 238 non...dicebatur] Heb. 12:20. 239 quod...potuimus] Act. 15:10. 254 ex...255 caro] Rom. 3:20. 256 exclusa...257 non¹] Rom. 3:27. 257 non²...258 legis] Gal. 2:16. 258 nam...259 promissione] Gal. 3:18. 260 misit...261 reduceret] Gal. 4:4-5 (reduceret) redimeret *Vulg.*) 262 non...263 mortuis] Heb. 6:1. 263 reprobatio...265 lex] Heb. 7:18, 19 (duxit) adduxit *Vulg.*) 265 in²...testamenti] Heb. 7:22. 266 lex...267 habentes] Heb. 7:28. 267 Vmbram...269 rerum] Heb. 10:1. 269 impossibile...270 peccata] Heb. 10:4.

236 causa] enim *F* | quod] quia *F* 244 dicebant] add. de *P* exp. 247 deus] om. *F* 252 glorie salutaris] gratie secularis *F*

237 illud|fol. 46vb *P* 240 uetus|fol. 35v *F* 261 sub|fol. 47ra *P*

---

1) This fourth book is missing in both manuscripts. It was likely never even begun.

hyrcorum auferri non potest peccata etcet. ex hiis ergo patet quod uetus testamentum uarios habuit defectus.

Catholicus: Responsio. dico quod uetus testamentum habuit defectus absque dubio. alioquin non opportuisset uenire christum in mundum cum gratia noue legis. nec tamen sequitur. quod propter hoc fit malum. immo ex hoc quod dicitur imperfectum uetus testamentum reliquitur eum fuisse bonum. ubi enim nullum est bonum nullum est imperfectum. ubi autem imperfectum est ibi et bonum est. exemplum de libro qui non est perfectus. quia non est perfectus. quia non sequitur propter hoc quod ideo quod factum est de ipso malum sit. sed potius arguitur ut sit bonum et nota quod tribus modis dicitur uetus testamentum fuisse imperfectum. seu legem moysi. primo quia opera eius operantia in se indifferentia erant. quia nihil gratie conferebant. quantum in se erat. secundo quia opera operata nullo modo gratia dabant. tertio quia ianua celi aperire non poterat de uirtute sui. donec ueniret sanctum id est christus cui repromiserat deus.

[Patarenus:] Quinta causa est quia nouum testamentum dicit uetus testamentum et finitum seu terminatum. unde mattheus. xi. nemo immittit commissuram panni rudis in uestimentum uetus etcet. mattheus. vii. prophete et lex usque ad iohannem. item. iohannes. xviiii. consummatum est etcet. Item. ad romanos. x. finis enim legis christus etcet. item. ii^a. ad corinthios. v. uetera transierunt. et ad Galathas. iiii^o. quomodo conuertimini iterum ad infirma et egena elementa quibus denuo seruire uultis. dies obseruatis et menses et tempora et annos etcet. et v^o. omnis enim lex uno sermone impletur. diliges proximum tuum sicut teipsum. item ad ephesios. ii^o. legem emandatorum euacuans etcet. item ad hebreos. viii. quod enim antiquatur et senescit prope interitum est etcet. et ix. habuit quidem et prius iustificationes culture et sanctum seculare etcet. item usque ad tempus correctionis impositis etcet. ex quibus patet quod uetus testamentum etiamsi alioquin potuisset tollerari. tamen prius aduentum christi terminatum est. et ideo malum est ipsum modo seruare et credere.

Catholicus: Respondeo quod terminatum est uetus testamentum. ubi est impletum sicut in his que de christo loquebantur. quia ipse confirmauit ea adimplendo illa. item consummatum est quantum ad cerimonialia. non tamen sequitur quod non sit credendum bonum fuisse suo tempore illa seruare ad litteram et modo spiritualiter. nec etiam sequitur quod alia

with the blood of oxen and goats sin should be taken away." From these it is clear that the Old Testament had various defects.

Cath: Response. I say that the Old Testament had defects, without a doubt, otherwise it would not have been required for Christ to come into the world with the grace of the New Law, nor yet does it follow that on account of this it was evil. Indeed on account of this Old Law is called imperfect, yet it remains that it was good. For where there is no good there is no imperfection, yet where there is imperfection, there is also good. Take for example a book that is not yet completed, because it is not finished it does not follow that what is [already] done in it is bad, but rather it proves that it is good. And note the three ways of saying the Old Testament, or the Law of Moses, might have been imperfect: in the first place that the deeds done in it were indifferent in themselves, since they did not confer any grace, insomuch as they existed in themselves. The second is that the deeds done did not give any grace. The third that the gate of heaven was not able to be opened by its power until the holy one had come, that is, Christ, whom God had promised.

[Pat:] The fifth reason is that the New Testament says that the Old Testament is finished or completed. Whence Matthew 11 (9:16) "And nobody sews a piece of raw cloth into an old garment." Matthew 7 (11:13) "For all the prophets and the law prophesied until John." Also John 19 (19:30) "it is finished." Also Romans 10 (10:4) "For the end of the law is Christ." Also 2 Corinthians 5 (5:17) "the old things have passed away." And Galatians 4 (4:9) "how can you turn again to the weak and needy elements, which you desire to serve again? You observe days, and months, and times, and years." And 5 (5:14) "For all the law is fulfilled in one word, you shall love your neighbor as yourself." Also Ephesians 2 (2:15) "Making void the law of commandments." Also Hebrews 8 (8:13) "And that which decays and grows old, is near its end," and 9 (9:1) "The former indeed had also justifications of divine service, and a worldly sanctuary," also (9:10) "until the time of correction." From these it is plain that the Old Testament, even if it otherwise was able to be tolerated before the coming of Christ, was completed and so is evil in the same way as it is evil to observe and believe it.

Cath: I reply that the Old Testament is completed where it has been fulfilled just as in those things which spoke of Christ because He confirmed the Law by fulfilling them. Also it is completed as regards the ceremonial law, yet it does not follow that one should not believe that it was good to observe it literally during its time, and in a spiritual way, nor also does it follow that otherwise it

---

292 nemo...293 uetus] Matt. 9:16.   294 prophete...iohannem] Matt. 11:13.   295 consummatum est] Ioh. 19:30.   296 finis... christus] Rom. 10:4.   297 uetera transierunt] 2 Cor. 5:17.   298 quomodo...300 annos] Gal. 4:9-10.   300 omnis...302 teipsum] Gal. 5:14.   302 legem...303 euacuans] Eph. 2:15.   303 quod...304 est] Heb. 8:13.   305 habuit...306 seculare] Heb. 9:1.   306 usque... 307 impositis] Heb. 9:10.

275 quod] quia *P*   276 immo] nonne *P*   278 nullum^1] malum *F*   279 bonum] bonorum *P*   280 quia^1...perfectus^2] om. *F*   281 ideo] id *F*   282 arguitur] argumentatur *F*   284 moysi] moysy *F*   289 ueniret] om. *P*   290 Quinta] **sic** *PF* **leg. quarta**   296 enim] add. tantum *P* | iia] add. ii^o *P*   312 his] hiis *F*   313 confirmauit] consumauit *F*   314 item] iterum *F*

288 celi|fol. 47rb *P*   299 obseruatis|fol. 36r *F*

uiuificatur que non sunt adimpleta. scire namque debes quod interest nunc precepta uite agende et precepta uite figurande. prima namque debemus seruare hodie namque ad litteram usque ad unguem. sicut honora patrem tuum etcet. moralia et de istis dicit dominus. si uis ad uitam ingredi serua mandata etcet. alia uero debemus credere et seruare. credere in quam quod ad litteram debuerunt seruari usque ad aduentum noue gratie figurate per illa. seruare autem debemus ea spiritualiter adimplenda mandata. nec obstat illud. mattheo. nemo pannum nouum etcet. quia ille pannum nouum uestimento ueteri assuit qui conscientiam uult habere spiritualem et non deposuit carnalem. intellige autem ydiota quod quando dominus dixit. nemo. etcet. interrogatus erat de ieiunio quod credebat debere seruare et facere. more iudeorum intentione carnali.

Quarta ratio

[Patarenus:] Quarta ratio est quare uetus testamentum malum esse credatur quia a malo deo ipsum traditum inuenitur. ut supra in proxima rubrica probauimus.
Catholicus: Respondeo istam falsam esse rationem supra in predicto tractatu tam in parte nostra quam in tua euidenter ostendimus.

Quod qui fuerit sub ueteri testamento non sunt salui

[Patarenus:] Mattheus. xx. sic erunt nouissimi primi et primi nouissimi. sed primi sunt qui fuerunt sub ueteri testamento. ergo non sunt salui.
Catholicus: Respondeo immo per hoc habetur contrarium. quia si sunt nouissimi ad salutem. ergo sunt salui et expressim dicit ibi dominus quod isti primi receperunt denariam cum aliis.
[Patarenus:] Item iohannes. vi. patres nostri manducauerunt manna in deserto et mortui sunt etcet. ergo sunt dampnati.
Catholicus: Respondeo quod multi sunt dampnati de filiis israel sine dubio qui manducauerunt manna sed non dicit quod omnes sint mortui uel loquitur de morte naturali.
[Patarenus:] Item idem vii°. nondum enim erat spiritus datus quia ihesus nondum erat glorificatus etcet. sed sine spiritu sancto nullus potest saluari. ergo ante glorificationem christi nullus fuit saluus.
Catholicus: Respondeo non dicit quod nullus datus fuit spiritus sanctus antea. sed dicit quod ille spiritus quem credentes erant accepturi post resurrectionem

would give life when it was not fulfilled. In fact you ought to know the difference between the precepts for life now and the precepts for the life to come. In fact the first we ought to observe today, literally with perfect accuracy,[1] such as (Dt 5:16) "honor your father," the moral laws, of these the Lord says (Mt 19:17) "if you wish to enter into life, keep the commandments," yet others we ought to believe and observe, to believe in them literally, they ought to be observed up until the coming of the new grace prefigured by them. Yet we ought to observe them by fulfilling the commands spiritually, neither does that passage in Matthew contradict it (9:16) "new cloth," since the new cloth sewed on to an old garment which one wishes to have spiritual knowledge of and yet not give up the flesh. But understand, O Fool, when the Lord says "no one," He was asked about fasting, which He believed that one ought to observe and do, after the manner of the Jews with a fleshly intention.

The fourth reason

[Pat:] The fourth reason why the Old Testament is believed to be evil is because it was found to be handed on by an evil God, as we proved above in the foregoing section.
Cath: I replied that argument was false above in that section, which we proved as much in our part as in yours.

That those who were under the Old Testament were not saved

[Pat:] Matthew 20 (20:16) "So shall the last be first, and the first last," but those who were under the Old Testament were first, therefore they are not saved.
Cath: I answer no indeed, for the reason is exactly to the contrary, because if they are the last to be saved then they are saved and the Lord clearly says that these first received the same pay the others.
[Pat:] Also John 6 (6:31) "our fathers ate manna in the desert and they died," therefore they are damned.

Cath: I respond that without a doubt many are damned among the sons of Israel who ate manna, but it does not say that all might be damned, or because it is merely speaking about natural death.
[Pat:] Also in the same in 7 (7:39) "for as yet the Spirit was not given, because Jesus was not yet glorified." But without the Holy Spirit no one can be saved, therefore before the glorification of Christ no one was saved.
Cath: I reply that He did not say that no one was given the Holy Spirit before, but He said that the Spirit whom they trusted they would be able to receive after His

---

322 honora...tuum] Deut. 5:16.   323 si...mandata] Matt. 19:17.   328 nemo...nouum] Matt. 9:16 paraphrase.   VII.24.3 sic...4 nouissimi] Matt. 20:16.   10 patres...11 sunt] Ioh. 6:31.   17 nondum...18 glorificatus] Ioh. 7:39.

318 uiuificatur] transierat F 319 nunc] inter F 320 debemus] debetis F 327 adimplenda mandata] adimplendo ipsa F VII.23.4 rubrica] rubricella F | probauimus] probaui F VII.24.9 denariam] de natura P 22 fuit] fuerat P 23 accepturi] add. erant P exp.

318 scire|fol. 47va P VII.24.7 contrarium|fol. 47vb P

---

[1] Literally "to the nail", a sculptor's expression for "exactly alike". See Horace, Sat. I. 5. 32. "ad unguem factus homo."

eius id est ad illum usum nondum erat datus. hoc est quod dicit ibi. hoc autem dixit de spiritu quem accepturi erant credentes in eum etcet. quia autem spiritus sanctus. fuerit in sanctis ueteris testamenti prosequere ut supra. in parte nostra huius tractatus notatum est.

[**Patarenus:**] Item. iohannes. x. omnes quotquot uenerunt fures sunt et latrones etcet. ergo omnes qui fuerunt ante aduentum christi sunt dampnati.

Catholicus: Respondeo quod illi intelliguntur uenisse qui non erant a domino missi. sed sua auctoritate prophetabant aut alia faciebant. de quibus dicit deus in ieremia. xxiii. nolite audire uerba prophetarum qui prophetant uobis et decipiunt uos. uisionem cordis sui loquuntur et non de ore domini et infra. mendacium ipsi loquuntur uobis quia non misi eos etcet. simile est quod dicit iohanne. v. ego ueni in nomine patris mei et non accepitis me. si alius uenerit in nomine suo illum accipietis etcet. et apostolus ii^a. ad corinthios. xi. nam si is qui uenit alium christum predicat etcet. multi enim non uenire sed mitti dicitur. Iohanne. xx. sicut misit me pater et ego mitto uos etcet.

[**Patarenus:**] Item ad romanos. iii^a. causati enim sumus iudeos et grecos omnes sub peccato esse etcet. ergo omnes sunt dampnati qui fuerunt ante aduentum christi.

Catholicus: Respondeo comprehendit genera singulorum et non singula genera id est comprehendit iudeos et gentes. uel omnes erant sub peccato id est sub pena peccati.

[**Patarenus:**] Item ad Galatas. iii. quicumque ex operibus legis sunt sub maledicto sunt etcet. ergo sunt omnes dampnati qui fuerunt sub lege.

Catholicus: Respondeo non dicit quod sint dampnati. sed dicit quod sunt sub maledicto. non omne maledictum est dampnatio. nam et ihesus dominus noster fuit maledictum ut dictum est supra. fuerunt namque sub maledicto legis id est sub penalibus preceptis legis et sub defectibus eius.

[**Patarenus:**] Item ad hebreos. viii. uituperans eos dicit etcet. ergo sunt omnes dampnati qui fuerunt sub ueteri testamento si deus uituperat eos.

Catholicus: Respondeo quia de transgressoribus loquitur uel erant omnes in statu uituperii. quia sub seruitute legis premebantur quia non poterant eos ducere in patrie libertatem.

Resurrection, that is, since this was not yet given. This is what He says there (7:39) "Now this he said of the Spirit which they should receive, who believed in him." Because indeed the Holy Spirit had been in the saints of the Old Testament, as described above, as noted in our part of this work.

[**Pat:**] Also John 10 (10:8) "All others, as many as have come, are thieves and robbers." Therefore all who lived before the coming of Christ were damned.

Cath: I reply that these words are to be understood as referring to those who were coming and were not sent by the Lord, but by their own authority prophesied or did other things of which God speaks in Jeremiah 23 (23:16) "Do not listen to the words of the prophets that prophesy to you, and deceive you. They speak a vision of their own heart, and not out of the mouth of the Lord." And later (27:14–15) "for they tell you a lie, for I have not sent them." It is similar to what he says in John 5 (5:43) "I have come in the name of my Father, and you do not receive me, if another shall come in his own name, him you will receive." And the Apostle in 2 Corinthians 11 (11:4) "For if he who comes preaches a different Christ." For many will not come, but they are said to be sent, in John 20 (20:21) "As my Father has sent me, so I send you."

[**Pat:**] Also Romans 3 (3:9) "For we have charged both Jews and Greeks, that they are all under sin." Therefore all those who lived before the coming of Christ were damned.

Cath: I reply that it includes classes of each, and not a single class, that it, it includes Jews and Gentiles, or all who were under sin, that is, under the penalty of sin.

[**Pat:**] Also Galatians 3 (3:10) "For as many as are of the works of the law, are under a curse," therefore all those who were under the law were damned.

Cath: I respond that he did not say that they might be damned, but that they were under a curse, for not every curse is damnation. For instance Jesus our Lord was cursed as it was said above. They were in fact under the curse of the law, that is, under the penalties of the commands of the law and under its defects.

[**Pat:**] Also Hebrews 8 (8:8) "For finding fault with them:" therefore all those who were under the Old Testament were damned if God found fault with them.

Cath: I reply that he was speaking of transgressors or that they were in a state of reproach, since they were pressed down by servitude to the law, since it was not able to lead them into the freedom of the native land.

---

25 hoc...26 eum] Ioh. 7:39.   **30** omnes...31 latrones] Ioh. 10:8.   **36** nolite...38 domini] Ier. 23:16.   **38** mendacium...39 eos] Ier. 27:14-15.   **40** ego...42 accipietis] Ioh. 5:43.   **42** nam...43 predicat] 2 Cor. 11:4.   **44** sicut...45 uos] Ioh. 20:21.   **46** causati...47 esse] Rom. 3:9.   **54** quicumque...55 sunt^2] Gal. 3:10.   **63** uituperans...dicit] Heb. 8:8.

44 enim] om. P   **61** maledicto] add. d F exp.   **68** premebantur] premebantur premebant P | quia] que F

27 spiritus|fol. 36v F   **37** decipiunt|fol. 48ra P   **67** erant|fol. 48rb P

De Abel. quod patres et prophete ueteris testamenti non sunt salui

[**Patarenus:**] Ad hebreos penultimo. melius loquentem quam abel etcet. hic inuenit quod Abel non fuit bonus si christus melius locutus est quam ipse.

Catholicus: Respondeo secundum hoc nullus erit saluus. quia in omnibus omnis excedit ihesus. obmutesce sanctorum detractor quem diabolus infatuauit. potius enim debuisti dicere quod ex hoc solo potest intelligi quod abel fuerit sanctus. si aliunde nulla de sua sanctitate haberetur quia domino ihesu christo utrumque comparatur ab apostolo.

De enoc

[**Patarenus:**] De enoc legitur quod ipse ambulant cum deo et nusquam comparuit a principio mundi quando nullus intrabat in regnum celorum etiam secundum omnis quare uidetur quod fuerit illusus sicut malus homo a deo illo qui decepit multos.

Catholicus: Respondeo quod ambulauit cum deo quo deus uoluit .licet non in paradisum celestem. tu atque detrahis ei. unde deberes illum comendare scilicet quia legitur eum cum deo ambulasse.

De noe

[**Patarenus:**] Noe inebriatus et denudatus. ergo malus fuit.

Catholicus: Respondeo non enim omnis ebrietas est mortale peccatum. Alioquin et tu forte sepissime peccasti mortaliter.

De melchisedech

[**Patarenus:**] De Melchisedech legitur quod non habuit principium neque finem. quare uidetur quod fuerit malus et uidetur quod fuerit diabolus.

Catholicus: Respondeo. sed hoc nullo mali conicitur in eo. quidem dictum ut supra. titulum in primo. in parte tua notatum inuenies.

De loth

Patarenus: Loth inebrietatus est et comisit incestum cum filiabus.

Catholicus: Respondeo quia illa ebrietas non fuit ei mortale peccatum. cum prima et ultima fuerit. quia nusquam legitur ipsum alias inebriatum fore. et per consequentiam nec ille coitus fuit ei incestus quia non discernebat quid faceret.

De Job

[**Patarenus:**] Job fuit impatiens et blasphemus.

On Abel, that the fathers and prophets of the Old Testament were not saved

[**Pat:**] In the penultimate chapter of Hebrews (12:24) "which speaks better than that of Abel." Here one discovers that Abel was not good if Christ was spoken of as better than he.

Cath: I reply that according to this no one at all will be saved since Jesus exceeds all others. Silence then, O disparager of the saints, whom the devil made a fool of, for you ought rather to say that by this that one is only able to understand that Abel was a saint, if there is no other with such sanctity, as to be compared to the Lord Jesus Christ by the Apostle.

On Enoch

[**Pat:**] Regarding Enoch it is read that he walked with God and on no occasion is there evidence from the beginning of the world when no one at all entered into the kingdom of heaven, also according to all, whence it seems that he was mocked as an evil man by that god who deceived many.

Cath: I reply that he walked with God by that which God willed, although not in the celestial paradise. Whereas you disparage him, when you ought to commend him, namely, because it is read that he walked with God.

On Noah

[**Pat:**] Noah was drunk and naked, therefore he was evil.

Cath: I reply that not all intoxication is a mortal sin, otherwise you also would by chance have often sinned mortally.

On Melchizedek

[**Pat:**] Regarding Melchizedek it is read that he had neither beginning nor end, whence it seems that he was evil and it seems that he was the devil

Cath: I respond. But to this no evil was attributed in him, indeed as was said above in the first section, which you may find noted in your part.

On Lot

Pat: Lot was drunk and committed incest with his daughters.

Cath: I reply that his drunkenness was not a mortal sin for him since it was his first and last time, because it is never read that any other episode of drunkenness for him exists, and as a consequence neither was that intercourse incest for him since he could not distinguish what it was he was doing.

On Job

[**Pat:**] Job was impatient and blasphemous.

VII.25.3 melius...4 abel] Heb. 12:24.

VII.26.2 enoc] noe *P*   5 illusus] illius *F*   VII.28.5 sed] de *F*   6 dictum] om. *F*   VII.29.1 De loth] om. *P*   6 inebriatum] sui *P* exp.
VII.30.2 blasphemus] blasfemus *P*

VII.27.4 ebrietas|fol. 37r *F*   VII.28.6 quidem|fol. 48va *P*

Catholicus: Respondeo quod ipse fuit patientissimus licet fuerit turbatus. Non enim omnis turbatio iudicatur impatientia. de domino enim legitur cum tristitia et furore respexit. item non blasphemauit diem uel noctem naturalem. sed tantum diem et noctem peccati. preterea non omnis maledictio peccatum est. nam et dominus maledixit ficui.

De abraham et moyses et samuel et dauid

[**Patarenus:**] Abraham et moyses et samuel et dauid et alii reges et helyseas fuerunt homicide.
Catholicus: Respondeo quod falsum est. Sed iustitie fuerunt ei executores sicut dei ministri contra filios iniquitatis.

De iacob

Patarenus:] Iacob fuit mendax et deceptor fratris.
Catholicus: Respondeo quod hoc falsum est. quoniam uerum dicebat quando dicebat se esse esau scilicet quantum ad id quod pater querebat id est ad benedictionem recipiendam. Nec deceptor fratrem. quia ius erat suum quod uendicabat. qua esau iam dudum ius progenitorum uendiderat illi.
[**Patarenus:**] Item abraham et dauid consimiles habuerunt concubinas pariter cum uxoribus ergo fuerunt adulteri.
Catholicus: Respondeo quod omnes que dicuntur concubine illorum uxores erant que dicebatur minores uxores et concubine et licebat tunc temporis habere plures uxores.

De heliseo

[**Patarenus:**] Helyseus impetrauit mortem pueris per lacerationem ursorum.
Catholicus: Respondeo quia uidebat per spiritum sanctum. ita debere contingere illis a domini uindictam propter illorum peccatum et ideo non fuit. imprecatio uel maledictio sed prophetia. Tu autem sanctorum obtrectator noli sanctos dei blasfemare sed conuertere ad aliquid sanctorum illorum humiliter. ut pro tua salute deum ponetur in celis.

De beata uirgine Maria quod fuerit mulier

Tractatum est supra de natura diuinitatis et de ueteri testamento. subsequenter tractande est de humana natura quam deus assumpsit et de fide noui testamenti. sed quia mater precedit filium. primus uidenda est de benedicta matre cuius filius extitit deus. hoc est de beata uergine maria. Circa quam periclitantur patareni miserabiliter ipsam negantes feminam fuisse et per consequentiam matrem esse dei minime recognoscunt.

Cath: I reply that he was most patient although he was troubled. For not all disturbances of the soul are judged as impatience. Of the Lord it is read that He looked back with sadness and anger. Also he did not blaspheme natural day or night, but only the day and night of sin. Further not every curse is a sin, for example, when the Lord cursed the fig tree.

On Abraham and Moses and Samuel and David

[**Pat:**] Abraham and Moses and Samuel and David and other kings, and Elijah, were killers.
Cath: I answer that it is false, rather they were executors of justice as ministers of God against the sons of iniquity.

On Jacob

[**Pat:**] Jacob was a liar, a deceiver of his brother.
Cath: I say that this is false, because he spoke truly when he called himself Esau, namely, insofar as that which his father asked, that is, for the reception of the blessing. Neither was he a deceiver of his brother, since the right was his to sell, by which Esau had long since sold to him the right of his parents.

[**Pat:**] Also Abraham and David similarly had concubines together with wives, therefore they were adulterers.

Cath: I reply that all those who are called their concubines were their wives who were called lesser wives and concubines, and it was permitted at that time to have many wives.

On Elisha

[**Pat:**] Elisha prayed for the death of boys by the mauling of bears.
Cath: I reply that he foresaw by the Holy Spirit, so it ought to happen to them in vindication from the Lord on account of their sins, and so it was not an imprecation or curse, but a prophecy. Yet you, O Critic of the saints, cease to blaspheme the saints of God but turn humbly towards some of those saints, so that for your salvation they may pray to God that you might be admitted in heaven.

That the Blessed Virgin Mary was woman

The section above was on the nature of divinity and of the Old Testament, the following section will treat of the human nature which God assumed, and of the faith of the New Testament, but since the Mother precedes the Son, the first thing one ought to look at is the Blessed Mother whose Son came forth as God. This is the Blessed Virgin Mary, about whom the Pataranes miserably attempt to deny that she was a woman and, consequently, they do not

---

5 de] ut *F* 6 blasphemauit] blasfemauit *P* **VII.31.1** abraham] abraam *P* 2 Abraham] Abraam *P* **VII.32.7** erat suum] transp. *F*
12 omnes] add. ille *F* **VII.23.2** impetrauit] imprecauit *P* 5 domini] *sic PF* **leg. domino** 9 aliquid] aliquam *F* | sanctorum] om. *F*
illorum] om. *P* 10 ponetur] deponetur *F* **VIII.1.8** ipsam negantes] transp. *F*

VII.32.11 adulteri|fol. 48vb *P*

delirant namque blasphemantes. ipsam esse angelum nomine Marinum. quorum imprudentiam obmutescere faciemus per testimonia scripturarum sanctarum. Mattheus. i°. jacob autem genuit ioseph uirum marie de qua natus est ihesus qui uocatur christus. cum dicit ipsam mariam innuit eam non fuisse angelum marinum prout blasphematis pessimi demoniaci. Item cum eam dicit fuisse uxorem ioseph sicut et plurisquam locis sancti euangelii leguntur manifeste declarat eam mulierem fuisse. mulierum enim est nubere et non angelorum. presertim cum dominus dicit de sanctis hominibus. neque nubent neque nubentur. sed erunt sicut angeli dei etcet. item cum dicit de quam euidenter denominant fuisse eam feminam non angelum. qui enim uel qua femini sexus est significatio in humana natura. alioquin si angelis fuisset dixisset de quo. quia angeli semper in scripturis sacris nominibus masculinus nominantur. Item in eodem. antequam conuenirent in utero habens etcet. et in lucam. ii°. legitur de ioseph quod ascendit in betleem ut profiteretur cum maria sibi desponsata uxore pregnante etcet. igitur fuit mulier beata uirgo et non angelis. Quis enim audiuit umquam o insensate gazare angelum esse pregnante. Item lucam. i°. ecce helysabeth cognata tua etcet. ergo non fuit angelus. sed mulier. angelus enim non est cognatus uel cognata. cum inter angelos uel inter homines et angelos non sit gradus consanguinitatis. nisi forte insaniendo uelles dicere inter eos carnalem esse coitum. Item in eodem supra. aue gratia plena dominus tecum benedicta tu in mulieribus et benedictus etcet. et infra. benedicta tu inter mulieres et benedictus fructus uentris tui etcet. Si enim non esset mulier. non uideo qua ratione uel quo priuilegio benedicta inter mulieres spiritualiter diceretur. item in eodem. et ait Maria. Magnificat anima mea dominum etcet. ibi quia respexit humilitatem ancille sue etcet. et supra in eodem dixerat ad angelum. ecce ancilla domini etcet. in quibus uerbis ipsamet profitetur se feminam esse. item infra. xi. extollens uocem quedam mulier de turba dixit illi. Beatus uenter qui te portauit et ubera que supsisti etcet. ista uerba numquam angelice nature conuenire possunt. angeli enim neque in uentre portant neque habent ubera. sed tantum proprium est femine. igitur femina fuit. item. xviiii. cum uidisset ergo ihesus matrem et discipulum stantem quem diligebat dicit matri sue. mulier etcet. non dixit angele uel uir. sed aperte apellauit eam ueritas mulierem et euangelista scripsit eam esse matrem

recognize her to be the Mother of God. For instance they rave blasphemously that she was an angel named Marinum.[1] Their ignorance we will make silent by the testimony of the Holy Scriptures. Matthew 1 (1:16) "And Jacob begot Joseph the husband of Mary, of whom was born Jesus, who is called Christ." When he calls her "Mary" he nods to the fact that she was not the angel Marinum, just as you wicked demoniacs blaspheme. Also when he says she was the wife of Joseph, just as is read in many places in the holy Gospels, it manifestly declares her to be a woman. For to marry belongs to women and not angels, especially when the Lord says of holy men (Mt 22:30) "neither shall they marry, or be given in marriage, for they shall be like the angels of God." Also when He plainly says that they always called her a woman and not an angel, for the female sex is signified only in human nature, He would have said otherwise if the angels were what He was speaking of, since angels are always called in the Sacred Scriptures by masculine names. Also in the same (Mt 1:18) "before they came together, she was found with child," and in Luke 2 it is read (Lk 2:4–5) "And Joseph also went up from Galilee, out of the city of Nazareth into Judea, to the city of David, which is called Bethlehem, because he was of the house and family of David, to be enrolled with Mary his espoused wife, who was with child." Therefore the Blessed Virgin was a woman and not an angel. For who ever heard, O senseless Cathar,[2] an angel to be pregnant? Also Luke 1 (1:36) "Behold Elizabeth your cousin," therefore she was no angel but a woman, for there are no male or female relations between angels, or between men and angels there is no grade of consanguinity, except perhaps in your insanity you wish to say that there is carnal intercourse between them. Also in the same above (1:28) "Hail full of grace, the Lord is with you, blessed are you among women, and blessed," and later (1:42) "blessed are you among women, and blessed is the fruit of your womb." If she had not been a woman, I cannot see by what reason or what privilege one might spiritually call her 'blessed among women.' Also in the same (Lk 1:46,48) "and Mary said, 'My soul magnifies the Lord,'" and "'because he has looked upon the lowliness of his handmaid.'" Also in the same (1:38) "She said to the angel, 'Behold the handmaid of the Lord.'" In these words especially it declares her to be a woman. Also later 11 (11:27) "a certain woman from the crowd, lifting up her voice, said to him, 'Blessed is the womb that bore you, and the breasts that nursed you.'" One cannot harmonize these words with an angelic nature, for angels neither carry in their wombs nor have breasts, but these are only proper to women, therefore she was a woman. Also 19 (Jn 19:26) "When Jesus therefore had seen his mother and the

---

VIII.1.13 jacob…14 christus] Matt. 1:16. 21 neque¹…22 dei] Matt. 22:30. 28 antequam…habens] Matt. 1:18. 29 de…31 pregnante] Luc. 2:4-5. 33 ecce…34 tua] Luc. 1:36. 39 aue…40 benedictus] Luc. 1:28. 40 benedicta…41 tui] Luc. 1:42. 44 et…46 sue] Luc. 1:46, 48. 46 dixerat…47 domini] Luc. 1:38. 48 extollens…50 supsisti] Luc. 11:27. 54 cum…55 mulier] Ioh. 19:26.

---

16 blasphematis] blasfematis P 23 denominant] om. P 24 femini] feminini F 27 masculinus nominantur] transp. P 32 umquam] unquam P 34 sed] ergo P 44 item…46 supra] om. P 51 conuenire] add. non P exp.

VIII.1.11 imprudentiam|fol. 37v F 13 ioseph|fol. 49ra P 39 aue|fol. 49rb P

---

1) Burci, 313; Sacconi, c. 17, 24, 25. | 2) Could perhaps be *gazare* "sorcerer." See du Cange, t. 4, col. 049a.

ihesu. ergo mulier fuit uirgo maria. item paulus ad galatas. iiii. misit deus filium suum factum ex muliere etcet. non dixit ex angelo. ex hiis patet euidenter quod beata uirgo maria fuit femina secundum quam naturam fuit mater dei que fuit eius gloria pariter et nostra. a quam pessimi canes patareni dogmatizant fore priuatam. Sunt autem inter eos aliqui qui dicunt ipsam mulierem fuisse. qui tamen negant. sicut et alii. Christum de ipsa carnem traxisse et nota quod omnes auctoritates faciunt ad probandam beatam uirginem fore mulierem. quas introducemus infra de christi humanitate.

Quod beata uirgo maria non fuit mulier

[**Patarenus:**] Lucam. xi. at ille dixit. quin immo beati qui audiunt uerbum dei etcet. uide quia cum illa dixerat de maria. beatus uenter qui te portauit ubera etcet. Christus dixit quin immo etcet. quasi diceret. non me portauit uenter. sed beati qui audiuit etcet.
Catholicus: Respondeo quod non referuntur uerba christi ad illa uerba et substantia sed ad illud. sed ad uerbum scilicet beatus etcet. ac si diceret. non solum est beatus uenter cum suis uberibus qui me portauit sed etiam omnis qui audiunt uerbum dei. sed dic tu heretice que nam illatio esset illa non portauit me uenter nec suxi ubera immo beati qui audiuit uerbum dei etcet. nimis enim aliena esset et peregrina.

[**Patarenus:**] Item actus. i°. hi omnes erant perseuerantes unanimiter in oratione cum mulieribus et maria matre ihesu etcet. ecce quod segreganti a mulieribus nominat mariam matre ihesu. igitur non fuit mulier.

Catholicus: Respondeo quod tale est hoc locutio quale fuit angelica illa. marco ultimo dicite discipulis eius et petro etcet. non sequitur propter hoc quod petrus non fuerit discipulis. uocat ergo per se a mulieribus beatus lucas matrem dei nomine suo propter exellentem dignitatem ipsius. proprie enim mulieres dicuntur corrupte. hinc est quod ipse lucam. scripsit in euangelio suo. primo. Missus est angelis gabriel etcet. ibi. ad uirginem etcet. non dixit ad mulierem. sed tu respondeas mihi. hic dicit lucam cum maria matre ihesu etcet. ergo dicit eam esse feminam et non angelum. nusquam enim angelis nuncupatur mater.

disciple standing whom he loved, he said to his mother, 'Woman'" He did not say 'angel' or 'man,' but clearly called her true woman and the evangelist wrote that she was the mother of Jesus. Therefore the Virgin Mary was a woman. Also Paul to the Galatians 4 (4:4) "God sent his son, born of a woman," he did not say from an angel. From these it is plainly evident that the Blessed Virgin Mary was a woman according to which nature she was the Mother of God which was her glory equally and ours, about whom wicked Patarene dogs teach in private.[1] There are yet among them some who say that she was a woman, who yet deny, just like the others, that Christ took flesh from her.[2] And note that all authorities adduced for proving the Blessed Virgin to be a woman which we shall introduce below regarding the humanity of Christ.

That the Blessed Virgin Mary was not a woman

[**Pat:**] Luke 11 (11:28) "he said to her, 'Rather how much more blessed are they who hear the word of God,'" see that since He is speaking of Mary "blessed is the womb that bore thee and the breasts," Christ said 'rather,' as if to say, "no womb bore me, but blessed are they who hear."
Cath: I reply that the words of Christ do not refer to that word and substance, but rather to this word, namely, 'blessed,' as if He might have said "not only is the womb blessed with her breasts who bore me, but also all who hear the word of God." But tell me, you heretic, what would be the inference, "she did not bear me in her womb, nor nurse me with her breasts, rather blessed is he who hears the word of God," for it would be exceedingly strange and foreign.

[**Pat:**] Also Acts 1 (1:14) "These all were persevering with one mind in prayer with the women and with Mary the mother of Jesus." See that she is separated from the women, by naming Mary the mother of Jesus, therefore she was not a woman.

Cath: I reply that this phrase is just like that of the angel at the end of Mark (Mk 16:7) "But go, tell his disciples and Peter." It does not follow on account of this that Peter was not a disciple, therefore blessed Luke calls on her by name particularly among the women, the Mother of God, on account of her preeminent dignity, for women are properly called corrupt. Hence this is what Luke himself wrote in his gospel in the first chapter (1:26) "the angel Gabriel was sent," and "to a virgin," he did not say "to a woman." But answer me this, Luke says here "with Mary the mother of Jesus," therefore he calls her woman and not angel, for never is an angel called mother.

---

59 misit...muliere] Gal. 4:4.   VIII.2.2 at...3 dei] Luc. 11:28.   15 hi...17 ihesu] Act. 1:14.   20 dicite...21 petro] Mar. 16:7.
26 Missus...gabriel] Luc. 1:26.

63 nostra] materia F | dogmatizant] devorant P   VIII.2.3 illa] add. mulier F   6 non me] nonne F   7 referuntur] add. illa P exp.
8 substantia] verba P | sed² ...9 uerbum] om. F   11 dei] om. P   23 exellentem] exxellentiam P   24 ipsius] om. P   30 nuncupatur mater] transp. F

63 pessimi|fol. 49va P   VIII.2.3 audiunt|fol. 38r F   19 tale|fol. 49vb P

---

1) Mary was such a popular figure among medieval Catholics, that Cathars made known these doctrines only among their inner circles. | 2) A doctrine of the mitigated dualists, see Sacconi, c. 25.

[Patarenus:] Preterea nusquam in scripura noui testamenti uel etiam ueteris legitur. quis eius pater uel mater fuerit. quare uidetur quod fuerit angelis.
Catholicus: Respondeo. nec de parentibus symonis et iude ac baratholomeum. et quam plurimum aliorum apostolorum et discipulorum in testamentis legitur et tamen propter hoc non negas eos homines fuisse. sed intellige stulte. quod non omnia que fuerit. non dico de beata uirgine. sed etiam de ipso christo. scripta sunt in nouo uel ueteri testamento. per euangelium satis innuitur quod beata uirgo carnale habuit genealogiam. ut mattheus. i° liber generationis ihesu christi etcet. et postea iacob genuit ioseph uirum marie de qua natus est ihesus qui etcet. quia posito quod illa genealogia christi de qua fuit ioseph. et de ioseph christus non sit natus et posito quod de uirgine maria natus est. intelligitur poni manifeste quod beata uirgo fuit de genealogia ioseph. item cum ipsa dicatur cognata helisabeth ut supra probauimus aperte. patet ipsam habuisse genealogiam et per consequentiam eam habuisset patrem et matrem. quod legimus alibi. fuisse ioachim et annam. sed dic mihi tu miser ypocrita quare negas beatam uirginie mulierem esse? eo quod in ueteri testamento uel nouo de parentibus eius non legatur. cum utriusque testamenti scriptura clamitet uniuersa. de parentibus ihesu christi scilicet de deo patre et marie uirgine ipsius matre et tamen ipsum dei et uirginis filium esse minime recognoscas.

[Pat:] Further never it is read in the Old or New Testaments who her father or mother was, so it seems she was an angel.
Cath: I respond that it is never read of the parents of Simon and Jude and Bartholomew and many other Apostles and disciples in the testaments, and yet on account of this you do not deny that they were men, but understand, O fool, that not all things were written in the Old or New Testaments, I speak not only of the Blessed Virgin, but also of Christ Himself. In the gospels it is enough to mention that the Blessed Virgin had an earthly genealogy, as in Matthew 1 (1:1) "The book of the generations of Jesus Christ." and later (1:16) "Jacob begot Joseph, the husband of Mary, from whom was born Jesus." Since it is established that the genealogy of Christ of which He was of Joseph, and Christ was not born from Joseph, and it is established that He was born of the Virgin Mary. It is understood plainly to be established that the Blessed Virgin was of the genealogy of Joseph. Also since she is called the cousin of Elizabeth, as we proved above, it is clear that she had a genealogy and, consequently, she had a father and mother, whom we read elsewhere were Joachim and Anne. But tell me you miserable hypocrite, why do you deny that the Blessed Virgin was a true woman for the reason that her parents are not mentioned in either the Old or New Testaments, since both scriptures might cry out universally of the parents of Jesus Christ, namely, of God the Father and of the Virgin Mary, His mother, and you ought to at least recognize Him to be the Son of God and of the Virgin.

De beato Iohanne baptista quod fuerit bonus et saluus et quod fuerit angelus bonus annunciator eius

Quoniam beatus Iohannes baptista precursor fuit filii hominis. prius de ipso discutiamus. Quem quidam ex patarenis blasfemant fuisse diabolum quemdam. quidam autem ex illis delirant quod fuerit unus de spiritibus saluandis credunt quod fuerit spiritus helie qui non fuerit tunc saluus. sed in fine mundi saluabitur. et dicunt isti quod ipse missus a diabolo ad impediendam uiam Christi. alii uero garriunt quod fuerit angelus bonus a deo missus. in hoc tamen omnes concordant quod non fuerit homo sed angelus. de angelo uero annunciatione. ipsius quidam aiunt ipsum bonum. quidam uero ipsum malum fuisse. Nos autem

IX On Blessed John the Baptist, that he was good and saved, and that the angel that announced his birth was good

Because Blessed John the Baptist was the forerunner of the Son of Man, we will examine him first. Certain of the Patarenes blaspheme that he was a particular devil.[1] Yet others among them rave that he was one of the saved spirits, they believe that he was the spirit of Elijah who was not then saved, but who shall be saved at the end of the world. And these say that he was sent by the devil to hinder the way of Christ. Others yet babble that he was a good angel sent by God, yet all agree that he was no man, but an angel.[2] Of the angel of the annunciation, regarding him certain ones say he was good, yet others that he was evil.[3] We shall

---

42 liber...christi] Matt. 1:1.   43 iacob...44 qui] Matt. 1:16.

---

35 ac] ad P   38 intellige] add. eos P exp. | quod] quia F   49 probauimus] probamus F   51 et matrem] om. P   55 testamenti] om. P
IX.1.1 fuerit] fuit F   6 patarenis] parentibus F   8 credunt] et dicunt F   9 sed in] add. marg. sin. alia manu P privilegia et laudibile joh. babte et de conceptionem suam   12 in...13 angelus] om. P   14 annunciatione] sic PF leg. annunciationis

42 etcet|fol. 50ra P   IX.1.9 fine|fol. 50rb P   10 et|fol. 38v F

---

1) Sacconi, c. 17; Moneta, 227ff. | 2) The mitigated dualists of Concorezzo, Sacconi, c. 24; Moneta, 231. | 3) Moneta, 225ff.

ea que in rubrica de ipso continentur. per sacras scripturas testamenti probabimus euidenter.

Quod beatus iohannes fuit bonus et sanctus

Quod autem beatus iohannes fuerit bonus et sanctus per xviii. priuilegia que habuit potest manifeste probari. quorum primum occurrit quod per sanctos prophetas scilicet ysaia et malachi. fuit dudum antea preuisum et prenuntiatum eius sanctitatis officium. Mattheus. iii. hic est enim qui dictus est per ysaiam prophetam. uox clamantis in deserto etcet. quod enim in ysaias xl. uox clamantis in deserto parate uiam domini etcet. mattheus. xi. hic est enim de quo scriptum est ecce ego mitto angelum meum ante faciem tuam qui preparabit uiam tuam ante te. et hoc in malachia. iiiº. ecce ego mitto angelum meum etcet. secundum est. quia de sanctis parentibus ortus est. lucam. iº. erant ambo iusti ante deum incendentes in omnibus mandatis et iustificationibus sine querela etcet. tertium est quia ab illo celesti paranimfo. scilicet angelo gabriele. eius conceptio et natiuitas prenuntiata est. a quo filii dei incarnatio et natiuitas nascitur annuntiata. lucam. iº. ait autem ad illum angelus. Ne timeas zacharia quoniam exaudita est deprecatio tua et helisabeth uxor tua pariet tibi filium et uocabitur nomen eius iohannes etcet. et infra. ego sum gabriel qui asto ante deum etcet. et quod fuerit ille qui adnuntiauerit christi aduentum. lege in eodem capitulo lucam. ibi. in mense autem sexto. missus est angelus gabriel a deo in ciuitate galilee etcet. Quartum est quia miraculose conceptus et natus est. quia de sterili et senibus. lucam. iº. non erat filius eo quod esset helisabeth sterilis et ambo processent in diebus suis etcet. Quintum est quia repletus est spiritu sancto ex utero matris sue. lucam. iº. et spiritu sancto replebitur adhuc ex utero matris sue etcet. Sextum est quia in uentre matris existens cognouit matrem filii dei et ipsum dei filium ad uocem maternam exaltauit pre gaudio et in eius exclamatione. mater ipsius repleta est spiritu sancto ut cognosceret et ipsa matrem dei una cum eius filio. lucam. iº. et factum est ut audiuit salutationem marie helisabeth exaltauit in gaudio infans in utero eius et repleta est spiritu sancto helisabeth exclamauit uoce magna dixit. Benedicta tu inter mulieres et benedictus fructus uentris tue. unde hoc mihi ut ueniat mater domini mei ad me? ecce enim etcet. Septimum est de nomini excellenti et quod ei ab angel fuit imponitum et uocabitur nomen eius iohannes etcet. Octauum est. quia factum est

That Blessed John was good and holy

That Blessed John was good and holy is absolutely able to be proven by the eighteen privileges that he had. Of these, the first that comes to mind is that through it was through the holy prophets, namely, Isaiah and Malachi, that his holy office was formerly foreseen and prophesied. Matthew 3 (3:3) "For this is he who was spoken of by Isaiah the prophet, saying, 'A voice of one crying in the desert.'" For this is in Isaiah 40 (40:3) "A voice crying in the desert, prepare the way of the Lord." Matthew 11 (11:10) "For this is he of whom it is written, 'Behold I send my angel before your face, who shall prepare your way before you.'" And this in Malachi 3 (3:1) "Behold I send my angel." The second is that he had his origin from holy parents. Luke 1 (1:6) "And they were both just before God, walking in all the commandments and ordinances of the Lord without blame." The third is because of that heavenly witness, namely, the angel Gabriel. For his conception and birth was foretold by him whom the incarnation and birth of the Son of God came to be announced. Luke 1 (1:13) "But the angel said to him, 'Fear not, Zachariah, for your prayer is heard and your wife Elizabeth will bear you a son, and you shall call his name John.'" And later (1:19) "I am Gabriel, who stands before God," and that it was he who announced the coming of Christ, is read in the same chapter of Luke (1:26) "In the sixth month, the angel Gabriel was sent by God to a city in Galilee." The fourth is his miraculous conception and birth, from an old, barren woman. Luke 1 (1:7) "As there was no son because Elizabeth was barren" and (1:18) "and both are advanced in years." The fifth is that he was filled with the Holy Spirit from the womb of his mother. Luke 1 (1:15) "and he shall be filled with the Holy Spirit, even from his mother's womb." The sixth is that while still in his mother's womb he recognized the mother of the Son of God, and the Son of God Himself and exulted from the voice of His mother for joy and in her exclamation. The mother herself was filled with the Holy Spirit since she had recognized the Mother of God along with her Son. Luke 1 (1:41–44) "And it came to pass, that when Elizabeth heard Mary's greeting, the infant leaped in her womb. And Elizabeth was filled with the Holy Spirit and she cried out with a loud voice, and said, 'Blessed are you among women, and blessed is the fruit of your womb, and how does it come to be that the mother of my Lord should come to me? For behold.'" The seventh is of the excellent name that the angel gave to him (1:13) "and you shall call his name John." The eighth is that a great miracle was worked at the

---

IX.2.7 hic…8 deserto] Matt. 3:3.   9 uox…10 domini] Is. 40:3.   10 hic…12 te] Matt. 11:10.   13 ecce…meum] Mal. 3:1.   15 erant…16 querela] Luc. 1:6.   20 ait…23 iohannes] Luc. 1:13 (iohannes) iohannem *Vulg.*)   23 ego…24 deum] Luc. 1:19.   26 in…27 galilee] Luc. 1:26.   30 ambo…31 suis] Luc. 1:18.   32 et…33 sue] Luc. 1:15.   38 et…44 enim] Luc. 1:41-44.   45 et…46 iohannes] Luc. 1:13.

IX.2.1 fuit] om. *P*   4 quod] quia *F*   14 est²] add. sanctorum *P*   15 ambo iusti] transp. *F*   16 iustificationibus] alia manu, sup. domini *P*   17 paranimfo] paranimpho *F (from paranymphus, a groomsman, see Augustine,* De civ. Dei, *14.18)*   20 annuntiata] adnuntiata *P*   22 helisabeth] elysabet *F*   26 sexto] vi *P*   34 cognouit] cognoscens *P*

IX.2.19 incarnatio|fol. 50va *P*   42 et|fol. 50vb *P*

miraculum magnum in eius nominis manifestatione quia locus est mutus et prophetauit. lucam. i°. postulans pugillarem scriptsit dicens. iohannes est nomen eius. et mirati sunt uniuersi. apertum est autem illico os eius et lingua eius et loquebatur etcet. et infra. repletus est spiritu sancto et prophetauit dicens. benedictus dominus deus israel etcet. Nouum est gaudium et congratulatio et timor que apparuerunt circa manifestationem ipsius lucam. i°. tunc gaudium erit et exultatio et multi in natiuitate eius gaudebunt etcet. et infra. audierunt uicini et cognati eius quia magnificauit dominus misericordiam suam cum illa etcet. et infra. et factus est timor super omnes uicinos eorum etcet. Decimum est asperitas uite que fuit in eo speciale in cibo et potu et uestibus et in stramine et in domo et per consequentiam pura castitas. lucam. i°. uinum et siceram non bibet et vii sed quid existis in desertum uidere hominem mollibus uestibus indutum. ecce qui in ueste pretiosa sunt et in deliciis in domibus regum sunt. etcet. Et infra. uenit enim iohannes baptista neque manducans panem neque bibens uinum. etcet. et Mattheus. iii. ipse autem iohannes habebat uestimentum de pilis camellorum et zonam pelliceam circa lumbos eius. escam autem eius erat locuste et mel siluestre. undecimum est prerogatiua precursionis celestis imperatoris et saluatoris mundi quia fuit precursor eius in spiritu et uirtute helie. lucam. i°. et ipse precedet ante illum in spiritu et uirtute helie. ut conuertat corda patrum in filios et incredulos ad prudentiam iustorum parare domino plebem perfectam etcet. et mattheus xi. ecce ego mitto angelum meum ante faciem tuam qui preparabit uiam tuam etcet. Duodecimum est dignitas baptizandi saluatorem. Mattheus. iii°. Tunc uenit ihesus a galilea in iordanem ad iohannem ut baptizaretur ab eo etcet. et marcum. i°. uenit ihesus a nazareth galilee et baptizatur est a iohanne etcet. Tertium decimum est. elegans officium predicationis quod excercuit tam ueraciter quam utiliter quod apparuit maxime in tribus scilicet in predicando baptismum propter assuefactionem ad christi baptismam et propter penitentiam ad quam uenientes inuitabat. secundo in reprehendendo uitia et peccatam et ad regnum celorum ortando penitentes. tertio in fide domini nostri ihesu christi docenda. ut leguntur. mattheum. iii°. et baptizabantur ab eo in iordane confitentes peccata sua. uidens autem multos phariseorum et sadduceorum uenitentes ad baptismum suum dixit eis. Gemina uiperarum etcet. usque ibi. tunc uenit ihesus etcet. lucam. i°. et multos filiorum israel conuertet ad dominum deum ipsorum

revelation of his name, by which the mute spoke and prophesied. Luke 1 (1:63–64) "And demanding a writing tablet, he wrote, saying, 'John is his name.' And they all marveled and immediately his mouth was opened, and his tongue loosed, and he spoke, blessing God." And later (1:67–68) "And he was filled with the Holy Spirit; and he prophesied, saying, 'Blessed be the Lord God of Israel.'" The ninth is the joy and well wishes and fear which appeared around his manifestation, Luke 1 (1:14) "And you will have joy and gladness, and many shall rejoice in his nativity," and later (1:58) "And her neighbors and kinsfolk heard that the Lord had shown his great mercy towards her," and later (1:65) "And fear came upon all their neighbors." The tenth is the austerity of life that he demonstrated, particularly in food and drink, in clothing, and in bedding, and in housing, and, consequently, in perfect chastity. Luke 1 (1:15) "he shall drink no wine nor strong drink," and 7 (7:25) "But what did you go out to see? A man clothed in soft garments? Behold those who are in costly apparel and live delicately are in the houses of kings." And later (7:33) "For John the Baptist came neither eating bread nor drinking wine." And Matthew 3 (3:4) "And the same John had his garment of camel's hair, and a leather girdle about his loins, and his meat was locusts and wild honey." The eleventh was the prerogative of being the forerunner of the heavenly emperor and savior of the world since he was his precursor in the spirit and power of Elijah. Luke 1 (1:17) "And he shall go before him in the spirit and power of Elijah, so that he may turn the hearts of the fathers to the children, and the incredulous to the wisdom of the just, to prepare for the Lord a perfect people." And Matthew 11 (11:10) "Behold I send my angel before my face who will prepare your way before you." The twelfth is that he had the dignity of baptizing the Savior. Matthew 3 (3:13) "Then Jesus came from Galilee to the Jordan, to John, to be baptized by him." And Mark 1 (1:9) "Jesus came from Nazareth in Galilee and was baptized by John." The thirteenth is the fine office of preaching that he exercised, that it was as true as it was useful, which is apparent especially in three ways, namely, in preaching baptism so as to accustom people to the baptism of Christ, and on account of penitence towards which he invited those who came. The second in upbraiding vices and sins and in exhorting penitents to the kingdom of heaven. The third in teaching the faith of our Lord Jesus Christ, as is read in Matthew 3 (3:6–7) "And they were baptized by him in the Jordan, confessing their sins, and seeing many of the Pharisees and Sadducees coming to his baptism, he said to them, 'You brood of vipers,'" up to there (3:17) "then Jesus came." Luke 1 (1:16) "And he shall convert many of the children of Israel to the Lord their God." And 3 (3:7) "He said therefore to the

---

49 postulans...51 loquebatur] Luc. 1:63-64.   52 repletus...53 israel] Luc. 1:67-68.   55 tunc...56 gaudebunt] Luc. 1:14. 57 audierunt...58 illa] Luc. 1:58.   59 et²...60 eorum] Luc. 1:65.   63 uinum...bibet] Luc. 1:15. | sed...66 sunt] Luc. 7:25 (in desertum] om. *Vulg.*)   68 autem...71 siluestre] Matt. 3:4 (eius) suos | escam] esca *Vulg.*)   74 et¹...77 perfectam] Luc. 1:17. 77 ecce...79 tuam] Matt. 11:10 (tuam) add. ante te *Vulg.*)   80 Tunc...81 eo] Matt. 3:13.   82 uenit...83 iohanne] Mar. 1:9.   91 et... 94 uiperarum] Matt. 3:6-7 (Gemina) progenies *Vulg.*)   95 tunc...ihesus] Matt. 3:17. | et...96 ipsorum] Luc. 1:16.

---

68 ipse] ipsa *P*   81 iordanem] add. ut *P* exp.   91 ut] add. hec *P*

57 infra|fol. 39r *F*   66 etcet|fol. 51ra *P*   92 in|fol. 51rb *P*

etcet. et iii. dicebat ergo turbas qui exibant ut baptizarentur ab ipse. genimina uiperarum etcet. usque ibi. factum est autem etcet. et. iohanne. iº. fuit homo missus a deo cui nomen erat iohannes hic uenit in testimonium etcet. usque ibi. altera die etcet. Quartum decimum est profunda hu-militas que in eo fuit que apparuit. mattheus. iiiº. cum dixit ego quidem uos baptizo in aqua in penitentiam. qui autem post me uenturus est fortior me est. cuius non sum dignus calciamenta portare. etcet. et infra. iohannes prohibebat eum dicens. ego a te debeo baptizari et tu uenis a me etcet. et marcum. iº. et predicabat dicens uenit fortior post me cuius non sum dignus procumbens soluere corrigiam calciamentorum eius. et lucam. iiiº. ueniet autem fortior me etcet. et iohannes. iº. qui post me uenturus est ante me factus est etcet. et infra. et confessus est quia non sum ego christus etcet. et infra. quid dicis de teipso ait. ego uox clamantis in deserto. Quintum decimum est claritas et firmitas fide quam habuit de christo tam prophetando quam euangelizando. de fide quam habuit de christo prophando habes. Mattheus. iiiº. ubi dixit. qui autem post me uenturus. idem dicit mattheus. iº. et iohannes. iº. de fide autem quam habuit de christo euangelizando habes. iohannes. iº. ubi dicit ego uidi et testimonium perhibui quia hic est filius dei. altera die iterum stabat iohannes et ex discipulis eius duo et respiciens ihesum ambulantem dicit ecce agnus dei etcet. et. iiiº. respondit iohannes et dixit. non potest homo accipere quicquam etcet. usque ad finem capituli et propter hoc dicit dominus de ipso. sed quid existis uidere. prophetam etiam dico plusquam prophetam etcet. et lucam. vii. est idem. Sextum decimum est singularitas famili-aritas et amicitia quam habuit cum christo. unde ipse dicit in iohanne. iiiº. qui habet sponsam sponsus est. amicus autem sponsi qui stat et audit eum gaudio gaudet propter uocem sponsi. in hoc gaudium meum impletum est etcet. Septimum decimum est martirii felicitas ad quam peruenit propter iustitiam. lucam iiiº. herodes autem tetrarcha cum corriperetur ab illo. de herodiade uxore fratris sui. et de omnibus malis que herodes adiecit et hoc super omnia. inclusit iohannem in carcere etcet. et mattheus. xl. herodes tenuit iohannem et alligauit eum. etcet. et infra. misitque et decollauit iohannem in carcere et allatum est caput eius in disco. Octauum decimum priuilegium est canonizatio ipsius quam meruit habere a summo pontifice celesti domino ihesu christo quam fecit de ipso tam in uita eius quam post mortem collaudando eum et in cathologo sanctorum approban-

multitudes that went forth to be baptized by him, 'You offspring of vipers, who has showed you how to flee from the wrath to come?'" up to (3:21) "Now it came to pass." And John 1 (1:6–7) "There was a man sent by God whose name was John, he came to bear witness," up to (1:29) "the next day." The fourteenth is the profound humility that was in him whe He appeared, Matthew 3, when he said (3:11) "I indeed baptize you in the water for penance, but he who shall come after me is mightier than I, whose shoes I am not worthy to carry," and later (3:14) "But John tried to stop him, saying, 'I ought to be baptized by you, and you come to me?'" And Mark 1 (1:7) "And he preached, saying, 'There will come after me one mightier than I, the lace of whose shoes I am not worthy to stoop down and untie.'" And Luke 3 (3:16) "but there shall come one mightier than I." And John 1 (1:27) "The same is he who shall come after me, who was before me." And also (1:20) "and he confessed, 'I am not the Christ,'" and later (1:22–23) "'What do you say about yourself?' He said, 'I am the voice of one crying out in the wilderness.'" The fifteenth is the clarity and firmness of faith which he had regarding Christ, as much in prophesying as in evangelizing regarding the faith which he had in Christ. In prophesy-ing, you have Matthew 3 (3:11) where he said, "yet he who will come after me," the same thing Matthew says in chapter one and John in chapter one. Also of the faith which he had in Christ in evangelizing, you have John 1, where he says (1:34–36) "And I saw, and I gave testimony, that this is the Son of God. The next day again John stood with two of his disciples, and beholding Jesus walking, he said, 'Behold the Lamb of God.'" And in 3 (3:27) "John answered and said, 'A man cannot receive anything,'" up to the end of the chapter, and on account of this the Lord says of him (Mt 11:9) "But what did you go out to see? A prophet? Yes I tell you, and more than a prophet." And Luke 7 (7:26) is the same. The sixteenth is the singular familiarity and friendship which he had with Christ, whence he says in John 3 (3:29) "He who has the bride, is the bridegroom, but the friend of the bridegroom, who stands and hears him, rejoices with joy because of the bridegroom's voice. In this my joy is fulfilled." The seventeenth is the happy martyrdom which came to him on account of justice. Luke 3 (3:19–20) "But Herod the tetrarch, when he was reproved by him for Herodias, his brother's wife, and for all the evils which Herod had done, he added this also above all, and shut up John in prison." And Matthew 40 (14:3) "For Herod had apprehended John and bound him," and later (14:10–11) "And he sent and beheaded John in the prison, and his head was brought in a dish." The eighteenth privilege is his canoniz-

---

97 dicebat…98 uiperarum] Luc. 3:7. 99 factum…autem] Luc. 3:21. | fuit…101 testimonium] Ioh. 1:6-7. 101 altera die] Ioh. 1:29. 103 ego…106 portare] Matt. 3:11. 106 iohannes…107 me] Matt. 3:14. 108 et²…110 eius] Mar. 1:7. 110 ueniet…111 me¹] Luc. 3:16. 111 qui…112 est²] Ioh. 1:27. 112 et²…113 christus] Ioh. 1:20. 113 quid…114 deserto] Ioh. 1:22-23. 118 ubi…uenturus] Matt. 3:11. 121 ego…124 dei] Ioh. 1:34-36. 124 respondit…125 quicquam] Ioh. 3:27. 127 sed…128 prophetam] Matt. 11:9. 130 qui…133 est] Ioh. 3:29. 135 herodes…138 carcere] Luc. 3:19-20. 139 herodes…eum] Matt. 14:3. 140 misitque…141 disco] Matt. 14:10-11.

---

115 claritas…116 christo] om. F   129 amicitia] annotitia F   139 xl] sic FP   142 canonizatio] canonicatio F

119 iohannes|fol. 51va P   121 perhibui|fol. 39v F   145 approban-do|fol. 51vb P

do. de laude uite beati iohannis quam fecit ihesus christus. habes. mattheus. xi. amen dico uobis inter natos mulierum non surrexit maior iohanne baptista propterea nemo est. etcet. sileat ergo o heretice falsa glosa tua. quam facis super mattheus. maior iohanne baptista. etcet. ubi exponit dicens. maior propheta. uero de laude beati iohannes quam fecit christus post mortem eius. habes in iohannes. v°. uos misistis ad iohannem et testimo-nium perhibuit ueritati etcet. et infra ille erat lucerna ardens et lucens. uos autem uoluistis exultare ad horam in lucem eius etcet. et mattheus. xxi. uenit enim iohannes ad uos in uia iustitie et non credidistis ei. plublicani autem et meretrices crediderunt ei. uos autem uidentes nec penitentiam habuistis postea ut crederetis ei. etcet. ex hiis priuilegia quibus similia nullus sanctorum legitur habuisse. probatur aperte beatum iohannem sanctissi-mum fuisse quod quicumque negauerit contumaciter anathema sit. anathema ergo patarenus.

ation,[1] which he merited to have from the Supreme Pontiff of Heaven, the Lord Jesus Christ, which He did for him just as much as for his life as for his praise after death, and by approving him in the catalog of the saints. Of the praise which Jesus Christ made regarding the life of Blessed John, you have Matthew 11 (11:11) "Amen I say to you, there has not arisen among those that are born of women a greater than John the Baptist." Therefore may your false interpretation fall silent, O Heretic, which you make regarding [the passage in] Matthew, "greater than John the Baptist," where you explain saying "a greater prophet." Yet of the praise of Blessed John which Christ made after his death, you have John 5 (5:33) "You sent to John, and he gave testimony to the truth," and later (5:35) "He was a burning and a shining light, and you were willing for a time to rejoice in his light." And Matthew 21 (21:32) "For John came to you in the way of justice, and you did not believe him. But the publicans and the harlots believed him, but you, seeing it, did not even afterwards repent, that you might believe him." From these privileges, of which none of the saints is read to have had, it is plainly proven that Blessed John was sanctified, and that whoso-ever denies this is contumacious and anathema, therefore, so is the Patarene anathema.

Quod beatus iohannes fuerit homo

Quod beatus iohannes fuerit homo tribus rationibus probatur. prima est quia scriptura appellerat eum hominem. secundo quia necessitatibus humane nature fuerit usus. ut puta cibus et potibus et uestibus et huiusmodi. Tertia est quod legitur captus et occisus ut hec omnia superius sunt scripta.

That blessed John was a man

That Blessed John was a man can be proven by three arguments. The first is that Scripture calls him 'man.' The second is that he made use of the necessities of human nature, for example, in food and drink and clothing and the like. The third is that it is read that he was taken and killed, as all these things are written above.

Quod angelus annuntiatio eius fuerit bonus

Quod angelus annunciator conceptionis et natiuitatis beati iohannis fuerit gabriel archangelus annuntiator dominice incarnationis probatur duabus rationibus. una est quia ipse angelus hoc dixit. secunda quia lucam euangelista ita scripsit. nec contrarium posuit ut hoc patent in lucam prima.

That the angel of his annunciation was good

That the announcing angel of the conception and birth of Blessed John was the archangel Gabriel, the proclaimer of the Lord's incarnation, is proven by two arguments. One is that the angel himself said this. The second is that Luke the Evangelist wrote thusly. Neither can one deny this, as is well known from Luke 1.

Quod iohannes baptista non sit saluus et quod fuerit angelus uel spiritus helie et quod angelus annuntiator eius non fuit bonus

Mattheus. xi. iohannes cum audisset opera christi mittens duos de discipulis suis ait illi. Tu es qui uenturus es an alium exspectamus. etcet. ergo dubi-tauit iohannes baptista de christo. igitur fuit malus et quod fuerit dubitatio iohannis ostendit christus in res-ponsione sua. unde subditur. ibi. et respondens ihesus

That John the Baptist was not saved and that he was an angel or the spirit of Elijah and that the angel of his annunciation was not good

Matthew 11 (11:2–3) "Now when John had heard in pris-on the works of Christ, sending two of his disciples he said to him, 'Are you he that is to come, or should we look for another?'" Therefore John doubted Christ, and there-fore was evil. Christ shows in his response that John doubted, whence it adds there (11:3) "And Jesus answering, said to

---

147 amen...149 est] Matt. 11:11.   153 uos...154 ueritati] Ioh. 5:33.   155 ille...156 eius] Ioh. 5:35.   157 uenit...160 ei] Matt. 21:32.   IX.5.4 iohannes...6 exspectamus] Matt. 11:2-3.   9 et...11 uidistis] Matt. 11:4.

149 propterea...est] om. F | falsa] om. F   151 exponit dicens] om. P | add. exponis maior. scilicet. diabolus. quia veritas exponit F   152 uero] om. F | laude] add. uero F   161 hiis] add. ergo F   162 sanctissi-mum] sanctificatum P   163 negauerit] add. a P exp.   164 sit] om. P   IX.3.6 quod] quia F   IX.4.3 beati] beata P   IX.5.2 helie] helye F

IX.3.6 est|fol. 52ra P   IX.5.8 dubitatio|fol. 40r F

---

1) An early and innovative use of "canonization" especially as it was being reserved to the papacy at that time.

ait illis. Euntes et renuntiate iohanni. que audistis et uidistis etcet. et antequam redirent nuntii decollatus est iohannes et ideo non potuit scire ueritatem. Vnde et dominus uituperans eum dixit. beatus est qui non fuerit scandalizatus in me etcet. quasi diceret iohannes non beatus quia in me scandalizatus est de me dubitando qui prius credere uidebatur. et ideo comperat eum arundinem uento agitate. unde dicit. Quid existis in desertum uidere arundinem uento agitatam etcet. unde ostendit quod non habet partem in regno celorum dicens qui autem minor est in regno celorum maior est illo etcet. quasi dicat non est paruus in regno celorum qui non sit maior eo in regno dei quia ipse nulla est ibi.

Catholicus: Respondeo quod illa dubitatio non fuit iohannes set discipulorum eius. quos non uolens aduertere a sua dubitatione misit eos ad ihesum ut oculata fide uiderent de quo dubitabant et eis more boni magistri interrogatorem ex nomine suo ordinauit. et ideo dicitur quod misit illos. Quod autem iohannes non dubitauit. sed discipuli eius habes in iohannes. tertio. ubi dicitur facta ergo questio ex discipluis iohannis etcet. et infra. respondit iohannes et dixit. non potest homo accipere quicquam nisi fuerit ei datum a deo ipsi uos mihi testimonium perhibetis quod dixerim non sum ego christus. sed quia missus sum ante illum. qui habet sponsam etcet. uel dubitauerint de descensu christi ad inferos et secundum hoc descensus nondum erat articulus fidei. uel possunt legi uerba beati iohannis assertiue. sic. tu es qui uenturus es. an alium expectamus. simile in ysaias. viiii. secundum unam lecturam. ibi. multipli-casti gentes non magnificasti letitiam. etcet. quod autem christus misit responsionem iohanni. dicimus quod hoc fecit ad congratulationem eius de illo quod dixisti quod decollatus est. iohannes ante reuisionem discipulorum. dic mihi unde habes hoc. potius tamen uidetur ex uerbis dei quod ad huc uiueret. cum dicit euntes nuntiate iohanni. alias enim legatio quam chris-tus mittebat esset uana et otiosa. quod tale cogitare de domino nefas est. illam autem lecturam quam fecisti super illo uerbo. quid existis in desertum uidere etcet. probat ueritas esse falsam. quia ibi ponit duas clausulas eodem modo scilicet illam de arundine et illam de mollitie uestium et constat quod illa de mollitie uestium sic legitur. sed existis quod uidere? hominem mollibus uestimentum etcet. quod sic intelligitur? se credidistis iohannem mollibus esse uestitum in domibus regum sunt etcet. et iohannes erat in domo

them, 'Go and tell John what you have heard and seen.'" And before the emissaries returned John had been beheaded and so he was not able to know the truth. Whence the Lord, reproaching him, said (11:6) "And blessed is he who is not scandalized by me," as if to say that John was not blessed since he was scandalized by me by doubting Him who before he had seemed to believe, and so he was compared to (11:7) "a reed shaken with the wind" whence He says "What do you go out into the desert to see? A reed shaken with the wind?" Whence He shows that he did not have a share in the kingdom of heaven, saying (Lk 7:28) "He that is least in the kingdom of God, is greater than he." As if to say that there is not the least person in the kingdom of heaven who is not greater than he in the kingdom of God, since he is in no way there.

Cath: I reply that the doubt was not John's but that of his disciples which, not willing to draw attention to their doubts, sent them to Jesus so that by the eyes of faith they might see Him of whom they doubted, and asking them, after the manner of a good teacher, commanded in his name and so it is said that he sent them. Yet that it was not John who doubted, but his disciples, you have in John 3 where he says (3:25) "And there arose a question between some of John's disciples," and later (3:27-29) "John answered, and said, 'A man cannot receive anything, unless it is given to him from heaven. You yourselves do bear me witness, that I said, I am not Christ, but that I am sent before him. He who has the bride.'" Or they were doubting the descent of Christ to hell and according to this, the descent was not yet an article of faith. Or they are able to read the words of blessed John stating, (Lk 7:19) "are you he who is to come, or should we look for another?" Similar [to this is found] in Isaiah 9 according to one reading there (9:3) "You have multiplied the nation, and have not increased the joy." Yet that Christ sent an answer to John, we say that He did this as good wishes regarding him that you said had been beheaded — John before the return of his disciples. Tell me how you have it thus, yet rather from the words of God it seems that he still lived, when He says, "Go tell John" for otherwise the embassy which Christ sent was vain and pointless, and to think this of the Lord is impious. Yet that reading which you have regarding that passage (7:24) "What did you go out into the desert to see?" The truth proves this to be false, for there one places two clauses in the same manner, namely, that of the reed and that of the soft garments, and it happens that it is the soft garments that is read (7:25) "what did you go out to see, a man clothed in soft garments?" How is that understood? If you believed John to be in soft garments and in the houses of kings, and John was in the home of beasts, that is, in the desert clothed in

---

13 beatus...**14** me] Matt. 11:6. **17** arundinem...**18** agitatam] Matt. 11:7. **20** qui...**21** illo] Luc. 7:28. **31** facta...**32** iohannis] Ioh. 3:25. **32** respondit...**36** sponsam] Luc. 3:27-29 (a deo) om. add. de caelo *Vulg.*) **39** tu...**40** expectamus] Luc. 7:19. **41** multipli-casti...**42** letitiam] Is. 9:3 (gentes) om. add. gentem et *Vulg.*) **51** quid...uidere] Luc. 7:24. **55** sed...**56** uestimentum] Luc. 7:25.

16 prius] postea *P* | comperat] computat *F* **19** ostendit] add. arundi *P* exp. | non] si *P* **25** uolens] ualens *F* **26** ihesum] christum *F* **27** oculata fide] translated as "the eyes of faith," see Thomas, *Summa Theologiae* III. 55.2, ad. 1. **38** nondum] add. non dicit *P* **42** quod] uel *F* **46** unde] om. *F* | unde habes] add. unde *P* **48** nuntiate] renuntiate *F* **53** arundine] harudine *F*

18 desertum|fol. 52rb *P* **45** iohannes|fol. 52va *P*

bestiarum id est in deserto indutus pile camelorum ut testificantur euangeliste. eodem modo ergo legitur illa de arundine scilicet quid existis in desertum uidere? arundinem uento agitatam etcet. quasi dicat non fuit iohannes arundo uento agitata et per istas comendationes quas fecit dominus de iohanne post interrogationem discipulorum eius et recessum patet expressius quod ipse minime dubitauit. numquam enim postea commendasset illum ueritatis sed potius uituperasset. illud autem uerbum scilicet beatus qui non fuerit scandalizatus in me etcet. non dixit propter iohannem. sed discipulos eius et aliquos de turba et illud uerbum scilicet qui minor est in regno celorum propter humilitatem passionis sicut dicit apostolus ad hebreos. ii. eum autem qui modico quam angeli minoratus est uidemus ihesum propter passionem mortis etcet. et si uis illud intelligere de iohanne. habeo ex hoc quod ipse beatus fuit quia comparatum ponitur ratione positiui. si ergo qui minor erat in regno celorum maior erat illo. iohannes ergo aliquid erat in regno celorum. qui minor erat in regno celorum existentium in patria dum adhuc uiueret propter periculum uite.

[Patarenus:] item. iohannes. i°. non erat ille lux etcet. ergo malus erat.

Catholicus: Respondeo non ille lux de qua dicit euangelista ibi. qui illuminat omnem hominem uenientem in hunc mundum. erat tamen aliqua bona lux. sicut dicit dominus alibi. ille erat lucerna ardens et lucens etcet.

[Patarenus:] Item. idem. ii°. propheta es tu? respondit non etcet. sed christus dicit quod ipse est propheta. ergo mentitus est iohannes et sic malus fuit. uel si uerum dicit intelligitur sic quod christus dixerat eum prophetam scilicet malum. ipse autem negat se esse prophetam scilicet bonum.

Catholicus: Respondeo quod iohannes negauit se esse prophetam scilicet de illo de quibus dicitur. in iohanne viii. abraam mortuus est et prophete mortui sunt. etcet. putabant enim interogantes quod iohannes esset unus de prophetis mortuis qui resurexisset uel negauit se esse prophetam scilicet helyseum qui antonomasice apud iudeos dicebantur propheta. uel negauit se esse prophetam causa humilitatis et uerum dixit quia ex uirtute sua non erat propria sed ex deo bonitate. simile docet nos ueritas dicere. lucam. xvii. cum feceritis omnia que precepta sunt uobis dicite serui inutiles sumus.

camel hair, as the evangelists testify. In the same way therefore that is read of the reed, namely, (7:24) "What did you go into the desert to see? A reed shaken by the wind?" As if to say John was not a reed blown by the wind and through those commendations which the Lord made regarding John after the questioning by his disciples and their departure, it is most clear that He in no way doubted, for He afterwards never commended him, but rather condemned him, also that passage, (7:23) "blessed is he who is not scandalized in me." He did not say this on account of John, but of his disciples and those of the crowd and that passage, namely (7:28) "But he that is the least in the kingdom of God," on account of the humiliation of the passion, just as the Apostle says in Hebrews 2 (2:9) "But we see Jesus, who was made a little lower than the angels, for the suffering of death," and if you wish to argue that was spoken of John, I take it from this that he was blessed, since the comparison is made for the posited reason. If therefore he who was least in the kingdom of heaven was greater than he, therefore John was to some degree in the kingdom of heaven, he who was least in the kingdom of heaven of those who are in heaven, since he was still alive, in near danger of life.

[Pat:] Also John 1 (1:8) "he was not the light," therefore John was evil.

Cath: I reply that he was not the light of which the Evangelist spoke there, who illuminates all men coming into this world. Yet he was some good light, as the Lord says in another place (5:35) "He was a burning and a shining light."

[Pat:] Also in the same in 2 (1:12) "Are you a prophet? He said no." But Christ said he was a prophet, therefore John lied and so is evil, or if he was speaking truly, and it is interpreted thus that Christ called him to be a prophet, namely, evil. Yet he denied himself to be a prophet, that is to say, good.

Cath: I reply that John denies he is a prophet, namely, of that of which it is said in John 8 (8:52) "Abraham, who is dead, and the prophets are dead." For those asking think that John was one of the dead prophets who had been raised up, or he denied himself to be a prophet, namely, Elisha, who by title was called a prophet among the Jews. Or he denied himself to be a prophet on account of humility and spoke truly since he was not a prophet by his own power but rather from the goodness of God. Similarly he taught us to speak the truth. Luke 17 (17:10) "when you will have done all these things that you are commanded, say, 'We are unprofitable servants.'"

---

61 quid...62 agitatam] Luc. 7:24. 68 beatus...69 me] Luc. 7:23. 71 qui...celorum] Luc. 7:28. 73 eum...74 mortis] Heb. 2:9. 81 non] Ioh. 1:8. 86 ille...87 lucens] Ioh. 5:35. 88 propheta...89 non] Ioh. 1:21. 96 abraam...sunt] Ioh. 8:52. 103 cum...105 sumus] Luc. 17:10.

---

59 camelorum] camellorum P 65 expressius] expressim F 69 dixit] add. christi F 76 beatus] bonus F | positiui] †† unclear in mss. 80 uite] uitem F 81 non...lux] *ante corr.* erat lux uera P 90 si] om. P 99 helyseum] helysabeth P 102 ex] om. P 103 docet] dixit P exp. | ueritas] add. docet P

67 sed|fol. 52vb P 75 intelligere|fol. 40v F 92 esse|fol. 53ra P

Quod iohannes fuerit angelus

[**Patarenus:**] Mattheus. xi. hic est enim de quo scriptum est. Ecce mitto angelum meum etcet.
Catholicus: Respondeo quod iohannes fuit angelus per officium. fuit enim nuntius christi sicut legitur tam in propheta malachias quam in euangelio mattheum et lucam. qui preparabit uiam tuam ante te. etcet.

Quod iohannes fuit helias

[**Patarenus:**] Mattheus. xvii. Dico autem uobis quia heliam uenit et non cognouerunt eum etcet. et infra. Tunc intellexerunt discipuli quia de iohanne baptista dixisset eis etcet.
Catholicus: Respondeo quod iohannes fuit helias per officium. quia processit christum. primo aduentu in spiritum et uirtute helie sicut dicit angelus gabriel. lucam. io. ipse ante illum in spiritu et uirtute helye ut conuertat corda patrum et filios etcet. ergo non fuit helias ad litteram. quia quod fuit in alterius uirtute non est illud.

De Christi humanitate

Circa humanam naturam christi uariis erroribus naufragantur patareni. quidam enim illorum delirant quod ipse attulit carnem de celo. non de nostra natura. quem errorem traxerunt a martionistis et utices qui antiquitus hoc disseminarunt. alii uero latrant quod nullam carnem habuit in ueritate. nisi quia uidebatur hominibus et hanc dementiam habent a manicheis et ualentinis. qui in hac doctrina falsa fuerunt. Sunt et alii inter eos qui demoniace loquuntur dicentes usque ad crucem sine passione in carne humana sed tunc transfiguratus fuit ponens quemdam demonem ad passionem loco sui et hoc est unum de suis secretis et hanc pestilentiam subripuerunt a saracenis qui ita blasfemant. In quem errorem pestiferum ducti sunt nestorii simul cum iacobitis. Sunt et alii inter eos qui estimant christum non tantum semel sed etiam pluries mortuum fuisse ad eo ut dicant quod in VII celis fuerit passus et occisus cuius sunt ipsum auctores uesanie. De anima uero Christi sunt similiter dissentientes. Qui-

6 That John was an angel

[**Pat:**] Matthew 11 (11:10) "For this is he of whom it is written, 'Behold I send my angel.'"
Cath: I reply that John is an angel by reason of his office, for he was the messenger of Christ, as is read as much in the prophet Malachi as in the gospels of Matthew and Luke (Mt 11:10 and Lk 7:27) "who shall prepare your way before you."

7 That John was Elijah

[**Pat:**] Matthew 17 (17:12) "But I say to you that Elijah has already come, and they did not know him," and later (17:13) "Then the disciples understood, that he had spoken to them of John the Baptist."
Cath: I reply that John was Elijah by reason of his office, since he went before Christ, in his first coming in the spirit and power of Elijah, as the Angel Gabriel says in Luke 1 (1:17) "And he shall go before him in the spirit and power of Elijah, that he may turn the hearts of fathers to their children." Therefore he was not literally Elijah, since that was in another's power, not in his.

X On the humanity of Christ

Regarding the human nature of Christ, the Patarenes make shipwreck of their faith by various errors. For certain of them rave that He brought flesh from heaven, not of our nature, which error was derived from the Marcionites and Eutychians[1] which they have spread about since antiquity. Yet others bark that He had no true flesh, except that which was seen by men and this madness they have from the Manichees and Valentinians, who held this false teaching.[2] And there are others among them who speak demonically, saying that up until the cross, He was without passion in His human flesh,[3] but then He was transfigured, putting a certain demon to suffer in His place and this is one of their secrets, and this pestilential idea they stole from the Saracens,[4] who blaspheme in the same manner, in which destructive error they are led by the Nestorians and also by the Jacobites. There are also others among them who consider that Christ did not die once only, but [assert] He died many times, as they say that He suffered and was killed in the seventh heaven, of which idea they themselves

---

IX.6.2 hic...3 meum] Matt. 11:10. 7 qui...te] Matt. 11:10, Luc. 7:27. IX.7.2 Dico...3 eum] Matt. 17:12. 4 Tunc...5 eis] Matt. 17:13. 9 ipse...10 filios] Luc. 1:17.

IX.6.1 fuerit] fuit *F* IX.7.1 helias] helia *P* 8 helie] helye *F* 11 helias] helyas *F* | fuit] fit *P* X.1.4 nostra] add. omni *P* 5 martionistis] martioniscis *F* | utices] unus *P* 8 hominibus] homine *P* 10 inter] autem *F* | loquuntur] locuntur *P* 16 nestorii] nestarii *P* | iacobitis] iacobinis *F* 17 semel] om. *P* 18 VII] et hoc *P*

IX.7.6 fuit]fol. 53rb *P* X.1.17 christum|fol. 53va *P* 18 dicant|fol. 41r *F*

---

1) The reading is difficult here; I propose *Eutychians* from *utices* provided by the mss. It would be unusual for these to be aligned with Marcionites, but in light of their doctrine of a single Divine nature, not out of the realm of possibility. | 2) On the various Docetistic tendencies in Catharism see: Burci, 313-314; Sacconi, c. 17; Moneta, 5, 6, 233, 246-248; Georgius, 1705. | 3) Perhaps a type of the Catharism of Bagnolo, see Georgius, 1748. | 4) e.g. Qur'ān 4: 135.

dam enim illorum dicunt quod nullam habuit animam humanam. quam sectam perditionis tenent traditam apolinaristis. Sunt et alii qui garriunt de illis quod in ipso fuerint duo spiritus. simul a principio mundi uel ante creati. quorum unum proprie spiritum uocant. nos autem fides ihesu christi. de ipso uere sentientes credimus et tenemus quod sicut fuit uerus deus ita et uerus extitit homo habens humanam animam. unam tantum in suis uiribus et passionibus tempore sue conceptionis creatum et quod habuit carnem humane nature de massa ade deriuatam in quam carne esuriunt et sitiuit comedit et bibit uestibus est usus. et domibus laborauit et laxatus est. dormiuit atque quieuit dolores sustinuit et mortem et quod tantum semel mortuus est et quod sepultus est et resurrexit. descendit ad inferos et ascendit in celum. et inde uenturus est iudicare uiuos et mortuos. quia tam per rationes ueridicas quam per scripturas sacras aperte probatur.

Probatio per rationes naturales de humanitate christi. et quod christus fuit homo

Cum deus esset beatus decuit eum facere bona opera per que laudaretur opifex. unde fecit celum et terram et creauit animas et similia. et cum esset summe bonus decuit eum summum bonum facere opus. ut in summo bono opere. magistri summa bonitas cognosceretur. sed deum pati mortem pro sua creatura redimenda in qua erat eius ymago summum bonum opus erat. quo nullum melius. nullum sanctius. nullum dulcius. nullum insuper quod magis a creatura diligeretur. creator agnosceretur auctor. coleretur redemptor quam per istud. igitur decens fuit deum naturam humanam recipere in qua mortem pro genere sustineret humano. sed deus fecit quicquid eum decuit igitur et hominem. item dicit phylosophus quod natura id est deus facit in rebus passibilibus semper id quod melius est. sed deus uoluit redimere hominem quod melius quam per amorem non potuit fieri. sed amor melior et maior est cum pro amico mors suscipere. ergo deus in nostra redemptione homo factus est. et mortuus quo tangit ipse in euangelio iohannis xv. maiorem hac dilectionem nemo habet ut animam suam ponat qui pro amicus suus etcet. Item non decuit hominem redimi nisi per maiorem sui. quia dedecuisset eum seruum esse minoris uel equalis. sed in creaturis nulla nobilius

are the mad authors.[1] Regarding the soul of Christ they similarly differ. For certain of them say that He had no human soul, which they hold as passed on from that sect of perdition, the Apollinarians.[2] There are others who babble among themselves that there were two spirits in Him, at the same time from the beginning of the world or before creation, of which one they properly call spirit. Yet we of the faith of Jesus Christ, thinking of Him in a true manner, we believe and hold that just as He was true God so also He was true man, having one human soul only in His powers and passions, created at the time of His conception and that He had the flesh of human nature, derived from the stock of Adam in which flesh He hungered and thirsted, ate and drank, and used clothing, and He worked in the house and relaxed. He slept and rested. He suffered sorrows and death, and that He died only once and that He was buried and rose. He descended to hell and ascended to heaven, and He will come again to judge the living and the dead, which shall be plainly proven as much by truthful arguments as by the Holy Scriptures.

Proof by natural arguments of the humanity of Christ, and that Christ was a man

Since God was blessed it befitted Him to do good works, through which He might be praised as the architect, so He made heaven and earth and He created souls and similar things, and since He was good in the highest degree, it befitted Him to do the highest good work, that in the highest good work the supreme goodness of the master might be recognized. But that God should suffer death for the redemption of His creature which bore His image, was the highest good work, than which there is none better, none holier, none more delightful, none, moreover, through which He might be loved more by His creature as creator, that He might be acknowledged as author, that He might be worshipped as redeemer, than through that [act]. Therefore it was fitting for God to receive a human nature in which He might suffer death for the human race. But God does whatsoever is fitting for Him, therefore also man. Also the Philosopher says that nature, that is, God acts in passible things [that which] is always for the best.[3] But God wished to redeem man, which could not have been done better than by love, but that love is better and greater that undergoes death for a friend, therefore God became man for our redemption, in which He Himself touched upon in the Gospel of John 15 (15:13) "There is no greater love than this, that one give up one's life for one's friend." Also it was not fitting for man to be redeem-

---

X.2.16 deus... 17 est] Aristotle, *On Generation and Corruption* II, 10, 336. and *De Caelo*, II 5, 288 a 2, also *Physics*, II.1, "quod natura semper facit de possibilibus quod melius est." **22** maiorem... 24 suus] Ioh. 15:13.

---

27 deus] om. *F* **29** sue] om. *P* **31** ade] om. *P* | deriuatam] deriuatum *P* **34** sustinuit] substinuit *P* **X.2.2** et...homo] om. *F* **3** beatus] bonus *F* **11** insuper] add. per *P* **12** agnosceretur] cognosceretur *P* **17** semper] scivit *P* **19** non...fieri] fieri non potuit *F* sed] et *F* **25** dedecuisset] decuisset *F*

X.2.1 2|fol. 53vb *P* **22** dilectio-nem|fol. 54ra *P*

---

1) The doctrine of John of Lugio, see Sacconi, c. 22. | 2) The mitigated dualists of Concorezzo, Sacconi, c. 24, Moneta, 260. 3) A paraphrase of *On Generation and Corruption* II, 10. 336; and *De Caelo*, II 5, 288 a 2 "always does that which is best among the things that are possible".

erat homine ergo debuit esse deus redemptor eius. sed in uenditione et emptione datur pretium pluris quam sit res que uendatur. sed nichil erat maius uita hominis. quam uita dei. ergo decuit eum uitam suam pro nostra redemptione quod in sui natura facere non poterat. unde debuit assumere aliam. sed conuenientius fuit assumere illam que peccauerat ut ubi habundauit delictum super habundaret et gratia. ergo deus assumpsit uitam humane nature quam pro nobis tradidit morti. et hoc ratio assignatur. apocalypsis. v. ubi dicitur nemo poterat in celo neque in terra neque subtus terram aperire librum neque respicere illum etcet. et postea. ecce uicit leo de tribu iuda radix dauid aperire librum etcet. item. quodammodo per occisionem dei genus humanum cecidit in ruinam et maxime occisione filii dei. hoc modo. quia lucifer superbiuit in deum. dum dixit. ero similis altissimo quod maxime de filio dei intelligitur et cui inuidit. unde de celo proiectus est. unde inuidia eius exarsit in hominis interitum scriptum sicut est. sapientia. iiiº. inuidia autem diaboli mors introiuit in orbem terrarum etcet. sed interitus hominis accidit per summam superbiam. luciferi occasionaliter ut dictum est. et etiam per causam ipsius hominis. quia ipse ut deus uoluit esse. item contigit per maxima diaboli inuidiam. unde decuit quod per summam dei humilitate et ipsius dilectionis exellentiam liberaretur homo. ut tanta esset medicina. quanta fuit infirmitas. tanta humilitas quanta et superbia. tanta denique inueniretur et caritas quod et inquanta et inuidia fuerat reperta quod non potuit aliter esse nisi per dei humanitate et mortem sumere. ergo factum est. hanc rationem reddit deus per ionam. iº. ione dicens tollite me et mittite in mare et cessabit mare a uobis scio enim ego quoniam propter me hec tempestas grandis est super uos etcet.

Probatio per scripturas de humanitate christi

prima ad corinthios. xv. quoniam quidem per hominem mors et per hominem resurrectio mortuorum etcet. et infra. primus homo de terra terrenus. secundus homo de celo celestis etcet. et primum ad timotheus. iiº. unus enim mediator dei et hominum homo christus ihesus. et ad timotheus. iiiº. cum autem benignitas et humanitas apparuit saluatoris

ed except by something greater than He, since it would not have been fitting Him to be a servant of lesser or equal things. But among creatures there is none more noble than man, therefore it was fitting for God to be his redeemer. But in buying and selling, a price is given which is more than the cost of the thing which is sold, but nothing was greater than a human life besides the life of God, therefore it was fitting for Him to give His life for our redemption, since according to His nature He was not able to do it, whence He was obliged to assume another, but it was more convenient to assume that which sinned, since (Rm 5:20) "where sin abounded, grace abounded all the more." Therefore God took on the life of human nature which He handed over to death for us, and this is the argument used in Apocalypse 5, where it says (5:3) "And no man was able, neither in heaven, nor on earth, nor under the earth, to open the book, nor to look on it," and later (5:5) "behold the lion of the tribe of Judah, the root of David." In a certain way through the killing of God the human race fell into ruin, and especially in the killing of the Son of God. In this way, for Lucifer disdained God when he said, 'I am like the most high,' and especially it is to be understood of the Son of God, whom he envied. Whence he was cast out of heaven, since his envy blazed forth unto the ruin of men, it was written thusly in Wisdom 3 (2:24) "But by the envy of the devil, death came into the world." But the ruin of man happened through the highest pride of Lucifer as has been spoken of periodically, and also through the cause of man himself, since he wished to be like God. Also it happens especially through the envy of the devil, whence it was fitting that through the supreme humility of God, and of His excelling love, that man might be delivered. For the medicine must match the sickness, and that such humility offset the pride. That such great humility and charity might be found and insofar as the envy was discovered, since it was not able to be otherwise except through the assumption of humanity and death by God, therefore it came to pass. God gave this reason though Jonah 1, with Jonah saying (1:12) "Take me and cast me into the sea, and the sea shall be calm to you, for I know that for my sake this great storm is upon you."

Proof from the Scriptures regarding the humanity of Christ

1 Corinthians 15 (15:21) "For by a man came death, and by a man the resurrection of the dead," and later (15:47) "The first man was of the earth, earthly. The second man, from heaven, heavenly." And 1 Timothy 2 (2:5) "For there is one mediator between God and man: Christ Jesus." And Timothy 3 (Tit 3:4) "But when the goodness and kindness

---

33 ubi…34 gratia] Rom. 5:20.   37 nemo…38 illum] Apoc. 5:3.   39 ecce…40 librum] Apoc. 5:5.   46 inuidia…47 terrarum] Sap. 2:24.   59 tollite…61 uos] Ion. 1:12.   **X.3.2** quoniam…4 mortuorum] 1 Cor. 15:21.   4 primus…5 celestis] 1 Cor. 15:47.   6 unus…7 ihesus] 1 Tim. 2:5.

28 in] om. *P*   29 nichil] nulla *P*   30 ergo] igitur *F*   32 debuit] om. *P*   36 tradidit] tradiderat *F*   38 neque…40 etcet] om. *F*   43 dum…44 inuidit] om. *F*   48 interitus] interit *F*   50 quia] et *F*   53 exellentiam] exxellentiam *P*   55 quanta] quam *F*   58 sumere] om. *F*   **X.3.7** timotheus iiio] *sic FP*

41 genus|fol. 41v *F*   44 inuidit|fol. 54rb *P*   **X.3.8** humanitas|fol. 54va *P*

nostri dei etcet. et actus. ii°. uirum approbatum a deo etcet.

De anima christi

Mattheus xxv. cepit contristari et mestus esse. tunc ait illis. tristis est anima mea usque ad mortem. etcet. ergo christus habuit animam cum passione tristitie.

Item in eodem. mi pater si possibile est transeat a me calix iste. uerumptamen non sicut ego uolo sed sicut tu etcet. ergo habuit dei filius aliam in aliquo uoluntatem a patre quod secundum angelicam naturam non potuit esse. neque secundum diuinam. igitur secundum sensualitatem anime fuit. item secundum angelicam naturam non orasset ut calix passionis ab eo transiret quia angelus impassibilis est. idem. xxvi. ut quid dereliquisti me etcet. sed non dixit corpus per se quia corpus per se non loquitur. Nec etiam angelicam naturam potuit esse. quia ad quid secundum illam fuisset in cruce derelictus. uel in quo. non uideo. igitur secundum spiritum humane nature quem habuit locutus est quia in passione crucis cum corpore suo fuit derelictus id est penis expositus. idem in eodem. ihesus autem iterum clamans emisit spiritum etcet. ergo habuit spiritum. item aliud est quod emittitur et aliud quod emittit ergo in christo fuit spiritus emissus a corpore et corpus emittens illum. ergo humanum spiritum habuit. que est anima. item. Marci. iii°. et circumspiciens eos cum ira contristatus super cecitate cordis eorum etcet. sed ira et tristitia sunt passiones anime humane tantum. ergo christus habuit animam. idem. xiiii. et cepit pauere et tedere. et ait illis. Tristis est anima mea etcet. ergo manifeste habuit animam christus. cum pauor et tedium tristitia fuit in passione anime scilicet humane. item lucam. xxii. apparuit illi angelus de celo confortans eum etcet. hoc dic mihi heretice. si christus fuit angelus et maxime altior et dignior ut tu fabulas. ad quid quomodo alius angelus minor uenit confortare illum. presertim cum nec ipsum uere passum existimes. ergo deus habuit humanam animam secundum cuius sensualitatis infirmitatem ab angelo de celo confortatus est. idem. xxiii. ait illis ihesus. pater in manus tuas commendo spiritum meum etcet. Ecce quomodo dicit quod christus habuit spiritum et cum dicit exspirauit innuit quod spiritus est anima. quia spiratio uite anime. ergo christus animam humanam qui dicitur anima et spiritus. anima uero dicitur quia animat corpus. spiritus autem quia spirat in corpore. iohanne. x. Ego sum pastor bonus. bonus pastor animam suam dat pro ouibus suis etcet. et infra. propterea me pater diligit quia pono animam

of God our Savior appeared." And Acts 2 (2:2) "A man approved by God."

On the Soul of Christ

In Matthew 25 he began to be saddened and mournful, (26:38) "Then he said to them, 'My soul is sorrowful even unto death.'" Therefore Christ had a soul with the passion of sadness.

Also in the same (26:39) "My Father, if possible let this chalice pass from me, yet not as I will but as you will." Therefore the Son of God had another will in Him separate from that of the Father, which could not have been according to angelic nature, neither according to His divine nature, therefore it was according to a sensuality of soul. Also according to angelic nature He would not have prayed that the chalice of the passion might pass from Him, since an angel is impassible. In the same 26 (27:46) "why have you forsaken me," but the body did not say this of itself, since the body does not speak of itself, nor also was it possible that it was an angelic nature; to what, or in what, He would have been abandoned on the cross according to that [nature], I do not see. Therefore according to the spirit of human nature which He had, He said that in the Passion of the cross He was abandoned with His body, that is, abandoned to punishment. Also in the same (27:50) "and Jesus letting forth a loud cry, gave up the spirit," therefore He had a spirit. Also one thing is given forth, and another thing gives forth, therefore there was a spirit in Christ, given forth from the body, and the body giving it forth, therefore He had a human spirit, which is the soul. Also in Mark 3 (3:5) "And looking around at them with anger, being grieved for the blindness of their hearts." But anger and sadness are passions of the human soul only, therefore Christ had a soul. The same in 14 (14:33–34) "and he began to fear and to be heavy of heart, and he said to them, 'My soul is sorrowful even unto death.'" Therefore Christ clearly had a soul, since fear and the grief of sadness were in the passions of the soul, namely, the human soul. Also Luke 20 (22:43) "An angel appeared to him, comforting him." Tell me this, O Heretic, if Christ was an angel, and especially one as high and exalted as you falsely speak, for what reason would another lesser angel come to comfort Him, since you do not think that He could truly suffer? Therefore God had a human soul according to which He was able to feel weakness and be comforted by an angel from heaven. Also 23 (23:46) "Jesus then said, 'Father, into your hands I commend my spirit.'" See in what way Christ says that He has a spirit and when it says He expired, it notes that the spirit is the soul, since by breathing is of life of the soul. Therefore Christ had a human soul which is called soul and spirit. Yet soul is said to be that which animates the body, spirit that which breathes in the body. John 10

---

9 uirum...deo] Act. 2:2.   **X.4.2** tunc...3 mortem] Matt. 26:38   5 mi...6 tu] Matt. 26:39.   12 ut...13 me] Matt. 27:46.   20 ihesus...spiritum] Matt. 27:50.   24 et...26 eorum] Mar. 3:5.   28 et¹...29 mea] Mar. 14:33–34.   31 apparuit...32 eum] Luc. 22:43.   38 ait...40 meum] Luc. 23:46.   45 Ego...46 suis] Ioh. 10:11.   47 propterea...48 eam] Ioh. 10:17 (quia add. ego *Vulg.*)

X.4.1 De...christi] om. *F*   4 tristitie] tristitia *P*   6 uolo] om. *P*   7 filius] add. animam *P* exp.   14 etiam] add. est *P*   19 fuit derelictus] transp. *F*   27 tantum] om. *P*   31 xxii] xx *P*   34 fabulas] fabularis *F*   42 uite...45 spirat] om. *F*   46 bonus] add. anima *P* exp.

X.4.24 item|fol. 54vb *P*   33 et¹|fol. 42r *F*   47 infra|fol. 55ra *P*

meam ut iterum sumam eam etcet. item. xii. fremuit spiritu et turbauit semetipsum etcet. et ista prima sunt anime. item. xviiii. inclinato capite tradidit spiritum etcet. ad idem. ex hiis patet quod christus habuit animam humanam cum passionibus suis et quod anima eius et spiritus idem fuit. quid illi quam tradidit in morte pro nobis.

Quod christus habuit carnem humanam passibilem de massa protoplausti deriuatam ade

Mattheus. i°. liber generationis ihesu christi filii dauid. filii adam. filii abraham. etcet. et frequenter dicitur filius dauid et abrahe. et infra de iuda ad hebreos. vii. manifestum est enim quod ex iuda ortus sit dominus noster etcet. et Apocalypsis. v. ecce uicit leo de tribu iuda. etcet. sed illi fuerunt homines de massa ade sicut nos. ergo et christus de eadem fuit. item. mattheus. viii. filius autem hominis non habet ubi caput suum reclinet etcet. ergo habuit defectum circa caput ergo habuit penam carnalem. qui est de massa ade. idem. xiii. turbati sunt dicentes quia fantasma est. et per timore clamauerunt statim ihesus locutus est illi dicens. habete fiduciam nolite timere ego sum. etcet. ecce quomodo aperte dominus ostendit se non habere corpus fantasticum sed uerum. idem. xxvi mittens enim hac mulier unguentum hoc in corpus meum ad sepelliende me fecit. et ultimo. tunc pilatus iussit reddit corpus. et accepto corpore ioseph inuoluit illud in syndone munda et posuit iillud in monumento suo nouo etcet. ergo habuit corpus nostre nature quod ungitur et sepellitur. item. marcum. i°. Baptizatus est in iordane etcet. ergo habuit corpus quod baptizatum est in aqua. idem. xvii. Tradidit ihesum flagellis cesum. ergo habuit corpus humanum passibile. item lucam. ii°. ut circumcideretur puer etcet. ad idem. item idem. iii°. eodem et ipse ihesus erat incipiens quasi annorum. triginta. quod numquam nisi sercundum humanam naturam potest intelligi. hoc etiam probatur quod nouam animam et nouam carnem habuit christum. item in eodem. qui fuit adam etcet. ergo christus fuit de genealogia ade. item ultimo. et dixit eis uidete manus meas et pedes meos quia ipse sum. palpate et uidete quia spiritus carnem et ossa non habet sicut me uidetis habere etcet. hoc aperte demorant. dominus se habere carnem humanam et ossa non fantastice sed in ueritate. iohannes. ii°. soluite templum hoc etcet. et infra. ille autem dicebat de templo corporis sui. etcet.

(10:11) "I am the good shepherd. The good shepherd gives his life for his sheep," and later (10:17) "Therefore so does the Father love me, because I lay down my life, that I may take it up again." Also 12 (11:33) "he groaned in spirit, and was himself troubled." And this first pertains to souls. Also 19 has the same, (19:30) "Bowing his head, he gave up the spirit." From these it is plain that Christ had a human soul with its passions and that His soul and spirit were the same, which He gave up in death for us.

That Christ had passible human flesh taken from the descendants of Adam, the first man

Matthew 1 (1:1) "The book of the genealogy of Jesus Christ, Son of David, Son of Adam, Son of Abraham," and He is frequently called Son of David and Abraham, and later of Judah, in Hebrews 7 (7:14) "For it is evident that our Lord took His origin from Judah." And Apocalypse (5:5) "behold, the Lion of the tribe of Judah conquers." But those were men of the stock of Adam, like us, so also was Christ. Also Matthew 8 (8:20) "yet the son of man has nowhere to lay his head." He had a defect regarding the head, so He had bodily pains, which is proper to the descendants of Adam. Also 13 (Mt 14:26–27) "And they were troubled, saying, 'It is a ghost.' And they cried out for fear. And immediately Jesus spoke to them, saying, 'Have trust. It is I, do not fear.'" See how plainly the Lord shows Himself not to have an imaginary body, but a true one. Also 26 (Mt 26:12) "For this woman in pouring this oil on my body, has prepared me for burial," and at the end (Mt 27:58–60) "Then Pilate commanded that the body should be returned and Joseph, taking the body, wrapped it up in a clean linen cloth and laid it in his own new tomb." Also Mark 1 (1:9) "He was baptized in the Jordan." therefore He had a body that was baptized in water. Also 17 (15:15) "and he handed over Jesus to be scourged," therefore He had a passible human body. Also Luke 2 (2:21) "that the child might be circumcised," to the same in 3 (Lk 3:23) "And Jesus himself began his ministry about the age of thirty years," that would be impossible to understand except according to human nature. Also it is proven that Christ had a new soul and a new body in the same (3:38) "who was of Adam," therefore Christ was of the lineage of Adam. Also at the end (24:39) "And he said to them, 'See my hands and feet, that it is I myself, touch and see, for a spirit does not have human flesh and bones, as you see me I have.'" He shows this clearly. The Lord Himself had human flesh and bones not as a phantom, but in reality. John 2 (2:19) "destroy this temple," and later (2:21) "but he was speaking of the temple of his body." Therefore His body was able to be destroyed, and so he was human. In

---

49 spiritu...semetipsum] Ioh. 11:33 (fremuit) infremuit | semetipsum] seipsum *Vulg.*)   50 inclinato...spiritum] Ioh. 19:30. X.5.4 liber...5 adam] Matt. 1:1 (filii adam) om. *Vulg.*   7 manifestum...8 noster] Heb. 7:14.   8 ecce...9 iuda] Apoc. 5:5.   11 filius...12 reclinet] Matt. 8:20.   14 turbati...16 sum] Matt. 14:26-27 (illi) eis *Vulg.*)   18 mittens...20 fecit] Matt. 26:12.   20 tunc...23 nouo] Matt. 27:58-60.   24 Baptizatus...25 iordane] Mar. 1:9.   26 Tradidit...cesum] Mar. 15:15.   28 ut...puer] Luc. 2:21.   29 eodem...30 triginta] Luc. 3:23.   33 qui...adam] Luc. 3:38.   34 et...37 habere¹] Luc. 24:39.   39 soluite...hoc] Ioh. 2:19.   40 ille...sui] Ioh. 2:21.

53 illi] uel P   X.5.2 deriuatam...3 ade] transp. F   8 Apocalypsis v] mattheus. v P   9 illi] illa P   10 christus] eius P   18 xxvi] xxvii P 33 ergo] item P   34 ade] add. etcet P   37 demorant] *sic* PF **leg. demonstrat**   40 dicebat] add. eis P exp.

X.5.18 uerum]fol. 55rb P

ergo habuit corpus solubile. ergo humanum etcet. idem. viiii. hec cum dixisset expuit in terram et fecit lutum ex sputo etcet. hoc tantum corpori humano conuenit. idem. xviii. quid me cedis etcet. ergo habuit carnem passibilem. idem xix. non fregerunt eius crura etcet. et postea. sed unus militum lancea latus eius aperuit et continuo exiuit sanguis et aqua etcet. et infra. uidebunt in quem transfixerunt etcet. et infra acceperunt ergo corpus ihesu etcet. ex hiis patet quod habuit corpus tractabile et passibile. item. idem. xx. deinde dicit thome. infer digitum tuum huc et uide manus meas et aufer manum tuam et mitte in latus meum etcet. audi patarene quam manifeste dominus demonstrat se habuisse manus perforatas et latus. ergo carne habuit passibilem. noli ergo amplius esse incredulus sed fidelis cum thoma dominus meus et deus meus. etcet. item ad romanos. primo. qui factus est ei ex semine Dauid secundum carnem. etcet. ergo habuit carnem humanam. item x. dampnauit pec-catum in carne etcet. item ad Galathas. iii°. Christus nos redemit de maledicto legis factus pro nobis maledic-tum etcet. sed christus non habuit maledictio-nem culpe. igitur pene. ergo carne penalem habuit que est nostra. item ad ephesios. i°. in quo habemus redem-tionem per sanguinem etcet. sed sanguis non est nisi in carne penali. ergo habuit eam. ad hoc est. ad colosenses scilicet per sanguinem crucis eius etcet. et ad hebreos. viiii°. sed per proprium sanguinem introuit etcet. et infra. quanto magis sanguis christi etcet. et postea. petrus primo. per aspersionem sanguinis ihesu christi etcet. et infra. pretioso sanguine agni quasi incontami-nati et immaculati ihesu Christi etcet. et apocalypsis. i°. qui dilexit nos et lauit nos a peccatis nostris in sanguine suo etcet. item ad ephesios. secundo. ipse enim est pax nostra qui fecit utraque unum et medium parietem macerie soluens inimicitias in carne sua etcet. ergo habuit carnem humanam. item ad phylippenses ii°. sed semetipsum exinaniuit formam serui accipiens etcet. ad idem. ad hebreos iiii°. non enim habemus pontificem qui non possit compati infirmitatibus nos-tris tentatum autem per omnia per similitudine absque peccato etcet. ergo habuit carnem nostram cum omnibus suis penis absque peccato. item idem. v. qui in diebus carnis sue preces supplicationesque ad eum qui possit illum saluum facere a morte cum clamore

the same in (9:6) "When he had said these things, he spat on the ground:" this act pertains only to a human body. In the same in 18 (18:23) "why do you strike me?" Therefore He had passible flesh. The same in 19 (19:33) "they did not break his legs," and after (19:34) "But one of the soldiers opened his side with a spear, and immediately there came out blood and water," and later (19:37) "they looked upon him whom they had transfixed," and later (19:40) "They received the body of Jesus," from these passages it is clear that He had a body that was passible and able to be touched. Also 20 (20:27) "then he said to Thomas, 'Put in your finger here, and see my hands, and bring your hand here, and put it into my side.'" Hear, O Patarene, how undoubtedly the Lord shows Himself to have had His hands and side pierced, therefore He had passible flesh, therefore (Paschal Sequence) do not be further unbeliev-ing,[1] but believe with Thomas (20:28) "My Lord and my God." Also Romans 1 (1:3) "who was made for him of the seed of David, according to the flesh." Therefore He had human flesh. Also 10 (8:3) "he has condemned sin in the flesh." Also Galatians 3 (3:13) "Christ has redeemed us from the curse of the law, being made a curse for us." But Christ does not have the guilt of the curse, and therefore no penalty, so the penalty He has of the flesh is ours, but there is no blood unless in fleshly punishment, therefore He had it. Colossians speaks to this, namely (1:20) "making peace through the blood of his cross," and Hebrews 9 (9:12) "but by his own blood, he entered." and later (9:14) "How much more shall the blood of Christ." And after 1 Peter (1:2) "through the sprinkling of the blood of Jesus Christ," and later (1:19) "But with the precious blood of Christ, as of a lamb unspotted and undefiled." And Apocalypse 1 (1:5) "who has loved us, and washed us from our sins in his own blood." Also Ephesians 2 (2:14) "For he is our peace, who has made both one, and breaking down the middle wall of partition, the enmities in his flesh." Therefore He had human flesh. Also Philippians 2 (2:7) "But he emptied himself, taking the form of a slave." Also Hebrews 4 (4:15) "For we do not have a high priest who cannot have compassion on our infirmities, but one tempted in all things like as we are, without sin." Therefore He had our flesh, with all its punishments, but without sin. Also the same in 5 (5:7) "Who in the days of his flesh, with a strong cry and tears, offering up prayers and supplications to him who was able to save him from death." But shouts and tears are cor-

---

42 hec...43 sputo] Ioh. 9:6.   44 quid...cedis] Ioh. 18:23.   45 non...crura] Ioh. 19:33.   46 sed...47 aqua] Ioh. 19:34.   48 uidebunt...transfixerunt] Ioh. 19:37.   49 acceperunt...ihesu] Ioh. 19:40.   51 deinde...53 meum] Ioh. 20:27 (aufer) affer *Vulg.*)   55 noli...56 fidelis] Paschal sequence.   56 dominus...57 meus] Ioh. 20:28.   57 qui...58 carnem] Rom. 1:3.   59 dampnauit...60 carne] Rom. 8:3.   60 Christus...62 maledic-tum] Gal. 3:13.   64 in...65 sanguinem] Eph. 1:7.   67 per...eius] Col. 1:20.   68 sed...introuit] Heb. 9:12.   69 quanto...christi] Heb. 9:14.   70 per...christi] 1 Pet. 1:2.   71 pretioso...72 Christi] 1 Pet. 1:19.   73 qui...74 suo] Apoc. 1:5.   74 ipse...76 sua] Apoc. 2:14.   78 sed...accipiens] Php. 2:7.   79 non...82 peccato] Heb. 4:15.   83 qui...86 lacrimis] Heb. 5:7.

---

45 xix] xviiii *P*   53 patarene] patarine *P*   54 demonstrat] om. *P* | et latus] om. add. cum clavis *P* | ergo] igitur *F*   77 phylippenses] ephesios *F*

44 conuenit|fol. 55va *P*   46 lancea|fol. 42v *F*   66 habuit|fol. 55vb *P*

---

1) Peter of Verona sang this during his last journey on the day of his martyrdom.

ualido et lacrimis etcet. sed clamore et lacrime penalis corporis sunt. ergo habuit penale corpus. ab hec est in iohanne. xi. lacrimatus est ihesus. etcet. item ad hebreos. x. corpus autem adaptasti mihi etcet. ergo habuit corpus in ueritate et non fantastice. quia deus non adaptasset fantasiam quia esset illusor. item i° petri. iiii°. Christo igitur passo in carne et uos eadem cogitatione armamini etcet. ergo uere carnem passibilem habuit christus. alias si talem enim non habuisset uiueret nobis petrus quod non adueras passiones debemus armari. sed tamen ad simulatas. item prima iohanne. iiii. omnis qui confitetur ihesum christum in carne uenisse ex deo est. et omnis spiritus qui soluit ihesum ex deo non est. hic est antichristus ergo uos patareni qui negatis incarnationem christi estis antichristos qui iam uenit et estis seductores animarum. de quibus dicit. iohannes. in secunda. multi seductores exierunt in mundum qui non confitentur ihesum christum uenisse in carnem. hic est seductor et antichristus etcet. item actus. xxvi. si passibilis christus si primus ex mortuorum resurrectione lumen annuntiaturus etcet. ergo christus habuit carnem passibilem et supra de hac materia. titulum iii°. in rubricella quod christus duas habuit naturas.

poreal punishments, therefore He had punishments of the body, and this is in John 11 (11:35) "And Jesus wept," also Hebrews 10 (10:5) "You have fitted a body for me," therefore He had a body in reality and not in fantasy, since God does not make use of fantasies, since then He would be a scoffer. Also 2 Peter 4 (1 Pt 4:1) "Christ therefore having suffered in the flesh, you also be armed with the same thought," therefore Christ had true, passible flesh, for otherwise if He did not have it in life, Peter would not have warned us that we ought to be armed with the Passion, but only its imitation. Also 1 John 4 (4:2–3) "Every one who confesses that Jesus Christ has come in the flesh is of God and every spirit that denies Jesus is not of God, and this is Antichrist," therefore you Patarenes who deny the Incarnation of Christ are Antichrist who has already come and you are the seducers of souls of which John speaks in his second epistle (2 Jn 1:7) "many seducers have gone out into the world, who do not confess that Jesus Christ has come in the flesh, such a one is a seducer and an Antichrist." Also Acts 26 (26:23) "That Christ should suffer, and that he should be the first who should rise from the dead, and should show light." Therefore Christ had passible flesh and there is more material on this in the third section, in the subsection that Christ has two natures.

Quod christus habuit carnem suam de carne beate marie uirginis

Mattheus i°. de quo natus est ihesus qui uocatur christus etcet. et infra. donec peperit filium suum primogenitum filium tuum etcet. et ii°. angelus domini apparuit in somnis ioseph dicens. surge et accipe puerum et matrem eius etcet. et xii°. ecce mater tua etcet. et lucam. ecce concipies in utero et paries filium et uocabis nomen eius ihesum etcet. et infra. et unde hoc ut ueniat mater domini mei ad me. etcet. et ii°. et peperit filium suum primogenitum etcet. et infra. et dixit mater eius ad illum etcet. et xi. beatus uenter qui te portauit et ubera que suxisti etcet. et iohannes. xviiii. cum uidisset ergo ihesus matrem et discipulum stantem quem diligebat dicit matri sue etcet. et paulus ad Galathas. iiii°. misit deus filium suum factum ex muliere. ergo beata maria fuit mater christi concepit et peperit et lactauit eum igitur de carne sua fuit caro christi.

That Christ took his flesh from the flesh of the Blessed Virgin Mary

Matthew 1 (1:16) "of whom was born Jesus, who is called Christ," and later (1:25) "And he did not know her until she brought forth her firstborn son," and 2 (2:12) "The angel of the Lord appeared in a dream to Joseph, saying, 'Arise and take the child and his mother,'" and 12 (12:47) "behold your mother." And Luke (1:31) "Behold you shall conceive in your womb and bear a son, and you will call his name Jesus,'" and later (1:43) "And how is it, that the mother of my Lord should come to me?," and 2 (2:7) "And she brought forth her firstborn son," and later (2:48) "And his mother said to him," and 11 (11:27) "blessed is the womb that bore you and the breasts which nursed you," and John 19 (19:26) "Therefore when Jesus saw his mother and the disciple standing whom he loved, he said to his mother." And Paul in Galatians 4 (4:4) "God sent his son, born of a woman." Therefore the Blessed Mary was the Mother of Christ. She conceived and bore and nursed Him, therefore the flesh of Christ is from her body.

De esurie et siti ihesu Christi

Mattheus. iiii. Cum ieiunasset xl diebus et xl noctibus postea esuriit. et iohanne. xviiii. sciens ihesus etcet. ibi

On the hunger and thirst of Jesus Christ

Matthew 4 (4:2) "After he had fasted for forty days and forty nights, he was hungry," and John 19 (19:28) "Jesus

sitio etcet. ex hiis patet quod dominus esuriit et sitiuit in carne humana.

De esu et potu christi

Mattheus. viiii. multi publicani et peccatores uenientes discumbebant cum ihesu et discipulis eius et uidentes pharisei dicebant. quare cum publicanis et peccatoribus manducat magister uester etcet. et infra. uenit enim filius hominis manducans et bibetis et dicitis ecce homo uorax et potator uini publicanorum amicus et peccatorum etcet. Item. xxvi. uespere autem facto discumbebat cum duodecim discipulis suis etcet. et infra. Qui intingit mecum manum in passide hic me tradet. etcet. item mattheus. ii. multi publicani et peccatores simul discumbebant cum ihesu etcet. et infra. scribe et pharisei dicentes quia manducaret cum publicanis et peccatoribus dicebant etcet. Item lucam v. et fecit ei conuiuium magnum leui in domo sua etcet. idem. vii. uenit filius hominis manducans et bibens etcet. idem xiiii. cum intrasset ihesus in domum cuiusdam principis phariseorum sabbato manducare panem etcet. idem xv. et murmurabant pharisei et scribe dicentes. quia hic peccatores recipit et manducat cum illis. Ex hiis patet expressim quod dominus comedit temporaliter ante passionem suam. De potu autem suo habes in marcho. xiiii. amen dico uobis quod iam non bibam de hoc genimine uitis usque in diem illum cum illud bibam nouum in regno dei.

Patarenus: Dico quod christus uidebatur comedere sed non comedebat.

Catholicus: mentiri te probat ipse christus qui dicit expressim quod ipse comedit et bibit cui sancti euangeliste testimenti perhibent.

Quod christus comedit carnes

lucam. xxii. uenit autem dies azimorum in quo necesse erat occidi pascha etcet. et infra. parate nobis pascha ut manducemus etcet. et infra. dicit tibi magister. ubi est diuersorium ubi pascha cum discipulis meis manducem etcet. et infra. et parauerunt pascha etcet. et infra. ait. desiderio desideraui hoc pascha manducare uobiscum antequam patiar. dico enim uobis quia ex hoc non manducabo istud donec impleatur in regno dei etcet. ergo christus comedit pascha id est agnum paschalem. sic enim sonat hoc uerbum in ueteri testamento unde sumptum est.

On the eating and drinking of Christ

Matthew 9 (9:10–11) "And it happened that as he was reclining in the house, behold many publicans and sinners came, and sat down with Jesus and his disciples and the Pharisees seeing this said to his disciples, 'Why does your master eat with publicans and sinners?'" And later (11:19) "The Son of man comes eating and drinking, and they say, 'Behold a man who is a glutton and a wine drinker, a friend of publicans and sinners.'" Also 26 (26:20) "Evening having come, he reclined with his twelve disciples," and later (26:23) "He who dips his hand with me in the dish, he will betray me." Also Matthew 9 (9:10) "Many publicans and sinners likewise reclined with Jesus," and later (Mk 2:16) "And the scribes and the Pharisees, seeing that he ate with publicans and sinners." Also Luke 5 (5:29) "And Levi made him a great feast in his own house," also 7 (7:34) "The Son of man comes eating and drinking," also 14 (14:1) "when Jesus went into the house of one of the chiefs of the Pharisees on the Sabbath day to eat bread." The same in 15 (15:2) "And the Pharisees and the scribes murmured, saying, 'This man receives sinners, and eats with them.'" From these it is patently clear that the Lord ate in an earthly manner before His Passion. Also of drinking you have in Mark 14 (14:25) "Amen I say to you, that I will drink no more of the fruit of the vine, until that day when I shall drink it new in the kingdom of God."

Pat: I say that Christ seemed to eat, but He did not eat.

Cath: You lie, Christ Himself proves it when He says plainly that He ate and drank, to which the holy evangelists bore witness.

That Christ ate meat

Luke 22 (22:7) "and the day of the unleavened bread came, on which it was necessary that the pasch should be killed," and later (22:8) "Prepare the pasch for us, that we may eat," and later (22:11) "The master says to you, 'Where is the guest chamber, where I may eat the pasch with my disciples?'" And later (22:13) "and they prepared the pasch," and later (22:15–16) "he said, 'With great desire I have desired to eat this pasch with you before I suffer. For I say to you, that from this time I will not eat it, until it be fulfilled in the kingdom of God.'" Therefore Christ ate the pasch, that is, the paschal lamb. For that is what the word means in the Old Testament, whence it was consumed.

X.8.2 multi...5 uester] Matt. 9:10-11. 5 uenit...8 peccatorum] Matt. 11:19 (bibetis) bibans | dicitis] dicunt *Vulg.*) 8 uespere...9 suis] Matt. 26:20. 10 Qui...11 tradet] Matt. 26:23 (passide) paropside *Vulg.*) 11 multi...12 ihesu] Matt. 9:10. 13 scribe...14 dicebant] Mar. 2:16 (dicentes) uidentes *Vulg.*) 15 et...sua] Luc. 5:29. 16 uenit...bi-bens] Luc. 7:34. 17 cum...19 panem] Luc. 14:1 (intrasset) intraret *Vulg.*) 19 et[1]...21 illis] Luc. 15:2. 23 amen...25 dei] Mar. 14:25 (quod) quia *Vulg.*) X.9.2 uenit...3 pascha[1]] Luc. 22:7 (quo) qua *Vulg.*) 3 parate...4 manducemus] Luc. 22:8. 4 dicit...6 mandu-cem] Luc. 22:11. 6 et[2]...pascha] Luc. 22:13. 7 ait...9 dei] Luc. 22:15-16 (istud) illud *Vulg.*)

X.9.1 Quod...carnes] om. *F* 10 pascha] pasca *P*

X.8.5 manducant|fol. 56va *P* 25 dei|fol. 56vb *P* X.9.8 quia|fol. 43v *F*

Patarenus: Dico quod per pascha intelligitur dies illa uel consolatio quam habuit christus cum discipuli in sero illo. uel ipse christus.

Catholicus: Sed euangelista reprobat tuos intellectus omnes. primos duos reprobat in illo uerbo cum dicit. uenit autem dies azimorum in qua necesse erat occidi pascha. quia nec dies occiditur nec consolatio christi quam fecit discipulis erat mortua. sed uita eterna plena. tertium uero intellectum reprobat in illo uerbo scilicet et parauerunt pascha etcet. quia apostoli non parauerunt passionem christo. immo uehementer doluerit. preterea quoniam staret quod dicit dominus. desiderio desideraui hoc pascha manducare uobiscum antequam patiar etcet. ergo aliud fuit pasca illud et aliud pasca christi.

De comestionem et potu christi post resurrectionem eius

lucam. ultimo. adhuc autem illis non credentibus prae gaudio dixit. habetis hic aliquid quod manducetur. at illi optulerunt ei partem piscis assi et fauum mellis et cum manducasset coram eis sumens reliquias dedit eis etcet. item actus. i°. et conuescens id est simile uescens etcet. item. in eodem. x. ubi dicit petrus. nos qui manducauimus et bibimus cum illo postquam resurrexit a mortuis etcet. et nota quod dominus comedit carnes et pisces panem fermentatum et mel et bibit uinum uitis qui sunt meliora cibaria et potus et magis nature conuenientia. ut ostenderet se ueram et solidam naturam humanam habere.

De vestibus et calciamentis christi

Mattheus. viiii. tetigit fimbriam uestimenti eius etcet. et xxvi. et exuentes eum clamadem coccineam circumdederunt illi. et infra. exuerunt eum clamide. et induerunt eum uestimentis eius etcet. et infra. diuiserunt uestimenta eius sortem mittentes etcet. et marco. i. cuius non sum dignus procumbens soluere corrigiam calceamentorum eius. item lucam. xxiii. illuxit indutum ueste alba etcet. et iohannes xiii. surgit a cena et ponit uestimenta sua et cum accepisset linteum precinxit se etcet. et infra. postquam lauit pedes discipulorum suorum accepit uestimenta sua etcet. et xviiii et ueste purpurea circumdederunt eum etcet. et infra acceperunt uestimenta eius et fecerunt quatuor partes unicuique militi partem et tunicam. erat autem tunica inconsutilis desuper contexta per

---

Pat: I say that by 'pasch' it is to be understood of the day, or of the consolation[1] which Christ had with His disciples at that late hour, or it refers to Christ Himself.

Cath: But the evangelist rebukes your entire conception. The first two he reproves in the passage where he says "and the day of the unleavened bread came, on which it was necessary that the pasch should be killed." Because neither the day is killed, nor was the consolation of Christ killed, which He prepared for the disciples that was a dead thing, but the fullness of eternal life. Also he rebukes the third interpretation in that phrase, namely (22:13) "and they prepared the pasch," for the Apostles did not prepare the Passion of Christ, no indeed they gravely sorrowed over it. Further because it remains that the Lord says, "with desire I have desired to eat this pasch with you before I suffer," therefore that pasch was one thing, and the pasch of Christ another.

On Christ's eating and drinking after His resurrection

At the end of Luke (24:41–43) "But while they yet did not believe for joy, he said, 'Have you anything to eat?' And they offered him a piece of a boiled fish, and a honeycomb. And when he had eaten before them, taking the leftovers, he gave to them." Also Acts 1 (1:4) "and eating together," that is, 'eating.' Also in the same in 10 where Peter says (10:41) "even to us, who did eat and drink with him after he arose again from the dead." And note that the Lord eats meat, fish, leavened bread, and honey, and drinks wine from grapes which are better foods and drinks and more suitable to nature, as He shows Himself to have a true and solid human nature.

On the shoes and garments of Christ

Matthew 9 (8:44) "she touched the hem of his garment," and 26 (Mt 27:28) "And stripping him, they put a scarlet cloak around him," and later (27:31) "they took the cloak off of him, and put his own garments on him," and later (27:35) "they divided his garments, casting lots." And Mark 1 (1:7) "the strap of whose shoes I am not worthy to stoop down and loosen." Also Luke 23 (23:11) "putting on him a white garment." And John 13 (13:4) "He arose from supper and, laying aside his garments and having taken a towel, girded himself," and after (13:12) "Then after he had washed their feet, and he took his garments," and 19 (19:2) "they put a purple garment on him," and later (19:23) "They took his garments, and they made four parts, each soldier taking a part, and also his coat. Now the coat

---

22 et...pascha] Luc. 22:13.   X.10.3 adhuc...6 eis²] Luc. 24:41-43 (credentibus) add. et mirantibus *Vulg.*)   7 et...uescens] Act. 1:4.   8 ubi...10 mortuis] Act. 10:41 (nos) nobis *Vulg.*)   X.11.2 tetigit...eius] Luc. 8:44.   3 et²...4 illi] Matt. 27:28 (illi) ei *Vulg.*)   4 exuerunt...5 eius] Matt. 27:31.   6 diuiserunt...mittentes] Matt. 27:35.   7 cuius...8 eius] Mar. 1:7.   9 illuxit...alba] Luc. 23:11 (illusit) illuxit *Vulg.*)   10 surgit...11 se] Ioh. 13:4.   11 postquam...12 sua] Ioh. 13:12 (suorum) eorum *Vulg.*)   13 et²...eum] Ioh. 19:2.   14 acceperunt...17 totum] Ioh. 19:23.

19 nec¹] om. *P*   X.10.2 eius] om. *F*   11 fermentatum] furmentiuum *F*   14 naturam humanam] transp. *F*

18 dies|fol. 57ra *P*   X.10.13 solidam|fol. 57rb *P*

---

1) This perhaps refers to the Cathar ceremony of "Consolation".

totum etcet. ecce quomodo habes quod dominus usus est uestibus humanis et calciamentis et quod simile portauit plures uestes et maxime uestem pretiosam.

Quod christus usus est domibus

Mattheus. ix. et factum est discumbente eo in domo. ecce multi publicani etcet. et xii. cum intrasset uenit in sinagogam eorum etcet. et xii. exiens ihesus de domo etcet. et marcum iii. et introiuit iterum in synagogam etcet. et infra. et ueniunt ad domum etcet. et lucam. vii. quia dignus est ut hoc illi prestes diligit enim gentem nostram et synagogam ipse edificauit nobis etcet. et infra eodem. et ingressus domum pharisei discubuit etcet. et xiiii. cum intrasset ihesus in domum cuiusdam principis etcet. et xviiii et dixit ad eum zachee festina descende quia hodie in domo tua oportet me manere et iohannes. io. et uidentes eos sequentes se dicit eis. Quid queritis. qui dixerunt ei. Rabbi quod dicitur magister. ubi habitas. dicit eis. uenite et uidete. uenerunt et uiderunt ubi maneret et apud eum manserunt die illo etcet. et xiiii. et domus impleta est ex odore unguenti etcet. Ostensum est ergo ex predictis quod dominus ihesus usus fuit domibus materialibus.

De laxione et labore christi

Lucam xxii. et factus in agonia prolixius orabat et factus est sudor eius sicut guttae sanguinis defluentis in terram. etcet. et iohannes iiii. ihesus ergo fatigatus ex itinere etcet. ergo laxatus et laborat ihesus.

De dormitione et requie christi

Mattheus viiio. ipse uero dormiebat etcet. et lucam. viii. nauigantibus illis obdormiuit etcet. et iohannes. iiii. sedebat sic supra fontem etcet. ergo dormuit et requieuit dominus.

De passione et crucifixione et morte et sepultura et resurrectione ihesu christi

Mattheus. xvi. Exinde cepit ihesus ostendere discipulis suis quia oporteret eum ire ierosolymam et multa pati a senioribus et scribis et principibus sacerdotum et occidi et tertia die resurgere etcet. xvii sic et filius hominis passurus est ab eis id est. sicut ioannis baptista de quo dixerat. item. xx. ecce ascendimus ierosolymam et filius hominis tradetur principibus sacerdotum et condemnabunt eum morte. et tradent eum gentibus ad illudendum et flagellandum et tertia die resurget. etcet.

---

was without seam, woven from the top throughout." See how you have it that the Lord used human clothing and shoes and that similarly He wore many clothes and certainly even expensive clothes.

That Christ made use of houses

Matthew 9 (9:10) "And it came to pass as he was reclining in the house, behold many publicans," and 12 (12:9) "And when he had entered from there, he came into their synagogues," and 13 (13:1) "Jesus going out of the house." And Mark 3 (3:1) "And again he entered into the synagogue," and later (3:20) "And they came to a house." And Luke 7 (7:4-5) "He is worthy that you should do this for him for he loves our nation, and he has built us a synagogue," and in the same (7:36) "and going into the house of the Pharisee, he reclined," and 14 (14:1) "he went into the house of one of the chiefs," and 19 (19:5) "and said to him, 'Zacchaeus, make haste and come down, for this day I must stay in your house.'" And John 1 (1:38–39) "And seeing them following him, said to them, 'What do you seek?' They said to him, 'Rabbi, Master, where do you live?' He said to them, 'Come and see.' They came, and saw where he lived, and they stayed with him that day," and 14 (12:3) "and the house was filled with the odor of the ointment." Therefore the foregoing demonstrate that the Lord Jesus made use of material houses.

On the leisure and labor of Christ

Luke 22 (22:43–44) "And being in an agony, he prayed longer, and his sweat became like drops of blood, trickling down upon the ground." And John 4 (4:6) "Jesus therefore being wearied by his journey." Therefore Jesus had leisure and labored.

On the sleep and rest of Christ

Matthew 8 (8:24) "but he was asleep." Luke 8 (8:23) "And while they were sailing, he slept." And John 4 (4:6) "he sat thus on the well." Therefore the Lord slept and rested.

On the passion and crucifixion and death and burial and resurrection of Jesus Christ

Matthew 16 (16:21) "From that time Jesus began to show to his disciples that he must go to Jerusalem, and suffer many things from the elders and scribes and chief priests, and be put to death, and the third day rise again," and 17 (17:12–13) "So also the Son of man shall suffer from them. Then the disciples understood that he had spoken to them of John the Baptist." Also 20 (20:18-19) "Behold we go up to Jerusalem, and the Son of man shall be betrayed to the chief priests and the scribes, and they shall condemn him

---

X.12.2 et...3 publicani] Matt. 9:10. 3 cum...4 eorum] Matt. 12:9 (cum intrasset) cum inde transisset *Vulg.*) 4 exiens...domo] Matt. 13:1. 5 et²...synagogam] Mar. 3:1. 6 et²...domum] Mar. 3:20. 7 quia...8 nobis] Luc. 7-4-5. 9 et²...10 discubuit] Luc. 7:36. 10 cum...11 principis] Luc. 14:1 (intrasset) intraret *Vulg.*) 11 et²...13 manere] Luc. 19:5 (festina) festinans *Vulg.*) 13 et²...17 illo] Ioh. 1:38-39 (uidentes) uidens | dicitur) interpretatum *Vulg.*) 17 et²...18 unguenti] Ioh. 12:3. X.13.2 et¹...4 terram] Luc. 22:43-44 (defluentis) decurrentis *Vulg.*) 4 ihesus...5 itinere] Ioh. 4:6. X.14.2 ipse...dormiebat] Matt. 8:24. 3 nauigantibus...obdormiuit] Luc. 8:23. 4 sedebat...fontem] Ioh. 4:6. X.15.3 Exinde...6 resurgere] Matt. 16:21. 6 sic...8 dixerat] Matt. 17:12-13. 11 resurget] Matt. 20:18-19 (flagellandum) add. et crucifigendum *Vulg.*)

X.12.10 xiiii] om. P   X.14.4 dormuit] laxatus F   X.15.1 crucifixione] cruce F

X.12.2 eo|fol. 57va P   11 principis|fol. 44r F   X.14.2 dormiebat|fol. 57vb P

item xxvi mitte enim hec unguentum hoc in corpus meum ad sepelliendum me fecit. etcet. et xxvii. post-quam autem crucifixerunt eum etcet. infra ihesus autem iterum clamans uoce magna emisit spiritum etcet. et in eodem. et accepto corpore ioseph inuoluit illud in sindone munda et posuit in monumento nouo etcet. et ultimo. scio enim quod ihesum qui crucifixus est queritis. non est hic. surrexit enim sicut dixit. uenite et uidete locum ubi positus fuerat dominus etcet. item. pilatus autem mirabatur si iam obiisset et accersito centurione interrogauit eum si iam mortuus esset et cum cognouisset a centurione donauit corpus Ioseph. item lucam. ii°. ecce positus est hic in ruinam et in resurrectionem multorum in israel et in signum cui contradicetur etcet. ultimo. quid turbati estis. et cogitationes ascendunt in corda uestra. uidete manus meas et pedes meos quia ego ipse sum. palpate et uidete etcet. iohannes xviiii. acceperunt ergo corpus ihesu. etcet. item ad romanos. vi. christus resurgens ex mortuis iam moritur etcet. item apocalypsis. i°. et uidebit eum omnis oculus et qui eum pupugerunt etcet. et infra. ego sum primus et nouissimus et sum uiuus et fui mortuus. etcet. item actus. ii°. hunc definito consilio et presciencia dei traditum per manus iniquorum affligentes interemistis quem deus suscitauit etcet. ex hiis ergo scripturis et ex multis aliis quas propter prolixitatem dimisi inserere. patet euidenter quod dominus noster ihesus christus. uere passus et mortuus et sepultus fuit uere etiam resurrexit.

Patarenus: Dico quod in omnibus scripturis que locuntur de christi passione et morte ac sepultura. seu de resurrectione intelligitur ut putabatur uel ut uidebatur.
Catholicus: sed dicite mihi o crudeles belue. quid laceratis dei karitatem et scripture ueritatem? quare conquerimini de ecclesia romana.
Patarenus: Quia nos uariis tormentis perimit.
Catholicus: non est ita sed ita uidetur uobis.
Patarenus: immo est.
Catholicus: quis sunt hoc dicit.
Patarenus: nos dicimus qui sentimus.
Catholicus: Quomodo credendam hoc uobis? qui non uultis credere euangelistis et apostolis et angelis et ipsi christo perhibentibus testimonium de ipsius passione et morte ac sepultura et resurrectione. numquid estis pura et simplex ueritas et illi sunt fallax mendacium. obmutescite filii diaboli. stipula dampnationis eterne. et attende quod christus stultos apellerat non solum

to death and shall deliver him to the Gentiles to be mocked, and scourged, and crucified, and the third day he shall rise again." Also 26 (26:12) "For she in pouring this ointment upon my body, has done it for my burial." And 27 (27:35) "And after they had crucified him," and later (27:47) "and Jesus, crying out in a loud voice, gave up the spirit," and in the same (27:59-60) "And Joseph taking the body, wrapped it up in a clean linen cloth and laid it in his own new monument," and at the end (28:5-6) "for I know that you seek Jesus who was crucified. He is not here, for he is risen, as he said. Come, and see the place where the Lord was laid." Also (Mk 15:44) "But Pilate marveled that he should be already dead. And sending for the centurion, he asked him if he were already dead, and when he had understood it from the centurion, he gave the body to Joseph." Also Luke 2 (2:34) "Behold this child is set for rise and fall of many in Israel, and for a sign which shall be contradicted." And at the end (24:38-39) "Why are you troubled, and why do thoughts arise in your hearts? See my hands and feet, that it is I myself, touch and see." And John 19 (19:40) "They took therefore the body of Jesus." Also Romans 6 (6:9) "Christ rising again from the dead, dies now no more." And Apocalypse 1 (1:7) "and every eye shall see him, and those also who pierced him,' and later (1:17-18) "I am the first and the last, and was alive, and was dead." And also Acts 2 (2:23-24) "this same being delivered up, by the determinate counsel and foreknowledge of God, you have crucified and slain by the hands of wicked men, whom God has raised up." From these therefore and from many other passages, which I have not included so as not to be long-winded, it is plainly evident that our Lord Jesus Christ truly suffered, died, and was buried, and also truly rose again.

Pat: I say that all the passages which speak about the passion, death, and burial or Christ, or of His resurrection, are to be understood 'as it was thought' or 'as it seemed.'
Cath: But tell me, O savage beast, you who slander the charity of God and the truth of scripture, why do you complain about the Roman Church?
Pat: Since it kills us with various tortures.
Cath: That is not so, but it seems so to you.
Pat: On the contrary, it is so.
Cath: Who says this?
Pat: We say it, who experience it.
Cath: How can I believe you, who do not wish to believe the evangelists and apostles and angels and Christ Himself, bearing witness to His passion, death, burial, and resurrection? Is it possible that you are true, pure and simple, and all these are deceitful liars? Be silent, offspring of the devil, stubble prepared for eternal damnation! And listen that Christ calls fools not only those who

---

12 enim…**13** fecit] Matt. 26:12 (mitte) mittens *Vulg.*)   **13** post-quam…**14** eum] Matt. 27:35.   **14** ihesus…**15** spiritum] Matt. 27:47.   **16** et² …**17** nouo] Matt. 27:59-60 (posuit) add. illud | monumento) add. suo *Vulg.*)   **18** scio…**20** dominus] Matt. 28:5-6 (fuerat) erat *Vulg.*)   **21** pilatus…**24** Ioseph] Mar. 15:44.   **24** ecce…**26** contradicetur] Luc. 2:34.   **26** quid…**29** uidete] Luc. 24:38-39 (meos) om. *Vulg.*)   **29** acceperunt…**30** ihesu] Ioh. 19:40.   **30** christus…**31** moritur] Rom. 6:9 (iam) add. non *Vulg.*)   **31** et…**32** pupugerunt] Apoc. 1:7.   **33** ego…**34** mortuus] Apoc. 1:17-18.   **34** hunc…**37** suscita-uit] Act. 2:23-24.

23 donauit] lavit *P*   **31** apocalypsis] lucam *P*   **37** ex²] om. *F*   **45** Catholicus] om. *P*   **47** romana] christiana *P*   **59** attende] actendite *P*

X.15.21 iam|fol. 58ra *P*   **44** uidebatur|fol. 58rb *P*   **45** dicite|fol. 44v *F*

illos qui hoc contumaciter negant. sed etiam illos qui de his pie dubitant. dicens in lucam. ultimo. O stulti et tardi corde ad credendum in omnibus que locuti sunt prophete. nonne hec oportuit pati christum et ita intrare in gloriam suam? etcet. uidete quod de uobis hanc uesaniam amplectentibus apostolus. ii^a. ad corinthios. i^o. uerbum enim crucis pereuntibus quidem stultitia est. his autem qui salui fiunt id est nobis uirtus dei est. etcet. et infra. nos autem predicamus christum crucifixum. iudeis quidem scandalum gentibus autem stultitiam. ipsis autem uocatis etcet. et ad phylippenses. iii. nunc autem et flens dico inimicos crucis christi. ergo uos estis pereuntes et estis sicut iudei et gentiles insuper inimici sancte crucis. qui passionem crucis negatis salutarem.

Patarenus: Dicam ergo quod christus fuit passus et mortuus et sepultus. ac resurrexit in carne celesti quam de celo portuit.

Catholicus: Hoc non potes uere dicere quia paulus infrenat os tuum. i^a. ad timotheus. ii^o. dicens. memor esto dominum ihesum christum resurrexisse a mortuis ex semine dauid. etcet. et in actus. xiii. inueni dauid filium iesse etcet. et infra. Cuius deus ex semine secundum promissionem eduxit israel saluatorem ihesum etcet. ergo dominus ihesus mortuus est et resurrexit in ea carne quam traxit de de genealogia dauid filii iesse quam texunt mattheus et lucam in euangeliis suis.

Quod christus semel tantum passus est

Ad romanos. vi. quod enim mortuus est peccato mortuus est semel et ad hebreos. ix. christus autem assistens pontifex etcet. ibi per proprium sanguinem introiuit semel in sancta eterna redemptionem inuenta. et infra quemadmodum pontifex etcet. ibi alioquin oportebat eum frequenter pati ab origine mundi. nec autem semel in consummatione seculorum ad destruxionem peccati per hostiam suam apparuit et quemadmodum statutum est hominibus semel mori post hoc autem iudicium sic et christus semel oblatus est ad multorum exhaurienda peccata etcet. item. x. una enim oblatione consummauit in sempiternum sanctificatos etcet. ergo christus tantum mortuus est.

De descensu christi ad inferos

Ad romanos. x. ne dixeris in corde tuo quis ascendet in celum id est christum deducere. quasi dicat. non dicis quod nullus ascendit. quia hoc dicere est christum deducere id est inde sequitur hoc inconueniens quod

contumaciously deny Him, but also those who respectfully doubt, saying in Luke at the end (24:25–26) "O foolish and slow of heart to believe in all things which the prophets have spoken. Ought not Christ to have suffered these things, and so to enter into his glory?" See that the Apostle also includes you in this insanity, 2 Corinthians 1 (1 Cor 1:18) "For the word of the cross to those indeed that perish is foolishness, but to those who are saved, that is, to us, it is the power of God." and later (1:23–24) "But we preach Christ crucified, unto the Jews indeed a stumbling block, and unto the Gentiles foolishness, but unto those who are called." And Philippians 3 (3:18) "I now tell you weeping, that they are enemies of the cross of Christ." Therefore you are perishing and you are like the Jews and Gentiles, above all enemies of the Christ, who deny His saving passion on the cross.

Pat: Therefore I would say that Christ suffered, died, was buried, and rose in His spiritual flesh, which He carried from heaven.

Cath: This you cannot say to be true since Paul restrains your mouth, saying in 1 Timothy 2 (2 Tim 2:8) "Be mindful that the Lord Jesus Christ has risen again from the dead, of the seed of David." And in Acts 13 (13:22) "I have found David, the son of Jesse," and later (13:23) "Of this man's seed God, according to his promise, has raised up to Israel a Savior, Jesus." Therefore the Lord Jesus died and arose in that flesh which He took from the line of David, the son of Jesse, which line Matthew and Luke carefully traced in their gospels.

That Christ suffered only once

Romans 6 (6:7) "For he that is dead in sin," one dies but once only. Hebrews 9 (9:11) "But Christ, having come as a high priest," here (9:12) "but by his own blood, entered once into the holies, having obtained eternal redemption," and later (9:25–26) "as the high priest," there "for then he ought to have suffered often from the beginning of the world, but now once at the end of ages, he has appeared," and (9:27–28) "And as it is appointed for men to die once, and after this the judgment so also Christ was offered once to bear the sins of many." Also 10 (10:14) "For by one oblation he has perfected forever those who are sanctified." Therefore Christ died only once.

On the descent of Christ into hell

Romans 10 (10:6–8) "Do not say, who shall ascend into heaven? That is to bring Christ down," as if to say, do not say that no one ascends, for this is to bring Christ down, that is, thence inconsistent with what follows, "who shall

quis descendet in abyssum. esset dicere quod christus non descendit. quid falsum esset dicere. quia ipse descendit in abyssum. ad hoc est quod dicit beatus petrus in actibus. ii°. uiri israelitice etcet. ibi. quem deus suscitauit solutis doloribus inferni iuxta quod impossibile erat teneri illum ab eo etcet. et infra. quoniam non derelinques animam meam in inferno etcet. et infra. prouidens. scilicet Dauid. locutus est de resurrectione christi. quia neque derelictus est in inferno etcet. ergo christus descendit ad inferos. intellige scilicet secundum animam.

De ascensu christi in celum

Marcum. ultimo. et dominus quidem ihesus postquam locutus est eis assumptus est in caelum. et sedet a dextris dei etcet. item lucam. ultimo. et factum est dum benediceret illis recessit ab eis et ferebatur in caelum etcet. et actus primo. cum hec dixisset uidentibus illis eleuatus est et nubes suscepit eum ab oculis eorum etcet. et infra. hic ihesus qui assumptus est a uobis in celum etcet. et nota quod tam in euangelius matheus et lucam. quam in actibus dicit. ihesus quod nomen est humanitatis christi et dicit assumptus uel ferebatur que sunt uerba pertinentia ad eius humanitatem. quasi dicat. ex uirtute humanitatis non ascendit. sed asumptus est scilicet a diuinitate id est ex uirtute diuinitatis. magnificentia humanitatis christi eleuata est in celum.

De aduentu christi in fine mundi ad iudicium

Mattheus. xiii. sic erit in consummatione seculi mittet filius hominis angelos suos etcet. et xxiii. sicut enim fulgur exit ab oriente et paret usque in occidentem ita erit et aduentus filii hominis etcet. et infra. et tunc apparebit signum filii hominis in caelo et tunc plangent se omnes tribus terrae et uidebunt filium hominis uenientem in nubibus celi cum uirtute multa et maiestate et mittet angelos suos cum tuba et uoce magna et congregabunt electos eius a iiii^{or} uentis a summis celorum usque ad terminos eorum. etcet. et infra ita erit aduentus filii hominis. etcet. et postea. quia qua nescitis hora filius hominis uenturus est etcet. item. xxv. cum autem uenerit filius hominis in maiestate sua et omnes angeli eius cum eo tunc sedebit super sedem maiestatis sue et congregabuntur ante eum omnes gentes et segregabit eos etcet. idem. xxvi amodo uidebitis filium hominis sedentem a dextris uirtutis dei et uenientem in nubibus caeli etcet. item lucam. xvii. ita erit filius hominis in die sua etcet. et

descend into the deep," this is to say that Christ did not descend, which is false, since he descended into the abyss, this is what Blessed Peter says in Acts 2 (1:11) "Men of Israel," there (2:24) "Whom God has raised up, having loosed the sorrows of hell, as it was impossible that he should be held by it," and later (2:27) "Because you will not leave my soul in hell," and later (2:31) "Foreseeing this," namely, David, "he spoke of the resurrection of Christ. For neither was he left in hell," therefore Christ descended into hell, understood, namely, according to the soul.

On the ascent of Christ into heaven

At the end of Mark (16:19) "And the Lord Jesus, after he had spoken to them, was taken up into heaven, and sits at the right hand of God." Also at the end of Luke (24:51) "And it happened that while he blessed them, he departed from them, and was carried up to heaven." And Acts 1 (1:9) "And when he had said these things, while they looked on, he was raised up, and a cloud received him out of their sight." And later (1:11) "This Jesus who is taken up from you into heaven," and note that just as in the gospels of Matthew and Luke, so it says in Acts, Jesus — which is the name of Christ in His humanity — and it says assumed or brought, which are words pertaining to His humanity, as if to say, He did not ascend by virtue of His humanity, but was assumed, namely, by divinity, that is, by the strength of divine power. The grandeur of the humanity of Christ was taken up to heaven.

On the coming of Christ at the end of the world for judgment

Matthew 13 (13:40–41) "so shall it be at the end of the world, the son of man shall send his angels," and 23 (24:27) "For as lightning comes out of the east, and appears even into the west, so shall the coming of the Son of man be," and later (24:30–31) "And then shall appear the sign of the Son of man in heaven, and then shall all tribes of the earth mourn and they shall see the son of man coming in the clouds of heaven with much power and majesty, and he shall send his angels with a trumpet, and a great voice, and they shall gather together his elect from the four winds, from the farthest parts of the heavens to their utter ends," and later (24:27) "so shall the coming of the son of man be," and later (24:44) "because at what hour you do not know the Son of man will come." Also 25 (25:31–32) "And when the Son of man shall come in his majesty, and all his angels with him, then shall he sit upon the seat of his majesty, and all nations shall be gathered together before him, and he shall separate them one from another." The same in 26 (26:64) "hereafter you shall see the Son of man sitting on the right hand of the power of

---

9 uiri israelitice] Act. 1:11 (israelitice) galilaeae *Vulg*.) | quem…11 eo] Act. 2:24. 12 quoniam…inferno] Act. 2:27. 13 prouidens…15 inferno] Act. 2:31. **X.18.2** et…4 dei] Mar. 16:19. 4 et…6 caelum] Luc. 24:51. 6 cum…8 eorum] Act. 1:9. 8 hic…9 celum] Act. 1:11. **X.19.2** sic…3 suos] Matt. 13:40-41. 3 sicut…5 hominis] Matt. 24:27. 5 et³…11 eorum] Matt. 24:30-31 (apparebit] parebit | se] om. *Vulg*.) 12 ita…hominis] Matt. 24:27. 13 quia…est] Matt. 24:44. 14 cum…17 eos] Matt. 25:31-32 (eius] om. | segregabit] separabit *Vulg*.) 18 amodo…19 caeli] Matt. 26:64. 20 ita…sua] Luc. 17:24.

6 quis…8 abyssum] repet. *F* 15 etcet…inferos] om. *P* **X.18.11** assumptus] adsumptus *P*

X.17.8 hoc|fol. 45r *F* **X.18.7** suscepit|fol. 59ra *P* **X.19.17** xxvi|fol. 59rb *P*

xxi. et tunc uidebunt filium hominis uenientem in nube etcet. item. iohannes. v. neque enim pater iudicat quemquam sed omne iudicium dedit filio etcet. et infra. et potestatem dedit ei iudicium facere quia filius hominis est. nolite mirari hoc quia uenit hora in qua omnes qui in monumentis sunt audient uocem filii dei etcet. item. ii^a. ad corinthios. v. omnes enim nos manifestari oportet ante tribunal christi etcet. item ad phylippenses. ii^o. ut in nomine ihesu omne genuflec-tatur etcet. et ii^o. ad thimotheus. iiii^o. testificor coram deo. et christo ihesu qui iudicaturus est uiuos et mortuos etcet. et apocalypsis. xix. et de ore ipsius procedebat gladius ex utraque parte acutus ut in ipso percutiat gentes etcet. idem ultimo. ecce uenio cito et merces mea mecum est etcet. item actus. i^o. sic ueniet quemadmodum uidistis eum etcet. supple de hac materia ut supra titulus i^o. in rubricella quod pene omnis sunt a deo etcet. et infra in tractatu de iudicio uniuersali et fine mundi notatum inuenies. et sic patet ex premissis. quod dominus ihesus christis iudicabit in fine mundi uiuos et mortuos in carne humana. in qua iudicatus fuit ipse.

Quod christus non fuit uerus homo

Patarenus: Ad phylippenses. ii^o. in similitudinem hominum factus et habitu inuentus ut homo etcet. sed quod est simile alteri non est illud. ergo christus non fuit homo. si fuit similis homini.

Catholicus: Respondeo quod duplex est similitudo scilicet per naturam et per accidens. primam uero non habuit christus. quia uere naturam assumpsit humanam. secundam autem habuit. quia non fuit peccator sed fuit similis peccatori propter penam peccati quam portauit. Vnde ad romanos. viii. Deus filium suum mittens in similitudinem carnis peccati etcet. et sic intelligitur istud scilicet in similitudinem hominum factus etcet. uel est hoc accomoda distributio et est sensus. christus factus est in similitudinem hominum id est talis qualis est unusquisque homo scilicet per naturam hoc animal rationale et mortale.

Patarenus: Item apocalypsis. i^o. in medio septem candelabrorum aureorum similem filio hominis etcet.

Catholicus: Christus dicitur similis filio hominis prout supra tibi exposui uel dicitur similis filio hominis scilicet post resurrectionem eius postquam non erat passibilis. sed quasi passibilis apparuit in uisione beato iohanni. uel uerius dico quod ille qui apparuit erat

God, and coming in the clouds of heaven." Also Luke 17 (17:24) "so shall the Son of man be in his day," and 21 (21:27) "and then they shall see the Son of man coming in the clouds." Also John 5 (5:22) "For neither does the Father judge any man, but has given all judgment to the Son," and later (5:27–28) "And he has given him power to execute judgment, because he is the Son of man. Do not wonder at this; for the hour is coming, in which all who are in the graves shall hear the voice of the Son of God." Also 2 Corinthians 5 (5:10) "For we must all stand before the judgment seat of Christ." Also Philippians 2 (2:10) "That at the name of Jesus every knee should bend." And 2 Timothy 4 (4:1) "I charge you before God and Jesus Christ, who shall judge the living and the dead." And Apocalypse 19 (19:15) "And out of his mouth comes a sharp two edged sword, that with it he may strike the nations," also at the end (22:12) "Behold, I come quickly, and my reward is with me." Also Acts 1 (1:11) "So he shall come, as you have seen him going into heaven." This material is supplied above in book 1, in the section that nearly all is from God, and later you will find it noted in the section on the universal judgment and the end of the world, and so it is plain from the foregoing that the Lord Jesus Christ will judge the living and the dead at the end of the world in His human flesh, in which He Himself was judged.

That Christ was not truly a man

[Pat:] Philippians 2 (2:7) "being made in the likeness of men, and in form found as a man." But because what is similar to another, does not make it that thing, therefore Christ was not a man if he was similar to a man.

Cath: I reply that similitude can be taken in two senses, namely, naturally or accidentally. The first Christ did not have, since He assumed a true human nature, yet the second He had, since He was not a sinner but was like sinners on account of the penalty for sin which He bore. Whence Romans 8 (8:3) "God sending his own Son, in the likeness of sinful flesh," and this it is to be interpreted thusly, namely, "being made in the likeness of men," or it is adapted to the division, and this is the sense of Christ "being made in the likeness of men," that is, such as to each man, namely, through the nature of this rational and mortal animal.

Pat: Also Apocalypse 1 (1:13) "And in the midst of the seven golden candlesticks, one like the Son of man."

Cath: Christ is said to be like the son of man just as I explained above, or He is said to be similar to the son of man, namely, after His resurrection He was no longer passible, but He appeared as passible in the vision of Blessed John, or more truly I say that he who appeared was an

---

21 et...22 nube] Luc. 21:27.   22 neque...23 filio] Ioh. 5:22.   24 et...26 dei] Ioh. 5:27-28.   27 omnes...28 christi] 2 Cor. 5:10.   29 ut...genuflec-tatur] Php. 2:10.   30 testificor...32 mortuos] 2 Tim. 4:1.   32 et^2...34 gentes] Apoc. 19:15 (ipsius) eius *Vulg.*)   34 ecce...35 mea] Apoc. 22:12.   35 sic...36 eum] Act. 1:11.   X.20.2 in...3 homo] Php. 2:7.   11 Deus...12 peccati] Rom. 8:3.   19 in...20 hominis] Apoc. 1:13.

X.19.30 thimotheus] tymotheus *F*   32 xix] xviiii *P*   34 idem] quod *F*   35 mecum est] om. *P*   39 patet] add. ei *F*   X.20.1 uerus] uere *F*   5 fuit^1] add. similis *P*   7 non] om. *F*   19 Patarenus] om. *F* | septem] vii *F*   21 prout...22 hominis] om. *P*

32 mortuos|fol. 45v *F*   41 mundi|fol. 59va *P*

angelus qui habebat formam filii hominis sicut et angelis ueteris testamenti tenebat formam dei in ideo dicitur similis filius homini.

Quod christus non habuit carnem uel saltem nostre conditionis

[Patarenus:] Mattheum iiii. Cum ieiunasset xl. diebus et xl. noctibus etcet. ergo non habuit carnem terrestrem. quia secundum illam non potuisset tantum ieiunare.

Catholicus: Respondeo quod tantum ieiunauit miraculum fuit quale et deus fecit per moysen et heliam quod carne terrestre habuisse non inficiaris. sed audi quod sequitur ibi postea exuriit etcet. ergo habuit carnem nostre conditionis que esuriit.

[Patarenus:] Item idem xii. at ipse respondens dicenti sibi ait que est mater mea et qui sunt fratres mei. etcet. ecce quod christus negauit mariam esse matrem suam carnalem et illos carnales fratres esse. ergo non habuit carnem humanam.

Catholicus: Respondeo non est uerum. quod ipse negauerit hoc sed addidit quod et illi sunt frater et soror et mater eius. qui faciant uoluntatem patris sui. similiter in iohanne. xx. beati qui non uiderunt et crediderunt etcet.

[Patarenus:] Item. idem. xvii. ducit illos in montem excelsum seorsum et transfiguratus est ante eos et resplenduit facies eius sicut sol etcet. hic apparuit qualem carnem habuit christus. quia non de nostra condictione sed de celo gloriosam.

Catholicus: respondeo quod christus ostendit ibi carnem quam habebat sed non talem in ideo dicit. transfiguratus est et illustrauit enim eam lumine sue diuinitatis ad horam. in argumentum sue resurrectionis et nostre. sicut et post resurrectionem eandem obfuscauit gloriosam. ut sui discipuli morose possent eum intueri.

Patarenus: Item lucam. iiiº. ut putabatur filius ioseph etcet. a simili dicendum est ut putabatur filius marie. et sic non habuit carnem uere.

Catholicus: Respondeo immo ex hoc quod dicit de ioseph ut putabatur christus filius eius et dixerat de eo et de uirgine maria parentes eius etcet. innuit quod uerus filius fuit beate uirginis cum de illa numquam dicat ut putabatur filius marie. quia excepto aliquo de regula. omnia que intra regulam concluduntur in suo statu relinquuntur. presertim cum expressim legatur beatam uirginem matrem esse deum.

21 That Christ did not have flesh or at least [a body] subject to our conditions

[Pat:] (Mt 4:2) "After he had fasted for forty days and forty nights," therefore He did not have earthly flesh, since according to such human flesh no one would be able to fast in such a manner.

Cath: I reply that He had fasted in such a manner, and it was a miracle the like of which God also performed for Moses and Elijah, and that they had human flesh you do not deny, but hear what follows thereafter "he was hungry," therefore he had the flesh like ours which hungers.

[Pat:] Also the same in 12 (12:48) "But he answering him who spoke, said, 'Who is my mother, and who are my brethren?'" See that Christ denies Mary to be his carnal mother, and denies his carnal brothers, therefore he had no human flesh.

Cath: I reply that it is not true that he denied this, but he adds to that "he is my brother, and sister, and mother who do the will of my Father." Similarly is John 20 (20: 29) "Blessed are those who have not seen, and believed."

[Pat:] Also the same in 17 (Mt 17:1–2) "And after six days Jesus took Peter and James, and John his brother with him, and brought them up apart into a high mountain, and he was transfigured before them. And his face did shine like the sun and his garments became white as snow." Here Christ appears to have such flesh that is not like ours, but rather of the glory of heaven.

Cath: I reply that Christ shows here the flesh which He had, but not of such a kind, as He says, it was transfigured, for He shows it forth in it the light of His divinity at that time, foretelling His resurrection and ours, just as after His resurrection He hid His glory, so that His fretful disciples might be able to look at Him.

Pat: Also Luke 3 (3:23) "being as it was supposed the son of Joseph," which is similar to saying "being as it was supposed the son of Mary," and so He did not have true flesh.

Cath: I reply to the contrary from this because it says that it was supposed that Christ was the son of Joseph, and it spoke of him and of the Virgin Mary as "his parents." This implies that He was the true son of the Blessed Virgin since it never says "being as it was supposed the son of Mary," for when an exception has been made from a rule, all the things which are contained within the rule are left in their own state, especially since it is plainly read that the Blessed Virgin is the mother of God.

X.21.3 Cum...4 noctibus] Matt. 4:2.   12 at...13 mei] Matt. 12:48.   20 beati...21 crediderunt] Ioh. 20:29.   22 xvii...24 sol] Matt. 17:1-2.   34 ut...ioseph] Luc. 3:23.

28 similis] om. *P*   X.21.1 christus] christo *F*   9 heliam] helyam *F*   15 ergo] add. ha *P* exp. | habuit...16 carnem] transp. *P*   20 similiter] similis *F*   22 ducit] duxit *P* | illos] eos *F*   31 et post] om. *P*   32 morose] moto se *P* | possent] posse *P*   34 Patarenus] om. *F*

X.20.26 habebat|fol. 59vb *P*   X.21.22 xvii|fol. 60ra *P*   36 habuit|fol. 46r *F*   43 presertim|fol. 60rb *P*

Patarenus: Item xx. quomodo dicunt christum filium esse dauid etcet. uidete o romani quomodo christus ostendit quod non fuit filius dauid. ergo non habuit carnem nostre condicionis.

Catholicus: Respondeo loquitur dominus secundum intellectum iudeorum. qui intelligebant christum tantum unam naturam habere debere scilicet humanam sicut et hodie faciunt et ipse probat quod et aliam habuit hoc est diuininam et probat hoc per dauid. qui notat christum dominum suum ante quam ueniret in carnem. nec est putandum quod dominus dicat hic contra euangelistam suum mattheum qui scribit libro generationis ihesu christi filii dauid etcet. quod et in plerisque locis euangeliorum legitur.

Patarenus: Item. iohannes. secundo. dicit ei ihesus quid mihi et tibi est mulier? ergo non fuit filius eius et sic non habuit carnem humanam.

Catholicus: Respondeo quod nil christo et beate marie fuit de hoc quod ipsa querebat scilicet de uirtute conuertendi aquam in uinum quam non habebat ex natura humanitatis quam ab illa contraxerat. sed ex natura diuinitatis de uino uero quidem elicere debebat de natura humanitatis quam a matre contraxerat subdit. nondum uenit hora mea etcet. hora. scilicet passionis uel aliter. nil mihi et tibi est mulier de uino procurando conuiuis sed modo intelligis dicta ibi enim statim sequitur. dicit ministris etcet. et supra dixerat dicit mater ihesu ad eum etcet. ergo christus fuit filius uirginis secundum carnem.

Patarenus: item idem. iii°. nemo ascendit in celum nisi qui de celo descendit filius hominis qui est in celo etcet. ergo filius hominis descendit de celo apportauit carnem suam.

Catholicus: Respondeo quod tanta est unio diuinitatis et humanitatis christi quod totus dicitur deus et totus dicitur filius hominis siue homo. est ergo sensus filius hominis qui est deus descendit de celo id est qui latebat in diuinitate. quod est esse deum in celo. apparuit nobis per assumptam humanitatem in terris. quod fuit eius descendere. sed modo audias tu. hoc dicit filius hominis qui est in celo. sed tunc illa caro christi quam gestabat not erat in celo. ergo intelligitur qui est in celo scilicet per naturam diuinitatis. sic et istud intelligitur. descendit de celo filius hominis scilicet in quantum deus.

Patarenus: item idem. vi. uiderunt ihesum ambulantem supra mare etcet. ergo non habebat carnem humanam. sed fantasticam. uel de celo.

---

45 quomodo...46 dauid] Luc. 20:41.   56 libro...57 dauid] Matt. 1:1.   59 dicit...60 mulier] Ioh. 2:4.   68 nondum...mea] Ioh. 2:4.   71 dicit ministris] Ioh. 2:5.   72 dicit...eum] Ioh. 2:3.   74 nemo...75 celo²] Ioh. 3:13.   90 uiderunt...91 mare] Ioh. 6:19 (uiderunt] uident *Vulg.*)

47 ergo] igitur *F*   52 quod...53 diuininam] om. *F*   54 notat] negat *F*   58 legitur] add. etcet *P*   66 de...67 humanitatis] om. *F*   69 uino] humo *P*   70 conuiuis] conuiuis cumuiit *F*   74 Patarenus] om. *F; al. man. marg. sin P*   79 totus¹] totum *P* | totus² totum *P*   90 Patarenus] om. *F; al. man. marg. sin P*

68 subdit|fol. 60va *P*

Catholicus: respondeo sicut tibi respondi supra de obiectione ieiunii item est instantia contra tuam argumentationem de helia et heliseo qui ambulauerunt supra aquam et tamen habuerunt carnem sicut nos habemus.

Patarenus: Item. idem. vi°. ego sum panis uiuus qui de celo descendi etcet. ergo caro eius descendit de celo.

Catholicus: Respondeo quod christus descendit de celo in quantum deus et secundum quod est deus dicitur panis. quia sicut panis exit non de carne. ita christus in quantum deus non exiuit de carne humana. secundum uero corpus sue humanitatis dicitur caro quia caro fuit et de carne exiuit. de qua subdit. caro mea uere est cibum. etcet.

Patarenus: item. prima. ad corinthios. xv. secundus homo de celo celestis etcet. ergo christus in quantum fuit homo fuit celestis. igitur de celo portauit carnem suam.

Catholicus: Respondeo quod ideo dicitur de celo christus. quia quicquid in eo fuit desuper habuit unde uenit omne bonum. nichil enim terrenitatis in eo fuit. simile. apocalypsis. xxi. ubi legitur israele de celo descendisse.

Patarenus: item ad ii^a. ad corinthios. v°. si cognouimus secundum carnem christum sed nunc iam non nouimus etcet. ergo non habuit carnem christus. nisi quia ita uidebatur.

Catholicus: Respondeo hoc intelligitur si cognouimus christum secundum carnem id est secundum cerimonialia ambulasse usque ad mortem suam. nunc iam non nouimus ipsum in nobis ambulare. secundum illa postquam in passione dixit. consummatum est. unde subdit. hic apostolus. si qua ergo in christo noua creaura est. uetera transierunt. ecce facta sunt noua etcet. uel aliter. si cognouimus secundum carnem christum. carnem scilicet mortalem. quandoque immo iam scilicet resurrectione facta non nouimus eum secundum carnem mortalem. quia christus resurgens a mortuis iam non moritur. nec potest intelligi hoc auctoritas secundum uestrum errorem. quia non dicit si opinati sumus secundum carnem christum. in opinione enim cito potest errari. sed pro constanti ponit si cognouimus etcet. in cognitione autem numquam erratur. ergo aliquando fuit uerum apostolum et illos fideles quibus loquebatur nouisse christum secundum carnem. ergo uerum est quod christus carnem habuit. quia quod semel est uerum semper erit uerum.

Cath: I reply just as I answered above regarding the objection to fasting, again an instance against your argument is that about Elijah and Elisha who walked on water, and yet had flesh like us.

Pat: Also the same in 6 (6:41) "I am the living bread come down from heaven," therefore his flesh descended from heaven.

Cath: I reply that Christ descended from heaven inasmuch as He was God, and according to this God is called bread, since just as bread does not emerge from flesh, so Christ, insofar as He is God, does not come forth from human flesh, just as according to the body of His humanity He is called flesh, since it was flesh and proceeded forth from flesh, about which He adds (6:56) "for my flesh is food indeed."

Pat: also 1 Corinthians 15 (15:47) "the second man, from heaven, heavenly." Therefore Christ, insofar as He was a man, was heavenly, as a result He carried his flesh from heaven.

Cath: I reply that Christ is said to be from heaven, since whatever was in Him was from above, whence comes every good thing, for there was nothing earthly in Him, similar in Apocalypse 21 (21:10 paraphrase) where it is read of Israel descending from heaven.

Pat: Also 2 Corinthians 5 (5:16) "And if we have known Christ according to the flesh, but now we know him so no longer." Therefore Christ did not have flesh, unless He only seemed to have it.

Cath: I reply that this is to be interpreted if we knew Christ according to the flesh, that is, according to the ceremonial law to be followed even to His death, now we do not know Him walking among us according to that flesh, as He spoke after His passion, "It is finished," whence the Apostle adds here (2 Cor 5:17) "If then any be in Christ a new creature, the old things have passed away, behold all things are made new." Or otherwise (5:16) "If we have known Christ according to the flesh," namely mortal flesh, "but now we know him so no longer, whereas on the contrary now" — the resurrection having been accomplished — "we do not know him according to mortal flesh," (Rm 6:9) "that Christ rising again from the dead, dies now no more." Neither is one able to understand this passage according to your error, since it does not say if by supposing we are according to the flesh of Christ, for in an opinion one is easily able to err, but for constancy he puts it thus "if we have known." For in cognition one can never err. Therefore at some time it was true that the apostle and those faithful to whom he was speaking knew Christ according to the flesh, therefore it is

---

98 ego...99 descendi] Ioh. 6:41.   105 caro² ...106 cibum] Ioh. 6:56.   107 secundus...108 celestis] 1 Cor. 15:47.   114 ubi...115 descendisse] Apoc. 21:10 paraphrase.   116 si...118 nouimus] 2 Cor. 5:16.   125 si...126 noua] 2 Cor. 5:17.   127 si...129 nouimus] 2 Cor. 5:16.   130 quia...131 moritur] Rom. 6:9.

---

95 helia] helya F | heliseo] helyseo F   102 exit non] transp. F | ita...103 humana] om. F   107 Patarenus] om. F; al. man. marg. dex. P   116 Patarenus] om. F; al. man. marg. dex. P   118 habuit] om. P   123 ipsum] add. ambulare P | in...ambulare] transp. P   132 errorem] om. P   133 opinati] oppinati P   134 opinione] oppinione P   135 cognitione] add. marg. sin. P exclamation point.   138 est] add. semper F

94 contra|fol. 60vb P   110 suam|fol. 46v F   123 nouimus|fol. 61ra P

140 **Patarenus:** Item ad ephesios. ultimo. in finem cum omnibus qui diligunt dominum nostrum ihesum christum in incorruptione etcet. ergo nobiscum o romani non erit gratia. quia non creditis christum fuisse sine corruptione.

145 **Catholicus:** Respondeo non dicit quod christus fuerit sine corruptione. sed dicit quod diligunt eum fideles in incorruptione. quia habent eum iam impassibilem. uel fuit christus sine corruptione peccati. sicut dicit petrus in prima. secundo. qui peccatum non fecit nec
150 inuentus est dolus in ore eius etcet. et fuit etiam sine corruptione putrefactionis carnis in sepultura. ut legitur actus. ii°. neque caro eius uidit corruptionem etcet. uel dicit incorruptione id est in uita eterna ubi nulla erit corruptio.

155 [**Patarenus:**] Item prima iohanne. iiii. omnis qui qui confitetur Iesum Christum in carne uenisse etcet. sed bene sequitur. iste uenit de monte inueste. ergo portauit uestem. et sic patet quod christus carnem suam portauit de celo.

160 **Catholicus:** Respondeo quod christus inde portauit carnem suam. unde eam accepit id est de utero beate uirginis. sicut ostendit apostolus ad Galathas. iiii°. misit deus filium suum factum ex muliere etcet. et est tale istud id est deus inuisibilis existens in diuinitatis
165 natura. factus est nobis uisibilis per carnem assumptam. quod fuit uenire nobis. unde apostolus. ad titum. ultimo. cum autem benignitas et humanitas apparuit saluatoris nostri dei etcet. et iohannes. i°. uerbum caro factum est et habitauit in nobis etcet. uel dicam quod
170 uerum est. quia uera littera non est in carne uenisse. sed est in carnem uenisse et sic est per fidem catholicam.

Patarenus: Preterea quomodo possum credere quod christus tam turpe quod sumpsisset et tam turpia
175 egisset prout natura exigit humana.

Catholicus: Respondeo quod nichil turpe est in conspectu non solum dei sed et filiorum eius. nisi peccatum. et unde stulta est incredulitas tua. audi enim apostolum loquente de infirmitate humane
180 nature quam christus assumpsit unde prima ad corinthios. i°. quod infirmum est dei fortius est hominibus etcet.

Quod christus non comedit temporaliter

Patarenus: Lucam ultimo. sumens reliquias dedit eis et dixit ad eos hec sunt uerba que locutus sum ad uos

true that Christ had flesh, since what is once true always will be true.

Pat: Also Ephesians at the very end (6:24) "With all those who love our Lord Jesus Christ in incorruption," Therefore with us, O Roman, for with you there will not be grace, since you do not believe that Christ was without corruption.

Cath: I reply that it does not say that Christ was without corruption, but it says that "the faithful love him in incorruption," since they hold Him now as impassible. Or Christ was without the corruption of sin as 1 Peter 2 says (2:22) "Who did no sin, neither was guile found in his mouth." And also He was without the decomposition of the flesh in the tomb, as is read in Acts 2 (2:31) "neither did his flesh see corruption." Or he says 'incorruption,' that is, in eternal life, where there will be no corruption.

[**Pat:**] Also 1 John 4 (4:2) "all those who confess that Jesus Christ is come in the flesh." But it well follows, He came from the mountain unclothed, therefore He carried clothing, and thus it is plain that Christ carried His flesh from heaven.

Cath: I reply that Christ bore His flesh from whence He received it, that is, from the womb of the Blessed Virgin, just as the Apostle shows in Galatians 4 (4:4) "God sent his son, born of a woman," and this is such, that is, the invisible God living in the divine nature, was made visible for us by the assumption of flesh, which was to come to us, whence the Apostle says at the end of Titus (3:4) "But when the goodness and kindness of God our Savior appeared." And John 1 (1:14) "The word became flesh and dwelt among us." Or I might say that it is true, since the true literal meaning is not He has come in the flesh, but rather has come into flesh, and this is the Catholic faith.

Pat: Further in what manner can I believe that Christ was so base that He might take in or expel such nasty things as is necessary for human nature.

Cath: I reply that nothing is base in the sight of not only God, but also of his Son, except for sin, and so your disbelief is foolish. For hear the Apostle speaking about the infirmity of the human nature which Christ assumed, whence 1 Corinthians 1 (1:25) "the weakness of God is stronger than men."

That Christ did not eat in time

Pat: At the end of Luke (24:43–44) "taking the remains, he gave to them and he said to them, 'These are the words

---

140 cum...142 incorruptione] Eph. 6:24.   149 qui...150 eius] 1 Pet. 2:22.   152 neque...corruptionem] Act. 2:31.   155 omnis...156 uenisse] 1 Ioh. 4:2 (qui) om. add. spiritus *Vulg.*)   163 misit...muliere] Gal. 4:4.   167 cum...168 dei] Tit. 3:4.   168 uerbum...169 nobis] Ioh. 1:14.   181 quod...182 hominibus] 1 Cor. 1:25.   **X.22.2** sumens...3 uos] Luc. 23:43-44.

142 nobiscum...143 romani] nobiscum o romani vobiscum ordinari F   143 gratia] add. ergo F   171 per...172 catholicam] pro fide catholica F   173 Patarenus] om. F; *al. man. marg. dex.* P   178 et] om. F

150 sine|fol. 61rb P   179 apostolum|fol. 61va P   **X.22.3** ad²|fol. 47r F

etcet. hic apparet qualem cibum manducauit christus id est uerba sua.

Catholicus: respondeo stulte non dicit quod christus manducasset uerba sua. sed quod manducauit piscem et mel dicit autem quod illa comestione est probatio et effectus uerborum que consueuerat illi dicere de sua resurrectione ante passionem eius. unde subdit ibi. locutus sum ad uos cum adhuc essem uobiscum. quoniam necesse est impleri omnia que scripta sunt etcet. et infra. quoniam scriptum est et sic opportebat pati christum et resurgere a mortuis die tertia etcet.

Patarenus: item iohannem. v. ille autem dixit eis. Ego cibum habeo manducare quem uos nescitis etcet. et quis sit ille cibum subdit. meus cibus est ut faciam uoluntatem eius qui misit me etcet. ecce quod non temporaliter sed spiritualiter dicit christum se comedisse.

Catholicus: Respondeo quod christus non negat quin temporaliter comederit. sed potius innuit cum dicit. ego cibum habeo manducare quem uos nescitis. quasi dicat non solum habeo manducare cibum temporale quem uos scitis. sed etiam manducare habeo potuisse alium cibum quem adhuc nescitis. nam hoc etiam de puro homine dicit ipse dominus quod duplici cibo uiuere debeat. mattheus. iiii. non in solo pane uiuit homo sed in omni uerbo quod procedit de ore dei etcet.

Quod christus non fuit uere passus

Patarenus: Apocalypsis v. et uidi et ecce in medio throni et quatuor animalium et in medio seniorum agnum stantem tamquam occisum etcet. ergo non fuit uere occisus christum sed ita uidebatur.

Catholicus: Respondeo quod quando in hac uisionem uidit eum beatus iohannes non erat occisus quia iam dudum resurrexerat non amplius moriturus. sed apparuit tamquam occisus propter electos suos. in quibus quasi tota die occiditur. iuxta illud actus. ix. saule quid me persequeris etcet. potest et aliter intelligi quod christus non fuit occisus sicut alii homines. quia in aliis erat mors necessitas. in christo uero fuit uoluntas. item in aliis erat potestas diaboli ad deducendum eos in infernum. uel in limbum. in christo uero fuit potestas super diabolum in morte eius ad religandum ipsum et ideo dicit tamquam occisum etcet. Sed dicite mihi heretici pessimi. quare negatis incarnationem christi et eius passionem? In potentia enim eius non repugnat quia cum omnia possit potuit istud. neque ignorantia eius repugnat et benignitas eius hoc exigebat ut probamus supra in parte nostra huius tractatus in rationibus naturalibus scriptura etiam tota

which I spoke to you.'" Here appears the kind of food that Christ ate, that is, His words.

Cath: I reply, Fool, it does not say that Christ ate His words, but that He ate fish and honey, and it also says that this eating is the proof and effect of the words which He left for them to speak of His resurrection before His passion, whence it adds there (24:44) "which I spoke to you while I was yet with you, that all things must be fulfilled, which are written." And later (24:46) "Thus it is written, and thus it was fitting for Christ to suffer, and to rise again from the dead on the third day."

Pat: Also John 5 (4:32) "But he said to them, 'I have food to eat, of which you do not know.'" And what that food might be, it continues (4:34) "My food is to do the will of Him who sent me." Behold Christ speaks about Himself eating not in time but spiritually.

Cath: I reply that Christ does not in fact deny eating in time, but rather alludes to it when He says "I have food to eat, of which you do not know," as if to say that I do not only have earthly food to eat which satisfies you, but also I have another food I am able to eat which you know, for this also speaks of man simply considered [e.g. of the humanity of Christ], that the Lord himself ought to live by means of two kinds of food. Matthew 4 (4:4) "Man does not live by bread alone, but by every word that comes from the mouth of God."

That Christ did not truly suffer

Pat: Apocalypse 5 (5:6) "And I saw, behold in the midst of the throne and of the four living creatures, and in the midst of the ancients, a Lamb standing as if it were slain." Therefore Christ was not truly killed, but it only seemed that way.

Cath: I reply that when Blessed John saw Him in this vision, He had not been killed since He had formerly been resurrected, no more to die, but He appeared like one killed on account of His elect, in whom He was being killed all the day through, according to that in Acts 9 (9:4) "Saul, why do you persecute me?" Or one is otherwise able to construe it that Christ was not killed like other men, since in others death is necessary, yet in Christ it was voluntary. Also in others the devil has power to lead them to hell or into limbo, yet in Christ there was power over the devil through His death for binding him anew, and so he says (Apoc 5:6) "as if it were slain." But tell me, O most wicked heretics, why you deny the incarnation of Christ and His passion? For it is not opposed to His power, for since He is capable of everything, He was capable of this, nor is His lack of knowledge opposed to it, and His kindness was demanding it, as we proved above in the section in this work of ours by natural reason, also the entirety of the Old and New Testaments plainly assert it in

---

11 locutus…12 sunt] Luc. 24:44.   13 quoniam…14 tertia] Luc. 24:46.   15 ille…16 nescitis] Ioh. 4:32.   17 meus…18 me] Ioh. 4:34.   28 non…29 dei] Matt. 4:4.   X.23.2 et¹…4 occisum] Apoc. 5:6.   11 saule…persequeris] Act. 9:4.   17 tamquam occisum] Apoc. 5:6.

X.22.15 Patarenus] om. F; al. man. marg. sin. P   22 dicit] add. non P exp.   23 quasi…26 nescitis] om. P   26 de] om. P
X.23.15 limbum] lunbum F

22 comederit|fol. 61vb P   X.23.16 uero|fol. 62ra P

ueteris et noui testamenti hic asseruit euidenter.
scriptura etiam mundanorum sapientum et istud ait
enim aperte uaticinatrix sibilla. deus qui in ligno
perpendit etcet. et alibi celo rex aduenit per secula
futurus scilicet in carne presens ut iudicet orbem. unde
deum cernent. incredulis atque fidelis etcet. philosophus etiam seneca dicit. deus ad homines uenit. immo
plus quia in homines uenit. Virgilius etiam poeta
cecinit. iam noua progenies de celo mittitur alto etcet.
et lucanus etiam dicens hic pax cum domino uenit
etcet. ecce qualiter mundani sapientes confessi sunt
antea prouidentes incarnationem christi et eius
passionem atque ipsius in carne iudicium. bestia etiam
illa crudelis machomectus uidelicet in sua lege fatetur
dicens. tria miracula fecit deus. quia mundum de
nichilo fecit. et ysaac de sterili et christum de uirgine
nasci etcet. demones etiam in euangelius clamitant
licet inuiti. ihesu. filii dei quid uenisti ante tempus
torquere nos etcet. quid est enim christum in mundum
uenisse nisi per assumptam humanitatem in mundo
apparuisse?

Patarenus: Dicimus diabolum carnem humanam
fecisse et hoc est causa quare negamus christum illam
assumpsisse.
Catholicus: Sed legite supra in titulum. primo. in
rubricella quod corpora sunt a deo et scietis carnem
humanam non a diabolo esse factam sed a deo.

Quod christus pluries quam singulo passus est

[**Patarenus:**] Apocalypsis. xiii. in libro uite agni qui
occisus est ab origine mundi etcet. ergo christus bis
fuit occisus scilicet semel ab origine mundi et semel
sub pontio pilato et sunt quidam ex nostris qui dicunt
quod ipse fuit septies passus in septem celis id est
unoquoque celo semel.
Catholicus: Respondeo quod sic intelligitur istud.
quod agnus est occisus ab origine recreationis et
redemptionis mundi. de quam origine dicit ipse in
apocalypsis. xxi. ecce noua facio omnia etcet. uel fuit
occisus agnus ab origine mundi scilicet in
predestinatione dei. immo ab eterno et est tale illud in
prima petri. primo. agni incontaminati et immaculati
ihesu christi. precogniti quidem ante constitutionem
mundi. etcet. uel fuit occisus ab origine creationis ade
per occisionem. non enim fuisset occisus deus nisi

both scriptures, also men learned in profane studies. For this is apparent by the Sibylline prophetess (Sibylline Oracles VI, 33–35) "the God who was suspended on the wood," and in another place (VIII, 285–286) "from heaven shall come the King who for the ages is to be," namely, (287–288) "present to judge all flesh and the whole world, the disbelievers and the faithful." The philosopher Seneca says (Book II, Letter 73.16) "God comes to men, yet even more, he comes into men." Also the poet Virgil foretells (Fourth Eclogue, 7) "Now from high heaven a new generation comes down." And also Lucan, saying (Pharsalia, 1.670) "with the lord comes peace." Behold how the wise men of the world confessed, seeing beforehand the incarnation of Christ and His passion, as well as his coming in the flesh for judgment. Also that savage beast Muhammad in his law admitted it, saying "God performed three miracles: that he made the earth from nothing, that he made Isaac from the barren woman, and that Christ was born to a Virgin." Even the demons in the gospels call out, though reluctantly, (Mt 8:29) "Jesus, son of God, why do you come here before the hour to torment us." For what has Christ come into the world for, unless that He might appear to the world by his assumption of humanity?

Pat: We say that the devil made human flesh and this is the reason that we deny that Christ assumed it.

Cath: But read above in the first section, in the part that bodies are from God and learn that human flesh is not made by the devil, but by God.

That Christ suffered many times, rather than once

[**Pat:**] Apocalypse 13 (13:8) "the book of life of the Lamb, who was slain from the beginning of the world." Therefore Christ was killed twice, namely, once at the beginning of the world, and once under Pontius Pilate and there are some among us who say that He suffered seven times in the seven heavens, that is, once in each of the heavens.

Cath: I respond that it is to be interpreted thusly, that the Lamb is slain from the beginning of the recreation and redemption of the world, of which origin he says in Apocalypse 21 (21:5) "behold I make all things new." or the lamb was slain from the beginning, namely, in the predestination of God, more correctly, from eternity, and this is the interpretation in 1 Peter 1 (1:19–20) "Jesus Christ, as of a lamb unspotted and undefiled, foreknown indeed before the foundation of the world." Or He was killed from the beginning of creation of Adam, by killing, for God would not be killed, except that man had committed a

---

26 deus…27 perpendit] *Sibylline Oracles* VI, 33–35.   27 celo…28 futurus] *Sibylline Oracles* VIII, 285-86.   28 in…29 fidelis] *Sibylline Oracles* VIII, 288.   30 deus…31 uenit] Seneca, *Epistulae morales ad Lucilium*, Book II, Letter 73. 16, "Immo quod est propius, in homines uenit."   32 iam…alto] Virgil, *Fourth Eclogue*, 7.   33 hic…uenit] Lucan, *Pharsalia*, 1. 670.   41 ihesu…42 nos] Matt. 8:29.   X.24.2 in…3 mundi] Apoc. 13:8.   11 ecce…omnia] Apoc. 21:5.   14 agni…16 mundi] 1 Pet. 1:19-20 ("agni immaculati Christi, et incontaminati praecogniti quidem ante mundi constitutionem," *Vulg.*)

26 sibilla] sybylla *F*   29 philoso-phus] phylosophus *F*   45 humanam] add. habuisse *P* exp.   47 assumpsisse] sumpsisse *P*   50 esse… deo] sed a deo esse factam *F*   **X.24.1** Quod…est] Quod pluries quam. vii. passus est *F*   6 septem] vii *F*   7 celo] om. *P*   14 prima] secunda *F*   17 occisionem] occasionem *F*

37 machomectus|fol. 62rb *P*   39 et²|fol. 47v *F*   **X.24.12** occisus|fol. 62va *P*

fuisset homo factus reus. unde dixit in Genesis. penitet me fecisse hominem id est. penam me tenebit quia feci hominem. pena scilicet passionis crucis. uel ab origine mundi id est a peccato ade quod fuit ab origine generis humani. tunc enim fuit parata mors christi per causam. quia peccatum ade fuit causa dominice passionis. quod autem sine aliqua ratione uel auctoritate christum septies passum fuisse eadem recuso facilitate qua dicitis.

crime. Whence He said in Genesis (6:7) "I repent that I have made them," that is, "I will hold it as a punishment for me that I made men." A punishment, namely, of the passion of the cross. Or from the beginning of the world, that is, from the sin of Adam that was from the origin of the human race, for then the death of Christ was prepared because of this cause, since the cause of the Lord's passion was from Adam. Yet there is no argument or authority that Christ suffered seven times, and for that reason I easily refute what you say.

XI

Quod lucifer de aliquo loco non ascendit in celum. et quod angeli qui ceciderunt sunt eternaliter dampnati

That Lucifer did not ascend from someplace to heaven and that the angels who fell are eternally damned

Dictum est supra de causa salutis. que fuit humanitas Christi. Nunc autem uidendum est quibus non profuit. et quibus autem fuerit effectuosa. et primo de illis quibus nullius fuit utilitatis. hoc est de cacodemonibus circa quos patareni mortaliter errant. tam in uno capitulo diuersi diuersa sentiunt. sicut et in ceteris faciunt omnibus. Quidam enim illorum autumnant quod diabolus ascendit de sua terrestri habitatione cum angelis suis et omni uirtute sua in celum et quod deus eiecerit illum cum angelis suis per prelium fortissimum facta strage occisorum hinc inde non modica et sanguinis effusione in tanta quantitate diffusa. quod usque ad frenos equorum inundabat. Dicunt enim quod angeli habebant corpora que sunt ibi prostrata et aiunt quod diabolus in illo casu traxit tertiam partem bonorum angelorum in terram. Et nota quod isti dissentiunt de ascensu diaboli et de casu angelorum et de ascensu eius dicunt quidam ex eis quod diabolus ascendit in celum deo ignorante. quidam autem quod deo sciente et non ualente illi resistere. alii uero deo sciente et consentiente. de casu angelorum dicunt quidam eorum quod diabolus traxit illos uiolenter. deo penitus et non ualente defendere illos. alii uero asserunt in contrarium scilicet quod per deceptionem eos aduxerit permittente deo. alii uero qui negant duo esse principia. scilicet tam illi qui dicunt diabolum esse natum in machina mundi quam

It was stated above that the cause of salvation was the humanity of Christ. Yet now it remains to be seen for whom it was not beneficial and for whom it was efficacious. And first concerning those for whom it was of no usefulness whatsoever. This is regarding the Cacodemons[1] about which the Patarenes mortally err. Different men hold such different opinions in one chapter as they do even in all the rest. For some among them assert that the devil ascended from his earthly habitation with his angels and all his power and that God cast him down with his angels through a most bitter battle, and a great slaughter ensued, and not a little blood was spilled, indeed in such quantity that it was spread around up to the bridles of the horses.[2] For they say that the angels had bodies which are there laid low, and they claim that the devil carried off a third part of the good angels to earth. And note that these disagree about the ascent of the devil and of the case of the angels,[3] and of his ascension certain ones from these say that the devil ascended to heaven without God's knowledge. Yet some say that God did know and was not able to prevent it, yet others say God knew and consented. Regarding the case of the angels, regarding their ascent some of them say that the devil carried them off by violence, and God was absolutely unable to defend them, others yet claim the contrary, namely that they were led through deception by the permission of God, others, while they deny there to be two principles,[4] namely those who say that the devil is

---

18 penitet...19 hominem] Gen. 6:7 ("poenitet enim me fecisse eos," *Vulg.*)

---

21 quod...23 fuit] om. *F*   **XI.1.2** ceciderunt...3 dampnati] occiderunt sunt enum aliter dampnati *F*   6 autem] ante *P*   10 autumnant] auctumnant *F*   12 et¹...13 suis] om. *P*   22 ignorante...24 deo] om. *F*   27 asserunt] adsunt *P*

XI.1.13 per|fol. 62vb *P*   29 principia|fol. 48r *F*

---

[1] Κακόδαίμων, a term from classical Greece, was a term used in demonological lore, to varying effects; cp. Petrus Comestor, *Historia scholastica*, Genesis 7: "Nota quia ex hoc quod dictum est, creavit volatile coeli super terram, erravit Plato, qui descendens in Aegyptum libros Moysi legit, et putavit Moysen sensisse volatilia esse ornatum aeris tantum circa terram, ornatum vero aeris superioris calodaemones, et cacodaemones: sed non ita est" (PL 198, 1053–1722, at 1061D; Note that since from the way this is said, *He created the flying creatures of the heavens above the earth*, Plato was led into error: he had traveled to Egypt and there read the books of Moses, and thought Moses meant that the birds were the adornment of the air close to the earth, and the adornment of the upper air were the *calodemons* and the *cacodemons* — but it is not so). | [2] The Albanenses, Burci, 313, 335; Moneta, 4, 36; Sacconi, c. 17; Douais, 117. | [3] On this dissention, see Moneta, 41ff. | [4] Burci, 292, 314, 339; Sacconi, c. 24; Moneta, 110.

illi qui dicunt eum in celo a deo esse creatum simul opinantur quo deos preposuerit eum aliis angelis in prelatum. sed quia male se habuit in illa prepositura uolebat eum eicere deus et ille petiit a deo misericordiam sed eo postea se non corrigente per prelium magnum eiectus est a deo cum omnibus angelis qui eum diligere uidebantur et iste eiectus in machina mundi fabricauit in ea duo corpora humana. sed cum per XXX annos uitalem spiritum istis corporibus infundere non posset. deus duos angelos de suis qui diabolum occulte diligere uidebantur. ad preces illorum et diaboli concessit eisdem. premonens eos ut a dormitione cauerent ne post soporem uiam reuertendi traderent obliuioni. quibus ipse promisit quod si ipsi dormirent quod post. vi. milia annorum ad illos liberandos transmitteret. qui uenerunt et dormierunt et errantes per corpora ade et eue et enoc et noe et abraham et patriarcharum et omnium prophetarum errantes numquam salutem reperire potuerunt. deinde in symeonem et annam secundum promissionem in paradiso factam saluati sint in aduentu christi. unde symeon dixit. nunc dimittis seruum tuum domine secundum uerbum tuum in pace etcet. sic etiam omnes spiritus qui de celo ceciderunt in diuersa corpora intrant et saluantur in fide patarenorum et si non saluantur in uno corpore intrant aliud donec ueniant ad salutem. sunt tamen aliqui inter istos qui distinguunt subtiliçantes inter angelos delinquentes dicunt enim quod quidam eorum erant capita ordinum qui uoluntarie diabolo consenserunt et istos dicunt numquam posse saluari. alii uero fuerunt inter eos qui dixerunt minores. quos dicunt omnes more supradicto debere saluari. et attende lector quod patareni predicti in iiii^{or} dissentiunt circa factum angelorum de celo ruentium et in tribus consentiunt simul. dissentiunt autem in ascensu luciferi. quia qui dicunt duo esse principia dicunt eum de terrestri habitatione in celum ascendisse. alii uero negant. secundo dissentiunt in casu angelorum quia primi dicunt tertiam partem angelorum dei per diabolam de celo in terram tractam. alii uero dicunt deum illos deiecisse. in hoc ipso dissentientes prout superius posuimus. tertio uero dissentiunt in quantitate preliorum. quia quidam dicunt multa fuisse prelia inter angelos et inter deum et luciferum quidam uero tantum unum fuisse fatentur. dissentiunt et in quarto scilicet in statu spirituum in celo prius existentium. quidam enim illorum dicunt quod erant spiritus et anime et corpora in illis spiritus dicunt in aerem

born into the world system, as also those who say he was equally created by God in heaven both at the same time, are of the opinion that God placed him in leadership over the other angels, but because he performed poorly in that command, in that he wished to overthrow God and [then] he sought mercy from God, but afterwards, not having been corrected, was cast out by God in a great battle, along with all the angels who seemed to love him.[1] And this one, cast out into the world system, made two human bodies in it, but when for 30 years he was unable to infuse a vital spirit into these bodies, God sent two of his angels, who seemed secretly to love the devil by their prayers and gave them to the devil, forewarning them to beware of sleep, lest after their rest they might be handed over to the way of oblivion, in which he promised that if they might have slept after 6,000 years they might cross over to freedom. These who came and slept, and having erred through the bodies of Adam and Eve and Enoch and Noah and Abraham and the patriarchs and all the prophets, were never able to recover salvation. Afterwards in Simeon and Anna, according to the promise made in paradise, they would be saved at the coming of Christ, whence Simeon said (Lk 2:29) "Now let your servant depart in peace, according to your word." So also all spirits that fell from heaven enter into diverse bodies and are saved in the faith of the Patarenes, and if they are not saved in one body, they go into another until they come to salvation. Yet there are some among those who make subtle distinctions between the erring angels, for they say that certain of them were heads of orders who voluntarily consented to the devil, and these they claim are never able to be saved. Yet others were among those whom they call lesser, whom they say must be saved in the aforementioned way. And pay attention, O reader, that the aforementioned Patarenes dissent in four things regarding the fact of the overthrow of the angels from heaven, and in three they agree together. They disagree on the ascent of Lucifer, since those who say there are two principles say that he ascended to heaven from an earthly habitation, but others deny it. In the second place they dissent on the fall of the angels because the first say the third part of the angels of God were dragged by the devil from heaven to earth, yet others say that God overthrew them, in this dissenting just as we detailed above. In the third place they dissent on the number of the battles, since certain of them say that there were many battles between the angels, and between God and Lucifer, yet certain others confess that there was but one. And they disagree on the fourth point, namely, on the state of the spirits in heaven already existing. For some of them say that there were spirits and souls and bodies in

---

XI.1.52 nunc...53 pace] Luc. 2:29.

31 esse] om. P 32 opinantur] opponuntur P 42 eisdem] eidem P | ut] om. F 48 abraham] abraam P 49 reperire] repperire F 62 qui dixerunt] om. F | quos] qui P 63 attende] actende P 66 ascensu] assensu F 71 tractam] tractum F 75 luciferum] add. dissentiunt P

36 omnibus|fol. 63ra P 61 inter|fol. 63rb P

---

[1]) Georgius, 1719ff.

cecidisse animas uero in terram et corpora in celo remansisse prostrata et dicunt quod spiritus uadunt per aerem querendo animas suas et quando congnoscunt illas confortant eas ut faciant uitam patarenorum et tunc faciant eam et saluantur. alii uero dicunt quod non fuerunt nisi spiritus qui et anime nuncupatur et de corporibus in celo prostratis nichil credunt. Item quidam ex illis dicunt quod deus et diabolus creauerunt angelos et animas. quidam uero quod tantum angelos. consentiunt autem omnes prelium in celis fuisse et angelos deiectos esse saluandos et quod per diuersa transeunt corpora et ita in hoc articulo sicut et in aliis ducuntur per diuersas et diabolicas fantasias. Nos uero discipuli ueritatis dicimus quod diabolus angelus creatus a deo superbiuit contra deum cum multis angelis et quod deus in ictu oculi de celo empireo eiecerit illos absque redemptione salutis et hic est sathanas et illi sunt demones. qui pro inuidia fatigauit seducere humanas animas ne illuc ascendant unde illi ruerunt. quod tam rationibus quam scripturis sacris per dei gratiam possumus ostendere de plano.

Probatio per rationem quod diabolus non adscendit in celum de terrestri habitatione ad decipiendum angelos dei

Aut diabolus ascendit ad decipiendum angelos dei. deo nesciente et tunc fuit ignorans. quod stultum est de deo sompniante. aut ascendit deo sciente et tunc aut deus potuit ei resistere et non fecit et sic fuit stultus uel iniquis. aut non potuit et tunc fuit impotens que sunt impossibilia de deo et sic patet quod nichil fuit de ascensu luciferi.

Probatio per rationes de dampnatione eterna cadentium angelorum

angeli peccauerunt non dante occasionem peccato eorum fragilitate nature. quia in optimis naturalibus creati erant. neque alterius suggestione quam decepti non fuerit. sed ex propria malitia peccauerunt. et ideo peccatum eorum est inremmisibile. quam rationem tangit beatus paulus ad hebreos. ii°. dicens. Quia ergo pueri communicauerunt carni et sanguini et ipse similiter participauit eis ut per mortem destrueret eum qui habebat mortis imperium id est diabolum et liberaret eos qui timore mortis per totam uitam obnoxii erant seruituti. Nusquam enim angelos apprehendit etcet.

those,[1] they say the spirits fell into the aether, the souls onto earth, and the bodies remained prostrate in heaven, and they say that the spirits go through the aether seeking their souls and when they recognize them, they comfort them so that they might follow the life of the Patarenes and, by living it, be saved. Yet others say that there were none but spirits which were called souls, and they do not believe that there are prostrated bodies in heaven. Also certain of them say that God and the devil created angels and souls, yet certain others that they created only angels. Yet all agree that there was a battle in heaven, and that the overthrown angels are saved and that they went into diverse bodies and so in this belief, as in others, they are led to a variety of diabolical fantasies. Yet we disciples believe that the devil was an angel created by God, who struggled against God with many angels, and that God, in the blink of an eye, cast them out from the empyreum without the redemption of salvation and that this is Satan, and the others are demons, who on account of jealousy tirelessly seek to seduce human souls, lest such ascend there from whence they were overthrown. This we are able to plainly prove as much from natural arguments as from the holy scriptures by the grace of God.

Proof from reason that the devil did not ascend into heaven from a terrestrial habitation for the purpose of deceiving the angels of God

Either the devil ascended for the purpose of deceiving the angels of God, with God being ignorant of it, and then He was ignorant which is as foolish to say as God sleeps, or he ascended with the knowledge of God and then either God was able to resist him and did not do it, and this is foolish or wicked, or He was not able to resist him and then He was impotent, which is impossible to say of God, and thus it is clear that there is nothing to this ascent of Lucifer.

Proof from reason about the eternal damnation of the fallen angels

The angels sinned, not by giving an occasion for their sin because of fragility of nature, since they were created with the best natures, neither can there be an alternate suggestion in which they were deceived since no one did it to them, but rather it was on account of their own malice that they sinned, and so their sin is unforgivable, for which reason Blessed Paul touches upon in Hebrews 2, saying (2:14–16) "Therefore because the children are partakers of flesh and blood, he also himself in like manner has been partaker of the same, that, through death, he might destroy him who had the empire of death, that is to say, the devil, and might deliver them, who through the fear of death were all their life subject to servitude. For nowhere does he aid the angels."

XI.3.8 Quia...14 apprehendit] Heb. 2:14-16 (eis) eisdem *Vulg.*)

95 angelis] add. dei *F* **XI.3.4** fragilitate] add. eorum *P* exp. 5 suggestione] subgestione *F* 8 tangit] om. *P* 13 Nusquam] numquam *F*

88 creauerunt|fol. 63va *P* 92 aliis|fol. 48v *F* **XI.3.2** angelorum|fol. 63vb *P*

---

1) The Albanenses, Burci, 313, 321; Moneta, 105ff.

Item angeli semper peccant. immo potius aggrauatur eorum iniquitas. iuxta illud Dauid. superbia eorum qui te oderunt ascendit semper. et ideo semper debent dampnari.

Item ipsi sunt dampnati in inferno ubi nulla est redemptio et ideo non possunt saluari.

Item ipsi peccauerunt in suo mundo id est in celo nec ibi penitentiam fecerunt. unde in alio non est eis remedium. sicut est de hominibus qui se non faciunt hic penitentiam de suis peccatis in alio uenia carent.

Preterea ipsi peccauerunt in suo eterno id est donec uixerunt in sua uita id est in celo peccauerunt dico deum offendendo. ideo iustum est ut penam reportent donec durabit dei eternum.

Patarenus: Dico quod angeli qui ceciderunt de celo non peccauerunt. quia fuerunt tracti uiolenter a diabolo uel seducti et ideo non habent locum oppositiones tue.

Catholicus: Si autem deus potuit eos defendere et non fecit et tunc fuit iniquus quod falsum est quia iniquitas non est apud deum. aut non potuit et sic fuit impotens. quod est contra scripturas diuinas que dicunt esse omnipotentem etcet. etiam contra tuam opinionem patarene qui dicis eum esse omnipotentem in regno suo. quod est celum empyreum. et sic patet quod omnis illi angeli peccauerunt.

Patarenus: Dicam ergo quod ipsi offenderunt non tamen peccauerunt et propter illam offensam debuerunt temporali pena puniri. uel si peccauerunt quia habuerunt causam a diabolo non debent puniri eternaliter sed temporaliter.

Catholicus: aut ipsi compulsi obedierunt diabolo et tunc non peccauerunt quia nullus tenetur ad impossibile et sic restat quod deus fuit iniquis uel impotens qui permissit indebite puniri quod improbatum est superius. aut uero ipsi consenserunt et ille consensus fuit ab eis et sic habemus quod a libero arbitrio potuit esse peccatum angelorum quod tu inficiaris. preterea omnis peccant per suggestionem uel aliquem instructum diaboli maxime secundum tuam sectam. ergo omnis spiritus saluabuntur. quod est contra sententiam christi qui dicturus est peccatoribus. discedite a me maledicti in ignem eternum etcet. et sic per istas inconuenientias relinquitur rationibus in eis esse consentiendum.

Probatio per scripturam quod lucifer non ascendit in celum neque aliqui angeli eius

Iohannes. iii. nemo ascendit in celum nisi qui descendit de celo filius hominis qui est in celo. ergo neque lucifer neque alii angeli ascenderunt de aliqua terrestri habitatione in celum.

Also the angels always sin, indeed that rather aggravates their wickedness, according to David (Ps 73:23) "the pride of those who hate you goes up continually." Therefore they ought always to be damned.

Also these are damned in hell where there is no redemption, and so they are not able to be saved.

Also they sinned in their world, that is, in heaven, and they did not do penance, whence in no other place is there remedy for them, just as men who do not do penance here for their sins shall lack mercy in the other.

Further they sinned in His eternity, that is, as long as they lived in His life, that is, in heaven. They sinned, I say, in offending God. Therefore it is just that they should suffer their punishment as long as the eternity of God endures.

Pat: I say that the angels who fell from heaven did not sin, since they were dragged from thence violently by the devil, or were seduced and so your arguments do not hold water.

Cath: Yet if God was able to defend them and He did not do it, then He was wicked, which is false since wickedness does not pertain to God, or otherwise He could not do it, and so He was impotent, which is contrary to the divine scriptures, which call Him omnipotent, and this also against your opinion, Patarene, by which you call Him omnipotent in His kingdom, which is the heavenly empyreum, and so it is clear that all those angels sinned.

Pat: I might say therefore that they offended, but they nevertheless did not sin, and for that offense they ought to be punished in time, or if they did sin, it was because they had cause from the devil, and ought not to be punished eternally, but only for a time.

Cath: Either they were compelled to obey the devil, and so did not sin since no one is obliged to do the impossible, and so it remains that God was wicked or impotent who permitted those to be punished to whom it was not due, which was disproven above, or yet they consented and the consent was from them, and so we have it that by free will the sin of the angels is possible, which you deny. Further all sin through suggestion or by some instruction of the devil, especially according to your sect, therefore all spirits shall be saved, which is against Christ's way of thinking who will say to sinners (Mt 25:41) "Depart from me, you accursed ones, into everlasting fire." And so through these inconsistencies it remains that they consented to these things in their reason.

Proof by the scriptures that Lucifer did not ascend into heaven, neither did any of the other angels

John 3 (3:13) "And no one has ascended into heaven, but he who descended from heaven, the Son of man who is in heaven." Therefore neither did Lucifer nor any other angel ascend from any earthly habitation into heaven.

Patarenus: respondeo quia per hoc enim non excluditurus luciferi et angelorum eius ascensus. nemo enim componitur ex nullus et homo quasi dicat nullus homo. in carne humana in celum ascendit nisi filius hominis etcet.

Catholicus: Modo respondeas nemo est signum uniuersale. uniuersalis est ergo propositio hec. nemo ascendit in celum etcet. sed ibi ponitur hoc exceptio nisi filius hominis etcet. sed omnis exceptio debet esse eiusdem nature cum suo uniuersali. summi cum suo genere. uerbi gratia. omnis homo est excepto petro. uniuersalitas est homo et petrus est exceptio et exceptio est eiusdem nature cum suo genere quia petrus est homo et ideo congrua est locutio. sed modo pone contrarium. omnis homo currit excepto asino. hoc locutio est inconueniens quia exceptio discrepat a suo genere. cum asinus non sit homo. modo reuertamur ad propositum. nemo id est nullus homo ut tu exponis uniuersale hoc est de quo sit hoc exceptio nisi filius hominis qui est christus. fuit eiusdem nature nobiscum et sic conuinceris de maiori errore. et ita uitando scillam incidis in caritdin. tamen de deducto ad inconueniens de tua inani sophysticatione quod hoc dictio nemo dicimus quod simpliciter ponitur in diuina pagina id est nullus. unde in euangelio iohannis. xv. maiorem hac dilectionem nemo habet etcet. et in apocalypsis. v. nemo poterat in celo neque in terra neque subtus terram etcet. id est neque angelus neque homo neque demon. Perfa. christus nondum ascenderat in celum quando hic dixit secundum humanitatem. ergo hoc exceptio nisi filius hominis non refertur ad eius humanitatis ascensum et per consequentiam uniuersale hoc scilicet nemo ascendit in celum non ad homines sed ad angelos refertur.

Probatio per scripturam quod eternaliter sunt dampnati angeli de celo cadentes

Mattheus. xxv. discedite a me maledicti in ignem eternum qui paratus est diabolo et angelis eius etcet. ergo alii sunt angeli diaboli quibus preparatus est ignis eternus ab origine mundi et alii sunt maledicti qui descendent a domino ituri cum angelis diaboli in ignem eternum. sed primi autem sunt angeli diaboli ab eo creati ut dogmatizati et secundi sunt angeli uel homines a deo creati. sed angeli uel homines a deo creati non possunt dampnari secundum uestram sectam et sic patet quod intellectus uester stare non potest. igitur noster est uerus qui dicimus quod primi

Pat: I reply that though this will not exclude an ascension of Lucifer and his angels, for 'no man' is composed of 'nothing' and 'man', as if to say, no man in human flesh ascends into heaven except the Son of Man.

Cath: How could you reply no man is a universal term. Therefore 'no man has ascended into heaven' is a universal proposition. But here this exception is posed, 'unless the Son of Man.' But every exception has to be of the same nature as its universal, above all with its own kind. For example, the kinds, 'every man exists except Peter,' 'man' is the universal term, and 'Peter' the exception, and the exception is of the same nature with its own kind because Peter is a man and therefore the sentence is logically consistent. But now suppose the opposite, 'every man runs with the exception of an ass.' This expression is inconsistent, since the exception differs in genus, since an ass is not a man. Now go back to the proposition, 'no man,' that is, no man at all, as you explain. This is the universal of which there is an exception, "the Son of Man," who is Christ. He was of the same nature as us, and so you are guilty of a grave error, and so by avoiding Scylla, you fall upon Charybdis.[1] Yet deducing from your inconsistency, regarding your inane sophistries about this utterance 'no man,' we say that it is proposed simply in the divine scripture, that is, 'no one.' Whence in the gospel of John 15 (15:13) "Greater love than this no man has," and in Apocalypse 5 (5:3) "And no man was able, neither in heaven, nor on earth, nor under the earth," that is, neither angel, nor man, nor the aforementioned demon. Christ had not yet ascended into heaven according to His humanity when He said this. Therefore this exception "except the Son of Man," does not refer to His ascended humanity and consequently this is universal, namely "no one has ascended into heaven," is referring not to men but to angels.

Proof from scripture that the angels who have fallen from heaven are eternally damned.

Matthew 25 (25:41) "depart from me you cursed ones into the everlasting fire which is prepared for the devil and his angels." Therefore the angels of the devil — for whom the eternal fire is prepared from the beginning of the world — are one thing, and the damned who go down from the Lord by going with the angels of the devil into eternal fire are another. But yet the first are the angels of the devil created by him as has been asserted and the second are angels or men created by God, but the angels or men created by God are not able to be damned according to that sect and it is clear that your interpretation cannot

---

32 maiorem...habet] Ioh. 15:13.   33 nemo...34 terram] Apoc 5:3 (poterat) add. neque *Vulg.*)   XI.5.3 discedite...4 eius] Matt. 25:41.

7 non] om. *P*   25 uniuersale...est] hoc est universale *F*   29 sophysticatione] add. dicimus *F*   32 xv] xi nemo *P* exp.   35 Perfa] †† unclear in mss.   40 sed] set *P*   XI.5.5 ignis] cibus (!) *F*   6 et] om. *F*   9 dogmatizati] dogmatizans *P*   11 uestram] ipsam *P*   12 sic] hoc *P*   13 igitur] add. non *P* exp.

XI.4.15 nisi|fol. 64va *P*   XI.5.1 eternaliter|fol. 64vb *P*

---

1) Ovid, *Metamorphoses*, XIV, 51–52. Scylla and Charybdis, likely a common saying not a citation, especially given the vernacularized spelling.

sunt angeli qui ceciderunt de celo qui dampnati sunt eternaliter et secundi sunt homines qui recessunt a deo per malam operationem. qui similiter eternaliter dampnabuntur. Item lucam. ix. filius hominis non uenit animas perdere sed saluare etcet. non dixit angelos sed animas. angelos enim nomen est spiritus qui non incorporatur. anima uero nomen est spiritus humanis corpus. uel qui corpus habuit spiritus uero utriusque nomen est. et manifestum est quod numquam in diuina pagina uocantur angeli anime. et numquam legitur de salute angelorum peccantium. sed tamen de salute animarum. ergo anime humane possunt saluari et angeli qui peccauerunt eternaliter. item dampnati. de quorum eterna dampnatione dicit beatus petrus euidenter in ii^a. ii^o. si deus angelis peccantibus non pepercit sed rudentibus inferni detractos in tartarum tradidit iudicium cruciandos reseruari. cui concordat beatus iudas manifeste in primo dicens quoniam ihesus populum de terra egypti saluans secundo eos. qui non crediderunt perdidit. angelos uero qui non seruauerunt suum principatum. sed dereliquerunt suum domicilium. iudicium magni diei uinculis eternis sub caligine reseruauit etcet. idem in eodem. sicut sodoma et gomorra etcet. ergo alii sunt angeli qui de celo ceciderunt qui sunt dampnati in eternum. de quibus dixit angelos uero. etcet. et alii sunt sodomite et gomorroite et illi de ciuitatibus finitimis qui ex fornicantes et abeuntes post carnem alteram. facti sunt exempla ignis eterni penam sustinentes. de quibus hoc assimilat dicens. sicut sodoma et gomorra etcet. et alii sunt qui secuntur illos de quibus subdit similiter et hi carnem quidem maculant etcet. et alii sunt increduli de quibus superius dixerat. secundo eos qui non crediderunt perdidit etcet. sed constat secundum te o heretice quod omnis spiritus sunt angeli uel dei uel diaboli. sed illi de quibus dicit angelos uero etcet. aut sunt angeli dei et alii sunt diaboli uel econtrario. sed illi et isti eternaliter sunt dampnati. ergo angeli dei et diaboli sunt perditi. quod est etiam contra tue secte prauitatem et sic reliquitur quod illi fuerunt angeli qui ceciderunt de celo per eorum superbiam. et isti sunt homines finaliter peccantes qui omnis erunt eiusdem dampnationis participes.

Patarenus: Respondeo quod ubicumque scriptura loquitur de dampnatione angelorum intelligitur de angelis diaboli qui secum ascenderunt in celum quos eternaliter dampnatos esse non inficior et hoc secundum opinionem quorumdam ex nostris. uel secundum alios intellgitur de capitibus ordinum. sunt et alii ex nobis qui intelligunt eum loqui de angelis qui

stand. Therefore ours is true, we who say that the first are angels who fell from heaven, and are damned eternally, and that the second are men who departed from God through bad works, who are also damned eternally. Also Luke 9 (9:56) "The Son of man did not come to destroy souls, but to save." He did not say angels, but souls. For the name 'angels' is a spirit that is disembodied, yet 'soul' is the name of the spirit of the human body, or whose bodies have spirits, yet both names are apt, and it is clear that angels are never called souls in divine scripture, and the salvation of a sinning angel is never read about, but nevertheless the salvation of souls is, therefore human souls are able to be saved and the angels who sinned are damned eternally, of which eternal damnation Blessed Peter plainly speaks in 2 Peter 2 (2:4) "For if God did not spare the angels who sinned, but delivered them, drawn down by infernal ropes to the lower hell, unto torments, to be reserved unto judgment." To which Blessed Jude plainly agrees in his first chapter, saying (1:5–6) "that Jesus, having saved the people out of the land of Egypt, did afterwards destroy those who did not believe, and the angels who did not keep their principality, but forsook their own habitation, he has reserved under darkness in everlasting chains, unto the judgment of the great day." Also in the same (1:7) "As Sodom and Gomorrah," therefore the angels who fell from heaven and are damned eternally are one thing, of which he said "and the angels," and the inhabitants of Sodom and Gomorrah — and to the limits of those of the cities — are another, who "for fornicating and going after other flesh," were made examples of eternal fire, suffering a punishment of which he speaks similarly, saying, "As Sodom and Gomorrah." And those who follow them are one thing, of which he adds (1:8) "In a similar way these men also defile the flesh." And those disbelievers which he spoke of above are another, regarding those whom He "did afterwards destroy those who did not believe." It remains according to you, O Heretic, that all spirits are either angels or devils, but those of which he says "therefore the angels," are either angels of God or are of the devil, on the contrary, but these and those are eternally damned, therefore angels of God and of the devil are lost, which is also against your depraved sect, and thus it remains that those were angels who fell from heaven on account of their pride, and these are men who, hardened in final impenitence, shall all be partakers of their same damnation.

Pat: I reply that wherever the scriptures speak of the damnation of the angels, one is to understand it as speaking of the angels of the devil who ascended with him into heaven. That these are eternally damned I do not deny, and this is according to the opinion of certain ones among us, or according to others, it is to be understood of the heads of the orders, and there are others among us who

---

17 filius...18 saluare] Luc. 9:56.   28 deus...31 reseruari] 2 Pet. 2:4 (si] add. enim | tradidit] cruciandos, in iudicium reseruari *Vulg.*)   32 quoniam...36 reseruauit] Iud. 1:5-6 (domicilium] add. in *Vulg.*)   37 sicut...39 uero] Iud. 1:7.   45 similiter...46 maculant] Iud. 1:8.

15 sunt] om. *F* | recessunt] resurexerunt *F*   17 ix] viiii *P*   45 hi] hii *F*   51 eternaliter...52 sunt^1] transp. *F*   52 sunt^2] essent *F*   53 prauitatem] uirtutem *F*   54 ceciderunt] add. eorum per *P*   62 opinionem] oppinionem *P*   64 et] om. *F*

16 eternaliter|fol. 49v *F*   27 eterna|fol. 65ra *P*   51 diaboli|fol. 65rb *P*

fuerunt uiolenter uel seducti qui in tartarum istius mundi sunt eternaliter dampnati.

Catholicus: Sed hunc triplicem intellectum reprobat. scriptura sancta. primum uero reprobat iudas cum dicit de illud angelis dampnatus. angelos uero qui non seruauerunt suum principatum sed reliquerunt suum domicilium etcet. quia innuit quod causa dampnationis eorum fuit peccatum hoc scilicet quia non seruauerunt suum principatum. sed reliquerunt suum domicilium sed constat quod si esset uera opinio tua quod diabolus et angeli eius ascendissent in celum dei. uolentes rapere illud ei. quod peccatum eorum esset rapina alterius quod non fuisset illorum. ergo loquitur de angelis dei qui per superbiam reliquerunt et perdiderunt celibus empireum ubi erat principatus et domicilium eorum. preterea si ascendissent angeli diaboli in celum ad rapiendum illud. quare et quomodo ligassent eos catenis eternis? si enim naturaliter essent mali non potuissent facere nisi malum. iniuste ergo punisset illos deus. nec in illos etiam aliquid potuisset cum de regno suo minime fuissent. secundum uero intellectum reprobant ambo apostoli predicti scilicet petrus et iudas qui de dampnatione angelorum locuuntur qui non distingunt inter capita et caudas. fuit inter maiores et minores sed simpliciter dicunt angelos esse dampnatos qui peccauerunt et eorum domicilium reliquirunt. ergo omnes angeli sunt dampnati qui de celo ceciderunt. presertim cum nulla memoria fiat in scriptura diuina de salute aliquorum. Tertium autem intellectum reprobant tres apostoli scilicet petrus. iudas et iohannes. petrus autem cum dicit angelus peccantes in tartarum in iudicium cruciandos reseruari. iudas uero cum dicit quod uinculis eternis sub caligine reserauantur. iohannes uero cum dicit in apocalypsis. xii. draco pugnabat et angeli eius et non ualuerunt neque locus inuentus est amplius eorum in celo etcet. ergo non temporaliter sed eternaliter sunt dampnati angeli qui de celo ceciderunt et notauit bene quod dicit beatus iohannes diligente scilicet locus eorum. etcet. ubi dat manifeste intelligere quod celum empyreum fuit locus proprius angelorum apostatantium et per consequentiam fuerunt angeli dei per creationem et naturalium bonorum collocationem. qui facti sunt angeli draconis per superbie imitationem. preterea audite o uos omnes patareni quodcumque opinionem teneatis pro defensione angelorum de celo ruentium quidem de illis dicat apostolus ad hebreos. vi. impossibile est enim eos qui semel sunt illuminati gustauerunt etiam donum celeste et participes facti sunt spiritus sancti. gustauerunt nihilominus bonum

understand him to speak of the angels who, taken by violence or seduction into the Tartarus of this world, are eternally damned.

Cath: But this can be disproved by three interpretations in Holy Scripture. The first is that Jude denies [it] where he speaks of those damned angels (1:6) "and the angels who did not keep their principality, but forsook their own habitation," since he intimates that the cause of their damnation was this sin, namely, that they "did not keep their own principality, but forsook their own habitation," but it happens that if your opinion were true that the devil and his angels ascended into the heaven of God wishing to steal it from Him, then their sin would have been robbery of another's of that which was not their own. Therefore he is speaking of the angels of God, who through pride left and lost the empyrean heavens where their principality and habitation was. Further if the angels of the devil had ascended into heaven to capture it, why and how were they bound with eternal chains? For if they were evil by nature they would not have been able to do anything but evil, therefore God would have punished them unjustly, nor would He even have been capable of anything towards them, since they would not have been of His kingdom. The second interpretation is denied by both of the foregoing Apostles, namely Peter and Jude, who when speaking of the damnation of the angels did not distinguish between heads and tails. There was among them greater and lesser angels but they simply say that the angels are damned who fell from heaven and left their abode, therefore all the angels who fell from heaven are damned, particularly since no mention was made in the Holy Scriptures about the salvation of any. The third understanding is denied by three Apostles, namely, Peter, Jude, and John. Peter when he says (2 Pt 2:4) "the sinning angels drawn down by infernal ropes to the lower hell, unto torments, to be reserved unto judgment." Jude when he says (1:6) "he has reserved under darkness in everlasting chains." And John when he says in Apocalypse 12 (12:7–8) "and the dragon fought and his angels, and they did not prevail, neither was their place found any more in heaven." Therefore the angels are not temporally damned but eternally, who fell from heaven, and one noted well what Blessed John carefully says, namely "their place," where he gives a plain interpretation that the empyrean heaven was the proper place of the angels, and consequently they were angels of God by creation and ordered with a good nature, who were made angels of the dragon by imitation of his pride. Further hear, O all you Patarenes of whatsoever opinion you might hold for defense of the angels overthrown from heaven, certain of those the Apostle says to the Hebrews in chapter 6 (6:4–6) "For it is impossible for those who were once illuminated, and have tasted also the heavenly gift, and were made partakers of the Holy Spirit,

---

69 angelos...71 domicilium] Iud. 1:6.   96 angelus...97 reseruari] 2 Pet. 2:4.   98 uinculis...reserauantur] Iud. 1:6.   99 draco...101 celo] Apoc. 12:7-8.   112 impossibile...120 sunt] Heb. 6:4-6.

71 quia] qui *F*   74 opinio] oppinio *P*   81 illud] add. deo *F*   82 catenis] cathenis *P* | naturaliter] similiter *F*   86 secundum] add. in *F*   89 caudas] iudas *P*   103 notauit] add. ubi *P*   104 ubi] add. dicit *P* exp.   106 apostatantium] apppostatantium *P*   107 collocationem] collationem *F*   110 opinionem] oppinionem *P* | pro] quod *P*

78 superbiam|fol. 65va *P*   79 erat|fol. 50r *F*   102 eternaliter|fol. 65vb *P*

dei uerbum uirtutesque seculi uenturi. et prolapsi sunt rursus renouari ad penitentiam. et constat quod de angelis diaboli per creationem non loquitur. quia illi numquam aliquid boni de deo gustassent. et loquitur in genere de omnibus qui gustauerunt dona dei et prolapsi sunt quod numquam possunt saluari. ergo loquitur de angelis dei tam de maioribus quam de minoribus qui peccauerunt. ergo omnes sunt eternaliter dampnati.

Patarenus: uerum est quod multi ex nobis intelligunt auctoritatem pauli de peccato angelorum quod in celo fecerunt. quos defendere non possum propter tuas insultationes. alii tamen intelligunt eam de peccato quod faciunt fratres nostri post manus impositionem qui possunt saluari postea scilicet per eum modum per quem receperunt prius spiritum sanctum. uel non possunt saluari scilicet in hoc corpore saluabuntur tamen in alio sed miror quomodo predictam auctoritatem introducis contra nos de peccato angelorum in celo. cum ecclesia tua intelligat ipsam de peccato quod faciunt homines post baptismum.

Catholicus: Et in hac fuga comprehendam te uelociter. scio enim quod uos patareni non habetis alium modum ad salutem nisi per manus impositionem. ergo si peccant aliqui per manus ipsorum. non est eis aliquis modus salutis. preterea fratribus uestris ad nos uenientibus post manus impositionem uestra et postea ad uos reuertentibus facitis iterum manus impositionem. qui post primam necauerunt. ergo decipitis eos cum uos dicatis quod possunt renouari ad penitentiam per secundam manus impositionem qui post secundam peccauerunt nec ualet etiam illud quod dixisti quod licet non possint saluari in illo corpore saluabuntur tamen in alio. quia apostolus dicit expressim quod impossibile est rursus renouari ad penitentiam nec determinat in isto corpore uel in alio. ergo eternaliter dampnbuntur nec etiam transeunt spiritus de corpore in corpus prout in sequenti rubrica declarabitur. nec mireris si aliter expono auctoritatem presentem quam eam sancti doctores nostri exponunt. quia hoc facio secundum tue praue doctrine documentum. ut ex prauis tuis iaculis te feriam uituperabilius. aut in foueam te proiciam ineuitabiliter maioris ruboris et confusionis. sin autem uelles consentire nostre doctrine gauderem utique uehementer et dicerem factus est lupus agnus.

and have moreover tasted the good word of God, and the powers of the world to come, and are fallen away, to be renewed again to penance." And it seems that he does not speak of the angels of the devil through creation, since they never tasted any good thing of God, and he speaks generally of all who tasted the gifts of God and have fallen away, saying that these are never able to be saved. Therefore he speaks of the angels of God, both the greater and the lesser, who sinned. Therefore all are eternally damned.

Pat: It is true that many among us understand the passage of Paul to be about the sin of the angels which they committed in heaven, which I am unable to defend on account of your mockery. Nevertheless others interpret the passage as speaking of sin that our brothers commit after the imposition of hands, who afterwards are able to be saved, namely, through the manner in which they had before they received the Holy Spirit; or they are not able to be saved in this body, but they will be saved in another body. I am surprised how you adduce the foregoing authority against us regarding the sin of the angels in heaven, since your church understands these passages to refer to the sin that men commit after baptism.

Cath: And in this retreat I quickly overtake you, for I know that you Patarenes have no other path to salvation save by the imposition of hands. Therefore if some people sin after the imposition of hands, there is no other way that they can be saved. Further your brethren who have come to us after the imposition of your hands and who have later gone back to you, you make them again receive the imposition of hands, as they had destroyed [the effect of] the first imposition. Therefore you deceive those when you say that they are able to be renewed to penance by a second imposition of hands, who sinned after the second time. Nor also does it avail that you say that although they are not able to be saved in this body, yet they will be saved in another one, since the Apostle says plainly that this is impossible (Heb 6:6) "to be renewed again to penance," neither does he determine whether in this body or in another. Therefore they will be damned eternally. Nor also do the spirits cross from body to body, just as is established in the following section. Nor ought you to be amazed if I explain the present passage otherwise than in the manner that our Holy Doctors construe it, since I do this as instruction to your wicked doctrine, so that I might strike you from your own wicked arrows, or I shall inevitably drive you into the pit with greater shame and confusion, or yet if you would wish to consent to our teaching I would certainly rejoice exceedingly and would say that the wolf has become a lamb.

---

149 rursus...150 determinat] Heb. 6:6.

---

120 ergo] igitur *F* 121 dei] om. *P* 126 fecerunt] fuerunt *F* 134 tua] mea *P* 136 fuga] om. *P* 138 ergo...139 ipsorum] om. *F* 143 qui...necauerunt] om. *F* | ergo...146 peccauerunt] om. *P* 156 aut] utrum *F* 158 doctrine] om. *P*

125 auctoritatem|fol. 66ra *P* 146 dixisti|fol. 50v *F* 151 transeunt|fol. 66rb *P*

Quod lucifer de terrestri habitatione ascendit in celum cum angelis suis et quod angeli qui ceciderunt de celo saluabuntur uel per incorporationem de ascensu luciferi

[**Patarenus:**] Ys. xiiii. Quomodo cecidisti de celo lucifer qui mane oriebaris? etcet. et postea Qui dicebas in corde tuo in caelum ascendam super astra celi exaltabo solium meum etcet. ergo de terrestri habitatione ascendit lucifer in celum aliunde enim ascendere non potuit.

Catholicus: Respondeo quod hystorialter loquitur de rege babilonis. unde supra in eodem dicit. sumes parabolam istam contra regem babillonis et dices etcet. qui fuit nabuchadnezzar qui dicitur lucifer per similitudinem. quia sicut stella lucifer cunctis aliis astris lucidior apparet. iam ille clarior potentia super omnis erat mortales. qui dicitur etiam ascendisse in celum per dignitatis et potentatus altitudinem. nec umquam de diabolo potest ad litteram intelligi dictum ysaie. quia dicit ibi de illo lucifero. concidit cadauer tuum etcet. diabolus enim numquam habuit corpus et si uellem dicere quod lucifer diabolus fuerit. non propter hoc habes quod ipse in celum ascendit. quia ysaias non dicit hoc sed dicit quod lucifer hoc dicebat in corde suo et ipse mentitus est sicut solet. sicut et dominus dicit ipse est mendax etcet. dicebat enim se uelle ascendere in celum id est in dei equalitatem. unde subdit. ero similis altissimo etcet. et hoc dicens deceptus est et factus est uilissimus inter omnes creaturas. unde ysaias insultans ei dicit. tu autem proiectus es de sepulcro tuo quasi stirps inutilis fame pollutus. et superius dixit et operimentum tuum erunt uermes id est angeli facti demones qui prius erant tibi ad decorem decentio erunt ad confusionem. sed attende patarene quid dicit ysaias de lucifero ibi proiectus est de sepulcro tuo etcet. sed patet quod lucifer non fuit proiectus de mundo sed de celo empireo. ergo celum empyreum erat locus eius proprius. et sic patet quod ipse fuit de bona creatione.

De prelatione luciferi super angelos

[**Patarenus:**] Item. ezechielis. xxviii. Tu cherub signaculum similitudinis plenus sapientia et perfectus decore in delitiis paradisi dei fuisti etcet. et infra et posui te in monte santo dei etcet. ergo lucifer in celum ascendit et ibi constitutus est et prelatus a deo super angelos. secundum quia male se habuit in illa prelatione deiectus est inde per deum. unde sequitur et peccasti et eieci te de monte sancto dei etcet. et est hic

That Lucifer ascended from an earthly habitation into heaven with his angels and that the angels who fell from heaven shall be saved or through assuming a body by the ascent of Lucifer

[**Pat:**] Isaiah 14 (14:12) "How are you fallen from heaven, O Lucifer, who did rise in the morning?" And later (14:13) "And you said in your heart, 'I will ascend into heaven, I will exalt my throne above the stars of God.'" Therefore Lucifer ascended from an earthly habitation into heaven, for he would not have been able to arise from any other place.

Cath: I reply that this passage is speaking historically of the king of Babylon, whence above in the same place he says (14:4) "You shall take up this parable against the king of Babylon, and shall say." This was Nebuchadnezzar who is called Lucifer by resemblance, since just as the star Lucifer appears brighter than all the other stars, so was he more glorious in power above all mortals, who is said also to ascend into heaven by dignity and height of kingship. Nor ever is one able to understand the saying of Isaiah to be literally about the devil, since he speaks there about Lucifer (14:11) "your corpse is fallen down." The devil never had a body, and if you wish to say that Lucifer was the devil, not on account of this do you have it that he ascended into heaven, because Isaiah did not say 'this' but he said that Lucifer said this in his heart and he is a liar as usual. Just as the Lord says (Jn 8:44) "he is a liar." For he was saying that he wished to ascend to heaven, that is, unto equality with God, whence he adds (Is 14:14) "You will be like the most high," and saying this, he is deceived and is made most worthless among all creatures, whence Isaiah, insulting him, says (14:19) "But you are cast out of your grave, like an unprofitable branch defiled." And above he said (14:11) "and worms shall be your covering," that is, of the angels made demons who before were with you for your adornment shall be unto your shame. But pay attention, O Patarene, to what Isaiah says of Lucifer there "cast out of your grave," but it is clear that Lucifer was not cast out of the world, but out of empyrean heaven, therefore empyrean heaven was his proper abode, and thus it is clear that he was created good.

On the rule of Lucifer over the angels

[**Pat:**] Also Ezekiel 28 (blend of 28:14 and 12-13) "You a cherubim, You were the signet of perfection, full of wisdom and perfect in beauty, in the pleasures of the paradise of God." And later (28:14) "I set you in the holy mountain of God." Therefore Lucifer ascended into heaven and there was made leader by God over the angels. But because he performed poorly in that leadership position he was overthrown from thence by God, whence it adds (28:16) "and you have sinned and I cast you out from the

---

XI.6.5 Quomodo...6 oriebaris] Is. 14:12.   6 Qui...8 meum] Is. 14:13 (ascendam) conscendam | celi] add. dei *Vulg.*)   12 sumes...13 dices] Is. 14:4 (sumes) sumens | istam] ista *Vulg.*)   20 concidit...21 tuum] Is. 14:11.   26 est mendax] Ioh. 8:44.   28 ero...30 creaturas] Is. 14:14 (eris)ero *Vulg.*)   30 tu...32 pollutus] Is. 14:19 (fame) om. *Vulg.*)   32 et²...33 uermes] Is. 14:11.   XI.7.2 Tu...4 fuisti] conflation of Ez. 28:14 and 28:12-13.   4 et²...5 dei] Ez. 28:14.   8 et...9 dei] Ez. 28:16.

XI.6.4 incorporationem] corporationem *P* | de...luciferi] om. *F*   11 hystorialter] ystorialter *F*   12 babilonis] babylonis *F*   28 ero] eris *P*   29 est²] om. *P*   35 attende] actende *P*   36 est...37 proiectus] om. *F*   XI.7.9 eieci] eiecite *F*

XI.6.19 diabolo|fol. 66va *P*   XI.7.7 secundum|fol. 66vb *P*

pro illis de nostris qui dicunt quod diabolus de mundo ascendit in celum et ibi constitutus est a deo prelatus angelorum et est etiam pro illis qui dicunt quod ibi fuit creatus a deo et ab eo preponitus angelorum factus.

Catholicus: Respondeo quod loquitur de rege tyri. qui fuit homo. unde dicit ibi. factus est sermo domini ad me dicens. fili hominis leua planctum super regem tyri et dices ei etcet. et numquam loquitur de lucifero hystorialiter quod patet ex multis uerbis huius capituli. maxime ex illi superiorem cum sit homo et non deus etcet. et infra. dabo te in cinerem super terram etcet. et postea non eris in perpetuum etcet. diabolus enim non est homo. nec habet corpus ut cinerem redigatur. nec desiit esse preterea esto quod lucifer intelligatur. non dicit quod ascenderit in celum nec quod deus fecerit eum prelatum angelorum. item ex hiis uerbis et ex aliis quam pluribus istius capituli constat quod ille de quo loquitur ezechielis fuit quandoque in statu innocentie et quod postea peccauerit et quod dampnatus sit eternaliter et quod non sit deus. igitur si de lucifero loquitur. ergo fuit dei creatura et innocens et peccans per superbiam dampnatus est eternaliter secundum sententiam ecclesie nostre.

Patarenus: Item. lucam. xvi. homo quidem erat diues qui habebat uillicum etcet. hoc patet quod lucifer fuit in celo preponitus a deo super angelos sed quia male se habuit in illo officio deus eiectus illum de celo.

Catholicus: Respondeo quod illa fuit parabola in qua dominus significauit diuites huius seculi. quod patet ex illis uerbis qui subiecit scilicet quia filii seculi huius prudentiores filius lucis sunt in generatione sua etcet. quod non loquatur de lucifero probatur aperte quia dicit ibi et laudauit dominus uillicum iniquitatis quia prudente fecisse etcet. non enim lucifer prudenter fecit illam fraudem comittendo. per quam nulla est lucratus et de paradiso dei est deiectus. immo stultissime fecit. preterea illi debitores erant angeli dei ut dicitis et erant tunc sine peccato. que nam ergo debita habebat ipsi que dimiserit eis lucifer? dicite nobis. item in quas domos suas debuerunt ipsi recipere luciferum. cum remotus esset a sua uillicatione. sicut dixit uilicus ibi? et hic nobis ennarate. preterea quomodo diceret dominus ihesus facite uobis amicos etcet. quasi diceret sicut fecit lucifer ita faciatis et uos. sed lucifer in illo facto sicut dicitis ammisit bonum et meruit malum. sic ergo daret nobis consilium mortis. quod falsum est. quia uerba uite eterne habet. ergo non loquitur christus de illa uestra fantasia per uos mendaciter composita.

mountain of God." And it this for those of us who say that the devil ascended from the world into heaven, and there was made the leader of the angels by God, and it is also for those who say that there he was created by God and from Him was made commander of the angels.

Cath: I reply that he was speaking of the king of Tyre, who was a man, whence he says there (28:11) "And the word of the Lord came to me, saying, 'Son of man, take up a lamentation upon the king of Tyre, and say to him.'" And never was he speaking historically of Lucifer, that is clear from many of the words in this chapter, especially from those above (28:2) "whereas you are a man, and not God." And later (28:19) "and I will make you like ashes upon the earth," and after (29:19) "and you shall never be any more." For the devil is no man, neither does he have a body which might be reduced to ashes, nor has he ever ceased to be. Further, even if we understand that it is Lucifer; he did not say "that might have ascended into heaven" neither that God made him leader of the angels. Also from these words and from many others in this chapter it remains that he of whom Ezekiel speaks was at some point in the state of innocence and that later he had sinned and was damned eternally and that he is not God. Also if it were speaking of Lucifer, therefore he was a creature of God, and was innocent and, sinning by pride, was damned eternally according to the opinion of our church.

Pat: Also Luke 16 (16:1) "There was a certain rich man who had a steward," This is clear that Lucifer was in heaven, placed as leader by God over the angels, but because of the evil he did in that office, God cast him out of heaven.

Cath: I reply that that was a parable in which the Lord was speaking of the rich of this world, which is clear from those words that follow, namely, (Lk 16:8) "for the children of this world are wiser in their generation than the children of light." That it does not speak of Lucifer is plainly proven since he speaks of the Lord there praising the wicked steward "for he had done wisely." For Lucifer did not do wisely in committing that offense, through which he gained nothing and was cast out of paradise by God, rather he acted most stupidly. Further the debtors were the angels of God, as you say and they were without sin. What therefore are the debts they had towards Him who dismissed Lucifer from them? Tell us. Also in what houses ought they to receive from Lucifer, when he had been removed from his stewardship, as the steward says there? And here tell the story for us. Further how could the Lord Jesus have said (16:9) "Make friends to yourselves," as if to say just as he did, do likewise, but Lucifer by this fact, as you say, lost the good, and merited evil, so Lucifer would give us a counsel of death, which is false. Because instead He has the words of eternal life, therefore Christ is

---

16 factus...18 ei] Ez. 28:11.   20 cum...deus] Ez. 28:3.   21 dabo...terram] Ez. 28:18.   22 non¹...perpetuum] Ez. 28:19.
34 homo...35 uillicum] Luc. 16:1.   40 quia...41 sua] Luc. 16:8.   53 facite...amicos] Luc. 16:9.

14 factus] om. P   23 ut] **sic** PF **leg. in**   24 lucifer] lucifero P   27 ille] illo F   45 illam] add. laudem P exp.   49 in quas] iniquias P
50 debuerunt] debita habebant F   56 nobis] add. exemplum P | quod] quid P

11 ascendit|fol. 51r F   34 diues|fol. 67ra P   58 fantasia|fol. 67rb P

De prelio quod dicunt in celo fuisse

[**Patarenus:**] Item in apocalypsis. xii. factum est praelium magnum in celo michael et angeli eius preliabantur cum draconem et draco pugnabat et angeli eius etcet. ecce quod diabolus comisit prelium magnum in celo sicut nos dicimus in quo prelio fuit mirabilis sanguinis effusio ut dicitur infra. xiiii. et exiuit sanguis de lacu usque ad frenos equorum per stadia mille sexcenta etcet.

Catholicus: Respondeo quod illud prelium est cotidie in celo mistico in ecclesia ubi pugnabat diabolus et angeli eius id est demones et mali homines ex una parte. ex alia uero pugnant michael et angeli eius id est sibi deputati ad auxilium electorum hominum et ipsi electi et nota quod per angelos intelliguntur hic et angeli et homines quia per dignius intelligitur et illud quod minus dignum est id est angeli et homines et quod de isto prelio intellexerit beatus. iohannes. ex eo quod subdit. et ipsi uicerunt illam propter sanguinem agni. et propter uerbum testimonii sui etcet. omnia enim que beatus iohannes scripsit in apocalypsis fuerunt reuelationes de futuris. sicut innuit in principio libri ubi dicit apocalypsis ihesu christi. quam dedit ei deus palam facere seruis suis que oportet fieri cito. preterea esto quod loquatur de prelio quod fuit in celo inter beatos angelos et malos non dicit quod fuerit male prelium. fuit enim prelium uoluntatum tamen. quia lucifer et aliqui angeli superbierunt. et alii per humilitatem deo adheserunt. nec obstat quod opposuisti de sanguinis effusione. quia illa effusio non fuit in celo sed in mundo isto est uel erit ad litteram. uel spiritualiter. quod patet ex tribus. primo quia beatus iohannes ponit illam fuisse longe post prelium celeste et post deiectionem draconis et angelorum eius. secundo quia ponit manifeste eam in terra fuisse. unde et dicit et misit angelis falcem suam in terram et uindemiauit uineam terre et misis in lacum ire dei magnum etcet. tertio quia dicit eam fuisse in lacum qui est extra ciuitatem et exiuit sanguinis de lacu. unde subdit. et calcatus est lacus extra ciuitatem et exiuit sanguis de lacu etcet. sed prelium illud fuit in ciuitate celi secundum tuam oppinionem. ergo sanguinis effusio illa non fuit in celo.

On the battle that they say was in heaven

[**Pat:**] Also Apocalypse 12 (12:7) "And there was a great battle in heaven, Michael and his angels fought with the dragon, and the dragon fought and his angels." See that the devil engaged in a great battle in heaven as we say, in which there was much spilling of blood, as is said later in 14 (14:20) "and blood came out of the press, up to the horses' bridles, for a thousand and six hundred furlongs."

Cath: I reply that this battle is fought daily in the mystical heaven of the Church, where the devil fights with his angels, that is, demons and evil men on one part, and on the other are fighting Michael with his angels, that is, he has charge of those to the aid of elect men and the elect themselves. And note that through 'angels' here are to be understood both angels and men, because by the more worthy thing is also understood that which is less worthy, that is, angels and men. And that Blessed John is speaking of this battle is clear from what comes next (12:11) "And they overcame him by the blood of the Lamb, and by the word of the testimony." For all that Blessed John wrote in Apocalypse were revelations about the future, just as he indicates at the beginning of the book where he says (1:1) "The Revelation of Jesus Christ, which God gave to him, to make known to his servants the things which must shortly come to pass." Further, suppose that he was speaking of the battle that was in heaven between the blessed angels and the evil ones, he did not say that it was an evil battle, for it was a battle of will nevertheless, since Lucifer and some angels were prideful, and others cleaved to God through humility, neither does it matter what you present concerning the shedding of blood, since that shedding was not in heaven but on this earth, or will be in the future, either literally or spiritually. This is clear for three reasons. The first is that Blessed John puts it happening long after the heavenly battle and after the overthrow of the dragon and his angels. The second that he plainly puts it as happening on earth, whence he says (14:19) "And the angel thrust in his sharp sickle into the earth, and gathered the vineyard of the earth, and cast it into the great press of the wrath of God." The third is that he says it was in the press which is outside the city, and blood flowed from the press, whence he adds (14:20) "And the press was trodden outside the city, and blood came out of the press." But that battle was in the city of heaven according to your opinion, therefore the shedding of blood was not in heaven.

XI.8.2 factum...5 eius] Apoc. 12:7.   7 et...9 sexcenta] Apoc. 14:20.   19 et...20 sui] Apoc. 12:11 (illam] eum *Vulg.*) 23 apocalypsis...25 cito] Apoc. 1:1 (ei] illi *Vulg.*)   36 et²...38 magnum] Apoc. 14:19.   40 et¹...41 lacu] Apoc. 14:20.

XI.8.1 De...fuisse] om. *F*   7 mirabilis] mutabilis *F* | sanguinis] sanguis *P*   11 mistico] add. id est *F*   14 ad] in *P*   31 isto] om. *P* 38 magnum] add. dei *P* exp.   39 exiuit...lacu] *P* exp.

XI.8.17 homines|fol. 51v *F*   28 alii|fol. 67va *P*

Probatio per scripturam quod angeli qui ceciderunt debeant saluari per corpora

[**Patarenus:**] Dauid. heu mihi quia incolatus meus prolongatus est etcet. ergo alibi habitauit quandoque spiritus dauid scilicet in celo.

Catholicus: Respondeo quod dauid appelerat celum incolatum suum non quia ibi fuerit anima. sed quia per ueram spem suus erat. sicut dicit apostolus in persona sanctorum omnium.

Catholicus: Non habemus hic manentem ciuitatem sed futuram inquirimus etcet. et est ista spes maxime ex promissione filii dei dicentis. lucam. xxii. Ego dispono uobis sicut disposuit mihi pater meus regnum etcet.

[**Patarenus:**] Item. ysaias. xxiiii. et erit in die illa uisitabit dominus super militiam celi in excelso et super reges terre qui sunt super terram et congregabuntur in congregatione unius facis in lacum et claudentur ibi et post multos dies uisitabuntur etcet. ergo militia celi que est congregatio angelorum de celo cadentium saluabuntur.

Catholicus: Respondeo quod dicimus per ysaias uocat militiam celi iudeos de ierusalem. que scilicet ierusalem dicitur celum eo quod in alto sita est. uel quia de celo tantum erat ei aqua ad uitam habitantium in ea. uel dicitur populus iudeorum militia celo eo quod uni dominus celi militabat per fidem. reges uero terre dicuntur maiores iudeorum uel reges gentium que erant circa ierusalem. uisitauit ergo dominus super ierusalem et iudeam et super gentes terre non habitantes per nabucho et per eum congregauit illos et incarcerauit in babillonia ubi erat lacus per. lxx annos et post illos multos annos uisitauit eos per cyrum a quo licentia data redierunt ad propria et hic dicit hoc dominus per ysaiam. uel spiritualiter loquitur de bonis et malis hominibus qui significatur per militiam celi scilicet boni et per reges terre scilicet mali qui tribulabuntur in hoc mundo sed in die iudicii uisitabuntur per aduentum filii dei. alii uisitatione maioris glorie. alii uero uisitatione maioris pene. iohannes. v. nolite mirari hoc quia uenit hora etcet. et daniel. xii. et multi de his qui dormiunt puluere euigilabunt. alii in uitam eternam et alii in opprobrium ut uideant semper etcet. potest etiam istud ysaia. intelligi de bonis hominibus. et si de angeli qui ceciderunt uis intelligere dico quod ipsi uisitabuntur in die iudicii uisitatione maioris pene de qua legitur in ysaias. xxvii. in die illa uisitabit dominus in gladio suo duro et grandi et forti super leuiathan serpentem uectem et super leuiathan serpentem tortuosum etcet. et petri. secunda. ii°. Tra-

Proof from scripture that the angels who fell ought to be saved through bodies

[**Pat:**] David (119:5) "Woe is me, that my sojourning is prolonged!" Therefore there is another place where the spirit of David dwelt at some time, that is, in heaven.

Cath: I reply that David called heaven his dwelling, not that he was there in soul but rather by true hope, he was as the Apostle speaks in the person of all the saints.

Cath: (Heb 13:14) "For we do not have here a lasting city, but we seek one that is to come." And this is especially hope in the promise that the Son of God was speaking of in Luke 22 (22:29) "and I assign to you, as my Father assigned to me, a kingdom."

[**Pat:**] Also Isaiah 24 (24:21–22) "And it shall come to pass, that in that day the Lord shall visit upon the host of heaven on high, and upon the kings of the earth, on the earth, and they shall be gathered together as in the gathering of one bundle into the pit, and they shall be shut up there in prison, and after many days they shall be visited." Therefore the army of heaven, which is the brotherhood of angels fallen from heaven, shall be saved.

Cath: I reply that we say that what Isaiah calls the army of heaven is the Jews of Jerusalem which, 'Jerusalem' is called 'heaven' because it is situated on a high place, or because only from heaven was there water for the life of those who lived in it, or it refers to the Jewish people as the army of heaven by him, since the Lord of heaven made them one to fight for the faith. Indeed the kings of the earth are called greater than the Jews, or the kings of the gentiles who were around Jerusalem, therefore the Lord visited over Jerusalem and Judah and over the peoples of the earth, not living through Nebuchadnezzar and through him gathered and imprisoned in Babylon, where there was a press, for 70 years, and after those many years they were visited by Cyrus, by whom they were given permission to return to their own land. This the Lord says by Isaiah. In the spiritual sense it is to be interpreted as regarding good and bad men, which are signified by the army of heaven, namely, the good, and through the kings of the earth, the evil, those who are troubled in this world but shall be visited on the day of judgment at the coming of the Son of God, some by a visitation of greater glory, yet others will be visited with a greater punishment. John 5 (5:28) "Do not wonder at this, for the hour comes," and Daniel 12 (12:2) "And many of those who sleep in the dust of the earth, shall awake, some unto life everlasting, and others unto reproach, that they may see it always." Also one can interpret that passage in Isaiah as referring to good men, and if you wish to interpret it as the angels who fell, I say that they shall be visited in the day of judgment with a greater punishment, as one reads in Isaiah 27 (27:1) "In

---

XI.9.3 heu...4 est] Ps. 119:5.   10 Non...11 inquirimus] Heb. 13:14.   12 Ego...13 regnum] Luc. 22:29.   15 et...19 uisitabuntur] Is. 24:21-22 (ibi) add. in carcere *Vulg.*)   41 nolite...hora] Ioh. 5:28. | et²...43 semper] Dan. 12:2 (dormiunt) add. in terre *Vulg.*)   47 in²...50 tortuosum] Is. 27:1.   50 Tra-didit...51 reseruari] 2 Pet. 2:4.

XI.9.29 uisitauit...30 ierusalem] om. *P*   30 non] add. circum *F*   32 lxx] xlxx *P*   34 dicit] prodicit *P*   38 uisita-buntur] add. in die iudicii *P* exp.   39 alii...40 glorie] om. *F*   44 etiam] add. totum *F*

XI.9.12 dicentis|fol. 67vb *P*   38 tribulabuntur|fol. 68ra *P*   45 intelligere|fol. 52r *F*

didit iudicium cruciandos reseruari etcet. ergo seruatur ad maiorem penam. unde et dicebant in euangelio. ihesu christi. filli dauid quid ante tempus torquere nos etcet.

[Patarenus:] Item ieremias. ii°. populus uero meus oblitus est mei diebus innumeris etcet. isti sunt angeli qui ceciderunt quibus dicit deus in sequenti capitulo tamquam multe adultere reuertere ad me dicit dominus et ego suscipiam te etcet. ergo possunt saluari.

Catholicus: Respondeo hoc de iudeis loquitur qui inumeris diebus id est multis peccauerant contra deum. similis est locutio ad romanos. iiii°. sic erit semen tuum sicut stelle celi sicut arena qui est in littore maris id est multum quia neque homines neque angelos omnes sunt tot quot sunt sidera celi et arena maris. ad hoc est illud. ad hebreos. xi. et hoc emortuo tamquam sidera celi in multitudine etcet. et lucam. ii°. ut describeretur uniuersus orbis etcet. nec potest intelligi de angelis hoc dictum ieremie. quia dicit quod peccatum populi huius fuit ydolatria. quod nequaquam fuit peccatum angelorum. set superbia.

[Patarenus:] Item in trenis iiii°. filii syon incliti et amicti auro primo. quomodo computata sunt in uasa testea opus manuum figuli etcet. ergo spiritus qui de celo uenerunt incorporantur. sed qui in corpore sunt penitentiam faciunt et saluantur. ergo illi saluantur.

Catholicus: Respondeo non dicit quod sint computati in uasis testeis sed dicit in uase testea. loquitur enim de iudeis captiuitatis in babillonia qui computabantur a gentibus sicut uasa testea qui sunt fragilia et ideo bene dicit computati. non dicit positi. sed audi quid ibi dicitur scilicet opus manuum figuli etcet. ergo deus facit uasa testea que sunt corpora. quid est contra alium errorum tuum.

[Patarenus:] Item baruch. iii°. quid est israel. quod in terra inimicorum es etcet. et infra disce ubi sit sapientia. etcet. quis autem sit iste israel. dicitur ad Galathas. ultimo. pax super illos et misericordia et super israel dei etcet. ergo angeli qui ceciderunt sunt israel dei. qui fuerunt tracti in mundum que est terra demonum. quibus dicit supra. audi israel mandata uite etcet. et sic patet quod ipsi possunt saluari.

Catholicus: Respondeo quod loquitur de iudeis qui dicuntur israel. qui propter malitia peccata que fecerunt sepe fuerunt captiuati et dispersi in terris gentium. paulus uero loquitur ad galathas de duobus

that day the Lord with his hard and great and strong sword shall visit leviathan the fleeing serpent, and leviathan the crooked serpent," and 2 Peter 2 (2:4) "unto torments, to be reserved unto judgment," therefore to a greater punishment, whence as they say in the gospel (Mt 8:29) "Jesus Christ, Son of David, why have you come to torment us before the time."

[Pat:] Also Jeremiah 2 (2:32) "but my people have forgotten me days without number." And these are the angels who fell, of which God says in the next chapter, just as many adulterers (3:1) "return to me, says the Lord, and I will receive you."

Cath: I reply that this is spoken regarding the Jews who "for days without number," that is, sinned against God. There is a similar expression in Romans 4 (4:18) "So shall your seed be," (Heb 11:12) "like the stars of the heavens, like the sand which is on the shore," that is, 'many,' since neither men nor all angels are as many as the stars of the heavens or the sand of the sea. On this point is Hebrews 11 (11:12) "and him as good as dead, as the stars of heaven in multitude," and Luke 2 (2:1) "that the whole world be enrolled," nor are you able to interpret this passage of Jeremiah as speaking about the angels, since he says that the sin of this people was idolatry, which by no means was the sin of the angels, but rather pride.

[Pat:] Also in Lamentations 4 (4:2) "The noble sons of Zion, and they who were clothed with the best gold, how are they considered as earthen vessels, the work of the potter's hands?" Therefore the spirits which came from heaven are embodied, but he who is in the body can do penance and be saved, therefore they are saved.

Cath: I reply that he does not say that they might be considered as in earthen vessels, but he says "as earthen vessels," for he is speaking of the Jews during the Babylonian captivity who were considered by the gentiles as earthen vessels which are fragile and so he well says 'considered,' he did not say 'put.' But hear what he is saying there, which is against another of your errors.

[Pat:] Baruch 3 (3:10) "How did it happen, O Israel, that you are in your enemies' land?" And after (3:14) "Learn where is wisdom," Yet who is meant by this Israel is spoken of at the end of Galatians (6:16) "peace on them, and mercy, and upon the Israel of God." Therefore the angels who fell are the Israel of God, who were dragged into the world which is the land of demons, of which it speaks above (Bar 3:9) "Hear, O Israel, the commandments of life." And so it is plain that they are able to be saved.

Cath: I reply that he is speaking of the Jews, who are called Israel, who, on account of the sins which they frequently committed, were captured and dispersed among the lands of the gentiles, yet Paul speaks to the Galatians about two

populis saluatis per christum scilicet de gentili et de israel. quare patet quod non loquitur de angelis qui ceciderunt. quia illi non sunt nisi unus populus.

Patarenus: Item mattheus. xv. respondens ait. non sum missus nisi ad oues que perierunt domus israel etcet. hoc numquam potest intelligi de israel carnali quia secundum uos o romani christus uenit saluare omnes homines. ergo de angelis qui ceciderunt intelligitur.

Catholicus: Respondeo quod christus loquitur de israel id est de iudeis qui exierunt de iacob qui dictus est israel. quos uenit saluare in propria persona et principaliter ad gentes autem nec in propria persona predicauit scilicet in terris eorum nec principaliter uenit pro eis. saluauit autem gentes per apostolos suos. seruato primo ordine reuerentie populo digniori. hoc est israelitico. unde dixit apostolis primo. mattheus. x°. in uiam gentium ne abieritis et in ciuitates samaritanorum ne intraueritis. sed potius ite ad oues que perierunt domus israel etcet. et postea in ascensionem dixit eis. Mattheus ultimo. euntes ergo docete omnis gentes. unde et paulus et barnabas dicerunt in actibus. xiii. uobis oportebat primum loqui uerbum dei. sed quoniam repulistis illud et indignos uos iudicatis uite eterne ecce conuertimur ad gentes etcet. nec umquam potest hoc euangelium intelligi de angelis qui ceciderunt. quia christus saluauit filiam cananee que non erat de illi ouibus et uos dicitis quia non debent saluari nisi illi spiritus qui ceciderunt. ergo christus non loquitur de illis. preterea dic mihi heretice quis est iste israel. cuius sunt oues iste saluande. si dicis quod est deus. sed israel interpretatur uir uidens deum. ergo deus est uir. et est uidens alium deum. quid nulla est dictum. si autem dicis quod christus est. sed iste oues fuerunt eius antequam ueniret in mundum. quod nullo alio modo quam per creationem et sic patet quod christus creauit angelos. et sic est deus per naturam quod uos negatis.

[**Patarenus:**] Item lucam. xv. quis ex uobis homo qui habet centum oues etcet. et infra. aut que mulier habens dragmas. x. etcet. ergo saluabuntur angeli qui perierunt de celo cadentes qui significantur per ouem centesimam et per decimam dragmam perditam et recuperatam.

Catholicus: Respondeo quod sunt due similtudines pro salute peccatorum introducte a domino quod patet ibi supra et ait ad illos parabolam istam etcet. et infra congratulamini mihi quia inueni ouem meam que perierat. dico autem uobis quod ita gaudium erit in celo super uno peccatore penitentiam agente quam super xc.viiii iustis etcet. nec possunt intelligi hystorialiter de angelis qui ceciderunt. quia illi non

peoples saved through Christ, namely, the gentiles and Israel, hence it is plain that he is not speaking of the angels who fell, since they are not but one 'people.'

Pat: Also Matthew 15 (15:24) "And he answering, said, 'I was not sent except to the sheep that are lost of the house of Israel.'" You are unable to interpret this as carnal Israel since according to you, O Roman, Christ came to save all men, therefore it is understood as relating to the angels who fell.

Cath: I reply that Christ is speaking of Israel, that is, of the Jews who went with Jacob, who is called Israel, which He came to save in His own person, and principally to preach to the people, namely, in their territory, neither did He principally come for them, yet He saved the gentiles through His Apostles, by saving the first in order of reverence to the more worthy people, that is Israel, whence He says to the Apostles first in Matthew 10 (10:5–6) "Do not go into the way of the Gentiles, and into the city of the Samaritans do not enter, but go rather to the lost sheep of the house of Israel." And later at the Ascension he said to them at the end of Matthew (28:19) "Go, teach all nations," whence Paul and Barnabas say in Acts 13 (13:46) "It was necessary that the word of God should be spoken first to you. Since you thrust it away from you, and judge yourselves unworthy of eternal life, behold, we turn to the Gentiles." Nor is this gospel ever to be interpreted in light of the angels who fell, because Christ saved the daughter of the Canaanite who was not of those sheep, and you say that He should save none except those spirits who fell. Therefore Christ is not speaking of them. Further, tell me, O Heretic, who is this Israel, of whose sheep shall be saved? If you say that it is God, but Israel is interpreted as man seeing God, therefore God is a man, and is seeing another God, which is never said. But yet if you say it is Christ, but these sheep were His before He came into the world, and in no other way than by creation, and so it is clear that Christ created the angels, and so is God by nature, which you deny.

[**Pat:**] Also Luke 15 (15:4) "who among you who has one hundred sheep," and later (15:8) "or what woman having ten drachmas," therefore the Angels who fell from heaven shall be saved, falling, which is symbolized by the one hundred sheep and by the two drachmas lost and recovered.

Cath: I reply that these are two parables for the salvation of sinners, introduced by the Lord which is clear from above (15:3) "And he spoke to them a parable," and later (15:6–7) "Rejoice with me, because I have found my sheep that was lost. I say to you, that even so there will be joy in heaven upon one sinner who does penance, than upon ninety-nine just who do not need penance." Nor are you able historically to understand this as relating to the angels

---

101 respondens...102 israel] Matt. 15:24. 115 in¹...117 israel] Matt. 10:5-6. 118 euntes...119 gentes] Matt. 28:19. 120 uobis...122 gentes] Act. 13:46 (repulistis) repellitis *Vulg.*). 135 quis...136 oues] Luc. 15:4. 136 aut...137 x] Luc. 15:8. 143 et¹...istam] Luc. 15:3. 144 congratulamini...147 iustis] Luc. 15:6-7.

98 populis] prophetis *F* 103 intelligi] om. *P* 104 christus] om. *P* | saluare] salvari *P* 110 ad...persona] om. *F* 130 deum] de uiro *F* | dictum] dictu *P* 139 centesimam] centesima *F*

118 dixit|fol. 68vb *P* 120 oportebat|fol. 52v *F* 143 infra|fol. 69ra *P*

fuerunt centesima pars tantum angelorum immo. x. secundum nos. secundum autem errorem uestrum tertia.

[Patarenus:] Item ad Romanos. xi. conclusit enim deus omnia in incredulitate ut omnium misereatur etcet. ergo saluabuntur angeli qui peccauerunt.

Catholicus: Respondeo. quia non loquitur de angelis. quia peccatum angelorum non fuit incredulitas sed superbia. sed loquitur de duobus populis iudeo scilicet et gentili. ut patet ex sequentibus uerbis ibidem. comprehendit enim genera populorum. sin autem uelles intelligere largissime sic saluarentur omnis iniqui. quid falsum est. et nota quod ex ista auctoritate et ex illa ysaias supradictum? uoluit dicere origenes quod demones debeant ad huc saluari. et inde forte traxerunt patereni errorem suum in hac parte.

Patarenus: Item apocalypsis. ii°. ecce missurus est diabolus aliquos ex uerbis in carcerem ut temptemini et habebitis tribulationem diebus decem etcet. ergo angelis missi ad tempus in carcerem istorum corporum a diabolo. sed tandem saluabuntur.

Catholicus: Respondeo. non loquitur de angelis sed de hominibus qui peccauerunt et penitentiam faciunt. contra quos diabolus suscitat temptationes et pressuris et ista dicuntur carcer. dicuntur autem tribulari diebus. x. preceptorem decalogi. quod autem de angelis non loquatur probo quia dicit missurus est etcet. sed angeli iam missi erant in suum carcerem per quinque milia annorum antea. item quoniam stabit diebus x etcet. secundum tuum intellectum dic mihi si nosti.

[Patarenus:] Preterea uidemus quod spiritus humanam desiderant ire in celum. opinantur etiam multa secreta celestia. sicut dicit apostolus. prima. ad corinthios. ii°. spiritus enim omnia scrutatur etiam profunda dei etcet. quare uidetur quod quandoque fuerunt ibi et uiderint. et experti sint illa et sic patet rationabiliter quod de celo uenerunt. sed talis istis datur remissio peccatorum. et uita restituitur eterna. igitur saluantur spiritus qui de celo ceciderunt.

Catholicus: Respondeo. quod hoc ideo est ex parte quia spiritualis sunt et quia uero naturaliter a deo sunt per creationem et ideo ad spiritualia. et ad deum tendunt. ipsaque quandoque subtiliter perscrutantur. est etiam propter eruditionem doctrine sancte sicut dicit apostolus ad romanos. x. quomodo ergo credent ei quem non audierunt etcet. et postea. fides ex auditu etcet. item est etiam per gratiam spiritus sancti. unde. i^a. iohannes. ii°. sed sicut unctio eius docet uos de omnibus etcet. quandoque uero et multi multa falsa

who fell, since they were not a hundredth part only of the angels, no more than a 10th according to us, yet according to your error a third.

[Pat:] Also Romans 11 (11:32) "For God has consigned all men to unbelief, that he may have mercy upon all." Therefore all the angels who sinned shall be saved.

Cath: I reply that he is not speaking of the angels, since the sin of the angels was not unbelief by pride, but he speaks of the two peoples, namely, the Jews and Gentiles, that is clear from the following words there, for it includes both kinds of people, but if on the contrary you yet wish to interpret more broadly, thus all wicked ones shall be saved, which is false. And do you note what this authority and that passage of Isaiah above say? Origen wanted to say that the demons ought to be saved,[1] and from him perhaps the Patarenes drew their error on that point.

Pat: Also Apocalypse 2 (2:10) "Behold, the devil will cast some of you into prison that you may be tested, and you shall have tribulation for ten days." Therefore the angels are sent into the prison of these bodies for a time, but shall be saved in the end.

Cath: I reply that he is not speaking of the angels but of men who sinned and then did penance, against which the devil rouses temptations and distresses, and these are called 'prison.' Yet they say that the tribulation of ten days is the 10 commandments of the decalogue, yet I prove that the angels are not spoken of because he says he "is sent," but the angels were already sent into their prison five thousand years before that. Also because it will last "for ten days." According to your understanding, tell me if you knew.

[Pat:] Further we see that the human spirit desires to go to heaven, also they also are privy to many heavenly secrets, as the Apostle says in 1 Corinthians 2 (2:10) "For the Spirit searches all things, even the deep things of God." So it does sometimes seem that they were there and saw, and experienced it, and so it is rationally plain that they came from heaven, but to such as these shall be given remission of sins and shall be restored to life, and so the spirits who fell from heaven shall be saved.

Cath: I reply that the reason for this is on account of the fact that they are spiritual and that also they naturally tend to God by [reason of] their creation, and for that reason those spiritual things tend towards God, so sometimes they subtly look towards there, and this is on account of learning in holy doctrine, as the Apostle says in Romans 10 (10:14) "How shall they believe him, of whom they have not heard," and after (10:17) "faith comes through hearing," also through the grace of the Holy Spirit, as in 1 John 2 (2:27) "but as his anointing teaches you about all things." But sometimes in fact many persons hold many false

---

152 conclusit...153 misereatur] Rom. 11:32. 165 ecce...167 decem] Apoc. 2:10. 182 spiritus...dei] 1 Cor. 2:10. 193 quomodo...194 audierunt] Rom. 10:14. 194 fides...195 sancti] Rom. 10:17. 196 sed...197 omnibus] 1 Ioh. 2:27.

168 missi] add. v *P* exp. 175 sed] set *P* 177 x] om. *P* 180 opinantur] oppinantur *P* 185 talis] om. *P* 186 uita] rata *P* | saluantur] solvantur *P* 189 naturaliter] mirabiliter *P* 191 quandoque] om. *P* | perscrutantur] perscruptantur *P* 197 multi] add. etiam *P* exp.

170 loquitur|fol. 69rb *P* 186 uita|fol. 53r *F*

---

[1] Origen's doctrine of ἀποκατάστασις was that all, including the demons, would be saved at the end of time.

opinantur de quibus uos estis et decipimini more freneticorum. sed modo respondeas mihi. anime dampnatorum diligunt bona celestia. sed ad hic non mouet eos gratia. ergo natura bona mouet eos et sic incidis in confusionem illius erroris que negas dampnatorum spiritus esse dei creaturas.

Attende catholice quod in nulla auctoritate ab heretico allegata sit aliqua mentio de salute angelorum de celo cadentium sed in illis quas induximus expressim agitur de illorum eterna dampnatione.

opinions – you all belong to this group – and you are deceived in the manner of madmen. But how can you respond to me? The souls of the damned love the good things of heaven, but to this they are not moved by grace, therefore good nature moves them, and thus you fall into the confusion of the errors of those who deny that the spirits of the damned are creatures of God.

Pay attention, O Catholic, that in no authority adduced by heretics is there any mention of the salvation of angels fallen from heaven, but in these which we bring forward it expressly establishes their eternal damnation.

Quod spiritus humani cotidie de nouo creantur neque ueniunt ex traduce neque transeunt de corpore in corpus et quod sancti homines finita uita corporis ascendunt in celum cotidie

Dictum est supra de angelis apostatis quibus non profuit humanitas Christi. Nunc autem uidendum est de hominibus qui per ipsam ueraciter redempti sunt et primo dicendum est de animabus circa quarum statum patareni uidentur errare tripliciter scilicet in creatione ipsarum et incorporatione atque in glorificatione. Verumptamen in primis duobus diuersimode sentiunt ad inuicem. De creatione uero illarum quia omnes anime siue sint angeli siue non fuerunt create simul a principio mundi siue a deo et diabolo siue a deo tantum. secundum diuersas in hoc ipso sectas eorum. Alii uero ex ipsis dicunt quod spiritus humani a deo et diabolo ex traduce fiunt. Alii tamen inter illos dicunt omnes spiritus esse eternos. de incorporatione uero spirituum dicunt quidam ex predictis hereticis quod omnes uadunt de corpore in corpus et qui debent saluari. si non saluantur in illo corpore uariantur per diuersa corpora donec faciendo uitam illorum in aliquo saluantur. et dicunt isti quod spiritus intrant omnia corpora animalium. Alii uero dicunt ex illis quod licet spiritus transeant per diuersa corpora. quod non tamen intrant corpora animalium nisi domesticorum et habentium sanguinem. de glorificatione uero animarum autumnant omnes patareni quod nulle sanctorum anime ascendant in celum usque ad finem mundi. quorum primum errorem traxisse uidentur ab

XII That the spirits of humans are daily created from nothing, neither do they come from traducianism,[1] neither do they cross from body to body, and that holy people at the end of bodily life ascend into heaven daily

We[2] spoke above about the apostate angels for whom the humanity of Christ was of no benefit. Yet now it remains to be seen regarding men who through it are truly redeemed and first the situation of souls must be discussed, regarding the condition of which the Patarenes seem to err in three ways: namely, in their creation, and embodiment, and in their glorification. Still, regarding the first two, they differ considerably among themselves. Regarding their creation, since all souls either are angels or they were not created together with the beginning of the world, by God and the devil, or by God alone,[3] they differ on this point in their sects. In truth, some of them say that the human spirit was made by God and the devil in the manner of traducianism.[4] Nevertheless, others among them say that all spirits are eternal.[5] Yet regarding embodiment of spirits, certain ones among the foregoing heretics say that all cross from one body to the next, and that they ought to be saved.[6] If they might not be saved in one body, they go wandering into different bodies until they are saved by finding life in another. And these say that spirits go into all animal bodies. Yet others among them say that though the spirits cross into different bodies, nevertheless that they do not go into animal bodies, except of domestic animals, and those having blood.[7] Also regarding the glorification of souls all Patarenes rave that no soul of a holy person ascends to heaven until the end of the world,[8] of which the

---

198 opinantur] oppinantur *P*   **203** dei] om. *P*   **204** Attende] Adtende *P*   **XII.1.7** redempti] redempta *F*   **12** quia] quod *F*   **20** qui] *sic PF leg.* quod

198 quibus|fol. 69va *P*   **XII.1.14** siue²|fol. 69vb *P*

---

1) An opinion among the early Latin theologians, notably Tertullian, that the soul originates from the act of natural generation by the parents, i.e. the soul comes from a part of the parents' souls. Augustine wavered regarding this position, and it was later universally rejected. | 2) The author here pauses the dialogue format and begins writing his work more directly as a theological tract. The dialogue will resume below. | 3) This belief attributed by Sacconi to the Bagnolenses, see. Sacconi, c. 26; Georgius, 135. | 4) The Concorezzans, Sacconi, c. 24; Burci, 340ff. | 5) John of Lugio espouses this, Sacconi, c. 21-22; Douais, 116; Burci, 335. | 6) Absolute dualism, Burci, 335; Sacconi, c. 17; Moneta, 61; Georgius, 134ff. | 7) This belief seems to have been a predilection of the French Cathars, Sacconi, c. 17. | 8) Sacconi limits this to the Concorezzans, c. 25; Moneta, 375ff. This doctrine of "soul sleep" was however in the air in the thirteenth century.

origine. qui dixit animas simul a principio mundi esse creatas alium uero deduxerunt ab antiqua heresi luciferanorum qui dixerant animas ex traduce prouenire. tertium autem errorem uidentur contraxisse a quibusdam philosophis antiquis qui dixerunt omnes spiritus rationales fuisse eternos. Quartum uero acceperunt scilicet de transitu spirituum de corpore in corpus. a pictagora philosopho qui hoc dicere non erubuit. Quintum autem errorem ipsi ex se adinuenerunt. nos autem dicimus reiectis istis erroribus quod deus spiritus humanos cotidie creat et eos nouis corporibus propagatis infundit et infundendo creat et quod nulli spiritus sunt ex traduce. sed omnes sunt de nichilo creati et quod spiritus non nisi unum corpus habet. item quod sanctorum anime uita corporis solute de die ascendunt in gloriam celorum sempiternam que tam rationibus quam scripturis diuinis gratia faciente probabimus in hoc loco.

Quod spiritus humani cotidie de nouo creantur probatur rationibus similibus

Constat quod spiritus nostri non opinantur nec meditantur aliqua que fuerit antequam nascerentur in hac uita nisi dicta sint eis. uel nisi per rationes uisibiles possint illa conspicere. ergo spiritus quod nunc sunt in corporibus hominum non sunt antiqui sed noui. nec possunt dicere patareni quod hoc ideo sit qui spiritus domuerunt uel quasdam biberint aquas quia uidemus sepissime quod dormiunt homines et bibunt non solum aquam sed etiam uinum et tamen non obliuiscuntur que uiderunt aut scierunt antea. preterea in qua scriptura habent ipsi de isto sompno et de hac potatione et de ista obliuisione dicant si noscunt. Item legitur in scripturis homines alios iuniores. alios antiquiores esse igitur non sunt pariter creati sed per diuersa tempora. item antequam spiritus istis corporibus fuissent incorporati sepissime tam bona quam mala fecissent. sed hic numquam legitur quod aliquid fecerunt antea. immo contrarium reperitur ut inferius patebit. igitur non sunt antiquiores corporibus suis. ergo sunt noui. preterea legimus frequenter antiquos dampnatos quia fecerint illa uel illa. ergo non sunt illi spiritus qui sunt modo in carne sed transierunt de hoc mundo aliis post eos de nouo creatis. alias enim non essent tam cito dampnati. quia si non fecissent tunc illa uel habuissent possent modo uel alio tempore ipsa facere uel habere.

Quod spiritus non ueniuntur ex traduce probatur naturaliter

corpus generatur ex semine utriusque et tunc usque ad plures menses non est in eo spiritus et postea spiritus

That human spirits are daily created from nothing is proven by similar reasons

It happens that our spirits do not know or meditate on anything before they are born into this life, unless it were told to them, or unless they might be made plain to them by visible argument. Therefore the spirits that are now in human bodies are not ancient, but new. Nor are they Patarenes able to say that rather it might be that the spirits slept or drank some certain water because we often see that men sleep and drink not only water but also wine and yet they do not forget what they saw or knew beforehand. Further in what passage of scripture do they have this, of this sleeping, or of this drinking and of this forgetting? Let them speak if they know. Also it is read in the scriptures that some men are younger, some older, therefore they were not created at the same time, but at different times, likewise very often the spirits that were infused into these bodies had done both good and evil. But here it is never read that they did anything previously, rather the contrary is discovered, as will be shown plainly below. Their bodies are not old ones, but are new. Further, we frequently read of those damned of old that they did this or that, therefore they are not those spirits who are only in flesh, but they have passed from this world, with others created anew after them, for otherwise they would not have been so swiftly damned since if they might not have then done or had those things, they would be able in a way, or at another time to do or to have those things.

That spirits do not come from traducianism is proven by natural reason

The body is produced from the seed of both and then for a few months there no spirit in it, and later the spirit is

---

XII.1.31 origine] Origen, *Peri Archon*, I, 7, 8.

31 origine] orrigine *P* 32 alium] alii *F* | antiqua] antiquo *F* 44 creati] creata *P* XII.2.2 similibus] filiorum *F* 3 opinantur] oppinantur *P* 4 antequam] ante quod *P* 5 dicta sint] dictum fuit *P* 8 dicere] add. quod *P* exp. 15 alios¹] altios *P* add. t exp. 18 fuissent] om. *P* 19 numquam] nusquam *F* 22 legimus] legitur *P* 26 fecissent] fuissent *F* 27 possent] om. *F*

39 erubuit]fol. 70ra *P* 43 spiritus]fol. 53v *F* XII.2.15 scripturis]fol. 70rb *P*

adest quandoque et quandoque non. sed spiritus non sit ex semine. quia si hoc esset statim cum generatur corpus fieret spiritus. item ex quocumque semine fieret corpus. fieret spiritus. sed hoc non sunt quia neque cum generatur corpus procreatur spiritu neque adest spiritus semper in corpore propagato ex semine. item ex anima uiri non potes dicere quod spiritus filii procedat. quia quandoque non adest pater in prouintia cum corpus pueri uiuificatur ex anima autem mulieris non potes dicere quod spiritus filii traducatur. quia tunc secundum spiritum semper filius esset filius matri in omnibus. nec uales etiam dicere quod in procreatione corporis procreetur spiritus. aut quedam uis eius ad instar ouorum in calcatione galline. quia anima humana uiuificat corpus suum. et quicquid uiuificat mouet et corpora puerorum non mouentur in uentribus matrum usque ad multa tempora. ergo sunt tunc sine anima et sic patet quod ex traduce non ueniunt spiritus.

Item spiritus non fit per modum cogitatus quod manifestum est. nec per modum seminis ut probatum est et alium modum nullis potest assignare. ergo a solo deo creatur ex nichilo.

Quod anime non transeant de corpore in corpus probatio rationabiliter

aut sua auctoritate et potestate anime intrent corpus unum uel aliud aut alius immitteret illas. Si sint autem sua auctoritate et potestate hoc facerent intrarent utique in melius corpus et uicinius saluti. sed nos uidemus quod secundum uestram sectam intrent corpus bestiale ubi non possunt saluari prout deliratis. item intrant in corpus humanum quandoque ualde deforme et ineptum ad salutem. quod non facerent si esset in sua potestate intrare prout uellent. igitur alius immittit eas statim in corpus qui est uel deus uel diabolus. deus non est quia immitteret eas statim in corpus in quo possent saluari. item nec diabolus est qua semper immitteret eas in corpus in quo non possent saluari. igitur non transeunt de corpore in corpus.

Item nusquam legitur aliquem spiritum diuersa uel plura corpora habuisse. nec aliquam secundum carnem pluries natum uel nasci debere. igitur diabolica est hoc uestra o heretici uere illi estis de quibus dicit. apostolus. prima ad timotheus. iiii. spiritus manifeste dicit. quia in nouissimis temporibus discedent quidam a fide actendentes spiritibus erroris et doctrinis demoniorum. etcet.

Preterea si spiritus intrarent corpora bestiarum bestie essent ita rationales ita ut intellectuales sicut homines. quia eiusdem nature sunt corpora omnia et si essent

infused at some point, and if at some point there was no spirit, then it was not from the seed, since if this would have happened immediately when it was generated then the body and spirit might come to be. Also from whatever seed a body arises from, so also does a spirit, but this is not true, because neither when a body is generated it is procreated by a spirit, nor is the spirit always present in the body that arises from seed. Also you cannot say that the spirits of sons proceed from the spirits of men, since sometimes the father is not near when the body of the child is quickened by the soul, yet you are not able to say that the spirit of the son is taken from the woman, because then the son would be the son of the mother in all things according to the spirit. Neither also are you able to say that in procreation of the body, the spirit is procreated, according to the likeness of eggs in a hen's brooding, since the human soul quickens its body, and whatever is quickened moves, and the bodies of children do not move in their mother's wombs for a long time, therefore they are then without a soul and so it is clear that spirits do not come through traducianism.

Also a spirit is not made by the act of thinking, as is clear, nor through the manner of seed as was proven, and one cannot assign any other way for it to come into being. Therefore from God alone is it created 'ex nihilo.'

That souls do not cross over from one body to another, by rational arguments

Either souls enter one body by their own authority and power, or another's, or another infuses them in bodies. Moreover, if by its own authority and power they do this, by all means they go into a better body and one closer to salvation. Yet we see that according to your sect they go into animal bodies where they are not able to be saved, just as you rave. Also they enter into human bodies sometimes that are gravely deformed and unsuitable for salvation, which they would not do if it were in their power to go about as they pleased. He who infuses them is either God or the devil. It is not God, because he might infuse them immediately into a body in which they are able to be saved, also neither is it the devil because by him he would always infuse them into a body in which it was impossible to be saved. Therefore they do not cross from one body to the next.

Also it is never read of any opposed spirit or one having many bodies, neither is any born many times according to the flesh or which ought to be born many times. Therefore your position is diabolical, O Heretic, you are truly those of which the Apostle says in 1 Timothy 4 (4:1) "Now the Spirit plainly says that in the last times some shall depart from the faith, giving heed to spirits of error, and doctrines of devils."

Further if spirits might go into animal bodies, they are animals, and so, rational, and so intellectual beings like men, because all the bodies are of the same nature, and if

---

XII.4.21 spiritus...23 demoniorum] 1 Tim. 4:1.

XII.3.7 corpus] add. et spiritus *F* | item...8 spiritus] om. *F* 18 ouorum] mirorum *P* XII.4.1 anime] autem *P* 2 probatio] om. *P* 4 Si] om. *F* | sint] om. *F* 12 statim...corpus] *P* exp.

XII.3.17 procreetur|fol. 70va *P* XII.4.10 salutem|fol. 54r *F* 15 non|fol. 70vb *P* eiusdem nature spiritus essent utique et eiusdem potentie.

Item quare non possunt spiritus ita penitentiam facere in corporibus animalium brutorum sicut in corporibus humanis possunt. et causa nulla ratio diuersitatis possit a nobis assignari secundum stultitiam uestre opinionis. o infatuati cathari nolite ergo insanire miseri heretici.

Quod sanctorum anime cotidie ascendunt in celum

Constat quod anime perfectorum nisi habent impedimenti in se uel contrarietatis post carnis obitum. propter quod debeat differi eorum retributio. igitur cum deus sit iustus statim dat illis mercedem suam que est uita eterna. alias enim si differret cruciarentur ille. quia spes que differtur affligit animam et sic illas iniuste puniret. quid est impossibile. preterea anime sanctorum seruierunt deo usque ad finem in suo mundo. igitur conueniens est quod statim finito suo mundo consolentur in mundo dei qui est eterne glorie participatio.

probatio quod deus creat cotidie nouos spiritus

Mattheus. xx. sic erunt nouissimi primi et primi nouissimi etcet. ergo alii primi et alii postmodum creantur spiritus. item lucam. primo. exsultauit in gaudio infans in utero meo etcet. et infra. audierunt uicini et cognati eius. quia magnificauit dominus misericordiam suam cum illa etcet. ergo non erat v milia annorum o heretici falsi. si erat infans nec etiam aliquid miraculum esse tantorum annorum spiritum exultari posse. item auditis quod dominus fecit hac misericordia cum matre. iohannes. baptista. quia ipsum habuit conceptum et natum. igitur nouus spiritus fuit suus. idem. iiº. et uenerunt festinantes et inuenerunt mariam et ioseph et infantem positum in presepio etcet. et hic dicite quomodo erat infans nisi ratione humanitatis eius. ergo de nouo fuerat ihesus creatus ergo quantum ad animam. et propagatus quantum ad corpus. quod idem de aliis hominibus credere non erubescas. idem in eodem. et cum factus esset ihesus annorum duodecim. etcet. et iii. ipse erat incipiens quasi annorum triginta. etcet. ad idem. item. iohannes. v. pater meus usque modo operatur et ero operior etcet. cum dicit dominus in presenti ego operior et non determinat creatum finem temporis. patet quod usque ad finem temporis operatur et si operatur quid nisi nouas creaturas scilicet animas et nouas facturas scilicet corpora cum non sint alie noue creature uel noue alie facture? nec potes dicere quod loquitur de operatione salutis generis humani. quia

they are of the same nature, they are spirits at any rate, and of the same power.

Also therefore spirits are not able to do penance in the bodies of brute animals, just as they are able to in human bodies. And no cause of rational difference can be assigned by us, according to your foolish opinion, O idiot Cathar, therefore refuse to be deranged, miserable heretic.

That the souls of holy people daily ascend into heaven

It happens that souls of the perfect — unless they have some impediment in themselves or trouble after bodily death on account of which they ought to postpone their reward — since God is just, He immediately gives them their recompense, which is eternal life. Otherwise if [their reward might be] postponed, it might torment them, because a hope which is delayed afflicts the soul, and thus they are unjustly punished, which is impossible. Further the souls of the saints have served God even to the end in their world, therefore it is appropriate that immediately after their deaths in this world that they be consoled in the world of God, which is participation in eternal glory.

Proof that God daily creates new spirits

Matthew 20 (20:16) "And the last shall be first, and the first, last," therefore some spirits are created first and others later. Also in Luke 1 (1:44) "the infant in my womb leapt for joy," and later (1:58) "And her neighbors and kinsfolk heard that the Lord had showed his great mercy towards her." Therefore it was not 5,000 years for him, O false Heretic, if he was an infant, nor also was it by some miracle that he was able to rejoice for so many years. Also you hear that the Lord showed this mercy to the mother of John the Baptist, because she had conceived and bore, therefore his was a new spirit. In the same 2 (2:16) "And they came with haste and they found Mary and Joseph, and the infant lying in the manger." And this shows how He was an infant, except in His human reason, therefore Jesus was newly created, insofar as His soul is concerned, and was propagated in body, and you are not ashamed to believe this regarding other men. Also in the same (2:42) "And when Jesus was twelve years of age," and 3 (3:23) "he was beginning around the age of thirty." To the same point is John 5 (5:17) "My Father is working still, and I work." Since the Lord speaks in the present tense 'I work,' and does not delimit an end of created time, it is clear that He is working until the end of time, and if He is working, what is He doing except making new creatures, namely, souls and new handiworks, namely, bodies since they might not be other new creatures or newly made handiworks? Nor are you able to say that He is speaking of the work of the salvation of the human race, since according to

---

XII.6.2 sic...3 nouissimi] Matt. 20:16.   4 exsultauit...5 meo] Luc. 1:44.   5 audierunt...7 illa] Luc. 1:58.   13 et¹...15 presepio] Luc. 2:16.   19 et...20 duodecim] Luc. 2:42.   20 erat...21 triginta] Luc. 3:23 (vulg. ipse] ipse Iesus *Vulg.*)   22 pater...23 operior] Ioh. 5:17.

30 penitentiam] presentiam *P*   32 et causa] item cum *P*   33 opinionis] oppinionis *P*   34 cathari] katari *P*   **XII.6.1** probatio...spiritus] probatio per scripturas quod spiritus humani cotidie de nouo creantur *F*   3 primi] primo *F*   7 v] ei *P*   10 hac] hanc *P*   24 creatum] add. u *P* exp.   27 noue] om. *P*

XII.5.8 que|fol. 71ra *P*   **XII.6.21** incipiens|fol. 71rb *P*

secundum hoc et pater fuisset operatus eam a principio mundi usque ad christi aduentum quod est contra tua sectam quam negas aliquos in statu salutis fuisse ante aduentum christi. Nec etiam potes dicere quod loquatur de operatione miraculorum. quia tu negas christum fecisse miracula carnalia. loquitur ergo de operatione creationis et factionis et sanitatis et uite et de omni uirtute diuinitatis quod etiam iudei intellexerunt. unde subdit iohannes propterea ergo magis querebant eum iudei interficere. quia non solum soluebant sabbatum sed et patrem suum dicebat deum equalem se faciens deo etcet. quod et ipse dominus confirmat. unde dicit. quecumque enim ille fecerit hec et filius similiter faciet etcet. item ad romanos. viiii. cum enim nondum nati fuissent ut aliquid boni egissent aut mali ut secundum electionem etcet. ergo noui erant spiritus qui alias si antiqui fuissent et multa mala et bona fecissent quod alterum necesse est illos fuisse. item. secunda ad corinthios. v. si qua ergo in christo noua creatura est etcet. ergo in christo sunt noui spiritus creati.

Probatio per scripturas quod spiritus scilicet non ueniunt ex traduce sed ex nichilo creatur a deo

Dauid. qui finxit singillatim corda eorum etcet. ergo deus animas que per corda intelliguntur finxit singillatim igitur non fiunt per decisionem. item ysaias. xlii. hec dicit dominus deus etcet. ibi dans flatum populo qui est super eam et spiritum calcantibus eam etcet. ecce quam manifeste innuit ysaias. quod solus deus creat spiritum. ergo non est per traducem. item ad romanos. viii. uanitati enim creatura subiecta est non uolens. etcet. uanitati id est corruptioni carnis creatura id est anima sequitur propter eum qui subiecit eam in spe. hac scilicet quia liberabitur a seruitute corruptionis etcet. sed creatura est res non ex preiacenti materia facta. ergo anima de nichilo creatur a deo et ipse eam creando infundit corpori uitioso et infundendo creat. unde dicit. sed propter eum qui subiecit eam in spe etcet. item prima ad timotheus. ii°. adam enim primus formatus est deinde eua etcet. sed in adam in primo formauit deus corpus. deinde spirauit in eum animam per quam corpus spirat prout hoc leguntur in Genesis. ii°. Item etiam leguntur ibi. primo. ad ymaginem suam creauit illum etcet. quod numquam de corpore intelligitur. quia secundum corpus homo non est factus ad ymaginem dei. sed secundum animam. et ideo dicit de anima eue unde subdit.

masculum et feminam creauit illos. etcet. sed cum eadem sit ratio nostrarum animarum ad animas prothoplaustrorum patet quod sicut illas de nichilo creauit deus. ita et nostras. causa ratio diuersitatis non possit assignari. quia ubi eadem est ratio eadem debet esse et iuris sententia. item ad hebreos. xii. deinde patres quidem carnis nostre habuimus eruditores et reuerebamur eos. non multo magis obtemperabimus patri spirituum et uiuemus etcet. non dicit patres quidem habiturus spirituum nostrorum sicut dicit carnis nostre. igitur non sunt spiritus ex traduce. sed tantum ex nichilo creati a deo. unde dicit. multo magis obtemperabimus patri spirituum etcet. quasi dicat carnem habemus a deo mediante opere patrum nostrorum sed spirituum solus deus est pater id est creator. item actus. xvii. hic celi et terre cum sit dominus non in manufactis templis habitat. nec in manibus humanis colitur indigens aliquo. cum ipse det omnibus uitam et inspirationem et omnia fecitque ex uno omni genus hominum inhabitare super uniuersam terram faciem etcet. non dixit apostolus quod deus det angelum sed dixit uitam et inspirationem id est animam que dicitur uita. quia uiuificat corpus. unde etiam dicitur anima quasi inanimans corpus et dicitur etiam uita quia uiuit in sempiternum. dicitur uero inspiratio quia spirat per corpus. item non dixit quod deus eam traducat de anima alius sicut dixit de corporibus de quibus dixit quod omnia fecit deus. de primo corpore scilicet ade. sed dixit quod deus eam dat in nobis quod est dicere quod ipse eam creando infundit corpori et infundendo creat ipsam et sic patet expressim quod anime non sunt ex traduce. sed quod a deo cotidie creantur ex nichilo.

Probatio per scripturam quod spiritus non transeunt de corpore in corpus

Iohannes. iii°. Respondit ihesus et dixit ei. amen amen dico uobis nisi quis renatus fuerit denuo non potest intrare regnum dei. dicit ad eum nichodemus. Quomodo potest homo nasci cum sit senex? numquid potest in uentrem matris sue iterato introire et renasci? respondit ihesus. amen amen dico uobis nisi quis renatus fuerit ex aqua et spiritu sancto non potest introire in regnum dei etcet. audi heretice quid ueritas respondit nichodemo simpliciter intelligenti. de secunda natiuitate spiritus de qua dixerat. nisi quis renatus fuerit denuo etcet. respondit enim quod de spirituali natiuitate intelligebat que sit per baptismum et hoc est quod dicit. nisi quis renatus fuerit ex aqua et spiritu sancto etcet. ac si diceret primo nascitur homo secundum carnem et secundo oportet illum nasci secundum spiritum genere baptismalis per aquam. unde etiam postea subdit. sicut est omnis qui natus est ex spiritu

them." But since by the same reason of the relation of our souls to the souls of our first parents, it is clear that just as God created these *ex nihilo*, so also He created ours, since a reason for difference [between our natures and theirs] cannot be posited, because where the reason is the same there ought also to be the same sentence of the Law. Also Hebrews 12 (12:9) "Moreover we have had fathers of our flesh as instructors, and we reverenced them. Shall we not much more obey the Father of spirits, and live?" He did not say fathers who will have our spirits, just as he said our flesh, therefore spirits do not arise from traducianism, but are only created *ex nihilo* by God, whence he says "shall we not much more obey the Father of spirits," as if to say we have flesh from God, by means of the work of our fathers, but of spirits only from God the Father, that is, the creator. Also Acts 17 (17:24–26) "he, being Lord of heaven and earth, does not dwell in temples made with hands, neither is he served by men's hands, as though he needed anything, seeing it is he who gives life, and breath, to all and to all things, and has made of one, all mankind, to dwell upon the whole face of the earth." The apostle did not say that God gave an angel, but he said life and breath, that is, the soul which is called life, since it gives life to the body. Whence also one says the soul, as of a lifeless body, and it also says life, since it lives immortally. Yet it says breathed, since it breathes through the body. Also God did not say one is propagated by traducianism from another soul, just as He said of bodies, of which it said that God made all of them from the first body, namely, Adam. But God said that He gave it to us, which is to say that He by creating it, infused it into the body and by infusing, created him, and thus it is plainly clear that souls do not derive from traducianism, but that they are daily created by God 'ex nihilo.'

Proof from scripture that spirits do not cross from body to body

John 3 (3:3–5) "Jesus answered, and said to him, 'Amen, amen I say to you, unless a man be born again, he cannot enter the kingdom of God.' Nicodemus said to him, 'How can a man be born when he is old? Can he enter a second time into his mother's womb, and be born again?' Jesus answered, 'Amen, amen I say to you, unless a man be born again of water and the Holy Spirit, he cannot enter into the kingdom of God.'" Hear, O Heretic, that Truth replies to Nicodemus with a simple interpretation of the second birth of the spirit of which He spoke, "unless a man be born again." For He replied that He understood it as a spiritual birth, which is through baptism, and this is what He says "unless a man be born again of water and the Holy Spirit," as if to say one is born a man first by flesh, and second it befits him to be born according to the Spirit by means of the baptism of water, whence also later it adds (3:8) "so is everyone who is born of the Spirit." Therefore

---

28 masculum…illos] Gen. 1:27 (illos) eos *Vulg.*)   33 deinde…36 uiuemus] Heb. 12:9.   43 hic…48 faciem] Act. 17:23-26 (terram) terrae *Vulg.*)   XII.8.3 Respondit…10 dei] Ioh. 3:3-5 (uobis) tibi | intrare) uidere | uobis²) tibi *Vulg.*)   19 sicut…spiritu] Ioh. 3:8.

29 ad animas] om. P   31 causa ratio] cum ratio F   48 apostolus] om. P   XII.8.1 scripturam] scripturas F

48 dixit|fol. 72ra P   51 inanimans|fol. 55r F   XII.8.13 enim|fol. 72rb P

etcet. igitur non nisi semel nascitur carnaliter homo. item prima. ad corinthios. viiii. numquid de bobus cura est deo etcet. hoc dic mihi heretice fatue quare non esset cura deo de bobum si eosdem spiritus haberent quales sunt in humanis corporibus. item ad hebreos. viiii. quemadmodum statutum est hominibus semel mori etcet. audi asine patarene quod non nisi semel moriuntur homines id est separatur a carne. igitur spiritus humani non transeunt de uno corpore in aliud.

one is not born carnally as a man except once. Also 1 Corinthians 9 (9:9) "Does God care for the oxen?" Tell me this, O foolish Heretic, why does God not have a care for the oxen if they might have spirits such as those which are in human bodies? Also Hebrews 9 (9:27) "And as it is appointed unto men to die once." Hear, you blockheaded Patarene, that men do not die but once — that is, are separated from the body — therefore the spirit of humans does not cross over from one body to another.

Probatio per scripturam quod sanctorum anime cotidie ascendunt in celum

9 Proof from scripture that the souls of holy people daily ascend into heaven

ad ephesios. iiii°. ascendens in altum captiuam duxit captiuitatem dedit dona hominibus etcet. ecce quod dicit quod christus ascendens in altum id est in celum duxit secum captiuam captiuitatem id est illos quos de inferno eduxerat ergo multorum sanctorum anime sunt nunc in celo. item ad hebreos. i°. decebat enim eum propter quem omnia et per quem omnia qui multos filios in gloriam adduxerat etcet. idem iiii°. itaque relinquitur sabbatissimus populo dei qui enim ingressus est requieuit dei etiam ipse requieuit ab operibus suis. sicut a suis deus. festinemus ergo ingredi in illam requiem etcet. Dicit ergo quod nunc est sabbatissimus id est requies populo dei. quale autem requies sit dicit cum subinfertur quod ita requiescit sic deus cum hortatur nos festinare ingredi in illam. igitur illa requies est uita eterna. in quam ostendit aliquos esse ingressos. item apocalypsis. vi. et date sunt illis singule stole albe etcet. sed iste stole significant animam glorificationem quam habent sancti in celo. ergo sancti omnes sunt in celo. item. vii. et audiui numerum signatorum. cxliiii°r. millia signati ex omni tribu filiorum israel. et infra. post hec uidi turbam magnam quam dinumerare nemo poterat ex omnibus gentibus et tribubus et populis et linguis stantes ante thronum in conspectu agni. amicti stolis albis et palme in manibus eorum et clamabant uoce magna dicentes. salus deo nostro qui sedet super thronum et agno et omnes angelis stabant in circuitu thronum etcet. et infra. et dixit mihi. hi sunt qui uenerunt de tribulatione magna et lauerunt stolas suas in sanguine angi et dealbauerunt eas. ideo sunt ante thronum dei et seruiunt ei die ac nocte in templo eius et qui sedet super thronum habitabit super illos ergo multi sancti homines ante thronum dei. in templo eius cum agno et angelis dei. ergo sunt in uita eterna. idem xiiii. et uidi et ecce agnus stabat supra montem syon et cum eo cxliiii°r millia etcet. et infra. et nemo poterat dicere canticum nisi illa. cxliiii°r. millia. qui empti sunt de

Ephesians 4 (4:8) "Ascending on high, he led captivity captive, he gave gifts to men." See that he says that Christ ascends on high, that is, into heaven, where He leads captivity captive with Him, that is, those which were taken out of hell, therefore there are many souls of holy people that are now in heaven. Also Hebrews 1 (2:10) "For it was fitting for him, for whom are all things, and by whom are all things, who had brought many children into glory." Also 4 (4:9–11) "There remains therefore a day of rest for the people of God, for he who has entered into his rest, the same also has rested from his works, as God did from his. Let us hasten therefore to enter into that rest." He says therefore that now is the day of rest, that is, the rest of the people of God, which moreover is called 'rest' since it is enjoined that one indeed rest, so God exhorts us to rejoice by going into it, therefore that rest is life eternal, in which He shows that some have entered. Also Apocalypse 6 (6:11) "And white robes were given to every one of them." But this robe signifies the glorified soul which the saints have in heaven, therefore all saints are in heaven. Also 7 (7:4) "And I heard the number of them that were signed, a hundred forty-four thousand were signed, of every tribe of the children of Israel," and later (7:9–11) "After this I saw a great multitude, which no man could count, of all nations, and tribes, and peoples, and tongues, standing before the throne, and in the sight of the Lamb, clothed with white robes, with palms in their hands, and they cried with a loud voice, saying, 'Salvation to our God, who sits upon the throne, and to the Lamb.' And all the angels stood around the throne," and later (7:14–15) "And he said to me, 'These are they who have come out of great tribulation, and have washed their robes and have made them white in the blood of the Lamb.' Therefore they are before the throne of God, and they serve Him day and night in his temple, and he, who sits on the throne, will dwell over them." Therefore many holy men are before the throne of God, in His temple and with the Lamb and the angels of God, therefore they are in eternal life. The same 14 (14:1) "And I saw, and behold a lamb stood upon mount Zion, and with him a hundred forty-four

---

21 numquid...22 deo] 1 Cor. 9:9.   **25** quemadmodum...26 mori] Heb. 9:27.   **XII.9.3** ascendens...4 hominibus] Eph. 4:8.   **8** decebat...10 adduxerat] Heb. 2:10.   **11** itaque...14 requiem] Heb. 4:9-11.   **19** et...20 albe] Apoc. 6:11.   **22** et...24 israel] Apoc. 7:4.   **24** post...30 thronum] Apoc. 7:9-11.   **31** et...35 illos] Apoc. 7:14-15 (super thronum] in throno *Vulg.*)   **37** et²...39 millia] Apoc. 14:1.   **39** et²...43 ierit] Apoc. 14:3-4.

---

28 uno...29 aliud] corpore in corpus *P*   **XII.9.16** sic] sicut *F*   **17** hortatur] ortatur *P*   **20** singule] singulis *P* exp.   **27** et] add. sti *P* exp.

XII.9.14 Dicit|fol. 72va *P*   **32** stolas|fol. 55v *F*   **40** qui|fol. 72vb *P*

terra. hii sunt qui cum mulieribus non sunt coinquinati uirgines enim sunt. hii sequuntur agnum quocumque ierit etcet. et infra. sine macula enim sunt ante thronum dei etcet. ergo sancti qui fuerunt uirgines qui sunt empti de terra sunt in celo gloriosi. si ipsi sunt in monte syon nisi stat agnus qui sine ulla contradictione habet locum suum in celo et sic sequuntur eum quocumque ierit etsi sunt ante thronum dei. idem in eodem. et audiui uocem de celo dicentem. scribe beati mortui qui in domino moriuntur. amodo iam dicit spiritus. ut requiescant a laboribus suis.

Quod spiritus humani fuerunt simul creati ab initio mundi. uel quod ueniant ex traduce secundum alios et quod uadunt per diuersa corpora et quod anime sanctorum non ascendunt in celum usque ad finem mundi

Hec quidem que in rubrica posuimus per testimoniam scripturarum probabimus.

quod omnis spiritus fuerint simul creati ab initio mundi

[Patarenus:] Ecclesiastes. i°. Quid est quod fuit? ipsum quod futurum est et quod factum est? ipsum quod faciendum est. nichil sub sole nouum. nec ualet quisquam dicere ecce hoc recens est. etcet. ergo nullus spiritus est nouus.
Catholicus: Respondeo quod hoc intelligitur quantum ad dei presentiam uel prescientiam quasi dicat omnia sunt in mente diuina scilicet preterita. presentia et futura. uel loquitur de similitudibus rerum. quasi dicat nulla est cui simile non fuerit. nichil enim prohibet quin alia in substantiis esse possunt quam fuerint aliquando. immo uno innuit manifeste quod alii homines quandoque fuerant quam aliquando sint futuri et econtrario. unde dicit generatio preterit et generatio aduenit etcet.
[Patarenus:] Item ecclesiasticus. xviii. qui uiuet in eternum creauit omnia simul etcet. ergo spiritus omnis sunt antiqui.
Catholicus: Respondeo quod deus creauit omnia simul in materia uel in forma. in materia concreauit machinam mundi constantem ex iiii^or. elementis dicitur creasse omnia elementa id est corporea quia omnia de elementis facta sunt. in forma dixi quia cum deus creauit angelos quos simul cum machina mundi et cum celo empyreo et cum tempore creauit omnis spiritus humanos dicitur creasse. quia talem formam

thousand," and later (14:3–4) "and no man could sing the canticle, but those hundred forty-four thousand, who were purchased from the earth. These are they who were not defiled with women, for they are virgins. These follow the Lamb wherever he goes," and later (14:5) "for they are without spot before the throne of God." Therefore the saints who were virgins, who were purchased from the earth, are in glorious heaven. If these are on Mount Zion, unless the Lamb stands, who without any contradiction has His place in heaven, and thus they follow Him wherever He goes if they are before the throne of God. Also in the same (14:13) "And I heard a voice from heaven, saying to me, 'Write: Blessed are the dead who die in the Lord. From henceforth now, says the Spirit, that they may rest from their labors.'"

That human spirits were all created together at the beginning of the world, or that they came by means of traducianism, according to others, and that they go through different bodies and that the souls of the saints do not ascend into heaven until the end of the world

This we will prove by the testimony of scripture, those things we have put in the section.

That all spirits were created together at the beginning of the world

[Pat:] Ecclesiastes 1 (1:9–10) "What is it that has been? The same thing that shall be. What is it that has been done? The same that shall be done. Nothing is new under the sun, neither is any man able to say, 'Behold this is new.'" Therefore no spirit is new.
Cath: I reply that this is to be interpreted as referring to the present of God, or prescience as if to say, all things are in the mind of God, namely, past, present, and future, or he is speaking about the similarity to things, as if to say, nothing is like something else which never existed, for nothing prevents things different in substance to be able to be other than they were at some time, for one clearly knows that some men sometimes were [in the past] and other men sometimes shall be in the future, and vice versa. Whence it says (1:4) "One generation passes away, and another generation comes."
[Pat:] Also Ecclesiasticus 18 (18:1) "He who lives forever created all things together." Therefore all spirits were created from of old.
Cath: I reply that God created all things at once in terms of matter or form. In matter He created the world system from the four elements. It is said that He created all primary elements, that is, bodily things, since they are made from all the elements. I said 'in form' because since God created the angels and time together. It is said that He created all human spirits since they have a form like the angels. Or explain that passage as we explained the words

---

43 sine…44 dei] Apoc. 14:5.   49 et…51 moriuntur] Apoc. 14:13.   XII.11.3 Quid…6 est] Eccl. 1:9-10.   16 generatio…17 aduenit] Eccl. 1:4.   18 qui…19 simul] Ecclesiastic. 18:1.

XII.10.4 anime sanctorum] transp. *F*   6 testimoniam…7 scripturarum] testimonia scriptura *P*   XII.11.1 quod…2 mundi] om. *F*   14 immo uno] transp. *F* | uno] om. *P*   23 elementis] helementis *F*   25 elementis] helementis *F*   27 empyreo] empireo *F*

XII.11.8 quantum|fol. 73ra *P*

habent sicut angeli uel expone ista uerba sicut exposuimus uerba ecclesiastes supra proxime. sed responde tu mihi de isto teste. quomodo intelligis uerba eius? quia aut spiritualiter. aut generaliter. si quid spiritualiter ergo non habes quod omnia sint simul creata. si uero generaliter intelligis contradicit tibi idem testis supra. xiiii. ubi dicit. omnis caro sicut fenum ueterascet et sicut folium fructificans et sicut solium in arbore uiridi. alia generantur et alia deiiciuntur sic generatio carnis et sanguinis. alia fit et alia nascitur etcet. nec potes intelligere quod loquatur de creaturis dei quasi ille sint simul create. et quod creature quas dicis esse diaboli non sint simul create. quia dicit apostolus. secunda ad corinthios. v°. si qua igitur in christo noua creatura etcet. ergo non creauit deus omnis creaturas suas simul. immo adhuc aliquas de nouo creat.

Patarenus: Item. iohannes. vi. unus ex uobis diabolus est. etcet. ergo iudas non erat nouus si erat diabolus quod eadem ratione uidetur posse dici de aliis.

Catholicus: Respondeo. sic erat iudas diabolus sicut cananei erant canes. de quibus dominus dicit. Mattheus. xv. non est bonum sumere panem filiorum et mittere canibus. etcet. erant illi canes per imitationem sic et iudas diabolus erat. quod autem non fuerit per naturam diabolus sed homo ostendit dominus. mattheus. xxvi. ue autem homini illi per quem filius hominis tradetur. bonum erat ei si natus non fuisset homo ille. etcet.

Patarenus: Item ad Romanos v. propterea sicut per unum hominem peccatum in hunc mundum intrauit et per peccatum mors et ita in omnes homines mors pertransiit. in quo omnes peccauerunt. adam. quia non potuissent in eo id est in peccato eius nisi fuissent.

Catholicus: Respondeo. quia ideo dicit apostolus quod omnes peccauerunt in peccato ade. quia omnes puniuntur per illud peccatum propter originale quod tamen traxerunt. unde subdit. sed regnauit mors ab adam usque ad moysen. etiam in eos qui non peccauerunt in similitudinem preuaricationis ade etcet. preterea possum dicere quod omnes homines secundum corpus unum contrahitur peccatum in adam id est in lumbe eius. simile est. ad hebreos. vii. quamquam et ipsi exierint de lumbis abrahe etcet. et infra. adhuc enim in lumbis patris erat. quando obuiauit ei melchisedech etcet. unde ipse apostolus dicit in actibus. fecitque ex uno omne genus hominum inhabitare super uniuersam faciem terre etcet.

of Ecclesiastes above. But answer me this about this witness, in what way do you understand his words? They can be understood spiritually or generally, if spiritually, then you will not have it that everything is created at once, but if [you understand it] generally you will be contradicted by the witnesses above in chapter 14 where it says (14:18–19) "All flesh shall grow old as grass, and like the leaf that springs out on a green tree, some grow, and some fall off. So is the generation of flesh and blood, one comes to an end, and another is born." Nor are you able to interpret that he is speaking of the creatures of God, as if they were created at the same time, and that the creatures which you say to be from the devil, they are not created at the same time, since the Apostle says in 2 Corinthians 5 (5:17) "If then any be in Christ a new creature," therefore God did not create all His creatures together, rather until now He newly creates some.

Pat: Also John 6 (6:71) "one of you is a devil," therefore Judas was not new, since he was the devil, and by that same reason it seems one can say it of others.

Cath: I reply that Judas was the devil in the same manner that the Canaanites were the dogs of which the Lord speaks in Matthew 15, (15:26) "it is not good to take the bread of the children and to cast it to the dogs." They were dogs in the manner of likeness, and so was Judas similar to the devil, moreover that he was not the devil by nature, but a man, the Lord shows in Matthew 26 (26:24) "woe to that man by whom the son of man is betrayed, it would have been good if that man had never been born."

Pat: Also Romans 5 (5:12) "Wherefore as by one man sin entered into this world, and by sin death, and so death passed upon all men, in whom all have sinned." Adam. For they would not be able to be in him — that is, in his sin — unless they had existed.

Cath: I respond that the Apostle says that all have sinned in the sin of Adam, since all are punished because of that sin on account of original sin, since they have also inherited it, whence he adds (5:14) "But death reigned from Adam to Moses, even over those also who have not sinned after the likeness of the transgression of Adam." Further I might be able to say that all men are like one body from which they acquired the sin from Adam, that is from his loins, similar is Hebrews 7 (7:5) "though they themselves also came out of the loins of Abraham," and later (7:10) "For he was yet in the loins of his father, when Melchizedek met him." Whence the Apostle himself says in Acts (17:26) "And He has made one all mankind to dwell upon the whole face of the earth."

---

35 omnis...38 nascitur] Ecclesiastic. 14:18-19 (fit) fintiur *Vulg.*) 42 si...43 creatura] 2 Cor. 5:17 (igitur) ergo *Vulg.*) 46 unus...47 est] Ioh. 6:71. 51 non...52 canibus] Matt. 15:26. 55 ue...57 ille] Matt. 26:24. 58 propterea...61 peccauerunt] Rom. 5:12. 66 sed...68 ade] Rom. 5:14. 72 quamquam...abrahe] Heb. 7:5. 73 adhuc...74 melchisedech] Heb. 7:10. 75 fecitque...76 terre] Act. 17:26.

36 sicut²] add. o *P* exp. 50 cananei] chananei *F* 58 Romanos] corinthios *P*

36 solium|fol. 73rb *P* 51 est|fol. 56r *F* 64 omnes²|fol. 73va *P*

Quod spiritus ex spiritu fit sicut caro de carne

[Patarenus:] Iohannes. iii°. quod natum est ex carne caro est. quod natum est ex spiritu spiritus est. etcet. ergo sicut caro fit ex traduce ita et spiritus.

Catholicus: Respondeo. fatue ydiota nullam mentionem facit hic dominus de natiuitate spirituum nostroum in mundo. sed loquitur qualiter nascantur dominus et quomodo spiritus sanctus nascitur in nobis per effectum gratie sue. unde dicit supra. nisi quis renatus fuerit ex aqua et spiritu sancto non potest introire in regnum dei. ecce de qua natiuitate spirituum loquitur. quasi dicat. si uolumus intrare in regnum dei. oportet ut renascamur ex spiritu sancto. qui datur in baptismo aqua debite celebrato. et quod subdit postea scilicet quod natum est ex carne etcet. tale est. ac si diceret. non sufficit homini nasci secundum carnem tamen. quia illa natiuitas caro est id est fragile. sed oportet ut ex spiritu sancto nascatur qui natiuitatis spirituale est. et ideo efficax. hoc est quod subdit. quod natum est ex spiritu spiritus est etcet. et quod nulla dubitatio sit quin de spiritu sancto loquatur et eius natiuitate in nobis et de nostram per eum factam deo subicit. non mireris quia dixi tibi. oportet uos nasci denuo. spiritus ubi uult spirat et uocem eius audis et nescis immo ueniat aut quo uadat. sic est omnis qui natus est ex spiritu etcet.

Quod spiritus transeunt de corpore in corpus

[Patarenus:] Dauid. transiuimus per ignem et aquam et eduxisti nos in refrigerium etcet. et illud. super flumina babillonis illic sedimus et fleuimus etcet. sed dauid in illo corpore in quo erat cum hoc dixit non transiuit per ignem et aquam nec fuit babylonie. ergo in alio corpore acciderunt ei hoc. igitur transeunt spiritus per diuersa corpora.

Catholicus: Respondeo quod dauid loquitur prophetando de tribulationibus que debebant accidere israel carnali uel spirituali. sed tu respondeas mihi de uerbis dauid. dicit enim et induxisti nos in refrigerium etcet. ergo in illo corpore in quo erat quando dixit hoc fuit in refrigerio. quod tu negas.

[Patarenus:] Item. ad romanos. xi. numquid sic offenderunt ut caderent? absit etcet. et infra. quod si aliqui ex ramis fracti sunt etcet. et infra. sed illi si non permanserit in incredulitate inserentur etcet. ergo spiritus fuerunt in aliis corporibus quandoque ante christi aduentum. in quibus non fuerint salui. sed postea in aliis salui fuerit post christi aduentum. si credunt ergo spiritus transeunt de corpore in corpus.

That spirits are made from spirit, as flesh from flesh

[Pat:] John 3 (3:6) "what is born of the flesh is flesh. What is born of the spirit, is spirit." Therefore just as flesh is fashioned from traducianism, so also are spirits.

Cath: I respond, O blockheaded Idiot, the Lord makes no mention here of our spiritual birth in the world, but He is speaking about what manner the Lord is born, and how the Holy Spirit is born in us by the effect of His grace. Whence He says above "he who is not born again of water and the Holy Spirit cannot enter into the Kingdom of God." See how He is speaking of spiritual births, as if to say, if we wish to enter into the Kingdom of God, it is fitting that we be reborn by the Holy Spirit, who is given in the water of baptism, correctly celebrated, and that He adds after, namely (3:6) "what is born of flesh," such as if to say, it does not suffice for a man to be born of the flesh alone, since that birth is fleshly, that is, fragile. But it befits that he is born from the Holy Spirit, whose birth is spiritual, and so efficacious. This is what He adds "that which is from the spirit, is spirit," and that there might be no doubt whether He is speaking of the Holy Spirit and His birth in us, and of us made subject to God through Him, (Jn 3: 7–8) "Do you not wonder that I said to you, you must be born again. The Spirit breathes where he will, and you hear his voice, but you do not know from whence he comes, or where he goes. So is every one who is born of the Spirit."

That the spirits cross from body to body

[Pat:] David (Ps 65:12) "We have passed through fire and water, and you have brought us out into a refreshment." And again (136:1) "By the waters of Babylon, there we sat and wept," but David, in that body which he inhabited when he said this, did not pass through fire and water, nor was he in Babylon, therefore there had been another body for him, therefore spirits cross through different bodies.

Cath: I reply that David is speaking by prophesy of the tribulations which ought to befall carnal or spiritual Israel. But answer me this regarding the word of David, for he says and "you have brought us out into a refreshment." Therefore in that body in which he was when he said this, he was in refreshment, which you deny.

[Pat:] Also Romans 11 (11:11) "that they should stumble? God forbid," and later (11:17) "And if some of the branches be broken," and later (11:23) "And they also, if they do not abide still in unbelief, shall be grafted in." Therefore sometime before the coming of Christ the spirits were in other bodies in which they were not saved, but then after the coming of Christ they were saved in other bodies, if they believe. Therefore the spirits cross from body to body.

XII.12.2 quod…3 est³] Ioh. 3:6. **15** quod…carne] Ioh. 3:6. **23** non…26 spiritu] Ioh. 3:7-8. **XII.13.2** transiuimus…3 refrigerium] Ps. 65:12. **3** super…4 fleuimus] Ps. 136:1. **15** numquid…16 absit] Rom. 11:11. **16** quod…17 sunt] Rom. 11:17. **17** illi…18 inserentur] Rom. 11:23 (sed) add. et *Vulg.*

XII.12.**5** fatue] add. et F **13** oportet] opportet P **21** dubitatio] add. e P exp. **22** de] om. P **23** factam] sitam P XII.13.**6** babylonie] babillonie P

XII.12.**15** postea|fol. 73vb P **XII.13.13** etcet|fol. 74ra P

Catholicus: Respondeo quod loquitur apostolus in persona duorum populorum scilicet israelitici et gentilis. quorum alter ceciderat per incredulitatem ex magna parte scilicet israeliticus et alter scilicet. gentilis de infidelitate nuper insertus erat in fide christi. et hoc est quod dicit ibi. illorum delictum saluus est gentibus etcet. et infra quod si aliqui ex ramis fracti sunt tu autem cum oleaster. insertus es in illis etcet. et ostendit postea apostolus quod gentiles facti christiani possent dampnari. si de gratia fidei superbirent et iudei possent saluari. si de sua incredulitate uellent exire. unde subdit. si enim deus naturalibus ramis non pepercit id est filius israel qui erant naturati in fide unius dei per antiquam credulitatem ne forte nec tibi parcat etcet. et infra. sed illi. si non permanserint in incredulitate inserentur etcet. sed tu responde mihi heretice. dicit enim apostolus in hoc capitulo quod si aliqui ex ramis fracti sunt etcet. ergo quidam spiritus. qui erant in corporibus ante christi aduentum peccauerunt et quidam non. et sic innuit quod aliqui immo multi in illis corporibus saluati sunt. preterea dicit quod illi propter incredulitatem fracti sunt et deus seuere id est iuste se habuit ad illos iudicando eos. unde dicit propter incredulitate fracti sunt etcet. et postea si non fuissent increduli et poterat ipsi credere et sic saluari et sic poterant saluari homines ante christi aduentum quod tu negas. uel si non poterant credere deus fuit iniquis eos iniuste dampnando. quod absit.

Patarenus: Dico quod isti rami fracti fuerunt angeli qui ceciderunt de celo. qui peccauerunt in celo uel offenderunt et qui ideo fuerunt iudicati ad penas istius mundi. nec potuerunt saluari ante christi aduentum. sed modo saluantur per fidem et doctrinam eius et dicuntur isti rami naturales quia sunt creature dei.

Catholicus: Sed audi quid dicit apostolus hic. Nam si tu ex naturali excisus es oleastro insertus es in bonam oliuam. quanto magis hii secundum naturam inserentur sue oliue etcet. ergo saluabuntur. non solum illi spiritus qui sunt creature dei. sed etiam illi qui sunt creature diaboli secundum hominem brutalem loquor id est secundum te qui dicis aliquos spiritus creatos esse a diabolo. et tu illos dicis saluari non posse et sic es tibi ipsi contrarius in hac tua expositione et ideo merito repellendus et non mireris catholice si non sum prosecutus in hoc tractatu. opinionem illorum patarenorum qui dicunt omnis spiritus esse eternos quia de illa materia satis est dictum. supra. titulum. primo. et dicetur infra. libro secundo. titulum de predestinatis.

Cath: I reply that the Apostle is speaking in the person of the two peoples, namely, Israel and the gentiles, of whom one fell by the unbelief of the greater part, namely Israel, and the other, namely, the gentiles, recently were grafted from unbelief onto the faith of Christ. And this is what he says there (11:12) "But by their offence, salvation has come to the Gentiles," and later (11:17) "And if some of the branches be broken, and you, being a wild olive, are engrafted in them." And the Apostle later shows that the Gentiles who have been made Christian are able to be damned, if they become haughty regarding the grace of faith, and that the Jews are able to be saved, if they wish to depart from their unbelief, whence he adds (11:21) "For if God has not spared the natural branches," that is, the sons of Israel who were natural to the faith of the one God by ancient belief, "fear lest perhaps he also not spare you," and later (11:23) "And they also, if they do not abide still in unbelief, shall be grafted in." But answer me this, O Heretic, for the Apostle says in this chapter that "if some of the branches be broken" therefore certain spirits who were in bodies before the coming of Christ sinned and certain ones did not, and so he indicates that they are broken on account of their unbelief and God severely, that is, justly behaved towards them by judging them, whence he said (11:20) "because of unbelief they were broken off." And after if they had not been disbelieving and were able to believe Him, and so to be saved, and thus men were able to be saved before the coming of Christ, which you deny, or if they were unable to believe, God was wicked because He unjustly damned them, which God forbid!

Pat: I say that these broken branches were the angels who fell from heaven, who sinned in heaven or who offended, and who for that reason were sentenced to the punishment of this world, nor are they able to be saved before the coming of Christ, they can only be saved by His faith and teaching and it is said that these are natural branches since they are the creatures of God.

Cath: But hear that the Apostle says here (11:24) "For if you were cut out of the wild olive tree, which is natural to you, and, contrary to nature, were grafted into the good olive tree, how much more shall those who are the natural branches be grafted into their own olive tree?" Therefore they shall be saved, not only those spirits who are creatures of God, but also those who are creatures of the devil, I am speaking according to that brutal man, that is, according to you, who say that certain spirits have been created by the devil, and you say that they are not able to be saved, and thus you have contradicted yourself in this explanation, and so with good reason you are to be rebuffed, and do not be surprised, Catholic, if I do not pursue in the present work the opinion of those Patarenes who say that every spirit is eternal, since enough material on that topic has been discussed above in the first section, and will be

---

28 illorum...gentibus] Rom. 11:12 (saluus est gentibus] om. *Vulg.*)   29 quod...30 illis] Rom. 11:17 (oleaster] add. esses *Vulg.*)   34 si...pepercit] Rom. 11:21.   37 sed...38 inserentur] Rom. 11:23 (sed] add. et *Vulg.*)   46 propter...sunt] Rom. 11:20.   57 Nam... 60 oliue] Rom. 11:24.

44 et...45 dicit] om. *F*   47 et¹] add. si *P* exp. | poterat ipsi] transp. *F*   56 sunt] om. *P* | dei] add. sunt *P*   59 secundum] add. sic *P* exp.   62 hominem] Iohannem *F*   63 te] ente *P*   64 illos dicis] transp. *F*   66 repellendus] repellendi *P*   67 opinionem] oppinionem *P*

23 Respondeo|fol. 56v *F*   37 infra|fol. 74rb *P*   61 etiam|fol. 74va *P*

Quod nulle anime sanctorum ascendunt modo in celum

[**Patarenus:**] Ad colosenses. iii°. Cum christus apparuerit uita uestra tunc et uos apparebitis cum ipso in gloria etcet. ergo cum christus tamen in fine seculi debeat apparere patet quod sancti ante non erunt in celi gloria.
Catholicus: Respondeo loquitur de gloria resurrectionis corporis christi. quam non habemus in nostris corporibus nisi in aduentu eius in nouissimo die. et hoc est quod tangit. ibi. igitur si consurrexistis cum christo que sursum sunt querite etcet. uel loquitur de apparitione christi qui apparet animabus sanctorum cotidie. quando egresse de corporibus assumuntur in celum.
Patarenus: Item. iiª. ad tessaloncenses iiii° Deus eos qui dormierunt per ihesum adducet cum eo etcet. ergo non ante aduentum domini ihesu qui dormierunt adducentur in gloria.
Catholicus: Respondeo quia secundum corpus loquitur. unde sequitur. quoniam ipse dominus in iussu et in uoce archangeli et in tuba dei descendet de celo et mortui qui in christo sunt resurgent primi etcet. sed dic mihi heretice si sancti non ascendunt in celum usque ad finem mundi ubi sunt interim? in inferno non. quia ibi non sunt nisi dampnati. si autem in mundo stant. ergo adhuc sunt in carcere diaboli secundum uestram perfidiam loquor qui dicitis mundum esse diaboli domum ubi incarcerat sanctorum animas. quomodo ergo implentur scripture que dicunt animas sanctorum requiescere cantare et letari.

Patarenus: Dicimus quod requiescunt in quodam ameno et delectabili.
Catholicus: Sed aut iste locus est supra celum et tunc sunt in regno dei. aut est infra et tunc sunt adhuc in regno diaboli et sic non habent quiescere nec letari.

De resurrectione corporum mortuorum

Improbatis erroribus patarenorum in superiori tractatu quem habent statum humanorum spirituum. sequitur in presenti reprobare dementiam eorum. quam tenent circa corporum resurrectionem. dicunt enim quod ista corpora uisibilia que hic gestamus. numquam debeant resurgere. addentes quidam ex eis quod deus noua corpora sit facturus electis in quibus debeant remuniari.

mentioned below in the second book, in the section on the Predestinarians.

That no souls of holy people ascend in any way into heaven

[**Pat:**] Colossians 3 (3:4) "When Christ shall appear, who is your life, then you also shall appear with him in glory." Therefore since they shall appear only with Christ at the end of the world, it is clear that the saints will not be in the glory of heaven before then.
Cath: I reply that he is speaking of the glory of the risen body of Christ, which we will not have in our bodies except at His coming on the last day, and this is what he touches on there (3:1) "if you be risen with Christ, seek the things that are above," or he is speaking of the vision of Christ who appears to holy souls daily, when, leaving their bodies, they are taken into heaven.

Pat: Also 2 Thessalonians 4 (1 Thes 4:14) "even so those who have slept in Jesus, will God bring with him," therefore not before the coming of Christ shall those who sleep be led to glory.
Cath: I reply that he is speaking about the body, whence he adds (4:16) "For the Lord himself shall come down from heaven with command, and with the voice of an archangel, and with the trumpet of God, and the dead who are in Christ, shall rise first." But tell me, O Heretic, if the saints do not ascend to heaven until the end of the world, where are they in the meantime? Not in hell, since no others reside there except the damned. Yet if they remain in the world, even so are they imprisoned by the devil, for I am now speaking according to your perfidy since you say that the world is the domain of the devil, where he imprisons holy souls. In what way therefore would the scripture be fulfilled which says that the souls of the dead rest, sing, and rejoice?
Pat: We say that they rest in some pleasant and delightful place.
Cath: But either this place is above heaven, and then they are in the kingdom of God, or it is below, and then they are in the kingdom of the devil, and thus they have no rest or joy.

On the resurrection of dead bodies

We disproved the errors of the Patarenes regarding the state of human spirits in the foregoing work. It remains in the present section to condemn their madness which they hold regarding the resurrection of bodies. For they say that this visible body, which we bear here, should never be risen. Certain ones go on from this that God shall make new bodies for the elect, in which they ought to be

---

XII.14.3 Cum...5 gloria] Col. 3:4.   11 igitur...12 querite] Col. 3:1.   16 Deus...17 eo] 1 Thes. 4:14.   21 quoniam...23 primi] 1 Thes. 4:16.

XII.14.1 modo...2 celum] in celum modo F   16 iia] **both PF incorrect, leg. ia.**   17 adducet] adducent P   32 Patarenus] Catholicus F   36 non] om. F | habent] add. nec F

XII.14.22 archangeli|fol. 74vb P   23 resurgent|fol. 57r F

secundum uniuscuisque merita uite. alii autem autumnant quod fuerunt quedam corpora illorum qui ceciderunt de celo. ibidem prostrata in prelio magno que dicunt debere resurgere in fine mundi. sunt et alii inter illos qui dicunt nullas animas bonas uel malas habituras esse corpora carnis in celo uel in inferno. Nos uero tam per rationes naturales quam per scripturas ueteris ac noui testamenti quod ista corpora qui hoc habemus et non alia. resurgent in fine seculorum ostendere euidenter possimus.

Probatio per rationes naturales de resurrectione corporum

Constat quod deus uult iustitiam facere et potest et nouit ergo faciet illam. sed iustitia est ut in quo peccauit uel meruit quis recipiat premium suum. ergo in istis corporibus in quibus bona uel mala fecimus recipiemus premia et sic resurgent ista corpora et non alia. in quibus nec bona nec mala facta sunt. item arbores maxime ex modico surgunt semine. item corpora brutorum animalium resurgunt quandoque ut auis que dicitur fenix que postquam combusta est de suo puluere resurgit et auis que dicitur pellicanus mortua resurgit ad tactum sanguinis paterni. item leo resurgit post tres dies a sua natiuitate ad rugitum paternum. quod tantum operatur natura naturans in signum resurrectionis nature. que ut ait phylosophus nichil facit otiose. sed cum resurgunt bruta animalia que propter hominem facta sunt. multo fortius debet resurgere homo propter quem sunt facta. item deus facit corpus hominis de uili materia et modica et in eo creat animam de nichilo et sic procedit uiuus homo integer. sed multo abilius potest facere et credende est quod faciat de honestiori materia et maioris quantitatis corpus resurgere et in eo reducere animam iam dudum existentem. ut sic remaneat homo integer semper. preterea scimus quod deus iam multa corpora resurgere fecit licet iterum moritura. et aliqua resurgere fecit que non forte fuerunt iterum in cinerem redacta. quod uidetur manifeste cum fecisse in signum resurrectionis uniuersalis.

Probatio de resurrectione corporum per uetus testamentum

Iob. xix. scio enim quod redemptor meus uiuit et in nouissimo die de terra surrecturus sum et in rursum circum dabor pelle mea et in carne mea uidebo deum saluatorem meum. quem uisurus sum ego ipse et oculi

rewarded, each according to his own merits in life,[1] but others assert that there were certain bodies of those who fell from heaven, there fallen in the great battle, which they say should be raised at the end of the world. And among them there are others who say that no good or bad souls will have fleshly bodies in heaven or hell.[2] Now indeed we are able to show clearly both by natural reason as by the scriptures of the Old and New Testaments that these bodies which we possess here and no other shall be raised at the end of time.

Proofs from natural reasons for the resurrection of the body

It is evident that God wishes to do justice and He has the capability and knowledge to do so, therefore He shall do so, but justice demands that whoever sins or merits receive the reward of his good or evil, therefore [this will happen] in this body and not in another — for in such neither good nor evil deeds were done. Further trees grow from a small seed and the bodies of brute animals arise sometimes, for example, the Phoenix which, after being burned, arises from his ashes,[3] and the bird called the Pelican rises from the dead at the touch of its parent's blood.[4] Similarly a lion arises three days after its birth at the roar of its father,[5] because only nature doing what nature does effects a foreshadowing of resurrection in nature, as the Philosopher says, "nature does nothing in vain."[6]. Yet since brute animals are raised, which are made for man's sake, how much greater reason ought there be that man be raised, for God fashioned man's body from a bit of common matter and creates a soul in him from nothing and so a whole man comes forth, but He can do even more, and it is to be believed that He shall make the resurrected body of more honorable material and of a greater quantity, and in it He will restore the soul already in existence, so that the man shall remain complete. Further we know that God has already caused many bodies to rise again, though naturally they will again die and some which He again caused to rise perhaps had not been reduced to ashes, which is clearly apparent He accomplished as a sign of the universal resurrection.

Proof of the resurrection of bodies from the Old Testament

Job 19 (19:25–27) "for I know that my Redeemer lives, and on the last day I shall arise out of the earth and I shall be clothed again with my skin and in my flesh I will see God my savior. Whom I myself shall see, and my eyes shall

---

XIII.2.17 nichil...otiose] Aristotle, *De generatione animalium* II, 6: 743.   XIII.3.3 scio...7 alius] Iob 19:25–27 (saluatorem) om. *Vulg.*)

XIII.1.18 euidenter possimus] transp. *F*   XIII.2.26 deus iam] transp. *F*   XIII.3.1 per...2 testamentum] om. *P*   3 xix] xviiii *P*   4 in] add. carne *P* exp.

XIII.1.10 corpora|fol. 75ra *P*   XIII.2.17 animalia|fol. 75rb *P*   XIII.3.5 circum|fol. 57v *F*

---

1) The Albanenses. Burci, 319; Sacconi, c. 20; Moneta, 353. | 2) The Concorezzans. Burci, 339; Moneta, 355. 3) Common from ancient world, also from Isidore, *Etymologies*, 12, 7:22. | 4) Isidore, *Etymologies*, 12, 7:26. | 5) A common medieval belief, perhaps from Isidore, *Etymologies*, 12, 2:3–6. | 6) Aristotle, *De generatione animalium* II, 6: 743.

mei conspecturi sunt et non alius. ezechielis. xxxvii. et dimisit me in medio campi qui erat plenus ossibus mortuorum etcet. et infra. hec dicit dominus deus ossibus hiis et ecce ego intromittam in uos spiritum et uiuetis et dabo super uos neruos et succrescere faciem super uos carnes etcet. et infra. ecce ego aperiam tumulos uestros et educam uos de tumulis uestris. etcet. item daniel. xii. et multi de hiis qui dormiunt in puluere terre. euigilabunt. alii in uitam eternam et alii in opprobrium ut uideant semper. etcet. et ii^a. machabeorum. xii. et facta collatione. xiic. milia drachmas argenti misit ierosolimam offeri pro peccatis mortuorum sacrificium. bene et religiose de resurrectione cogitans. nisi enim eos qui ceciderant resurrecturos speraret superfluum uideretur et uanum orare pro mortuis. etcet. ecce quam euidenter probatur per uetus testamentum quod ista corpora resurgent.

Probatio de resurrectione corporum per nouum testamentum

Mattheus. xxii. accesserunt ad eum saducei. qui dicunt non esse resurrectionem etcet. et infra. respondens autem iesus ait illis. erratis nescientes scripturas neque uirtutem dei. in resurrectione enim neque nubent etcet. et infra. de resurrectione autem mortuorum non legistis quod dictum est a deo dicente uobis. ego sum deus abraam et deus ysaac et deus iacob. non est autem mortuorum sed uiuentium. ecce quomodo ex his uerbis conclusit dominus saduceis qui negabant resurrectionem quorum errorem uos patareni tenetis. item idem. xxvii. et multa corpora sanctorum qui dormierant surrexerunt. et exeuntes de monumentis post resurrectionem eius uenerunt in sanctam ciuitatem et apparuerunt multis. etcet. hic aperte loquitur de resurrectione corporum que hic iacebant in monumentis. item iohannes. v. Nolite mirari hoc. quia uenit hora in qua omnes qui in monumentis sunt audient uocem filii dei et procedent qui bona fecerunt in resurrectionem uite. qui uero mala egerunt in resurrectionem iudicii etcet. item idem vi. hec est autem uoluntas eius qui misit me. ut omne quod dedit mihi pater id est animam et corpus non perdam ex eo sed resuscitem illud in nouissimo die. etcet. ad idem. x. dicit illi ihesus. resurget frater tuus etcet. quod de corporali resurrectione lazari intelligitur quam statum operatus est dominus in signum nostre resurrectionis. item. i^a. ad corinthios. vi. deus uero et dominum suscitauit et nos suscitabit per uirtutem suam etcet. ergo deus suscitabit nos sicut suscitauit dominus ihesus. sed illum suscitauit secundum carnem. ita

behold, and not another." Ezekiel 37 (37:1) "and he placed me in the midst of a plain that was full of bones of the dead." And later (37:5–6) "thus says the Lord God to these bones, 'and behold, I will send a spirit into you and you shall live and I will place muscles upon you, and will cause flesh to grow over you,'" and further on (37:12) "Behold I will open your graves and will bring you out of your tombs." Daniel 12 has it (12:2) "And many of those that sleep in the dust of the earth shall awake, some unto life everlasting and others unto reproach that they might see it always." And in 2 Maccabees 12 (12:43–44) "And taking up a collection, he sent twelve thousand silver drachmas to Jerusalem for sacrifice to be offered as a sacrifice for the sins of the dead, thinking well and piously concerning the resurrection, for unless he had not hoped that they who fell should rise again, it would have seemed superfluous and vain to pray for the dead." Look how obviously the Old Testament establishes that bodies shall be raised!

Proof of the resurrection of bodies from the New Testament

Matthew 22 (22:23) "That day the Sadducees came to him, who say there is no resurrection," and further on (22:29–30) "and in response Jesus said to them, 'you err, not knowing the Scriptures, nor the power of God. For in the resurrection they shall neither marry nor be married,'" and further (22:31–32) "concerning the resurrection of the dead, have you not read that which was spoken by God saying to you, 'I am the God of Abraham, and the God of Isaac, and the God of Jacob? He is not the God of the dead, but of the living.'" See how the Lord silences the Sadducees who denied the resurrection with these words, and yet you Patarenes cling to their error. Further in 27 (27:52–53) "and many bodies of the saints that had slept arose, and coming out of the tombs after His resurrection came into the holy city and appeared to many." This manifestly speaks of the resurrection of bodies who had laid in the tombs. John 5 (5:28) "Do not wonder at this for the hour is coming when all who are in tombs shall hear the voice of the Son of God, and they who have done good shall come into the resurrection of life but they who have done evil, unto the resurrection of judgment." And in chapter 6 (6:39) "Now this is the will of He who sent me: that of all that he has given me" — that is, soul and body — "I should lose nothing, but should raise it up again in the last day." Also in chapter 10 (11:23) "Jesus said to her, 'Your brother shall rise again,'" so that the bodily resurrection of Lazarus, which the Lord immediately wrought, was done as a sign of our resurrection. Further in 1 Corinthians 6 (6:14) "Now God has both raised up the Lord and will raise us up also by his power," therefore God will raise us just as he raised the Lord Jesus, but He raised

---

7 et² ... 9 mortuorum] Ez. 37:1 (mortuorum] om. *Vulg.*)   9 hec ... 12 carnes] Ex. 37:5-6 (hiis] his *Vulg.*)   12 ecce ... 13 uestris] Ez. 37:12 (tumulis] sepulchris *Vulg.*)   14 et ... 16 semper] Dan. 12:2 (hiis] his *Vulg.*)   17 et ... 22 mortuis] 2 Macc. 12:43-44. XIII.4.3 accesserunt ... 4 resurrectionem] Matt. 22:23.   4 respondens ... 6 nubent] Matt. 22:29-30.   7 de ... 10 uiuentium] Matt. 22:31-32.   13 et ... 16 multis] Matt. 27:52-53.   18 Nolite ... 22 iudicii] Ioh. 5:28-29.   22 hec ... 25 die] Ioh. 6:39 (me] add. patris *Vulg.*)   26 dicit ... tuus] Ioh. 11:23.   29 deus ... 30 suam] 1 Cor. 6:14.

17 machabeorum] malachias *F*   XIII.4.1 per ... 2 testamentum] om. *P*

14 dormiunt|fol. 75va *P*   XIII.4.18 Nolite|fol. 75vb *P*

igitur et nos. idem. xv. si autem christus predicatur quod resurrexit a mortuis. quomodo quidam dicunt in nobis. quoniam resurrectio mortuorum non est. si autem resurrectio mortuorum non est. neque christus resurrexit. etcet. et infra. alioquin quid facient qui baptizantur pro mortuis si mortui non resurgunt etcet. et infra. si secundum hominem ad bestias pugnaui ephesi. quid mihi prodest si mortui non resurgunt etcet. ex hiis aperte ostendit resurrectionem corporum. item ii^a. ad corinthios. v. Nam et in hoc tabernaculo ingemiscimus grauati eo quod nolumus expoliari sed superuestiri ut absorbeatur quod mortale est a uita etcet. ergo corpus mortale fuit vitale. idem. in eodem. omnes enim nos manifestari oportet ante tribunal christi ut referat unusquisque prout gessit siue bonum siue malum etcet. ergo resurgent corpora alia ad premium. alia ad penam. ad phylippenses. iii^o. unde et saluatorem exspectamus dominum nostrum ihesum christum qui reformabit corpus humilitatis nostre configuratum corpori claritatis sue secundum operationem qua possit subici sibi omnia etcet. audi nequam quod ihesus christus reformabit corpus nostrum quod est passibile sicut aliquando suum fuit et non uideatur tibi impossibile quia ipse omnia potest et per consequentiam dicit apostolus hoc poterit scilicet fuerit corpora ut mortua resurgant. item. i^a. ad tessalonicenses. iiii^o. nolumus autem uos ignorare fratres de dormientibus ut non contristemini sicut et ceteri qui spem non habent. Si enim credimus quod ihesus mortuus est et resurrexit ita et deus eos qui dormierunt per ihesum adducet cum eo. etcet. item. idem. ultimam. ut integer spiritus uester et anima et corpus sine querela in aduentu domini nostri ihesu christi saluetur etcet. ergo corpus cum anima pariter erit in die iudicii. item. i^a. ad timotheus. ii^o. multum enim proficiunt ad impietatem et sermo eorum ut cancer serpit quibus est phyletus et ymeneus. qui a ueritate exciderunt dicentes resurrectionem esse iam factam etcet. ergo uos patareni excidistis a ueritate. qui dicitis quod iam resurrectio mortuorum sit facta ut scripture qui loquitur de resurrectione mortuorum intelligantur de spirituali que facta est. item iude. i^o. cum michael archangelis cum diabolo disputans altercaretur de moysi corpore etcet. audi stulte quare michael et diabolus fuissent alterati de corpore moysi postquam plusquam de alia ratione particula si resurgere non debuerat. item apocalypsis. i^o. primogenitus mortuorum etcet. pro resurrectione.

Him according to the flesh, so also will it be with us. See chapter 15 (15:12–13) "if Christ is preached that he arose from the dead, how do some among you say that there is no resurrection of the dead? But if there be no resurrection of the dead, then Christ is not risen." And further (15:29) "Otherwise what shall they do that are baptized for the dead, if the dead do not rise again." And (15:32) "if according to man I fought with beasts at Ephesus, what does it profit me if the dead do not rise again?" These passages clearly demonstrate the resurrection of bodies. Further 2 Corinthians 5 (5:4) "for we groan, who are in this tabernacle, being burdened, because we would not be unclothed but clothed over, so that what is mortal may be swallowed up by life." Therefore the mortal body was able to live. In the same place (5:10) "for we must all be manifested before the tribunal of Christ, that every one may receive the proper things of the body, according as he has done whether it be good or evil." Therefore bodies shall arise, one to rewards, one to punishment. Philippians 3 (3:20–21) "from there also we look for the Savior, our Lord Jesus Christ, who will reform the body of our humility, made like the body of his glory, according to the operation by which also he can subdue all things." Hear me, O evildoer, that Jesus Christ shall reform our body, which is able to suffer, just as was His own, and just as it does not seem impossible to you that He can do all things and, consequently, the apostle says He can do this, namely, that the bodies of the dead are to rise again. 1 Thessalonians 4 (4:12–13) "but we will not leave you ignorant, brethren, about those who are asleep, that you not be sorrowful, like others who have no hope. For if we believe that Jesus died and rose again, God will bring with him even those who have fallen asleep in Jesus." In the same letter at the end (5:23) "that your whole spirit, and soul, and body, may be saved at the coming of our Lord Jesus Christ." Therefore the body with the soul shall be together at the last day. 1 Timothy 2 (2:16–18) "for they grow much towards impiety. And their speech spreads like a cancer, of whom are Hymenaeus and Philetus, who have erred from the truth, saying that the resurrection is past already." Therefore you Patarenes hew down truth, who say that the resurrection of the dead has already been accomplished, so that when scripture speaks of the resurrection of the dead they are to be understood as having been spiritually accomplished. As in Jude 1 (1:9) "when Michael the archangel, disputing with the devil, fought over the body of Moses." Listen, fool, why would Michael and the devil have contended over the body of Moses, more than any other particular reason, if he would not have risen again? Apocalypse 1 (1:5) "firstborn of the dead," for the resurrection. In the same place (1:7) "and every people

---

33 si…37 resurrexit] 1 Cor. 15:12-13 (nobis) uobis *Vulg.*)   37 alioquin…38 resurgunt] 1 Cor. 15:29.   39 si…40 resurgunt] 1 Cor. 15:32.   42 Nam…44 uita] 2 Cor. 5:4.   46 omnes…48 malum] 2 Cor. 5:10.   49 unde…53 omnia] Php. 3:20-21 (subici) subiicere *Vulg.*)   59 nolumus…63 eo] 1 Thes. 4:12-13.   64 ut…66 saluetur] 1 Thes. 5:23 (saluetur) seruetur *Vulg.*)   67 multum…71 factam] 1 Tim. 2:16-18.   75 cum^1…76 corpore] Iud. 1:9.   80 primogenitus mortuorum] Apoc. 1:5.

43 sed] sed set *P*   45 vitale] mortale *P*   54 ihesus] om. *F* | nostrum] mundi *P*   67 timotheus] tymotheus *P*   76 audi…78 postquam] om. *P*   78 ratione] terra *P*

42 ad|fol. 76ra *P*   46 manifestari|fol. 58r *F*   65 sine|fol. 76rb *P*

idem in eodem. et uidebit eum omnes populus qui eum pupugerunt etcet. ad idem. xi. et corpora eorum non sinent poni in monumento etcet. et infra. et post duos et dimidium spiritus uite a deo intrauit in eos et steterunt super pedes suos etcet. idem. xx. et dedit mare mortuos qui in eo erant etcet. sed constat quod in mari non sunt anime humane. igitur corpora qui sunt in mari resurgent et alia eodem modo. item. actus. xxiii. de spe et resurrectione mortuorum ego iudicor etcet. quod nequaquam uos patareni iudicamini de illa. sed quia cum saduceis blasphematis ipsam idem. xxvi. quid incredibile iudicatur apud uos. si deus mortuos suscitat. etcet. non ergo incredibile uideatur uobis pessimi heretici. si dicimus quod deus qui omnia potest suscitabit corpora mortuorum.

Patarenus: Responsio. Dico quod omnes auctoritates quas induxisti de resurrectione secundum illos ex nostris qui dicunt non esse corpora in alia uita intelliguntur de resurrectione spirituali que hic fit per gratiam ihesu christi quando resurgunt anime de morte peccati. nec obstat quod in scriptura dicatur de resurrectione corporum. quia anime dicuntur corpora. quia cum sint substantie. et omnis substantia quodam modo corpus sit. non inepte corpora nuncupantur. secundum uero alios ex nobis qui dicunt corpora esse prostrata in celis. intelliguntur de corporum resurrectione quam expectant in fine mundi. per aduentum filii dei esse faciendam. Secundum uero illorum de gente uestra qui dicunt noua corpora debere dari electis in fine seculorum intelliguntur obiecta tua de resurrectione illorum.

Catholicus: Sed primum intellectum tuum tollit beatus paulus in actibus. xxiiii. ubi dicit spem habens in deum quam et ipsi exspectant resurrectionem futuram iustorum et iniquorum etcet. quia de resurrectione corporum necesse est tantum intelligere. quia iniqui spiritualiter non resurgunt. preterea eadem resurrectio non potest esse iustis et iniquis nisi corporale. Secundum autem intellectum ostendit esse fatuum. idem. beatus paulus ad romanos. viii. ubi ait. qui suscitauit ihesum christum a mortuis uiuificabit et mortalia corpora nostra etcet. non ergo loquitur de corporibus prostratis in celis. quia illa non sunt mortalia. sed mortua secundum uestram fatuitatem loquor. igitur loquitur de corporibus istis que quidem uiuunt sed morti dedita sunt et hic est dictum mortalia. ad hoc est quod dicit. ii^a. ad corinthios. iiii^a. ibi. semper mortificationem ihesu in corpore nostro circumferentes ut et uita ihesu in corporibus nostris manifestetur. semper enim nos qui uiuimus in mortem

shall see him, and they also who pierced him." And in 11 (11:9) "and they shall not suffer their bodies to be laid in tombs." And further (11:11) "And after two days and a half, the spirit of life from God entered into them and they stood on their feet." Similarly 20 (20:13) "And the sea gave up the dead that were in it." But it is clear that human souls are not in the sea, therefore the bodies which are in the sea shall arise in the same manner. Moreover Acts 23 (23:6) "concerning the hope and resurrection of the dead I am called into question." But are not you Patarenes to be judged of that, since you blaspheme like the Sadducees? See Acts 26 (26:8) "Why should it be judged incredible among you, if God should raise the dead?" Therefore it should not seem incredible to you miserable heretics if we say that God, for whom all things are possible, shall raise the bodies of the dead.

Pat: Response. I say regarding all the authorities which you cite in favor of the resurrection, that according to those among us who say that it is not these [earthly] bodies, rather they interpret a spiritual resurrection accomplished by the grace of Jesus Christ when souls arise from mortal sin in another life. Nor does it matter what is said in scripture about the resurrection of bodies, because souls are called bodies, since they are substances and all substances are in a certain way bodies, and are not inappropriately called bodies. Yet according to others among us who say that bodies are prostrate in the heavens, these are understood concerning the resurrection of bodies which they await at the end of the world, that is to be accomplished by the advent of the Son of God. Yet according to those of your people who say that new bodies ought to be given to the elect at the end of time, your objections are understood regarding their resurrection.

Cath: But Blessed Paul destroys your first contention in Acts 24 where he says (24:15) "having hope in God, which these also themselves look for, that there shall be a future resurrection of the just and unjust," because for the resurrection of bodies it is necessary at least to understand that only the unrighteous will not be raised spiritually. Furthermore the same resurrection cannot be for the just and for the unjust unless it is bodily. Your second contention is also shown to be foolish, in the same Blessed Paul in Romans 8, where he says (8:11) "he that raised up Jesus Christ from the dead shall give life also to our mortal bodies." He is not speaking of prostrate bodies in heaven. For those are not mortal, but dead. I speak according to your foolishness. Therefore it says of these bodies here that certain ones live but are abandoned to death and this is called mortality. 2 Corinthians 4 speaks to this (4:10–11) "Always bearing about in our body the mortification of Jesus that the life of Jesus may be made manifest in our bodies. For we who live are always delivered unto death for

---

81 et...82 pupugerunt] Apoc. 1:7 (populus) oculus *Vulg.*) 82 et...83 monumento] Apoc. 11:9. 83 et^2...85 suos] Apoc. 11:11 (duos) tres *Vulg.*) 85 et...86 erant] Apoc. 20:13. 89 de...iudicor] Act. 23:6. 92 quid...93 suscitat] Act. 26:8. 113 spem...115 iniquorum] Act. 24:15 (et) add. hi *Vulg.*) 121 qui...122 nostra] Rom. 8:11 (nostra) uestra *Vulg.*) 128 semper...132 mortali] 2 Cor. 4:10-11.

91 blasphematis] blasfematis *P* 100 quando] add. resurrectione *P* exp. 106 corporum] corpore *P* 108 illorum] both *PF* incorrect, leg. illos. 112 Sed] Si *P* 115 quia] quid *F* 118 iniquis] iniquitatis *P* 123 quia] primo *P* 125 quidem] add. a *P* exp.

90 illa|fol. 76va *P* 113 beatus|fol. 58v *F* 119 ostendit|fol. 76vb *P*

tradimur propter ihesum ut et uita ihesu manifestetur in carne nostra mortali etcet. ecce quam manifeste demonstrat quod corpora que hic mortificatur et moriuntur debent uiuificari. primum autem et secundum intellectum remouet. i^a. ad corinthios xv. ubi scribit. omnes quidem resurgemus sed non omnes immutabimur etcet. hic remouet primum. quia non omnes spiritualiter resurgunt. ergo loquitur de corporali resurrectione. sequitur in momento in ictu oculi in nouissima tuba. canet enim tuba et mortui qui in christo sunt resurgent incorrupti et nos immutabimur. oportet enim corruptibile hoc induere incorruptionem. et mortale hoc induere immortalitatem etcet. hic remouet secundum quia dicit hoc et non dicit illud corruptibile et non corruptum et mortale et non mortuum. quare ostendit quod ista corpora uisibilia tantum que hic corrumpuntur et moriuntur debeant resurgere. Tertius autem intellectus duobus modis reprobatur. primo quia scriptura dicit ut ostensum est quod corpora debent resurgere sed nichil resurgit nisi prius mortuum fuerit et illa corpora que dicit non sunt mortua cum nichil sit inter natura. secundus modus est quia scriptura dicit quod corpora resurgent que nunc dormiunt et que sunt mortalia sed illa corpora noua de quibus asseris neque dormiunt cum nichil fuit. neque mortalia sunt aut erunt quia secundum opinionem tuam numquam morientur et sic patet neccesario. quia scriptura loquitur de resurrectione corporum istorum uisibilium.

Quod corpora ista uisibilia non debeant resurgere probatio per rationes contra resurrectionem

[Patarenus:] Quod corpora non debeant resurgere rationibus et scripturis ostendemus. Quomodo posset esse quod una manus que est ultra mare et per qui est citra. conuergerentur simile et illa corpora que sunt a bestiis comesta uel combusta resurgerent. et quia non uidetur possibile ideo non credo resurrectionem esse corporum.

Catholicus: solutio ut supra. in parte nostra ad phylippenses. ii°. unde saluatorem exspectamus etcet.
Patarenus: Item aut costa ade de qua formata est eua. fuit de necessitate humane nature. ergo resurget in adam et non in euam. cum tota ueritas humane nature debeat resurgere. uel alias adam non resurgeret integre. et secundum hic eua non resurgeret. uel resurgeret in corpore ade. uel saltem sine una costa. si uero non fuit de ueritate humane nature. ergo non potest dici quod uere formata fuerit eua de costa ade. quia non fuit ade. si non de ueritate substantie eius. similis est obiectio de

Jesus' sake, so that the life of Jesus may be made manifest in our mortal flesh." See how clearly this shows that the bodies, which are here destroyed and decayed, ought to be given life. So your first and second contentions are removed. See 1 Corinthians 15, where it is written (15:51–53) "We shall all indeed rise again, but we shall not all be changed." This removes the first, that not all shall arise spiritually. Therefore he speaks of a bodily resurrection. He continues, "In a moment, in the blink of an eye, at the last trumpet, for the trumpet shall sound, and the dead, who died in Christ, shall rise again incorruptible, and we shall be changed. For this corruptible body must put on incorruption, and this mortal must put on immortality." This removes your second contention since he says this and not that, corruptible and not corrupt, mortal and not dead. Whence does he show only that these visible bodies that are here corrupted and died, and ought to rise again. Moreover the third contention can be disproved in two ways. First, because scripture says that it has been shown that bodies ought to rise, but nothing rises unless it first be dead, and those bodies of which it speaks have nothing of the nature [of death] within them. The second way is that scripture says that bodies shall arise which now sleep and that they are mortal, but those new bodies which you claim neither sleep — because they are nothing — are not nor will be mortal, since according to your opinion, they will never die and so it seems necessary that scripture speaks of the resurrection of those visible bodies.

That these visible bodies ought not to be resurrected, proven by arguments against the resurrection

[Pat:] We will demonstrate by reason and scripture that bodies ought not to be resurrected, for how could it happen that one hand is across the sea while the other is on this side, and they would have to come together, and in like manner those bodies which have been consumed by animals or burned would be raised, and it does not seem possible. Therefore I do not believe there to be a resurrection of bodies.
Cath: The solution is above. Where Philippians 2 takes our part (3:20) "whence we look for a Savior."
Pat: Further it was essential to human nature that Eve was formed from the rib of Adam, therefore it will be resurrected in Adam and not in Eve, since the whole of the human nature ought to be raised, for otherwise Adam shall not arise wholly, and according to this Eve shall not be raised, or she shall be raised in the body of Adam, or he shall arise without a rib, if it was not truly of his human nature, therefore I am not able to say that Eve was really formed out of the rib of Adam, since it was not Adam if not of his true substance. The objection is similar that whatever is

---

136 omnes¹ ... 144 immortali-tatem] 1 Cor. 15:51-53. XIII.5.12 unde...exspectamus] Php. 3:20.

133 et] om. *P* 143 incorruptionem] corruptionem *F* 144 secundum] seculum *F* 148 autem] aliter *P* 149 reprobatur] exprobatur *P* 150 ostensum...152 dicit] om. *F* 154 resurgent] resurgunt *P* 157 opinionem] oppinionem *P* XIII.5.2 probatio...3 resurrectionem] om. *F* 7 citra] add. erit *P* 12 phylippenses] Ephesios *F* 13 Patarenus] add. *al. man. marg. sin. P* 14 necessitate] necessitate ueritate *F*

145 corruptibile|fol. 77ra *P* XIII.5.15 cum|fol. 77rb *P*

quolibet nato diminuto et sic patet per istas inconuenientias quod ista corpora non resurgent.
Catholicus: solutio. Multiplex est ueritas humane nature scilicet ueritas essentie ut est substantia membrorum principalium seu radicalium sine quibus non potest esse homo et secundum hoc costa non fuit de ueritate humane nature et est ueritas integritatis ipsius indiuidui membra maxime officialia et etiam quemlibet sine quibus potest esse homo. sed non bene esse. hoc modo potest dici quod costa fuit de ueritate humane nature ante formationem mulieris. post formationem autem mulieris non. sed caro que coste repleuerat locum. unde illa caro resurget in adam sed costa in eua. quia in ea optimum suum esse habuit et est ueritas efficientie que facit ad conseruationem speciei. hanc non habuit natura humana ante formationem mulieris. quia tunc non habebat potestatem generandi feminam sed masculum tantum. sed formata muliere habuit utrumque et ita costa optima esse cepit in eua. unde in ea resurget et est ueritas de decentia ut capilli de quibus nullus peribit. qui pertinuerat ad decentiam hominis. et est ueritas perfectionis quam homo habet imperfectione sue quantitatis uel nature. natura non operante. uel aliter dicimus quod deus nouam costam formauit ade pro ea quam abstulit de qua formauit euam et secundum hoc sic intelligitur locus ille moysi scilicet et repleuit carnem pro ea etcet. repleuit scilicet deus carnem id est carnis uacuitatem ubi fuerat costa de qua fecit mulierem. repleuit dico aliam nouam costam ibi ponendo pro ea id est loco eius de qua mulierem formauerat et sic prima costa resurget in euam. secunda autem in adam. et resurget adam perfectus et mulier perfectam et secundum hoc nulla est opinio tua.

Probatio per scripturas contra resurrectionem

[**Patarenus:**] iª. ad corinthios. xv. sed dicet aliquis quomodo resurgent mortui. quali autem corpore uenient. insipiens tu quod seminas non uiuificatur nisi prius moriatur et quod seminas non corpus quod futurum est seminas sed nudum granum ut puta tritici aut alicuius ceterorum. deus autem dat illi corpus sicut uult et unicuique seminum proprium corpus. ergo ista corpora que hic gestamus non resurgent. sed alia noua que sumus a deo recepturi uel illa que dimisimus in celis.
Catholicus: Respondeo. quod ista uerba pauli pessime intelligis. Si enim questiones eius intelligeres forsitan et responsiones non ignorares quis conuenientes facit in ipsis questionibus namque sunt in persona nostra de duobus tamen scilicet de modo resurgendi et de

---

born is diminished, and thus it is apparent because of these inconsistencies that these bodies are not resurrected.
Cath: Solution. The truth of human nature is complex, the reality of the essence assuredly is the substance of the principal or radical members without which it cannot be a human being, and in this way the rib was not part of the reality of human nature, yet there is also the reality of the wholeness of the individual himself: the especially serviceable members and also whatever [members] without which a human being cannot be a human. But it cannot be maintained in this way that the rib was part of the reality of Adam's human nature before the formation of woman but not after. Rather the flesh which had filled the rib's place [is part of his substance], whence that flesh will rise again in Adam but the rib in Eve, because in her it had its fullest existence and it is the reality of the efficient power which acts for the conservation of the species. Human nature did not have this [power] before the formation of woman, because at that time it did not have the power of generating woman but only the male, but after the formation of the woman it had both, and it was fitting for Eve to be begun in a rib, which will arise again in her, for it is fitting that not one of their hairs be lost, regarding what concerns man's propriety and it is true of the perfection which man has in the imperfection in his quantity or nature, for nature does nothing [in vain], or otherwise we say that God formed a new rib for Adam from that which he took of that when he formed Eve, and this is understood by what Moses says (2:21) "and filled up flesh for it" namely God filled up the flesh, that is, of the empty space where the rib had been with which He had made the woman. I mean that He supplied another new rib there, putting it in that place from which the one that had formed the woman had been taken, and so the first rib shall arise with Eve but the second shall be resurrected with Adam, and Adam shall arise perfectly and the woman perfectly and by this is your position defeated.

Proof from the scriptures against resurrection

[**Pat:**] 1 Corinthians 15 (15:35-38) "but some will say: How do the dead rise again? or with what type of body will they come? You fool, what you sow does not come to life unless it dies first. And what you sow is not in the future body, but bare grain, as it happens with wheat or of some of the other crops. But God gives a body as He wills, and to every seed its proper body." Therefore these bodies which we here bear shall not be resurrected, but some new ones which we shall receive from God, or some other that we shall leave off in heaven.
Cath: I respond that you take Paul's words in the most wicked way. For perhaps if you understood his questions and you were not ignorant of all of his responses in those things which in our persons are dual, namely, on the manner of resurrection and of the quality of resurrected

---

48 et...ea] Gen. 2:21.   XIII.6.2 sed...8 corpus] 1 Cor. 15:35-38 (quali) qualiue *Vulg.*)

30 quemlibet sine] transp. *F*   32 nature] add. ade *F*   34 repleuerat] impleuerat *P*   35 ea] eua *P* | optimum] †† unclear in mss. perhaps opertum.   37 natura humana] transp. *F*   39 masculum] masculinum *P*   55 opinio] oppinio *P*   XIII.6.1 contra resurrectionem] de resurrectione *P*

24 solutio|fol. 59r *F*   42 qui|fol. 77va *P*   XIII.6.13 forsitan|fol. 77vb *P*

qualitate corporum resurgentium. Nam prima fuit ibi quomodo resurgent mortui. cui. respondit ibi. tu quod seminas non uiuificatur nisi prius moriatur etcet. ac si diceret hic modus quia prius corpora nostra putreficet in terra et postea resurgent in finem mundi ad uocem tube ut inferius postea ponit. secunda questio fuit ibi. quali autem corpore uenient? etcet. cui respondet ibi. Et quod seminas non corpus quod futurum est seminas id est non quale. ita etiam intelligitur illud. deus autem dat illi corpus sicut uult id est quale uult et quod ista ita sint intelligenda patet ex iiii^{or}. que hic colliguntur ex dictus apostoli. primo ex que omnibus quas ut dixi facit tantum de modo resurgendi et de qualitate corporum resurgendorum. numquam enim querit hic utrum resurgere debeant corpora. de illo uero dicet inferius. Ecce misterium. usque ibi. deo autem gratias etcet. secundo patet ex exemplo quod hic ponit comparat de grano cui resurrectionem corporum. nam manifestum est quod idem granum nascitur quid seminatur. licet in alia qualitate. quod idem ergo est de corporibus nostris. Tertio patet ex illo uerbo manifeste quod dicit hic. Tu quod seminas non uiuificatur nisi prius moriatur. ergo illud quod moritur postea uiuificatur. Quarto ostenditur ex illo uerbo tue obiectionis scilicet deus autem dat illi corpus etcet. ergo deus dat illi corpori seminato corpori id est corporis resurgentis substantialiter dat corporis qualitatem. igitur corpora natura mortua resurgent. et sic faciunt uerba ista potius per fide nostra quam pro heresi tua.

Patarenus: idem. in eodem. et corpora celestia et corpora terrestria etcet. ergo sunt corpora aliqua in celis que debemus recipere.

Catholicus: Respondeo quod corpora celestia uocat humana que ad hoc facta sunt in celum habitent. uel quia sunt de aere continendi. quia dicitur celum. corpora uero terrestria uocat brutorum animalium. que semper debent remanere in terra. de quibus omnibus dicit. non omnis caro eadem. sed alia quidem hominum. alia autem pecorum. alia autem uolucrum. alia autem piscium etcet. et quod ista corpora que uocat celestia sint ista que hic habent homines ostendit euidenter infra ubi dicit seminatur in corruptione surget incorruptione seminatur in ignobilitate surget in gloria etcet.

[**Patarenus:**] Item in eodem. si est corpus animale est et corpus spirituale etcet. ergo aliud est corpus quod recepturi simus quam istud animale quod uidetur.

Catholicus: Respondeo. non dicit quod sit aliud immo loquitur de hoc quod hic habemus quod modo dicitur animale quia communia habet cum omnibus animali-

bodies. For the first there was "How do the dead rise again," to which he replied, "what you sow does not come to life unless it dies first," as if to say in this way before our bodies decay in the earth and later they arise at the end of the world at the sound of the trumpet, as he later asserts. The second question is here, "what type of body will they have?" to which he responds, "you do not sow in the future body" that is, not what kind, but that is to be understood as "God gives a body as He wills" that is, of what kind He wills and those should be understood in four ways, which are here collected from the teachings of the Apostle. The first of all things I spoke of is only regarding the mode of rising and the quality of resurrected bodies. He never asks whether bodies ought to be raised. He makes this clear later (15:54–57) "Behold I tell you a mystery," up to "But thanks be to God." The second is clear by the example that he poses when he compares the grain to the resurrection of bodies, for it is clear that the identical grain that was born was sown, though in another quality, therefore that is the same with our bodies. The third is made clear when he says this: "what you sow does not come to life unless it dies first," Therefore that which does die is later given life. The fourth is clear from the words of your objection, namely "but God gives a body." Therefore God gives that sown body — body, that is, of the risen body — He substantially gives the quality of a body, therefore natural bodies arise from the dead, and so these passages argue rather more for our faith rather than your heresy.

Pat: Look in the same place (15:40) "and there are heavenly bodies and earthly bodies." Therefore there are some bodies in heaven which we are destined to receive.

Cath: To this I answer that one terms human bodies as 'heavenly bodies,' that are made so that they might dwell in heaven or because they are filled with air, which is called heaven. One rather calls the bodies of brute animals 'earthly' for they always remain on the earth. Paul speaks of all these when he says: (15:39) "All flesh is not the same, but one is the flesh of men, another of beasts, another of birds, another of fishes." And that he calls 'heavenly bodies' those of men is shown clearly below where he says (15:42–43) "what is sown in corruption, shall rise in incorruption. What is sown in dishonor, shall rise in glory."

[**Pat:**] In the same place (15:44) "What is sown a natural body, shall rise a spiritual body." Therefore it seems that the body that we shall receive is something other than an animal one.

Cath: I respond that he did not say it would be other, on the contrary, he speaks of those things that are called 'animal' that are possessed in common with all animals,

---

32 Ecce...33 gratias] 1 Cor. 15:54-57.   41 deus...corpus] 1 Cor. 15:38.   47 et¹...48 terrestria] 1 Cor. 15:40.   59 seminatur...61 gloria] 1 Cor. 15:42-43.   62 si...63 spirituale] 1 Cor. 15:44.

19 nisi...moriatur] om. F   33 ex] om. F   34 comparat...cui] cui comparat F | de grano] om. P   43 resurgentis] resurrectionem P   52 quia²] qui F   59 seminatur...60 incorruptione] om. P   64 simus] sumus F

33 gratias|fol. 59v F   37 ex|fol. 78ra P   64 recepturi|fol. 78rb P

bus scilicet comedere et bibere et corre et grossitudinem et pati et mori et huius. In resurrectione uero erit spiritale. quia in naturam spiritus transibit. sicut dicit dominus. In resurrectione neque nubent neque nubentur sed erunt sicut angeli dei in celo etcet. sed non prius quid spiritale est. sed quod animale. deinde quod spiritale etcet.

Patarenus: Item. in eodem. Caro et sanguis regnum dei possidere non possunt etcet. ergo ista corpora que sunt de carne et sanguine non possidebunt regnum dei.

Catholicus: Respondeo. quod per carnem et sanguinem corruptionem intelligit corporis. que non erit in patria. unde subdit exponendo. neque corruptio incorruptelam possidebit etcet. uel caro et sanguinis dicuntur. qui sunt uitiis dediti. que scilicet uitia ideo dicuntur caro et sanguis quia de carne et sanguine oriuntur. licet enim omnes resurgamus. tamen soli boni immutabuntur in incorruptionem uite. unde sequitur. omnes quidem resurgemus sed non omnes immutabimur etcet. Et quod de tali corruptione loquatur apostolus patet ex hoc quod dixerat superius. primus homo de terra terrenus. secundus homo de celo celestis. Qualis terrenus tales et terreni et quale celestis tales et celestes. ergo sicut portauimus ymaginem terreni. portemus et ymaginem celestis etcet.

namely: to eat and drink, to run and grow, to suffer and die, and suchlike. In the resurrection it shall be spiritual, for the spirit shall change in nature, as the Lord says (Mt 22:30) "At the resurrection they shall neither marry nor be married, but shall be like the angels of God in heaven." And that the Apostle understands similarly about the body is made clear in the passage that follows, (1 Cor 15:46) "Yet that which was not first spiritual, but that which is animal, afterwards it shall be spiritual."

Pat: But in the same place he says (15:50) "that flesh and blood cannot possess the kingdom of God." Therefore this body which is composed of blood and flesh shall not possess the kingdom of God.

Cath: I respond that 'flesh and blood' is meant to convey the corruption of the body, of which there will be none in heaven, as he explains below (15:50) "neither shall corruption possess incorruption." Or those addicted to vice are called 'flesh and blood,' that is, the vices of flesh and blood since they arise on account of flesh and blood. For although we all rise, yet only the good shall rise to immortality and incorruption of life. So he continues (15:51) "We shall all indeed rise again, but we shall not all be changed." And let what the Apostle said earlier of such corruption be clear (15:4749) "The first man was of the earth, earthly, the second man, from heaven, heavenly. Such as is the earthly, such also are the earthly: and such as is the heavenly, such also are they that are heavenly. Therefore as we have borne the image of the earthly, let us bear also the image of the heavenly."

Quod erit iudicium uniuersale et quod mundus destruetur secundum formam exteriorem et non secundum essentiam suam et quod infernus est et erit alibi quam in mundo isto

XIV In what the universal judgment shall consist, and that the world shall be destroyed according to its external form and not according to its essence and that hell exists and shall exist in that other world

Post resurrectionem corporum. sequitur uidere de iudicio uniuersali ac de fine mundi et de loco inferni. que sunt comitantia corporum resurrectioni. circa que sepe dicti heretici errant diuersimode. Dicunt namque quidam ex illis quod nullum iudicium debet unquam fieri nec uniuersale nec particulare. sed tamen cum ascenderint in celum omnes saluandi in aduentu filii dei quem dicunt uenire pro illis. tunc stabit ita mundus in peccatoribus sicuti nunc est et intrabunt spiritus de corpore in corpus et erunt ita homines et mundus semper sicuti nunc sunt et de inferno nichil credunt. alii uero aiunt quod iudicium singulare cotidie fit sed de uniuersali nichil credunt. sed dicunt quod cum erunt salui omnes qui debent saluari. tunc deus ponet ignem in mundum et comburetur totus ita quod nichil de ipso remanebit. et peccatores erunt in inferno. alii

After the resurrection of bodies, it follows that we should consider the universal judgment and of the end of the world and of hell, [things] which accompany the resurrection of the body, and about which the heretics err in diverse ways. For some among them say that there is never any universal or particular judgment, but yet some say when they are taken up to heaven are all saved at the advent of the Son of God whom they say is coming for them. Then the world will remain with sinners just as now and the spirits shall go from body to body and men will be just as the world is now and always, and they believe nothing of hell. Others say that the judgment occurs every single day but do not believe in the universal judgment, but they say that all are saved who ought to be saved, then God shall cast fire upon the earth and shall burn it wholly until nothing of it remains, so that the sinners shall be in

autem credunt quod mundus debeat comburi ita quod semper sit et dicunt quod ibi cruciabuntur mali et non erit alius infernus. quia mundus semper ardens infernus erit. alii uero referunt quod tantum secundum formam exteriorem comburendus sit mundus quem dicunt esse a diabolo. Idem de iudicio ergo uniuersali concordant omnes patareni quod non debeat fieri. de iudicio uero singulari utrum fiat uel non fiat et de inferno utrum sit uel non sit et ubi sit et de mundo quomodo sit destruendus sunt diuersi. Nos autem fidem orthodoxam tenentes credimus et per sacras scripturas probamus quod iudicium uniuersale fiet a domino ihesu christo et in finem seculi et quod cotidie fiat ab ipso singulare iudicium et quod infernus sit. in quo dampnati cruciari debunt in sempiternum et sit alibi quam in hoc mundo et quod mundus sit exurendus secundam formam exteriorem. secundum uero essentiam elementorum stabit semper.

De iudicio uniuersali

Mattheus. xxv. cum uenerit filius hominis in maiestate sua etcet. et infra. congregabuntur ante eum omnes gentes et segregabit eos ab inuicem etcet. et infra. tunc dicet rex hiis qui a dextris eius erunt etcet. et infra esuriui enim et dedistis mihi manducare etcet. usque ad finem capituli. ex hiis patet expressim quod filius dei iudicabit omnes in fine mundi per solempne iudicium. item. lucam. xvii. qua die exiit loth a sodomis pluit ignem et sulphur de celo et omnes perdidit. sic erit qua die filius hominis reuelabitur etcet. item. ad idem. item. ad Romanos. ii°. thesaurizas tibi iram in die ire et reuelationem iusti iudicii dei. qui reddet unicuique secundum opera eius. etcet. ergo erit iudicium uniuersale. iudicabit deus de meritis singulorum. item ii^a. petri. ii°. nouit dominus pius de temptatione eripere iniquos uero in diem iudicii cruciandos reseruare etcet. et supra dixerat de demonibus. Si enim deus angelis peccantibus non pepercit sed rudentibus inferni detractos in tartarum tradidit cruciandos reseruari dixerat de demonibus. Si enim deus angelis peccantibus non pepercit sed rudentibus inferni detractos in tartarum tradidit cruciandos reseruari etcet. ergo omnis iniqui tam mali homines quam demones erunt in iudicio uniuersali. de maiori cruciatu reportaturi sententiam. idem in eadem. iii°. igni reseruati in diem iudicii et perditionis impiorum hominum et infra adueniet dies domini ut fur etcet. ad idem. idem. iudas. ii°. ecce uenit dominus in sanctis milibus suis facere iudicium contra omnes de omnibus operibus impietatis eorum quibus impie gerunt et de omnibus duris uerbis que locuti sunt contra deum

On the universal judgment

the inferno. But others believe that the world ought to be burned eternally and they say that the evildoers will be tormented there so that there is no other Hell, for the world always shall burn in fire. Others contend that only the external form of the world shall be burned which they say is from the devil. Further all of the Patarenes agree that there will not be a universal judgment, regarding whether there is or is not a particular judgment or whether hell exists or not, or whether the world will be destroyed, they are divided. But we keepers of the orthodox faith believe — and shall prove from the sacred scriptures — that the universal judgment shall be given by the Lord Jesus Christ at the end of time, and that daily particular judgments are rendered by Him and that Hell exists, in which the damned shall be tormented eternally and which is elsewhere than in this world, and that the world shall burn according to its external form, though in its essential elements it will always exist.

On the universal judgment

Matthew 25 (25:31) "Then shall the son of man come in his majesty," and further (25:32) "he shall gather before him all the peoples and shall separate them, one from another," and also (25:34) "then shall the king say to those on his right," and (25:35) "for I was hungry and you gave me to eat," all the way to the end of the chapter. From these words it is exceedingly clear that the Son of God shall judge all men at the end of the world by a solemn judgment. See Luke 17, (17:29–30) "On the day that Lot left Sodom, it rained fire and brimstone from heaven, and destroyed them all. Even so will it be in the day when the Son of man shall be revealed." More on the same subject in the second chapter of Romans (2:5–6) "You store up a wealth of wrath for yourself against the day of wrath, and revelation of the just judgment of God, who will render to every man according to his works." So there will be a universal judgment, and God will judge each on his merits. 2 Peter 2 (2:9) "The Lord knows how to deliver the godly from temptation, but to reserve the unjust for the day of judgment to be tormented." And above he spoke of the demons (2:4) "For if God did not spare the angels that sinned, but delivered them, drawn down by infernal ropes to the lower hell, unto torments, to be reserved unto judgment." Therefore shall all evildoers — be they bad men or demons — be tried in the universal judgment to receive a sentence concerning greater torments. In the same letter see what he says, (3:7) "reserved in fire against the day of judgment and perdition of ungodly men," and later (3:10) "but the day of the Lord shall come like a thief." Jude has the same sentiment: (1:14–15) "behold, the Lord will come with thousands of his saints to execute judgment upon all, for all the works of their ungodliness, by which they have wrought impiety, and of all the hard

---

XIV.2.2 cum...6 manducare] Matt. 25:31-32, 34-35 (segregabit) separabit | hiis] his *Vulg.*)   9 qua...11 reuelabitur] Luc. 17:29-30.   12 thesaurizas...14 eius] Rom. 2:5-6 (reuelationem) reuelationis *Vulg.*)   16 nouit...18 reseruare] 2 Pet. 2:9.   21 reseruari...23 reseruari] 2 Pet. 2:4 (cruciandos) add. in iudicium *Vulg.*)   26 igni...28 hominum] 2 Pet. 3:7.   28 adueniet...fur] 2 Pet. 3:7.   29 ecce...33 impii] Iud. 1:14-15 (uerbis) om. *Vulg.*)

---

24 referunt] refertur *F*   26 Idem] om. *F* | de] om. *P*   29 sit^1] om. *P*   30 destruendus] dextruendus *F*   XIV.2.5 hiis] ipsis *F*

27 fieri|fol. 78vb *P*   XIV.2.13 die|fol. 79ra *P*

peccatores impii etcet. ecce quam aperte ostendit beatus iudas quod omnes peccatores in iudicio uniuersali arguentur et iudicabuntur a deo. item. apocalypsis. xx. et uidi thronum magnum et candidum et sedentem super eum etcet. et infra. et uidi mortuos magnos et pusillos stantes in conspectu throni et libri aperti sunt et alius liber apertus est qui est uite et iudicati sunt mortui ex hiis que scripta erant in libris secundum opera ipsorum etcet. Ex quibus patet expressim quod erit iudicium uniuersale in fine mundi. in quo omnes peccatores et iusti iudicabuntur uel ad maiorem confusionem. uel ad maiorem exaltationem secundum merita ipsorum et supple de hac materia. prout supra. titulum. i°. in rubricella quod omnes pene temporales et eterne sunt a deo et supra de humanitate christi in rubricella de aduentu filii dei in fine mundi ad iudicium notatum inuenies.

De singulari iudicio

Lucam. xvi. eleuans autem oculos suos cum esset in tormentis etcet. item apocalypsis. xiiii. beati mortui qui in domino moriuntur. amodo iam dicit spiritus ut requiescant a laboribus suis opera enim illorum sequuntur illos etcet. et xx. et infernus dederunt mortuos etcet. Ex quibus tribus auctoritatibus et ex multis aliis quas non oportet hic prosequi patet quod cotidie iudicatur anime malorum uel bonorum ad infernum uel ad requiem eternam secundum merita uniuscuiusque.

Quod infernus est et alibi quam in mundo isto

Mattheus. xiii. mittet dominus angelos suos et colligent de regno eius omnia scandala et eos qui faciunt iniquitatem et mittent eos in caminum ignis ibi erit fletus et stridor dentium etcet. Item tunc dixit rex ministris. ligatis pedibus et manibus mittite illum in tenebris exteriores ibi erit fletus et stridor dentium etcet. idem. xxv discedite a me maledicti in ignem eternum etcet. ergo est pena eterna dampnatis. que dicitur a domino caminum ignis et locus fletus et stridoris et ignis eternus et infernus et huiusmodi et patet per id quod dicit mittent et mittite et discedite et huiusmodi uerba que significant separationem a mundo. item lucam. xvi. sepultus est in inferno etcet. ergo est infernus et alibi quam in mundo isto. quia non dum comburebatur nec adhuc combuntur mundus. nec potes dicere quod fuerit parabola cum ibi nominetur spiritualis persona lazari. ergo fuit exemplum.

---

things which ungodly sinners have spoken against God." Look how plainly blessed Jude demonstrates that all sinners shall be convicted and judged by God. See also Apocalypse 20 (20:11) "And I saw a throne, mighty and white, and one sitting upon it," and further (20:12) "And I saw the dead, both great and small, standing in the sight of the throne, and the books were opened; and another book was opened, which is the book of life, and the dead were judged by those things which were written in the books, each according to their works." From these passages it is clear that there shall be a universal judgment and the end of the world, in which all the sinners and the just will be judged, either to their great confounding or to their great triumph according to their merits. Let this be in addition to the above material in title 1, in the section concerning whether all temporal and eternal punishments be from God and above about the humanity of Christ, you will find noted in the section on the coming of the Son of God at the end of the world for judgment.

On the particular judgment

Luke 16 (16:23) "And lifting up his eyes when he was in torment." Apocalypse 14 (14:13) "Blessed are the dead, who die in the Lord. From now on, says the Spirit, that they may rest from their labors, for their works follow them." And 20 (20:13) "and hell gave up its dead." From these three authorities and from many others which I will not describe in detail here, it is clear that the good or evil souls of the dead are daily judged, and proceed to hell or to eternal rest according to the merits of each.

That hell exists and is in another place than this world

Matthew 13 (13:41–42) "The Son of man shall send his angels, and they shall gather from his kingdom all scandals, and they that work iniquity and shall cast them into the furnace of fire, there shall be weeping and gnashing of teeth." Further (22:13) "Then the king said to the waiters, 'Bind his hands and feet and cast him into the outer darkness: where there shall be weeping and gnashing of teeth.'" Further 25 (25:41) "Depart from me, you cursed ones, into everlasting fire," therefore damnation is an eternal punishment, such as when the Lord says things like "fiery furnace" and a place with "weeping and gnashing of teeth" and "eternal fire" and "hell" and similar terms that signify a distinction from the world. Also Luke 16 (16:22) "and was buried in hell," therefore hell is other than in this world, since the world was not yet burned, nor has it yet burned up to now, neither are you able to say that it was

---

36 et¹…37 eum] Apoc. 20:11.   37 et²…41 ipsorum] Apoc. 20:12.   **XIV.3.2** eleuans…3 tormentis] Luc. 16:23.   3 beati…4 moriuntur] Apoc. 14:13.   6 et²…7 mortuos] Apoc. 20:13.   **XIV.4.2** mittet…5 dentium] Matt. 13:41-42 (dominus] filius hominis *Vulg.*)   5 tunc…7 dentium] Matt. 22:13 (illum] eum *Vulg.*)   8 discedite…9 eternum] Matt. 25:41.   14 sepultus…inferno] Luc. 16:22.

45 supple] suple *F*   **XIV.3.1** iudicio] add. m. *P*   **XIV.4.8** xxv] xxx. *P*   17 cum] add. e *P* exp.

37 magnos|fol. 79rb *P*   **XIV.3.1** iudicio|fol. 60v *F*   **XIV.4.5** stridor|fol. 79va *P*

Quod mundus destruetur secundam formam exteriorem et non secundam materiam elementorum

Mattheus. iii°. cuius uentilabrum in manu sua et permundabit aream suam etcet. ergo non destruetur mundus totaliter. sed ad modum aree permundabitur. Item ad hebreos. i°. et tu in principio domine terram fundasti et opera manuum tuarum sunt celi. ipsi peribunt tu autem permanebis et ut uestimentum uestrascent et uelud amictum mutabis eos et mutabuntur etcet. ergo mundus tantum peribit secundam formam exteriorem. secundum uero elementorum substantiam mutatus in melius stabit in sempiternum. terra uero in eternum stat. etcet. et eccesiasticus. xlii°. Quam desiderabilia omnia opera eius etcet. et infra. omnia hec uiuunt et manent in seculum seculi.

Quod non erit iudicium uniuersale nec etiam singulare secundum aliquos et quod mundus destruetur totaliter uel quod conburetur in sempiternum et erit ibi infernus et non alibi

De iudicio uniuersali concordant omnes patareni quod non debeat fieri.

Contra iudicium uniuersale

[Patarenus:] Dauid. ideo non resurgent impii in iudicio neque peccatores in concilio iustorum etcet. ergo non erit uniuersale iudicium.

Catholicus: Respondeo quod non resurgent impii et peccatores in iudicio et consilio iustorum id est cum iustis iudicentur ad regnum. simile est quod dicit apostolus. prima ad corinthios. xv. quiquid resurgemus sed non omnes immutabimur etcet. licet loquitur de infidelibus et hereticis qui non resurgent in iudicio examinationis. quia soli fideles examinabuntur de bonis operibus qui neglexerunt. Resurgent tamen in iudicio maioris confusionis et dampnationis.

[Patarenus:] Item. iohannes. iii°. qui credit in eum non iudicatur. qui autem non credit iam iudicatus est etcet. sed credere intelligitur cum effectu. igitur omnis malus homo iam iudicatus est. unde non fiet aliud iudicium.

Catholicus: Respondeo. illud intelligitur de infidelibus et de iudicio excecationis et est sensus qui non credit iam iudicatus est id est excecatus est. et subdit

---

an allegory about a spiritual person named Lazarus, for he was an example.

That the world shall be destroyed according to its external form but not according to its material constitution

In the third chapter of Matthew (3:12) "Whose threshing fan is in his hand and he will thoroughly cleanse his floor," therefore the world shall not be completely destroyed, rather in the manner of the floor being totally cleansed. Further Hebrews 1 (1:10–12) "and you in the beginning, O Lord, founded the earth and the works of your hands are the heavens. They shall perish, but you will remain, and they shall all grow old like a garment. And like an outfit you will change them." Therefore the world shall only be destroyed according to its external form, but according to the substance of its elements it shall be changed for the better, and it will endure forever. (Ecc 1:4) "The earth shall stand forever," and Ecclesiasticus 42 (42:23) "how desirable are all your works," and further (42:24) "All these things live, and remain forever."

That there will not be either a universal or particular judgment according to some and that the world will be totally destroyed or that it shall burn forever and that hell will be here and not elsewhere.

All the Patarenes agree that there will be no universal judgment.

Against the universal judgment

[Pat:] David says (Ps 1:5) "Therefore the wicked shall not rise again in judgment, neither shall sinners be in the council of the just." Therefore there shall be no universal judgment.

Cath: I respond that wicked men and sinners shall not arise and be admitted to the council of the just, that is, when they will be judged with the just in the kingdom. Similar is that which the Apostle says in 1 Corinthians (15:51) "We shall all indeed rise again, but we shall not all be changed," clearly he is speaking of unbelievers and heretics who are not resurrected in the judgment of examination, because only the faithful shall be weighed regarding good works, which these neglected. Yet they shall arise at the judgment in greater confusion and damnation.

[Pat:] In John 3 (3:18) "he who believes in him is not judged, but he who does not believe is already judged." But 'to believe' is understood here as already effected, therefore all wicked men are already judged, so there is no need for another judgment.

Cath: I respond that is to be understood in relation to unbelievers by the judgment of blindness and the sense is that he who does not believe has already been judged, that is, he has been blinded, and thence follows the reason:

XIV.5.4 cuius…5 suam] Matt. 3:12. 7 et…11 mutabuntur] Heb. 1:10-12 (et) add. omnes *Vulg.*) 14 terra…stat] Eccl. 1:4. 15 Quam…16 eius] Ecclesiastic. 42:23. 16 omnia…17 seculi] Ecclesiastic. 42:24 (seculi) om. *Vulg.*) XIV.7.2 ideo…3 iustorum] Ps. 1:5. 8 quiquid…9 immutabimur] 1 Cor. 15:51. 14 qui…15 est] Ioh. 3:18.

XIV.5.1 destruetur] dextruetur *F* 2 materiam] naturam *F* 5 destruetur] dextruetur *F* XIV.6.3 destruetur] dextruetur *F* XIV.7.2 Dauid] om. *F* 6 est] add. ut *P* 13 confusionis] consumati omnis *P*

XIV.5.16 manent|fol. 79vb *P* XIV.7.20 et¹|fol. 80ra *P*

rationem quia non credit in nomine unigeniti id est non credit in lucem.

Patarenus: Item ad quid fieret iudicium cum deus sciat omnia et apud eum sint certa et determinata merita omnium.

Catholicus: Respondeo quia iudicabit propter malos ad confusionem illorum et propter bonos ad maiorem illorum exaltationem sicut legitur apocalypsis. i°. et uidebit eum omnis oculus et qui eum pupugerunt et tunc plangent se super eum omnes tribus terre etiam amen etcet. et xviii. exulta super eam celum et sancti apostoli et prophete quoniam iudicauit iudicium uestrum uerum de illa etcet. et letabitur iustus cum uiderit uindictam etcet. et sapientiam. v. tunc stabunt iusti in magna constantia aduersus eos qui se angustiauerunt etcet.

Contra utrumque iudicium generale et singulare

[**Patarenus:**] Dicimus quod omnis spiritus sunt creature dei uel diaboli et deus nichil habet facere de creaturis diaboli et econtrario. ad quid ergo fieret aliquid iudicium.

Catholicus: Respondeo si dicis quod aliqui spiritus sint creatura diaboli errorem dicis et dicis quod tuum est quia hereticus es et hunc errorem ego reprobaui per rationes naturales et scripturas diuinas supra titulum. i°. Sed dic mihi tu qui negas utrumque iudicium. quomodo respondebis ad sacras scripturas que de utroque scilicet uniuersali et singulari loquitur quas contra te supra posui.

Quod Mundus semper comburetur et infernus ibi erit et non alibi

[**Patarenus:**] Mattheus. xxii. et missis exercitibus suis et perdidit homicidas illos et ciuitatem succendit etcet. ergo deus ponet ignem in mundum et non alibi postquam salui fuerunt electi et comburetur semper et erit peccatorum infernus et non erit infernus alius.

Catholicus: Respondeo loquitur de ciuitate iudeorum que erat ierusalem que combusta fuit post obstinationem eorum per titum et uespasianum imperatores romanorum. uel si de mundo uis intelligere non dixit quod semper debeat comburi. nec dicit quod ibi sit infernus qui dicitur ciuitas malorum eo quod ibi facti sunt mali.

Quod mundus totaliter destruetur

[**Patarenus:**] ii^a. petri. iii°. adueniet autem dies domini ut fur in quo celi magno impetu transient et elementa uero calore soluentur. et terra et que in ipsa sunt opera

because he does not believe in the name of the only begotten Son, i.e., he does not believe in the light.

Pat: To what end might justice obtain since God knows all things and before Him the merits of all are certain and defined?

Cath: I respond that He will judge the evil to their shame and the good to their greater glory, as it is read in Apocalypse 1 (1:7) "and every eye shall see Him, and even those who pierced him. And all the tribes of the earth shall weep over themselves on account of Him. Even so. Amen." And 18 (18:20) "Rejoice over her, heaven, and you holy apostles and prophets; for He has judged your judgment on her." (Ps 57:11) "The just shall rejoice when He sees vengeance." And Wisdom 5 (5:1) "Then shall the just stand with great constancy against those who have afflicted them."

8 Against both the universal and particular judgment

[**Pat:**] We say that all spirits are creatures of God or of the devil and God has nothing to do with diabolic creatures, and vice versa. To what purpose then would any judgement be?

Cath: I respond if you say that some spirits might be diabolic creatures, you speak wrongly, and you say that your position is true because you are a heretic and I have already confuted you by natural proofs and the divine scriptures above in Title 1. But tell me, you who deny both judgments, how you will respond to the sacred scriptures about both, namely those that speak of the universal and particular judgments, which above I cited against you?

9 That the world shall always be burned and that Hell is there and not elsewhere

[**Pat:**] Matthew 22 (22:7) "and sending his armies, he destroyed those murderers and burnt their city." Therefore God shall send fire upon this world and no other, after the elect are saved and it shall burn forever and it will be Hell for sinners and there shall not be another Hell.

Cath: I respond by saying that the city of the Jews, Jerusalem, was burned after their stubbornness by the Roman emperors Titus and Vespasian, or if you wish to understand this as referring to the world, He did not say that it ought always to be burned, neither did He say that there would be Hell, which He called the city of the wicked, because there they were made wicked.

10 That the world shall be utterly destroyed

[**Pat:**] 2 Peter 3 (3:10) "But the day of the Lord shall come as a thief, in which the heavens shall pass away with great violence, and the elements shall be melted with heat, and

---

29 et…32 amen] Apoc. 1:7 (tunc) om. *Vulg.*) 32 super…34 illa] Apoc. 18:20 (exulta | exsulta | iudicauit] add. deus *Vulg.*) 34 et…35 uindictam] Ps. 57:11. 35 tunc…37 angustiauerunt] Sap. 5:1. XIV.9.3 et…4 succendit] Matt. 22:7. XIV.10.2 adueniet…5 exurentur] 2 Pet. 3:10.

XIV.9.3 missis] missit *P* 5 et…alibi] om. *P* 6 postquam] add. liberati *P* exp. | salui fuerunt] transp. *P* 11 dixit] dicit *P*
XIV.10.1 destruetur] dextruetur *F*

29 illorum|fol. 61r *F* XIV.8.9 reprobaui|fol. 80rb *P*

exurentur etcet. ad hec est quod dicit dominus.
matheus. v. donec transeat celum et terra etcet. et
matheus. xxiiii. celum et terra transibunt etcet. ergo
mundus totaliter destruetur. et apocalypsis. xxi. uidi
celum nouum et terram nouam. primum enim celum
et prima terra abiit et mare iam non est etcet.

Catholicus: Respondeo dicimus quod mundus
transibit et comburetur ac destruetur secundum formam exteriorem et maxime duo elementa que magis
fedata sunt ab usu peccatorum hominum scilicet aer et
aqua purgabuntur quantum uero ad suberam puram
elementorum mundus stabit in sempiternum. quid
patet ex hoc quod dicit beatus. iohannes. apocalypsis.
xi. factum est regnum huius mundi domini nostri
ihesu christi etcet. et quod dicit mattheus xiii. Et
colligent de regno eius omnia scandala etcet. quia si
post iudicium uniuersale mundus fiet de regno christi
et erit regnum eius. ergo non destruetur substantialiter.
Et attende catholice quod de materia huius tractatus
non multum nos exercere oportet. quia de leui non est
cum hereticis de hac disputatione.

the earth and the works which are in it shall be burnt up."
The Lord speaks about these things in Matthew 5 (5:18)
"until heaven and earth pass away," and Matthew 24
(24:35) "heaven and earth shall pass away." Therefore the
earth shall be wholly destroyed. And Apocalypse 21 (21:1)
"I saw a new heaven and a new earth, for the first heaven
and the first earth was gone, and the sea is now no more."

Cath: I respond that we say that the world shall pass away
and be burned and destroyed according to its exterior
form, and especially the two elements which have been
defiled to a greater extent from the use of sinful men,
namely, air and water, will be purged But so far as pertains
to the pure substance/substratum of the elements, the
world will endure forever. This is clear from what Blessed
John says in Apocalypse 11 (11:15) "The kingdom of this
world has become that of our Lord Jesus Christ," and what
he says in Matthew 13 (13:41) "and they shall gather out
of his kingdom all scandals." For if after the universal
judgment the world shall be for the reign of Christ, and
shall be His kingdom, then it shall not be essentially
destroyed. Pay attention to this, O Catholic, that it is not
proper that we be troubled much over the subject of this
treatise, for this debate with the heretics is a trivial matter.

Quod peccata et supplicia et merita non sunt equalia

Dictum est supra de iudicio. Sequitur uidere de meritis
et premiis secundum que et de quibus fiet iudicium.
ubi sciendum quod patareni dicunt errando quod
peccata et supplicia sunt equalia quorum uesanie
testimonio scripturarum de facili possumus obuiare.

XV That sins and sufferings and merits are not equal

This was discussed above regarding judgment. It remains to
examine merits and rewards according to which and in
which one will have judgment, knowing that the Patarenes
errantly claim that sins and sufferings are equal,[1] with the
testimony of the scriptures we are easily able to confront
their madness.

Quod peccata et supplicia non sunt equalia

Mattheus. xi. tyro et sydoni remissius erit in die iudicii
quam uobis etcet. ergo magis peccant unus quam alius
et grauius torquatur. idem xii. uiri niniuite surgent in
iudicio cum generatione ista et condemnabunt eam
etcet. et infra. regina austri surget in iudicio etcet.
quod intelligitur comparatione minoris peccati et
minoris pene. idem. xxiii. ue uobis scribe et pharisei
etcet. magis grauat illos ergo plus peccant et infra.
facitis eum filium gehene duplo quam uos etcet. ergo
in gehena est inequalitate penarum. item. marcum. iii°.
omnia dimittentur filiis hominum peccata et blasphemie quibus blasphemauerit. qui autem blasphemauerit
in spiritum sanctum non habebit remissionem in

2 That sins and sufferings are not equal

Matthew 11 (11:22) "it shall be more tolerable for Tyre
and Sidon on the day of judgment, than for you," therefore the more one man sins than another, the more gravely
he shall be tormented. See also chapter 12 (12:41) "The
men of Nineveh shall rise in judgment with this generation, and shall condemn it," and further (12:42) "The
queen of the south shall rise in judgment," which is understood as a comparison of lesser sins and lesser punishments, further (23:13) "woe to you scribes and Pharisees,"
the condemnation lies more heavily upon them, therefore
they sinned more seriously, and later (23:15) "you make
him the child of hell twice more than yourselves," therefore in hell there is an inequality of punishments. See also
Mark 3 (3:28–29) "all sins shall be forgiven for the sons of

---

6 donec…terra] Matt. 5:18.   7 celum…transibunt] Matt. 24:35.   8 uidi…10 est] Apoc. 21:1.   18 factum…19 christi] Apoc. 11:15.
19 Et…20 scandala] Matt. 13:41.   **XV.2.2** tyro…3 uobis] Matt. 11:22.   4 uiri…5 eam] Matt. 12:41.   6 regina…iudicio] Matt.
12:42.   8 ue…9 peccant] Matt. 23:13.   10 facitis…uos] Matt. 23:15.   12 omnia…15 eternum] Mar. 3:28-29.

12 destruetur] dextruetur F   **13** duo] om. P   **15** suberam] sic PF leg. substantiam   **22** destruetur] dextruetur F   **23** attende] actende P
24 non²] **leg. om.**

XIV.10.9 celum²|fol. 80va P   **XV.2.5** et|fol. 80vb P   6 iudicio|fol. 61v F

---

1) Mitigated dualism. Burci, 320, 338; Moneta, 383.

eternum. ergo maius est unum peccatum quam aliud. item. lucam. xii. ille autem seruus qui cognouit uoluntatem domini sui et non se preparauit et non fecit secundum uoluntatem eius plagis uapulabit multis. qui autem non cognouit et fecit digna plagis uapulabit paucis. ergo magis puniteur et lucam. xx. hi accipient dampnationem etcet. ergo magis punietur unus quam alius. item. iohannes. xviiii. propterea qui tradidit me tibi maius peccatum habet. ergo unum peccatum est maius quam aliud. item. ii^a. petri. ii^o. iniquos uero etcet. et infra. magis autem eos qui post carnem etcet. ergo magis peccat unus alio et magis cruciabitur. item. apocalypsis. xviii. in poculo miscuit miscete illi duplum. quamtum glorificauit se et in deliciis fuit tantum date illi tormentum et luctum. etcet. ergo secundum mensuram delictorum maiorem uel minorem erit mensuratio tormentorum. preterea deus est iustus igitur unum puniet magis quam alium quia sic exigat iustitia.

Quod merita et premia non sunt equalia

Mattheus. xiii. alia autem ceciderunt in terram bonam et dabant fructum aliud etcet. et aliud. lxam. aliud. xxxm. etcet. idem xviii. quicumque ergo humiliauerit se sicut paruulus iste. hic maior est in regno celorum etcet. idem xviiii. amen dico uobis quod uos qui secuti estis me in regeneratione cum sederit filius hominis in sede maiestatis sue sedebitis et uos super sedes iudicantes. xii. tribus israel etcet. item. lucam. vi. eadem quippe mensura qua messi fueritis remetietur uobis etcet. idem. vii. remittuntur ei peccata multa. quoniam dilexit multum. cui autem minus dimittitur munus diligit etcet. item ultimo. dicit simoni petro ihesus. simon iohannis diligis me plus his? etcet. item. prima ad corinthios. iii^o. uniusquisque autem propriam mercedem accipiet secundum suum laborem. idem. xv. alia claritas solis alia claritas lune et alia claritas stellarum. stella autem a stella differt in claritate sic et resurrectio mortuorum etcet. item ii^a. ad corinthios. viiii. qui parce seminat parce et metet et qui seminat in benedictionibus de benedictionibus et metet uitam eternam etcet. item ad Galathas. ultimo. que enim seminauerit homo hec et metet. item ad ephesios. iiii^o. Vnicuique autem nostrum data est gratia secundum mensuram donationis christi etcet. idem. ultimo. scientes quoniam unusquisque quodcumque fecerit bonum hoc percipiet a domino etcet. prima. ad

men, and the blasphemies by which they blaspheme, but he who shall blaspheme against the Holy Spirit shall never have forgiveness." Therefore one sin is greater than another. See also Luke 12 (12:47–48) "And that servant who knew the will of his lord, and did not prepare himself, and did not do according to his will, shall be beaten much, but he that didn't know, and did things worthy of a beating, shall be beaten only a little." Therefore some are punished more. Luke 20 (20:47) "These shall receive greater damnation." Therefore one is punished more than another. See also John 19 (19:11) "Therefore, he who has delivered me to you has the greater sin," Therefore one sin is more serious than another. Further see 2 Peter 2 (2:9) "reserve the wicked," and further (2:10) "and especially those who walk after the flesh." Therefore one sins more than another and so shall be punished more severely. Further Apocalypse 19 (19:6–7) "in the cup in which she has mixed, mix double unto her. As much as she has glorified herself, and lived in delicacies, so much torment and sorrow give to her." Therefore according to the degree of the faults there will be greater or lesser torments. Further, God is just because He punishes one more than another, as justice demands.

That merits and rewards are not equal

Matthew 13 (13:8) "And others fell upon good ground and they brought forth fruit, some a hundredfold, some sixtyfold, and others thirtyfold," and the same in 18 (18:4) "Whoever therefore shall humble himself just as this little child, he is the greater in the kingdom of heaven." See also 19 (19:28) "Amen, I say to you, that you who have followed me, in the regeneration, when the Son of man shall sit on the seat of his majesty, you shall also sit on twelve seats judging the twelve tribes of Israel." Also Luke 6 (6:38) "For with the same measure that you measured, it shall be measured to you again." Further 7 (7:47) "Many sins are forgiven her, because she has loved much. But to he who loves less, less is forgiven." See also the last chapter of John (21:15) "Jesus said to Simon Peter: 'Simon son of John, do you love me more than these?'" Further in 1 Corinthians 3 (3:8) "And every man shall receive his own reward, according to his own labor." Further 15 (15:41–42) "One is the glory of the sun, another the glory of the moon, and another the glory of the stars. For star differs from star in glory." Also 2 Corinthians 9 (9:6) "He who sows sparingly, shall also reap sparingly, and he who sows in blessings, shall also reap blessings in eternal life." In the last chapter of Galatians (6:8) "what things a man shall sow, those also shall he reap." Ephesians 4 (4:7) "But to every one of you is given grace, according to the measure of the giving of Christ." Again at the end (6:8) "Knowing that whatever good thing any man shall do, the same shall he receive from the Lord." 1 Timothy 5 (5:17) "Let the

---

16 ille...20 paucis] Luc. 12:47-48 (fecit) facit | plagis] om. *Vulg.*) 20 hi...21 dampnationem] Luc. 20:47. 22 propterea...23 habet] Ioh. 19:11. 24 iniquos...25 carnem] 2 Pet. 2:9-10. 27 in...29 luctum] Apoc. 18:6-7 (poculo) add. quo *Vulg.*) XV.3.2 alia...3 aliud^1] Matt. 13:8. 4 quicumque...5 celorum] Matt. 18:4. 6 amen...9 israel] Matt. 19:28. 9 eadem...10 uobis] Luc. 6:38 (messi) mensi *Vulg.*) 11 remittuntur...13 diligit] Luc. 7:47. 13 dicit...14 his] Ioh. 21:15. 15 uniusquisque...16 laborem] 1 Cor. 3:8. 17 alia^1...19 mortuorum] 1 Cor. 15:41-42. 20 qui^1...22 eternam] 2 Cor. 9:6 (uitam eternam) om. *Vulg.*) 22 que...23 metet] Gal. 6:8. 24 Vnicuique...25 christi] Eph. 4:7. 26 scientes...27 domino] Eph. 6:8 (percipiet) recipiet *Vulg.*)

XV.2.29 etcet] om. *P* XV.3.24 nostrum] vestrum *P*

27 apocalypsis|fol. 81ra *P* XV.3.17 claritas^3|fol. 81rb *P*

timotheum. v. Qui bene presunt presbyteri duplici honore digni habeantur maxime qui laborant in uerbo et doctrina etcet. preterea deus est iustus et reddit unicuique secundum opera sua. ergo plus uel minus reddet unicuique de premio. cum diuersa sint merita uniuscuiusque. Ex hiis patet expressim quod peccata et supplicia non equalia neque premia et merita.

Quod peccata et supplicia et premia et merita sunt equalia

[Patarenus:] Ad romanos. iii°. non enim est distinctio. omnes enim peccauerunt et egent gloria dei etcet. ergo equalia sunt peccata.

Catholicus: Respondeo. non loquitur de equalitate peccatorum sed ostendit omnes populos peccasse scilicet iudeum et gentilem et omnes egere gratia christi.

[Patarenus:] Item. jacobum. ii°. qui autem totam legem obseruauerit offendat autem in uno factus est omnium reus etcet. ergo tantum punitur quis pro uno peccato quantum pro multis. ergo peccata et supplicia sunt equalia.

Catholicus: Respondeo quia factus est omnium reus pro tanto quia uitam eternam non habebit. Sicut non habuisset si nullum seruasset et quia intrabit ignem eternum. nec dixit beatus iacobus quod tantum dampnetur uel quod tantum peccauerit.

[Patarenus:] Preterea uos romani dicitis quod in baptismo equaliter peccata et pene dimittuntur. nec aliquam penitenciam baptizatis imponitis. quod idem nos dicimus et seruamus de manus impositione ergo concordare uidetis nobiscum quod peccata sunt equalia cum penis eorum si equaliter dimittuntur.

Catholicus: Respondeo. quia equaliter dimmituntur peccata et pene in baptismo non est ideo quod equalia fuerit sed est ex uirtute baptismi et spirituali prerogatiua sacramento a ihesu christo collata. Sed respondete mihi uos patareni. Nonne plus punitis uos ad inuicem de uno maiori peccato quam de uno minori. et scio quod facitis. Sed aut iniuste facitis aut iuste. siquidem iniuste ergo estis iniusti. Si autem iuste facitis ergo deus est iniustus qui hic non facit cum iustitia non seruet. et sic uos super luciferiam facitis uos iustiores domino. Sed lucifer non fecit. suffecit ei ad culmen superbie sue facere se equale deo. et ideo magis debetis cruciari quam ille qui altius superbitis. hinc est quod beatus petrus in secunda. ii°. dicit de uobis magis autem eos qui post carnem in concupiscentia immunditiae ambulant dominationem contempnunt. audaces sibi placentes ... ubi angeli fortitudine et uirtute cum sint maiores non portunt aduersus

priests who rule well be considered worthy of double honor, especially those who labor in the word and doctrine." Further God is just, and renders to each according to his works, therefore to each one shall He mete out more or less of rewards, since the merits of each are different. From these passages it is completely clear that sins and punishments are not equal, nor are rewards and merits.

That sins and sufferings and rewards and merits are equal

[Pat:] Romans 3 (3:22) "for there is no distinction, For all have sinned, and are in need of the glory of God." Therefore sins are equal.

Cath: I respond. This is not speaking of equality of sins but rather is demonstrating that all peoples have sinned, namely, that the Jews and the gentiles are all in need of the grace of Christ.

[Pat:] See James 2 (2:10) "And whoever shall keep the whole law, but offend in one point, has become guilty of all." Therefore one is punished for one sin as much as for many, so sins and punishments are equal.

Cath: I respond that he has been made guilty of all things, to the extent that he shall not have eternal life, just as he would not have had it if he had observed nothing, and therefore he shall enter into eternal fire. Neither did Blessed James say that one is so much damned nor that one has much sinned.

[Pat:] Further you Romans say that in baptism sins and punishments are equally remitted, nor is any penance imposed on the baptized. We all say and hold the same thing concerning the imposition of hands, therefore you seem to agree with us that sins are equal if their penalties are equally remitted.

Cath: I reply that while sins and punishments are equally remitted in baptism, it is not because they are all equal but rather it is by the power of baptism and of the spiritual privileges conferred on the sacrament by Jesus Christ. But answer me this, you Patarenes. Why do you punish one another more for a greater sin, than for a lesser one? And I know that you do this. But either you do it justly or unjustly. So if you do it unjustly then you are unjust. But if you do it justly then God is unjust who does not do this, for He does not observe this with justice, and thus you, who are more just than God, do more than Lucifer, but Lucifer does not do this, for he considered it sufficient to make himself equal to God in the height of his pride, and so you ought to be tortured worse than he, since you demonstrate an even higher pride. Hence Blessed Peter says in his second letter about you (2:10–11) "And especially them who walk after the flesh in the lust of uncleanness, and despise government, audacious, self willed ... Where angels, who are greater in strength and

---

28 Qui...30 doctrina] 1 Tim. 5:17.   XV.4.3 non...4 dei] Rom. 3:22-23.   10 autem...12 reus] Iac. 2:10 (qui] quicumque | obseuauerit] seruauerit *Vulg.*)   39 magis...44 iudicium] 2 Pet. 2:10-11 (aduersus] aduersum *Vulg.*)

XV.4.17 seruasset] add. ei *F*   22 baptizatis] baptismatis *F*   24 uidetis] om. *F* with space left.   25 si] sed *P*   26 quia] add. quod *P*   28 uirtute] add. et *P* exp.   32 Sed...facitis²] om. *P*   38 est] om. *P*

XV.4.5 sunt|fol. 62r *F*   13 ergo|fol. 81va *P*   38 altius|fol. 81vb *P*

execrabile iudicium etcet. hoc est dictum quod non puniuntur quasi demones in respectu uestri.

Patarenus: Mattheus. xx. uenientes autem et primi arbitrati sunt quod plus essent accepturi. acceperunt autem et ipsi singulos denarios etcet. ergo equalia sunt premia et per consequentiam paria sunt et merita.

Catholicus: Respondeo quod fuit parabola quam induxit dominus ad ostendende quod non minoris meriti et premii essent christiani quam fuerunt iudei. unde supra in proximo capitulo dixerat de apostolis. uos qui secuti estis me etcet. et omnis qui relinquerit domum etcet. et infra conclusit. multi autem erunt primi nouissimi et nouissimi primi etcet. et postea inmediate adiecit parabolam istam ut ostenderet quod de statu christianorum loqueretur ad statum iudeorum redit infra. ad eandem conclusionem dicens. sic erit nouissimi primi et primi nouissimi etcet. et quod fuerit parabola patet ex illo uerbo et accipientes murmurabant aduersus patremfamilias etcet. in patria enim eterna ubi mensurabuntur merita non quod erit murmure. Et quod iste fuerit intellectus domini ostendit illico in lucam xiiii. ubi dicit cum uideritis abraam et ysaac et iacob. et omnes prophetas in regno dei uos autem expelli foras et uenient ab oriente et occidente et aquilone et austro et accumbent in regno dei. et ecce sunt nouissimi qui erant primi et sunt primi qui erant nouissimi etcet. uel fuit parabola contra presumentes de longitudine temporis in quo penitenciam egerunt et contempnentes illos qui tardius inceperunt quasi diceret. Non superbiant aliquid de penitentia multi temporis. quia possunt fieri equales illis propter maiorem feruorem qui tardius incipiunt. uel loquitur de denario increato quem omnes sancti simile recipiunt qui dicitur in singulari et in plurali propter unitatem essentie et trinitatem personarum. uel quia bonus est essentialiter et plures in nobis operatur effectus. Nec obstat quod legitur arbitrati sunt quod plures essent accepturi.

Patarenus: idem. xxv. accedens autem et qui duo talenta acceperat etcet. et infra. ait illi dominus Euge serue bone et fidelis. quia super pauca fuisti fidelis super multa te constitutam. intra in gaudium domini tui etcet. ecce quod tantum recepit ille qui minus fecit quantum qui plus. ergo sunt equalia premia.

Catholicus: Respondeo. non plus fecit si recte confideas. uel non dicitur quod tantum receperit. sed quod recepit gaudium domini sui. quod alius receperat id est uitam eternam.

power, do not bring against themselves an accursed judgment." Hence it is said that they are not punished like the demons in your conception.

Pat: Matthew 20 (20:10) "But when the first men also came, they thought that they should receive more, and they also each received a denarius." Therefore rewards are equal and, as a consequence, merits are also equal.

Cath: I respond that the parable which the Lord gave was to show that those who were Christians would receive no fewer rewards and merits than the Jews. So above in the next chapter He spoke to the apostles (Mt 19:28) "you who have followed me." (19:29) "and all who have left home" and He concludes (19:30) "but many who are first shall be last, and the last shall be first." And immediately after He added that parable that He might clarify that He is speaking about the state of the Christians, He returns to the state of the Jews below, coming to the same conclusion, saying "that the first shall be last and the last shall be first." and that the parable was clear from that passage (Mt 20:11) "And receiving it they murmured against the master of the house." For in the eternal fatherland where merits shall be measured, there shall be no murmuring. And that this was the Lord's understanding is shown in Luke 14 where he said (13:28–30) "when you shall see Abraham, Isaac and Jacob and all the prophets in the kingdom of God and you yourselves thrust out. And there shall come from the east and the west, and the north and the south, and they shall sit down in the kingdom of God. And behold, those who are last shall be first, and those who are first that shall be last." Or there was the parable against those who made presumptions from the length of time in which they had done penance and condemned those who came later, as if to say, let them not glory at all in their long-lasting penance, for they have become equal to them on account of the great fervor of those who began later, or he was speaking of the uncreated 'denarius' by which all saints shall receive similarly which is called in the singular on account of the unity of essence and in the plural by the Trinity of Persons, or because the good is one, yet in us it is plural in its worked effects. Nor does it oppose what we read that they thought that they should have received more than one.

Pat: In the same chapter 25 (25:22) "And he also that had received the two talents," and further the Lord said (25:23) "Well done, good and faithful servant. Because you have been faithful in small things, I will place you over many things, enter into the joy of your Lord." See how he who did less received the same as he who did more. Therefore rewards are equal.

Cath: I respond. He did not do more if you rightly consider it, or rather it is not said that he received so much, but that he received the joy of his Lord which another had received, that is, eternal life.

---

46 uenientes…48 denarios] Matt. 20:10.   54 uos…56 primi²] Matt. 19:28-30.   61 et…62 patremfamilias] Matt. 20:11.   65 cum… 70 nouissimi] Luc. 13:28-30 (erant¹] erunt | erant²] erunt *Vulg.*)   82 et…83 acceperat] Matt. 25:22 (accedens] accessit *Vulg.*)   83 ait… 86 tui] Matt. 25:23 (dominus] add. deus *Vulg.*)

51 minoris] om. *F*   57 istam] add. et *P*   65 illico] om. *F* | in lucam] om. *P*   67 foras] om. *P*   72 inceperunt] ireceperunt *P*   73 de] om. *P*   78 uel…81 accepturi] om. *F*

61 patet|fol. 82ra *P*   73 superbiant|fol. 62v *F*   86 tantum|fol. 82rb *P*

De septem ecclesie sacramentis. quomodo et qualiter spiritus sanctus datur

Tractauimus supra de articulis fidei et de erroribus quos habent patareni circa illos. excepto de illo articulo scilicet credo in sanctam ecclesiam catholicam etcet. quem dimittimus ex certa scientia in librum tertium. ubi agitur de communibus erroribus hereticorum eo quod omnes circa illum naufragium patiuntur. subsequenter autem uidendum est de. vii. ecclesie sacramentis et quomodo et qualiter spiritus sanctus datur in illis. ubi sciendum est primo quomodo kathari errent circa ista. dicunt enim non esse nisi duo sacramenta fidei scilicet manus impositionem quam confirmationem apellamus et manus impositionem que fit in sacrorum ordinem datione et sunt quidam ex eis qui non nisi unum sacramentum ipsam uocant habentem officia duo. cetera uero negant sacramenta et per consequentiam asserunt quod in eis non datur spiritus sanctus. de datione uero spiritus sancti equaliter errant. Dicunt enim quod essentialiter datur et ab homine et in his concordat omnes. quotiens autem detur. discordant ad inuicem quia quidam dicunt quod numquam datur nisi semel et quod semel datus nunquam potest amitti. Alii uero dicunt quod pluries potest dari. potest perdi et iterum recuperari. Nos autem per uiam ueritatis ambulantes dicimus quod. vii. sunt ecclesiastica sacramenta et quod in eis omnibus datur spiritus. paraclitus prout hic inferius in singulis eorum rubricis ostendemus. spiritum autem sanctum dicimus non substantialiter sed per carismata dari. et non ab homine sed a solo deo. et quod pluries datur perditur et recuperatur. prout ista in presenti rubrica tam per rationes naturales quam scripturas diuinas per singula declarabimus.

Probatio per rationes naturales quod spiritus sanctus non datur substantialiter

Cum spiritus sanctus datur aut aliud sit quam prius erat. aut non sit aliud. siquidem est aliud sit. aut quid sit aliud circa substantiam eius aut non. siquidem aliud sit circa substantiam eius. ergo est localis et mutabilis et sic non esset deus. quod falsum est. prout probatum est supra in iiii^a. rubrica. siquidem aliud non sit circa substantiam eius. sed tantum in effectu in nobis ab ipso operatio. ergo non datur substantialiter sed per carismata tamen. siquidem dicas quod in datione spiritus sancti non aliud fiat quam erat antea. non ergo potest dici quod spiritus sanctus detur. et sic patet per istas inconuenientias quod spiritus sanctus non substantialiter sed per carismata datur. item si spiritus sanctus datur omnibus bonis hominibus

On the Seven Sacraments of the Church, how and in what manner the Holy Spirit is given

We have treated above the articles of faith and the errors which the Patarenes hold about them, with the exception of that article, namely "I believe in the holy Catholic Church," which from certain knowledge we confined to the third book, where the subject is the common errors of the heretics in which they all make shipwreck of their faith. But now one must turn attention to the seven sacraments and in what way and manner the Holy Spirit is given in them. It should be noted first how the Cathars err concerning this, for they say there are none other than two sacraments of faith, namely the imposition of hands — what we call confirmation — and the imposition of hands which results in the granting of sacred orders. There are some of them who say that there is but one sacrament, which has two purposes. Others yet deny sacraments and, as a consequence, assert that in them the Holy Spirit is not given, yet they equally err about the giving of the Holy Spirit. For they say that He is essentially given and by man, and in this they all agree, but as to how often He is given they disagree among themselves, for certain of them say that He is not given but once and that, once given, He cannot be lost.[1] Yet others say that He can be given many times, for He can be lost and later recovered.[2] But we who walk in the way of truth say that the ecclesial sacraments are seven and that the Spirit is granted in all of them, the Paraclete, as we shall show in every single rubric below, but we say that the Holy Spirit is not given according to His substance, but through His grace, and not by man, but only by God alone, and that which is given can be lost and recovered many times, and these concepts will be made plain in the present rubric equally through natural reason as by the divine scriptures.

Proof that the Holy Spirit is not given substantially from natural arguments

When the Holy Spirit is given, either He would be other than He was before, or He would not be other. Accordingly, if other [than He was], then either what He is, is another according to His substance or not. So if it is according to His substance, then He is local and changeable, and so He could not be God. This is false, just as was established above in the fourth rubric. He is not another however, but only in His effect in us by His own operation. He is not given substantially but only through the sacraments. If you say that in the giving of the Holy Spirit, a man is no other than what he was before, then you cannot say that it is the Holy Spirit that is given and so it is clear by these inconsistencies that the Holy Spirit is given through grace and not substantially. Yet if the Holy

---

XVI.1.1 De...2 datur] De sacramentis. vii fidei et de datione spiritus sancti. *F* **7** eo] om. *P* **11** kathari] katari *P* **20** equaliter] add. detur et *PF* **21** omnes] homines *F* **24** amitti] admitti *P* **30** carismata] karismata *P* XVI.2.3 aut] ad *P* **9** ab] add. o *P* exp. **11** carismata] karismata *F* **12** non ergo] transp. *P*

XVI.1.25 potest¹|fol. 82va *P*

---

1) Moneta, 74ff. | 2) Sacconi, c. 6.

substantialiter. ergo omnes boni homines habent in se spiritum sanctum sed spiritus sanctus datur in ipsum hominem. ergo spiritus sanctus totius incarnatur et in tot hominibus quotiens et a quo datur atque recipitur quod absurdum est sompniare. igitur tamen per carismata datur.

Probatio per rationes naturales quod sanctus spiritus non datur ab homine sed a deo solo

Omne dans procedit datum uirtute uel auctoritate. aut saltem equalitatem habet cum illo. ergo spiritus sanctus non ab homine. quia homo non procedit illum. nec uirtute nec auctoritate. igitur a patre et filio procedit tantum. apud quos ipsius processionis est auctoritas et cum quibus eius maiestatis adoratur equalitas. item quod datur habet originem ab eo a quo datur ergo homo spiritus sanctus esset origo. sed spiritus daretur ab ipso quod fatuissimum esset dicere.

Item si spiritus sanctus daretur ab homine. homo esset causa dationis spiritus sancti. sed qualis est effectus talis est et causa. sed datio spiritus sancti est purissima. ergo et homo purissimus esset. quod non est uerum.

Item possibile est quod iste homo non habet in se spiritum sanctum. ergo non potest mihi dare illum. secundum opinionem tuam loquor qui dicis spiritum sanctum ab homine dari. sed scire statum hominis est inhumanum et sic esset salus semper incerta. si esset in homine quod stultum est cogitare.

Item potest esse quod impossibile est huic homini habere spiritum sanctum. ergo impossibile esset ei habere salutem. quod falsum est. quia christus dicit. uenite a me omnes qui honerati et laborati estis etcet. preterea plus posset homo quam deus si hoc esset. quia per bonam uoluntatem ad quam respicit deus. non posset quis habere salutem. et posset habere illam per hominis tactum et non sine illo. quod absurdissimum est.

Item qua ratione per hominem solum daretur. spiritus sanctus eadem ratione dat perderetur. siquidem ille qui dedit perderet illum. quod etiam creditis. sed impossibile est quod aliquis illorum qui uisus est dare non amiserit illum. aut non fuerit sine illo et sic nullus esset saluus in terra. preterea hoc dicendo tota spes salutis in homine ponitur quod est contra sacram scripturam quam dicit. maledictus homo qui ponit spes suam in homine.

Spirit would be given substantially to all men, therefore all good men have the Holy Spirit in them. But the Holy Spirit is given into the man himself, therefore the Holy Spirit is wholly incarnated in each and every man as often and by whom He is given and received, which is absurd to contemplate. Therefore He is given by grace.

Proof by natural reasons that the Holy Spirit is not given by man but by God alone

All giving proceeds by being given either by power or authority, or at least has equality with its giver. Therefore the Holy Spirit is not given by man, for man does not go before Him by either power or authority. Therefore He proceeds only from the Father and Son, by whom is the authority for His procession and with whom the equality of His majesty is adored. Further something that is given has its origin from that by which it is given, therefore man would be the origin of the Holy Spirit. But the Holy Spirit would then be given by the same man himself which thing is totally foolish to say.

Further, if the Holy Spirit were given by man, then man would be the cause of the conferral of the Holy Spirit. But the effect is like the cause. Yet the giving of the Spirit is most holy and most pure, therefore man is most pure, which is not true.

Further it is possible that that man does not have the Holy Spirit in himself, therefore he cannot give Him to me. I speak according to your opinion who say that the Holy Spirit is to be given by man. But to know the state of a man is itself inhuman, and thus the salvation of a man would be always uncertain, if it were dependent upon a man, which is stupid to think.

Further, can it be that it is impossible for this man to have the Holy Spirit? Therefore it would be impossible for him to have salvation. That is false, because Christ said: (Mt 11:28) "come to me all you who labor and are burdened." Further, man would be able to do more than God if this were the case, since through a good will, which God regards, one would not be able to be saved, and would be able to have it by the touch of man and not without it, which is most absurd.

Further, by what method could the Holy Spirit be given by man alone? By the same method he gives [the Holy Spirit], [the Holy Spirit] would be lost, if in fact he who has given [the Holy Spirit] might lose Him, which you all also believe, but it is impossible that any of them who is seen to give might not lose Him. Or else he would not have been without Him and thus no one would be saved on earth. Further in saying this all hope of salvation is put in man which is contrary to the sacred scriptures that say (Jr 17:5) "cursed is the man who puts his hope in men."

XVI.3.25 uenite...estis] Matt. 11:28 (a) ad *Vulg.*)   38 maledictus...39 homine] Ier. 17:5 (ponit spes suam in homine] confidunt in homine *Vulg.* Common reading in medieval sermons.)

19 totius] totus F   20 quo] quot F   XVI.3.2 deo solo] transp. P   7 quos] quod P   10 sanctus] sancti F   12 homo] add. non P exp.   18 opinionem] oppinionem P   22 homini...23 habere] habere hominem habentem P

XVI.2.20 et|fol. 82vb P   XVI.3.2 solo|fol. 63r F   23 impossibile|fol. 83ra P

Probatio per scripturas quod spiritus sanctus non datur substantialiter sed per carismata

Lucas ultimo. Ego mittam promissum patris mei in uos. uos autem sedete in ciuitate quo usque induamini uirtute ex alto etcet. ecce quod non dixit christus quod apostoli recepturi essent spiritum sanctum substantialiter sed uirtutem eius tantum. Item. prima. ad corinthios. xii. diuisiones uero gratiarum sunt. idem autem spiritus et diuisiones ministrationum sunt idem autem dominus et diuisiones operationem sunt idem autem deus qui operatur omnia in omnibus. unicuique autem datur manifestatio spiritus ad utilitatem. alii quidem per spiritum datur sermo sapientie alii autem sermo scientie etcet. et infra. emulamini autem karismata meliora etcet. ecce quomodo apostolus dicit quod idem spiritus idem dominus. idem deus operatur in factis diuersos effectos gratiarum et dat eis diuersa carismata et non dicit quod ipse detur substantialiter. item. actus. ii°. baptizetur unusquisque uestrum in nomine ihesu christi in remissionem peccatorum uestrorum et accipietis donum spiritus sancti etcet. Non dixit quod ipsi acciperent substantialiter spiritum sanctum. sed dixit. accipietis donum spiritus sancti. ergo spiritus sanctus non substantialiter. sed per karismata datur.

Probatio per scripturas quod spiritus sanctus datur a solo deo

johannes. i°. Qui misit me baptiçare in aqua ille mihi dixit. Super quem uideris spiritum descendentem et manentem super eum. hic est qui baptizat in spiritu sancto etcet. ergo quicumque homo baptiszat exterius uel aliud det sacramentum solus deus dat gratiam spiritus sancti interius. idem xiii. et quodcumque petieritis patrem in nomine meo. hoc faciam etcet. ergo omne bonum facit deus. Non ergo petrus gallus dat spiritum sanctum. sed dedit spiritum galli filie conradi de mario confratris sui. Item ad romanos x. si autem gratia iam non ex operibus etcet. ad idem. item. i^a. ad corinthios. i°. Hoc autem dico quod unusquisque uestrum dicit. Ego sum pauli. ego autem appollo. ego uero cephe. ego autem christi. Diuisus est christus. numquid paulus crucifixus est pro nobis. aut in nomine pauli baptizati estis. quasi dicat non? Redarguit ergo paulus corinthios qui de gratia baptismi. non totum honorem attribuerant christo deo. sed parte attribuebant hominibus. igitur tota a

Proof from the scriptures that the Holy Spirit is not given substantially, but by grace

In the last chapter of Luke (24:49) "And I send the promise of my Father upon you, but stay in the city until you are endowed with power from on high." See that Christ did not say that the Apostles were about to receive the Holy Spirit substantially but His power only. Further 1 Corinthians 12 (12:4–8) "Now there are varieties of graces, but the same Spirit, and there are varieties of ministries, but the same Lord, and there are varieties of operations, but the same God, who works all in all. And the manifestation of the Spirit is given to every man for profit. To one indeed, by the Spirit is given the word of wisdom, and to another, the word of knowledge, according to the same Spirit," and later (12:31) "be zealous for the better graces." See how the Apostle says that the same Spirit of the Lord — the same God — works in diverse ways in the effects of graces and gives diverse gifts to them and he does not say that the Spirit is given substantially. Further Acts 2 (2:38) "let each one of you be baptized in the name of Jesus Christ, for the remission of your sins and you shall receive the gift of the Holy Spirit." But he said receive the gift of the Holy Spirit, therefore the Holy Spirit is not given substantially, but is given through grace.

Proof from the scriptures that the Holy Spirit is given by God alone

John 1 (1:33) "he who sent me to baptize with water said to me, 'He upon whom you will see the Spirit descending, and remaining upon him, is he who baptizes with the Holy Spirit." So whatever man baptizes exteriorly or lets another give the sacrament, God alone gives the interior grace of the Holy Spirit. Further in 14 (14:13) "and whatsoever you shall ask the Father in my name, that will I do." Therefore God causes all good. It is not Peter Gallus,[1] then, giving the Holy Spirit, but he gives the spirit of Gallus to the daughter of his confrere Conrad de Mario. As Romans 10 has it (11:6) "And if by grace, it is not now by works." On the same topic is 1 Corinthians 1 (1:12–13) "Now I say, that every one of you declares, 'I am of Paul, and I am of Apollo, and I am of Cephas, and I of Christ.' Is Christ divided? Was Paul then crucified for us? or were you baptized in the name of Paul?" As if to say 'no.' Paul therefore convicts the Corinthians, who did not attribute the whole of their honor of the grace of baptism to Christ who is God, but partly attributed it to men. Therefore all

---

XVI.4.3 Ego...5 alto] Luc. 24:49 (mittam) mitto *Vulg.*) 8 diuisiones...14 scientie] 1 Cor. 12:4-8. 14 emulamini...15 meliora] 1 Cor. 12:31. 19 baptizetur...21 sancti] Act. 2:38. XVI.5.3 Qui...6 sancto] Ioh. 1:33. 8 et...9 faciam] Ioh. 14:13. 12 si...13 operibus] Rom. 11:6. 14 Hoc...18 non] 1 Cor. 1:12-13 (nobis) uobis *Vulg.*)

XVI.4.2 sed] si *F* | carismata] karismata *P* 6 essent] tenent *P* 22 acciperent] inciperent *F* XVI.5.1 sanctus] add. a solo deo *F* 2 a...deo] om. *F* 20 attribuerant] actribuerant *P* 21 attribuebant] actribuebant *P*

XVI.4.10 autem|fol. 83rb *P* XVI.5.14 unusquisque|fol. 83va *P* 15 uestrum|fol. 63v *F*

---

[1] Peter Gallus was a Cathar bishop with whom the author likely had personal contact. For Gallus as interlocutor, see Käppeli, 305-311.

deo est. qui pro nobis passus est et cuius nomine recepimus illam. ad hoc est quod dicit infra. iii°. nonne carnales estis et secundum hominem ambulatis? cum enim quis dicat. ego quidem sum pauli. alius autem ego sum appoli. nonne homines estis etcet. et infra. ego plantaui appolo rigauit. sed deus incrementum dedit. itaque neque qui plantat est aliquid neque qui rigat. sed qui incrementum dat etcet. et infra. neque itaque glorietur in hominibus etcet. et prophetam dicitur maledictus qui confidit in homine etcet. uere ergo maledicti eritis uos miseri patareni. qui non in dei misericordia sed in hominis superbia confiditis. idem. iiii°. sic nos existimet homo ut ministros christi. ergo non ut deus. idem xii. hec autem omnia operantur unus atque idem spiritus diuidens singulis prout uult. non ergo patarenus. qui non potest facere unum capillum nigrum aut album. idem xv. gratia autem dei sum id quod sum etcet. non dixit gratia hominis. item. ii^a. ad corinthios. iii. non quod sufficientes simus cogitare aliquid a nobis quasi ex nobis sed sufficientia nostra ex deo est. non dixit ex homine. item ad ephesios. ii°. cuius gratia uos estis saluati etcet. et infra. gratia estis saluati per fidem hoc non ex uobis. dei enim donum est. non ex operibus enim quis glorietur etcet. ergo a solo deo est gratia salutis. item. ad phylippenses. ii°. deus est enim qui operatur in uobis et uelle et perficere etcet. non ergo homo. item actus. iii°. uiri israelite quid admiramini in hoc aut uos intuemini quid? aut potestate fecimus hunc ambulare. deus abraam. deus ysaac. deus iacob. etcet. et iiii°. nec enim aliud nomen est sub celo datum hominibus in quo oporteat nos saluos fieri etcet. ergo nulla saluus est nisi per ihesum christum. idem in eodem. qui cum orassent motus est locus in quo erat congregati et repleti sunt omnes spiritu sancto etcet. non ergo dabant eum apostoli sed orabunt deum ut ipse daret illum. idem. xi. si ergo eamdem gratiam dedit illis deus sicut et nobis qui credidimus in dominum etcet. ergo manifestum est quod solus deus dat gratiam sancti spiritus. idem. xiiii. ubi audierunt apostoli barnabas et paulus cum scissis tunicis suis etcet. et infra. nos mortales sumus similes uobis etcet. ergo tota gloria deo danda est. ad hoc est illud ibi. ad timotheus. i°. Regi autem seculorum immortali inuisibili deo soli honor et gloria in secula seculorum amen. etcet. et apocalypsis. xiiii. timete dominum et date illi honorem etcet. ergo omnis honor deo dandus est et omnis gloria ei referenda est. item in ysaias. xlii. dicit dominus. Ego

things are of God, who suffered for us and in whose name we receive it, as it has further down (3:3–4) "are you not carnal, and walk according to man? For while one says, I indeed am of Paul, and another, I am of Apollo, are you not men?" and later (3:6–7) "I have planted, Apollo watered, but God gave the increase. Therefore, neither he who plants is anything, nor he who waters, but God who gives the increase." And later (3:21) "therefore let no man glory in men." And the prophet says (Jr 17:5) "Cursed is he who trusts in men." Therefore truly cursed are you miserable Patarenes, since you place trust not in the mercy of God, but in the pride of men. See also chapter 4 (4:1) "Let a man consider us as the ministers of Christ." Therefore not as God. Later in 12 (12:11) "But all these things one and the same Spirit works, dividing to every one according as he will." Therefore not the Patarene, who cannot make one hair black or white, for see 15 (15:10) "But by the grace of God, I am what I am." He did not say by the grace of man. Further 2 Corinthians 3 (3:5) "Not that we are sufficient to think anything of ourselves, as of ourselves, but our sufficiency is from God." He did not say from man. Also Ephesians 2 (2:5) "by whose grace you are saved." and later (2:8) "For you are saved by grace through faith, and that not of yourselves, for it is the gift of God. Not of works, that no man may glory." Therefore the grace of salvation is from God alone. Further in Philippians 2 (2:13) "For it is God who works in you, both to will and to accomplish." Therefore not man. Also Acts 3 (3:12–13) "O men of Israel, why do you wonder at this? Or why look you upon us, as if by our strength or power we had made this man walk? The God of Abraham, and the God of Isaac, and the God of Jacob." And in chapter 4 (4:12) "For there is no other name under heaven given to men, by which we must be saved." Therefore no one at all is saved unless through Jesus Christ. In the same place (4:31) "Who, when they had prayed, the place where they were gathered was moved, and they were all filled with the Holy Spirit." Therefore the Apostles did not give Him but they prayed that God might give Him. Also 11 (11:17) "If then God gave them the same grace, just as to us also who believed in the Lord." Therefore it is clear that God alone gives the grace of the Holy Spirit. See also 14 where (14:13) "when the apostles Barnabas and Paul had heard, rending their clothes." And further (14:14) "We are also mortals, men like you." Therefore all glory is to be given to God, and 1 Timothy has it there (1:17) "Now to the king of ages, immortal, invisible, the only God, be honor and glory forever and ever. Amen." And Apocalypse (14:7) "Fear the Lord, and give him honor," therefore all honor is to be given to God and all glory is to be rendered to him.

---

23 nonne…26 estis] 1 Cor. 3:3-4. 27 ego…29 dat] 1 Cor. 3:6-7. 29 neque…30 hominibus] 1 Cor. 3:21. 31 homine] Ier. 17:5 (maledictus) add. homo *Vulg.*) 34 sic…christi] 1 Cor. 4:1. 35 hec…36 uult] 1 Cor. 12:11. 38 gratia…39 hominis] 1 Cor. 15:10. 40 non…42 est] 2 Cor. 3:5. 43 cuius…saluati] Eph. 2:5 (uos) uobis *Vulg.*) 44 gratia…45 glorietur] Eph. 2:8-9 (enim) add. ut ne *Vulg.*) 47 deus…48 perficere] Php. 2:13. 49 uiri…51 iacob] Act. 3:12-13 (uos) nos | fecimus] fecerimus *Vulg.*) 51 nec…53 fieri] Act. 4:12. 54 qui…56 sancto] Act. 4:31. 58 si…59 dominum] Act. 11:17. 61 audierunt…62 suis] Act. 14:13 (cumscissis) conscissis *Vulg.*) 62 nos…63 uobis] Act. 14:14. 64 Regi…66 amen] 1 Tim. 1:17. 67 timete…honorem] Apoc. 14:7. 69 dicit…70 me] Is. 43:25.

32 miseri] uniuersi P

39 hominis|fol. 83vb P 62 tunicis|fol. 84ra P

70 sum qui deleo iniquitates tuas propter me etcet. et in matheo. ii°. legitur solus deus dimittit peccata etcet. ergo peccatorum remissio non est ab homine sed a solo deo et sic patet ex superioribus quod gratia. spiritus. sancti non est ab homine sed a solo deo.

Quod gratiam spiritus sancti sepius potest dari et perdi et recuperari

Mattheus.v. uos estis sal terre etcet. et infra. uos estis lux mundi etcet. et x. non enim uos estis loquimini sed
5 spiritus patris uestri qui loquitur in uobis et iohannes. xv. uos mundi estis propter sermonem quem locutus sum uobis etcet. et infra sicut dilexit me pater et ego dilexi uos. manete in dilectione mea etcet. et infra. ego elegi uos de mundo etcet. Ex hiis patet expressim quod
10 apostoli habuerunt spiritum sanctum ante passionem domini quem postea circa ipsam amiserunt. maxime petrus in negatione saluatoris. Sed iterum receperunt eum post resurrectionem christi. ut legitur. iohannes. xx. hec cum dixisset insufflauit et dixit eis. accipite
15 spiritum sanctum etcet. et actus. ii°. et cum complerentur dies pentecostes etcet. igitur spiritus sanctus habitus potest perdi et iterum recuperari. item ad romanos. xi. uide ergo bonitatem et seueritatem dei in eos qui ceciderunt seueritatem. in te autem bonitatem
20 dei se permanseris in bonitate alioquin et tu excideris. sed illi si non permanserint in incredulitate inserentur etcet. igitur gratia perdita potest recuparari et habita potest amicti. item. iª. ad corinthios. v. omnino auditur inter uos fornicatio et talis fornicatio qualis nec
25 inter gentes ita ut uxorem patris sui aliquis habeat et uos inflati estis etcet. et de istis omnibus dixerat supra. iii°. Nescitis quia templum dei estis et spiritus dei habitat in uobis etcet. ergo isti corinthi habuerant spiritum sanctum quem postea amiserant per disen-
30 siones et alia peccata et istos amonet apostolus ad penitentiam ergo poterant recuperare gratiam spiritus sancti perditam sicut fecit ille incestuosus. de quo ibi dicit. quem in secunda epistola protestatur recepisse correctum. quod idem est de aliis hominibus ad hec
35 sunt. iiª. ad corinthios. vii. etsi ad horam uos contristauit nunc gaudeo. non quia contristati estis ad penitentiam. idem xii. et lugeam multos ex his qui ante peccauerunt et non egerunt penitentiam super immunditia et fornicationem etcet. Item ad Galatas. i°.

Further in Isaiah (43:25) "Thus says the Lord, 'I am he who blots out your iniquities for my own sake.'" And in Matthew 2 it is read (Mk 2:7 and Lk 5:21) "God alone remits sins." Therefore the remission of sins is not from men but from God alone, and it is clear from the foregoing that the grace of the Holy Spirit is not from men but from God alone.

That the grace of the Holy Spirit can be given and lost and recovered several times

Matthew 5 (5:13) "You are the salt of the earth," and further (5:14) "you are the light of the world," and in 10 (10:20) "For it is not you who shall speak but the spirit of your Father who shall speak in you." And John 15 (15:3) "Now you are clean by reason of the word, which I have spoken to you." And later (15:9) "I have chosen you out of the world." From these passages it is clear that the apostles had the Holy Spirit before the passion of the Lord, which they later lost, especially Peter in his denial of the Savior. But later they received Him after the resurrection of Christ, as is read in John 20 (20:22) "having said this he breathed on them and said to them, 'Receive the Holy Spirit.'" And Acts 2 (2:1) "and when the days of Pentecost were completed." Therefore the habit[1] of the Holy Spirit can be lost and later regained. See also Romans 11 (11:22–23) "See then the goodness and the severity of God towards those indeed that are fallen, the severity, but towards you, the goodness of God, if you abide in goodness, otherwise you also shall be cut off. And they also, if they do not remain in unbelief, they shall be grafted in." So then grace that has been lost can be recovered and one can be reclothed in the habit of grace. Further, 1 Corinthians 5 (5:1–2) "It is absolutely heard that among you there is fornication, and such fornication as the like is not among the heathens, that one should have his father's wife. And you are puffed up." And about all these things he said above (3:16) "Do you not know that you are the temple of God, and that the Spirit of God dwells in you?" Therefore these Corinthians had the Holy Spirit, which they later lost through dissensions and other sins, and these the Apostle counsels towards repentance, therefore they are able to recover the lost grace of the Holy Spirit, just like those incestuous ones. Of these he speaks in his second letter as having received correction, and it is the same for all men as he has in 2 Corinthians 7 (7:8–9) "although but for a time did make you sorrowful. Now I rejoice, not because you were made sorrowful, but because you were made sorrowful unto penance." The same is in 12 (12:21) "and I mourn many of them who sinned before, and have

---

71 solus...peccata] Conflation of Mar. 2:7 and Luc. 5:21. XVI.6.3 uos¹...terre] Matt. 5:13. | uos²...4 mundi] Matt. 5:14. 4 non...5 uobis] Matt. 10:20. 6 uos...7 uobis] Ioh. 15:3. 7 sicut...8 mea] Ioh. 15:9. 8 ego...9 mundo] Ioh. 15:19. 14 hec...15 sanctum] Ioh. 20:22. 15 et²...16 pentecostes] Act. 2:1. 18 uide...21 inserentur] Rom. 11:22-23. 23 omnino...26 estis] 1 Cor. 5:1-2. 27 Nescitis...28 uobis] 1 Cor. 3:16. 35 etsi...37 penitentiam] 2 Cor. 7:8-9. 37 et...39 fornicationem] 2 Cor. 12:21 (fornicationem) fornicatione *Vulg.*).

---

72 solo...73 deo] transp. F XVI.6.1 sepius] septies F 2 et¹] om. F 6 xv] iiii P 12 saluatoris] saluationis P 22 perdita] add. non P 23 amicti] amitti F 29 amiserant] ammiserant P 32 incestuosus] incetuosus P 39 immunditia] immunditiam P

XVI.6.8 manete|fol. 64r F 12 saluatoris|fol. 84rb P 39 immunditia|fol. 84va P

---

1) In the sense of the graced condition.

miror quod sic tam cito transferimini ab eo qui uos uocauit in gratiam christi etcet. et iii°. O insensati galathe quis uos fascinauit non obedire ueritati etcet. et infra qui ergo tribuit uobis spiritum et operatur uirtutes in uobis etcet. et vi. si preoccupatus fuerit homo in aliquo delicto uos qui spirituales estis huiusmodi instruite in spiritu lenitatis. considerans teipsum ne et tu tenteris etcet. et prima ad thessalonicenses ultimum. spiritum nolite extinguere etcet. et ii^a. ultimo si quis non obedit uerbo nostro per epistolam hunc notate et ne commisceamini cum illo ut confundatur et nolite quasi inimicum existimare sed corripite ut fratrem etcet. Item jacobum ultimo in finem. si quis ex uobis errauerit a ueritate et conuerterit quis eum etcet. item iude. ii°. arbores auptumnales bis mortue etcet. item. apocalypsis. ii°. memor esto unde excideris et age penitentiam et prima opera fac etcet. et iii°. tene quod habes ut nemo accipiat coronam tuam etcet. ex supradictis scripturis et ex aliis quasi innumeris probatur aperte quod gratiam spiritus sancti sepe et sepius potest haberi. perdi et iterum recuperari.

not done penance for uncleanness and fornication." Also in Galatians 1 (1:6) "I wonder that you are so soon removed from him who called you into the grace of Christ," and in 3 (3:1) "O foolish Galatians, who has bewitched you that you should not obey the truth." And later (3:5) "He therefore who gives to you the Spirit, and works miracles among you." And in chapter 6 (6:1) "if a man be worried over any fault, you who are spiritual, instruct him in the spirit of meekness, considering yourself, lest you also be tempted." And in the last chapter of 1 Thessalonians (5:19) "Do not extinguish the spirit." And 2 Thessalonians at the end (3:14–15) "if any man does not obey our word by this epistle, note that man and do not mix with him, that he may be ashamed. Yet do not consider him as an enemy, but admonish him as a brother." And in the last chapter of James, at the end (5:19) "if any of you err from the truth, and one convert him." Also Jude 2 (1:12) "trees of the autumn twice dead." And Apocalypse 2 (2:5) "Be mindful therefore from where you are fallen and do penance and do the first works." And 3 (3:11) "hold to what you have, so that no man might take your crown." From these scriptures here and from an innumerable amount of others it is clearly established that the grace of the Holy Spirit is often and many times able to be gained, lost, and thereafter recovered.

Quod spiritus sanctus datur substantialiter et ab homine et quod semel datus non potest recuperari uel secundum quosdam uel secundum alios semel datus non potest amplius perdi

Sicut distulisti tractare de septem sacramentis per singulas rubricas. sic et ego differo ibidem respondere tibi.

Patarenus: Iohannes xx. et dixit eis. accipite spiritum sanctum etcet. et sepe dixit dominus in euangelio quod mitteret apostolis spiritum paraclitum et in actibus apostolorum legitur in primo quod ipsi de celo receperunt spiritum sanctum et pluries inuenitur. quod alii fideles multi acceperunt et habuerunt spiritum sanctum. ergo spiritus sanctus datur substantialter.

Catholicus: Respondeo quod non est ibi illa glosa substantialiter. sed datur per carismata. quam glosam probaui in superioribus ueram esse. et est simile quod dominus ihesus christus loquitur de persona sua in mattheus ultimum. in fine dicens. et ecce uobiscum sum omnibus diebus usque ad consummationem seculi. constat enim quod in celum ascendebat. non amplius in terra personaliter moraturus. sed est cum fidelibus suis usque ad consummationem seculi per gratiam suam.

7 That the Holy Spirit is given substantially and by man and that, once given, cannot be recovered or — according to those or others — once given is not able any more to be lost

Just as you have deferred a treatment of the seven sacraments until the distinct sections, so I have deferred answering you.

Pat: John 20 (20:22) "and he said to them, 'receive the Holy Spirit," and the Lord often said in the gospels that He would send the Spirit Paraclete and in the Acts of the Apostles one reads in the first chapter that they received the Holy Spirit from heaven and found it many times, and that many others of the faithful received and possessed the Holy Spirit, therefore the Holy Spirit was granted substantially.

Cath: I respond that the gloss here is not 'substantially' but 'given in grace' just as I proved with the commentary above to be true, and that the Lord Jesus Christ speaks in a similar manner about His person in the last chapter of Matthew, at the end (28:20) "and behold I am with you always even unto the end of the age." For it remains that He ascended into heaven, not any longer remaining personally upon the earth, but He is with his faithful unto the end of the age through His grace.

---

40 miror...41 christi] Gal. 1:6.   41 O...42 ueritati] Gal. 3:1.   43 qui...44 uobis] Gal. 3:5.   44 si...47 tenteris] Gal. 6:1.   48 spiritum...extinguere] 1 Thes. 5:19.   49 si...52 fratrem] 2 Thes. 3:14-15.   53 si...54 eum] Iac. 5:19.   54 arbores...55 mortue] Iud. 1:12.   56 memor...57 fac] Apoc. 2:5.   57 tene...58 tuam] Apoc. 3:11.   **XVI.7.7** et...8 sanctum] Ioh. 20:22.   18 et...20 seculi] Matt. 28:20.

XVI.7.2 potest] add. amplius *F*   **8** dixit] om. *F* | dominus] add. dixit *F*   **9** mitteret] mittet *F*   **15** carismata] karismata *P*   **16** est simile] consimile *F*   **21** moraturus] moriturus *F*   **23** gratiam] generationem *P*

XVI.7.4 perdi|fol. 84vb *P*   **16** superioribus|fol. 64v *F*

Quod spiritus sanctus datur ab homine 8

Item idem in eodem. quorum remiseritis peccata etcet. sed remissio peccatorum nulla aliud est quam gratia spiritus sancti. ergo apostoli dederunt spiritum sanctum.

Catholicus: Respondeo. sic intelligitur illud. quorum remiseritis peccata id est remissa ostenderitis non errantibus clauibus. uel loquitur de pena peccatorum temporali ad quam tenentur peccatores dimissa eis a deo culpa per contritionem et pena eterna mutata in temporalem. quando contritio non fuit sufficiens ad illam totaliter delendam. Illam dico penam temporalem possunt dimittere sacerdotes totam uel partem potestate eis a christo tradita clauium et supple de hac materia infra libro iii°. in tractatu quod malus prelatus seu sacerdos uel predicator potest suo fungi officio in oppositione de hac auctoritate nobis ab hereticis facta.

Patarenus: Actus. viii. tunc imponebant manus super illos et accipiebant spiritum sanctum. cum uidisset autem symon quia per impositionem manus apostolorum daretur spiritus sanctus optulit eis pecuniam dicens date et mihi hanc potestatem etcet. ergo apostoli dabant spiritum sanctum.

Catholicus: Respondeo. Non dicit quod apostoli dedissent immo dicit ibi. quod orauerunt scilicet domini ut illi acciperent eum. ergo ipsi non dabant. sed deus per orationes eorum. Nec obstat quia dabatur in manus impositione ipsorum quia propter hoc non sequitur quod illi darent eum. sicut cum ex eo ad solere et calefio a sole. et fit hoc in exitu meo ad solem. et tamen ego non facio illum calorem sed soli et sicut cum dicitur. aqua transit per canalia ad prata et tamen de canalibus non procedit nec exit aqua illa. sed a fonte uel fluuio. sic gratia spiritus sancti datur per manus impositionem debite factam. non tamen ab homine sed a solo deo. Nec obstat dictum Symonis magi. qui errabit credens quod potestate hominum daretur spiritus sanctus. cuius locum uos cathari optinetis. quod ostendit beatus petrus cum dixit Existimasti enim donum dei pecunia possideri etcet. Non est ergo donum petrus galli spiritus sanctus. quod non fuit symonis petri sed dei benedicti et sublimis.

Quod spiritus sanctus semel datus et perditus non potest amplius recuperari 9

Matheus xii. qui autem dixerit contra spiritum sanctum non remittetur et neque in hoc seculo neque in futuro etcet. ergo peccatum in spiritum sanctum est irremiscibile quod intelligo de illo quod fit post

That the Holy Spirit is given by man

In the same place (20:23) "whose sins you shall forgive." But the remission of sins is nothing other than the grace of the Holy Spirit, therefore the Apostles gave the Holy Spirit.

Cath: I respond that it is understood thusly: whose sins you shall have forgiven, that is, shall have declared forgiven with the inerrant keys; or rather He speaks concerning the temporal punishment of sins to which sinners are held: their guilt has been forgiven by God and eternal punishment changed into temporal, since their contrition was not sufficient to erase the punishment entirely. I say that that penalty can be remitted totally or partly by a priest, on account of the power of the keys given to him by Christ, and this material is treated of in book 3, in the section about whether a bad prelate or priest can exercise his office, in opposition to this authority of ours made by the heretics.

Pat: Acts 8 (8:17–19) "Then they laid their hands upon them and they received the Holy Spirit. And when Simon saw that the Holy Spirit was given by the imposition of the hands of the apostles, he offered them money, saying, 'Give me this power too.'" Therefore the Apostles give the Holy Spirit.

Cath: I respond, he does not say that the Apostles gave, on the contrary he said that they prayed, namely, to the Lord that they might receive Him. Therefore they did not give Him, but it was God who granted Him by their prayers. Neither does the fact that they gave the Spirit by the imposition of hands make any difference, because on account of this it does not follow that they gave Him, just as for example, the sun, and from the sun heat which is caused by my moving towards the sun, and yet I do not make that heat but the sun. Similarly when it is said that water passes through canals to the meadows and yet water has neither proceeds nor comes from canals, but rather from a spring or a river. So the grace of the Holy Spirit is given through the duly made imposition of hands, yet not by man, but only by God. Nor does the fact that Simon Magus — whose place you Cathars today hold — who erred by believing that the Holy Spirit was given by the power of men, make any difference, as Blessed Peter shows when he says (8:20) "you have thought that the gift of God may be purchased with money." Therefore the Holy Spirit is not the gift of Peter Gallus, since it was not of Simon Peter but of the blessed and sublime God.

That the Holy Spirit, once given and lost, can never be recovered again

Matthew 12 (12:32) "but he who shall speak against the Holy Spirit, it shall not be forgiven him, neither in this world, nor in the world to come." Therefore the sin against the Holy Spirit is unforgivable, which is understood to be

---

XVI.8.2 quorum...peccata] Ioh. 20:23.   18 tunc...22 potestatem] Act. 8:17-19.   39 Existimasti...40 possideri] Act. 8:20.
XVI.9.3 qui...5 futuro] Matt. 12:32.

XVI.8.1 Quod...homine] om. F   16 fungi] frangi F   26 domini] deum P   30 solere] saleo F | solem] salem F   32 cum] non P   38 cathari] katari P   39 Existimasti] estimasti F   42 petri] petrus P

XVI.8.10 contritionem|fol. 85ra P   34 manus|fol. 85rb P

acceptionem spiritus sancti. et intelligo quod est inremiscibile scilicet in hoc corpore.

Catholicus: Respondeo. intelligitur illud de peccato finali. uel subauditur scilicet de facili. alias enim omne peccatum remiscibile est quamdiu homo in hoc corpore uiuit. et spiritualiter probatum est tibi supra in parte nostra quod qui peccant post acceptionem spiritus sancti. potest iterum recuperare illum.

Patarenus: Item ad hebreos. vi. impossibile est enim eos qui semel sunt illuminati etcet. et x. uoluntarie enim peccantibus nobis post acceptam notitiam ueritatis iam non reliquitur pro peccatis hostia etcet. ergo non potest quis amplius recuperare spiritum sanctum. postquam illum semel amiserit.

Catholicus: Respondeo quod utriusque auctoritatis sententia apostoli intelligitur de illis qui mortui sunt in mortali peccato. quia in alia uita non possunt renouari ad penitentiam nec oblatio alicuius hostie ualet eis ad salutem. unde dominus dicit in euangelio uidete autem ut ne fiat fuga uestra in yieme uel sabbato etcet. et quod dicitur in hac prima auctoritate. rursus crucifigentes sibimetipsis etcet. sic intelligitur id est non possunt facere isti talis quod crucifixio christi eis ualeat amplius. uel ut pro eis crucifigatur in alio seculo. uel aliter non possunt renouari qui post gratiam baptismi peccauerunt scilicet per eumdem modum per quem fuerunt prius illuminatia. per baptismum in quo penitentia exigitur id est contritio de peccatis cum uoluntate cauendi a futuris. illud autem quod est in alia auctoritate. scilicet uoluntarie etcet. sic intelligitur secundam primam expositionem. non. peccat id est uoluntarie in peccatis manentibus usque ad finem uite. non prodest christus qui est hostia etcet. uel secundum aliam non reliquitur hostia id est non datur amplius baptismus qui uirtutem recepit per hostiam oblatis pro peccatis. qui fuit christus in cruce morti pro nobis oblatus.

Item prima iohannis. ultimo. est peccatum ad mortem non pro illo dico ut roget quis etcet. sed istud est illud quod facit quis post acceptionem spiritus sancti. ergo non post amplius. spiritus sanctus. amissus recuperari.

Catholicus: Respondeo. loquitur de finali peccato pro quo postea non est orandus. uel uocat peccatum ad mortem heresim. de isto non dicit id est non imperat orare. simile de paulo qui noluit orare pro laxando errario. ii^a ad timotheus. ultimo. alexander erarius multa mala mihi ostendit. reddet illi dominus

that which is committed after the acceptance of the Holy Spirit, and I understand that is unforgivable, namely, in this body.

Cath: I respond: that is understood as final impenitence or, omitting a word, 'easily [forgiven],' for every other sin can be forgiven, as long as man is living in this body, and is spiritually proven to you above in our section that those who sin after accepting the Holy Spirit, are able later to recover Him.

Pat: Further Hebrews 6 (6:4) "For it is impossible that those who were once illuminated," and 10 (10:26) "For if we sin willfully after having the knowledge of the truth, there is now left no sacrifice for sins." Therefore there cannot be any further recovery of the Holy Spirit, after having once lost Him.

Cath: I respond that both of these Apostolic authorities are able to be understood in reference to those who die in mortal sin, since in the next life it is not possible to be (Heb 6:6:) "renewed again to penance" for neither oblation nor any sacrifice is able to benefit them unto salvation, as the Lord says in the Gospel (Mt 24:20) "Beware lest your flight be in the winter, or on the Sabbath," and, as is spoken of in that first authority (Heb 6:6) "to be renewed again to penance, crucifying again to themselves." It is to be understood in this way, that is, they are not able to do such a thing since the crucifixion of Christ is no longer able to benefit them, or that He might be crucified for him in the next world, or again that one who had sinned after receiving the grace of baptism might not be able to be renewed, namely, in the same way that he had been first illuminated through baptism after which penance is required, that is, by the contrition for sins with the will to avoid them in the future, and this is in another authority (Heb 10:26) "voluntarily," which is to be understood according to the first explanation: do not sin, that is, Christ, who is the victim, cannot benefit those voluntarily remaining in sins until the end of life. Or according to another interpretation, a victim does not remain, that is, a further baptism in not given to those who received grace by the victim offered for sins, who was Christ offered on the cross unto death for us.

Also 1 John, in the last chapter (5:16) "There is a sin unto death, for that I do not say that any man ask." But that is one which is committed after the reception of the Holy Spirit, therefore not after the Holy Spirit has been later lost and recovered.

Cath: I respond: He is speaking of final impenitence after which one cannot pray, or he terms deadly sin a heresy. This He did not say, that is, He did not command to pray, just as Paul did not wish to pray for the loosening of the coppersmith. 2 Timothy, at the end (4:14) "Alexander the coppersmith has done much evil to me, the Lord will

---

15 impossibile...16 illuminati] Heb. 6:4.   16 uoluntarie...18 hostia] Heb. 10:26.   23 renouari...25 salutem] Heb. 6:6.   25 uidete... 26 sabbato] Matt. 24:20 (uidete | orate | ne] non *Vulg.*)   28 sibimetipsis] Heb. 6:6 (rursus] renouari ad penitentiam *Vulg.*) 36 uoluntarie] Heb. 10:26.   44 est...45 quis] 1 Ioh. 5:16.   52 alexander...54 eius] 2 Tim. 4:14.

XVI.9.11 remiscibile est] transp. *F*   22 sententia apostoli] transp. *P*   25 euangelio] om. *P* | uidete] Cavete *F*   27 prima] secunda *F*   29 possunt] possum *P*   35 illud] quid *P*   37 primam] propriam *P*   41 oblatis] ablatas *F*   44 Item] ita *P*   45 istud est] transp. *P* 48 Catholicus] Cauete *P*   50 mortem] morte *F*   51 simile...orare²] om. *P*

XVI.9.20 amiserit|fol. 65r *F*   21 utriusque|fol. 85va *P*   48 finali|fol. 85vb *P*

secundum opera eius etcet. sed nunc respondete mihi qui tenetis hanc opinionem quare non potest quis gratiam dei recuperare ammissam. sicut eam potuit adipisci a principio non habitam. Cum eadem enim ratio sit in utroque casu. idem est et rationis effectus. Preterea quare uestros amplius recipitis postquam ad nos uenerunt. cum secundum uos saluari nullo modo possint. saltem in hoc corpore. Item sic dicendo miseri desperati peccatis. et peccare facitis in spiritum sanctum. cum dicitis aliquod peccatum esse maius quam sit dei bonitas que non possit illud delere et uos miserrimi quare cum illis permanetis? exi igitur. petre galle. de medio babillonis. quia secundum doctrinam quam docuisti dampnatus es sine alicuius spei redemptione et ueni ad ecclesiam dei ubi est bonitas eius que maior apparebit quam fuerit iniquitas tua.

Quod spiritus sanctus semel datus non potest perdi amplius

Prima iohannes. ii°. Ex nobis prodierunt. sed non erant ex nobis nam si fuissent ex nobis permansissent utique nobiscum etcet. et iii°. omnis qui natus est ex deo peccatum non facit. quoniam semen ipsius in eo manet et non potest peccare. quoniam ex deo natus est etcet. et infra ultimam. omnis qui natus est ex deo non peccat. set generatio dei conseruat eum. et malignus non tangit eum etcet. ergo non potest ammittere spiritum sanctum qui semel habet illum.

Catholicus: Respondeo. prima uerba. iohanne. sic intelliguntur non erant ex nobis id est noluerunt esse. ex nobis per gratie conseruatorem. poterant enim esse si uoluissent sicut innuit apostolus. ubi dicit. Cauete nequis uestrum desit gratie dei etcet. uel non erant ex nobis scilicet per predestinationem ad alia uerba. iohannes. Respondi supra. titulo. i°. in contraria rubricella de creatione et factione diaboli. item. i^a. iohannes. iii°. omnis qui natus est etcet. Sed respondete mihi qui tenetis hanc sectam. constat quod isti qui receperunt a uobis manus impositionem et quibus post ipsam peccantibus et ad uos reuertentibus secundam facitis quod omnia in prima manus impositione habuerunt et fecerunt que uos ipsi qui remansistis scilicet habuistis et fecistis. quare ergo non receperunt spiritum sanctum ergo nec uos. preterea utrum uos receperitis spiritum sanctum nescitis. quia qua ratione dicitis illos non recepisse. eadem ratione potest probari quod uos non receperitis. quia ratio quam assignatis est quia ipsi peccauerunt postea. sed uos potestis peccare cum estis omnino incerti utrum debeatis peccare uel non. ergo uel uos non recepistis spiritum sanctum uel saltem estis in uehementi dubitatione an receperitis illum et sic debetis existimare quod

reward him according to his works." But now answer me, you who hold this opinion, why one cannot recover the lost grace of God, just as one could gain it when one did not have it from the beginning. For since the reason is the same in both cases, so is the effect the same. Further why do you receive your own back again after they came to us, since according to you they are in no manner able to be saved, at least not in this body? Also by saying they are poor, desperate sinners and they sin against the Holy Spirit, since you say that some sins are so great that the beneficence of God cannot remit them, why do you continue to remain with these miserable ones? So come out, Peter Gallus, from the midst of Babylon, since according to the doctrine which you taught, you are damned without any hope of redemption and come to the Church of God wherein exists His beneficence, which will seem far greater than shall have been any of your iniquity.

That the Holy Spirit, once given, cannot be lost any more

1 John 2 (2:19) "They went out from us, but they were not of us, for if they had been of us, they would no doubt have remained with us." And 3 (3:9) "Every one who is born of God does not commit sin, for his seed remains in him, and he cannot sin, because he is born of God." And at the end (5:18) "We know that whoever is born of God, does not sin, but the generation of God preserves him, and the wicked does not touch him." Therefore one who has once had the Holy Spirit cannot lose Him.

Cath: I respond, the first words of John are understood thus: they were not of us, that is, they were unwilling to be of us by the preservation of grace, for they would have been able to be if they had wished, as the Apostle indicates when he says (Heb 12:15) "Beware lest any man be wanting in the grace of God," or that it was not from us, namely, by predestination. To the other passage of John, I responded above in the first title, in the contrary rubric on the creation and fashioning of the devil. See 1 John 3 (3:9) "Every one who is born." But answer me, you who hold with this sect, it happens that these who receive the imposition of hands from you and which, after sinning and returning to you, you cause it that all things which they had and did in the first imposition of hands [to be repeated] a second time, which you who remained had and did, hence they did not receive the Holy Spirit, therefore neither did you. Furthermore you do not know whether you received the Holy Spirit, since by that reason you say that they did not receive Him, by the same reason one can prove that you might not have received Him, because by the reason that you asserted is that they sinned after, but you are able to sin when you are entirely uncertain whether you ought to sin or not. Therefore either you have not received the Holy Spirit, or at the very least you are in vehement doubt as to whether you have received Him and

---

XVI.10.3 Ex...5 nobiscum] 1 Ioh. 2:19.   5 omnis...7 est] 1 Ioh. 3:19.   8 omnis...10 eum] 1 Ioh. 5:18.   16 nequis...dei] Heb. 12:15.   20 omnis...est] 1 Ioh. 3:9.

55 opinionem] oppinionem P | quis] add. recuperare P   64 delere] deleri P   XVI.10.15 Cauete] evicte ne quis F   26 non...27 uos] aut si non receperunt ergo nec nos F   27 ergo...uos] sicut et uos F

XVI.10.5 utique|fol. 86ra P   22 isti|fol. 65v F   29 eadem|fol. 86rb P

nulli premii a deo recipietis. dicit enim iacobus. i°. qui enim hesitat similis est fluctui maris qui a uento mouetur et circumfertur. non enim existimet homo ille quod accipiat aliquid a domino. uir duplex animo inconstans est in omnibus uiis suis. preterea uos de utraque opinione nescitis utrum ille qui fecit uobis manus impositionem habuit spiritum sanctum uel an amissurus sit eum per mortale peccatum et semper ignoratis utrum spiritum sanctum habetis. et ideo miserabiles persone semper in tenebris ambulatis.

thus you ought to consider that you will receive no rewards from God. For James 1 says (1:6–8) "For he that wavers is like a wave of the sea which is moved and carried about by the wind. Therefore do not let that man think that he will receive anything of the Lord. A double minded man is inconstant in all his ways." Further, no matter which opinion you have, you do not know whether he who imposed hands on you had the Holy Spirit or whether he might have lost Him by a mortal sin, and so you are always in doubt whether you have the Holy Spirit. And so like miserable persons, you are always walking in darkness.

De baptismo aque. quod sine eo non est salus et quod in eo debite celebrato datur spiritus sanctus et quod paruuli saluantur per eum

Quoniam baptismus primum est sacramentum. prius de illo dicendum est circa quod dampnabiliter patareni periclitantur dicentes quod in baptismo aque quocumque sit celebratus nullatenus datur spiritus sanctus. asserentes etiam quod nullius sit prorsus utilitatis. et maxime prauis. qui usu rationis non mouentur. quibus gratia sancti spiritus inuocata obuiare testificationis sacrarum scripturarum possumus euidenter.

XVII On the baptism of water, that without it there is no salvation and that in its appropriate celebration the Holy Spirit is given, and that little children are saved through it

Since baptism is the first sacrament, it must be said first of all that the Patarenes damnably attempt to say that in the baptism of water, by whomever it might be celebrated, the Holy Spirit is not given in any manner, while also asserting the fact that it is wholly without use, and exceedingly evil for those who have not arrived at the use of reason, upon whom the grace of the Holy Spirit is invoked. We are able to refute them with the obvious testimony of the sacred scriptures.

Quod sine baptismo aque non est salus et quod in eo debite celebrato datur spiritus sanctus

Mattheus. ultimo. euntes ergo docete omnes gentes baptizantes eos in nomine patris et filii et spiritus sancti docentes eos seruare omnia quecumque mandaui uos etcet. et marci ultimo. Euntes in mundum uniuersum predicate euangelium omni creature. qui crediderit et baptizatus fuerit saluus erit. qui uero non crediderit condemnabitur etcet. ecce quomodo dominus dicit ipsemet quod baptisma est ad salutem et quod qui non credit doctrinam baptismi condempnabitur. quod de baptismate aque et spiritus sancti intelligere necesse est. quia de doctrina non potest intelligi eo quod de illa dixerat docete et predicate etcet. neque de manus impositione. quia ut inferius apparebit aliud est baptisma et aliud manus impositio. Item lucam. iii°. factum est autem cum baptizaretur omnis populus et ihesu baptizato etcet. hoc numquam de predicatione potest intelligi uel manus impositione. quia tunc non predicabatur christus. neque ei uel populo manus imponebatur. nisi per baptismum aque. igitur de baptismate aque intelligitur quod si malum fuisset et de doctrina diaboli numquam eo magister

That without the baptism of water there is no salvation and that in its appropriate celebration the Holy Spirit is given

Matthew, in the last chapter (28:19–20) "Go therefore, teach all nations, baptizing them in the name of the Father, and of the Son, and of the Holy Spirit, teaching them to observe all things whatsoever I have commanded you." and in the last chapter of Mark (16:15–16) "Go into the whole world, and preach the gospel to every creature. He who believes and is baptized shall be saved, but he who does not believe shall be condemned." See how the Lord Himself said that baptism is unto salvation and that he who does not believe the doctrine of baptism shall be condemned. It is necessary to understand that by the baptism of water and the Holy Spirit one cannot interpret the doctrine that He was speaking as 'teach and preach,' neither did He speak of the imposition of hands, since, as will be clear below, baptism is one thing and the imposition of hands another. See Luke 3 (3:21) "Now it came to pass, when all the people were baptized, that Jesus was also baptized." This could never be understood to be preaching or the imposition of hands, since Christ was not then preaching, neither was He laying hands on people, except by the baptism of water. Therefore if the baptism of water were

---

36 qui...40 suis] Iac. 1:6-8 (existimet] estimet *Vulg.*)   XVII.2.3 euntes...6 uos] Matt. 28:19-20.   6 Euntes...9 condemnabitur] Mar. 16:15-16.   17 factum...18 baptizato] Luc. 3:21.

36 nulli premii] sic *PF* reading 'nulla premia'   41 opinione] oppinione *P*   XVII.1.5 dicendum] discutiendum *F*   6 baptismo] add. per eum *F*   7 nullatenus] add. n *P* exp.   9 rationis] ratione *P*

XVII.1.9 rationis|fol. 86va *P*

ueritatis usus fuisset qui dicit in iohanne. xiiii°. uenit enim princeps mundi huius et in me non habet quidquam etcet. de qui dicit. iohannes. i\ª. iii°. in hoc apparuit filius dei ut dissoluat opera diaboli etcet. item. iohannes. iii°. respondit ihesus. amen amen dico tibi nisi quis renatus fuerit ex aqua et spiritu sancto non potest introire in regnum dei etcet. ergo necessarium est baptisma aque ad salutem et datur in eo spiritus sanctus. idem. iiii°. post uenit ihesus et discipuli eius in terram iudeam terram et illic morabatur cum eis et baptizabat etcet. et iiii°. ut ergo cognouit ihesus quia audierunt pharysei quod ihesus plures discipulos facit et baptizat quam iohannes. quamquam ihesus non baptizaret sed discipulos eius etcet. ergo baptisma aque salutare est. quod dominus ihesus faciebat per apostolos suos. nec potest intelligere hoc de manus impositione. quia illi non dum fiebat secundum opinionem tuam nec etiam de baptismate doctrine potest intelligi quia sic esset datum quod ihesus christus non predicaret. quod summum mandatum esset. item. ad romanos. vi. quicumque baptizati sumus in christo ihesu in morte ipsius baptizati sumus etcet. ad idem. item. i\ª. ad corinthios. i°. gratias ago deo meo quod neminem uestrum baptizaui nisi crispum et gaium etcet. et infra. non enim misit me christus baptizare set euangelizare etcet. ex hiis patet quod baptisma aque sit faciendum. si enim non esset bonum. eos manifeste reprehendisset. quod baptizaretur illo. quod nequaquam fecit. sed de hoc tantum quod ei in cuius nomine baptizati fuerant a christo non uere actribuebant cum de baptistis iactarent. Item si non esset faciendum. numquam fecisset illud et numquam de predicationem uel manus impositione possunt pauli uerba intelligi. quia secundum hoc numquam nisi duos homines et unam familiam baptizasset uel manus eis imposuisset. item quod differentia sit inter baptisma et doctrinam. ostendit manifeste cum dicit. Non enim misit me christus baptizare sed euangelizare etcet. idem. iii°. ego plantaui scilicet predicatio. apollo rigauit scilicet baptizando sed deus incrementum dedit etcet. ad idem. item ad ephesios. iiii°. unus dominus. una fides. unum baptisma etcet. ergo baptisma aque et spiritus sancti unum baptisma sunt. idem. v. diligite uxores uestras sicut et christus dilexit ecclesiam et semetipsum tradidit pro ea. ut illam sanctificaret mundans eam lauacro aque. in uerbo uite id est in inuocatione trinitatis. ergo in baptismo aque datur remissio peccatorum et per consequentiam. spiritus sanctus.

---

24 uenit...26 quidquam] Ioh. 14:30.   26 in...27 diaboli] 1 Ioh. 3:8.   28 respondit...30 dei] Ioh. 3:5.   32 uenit...34 baptizabat] Ioh. 3:22 (post) add. haec | morabatur] demorabatur *Vulg.*)   34 ut...37 eius] Ioh. 4:1-2.   44 quicumque...45 sumus²] Rom. 6:3.   46 gratias...48 gaium] 1 Cor. 1:14.   48 non...49 euangelizare] 1 Cor. 1:17.   61 Non...62 euangelizare] 1 Cor. 1:17.   62 ego...64 dedit] 1 Cor. 3:6.   65 unus...66 baptisma¹] Eph. 4:5.   67 diligite...70 aque] Eph. 5:25-26 (semetipsum) seipsum *Vulg.*)

XVII.2.28 dico] add. uobis *P* exp.   40 secundum] om. *P*   41 opinionem] oppinionem *P*   51 manifeste] manifestare *F* | quod...52 fecit] om. *P*   53 cuius] eius *F*   57 pauli] add. et *P* | uerba] scribi *P*   58 duos] duo *F*   59 eis] ei *F*   68 ecclesiam] ecclesia *P*

XVII.2.27 dissoluat|fol. 86vb *P*   35 discipulos|fol. 66r *F*   54 actribuebant|fol. 87ra *P*

item ad hebreos. x. accedamus cum uero corde in plenitudine fidei aspersi corda a consciencia mala et abluti corpus aqua munda etcet. ecce quoniam apostolus appellat aquam baptismatis que lauet corpus aquam mundam eo quod spiritus sanctus detur cum ea in remissionem peccatorum. item. i^a. ad petri. iii^o. in diebus noe cum fabricaretur archa. in qua pauci id est octo anime salue facte sunt per aquam quod et nunc uos similis forme saluos facit baptisma etcet. id est sicut aquam diluuii subleuantes archam saluos fecerunt illos ne perirent cum submersis. ita aqua baptismi nos saluat ne pereatis cum dampnatis. ergo baptismis aque necessarius est ad salutem. item actus. ii^o. petrus uero dixit ad illos. penitentiam inquid agite et baptizetur unusquisque uestrum in nomine ihesu christi in remissionem peccatorum uestrorum et accipietis donum spiritus sancti. ergo in baptismo aque datur remissio peccatorum et gratia spiritus sancti. Nec potes dicere quod baptismus appelletur hic predicatio uel penitentia. quia de predicatione dicit primo ibi superius stans autem petrus cum. xi. et leuauit uocem et locutus est eis etcet. de penitencia dicit hic. penitenciam in quid agite etcet. et postea subdit de baptismate per se. dicens. et baptizetur unusquisque etcet. idem. viii. cum uero credidissent phylippo euangelizanti regnum dei et in nomine ihesu christi baptizarentur uiri ac mulieres etcet. ad idem. idem in eodem. et ait eunucus. ecce aqua quis prohibet me baptizari etcet. et infra. et descenderunt uterque in aquam phylippus et eunuchus et baptizauit eum etcet. quod manifeste de aqua baptismate necesse est intelligi. idem. viiii. et surgens baptizatus est etcet. scilicet paulus. sed de manus impositione minime potest hoc intelligi cum superius dicatur et abiit ananias et imponens ei manus dixit etcet. ergo post manus impositionem baptizatus est in aqua materiali. idem. x. in finem. tunc respondit petrus. numquid aquam quis prohibere potest ut non baptizentur hii qui spiritum sanctum acceperunt sicut et nos et iussit eos baptizari in nomine ihesu etcet. sed constat secundum uos heretici quod spiritus sanctus non datur nisi per manus impositionem igitur antea facta erat manus impositio illis et tamen postea baptizauit eos petrus. ergo baptisma aque necessarium est ad salutem. quod autem dico per manus impositionem tantum dari spiritum sanctum secundum uestram loquor stultitiam. quia et ipsis datus est a deo sine manus impositione prius. idem. xvi. et extollens eos in illa hora noctis lauit plagas eorum et baptizatus est et omnis domus eius continuo. etcet. idem. xviiii. dixit

baptism of water and, consequently, the Holy Spirit. Also Hebrews 10 (10:22) "Let us draw near with a true heart in fullness of faith, having our hearts sprinkled from an evil conscience, and our bodies washed with clean water." See how the Apostle calls the water of baptism that washes the body with clean water for the reason that the Holy Spirit might be given with it unto the remission of sins. As 1 Peter 3 has it (3:20–21) "in the days of Noah, when he was building the ark in which a few, that is, eight souls, were saved by water, and now you similarly are saved through baptism being a similar type." That is, just as those were saved from the rising water of the flood, lest they perish when it came, just so does the water of baptism save us lest we perish with the damned, therefore baptism of water is necessary for salvation. See Acts 2 (2:38) "But Peter said, 'Do penance, and be baptized every one of you in the name of Jesus Christ, for the remission of your sins and you shall receive the gift of the Holy Spirit.'" Therefore in baptism one is given the remission of sins and the grace of the Holy Spirit. Neither are you able to say that baptism is here called preaching or penance, since above it speaks of preaching (2:14) "But Peter, standing with the eleven, raised his voice and spoke to them." And of penance he speaks here, (2:38) "Do penance" and later adds baptism itself, saying "and be baptized every one of you." Also 8 (8:12) "But when they had believed Philip preaching of the kingdom of God, they were baptized in the name of Jesus Christ, both men and women." And in the same place (8:36) "See, here is water. What prevents me from being baptized?" And (8:38) "and they went down into the water, both Philip and the eunuch, and he baptized him." So it is understood that baptism of water is clearly necessary. Also 9 (9:18) "and arising, he was baptized." But one cannot interpret that the imposition of hands is meant here, since above it says (9:17) "And Ananias went away and laying his hands upon him, said. . ." Therefore after the imposition of hands he was baptized in material water. Also 10, at the end (10:47–48) "Then Peter answered, 'Can any man forbid water, that these should not be baptized, who have received the Holy Spirit, like us?' And he commanded them to be baptized in the name of Jesus." But it is obvious that according to you heretics that the Holy Spirit is only given by the imposition of hands, but in that case the imposition of hands was granted to them before, and yet Peter still baptized them after, therefore the baptism of water is necessary for salvation. Thus I say that the giving of the Holy Spirit only by the imposition of hands according to your [practice] is idiocy, since He had been given by God without a prior imposition of hands. Also 16 (16:33) "And he, taking them the same hour of the night, washed their wounds, and was himself baptized

---

73 accedamus...75 munda] Heb. 10:22.   78 in^2...81 baptisma] 1 Pet. 3:20-21 (facit) fecit *Vulg.*)   85 petrus...89 sancti] Act. 2:38 (inquid) inquit *Vulg.*   93 stans...94 eis] Act. 2:14.   97 cum...99 mulieres] Act. 8:12 (regnum) de regno | baptizarentur] baptizabantur *Vulg.*)   100 et...101 baptizari] Act. 8:36.   101 et^2...102 eum] Act. 8:38.   104 et...est] Act. 9:18.   106 et^1...107 dixit] Act. 9:17. 109 tunc...112 ihesu] Act. 10:47-48 (hii) hi *Vulg.*)   120 et...122 continuo] Act. 16:33 (extollens) tollens *Vulg.*)   122 dixit...125 estis] Act. 19:2-3 (dixit) dixitque *Vulg.*)

82 saluos] salua *P*   83 ita] in *F*   103 necesse] add. it *P* exp.   105 hoc] om. *F*

79 fabricaretur|fol. 87rb *P*   103 intelligi|fol. 66v *F*   107 imponens|fol. 87va *P*

ad eos. si spiritum sanctum accepistis credentes? at illi dixerunt ad eum sed neque si spiritus sanctus est audiuimus. ille uero ait. in quo ergo baptizati estis etcet. et infra. hiis auditis baptizati sunt in nomine ihesu cum imposuisset manus etcet. ergo prius eos predicauit cum dixit. in quo baptizati estis et postea baptizauit eos. demum manus illis imposuit. igitur baptisma non est predicatio neque manus impositione ergo aqua materiali baptizati sunt. preterea patet ex istis uerbis pauli manifeste quod spiritus sanctus dabatur in baptismo aque facto in nomine ihesu christi. licet non daretur in baptismo. iohannes baptista. idem. xxii. et nunc moraris. exsurge et baptizare et ablue peccata tua inuocato nomine ipsius etcet. ergo in baptismo aqua lauantur peccata. patet ergo ex premissis quod baptisma aque necessarium est ad salutem et quod in eo debite celebrato dat remissionem peccatorum et gratiam spiritus sancti.

Quod pueri paruuli baptizati saluantur

Mattheus. viii. et dixit ihesus centurioni. uade et sicut credidisti fiat tibi. et sanatus est puer in illa hora etcet. idem. viiii. et ecce offerebant ei paraliticum muto iacentem in lecto et uidens ihesus fidem illorum dixit paralitico. confide fili remittuntur tibi peccata tua etcet. idem. xv. tunc respondens ihesus ait illi. o mulier magna est fides tua. fiat tibi sicut uis et sanata est filia eius ex illa hora etcet. item. marcum. viii. at ille ait ibi. sed si quid potes adiuua nos misertus nostri. ihesus autem ait illi. si potes credere omnia possibilia sunt credenti. etcet. ex quibus auctoritatibus patet quod in fide aliorum alios saluauit ihesus tam in corpore quam in anima. ergo simili et pueri baptizati saluantur in fide ecclesie. item. xviii. et aduocans ihesus paruulum statuit eum in medio eorum et dixit. amen dico uobis nisi conuersi fueritis et efficiamini sicut paruuli non intrabitis in regnum celorum etcet. et infra. et qui susceperit unum paruulum talem in nomine meo me suscepit. qui autem scandalizauerit unum de pusillis istis qui in me credunt expedit ei ut suspendatur mola asinaria in collo eius etcet. et infra. uidete ne contemnatis unum ex hiis pusillis. dico enim uobis quia angeli eorum in celis semper uident faciem patris mei qui in celis est etcet. Item. Marcum. viiii. et accipiens puerum statuit eum in medio eorum me recepit etcet. item apocalypsis. vii. et audiui numerum signatorum c. xliiiior millia signati etcet. et xiiii. et nemo poterat dicere canticum nisi illa. c.xliiiior. millia. qui empti sunt de terra. hi sunt qui cum mulieribus non sunt coinquinati uirgines enim sunt etcet. ex quibus habes quod pueri paruuli saluantur et credunt

immediately, along with all his household." And 19 (19:2–3) "And he said to them, 'Have you received the Holy Spirit since you believed?' But they said to him: 'We have not so much as heard about a Holy Spirit.' And he said: 'In what then were you baptized?'" Therefore he preached to them first, when he said "In what then were you baptized?" and then he later baptized them. At the end he laid hands on them. Then baptism is not preaching nor is it the laying of hands, therefore they are baptized in material water. Further it is plain from these words of Paul that the Holy Spirit was given in by a baptism of water in the name of Jesus Christ, although He was not given in the baptism of John the Baptist. See 22 (22:16) "And now why do you delay? Rise up, and be baptized, and wash away your sins, invoking his name." Therefore it is clear from the foregoing passages that baptism of water is necessary for salvation and that, when it is rightly celebrated, it gives the remission of sins and the grace of the Holy Spirit.

That baptized little children are saved

Matthew 8 (8:13) "and Jesus said to the centurion, 'Go and just as you have believed, it shall be done unto you,' and the child was healed at that very hour." Also 9 (9:2) "And behold they brought to him a paralyzed man lying in a bed. And Jesus, seeing their faith, said to the paralytic, 'Be of good cheer, son, your sins are forgiven.'" And 15 (15:28) "Then Jesus answered and said to her, 'O woman, your faith is great: let it be done as you wish,' and her daughter was cured from that hour." And Mark 8 (9:21–22) "And he said there, 'but if you can do anything, help us, have compassion on us.' And Jesus said to him: 'If you can believe, all things are possible to him who believes.'" From these authorities it is clear that Jesus saved some through the faith of others, some in body and others in soul, so baptized children are similarly saved through the faith of the Church. See 18 (18:2–3) "And Jesus called a little child to him, and set him in the midst of them, and said, 'Amen I say to you, unless you be converted, and become as little children, you shall not enter into the kingdom of heaven.'" And later (18:5) "And he who receives one of these little ones in my name, receives me, but whosoever might scandalize one of these little ones who believe in me, it is better for him that a stone be hung around his neck." And further on (18:10) "See that you do not despise these little ones, for I say to you that their angel in heaven always beholds the face of my Father who is in heaven." See also Mark 9 (9:35–36) "and taking a child he stood him in the midst of them, whoever receives one of these." And Apocalypse (7:4) "and I heard the number of the signed, and it was 144,000 signed." And 14 (14:3–4) "and no man could say the song, but those 144,000, who were purchased from the earth. These are they who were not defiled with women, for they are

---

126 auditis...127 manus] Act. 19:5 (hiis) his *Vulg.*)   135 et¹...136 ipsius] Act. 22:16.   XVII.3.2 et¹...3 hora] Matt. 8:13.   4 et...6 tua] Matt. 9:2 (muto) om. *Vulg.*)   7 tunc...9 hora] Matt. 15:28.   9 at...12 credenti] Mar. 9:21-22.   15 et...18 celorum] Matt. 18:2-3. 18 et²...22 eius] Matt. 18:5-6.   22 uidete...25 est] Matt. 18:10.   25 et...27 recepit] Mar. 9:35-36 (eorum) add. in nomine meo *Vulg.*) 27 et...28 signati] Apoc. 7:4.   28 et²...31 sunt²] Apoc. 14:3-4.

XVII.3.19 paruulum] om. P   21 ei] om. P   23 hiis] om. P

135 exsurge|fol. 87vb P   XVII.3.17 et|fol. 88ra P   27 apocalypsis|fol. 67r F

secundum in sua fide non saluantur cum ea non moueantur propter etatis debilitatem. igitur in fide patrinorum uel aliorum fidelium. sed nulli saluantur sine baptismo ergo pueri paruuli baptizati saluantur per aliorum fidem et dicuntur credere quia per alios credunt.

Quod baptismus aque nullius est utilitatis nec quo ad remissionem peccatorum nec quo ad acceptionem spiritus sancti et maxime baptismus paruulorum

[Paterenus:] Mattheus. i°. ego quidem baptizo uos in aqua etcet. et infra. ipse uos baptizauit in spiritu sancto et igni etcet. ergo pro nichilo reputauit ipse. iohannes baptista. aqua baptismum ostendens quod in eo non datur spiritus sanctus.

Catholicus: Respondeo quod in baptisma. iohannes. sine dubio non dabatur spiritus sanctus. quia non dum aque receperant ueri regeneratiuam per tactum mundissime carnis christi.

[Paterenus:] Item iohannes. vii. qui credit in me sicut dicit scriptura flumina de uentre eius fluent aque uiue. hoc autem dixit de spiritu quem accepturi erant credentes in eum etcet. Ex istis uerbis colligitur manifeste quod per aquam intelligitur spiritus sanctus et quod aque materiales baptisma nullius est utilitatis ad salutem.

Catholicus: Respondeo quod christus non dixit quod semper per aquam intelligatur spiritus sanctus. nec ego dico quod aliquando non intelligatur spiritus sanctus. per aquam ut hic habetur. nec propter hoc sequitur quod aque baptismalis. non sit baptisma et quod non sit utile et neccesarium ad salutem. uel uocat dominus aquas baptismales spiritum sanctum eo quod spiritus sanctus datur in illis.

[Paterenus:] Item ad hebreos. vi. non rursum iacientes fundamentum ab operibus mortuis et fidei ad deum. baptismatum doctrine etcet. ergo doctrina est baptisma de quo dicitur in scripturis quo debemus baptizari.

Catholicus: Respondeo quod ex hoc non inficior quidem per baptisma non intelligatur doctrina quandoque ut hic sed simpliciter uerbum baptismi prolatum. nichil aliud significat quam aque et sancti spiritus baptisma. et maxime quando expressim aqua nominatur. uel melius uocat apostolus sacramentum baptismi doctrine baptisma eo quod ad spiritualem christi doctrinam pertinet sicut ipse dicit. Euntes docente omnes gentes baptizantes eos in nomine patris

virgins." From these you have it that small children are saved and they believe, for they are not saved by their own faith, for they are not moved to it on account of want of age, therefore they believe through the faith of the godparents, or of others of the faithful. But no one is saved without baptism, therefore small baptized children are saved by the faith of another, and they are said to believe, because they believe through others.

That the baptism of water is of no use, neither for the remission of sins nor for the reception of the Holy Spirit and especially the baptism of children

[Pat:] Matthew 1 (3:11) "I baptize you in water," and later "but he will baptize you with the Holy Spirit and with fire," therefore he held the baptism of John the Baptist as for nothing, showing in the baptism of water the Holy Spirit is not given.

Cath: I respond that in the baptism of John the Holy Spirit was, without a doubt, not given, for the water had not yet received the touch of true regeneration by the most pure flesh of Christ.

[Pat:] See John 7 (7:38–39) "He who believes in me, as the scripture says, 'Out of his stomach shall flow rivers of living water.' Now this He said of the Spirit which they would receive, who believed in him." From these passages it is plainly inferred that 'by water' is understood to be the Holy Spirit, and that material water of baptism is of no use for salvation.

Cath: I respond that Christ did not say that the Holy Spirit is always understood by water, nor for this reason does it follow that the baptismal water is not a baptism and that it is not useful and necessary for salvation; or rather the Lord calls the baptismal waters the Holy Spirit because the Holy Spirit is given in them.

[Pat:] See Hebrews 6 (6:1) "not laying again the foundation from dead works, and of faith towards God, of the doctrine of baptisms." Therefore 'doctrine' is the baptism of which it is said in the scriptures in which we ought to be baptized.

Cath: I respond that I certainly do not deny the fact that through baptism one does not understand 'doctrine,' as is sometimes the case but, simply said, baptism signifies nothing other than baptism of water and the Holy Spirit, and especially whenever water is expressly mentioned. Or it is even better the apostle calls the sacrament of baptism the doctrine of baptism, for the reason that it belongs to the spiritual doctrine of Christ, as he says (Mt 28:19) "Go forth and teach all men, baptizing them in the name of the

---

XVII.4.5 ego…7 igni] Matt. 3:11.   14 qui…17 eum] Ioh. 7:38-39.   29 non…31 doctrine] Heb. 6:1 (fundamentum) poenitentiae Vulg.)   41 Euntes…43 sancti] Matt. 28:19.

35 patrinorum] patarinorum F   XVII.4.5 i°.] sic PF   12 per] quod P   14 in me] om. P   25 non¹] add. natura F   31 baptismatum] aptissimum F   35 baptisma] aptissima F   36 sed] set P

XVII.4.3 maxime|fol. 88rb P   37 aliud|fol. 88va P

et filii et spiritus sancti. etcet. uel quia in eo docentur baptizandi seu baptizanti fide catholica.

[**Patarenus:**] Item prima petri. iii. quod et nunc uos similis forme saluos facit baptisma non carnis depositio sordium etcet. ergo nichil facit per baptizationem aque lauare corpus.

Catholicus: Respondeo quod uerum est nisi sint ibi duo que sunt necessaria in baptismo adultorum scilicet conscientia bona hoc est contritio peccatorum et benefaciendi propositum. ecce unum. aliud est fides catholica et hoc est quod subdit ibi petrus. sed conscientie bone interrogatio in deum per resurrectionem domini nostri ihesu christi qui est in dextera dei patris etcet. et actus ii°. penitentiam inquit agite et baptizetur unusquisque uestrum in nomine ihesu christi.

[**Patarenus:**] Item actus. i°. uos autem baptizabimini spiritu sancti non post multos hos dies etcet. ergo spiritus sanctus quem receperunt apostoli in die pentecosten sine aqua dicitur baptisma.

Catholicus: Respondeo uerum est quod acceptio spiritus sancti dicitur baptisma proprie et realiter. eo quod lauat peccata et peccatorum penas non tamen propter hoc sequitur quod baptismus aque non dicatur baptisma sacramentaliter. scire enim debes quod fuit quandoque figura et non sacramentum neque res baptizatio ut fuit baptisma. iohannis baptiste. quandoque uero est sacramentum baptismi et non res ut infinite baptizatis et quandoque res et non sacramentum ut in illis qui recipiuntur gratiam spiritus sancti scilicet per contrintionem tantum. uel per martyrium. uel sicut receperunt apostoli post resurrectionem et in die penthecosten. et quandoque uero est sacramentum et res ut in bona conscientia baptizatis in aqua secundum formam a saluatore traditam. sed uos respondete mihi facio uobis unam questionem ad similitudinem illius quam dominus fecit principibus sacerdotum et senioribus populi iudeorum. de baptismate. iohanne. quero enim a uobis utrum baptismis aque sit doctrina dei uel doctrina hominum. siquidem dicitis quod est doctrina dei. ergo ecclesia romana est ecclesia dei que facit doctrinam et opus eius. et uos non estis ecclesia dei qui non seruatis et non facitis doctrinam ipsius. constat enim quod ecclesia dei totam eius doctrinam debet seruare et facere. ait enim beatus iacobus apostolus. quicumque autem totam legem seruauerit offendat autem in uno factus est omnium reus etcet. siquidem dicitis quod sit doctrina humana et non diuina non debetis participes eius fieri. scriptum est enim de illis qui doctrinam humanam seruant que non est diuina. mattheus. xv. populus hic labiis me honorat

Father and of the Son and of the Holy Spirit." Either because those about to be baptized or those baptizing are instructed in the Catholic faith.

[**Pat:**] Also 1 Peter 3 (3:21) "So baptism being of the like form, now saves you also, not the putting away of the filth of the flesh." Therefore nothing is accomplished by the baptism of water, save the washing of the body.

Cath: I reply that it is true that unless there are two things are present, which are necessary for the baptism of adults, namely a good conscience — which is sorrow for sins and a purpose of amendment for one — and another is the Catholic faith which Peter adds (3:21–22) "but the examination of a good conscience towards God by the resurrection of Jesus Christ who is on the right hand of God." And Acts 2 (2:38) "he said do penance and be baptized, every one of you, in the name of Jesus Christ."

[**Pat:**] And Acts 1 (1:5) "but you shall be baptized with the Holy Spirit, not many days from now." Therefore the Holy Spirit whom the Apostles received on the day of Pentecost, without water, was called baptism.

Cath: I respond that it is true that the reception of the Holy Spirit is called baptism properly and really, and by it sins are cleansed as well as the punishments for sins, but on account of this it does not follow that the baptism of water is not called sacramental baptism, for you ought to know that there was sometimes a type and not a sacrament or the reality of baptism, as was the baptism of John the Baptist, but sometimes there is a sacrament of baptism and not the reality as for those imperfectly baptized, and sometimes there is the grace but not the sacrament as in those who received the grace of the Holy Spirit, namely, by contrition alone or through martyrdom, or in the manner that the apostles received Him after the Resurrection on the day of Pentecost. And those who receive the sacrament and its grace in good conscience in water according to the form handed on by the Savior [receive it truly]. But answer me this, I pose one question for you similar to that which the Lord proposed to the princes, priests, and elders of the Jewish people, about the baptism of John. For I ask you whether the baptism of water is the teaching of God or a human doctrine. Supposing that you say that it is a teaching of God, therefore the Roman Church is the Church of God, which follows His teachings and works and yours is not the Church of God since you neither observe nor perform His teachings, for the Church of God holds all of his teachings and one ought to follow and accomplish them. As Blessed James the Apostle says (2:10) "And whosoever shall keep the whole law, but offend in one point, has become guilty of all." But if you say that it is a human doctrine and not a divine one, you ought not to participate in it, for it is written that one should not observe the precepts of men which are not divine. Matthew 15 (15:8–9) "This people honors me with their

---

45 quod...47 sordium] 1 Pet. 3:21 (facit) fecit *Vulg*.) 53 sed...56 patris] 1 Pet. 3:21-22. 56 penitentiam...58 christi] Act. 2:38. 59 uos...60 dies] Act. 1:5. 88 quicumque...89 reus] Iac. 2:10. 93 populus...95 hominum] Matt. 15:8-9.

43 sancti] add. amen *P* (*scribe perhaps not a priest, "amen" not in gospel or in the sacramental formula*) 54 interrogatio] om. *F with space left for word* 70 infinite] infute *P* 72 recipiuntur] recipuint *F* 77 uos] om. *P*

64 baptisma|fol. 67v *F* 68 res|fol. 88vb *P*

cor autem eorum longe est a me. sine autem causa colunt me docentes doctrinas et mandata hominum etcet. et ii^a. ad corinthios. vi. nolite iugum ducere cum infidelibus. que enim participatio iustitie cum iniquitate etcet. et ad romanos. ultimo. dicit. quoniam qui talia agunt digni sunt morte. non solum qui faciunt ea sed etiam qui consentiuit facientibus etcet. ergo uos peccatis mortaliter cum mittitis filios uestros et alios ad baptismum aque ab ecclesia romana recipiendum.

Patarenus: Respondeo quia facimus hoc ad simulationem ut sic cooperiamur ne nos ecclesia romana cognoscat sicut et paulus intrans templum iudeorum purificationem eorum seruauit et circumcidi fecit tymotheus.

Catholicus: sed non debetis uti simulationem in doctrina fidei. quia mortale peccatum est. nec obstat obiectio de paulo quia ipse diuinam doctrinam seruauit que hoc esset ad litteram finita tamen non erit peccatum illam seruare circa mortem synagoge matris. dum tamen in cortice fides non exponeretur. quia mater synagoga cum honore dicenda erat ad tumulum. sed dicite mihi quare non comeditis carnes et oua et caseum ad simulationem et quare non iuratis? que utique minoris esset peccati. quam seruare baptismum aque. si utrumque peccatum esset.

Patarenus: Facimus ergo causa exhibendi quadam honorem temporalem ecclesie romane in signum nostre humilitatis.

Catholicus: Sed et in hoc restant obiectiones supradicte. preterea apostoli ihesu christi baptizauerunt in aqua et ipse ihesus christus per eos quod numquam legitis fecisse iudeos. ergo baptizare in aqua est honor ecclesie sancte dei et filii uestri iudices uestri erunt quia fecistis illos recipere et seruare doctrinam ecclesie romane. nec tamen credidistis ei.

Quod pueri paruuli non saluantur per baptismum neque per aliquid

[**Patarenus:**] Marcus ultimo. qui uero non crediderit condemnabitur. etcet. sed pueri non credidit. ergo dampnatur.

Catholicus: Respondeo quia ipsi credunt per fidem patrinorum et aliorum fidelium. Nec dixit dominus qui non crediderit scilicet per se tamen. potest enim quis facere aliquid et per se et per alium. Nec mireris si

lips, but their heart is far from me, and in vain do they worship me, teaching doctrines and commandments of men." And 2 Corinthians 6 (6:14) "Do not bear the yoke with unbelievers, for what does justice have to do with injustice?" In the last sentence of the first chapter of Romans (1:32) "they who do such things are worthy of death, and not only they who do them, but also they who consent to them who do them." Therefore you sin mortally when you send your sons and others to receive the baptism of water from the Roman Church.[1]

Pat: I respond that we do this as silly play acting, lest the Roman Church might find us out, just as Paul, entering into the temple of the Jews, observed their purification and caused Timothy to be circumcised.

Cath: But one ought not to use dissimulation in the doctrines of the faith, since that is a mortal sin, neither is the objection about Paul relevant since he was observing a divine teaching, that this was literally the end, for it was no sin to observe the funeral rites of mother synagogue, since the faith as yet had not emerged from the cocoon, for "the mother, the synagogue, was destined to be brought in honor to the grave." (Augustine, Ep. 82, c. 16). But tell me why you do not play act by eating meat and eggs and cheese and why do you not swear? These would be a lesser sin that observing the baptism of water, if indeed both of those were sinful.

Pat: We do this therefore in order to demonstrate a certain temporal honor for the Roman Church, as a sign of our humility.

Cath: But yet there remains the above objections. Further the Apostles of Jesus Christ baptized in water and [so did] Jesus Christ Himself through them, a thing which you nowhere read that the Jews did. Therefore to baptize in water is to honor the holy Church of God and your sons are your judges since you cause them to receive and observe the doctrine of the Roman Church, though you do not believe her.

That little children are not saved by baptism nor in any other way

[**Pat:**] (Mk 16:16) "He who believes and is baptized shall be saved, but he who does not believe shall be condemned." But children do not believe, therefore they are damned.

Cath: I reply that they believe by the faith of their godparents and of others of the faithful. For the Lord did not say those who do not believe by themselves. For one can do something both by himself and through another.

---

96 nolite...98 iniqui-tate] 2 Cor. 6:14.   98 dicit...100 facientibus] Rom. 1:32 (consentiuit) consentiunt *Vulg.*)   113 quia...114 tumulum] Augustine, *Epistulae*, 82. c. 16.   **XVII.5.3** qui...4 condemnabitur] Mar. 16:16.

103 facimus] fatuus *P* | simu-lationem] similitudinem *F*   110 diuinam] om. *P*   112 peccatum] om. *P* | synagoge] sinagoge *P*   113 exponeretur] poneretur *F*   115 comeditis] comedistis *F* | carnes] canes (!) *P*   **XVII.5.2** aliquid] add. aliud *P*   3 Marcus ultimo] om. *P*

95 colunt|fol. 89ra *P*   119 exhibendi|fol. 89rb *P*   **XVII.5.2** aliquid|fol. 68r *F*

---

1) The Cathars followed the external celebration of the Catholic sacraments because they did not believe them to have efficacy and in order to avoid the suspicions of their orthopractic neighbors. This also points to conventionalization of Cathar practice.

dicimus quod in fide multorum id est totius ecclesie possit unus puer talis saluari. quia uidemus quod peccatum unius scilicet ade transiuit in omnes. ad romanos. v. per unum hominem peccatum in mundum intrauit et per peccatum mors et ita in omnes homines mors pertransiit in quo omnes peccauerunt etcet. et infra. sed regnauit mors ab adam usque ad moysen etiam in eos qui non peccauerunt in similitudinem preuaricationis ade. sed cum deus sit pronior ad gratiam dandam et uitam quam ad penam et mortem. multo fortius non dico per multos sed per unum tantum debet unus saluari et liberari. hanc enim argumentationem facit apostolus in predicto capitulo ubi dicit. si enim unius delicto mors regnauit per unum multo magis abundantiam gratie Christi et donationis et iustitie accipientes in uita regnabunt per unum ihesum christum. etcet. preterea uos heretici dicitis quod per peccatum illius qui per manus impositione dedit spiritum sanctum ammittit eum qui accepit illum et dampnatur. et tamen iste qui consolatus est ab illo laborat benefacere prout potest. multo ergo fortius debetis credere quod per fidem patrini immo totius ecclesie dei salueutr puerculus. propter etiam aliter intelligi dominicum illud uerbum qui non credidit scilicet qui credere potest. non enim impossibile requirit deus. intelligitur ergo de adultis. simile est illud. Jacobi. iii°. si quis in uerbo non offendit hic perfectus est uir etcet. quod de hiis qui peccare possunt intelligitur. Muto enim in uerbo non offendere meritorium non est. potest etiam tertio modo exponi qui non crediderit id est credere noluerit et refertur hoc ad illud uerbum scilicet predicate euangelium omni creature etcet. et iste fuit intellectus deum. simile dicit. mattheus. x. et quicumque non receperint uos et nec audierint sermones uestros exeuntes de domo uel ciuitate excutite puluerum de pedibus uestris. amen dico uobis tolerabilius erit terre sodomorum et gomorrorum in die iudicii quam illi ciuitate etcet.

[**Patarenus:**] Item ad hebreos. xi. sine fide impossibile est placere deo. etcet. ergo pueri non possunt placere deo.

Catholicus: solutio ut supra proxime.

Patarenus: Item. ad Galathas. ultimo. unusquisque enim honus suum portabit etcet. ergo pueri non saluantur cum nichil boni faciant.

Catholicus: Respondeo quia illa ratio est in corona quam in pena. quia peccata unius alteri non rei imponuntur iuxta illud ezechiel. filius non portabit iniquitatem patris etcet. et ad romanos. xiiii. itaque unusquisque nostrum pro se rationem reddit deo etcet.

Neither wonder if we say that it can come through the faith of many, that is, the whole of the Church can save such a child, since we see that by Adam's sin, it passed to all, as in Romans 5 (5:12) "Wherefore as by one man sin entered into the world, and by sin death, and so death passed to all men, in whom all have sinned." And later (5:14) "But death reigned from Adam to Moses, even over them also who have not sinned in the manner of the transgression of Adam." But since God is more prone to give grace and life than punishment and death, how much more strongly — I do not say for many but for one only — ought he to save and free that one. For the Apostle makes this argument in the same place where he says (5:17) "For if by one man's offence death reigned through one, how much more they who receive abundance of grace, and of the gift, and of justice, shall reign in life through one Jesus Christ." Further, you heretics say that through the sin of he who gave the Holy Spirit by the imposition of hands, the one who received the Holy Spirit loses Him and is damned. Yet he who is consoled by Him labors to do as well as he is able, how much more strongly ought you to believe that a little child might be saved by the faith of the godparents, or more correctly, of the [faith of the] whole Church of God. That saying of the Lord cannot be understood any other way "he who did not believe" — more properly — "who was able to believe," for God does not demand the impossible, therefore it is to be understood of adults. Similar sentiments to these are found in James 3 (3:2) "If any man does not offend in word, he is a perfect man." These are understood to be those who are able to sin. For [to be] a mute, who cannot offend by words is not meritorious. But I am able to explain those who do not believe in a third manner, that is, they do not wish to believe, and this passage speaks to that idea, (Mk 16:15) "Preach the gospel to all creatures," and this was God's meaning. Matthew speaks similarly (10:14-15) "And whoever will not receive you, nor hear your words, go forth out of that house or city and shake off the dust from your feet. Amen I say to you, it will be more tolerable for the land of Sodom and Gomorrah on the day of judgment, than for that city."

[**Pat:**] Also Hebrews 11 (11:6) "without faith it is impossible to please God." Therefore children are unable to please God.

Cath: The solution is like that given above.

Pat: See the last chapter of Galatians (6:5) "For every one shall bear his own burden." Therefore children are not saved since they have never done any good works.

Cath: I respond that the reason is more in the crown than the punishment, since the sins of another are not imputed, just as Ezekiel has it (18:20) "the sons will not bear the iniquity of the father." And Romans 14 (14:12) "Therefore

---

13 per...16 peccauerunt] Rom. 5:12.   16 sed...18 ade] Rom. 5:14.   23 si...26 christum] Rom. 5:17 (Christi) om. *Vulg.*   36 si...37 uir] Iac. 3:2.   41 predicate...42 creature] Mar. 16:15.   43 et...48 ciuitate] Matt. 10:14-15.   49 sine...50 deo] Heb. 11:6.   53 unusquisque...54 portabit] Gal. 6:5.   58 filius...59 patris] Ez. 18:20.   59 itaque...60 deo] Rom. 14:12.

18 cum] non *P*   24 Christi] christo *P*   27 illius] illi *F*   32 saluetur] saluatur *P*   38 possunt] nolunt *F*   56 illa] alia *P*   58 imponuntur] ponuntur *P*

22 apostolus|fol. 89va *P*   50 placere²|fol. 89vb *F*

sed fidei meritis unius. alter saluatur et est hoc ex larga dei misericordia.

Patarenus: Item apocalypsis. ultimo. ecce uenio cito et merces mea mecum est reddere unicuique secundum opera sua etcet. sed pueri nulla opera faciunt. igitur nullum recipiunt premium.

Catholicus: Respondeo quia loquitur de illis qui facere possunt.

Patarenus: Sed quare saluantur se nichil boni faciunt? Nonne deus iustus est? quare sine causa daret illis regnum suum.

Catholicus: Respondeo. quia iustus est. ideo saluat illos. Nec sine causa est. bonitas enim sua causa est. quia uult creaturas suas ad ymaginem et similitudinem suam creaturas frui sua bonitate. cum non habeant obstaculum peccati actualis uel originalis. actuale enim non habent pueri baptizati. quia non comiserunt illud. neque originale. quia deletum est per baptismum. Sed dicite mihi uos heretici quare debent dampnari pueri baptizati. creatura enim dei sunt. neque peccatum habent. quod est omnis dampnationis causa. quare enim deus sine causa perderet quod suum est. obmutescite igitur et desinite persequi puerculos innocentes et seuire in eis. qui iam requiescunt in brachiis patrinis. o uos lamie crudeles monstra utique diabolica.

De manus impositione XVIII

Catholicus: Sequitur de manus impositione in qua datur spiritus sanctus ad confirmationem recepte gratie baptismalis in qua quadrupliciter infatuantur patareni nefandi. Primo quia dicunt sine illa nullum aliquo modo posse saluari. secundo quia delirant in ipso spiritum sanctum dari ad peccatorum remissionem. tertio quia autumant in ipsa per homines dari spiritum sanctum. quarto uero putant quod ipsa possit per alios quam per episcopos fieri. quorum tertium errorem elisimus supra. in tractatu de septem sacramentis et datione spiritus sancti. alios uero tres confutabimus sub hac rubrica per testimonia scripturarum sacrarum ubi primo sciendi est quod tres sunt manus impositiones. de quibus in nouo testamento legitur. prima est illa solempnis quam confirmationem appellamus de qua proprius est hic tractatus. de qua etiam legitur in actibus apostolorum in pluribus locis et ista sit post baptismum in confirmationem et robur recepte gratie in baptismo. de qua legitur. actus. xviii. dixitque ad

every one of us shall render account for himself to God." So one is saved by the generous mercy of God.

Pat: See the last chapter of Apocalypse (22:12) "Behold, I come quickly and my reward is with me, to render to every man according to his works." But children have done no works, therefore they shall receive none of the reward.

Cath: I reply that he is speaking of those who are able to perform such works.

Pat: But why are they saved if they have done no good work? Isn't God just? Why should He give them his kingdom without cause?

Cath: I respond that it is just for God to save them, neither is He without cause, for His Goodness is the cause, since He wishes creatures created in His image and likeness to enjoy His goodness, since they have no obstacles of actual or original sin. Baptized children have no actual sin, since they have not committed any, neither do they have original sin, since it was removed by baptism. But tell me, you heretics, why baptized children ought to be damned, for they are servants of God. Neither do they have any sin, which is the cause of all damnation. For why would God lose them without cause, since they are His. Therefore be silent and refrain from persecuting innocent little children and railing against them, who rest in the arms of their godparents. O you cruel monsters and jackals! You are certainly from the devil!

On the imposition of hands [Confirmation]

Cath: Now follows the laying on of hands, by which the Holy Spirit is given for the confirmation of baptismal grace, regarding which the Patarenes err foolishly in four ways. In the first place, they say that without it no one at all can be saved. Secondly, they rave that in it the Holy Spirit is given for the remission of sins. Thirdly, they assert that in it the Holy Spirit is given through men. And fourthly they consider that it can be conferred by those other than bishops.[1] We destroyed the third error above in the section on the seven sacraments and the granting of the Holy Spirit. The other three we will refute under this rubric by the testimony of the sacred scriptures, where three impositions of hands are first made known. One reads of these in the New Testament. The first is the solemn imposition, which we call confirmation, of which this section is really about, and of which is read in the Acts of the Apostles, in numerous places, and that it is given after baptism and reinforces the graces received in baptism. About this one reads in Acts 19 (19:2) "And he said to

---

63 ecce…65 sua] Apoc. 22:12. **XVIII.1.20** dixitque…21 credentes] Act. 19:2.

83 desinite] desine *F* **XVIII.1.1** De…impositione] Title om. *P* 5 Primo] secundo *F* 8 autumant] auptumant *P* | per] pariter *F* 9 uero] add. quia *F* 11 septem] vii *F* 16 solempnis] sollempnis *F* 18 apostolorum] appostolorum *P*

79 dicite|fol. 90ra *P* 82 perderet|fol. 68v *F* **XVIII.1.19** robur|fol. 90rb *P*

---

1) These errors are discussed in Moneta, 293; Sacconi, c. 4.

eos. si spiritum sanctum acceptistis credentes etcet. et infra. hiis audistis baptizati sunt in nomine ihesu domini. et cum imposuisset manus paulus. uenit spiritus sanctus super eos et loquebantur linguis et prophetabant etcet. secunda uero est qui sit in sacris ordinibus. vii. unde prima ad timotheus. iiii°. noli negligere gratiam dei que est in te que data est tibi per prophetiam cum impositione manuum presbiteri etcet. de qua dicit in secunda id est propter quam causam amoneo te. ut per impositionem manuum mearum etcet. Tertia sit in unctione extrema. de qua. Iacobum. ultimo. infirmatur quis in uobis inducat presbiteros ecclesie et orent super eum ungentes eum oleo in nomine domini. etcet. Et in istis duabus datur spiritus sanctis. Tertia uero est que sit per infirmos ad expellendas egritudines corporales. de qua dicit Marcum. ultimo. super egros manus imponet et bene habebunt etcet. in ista non datur spiritus sanctus et sit hic per quoslibet fideles christi. ut dicit dominus in predicto capitulo. signa autem eos qui crediderint hec sequentur etcet. Quarum due prime per episcopos et tertia presbiteros tantum fieri possunt ut hoc suis locis ostendemus.

Quod sine manus impositione potest esse saluus

Mattheus. xi. uenite ad me omnes qui laboratis et honorati estis et ego reficiam uos. etcet. et infra. jugum enim meum soaue est et onus meum leue etcet. cum dominus uocet omnes peccatores ad refectionem nec aliquem excludat et cum dicat iugum et honus suum esse suaue atque leue patet quod per fidem et contritionem omnes saluari possunt. cum aliud non possunt. atque nullus pauper esse potest. sin autem non possent saluari. nisi haberent hominem qui eis penitentiam daret uel baptizaret seu manus imponeret. tunc frustra uocaret multos dominus. qui per impossibilitatem ad eos uenire non possent. uel quia non possent illum inuenire hominem officia sicut hic. uel quia ille nolet aut non posset illi dare salutis sacramenta et uerum iugum domini nec suaue esset nec honus eius leue quia esset impossibile non dico tantum ad portandum sed salutem ad ipsum inueniendum. item. xviii. cum autem non haberet unde redderet etcet. et infra. procidens autem seruus ille rogabat eum dicens. patientiam habe in me et omnia reddam tibi. misertus autem dominus serui illius dimisit eum et debitum dimisit ei etcet. ergo sufficit in necessitate sola bona uoluntas ingredi serua mandata etcet. ergo sine manus impositione potest quis habere

them, 'Have you received the Holy Spirit since you believed?'" and later (19:5–6) "Having heard these things, they were baptized in the name of the Lord Jesus. And when Paul had laid his hands on them, the Holy Spirit came upon them, and they spoke with tongues and prophesied." The second is that which is given in the seven Holy Orders. 1 Timothy 4 (4:14) "Do not neglect the grace that is in you, which was given you by prophecy, with imposition of the hands of the priesthood." The third laying of hands is given in Extreme Unction, spoken of in the last chapter of James (5:14) "Is any man sick among you? Let him bring in the priests of the church, and let them pray over him, anointing him with oil in the name of the Lord." And in these two the Holy Spirit is given. Yet the third [fourth] is that which is given to the sick for the driving out of physical illness. Mark speaks of this at the end of his gospel (16:18) "they shall lay their hands upon the sick, and they shall recover." In this the Holy Spirit is not given, and that this might be for all the Christian faithful, as the Lord says in the foregoing passage (16:17) "And these signs shall follow those who believe." The first two are able to be conferred by bishops and the third by priests also, as we shall demonstrate in their respective sections.

That one can be saved without the imposition of hands

Matthew 11 (11:28) "Come to me all you who labor and are heavily burdened and I will refresh you." And later (11:30) "my yoke is sweet and my burden is light." Since the Lord calls all sinners to refreshment, neither does He exclude anyone, and when He says that His yoke and burden are sweet and light, it is clear that all are able to be saved through faith and contrition, and since they cannot be otherwise, and no-one might be [rendered] poor (without which they cannot be saved), unless there should be a man who might give penance to them, or baptize, or lay hands on them, then the Lord would be calling many in vain who because of impossibility would not be able to come to such, whether because they would not be able to find that man [who might perform them], either because he was unwilling or unable to give him the sacrament of salvation, and then the true yoke of the Lord would be neither sweet nor would the burden be light, rather it would be impossible not, I say, only bearing but finding the salvation for himself. See 18 (18:25) "And as he didn't have anything to pay for it with." And later (18:26–27) "But that servant threw himself down, and begged him, saying, 'Have patience with me, and I will pay you everything.' And the lord of that servant being moved with pity, let him go and forgave him the debt." Therefore in necessity good will alone suffices. (19:17) "To enter into

---

22 hiis...25 prophetabant] Act. 19:5-6 (hiis audistis] his auditis *Vulg.*)   26 noli...28 presbiteri] 1 Tim. 4:14.   29 propter...30 mearum] 2 Tim. 1:6.   35 uero...37 egros] Iac. 5:14.   37 super...habebunt] Mar. 16:18.   40 signa...sequentur] Mar. 16:17. XVIII.2.3 uenite...4 uos] Matt. 11:28.   4 jugum...5 leue] Matt. 11:30.   20 cum...21 redderet] Matt. 18:25.   21 procidens...24 ei] Matt. 18:26-27 (rogabat] orabat *Vulg.*)   25 ingredi...mandata] Matt. 19:17.

26 vii] om. *F*   31 Tertia...34 etcet] om. *F* | Tertia...35 sanctis] ante. corr. *P*, sup. uacat.   35 Tertia] sic *PF* reading 'quarta' XVIII.2.9 cum...10 potest] †† unclear in mss.   10 atque] ad que *F*   18 dico] om. *P*   19 portandum] add. dico *P*

XVIII.2.4 estis|fol. 90va *P*

uitam. item. lucam. xxiii. dixit illi ihesus. amen dico tibi. hodie mecum eris in paradiso etcet. ad idem. item. ad Romanos. ii°. non est enim personarum acceptio apud deum etcet. et infra. cum autem gentes que legem non habent naturaliter ea que legis sunt faciunt. eiusmodi legem non habentes ipsi sibi sunt lex. quia ostendunt opus legis scriptum in cordibus suis. testimonium reddente illis conscientia ipsorum et inter se inuicem cogitationum accusatum aut etiam defendentium etcet. ergo omnino homo potest saluari ex sola bona uoluntate. cum aliud non potest. idem. iii°. iustitia autem dei per fidem ihesu christi in omnes et super omnes qui credunt in eum etcet. et infra. iustificati gratis per gratiam ipsius etcet. et iiii°. ei uero qui non operatur id est qui non habet tempus operandi. credenti autem in eum qui iustificat impium reputatur fides eius ad iustitiam secundum propositum gratie dei etcet. idem. v. iustificati ergo ex fide pacem habeamus ad deum etcet. idem. x. corde enim creditur ad iustitiam etcet. et infra. non enim est distinctio iudei et greci. Nam idem dominus omnium diues in omnes qui inuocant illum. non enim quicumque inuocauerit nomen domini saluus erit. item ad Galathas. secundo. Nos in christo ihesu credimus ut iustificemur ex fide christi etcet. item actus. vi°. crede in dominum ihesum et saluus eris tu et domus tua etcet. ex hiis et ex multis aliis scripturis sacris probatur quod in neccessitate sola fides cum bona uoluntate sufficit ad salutem. non solum sine manus impositione sed etiam sine quolibet alio sacramento. preterea apostoli habuerunt spiritum sanctum sine manus impositione et non solum illi sed etiam alii. ut legitur. actus iiii°. et cum orassent motus est locus in quo erant congregati et repleti sunt omnes spiritu sancto etcet. et x. adhuc loquente petro uerba hec cecidit spiritus sanctus super omnes qui audiebant uerbum etcet. item. multi in ueteri testamento habuerunt spiritus sanctus et fuerint salui sine manus impositione. ergo spiritus sanctus datur et saltem homini potest sine manus impositionem dum tamen non condempnatur.

Quod spiritus sanctus non datur in manus impositione ad remissionem peccatorum sed tantum ad confirmationem et robur recepte gratie baptismalis

Quod autem in manus impositione non detur spiritus sanctus ad remissionem peccatorum sed tantum ad robur et confirmationem gratie recepte in baptismo.

life, keep the commandments." Therefore one can have life without the laying on of hands. Luke 23 (23:43) "Jesus said to him 'Amen I say to you, today you will be with me in paradise.'" Romans 2 is about the same idea (2:11) "there is no respect of persons with God," and later (2:14–15) "For when the Gentiles, who do not have the law, do by nature those things that are of the law, these having not the law are a law to themselves, who show the work of the law written in their hearts, their conscience bearing witness to them, and their thoughts between themselves accusing, or also defending one another." Therefore no man can be saved from good will alone, since another is not able. In the same book (3:22) "Even the justice of God, by faith of Jesus Christ, for all and upon all who believe in him." And later (3:24) "justified freely by his grace." And 4 (4:5) "But to him who does not work" — that is, who does not have the time for works — "yet believes in him who justifies the ungodly, his faith is reputed to justice, according to the purpose of the grace of God." Also 5 (5:1) "Being justified therefore by faith, let us have peace with God." And 10 (10:10) "For, with the heart we believe unto justice." And later (10:12–13) "For there is no distinction between Jew and Greek: for the same is Lord over all, rich to all who call upon him. For whosoever shall call upon the name of the Lord, shall be saved." Also Galatians 2 (2:16) "We also believe in Christ Jesus, that we may be justified by the faith of Christ." Also Acts 6 (16:31) "Believe in the Lord Jesus and you shall be saved and also your house." From these and many other passages of Sacred Scripture it is established that faith alone, with a good will, justifies in necessity unto salvation. Not only without the laying on of hands but also without any other sacrament. Further the Apostles had the Holy Spirit without the imposition of hands and not only them but also others as is read in Acts 4 (4:31) "And when they had prayed, the place where they were gathered was moved, and they were all filled with the Holy Spirit." And 10 (10:44) "While Peter was still speaking these words, the Holy Spirit fell on all them who heard the word." And many in the Old Testament had the Holy Spirit and were saved without the imposition of hands, therefore the Holy Spirit is given and a man can at least be saved without imposition of hands, provided that he was not condemned.

That the Holy Spirit is not given in the imposition of hands for the remission of sins but only for the confirmation and strengthening of the grace received in baptism

For it is clear that the Holy Spirit is not granted in the laying of hands for the remission of sins but only for the

patet quia in baptismo remissa sunt omnia peccata et data est ibi gratia spiritus sancti. debite recipientibus illum et probatum est supra in tractatu de baptismo. Si igitur manus impositione remitteret peccata et gratiam conferret de nouo esset utique plerumque inanis et uana. cum non inueniret peccata que remitteret et gratiam inuenisset iam datam. presertim cum iuxta baptismum daretur. sic dedit eam paulus actus xix. his auditis baptizati sunt in nomine domini ihesu. et cum imposuisset manus paulus etcet. preterea haberet idem officium cum baptismate et sic non esset diuersitas inter unum sacramentum et aliud. quod absurdum est cogitare. preterea in nulla auctore inuenitur quod in manus impositione fiat peccatorum remissio. sed semper ubi legitur de ipsa et datione spiritus sancti in ea inuenies aliqua uerba ostendentia quod cum spiritus sanctus datur in illa. datur utique ad aliquod robur et uigorem est aliquod. uerbi gratia. ut habes. actus. xix. et cum imposuisset manus paulus uenit spiritus sanctus super eos et loquebantur linguis et prophetabatur etcet. Non dixit quod spiritus sanctus datur per impositionem manuum pauli. uenisset super illos ad remissionem peccatorum uel gratie collationem sed ostendit quod uenit super eos ad usum loquendi linguis et prophetandi. qui sunt duo effectus roboris accepte gratie.

Quod manus impositio que dicitur confirmatio non potest fieri nisi per episcopos

Actus viii. cum uero credidissent phylippo euangelizanti de regno dei et in nomine ihesu christi baptizaretur uiri ac mulieres etcet. et infra. cum autem audissent apostoli qui erant ierosolimis. miserunt ad illos petrum et ioannem etcet. et infra. tunc imponebant manus super illos etcet. ex quo patet quod solis episcopis data est auctoritas faciendi manus impositionem. Si enim licuisset aliis fecisset utique ipsam samaritanis phylippus quos predicauerat et baptizauerat. Nec pro apostolis missum fuisse ut facerent illam. Non enim poterat eam facere phylippus diaconus. de quo legitur supra. vi. ubi dicitur et elegerunt stephanum uirum plenum de fide et spiritu sancto et phylippum etcet. et quod iste non fuerit phylippus apostolus habetur ex principio istius capituli ibi cum dicitur. facta est autem in illa die persecutio magna in ecclesia que erat ierosolimis et omnes dispersi sunt per regiones iudee et samarie preter apostolos etcet. ergo phylippus apostolus remanserat ierosolimis et ille phylippus qui predicabat samarie erat diaconus de quo dictum est supra. et ideo non licebat ei facere manus impositionem cum non esset episcopus. preterea nusquam inuenitur in aliquam scriptura quod aliqui-

confirmation of the graces received in baptism, because baptism forgives all sins and in it the grace of the Holy Spirit is given to its worthy recipients is proven in the section above on baptism. For if the laying of hands might remit sin and confer grace anew it would be almost entirely empty and meaningless, since one could not find sins already forgiven and grace already given, especially since it had already been granted in baptism. So Paul gave it (19:5–6) "Having heard these things, they were baptized in the name of the Lord Jesus, and when Paul had imposed his hands on them." Furthermore it would have had the same role as baptism and thus there would not be a distinction between one sacrament and the other, which is absurd to think. Further one discovers in no author that the laying of hands effected the remission of sins, but one always reads of the sacrament and the granting of the Holy Spirit in it, finding some words showing that the Holy Spirit is given therein, and is certainly conferred so that the word of grace might be strengthened and given vigor. You have for example Acts 19 (19:6) "and when Paul had imposed his hands on them, they began speaking in languages and prophesying," and these are two of the effects of receiving strengthening grace.

That the imposition of hands which is called Confirmation cannot be conferred but by a bishop

Acts 8 (8:12) "But when they had believed Philip preaching of the kingdom of God in the name of Jesus Christ, they were baptized, both men and women." And later (8:14) "Now when the apostles heard, who were in Jerusalem, they sent Peter and John to them." And later (8:17) "Then they laid hands on them." From this it is clear that only bishops are given the authority of making the imposition of hands. For if it were permitted for others to do so, why not Philip who had preached and baptized the same Samaritans? Nor was he deputed by the Apostles to do so. Nor could he confirm them, since Philip was a deacon, as is read above in 6 where it says (6:5) "And they selected Stephen, a man full of faith and the Holy Spirit and Philip." That that this was not Philip the Apostle is shown from the head of this chapter when it says (8:1) "And at that time there arose a great persecution against the church which was at Jerusalem, and they were all dispersed through the regions of Judea, and Samaria, except the apostles." Therefore Philip the Apostle remained at Jerusalem and that Philip who preached in Samaria was the deacon mentioned above, and therefore it was not permitted for him to lay hands since he was no bishop. Further nowhere is it to be found in any passage of

---

XVIII.3.15 his...17 paulus] Act. 19:5-6 (imposuisset] add. illis *Vulg.*) 26 et...27 prophetabatur] Act. 19:6 (imposuisset] add. illis | prophetabatur] prophetabant *Vulg.*) XVIII.4.3 cum...5 mulieres] Act. 8:12 (baptizaretur] baptizabantur *Vulg.*) 5 cum...7 etcet] Act. 8:14 (illos] eos *Vulg.*) 7 tunc...8 illos] Act. 8:17. 14 et...16 phylippum] Act. 6:5. 18 facta...20 apostolos] Act. 8:1.

12 et] add. vacua P exp. 15 xix] xviiii P 17 preterea] postea F 25 xix] xviiii P XVIII.4.22 quo] qua F

XVIII.3.20 nulla|fol. 91rb P XVIII.4.2 episcopos|fol. 69v F 18 persecutio|fol. 91va P

Quod sine manus impositione non potest esse saluus et quod per solam manus impositionem datur spiritus sanctus et quod ipsa potest fieri etiam per non episcopos

[Patarenus:] Actus. viii. qui cum uenisset orauerunt pro ipsis ut acciperent spiritum sanctum. nondum enim in quemquam illorum uenerat. sed baptizati tamen erant in nomine domini ihesu. tunc imponebant manus super illos et accipiebant spiritum sanctum. Ecce quomodo habes quod spiritum sanctum non dabatur per baptismum sed sine spiritu sancto nulla est salus et dicitur hic quod datur in manus impositione et remittuntur peccata per spiritum sanctum datum in illa.

Catholicus: Respondeo quod ista uerba sic intelliguntur. nondum enim in quemquam illorum uenerat etcet. scilicet ad robur et confirmationem. uenerat utique ad remissionem peccatorum et gratie collationem sicut per multas auctores probatum est supra. titulum de baptismo scilicet manifeste uidentibus astantibus. consueuerat enim uenire spiritus sanctus uidentibus hominibus plerumque quando dabatur per manus impositionem et quandoque etiam quando alio modo ueniebat. Sed modo respondete mihi de hac uestra perfidia quos multiplicatur ad inconueniens deducere possum. et primo sic. Dicitis enim et uerum est quod ex sola mala uoluntate incurrit in dei indignationem. ergo multo fortius ex sola bona uoluntate ipsius igitur potest inueniri ut probat apostolus ad romanos. v. non sicut delictum ita et donum. Si enim unius delicto multi mortui sunt multo magis gratia dei et donum in gratia unius hominis ihesu christi in plures habundauit et dominus dicit. mattheus. xii. si autem sciretis quid est misericordiam uolo etcet. ubi ostendit quod pronior est ad saluandum quam ad condempnandum. unde et Jacobum. iiº. dicit superexaltat autem misericordia iudicium etcet. ergo si deus condempnat ex sola mala uoluntate hominem. multo fortius ex sola bona uoluntate iustificat illum. ergo sine manus impositione potest esse saluus et potest dari spiritus sancti. preterea. non est in hoc mundo adeo rusticus homo. et adeo sceleratus qui non reputet illum sibi amicum. quem se diligere nouit. licet ei seruire non possit. sic ergo deus esset secundum uestram blasphemiam omni rustico rusticior et omni iniquorum peior.

audite miseri quid dicit apostolus ad romanos. viiii. numquid iniquitas apud deum. absit. etcet. iterum

That without laying of hands one cannot be saved and that only through the laying of hands is the Holy Spirit granted and that it can be done also by those who are not bishops

[Pat:] Acts 8 (8:15–17) "Who, when they had come, prayed for them, that they might receive the Holy Spirit, for he had not yet come upon any of them, but they were only baptized in the name of the Lord Jesus. Then they laid their hands upon them, and they received the Holy Spirit." See how you have it that the Holy Spirit was not given by baptism, but without the Holy Spirit none at all can be saved, and it says here that the Spirit is given in the laying of hands and sins are forgiven by the Holy Spirit given in that act.

Cath: I reply that the passage "for he had not yet come upon any of them" is to be interpreted thusly, namely in the strength of confirmation, and He came by the conferral of grace for the forgiveness of sins, as was proven above by many authorities in the section on baptism, or "for he had not yet come upon any of them" namely to those standing and looking, for the Holy Spirit had been accustomed to come by appearing to men for the most part when He was given through laying of hands and sometimes also when He came in other ways. But now answer me regarding this faithlessness of yours, in which I can detect many inconsistencies. The first is this: for you say, and it is true, that one incurs the wrath of God by a bad will alone, therefore how much more from a good will alone [will one find favor]. One can find it as proven by the Apostle in Romans 5 (5:15) "But not as the offence, so also the gift. For if by the offence of one, many died, how much more the grace of God, and the gift, by the grace of one man, Jesus Christ, has abounded unto many." And the Lord says in Matthew 12 (12:7) "And if you knew what this means, 'I will have mercy.'" Where he shows that he is more inclined to salvation than to condemnation. Also James 2 says (2:13) "And mercy exalts itself above judgment." So if God condemns solely based on a man's bad will, how much more from just a good will shall He justify him? Therefore one can be saved without the laying of hands and the Holy Spirit can be given. Further there is no man in this world so boorish and so wicked that he does not think him who he knows loves him is a friend to himself, although he be unable to serve him. So God would be — according to your blasphemy — more rustic than every peasant and worse than all evildoers.

Listen you miserable wretch, what the Apostle says to the Romans in chapter 9 (9:14) "Is there injustice with God?

miseri uos sic dicendo asseritis non in deo qui ad cor respicit salutem esse uite eterne. sed in homine qui tactu corporis sui det illam. et constitutus uos deo sanctiores et potentiores esse. immo spiritum prophetam que non est licitum reputatis. quidem est omne scelerus superans. preterea proponitis quod minus est maiori scilicet manus impositionem baptismati et penitentie. immo illa pro nichilo reputatis. sed dicite mihi ubi umquam dixit ueritas. dixit. nisi quis renatus fuerit per manus impositionem non intrabit in regnum dei. et item qui crediderit et manus impositione habuit saluus erit. et accipite manus impositionem et appropinquabit regnum celorum et nisi manus impositione habueritis omnes simile peribitis. sicut hoc dicit. de baptismate et de penitencia. Obmutescite igitur fere belue et nolite lacerare facta dei.

Quod manus impositioni tota potest fieri per non episcopos

[**Patarenus:**] Actus viii. et abiit ananias et introiuit in domum et imponens ei manum et dixit. Saule frater dominus misit me qui apparuit tibi in uia qua ueniebas ut uideas et implearis spiritu sancto. etcet. sed ille ananias non erat episcopus. ergo per non episcopum potest fieri manus impositio.

Catholicus: Respondeo quod ananias fecit manus impositionem paulo de spirituali mandato christi. et quod est spirituale non trahitur ad consequentiam et est simile de moyse. qui de spirituali mandato dei. licet esset laicus consecrauit aaron in summum sacerdotem ut legitur. exodus ultimo. et tamen non licet alius laicis episcopos consecraret. preterea ubi habes quod ananias non fuerit episcopus. ego tamen habeo presumptionem quod episcopus fuit propter rationes quas superius in nostra parte allegaui. possum etiam dicere et uerum est quod non loquitur ibi in actibus. de manus impositione sacramentali. Sed de illa que sit ad expellendas egritudines. erat enim paulus excecatus ut legitur in superius. sed surrexit autem saulus de terra. aperitsque oculis nihil uidebat etcet. et postea et erat tribus diebus non uidens etcet. ad duo enim missus fuit ananias ad non ad paulum scilicet ut imponeret illi manus in nomine eius. et sic ille uisum reciperet. et ut spiritus sanctus per baptismum reciperet. et hoc est quod ibi sequitur. et confestim ceciderunt ab oculis eius tamquam squame et uisum recepit. et surgens baptizatus est etcet. nec dixit ananias quod per manus impositionem eius paulus deberet accipere. spiritus sanctus. sed dixit per manus impositionem eius reciperet uisum. et dixit quod christus uolebat quod

God forbid!" Again you would be miserable by speaking thus, you do not claim that salvation does not flow from God who considers the heart, but rather from men who might give them a physical touch, and make yourselves holier and more powerful than God, indeed even the spirit of prophecy, which is not permitted, for this exceeds all wickedness. Further you propose that the lesser is greater, namely, the imposition of hands [as greater than] baptism or penance, indeed you do not value either of those. But tell me where this truth was ever spoken. "He said, unless you be born again through the laying of hands you shall not enter the kingdom of God." And further "he who shall believe in the laying of hands shall have salvation." and "Receive the laying of hands and one shall approach the kingdom of heaven" and "unless you receive the laying of hands, you shall all perish likewise." Just as He said of baptism and penance. Keep silent, then, you wild beast, and do not mangle the deeds of God.

That the imposition of hands can be entirely accomplished by those who are not bishops

[**Pat:**] Acts 8 (9:17) "And Ananias went his way, and entered into the house, and laying his hands upon him, he said, 'Brother Saul, the Lord has sent me, he who appeared to you in the way in which you came, that you might see, and be filled with the Holy Spirit.'" But that Ananias was not a bishop. Therefore the laying of hands can be done by one not a bishop.

Cath: I reply that Ananias laid hands on Paul by the spiritual command of Christ and that from spiritual things one does not draw conclusions, and it is similar to Moses who, by a certain spiritual command of God and though he was a layman, was able to consecrate Aaron as the High Priest as is read in the last chapter of Exodus, yet it was not allowed that any other layman might consecrate bishops. Further, while you consider that Ananias was not a bishop, yet I presume that he was a bishop on account of the reasons I detailed above. Also I am able to say, and it is true, that he is not speaking there in Acts of the sacramental imposition of hands, but of that by which sickness is driven out, for Paul had been struck blind, as is read above. But (Acts 9:8) "And Saul arose from the ground, and when his eyes were opened, he saw nothing." and after (9:9) "and he was blind for three days." For Ananias was sent to the two and not to Paul, namely so that he might lay hands in His name, and so that Paul might recover his sight, and so that he might receive the Holy Spirit in Baptism, and this follows (9:18) "And immediately things like scales fell from his eyes, and he received his sight, and rising up, he was baptized." Neither did Ananias say that Paul ought to receive the Holy Spirit by the imposition of hands, but he said that he would receive sight through the laying of his hands, and he said that Christ wished that he

---

XVIII.6.3 et¹...6 sancto] Act. 9:17 (manum] manus *Vulg.*)   22 surrexit...23 uidebat] Act. 9:8.   23 et²...24 uidens] Act. 9:9.
28 et...30 est] Act. 9:18.

49 non] add. ideo *P* exp.   52 spiritum prophe-tam] ipsum quod hoc *F*   53 est¹] add. litteram *P* exp.   57 umquam] numquam *F*
XVIII.6.6 ille] iste *F*   15 episcopos] om. *F*   26 et²...27 reciperet] om. *P*   30 per] om. *F*   32 sed] set *P*

49 dicendo|fol. 70r *F*   50 qui|fol. 92ra *P*   **XVIII.6.15** quod|fol. 92rb *P*

ille impletur spiritu sancto quod intelligo factum per sacramentum baptismatis. de manus autem impositione sacramentali factam paulo legitur actus. xiii. dixit illi spiritus sanctus segregate mihi barnabam et saulum in opus ad quod asumpsi eos. Tunc ieiunantes et orantes imponentesque illis manus dimiserunt illos etcet.

might be filled with the Holy Spirit, and that I understand to be caused by the sacrament of baptism rather than the sacramental imposition of hands made to Paul, as is read in Acts 13 (13:2–3) "the Holy Spirit said to them, 'Separate me Saul and Barnabas, for the work which I assign to them.' Then, fasting and praying, and imposing their hands upon them, they sent them away."

De sacramento penitentie

XIX

On the Sacrament of Penance

Sequitur de penitentia. cuius tres sunt partes. scilicet contritio. confessio et satisfactio. circa quas omnes errant patareni. Sed quia de confessione omnes errant heretici. dimittimus eius tractatam in tertium librum. De contritione uero duobus modis errare uidentur de quibus in hoc tractatu discutiemus. Primo quia dicunt non esse illam habendam nisi de peccatis que dicunt se in celis commisisse. secundo uero quia delirant se tria in celis habuisse scilicet corpus et animam et spiritum. Corpus autem dicunt in celis iacere prostratum. animam uero dicunt in terram esse proiectam et cotidie ipsam de corpore in corpus pertransire. spiritum autem aiunt in aere peruagari donec animam suam in terris cognoscens alloquitur et confortat illam de penitentia patarenorum facienda et tunc anima cognoscens eius spiritus inspirationem. conuertitur de peccatis que fecit in celis et per manus impositionem patarenorum uitam eorum faciens saluatur. prout tetigimus supra in titulo de angelis de celo cadentibus. in principio. Verumtamen in istis duobus predictis ipsi diuersa sentiunt ad inuicem. alii alia sentientes et dicentes quod et de peccatis que commiserunt in terra oporteat eos habere contritionem et penitentiam facere et quod non habeant nisi unum spiritum qui anima dicitur. Errant autem et in tertio circa contritionem. scilicet quod per ipsam sine manus impositione non possit aliquo modo aliquis saluari. prout hoc in superiori tractatu discussimus diligenter. De satisfactione autem tandem credunt que de contritione diximus similiter et in illa ad inuicem sibi contradicentes. preterquam de restitutione male ablatorum. de qua concordat communiter omnes quod ad illam minime teneantur addentes quod usura nunquam sit mortale peccatum. Nos uero deo dante huiusmodi opiniones errores esse dampnatos. in hoc tractatu declarabimus manifeste.

Here follows penance, of which there are three parts, namely contrition, confession, and satisfaction. All the Patarenes err concerning these. But since all the heretics err about confession, we will forego treating it until book three. Regarding contrition they are seen to err in two ways, of which we shall treat in this section. The first is that they say that there are no sins except those which are said to be committed in heaven. In the second place, because they delude themselves that they have three things in heaven: the body, the soul, and the spirit. But they say that the body lies prostrate in heaven, yet they say the soul is cast down on earth and daily goes from body to body, but the spirit wanders about in the air until, knowing its soul on earth, calls and consoles the soul by the performance of the Patarene penance. And then, knowing its soul, the spirit is breathed in, and is converted from the sins which it did in heaven and its life is saved by the Patarene imposition of hands,[1] just as we touched on above at the beginning of the section on the fallen angels. However they differ among themselves about these two issues, with some of them thinking and saying that for those sins committed on earth, one ought to have contrition and to do penance, and that they have nothing but one spirit which is called the soul. Yet they err in the third issue about contrition, for they say that no one can be saved except by the imposition of hands, as we have diligently treated in the above sections. Finally, about satisfaction they believe similarly about what we said about contrition and there are contradictions between them. Further on the restoration of ill-gotten goods, about which they all agree together, adding that they hold that usury is never a mortal sin. Yet we, God willing, hold those errors to be damnable, as we shall declare plainly in that section.

---

37 dixit... 40 illos] Act. 13:2-3 (illi] illis | illis] eis *Vulg.*)

XIX.1.3 circa] add. sarai *P* **11** prostratum] prostratis *P* **12** animam] naturam *F* **14** aiunt] om. *P* **15** alloquitur... 17 cognoscens] om. *F* **22** sentiunt... inuicem] transp. *F* | alia] aliud *F* **24** oporteat] opporteat *P* **27** per] add. ma *P* exp. **30** tandem] eadem *F* **32** male] mala *P* **34** addentes] om. *P* **35** opiniones] oppiniones *P* **36** esse] om. *P*

XIX.1.8 habendam|fol. 92va *P* **24** oporteat|fol. 70v *F* **37** manifeste|fol. 92vb *P*

---

1) The doctrine of the absolute dualists.

Quod oportet hominem contritionem habere et penitentiam facere de omnibus peccatis que fecit in hac uita et non de aliquibus celestibus que numquam fuerunt

Mattheus. iiii°. penitentiam agite appropinquabit enim regnum celorum etcet. et vii. nolite iudicare et non iudicabimini. in quo enim iudicio iudicaueritis iudicabimini. etcet. per totum capitulum. et xii. dico autem uobis quoniam omne uerbum otioso quod locuti fuerint homines reddent rationem de eo in die iudicii. ex uerbis enim tuis iustificaberis et ex uerbis tuis condemnaberis. etcet. et xiii. mittet enim angelos suos et colligent de regno eius omnia scandala et eos qui faciunt iniquitatem et mittent eos in caminum ignis etcet. et xvi. et tunc reddet unicuique secundum opera eorum etcet. et xviiii. ihesus autem discipulis suis. amen dico uobis quia diues difficile intrabit in regnum celorum. etcet. et xx. quid hic statis tota die otiosi. et xxi. uos autem fecistis illam speluncam latronum. et xxiii. super cathedram moysi sederunt scribe et pharisei. et per totum capitulum ubi reprehendit scribas et phariseis eos de multis peccatis que super faciebant et propter hoc cominatur eis dampnationem eternam. item. marcum. vi. et exeuntes predicabant ut penitentiam agerent. et xi. quod si uos non dimiseritis nec pater uester dimittet uobis peccata uestra. Item lucam. xiii. respondens dixit illis. putatis quod hii galilei prae omnibus galileis peccatores fuerint quia talia passi sunt non dico uobis sed nisi penitentiam habueritis omnes similiter peribitis etcet. idem. xvi^a. homo quidam erat diues qui induebatur purpura et bisso et epulabatur quotidie splendide etcet. et postea et sepultus est in inferno etcet. item iohannes. x. multa bona opera ostendi uobis ex patre meo. propter quod eorum opus me lapidatis. etcet. item ad romanos. i°. reuelatur enim ira dei de celo super omnem impietatem et iniustitiam hominum eorum qui ueritatem dei in iniustitia detinent etcet. per totum maxime in finem. quoniam qui talia agunt digni sunt morte et non solum qui ea faciunt sed etiam qui consentiunt facientibus etcet. et ii°. ignoras quoniam benignitas dei ad penitentiam te adducit etcet. et infra. per totum. et vi. sicut enim exibuistis membra uestra seruire immunditie et iniquitati ad iniquitatem ita nunc exhibete etcet. et infra. quem ergo fructum habuistis tunc in illis in quibus nunc erubescitis? nam finis illorum mors est etcet. item. prima. ad corinthios.

That it is fitting that a man should have contrition and do penance for all of the sins he committed in this life, and not about those what never happened in another heavenly place

Matthew 4 (4:17) "Do penance, for the kingdom of heaven is approaching," and 7 (7:1–2) "Judge not, so that you may not be judged, for with the judgment you judge, you shall be judged," and through the whole chapter. And 12 (12:36–37) "But I say to you, that every idle word that men will speak, they will render an account for it in the day of judgment. For by your words you will be justified, and by your words you will be condemned." And 13 (13:41–42) "The Son of man will send his angels, and they will gather all scandals out of his kingdom, and those who work iniquity and shall cast them into the furnace of fire." And 16 (16:27) "and he will render to each according to his works," and 19 (19:23) "And Jesus said to them, 'Amen I say to you, it is very difficult for a rich man to enter the kingdom of heaven.'" And 20 (20:6) "Why do you stand here idle all day?" And 21 (21:13) "but you have made it a den of thieves." And 23 (23:2) "The scribes and the Pharisees sit on the chair of Moses," and throughout the chapter where He reprimands what the scribes and Pharisees have done and on account of which He threatens them with eternal damnation. Further Mark 6 (6:12) "And going forth they preached that men should do penance." And 11 (11:25) "forgive, if you have anything against any man; that your Father also may forgive you your sins." Also Luke 13 (13:2–3) "he answering, said to them, 'do you think that these Galileans were sinners worse than all the men of Galilee, because they suffered these things? No, I say to you, but unless you do penance, you will all likewise perish.'" And in 16 (16:19) "There was a certain rich man, who was clothed in purple and fine linen and feasted sumptuously every day." And later (16:22) "and he was buried in hell." And John 10 (10:32) "I have shown you many good works from my Father, for which of these works do you stone me?" Also Romans 1 (1:18) "For the wrath of God is revealed from heaven against all ungodliness and injustice of those men that detain the truth of God in injustice." And this continues throughout, especially at the end (1:32) "that those who do such things, are worthy of death, and not only those who do them, but those also who consent to those who do them." And 2 (2:4) "Do you not know that the benignity of God leads you to penance?" And so on through the rest. And 6 (6:19) "For as you have yielded your members to serve uncleanness and iniquity, for iniquity, so now yield your members to serve justice, unto sanctification." And later (6:21)

XIX.2.5 penitentiam...6 celorum] Matt. 4:17.   6 nolite...8 iudicabimini] Matt. 7:1-2.   8 dico...12 condemnaberis] Matt. 12:36-37 (otioso) otiosum | fuerint] sunt *Vulg.*)   12 mittet...15 ignis] Matt. 13:41-42 (enim) add. filius hominis *Vulg.*)   15 et²...16 eorum] Matt. 16:27 (eorum) eius *Vulg.*).   16 ihesus...18 celorum] Matt. 19:23 (autem) add. dixit *Vulg.*)   18 quid...19 otiosi] Matt. 20:6.   19 uos...20 latronum] Matt. 21:13.   20 super...21 pharisei] Matt. 23:3.   24 et...25 agerent] Mar. 6:12.   25 quod...27 uestra] Mar. 11:25 (uester) add. qui in caelis est *Vulg.*).   27 respondens...30 peribitis] Luc. 13:2-3.   31 homo...32 etcet] Luc. 16:19.   33 et... inferno] Luc. 16:22.   34 multa...35 lapidatis] Ioh. 10:32.   36 reuelatur...38 detinent] Rom. 1:18.   39 quoniam...41 facientibus] Rom. 1:32.   41 ignoras...42 adducit] Rom. 2:4.   43 sicut...45 exhibete] Rom. 6:19.   45 quem...47 est] Rom. 6:21.

XIX.2.1 hominem] om. *P*   20 cathedram] cathedra *P*   36 dei] add. ce *P* exp

XIX.2.26 dimiseritis|fol. 93ra *P*

vᵒ omnino auditur inter uos fornicatio etcet. et infra. et uos inflati estis et non magis luctum habuistis etcet. Item. iia. ad corinthios. viiᵒ. mundemus nos ab omni inquinamento carnis et spiritus etcet. item. ad Galathas. v. manifesta sunt opera carnia que sunt fornicatio immundicia impudicitia luxuria auaritia etcet. et postea. quoniam que talia agunt regnum dei non consequentur. item ad ephesios. v. omnis fornicator aut immundus aut auarus quod est ydolorum seruitus non habet hereditatem in regno christi et dei etcet. item ad phylippenses. iiiᵒ. nunc autem et flens dico inimicos crucis quorum finis interitus quorum deus uenter est et gloria in confusione ipsorum qui terrena sapiunt. Item. prima ad thessolonicenses. iiiiᵒ. hec est enim uoluntas dei sanctificatio uestra ut abstineatis uos a fornicatione etcet. item. iiª. iiᵒ. ut iudicentur omnes qui non crediderunt ueritati etcet. item ad phylippenses. iiiᵒ. propter que uenit ira dei super filios incredulitatis etcet. item iª ad timotheus. iiiiᵒ. in nouissimis temporibus discedent quidam a fide etcet. item iiª. iiᵒ. nemo militans deo implicat se negotiis secularibus etcet. Item ad titum. iᵒ. confitentur se nosse deum factis autem negant ab honorabiles et incredibiles et ad omne opus bonum reprobi etcet. item ad hebreos. ultimo. fornicatores enim et adulteros iudicabit deus. Item. jacobus. iiiiᵒ. unde bella et lites in uobis nonne ex concupiscentiis uestris que militant in membris uestris etcet. item iiª petri. iiᵒ. magis autem eos qui post carnem in concupiscentia immunditie ambulant etcet. per totum. item. iª. iohannes iᵒ. qui autem odit fratrem suum in tenebris est. etcet. item iudas. iiᵒ. ecce uenit dominus in sanctis milibus suis facere iudicium contra omnes per totum etcet. item actus. iiᵒ. ihesum nazarenum etcet. et postea. penitentiam inquit agite etcet. et iiiᵒ. auctorem uite interfecistis etcet. et infra. penitemini igitur et conuertimini ut deleantur peccata uestra etcet. Item apocalypsis. ix. non egerunt penitentiam ab homicidiis suis neque a ueneficiis suis. neque a fornicatione sua neque a furtis suis etcet. Ex hiis patet et ex multis aliis scripturis noui testamenti. immo quasi ex toto nouo et ueteri testamento quod deus prohibet peccata fieri in hac uita et quod facientibus illa comminatur et dat eternam dampnationem et quod de illis predicauit et predicari fecit penitentia et quod de illis penituerant multi et penitere possunt omnis. et quod illi qui penitentiam faciunt de illi saluantur. et quod scriptura

"What fruit therefore did you have then in those things of which you are now ashamed? For the end of them is death." And 1 Corinthians (5:1) "It is absolutely heard that there is fornication among you." And later (5:2) "And you are puffed up, and have not rather mourned." Also 2 Corinthians 7 (7:1) "let us cleanse ourselves from all defilement of the flesh and of the spirit." Also Galatians 5 (5:19) "Now the works of the flesh are clear, which are fornication, uncleanness, immodesty, luxury." And later (5:21) "those who do such things shall not obtain the kingdom of God." And Ephesians 5 (5:5) "no fornicator, or unclean or covetous person — which is a serving of idols — has an inheritance in the kingdom of Christ and of God." Also Philippians 3 (3:18–19) "and I now tell you weeping, that they are enemies of the cross of Christ, whose end is destruction, whose God is their belly, and whose glory is in their shame, who mind earthly things." Also 1 Thessalonians 4 (4:2) "For this is the will of God: your sanctification, so that you might restrain yourselves from fornication." Also 2 Thessalonians 2 (2:12) "That all may be judged who have not believed the truth." And Philippians 3 (Colossians 3:6) "For which things the wrath of God comes upon the children of unbelief." Also 1 Timothy 4 (4:1) "For in the last days some will depart from the faith." And 2 Timothy 2 (2:4) "No man, being a soldier of God, entangles himself in secular affairs." Also Titus 1 (1:16) "They profess that they know God: but in their works they deny him, being abominable, and incredulous, and to every good work reprobate." And in the last chapter of Hebrews (13:4) "For God will judge fornicators and adulterers." Also James 4 (4:1) "From where arise wars and contentions among you? Are they not from your concupiscences, which war in your members?" And 2 Peter 2 (2:10) "And especially those who walk after the flesh in the lust of uncleanness." and 1 John 1 (2:11) "But he who hates his brother is in darkness." Also Jude 2 (1:14–15) "Behold, the Lord comes with thousands of his saints to execute judgment upon all." Also Acts 2 (2:22) "Jesus of Nazareth," and after (2:38) "'Do penance,' he said." And 3 (3:15) "But you killed the author of life." And later (3:19) "Be penitent, therefore, and be converted, so that your sins may be blotted out." Further Apocalypse 9 (9:21) "Neither did they do penance for their murders, nor for their sorceries, nor for their fornication, nor for their thefts." From these and many other passages in the New Testament — indeed from nearly the whole of the New and Old Testaments — it is clear that God prohibits the commission of sins in this life, and to those who commit them He threatens and gives eternal damnation, and that He preached to them and proclaimed penance, so that

---

48 omnino…fornicatio] 1 Cor. 5:1. 49 et¹…habuistis] 1 Cor. 5:2. 50 mundemus…51 spiritus] 2 Cor. 7:1. 52 manifesta…53 auaritia] Gal. 5:19 (auaritia) om. *Vulg.*) 54 quoniam…55 consequentur] Gal. 5:21. 55 omnis…57 dei] Eph. 5:5. 58 nunc…61 sapiunt] Php. 3:18-19 (crucis) christi *Vulg.*) 61 hec…63 fornicatione] 1 Thes. 4:3. 63 ut…64 ueritati] 2 Thes. 2:12. 65 propter…66 incredulitatis] Col. 3:6. 66 in…67 fide] 1 Tim. 4:1. 68 nemo…69 secularibus] 2 Tim. 2:4. 69 confitentur…71 reprobi] Tit. 1:16 (honorabiles] add. cum sint abominati *Vulg.*) 72 fornicatores…73 deus] Heb. 13:4. 73 unde…75 uestris] Iac. 4:1 (nonne] add. hinc *Vulg.*) 75 magis…77 ambulant] 2 Pet. 2:10. 77 qui…78 est] 1 Ioh. 2:11. 79 ecce…80 totum] Iud. 1:14-15. 81 ihesum nazarenum] Act. 2:22. 82 penitentiam…agite] Act. 2:38. | auctorem…83 interfecistis] Act. 3:15. 83 penitemini…84 uestra] Act. 3:19. 85 non…87 suis] Apoc. 9:21.

65 phylippenses] *sic PF* | filios] 66 incredulitatis] et diffidentie P. ms. this is confused with Eph 2:2 85 ix] viiii P

52 que|fol. 71r F | for-nicatio|fol. 93rb P 82 auctorem|fol. 93va P

diuina numquam de aliis peccatis hominum facit mentionem. nisi de illis que comiserunt in hac uita et numquam pena promittitur eis temporales uel eterna nisi propter peccata in hac uita comissa. Quare probatur necessario quod de omnibus peccatis que facit homo in hac uita oportet eum habere contritionem et penitentiam portare. et non de aliis que numquam fuerunt.

Quod homo non habet nisi unum spiritum qui et anima dicitur

iohannes x. ego pono animam meam. ut iterum sumam eam etcet. et xii. nunc anima mea turbata est etcet. et xviiii. inclinato capite tradidit spiritum. Ecce quod caput nostrum non habuit nisi unum spiritum qui et anima dictus est. nec habuit eum in aere uagantem sed in corpore suo. unde et in morte emisit illum. item. lucam. viiii. nescitis cuius spiritus estis filius enim hominis non uenit animas perdere sed saluare. Ecce idem sunt spiritus nostri quod et anime. Nec dicit quod spiritus nostri essent in aere. sed dicit quod nos sumus spiritus. ergo spiritus et anima idem est. nec umquam inuenio hanc abusionem quod homo habet duos spiritus quorum unus dicatur spiritus et altera anima. quorum unus sit in corpore et alter extra.

Quod non potest aliquis saluari nisi resistuat male ablata si potest

Mattheus. v. si ergo offers munus tuum ad altare et tibi recordatus fueris quod frater tuus habet aliquid aduersum te relinque ibi munus tuum ante altare et uade prius reconciliari fratri tuo etcet. sed non potest reconciliari fratri suo quem lesit auferendo suam nisi restituat ei illud si potest. ergo non potes placere dei nisi reddat alienum. idem. xvii. ut autem non scandalizemus eos. uade ad mare etcet. si ergo dominus propter scandalum uitandum uoluit quod non tenebatur multo fortius uult ut propter scandalum tollendum reddamus quod alienum est. et subdit generaliter. xviiii. ne scandalum detur alieni et penam minatur scandalum faciendi. unde dicit qui autem scandalizauerit unum de pusillis istis qui in me credunt. expedit ei ut suspendatur mola asinaria in collo eius etcet. et infra uerumptamen ue homini illi per quem scandalum uenit. etcet. ergo mortaliter peccant qui aliena non restituet. quia scandalum facit proximo suo et ideo dampnatur in eternum. idem xxii. tunc ait illis. reddite ergo que sunt cesaris et que sunt dei deo etcet. ergo omnibus debemus reddere que sua sunt. idem xxiii. ue uobis scribe et pharisei. ypocrite. quia mundatis quod deforis est calicis et intus autem

That man has but one spirit, which is called the soul

John 10 (10:17) "I shall lay down my life, so that I might take it up again," and 12 (12:27) "my soul is troubled," and 19 (19:30) "bowing his head, he gave up the spirit." See that our Head has but one spirit, which is called the soul, neither did He have it wandering about the air, but in His body, which He breathed forth at His death. Also Luke 9 (9:55-56) "you do not know of what spirit you are, for the Son of man came not to destroy souls, but to save them." But our spirits and souls are identical, neither did He say that our spirits were in the air, but He said that we are spirits. Therefore the spirit and the soul are the same reality. Neither do I ever find this improper usage, that man has two spirits, one called the soul and the other the spirit, or that one is in the body and the other outside of it.

That one cannot be saved unless one makes restitution concerning illgotten goods, if one can

Matthew 5 (5:23-24) "If therefore you present your gift at the altar, and you remember there that your brother has something against you, leave your offering there before the altar, and go first to be reconciled to your brother." But it is not possible to be reconciled with one's brother, whom one injured by taking his goods, unless he restore it to him if possible, therefore you are unable to please God unless you restore alienated goods. Further 17 (17:26) "But that we may not scandalize them, go to the sea." If therefore the Lord wished, in order to avoid scandal, to do that which He was not bound to do, how much more does He will that we remove scandal by returning that which was stolen. And it follows generally in chapter 18 lest one give scandal to another and be menaced with the penalty for causing scandal. Whence he says (Mt 18:6) "But he who shall scandalize one of these little ones who believes in me, it would be better for him that a millstone should be hanged about his neck," and later (19:7) "Truly, woe to that man by whom scandal comes." Therefore one sins mortally who will not restore stolen goods, since one causes scandal to his neighbor and therefore [that one] shall be damned eternally. Further 22 (22:21) "Then he said to them 'Render to Caesar what is Caesar's, and to God, what is God's.'" Therefore we all ought to return to

pleni estis rapina et immunditia etcet. ergo ue his qui rapinam tenent. item. marcus vii de corde enim male cogitatitiones procedunt adulteria fornicationes homicidia furta etcet. et mattheus xviiii. non facies furtum etcet. et ad romanos xiii. non furaberis etcet. ergo furtum et rapina prohibita sunt sed non sunt prohibita nisi propter duo scilicet propter auaritiam mali lucri et propter iniuriam dampni quod sit proximo. sed ista duo potius committuntur in retinendo quam in auferendo. ergo fures et latrones sunt qui aliena tenent et ideo non possunt saluari nisi restituant. unde apostolus dicit. prima ad corinthios. vi. sed uos iniuriam facitis et hoc fratribus etcet. et infra. neque fures neque auari neque ebriosi neque maledici neque rapaces regnum dei possidebunt etcet. item marcum x. filioli quam difficile est confidentes in pecuniis in regnum dei introire. etcet. item. lucam xii. uidete et cauete ab omni auaritia etcet. idem xviiii. stans autem zacheus dixit. ad ihesum. ecce dimidium bonorum meorum do pauperibus et si quid defraudaui reddo quadruplum etcet. ergo tenetur quis restituere alienum. presertim cum dominus dixerit ibi post dictum zachei. hodie salus domui huic facta est etcet. item ad romanos xiii. reddite ergo omnibus debita etcet. ergo tenetur quis alienum reddere. alioquin peccat mortaliter. quia caritatem impeditur. item i^a ad timotheus. ultimo. radix enim omnium malorum est cupiditas. quam quidam appetentes errauerunt a fide etcet. sed tenere alienum magna cupiditas est. quam patareni sequentes errauerunt a fide et errare fecerunt credentes eorum de quibus dicit beatus petrus. ii^a. i^o. in auaritia fictis uerbis de uobis negotiabuntur etcet. et infra. cor ex cecatum auaritia habentes. item. iacobus. iiii. miseri estote et lugete etcet. sed lugere precepit pro peccatis comissis. item dominus dicit. mattheus iiii^o. penitentiam agite etcet. quod intelligitur scilicet de peccatis. sed subripere rem alienam peccatum est. et si recte consideres si penitet aliquid de peccato quod fecit emendabit illud. ergo tenetur quis restituere aliena si recte uult lugere et penitere. preterea tenere rem alienam cum iactura proximi est contra illa duo precepta. naturalia scilicet quod tibi non uis etcet. et quicquid uultis ut faciant uobis homines. Item est

every man that which is theirs. Further 23 (23:24–25) "Woe to you scribes and Pharisees, hypocrites, because you clean the outside of the cup and the dish, but within you are full of robbery and uncleanness." Therefore woe to those who retain stolen goods. Also Mark 7 (7:21) "For from within the heart of men proceed evil thoughts, adulteries, fornications, murders, thefts." And Matthew 19 (19:18) "Do not commit theft," and Romans 13 (13:9) "you shall not steal." Therefore theft and robbery are forbidden, but they are not forbidden except on account of two things, namely, on account of the greed for filthy money and on account of the injury caused to one's neighbor, but these two are chiefly committed in the retaining of that which is taken, therefore thieves and robbers are those who retain those things and therefore they are unable to be saved unless they restore such goods. Just as the Apostle says in 1 Corinthians 6 (6:8) "But you do wrong, and that to your brethren." And later (6:10) "neither thieves, nor the covetous, nor drunkards, nor slanderers, nor extortioners, shall possess the kingdom of God." Also Mark 10 (10:24) "O children, how difficult it is for those who trust in wealth to enter the kingdom of God." Luke 12 (12:15) "Take heed and beware of all covetousness." The same in 19 (Lk 19:8) "But Zacchaeus stood up, and said to the Lord, 'Behold, Lord, half of my goods I give to the poor, and if I have wronged any man, I restore him four times over.'" Therefore one who holds stolen goods must restore them, particularly since the Lord said there after Zaccheus spoke (19:9) "Today salvation has come to this house." Also to the Romans 13 (13:7) "Render to each man their due." Therefore one who holds stolen goods must return them, otherwise he sins mortally, since he obstructs charity. Further in the last chapter of 1 Timothy (6:10) "the lust for money is the root of all evil, and the covetous have strayed from the faith." But to hold on to stolen goods is the greatest manifestation of the lust for money, the Patarene followers have erred from the faith and in erring they cause their believers to fall from the faith, of which blessed Peter speaks in his second epistle (2:3) "And through covetousness they will make merchandise of you with false speech." And later (2:14) "the heart having been blinded with covetousness." Also James 4 (4:9) "Be afflicted and mourn," but mourning is commanded for sins that have been committed, as the Lord says in Matthew 4 (4:17) "Do penance," by which is understood, namely, of sins. But to attempt to steal the goods of another is a sin, and if rightly considered, if you repent of some sin, you must make amends for it, therefore one is bound to restore stolen goods if you wish to mourn and to repent correctly. Further to retain stolen goods with injury to one's neighbor is against those two natural

---

27 de…29 furta] Mar. 7:21.   29 non…furtum] Matt. 19:18.   30 non furaberis] Rom. 13:9.   37 sed…38 fratribus] 1 Cor. 6:8 (facitis] add. et fraudatis *Vulg.*)   38 neque…40 possidebunt] 1 Cor. 6:10.   41 filioli…42 introire] Mar. 10:24.   42 uidete…43 auaritia] Luc. 12:15.   43 stans…46 quadruplum] Luc. 19:8.   48 hodie…est] Luc. 19:9.   49 reddite…debita] Rom. 13:7.   52 radix…53 fide] 1 Tim. 6:10.   57 in…negotiabuntur] 2 Pet. 2:3.   58 cor…habentes] 2 Pet. 2:14 (ex cecatum] exercitum *Vulg.*)   59 miseri…lugete] Iac. 4:9.   61 penitentiam agite] Matt. 4:17.   67 quod…uis] Ioh. 21:18.   68 quicquid…homines] Matt. 7:12.

27 vii] vii iii *P*   32 propter^2] add. ma *P* exp   36 restituant] restituantur *P*   40 marcum x] mattheus. i^o *P*   43 etcet] add. ad romanos. *P*   50 reddere] add. etcet. *F* exp. | peccat] peccant *P*   51 caritatem] karitatem *F*   64 aliena] alienum *F*   65 preterea tenere] om. *P*

42 xii]fol. 94rb *P*   68 ut]fol. 94va *P*

contra illud preceptum scilicet diliges proximum tuum sicut te ipsum etcet. Item est contra pietatem de quam dicit apostolus. quod ad omnia ualeat. ergo tenetur quis restituere alienum. Item tenetur quis dare proprium proximo suo in neccessitate multo fortius ergo quod illius est. preterea per que peccat homo per hoc torquendus est ut naturalis ratio dictat. et scriptum est. Cum ergo peccauerit quis male auferendo aliena. torquandus est in restituendo. igitur ex istis rationibus patet efficaciter quod non potest quis saluari nisi alienum restituat si potest.

Quod usuria est mortale peccatum

Usuria est contra illa precepta naturalia scilicet quod tibi non uis etcet. quecumque uultis etcet. item est contra legem moysi et uetus testamentum. deuteronomium xxiii. non fenerabis fratri tuo usuram pecuniam nec fruges nec quamlibet aliam rem etcet. et ezechiel. xviii. ubi loquitur de duodecimum partibus iustitie dicit. usuram et superabundantiam accepisti non accepit et psalmi domine quis habitabit in tabernaculo tuo etcet. ibi qui pecuniam suam non dederit ad usuriam etcet. et idem. non defecit de plateis eius usura et dolus etcet. et ii°. esdre. v. usuras ne singuli fratribus uestris exigitis etcet. et infra. insuper excussi meum et dixi. non est bona res quam facitis et infra insuper excuxi meum et dixi. sic excutiat deus meus omnem uirum qui non compleuerit uerum istud de domo sua. item est contra legem sancti euangelii. lucam. vi. mutuum date nichil inde sperantes etcet. item est contra preceptum caritatis. diliges proximum tuum sicut te ipsum etcet. item est contra pietatem. item facit comedere panem otiosum quid prohibitum est a domino. Genesis. iii°. in sudore uultus tui uesceris pane tuo etcet. et mattheus xx. et dixit eis quid hic statis tota die otiosi etcet. et infra. ite et uos in uineam meam etcet. item est ars uiuendi de eo quod malum est in se. item est contra statum omnem hominum. quod depauperat honestos homines ut non possint facere facta dei et cesaris. ex quibus patet quod usura est non solum mortale peccatum sed mortalissimum.

Quod non est penitentia habenda uel facienda nisi de peccatis in celo commissis et quod homo habet duos spiritus quorum unus spiritus uocatur et altera anima et quod non

precepts, namely, (Jn 21:18) "where you would not go," and (Mt 7:12) "what you wish men would do to you." Further it is against the precept, namely, (Mt 19:19) "Love your neighbor even as yourself." Likewise it is against the piety which the Apostle cites (1 Tm 4:8) that is "beneficial to all." Therefore one is obliged to restore stolen goods. Further since one is obliged to give one's own property to one's neighbor in times of necessity, how much more is one obliged to give back to him his own possessions. Further that through which man sins is what he should be punished for, as natural reason dictates, and as it is written [in law]. Then he will have sinned who carried off another's goods evilly, and should be tortured in exchange. Therefore for these reasons it is eminently clear that one cannot be saved unless he might restore stolen goods if he is able to.

That usury is a mortal sin

Usury is against the precept of natural law, namely (Mt 7:12) "that which you do not wish done." "Whatsoever you wish." Likewise it is against the law of Moses and the Old Testament, Deuteronomy 23 (23:19) "Do not lend to your brother money in usury, nor corn, nor any other thing." And Ezekiel 18, where he speaks of the twelve parts of justice, and says (22:12) "You have taken usury and excess," and in the Psalm (14:1) "O Lord, who shall dwell in your tabernacle." And there (14:5) "he who has not put out his money to usury." And on the same topic (Ps 54:12) "usury and deceit have not departed from the streets." And 2 Esdras 5 (Nehemiah 5:7) "Does every one of you exact usury of your brethren?" and later (5:9) "The thing you do is not good," and later (5:13) "Moreover I shook my lap, and said, 'So may God shake every man that shall not accomplish this word, out of his house.'" It is also against the law of the holy gospels. Luke 6 (6:35) "and lend, hoping for no return." And it is against the commandment of charity (Mt 19:19) "love your neighbor as yourself." It is also against piety, as when he caused [them] to eat the bread of idleness which was prohibited by the Lord. Genesis 3 (3:19) "by the sweat of your face shall you eat your bread" and Matthew 20 (20:6) "and he said to them, 'why do you stand idle all day?'" And later (20:7) "and go, all of you, into my vineyard." Likewise it is the art of living by the fact that it is evil in itself, for it is against the standing of all mankind that you impoverish honest men so that they are not able to fulfill their duties to God and Caesar. From the foregoing it is clear that usury is not only a mortal sin, but the most mortal of sins.

That one ought not to have penitence or to do penance save for sins committed in heaven and that man has two spirits, of which one is called spirit and

---

69 diliges…70 ipsum] Matt. 19:19. 71 quod…72 alienum] Perhaps a paraphrase of 1 Tim. 4:8. XIX.5.5 non…6 rem] Deut. 23:19. 8 usuram…9 accepit] Ez. 22:12 (accepit) accepisti *Vulg.*) 9 domine…10 tuo] Ps. 14:1. 10 qui…11 usuriam] Ps. 14:5 (dederit) dedit *Vulg.*) 11 non…12 dolus] Ps. 54:12. 12 usuras…13 exigitis] Neh. 5:7 (singuli) add. a *Vulg.*) 14 insuper…dixi] Neh. 5:9. | non…15 facitis] Neh. 5:13. 15 insuper…17 sua] Neh. 5:13. 18 mutuum…19 sperantes] Luc. 6:35. 20 diliges…ipsum] Matt. 19:19. 22 in…23 tuo] Gen. 3:19. 23 et² …24 otiosi] Matt. 20:6 (dixit eis) dicit illis *Vulg.*) 24 ite…25 meam] Matt. 20:7.

---

69 tuum] add. etiam *P* exp XIX.5.1 Quod…peccatum] De usuria *P* 7 duodecimum] xii *F* 14 insuper…dixi] al. man. sup. va……cat. *P* | excussi] excuxi *P* 26 se] add. et secundum se *F* 27 quod] quia *F* XIX.6.3 quorum] quod *P*

69 diliges|fol. 72r *F* XIX.5.17 istud|fol. 94vb *P*

tenetur aliquis aliena et quod usura non est mortale peccatum

Quia de confessione distulisti differam et ego.

Quod non est habenda penitentia uel facienda nisi de peccatis in celo commissis

[Patarenus:] Actus. ii°. penitentiam inquit agite et batpzizetur unusquisque uestrum in remissionem peccatorum etcet. ergo de nullo peccato facienda est penitenda penitentia. quod factum sit in hoc mundo. post acceptam gratiam spiritus sancti. sed legimus quod sancti postea fecerunt eam. igitur de peccatis que in celo comisserunt egerunt illam.

Catholicus: Solutio. Triplici de causa sit penitentia possit remissionem omnium peccatorum in baptismate. una est propter peccata mortalia uel uenalia que postea sunt comissa. secunda est propter exemplum dandum proximo. Tertia uero propter maius meritum acquirendum. Sed responde tu mihi dimissa sunt peccata alicui in gratie susceptione. Sed aut de illi intelligis que dicis facta esse in celis. quod non est uerum. quia adhuc de istis penitentiam fieri oportet. immo autumnas quod non nisi post gratiam fit penitentiam de istis. aut tu intelligis de his que facta sunt in hac uita et tunc concludo sic. ergo peccata illa fuissent imputata. ut fuissent per baptismum deleta et sic derisione dignum est totum quod dicis.

Quod homo habet duos spiritus. quorum unus spiritus uocatur et altera anima

[Patarenus:] prima ad tessalonicenses. ultimo. ipse autem deus pacis sanctificet uos per omnia. ut integer spiritus uester et anima et corpus sine querela in aduentu domini nostri ihesu christi etcet. ergo habemus animam que est in hoc corpore et spiritum qui est in aere. ad cuius inspirationem facit anima penitentiam et habemus corpus in celis prostratum.

Catholicus: Respondeo. quod spiritus ponitur multis modis et anima similiter. spiritus enim quandoque ponitur pro spiritu diuino. iohannes. iiii°. spiritus est deus quandoque uero pro angelico. ad hebreos. i°. qui facit angelos suos spiritus. quandoque uero pro humano. lucam. viiii. nescitis cuius spiritus estis etcet. quandoque pro superiori parte rationis ut hic et ad. i^a. ad corinthios. ii°. spiritus enim omnia scrutatur etiam profunda dei etcet. et psalmi defecit spiritus meus etcet. quandoque uero ponitur pro superbia. mattheus. v. beati pauperes spiritu etcet. similiter et anima ponitur multis modis. quandoque uero pro spiritu

the other soul, and that one ought not to retain any ill-gotten goods and that usury is not a mortal sin

I also disagree about what you have divulged about confession.

That one ought not to have penitence or to do penance save for sins committed in heaven

[Pat:] Acts 2 (2:38) "I say to you do penance and be baptized each one of you for the remission of your sins." Therefore there is no sin done in this world that one ought to repent of and do penance for after the acceptance of the grace of the Holy Spirit. But we read that the saints did penance later, therefore sins which are committed in heaven must be discharged.

Cath: Solution. There are three cases in which penance can be done after the remission of all sins in baptism. One is on account of mortal or venial sins which are later committed, the second is for the purpose of giving example to one's neighbor, and the third is on account of gaining greater merit. But answer me this: are sins remitted to anyone in the reception of grace? But either you understand [it to be] about those things that you say are done in heaven, which is untrue because it is still necessary to do pen-ance for them (You assert that one can do penance for these things only after receiving grace), or you understand penance to be about the things that are done in this life, thus then I conclude in the following manner, those sins have been imputed, so that they could be cancelled by baptism and thus [both the things] you say are worthy of complete scorn.

That man has two spirits, of which one is called the spirit and the other the soul

[Pat:] 1 Thessalonians, at the end (5:23) "And may the God of peace himself sanctify you in all things, so that your whole spirit, and soul, and body, may be preserved blameless at the coming of our Lord Jesus Christ." Therefore we have a soul which is in this body and a spirit which is in the air, at whose inspiration the soul does penance and we have a prostrate body in heaven.

Cath: I reply 'Spirit' is proposed in a number of ways and so is the 'soul.' For the 'spirit' is often presented as the divine spirit. John 4 (4:24) "God is spirit," and sometimes also it refers to an angel: Hebrews 1 (1:7) "He who makes his angels spirits," and again sometimes it is used to refer to humans: Luke 9 (9:55) "You do not know of what spirit you are." Sometimes it is used to refer to the superior, rational part as here in 1 Corinthians 2 (2:10) "for the spirit searches all things, even unto the profundity of God." And in the Psalms (76:4) "my spirit withered away." Sometimes it is used to describe pride: Matthew 5 (5:3) "Blessed are the poor in spirit." In a similar way soul is proposed in numerous ways. Sometimes it is used to

---

XIX.7.3 penitentiam...5 peccatorum] Act. 2:38. XIX.8.3 ipse...6 christi] 1 Thes. 5:23. 12 spiritus...13 deus] Ioh. 4:24. 13 qui...14 spiritus] Heb. 1:7. 15 nescitis...estis] Luc. 9:55. 17 spiritus...18 dei] 1 Cor. 2:10. 18 defecit...meus] Ps. 76:4. 20 beati...spiritu] Matt. 5:3.

XIX.7.1 Quod...2 commissis] om. *F* 6 penitentia] om. *F* 18 oportet] opportet *P* 19 autumnas] auptumnas *P* 20 aut] qui *P* | his] hiis *F* 21 concludo] conclude *P* XIX.8.7 hoc corpore] transp. *P* | corpore] om. *F*

XIX.7.5 facienda|fol. 95ra *P* XIX.8.8 facit|fol. 72v *F* 9 prostratum|fol. 95rb *P*

humano. lucam. viii. filius enim hominis animas perdere sed saluare etcet. quandoque uero pro uita corporis. iohannes. x. ego ponam animam meam etcet. et xii. qui amat animam suam perdet eam. quandoque uero ponitur pro interiori parte rationis. ut mattheus. xxvi. tristis est anima mea usque ad mortem etcet. et sic ponitur hic et ita ponit physicus. quandoque ponitur uero pro sensualitate carnali. i^a. ad corinthios. ii^o. animalis autem homo non percipit que spiritus dei sunt etcet. sed dic mihi heretice. ubi habes quod spiritus sit extra corpus et anima in corpore et quod spiritus sit in aere et quod spiritus loquatur anime ut penitentiam faciat nisi de spiritu dei uel angelico.

describe the human spirit: Luke 9 (9:56) "for the Son of Man has not come to destroy souls, but to save them." Sometimes it is used to describe the life of the body: John 10 (10:15) "I lay down my life," and 12 (12:25) "He who loves his life shall lose it." Sometimes again it is used for the interior aspect of reason, as in Matthew 26 (26:38) "my soul is sorrowful unto death." And so it is used here and so it is used in the natural sciences. Sometimes it is used to describe the sensuality of the flesh: 1 Corinthians 2 (2:13) "But the sensual man does not recognize these things that are of the Spirit of God." But tell me, O heretic, where do you have it that the spirit is outside of the body and the soul is in the body, and that the spirit is in the air and that the spirit might call the soul so that one might do penance, except [in reference to] the spirit of God or of an angel?

Quod non tenetur quis restituere aliena

[Patarenus:] Marcum ultimo. apparuit primo marie magdalene. de qua eiecerat septem demonia etcet. quod intelligitur de. vii. criminbus capitalibus inter que auaritia computatur et in conuersione illius non dixit ei ihesus. quod de auaritia satisfaceret reddendo male allata sed ut legitur in lucam. vii^o. fides tua te saluam fecit uade in pace etcet.

Catholicus: Respondeo quod auaritia potest esse solius cordis. sicut luxuria superbia et cetera uitia. ut dicitur in euangelio quod illa male habuit aliquid et esto quod habuit non dixit ei ihesus non debes reddere. sed fides tua te saluam fecit etcet. quia ex fide et uoluntate bona est salus. quare uestra si habuit male aliquid quod ipsa proposuerat reddere illud. alioquin fides sua informis non saluasset illam.

[Patarenus:] item. in eodem. qui crediderit et baptizatus fuerit saluus erit. qui uero non crediderit condempnabitur etcet. Non dixit qui aliena non reddiderit.

Catholicus: Nec dixerit qui manus impositionem non acceperit. disce autem stulte quod omnino non credit qui in peccatis mortalibus est. sed presumit. si ergo adultus est aut rapax et huiusmodi non habet fidem proprie loquendo sed presumptionem habere potest uel confidentiam.

[Patarenus:] item lucam. xvi. facite uobis amicos de mammona iniquitatis etcet. ergo potest homo dare mala ablata pauperibus. ergo non tenetur restituere illa quibus abstulit.

That one is not obliged to return other people's stolen goods

[Pat:] In the last chapter of Mark (16:9) "he appeared first to Mary Magdalene, from whom he had cast out seven demons," and one is to understand by that the seven capital sins, among which is counted avarice, and in her conversion Jesus did not say to her that regarding avarice she was to make satisfaction by giving back ill-gotten goods but as one reads in Luke 7 (7:50) "your faith has saved you, go in peace."

Cath: I respond that avarice can be of the heart alone, just as lust, pride, and the other vices, as is said in the Gospel; as for the fact that she had something ill gotten, and let it be granted that she did, Jesus did not say to her "you are not obligated to return it," but "your faith has saved you, etc." because salvation comes from faith and from a good will," therefore if this woman of yours had anything ill gotten, [it is clear] that she herself had proposed to give back, otherwise her dead faith would not have saved her.[1]

[Pat:] Further, on the same issue (Mk 16:16) "He who believes and is baptized shall be saved, but he who does not believe shall be condemned." He did not say he who does not restore ill-gotten goods.

Cath: Neither did He say, "who does not receive imposition of hands." But learn, fool, that he who is in mortal sins does not believe at all; rather he [merely] presumes [in his salvation]. Therefore if an adult is an extortioner or some such he does not have faith, properly speaking, but presumption, yet he can [still] have hope.

[Pat:] Luke 16 (16:9) "Make yourselves friends of the mammon of iniquity." Therefore a man can give ill-gotten gains to the poor so he is not obliged to restore those things to those he robbed.

---

22 filius...23 saluare] Luc. 9:56.   24 ego...meam] Ioh. 10:15 (ponam) pono *Vulg.*)   25 qui...eam] Ioh. 12:25.   27 tristis...mortem] Matt. 26:38.   30 animalis...31 sunt] 1 Cor. 2:14 (percipit) add. ea *Vulg.*)   XIX.9.2 apparuit...3 demonia] Mar. 16:9.   7 fides...8 pace] Luc. 7:50.   17 qui...19 condempnabitur] Mar. 16:16.   27 facite...28 iniquitatis] Luc. 16:9.

31 sed] set *P*   XIX.9.1 Quod] om. *F*   7 allata] illata *P*   12 debes] debbes *P*   20 reddiderit] crediderit *F*   22 non] om. *P*   28 dare...29 ablata] male allata dare *P*

XIX.9.4 criminbus|fol. 95va *P*

---

[1] "Fides informis" or "dead faith" means that faith which lacks charity, and is not salvific. See *Summa Theologiae*, II-II, q. 6. a. 2.

Catholicus: Respondeo non dixit quod essent male ablata. Non enim omnis mammona iniquitatis est male ablatum. Iniquitas enim idem est hic quod inequalitas siue superfluitas. est ergo dictum. facite uobis de diuitiis superfluis amicos sicut dicit. Verumptamen que superhabundat date elemosinas et omnia munda sunt uobis. Reprehendebat enim dominus phariiseos de auaritia elemosinarum. unde subdit ibi. audiebant autem omnia hec pharisei. qui erant auari. et deridebant eum etcet. uel si de male ablatus uis hec intelligere. sic exponitur. facite uobis amicos de mammona iniquitatis scilicet quos uobis feceratis inimicos id est restituite illi quibis abstulistis.
[Patarenus:] Item iohannem. viii. uade et noli iam peccare etcet. et huic non dixit quod deberet aliquid restituere.
Catholicus: Respondeo quia non legitur quod aliquid male abstulerit. de adulterio enim tantum infamata fuerat et si male aliquid abstulit. precepit dominus illam restituere illud. cum dicit. amplius noli peccare. peccat namque semper qui aliena retinet cum illa possit reddere.

Quod usura non est mortale peccatum

[Patarenus:] Deuteronomium. xxiii. ubi dicit. non fenerabis fratri tuo subdit de alieno etcet. ergo non est peccatum accipere usuram nisi a fratribus.
Catholicus: Respondeo quod illud scilicet. sed alieno fuit additio scribarum et phariseorum. uel concessit moyses iudeis fenerari extraneis ad duritiam cordis eorum quia nolebant etiam fratribus sicut concessit eis libellum repudii ne proprias uxories occiderit. uel melius concessit deus iudeis fenerari gentilibus non propter alienum lucrandus sed propter suum redimendus. abstulerant enim gentes bona eorum et labores et usura non est. nisi quando quis cum aliena iactura lucratur et isti fenerando gentibus non lucrabantur alienum sed suum utrumque redimebant. simile est de expoliatione egyptorum quam deus concessit iudeis.

[Patarenus:] item. mattheus. xxv. oportuit ergo te pecuniam meam committere numulariis et ego ueniens receissem utique quod meum est cum usuris etcet. et lucam. xviiii. quare non dedisti pecuniam meam ad mensam et ego ueniens cum usuris utique egissem illam etcet. ergo usura non est peccatum. si deus de illa ponit imitationis exemplum.
Catholicus: Respondeo. quod exemplum est imitationis non propter usura sed propter lucrum. similiter habes de parabola uilici iniquitatis. lucam. xvi.

Cath: I respond that He did not say that they were ill-gotten goods. For not all the mammon of iniquity is ill-gotten. For iniquity is the same as this: inequality or extravagance. Give of your excess riches to friends, as is said (Lk 16:11) "But yet of that which remains, give alms, and all things are clean unto you." The Lord upbraided the Pharisees for their stinginess in almsgiving, when He added (16:14) "Now the Pharisees, who were covetous, heard all these things and they mocked him." Or if you wish to understand this regarding stolen goods, it is thus explained, "make yourselves friends of mammon" that is, those whom you made enemies, that is, restore that which you have taken.

[Pat:] Further John 8 (8:11) "go and sin no more," and he did not say that one ought to restore anything.

Cath: I respond that it does not say that she stole anything for she had become infamous for her adultery only; and if she did steal something, the Lord commands her to restore it, when He says, "sin no more," for in fact one always sins who retains another's things when he can give them back.

That usury is not a mortal sin

[Pat:] Deuteronomy 23, where it says (23:19) "Do not lend to your brother money in usury," therefore it is not a sin to receive usury, unless it be from brothers.
Cath: I reply that namely, "but to foreigners" was an addition of the scribes and Pharisees. Perhaps Moses conceded usury to foreigners on account of their hardness of heart, because he did not wish them to lend at usury to their brethren, just as he conceded them the privilege of a bill of divorce lest they might kill their own wives. Or better, God conceded usury to the Jews towards the Gentiles not on account of profiting from foreigners, but rather for the redemption of their own [goods]. For the nations had carried off their goods and works, and so it was not usury, except when one is making money by other's loss and by charging usurious rates to those nations, they are not profiting off foreigners but really redeeming both their goods and labor. It is similar to the spoliation of the Egyptians which God conceded to the Jews.
[Pat:] As in Matthew 25 (25:27) "You ought therefore to have deposited my money to the bankers, and at my coming I should have received my own with interest." And Luke 19 (19:23) "And why then did you not put my money into the bank, so that at my coming, I might have exacted it with interest?" Therefore usury is no sin, if God proposed it as an example for imitation.
Cath: I reply that the meaning of the imitation is not on account of usury, but for the sake of profit, as you have in the parable of the dishonest steward in Luke 16 (16:8)

---

36 Verumptamen...37 uobis] Luc. 11:41.   39 audiebant...40 eum] Luc. 16:14 (eum) illum *Vulg.*)   44 uade...45 peccare] Ioh. 8:11.
XIX.10.2 non...3 alieno] Deut. 23:19.   18 oportuit...20 usuris] Matt. 25:27 (usuris) usura *Vulg.*)   21 quare...23 illam] Luc. 19:23 (egissem) exegissem *Vulg.*)

32 ablata] allata P   33 ablatum] allatum P   38 phariiseos] pharyseos P   41 ablatus] allatis P   XIX.10.7 extraneis...8 nolebant] om. F
27 uilici] uilicum F

33 idem|fol. 95vb P   45 deberet|fol. 73r F   XIX.10.7 iudeis|fol. 96ra P

laudauit dominus uilicum iniquitatis etcet. et infra. ego dico uobis facite uobis amicos de mammona iniquitatis etcet. et simile est de parabola iudicis iniquitatis. ut dicitur in eodem. xviii. ibi audite quid iudex iniquitatis dicit. deut autem non faciet uindictam electorum suorum etcet.

Patarenus: Preterea ex locatione et conductione habita non iudicantur ab ecclesia romana peccata. igitur eodem modo nec usura debet reputari peccatum esse. cum eadem sit ratio in utroque casu.

Catholicus: Respondeo non est uerum quod idem ius sit in utroque casu. quia in locatione et conductione res manet dantis et est periculum eius sed deterioratur uel huiusmodi interueniat sed pecunie uel alteri rei cum mutuatur transfertur dominium et periculum in accipientem.

Patarenus: Item pape et cardinales et alii prelati ecclesie romane accipiunt pecuniam sub usuris. quod si peccatum esset non facerent. uel peccant mortaliter. quia qui occasionem mali dat. malum facere intelligitur et constat quod non solum ipsi accipiunt pecuniam sub usuris sed etiam ipsos usuarios nutriunt et fouent et extollunt et multis priuilegiis faciunt splendescere. quare uidetur quod aut usura non sit peccatum. aut quod mortalissime peccant ipsi hoc facientes.

Catholicus: Respondeo quod in necessitate non est peccatum accipienti. licet sit peccatum danti. redimit enim sicut potest et conseruat dei honorem atque cultum uel uitam suam uel alienam. Sic ergo prelati ecclesie romane accipiunt pecuniam sub usuris pro defensione fidei christiane et ecclesiastice libertatis ab heretica prauitate uel tyrannorum iniquitate aut pro redemptione captiuorum aut pro substentatione uiduarum et pupillorum et aliarum miserabilium personarum in necessitate de gentium uel pro uita sua substentanda in ardua necessitate uel pro huiusmodi piis et necessariis causis non peccant. sed merendi potius habent occasionem.

"The lord commended the unjust steward," and later (16:9) "and I say to you, 'Make friends of the mammon of iniquity.'" And like it is the parable of the unjust judge, as it says in the same gospel 18 (18:6–7) "Hear what the unjust judge said, 'And will not God avenge his elect.'"

Pat: Furthermore since the renting and leasing of property is not considered a sin by the Roman Church, in the same way neither should usury be considered a sin, since in both cases the rationale is the same.

Cath: I respond that it is not true that it is the same in both cases, since in renting and leasing the property remains that of the provider but is at risk, for it may experience wear and tear, or likewise something else might befall [it], but with money or other things when they are borrowed the ownership and risk is transferred to the borrower.[1]

Pat: Further, the popes and cardinals and other prelates of the Roman church acquire money through usury, which if it were a sin, they should not do, lest they sin mortally. Since it is understood that those who give occasion of sin do evil, and it seems that not only do they acquire money by usury but also encourage and maintain and promote those usurers, and shower them with many privileges. Whence it seems either usury is no sin or that these sin most mortally by doing it.

Cath: I reply that it is no sin to receive it in times of need, although it may be a sin [for the lender] to redeem it. For one can redeem and keep it for the honor or worship of God, or to save one's own life or someone else's. Thus the prelates of the Roman Church acquire money by usury for the defense of the Christian faith and for the freedom of the Church from heretical depravity or from the iniquity of tyrants or for the ransom of captives or for the support of widows and orphans or of other pitiable persons, or for the maintenance of their lives in hard times, or for any other pious or necessary cause they do not sin, but rather that they might have an occasion of merit.

De sacris ordinibus   XX   On Holy Orders

Sequitur de sacris ordinibus qui sunt tres scilicet presbiteratus. diaconatus. et subdiaconatus. in quibus omnibus datur. spiritus sanctis. quorum duo primi insituti fuerant sacri a christo et apostolis eius in nouo testamento. Tertius autem id est subdiaconatus post nouum testamentum ab ecclesia consititutus est sacer et hunc negant patarenum esse ordinem saltem

One now proceeds to the sacred orders, which are three, namely, priesthood, diaconate, and subdiaconate, in all of which the Holy Spirit is conferred. The first two were instituted and sanctified by Christ and His Apostles in the New Testament, but the third was established after the New Testament by the Church and this the Patarenes deny even being a sacred order. But the other two they believe to

---

28 laudauit...iniquitatis] Luc. 16:8.   29 ego...30 iniquitatis] Luc. 16:9.   31 ibi...33 suorum] Luc. 18:6-7.

41 huiusmodi] homini *P*   48 ipsi] episcopi *F*   57 Sic] Si *P*   **XX.1.6** post...7 est] om. *F*

33 suorum|fol. 96rb *P*   60 prauitate|fol. 73v *F*   62 pupillorum|fol. 96va *P*

---

1) The translation here, from "but is at risk ..." (l. 41) is hypothetical.

sacrum. alios autem duos credunt esse sacros ordines et quod ipsi debeant ab episcopo conferri. et quod in eis detus spiritus sanctus. tantum ergo circa subdiaconatum est nobis questio cum illi. Sed quia de hoc errant communiter heretici dimittimus usque in librum tertium. eius tractatum titulum quod ecclesia romana est babyllonia et in tractatum de ecclesia romana et eius potestate.

Quod in ecclesia dei non sunt nisi duo sacri ordines scilicet presbiteratus et diaconatus

Quia distulisti tractare inferius de subdiaconatu quod sacer ordo debeat haberi. differo et ego reprobationem eius illuc faciendam.

Quod in sacramento eucharistie debite celebrato panis in corpus christi et uinum in sanguine eius transubstantiatur probatio per rationes naturales

Hoc credere et hoc dicere. scilicet corpus et sanguinem christi fideles ipsius recipere per modum sacramenti eucharistie. non est contra dei potentiam. quia cum omnia possit. potest et hoc nec est contra eius sapientiam. quia omnia scit facere que potest et est secundum benignitatem eius et ad laudem ipsius ut qui ex sue sanctitatis exellentia tantum nos dilexerit ut corpus suum pro nobis redimendis in mortem tradidit oridam. etiam nobis tradere uoluerit illud impassibile pro nobis mittendis. item ad salutem cedit animarum eum propter meritum fidei qua constituimus deum esse omnipotentem atque ueracem. eum propter reuerentiam quam ibi deo exhibemus et propter ipsius etiam cibi uirtutem. item est ibi misterium elegans quia forma panis exterior signifacat ipsum christum que recipimus uisibiliter qui est panis uiuus qui de celo descendit. preterea scriptura diuina dicit quod ipse deus hoc uoluit ut inferius apparebit. ergo ita est absque ulla contrarietate. Item fecerat deus hominem et redimerat. sed quia perfectum opus non fuisset scilicet fecisse et redemisse hominem nisi consubstentasset dignum fuit ut ei cibum sustentationis et uite preberet cum dei perfecta sint opera et sicut deus fecerat hominem creaturam qua nulla creatura dignior et melior est. et redemerat eum pretio quo nullum dignius nec melius esse potest. si conueniens fuit ut illo cibo pasceret eum atque nutriret. et cui similis uel equalis non potest inuenire id est corpore suo de quo in oratione dominica continetur. panem nostrum cotidianum etcet. item sicut per cibum temporalem mundus periit. sic per cibum spiritualem id est per corpus christi conuenienter saluari debuit.

That in the Church of God there are only two sacred orders, namely, priesthood and diaconate

Because you deferred treating of the subdiaconate till later, that one ought to hold it as a sacred order, I also defer making a repudiation of it till then.

Proof by natural reason that in the appropriate celebration of the Eucharist the bread is changed into the body of Christ and the wine into His blood

We believe and say this, that the fact that the body and blood of Christ is received by the faithful by means of the sacrament of the Eucharist is not against the power of God. For since He can do all things, He can do this, and neither is it against His wisdom since He knows what He does and is able to do so, and it is according to His kindness and to His praise that He loved us so much that from His superabundant holiness handed His body over to a horrible death that we might be redeemed. For He also wished to hand on to us that impassible body that was given for us. Further He granted it for the salvation of souls on account of the merit of faith by which we are convinced that God is omnipotent and truthful, and on account of the reverence for Him which we ought to have towards God and on account also of the power of this food. Further there is elegance in this mystery since the external form of bread signifies the same Christ that we receive visibly who is the living bread come down from heaven. Further the divine scriptures say that God wished that He might be present below. Therefore it is utterly without any contradictions. Furthermore, God had made and redeemed man, but because His work would not have been completed, that is, He would have made and redeemed man, but not supported him, it was right that He should furnish for him food for sustenance and life, since the works of God are perfect; and just as God had made man a such creature than which no other creature is worthier and better and had redeemed him with a ransom than which no other can be worthier or better, so it was fitting that He should feed and nourish him with that food to which one is unable to find anything similar or equal, that is, in His body, which is mentioned in the Lord's prayer, "our daily bread." So through

---

13 usque] om. *P* **14** titulum] uidetur *P* **15** babyllonia] babillonia *P* **XXI.1.3** probatio...4 naturales] om. *F* **11** exellentia] exxelentia *P* **14** nobis] add. auferendis *P* exp **20** uiuus] uite *F* **21** descendit] descendi *F* **26** sustentationis] sustentationis substantationis *P* **28** creatura] om. *F* **31** nutriret] add. sed *P*

XXI.1.5 sanguinem|fol. 96vb *P* **32** equalis|fol. 97ra *P*

Probatio per scripturas

Mattheus. xxvi. cenantibus autem illis accepit ihesus panem et benedixit ac fregit deditque discipulis suis et ait. accipite et comedite hoc est corpus meum. et accipiens calicem gratias egit et dedit illis dicens. bibite ex hoc omnes. hic est enim sanguinis meus noui testamenti qui pro uobis effundetur in remissionem peccatorum etcet. item marcus. xiiii. et manducantibus ait illis accepit ihesus panem et benedicens fregit et dedit illis et ait sumite hoc est corpus meum et accepto calice gratias agens dedit eis et bibite ex eo omnes. et ait illis. hic est sanguinis meus noui testamenti qui pro uobis effundetur etcet. lucam xxii°. et accepto pane gratias egit et fregit et dedit eis dicens. hoc est corpus meum quod pro uobis tradetur hoc facite in meam commemorationem. similiter et calicem postquam cenauit dicens. hic est calix nouum testamentum in meo sanguine qui pro uobis effundetur etcet. Ex hiis patet uerbis manifeste quod secundum institutionem domini nostri ihesu christi. quia panis conuertitur in corpus eius et uinum in sanguinem ipsius si in confectione teneatur forma ab ipso tradita.

Patarenus: Respondeo quod hoc uerbum est ponitur hic significantem et non essentialiter ut sit sensus est id est significat. similis de petra oreb. iᵃ ad corinthios. x. bibebant autem de spirituali consequente eos petra. petra autem erat christus etcet. et de duobus filiis abrahe. hec enim sunt duo testamenta etcet. Vel dicimus quod hoc uerba hoc est corpus meum referuntur ad corpus suum quod ibi erat. aliud enim accepit in manus id est panem et de alio dixit. hoc est corpus meum id est de se ipso quod non porrigebat neque dabat discipulis ad comedendum.

Catholicus: Sed utroque huiusmodi intellectus probatur falsus de primo patet quod dominus dixit expresse. hoc est corpus meum. non enim dixit hoc significat. Nec obstat oppositio de petra oreb et de duobus filiis abrahe. quia ut dicit apostolus. iᵃ. ad corinthios. x. hec omnia in figura contingebant illis. fuit enim primum testamentum figura secundi et figura precedit figuratum et ubi est figura ibi non est ueritas rei figuritate. sed aliud est hoc quod hic dicit dominus. non enim secundum testamentum debet figurare tertium et transierunt figure postquam uenit christus qui est figurata ueritas. et christi corpus ibi erat presentialiter. unde nulle fuisset decum. hic panis significat corpus meum quod hic est. quia nulle dicerem si accepto lapide uno dicerem hic me figurat cum essem ibi. preterea si uelles dicere quod christus

2

Proof from the scriptures

temporal food the earth is lost, but it is fitting that it ought to be saved by spiritual food — the body of Christ.

Matthew 26 (26:26–28) "And while they were at supper, Jesus took bread, and blessed and broke it, and gave to his disciples, and said, 'Take and eat, all of you, this is my body,' and taking the chalice he gave thanks, and gave to them, saying, 'drink all of this, for this is my blood of the new covenant, which will be shed for you for the remission of sins.'" Also Mark 14 (14:21–24) "And while they were eating, Jesus took bread and blessing it, broke and gave to them and said, 'Take all of you. This is my body.' And having taken the chalice, giving thanks he gave it to them. And they all drank of it. And he said to them, 'This is my blood of the new covenant, which shall be shed for you.'" Luke 22 (22:19–20) "And taking bread, he gave thanks, and broke it and gave to them, saying, 'This is my body, which is handed over for you. Do this in commemoration of me.' Likewise he took the chalice also after he had eaten, saying, 'This is the chalice, the new testament in my blood, which shall be poured out for you.'" From these plain words it is clear that according to the institution of our Lord Jesus Christ the bread is changed into His body and the wine into His blood if in the consecration one holds to the form handed on by Him.

Pat: I reply that these words are proposed here as signification and not essentially, that this might be the sense, that is, it means something like the rock of Horeb, 1 Corinthians 10 (10:4) "And they drank of the spiritual rock that followed them, and the rock was Christ." And (Gal 4:22) of the two sons of Abraham, and these were the two testaments. Or we say that this phrase "This is my body" refers to His body that was there, for another takes the bread in hand and another said "this is my body" that is, He did not distribute it Himself nor give it to His disciples to eat.

Cath: Yet both of these conceptions are false, of the first it is clear that the Lord expressly stated "This is my body." He did not say "this signifies." Neither can one hold up the rock of Horeb or the two sons of Abraham as an objection, since as the Apostle says in 1 Corinthians 10 (10:11) "Now all these things happened to them in allegory." For it was the first testament that prefigured the second, and the figure preceded the thing prefigured, and where there is a figure there is not the truth of the thing symbolized. But here the Lord is saying something else, for the second testament must not prefigure a third and the prefigurements passed away when Christ came, who is the form of truth, and the body of Christ was there face to face, therefore it would be in no way fitting for this bread to signify my body which is here, since no one would say if taking one rock I might say this symbolizes myself while I am present. Further if you wish to claim that Christ had it

---

XXI.2.2 cenantibus...8 peccatorum] Matt. 26:26-28 (illis] eis | uobis] multis *Vulg.*)   8 et...13 effundetur] Mar. 14:21-24 (illis] eis | uobis] multis *Vulg.*)   13 et...18 effundetur] Luc. 22:19-20 (tradetur] datur | effundetur] fundetur *Vulg.*)   26 bibebant...27 christus] 1 Cor. 10:4.   27 de...28 testamenta] Gal. 4:22.   39 hec...illis] 1 Cor. 10:11.

XXI.2.24 hic] om. P

XXI.2.10 dedit|fol. 74r F   22 teneatur|fol. 97rb P

habuit respectum ad tempus absentie sue. tunc debuit dicere hoc erit corpus meum. preterea postquam dixerat hic est calix etcet. et immediate subiunxit. uerumptamen ecce manus tradentis me mecum est in mensa etcet. ubi ostendit aperte quod illum sanguinem dabat apostolis quem iudas traditur iudeis. alia enim expositio nulla est. quia hoc pronomen hoc demonstratum est ad oculum et ad intellectum et ipse prius panem ostenderat et postea manifeste ponit de pane et de uino. et postea immediate dicit. hoc est corpus meum et hic est sanguis meis etcet. et subsequenter dicit. a modo non bibam de generatione uitis huius. etcet. inuenies expressim quod de illo uino dixerat hic sanguis. etcet. quod transubstantiatum erat in sanguinem eius. Item. iohannes. vi. Ego sum panis uiuus qui de celo descendi. si quis manducauerit ex hoc pane uiuet in eternum. et panis quem ego dabo caro mea est pro mundi uita etcet. et infra. amen amen dico uobis nisi manducaueritis carnem filii hominis et biberitis eius sanguinem non habebitis uitam in uobis. qui manducat meam carnem et bibit meum sanguinem habet uitam eternam et ego resucitabo eum in nouissimo die. Caro enim mea uere est cibus et sanguis meus uere est potus etcet. nescio qumodo apertius potuisset dominus exprimere quam quod in hac parte sancta credit ecclesia. ex quibus etiam uerbis declaratur quod. spiritus sanctus. datur ad remissionem peccatorum et augmentum gratie digne sumentibus corpus christi. ubi sciendum est quod in sacramento eucharistie tria sunt. primum est scilicet formule panis et uini et istud est sacramentum et non res. sacramentum enim est corpus christi ueri. secundam est ipsum corpus christi de uirgine tractum quod est res per se et est sacramentum corporis mistici id est unionis ecclesie et istud recipitur ab omnibus. uerumptamen a malis ut dicit apostolus sumitur in iudicium dampnationis et est ibi corpus christi misticum. quod est tertium et istud est tantum res et non sacramentum. et sumitur hoc tantum a sanctis fidelibus et ualet eis ad tria scilicet ad peccatorum mortalium occultorum absolutionem et ad uenialium dimissionem et ad gratie incrementum. item. prima ad corinthios. x. calix benedictionis cui benedicimus nonne communicatio sanguis christi est et panis quem frangimus nonne participatio corporis domini est etcet. nonne qui edunt hostias participes sunt altaris etcet. non potestis calicem domini bibere et calicem demoniorum etcet. non dixit figuratio sed communicatio et participatio. quare ostendit quod in sacramentis eucharistie. uerum est corpus christi. et innuit etiam quod in altari debet sacrificari. item. xi. ego accepi a domino quod et tradidi uobis quoniam dominus ihesus in qua nocte

in respect to the time of His absence, then He should have said that "this will be my body." Further, after He had said "this is the chalice" and immediately added (Lk 22:21) "nevertheless behold the hand of him who betrays me is with me on the table." Whence He showed clearly that He gave that [same] blood to the Apostles which Judas handed over to the Jews. There is no other explanation, since the pronoun shows to the eye and the intellect that He Himself first showed them the bread, and later clearly points out the bread and wine, and after immediately says "this is my body" and "this is my blood" and then adds, saying (Lk 22:18) "Henceforth I will not drink of the fruit of the vine." You will find explicitly that He had spoken of that wine as His blood, that was transubstantiated into His blood. Further John 6 (6:31) "I am the living bread which comes down from heaven." (6:59) "If someone shall eat of this bread they shall live eternally, and this bread which I give is my flesh for the life of the world," and later (6:54–56) "Amen, amen I say to you, unless you shall eat the flesh of the son of man and drink his blood you will have no life in you, for he who eats my flesh and drinks my blood will have eternal life, and I shall raise him up on the last day. For my flesh is meat indeed and my blood is drink indeed." I have no idea how the Lord could have been clearer saying and proclaiming what the holy Church believes about this matter, for by such words it is even declared that the Holy Spirit is given for the remission of sins and the growth of grace to those who worthily receive the body of Christ. Whence one should know that in the sacrament of the Eucharist there are three parts, the first is the form of bread and wine and this is the sacrament and not the reality, for the sacrament is the true body of Christ, the second is that body of Christ taken from the virgin, which is in itself the reality, and is the sacrament of the mystical body, that is, the union of the Church and this is received by all. Nevertheless the Apostle says that it is received by evildoers as a judgment of damnation. And there is the mystical body of Christ which is the third, and this is only the reality and not the sign, and this is only received by the holy faithful and benefits them in three ways, namely, for the absolution of hidden mortal sins, and the remission of venial sins, and for the augmentation of grace. Further 1 Corinthians 10 (10:16) "The chalice of benediction, which we bless, is it not the communion of the blood of Christ? And the bread, which we break, is it not the partaking of the body of the Lord?" (10:18) "Are not they, who eat of the sacrifices, partakers of the altar?" (10:21) "You cannot drink the chalice of the Lord, and the chalice of devils." He did not speak of symbol, but of communion and participation. Hence does he show that the true body of Christ is in the sacrament of the Eucharist, and he hinted also that it should be sacrificed on the altar. Further 11 (11:23) "For I have received from the Lord that which also I delivered to you, that the Lord Jesus, the

---

53 uerumptamen...54 mensa] Luc. 22:21.   61 a...huius] Luc. 22:18 (a modo] om. *Vulg.*)   64 Ego...65 descendi] Ioh. 6:31.   65 si... 67 uita] Ioh. 6:50.   67 amen¹...73 potus] Ioh. 6:54-56.   91 calix...94 est] 1 Cor. 10:16.   94 nonne...95 altaris] 1 Cor. 10:18. 95 non...96 demoniorum] 1 Cor. 10:21.   100 ego...104 meum] 1 Cor. 11:23.

---

74 dominus] add. dicere *P* exp   81 ueri...82 christi] om. *F*   82 uirgine] add. natum *P* exp

53 uerumptamen|fol. 97va *P*   79 panis|fol. 74v *F*   80 sacramen-tum|fol. 97vb *P*

tradebatur accepit panem et gratias agens fregit et dixit. accipite panem et gratias agens fregit et dixit accipite et manducate hoc est corpus meum etcet. ecce quomodo quod prius dixerat panem postea dixit corpus suum quod pro nobis in futurum debeat tradi. Si enim de corpore doctrine sue intellexisset dominus. prout uno modo uos blasphemi exponitis. qui dixisset in futuro tradetur. nonne semper tradebatur illa et tradita erat iam dudum? sequitur in littera. itaque quicumque manducauerit hunc panem et biberit calicem domini indigne. reus erit corporis et sanguinis domini etcet. dic ergo anathema qua ratione siquis comedit panem materialem et bibit materiale uinum reus sit corporis et sanguinis domini. cum nulla sit ibi de corpore et sanguine domini prout deliras. item quoniam per creaturam uel facturam diaboli scilicet panem et uinum sicut blasphemas posse tam pretiosum quid significari scilicet corpus et sanguis domini nostri ihesu christi. sequitur probet autem se ipsum homo et sic de pane illo edat et de calice bibat. qui enim manducat et bibit indigne. iudicium sibi manducat et bibit non diiudicans corpus domini etcet. ergo in hoc sumit sibi iudicem quia non diiudicat corpus domini cum indigne id est in peccato mortali. hunc panem manducat et de hoc calice bibit. ergo corpus domini nostri ihesu christi est in hostia debita et consecrata. quod ad salutem sumitur a fidelibus sanctis. sed respondete mihi patarenis. uos datis de hoc pane materiali more uestro sanctificato credentibus uestris quos scitis esse in multis peccatis mortalibus et scitis eos non esse purgatos quia cum non receperint manus impositionem non sunt ab aliquo peccato purgati secundam sectam uestram et ipsi cum indigne tractent panem predictum in iudicium et in dampnationem mortis hoc faciunt. ergo scienter facitis illos peccare mortaliter et per consequentiam uos mortalissime peccatis.

Quod panis non transubstantiatur in corpus christi. neque uinum in sanguinem eius

Quid autem panis non transubstantiatur in corpus christi. nec uinum in sanguinem eius. vii. rationibus probare possumus et per. v. auctoritates noui testamenti.

Probatio per rationes naturales

Si panis cotitde transubstantiatur in corpus chrisi ut dicitis uos romani. ergo panis cotidie mutatur in corpus christi. et corpus chrisi cotidie crescit que sunt due magne falsitates. quia nec res in aliam rem potest mutari. nec corpori christi accidit incrementum. item impossibile uidetur quod sub tam praua forma panis

---

same night in which he was betrayed, took bread and, giving thanks, broke, and said: 'Take and eat: this is my body.'" Behold the manner in which He first had said bread, then said His body that would be handed over in the future. For had the Lord understood your conception of the doctrine of the body just in the way you expose your blasphemy, how could He have said it will be handed over in the future? Has He not always been handed over as He was handed over long ago? It follows in the letter (1 Cor 11:27) "Therefore whosoever shall eat this bread, or drink the chalice of the Lord unworthily, shall be guilty of the body and of the blood of the Lord." Tell me for what reason this would be anathema, that if one ate the material bread and drank the material wine the he would be guilty of the body and blood of the Lord, since you rave that there is nothing there of the body and blood of the Lord. Further [how can it be that] it is through a creature, or rather a creation of the devil — namely the bread and wine as you blaspheme — that something so precious can be signified by them, that is, the body and blood of our Lord Jesus Christ. It follows (11:28–29) "But let a man prove himself, and so let him eat of that bread, and drink of the chalice. For he who eats and drinks unworthily, eats and drinks judgment to himself, not discerning the body of the Lord." Therefore in this he receives judgment unto himself for he is unworthy — that is, in mortal sin — since he does not discern the body of the Lord when he eats this bread and drinks this chalice. Therefore the body of our Lord Jesus Christ is in this appropriate and consecrated host, which is received unto salvation by the holy faithful. But answer me O Patarene, you give of this material bread, sanctified by your customs, to your believers whom you know to be [involved] in many mortal sins, and whom you know have not been purged of them, since they have not received the imposition of hands by which they are not cleansed of any other sins according to your sect, and so when they unworthily receive the said bread they do this for judgment and the damnation of death. Therefore you knowingly cause them to sin mortally and, on this account, you sin most seriously.

That the bread is not transubstantiated into the body of Christ, nor is the wine changed into His blood

That the bread is not transubstantiated into the body of Christ, nor the wine into his blood, we are able to prove by seven reasons and by five passages of the New Testament.

Proof from natural reasons

Regarding the bread daily transubstantiated into the Body of Christ as you say, O Romans, that the bread is daily changed into the Body of Christ, and that the Body of Christ daily grows, are two great falsehoods, since a thing cannot be changed into another thing, nor is there incremental growth in the body of Christ. So it seems impos-

---

110 itaque…112 domini] 1 Cor. 11:27.   120 probet…123 domini] 1 Cor. 11:28-29.

108 blasphemi] blasfemi *P* | qui] quomodo *P*   112 domini] add. nostri ihesu christi *F*   113 dic…120 christi] om. *F*   128 quod] quia *P*   136 scienter] om. *P*   XXI.3.2 sanguinem] sanguine *F*

107 doctrine|fol. 98ra *P*   134 secundam|fol. 98rb *P*

corpus christi possit latere. item non uidetur uisibile quod corpus christi in os hominis sumatur. cum ipso clauso modo exire non posse. item uos dicitis quod corpus christi diuiditur in tres partes quod est impossibile ut indiuisibile diuidatur. preterea asseritis quod ab immundis recipiatur quod est absurdum dicere. quia sic fedaretur corpus christi. quia qui tangit immundum sordescit. item quod apostolibus sumitur in pluribus locis diminitur et si christus esset ita mangus sicut unus magnus mons ita totus esset consumptus. preterea accidentia non possunt esse sine subiecto. sed in sacrificio uestro sunt formule panis et uini. ergo ibi est substantia panis et uini et sic nulla est quod de transubstantiatione uestra dicitis.

Catholicus: hec omnia de quibus opposuisti sunt in sacramento eucharistie non per naturam sed super naturam. sunt enim supernaturalia et non naturalia tamen et de illi exemplum possumus habere in naturis ad cognitionem licet non ad probationem uerbi gratia. primum est quia corpus christi fit de pane non mutatum manens id quod prius. hoc miraculosum est sicut cognitio mea mediante uoce fit tua manens mea. hoc exemplum in naturis est. ad cognitionem proponiti nostri. secundum est quod tanta magnitudo corporis christi est sub tam parua specie tota latens. hoc miraculum est. sicut in pupilla oculi totus motus recipitur quod naturale est. Tertium est quod totum corpus christi exit per os hominis clausum non diminitum eadem potentia. quo clauso utero uirginis exiuit et de sepulcro. quartum est. quia diuiditur idem indiuisibile sicut ab oculo uiror herbe diuisibiliter sumitur indiuisibil. Quintum est quod ab immundis tamquam et commeditur nec tamen polluitur. sicut radius sole lutum tangit sine macula sui. Sextum est quod apostolibus sumitur et in pluribus locis nec tamen diminuitur sicut ignis candele. viim. est quia ibi equalitas sine substantia. albedo sine albo. dulcedo sine dulci. pondus sine pondere et hiis similia. in apocalypsis. v. nemo dignus fuit aperire librum signacula vii. nisi leo de tribu iuda. quia nemo nouit ad plenum qualiter hec vii sint in corpore christi. nisi ipse filius dei et ideo dicit ysaias. xxviiii. et erit uobis uisio omnium sicut uerba libri signati. quem cum dederint scienti litteras dicent. lege istum et respondebit non possum. signatus est enim. et dabitur liber nescienti litteras diceturque ei. lege et respondebit nescio litteras. actende autem heretice animale homo brutum animali quid ea que de fide sunt. maxime de trinitate et de corpore christi sunt supra scientia naturalium et super

---

sible that the body of Christ was able to be hidden under such a corrupt form of bread. It does not seem that the body of Christ is visibly received in the human mouth, since He would not be able to go out were it closed. Further you say that the body of Christ is divided into three parts,[1] when it is impossible for an indivisible thing to be divided. Moreover you assert that the unclean receive Him, which is absurd to say, since on account of that the body of Christ would be polluted, because he who touches unclean things is polluted. Also what was received by the Apostles in many places it is diminished, and so even if Christ was so great as a mountain, He would already be wholly consumed. Further accidents are not able to exist without a subject, but in your sacrifice the appearance of bread and wine [remains], therefore there also is the substance of bread and wine and so nothing is transubstantiated as you say.

Cath: All of these things about which you have raised objections are not in the Eucharist according to nature, but rather are above nature. For they are supernatural realities and not natural ones, yet still we are able to see such examples in nature, but only in support of the doctrine, rather than as direct proofs. For example, the first is that the body of Christ is made out of bread, though [the body is] unchanged, remaining that which it was before. This is miraculous, just as if my knowledge by the medium of a voice becomes yours while remaining mine. This example is proposed to us in nature through knowledge. The second is that the great magnitude of the body of Christ is hidden under such a small species. The miracle is like this, just as every movement is received in the pupil of the eye, and this is natural. The third is that the whole body of Christ passes through the closed mouths of men, yet His power is not diminished, by which He passed through the closed womb of the Virgin and through the sepulcher. The fourth is that just as the greenness of the grass — which is indivisible — is received divisibly. The fifth is that it is eaten by the unclean and yet never polluted, just as the rays of the sun touch dirt without defilement. The sixth is that it was received by the Apostles in many places, yet it was never diminished, like the light of a candle. The seventh is that there is equality without substance, whiteness without white, sweetness with no sweet, heaviness without a weight, and similar such things, which is not found in any measure in nature, as blessed John says in Apocalypse 5 (5:4-5) "None was found worthy to open the book of the seven seals, save the Lion of the tribe of Judah." Since no one knows fully in what way these seven might be accomplished in the body of Christ, except the Son of God, as Isaiah says in 29 (29:11-12) "And the vision of all shall be to you as the words of a book that is sealed, which when they shall deliver to one that is learned, they shall say, 'Read this,' and he will answer, 'I cannot, for it is sealed.' And the book will be given to one who is

---

XXI.4.46 nemo...47 tribu] Apoc. 5:4-5 (fuit] inuentus est *Vulg.*) 49 et²...53 litteras²] Is. 29:11-12.

XXI.4.18 accidentia] om. *P* 19 et...20 uini¹] om. *P* 29 mea²] in ea *F* 31 nostri] mei *P* 53 litteras¹] add. dictura *P* exp

XXI.4.12 asseritis|fol. 75r *F* 20 nulla|fol. 98va *P* 50 dederint|fol. 98vb *P*

---

1) In reference to the Fraction rite at Mass.

intellectum nostrum. ideo oportet ut si fidem uolumus apprehendere ut extollamus nos super nos. unde dicit apostolus ad hebreos. xi. est autem fides sperandarum substantia rerum argumentum non apparentium etcet. et secunda ad corinthios. x. nam arma militie nostre non sunt carnalia sed potentia deo ad destructionem munitionum. consilia destruentes et omnem altitudinem extollentem se aduersus scientiam dei et in captiuitatem redigentes omnem intellecum etcet. et prima ad corinthios. ii°. animalis autem homo non percipit que spiritus dei sunt. stultitia enim est illi. et non potest intelligere quia spiritualiter examinantur. spiritualis autem iudicat omnia etcet.

Patarenus: Item si est corpus christi in hostia quare non uidetur et sentitur ab hominibus.

Catholicus: Respondeo dispensatum gratie dei est propter tres utilitates. prima est ne abhorreamus eum sumere quod esset si uideremus et sentiremus ipsum. et sic cibo uite eterne priuaremur. secunda est quia apparet in forma gloriosa sicuti est. non possemus sustinere presencia ipsius. licet finaliter appareret contempneremus ipsum et sic negligeremus utrobique naturam salutem. Tertia uero ratio est. ut nobis meritum fidei conseruetur. quia fides non habet meritum ubi humana ratio probet experimentum.

Probatio per scripturas

Patarenus: Lucam xxii. hoc facite in mean commemorationem etcet. quod idem dicit paulus. prima ad corinthios. xviiii. igitur misterium hoc quod dicit instituit de benedictione panis et uini. non fit nisi ad memoriam illius serotine cene. in qua captus et ductus est ad passionem. unde et apostolus dixit in predicto loco. quotiescumque enim manducabitis panem hunc et calicem hunc bibetis. mortem domini annuntiabitis donec ueniat.

Catholicus: Responsio. non dixit dominus hoc facite in meam commemorationem tantum nec dixit apostolis mortem deum tantum annuntiabitis. duo enim facimus in hoc sacrificio unum est. quia corpus christi uere recipimus nobis ad uitam si cum debita reuerentia tractemus illud. et hoc est quod dixit. hoc est corpus meum. etcet. et illud. Caro mea uere est cibus etcet. secundum est quia commemoramus passionem eius. que incepit a cena illa. et hoc est quod saluator dicit. hoc facite in meam commemorationem.

unlettered, and it will be said to him, 'Read,' and he will answer, 'I am illiterate.'" So pay attention, O heretic, the animal 'man' exceeds brute animals, those things which are of the faith, most especially that the Trinity and the body of Christ are beyond natural knowledge, and above our intellects, so it is proper that if we wish to understand it in faith we lift ourselves above our capacity, as the Apostle says to the Hebrews in 11 (11:1) "Now faith is the substance of things hoped for, the evidence of things that are not apparent." And in 2 Corinthians 10 (10:4–5) "For the weapons of our warfare are not carnal, but mighty to God for the pulling down of fortifications, destroying counsels and every height that exalts itself against the knowledge of God, and bringing into captivity every thought to the obedience of Christ." And 1 Corinthians 2 (2:14–15) "But the sensual man does not perceive these things that are from the Spirit of God, for it is foolishness to him and he cannot understand, because it is spiritually examined. But the spiritual man judges all things."

Pat: Then if the body of Christ is in the host, why is it not seen and perceived by men?

Cath: I reply that the dispensation of the grace of God is according to three useful principles. The first is lest we might abhor Him when receiving Him if we might see and sense Him [in His bodiliness], and thus we would be deprived of the food of eternal life. The second is that if He appeared in a glorious form, just as He is, we would not be able to withstand His presence. Finally, if He would habitually appear we might hold Him for nought and so we might neglect in both cases the nature of salvation. And the third reason is that we might preserve the merit of faith for ourselves, since faith has no merit where human reason proves the reality.

Proof from the scriptures

Pat: Luke 22 (22:19) "Do this in commemoration of me." Paul says the same thing, 1 Corinthians 19 (11:24), therefore this mystery that He instituted of the blessing of bread and wine is nothing else than the memory of His last supper, in which He was apprehended and lead to His passion, and as the Apostle says in the same place (11:26) "for whosoever shall eat this bread and drink this chalice will proclaim the death of the Lord until he comes."

Cath: Response. The Lord did not say do this only in commemoration of me, yet neither did the Apostle say you will only proclaim the death of God. For we do two things in this one sacrifice, since we truly receive the body of Christ unto eternal life if we treat it with due reverence, and that is what He said "this is my body." And that (Jn 6:56) "For my flesh is true food." The second thing is that we commemorate His passion, which began at that supper, and this is what the Savior said "Do this in commemor-

---

59 est…60 apparentium] Heb. 11:1.   61 nam…65 intellecum] 2 Cor. 10:4-5.   66 animalis…69 omnia] 1 Cor. 2:14-15.   XXI.5.2 hoc…3 commemorationem] Luc. 22:19.   4 xviiii] 1 Cor. 11:24.   8 quotiescumque…10 ueniat] 1 Cor. 11:26.   17 Caro…18 cibus] Ioh. 6:56.

---

71 sentitur] sumitur P   76 gloriosa] add. fci P exp   XXI.5.2 Patarenus] al. man. P   4 xviiii] sic PF

77 finaliter|fol. 75v F   78 negligeremus|fol. 99ra P

de quo dicit apostolus. quotiescumque enim etcet. manducabitis panem hunc etcet. sed dicite mihi uos ypocrite. quomodo facitis uos hoc in comemmorationem passionis christi. qui nichil de ipse creditis.

Patarenus: Item iohannes. vi. spiritus est qui uiuificat caro autem non prodest quidquam uerba que ego locutus sum uobis spiritus et uita sunt etcet. ergo caro christi non datur nec accipitur in hoc misterio.

Catholicus: Responsio. quod iudei et quidam discipuli domini uerba que dixerat de carne sua sumenda. erronee duobus modis intellexerunt. uno scilicet quod debent comedere carnem eius et lacerare passibiliter ad modum carnum animalium et quod sufficeret ad uitam simpliciter fuisse ipsam. quibus scandalizatis et recedentibus dominus exponit uerba hec apostolis remanentibus scilicet qualiter caro eius et sanguis summi debeat ad salutem dicens. caro mea scilicet sic sumpta ut illi bestialiter intellexerunt. qui scandalizati recesserunt. non prodest quicumque et postea subditur. uerba que ego locutus sum spiritus et uita sunt etcet. hoc est quod dixi de carne mea comedenda. spiritualiter est intelligendum et ad uitam quia caro mea spiritualiter sumenda est scilicet impassibiliter. inuisibiliter. et inlacerabiliter et ad uitam id est in tali statu quod sit tendens ad uitam. hoc est sicut dicit apostolus cum debita probatione uite. alioquin non proderat quicquam immo esset iudicium potius sumenti. caro enim christi et sanguis eius est sicut cibus nobilis et potus elegans qui ab infirmis receptus magis infirmat. sanos autem uel debiles saniores reddit et fortiores ut est caro perdicum et leporum et huiusmodi. et ut est unum bonum et puram. unde apostolus dicit contra illos qui indigne summunt eum infirmitatibus peccatorum prima ad corinthios. xi°. ideo inter uos multi infirmi et imbecilles et dormiunt multi etcet.

[**Patarenus:**] Item. i^a ad corinthios. xi. conuenientibus uobis in unum iam non est dominicam cenam manducare. unusquisque enim suam cenam presumit ad manducandum et alius quidem esurit. alius autem ebrius est etcet. ergo dominica cena fiebat in maxima quantitate panis et uini et in magna comessatione atque potatione. quod numquam est credendum de christi corpore et eius sanguine.

Catholicus: Responsio. Quia male faciebant reprehendit illos apostolus. uel aliter dico quod illa multitudo panis et uini de qua faciebant illa reprehensibilia non erat tota sacrificata. sicut nec totum quod fuit in cena domini fuit sacrificatum et reprehendit illos corinthios. de duobus scilicet de

ation of me," of which the Apostle said "for whosoever ... shall eat this bread" But tell me, you hypocrites, how can you make this in commemoration of the passion of Christ, which none of you believe in?

[**Pat:**] Further John 6 (6:64) "The spirit is that which gives life, but the flesh profits nothing. The words that I have spoken to you are spirit and life." Therefore the flesh of Christ is not given, nor is it received in this mystery.

Cath: Response. Since the Jews and certain disciples of the Lord took the words that He had spoken as referring to the eating of His flesh, they understood him wrongly in two ways: first, that they ought to eat His flesh and to tear it in a sensuous/material manner like [they tear] the flesh of animals and that it would suffice for life to consume it with prayers [i.e. like they do with an animal sacrifice]. After these were scandalized and as they were withdrawing, the Lord explains these words to the remaining apostles, namely what type of flesh and blood they ought to partake of for salvation — that is — what is so partaken of that those who left scandalized understood in an animalistic way, does not profit anyone, and later He added, (6:64) "The words that I have spoken to you are spirit and life." This is what I said of eating my flesh, it is to be understood spiritually and unto life since my flesh is to be received spiritually, namely, impassibly, invisibly, and with a good manner of life, that is, in such a state as that which tends towards [eternal] life. This is just as the Apostle says, "with the due testing of one's life," otherwise it would not profit for anything, rather one might have received judgment by reception. The flesh and blood of Christ. For the flesh of Christ and His blood is like rich food and fine drink which, when taken by the sick, further enfeebles them, but it renders healthy and weak [people] healthier and stronger, just as is the flesh of partridges and hares and the like. And as it were one good and pure thing, as the Apostle says against those who unworthily receive it with the infirmity of sins, 1 Corinthians 11 (11:30) "Therefore there are many infirm and weak among you, and many sleep."

[**Pat:**] Also 1 Corinthians 11 (11:20–21) "When you come therefore together into one place, it is not now to eat the Lord's supper, for every one takes his own supper before to eat, and one indeed is hungry and another is drunk." Therefore the Lord's Supper was instituted with a great quantity of bread and wine and amidst great merrymaking and drunkenness since it was never believed that it was the body of Christ or His blood.

Cath: Reply. Because they acted badly the Apostle reproved them, or I say they did those reprehensible things as regards a quantity of bread and wine which was not completely sacrificed, just as neither was everything a sacrifice at the Lord's supper and he reproved them regarding

---

25 spiritus…27 sunt] Ioh. 6:64.   40 uerba…sunt] Ioh. 6:64.   55 ideo…56 multi] 1 Cor. 11:30.   57 conuenientibus…61 est] 1 Cor. 11:20-21.

29 quidam] quida *F*   34 simplicter] suppliciter *F*   35 hec] est *F*   37 summi] *sic PF*   45 quod] *sic PF*   47 proderat] proderet *F*   50 infirmat] infirmatur *P*   51 leporum] leporis *F*   53 eum] cum *P*   67 panis…faciebant] de qua panis et uini fiebant *F* | faciebant] fiebant *F*

XXI.5.26 ego|fol. 99rb *P*   58 unum|fol. 99va *P*   67 faciebant|fol. 76r *F*

nimia comessatione et potatione quam faciebant post communionem et de inhumanitate inordinate karitatis. quod alius multum habebat ad comedendum et bibendum et alius esuriebat et sitiebat.

Patarenus: Item ad hebreos. x. hostiam et oblationem noluisti etcet. ergo ista hostia quam uos offeritis in modum sacrificium non placet deo.

Catholicus: Responsio. loquitur de hostia iudeorum. unde subdit infra. hostias et oblationem et holocautomata pro peccato noluisti nec placita sunt tibi que secundum legem offeruntur etcet. de qua dicit pro et contra et solutionem requiras supra in titulus de ueteri testamento. de natura autem hostia id est de corpore christi subdit in predicto capitulo. corpus autem adaptasti mihi etcet.

[**Patarenus:**] Item in eodem. una enim oblatione consummauit in sempiternum sanctificatos etcet. et infra. iam non relinquitur pro peccatis hostia etcet. ergo corpus christi non offertur amplius.

Catholicus: Responsio. quod loquitur de corpore christi passibili. quod numquam amplius offertur ad passionem. unde dicit supra. viiii. quemadmodum statutum est hominibus semel mori. post hoc autem iudicium. sic et christus semel ablatus est ad multorum exaurienda peccata etcet. Si autem obiciunt heretici de duabus auctoritatibus. augustini. in quibus uidetur dicere quod non corpus uisibile christi nec sanguis eius quem effuderunt iudei et quod christus sit in uno loco tantum id est in celo empyreo. secundum naturam humanitatis sic intelligitur. non corpus quod fuit uisibile id est non quale. et quem id est qualem. quia corpus eius et sanguinem non recipimus uisibiliter et passibiliter sicut fuit iudeis et dicimus quod ipse est tantum in celo. uerum est naturaliter est tamen in multis locis simul et semel miraculose et sic intellixit beatus augustinus. prout patet in multis aliis eius scripturis.

two things, namely, of excessive carousing and drunkenness which they indulged in after communion and of the inhuman charitable disorder, because they had much to eat and drink while others hungered and thirsted.

Pat: Further Hebrews 10 (10:5) "Sacrifice and oblation you did not want." Therefore that sacrifice which you offer as a sacrifice is not pleasing to God.

Cath: Reply. He is speaking of the sacrifices of the Jews, as he adds later (10:8) "Sacrifices and oblations and holocausts for sin you did not want, neither are they pleasing to you, those which are offered according to the law." As to that the pros and cons and the solution you can find above in the section on the Old Testament, on the nature of sacrifice — that is — on the Body of Christ in the foregoing chapter (10:5) "you have fitted a body for me."

[**Pat:**] And in the same place (10:14) "For by one oblation he has perfected forever those who are sanctified." And later (10:26) "there is now left no sacrifice for sins." Therefore the body of Christ is not offered any longer.

Cath: Reply. That speaks of the body of Christ which is subject to passibility, since He shall never again be offered as in the passion, as it says above in 9 (9:27–28) "And as it is appointed for men to die once, and after this the judgment, so also Christ was offered once to remove the sins of many." But if the heretics object with two authorities of Augustine,[1] in which it seems to say that neither body of Christ nor His blood is visible which the Jews spilled and that Christ is in one place alone, that is, in the empyrean heavens, according to the nature of His humanity it is understood as follows: it is not the body which was visible, that is, not that kind of body, for we do not receive his body and blood visibly and sensibly just as He appeared to the Jews, and we say that He Himself is only in heaven, it is true and natural to be in many places at the same time and this miraculously, and this is how Blessed Augustine understood it, just as is plain in many other of his writings.

De sacramento matrimonii   XXII   On the sacrament of marriage

De matrimonio sicut de duobus superioribus sacramentis concordant patareni ad inuicem preterquam de expositionibus scripturarum de ipso loquentium. in quibus sunt diuersi diuersa sentientes. omnis enim blasphemant matrimonium quod est

On the Sacrament of Marriage, just as in the two previous sacraments, the Patarenes are in agreement among themselves, with the exception of their understanding of the scriptures that speak of it, about which they have divergent interpretations. For all of they blaspheme against carnal

---

75 hostiam…76 noluisti] Heb. 10:5. 79 hostias…81 offeruntur] Heb. 10:8. 84 corpus…85 mihi] Heb. 10:5. 86 una…87 sanctificatos] Heb. 10:14. 88 iam…hostia] Heb. 10:26. 92 quemadmodum…95 peccata] Heb. 9:27-28 (ablatus est] oblatus est *Vulg.*)

74 et sitiebat] om. F 75 hostiam] sacrificium P 96 augustini] augustinus F 97 non] si P 98 iudei] ei P 99 empyreo] empireo F XXII.1.1 sacramento matrimonii] matrimonio sacramenti P

91 numquam|fol. 99vb P

---

1) Neither of these two authorities are certain. Augustine mostly wrote as a realist about the Eucharist, but there are passages which suggest a spiritualizing interpretation. As to the visible body of Christ, the heretics may be appealing to *Ennarationes in Psalmos* 98, 9 "You must understand what I have said in a spiritual sense. You are not going to eat this body which you see." As to the second regarding the body of Christ in heaven it perhaps refers to Sermon 131, 1, and the *Commentary on the Gospel of John*, 27, 5.

secundum carnem. Nos autem ipsum bonum et sanctum esse tam per naturales rationes quam per scripturas diuinas patefaciemus ad liquidum.

Probatio per rationales naturales

Deus uult animas in carne saluari et non aliter. ergo uult id per quod ad carnem ueniunt. qui est carnale coitus. Nam cum aliquid tam a deo quam ab homine conceditur aut datur et id domini uel concedi intelligitur sine quo datum uel concessum haberi non potest. igitur coitus matrimonialis a deo concessus intelligitur esse. Nec potes mihi arguere quod eadem ratione. omnis carnalis coitus intelligitur esse concessus. quoniam omnis alii leguntur spiritualiter esse prohibiti.

De matrimonio

Item coitus carnalis qui est in matrimonio secundum naturam est. nec honestati contrarium. nec aliquo inuenitur iure prohibitus. et nichil est peccatum quod est secundum cursum nature nisi inueniatur esse prohibitum. Item si non esset aliquis coitus uiri et mulieris concessus qui est matrimoniale. omnes fere homines uitio laborarent pessimo quod est contra naturam. preterea in diuina scriptura expressim conceditur et collaudatur et multi qui secundum ipsum uixerunt seu uiuunt sancti et iusti dicuntur et comprobantur. et ista ratio per multas scripturas declaratur. quare matrimonium carnis sanctum et iustum esse probatur

De matrimonio

Mattheus. i°. iacob autem genuit ioseph uirum marie de qua natus est ihesus qui uocatur christus etcet. et infra. cum esset desponsata maria mater ihesu ioseph etcet. et infra. et ecce angelus domini in somnis apparuit ei dicens. Joseph filii dauid noli timere accipere mariam coniugem tuam etcet. iohannes iii°. nuptie facte sunt in chana galilee et erat mater ihesu ibi. uocatus est autem et ihesus et discipuli eius ad nuptias etcet. ergo matrimonium sanctum est. si spiritus sanctus uoluit quod mater christi esset in eo et si christus stetit in nuptiis et nec illas reprehendit.

Patarenus: Respondeo quod matrimonio beate marie fuit uirginitas et tale matrimonium ego approbo. et christus iuit ad nuptias ut de illi eriperet. iohannes. euangelistam et per hoc habes potius quod matrimonium carnale malum sit.

marriage. But we hold it to be good and holy, as we will make clear as water from both natural reason and from the divine scriptures.

Proof from natural reasons

God wished souls to be saved in bodies and not in another way. Therefore He wished that men should come to be through bodies, which happens through sexual intercourse. In fact, since when a thing is granted or given by God to men, that is understood to be given or conceded by the Lord, [especially since] without which the given or conceded thing cannot be had. Therefore sex within marriage is to be understood as conceded by God, neither are you able to argue against me that by that rationale all human intercourse is to be understood as conceded, since all other types are read to be prohibited spiritually.

On Marriage

Further the carnal intercourse which is in marriage is according to nature, neither is it contrary to honor, neither is it found to be prohibited by any law. It is no sin at all since it follows the course of nature, except when it is found to be prohibited. Further if there is not some intercourse granted to men and women, which is of the matrimonial type, nearly all men would labor under terrible vices that are contrary to nature. Further in the divine scriptures marital intercourse is expressly conceded and praised and many who lived that way were later proven to be called saints and just people, and many passages attest to this idea about why carnal marriage is holy and just.

On Marriage

Matthew 1 (1:16) "Jacob begot Joseph the husband of Mary, of whom was born Jesus, who is called Christ." And later (1:18) "When his mother Mary was espoused to Joseph." And later (1:20) "behold the angel of the Lord appeared to him in his sleep, saying, 'Joseph, son of David, do not fear to take Mary as your wife.'" John 3 (2:1) "There was a marriage in Cana of Galilee, and the Mother of Jesus was there, and Jesus and his disciples were also invited to the wedding." Therefore marriage is holy, if the Holy Spirit wished that the Mother of Christ would be there and if Christ attended and did not hold it in contempt.

Pat: I reply that the marriage of Blessed Mary was a virgin one and I approve of such a union. Also Christ went to the marriage in order that He might deliver John the Evangelist,[1] and through this you have it rather that carnal marriage is evil.

XXII.4.2 iacob...3 christus] Matt. 1:16. 4 cum...ioseph] Matt. 1:18. 5 et² ...7 tuam] Matt. 1:20. 8 nuptie...10 nuptias] Ioh. 2:1.

XXII.2.1 rationales] add. m F exp. | naturales] add. *al. man. marg. dex.* angelorum ruinas per homines reparare P XXII.3.1 De matrimonio] om. F 11 seu uiuunt] om. F XXII.4.1 De matrimonio] Probatio per scripturas F 4 maria] om. F | ihesu] add. maria

XXII.2.5 domini|fol. 100ra P XXII.4.5 somnis|fol. 76v F 12 christus|fol. 100rb P

---

[1] A common medieval tradition was that the wedding was that of John the Evangelist, sometimes suggesting that the wife-to-be was Mary Magdalene. However that penetrating critic Jacobus of Voragine had his doubts. See *Golden Legend*, trans. William Granger Ryan, 2 Vols. (Princeton, NJ: Princeton University Press, 1993), Vol. 1, 375.

Catholicus: Non obstat quod replicasti de matrimonio beate marie in quo uirgo extitit. quia in omnibus aliis matrimoniis carnaliter erant ad inuicem uir et uxor et si malum fuisse matrimonium quod carnale copula sequebatur. omne namque matrimonium debet uitari propter scandalum et suspitiones. Nec obstat quod dicis quod christus de nuptiis eripuit iohannes quia non propter hoc nuptias uituperauit. licet ad maiorem gradum perfectionis educeret germanum. sed habeo manifeste quod illos approbauit cum eis amminiculum et obsequium preseterit dando conuiuis aquam uinum factam. si enim matrimonium esset peccatum. numquam ei deseruisset deus qui nulli seruit turpitudini.

Item. Mattheus. xix°. et accesserunt ad eum pharisei temptantes eum et dicentes. si licet homini dimittere uxorem suam quacumque ex causa. qui respondens ait illis. non licet quia qui fecit hominem ab initio masculum et feminam eos fecit. et dixit propter hoc relinquitur homo patrem et matrem et adherebit uxori sue et erunt duo in carne una. itaque iam non sunt duo sed una caro. quod ergo deus coniunxit homo non separet etcet. et infra. dico autem uobis quicumque dimiserit uxorem suam. nisi ob fornicationem et aliam duxerit mechatur et qui dimissam dixerit mechatur. Item lucam xvi. omnis qui dimittit uxorem suam et duxerit alteram mechatur et qui dimissam a uiro ducit mechatur. etcet. Ex hiis patet quod matrimonium sanctum et bonum est.

Patarenus: Nos qui dicimus scripturas exponi de matrimonio carnali. respondemus quod christus in uerbis istis non commendat matrimonium sed dicit quod deus ueteris testamenti ordinauit eum et quod secundum illius ordinationem qui dimittet uxorem suam. aut qui dimissam duxerit mechatur.

Catholicus: Hunc intellectum tuum reprobat dominus qui dicit hic. quos deus coniunxit homo non separet. ergo matrimonium est bonum et bene a bono deo ordinatum quod christus precipit non separari. alioquin dixisset dominus hic. separet illud. preterea dicitur ibi. dico autem uobis quia quicumque dimiserit uxorem suam etcet. ergo christus ex se matrimonium confirmat.

Patarenus: Respondebo ego secundum alios ex nostris qui scripturas intelligunt de matrimonio spirituali quod Christus precepit non separari scilicet de illo quod est inter episcopum et ecclesiam suam.

Catholicus: Et hunc intellectum reprobum esse pluribus modis potest probari. primo quia questio facta erat a phariseis de matrimonio carnali ut patet ex superioribus et maxime ex subsequentibus ubi dicitur dicunt illi quid ergo moyses mandauit dare libellum repudii et dimittere? ait illis. quoniam moyses ad

---

31 et...39 separet] Matt. 19:3-6. 39 dico...41 mechatur²] Matt. 19:9. 42 omnis...44 mechatur] Matt. 16:18. 53 quos...separet] Matt. 19:6. 68 dicunt...71 uestras] Matt. 19:7-8.

24 quod] om. F 26 habeo] habeo ab eo P 29 enim] add. vinum P exp 31 xix°] xviiii° P 60 ego] ergo F

39 autem|fol. 100va P 68 libellum|fol. 100vb P

duritiam cordis uestri permisit uobis dimittere uxores uestras etcet. ergo patet quod phariseis de matrimonio carnali respondit christus. preterea ipse dicit. ab initio autem non fuit sic. ergo ab initio mundi fuit matrimonium spirituale. inter episcopum et ecclesia quod uos negastis. preterea christus dicit quod qui dimittit uxorem mechatur. et qui dimissam duxerit mechatur. sed petrus gallus dimisit ecclesiam suam quod idem fecit iohannes iudeus. quod idem fecit iohannes de iudice. quod idem fecit garratus. quod idem fecerunt omnes episcopi uestri qui fuerunt primi in ytalia. ergo omnes mechati sunt et omnes alii episcopi qui ecclesias dimissas receperunt mechati sunt et sic omnes estis filii adulterorum. attende ad hoc. homo spiritualis.

Item lucam. i°. Erant autem iusti ambo ante deum incedentes in omnibus mandatis et iustificationibus domini sine querela et non erat illis filius etcet. Ecce qualiter euangelista laudat istos matrimoniales qui et carnaliter fuerunt simili et genuerunt partum ab angelo nuntiatum et a deo consecratum. ergo sanctum est et bonum carnale matrimonium. ad hoc est ad hebreos. xi. Fide et ipsa sara sterilis uirtutem in conceptionem seminis accepit etcet. et iª petri. iii°. sic enim aliquando et sancte mulieres sperantes in domino ornabant se subiecte propriis uiris. sicut sara obediebat abrahe dominum meum uocans. cuius estis filie benefacientes etcet. nec possunt hic intelligi de matrimonio spirituali. cum in ueteri testamento non fuissent spiritualia matrimonia secundum uestram perfidiam.

Catholicus: Item. iª. ad corinthios vii°. propter fornicationem autem unusquisque suam uxorem habeat etcet. igitur uitatur fornicationem propter matrimonium. ergo bonum est matrimonium.
Patarenus: Dicimus quod sic intelligitur. propter fornicationem scilicet faciendam.
Catholicus: Hec glosa doctorum uestrorum demonium est. numquam enim uas electionis predicaret homines ut fornicationem facerent. preterea dominus dicit ut superius demonstrauimus uir uxorem suam excepta causa fornicationis etcet. ergo secundum matrimonium uiuere non est fornicatio.
Patarenus: Dicam ergo quod de spirituali matrimonio loquitur.
Catholicus: Et hoc stare non potest. quia intelligis de matrimonio quod est inter ecclesiam et episcopum. sic apostolus precepit quod unusquisque fidelis sit episcopus habens unam ecclesiam quod est impossibile. Nec potes dicere quod de episcopis respondat hic apostolus. quod de illi non erat eis scriptum. De quibus dicit. de quibus autem scripsistis

He said to them, 'Because of the hardness of your hearts, Moses permitted you to put away your wives.'" Therefore it is clear that Christ was speaking about carnal marriage to the Pharisees. Further He said (19:8) "from the beginning it was not so." Therefore from the foundation of the world there was spiritual marriage between a bishop and the church, which you deny. Further Christ said that he who dismisses his wife commits adultery, and he who marries a divorced person commits adultery, but Peter Gallus divorced his church and John Judeus did the same, as did John Judice, as did Garratus, as likewise did all your bishops who first were in Italy. Therefore they all committed adultery, and all who received the divorced churches are adulterers and so you are all sons of adulterers. Pay attention to that, 'spiritual' man!

Further Luke 1 (1:6–7) "And they were both just before God, walking in all the commandments and ordinances of the Lord without blame, and they had no son." See then how the evangelist praises marriages which were in like manner carnal, and they gave birth to a son by the proclamation of an angel and by the blessing of God, therefore carnal marriage is holy and good. Hebrews speaks to this point in 11 (11:11) "By faith also Sarah herself, being barren, received the power to conceive seed," and in 1 Peter 3 (3:5–6) "For after this manner the holy women also, who trusted in God, adorned themselves, subjecting themselves to their own husbands, as Sarah obeyed Abraham, calling him lord, whose daughters you are, doing well." Neither are they able to understand spiritual marriage here regarding these passages since in the Old Testament there was no spiritual marriage according to your faithless interpretation.

Cath: Similarly, 1 Corinthians 7:2 "But on account of fornication, let every man have his own wife." So one avoids fornication by marriage, therefore marriage is good.

Pat: We say it is to be interpreted thusly, that "on account of fornication" it is to be done.

Cath: This gloss of your doctors is demonic, for the Vessel of Election never preached that men ought to fornicate, further the Lord says above (Mt 5:32) "whoever puts away his wife, excepting for the cause of fornication." Therefore to live in marriage is no fornication.

Pat: That is why I said that He is speaking of spiritual marriage.

Cath: And that cannot stand, since you understand that marriage is meant to be between a church and a bishop, so the Apostle commanded that each of the faithful might be a bishop having one church, which is impossible. Nor is one able to say that the Apostle was here replying about bishops, since he was not writing regarding them. About this he says (1 Cor 7:1) "Now about the things you wrote

---

72 ab...73 sic] Matt. 19:8.   85 Erant...87 filius] Luc. 1:6-7.   92 Fide...93 accepit] Heb. 11:11.   93 sic...96 benefacientes] 1 Pet. 3:5-6 (meum) eum *Vulg.*)   100 propter...102 habeat] 1 Cor. 7:2.   109 uir...110 fornicationis] Matt. 5:32.   120 de...121 mihi] 1 Cor. 7:1.

74 matrimonium] add. fuit *P* exp   90 ergo] igitur *F*   114 quia] quasi *P*   116 apostolus precepit] transp. *F*

76 duxerit|fol. 77r *F*   95 subiecte|fol. 101ra *P*

mihi etcet. immo de fornicatoribus maxime secundum opinionem tuam. Si uero intelligas de illo quod est inter christum et ecclesiam. uel ipsum et animam. ergo christo precipit apostolus uel consulit quod nichil est dictu. preterea dicit unamquamque suum uirum habeat etcet. quod sonat dicere illa habeat illum. et hic illum. ergo aut plures sunt christi quod falsum est. aut precipit uel consulit paulus quod una habeat christum. Alia uero alium partem christum quod ex parte mortis preceptum esset.

Probatio quod matrimonium est bonum et sanctum

Idem in eodem. uxori uir debitum reddat. similiter autem et uxor uiro. mulier sui corporis potestatem non habet. sed uir. etcet. ergo bonum est debitum quod est secundum carnem in matrimonio. presertim cum postea dicat et iterum reuertimini in idipsum ne temptet uos sathanas propter incontinentiam uestram etcet. ergo uitatur incontinentia propter carnale debitum matrimonii. igitur sanctum et bonum est.

Patarenus: dico quod est consilium minoris mali. quia melius quod cum uno quam cum pluribus fornicetur.
Catholicus: Sed hoc nichil est. numquam enim apostolus consuleret peccatum mortale fieri. qui dicit inferius. puto autem quod et ego spiritum dei habeam etcet. preterea sic exponendo mentiris. quia in tue secte prauitate est quod nullum peccatum est maius alio.
Patarenus: Dicam ergo tibi sectum meum quod paulus hic habuit os nimis latum.
Catholicus: Sanctior ergo os paulo. qui habes os ita strictum quod nulle diuini honoris. nichil reuerentie sanctorum nil denique ueritatis non potest audiri.
Patarenus: Dicam ergo quod de debito spirituale matrimonii loquitur.
Catholicus: Sed probo quod non potest intelligi de hoc debito quia statim de isto debito subdit. nolite fraudare inuicem nisi forte ex consensu ad tempus ut uacetis orationi etcet. ergo tempore orationis licet committere fraudem de debito spirituali quo tempore sanctius debet reddi quod nulla est decum. ergo de temporali loquitur.

to me." Indeed [it was to] the sexually immoral, especially according to your opinion. If in truth you understand it to be about the union of Christ and the Church, or Him and the soul, therefore the Apostle commands or counsels by Christ that nothing [further] is to be said. Further he says (7:2) "let every woman have her own husband," that seems to say that she might have Him, and He her, therefore either there are many Christs — which is false — or Paul commands or counsels that just one should have Christ. Indeed another woman [should have] another Christ as [her] share, which would be a command from the share of death.

Proof that marriage is good and holy

In the same place (7:2–3) "Let the husband render the debt to his wife, and the wife also in like manner to the husband. The wife does not have power over her own body, but the husband. And in like manner the husband also does not have power over his own body, but the wife." Therefore it is good to render the marriage debt according to the flesh in marriage, especially since he later says (7:5) "and come together again, lest Satan tempt you for your incontinency." So one avoids incontinency by the rendering of the carnal debt of marriage, therefore it is holy and good.

Pat: I say that it is a counsel for the lesser evil, since it is better to fornicate with one than with many.
Cath: But there is nothing to this, for the Apostle never counsels one to commit a mortal sin, as he later says (7:40) "I think that I also have the spirit of God." Further, by construing it in this manner you lie, since in your depraved sect no one sin is considered greater than another.
Pat: I might say therefore to you that in my sect Paul here has an extremely broad manner of speaking.[1]
Cath: Paul's speech is holier, you who have such a constricted mouth in which can be heard no divine honor, nor reverence for the saints, nor any truth at all.
Pat: I could say that the marriage debt is to be understood spiritually.
Cath: But I prove that one cannot understand the debt in this manner since he immediately subjoins (7:5) "Do not deprive one another, except perhaps by consent, for a time, so that you may give yourselves to prayer." Therefore it is permissible to be abstinent from the debt for a spiritual time of prayer during which one should become holier, and not render the debt unworthily, therefore he is speaking of temporal realities.

---

125 unamquamque...126 habeat¹] 1 Cor. 7:2 (unamquamque] unaqueque *Vulg.*)   XXII.5.3 uxori...5 uir] 1 Cor. 7:3-4.   7 et...8 uestram] 1 Cor. 7:5.   15 puto...habeam] 1 Cor. 7:40.   26 nolite...28 orationi] 1 Cor. 7:5.

122 opinionem] oppinionem *P*   124 christo] *sic PF leg.* Christus   125 dictu] dictum *F* | uirum] finem *P*   127 illum] *sic PF leg.* illam | sunt] om. *P*   129 Alia] alii *F* | partem] *sic PF leg.* parte | christum] *sic PF leg.* Christi   XXII.5.1 Probatio...2 sanctum] om. *F*   17 est²] add. e *P exp*   20 Sanctior] santior *F*   22 denique] add. quod *P*   25 Catholicus] Patarenus *P*   26 debito²] loco *F*

126 habeat²|fol. 101rb *P*   XXII.5.19 nimis|fol. 77v *F*   27 consensu|fol. 101va *P*

---

1) Perhaps even, "Paul has a big mouth"?

Probatio quod matrimonium est bonum

Item in eodem. hiis autem qui in matrimonio iuncti sunt precipio non ego sed dominus uxorem a uiro non discedere quod si discesserit manere innuptam. aut uiro suo reconciliari et uir uxorem non dimittat etcet. ergo bonum est carnale matrimonium. si preceptum domini est quod non separetur nec aliqua ratione de spirituali matrimonio potest intelligi quia secundum hoc sonaret quod siquis separaretur a christo uel a bono episcopo. postea esset sine christo illi sine episcopo quod falsum est. quia numquam dominus preceptum daret mortis.

De illo qui habet uxorem infidelem

Idem in eodem. nam ceteris ego dico non dominus. si quis frater uxorem habet et hec consentit habitare cum illo. non dimittat illam et si qua mulier habet uirum infidelem et hic consentit habitare cum illa non dimittat uirum. sanctificatus est mulier infidelis. per uirum fidelem. alioquin filii uestri immundi essent. nunc autem santi sunt etcet. Ex hoc spiritualiter non potest intelligi. quia numquam episcopus non debet habitare cum ecclesia infideli. nec etiam habet infidelem sub se. Nam hoc ipso non est ecclesia quo est infidelis.

Catholicus: Idem in eodem. alligatus es uxori noli querere solutionem. solutus es ab uxore noli querere uxorem etcet. ad idem.

De matrimonio

Idem in eodem. si autem acceperis uxorem non peccasti et si nupserit uirgo non peccauit. tribulationem tamen carnis habebunt huiusmodi. ego autem uos parco etcet. hoc de spirituali matrimonio non potest intelligi. quia secundum hoc diceret. apostolus uirginem esse animam que esset sine christo uel sine pastore et sic esset in meliori statu. iterum diceret animam habere tribulationem carnis cum esset cum christo uel cum pastore quam non esset alias habitura. qua indiget uenia quod falsum est. quia secundum hoc anima in meliori statu fuisset.

De matrimonio

Idem in eodem. si quis autem turpem se uideri existimat super uirgine sua quod sit superadulta et ita oportet fieri quod uult faciat. non peccat si nubat etcet. quod etiam de spirituali matrimonio non potest intelligere aliquas sani capitis.

Proof that marriage is good

In the same place (7:10–11) "But to those who are married, not I but the Lord commands that the wife depart not from her husband and if she depart, that she remain unmarried, or be reconciled to her husband. And let the husband not put away his wife." Therefore carnal marriage is good if the command of the Lord is that one should not separate for any reason. Nor is there any reason to understand it as a spiritual marriage, since according to this it might seem that whoever is separated from Christ or from a good bishop should later be without Christ or a bishop. This is false because the Lord would never give a precept of death.

On that one who has an unfaithful wife

In the same place (7:12–14) "For to the rest I speak, not the Lord. If any brother has an unbelieving wife, and she consents to dwell with him, let him not put her away. And if any woman has an unbelieving husband, and he consents to dwell with her, let her not put away her husband. For the unbelieving husband is sanctified by the believing wife and the unbelieving wife is sanctified by the believing husband, otherwise your children would be unclean, but now they are holy." This passage cannot be interpreted spiritually, since the bishop never ought to dwell with an unfaithful church, neither also does he have unfaithful people under his rule, for he himself is not that by which the Church is unfaithful.

Cath: In the same place (7:27) "Are you bound to a wife? Do not seek to be loosed. Are you free of a wife? Do not seek a wife."

On Marriage

In the same place (7:28) "But if you take a wife, you have not sinned. And if a virgin marries, she has not sinned, nevertheless, yet will have tribulation of the flesh. But I would spare you." This cannot be understood to be about spiritual marriage, for according to that reading, the Apostle would be saying that a virgin is a soul which, without Christ or without a pastor, would be in a better state. Further, he would be saying that the soul would have tribulation of the flesh when it was with Christ or with a pastor, which it would not otherwise have, because it lacked forgiveness, which is false, since according to this conception the soul would be in a better state.

On Marriage

In the same place (7:36) "But if any man think that he seems dishonored with regard to his virgin, because she is above the age, and so it must happen that he does what he will, he does not sin, if she marry." And it is also impossible for any sane understanding to interpret this as being about spiritual marriage.

XXII.6.2 hiis...5 dimittat] 1 Cor. 7:10-11.   XXII.7.2 nam...8 sunt] 1 Cor. 7:12-14 (mulier) add. fidelis *Vulg*.)   13 alligatus...15 uxorem] 1 Cor. 7:27.   XXII.8.2 si...5 parco] 1 Cor. 7:28.   XXII.9.2 si...4 nubat] 1 Cor. 7:36.

XXII.6.1 Probatio...bonum] om. *F*   7 nec...9 separaretur] om. *F*   XXII.7.1 De...infidelem] om. *F*   XXII.8.1 De matrimonio] om. *F*   5 matrimonio] add. hoc *P*   6 diceret] dicere *P*   XXII.9.1 De matrimonio] om. *F*

XXII.7.14 querere¹|fol. 101vb *P*

De matrimonio 10

item in eodem. Mulier alligata est legi quanto tempore uir eius uiuit. quod si dormierit uir eius liberata est. cui uult nubat tantum in domino. beatior autem erit si sic permanserit secundum consilium meum etcet. ergo temporale matrimonium bonum est. et mortuo priore uiro non est peccatum transire ad secundas nuptias. nec potest hoc intelligi spiritualiter. hoc spiritualis. quod secundum hoc mortuo uno uiro spirituali. beatior esset si staret sine alio. quod falsum est. quia aut secundus uir esset bonus et tunc non esset beata. necdum beatior si sine illo esset. si uero esset malus ergo esset beatior si esset sine illo. igitur esset beata si esset cum illo. cum comparatiuus positio comparetur.

Catholicus: Item. ad Galathas. v°. manifesta sunt opera carnia. que sunt fornicatio. immunditia etcet. audi quod inter opera carnis dampnata neque hic neque alibi matrimonium computatur. igitur non est malum sed bonum.

De matrimonio 11

Item. ad ephesios. v. mulieres uiris suis subdite sint sicut domino etcet. et infra. uiri diligite uxores uestras. et infra. ita uiri debent diligere uxores suas ut corpora sua qui suam uxorem diligit seipsum diligit. nemo enim umquam carnem suam odio habuit etcet. et infra propter hoc relinquet homo patrem et matrem et adherebit uxori sue et erunt duo in carne una. sacramentum hoc magnum est. Ego autem dico in christo et in ecclesia etcet. Ex hiis patet expressim quod matrimonium uiri et mulieris quod est secundum carnem. presertim cum sit sacramentum matrimonii spirituale quod est inter christum et ecclesiam.

De matrimonio 12

Item i^a. ad timotheus. ii°. Adam non est seductus. mulier autem seducta in preuaricatione fuit. saluabitur autem per filiorum generationem etcet. ergo saluus habetur per carnalem coitum. igitur ipse non est peccatum. Sed est occasio boni. nisi expressim inueniatur prohibitus. ergo matrimonialis non est peccatum. cum non inueniatur prohibitus sed concessus.

Catholicus: Idem. iiii°. spiritus autem manifeste dicit. quia in nouissimis temporibus discedent quidam a fide. actendentes spiritibus erroris et doctrinis demoniorum in ypocrisis loquentium mendacium et cauteriatam habentiam conscientiam prohibentium nubere etcet.

On Marriage 10

In the same place (7:39–40) "A woman is bound by the law as long as her husband is alive; but if her husband dies, she is freed. Let her marry whom she will, only in the Lord. But more blessed shall she be, if she so remains, according to my counsel." Therefore temporal marriage is good, and it is no sin to undertake a second marriage once the first husband has died. Nor can this be understood spiritually, because on that reading, when one spiritual husband has died, she would be more blessed if she remained without another, which is false, because either the second husband would be good and then she would not be blessed nor yet more blessed if she were without him, but if he were bad then she would be more blessed if she were without him, and so would be blessed if she were with him, if one compares the two.

Cath: Further in Galatians 5 (5:19) "Now the works of the flesh are manifest, which are fornication, uncleanness." Hear then that marriage is counted neither among the works of the flesh listed here, nor in any other place. Therefore it is not evil but good.

On Marriage 11

Further to the Ephesians 5 (5:22) "Let women be subject to their husbands, as to the Lord," and later (5:25) "Husbands love your wives," and later (5:28–29) "So also ought men to love their wives as their own bodies. He who loves his wife, loves himself, for no man ever hated his own flesh." And later (5:31–32) "Because of this a man shall leave his father and mother and shall cleave to his wife, and they shall be two in one flesh. This is a great mystery, and I speak it about Christ and the Church." From these words it is most clear that the marriage of men and women contracted according to the flesh is good, just like the spiritual sacrament of marriage between Christ and the Church.

On Marriage 12

Further 1 Timothy 2 (2:14–15) "And Adam was not led astray, but the woman was led astray in the lie. Yet she shall be saved through childbearing." So she will have salvation through carnal intercourse, therefore it is no sin, but an occasion of good, unless one finds it explicitly prohibited. So marriage is no sin, since it is not prohibited but conceded.

Cath: Also in chapter 4 (4:1–3) "Now the Spirit clearly says that in the last times some shall depart from the faith, giving heed to spirits of error and doctrines of demons, speaking lies in hypocrisy, and having their conscience

---

XXII.10.2 Mulier…5 meum] 1 Cor. 7:39-40.   15 manifesta…16 immunditia] Gal. 5:19.   XXII.11.2 mulieres…3 domino] Eph. 5:22.   3 uiri…uestras] Eph. 5:25.   4 ita…6 habuit] Eph. 5:28-29.   7 propter…10 ecclesia] Eph. 5:31-32.   XXII.12.2 Adam…4 generationem] 1 Tim. 2:14-15.   10 spiritus…14 nubere] 1 Tim. 4:1-3.

XXII.10.1 De matrimonio] om. *F*   12 malus] add. tunc *P* exp   13 igitur…14 illo] om. *F*   XXII.11.1 De matrimonio] om. *F*   XXII.12.1 De matrimonio] om. *F*   6 Sed est] om. *P*

XXII.10.10 beatior|fol. 102 ra *P*   19 bonum|fol. 78r *F*   XXII.12.6 peccatum|fol. 102rb *P*

ergo uos patareni per doctrinam diabolicam prohibetis matrimonium.
Patarenus: Dico quod loquitur de uobis qui prohibetis matrimonium spirituale.
Catholicus: Sed constat quod tempore apostoli erant plures quam sint hodie qui matrimonium spirituale prohibebant. quomodo ergo dicit apostolus. in nouissimis temporibus. uenient isti quasi non fuissent tunc? ergo loquitur de illis hereticis qui nondum apparuerant. nondum enim apparuerant aliqui negantes matrimonium carnale et isti debebant uenire circa finem mundi. ergo uos patareni estis illi de quibus dicit apostolus. quia uos soli estis inter omnes hereticos matrimonium blasphemantes.

Probatio quod matrimonium est bonum

adolescentiores uiduas diuita etcet. et infra. uolo autem iuniores nubere. filios procreare matresfamilias esse. nullam occasionem dare aduersario maledicti gratia etcet. Sed iste de quibus hic dicit apostolus. erant uidue et prohibet illas recipi in matrimonio spirituali et dicit quod uult quod nubant et filios generent. ne daret occasionem diabolo alicuius peccati. ergo matrimonium carnale sanctum est. presertim cum de uoluntate beati pauli fiat que non nisi bona et sancta fuit.

Item ad titum. ii°. adolescentulas ut uiros suos ament et filios suos diligant etcet.

De Matrimonio

Item. ad hebreos. ultimo. honorabile connubium et thorus in omnibus immaculatus. fornicatores etiam et adulteros iudicabit deus etcet. audi miser canis quod apostolus non uocat matrimonium adulterium uel fornicationem sed uocat eum honorabile et immaculatum et sine iudicio ultionis. quare patet quod sanctum et bonum est.
Patarenus: Dico quod loquitur de matrimonio spirituali. numquam enim matrimonium carnale est sine macula mortale peccati.
Catholicus: Sed probo quod mentiris. quia apostolus dicit. i^a. ad corinthios. vii°. nam qui statuit in corde suo firmus non habens necessitatem potestatem autem sue uoluntatis et hoc iudicabit in corde sui seruare uirginitatem bene facit. et qui non iungit melius facit. etcet. ergo sine macula peccati mortale potest esse matrimonium carnale. alias enim non benefaceret qui uirginem suam in illo ligaret.
Patarenus: Dico quod qui iungit uirginem suam matrimonio carnali benefacit id est minus male quam si faceret illam cum multis fornicari. et si non iungit conseruando eam in uirginitate melius facit.

seared, forbidding to marry." Therefore you Patarenes prohibit marriage by a devilish doctrine.
Pat: I say that he is speaking of those who would prohibit spiritual marriage.
Cath: But it remains that in the time of the Apostles there were many more than there are today who prohibited spiritual marriage, as the Apostle says (4:1) "in these last times." Such ones shall come, just as if they had not so far existed then? Therefore he speaks of these heretics who had not yet appeared, for when they would appear some would deny carnal marriage and that they would come at the end of the world. Therefore you Patarenes are those of which the Apostle spoke, since you alone among all the heretics blaspheme against marriage.

Proof that marriage is good

(5:11) "But avoid the younger widows." And later (5:14) "I wish therefore that the younger should marry, bear children, be mistresses of families, give no occasion to the adversary to speak evil." But about these the Apostle says here, there were widows and he prohibited them to be received in spiritual marriage and he says that he wished them to marry and bear children, lest they give occasion to the devil for some sins, so carnal marriage is holy, particularly since Paul would not have willed it unless it was good and holy.
Further in Titus 2 (2:4) "teach the young women to be wise, to love their husbands, to love their children."

On Marriage

Further in the last chapter of Hebrews (13:4) "Marriage honorable in all, and the bed undefiled, for God will judge fornicators and adulterers." Listen you miserable dog, the Apostle does not call marriage 'adultery' or 'fornication,' but he calls it honorable and immaculate and beyond reproach. Therefore it is clear that it is holy and good!

Pat: I say that he is speaking of spiritual marriage, for carnal marriage is never without the stain of mortal sin.

Cath: But I prove that you lie, since the Apostle says in 1 Corinthians 7 (7:37, 38b) "For he who has determined, being steadfast in his heart, having no compulsion, but having power of his own will, and has judged this in his heart, to keep his virgin, does well, and he who does not give her does better." Therefore one can be in a carnal marriage without the stain of mortal sin, for otherwise he does not do well who binds his virgin in marriage.

Pat: I say that he who gives his virgin in carnal marriage does well — that is — less badly than if he caused her to fornicate with many. And if she does not marry, she does better by preserving her virginity.

Catholicus: Sed apostolus dicit supra in eodem si nupserit uirgo non peccauit etcet. preterea peccata sunt equalia secundum te. ergo falsa est expositio tua.
[**Catholicus:**] Dicam igitur quod loquitur de matrimonio spirituali. ergo melius facit qui non iungit uirginem suam matrimonio spirituali quam qui iungit. et sic melius est uiuere carnaliter quam spiritualiter. quid dicit ad hunc homo spiritualis.
[**Patarenus:**] Ego sic istud intelligo caute. qui matrimonio scilicet spirituali iungit uirginem suam bene facit. et qui non iungit scilicet carnali melius facit.

Catholicus: Sed qui iungit matrimonio spirituali non iungit carnali et qui non iungit carnali benefaciendo iungit spirituali. ergo idem est unum quod reliquum. quomodo ergo iste illo melius facit cum nullum aliud faciat? preterea ubi dicit apostolus benefacit qui iungit et melius facit qui non iungit. sed non ponit nisi semel hoc uerbum matrimonio loquitur.

Patarenus: Dicam ergo sectam nostram expositionem que est hic. qui matrimonio uirginem suam scilicet episcopus cum non potest ecclesia suam tenere et custodire dando et committendo eam alteri episcopo benefacit et si non iungit scilicet cum possit ipsam commode tenere melius facit.

Catholicus: Sed hoc expositio tua diabolica est quod patet quia dominus dicit precipiendo quod nullus dimittat uxorem suam excepta causa fornicationis. sed hic de qua dicit apostolus non est adultera cum sit uirgo et si esset adultera oppone ut supra. idem. xix. et accesserunt ad eum pharysei etcet. notatum invenies. preterea quomodo melius facit tenendo eam cum commode possit tenere quam faceret illam a se dimittendo. cum si tenet eam facit quod debet si autem dimittat pessime faciat? inter bonum enim et pessimum nulla est de bonitate comparatio. nichil ergo valet hoc secretaria expositio. patet ergo ex predictis quod matrimonium secundum carnem sacramentum est ecclesie. bonum et sanctum. quod vivendo secundum ipsum potest esse salvus et ostensum est etiam quod conservat a peccato. et per consequentiam quod in eo detur spiritus sanctus ad confirmationem. cum a peccato conservare sit donum spiritus sancti.

Cath: But the Apostle says above in the same letter (7:28) "if he marries his virgin he does not sin." Further all sins are equal for you, therefore your interpretation is false.
[**Catholic**]:[1] So I might say that he is speaking of spiritual marriage, so he does better who does not bind his virgin in spiritual marriage, than he who does so, and thus it is better to live carnally than spiritually. What do you say to that, spiritual man.
[**Pat:**] And thus I understand this with due caution, who in marriage (that is, in spiritual marriage) joins his virgin does well, and he who does not join (that is, in carnal marriage) does better.

Cath: But he who joins [her] in spiritual marriage does not join [her] in a carnal one, and he who does not join [her] in a carnal one, does well by joining [her] in spiritual marriage. Therefore the same one that is left, how does this man do better than that man since he should do nothing else? Further where the Apostle says he does well who joins and does better who does not join, but one cannot posit except once for all that this word applies to marriage.

Pat: I would say therefore that our sect's interpretation is this, "who marries his virgin" — namely — the bishop who cannot keep and guard his church, and by giving and committing it to another bishop does well, and if he is not joined, namely, when he could do better by holding it properly.

Cath: But this explanation of yours is diabolical, because it is clear what the Lord says in commanding that no one ought to divorce his wife excepting the cause of fornication. But this about which the Apostle speaks is not an adulteress because she is a virgin, and if it were adultery, then the counterargument would be as above. In the same place (Mt. 19:3) "and the Pharisees came to him," you will find noted. Further, how does one do better by keeping her, when he could keep her properly than by dismissing her, since if he keeps her he does what he ought, but if he dismisses her he would do worse? For between good and the worst there is no comparison in goodness. There is then no value to this secret interpretation. Therefore it is clear from the foregoing that marriage according to the flesh is a sacrament of the Church, a holy and good thing, since in living according to it one can be saved, and it is clear that also in it one is preserved from sin, and consequently that in it the Holy Spirit is given for confirmation,

---

24 si...25 peccauit] 1 Cor. 7:28. 52 et² ...53 pharysei] Matt. 19:3.

29 uirginem] uirginitatem *F* 31 hunc] hoc *F* 32 Patarenus] Catholicus *P* 33 uirginem] uirginitatem *F* 36 et...carnali²] om. *F* 39 faciat] faciat *F* 40 sed] om. *P* 41 matrimonio] add. quod de uno eodemque matrimonio *F* 43 uirginem] uirginitatem *F* 52 oppone] appone *F* | xix] xviiii *P* 62 ipsum] episcopum *P*

XXII.14.24 eodem|fol. 102vb *P* 26 tua|fol. 78v *F* 52 oppone|fol. 103ra *P*

---

[1]) This and the next speaker attribution is speculative.

Quod matrimonium carnale sit dampnatum secundum patarenos

Quod matrimonium carnale sit dampnatum tam per naturales rationes quam per scripturas possumus comprobare.

Probatio per rationes naturales

In matrimonio carnali sunt tria mala scilicet luxuria. immunditia. et concupiscentia. igitur malum est ac pernitiosum.

Catholicus: Respondeo primum falsum est. quia non est ibi luxuria si ordo et modus debitus seruetur cum intentione recta. alias enim possum ibi esse luxuria. sicut et in potatione uini. ut dicit apostolus. ad ephesios. v. nolite inebriari uino in quo est luxuria et tamen non est luxuria in omni potatione uini. alia uero duo que ibi sunt scilicet immunditia et concupiscentia quia sunt naturalia non sunt peccata. non enim omnis immunditia peccatum est. o ypocrita pharisee ut dicit ueritas. mattheus. xv. non lotis autem manibus manducare non coinquinat hominem etcet. xxiii. ue uobis scribe et pharisei ypocrite. quia mundatis quod deforis est calicis et paropsidis etcet. nec omnis concupiscentia est dampnata. ut puta commendendi urinandi et huiusmodi que in necessitatibus et utilitatibus uite corporale uel spirituale habetur.

Patarenus: Mattheus. v. ego autem dico uobis quia omnis qui uiderit mulierem ad concupiscendum eam iam mechatus est eam in corde suo etcet. ergo matrimonium carnale mecha est cum sit ibi concupiscentia mulieris.

Catholicus: Respondeo et dominus prohibet in istis uerbis concupiscentiam adulterii. mecha enim idem est quod adulterium. et dominus dixerat superius. audistis quia dictum est antiquis non mechaberis etcet. que fuit inhibitio adulterii facta in. x. preceptis decalogi et scribe et pharisei docebant quod non esset prohibitum mecha cordis nisi tantum actuale. dominus ergo supplendo legem quantum ad prauum illorum intellectum dicit quod non solum mecha actuale prohibitum est sed etiam praue uoluntatis et secundum hunc modum procedit in omnibus aliis que in sermone illo continetur scilicet de prohibitione homicidii et huius et colliguntur hec ex duobus uerbis que dixerat superius scilicet non ueni soluere legem sed adimplere etcet. et nisi habundauerit iustitia uestra plusquam scribarum et phariseorum etcet. Ex quibus patet quod

That marriage according to the flesh is condemned according to the Patarenes

We are able to prove that marriage according to the flesh is condemned as much by natural reason as by scripture.

Proof from natural reasons

There are three evils in carnal marriage: indulgence, uncleanness, and concupiscence, therefore it is evil and pernicious.

Cath: I reply that the first is false, since there is no indulgence here if one observes the right order and manner with the right intention, otherwise there may be indulgence here, this is similar to the drinking of wine as the Apostle says in Ephesians 5 (5:18) "And do not be drunk with wine, wherein is indulgence," and yet there is not indulgence in every instance of wine drinking, yet the other two would be there, namely uncleanness and concupiscence which are natural things and are not sins. For not all uncleanness is a sin, you hypocrite Pharisee, when Christ says in truth, Matthew 15 (15:20) "But to eat with unwashed hands does not defile a man." (23:25) "Woe to you scribes and Pharisees, hypocrites, because you clean the outside of the cup and of the dish." Nor is all concupiscence damnable, for example, in eating and in urinating and the like one obtains the necessary and useful things for both bodily and spiritual life.

Pat: Matthew 5 (5:28) "But I say to you, that whoever shall look on a woman with lust has already committed adultery with her in his heart." So carnal marriage is adultery since there one has concupiscence for one's wife.

Cath: I respond that the Lord prohibits in these words the concupiscence of adultery. For 'mecha' means 'the adulterer' that the Lord has spoken about previously (5:27) "you have heard it said of old you shall not commit adultery." The prohibition of adultery was made in the ten commandments of the decalogue, and the scribes and Pharisees taught that adultery of the heart was not prohibited except when it was actually committed. So the Lord, in supplementing the law, supplied for their depraved understanding, said that not only actual adultery was prohibited but also a perverse will, and according to this manner He proceeds in all other instances which are mentioned in that sermon, namely, the prohibition on murder and the like, and these are summarized by the two sayings he made above, namely (5:17) "I come not to destroy the law but to fulfill it," and (5:20) "unless your justice surpass that of the scribes and the Pharisees." From these it is clear that in the

in subsequentibus non aliud dicit quam in lege continebatur sed interpretatur et supplet illam quantum ad prauum intellectum scribarum et phariseorum. possumus et aliter dicere quod loquitur hic de muliere in genere. de uxore uero excipit statum infra dicens. ego autem dico uobis quia omnis qui dimiserit uxorem suam excepta causa fornicationis facit eam mechari et qui dimissam duxerit adulterat. uel loquitur de concupiscentia mechare que prohibita est tam in propria quam in aliena. Si enim quis concupiscit uxorem suam tamquam alienam sine dubio mechatur. sicut dicit et beatus augustinus.

Patarenus: Idem. xviiii. sunt eunuchi qui seipsos castrauerunt propter regnum celorum etcet. ergo qui secundum carnalem matrimonium uiuunt non saluantur. quia non uiuunt caste.

Catholicus: Respondeo. quia loquitur de illis qui non possunt uti cum uxoribus suis propter earum impedimenta quos tamen oportet caste uiuere et habetur hoc ex illi uerbis scilicet dicunt ei discipuli eius. si ita est causa hominis cum uxore non expedit nubere etcet. dixerat enim dominus quod non licebat uiro repudiare uxorem suam. sicut consueuerant iudei repudiare illas. maxime quando propter impedimenta illarum non poterant uti carnali debito ex qui uidebatur sequi magna inconuenientia. quia necessario oportebat hominem uiuere caste et dominus ad hoc respondet ponens sequentia uerba de eunuchis quasi dicat. Qui in tali statu sunt cum uxoribus quia non possunt uti carnali debito cum illi propter illarum impotentiam oportet ut se in castitate custodiant ex uirtute. qui alias non sunt eunuchi ex natura uel ex accidenti. uel aliter consilium domini est ad perfectos qui uotum continentie faciunt quando licet eis propter maiorem perfectionem. qui tamen alias non tenentur. unde hic dicit dominus. non omnes capiunt uerbum istud sed quibus datum est etcet. et postea qui potest capere capiat etcet. simile est quia dicit infra in eodem. si uis perfectus esse uade et uende omnia que habes et da pauperibus et habebis thesaurum in celo etcet. alias enim sine illa perfectione poterat saluari. unde dixerat ei superius. si uis autem ad citam ingredi serua mandata etcet. uel possimus facere uim in hoc uerbo scilicet castrauerunt ut per hoc matrimoniales comprehendantur. est enim triplex castitas scilicet matrimonii continentie et uirginitatis.

Patarenus: Idem. in eodem. omnis qui reliquerit domum uel fratres aut sorores aut patrem aut matrem aut uxorem aut agros propter nomen meum

---

following passages He is not speaking of anything else than what is contained in the law, but it is interpreted and supplemented because of the perverse interpretation of the scribes and the Pharisees. We can even say differently that He spoke here of women in general. He excepts the condition of a spouse, saying later (5:31) "but I say to you that anyone who divorces his wife, except for the cause of fornication, makes her an adulteress, and he who takes a divorced wife commits adultery." Or He is speaking of the concupiscence of adultery which is prohibited just as much in one's own wife as in that of another. For if one desires one's own wife like that of another, one doubtless commits adultery, as blessed Augustine says.[1]

Pat: In the same place 19 (Mt. 19:12) "There are some eunuchs who have castrated themselves for the kingdom of heaven." Therefore those who live according to carnal marriage shall not be saved, since they do not live chastely.

Cath: I reply that He speaks of those who are not able to use their wives because of some impediment, for which however it is opportune to live chastely and this is evinced by those words, namely (19:10) "His disciples said to him, 'If the case of a man with his wife be so, it is not expedient to marry.'" The Lord said that it was not licit for a man to repudiate his wife as the Jews were accustomed to repudiate theirs. How much more when on account of those impediments they were not able to render the carnal debt, from which follow grave problems. Since it should be necessary for man to live chastely, and the Lord replied to this by positing the following words about eunuchs, as if to say, those who are in such a condition are not able to render the carnal debt to their wives because of their impotence ought to hold themselves in chastity on account of virtue. For such are not eunuchs by nature but because of some accident, or otherwise the counsel of the Lord for the perfect who made a vow of continence when they could [do so], on account of greater perfection, who nevertheless could not have it otherwise, whence the Lord says (19:11) "not all take this word, but those to whom it is given," and later (19:12) "let him who is able to receive it, take it." Similar is what He says later in the same passage (19:21) "if you wish to be perfect go and sell all you have, and give it to the poor, and you will have treasure in heaven." For besides, whose who do not have such perfection are able to be saved, as He had said above, (19:17) "if you would enter into life, keep the commandments." Or, that we may push the meaning thus, namely, 'they were castrated' so that through this married people are included. For there is a triple chastity, that is, marriage, continence, and virginity.

Pat: Also, in the same place (19:29) "And every one who has left house, or brothers, or sisters, or father, or mother, or wife, or children, or lands for my name's sake, shall

---

47 ego...49 adulterat] Matt. 5:32. 51 Si...52 mechatur] Probably Augustine, *De Nupt. et Concup.* 1.17. 54 sunt...55 celorum] Matt. 19:12. 61 dicunt...62 nubere] Matt. 19:10. 77 non...78 est] Matt. 19:11. 78 qui...79 capiat] Matt. 19:12. 79 si...81 celo] Matt. 19:21. 83 si...84 mandata] Matt. 19:17. 88 omnis...91 possibedit] Matt. 19:29.

44 phariseorum] pharyseorum F 50 concupiscentia] concupiscencia P 56 carnalem] carnale F 66 ex...71 debito] om. F

42 non|fol. 103va P 68 caste|fol. 103vb P

---

1) Probably referring to *On Marriage and Concupiscence*, 1.17.

centuplum accipiet et uitam eternam possidebit etcet. ergo qui uult habere uitam eternam debet uxorem reliquere. igitur matrimonium carnale malum est.
Catholicus: Respondeo. quod quis debet relinquare uxorem suam et omnes amicos et seipsum et omnia ne illa supra deum diligat. supra. x. Quo amat patrem aut matrem plusquam me non est me dignus etcet. uel debet dimittere uxorem et amicos id est quod in eis est ducens ipsum ad scandalum mortale peccati. in quo causa debet etiam odire illos. lucam. xiiii. si quis uenit ad me et non odit patrem suum aut matrem et uxorem et filios et fratres et sorores adhuc autem et animam suam non potest meus esse discipulus etcet. uel loquitur hic dominus de illis qui relinquunt uxores suas de communi consensu uel alias quando licite possunt propter maiorem uite perfectionem. alias enim non licet alicui dimittere uxorem suam secundum preceptum domini et quod ita debeat intelligi patet ex hoc quod dominus coniungat hic uxorem parentibus quibus paternum honorem subtrahere non licet nisi de illorum uoluntate aut de alia iusta occasione procedat ut dicit supra. xv. nam deus dixit. honora patrem et matrem tuam etcet.

Patarenus: Item lucam xiiii. et alius dixit uxorem duxi et ideo non possum uenire etcet. ergo matrimonium malum est si non sinet pergere ad cenam dei.

Catholicus: Respondeo. quod ille male dixit et mentitus est et ideo iuste a deo dampnatus est. alias enim uerum dixisset iniuste dampnasse eum deus. Sed tu respondeas mihi. nonne qui nullam emit et qui emit. v. iuga boum poterant saluari se nolebant et scio quod credis. ergo et qui uxorem duxerat saluari poterat si uolebat. cum sub eadem clausula de omnibus illis tribus concludatur et attende quod non ideo sunt dampnati illi duo quia uillam et v. iuga boum emerint et tertius quia uxorem duxerit. sed quia illa plusquam cenam domini dilexerunt et ego dico quod siquis uxorem plus diligit quam deum quod ipse priuabitur regno dei.

Patarenus: Item ad romanos. viii. Qui autem in carne sunt deo placere non possunt etcet. ergo matrimoniales deo non placent.

Catholicus: Respondeo. sic intelligitur in carne id est in carnalibus desideriis prohibitis. unde infra dicit. debitores sumus non carnui ut secundum carnem uiuamus etcet. alioquin comedere et bibere cum sint carnalia essent mortalia peccata.

Patarenus: Item prima ad corinthios. vi°. an nescitis quoniam qui adheret meretrici unum corpus efficitur. erunt enim inquit duo in carne una etcet. ergo

receive a hundredfold, and shall possess life everlasting." So he who wishes to have life everlasting must leave his wife. Therefore carnal marriage is evil.

Cath: I reply that one ought to leave his wife and all his friends and his very self and all things lest he love them more than God, as above (10:37) "He who loves father or mother more than me, is not worthy of me" or he who leaves wife and friends, that is, because by them one is lead to the scandal of mortal sin, in which case he ought also to hate them. Luke 14 (14:26) "If any man comes to me, and does not hate his father, and mother, and wife, and children, and brothers, and sisters, and even his own life also, he cannot be my disciple." Or the Lord is here speaking of those who left their wives by mutual consent, or others when they were licitly able to do so for the sake of greater perfection of life. For it was not permitted to others to dismiss their wives because of the command of the Lord and so it is clear that this ought to be understood from the fact that the Lord joined wives here with parents, from whom parental honor should not be removed, unless by their will or another just cause obtains, as it says above in 15 (Mt 15:3–4) "for God said, 'honor your father and mother.'"

Pat: Further Luke 14 (14:20) "And another said, 'I have married a wife, and therefore I cannot come.'" Therefore marriage is evil if it does not allow one to proceed to the banquet of God.

Cath: I reply that he spoke evil, and he lied, and that God is just and that he is condemned by God, for otherwise if he spoke the truth, God would have unjustly condemned him. For answer me, whether those who buy nothing or who buy five teams of oxen can be saved if they do not want to be, and I know what you believe. Therefore he who marries a wife can be saved if he wishes, since under the same clause all of these three are included. And listen carefully that therefore those two are not damned since they bought a farm and five teams of oxen and the third who took a wife, but because they loved those things more than the banquet of the Lord and I say that if one loves a wife more than God then one shall be deprived of the kingdom of God.

Pat: Further in Romans 8 (8:8) "They who are in the flesh are unable to please God." Therefore married people are unable to please God.

Cath: I reply that one should interpret "in the flesh" as under the power of prohibited carnal desires, as he says after (8:12) "we are debtors, not to the flesh, to live according to the flesh." Otherwise to eat and drink would be carnal and would be mortal sins.

Pat: Further 1 Corinthians 6 (6:16) "Do you not know that he who is joined to a harlot is made one body? For they shall be, he says, two in one flesh." Therefore marriage

matrimonium est fornicatio. cum ad probandam fornicationem inducat auctoritatem de matrimonio loquentem.

Catholicus: Respondeo quod illam auctoritatem inducat apostolus ad probandum quod fornicator et fornicaria sunt unum corpus ut per consequentiam probet quod fornicatio sit peccatum in primo corpore. sicut postea subdit. cum dicit. omne peccatum quodcumque fecerit homo extra corpus est. qui autem fornicatur in corpus suum peccat etcet. quasi dicat sicut uir et uxor dicuntur una caro eo quod unam carnem simul generant. uel quia in uno carnali opere conueniunt. sic fornicarius et fornicaria. sunt unum corpus quia hoc idem ipsi faciunt. sed non dicit apostolus quod sicut est peccatum opus fornicatoris sit. sic peccatum opus fornicatoris. unum enim idemque opus potest esse peccatum et non peccatum. sicut est comedere et bibere et hiis similia. Comedere enim suum non est peccatum. sed alienum sic ita et cognoscere uxorem suam peccatum non est. non suam uero cognoscere dampnabile est.

Patarenus: Idem. vii. de quibus qutem scripsistis bonum est homini mulierem non tangere etcet. ergo per consequentiam malum est tangere. et dicit mulierem ergo uxorem.

Catholicus: Respondeo quia statum excepit uxorem. unde sequitur propter fornicationem autem unusquisque suam uxorem habet.

Patarenus: Item. in eodem. hoc autem dico secundum indulgentiam etcet. ergo est peccatum. si indiget indulgentia.

Catholicus: Respondeo. immo non est peccatum si est indultum. potest tamen dicere quod triplex est indulgentia scilicet permissionis. mattheus. xviiii. moyses ad duritiam cordis uestri permisit uobis dimittere uxores etcet. et remissiones ut cum peccatum dimittitur a deo et a sacerdote. iii\(^a\). ut de moribus bonis ut hic quod autem ibi est indulgentia non semper sit peccatum habes. infra eodem. ubi dicit. si autem acceperis uxorem non peccasti. si nupserit uirgo non peccauit. tribulationem tamen carnis habebunt huiusmodi. ego autem uobis parco etcet. ecce quod dicit quia non peccant et tamen parcit. item. ad hoc est. ii\(^a\) ad corinthios. xii. parco autem ne quis me existimet supra id quod uidet in me etcet. uel dicit hic apostolis secundum indulgentiam propter peccatum ueniale. sine uel raro uel numquam illud opus. licet bonum fuit.

Patarenus: Idem in eodem. uolo enim omnes uos esse sicut meipsum etcet. sed ipse fuit sine uxore et uoluntas eius fuit bona. ergo contrariam uelle malum est.

is fornication, since for proving fornication he adduces a passage that speaks of marriage.

Cath: I reply that the Apostle adduces this authority to prove that the male and female fornicators are one body and, as a consequence, he establishes that fornication is a sin in the first body, as he later adds, saying (6:18) "Every sin that a man does, is without the body, but he who commits fornication, sins against his own body," as if to say that just as a husband and wife are one body, and for that reason they together generate one flesh, or that in one flesh they come together for the work, thus the male and female fornicators are one body since they do the same thing. But the Apostle does not say that just as a sin might be a work of fornication, so sin is a work of fornication, for one and the same deed can be a sin and not be a sin, just like eating and drinking and similar things. For to eat one's own food is no sin, but to eat another's is, so likewise to know one's own wife is no sin, yet to know another's is damnable.

Pat: In the same chapter (1 Cor 7:1) "Now concerning the things you wrote to me, it is good for a man not to touch a woman." So it follows that to touch one is an evil, and he says "woman" therefore, a wife.

Cath: I reply that this condition excepts a wife, for he continues (7:2) "for fear of fornication, let each one have his own wife."

Pat: Yet in the same place (7:6) "But I speak this by indulgence." Therefore it is a sin, if one requires an indulgence.

Cath: I reply, on the contrary it is no sin if one has permission, nevertheless it can be said that indulgence is threefold, namely, permissions: Matthew 19 (19:8) "Moses permitted divorce because of the hardness of your hearts;" remissions: as when sins are remitted by God and by the priest; and thirdly, as in good manners (as here) that although there is an indulgence it is not the case that you always have sin. He speaks below about the same topic. (7:28) "If you take a wife, you have not sinned. And if a virgin marries, she has not sinned, nevertheless, such shall have tribulation of the flesh. But I spare you." See that he says that they do not sin and yet he would spare them, to this is 2 Corinthians 12 (12:6) "But I forbear, lest any man should think of me above that which he sees in me." That is, he says here to the Apostles according to the indulgence on account of venial sin, without which rarely or never is that activity accomplished, though it was good.

Pat: In the same place (1 Cor 7:7) "I wish that all of you were like myself." But he himself was without a wife and his wish was a good one, therefore to wish contrariwise is evil.

---

148 omne...150 peccat] 1 Cor. 6:18. 162 de...163 tangere] 1 Cor. 7:1 (scripsistis) add. mihi *Vulg.*) 169 hoc...170 indulgentiam] 1 Cor. 7:6. 175 moyses...176 uxores] Matt. 19:8. 184 parco...185 me] 2 Cor. 12:6. 189 uolo...190 meipsum] 1 Cor. 7:7.

142 auctoritatem] auctoritates *F* 161 uero] add. non est *P* exp 165 ergo] igitur et *F*

154 faciunt|fol. 104va *P* 173 triplex|fol. 80r *F* 185 supra|fol. 104vb *P*

Catholicus: Solutio. loquitur de uoluntate conditionata uel conparantiam. unde statim terminat dicens. sed unusquisque proprium donum habet ex deo. alius quidem sic alius uero sic etcet.

Patarenus: Idem. in eodem. melius est nubere quam uri etcet. ergo malum est nubere cum comparatiuuo ratione positi fiat.

Catholicus: Respondeo. quod hic comparatiuus ponitur electem id est bonum est nubere et non uri. similiter. prima petri. iii°. melius est enim benefacientes si uelit uoluntas dei pati quam malefacientes etcet. alias enim secundum te qui putas malum esse nubere. falsum esset quod dicit apostolus. cum utrumque malum esset scilicet nubere et uri. immo quia contrarius est animam uri quam corpus debuerat dicere. melius est uri quam nubere.

Patarenus: Idem in eodem. reliquum est ut qui habent uxores tamquam non habentes sint etcet. ergo non debent aliqui carnaliter cognoscere uxores suas.

Catholicus: Respondeo. qui habent uxores debent esse tamquam non habentes quantum ad illud quid ibi subdit scilicet preterit enim figura huius mundi etcet. id est ut nec multum gaudeant. inde nec multum doleant sicut de re cito transitoria. Sed tu respondeas mihi ubi dicit de habentibus uxores quod debent esse tamquam non habentes subdit et de flentibus quod sint tamquam non flentes et de gaudentibus quod sint tamquam non gaudentes et de his qui emunt quod sint tamquam non possidentes et de his qui utuntur hoc mundo quod sint tamquam non utentes. ergo non licet flere neque gaudere neque possidere rem emptam. neque uti aliquam re huius mundi. uel si licet ergo uxore uti licet. quoniam ea ratione et eo ordine et eadem conclusione loquitur de uxore sicut de illis. item uos heretici gaudentis quandoque et fletis et tenetis res emptas et utimini rebus huius mundi in maxima habundantia et cum tenaci cupidite. ergo estis transgressores apostolici precepti.

Patarenus: Idem in eodem. Qui autem sine uxore est sollicitus est. que domini sunt. quomodo placeat deo etcet. ergo bonum est esse sine uxore et malum est esse cum illa si impedit diuinas cogitationes et a domino diuidit.

Catholicus: Respondeo. impedit ne sic libere cogitet homo de deo sicut faceret si esset solutus et diuidit a deo diuisione sollicitudinis que impedit contemplationem et non omnis diuisio est mortale peccatum. Nonne et uos hac diuisione diuisi estis sollicitudinem habentes de rebus uestris temporalibus. Et quod de ista diuisione. intelligat apostolus statim determinat dicens.

Cath: Solution. He speaks of a conditional wish or a comparison, for he immediately concludes saying (7:7) "but every one has his proper gift from God; one after this manner, and another after that."

Pat: Yet in the same place (7:8) "it is better to marry than to burn." Therefore it is evil to marry when one compares it to the arguments made.

Cath: I reply that this comparison is made in relation to the elect, that is, it is good to marry, rather than to burn, similarly 1 Peter 3 (3:17) "For it is better to suffer in doing good — if such be the will of God — than to do ill." For otherwise according to you who thinks it is evil to marry, what the Apostle says would be false, since both are evil, namely to marry and to burn. On the contrary it does not belong to the soul to be burned, rather [it belongs to] the body, he ought to say it is better to burn than to marry.

Pat: In the same place (1 Cor 7:29) "it remains that those also who have wives, let them be as if they had none." Therefore they ought not to know their wives in any carnal manner.

Cath: I reply, they who have wives should be as if they had none, just as that which he here adds, namely (7:31) "for the fashion of this world passes away." That is, so that they do not rejoice too much, neither will they sorrow too much, for these things quickly pass. But answer me where he says that those who have wives ought to be like those also not having them. He adds about those who weep that they ought to be like those not weeping and those joyful ought to be like those sorrowing, of those who buy that they should be like those who possess nothing, and of those who use the things of this world ought to be like those who do not use them. Therefore it is not permitted to weep or rejoice or possess any bought thing, nor to use anything of this earth, or if it is allowed, then it is also allowed to have a wife. For by that reason and that order and by that same conclusion it seems that it speaks of wives just as of the other things. But you heretics rejoice at times, and weep, and buy and hold things, and have made use of the things of this world in great abundance and with an obstinate avarice, therefore you transgress against an Apostolic precept.

Pat: The same thing in the same place (1 Cor 7:32) "He that is without a wife, is concerned for the things that belong to the Lord, how he may please God." Therefore it is good to be without a wife and evil to be with her, since she hinders holy thoughts and divides one from the Lord.

Cath: Response. She hinders her husband from thinking about God as freely as he would if he were freed, and she divides him from God by a division of solicitude which hinders contemplation, yet not every division is a mortal sin. Are not you also divided by this very division in as much as you have solicitude over your temporal affairs? And what the Apostle means concerning this division he

---

196 melius…197 etcet] 1 Cor. 7:8.   **201** melius…202 malefacientes] 1 Pet. 3:17.   **208** reliquum…209 sint] 1 Cor. 7:29.
213 preterit…mundi] 1 Cor. 7:31.   **230** Qui…231 deo] 1 Cor. 7:32.

192 con-ditionata] condictionata P **193** uel] seu F **211** uxores] add. ti P exp   **212** habentes] add. sint P **219** his] hiis F **220** his] hiis F **222** emptam] emitam P **223** licet] silicet P **231** domini] domino P **236** sicut…237 deo] om. F

215 doleant|fol. 105ra P **241** dicens|fol. 105rb P

Qui autem cum uxore sollicitus est que sunt mundi quomodo placeat uxori et diuisus est etcet. et infra. que autem nupta est cogitat que sunt mundi quomodo placeat uiro etcet. Et quod talis diuisio non sit peccatum ostendit dicens. porro hoc ad utilitatem uestram dico. non ut laqueum uobis initium. sed ad id quod honestum est et quod facultatem prebeat sine impedimento domino obseruandi etcet.

Patarenus: Item ad ephesios. v°. diligite uxores uestras sicut et christus dilexit ecclesiam etcet. igitur caste et sine carnis contagione.

Catholicus: Respondeo quod istud est sicut tale est quale est illud. mattheus. v. estote ergo uos perfecti sicut et pater uester celestis perfectus est. alioquin si esset per omnia sic impossibile esset hoc seruari.

item ad hebreos. ultimum. honorabile connubium in omnibus et thorus immaculatus etcet. ergo matrimonium carnale uituperabile est cuius thorus maculatus est.

Catholicus: Respondeo quod apostolus loquitur de macula peccati mortali. sine qua matrimonium est. siquis eo legitime uitatur. Nec quod ibi sit macula temporalis. non enim omnis macula peccatum est. quia in luto et fece potest esse homo et non peccat.

Catholicus: Item dicit decretum quod in opere coniugali non adest gratia spiritus sancti. etiam si inde propheta nascatur etcet. malum est ergo tale matrimonium. cuius opus est sine gratia spiritus sancti.

Catholicus: solutio. non est gratia spiritus sancti in opere coniugali quo ad usum prophetandi quod insinuatur cum dicit. etiam si inde propheta nascatur. uel ideo dicit quod non est gratia spiritus sancti in opere coniugali. quia non est pure propter ueniale peccatum quod ibi semper est uel quasi semper. uel dicitur secundum quosdam. spiritus sanctus. non est in opere coniugalia propter opus carnale quod prorsus diuersum est anima ipsius. Nec propter hoc sequitur quod malum sit. est enim indifferens quantum in se est.

Patarenus: Item ecclesia romana prohibet fieri nuptias aliquibus temporibus. igitur innuit quod male sint.

Catholicus: Respondeo. quod ideo facit quia multa licent que quandoque non expediunt. facit ergo ut illis temporibus uacent homines orationibus quod magis tunc expedit.

Patarenus: Item quare uos religiosi non accepistis uxores. si matrimonium bonum est?

immediately defines saying: (7:33) "But he that has a wife is worried for the things of the world, how he may please his wife, and he is divided." And later (7:34) "But she who is married thinks about the things of the world, how she may please her husband." And that this division is no sin, he shows saying (7:35) "And this I speak for your profit, not to cast a snare upon you, but for that which is decent, and which might give you power to wait upon the Lord without impediment."

Pat: But look to Ephesians 5 (5:25) "Love your wives just as Christ loved the Church," therefore chastely and without carnal contact.

Cath: I reply that this is just like that which is here, Matthew 5 (5:48) "Therefore be perfect, just as your heavenly Father is perfect," otherwise it would be impossible to observe this in all things.

Also in the last chapter of Hebrews (13:4) "Marriage honorable in all, and the bed undefiled." Therefore carnal marriage can be censured if the marriage bed can be defiled.

Cath: I reply that the Apostle speaks of the stain of mortal sin, which is outside of marriage, and which in it can be legitimately avoided. Neither that there be a temporal uncleanness, for not all uncleanness is a mortal sin, since man can be in mud and feces and still not sin.

Catholic [Patarene]: As the Decretum says, "in the marital act the grace of the Holy Spirit is not present, even if through it a prophet might be born." Therefore such marriage is evil, since the act is without the grace of the Holy Spirit.

Cath: Solution. The grace of the Holy Spirit is not in the conjugal act by which the use of prophecy comes about, as hinted when it says "even if a prophet might be born," or for that reason he says that the grace of the Holy Spirit is not in the conjugal act, since it is not blameless on account of venial sin which always or almost always accompanies it. Or it says, according to certain people, the Holy Spirit is not in the conjugal act because it is a carnal work which is totally distinct from the soul. Neither does it follow that because of this this is evil, for it is indifferent considering its moral essence.

Pat: But the Roman Church prohibits weddings during certain times, therefore she knows them to be evil.

Cath: I reply that it is for the reason that many things that are permitted are sometimes not expedient, therefore she determines that during these times men should be free for prayer since it is then more expedient.

Pat: Why do you religious not take wives, if marriage is good?

---

242 Qui…243 est] 1 Cor. 7:33.   244 que¹…245 uiro] 1 Cor. 7:34.   246 porro…250 Patarenus] 1 Cor. 7:35 (initium] iniiciam | domino] dominum | obseruandi] obsecrandi *Vulg.*)   250 diligite…251 ecclesiam] Eph. 5:25.   254 estote…255 est] Matt. 5:48. 257 honorabile…258 immaculatus] Heb. 13:4.   266 quod…268 nascatur] It is not clear where he might be citing this from. The anonymous "Summa contra Catharos" from Vat. Lat. 4255 also cites the same source.

242 est] om. *P* | add. saluatus est *F*   250 Patarenus] Catholicus *P*   256 sic] sicut *P*   266 Catholicus] *sic P* leg. Patarenus   267 coniugali] add. quo ad usum prophetandi qui in sumat cum dicit *F*   269 gratia] om. *P* | sancti] add. gratia *P*   270 solutio…273 sancti] om. *F* 278 est] add. non *P* exp

244 autem|fol. 80v *F*   274 est|fol. 105va *P*

Catholicus: Et uos heretici quare abstinetis a uino et a piscibus quandoque ergo discite ydiote stulti. quod est bonum et melius et optimum. Sed dicite mihi homines spirituales quibus matrimonium tam turpe uidetur peccatum. quare sodomitia amplectimini. que sunt omnibus sceleribus turpiora? nonne cotidie manibus uestris corpora uestra polluitis et tamen propter hoc spiritum sanctum dicitis uos non admittere. item multas immunditias circa alienas uxores comittitis et dicunt quidam ex uobis quod non est peccatum comittere illas nisi ad naturalem actum perueniatur. uere uos estis illi de quibus dominus ait. mattheus. vii. ypocrita eice primum trabem de oculo tuo etcet. et xxiii. duces ceci excolantes culicem camelum autem glutientes etcet.

Cath: And you heretics, why do you abstain from wine and from fish sometimes? So learn, you foolish ignoramus, that there is good, and better, and best. But explain to me, O Spiritual Men, to whom marriage seems to be such a vile sin, why do you embrace sodomy, which of all sins is most depraved? Do you not daily pollute your bodies with your hands and yet on account of this you say that you do not receive the Holy Spirit. Further you commit many impurities with the wives of others and they say certain of you don't think it a sin unless one arrives at the natural completion of the act. Truly you are those of which the Lord speaks in Matthew 7 (7:5) "Hypocrites! First remove the beam from your eye," and 23 (23:24) "Blind guides, who strain out a gnat, and swallow a camel."

De sacramento extreme unctionis XXIII

Sequitur uidere de sacramento unctionis extreme quod datur grauiter infirmitatibus ad liberationem infirmitatis corporalis et ad peccatorum dimissionem et per consequentiam datur in eo spiritus sanctus. et datur tantum a sacerdotibus ut hic dicit beatus iacobus ultimo. circa finem ubi dicit. infirmatur quis in uobis inducat presbyteros ecclesie et orent super eum ungentes eum cum olio in nomine domini et oratio fidei saluabit infirmum et alleuiabit eum dominus et si in peccatis sit dimittetur ei etcet. quod sacramentum institutum fuisse et seruatum ab apostolis legimus de uoluntate saluatoris. ut legitur. marcum. vi. et conuocauit duodecim et cepit eos mittere binos etcet. et infra. et ungebant cum oleo multos egros et saluabantur etcet. quod sacramentum penitus inficiantur patareni. et non quod in omnibus. vii. sacramentis datur. spiritus sanctus. hoc modo. in baptismate enim datur ad remissionem omnium peccatorum et penarum et gratie collationem. in manus impositione datur ad gratie confirmationem. in sacramento eucharistie datur ad peccatorum mortalium occultorum et uenialium dimissionem et gratie augmentum. in penitentia datur ad penarum et culparum dimissionem licet non ita plenarie sicut in baptismo et ad gratie reparationem. in sacris autem ordinibus datur ad gratie augmentum. in matrimonio uero datur ad bone uite conseruationem. in unctione uero extrema datur ad corporales egritudines expellendas et ad peccata dimittenda et ad robur gratie incrementum.

On the sacrament of Extreme Unction

Next it remains to look at the sacrament of extreme unction which is given in the case of grave illness for the liberation from bodily infirmities and for the remission of sins and, as a consequence, in it the Holy Spirit is given. And it is only given by priests as Blessed James says here in his last chapter, around the end where he says (5:14–15) "Is any man sick among you? Let him bring in the priests of the church, and let them pray over him, anointing him with oil in the name of the Lord and the prayer of faith shall save the sick man and the Lord shall raise him up, and if he be in sins, they shall be forgiven him." We read that the sacrament was instituted by the Apostles by the will of the Savior, as is read in Mark 6 (6:60) "And he called the twelve and began to send them in pairs," and later (6:13) "and they anointed many sick people with oil, and they were healed." This sacrament is thoroughly repudiated by the Patarenes, and that the Holy Spirit is not given in all seven sacraments. [He is given] in this manner: in baptism He is given for the remission of all sins and penalties and the granting of grace. In the imposition of hands He is given for the grace of confirmation. In the sacrament of the Eucharist He is given for the forgiveness of hidden mortal sins and of venial sins, and for the increase of grace. In penance He is given for a remission of penalties and guilt — though not so full as in baptism — and the grace of renewal. In sacred orders He is given for an increase of grace, in marriage He is given for the preservation of a good manner of life. In unction He is also given at the moment of death for the driving out of bodily infirmities and for the remission of sins and for the increase of strengthening graces.

---

301 ypocrita…tuo] Matt. 7:5.   302 duces…303 glutientes] Matt. 23:24.   **XXIII.1.7** infirmatur…11 ei] Iac. 5:14-15 (dimittetur] remittentur *Vulg.*)   14 conuocauit…binos] Mar. 6:7 (conuocauit] uocauit *Vulg.*)   15 et² …16 saluabantur] Mar. 6:13 (saluabantur] sanbant *Vulg.*)

296 spiritum…uos] dicitis uos spiritum sanctum *F*   298 peccatum] add. alias *P* exp   299 comittere illas] transp. *F*   302 culicem] pulicem *P* | add. esse *P*   **XXIII.1.27** ad¹…datur] om. *F*

303 glutientes|fol. 105vb *P*   **XXIII.1.16** saluabantur|fol. 81r *F*   28 in|fol. 106ra *P*

Contra unctionem extremam

2

Dicimus quod nichil est de unctionem extrema quem dicitis uos romani. nec obstat dictum iacobi. quia loquitur de manus impositione quam facimus credentibus nostris in articulo mortis. pro quibus oramus manus super capita eorum tenentes et ungimus cum oleo spiritus sancti. et sic omnia peccata eorum dimittuntur.

Catholicus: Sed beatus iacobus non nominat manus impositionem neque credentes patarenorum nec uocat spiritum sanctum oleum et facit differentiam inter salutem infirmi et peccatorum dimissionem. et uos non creditis quod in manus impositione sanetur corpora neque uirtute diuinia. preterea apostoli uiuente domino dederunt hoc sacramentum et sanabantur infirmi per illud et uos non credit quod manus impositio fuisset facta et salus fuisset in animabus nisi post christi passionem et resurrectionem. ergo beatus iacobus una cum euangelio loquitur de spirituali sacramento unctionis extreme et non de manus impositione.

Against Extreme Unction

We say that there is nothing to that which you Romans call Extreme Unction, nor does the saying of James matter, since he speaks of the laying of hands which we perform on our believers at the point of death, for which we pray holding our hands over their heads and we anoint them with the oil of the Holy Spirit, and so all sins are remitted to them.

Cath: But Blessed James does not name the imposition of hands, nor the believers of the Patarenes, nor does he call the Holy Spirit 'oil,' and he notes a difference between the health of the sick and the remission of sins. And you do not believe that in the laying of hands that bodies are healed, especially not by divine power. Further the Apostles, while the Lord was living, administered this sacrament and healed the sick by it and you do not believe that the laying of hands was done and that salvation was granted to souls except after the passion and resurrection of Christ, therefore Blessed James is one with the evangelists in speaking of a spiritual sacrament of extreme unction and not the laying of hands.

De quorumdam ciborum esu. scilicet carnium. ouorum et casei et huiusmodi in quibus patareni errant

XXIV On the eating of certain foods, namely of meat, eggs, cheese, and the like, in which the Patarenes err

Post tractatus articulorum et sacramentorum fidei sequitur nouissime de quorumdam ciborum esu scilicet carnium. ouorum et casei et huiusmodi pertractare. in quibus patareni errare uidentur. ut sicut hunc librum incepimus a creatore. sic terminemus in creaturis eundem. Dicunt enim predicti peccatum esse comedere predicta cibaria quem errorem triplici ratione uallare nituntur. prima est quia delirant quod quando factum est prelium magnum in celo. quod tunc erant ibi mulieres quedam pregnantes que propter pressuram uel propter rotationem celi quam ferre non potuerant abortiuos fecerunt et de illis carnibus asserunt esse factas carnes bestiarum et uolucrum. et ideo quia uidentur fuisse de humana carne compacte non esse comedendas dogmatizant. hunc autem errorem traxerunt ab heresi manicheorum et est illud unum de suis secretis archanis.

secunda est quia putant quod bestie et uolucres nate sint de peccato. eo quod de coniunctione sint nate. quam tam in brutis animalibus quam in hominibus adulterium communiter uocant. Tertia est quia dicunt quod sunt incentiua ad carnalia uitia et ideo se abstinent ab illis ex uoto propter maiorem abstinentiam et istam non credunt. tamen allegant ipsam coram illis quos simplices existimant esse. nos uero

After the sections on the articles and sacraments of the faith, here follows the last section on the eating of certain foods, to treat namely of meats, eggs, and cheese and the like, in which the Patarenes are seen to err. Just as we began this book with the Creator, so we shall end it with creatures. For they say that to eat the aforementioned foods is a sin, and this error they attempt to undergird by three reasons. In the first place they rave that when there was the great war in heaven, there were then certain pregnant women who on account of the pressure and rotation of the heavens, were not able to bear, and they had abortions, and they assert that from their flesh was made the flesh of beasts and birds, and therefore they proclaim as dogma those things are not to be eaten because it seems that they things were composed out of human flesh.[1] But this error they derive from the Manichaean heresy and it is one of their most arcane secrets.

The second is that they think that animals and birds are born of sin, by the fact that they are born of sexual union, which they commonly call adultery whether in brute animals or in men. The third is that they say that they are incentives to carnal vices and so they abstain from them on account of greater abstinence, and this they do not believe, yet they allege it in the presence of those they judge to be simpleminded. Yet we say, and have proven clearly in four

---

XXIII.2.7 oleo] olo *F* **20** non] om. *F* **XXIV.1.1** De…3 errant] om. *F (space left for title)* **12** quando] non *P*

XXIV.1.3 errant|fol. 106rb *P*

---

[1] Moneta, 139-141 discusses similar arguments except this one, which is unique to this Summa.

dicimus et probamus euidenter. iiii⁰ʳ. modis non esse peccatum comedere huiusmodi. quorum primus est quia non inuenimus rationem aliqua uel scriptura huiusmodi esse prohibita igitur non est transgressio comedere illa. secundus est quia sunt ad necessitatem fragilitatis humane releuande et necessitati lex non est imposita. Tertius est quia legimus quod magister totius bone doctrine ihesus christus. carnes agni pascale comedit. quare et nobis discipulis eius tradidit in exemplum. non esse notabile comedere huiusmodi. de cuius exemplo scripsimus supra. titulus de humanitate christi. in rubricella de comestione christi. quartus modus est quia expressim habemus in diuina pagina esse concessum ista comedere ut ecce. mattheus. xv. quare uos transgredimini mandata propter traditionem uestram etcet. et infra. non quod intrat in os coinquinat hominem etcet. ergo non est peccatum comedere quacumque cibaria et dicere contrarium de humana et superstitiosa doctrina procedit. item. lucam. x. in eadem domo manente edentes et bibentes que apud illos sunt etcet. et infra. et in quamcumque ciuitatem intraueritis et susceperint uos manducate que apponuntur uobis. etcet. ergo christus dat licentiam comedendi omnia que ab hominibus comedi consueuerunt. item ad romanos. xiiii. is qui manducat non manducantem non spernat et qui non manducat manducantem non iudicet etcet. per totum et loquitur spiritualiter de ydolatris que erant carnes pro maiori parte. item. iª. ad corinthios. viii. esca autem non commendat nos deo. etcet. ergo non est in cibis salus. idem x. omne quod in macello uenit manducate nichil interrogantes propter conscientiam. domini est terra et plenitudo eius. si quis uocat infidelium uos ad cenam et uultus ire omne quod uobis apponitur manducate nulla interrogantes propter conscientiam etcet. ergo non est peccatum comedere carnes que in macello ueniunt. non enim pisces aut cicera et huiusmodi uenduntur in macello. sed tantum carnes preterea dicit quod comedamus quicumque appoinitur nobis ab infidelibus in cena eorum et constat quod infideles non abstinebant a carnibus et huiusmodi. ergo licet nobis comedere carnes et omnia que ipsi comedunt. item ad colosenses. ii⁰. nemo uos iudicet in cibo aut in potu etcet. ergo uos patareni malefacitis. item. iª. ad timotheus. iii⁰. spiritus manifeste dicit quod in nouissimis temporibus discedent quidam a fide etcet. ibi abstinenere a cibis quis deus creauit ad percipiendem cum gratiarum actionem fidelibus et hiis qui cognouerunt ueritate. quia omnis creatura dei bona et nulla reiciendum quod cum gratiarum actione percipitur etcet. uidetis uos cathari quomodo paulus appellat uos hereticos quia prohibetis homines abstinere a cibis quos deus creauit uidelicet a carnibus

ways that it is no sin to eat such things. The first such reason is that we do not find any rational argument or scriptural passage of this type prohibiting it, therefore it is no transgression to eat them. The second is that they are necessary for the relief of our human fragility, and necessity knows no law. The third is that since we read that the master of all good doctrine, Jesus Christ, ate the meat of the paschal lamb, which He transmitted to us His disciples by example. It is no remarkable thing to eat in this manner. Regarding His example we have written above under the title of the Humanity of Christ, in the subsection on Christ's manner of eating. The fourth way is that we have it expressly conceded in the pages of divine scripture to eat such things, see Matthew 15 (15:3) "Why do you also transgress the commandment of God for your tradition?" And later (15:11) "That which goes into the mouth does not make a man unclean," therefore it is no sin to eat any kind of food whatsoever and to contradict that comes from a superstitious and human doctrine. Also Luke 10 (10:7) "And remain in the same house eating and drinking such things as they have," and later (10:8) "And into whatever city you enter and they receive you, eat such things as are set before you." Therefore Christ has given permission for eating all things which are accustomed to be eaten by men. Also Romans 14 (14:3) "Let not him who eats despise him who does not, and he that does not eat, let him not judge him who does." And so on through the whole of the chapter and he speaks spiritually of them who offered the greater part of the meat to idols. Further 1 Corinthians 8 (8:8) "But food does not commend us to God." Therefore there is no salvation in food. Also 10 (10:25–28) "Whatsoever is sold in the meat market, eat, asking no question for conscience's sake. The earth is the Lord's, and the fulness thereof. If any unbelievers invite you, and you are willing to go, eat anything that is set before you, asking no question for conscience' sake. But if any man says, 'This has been sacrificed to idols,' do not eat of it for his sake that mentioned it, and for conscience's sake." Therefore it is no sin to eat meat which comes from the butcher, for neither fish nor beans nor any other thing is sold at the butcher shop, but only meat. Further he says that we shall eat whatsoever is set before us by the gentiles in their meals, and it happens that the gentiles did not abstain from meat and the like. So it is permitted to us to eat meat, and indeed all things that they eat. Also in Colossians 2 (2:16) "Let no man therefore judge you in food or in drink." Therefore you Patarenes do evil. Also 1 Timothy 3 (4:1) "Now the Spirit clearly says that in the last times some shall depart from the faith." There, by abstaining from foods which God has created to be received with thanksgiving by the faithful and those who know the truth. (4:4) "For every creature of God is good, and nothing is to be rejected that is received with thanksgiving" See, you Cathars, how Paul calls you heretics since you hinder men by causing them to abstain from

et huiusmodi. Nec potestis uos spirituales homines uerba pauli spiritualiter exponere ut dicatis quod loquatur de spiritualibus cibis scilicet de uerbo dei. et de orationibus bonorum hominum quia statim subdit de huiusmodi cibo. sanctificatur autem per uerbum dei et orationem etcet. ergo alius est cibum qui debet comedi et aliud est uerbum et aliud est oratio. nec etiam potestis dicere quod uocet spiritum sanctum cibum. quia quoniam spiritus sanctus sanctificatur per uerbum et orationem hominis? numquid uerbum et oratio hominis sanctiora supra spiritum sanctum. sanctius enim est quod sanctificat. quam quod sanctificatur. De spiritualibus ergo cibis loquitur apostolus. obmutescite igitur spirituales uiri. quos spiritualis uoco. quia pleni estis spiritum superbie. quam a patre uestro diabolo habetis in uobis generatum. item pro nobis est actus. x. descendens uas quoddam uelud lintheum quattuor initiis submitti de celo in terram in quo erant omnia quadrupeda et serpentia terre et uolatilia celi et facta est uox ad eum. surge petre occide et manduca etcet. ergo non est peccatum comedere huiusmodi. Nec obstat quod fuerit figura conuersionis gentium. quia licet figura fuerit de gentium conuersione. tamen ipsa figura inducitur et indicitur comestabile et precipit petro quod a multis carnibus abstineat tamquam ab imundis. de quibus in lege mandatum fuerat. nec obstat quod mihi posses obicere quod nos non comedimus serpentes quia non est peccatum comedere illos. neque tenemur comedere si nolimus. serpentes nec etiam boues quia licentia tantum datur de cibis comedendis et non preceptum. serpentes etiam comedunt aliqui propter medicinam et absque peccato. licet communiter uitentur propter orrorem. ex hiis patet liquide quod non est peccatum comedere quecumque cibaria.

Quod sit peccatum predicta comedere. patarenus tribus rationibus uult probare

[**Patarenus:**] Quod sit peccatum predicta comedere cibaria tribus rationibus comprobamus. prima quarum est quia dicimus quod carnes animalium nate sunt de humanis carnibus prout in tuo prologo nos dicere inseruisti. et ideo tam illa quam ea que de illi sunt nobis inhumanum et orribile comedere uidetur.

Catholicus: Sed neque ratione aliqua naturali neque scriptura penitus ulla cauetur quod carnes animalium de humanis carnibus fuerint numquam et maxime de carnibus puerorum abortiuorum. naturalis enim ratio non uult. sed contrarium potius manifeste. quia uidemus de carne alicuius animali mortui aliqua bestia uel auis concreatur aliquando. in scriptura uero nulla inuenitur neque diuina neque humana. ista uestra blasphemia doctrina. sicut de archanis demoniorum qui uos sepe docent similia. ut dicit apostolus. i^a. ad timotheus. iiii°. ibi. in doctrinis demoniorum. etcet.

Patarenus: Item dicimus quo sunt nata de adulterio quia sint de coitu carnali nate. quia prohibitum est nobis illas et ea que de illi exeunt comedere. quia apostolus dicit ad colosenses. 3°. ne tetigeritis neque gustaueritis que sunt omnia in interitum ipso usu etcet.

Catholicus: Respondeo. quod falsum est quod dicit carnes de adulterio esse natas. nusquam enim repperitur mandatum de adulterio brutis esse datum et ut dixit apostolus. ad romanos. iiii°. ubi enim non est lex nec preuaricatio. immo contrarium dicit i^a. ad corinthios. viiii. numquid de bobus cura est deo etcet. an propter uos utique hoc dixit? nam propter uos utique scripta sunt etcet. et dominus dixit in mattheus. xv. quod de corde exeunt adulteria. de corde id est de proposito liberi arbitrii. quo bruta carent omnimodo. quare non est adulterium inter bruta animalia quia adulterium est ut ipsius uerbi ethimologia demonstrat alterius thori uiolatio. sed nulla lex inter bestias est apponita que dicat hic erit uxor istius et illa illius. Nec obstat auctoritas pauli apostoli ad colosenses. quia loquitur de omnibus ceremonialibus legis. que iam post nouam gratiam peccatum est seruare. Unde dixit in superioribus capitulo. nemo ergo uos iudicet in cibo aut in potu. aut in parte diei festi. aut neomenie aut sabbatorum que sunt umbra futurorum etcet. uel loquitur ibi apostolus de peccatis dimissis ad que reuerti non debemus. sed modo respondete mihi de ista uestra ratione. si hic est ratio quare non debetis comedere carnes bestiarum et uolucrum. quia sunt de coitu nate. et propter hoc sunt immunde. ergo ille que non sunt de coitu nate sunt munde. et debetis illas comedere. sicut sunt bufones et rane et huiusmodi. quare ergo non comedite illas. item aues de arboribus natas cum de coitu non sint. quare non comedistis? item si non uultis ore uestro tangere animalia de coitu nata tamquam immunda quomodo dicitis spiritum sanctum in uestris corporibus habitare que isto modo sunt nata similiter. nisi forte uos legem iustitie seruare dicitis et spiritum sanctum transgressorem esse. item quomodo aliqui uos tangere debeant et qualiter cum manu uestra uos spiritum sanctum dare potestis cum totum corpus uestrum sit de coitu natum. et si

neither divine nor human. This is your blasphemous teaching, just like the ancient teachings of the demons which teach you often similar things, as the Apostle says here in 1 Timothy 4 (4:1) "the doctrines of devils."

Pat: Further we say that they are born of adultery since they are born of carnal relations, so these things are forbidden to us is that come to be in such a manner, which the Apostle says in Colossians 3 (2:21–22) "Touch not, taste not, handle not, all those things which are unto destruction by their very use."

Cath: I reply that it is false to say that meat is born of adultery. For the commandment about adultery was never given to brute animals as the Apostle says in Romans 4 (4:15) "For where there is no law, there is no transgression." On the contrary he says in 1 Corinthians 9 (9:9–10) "Does God not care for oxen? Or does he say this indeed for our sakes? For these things are written for our sakes." And the Lord said in Matthew 15 (15:19) "from the heart come adulteries." "From the heart," that is, a volition of free will, which brute animals wholly lack. Hence that adultery among brute animals is different than adultery [in humans] is clear from the word's etymology that shows a violation of another's marriage bed, but there is no law among animals, whereby one can say here is apportioned this wife to one and the other to another. Neither does Paul in Colossians present a difficulty, since he is speaking of all the ceremonial laws, which now are sins to observe after the advent of grace. This he said in the prior chapter (2:16–17) "Let no man therefore judge you in meat or in drink, or in respect of a festival day, or of the new moon, or of the Sabbaths, which are a shadow of things to come." Or the Apostle speaks here of forgiven sins, to which we ought not to return. But in what way do you reply to me regarding your argument? If this be the reason why you do not eat the meat of animals and birds which are born of sexual union, and because of that, are unclean. Therefore those things not born of sexual union are cleam and you ought to eat those things, like toads and frogs and the like. Why do you not eat them? Also birds born of the trees are not from sexual union,[1] why not eat them? Also if you do not wish your mouth to touch animals born of sexual union since they are so unclean, how do you say the Holy Spirit dwells in your bodies, which are also born in a similar way, unless even more should you say you observe the law of justice and be a transgressor against the Holy Spirit. Also how are some of you able to touch, how is it that you are able to give the Holy Spirit by your hands, since your whole body was

---

XXIV.2.19 in…demoniorum] 1 Tim. 4:1.   23 ne…24 usu] Col. 2:21-22.   29 ubi…30 preuaricatio] Rom. 4:15.   31 numquid…33 sunt] 1 Cor. 9:9-10.   34 de¹…adulteria] Matt. 15:19 (quod] om. | corde] add. enim *Vulg.*)   43 nemo…45 futurorum] Col. 2:16-17

17 sicut] sed F   21 quia²] quare P   27 adulterio] add. alium P   38 thori] add. ad P exp   47 sed] set P   50 ergo…51 munde] om F   52 bufones] buffones P   59 dicitis] dicatis F   62 coitu] add. vestro P exp

XXIV.2.20 Patarenus|fol. 107va P   47 sed|fol. 107vb P   50 nate|fol. 82v F

---

1) The barnacle goose, which was thought to arise as the fruit of a particular tree which grew beside water-courses (the bird was therefore considered by some to be licit to eat during Lent, as it might be considered a type of vegetable, at least in origin); see Maike van der Lugt, "Animal légendaire et discours savant médiéval: la barnacle dans tous ses états", *Micrologus* 8:2 (2000), 351-93.

diceretis quod corpora uestra sint sanctificata a spiritu sancto et ideo iam sunt munda. dico quod antequam spiritum sanctum sanctificaret illa immunda erant. et sic spiritus sanctus tetigit immundum. quare ergo et uos immunde tangere non possumus. nonne spiritus sanctus potest sanctificare alias carnes sicut humanas. presertim cum hoc dicat apostolus. prima. ad timotheus. iiii°. sanctificatur enim per uerbum dei et orationem etcet. item quomodo spiritus sanctus potest sanctificare corpora uestra que dicitis opera esse diaboli? et sanctificat illa. quomodo non erunt in patria opera sanctificata? preterea uos dicitis quod per unum ouum comestum perditur spiritus sanctus ergo fortius est unum quam sit spiritus sanctus uidetur. item dicitis quod siquis comedit aliquid de carnibus uel de huiusmodi per ignorantiam amittit spiritum sanctum ergo non est in potestate uestra ex aliqua bona uita tenere illum. nec illius manere uobiscum sed quilibet seruiens uester aut alius homo ponendo aliquid de huiusmodi in ollere uestro. potest uobis auferre spiritum sanctum et quid scitis si iam sepius uobis factum sit hoc? Quedam uesania est hic. preterea sicut apostolus prohibet immunda gustari. sic prohibet illa tangi. ergo diabolis cum modica cortice lardi potest expellere de toto mundo spiritus sanctus ducendo illa per ora omnium qui illum habere uidentur et quilibet homo potest uobis auferre illum per hunc modum.

[**Patarenus:**] Item propter maiorem abstinentiam abstinemus quia sunt incentiua uitiorum carnalium. et ideo nos uoto astringimur ne huiusmodi comedamus. unde etiam si alias non esset peccatum comedere ista. nobis tamen peccatum esset propter uoti fractionem.

Catholicus: Respondeo quod non est uerum quod propter maiorem abstinentiam sit peccatum comedere huiusmodi. possum enim si bona et sana intentione quis faceret mereri magis comedendo quam abstinendo quandoque. quid autem falsum sit quod dicitis et quod hypocrisi loquimini mandatum probo. maior abstinentia est et minus uitia carnalia accenduntur per esum casei sicci et maxime modici quam per esum sturionum et huius piscium delicatorum cum piperatis et uinis electis et aquis speciebus plenis et tamen ab isto tamquam a mortali peccato abstinetis et super illi eructuatis et lasciuitis. uotum autem uestrum dicimus non tenere. quia factum fuit per errorem. quod alias etiam deberet frangi si factum esset bona intentione. cum ex causa probationis fidei ab ecclesia precipitur absolui. preterea eodem modo uouistis non occidere et tamen cotidie piscies et huiusmodi occiditis. et si forsitan diceretis quod in uoto generali de homicidio excepistis de piscibus et similibus dico quod eodem modo

born of sexual union? If you might say that your bodies have been sanctified by the Holy Spirit and so have become clean, I say that before the Holy Spirit might have sanctified it, they were unclean, and therefore the Holy Spirit touched unclean things. Hence then you are unable to touch unclean things. Isn't the Holy Spirit able to sanctify all flesh, including humans? Particularly since the Apostle says this in 1 Timothy 4 (4:5) "For it is sanctified by the word of God and prayer." Further how is the Holy Spirit able to sanctify your bodies, which you say are the work of the devil? And He yet sanctifies them. How will they not be sanctified by works in heaven? Further you claim that if one eats an egg one loses the Holy Spirit, therefore how much stronger is one egg than the Holy Spirit! Further you say that if anyone eats some bit of meat or the like through ignorance, then he loses the Holy Spirit therefore it is not in your power to hold him by any form of good life, nor in His [power] to remain with you, but any servant of yours or another person, by placing something of this kind in your pan is able to take the Holy Spirit from you and how do you know whether this has already been done to you very often? What insanity this is! Further just as the Apostle prohibited unclean eating, so did he prohibit such touching, therefore the devil can cast out the Holy Spirit from the whole world with only a small rind of bacon, by conveying it to everyone's mouth, from those who seemed to possess Him, and any man whatsoever can remove Him from you in this way.

[**Pat:**] Also, we abstain on account of a greater abstinence, since they are incentives towards carnal vices, and for that reason we are bound by a vow lest we should eat in this way, so if others ate in this way it would be no sin, yet for us it would be a sin on account of the broken vow.

Cath: I reply that it is not true that it is a sin to eat like this on account of greater abstinence, for I am able to merit more by eating than by abstaining sometimes, if done with a good and sound intention. But I will prove that you speak falsely and that you hypocritically utter commands. For greater is the abstinence and less are carnal vices ignited by eating dry cheese and especially in moderation than by eating sturgeon and such fish delicacies with spices and choice wines and with all manner of drinks, and yet you abstain from the former like it was a mortal sin, and over the latter you are wanton and are overthrown. But we say that your vow does not hold because it was made in error, and that others ought to be broken if they were made with a good intention, since on account of a testing of faith it can be ordered to be released by the Church. Further in the same manner you have vowed not to kill and yet daily you kill fish and the like, and if perhaps you might claim that in a general vow not to kill you have excepted fish and the like, I say that in the same way

---

70 sanctificatur...71 orationem] 1 Tim. 4:5.

---

75 comestum...76 quam] om. *F*   78 ignorantiam] add. quod *F* | amittit] admittit *P*   82 ollere] *an otherwise unknown word, although from the context, it has a probable connection to "olla" ('pot', 'pan')*   83 auferre] auferendo *P*   86 modica] modici *F*   87 illa] illam *P*   92 ne] ut *P*   98 mereri] add. n *P* exp   100 hypocrisi] ypocrisi *F*   110 uouistis] nouistis *P*

74 patria|fol. 108ra *P*   101 carnalia|fol. 108rb *P*

debuistis excipere in hoc uoto casum multiplicis necessitatis.

Patarenus: Item habemus auctoritates ad confirmationem nostrarum rationum ut ecce ad romanos. xiiii. bonum est non manducare carnem etcet. ergo malum est carnes manducare.

Catholicus: Responsio. Et eodem modo dixit ibidem. bonum est non bibere uinum. ergo mortaliter peccatis bibendo uinum. Disce autem pabulum mortis quia bonum est non manducare carnes et carnes manducare secundum intentionem bonam et secundum tempus et huius.

Patarenus: Item. iª petri iiº. obsecro uos tamquam aduenas et peregrinos abstinere uos a carnalibus desideriis etcet. ergo peccatum est desiderare carnes comedere.

Catholicus: Responsio. stulte non dixit a carnibus sed a carnalibus desideriis. que autem sint carnalia desideria conuenerat beatus paulus ad Galathas. v. ubi dicit. manifesta sunt opera carnis que sunt fornicatio immunditia impudicitia luxuria etcet.

[Patarenus:] Item actus. xv. ubi beatus iacobus dixit. ut abstineant se a contaminationibus simulacrorum et fornicationum et suffocatis et sanguine etcet. Et fornicatio dicuntur carnes quia de fornicatione nate sunt. suffocata uero dicuntur oua quia sub cortice inclusa sunt. caseus autem et lac et huiusmodi dicuntur sanguis de sanguine proueniunt ergo horum esus prohibitus est.

Catholicus: Respondeo quod ista est abusio demoniaca diuine scripture contraria. Scriptura enim diuina dicit quod non faciamus fornicationem et quod non committamus illam. ergo per fornicationem non intelliguntur carnes animalium. quomodo enim possemus facere aut committere carnes et dixit apostolus quod fornicatio est improprium corporis et hanc prohibet ne comedamus corpora nostra. item suffocatio appelatur quod prius fuit uiuum. ut mattheus. xviii. et tenens suffocabat eum. ergo oua non dicuntur suffocata. quia numquam habunt uitam et sanguis in diuina scriptura ipsa substantia sanguis non alterata.

[Patarenus:] Item moyses precepit abstinere a quibusdam carnibus ut puta porcinus et huiusmodi. ergo credebat esse peccatum comedere carnes.

Catholicus: Sed ex lege moysi argumentum accipere uis ab eo ergo quod licet comedere carnes. quia multas iudeis in figuram eorum que nobis erant futura.

Patarenus: Item quare abstinent aliqui de ecclesia romana a carnibus et huiusmodi comedendis immo

you ought to make an exception to this vow in case of many necessities.

Pat: Yet we have the authority and confirmation of our arguments in Romans 14 (14:21) "It is good not to eat meat," therefore it is evil to eat meat.

Cath: Response, and in the same way he says there (14:21) "it is good not to drink wine," therefore one sins mortally in drinking wine. But learn, O fodder of death, for it is good not to eat meat or to eat it according to a good intention and according to the occasion.

Pat: Also 1 Peter 2 (2:11) "I beseech you as strangers and pilgrims, to refrain from carnal desires." Therefore it is a sin to desire to eat meat.

Cath: Response. You fool, he did not say from meat, but from carnal desires, which are consistent with the carnal desires Blessed Paul speaks of to the Galatians in chapter 5, where he says (5:19) "Now the works of the flesh are clear, which are fornication, uncleanness, immodesty, luxury."

[Pat:] Also Acts 15, where Blessed James said (15:20) "that they refrain from the pollutions of idols, and from fornication, and from things strangled, and from blood." And fornication is called flesh meat since they are born of fornication, and eggs are said to be strangled since they are covered by a shell, and cheese and milk and the like are called blood since they arise from blood and therefore it is prohibited to eat of these things.

Cath: I reply that this is a demonic abuse contrary to the divine scriptures, for divine scripture says that we should not commit any fornication, nor should we do it. So by fornication is not understood the flesh of animals, for how would we be able to do or commit flesh? The Apostle said that fornication is an inappropriate use of the body and he prohibits this lest we should dissipate our bodies. Further strangling is thus called in relation to something formerly alive, as in Matthew 18 (18:28) "and holding him, he strangled him," therefore eggs are not termed suffocated things, since they never had life, and the substance blood in the divine scriptures is not changed.

[Pat:] Also Moses commanded abstinence from certain meats, for example, pork and the like, therefore he believed that it was a sin to eat meat.

Cath: But if you are willing to accept an argument from the law of Moses then from it one is allowed to eat meat, since many things prefigured for them were for us in the future.

Pat: Then why do certain ones of the Roman Church abstain from meat and like eating at certain times, and yet

---

118 bonum…carnem] Rom. 14:21.　　121 bonum…uinum] Rom. 14:21.　　126 obsecro…128 desideriis] 1 Pet. 2:11.　　133 manifesta…134 luxuria] Gal. 5:19.　　136 ut…137 sanguine] Act. 15:20 (fornicationum) fornicatione *Vulg.*)　　152 et…eum] Matt. 18:28 (suffocabat) suffocauit *Vulg.*)

142 prohibitus] add. eorum *P* exp　　160 eo] hemo *P*

115 necessitatis|fol. 83r *F*　　130 stulte|fol. 108va *P*　　159 argumentum|fol. 108vb *P*

tota romana ecclesia abstinet quandoque si non est peccatum comedere illas.
Catholicus: Responsio. qui abstinent de ecclesia romana ad huiusmodi bona et pura intentione faciunt propter maiorem abstinentiam non iudicando comedentes. parati etiam semper comedere de uoluntate prelatorum eccesie dei. et ecclesia abstinet quibusdam temporibus eadem ratione. sed dic mihi tu nonne et uos abstinetis a piscibus et a uino quibusdam temporibus. item respondete mihi de piscibus quos comeditis. nonne qui fecit bestias et uolucres fecit et pisces. scio quod creditis quod diabolus fecerit utrosque sed dicitis quod pisces sint non mediante coitu carnali. bestias autem et uolucres fecit illo mediante. ergo immundiores sunt pisces quam uolucres et bestie. quia magis apropinquant immundissimo. ergo magis peccatis pisces comedendo quam si carnes bestiarum et uolucrum comederetis. et si uelletis dicere quod pisces non sunt immundi quia sunt per uerbum et orationem sanctificati. dico quod eodem modo possunt et carnes non esse immunde. quia similiter per uerbum et orationem possunt sanctificari. aut si uelletis dicere quod non possint dicatis mihi diuersitatis rationem. quam in perpetuum non dicetis. uel si forsitan dicitis quod non comeditis carnes eo quod non legatur christum illas comedisse. arguo quod eodem modo nec cicera nec fabas nec aliquid huius comedere debetis. cum nichil de illi christum comedisse unquam legatur.
Hereticus: Comprehensus ergo a tuis obiectionibus manifestabo tibi secretam secretissimam nostram quam pauci etiam ex nostris consolatis sciunt. quia dicimus et credimus quod hec sit potissima ratio quare non comedimus carnes bestiarum et uolucrum quia in huiusmodi corporibus potuerunt habitare spiritus saluandorum quos dicimus intrare diuersa corpora animalium habentium sanguinem et ideo comedimus pisces. quia non intrant in eos cum careant sanguine.
Catholicus: Ista secreta uenit de puteo diaboli quia falsissimum est quod spiritus transeant de corpore in corpus siue humanum siue bestiale. ut probauimus supra in suo tractato. preterea aut spiritus erant in corporibus animalium sicut in carcere et tunc deberemus libenter destruere et comedere corpora illa in quibus fuerunt offensi. aut enim fuerunt in eis tamquam in locis consolationis et tunc deberemus libenter comedere propter reuerentiam eorum quas suo tactu sanctificassent. preterea de hoc quod dicis quod pisces non habent sanguinem mentiris per medium rostrum quia ego uidi oculis meis multos pisces habentes sanguinem de quibus tu libenter comederes et comedis frequenter.

sometimes the whole Roman Church abstains, if it is not a sin to eat them.
Cath: Response, they who abstain in the Roman Church from these things do so from a good and pure intention, on account of a greater abstinence, while not judging those who do eat. For they are ever ready to eat according to the will of the prelates of the Church of God. And the Church abstains in certain seasons for the same reason. But tell me whether your believers abstain from fish or wine at certain times. Also tell me which fish you eat, did not He who made the beasts also make birds and fish? I know that you believe that the devil has made both of them, yet you say that fish do not arise from act of sexual union, but animals and birds do come into being that way. Therefore fish are more unclean than animals and birds, since they more closely approach uncleanness, so it is a worse sin to eat fish than if one would eat the flesh of animals and birds, and if you would wish to say that fish are not unclean because of the words and prayers that sanctify them, then in the same way I say that meat is not unclean, since they are able to be sanctified similarly by word and prayer, or if you wish to say that they are not able to be consecrated, tell me the reason for the difference, which you consistently do not say. Or if perhaps you say that one should not eat meat because of the fact that it is not read that Christ ate it, I argue that by the same reasoning one ought not to eat chickpeas or beans, since one never reads anything of Christ eating them.

Heretic: Embracing therefore your objections, I share with you our secret of secrets which few even of our consoled brethren know, that we say and believe that this is the most powerful argument, by which we do not eat the flesh of animals and birds: the spirits of the saved are able to live in such bodies, by which we they say enter into the different bodies of animals that have blood, and that is why we eat fish, since they do not enter into them [the fish] since they lack blood.

Cath: This secret comes from diabolical depths, for it is most false that the spirit might cross over from body to body whether human or animal, as we have already proven above in this work. Further either the spirits are in the animal bodies as in a prison and then we ought to freely destroy them and eat those bodies in which they have offended, or they were in them just as in a place of consolation and so ought to be eaten on account of reverence for them by which they were sanctified by their touch. Further you lie through your nose when you say that fish do not have blood, since I have seen with my own eyes many fish that have blood, and of these you have freely eaten and you frequently do eat.

---

171 mihi tu] transp. *F* **186** dicatis] *sic PF* leg. dicari **189** quod] pro *F* **192** Hereticus] om. *F* **203** siue¹] suum *F* **206** destruere] dextruere *F* **207** in²] om. *P*

182 sunt¹|fol. 83v *F* **184** immunde|fol. 109ra *P* **208** come-dere|fol. 109rb *P*

LIBER II

De quinque aliarum heresim propriis naufragiis scilicet predestinationum. circumscisorum. speronistarum. pauperum leonistarum ac rebapticatorum

XXV

Diximus supra in superiori libro de patarenorum seu catharorum erroribus in quibus illi soli inueniuntur errare. Nunc autem in isto secundo dicemus de V aliarum heresum propriis naufragiis. scilicet predestinationum. circumscisorum. speronistarum. pauperum leonistarum ac rebapticatorum. Et quia predestinati grauius aliis hereticis cunctis deuiare uidentur post patarenos. ideo iuxta illorum tractatum primo discutiemus de ipsis. ubi sciendum est prius quare dicuntur predestinati et quot sunt genera predestinatorum et in quibus capitulis errant et unde suorum errorum habuerint originem. consequenter uero ipsorum uesanias reprobabimus modo supra posito prosecuto. Dicuntur autem predestinati quia dicunt omnia uenire sicut sunt preordinata uel predestinata. non quia sint ipsi predestinati ad uitam sed ut timeo potius sunt ad mortem ex parte maiori prescripti. Sunt autem pretestinatorum genera iiii^{or}. Quidam enim sunt qui dicunt bona omnia preordinata esse a deo bono. mala. uero a diabolo cuncta. quem errorem traxerunt a simone mago et a manicheis. qui hanc perfidiam disseminasse leguntur. alii uero delirant omnia inferiora regi secundum motum et cursum syderum aliorumque corporum superiorum. etiam animam ipsam dum tegitur carne. addunt etiam quod mundus sit eternus et quod adam non fuerit primus homo. quem errorem uidentur traxisse ex dictis aristotelis maxime. prout inferius in suis allegationibus patebit et sunt ex istis quidam qui dicunt quod deus mutat quandoque huiusmodi effectus. qui per naturam corporum superiorum procedere debent. Tertium uero genus predestinatorum est illorum qui autumant bona et mala omnia a bono principio id est a deo esse preordinata. Quartum uero genus est illorum qui blasphemant non esse angelos aliquos neque animas hominum ista uita finita cuius auctores stultitie. saducei primo fuerunt quam postea mutatus est quidam nomine arabs qui dogmaticauit cum complicibus suis. animam cum carne finiri. adiecit et quidam alius

Regarding five other heresies who make their own shipwrecks, namely, of the Predestinarians, of the Circumcisers, of the Speronists, of the Poor of Lyons, and of the Rebaptizers

We spoke above in the preceding book about the errors in which only the Patarenes or Cathars are found to err. But now in this second book we will speak of five other heresies who make their own shipwreck [of the faith],[1] namely the Predestinarians, the Circumcisers, the Speronists, the Poor of Lyons, and the Rebaptizers. And since the Predestinarians err more gravely than all other heretics, save the Patarenes, we shall begin by discussing them, where we first seek to inquire why they are called Predestinarians,[2] and how many types of Predestinarians there are, and in what articles of faith they err, and what the origin of their error was; after all this we will confute their madness by following the outline above. Now they are called Predestinarians because they say all things are preordained or predestined, not because they might be predestined to life but, as I fear, they are for the most part foreordained to death. There are four kinds of Predestinarians. For there are some who say that good things are preordained by the good God, yet all evil things [are preordained] by the devil. This error they derived from Simon Magus and from the Manichees who, it is read, spread this wickedness. But others rave that all things in the inferior world are ruled by the motion and course of the stars and other superior bodies, even the soul itself, while it inhabits the body. They seem to have taken this error principally from Aristotle, and this will become clear from their assertions below. And there are some of these who say that God sometimes changes effects of this kind, which ought to proceed from superior bodies. Yet a third sect of Predestinarians is of those who assert that all things, good and bad, come from the good principle, that is, preordained by God. The fourth group is made up of those who blaspheme by saying that there are neither angels nor human souls after this life. The origin of this stupidity was the Sadducees, later it was changed by a certain one, named Arabs,[3] who proclaimed, along with his followers, that the soul reached its end with that of the flesh. Another one named Zeno,[4] with his disciples, added that after a little while the soul will be

---

XXV.1.1 quinque … 2 scilicet] erroribus *F*   **4** leonistarum] lugdunensiam *F* | rebapticatorum] rebaptizatorum *F*   **6** catharorum] chatarorum *F*   **8** heresum] heresim *P*   **12** illorum] aliorum *F*   **21** maiori] maioris *F*   **25** simone] symone *F*   **42** complicibus] discipulis *P*

XXV.1.23 dicunt|fol. 109va *P*   **34** mutat|fol. 84r *F*

---

[1] Cf. 1 Tim. 1:19. | [2] No other source really identifies them as a discrete sect, though Moneta, 478-88, 496-500, and 549-559 discuss the errors listed here. | [3] "Arabs" as a name should, perhaps, be construed as "The Arab(ian)". Wakefield, 734, n. 38 speculates that this was a sect called "Arabici" who believed the soul to dissolve at death, but the body to be resurrected at the end of time. Both Eusebius and Augustine report this. However the idea is similar to some strains of Islamic eschatology as well, which may thus explain the nickname. | [4] Wakefield, 734, n. 39, proposes this as a scribal error for "Zarohen." He was listed by Moneta, 411 as holding these errors.

nomine zeno cum discipulis suis quod post modicum interuallum carne perempta perimatur et anima et dicunt isti predestinati qui proprie possunt uocari disperati. omnia ab eterno sic euenire et post finem anni quem magnum uocant iterum renouari. quem dicunt in xxx. milibus annorum usualium uel. xv. milibus consistere. De quibus desperatis adest multitudo in ciuitate sodomorum. que omnis turpitudinis merito dicitur esse sentina. que diuino iudicio percussa. dealbata nigrescet et flos in se ipsa marcescet. pene ad nichilum redigendi et isti quarti sunt qui nomen optinent predestinatorum. Et primo uidendum est de opinione illorum quam patareni sequuntur ut per hoc etiam totum quod illorum est proprium coniungamus. quam tam per rationes ueridicas quam per sacras scripturas improbamus.

destroyed with the flesh. These Predestinarians, who are properly able to be called the 'hopeless ones,' say that from eternity all things follow this course and after the end of a year, which they call 'Great',[1] shall again be renewed. This 'year' they say shall consist of 30,000 or 15,000 normal years. There were many of these desperate ones in the city of Sodom, which was rightly said to be the dregs of all infamy, and whose whitewash, when struck by divine judgment, turned black and its flower shriveled upon itself, and was reduced to almost nothing, and these are the fourth [group] who have acquired the name Predestinarians. We had to consider firstly the opinions which are accepted by the Patarenes,[2] and bringing together all that which was particular to them, and we have opposed them by natural reason and by the holy scriptures.

De libero arbitrio

Si boni et mali necessitate faciunt illa que gerunt. ergo non mouentur libero arbitrio. igitur nec boni merentur uitam eternam. nec mali penam et nichil suo uelle faciunt sed uelint nolint et incertus et cadunt in illa. sicut nec sol quia lucet remunerabitur gaudio eterno. nec terra. quia corrumpitur cruciabitur eterno igne. cum sol et terra necessario non uoluntarie nature sibi peragant impositum cursum. sed constat quia boni coronatur in celo et mali torquentur in inferno secundum opera uniuscuiusque igitur uoluntarie fecerunt. inde illi bona et isti mala recipiunt iuste.

Catholicus: preterea si faciunt homines bona et mala iuxta necessitatem impositam sibi imperantium ergo non ipsi faciunt illa. sed imperatores qui uelud instrumentis illis utuntur et secundum hec imperatores soli premium uel penam recipere debent.

Item secundum hoc boni non nisi bona facerent et mali non nisi mala peragerent. si omnia iuxta leges imperantium necessaria suis ordinatoribus obtemperarent. Non enim bonus deus indiceret sibi nisi bona. nec malus nisi mala suis. sed uidemus quod boni quandoque faciunt mala et mali bona quandoque igitur non sunt hoc hominibus necessario sic ordinata.

Catholicus: Ad hoc etiam occurit quia secundum hoc mali non possent benefacere nec saluari et boni non possunt facere mala. nec aliquo modo dampnati. et secundum hoc predicatio uel oratio aut bona operatio

On Free Will

If good and evil by necessity cause those things which they govern, then they are not moved by free will, therefore neither do the good merit eternal life nor the wicked punishment. And they do nothing by their own willing, but [are] uncertain whether they will or not, and they [simply] fall into those things. Just as neither the sun that shines is rewarded by eternal joy, nor is the corruptible earth tormented by eternal fire, since the sun and earth complete their courses not with a voluntary nature but by necessity. Yet it remains that the good are crowned in heaven and the evil are tormented in hell according to each one's works, therefore they do such things voluntarily. Thence these good receive good things and those evil receive evil things justly.

Cath: Furthermore if men do good and evil things under constraint which has been imposed upon them by rulers, then it is not the men themselves who do those things but their commanders who use them like instruments, and in this way those who command alone ought to receive reward or punishment.

But according to this good men are not good unless they do good things and bad men are not bad unless they pursue evil things. If all things are subject to the laws of unplanned necessity by those who ordained them such, a good God would not impose [anything] save good things, nor an evil God [anything] save evil things. But we see good men sometimes committing evils and evil men sometimes doing good works. Therefore these things are not thus ordained that to men by necessity.

Cath: To this it also happens that by this logic the evil are not able to do good nor can they be saved and the good are not able to do evil, nor in any way be damned, and according to this neither preaching or prayer or good

---

52 sentina] sententia *F*   56 opinione] oppinione *P*   57 sequuntur] secuntur *P*   **XXV.2.5** et incertus] om. *F*   15 imperatores] imperantes *P*   16 illis] add. uel *P* | imperatores] imperantes *P*   17 debent] debeat *F* | add. Catholicus *P*   20 necessaria] necessario *F*   21 Non] nunc *P*   26 benefacere] add. male *F* | nec…27 mala] om. *F*

48 uocant|fol. 109vb *P*   **XXV.2.13** Catholicus|fol. 110ra *P*

---

[1] Uncertain what is meant by the "great year" however Dondaine found a similar passage in the writings of Durand of Huesca, see Dondaine, "Durand de Huesca" *AFP* 29 (1959): 266. | [2] Referring to the 'Albanenses' or absolute dualist Cathars, whose beliefs demanded a denial of free will.

et industria seu uigilantia nichil ualeret. frustra ergo passus esset christus. et frustra quereretur deus. aut aliquid boni fieret aliquando. nichil etiam noceret diaboli malitia. nec obesset omnia facere mala. et sic melioris conditionis esset qui mala faceret. quam qui bona peragaret. quia ille utriusque uite gaudiis frueretur et iste uitam perderet istam propter quod nec melius aliqua lucraret. et forsitan tam istam quam illam perderet sicut stultus quod absurdum est cogitare. preterea isti qui hanc opinionem sequuntur mirabiliter se stultos esse demonstrant quod non illam dimittunt et nostram non imitantur. quia si eorum sententia uera esset. nec prodest eis sententiam tenere. nec nocet eis nostram amplecti. quia si sunt ad mortem proscripti. non possunt saluari per ipsorum fidem et uitam et sicut ad uitam predestinati. aliquo modo non possunt dampnari. si fidem nostram et uitam teneant et immitentur. at si nostra sententia uera est prout firmiter est stulti et insani undique apparebunt. quia uoluntarie eternam dampnationem inciderunt quam iurare potuerunt et uita eterna priuati erunt. quam utique habuissent nisi per eos remansissent.

Quod omnes homines saluari uel dampnati possunt secundum sua opera

Legimus in scripturis hanc sententiam. quod omnes homines possint saluari uel dampnari. secundum opera sua bona uel mala coadiuuante dei gratia seu deficiente. quare non uidetur quod ea qui hominibus eueniunt sint ordinata necessitate. ut ecce. ezechiel. iii°. si dicente me ad impium morte morieris. non adnuntiaueris ei. nec locutus fueris ut aduertatur a uia sua impia et uiuat. ipse impius in iniquitate sua morietur. etcet. et infra. sed et si conuersus iustus a iustitia sua fuerit et fecerit iniquitatem ponam offendiculum coram eo ipse morietur etcet. et mattheus. xi. quia si in sodomis facte fuissent uirtutes que facte sunt in te. forte mansissent usque in hanc diem etcet. et infra. uenite ad me omnes qui laboratis et honerati estis et ego reficiam uos etcet. idem. xiii. et corde intelligant et conuertantur et sanem eos etcet. item. ad romanos. x. non enim est distinctio iudei et greci. nam idem dominus omnium diues in omnes qui inuocant illum. omnis enim quicumque inuocauerit nomen domini saluus erit etcet. item. i^a. ad corinthios. iii°. unusquisque autem propriam mercedem accipiet secundum suum laborem. dei enim sumus adiutores etcet. idem. ix. sic currite ut comprehendatis etcet. item. ii^a. ad corinthios. v. omnes enim nos manifestari oportet ante tribunal christi ut referat unusquisque

That all men are able to be saved or damned according to their works

We read the following meaning in the scriptures, that all men are able to be saved or damned according to their good or evil deeds, either by the cooperating grace of God or its absence, hence it does not seem that those things which happen to men are ordered by necessity. See in Ezekiel 3 (3:18) "If, when I say to the wicked, 'You will surely die,' you do not declare it to him, nor speak to him, that he may be converted from his wicked way, and live, the same wicked man will die in his iniquity." And later (3:20) "Moreover if the just man turns away from his justice, and commits iniquity, I will lay a stumbling block before him, he shall die." And Matthew 11 (11:23) "For if in Sodom had been wrought the miracles that have been performed before you, perhaps it would be standing to this day." And later (11:28) "Come to me all who labor and are burdened and I will give you rest," and 13 (13:15) "and understand with their heart, and be converted, and I would heal them." Romans 10 (10:12–13) "For there is no distinction between Jew and Greek, for the same is Lord over all, rich to all who call upon him. For whoever will call upon the name of the Lord, will be saved." Also 1 Corinthians 3 (3:8–9) "And every man will receive his own reward, according to his own labor, for we are God's coadjutors." Also 9 (9:24) "So run that you may obtain." Also 2 Corinthians 5 (5:10) "For we must all be manifested before the judgment seat of Christ, so that

---

XXV.3.8 si...11 morietur] Ez. 3:18.   11 sed...13 morietur] Ez. 3:20.   14 quia...15 diem] Matt. 11:23.   16 uenite...17 uos] Matt. 11:28.   17 et^2...18 eos] Matt. 13:15.   19 non...22 erit] Rom. 10:12-13.   23 unusquisque...24 adiutores] 1 Cor. 3:8-9.   25 sic...comprehendatis] 1 Cor. 9:24.   26 omnes...28 malum] 2 Cor. 6:10.

---

29 ergo] igitur F   36 aliqua] aliam P   38 opinionem] oppinionem P | sequuntur] secuntur P   41 sententiam] suam P   48 inciderunt] add. quam dampnationem eternam P; leg. inciderunt pro incinerunt PF.   49 et...erunt] om. F   XXV.3.1 Quod...2 opera] om. F   5 uel] add. bo P exp.   6 ea] ei F   22 iii°] 3 P   25 ix] viiii P

36 forsitan|fol. 110rb P   40 eorum|fol. 84v F   XXV.3.11 morietur|fol. 110va P

propria corporis prout gessit. siue bonum siue malum etcet. idem. vi. adiuuantes autem exortamur ne in uacuum gratiam dei recipiatis. ait enim. tempore accepto exaudiui te etcet. item ad Galathas. ii°. deus personarum hominis non accipit etcet. item ad colosenses. v. propter que uenit ira dei super filios diffidentie etcet. item. i^a. ad timotheus. ii°. hoc enim bonum est et acceptum coram saluatore nostro deo. qui omnes homines uult saluos fieri. et agnitionem ueritatis uenire etcet. item. ad hebreos. xii. fili mi noli negligere disciplinam domini etcet. et infra. contemplantes ne quis desit gratie dei etcet. item. iacobum. ii°. uides quoniam ex operibus iustificatur homo. item prima. petri. primo. et si patrem inuocastis eum qui sine acceptione personarum iudicat secundum uniuscuiusque opus etcet. idem ii^a. iii°. non tardat dominus promissionem sed patienter agit propter nolens aliquem perire sed omnes ad penitentiam reuerti etcet. item actus. x. aperiens autem petrus os suum dixit. in ueritate comperi quoniam non est acceptor personarum deus. sed in omni gente qui timet eum et operatur iustitiam acceptus est illi etcet. ex hiis ergo scripturis et ex multis aliis quasi inueneris patet quod unusquisque potest saluari uel dampnari secundum sua opera bona uel mala. coadiuuante gratia dei. seu deficiente. et ideo que accidunt non sunt necessario preordinata et supple de hac materia ut supra titulo primo primi libri rubricella. quod dampnati sunt a deo. et titulo de sacramento penitentie. in rubricella i^a.

every one may receive the proper things of the body, according to what he has done, whether it be good or evil." Also 6 (6:1–2) "And we helping do exhort you, so that you do not receive the grace of God in vain. For he says, 'In the acceptable time have I heard you.'" Also Galatians 2 (2:6) "God is no respecter of persons." Also Colossians 5 (3:6) "For which things the wrath of God comes upon the children of unbelief." Also 1 Timothy 2 (2:3–4) "For this is good and acceptable in the sight of God our Savior, who wishes all men to be saved, and to come to the knowledge of the truth." Also Hebrews 12 (12:5) "My son, do not neglect the discipline of the Lord," and later (12:15) "Looking diligently, lest any man be wanting in the grace of God." Also James 2 (2:24) "You see then that man is justified by works." Also 1 Peter (1:17) "And if you invoke as Father him who, without respect of persons, judges according to every one's work," also in his second letter, chapter 3 (3:9) "The Lord does not delay his promise, as some imagine, but deals patiently for your sake, not willing that any should perish, but that all should return to penance." Also Acts 10 (10:34–35) "And Peter opening his mouth, said, 'In truth I see that God is not a respecter of persons but in every nation, he who fears him and works justice is acceptable to him.'" So from these scriptures and from many others you can find that it is clear that every man can be saved or damned according to his works, be they good or bad, with the help of the cooperating grace of God or the absence thereof, and so those things which happen are not by preordained necessity. This material is treated above in the first title of the book, in the section "Those damned by God" and in the title on the sacrament of penance, in the first rubric.

Contra errorem illorum qui dicunt omnia inferiora regi secundum motum et cursum corporum superiorum

Sequitur uidere contra illorum errorem qui dicunt omnia inferiora regi. secundum motum et cursum corporum superiorum. contra quos per naturales tantum rationes et philosophorum dicta procedemus. quoniam scripturas diuinas non admittunt.

De anima

anima est. ut ait philosophus. dignissima creaturarum id est qua nulla dignior est creatura. quod probat illa ratione. quia propter dignitatem rationabilis eius intellectus. ipsa est in confinio deitatis. unde cum dignior sit sole et omnibus astris. patet quod ab ipsis minime regitur.

Against the error of those who say that inferior bodies are ruled by the motion and course of superior ones

It remains to answer those who hold the error that says that inferior things are ruled according to the motion and course of superior bodies against whom we proceed only with natural arguments and the sayings of the philosophers, since they do not admit the [authority of the] divine scriptures.

On the soul

The soul is, as the philosopher says, that which nothing is worthier among creatures. That is, he proves that there is no creature with higher dignity by this reason, that on account of the dignity of its rational intellect it is akin to the divine nature. For this reason it has more worth than

---

29 adiuuantes...31 te] 2 Cor. 6:1-2.   31 deus...32 accipit] Gal. 2:6.   33 propter...34 diffidentie] Col. 3:6 (*F* confused with Eph. 5:6)   34 hoc...37 uenire] 1 Tim. 2:3-4.   37 fili...38 domini] Heb. 12:5.   38 contem-plantes...39 dei] Heb. 12:15.   40 quoniam...homo] Iac. 2:24 (uides uidetis *Vulg.*)   41 et...43 opus] 1 Pet. 1:17 (inuocastis inuocatis *Vulg.*)   43 non...45 reuerti] 2 Pet. 3:9 (non tardat Dominus promissionem suam, sicut quidam existimant, sed patienter agit propter uos, nolens aliquos perire, sed omnes ad poenitentiam reuerti *Vulg.*)   46 aperiens...49 illi] Act. 10:34-35 (quoniam quia *Vulg.*)

33 colosenses] ephesios *F*   **XXV.4.1** Contra...3 superiorum] om. *F*   **XXV.5.1** De anima] om. *F*

36 fieri|fol. 110vb *P*   **XXV.4.5** et|fol. 111ra *P*   8 diuinas|fol. 85r *F*

Item de eodem

Item anima supponit plato cum omnibus phylosophys et sanctis. habet liberum arbitrium. igitur non est legibus a stricta nature. et quod habet liberum arbitrium. possunt introduci omnes rationes quas superius diximus contra primum genus predestinatorum. item dicunt phylosophi quod anima est supra tempus. sed omnes uisibiles creature sunt sub tempore uel in tempore. ergo nichil possunt operari in anima principaliter. preterea nos uidemus quod sub uno sole uel sub una luna seu stella et in eodem solis motu seu lune uel stelle. et in eodem die et hora ac momento et eisdem concurrentibus omnibus huiusmodi due naues educuntur de portu et diuersimode contingit illis. quia alia prospere procedit. et altera subiungitur. eodem modo due gentes bella committunt et altera uincit et altera subcumbit. et duarum gentium uexilla dantur carrocia fiunt et exercitus exeunt locis. et huic bene et illi accedit male. et duo gemini fratres nascuntur et alii multi. superioribus concurrentibus in lucem uite huius producuntur et isti boni et illi reprobi. isti pauperes et illi diuites. isti sapientes et illi stulti. et huiusmodi reperiuntur. que exempla in omnibus posito possunt. que cotidie uariantur. ergo non ueniunt isti necessitate stellatoris. quia hoc est impossibile quod eadem res contrarios effectus per eadem uirtutem simul et semel operetur.

Dicta patarenorum

Item dicunt quod qui in tali puncto nascuntur omnes sunt piscatores et qui in tali sunt mercatores et sic de ceteris. sed constat quod alique terre sunt ubi nullus est piscator et alique ubi nullus est mercator. et alique ubi nullus est miles uel nullus clericus uel nullus pelleparius et sic de ceteris et etiam sunt iste terre contigue. ubi diuersi sunt status hominum cum ergo eedem stellationes et eadem puncta super utrasque concurrant. et tamen diuersi sunt status hominum in illis et uarie conditiones. constat quod mendatia sunt hec que in hac parte dicunt astrologi. item esto quod in puncto isto sit hec uirtus uel illa non potest aliquas uires habere quod non est uel desiit esse. sed punctum statim transiit. ergo eius uirtus nichil est. cum punctum iam non est. ergo mendacia sunt omnia que

Further on the same subject

Likewise Plato, along with all the philosophers and saints, supposes that the soul has free will, therefore it is not constrained by the laws of nature and has free will. All the arguments we gave above are able to be introduced against the first type of Predestinarians. Likewise the philosophers say (PseudoAristotle, *De Causis* II, 19) "the soul is beyond time" but all visible creatures are under time or in time, therefore they are not at all able to work in the soul principally. Further we see that under one sun or under one moon or star and in the same movement of the sun or moon or star, at the same day and hour and moment, with all of them running together, two ships depart from port and widely different things happen to them, since one proceeds with good luck, and the other is sunk. In the same way two nations wage war, one emerges victorious and the other is defeated, and the banners of the two nations are raised, and the 'Carroccio' deployed,[1] and the armies move to the battlefield. And it goes well for one and badly for the other. And two brother twins are born and the stars are aligned, so they are brought forth into this life and yet one is good and one is base, one is rich and the other poor, one is wise and the other stupid. And similar examples are able to be found in all things which vary from day to day. Therefore they are not compelled to necessity by the stars, since it is impossible that the same thing might be worked by the same power simultaneously and produce contrary effects.

The sayings of the Patarenes

Likewise they say that at one point in time all who are born are fishermen, and at another point are born merchants, and so on of others, but it remains that in some lands no one is a fisherman and in others where there are none who are merchants, and others where none are soldiers or none are clerics or none are skinners and so on, and there are also those contiguous lands, where there are different conditions of men, therefore since the same constellations and same points of time concur above both [lands] and yet there are different states and various conditions of men in them, it is established that these things which astrologers say in this regard are false. Likewise suppose that in this moment there be this or that power; it cannot have any strength because it does not exist or has ceased to exist; but the moment has immediately passed; therefore its power is nothing, since the moment

---

XXV.6.7 quod ... 8 tempus] Pseudo-Aristotle, *De Causis*, II. 19. Cited as *Liber de pura bonitate*. This was a collection by an anonymous Arab author who rearranged Proclus' *Elements of Theology*.

XXV.6.2 anima] add. ut *F* **18** carrocia] carroctia *P* **20** multi] add. superioribus *P* **21** reprobi] reprobasti *F* **23** reperiuntur] repperiuntur *F* **26** contrarios] contra nos *P* **XXV.7.1** Dicta patarenorum] om. *F* **11** conditiones] condiciones *F* **13** isto] om. *F* **16** mendacia] mendatia *P*

XXV.6.20 multi|fol. 111rb *P*

---

[1] The *carroccio* was a chariot on which the religious and civil standards of the northern Italian city-states were carried into battle. See: Hannelore Zug Tucci, "Il carroccio nella vita comunale," *Quellen und Forschungen aus italienischen Archiven und Bibliotheken* 65 (1985): 1-104.

dicunt. si in tali puncto uexilla dantur uincent inimicos etiam alio tempore. uel si in tali puncto uel in tali signo fiet hoc uel illud. continget alio tempore illud uel istud quia tunc non est punctum illud. uel signum istud. et etiam quandoque ex longo tempore desiit esse.

Catholicus: Item dicunt quod in omni puncto est uirtus. sed constat quod non sunt uirtutes in rerum naturis in tertia parte sicut puncta transierunt. ergo omnes uirtutes rerum naturalium necesse est dicere transiuisse quod falsum esse manifeste uidemus.

Item puncta et tempora in instanti et cito mutantur et transeunt. ergo omnis uirtus que per punctum est statim mutatur et transit. quia quale est causa. tale est eius effectus. ergo nulla est stabile quod per punctum temporis est. sed ea que ex animo ueniunt hominum uidemus quod diutius permanent et consistunt. ergo non ueniunt uel fuerit ex uirtute punctorum et temporum uelociter transeuntium.

Error patarenorum

Item dicut quod omnia puncta habent uirtutes suas uarias et contrarias et diuersas. sed unum punctum superueniet alio transeunte. et sic unum punctum semper expellit aliud et statim. sed omne quod desinit cum sua uirtute desinit. ergo omnis uirtus que est ex tempore expellitur una per aliam et sic nulla remanet.

Catholicus: Item uidemus quod sapientibus melius euenit quam stulti prout in pluribus et magis boni diliguntur quam reprobi et quod mutatur status et dignitates et conditiones hominum et hiis mutatis mutatur et eorum fortuna siue casus quod esse non posset si esset eis necessitas a lege corporum superiorum imposita. neque enim eorum possent status mutari. et si mutarent non tamen illorum mutaretur fortuna.

preterea si hoc sentencia uera esset. nulla pena imponeretur. et nullis bonis daretur premium. cum omnia necessario fierent. et sic aut deus non esset. aut esset non bonus cum iustus non esset. sed probatur deum esse et ipsum esse iustum. igitur secundum liberum arbitrium regitur anima. cui data sunt hoc iuste pro meritis. Item. si hoc deus necessario ordinasset per genesim. ergo ipse deus faceret ista. que et aliquo modo uitari non possent ab homine. sed constat quod ab homibius fiunt sodomitia. adulteria. proditiones et hiis similia infinita mala. igitur deus faceret illa principaliter et sic esset deus iniquiis quod omnis aures humane audire formidant. et mens omnis aborret.

Catholicus: preterea uidemus quod isti qui se astrologos dicunt aut diuinos hanc uesaniam tenentes. qui futura in aliis dicunt et occulta manifestant ut

no longer exists. Therefore all the things they say are lies, [that] if at such a moment the battle standards are raised they will conquer the enemy than at another time; or if at that moment or with such a sign this or that is done, this or that will happen at another time, for then that moment does not exist, or this sign; and sometimes even it has ceased to exist for a long time.

Cath: Likewise they say that power exists in all moments but it is evident in the third part that there are not powers in the natures of things just as moments have passed away. Therefore it is necessary to say that all powers of natural things have passed away, which we clearly see is false.

Further moments and times change and pass away quickly in an instant, therefore all power which is in a moment is changed and passes away, since the cause is just like the effect. Therefore nothing is stable that is for only a moment of time, but that which comes from the soul of men we see that it remains and stands for a considerable period of time, therefore they do not come into being or exist in virtue of moments and of quickly passing times.

Error of the Patarenes

Also they say that all moments have their own various powers and contraries and differences, but one moment rules, having superseded all others. And so one moment always drives out another at once, but all that ceases when that power ceases, therefore all power which exists from the time is driven out, together with another and so nothing remains.

Cath: Likewise we see that it goes better for the wise than for fools, just as in many things the good are loved more than the evil and that the status, dignity, and condition of men is changed and, in a similar way, their fortune or fall [occurs], which would be impossible if it were necessary for them to be subject to a law imposed by superior bodies. For neither would they be able to change their condition, and, if they changed, in any case they would be unable to change their luck.

Further if this interpretation were true, no punishment could be imposed, nor any reward given to the good, since all things happened of necessity. And so either God does not exist or if He exists He is not good, since He does not have justice, but it has been proven that God exists and that He is just, so the soul is governed according to free will, and to [the soul] this power is justly given for [obtaining] merits. Further, if this God ordained by necessity through one's origin, therefore that same God would cause these, and so it is impossible that man could sin in any way, but it remains that from men comes sodomy, adultery, treason, and such similar innumerable evils. Therefore God principally caused them, and so He is a God of iniquity that all human ears should dread to hear and all minds abhor.

Cath: Further we see that these, who call themselves astrologers or diviners, are holding this madness, telling the future to others and showing forth hidden things, as they

---

22 Catholicus] om. *F* 34 temporum] temporium *P* **XXV.8.1** Error patarenorum] om. *F* 7 tempore] parte *P* 17 nulla] add. pena *P* 20 sed...21 secundum] om. *P* 22 data] addita *P* 32 uesaniam] vexaniam *F*

XXV.7.23 constat|fol. 111va *P* **XXV.8.**4 sic|fol. 85v *F* 16 mutaretur|fol. 111vb *P*

aiunt. quod sibi uentura non prouident et occulta bona non inueniunt sibi ut ecce. nuntiant alienam mortem uel casum ut dicunt propriam autem penitus ignorantes aut si sciunt quare non precanent. et si omnia sciunt aliis quare non sibi? Si aliorum fortunas dirigunt et predicunt quare non suas. et si aliis thesaurum indicant. quare non sibi? que sibi non facere patet expresse. uidemus namque illos subito mortem et in casus alios incidere sicut et plusquam ceteros et fortunas illorum plenas miseriis intelligimus. et illos pauperes plures esse aliis et calamitatibus innumeris circumdatos conspicimus.

Catholicus: Quod mundus non sit eternus probatur sic. quia in se habet contrarietatem elementorum et quicquid ab originali corrumpitur destructabile est. et omne quod destuctabile principium habet et finem secundum sui naturam et adde per ista materia omnes rationes quas allegauimus supra in primo titulum. primi libri in prima rubricella. et infra in sua parte.

De illis qui oppinantur omnia tam mala quam bona preordinata esse a deo

Sequitur uidere de illis qui opinantur omnia tam mala quam bona preordinata esse a deo. et illa necessario euenire. contra quos fere omnes rationes possunt induci. que superius contra primos et secundos sunt allegate. et ideo sufficit unam tantum superinducere que locum suum optinet conuenientius. qua probatur quod deus saltem mala non ordinat. quia si deus ordinaret mala et necessario oporteret illa fieri. ergo non posset sine iniquitate facientis illa punire. immo potius deberet laudare sibi obtemperantes sed constat quod ipse punit delinquantes ergo uel ipse est iniquus quod falsum est. uel ipse non ordinat mala quod uerum est. immo prohibet suis legibus sanctis. hanc quidem rationem beatus paulus ad romanos. iii°. dicens. si autem iniquitas nostra iustitiam dei commendat. quid dicemus? numquid iniquus est deus qui infert iram? secundum hominem dico. absit. alioquin quomodo iudicabit deus hunc mundum? si dei ueritas in meo mendacio habundauit in gloriam ipsius. quid adhuc ego tamquam peccator iudicior etcet.

Contra illos qui hoc nomen predestinatorum occuparunt

Sequitur uidere contra illos qui hoc nomen predestinatorum occuparunt et primo probabimus quod angeli sunt quod illi negant. Aristoteles dicit quod sunt intelligentie a prima essentia emanantes. quas non angelos appellamus. item plato dicit quod sunt

say. But they cannot foresee things to come to themselves and they cannot find hidden goods for themselves, for see they announce the death of another or a fall just as they tell nothing of their own [fortune], or if they know why do they not foretell? And if they know all these things for others why not for themselves? Or if they are able to direct the fortunes of others and foretell them, why not their own? And if they can proclaim these treasures to others, why not to themselves? For it is clear they are unable to do it for themselves. We see on the other hand those [men] subject to sudden death, and finding themselves subject to other misfortunes just as more than other people we realize the full misery of their fortunes, and we see those many poor wretches to be surrounded by numerous other calamities.

Cath: That the world is not eternal is proven thusly, that since in it is found opposition of elements and so whatever is corruptible in its origins is destructible, and everything that is destructible has an origin and an end according to its nature and one can add regarding this topic all of the reasons we mentioned above in the first title of the first book in the first subsection, and below in its part.

On those who imagine that all things, both good and evil, are preordained by God

Next it follows to see those who imagine that all things, both good and evil, have been preordained by God and happen by necessity, against whom nearly all the arguments which were adduced above against the first and second can be employed. Therefore it is sufficient to bring forward in addition only one [argument], which obtains its own place rather more suitably, by which it is proven that God at least does not ordain evil, since if God ordained evil it would be necessary that it be done. Therefore He cannot punish the evildoer without iniquity. In fact, He ought rather to praise those working in obedience to Him, but it happens that He punishes wrongdoing therefore either He is iniquitous, which is false, or He Himself does not ordain evil which is true. In fact, He prohibits it by His holy laws, indeed this is the understanding that Blessed Paul has in his letter to the Romans 3, saying (3:5–7) "But if our injustice commends the justice of God, what shall we say? Is God unjust, who executes wrath? (I speak according to man.) God forbid: otherwise how shall God judge this world? For if the truth of God has more abounded through my lie, to his glory, why am I also yet judged as a sinner?"

Against those who claim this name of Predestinarian

Next we consider those who claim this name of Predestinarian, and first we will establish what angels are, whose existence they deny. Aristotle says that they are intelligences emanating from the first essence, which we do not term angels. Further Plato says that they are

---

XXV.9.17 si...22 iudicior] Rom. 3:5-7.

43 plenas] add. plures *P* 48 destructabile] dextructabile *F* | et...49 destuctabile] om. *F* XXV.9.1 De...2 deo] om. *F* 3 opinantur] oppinantur *P* 7 unam] una *F* XXV.10.1 Contra...2 occuparunt] om. *F* 6 emanantes] enuntiantes *F*

40 non²]fol. 112ra *P* XXV.9.14 est|fol. 112rb *P* XXV.10.6 intelligentie|fol. 86r *F*

Calodemons and demons,[1] and the divine scriptures of the Old and New Testaments almost all testify regarding the essence of angels' nature. But because of the above error that the human soul spiritually dies with the flesh, therefore they especially should pay attention to that chapter of proofs where we adduced, namely, that the soul is immortal.

On the soul

Everything which gives life to another thing lives in itself, just as the body is given life by the soul, therefore it gives life to itself, and whatever gives life to itself is immortal, therefore it is certainly immortal.[2] Whatever is immortal from the beginning is not corrupted and always endures. But the soul does not hold any contradictory elements within it, since it has not heat or cold, neither humidity or dryness, since it is not a body, but a whole spiritual substance, pure and simple. Therefore without a doubt it is immortal. Likewise all rational things that move themselves are immortal, but the rational soul moves itself, therefore it is immortal. Further we read that it is created in the image of God, hence just as its exemplar is immortal, so is it immortal, as is seen by clear reason, for it is in the image of its creator, it is unlikely to be different from Him.

That the soul is immortal

Further it was proven above in the first title of the first book that there is one sole God, the cause of all things, hence if God exists, it remains that He is found to be just, since otherwise God would not exist were He not just. (Pseudo-Clementines 3.40) "But we see some men who are blasphemers of God, leading their lives in injustice and pleasure and when they reach the end of life, die in their beds among their own and are buried honorably. Others yet worship God, keeping in their lives to all justice and sobriety, preserving temperance, perish in the desert for the preservation of righteousness, so that they are not accounted worthy even of a burial." Since therefore it has been determined that God is just, as a consequence it is necessary that there be another age in which each one is rewarded according to his merits and experiences the justice of God, therefore the soul does not perish with the body, but unendingly endures immortal. This indeed was the reason blessed Peter gave against Simon Magus in proof of the soul's immortality, just as is read in the Clementine books.

Cath: Likewise the true prophet Jesus Christ, who was proven to be the Truth by signs and prodigies from heaven, (Cassiodorus, *De Anima*, 22) "God will give continuous punishment to the evildoers and perpetual joy to the

---

[1] Plato, *Meno* or *Laws* 848D (see above, n. 1 to VII.22,118). [2] Cp. Cassiodorus, *De Anima*, IV. 20.

sit fas cum hesitatione recipi quod dignatur omnipotens diuinitas et hec ratio est cassiodori.

De immortalitate

Preterea legimus et inuenimus in sacris scripturis. tam christi animam quam sanctorum multorum nec non et aliquorum iniquorum post carnis interitum. uel cum suis propriis corporibus uel de nouo ad horam assumptis aetras apparuisse in hoc mundo. igitur immortale est anima. item anima in sui rationem apprehendit immortalitatem. sed nichil potest aliquid comprehendere nisi si tam quantum est comprehensum. cum ergo anima comprehendat immortalitatem utique et ipsa immortale est.

De illis qui non possunt inducere aliquam rationem seu auctoritate alicuius philosophi dicentis quod mundus sit eternus

De hoc quod dicunt quod mundus est eternus probatum est contrarium iam superius. de anno uero quem dicunt nec rationem inducunt penitus ullam. nec auctoritatem alicuius phylosophi. uel alicuius sani capitis dictum. sic dicimus. quia ea facilitate qua sua sola presumptione concludunt. eadem merito reicimus tamquam stultum. quia prorsus ueritate caret quod ratione uel auctoritate non probatur.

Quod secundum patarenum omnia sunt ordinata a deo et a diabolo

Quod omnia sunt ordinata a deo et a diabolo ab illo uero bona. ab isto mala et necessario sic eueniunt. probatur tam per rationes naturales. quam per scripturas.

Patarenus: Constat quod omnes homines sunt uel predestinati ad uitam uel presciti seu prescripti ad mortem. sed deus non presciret aliquos ad mortem. nec diabolus ullos predestinaret ad uitam. igitur boni a deo sunt ad uitam predestinati et mali a diabolo sunt presciti seu prescripti ad mortem. sed prescientia uel predestinatio maxime dei non potest esse nisi uera. igitur predestinati non possunt dampnari. nec saluari prescripti.

Catholicus: Respondeo quod male diuisisti et pessime conclusisti. cum enim diuisisti quod omnes homines aut sunt a deo predestinati. aut a diaboli prescripti. male posuisti. quia omnes sunt a deo predestinati et prescripti. nec obstat illa assertio tua scilicet quod deus non prescribet ad mortem quia falsa est. quia licet deus nullos presciebat ad dampnationem. omnes tamen dampnatos presciebit ad penam. et penam pro culpa infligere bonum est. conclusio autem tua quam fecisti scilicet si deus predestinauit uel prescripsit. ergo non potuit mutari non est uera. quia diuina prenotatio

good." Therefore the soul is immortal. "So it is wrong to accept with hesitation what the divine and all powerful One graciously promises." This is Cassiodorus' account.

On Immortality

Further we find and read in the holy scriptures that the soul of Christ and of the saints, as well as some of the unjust, appeared in this world after the destruction of the body, either with their own bodies, or having assumed a new body for a time from the aether. Therefore the soul is immortal. Further the soul apprehends immortality by its own reason, but nothing can comprehend anything unless it is in itself comprehensible. So since the soul can comprehend immortality, it is to that extent immortal.

On those who are not able to adduce any argument or give the authority of any philosopher saying that the world is eternal

Regarding those who say that the world is eternal, a contrary proof is already given above. About the [Great] Year of which they speak they do not have any argument at all, nor do they have the authority of any philosopher, or the sayings of any sane person, we say therefore for this reason they conclude it only on their own presumption, and on that merit we spurn it as foolish, since it utterly lacks truth since it is unproven by reason or authority.

That according to the Patarenes everything is ordained by God or by the devil

That everything is ordained either by God in the case of good things, or by the devil in the case of bad things, and so they happen by necessity. This is proven as well by natural argument as by the scriptures.

Pat: It is evident that all men are either predestined to life or they are foreknown and foreordained to death. But God does not foreknow those destined to death, neither does the devil predestine any to life, therefore the good are predestined by God to life and the evil are foreknown and foreordained by the devil to death. But the foreknowledge or predestination of God is especially not able to be false, therefore the predestined are not able to be damned, neither the reprobated to be saved.

Cath: I reply that you have distinguished badly and so you have concluded wickedly. For since you distinguished that all men either are predestined by God or reprobated by the devil, you specify badly, since all men are predestined and reprobated by God. Neither does your assertion apply, namely, that God does not reprobate unto death, which is false, because although He foreknows no one unto damnation, yet all the damned are foreknown unto punishment, and to inflict a punishment for a fault is good. So your conclusion which you have made, namely, if God predestined or reprobated therefore He cannot be changed, is not true, since the divine foreknowledge does

---

XXV.13.1 De immortalitate] om. *F* 6 aetras] aeris *F* XXV.14.1 De...3 eternus] om. *F* 5 anno] tertio *P* XXV.15.1 Quod...2 diabolo] om. *F* | add. hereticus. dicta patarenus *F* 7 Patarenus] om. *F* 8 predestinati] predestinata *P* 12 seu prescripti] om. *F* 18 prescripti] add. n *P* exp. 22 dampnationem] culpam *F* 23 culpa] dampnatum *P*

XXV.14.5 uero|fol. 113ra *P* XXV.15.5 rationes|fol. 86v *F* 20 assertio|fol. 113rb *P*

naturam rerum proprietatemque non mutat. Talia apud se presentia spectat. qualia in tempore olim pro futura prouenient. et nec rerum iudicia confundit. neque quia nouit omnia necessitatem sic ueniendi illis imposuit. nec aliter esse potest. ut nesciat omnia. quia aliter non esset deus nisi omnia sciat. et adde hoc de ista materia. ut notatum est in contraria primi titulum libri in rationibus naturalibus patarenorum.

Patarenus: Mattheus. xii. quomodo potestis bona loqui cum sitis mali etcet. ergo mali subiacent necessitati non loquendi bona.
Catholicus: Responsio. intelligitur quod mali non possunt bene loqui seu bene facere scilicet de facili. uel ex sua uirtute uel meritorie quam diu mali sint. uel ex mala intentione.
Patarenus: Idem. xv. omnis plantatio quam non plantauit pater meus celestis eradicabitur etcet. ergo necessario dampnatur omnis plantatio que ex deo non est.
Catholicus: Responsio. necessario dampnatur postquam non est dei plantatio. sed non necessario fuit. dei non plantatio. uoluntarie enim peccat homo. set necessario ex diuina iustitia recipit penam.
Patarenus: Idem xx. sedere autem ad dexteram meam uel sinistram non est meum dare uobis sed quibus paratum est a patre meo etcet. ergo sicut ordinatum est a deo regnum celorum. ita eum dari oportet.
Catholicus: Respondeo sic intelliguntur uerba illa. non est meum dare uobis id est non ego carnaliter ut putatis id est in quantum uidetur consanguineus suus. dabo eum uobis. sed quibus paratum est id est secundum merita uite. hoc enim non persone. sed uite paratum est. uel aliter. non est meum dare uobis scilicet superbis sicut ad huc estis. sed quibus paratum est id est humilibus.
Patarenus: Idem. xxvi. pater mi si possibile est transeat a me calix iste etcet. ergo mors christo fuit preordinata.
Catholicus: Responsio. poterat enim non mori si uoluit. ipse enim dixit. iohannes. x. potestatem habeo ponendi animam meam etcet. sed ipse uoluit mori ut mortem nostram destrueret. uoluit dico uoluntate diuina et etiam humana secundum rationem. licet sensualitas repugnaret et contra uoluntatem rationis assotiatam diuine. impossibile erat eum non mori.
Patarenus: Item lucam. xiii. dico uobis querunt intrare et non poterunt etcet. ergo non possunt homines saluari nisi sit eis ordinatum.

not change natural things and properties. He beholds in Himself in the presence of such things as at some point in time [i.e. in the future] will come forth; and He neither confounds His judgments of things nor, because He knows all things, has He imposed on them a necessity of happening thus. Neither could it be otherwise, that He might not know all things, for otherwise He would not be God unless He knew all. And add to this matter what was noted above in refutation in the first book on the natural arguments of the Patarenes.

Pat: Matthew 12 (12:34) "how can you speak good things, since you are evil." Therefore evil people are subjected to the necessity of not speaking good.
Cath: Response. It is understood that evil people are not able to speak well or to do well, namely, not easily, or they have been evil for a long time from their own power or merit, or from an evil intention.
Pat: Also 15 (15:13) "Every plant which my heavenly Father has not planted, shall be rooted up." Therefore of necessity every plant is damned which is not of God.

Cath: Response. It is necessary to damn later those plants not of God, but it was not necessary that they not be plants of God, for man voluntarily sinned, but it is necessary that they receive punishment on account of divine justice.
Pat: Also 20 (20:23) "But to sit on my right or left hand is not mine to give to you, but to them for whom it is prepared by my Father." Just as the kingdom of heaven is ordained by God so it must be given by Him.
Cath: I reply that this passage is to be understood thusly, 'it is not mine to give to you,' that is, I shall not give it to you according to the flesh, that is, in so far as he seems His kinsman, but [I shall give it] to him for whom it has been prepared; that is, according to the merits of his life. For this has been prepared not for a person, but for a life, or put differently, it is not mine to give to you, namely, to the proud, just as you still are, but to whom it has been prepared, the humble.
Pat: Also 26 (26:39) "Father, if it is possible let this chalice pass from me." Therefore the death of Christ was preordained.
Cath: Response. He was able not to die if He wished, for He Himself said in John 10 (10:18) "I have power to lay down my life." But He wished to die so that He might destroy our death. I say He willed it by His divine will and also by His human [will] according to reason, although His sensual nature resisted even against the wish of His reason joined to His divine [will]. [In this way] it was impossible for Him not to die.
Pat: Also Luke 13 (13:24) "for many, I say to you, shall seek to enter, and shall not be able." Therefore men are not able to be saved unless it be ordained for them.

XXV.15.35 quomodo...36 mali¹] Matt. 12:34. 42 omnis...43 eradicabitur] Matt. 15:13. 50 sedere...52 meo] Matt. 20:23. 62 pater...63 iste] Matt. 26:39. 65 potestatem...66 meam] Ioh. 10:18 (om. animam meam | add. eam *Vulg.*) 71 dico...72 poterunt] Luc. 13:24.

---

27 Talia] taliaque F 28 pro...29 futura] *may be a gloss on* in tempore olim. 30 ueniendi] venienda P 33 contraria] add. secundum F primi titulum] transp. F 56 id est] om. P 57 sed] scilicet F 64 non] add. non P 65 uoluit] voluisset P 67 nostram] naturam F

49 set|fol. 113va P 73 ordinatum|fol. 113vb P

Catholicus: Responsio. non possunt intrare in regnum dei qui rectam uiam non incedunt. que est artitudo uite. et quod possint ire per illam uiam et sic intrare. ostendit cum dicit ibi. contendite intrare per angustam portam.

Patarenus: idem xviii. impossibile est ut non ueniant scandala etcet. ergo scandala sunt ordinata cum non possint uitari. et hoc a diabolo. cum dominus dicat ibi. ue autem homini illi per quem scandalum uenit etcet.

Patarenus: Item. iohannes. iii°. non potest homo accipere quicquam nisi fuerit ei datum de celo etcet. et vi. omne quod dat mihi pater ad me ueniet etcet. et infra. nemo potest uenire ad me nisi pater qui misit me traxerit illum. etcet. ergo necessario saluatur qui saluari debet.

Catholicus: Responsio. quod a deo saluatur principaliter et auctoritate quicumque saluatur. quia dat ei deus gratiam per quam saluatur. et dicitur quod trahitur ideo. quia non est aliquis qui ex uitio nature corrupte uel temptationibus illectus non sit in aliquo sue saluti contrarius.

Patarenus: idem. xv. tui erant. etcet. ergo non poterant dampnari postquam dei erant.

Respondeo non dicit hec quod non possent dampnari. sed dicit quod erant dei per gratiam non solum per creationem.

Item ad romanos. viii. nam quos presciuit et predestinauit etcet. hoc dicit de omnibus electis. ergo bona bonis sunt preordinata. ad hoc est. ad ephesios. i°. qui predestinauit nobis in adoptionem filiorum etcet.

Catholicus: Responsio. prescit deus futuros bonos quia boni futuri sunt. bonitas ergo illarum causa est presciencie dei. et non prescientia dei est causa bonitatis illorum et cum prescit deus futuros bonos quod est ab eterno. preparat ei gratiam suam et postea uocat eos in tempore et cum inuenit eos paratos iustificat illos et sic postea glorificat eos. igitur ista prescientia dei et predestinatio et uocatio et iustificatio et glorificatio ex nobis dependet et sic intelligitur quod sequitur quos autem et predestinauit hos uocauit. etcet.

[**Patarenus:**] idem. 9. cum enim nondum nati fuissent aut aliquid boni egissent aut mali. ut secundum electionem propositum dei maneret. non ex operibus sed ex uocante dictum est ei quia maior seruiet minori. sicut scriptum est Jacob dilexit esau autem odio habuit. etcet. et infra. misereor cui miserebor igitur non uolentis neque currentis. sed miserentis dei est. etcet. Ex hiis patet expressim quod bona et mala ueniunt ex preordinatione.

Cath: Response. Those who do not follow the right path are unable to enter into the kingdom of God, which is the narrow life, and that they are able to go by that way and so to enter He indicates when he says there, "work to enter by the narrow gate."

Pat: Also 17 (17:1) "It is impossible that scandals not come." So scandals are ordained by God since they cannot be avoided, and this from the devil, when the Lord says there, "but woe to that man by whom scandal comes."

Pat: Also John 3 (3:27) "A man cannot receive anything, unless it be given him from heaven." And 6 (6:37) "All that the Father gives to me shall come to me." and later (6:44) "No man can come to me, except the Father, who has sent me, should draw him." Therefore it is necessary that one is saved who ought to be saved.

Cath: Reply. That one is saved primarily by God and by authority everyone is saved, since God gives him the grace to be saved. And it is said that 'he is drawn' for the reason that no one is such that, from the vice of a corrupt nature or temptations of allurement, he is not an opponent of his own salvation in some respect.

Pat: Also 15 (17:6) "they were yours" Therefore those are not able to be damned after they belonged to God.

I reply that he does not say there that they were not able to be damned, but he says that they were God's by grace and not only by creation.

Also Romans 8 (8:29) "those whom he foreknew he also predestined." This is said of all the elect, therefore the good are preordained to good things, to this pertains Ephesians 1 (1:5) "He who predestined us to the adoption of children."

Cath: Reply. God foreknows that they will be good because they are going to be good; therefore their goodness is the cause of God's foreknowledge, and God's foreknowledge is not the cause of their goodness, and when God foreknows that they will be good, which is so from eternity, He prepares His grace for them and later calls them in time, and when He finds them prepared He justifies them and thus later glorifies them. Therefore this foreknowledge of God and predestination and call and justification and glorification depends on us and so what follows is to be understood (Rom 8:30) "but those whom he predestined he also called."

[**Pat**] The same in 9 (9:11-13) "For when the children were not yet born, nor had done any good or evil – that the purpose of God, according to election, might stand – not from works, but of him who calls, it was said to her, 'The elder shall serve the younger.' As it is written: 'Jacob I have loved, but Esau I have hated.'" And later (9:15-16) "For he said to Moses, 'I will have mercy on whom I will have mercy,' So then it is not of him who wills, nor of him

---

79 impossibile...80 scandala¹] Luc. 17:1. 82 ue...uenit] Luc. 17:1 (om. scandalum uenit| add.ueniunt *Vulg.*) 83 non...84 celo] Ioh. 3:27. 85 omne...ueniet] Ioh. 6:37. 86 nemo...87 illum] Ioh. 6:44 (illum) eum *Vulg.*) 95 tui erant] Ioh. 17:6. 100 nam...predestinauit] Rom. 8:29. 102 qui...103 filiorum] Eph. 1:5 (nobis) nos *Vulg.*) 113 quos...uocauit] Rom. 8:30. 115 cum...119 habuit] Rom. 9:11-13. 120 misereor...121 est] Rom. 9:15-16 (om. misereor cui | miserebor] add/ cuius misereor *Vulg.*)

---

81 ibi] add. uerumtamen. F 89 Catholicus] om. F 90 quia...91 saluatur] om. P 95 Patarenus] om. F | idem...99 creationem] om. P 104 prescit] om. P | deus] add. presciuit P 105 illarum] illorum F 108 ei] sic PF, reading eis 110 igitur] ergo F 115 9] xx F

83 Item|fol. 87r F 103 etcet|fol. 114ra P

Catholicus: Responsio. non uult apostolus ostendere quod ex preordinatione ueniant bona et mala. sed quod bone ueniunt principaliter ex gratia dei. quam ipse dat quibus uult et quando uult. quia apud ipsum omnium est auctoritas et ex subtractione gratie eius fiunt mala. tamen in nobis est habere gratiam dei uel non habere. quia ipse paratus est nobis dare illam si uolumus. quia omnibus offert illam et omnibus contemptoribus subtrahit eam ut dicit apostolus. ii^a. ad timotheus. ii^o. si negauerimus et ille negabit nos. si non credimus. ille fidelis permanet negare se ipsum non potest etcet. et ad hebreos. xii. tamquam filiis offert se deus nobis. etcet. eodem modo soluitur idem. secunda. ad timotheus. i^o. non secundum opera nostra. sed secundum propositum suum etcet.
Patarenus: Item. ii^a. ad timotheus. ii^o. cognouit dominus qui sunt eius etcet. ergo sunt preordinati.
Catholicus: Responsio. cognoscit deus omnia et tamen non omnibus necessitate imponit.
Patarenus: Item ad titum. i^o. quam promisit qui non mentitur deus ante tempora secularia etcet. ergo ante tempora secularia preordinata est gratia bonis a deo.

Catholicus: Responsio. quod preordinata est ex dei bonitate igitur bonis id est dei bonitas uult bona bonis dare. non tamen preordinatum est a deo. quod ille non possit esse malus nec iste bonus.
Patarenus: Item. iude. i^o. subintroierunt enim quidam homines qui olim prescripti sunt in hoc iudicio etcet. ergo mali prescripti sunt ad mortem quod non nisi a male deo potest esse.
Catholicus: Responsio. quod mali sunt a deo non ad dampnatam culpam sed ad penam.
Patarenus: Item actus. v. si uero ex deo est non poteritis dissoluere illud etcet. ergo sic. necessitate preordinationis uallatum fuit.
Catholicus: Responsio. non sequitur propter hoc quod sit preordinatum sed sequitur quod sit consilium illud quod ex deo est. non potest ita redigi ad nichilum sicut consilium quod est ex hominibus.
Patarenus: Idem. xiii. et crediderunt quotquot erant preordinati ad uitam eternam etcet. ergo sunt preordinati qui sunt saluandi et non possunt alii saluari.
Catholicus: Responsio. non dicit quod alii qui non erant preordinati id est predestinati non possent saluari. uel dicitur preordinati. qui preordinari

who runs, but of God who shows mercy." From these it is plainly clear that good and evil come from preordination.
Cath: Response. The Apostle did not wish to show that good and evil came by preordination, but that good comes principally from the grace of God, which He gives to whom and when He wishes. And with Him is all authority to make one bad by the removal of grace, yet it remains in our power to have the grace of God or to not have it, since He is prepared to give it to us if we wish, since He offers it to all, and to all who despise it He withdraws it from them, as the Apostle says in 2 Timothy 2 (2:12–13) "If we deny him, he will also deny us. If we do not believe, he continues to be faithful, he cannot deny himself." And Hebrews 12 (12:7) "God deals with you as with his sons." It is resolved in the same way in 2 Timothy 1 (1:9) "not according to our works, but according to his own purpose and grace."

Pat: Also 2 Timothy 2 (2:19) "The Lord knows his own," therefore they are preordained.
Cath: Reply. God knows all things and yet does not impose necessity on all things.
Pat: Also Titus 1 (1:2) "which God, who does not lie, has promised before the ages of the world." Therefore before the foundations of the world grace was preordained to the good by God.
Cath: Reply. Those things preordained from the goodness of God are therefore good, that is, the goodness of God wills to give good things to the good, yet nevertheless it is preordained by God, since that one is unable to be bad nor is this one able to be good.
Pat: Also Jude 1 (1:4) "For certain men secretly entered in, who were written of long ago unto this judgment." Therefore the evil reprobate are destined to death for they are unable to do evil except by God.
Cath: I reply that the evil are not damned by God on account of guilt but on account of punishment.
Pat: Also Acts 5 (5:39) "But if it be of God, you cannot overthrow it." So thus it was of necessity established by preordination.
Cath: Reply. It does not follow on account of this that it is preordained, but it follows that it is that counsel which is from God cannot be reduced to nothing, unlike the advice which is from men.
Pat: Also 13 (13:48) "and as many as were ordained to life everlasting, believed." Therefore they are preordained who are to be saved and others cannot be saved.

Cath: Reply. It did not say that others who were not preordained, that is, the predestined, are unable to be saved, or did it say to the preordained, who wished to be

---

133 si^1...**135** potest] 2 Tim. 2:12-13. **135** tamquam...**136** nobis] Heb. 12:7 (nobis] uobis *Vulg.*) **137** non...**138** suum] 2 Tim. 1:9. **139** cognouit...**140** eius] 2 Tim. 2:19. **143** quam...**144** secularia] Tit. 1:2. **150** subintroierunt...**151** iudicio] Iud. 1:4 (iudicio] iudicium *Vulg.*) **156** si...**157** illud] Act. 5:39. **163** et...**164** eternam] Luc. 13:48.

127 et...uult^2] om. *F* **133** negauerimus] negaueritis *F* | negabit] negabimus *P* **143** titum] timotheum *F* **152** quod] qui *F* **155** culpam] om. *P* **158** fuit] erat *F*

131 uolumus|fol. 114rb *P* **159** Catholicus|fol. 114va *P* **165** saluandi|fol. 87v *F*

uoluerunt id est illi crediderunt qui sanum consilium recipere uoluerunt.

Patarenus: Item apocalypsis. vi. donec adimpleantur numerus conserui eorum etcet. et xxi. in finem. non intrabit in illa aliquod coinquinatum faciens abhominationem et mendacium nisi qui scripti sunt in libro uite agni. ergo non possunt saluari ultra certum numerum.

Catholicus: Responsio. numeris ille nichil aliud est nisi omnes qui saluari uoluint usque ad finem seculi. de quo numero omnes esse possumus. quia omnes possumus saluari si uolumus. qui omnes saluandi sunt scripti in libro uite agni id est in presciencia christi. quia ipse omnia nouit.

Nota catholice quod omnes argumentationes istorum hereticorum sumuntur in hac parte ex istis uel quia legitur quod deus scit quid facturi sunt omnes et quid in omnibus sit futurum. uel quia omnis gratia principaliter et auctore sit ab ipso. uel quia bonis bona et malis mala iustitia preparauit uel quia quidam secundum quasdam condiciones in quas uoluntarie uenitur necessitatem habuit hunc uel illum finem consequendi secundum rerum naturam.

[**Patarenus:**] quod autem omnia inferiora regantur secundum cursum superiorum corporum etiam anime probatur. pluribus rationibus. uidemus enim plerosque natos sub hoc signo uel sub illo. uel in hoc cursu alicuius corporis superioris uel in illo. item reperimus aliquos seruasse in suis negotiis horas et puncta secundum cursus corporum superiorum talia recepisse. qualia illorum factum esse naturi asserunt naturalis. igitur omnia inferiora secundum uirtutem corporum superiorem reguntur atque dicuntur.

Catholicus: Responsio. quia similiter uidistis aliis facientibus sua facta sub illis horis et punctis aliter accidisse. igitur non sunt ex illorum uirtute hominum casus.

Patarenus: item nos uidemus homines esse letiores et tristiores et anxiores atque magis timidos et planiores animi. uel magis irascibiles et acutioris ingenii uel pigroris esse uno tempore quam alio et una hora quam alia. et uno puncto quam alio. et ista scilicet letitia et tristitia. et huiusmodi sunt. nonne ergo anime dicuntur atque reguntur secundum uirtutem corporum superiorum.

Catholicus: Respondeo quod istud contingit occasione corporis in quo anima congluttinata est. in cuius complexionibus uirtus superiorum operatur. sicut contigit uinum in uegete positum affici uel infici. ex uasis qualitatibus bonis siue malis. uerumptamen anima humana potest aut uincere illas uirtutes

preordained, that is, those believed who wished to receive the saving counsel.

Pat: Also Apocalypse 6 (6:11) "until the number of the saved should be filled up." And 21 at the end (21:27) "There shall not enter into it anything defiled, or that works abomination or lies, but those who are written in the Lamb's book of life." Therefore there will be no salvation beyond a fixed number of people.

Cath: Reply. That number is nothing else except all those who wish to be saved until the end of the world, in which number we are all able to be included, since we are all able to be saved if we wish. All those to be saved are written in the Lamb's book of life, that is, in the foreknowledge of Christ, who Himself knows all things.

Note here Catholic, that all the arguments of these heretics are taken up in this section from these because it is read that God knows what all men are going to do and what is going to happen to everyone, or that all grace is principally and in origin from Him, or because He has prepared with justice good things for the good and bad things for the bad or because a certain person in accordance with certain conditions, in which His coming is voluntary, has had the necessity of attaining this or that end according to the natural order of things.

[**Pat:**] But since all inferior things are ruled according to the course of superior bodies also it is proved about the soul, by many reasons. For we see the majority of those born under this sign or that, or in the orbit of some superior body or of that. Further we find that some who have observed in their business dealings the hours and moments according to the courses of superior bodies, assert that they have received such things as have happened to them by nature, naturally. Therefore they say that all inferior things are ruled and commanded according to the power of superior bodies.

Cath: Reply. Since similarly you observe that it has happened differently to some going about their business under the same hours and conjunctions of stars, therefore the dealings of men are not under their power.

Pat: Further we see men to be happier and sadder and more anxious and more timid and simpler in soul, or to be angrier and of more brilliance or more slothful at one time than another, or at one hour rather than another, and at one [stellar] position rather than another, and these, namely, joy and sadness are also in this way. It is not therefore that the soul is named and ruled according to the influence of superior bodies?

Cath: I reply that this happens as a consequence of the body to which the soul is closely joined, in whose conjoining a higher power is at work, as happens to wine when it is placed in a cask is bettered or corrupted by the good or bad qualities it contains. Nevertheless the human soul can overcome the powers of superior bodies by the power of

---

172 donec...173 eorum] Apoc. 6:11 (adimpleantur) compleantur | numerus] om. *Vulg.*)   173 non...176 agni] Apoc. 21:27 (illa) eam *Vulg.*)

187 sit] scit *F*   191 habuit] om. *P*   197 reperimus] repperimus quod *P*   199 superiorum] add. qui *P* | talia...202 superiorem] om. *F*   203 Catholicus] om. *F*   207 Patarenus] om. *F*   212 nonne] om. *F*

188 bonis|fol. 114vb *P*   216 in¹|fol. 115ra *P*

corporum superiorum per potestatem liberi arbitrii. aut in illi defensione et maxime cum dei gratia uel per peccatum. sicut et uidemus per experientiam accidisse plerumque. unde et ypocras traditur dixisse. industria mutat naturam etcet. preterea uidemus quod illud idem tempus est uni ad letitiam est alteri ad tristitiam et modo et sic de aliis. quare patet quod etiam in corporibus inferioribus non semper in omnibus dominentur corpora superiora.

Patarenus: Item pluuia et tempestas nix. glacies. turbatio aquarum. frigus et calor et huiusmodi. sunt effectus signorum celestium seu corporum superiorum in inferiora corpora preuenientes. ergo omnis uirtus que in inferioribus est procedit a superioribus corporibus.

Catholicus: Respondeo quod istos effectus habent superiora corpora in inferioribus corporibus tantum et non in anima. nec etiam corpora inferiora habent omnes suo effectus a superioribus corporibus. neque corpora superiora neque inferiora dominantur in anima per potestatem liberi arbitrii maxime si a dei gratia adiuuatur.

Patarenus: Item magister uester christus dicit. nonne xii sunt hore diei etcet. ergo credebat quod in una hora esset alia uirtus quam in alia.

Catholicus: Responsio. stulte. magister noster sicut uere spiritualis est ita uere spiritualiter loquebatur. uocabat enim se diem. unde dixit alibi. Ego sum lux mundi et appostolos suos uocabit horas diei. unde alibi dixit de illis. uos estis lux mundi. etcet. quod horas diei uocat. quoniam ipsa accepta gratia per ipsum lucidi erant. et uocat eos. xii. quia tot miro fuerunt. ab ipso per electi. unde et dixit ego uos. xii^{cim}. elegi uel si ad litteram de die naturali et eius hominis uelitis intelligere ut per similitudinem illius de spirituali loquatur. planum est et hoc est quia xii^{cim}. sunt hore diei scilicet equinoctiali et in istis est ambulandum. sicut si homo non uult offendere pedes. unde subdit. ambulate dum lucem habetis ut uos tenebre non comprehendant. qui ambulat in tenebris offendit. etcet. De uirtute uero illarum horarum nichil aliud dixit. nisi quia sunt ad ambulandum in luce. Sed responde mihi patarenorum. nonne credis summo phylosopho naturalium uidelicet Aristoteli? et scio quod credis. sed ipse dixit in libro de pura bonitate quod deus benedictus influit bonitates suas in creaturis bonitate una. et in libro physicorum ait. quod deus gloriosus facit uenire pluuiam et platonium asserentis et scio quod asserentis sed ipse rogat in libro timeo. quod deus det ei gratiam scribendi ea que pertineant ad honorem eius et utilitatem hominum. ergo ipsi

free will, either in its own defense or especially with the grace of God or through sin, just as we see happening for the most part generally by experience. Hence Hippocrates is held to have said, "Diligent effort changes nature." Further we see that at the same moment one is overjoyed, while another is driven to sadness, and so of other states in the same way. Hence it is clear that even in inferior bodies, superior bodies might not always rule in all things.

Pat: Yet rain, storms, and snow, ice, sea tempests, cold and heat and the like are effects of the heavenly movements or of superior bodies prevailing upon inferior ones. So all power which proceeds in inferior things comes only from superior bodies.

Cath: I reply that superior bodies cause these effects only on inferior ones, and not on the soul. Not even do inferior bodies receive all their effects from superior bodies, nor do superior or inferior bodies dominate in the soul, on account of free will especially, if it be aided by the grace of God.

Pat: Also your master Christ says (Jn 11:9) "Are there not twelve hours in the day?" So He believed that at one hour there was more power than at another.

Cath: Response. You fool! Our master was speaking spiritually, since He was really spiritual. For He called Himself the day, wherefore He spoke elsewhere (8:13) "I am the light of the world." And He called his apostles the hours of the day, when He spoke about them in another place (Mt 5:14) "You are the light of the world," which one calls the hours of the day, because they had become luminaries, having accepted grace through Him. And He called them the twelve, since they bore such wonder from Him by their election, wherefore he said (Jn 6:71) "have I not chosen you twelve?" Or if you wish to interpret literally of the natural day and of His men, just as He spoke spiritually of them by resemblance, it is plain that this is because the twelve [Apostles] are the hours of the day, namely, the half of the day in which one walks [in the light]. Just as man does not wish to dash his foot, wherefore he adds (12:35) "Walk while you have the light, so that the darkness does not overtake you. And he who walks in darkness, does not know where he goes." He says nothing else about the power of those hours, except that they should walk in the light. But answer me this, O Patarene, why do you not believe the greatest of natural philosophers, namely Aristotle? And I know what you believe. But as he said in the book of Pure Goodness (Liber de Causis 22, 173-174) "that the blessed God infuses his goodness into creatures by one goodness," and in the book of Physics he says that (Aristotle, Meteorology, 1, 340a25)

---

243 nonne...244 diei] Ioh. 11:9.　248 Ego...249 mundi] Ioh. 8:12.　250 uos...mundi] Matt. 5:14.　253 ego...elegi] Ioh. 6:71.　259 ambulate...260 offendit] Ioh. 12:25 (om. offendit) nescit quo uadat Vulg. | this reading was common in 13th century, also in Hugh of St. Cher and St. Albert).　266 quod...267 una] Pseudo-Aristotle, *Liber de Causis* 22, 173-174.　267 deus...268 pluuiam] Aristotle, *Meteorology*, 1, 340a25. Likely an Islamic or Latin interpolation in the *translatio vetus*.　270 quod...271 hominum] Plato, *Timaeus*, 72d.

241 per] propter F　258 si] om. P

241 maxime|fol. 115rb P　248 uocabat|fol. 88r F　268 platonium|fol. 115va P

phylosophi attribuerunt gratiam donorum spiritualium et temporalium. deo benedicto et non uirtuti superiorum corporum. silete itaque infatuati astrologi.

Quod mundus est eternus

Patarenus: Deus est prima causa mundi. sed causa et creatum sunt relatiua. sed causa est eterna scilicet deus. ergo et creatum est eternum. ergo mundus est eternus.

Catholicus: Solutio hoc nomen causa de deo. non significit aliquam relationem ad creaturam. cum deus dicatur causa. in comparationem ad creaturam. sed significat solummodo diuinam essentiam et effectum in creatura. unde sensus est. deus est prima causa mundi id est diuina essentia est et mundus est ab eo.

Patarenus: Item prima causa omnino semper se habet. quia non cadit in ea mutabilitas. ergo semper facit idem. ergo si semel fecit mundum. ergo semper.

Catholicus: Solutio. dicimus quod duplex est principium uoluntatis et nature. causa uoluntaria dilatoria que operatur cum preliberatione. nulla autem non et illa proposito tua locum habet in naturali causa et non in uoluntaria et deus est causa uoluntaria mundi et non naturalis.

Patarenus: Item aut deus potuit ab eterno facere mundum. aut non. si non ergo impotens fuit. si sic. aut sciuit aut non. si non et postea uoluit. ergo uarietas in eo fuit. ergo ab eterno potuit sciuit et uoluit. ergo fecit.

Catholicus: Solutio dicimus quod deus uoluit facere mundum ab eterno. Sed hec determinatio ab eterno. determinet hoc uerbum uoluit. si autem determinet hoc uerbum facere falsa est.

Patarenus: Item omnis sapientia dei fuit eterna. similiter bonitas. similiter potentia et sic de aliis. ergo et omnis uoluntas. ergo uoluntas faciendi mundum. sed hoc sufficiebat ad hoc ut mundus esset. ergo sunt ab eterno.

Catholicus: Solutio. dicimus quod uoluntas duplicem habet respectum scilicet ad uolentem sicut est eternam et ad uolitum et sic non est eterna.

Patarenus: Item bonitatis et largitatis. est effluere. ergo summe bonitatis et summe largitatis est summe effluere. sed ab eterno fuit summe bonus et summe largitatis. ergo ab eterno summe effluxit. sed non est aliud fluxus iste quam mundi facturo ergo ab eterno.

"the glorious God causes rain to come," and you claim Plato and I know you claim him, but he asks in Timaeus (72d) that God give him the grace of writing those things which pertain to his honor and to the advantage of men. Therefore these philosophers ascribed the grace of spiritual and temporal gifts to God's blessing and not to the power of superior bodies, so silence, you foolish astrologers!

That the world is eternal

Pat: God is the first cause of the world, but cause and creation are related. The cause is eternal, namely, God. Therefore the creation is also eternal. Therefore the world is eternal.

Cath: Solution. This name 'cause' in regards to God does not signify a certain relation to creation, since God is called 'cause' in comparison to a creature, it means merely the Divine essence and its effect in creatures. The sense of this is: God is the first cause of the world – that is – He is the divine nature and the world comes from Him.

Pat: Also the first cause always entirely possesses Himself because He is not subject to change, therefore He always does the same thing. So if He once made the world, He therefore always makes it.

Cath: Solution. We say that the principle is twofold: of the will and of nature. The voluntary cause is not immediate and is worked in freedom, and that proposition of yours assigns it as a natural cause and not a voluntary, and God is the voluntary, not the natural, cause of the world.

Pat: Further, either God could make the world from all eternity, or not. If not, then He is impotent, if yes, either He knew or not, if not then He wished it later, therefore there was variance in Him, therefore from eternity He was able, He knew and He willed it, therefore He made it.

Cath: Solution. We say that God wills to make the world from all eternity. But this determination 'from all eternity,' is determined by the word 'wills.' But if it is determined by the word 'make,' the [solution] is false.

Pat: Yet all the wisdom of God was from eternity, also His goodness, also His power, and so on. Therefore so is all of His will, and His will caused the world to be made. But this sufficed to this point, that the world has existed, therefore it is from eternity

Cath: Solution. We say that will has a dual aspect, namely, to the one willing and that is eternal, and to the thing willed and this is not eternal.

Pat: Further it belongs to goodness and liberality to diffuse themselves, therefore the highest good and the greatest liberality is diffusive in the highest degree, but the highest good and greatest liberality was from eternity, therefore it has flowed out of Him in the highest degree, but there is no other outflowing than the creation of the world made by Him, therefore it is from eternity.

---

272 attribuerunt] actribuerunt *P* **XXV.16.**1 Quod...eternus] om. *F* 2 Patarenus] om. *F* 3 eterna] essentia *F* 5 Catholicus] om. *F* 6 ad creaturam] om. *P* 11 Patarenus] om. *F* 14 Catholicus] om. *F* 20 Patarenus] om. *F* 25 Catholicus] om. *F* 26 hec] Similiter *P* 34 Catholicus] om. *F* 35 scilicet] add. et *P* exp. | sicut...36 uolitum] om. *P* 37 Patarenus] om. *F*

XXV.16.23 potuit|fol. 115vb *P*

Catholicus: Responsio. dicimus quod largitatis proprium non est semper effluere. immo dare et non dare tempore et loco.

Patarenus: Item si mundus non fuit ab eterno. ergo deus erat otiosus antequam mundus fieret. quod inconueniens est cum otiositas sit uitium et contra aristotelem. qui dixit nulla substantia otiosa est etcet. quanto magis diuina?

Catholicus: Responsio. quod non fuit otiosus. non enim omnis cessatio est otium. sed illa quando est operandus. non est enim otiosa diuina essentia apud quam est uiuere et intelligere. licet hoc sit suum esse. uel secundum theologum. apud quem est eterna generatio et processio ab eterno.

Patarenus: Item antequam deus fecerit mundum. aut ille status bonus. aut non. si bonus erat quare ergo uariauit. si non secundum hoc non erat nisi propter solitudinem. ergo non erat bonum ipsum esse sine creaturis esse ergo ab eterno debuit ipsas producere. sed forte fecit quicquid debuit ergo ab eterno fecit mundum.

Catholicus: Respondeo quod bonus erat ille status antea et bonus quidem fuit postea.

Patarenus: Item si deus fecit mundum in tempore. uidetur quod penitetur de hoc quod non fecit eum ante cum de nouo fecerit. quasi uidens quod non erat bonum quod tam diu cessauerat.

Catholicus: Respondeo quod incepit non quasi penitens de cessatione. sed quasi incipiens quod ab eterno uoluerat. et uiderat esse faciendum. non enim affectiones cadunt in eo.

Patarenus: Item quare solum ante centum uel mille milia annorum. non fecit deus mundum cum tam modicum sit tempus ex quo fecit.

Catholicus: Responsio. quod nulla est hec questio. idem enim posset operari. si iam per centum milia uel mille milia durasset mundus. post quinque milia a creatione. Si autem queritur quare in tali tempore produxerit eum deus. Respondetur. O altitudo diuitiarum etcet. Sed responde tu mihi qui dicis mundum esse eternum. aut est creatus uel factus aut non. Si primum est. ergo non est eternus. Si secundam ergo non habet causam efficientem. ergo nec finalem. quia finale mouet efficientem. ergo nec formalem. quia finale finitur a fine. ut patet in singulo. qui motus finem operatur et secundum finem dat formam olle. item nec materialem. quia materia non est sine forma. quod patet falsum esse et primum falsum est. ergo mundus non est ab eterno. preterea gesta seculorum

---

XXV.16.48 nulla...est] This concept is found in Aristotle, *Metaphysics*, II, however that work had not yet been translated. Possible sources include Averroes or, more probably, St. John Damascene, *De Fide Orth.*, II.2. 80 O...diuiti-arum] Rom. 11:33.

42 Catholicus] om. *F* 45 Patarenus] om. *F* 47 contra] om. *P* 50 Catholicus] om. *F* 52 otiosa] om. *P* 59 esse] om. *P* 61 forte] om. *F* | fecit¹] om. *P* 63 Catholicus] om. *F* 65 Patarenus] om. *F* 66 penitetur] potuerit *P* 69 Catholicus] om. *F* 72 eo] deo *F* 73 Patarenus] om. *F* | solum] saltum *F* 74 tam] add. diu *P* exp. 76 Catholicus] om. *F* 79 queritur] om. *F* 82 est...factus] esse creatum uel factum *F* 84 finalem] formalem *F* | quia...86 finale] om. *F* | add. forma *F* 89 patet] om. *P*

51 omnis|fol. 116ra *P* 56 mundum|fol. 88v *F* 78 durasset|fol. 116rb *P*

per scripturas mittuntur ad posteros et inueniuntur scripture que narrant acta seculi a tempore quo fides asserit mundum esse factum et non antea et si dicis scripturas perisse in diluuio que narrabant anteriora facta. hoc nichil est. quia facta ante diluuium inueniuntur. per illos qui saluati fuerunt in archa. eodem modo et alia reseruari potuerunt ergo mundus non fuit antequam fides asserit catholici. item dicitur et probatur experientia quod montes propter sui grauitatem semper descendunt et ualles implentur. ergo si mundus fuisset ab eterno iam dudum terra fuisset adequata. sed hoc falsum est. ergo mundus non est eternus. preterea mons cadens defluit et saxum transfertur de loco suo. lapides excauentur aqua et alluuione paulatim terra consumitur. ergo si mundus fuisset ab eterno. riuuli et fontes qui fluunt in montibus tam diu est quod extrauassent lapides et saxa usque ad fundum et sic de aliis quod falsum est. ergo mundus non est eternus.

Quod omnia bona et mala sint preordinata a deo

Patarenus: Quod autem omnia sint a deo preordinata mala et bona et necessario eueniant omnia patet per casus et fortune status. quos uidemus cotidie mirabiliter et ineuitabili modo euenire.

Catholicus: Respondo quod in omnibus que conueniunt ratio est. quia nulla in terra sine causa. licet in omnibus eam comprehendere non possimus. eueniunt autem huiusmodi plerumque ex humana industria. quandoque autem cooperantibus naturalibus causis. plerumque uero ex dei iudiciis. uel ad probationem hominum uel ad correctionem. tamen necessario preordinata non sunt.

De illi qui dicunt non esse angelos et qui dicunt animam finiri cum corpore

Sequitur probare pro illis qui dicunt non esse angelos et qui aiunt animam finiri cum corpore et qui delirant omnia uariari ab eterno. secundum cursum anni magni quem dicunt. ubi sciendum est quod de angelis nichil allegant. uide et nos de illa materia respondere non possumus. cum nichil nobis opponatur.

Probatio secundum patarenum quod anima moritur cum corpore

anima inest corpori sicut forma subiecto. sed sicut non potest esse materia sine forma. sed nec forma sine materia. ergo dextructo corpore dextruitur anima. ergo perit cum corpore anima.

of errors. So the world is not from eternity. Further secular deeds are written and transmitted to future generations and are found in scripture, which narrate secular events in time by which faith asserts that the world is made, and did not exist previously, and if you say that the scriptures that recounted these early events perished in the flood. This makes no sense, they were able to be preserved in the same manner as those who were saved in the Ark, therefore the Catholic faith asserts that the world did not exist previously. Further it is said, and proven by experience, that mountains descend on account of their weight, and valleys are filled, so if the world were eternal, the earth would have long ago become flattened, but this is false, therefore the world is not eternal. Further the mountain flows out, falling down and the rocks are moved from their places. Stones are hollowed out by water and floods and, little by little, the earth is consumed. So if the world had been from eternity the rivers and fountains which flow from the mountains would have run for so long that they would have dislodged the stones and rocks all the way to the bottom, and that, like the others, is false. Therefore the world is not eternal.

That all good and bad things are preordained by God.

Pat: The fact that all good and evil things are preordained by God and happen by necessity is evident in the existence of chance and fortune, which we see daily happening in a wonderful and inevitable way.

Cath: I reply that there is a reason for all things that happen, for nothing on earth is without a cause, though we are unable to understand it for all things. Things happen for the most part by human industry, yet also by the cooperation of natural causes, and still others by the judgment of God, be they for the testing of men or for their correction. Yet they are not preordained by necessity.

On those who say that angels do not exist and who claim the soul's existence ends with that of the body

It remains to prove for those who say angels do not exist and who say that the soul dies with the body and who are deluded thinking that all things are random from eternity. According to the course of the 'Year' which they call 'Great,' where it must be known that they adduce nothing concerning angels. And see that we are unable to reply to these contentions, since they propose nothing against us.

Proof according to the Patarenes that the soul dies with the body

The soul belongs to the body just as a form to a subject, but just as matter cannot be without form, so neither form without matter, therefore in the destruction of the body the soul is also destroyed, so the soul perishes with the body.

---

94 narrabant] naturaliter *F*   97 reseruari] seruari *F*   104 et...105 alluuione] om. *P*   XXV.17.1 Quod...2 deo] om. *F*   3 Patarenus] om. *F*   7 Catholicus] om. *F*   13 correctionem] corruptionem *P*   XXV.18.1 De...2 corpore] om. *F*   3 pro] om. *F*   XXV.19.1 Probatio...2 corpore] om. *F*

103 preterea|fol. 116va *P*   XXV.19.3 inest|fol. 116vb *P*

Catholicus: Solutio dicimus quod quedam est supra essentiam. que est ita substantia quod nullo modo forma ut intelligentiam. quedam ita forma quod nullo modo substantia. scilicet per se stans. licet posset dici substantia sicut forma substantia uel dicitur substantia ut anima bruti. et quedam est forma et substantia ut anima rationale et de hac non sequitur quod licet destruatur in quantum forma quod simpliciter destruatur. quia habet naturam per se subsistendi.

Patarenus: Item dicit augustinus. in libro contra epistolam fundamenti. res ideo sunt corruptibiles. quia de nichilo etcet. sed anima de nichilo est ergo corruptibilis.

Catholicus: Solutio dicimus quod corruptibile dicitur duobus modis. uno modo quod non habet ex se causam sue permanentie. neque habet ex se subsistere. sic solus deus est incorruptibilis et omnia circa primum corruptibilia. alio modo dicitur corruptibile quod habet in se causam sue corruptionis. sicut conposita corporalia que constant. constituta ex contrariis sicut corporalia et etiam elementum. quod habet formam que habet contrarium et per hunc modum spiritus et corpus sunt corruptibilia. Magis autem res que habet quantitatem diuisibilem ut corpus celeste.

Patarenus: Item peccatum corrumpit bona naturalia anime. ergo tantum potest peccare homo quod omnia bona naturalia corrumpit. sed illis corruptis non remanet anima. ergo potest anima corrumpi.

Catholicus: Solutio dicimus quod licet peccatum adimat aliquid de bono naturali qui est habitus naturale. non tamen contingit totum illud corrumpi quia sunt ibi infiniti inseri in anima sicut in angelis recto sunt infiniti contingentie.

Patarenus: Item quicquid est citra primum secundum boetium est hoc et hoc. ergo compositum. ergo resolubile in suas partes. ergo corruptibile. sed anima est citra primum. ergo resolubile.

Catholicus: Solutio. dicimus secundum illos qui dicunt quod anima sit ex materia et forma spirituali simul cum anima congregata quod est resolubile in illa secundum rationem et non secundum rem. Non enim esse omne compositum resolubile est secundum rem in sua componentia. secundum alios uero qui dicunt quod est omnino simplex. dicimus quod est hoc et hoc id est multa non ex quibus fit sed que in ea sunt. unde notandum quod inter simplices substantias est substantia que caret partibus nec alicui componitur.

Cath: Solution. We say that some things are beyond essence, such as substances that are in no way forms such as intelligence, yet others of such forms that are in no manner substances, namely, those that are able to exist by themselves. Although substance may refer to the substantial form or substance may be used regarding the soul of a beast. And such is the form and substance of a rational soul, and from this it does not follow that insofar as it is destroyed as to form that it is absolutely destroyed, since it has the nature to subsist by itself.

Pat: Yet Augustine says in the book against the "Fundamental Epistle" (c. 38, 40), "yet because things are corruptible, they are from nothing." But the soul is from nothing therefore it is corruptible.

Cath: Solution. We say that a thing is corruptible in two ways: in one sense we mean that it does not in itself have the cause of its own existence in time, neither does it have from itself what it takes to subsist. Thus God alone is incorruptible and all things are corruptible in light of the first cause. In another sense, we speak of 'corruptible' about something that has in itself the cause of its own corruption, just as happens with corporeal things composed of contraries, like bodily things, and even an element which has a form which has a contrary, and in this way the spirit and the body are corruptible things. All the more something that has divisible quantity like a heavenly body.

Pat: Yet sin corrupts the natural good of the soul, therefore only man can sin, since all natural good things corrupt. But with everything being tainted this soul cannot remain untainted. So the soul can be corrupted.

Cath: Solution. We say that although sin takes something away of the natural good which is the natural condition of the soul, yet it does not happen that it is corrupted entirely since there are an infinity of things planted in the soul, just as in the good angels there are an infinite number of contingencies.

Pat: Also, whatever is besides the first thing according to Boethius (De Trinitate, 2) "it is this and that", therefore it is composed and able to be reduced to its parts, therefore corruptible, but the soul is less than the first thing, therefore it can be reduced to parts.

Cath: Solution. We say so far as concerns those who say that the soul is composed of matter and spiritual form, with the soul that can be reduced to these parts according to reason [mentally] and not according to the thing itself. For not every composite thing is resolvable into its component parts according to the thing itself. But so far as concerns the others who say that it is entirely simple, we say that "it is this thing and that," that is, many things not out of which it is made but which are in it. Therefore it must be noted that among simple substances there is a

---

XXV.19.17 res...18 nichilo¹] Augustine, *Contra epistolam manichaei quam vocant Fundamenti*, c. 38, 40. 41 est...hoc²] Boethius, *De Trinitate*, 2 (also cited in St. Albert, *De Trinitate* and *De Hebdomadibus*).

---

7 Catholicus] om. *F* 8 substantia] om. *P* | add. forma *P* 9 ut intelligentiam] substantia *P* | quedam...10 substantia] om. *P* 15 destruatur] dextruarur *F* 16 Patarenus] om. *F* 20 Catholicus] om. *F* 28 contrarium] contrariam *F* 31 Patarenus] om. *F* peccatum...32 anime] corrumpit bona peccatum naturalia animae *P* 33 naturalia] om. *P* | corrumpit] corrumpet *F* 35 Catholicus] om. *F* 37 totum illud] transp. *F* 38 inseri] om. *F* 39 infiniti] add. cinguli *P* 40 Patarenus] om. *F* 41 et hoc] om. *F* 44 Catholicus] om. *F* 46 congregata] concreata *P* 48 esse] om. *P* 53 alicui componitur] transp. *F*

9 intelligentiam|fol. 89r *F* 31 naturalia|fol. 117ra *P*

nec ei aliquid componitur ut primum. Est aliqua que caret partibus nec componitur alicui. sed aliquid id est accidens componitur ei ut intelligentia et hec minus simplex. Est et tertia que caret partibus tamen alicui componitur et ei aliquid et hec minus simplex.

Item de eodem

[**Patarenus:**] Item uix intellecta leditur et debilitatur a passionibus corporis ut patet in egris et sanis et senibus et morientibus ergo possibile est naturaliter ipsam posse anichilari sicut debilitari et infirmari.

Catholicus: Solutio diciums quod anima non leditur nec infirmatur nec debilitatur in illis casibus sed occupatur cura aliquod ut cum uidet exteriora ex illa occupatione accidit quod non potest illi operationi intellectuali uacare. sed ibi et quod certum sit sic patet. Nam sanat a uirtute animali. statim quasi nichil passa. libera redit ad suas operationes et si possibile esset ipsam statum ad aliquod corpus transferri bene dispositum. ita exerceret actiones suas quasi nichil passa.

[**Patarenus:**] Item anima sequitur conditionem corporis in crescendo ut in pueris. ergo sic in diminutione corporis ut etiam uidetur in senibus. ergo in deficiendo omnino ergo deficet cum corpore.

Catholicus: Solutio dicimus quod uis intellectiua nec crescit neque decrescit. nec essentia anime. unde si possibile esse uidere anima senis non appareret senior anima. pueri. secundum exercitium uero et actum profici in scientia posset tamen dici secundum naturales quod anima rationalis habet secundum quod rationalis est duas potentias. unam que dici potest intellectus inseparabilis qui dicitur etiam materialis. a qua potentia dicitur homo rationale. aliam que dicitur intellectus separabilis. et huius est consideratio species in fantasmatibus. potentia uero sensibilis. et ideo iste intellectus est media potentia inter sensibilem potentiam et intellectum separabilem et ideo dicitur anima secundum istum est in confinio trinitatis et temporis. secundum istum posset dici quod anima sequitur conditiones corporis et concedi potest quod iste est corruptibile. non tamen ideo essentia anime corruptibile est.

substance which lacks parts and is not composed for anything [else], nor is anything else, being first, composed for it. There is some [substance] which lacks parts and is not composed for anything [else]; rather something, that is, an accident, is composed for it, such as intelligence, and this is less simple. There is also a third [substance] which lacks parts, yet is composed of something [else] and something for it, and less simple.

More on the same

[**Pat.:**] When the power of the intellect is injured and weakened by bodily passions as happens in both the sick and the healthy, the old and the dying, therefore it is possible for it naturally to be annihilated just as it can be weakened and sickened.

Cath: Solution. We say that the intellectual power is not injured or weakened or sickened in those cases, but is occupied by some existing care so that it seems from which occupation it happens that it is unable to attend to that intellectual activity. But it is here and that is certain. For when it heals by a power of the soul, immediately it is as if it suffered no diminution in power, it returns freely to its proper operations and, if it were possible that it might be in that state transferred to some well disposed body, it would so pursue its activity as if nothing had happened.

[**Pat.:**] Further the soul follows the condition of the body in growth, as [it does] in children, so also in the weakening of the body as also is seen in the elderly. So in every single deficiency, it declines with the body.

Cath: Solution. We say that the intellectual power neither grows nor decreases, neither does the essence of the soul, whence if it were possible to see the soul of an old man, it would not appear as the older soul of a child. According to practice and action one can advance in knowledge, yet according to natural things that the rational soul has in itself are two powers, one which can be called the inseparable intellect which is also called the material intellect, by which power a man is called rational, and another which is the separable intellect, and this considers the forms through phantasms by its sensitive power, and so this intellect is a mediate power between the sensitive power and the separable intellect,[1] and so is called the soul according to which is the meeting of eternity and of time. According to this one can say that the soul follows the conditions of the body and concede that it is able to be corruptible, yet nevertheless the essence of the soul cannot be corrupted.

---

57 Est...58 simplex] om. *F* **XXV.20.1** Item...eodem] om. *F* 6 Catholicus] om. *F* 8 cura] circa *P* 10 uacare] uacaret *P* | sic] om. *F* 17 diminutione] dimmitione *P* 19 Catholicus] om. *F* 20 anime] amore *P* 25 duas] add. partes *P* exp. 26 qui...28 separabilis] om. *F* 28 consideratio] considerare *F* 29 sensibilis] add. fantasmata *P* | et] om. *F* 32 trinitatis] sic *PF* leg. eternity.

XXV.20.2 debilitatur|fol. 117rb *P* 31 intellectum|fol. 117va *P* 34 concedi|fol. 89v *F*

---

1) This section is very similar to that of an anonymous Arts master of Paris, ca. 1225 (also used by Albert and Thomas), see Robert Pasnau. *The Cambridge Translations of Medieval Philosophical Texts.* Volume 3 (Cambridge: Cambridge University Press, 2003), 30.

[Patarenus:] Item salomon dicit in ecclesiastes. iii°. nihil habet homo iumentis amplius. etcet. ergo cum carne anima moritur.

Catholicus: Solutio. uerum est. quantum ad mortalitatem. uel loquitur more contionatoris in persona stultorum quorum uerborum solomen facit in finem libri ubi dixit. finem loquendi pariter omnes audiamus. deum time et mandate eius obserua. hoc est omnis homo. cuncta que fiunt adducet deus in iudicium. pro omni errato siue bonum siue malum sit. etcet. simile sapientiam. ii°. dixerunt enim impii cogitantes apud se non recte etcet. et ii^a. petri. iii°. hoc primum scientes quod uenient in nouissimis diebus illusores etcet. Sed respondete uos mihi. si essentia intellectus dependet a corpore prout dicitis et confortatio sequitur confortationem debilitatio debilitationem sicut patet in uirtute alibi que dependet ex corpore econtraria uidemus. in senibus enim est debilitatio corporis et maior uigor intellectus. ergo essentia intellectus non dependet ex corpore. ergo non perit cum corpore. Item omne mortale sua duratione paulatim debilitatur et deficit donec ueniat ad finem ultimum qui est mors. uirtus autem intellectus ipsa sua duratione proficit et inualescit. ergo est immortalis. item nulla potentia naturalis inclinat suum subiectum ad non esse. nec mouet ad destructionem. alioquin natura destrueret se. sed uirtus intellectiua hoc facit. ergo est inmortalis. item aristotelum dixit in libro de anima loquens de intellectu et hoc solum contingit separari sicut per peccatum a corruptibili. etcet. et in quarto hoc solum immobile et perpetuum etcet. preterea secundum argumentationes uestras et mundus esset corruptibilis et dextructibilis. igitur non esset eternus quod uos negatis. et nota catholice. quod isti predestinati introducunt auctoritates et rationes ad probandum de dextruxione omne anime que loquuntur de anima secundum uires animales. unde propter hoc male concludunt quod uis eius intellectuale et essentia eius sit dextructibilis.

Probatio quod paradisus est et infernus

Quod autem non sit paradisus uel infernus nullam rationem uel auctoritatem habent. nos autem possumus probare de facili paradisum et infernum esse. tum propter scripturas que hoc dicunt tam diuinas quam humanas. de diuinis planum est. de humanis

[Pat:] Also as Solomon says in Ecclesiastes 3 (3:19) "man has nothing more than beast." So the soul perishes with the flesh.

Cath: Solution. It is true in reference to mortality, or to speak in the manner of a preacher of those stupid words, Solomon concludes at end of the book (12:13–14) "Let us all hear together the conclusion of the discourse. Fear God, and keep his commandments, for this is the office of every man. And God will bring into judgment all things that are done, for every error, whether it be good or evil." Similarly Wisdom 2 (2:1) "For they have said, reasoning with themselves, but not rightly." And 2 Peter 3 (3:3) "Knowing this first, that in the last days there shall come deceitful scoffers." But answer this for me, if the essence of the intellect depends on the body just as you say, and comfort follows comforting and weakness follows weakening just as is plain in some of those powers which depend on the body as we see on the contrary. For in the elderly we see weakness of body and greater vigor of intellect, therefore the essence of the intellect does not depend on the condition of the body, so neither does it perish with the body. Further all mortals are weakened by degrees during their lives and decline until they come to the end of all things, which is death, but still the intellectual power waxes and grows during life, so it is immortal. Further no natural power inclines its subject towards nonbeing, neither does it move towards destruction, for otherwise nature would destroy itself, but the intellectual power does this, and so it is immortal. Further Aristotle says in *De Anima* speaking of the intellect, "this alone is able to be separated, as through sin from corruptible things." And in 4, "this alone is unmoved and perpetual." Further by your arguments, the world is corruptible and capable of destruction, therefore it is not eternal, which you deny. And mark well, O Catholic, that these predestinarians introduce authorities and arguments for proving the destruction of all souls which spoke of the soul according to its animal powers. So thence they conclude wrongly that the soul's intellectual power and its essence is destructible.

Proof that paradise exists, and also hell

That the nonexistence of paradise or hell has no reason or authority. Yet we are able to easily prove that paradise and hell exist, since on this account the divine scriptures as well as human writers speak of this. Of divine scriptures it is plain. Of human writers you have Tully (*De Senectute*, 23)

XXV.20.38 nihil…amplius] Eccl. 3:19 (iumentis) iumento *Vulg.*)   43 finem² …46 sit] Eccl. 12:13-14 (est) add. enim | homo] add. et | malum] add. illud *Vulg.*)   47 dixerunt…48 recte] Sap. 2:1.   48 hoc…50 illusores] 2 Pet. 3:3.   65 loquens…66 corruptibili] Aristotle, *De Anima*, 2, 2l 413b 24-29. "De intellectu et perspectiua potentia nihil adhuc manifestum est, sed uidetur gens alterum animae esse, et hoc solum contingit separari, sicut aeternum a corruptibili. Relique autem partes animae manifestum ex his, quod non separabiles sunt, sicut quidam dicunt."   67 hoc…perpetuum] Again redolent of Aristotle, Metaphysics, 4.5, "immobile et perpetuum et separabile" but that was not yet translated, possibly also again from Averroes or St. John Damascene.

40 Catholicus] om. *F* | quantum] item *P*   63 destrueret] dextrueret *F*   71 auctoritates] auctates *F*   72 omne] om. *F* | que] om. *P*   74 uis] uix *P*   XXV.21.1 Probatio…infernus] om. *F*   5 tum] cum *P*

60 proficit|fol. 117vb *P*

habes unde tullius. si mortuis ut quidam censetur nihil esse sententiam. nonne uereor ut mortui phylosophi me irrideant. et cato dixit in salustio quod sunt campi ameni parati ad delectationem bonorum in alia uita et loca thetra et obscura ad cruciatum malorum. Seneca etiam ait in libro epistularum ad lucillum neronem. recipit nos locus quem putabamus amissum etcet. item plato. socrates et aristotelos et omnes phylosophi. detestabant peccata et predicabant uirtutes et dicebant quod peccatores de peccatis punirentur et uirtuosi premium de uirtutibus habent. sed hoc non fiebant in hac uita. ergo credebant aliam esse in quo complerentur ista. item hoc exigit iustitia dei que reddit uniuicuique secundum opera eius quod non facit in hac uita semper. ergo reliquitur quod sit alia in qua complere debeat. preterea naturalis ratio et communis opinio quasi omnium hominum est et fuit maxime sapientium et sanctorum quod ita sit et credo etiam quod conscientia remordet istos predestinatos quod ita est. sed sodomitia eorum et alia nefanda peccata ipsorum sub quibus grauiter premuntur induxerunt eos in desperationis profundum. ut ita contempnant de dei materiam pariter et iustitiam. et ad suam quedam excusationem ne saltem coram hominibus uituperentur. dicunt non esse predictam peccantes in spiritum sanctum. reuereuerantibus eos conscientiis suis et ideo in hoc tempore nec in futuro uenia sunt digni sed res sunt eternum delicti.

"But if when dead, as someone thinks, there is no sensation, I am not afraid of dead philosophers deriding my errors," and as Cato said in Sallust (52.8 paraphrase) that there are "pleasant fields prepared for the enjoyment of the good in the next life and gloomy, desolate places for the torment of the wicked." Also Seneca says in his book of letters to Lucilius Nero (Epistle 63, at the end) "there is a place to welcome us, then he whom we think we have lost has only been sent on ahead." Further Plato, Socrates, and Aristotle, and all philosophers abominated sins and preached the virtues and said that all sinners would be punished for their sins and the virtuous would have the reward of their virtue, but yet this would not happen in this life, therefore they believed there to be another in which this would be fulfilled. Similarly it happened that this divine justice, by which he renders to each according to his deeds, did not always occur in this life, therefore it remained that there be another in which it ought to be perfected. Further natural reason and common opinion, just as there is in all men, but especially in the most wise and holy among them, [confesses] that there is such a life, and I believe also that conscience nags those Predestinarians since it is so. But sodomy and their other abominable sins by means of which lead them into the depths of despair, so that they condemn God's material world as much as His justice and by way of excuse they say that the above sins are not against the Holy Spirit lest they be at all events slandered before them. Whence their consciences beat them back, so neither in the present age, nor in the future one, are they worthy of pardon, for these are things pertaining to everlasting sin.

De propriis erroribus circumcisorum. qui grauius errare uidentur quam alii heretici

XXVI Concerning the particular errors of the Circumcisers,[1] who seem to err more grievously than other heretics

Sequitur uidere de propriis circumcisorum erroribus qui post patarenos et predestinatos inter nobis notos hereticos grauius errare uidentur. affirmant namque circumcisionem et sacramenta legis ueteris. pariter cum noue legis sacramentis ad litteram debere seruari. quorum heresis omnibus aliis antiquiorem traditur habuisse originem. iam enim tempore apostoli pauli pullulabat in orbem. dicuntur autem isti cricumcisi a circumcisione quam predicant et obseruant quorum stultitias testimoniis scripturarum de facili possumus confutare et primo de circumcisione ait enim apostolus

Now we pass to the particular errors of the Circumcisers who, after the Patarenes and the Predestinarians, are known to us as the heretics who err more grievously. For instance, they affirm that circumcision and the sacraments of the old law are on par with the sacraments of the new law, and ought to be observed literally. These heretics are more ancient than all others, having their origins in antiquity, for they had already sprung up in the world at the time of the Apostle Paul. They are called the Circumcisers, from those of the Circumcision, since they preached and observed these follies, so that we are easily able to

---

XXV.21.7 si...9 irrideant] Cicero, *De Senectute*, XXIII. 85 "Sin mortuus - ut quidam minuti philosophi censet - nihil sentiam: non uereor ne hunc errorem meum philosophi mortui irrideant." 9 quod...11 malorum] Sallust, *Bellum Catilinae*, 52.13 paraphrase, "falsa credo, existimans quae de inferis memorantur; diverso itinere malos a bonis loca taetra, inculta, foeda atque formidolosa habere." 13 recipit...amissum] Seneca, *Ep. ad. Luc. Nero.*, 63.16. (locus) add. aliquis | putabamus ammissum] putamus periise praemissus est).

11 thetra] thetram P 12 epistularum] om. P 23 opinio] oppinio P 29 et²] om. P 33 ideo] iam F XXVI.1.1 De...2 heretici] om. F 10 pullulabat] pullubat P | a] om. P

XXV.21.11 obscura|fol. 118ra P 28 contempnant|fol. 90r F XXVI.1.2 heretici|fol. 118rb P

---

[1] A minor group, perhaps only in Lombardy. They may have been related to the Passagians, see *The 'Summa contra Hereticos' attributed to Praepositinus of Cremona*, eds. Joseph N. Garvin and James A. Corbett (Notre Dame Press, 1959). However the two groups had some differences, see Vacarius, 436–444.

ad Galathas. ii°. sed neque titus qui mecum erat cum esset gentilis compulsus est circumcidi sed propter subintroductos falsos fratres etcet. idem. v. Ecce ego Paulus dico uobis. quoniam si circumcidamini nichil christus proderit uobis etcet. et infra. nam in christo ihesu neque circumcisio aliquid ualet. neque preputium. sed fides que per caritatem operatur etcet. item ad phylippenses. iii°. uidete canes. uidete malos operarios. uidete circumcisionem nos enim sumus circumcisio qui spiritu dei seruiuimus et gloriamur in christo ihesu et non in carne fiduciam habentes etcet. item ad titum. i°. sunt enim inobedientes multi uaniloqui et seductores. maxime qui de circumcisione sunt. quos opportet redargui etcet. item actus. xv. surrexerunt autem quidam de heresi phariseorum qui crediderunt dicentes quia oportet circumcidi eos precipuere quoque seruare legem moysi etcet. et infra. nunc ergo quid temptatis deum imponere iugum super ceruicem discipulorum etcet. Ex hiis patet manifeste quod circumcisio nullius fuit utilitatis post passionem christi et quicumque seruauit eam postea ponendo fidem in illa peccauit mortaliter. potuit autem seruari circa passionem christi. propter aliquas causas utiles sicut paulus seruauit eam in tito sine peccato et meritorie. quia synagoga deducenda erat ad tumulum. dum tam fides non ponentur in illa.

Catholicus: Responsio. quod nomen circumcisionis ponitur pro circumcisis id est pro iudeis. ergo sensus est uerborum pauli qui uidetur prohibere circumcisionem quod non debemus circumcidi id est effici iudei et quod circumcisio pro iudeis ponatur habes ad Galathas. secundo. Destras dederunt mihi et barnabe societatis ut nos in gentes ipsi autem in circumcisionem. licet quandoque circumcisio pro ipsis obseruantibus circumcisionem ponatur ut puta quando ad differentiam gentilium ponitur ut in predicta auctoritate ad Galathas. tamen ubi ponitur simpliciter sine positione populi gentile pro ipsa sine circumcisione supponit. presertim ibi. si circumcidamini etcet. quis enim de hoc dubitabat aut modo dubitat quod christus nihil prodesse debet iudeis ipsum negantibus et blasphemantibus. sed aliud erat de quibusdam christianis. qui seducti uolebant seruare circumcisionis et sacramenta legis mosayice pariter cum sacramentis noue legis. nec propter hoc credebant amittere christum. quibus apostolus dicit. si circumcidamini etcet. et quod ipsa circumcisio facta sit prohibita. habes expressim ad colosenses. ergo ubi dixit. circumcisi estis circumcisione non manu facta in expoliatione

refute them by scriptural testimonies. In the first place the Apostle says this about circumcision to the Galatians in chapter 2 (2:3–4) "But neither Titus, who was with me, being a Gentile, was compelled to be circumcised on account of false brethren brought in unaware." Likewise in 5 (5:2) "Behold, I Paul tell you that if you be circumcised Christ will profit you nothing." And later (5:6) "For in Christ Jesus neither circumcision nor uncircumcision is of any use, but faith that works through charity." Also to the Philippians in 3 (3:2) "Beware of dogs, beware of evil workers, beware of the circumcisers. For we are the circumcision, who in spirit serve God and glory in Christ Jesus, not having confidence in the flesh." Also to Titus 1 (1:10–11) "For there are also many disobedient, vain talkers, and seducers: especially they who are of the circumcision who must be reproved." Also Acts 15 (15:5) "But there arose some of the sect of the Pharisees who believed, saying, 'They must be circumcised, and be commanded to observe the law of Moses.'" And later (15:10) "Now therefore, why do you tempt God to put a yoke upon the necks of the disciples." From these it is perfectly clear that circumcision is of no use after the passion of Christ and whoever observes it after putting faith in Him sins mortally, though it could be observed around the time of the passion of Christ. Paul was able observed it in certain useful cases, such as that of Titus, without sin and meritoriously, for he was leading the synagogue to the tomb, while they no longer put faith in it.

Cath: Reply. The name of circumcisers was applied for the circumcised, that is, for the Jews. Therefore the sense of Paul's words, who seemed to prohibit circumcision, was that we ought not be circumcised, that is, be made for the Jews, so circumcision is presupposed for the Jews, and that you have in Galatians 2 (2:9) "They gave to me and Barnabas the right hands of fellowship, so that we should go to the Gentiles, and they to the circumcision." Although sometimes 'the circumcision' is applied to those observing circumcision, for example when used to differentiate the gentiles, as one sees in the aforementioned quote from Galatians, however when it is applied simply without reference to the gentiles for themselves it applies without supposing the circumcision. Especially there (5:2) "if you be circumcised." For who regarding this doubted or still doubts that Christ is of no help, owes this to the Jews who denied and blasphemed Him. But it was another matter concerning certain Christians who, having been seduced, wished to observe circumcision and the sacraments of the Mosaic Law together with the sacraments of the new law. Nor for this reason did they believe that Christ dismissed it, to which the apostle says "if you be circumcised." And that he made a prohibition of this circumcision, you have it expressly asserted in Colossians, where he said (2:11–12)

XXVI.1.14 sed...16 fratres] Gal. 2:3-4.   16 Ecce...18 uobis] Gal. 5:2.   18 nam...20 operatur] Gal. 5:6.   21 uidete[1]...24 habentes] Php. 3:2-3 (circumciosionem] concisionem *Vulg.*)   25 sunt...27 redargui] Tit. 1:10-11.   28 surrexerunt...30 moysi] Act. 15:5.   31 nunc...32 discipulorum] Act. 15:10 (ceruicem] ceruices *Vulg.*)   45 Destras...47 circumcisio-nem] Gal. 2:9.   52 si circumcidamini] Gal. 5:2.   61 circum-cisi...64 baptismo] Col. 2:11-12.

20 caritatem] karitatem P   37 tito] nato F   38 tumulum] tumulum nichilum F   40 Catholicus] om. F   42 est] om. F | qui] ubi F   51 sine] facti F   53 modo] add. non P   55 blasphemantibus] blasfemantibus P   58 amittere] admittere P   62 manu facta] manifesta P

26 sunt|fol. 118va P   49 gentilium|fol. 118vb P   62 circumcisione|fol. 90v F

corporis carnis sed in circumcisione christi consepulti ei in baptismo. ergo ueri christiani o canes non estis qui circumcisi estis circumcisione manifesta que consistit in expoliandis carnalibus uestris pudendis. Et nota. catholice quod cum ista auctoritate conclusi euidenter per gratiam dei alberto bustigano circumciso in ciuitate pergamensi.

Quod christus seruauit circumcisionem

ad romanos. vii. scientibus enim legem loquor quia lex in homine dominatur quanto tempore uiuit etcet. et infra. nunc autem soluti sumus a lege mortis in qua detinebamur ita ut seruiamus in nouitate spiritus et non in uetustate. Item ii^a ad corinthios. iii^o. qui et ydoneos nos fecit ministros noui testamenti. non littera sed spiritu. littera enim occidit etcet. et ad Galathas. i^o. miror quod sic tam cito transferimini ab eo qui uocauit in gratiam christi in aliud euangelium etcet. idem. iii^o. quicumque enim ex operibus legis sunt sub maledicto sunt etcet. idem. v. qui in lege iustificamini a gratia excidistis et infra. modicum fermentum totam massam corrumpit etcet. et iii^o. lex pedagogus uester fuit in christo ut ex fide iustificemur. at ubi uenit fides iam non sumus sub pedagogo etcet. Item ad colosenses. ii^o. nemo ergo uos iudicet in cibo aut in potu. aut in parte diei festi etcet. item ad hebreos. vii. translatio enim sacerdotio necesse est ut et legis translatio fiat etcet. ergo transierint legalia. transeant ergo et circumcisorum errores et adde pro ista materia que supra in primo libro allegauimus pro parte patarenorum contra uetus testamentum. illa enim que contra unam heresim oportet nos laudare aliquando. necesse est contra aliam uilipendere sicut est de lege moysi quam contra patarenos oportet nos comendare. contra uero circumcisos per uipendere et nota etiam quod quicumque contra patarenos. allegauimus supra in alio libro in tractatu de carnibus et huiusmodi non comedendis possumus hic inducere contra circumcisos.

Mattheus. v. non ueni soluere sed adimplere etcet. item lucam. ii^o. postquam consummati dies viii^o. ut circimcideretur puer etcet. et infra. postquam impleti sunt dies purgationis marie secundum legem moysi. tulerunt illum in ierusalem ut sisterent eum domino. sicut scriptum est in lege domini etcet. idem xvii. quos

"you are circumcised with circumcision not made manifest in despoiling of the body of the flesh, but in the circumcision of Christ, buried with Him in baptism." So having been you are no true Christians, O dogs, who by the visible circumcision which consists of a spoliation of the flesh of your private parts. And mark this, Catholic, that with this evident authority I defeated — naturally by the grace of God — Alberto Bustigano, a Circumciser in the city of Bergamo.[1]

That Christ observed circumcision

Romans 7 (7:1) "for I speak to those who know the law, that the law has dominion over a man, as long as it lives?" And later (7:6) "But now we are loosed from the law of death, in which we were detained, so that we should serve in newness of spirit, and not in the oldness of the letter." Also 2 Corinthians 3 (3:6) "Who also has made us fit ministers of the new testament, not in the letter, but in the spirit. For the letter kills." And Galatians 1 (1:6) "I wonder that you are so soon removed from him who called you into the grace of Christ, to another gospel." And chapter 3 (3:10) "For as many as are of the works of the law, are under a curse." In the same book, chapter 5 (5:4) "you who are justified in the law are fallen from grace." And later (5:9) "A little leaven corrupts the whole lump." And 3 (3:24–25) "Wherefore the law was our teacher in Christ, so that we might be justified by faith. But after the faith is come, we are no longer under a teacher." Also Colossians 2 (2:16) "Let no man therefore judge you in meat or in drink, or in respect of a festival day." Also Hebrews 7 (7:12) "For the priesthood being translated, it is necessary that a translation also be made of the law." Therefore those things concerned with the law will pass away. Therefore the errors of the Circumcisers shall also pass away and in favor of this is what was presented in the first book against the Patarenes about the Old Testament, for it is sometimes necessary for us to praise those things in [one type] of heresy, and it is necessary to condemn in another, as is the case concerning the Law of Moses about which we must give praise in our works against the Patarenes above in another book in the section on meats in which way to eat them, here we can bring it to bear against the Circumcisers.

Matthew 5 (5:17) "I did not come to abolish but to fulfill." Also Luke 2 (2:21) "After the eighth day was completed that the boy might be circumcised." And later (2:22–23) "And after the days of her purification according to the law of Moses were accomplished, they carried him to Jerusalem, to present him to the Lord, as it is written in

---

XXVI.2.2 scientibus…3 uiuit] Rom. 7:1.   4 nunc…6 uetustate] Rom. 7:6.   6 qui…8 occidit] 2 Cor. 3:6.   9 miror…10 euangelium] Gal. 1:6.   11 quicumque…12 sunt²] Gal. 3:10.   12 qui…13 excidistis] Gal. 5:4.   13 modicum…14 corrumpit] Gal. 5:9.   14 lex…16 pedagogo] Gal. 3:24-25 (uester) noster *Vulg.*)   17 nemo…18 festi] Col. 2:16.   19 translatio…20 fiat] Heb. 7:12.   32 non…adimplere] Matt. 5:17.   33 postquam…34 puer] Luc. 2:21.   34 postquam…37 domini] Luc. 2:22-23.   37 quos…38 sacerdotibus] Luc. 17:14.

66 pudendis] pudenda P   XXVI.2.1 Quod…circumcisionem] om. F   24 enim] uero F | oportet] opportet P   32 Mattheus] add. Catholicus P *(although this is really the heretic speaking)*

XXVI.2.5 nouitate|fol. 119ra P   30 huiusmodi|fol. 119rb P

---

1) Bustigano is otherwise unknown, but the reference provides evidence that the author disputed in the city of Bergamo.

ut uidit dixit. ite ostendite uos sacerdotibus etcet. et xxii. uenit autem dies azimorum in qua necesse erat occidi pascha et misit petrum et iohannem etcet. item ad romanos. ii°. circumcisio quidem prodest si legem obserues etcet. idem. iii°. quoniam quidem unus est deus qui iustificat circumcisionem ex fide etcet. ecce habes quod christus seruauit circumcisionem et legalia et illa seruari mandauit et apostolos comendat circumcisionem quare patet quod ista seruanda sunt a christianis.

Catholicus: Responsio. quod christus seruauit circumcisionem non in exemplum doctrine seruande sed in testimoniuim doctrine uenerande et hoc est quod dicit apostolus ad romanos. xv. Dico enim ihesum christum ministrum fuisse circumcisionis propter ueritatem dei ad confirmandas promissiones patrum etcet. et idem dico de legalibus que seruauit usque ad mortem. post mortem autem suam. noluit circumcisionem uel legalia seruari. unde dixit in morte sua. iohannes. xviiii. consummatum est scilicet uetus testamentum. quo ad cerimonialia et in apocalypsis. xxi. Ecce noua facio omnia et mattheus. vii°. omnia ergo quecumque uultis ut faciant uobis homines et uos facite illis. hec est enim lex et prophete etcet. et lucam v. quia nemo commissuram a uestimento nouo immittit in uestimentum uetus etcet. hinc est quod apostolus. secunda ad corinthios. v°. si cognouimus secundum carnem christum. sed nunc iam non nouimus. si qua ergo in christo noua creatura est uetera transierunt. ecce facta sunt noua etcet. nec obstat mattheus. v. non ueni soluere legem etcet. loquitur ibi de lege moralium preceptorum ut patet in his que inferius subdit scilicet audite quid dictum est antiquis non occides etcet. et infra. non mechaberis. non periurabis etcet. et infra. diliges proximum tuum etcet. omnia enim illa precepta moralia sunt de quibus exemplificat. nec obstat illud pauli. circumcisio quidem prodest etcet. quia de spirituali circumcisione loquitur. non enim qui manifeste iudeus est. neque qui in manifesto in carne circumcisio. sed qui in abscondito iudeis est et circumcisio cordis in spiritu non littera. et est potius pro nobis quod nullius utilitatis et laudis sit circumcisio carnale. uel loquitur ibi apostolus secundum sua tempora. quando locum habuit circumcisio carnale. ante christi passionem quia et tunc parum ualuit sine spirituali que latet in corde. item non obstat illud qui iustificat circumcisionem etcet. quia uocat ibi circumcisionem iudeos. sicut et gentiles preputium et quos omnes fides christi iustificat

the law of the Lord." The same in 17 (17:14) "Who when he saw, said, 'Go, show yourselves to the priests.'" And 22 (22:7–8) "And the day of the unleavened bread came on which it was necessary that the pasch should be killed. And he sent Peter and John." Also Romans 2 (2:25) "Circumcision profits indeed, if you observe the law." The same in 3 (3:30) "For it is one God who justifies circumcision by faith." Behold you have it that Christ observed circumcision and the things pertaining to the law, and commanded it to be observed, and the apostles commended circumcision, hence it is clear that these things were observed by Christians.

Cath: Response. That Christ observed circumcision not as an example to be kept, but as testimony to a doctrine to be venerated, and this is what the Apostle says in Romans 15 (15:8) "For I say that Christ Jesus was minister of the circumcision for the truth of God, to confirm the promises made unto the fathers." And in the same way I speak also of the things pertaining to the law which He observed up to His death. Yet after His death, He did not wish circumcision and the things pertaining to the law to be observed, for He said at His death, John 19 (19:3) "It is consummated," that is, the Old Testament, by which He meant the ceremonial law, as Apocalypse has it in 21 (21:5) "Behold I make all things new." And Matthew 7 (7:12) "All things therefore whatsoever you wish that men should do to you, do also to them. For this is the law and the prophets." And Luke 5 (5:36) "That no man puts a piece from a new garment on an old garment." Hence the Apostle in 2 Corinthians 5 (5:16–17) "If we have known Christ according to the flesh, but now we know Him so no longer. If then any be a new creature in Christ, the old things are passed away, behold all things are made new." Neither is Matthew 5 opposed to this (5:17) "I have not come to abolish but to fulfill." He speaks there of the moral commands of the law, as is made clear in these words which later follow, namely (5:21) "You have heard of old it said 'you shall not kill'" and later (5:21) "you shall not commit adultery" (5:33) "you shall not bear false witness" and later (5:43) "love our neighbor" for He was a model of all these moral precepts. Nor does Paul oppose this here (Rm 2:25) "Circumcision profits indeed." Since he is speaking of spiritual circumcision, (2:2829) "but he is a Jew, that is one inwardly; and the circumcision is that of the heart, in the spirit, not in the letter." And it is rather for us that carnal circumcision is of no use or [receives no] praise. Or the apostle speaks here according to his times, when carnal circumcision was common before the passion of Christ, since then it had equal power even without a spiritual circumcision, which lies hidden in the heart. Neither is (3:30) "who justifies circumcision" an objection. Since there he is speaking the Jews as 'the circumcision.'

---

39 uenit...40 iohannem] Luc. 22:7-8. 41 circumcisio...42 obserues] Rom. 2:25. 42 quoniam...43 fide] Rom. 3:30. 51 Dico...54 patrum] Rom. 15:8. 57 consummatum est] Ioh. 19:3. 59 Ecce...omnia¹] Apoc. 21:5. | omnia²...61 prophete] Matt. 7:12. 62 quia...63 uetus] Luc. 5:36. 64 si...67 noua] 2 Cor. 5:16-17. 68 non...legem] Matt. 5:17. 70 audite...71 occides] Matt. 5:21. 71 non mechaberis] Matt. 5:27. 72 non periurabis] Matt. 5:33. | diliges...tuum] Matt. 5:43. 74 circumcisio...75 prodest] Rom. 2:25. 76 non...79 littera] Rom. 2:28-29. 84 qui...circumcisionem] Rom. 3:30.

---

59 omnia¹] om. P 83 et tunc] om. P 84 iustificat] iustificatus P 85 circumcisionem iudeos] videns P

59 xxi]fol. 119va P | omnia¹]fol. 91r F 86 quos]fol. 119vb P

et non preputium neque legalia cum dicit ibi. arbitramur enim iustificari hominem per fidem sine operibus legis et subdit quoniam quidem iustificat circumcisionem ex fide et preputium per fidem etcet. et sic est auctoritas illa potius pro nobis. preterea non fuit bona argumentatio quod fecisti scilicet quod circumcisio facta est in christo et legalia seruata sunt. uel quia ipse seruauit ea usque ad mortem ut propter hoc debeamus hoc facere et seruare quia non omnia que facta sunt in christo ut que ipse fecerit seruare tenemur. quia et in egypt ductus est et fauum melle et pisces comedit et tamen sine illis saluari possumus. Tenemur namque ad illa. que docuit aut apostoli eius. Sed numquam inuenies quod ipse unum uerbum fecerit aut apud eius de circumcisione seruanda nec de legalibus post mortem ipsius. desidie. ergo circumcisio arare in boue et asino et quiesce et noli contra legem moysi facere quam dicis amplecti.

Just as faith in Christ justifies all the uncircumcised gentiles and not circumcision nor the Law. as he says there (3:28) "For we consider a man to be justified by faith, without the works of the law." And he adds (3:30) "who justifies circumcision by faith, and uncircumcision through faith." And thus is that authority superior for us. Further, you do not make a good argument, namely, that since Christ was circumcised and followed the law, or that because He observed it until His death, so on account of this we ought to follow and observe it, yet we are not bound to observe all things that were done by Christ, for example He was taken to Egypt and ate honeycomb and fish, and yet we are nevertheless able to be saved without doing those things. We are held to those things which He or His Apostles taught, but you will never find that He or His Apostles uttered one word about observing circumcision nor about the things prescribed by the Law after His death, therefore stop going on about circumcision or plowing with the ox and ass (Dt. 22:10), they are idle questions. Do not act contrary to the Law of Moses, which you claim to embrace.

De erroribus speronistarum. quorum proprii sunt tres

Sequitur de erroribus speronistarum quorum proprii sunt tres. primus est quod omnes homines portant peccatum ade secundum carnem tantum et non secundum animam. secundus est quo inaniter fit baptismus paruulorum et quod sine ipso saluentur. tertius est quod boni ante christi aduentum ascenderunt ad gloriam. errant autem in sacramento eucharistie cum patarenis de quo diximus supra in primo libro. errant et in omnibus communibus erroribus de quibus dicemus infra in libro tertio. descenderunt autem isti a quodam iudice placentino qui uocabatur sperone a quo dicti sunt speroniste. et exierunt uno eodemque tempore cum pauperibus leonistis et sunt in ritu uite illis oppositi quia leoniste uiuunt absque proprio et de elemosinis et sine uxoribus. econtrario isti possessiones tenent et in matrimonio degunt. quorum tres errores proprios confutamus per sacras scripturas.

XXVII Concerning the errors of the Speronists,[1] of which three are particular to them

We proceed to the errors of the Speronists, of which three are particular to them. The first is that all men bear the sin of Adam according to the flesh only, and not according to the spirit. The second is that they consider the baptism of infants to be in vain, and that they may be saved without it. The third is that the good men before the coming of Christ ascended into glory. Also they err concerning the sacrament of the Eucharist with the Patarenes, of which we spoke before in book one. They err in all the common errors of which we will now discuss in book three. These heretics descend from a former judge in Piacenza who was called Speroni, from whom they are termed Speronists, and they arose around the same time as the Poor of Lyons though they are opposed in their manners of living, since the Leonists live without possessions, relying on alms and without wives. On the contrary these Speronists hold possessions and continue to marry. Their specific errors we will refute through the sacred scriptures.

De baptisma

Marco ultimo. predicate euangelium omni creature qui crediderit et baptizatus fuerit saluus erit. qui uero non credidit condemnabitur etcet. iohannes. iii°. amen amen dico uobis nisi quis renatus fuerit ex aqua et spiritu sancto non potest intrare in regnum dei etcet.

On Baptism

In the last chapter of Mark (16:15–16) "preach the gospel to every creature. He who believes and is baptized will be saved, but he who does not believe will be condemned." John 3 (3:5) "Amen, amen I say to you, unless a man be born again from water and the Holy Spirit, he cannot

---

88 arbitramur...89 legis] Rom. 3:28. 89 quoniam...90 fidem] Rom. 3:30. 103 arare...asino] Dt. 22:10 XXVII.2.2 predicate...4 condemnabitur] Mar. 16:15-16. 4 amen...6 dei] Ioh. 3:5 (uobis) tibi *Vulg.*)

87 cum] unde F 91 potius] patris P 93 sunt] add. in eo F 95 debeamus] desperamus P 96 ut] ut aut F 100 Sed...101 eius] om. P 102 circumcisio] circumcise F XXVII.1.1 De...2 tres] om. F 11 primo] secundo P | communibus] omnibus P XXVII.2.1 De baptisma] om. F 4 condemnabitur] dampnabitur P

XXVII.1.9 errant|fol. 120ra P XXVII.2.3 fuerit|fol. 91v F

---

1) For this group particularly see Vacarius.

nullum excipit christus cum dixit. qui non crediderit etcet. scilicet per se uel per alium condemnabitur et cum dicit nisi quis renatus fuerit ex aqua etcet. sed multi sunt qui non habet peccata actualia mortalia maxime pueri. et tamen priuantur uita eterna si non sunt baptizati. ergo peccatum ade ledit animas. item ad romanos. v. si ob unius delictum mors regnauit per unum hominem etcet. audi stulte quod apostolus dixit quod mors regnauit per adam in omnes homines et quod peccatores erant ex peccato ade et quod eo erant dampnati. sed per gratiam ihesu chrisi liberati sunt et constat quod peccata sunt in anima et quod anime sunt que condempnatur principaliter. ergo in animabus erat peccatum ade et est nisi per fidem baptismum ihesu christi sit deletum. item ad ephesios. ii°. eramus natura filii ire sicut et ceteri etcet. ergo secundum peccatum ade quod nature erat insitum. erant filii dampnationis ante christi gratiam et non potes dicere quod loquatur de ira id est de dampnatione corporis in mortem. quia adhuc morituri erant sicut prius. preterea subdit. deus autem qui diues est in misericordia propter nimiam karitatem suam qua dilexit nos quia cum essemus mortui peccatis conuiuificauit nos christo. cuius gratia uos estis saluati. resuscitauit etcet. igitur peccatum ade transierat in animas. a quo liberabit eas christus. item ad colosenses. iii°. expoliantes uos ueterem hominem cum actibus suis etcet. sed ueterem homine uocat id quod contraximus ex ade peccato. sed carnis mortalitatem non possumus exuere. igitur secundum animam ex eius peccato habemus tunicam id est peccatum qua debemus expoliari. preterea scripture clamant quod christus liberauit et redemit omnes homines a morte et a peccatis. sed constat quod a penis et morte corporis non liberauit nec redemit. igitur a peccatus et morte anime. item. quicquid in uas uitiatum ponitur uitiatur. ergo anima posita in corpore ade corruptio corrumpitur. ergo peccatum ade transiuit et transit in animas non solum in corpora. et ex predictis si bene aduertisti patet similiter. quod non inaniter sit paruulorum baptismus. cum sine illo uita priuarentur eterna. quod autem nullus in celum seu celestem gloriam ascendit et istud iam satis est euidenter probatum. quia alias ad quod christus uenisset mortem passurus et quomodo diceretur quod omnes homines liberasset a morte per passionem et aduentum ipsius. uerumptamen quasdam spirituales auctoritates. super adam in quibus continetur expressim quod nullus in celum ascenderit ante mediatoris aduentum.

---

13 si...14 hominem] Rom. 5:17. 22 eramus...ceteri] Eph. 2:3. 27 deus...31 resuscitauit] Eph. 2:4-6. 33 expoliantes...34 suis] Col. 3:9.

7 christus] add. quod P 12 sunt] om. P 15 per] in F | in] per F 22 ii°] iii F 32 item] om. P 34 sed] si F 43 anima] omnia F 52 per] propter F

15 homines|fol. 120rb P 44 corrumpitur|fol. 120va P

Ante aduentum chrisi nullus ascendit in celum

Iohannes. iii°. nemo ascendit in celum nisi qui de celo descendit filius hominis qui etcet. item ad ephesios. iiii°. ascendens christi in altum captiuam duxit captiuitatem etcet. item ad hebreos iiii°. nam si illis ihesus requiem prestitisset numquam de alia loqueretur post hanc diem. itaque relinquitur sabatissimus populo dei etcet. idem. xi. in finem et hii omnes testimonio fidei probati inuenti sunt non acceperunt repromissionem deo pro nobis melius aliquid prouidente ut non sine nobis consummarentur etcet. igitur nulli ante christi aduentum ascenderunt in gloriam. possumus ad hoc inducere illas auctoritates que inducuntur supra in primo libro titulus. de humanitate christi. in rubricella de descensu eius ad inferos et multas alias quas hic inserere non curaui proper operis prolixitate.

Probatio quod homines non portant peccatum ade

Quod secundum animam non portant homines peccatum ade probatur ad Galathas. ultimo. ubi dicitur. unusquisque enim honus suum portabit etcet. ergo non punietur anima pro peccato ade in quo non consensit et in hunc modum possumus reducere omnes auctoritates in quibus dicitur quod pro peccato alterius alter non punitur.

Catholicus: Respondeo quod ibi loquitur de honere et pena quod ex actuali peccato portat aliquis quod tam ex suo et non ex alieno reportat aliquis. preterea eodem modo secundum tuam rationem non deberet peccatum ade transire in aliquid aliud corpus quia nullum aliud consensit. in eius peccato.

Patarenus: prima ad corinthios. xiiii°. in finem. omnia autem honeste et secundum ordinem fiant in uobis. etcet. quis autem ordo debeat seruari in baptismate dominus dicit. mattheus. ultimo. docete omnes gentes etcet. sed pueri non possunt doceri quia non intelligunt quid doceantur. igitur nulla illis conferunt baptismus. quid autem propter hoc non dampnentur patet ad romanos. iiii°. ubi dicit. ubi non est lex nec preuaricatio etcet.

Catholicus: Respondeo quod loquitur de magis qui debet doceri. preterea pueri etiam docentur in suis patrinis uel in securis quod autem dicit apostolus ubi non est lex etcet. loquitur de gentilibus qui non tenebantur ad legem moysi obseruationem quia illis non fuerat data. secus est de lege baptismi que data est omnibus. sine qua dominus dicit. nullum in regnum dei introire posse.

Before Christ's coming no one ascended to heaven

John 3 (3:13) "And no man has ascended into heaven, but he who descended from heaven, the Son of man." Also Ephesians 4 (4:8) "Ascending on high, he led captivity captive." Also Hebrews 4 (4:8–9) "For if Jesus had given them rest, he would never have afterwards spoken of another day. So there remains a day of rest for the people of God." Also 11, at the end (11:39–40) "And all these being approved by the testimony of faith, did not receive the promise, God providing some better thing for us, that they should not be perfected without us." Therefore no one ascended to glory before the coming of Christ. We are able to deduce this from the authorities we introduced above in the first book, under the title "of the humanity of Christ" in the subsection "on His descent into hell" and many others which I do not care to adduce here on account of the elongation of this work.

Proof that men do not carry the sin of Adam

That men do not carry the sin of Adam in the soul is proven in the last chapter of Galatians where it says (6:5) "For every one shall bear his own burden." So the soul will not be punished for the sin of Adam which it did not consent to, and in this manner we are able to adduce all the authorities in which it is said that people will not be punished for the sins of another.

Cath: I reply that what is referred to here is the burden and penalty of actual [sin] that one carries, and which one bears for his own part and not on the part of another. Furthermore, in the same way according to your rationale, the sin of Adam would not transfer in any other body since no one else consented to his sin.

Pat: 1 Corinthians 14, at the end (14:40) "But let all things be done decently, and according to order." Yet those ought to observe the order observed in baptism, as the Lord says in the last chapter of Matthew (28:19) "teach all nations." Yet children are not able to be taught nor are they able to teach, since they do not understand what they might be teaching, therefore baptism should not be conferred upon them, yet on account of this they are not damned, as is clear from Romans 4, where it says (4:15) "for where there is no law, neither is there transgression."

Cath: I reply that it is speaking more of who ought to be taught, further children are taught by their godparents or by the rod, now the Apostle says "where there is no law," he is speaking of the gentiles who do not hold to the prescriptions of the law of Moses, since it was not given to them, they do follow the law of baptism which was given to all, without which the Lord says (Jn 3:5) "no one is able to enter the kingdom of God."

XXVII.3.2 nemo...3 qui] Ioh. 3:13. 4 ascendens...5 captiuitatem] Eph. 4:8. 5 nam...8 dei] Heb. 4:8-9 (post hanc diem] posthac die *Vulg.*) 8 et...11 consummarentur] Heb. 11:39-40. XXVII.4.5 unusquisque...portabit] Gal. 6:5. 16 omnia...17 uobis] 1 Cor. 14:40 (in uobis] om. *Vulg.*) 19 docete...gentes] Matt. 28:19. 23 ubi²...24 preuaricatio] Rom. 4:15 31 nullum...32 posse] Ioh. 3:5.

XXVII.3.1 Ante...celum] om. *F* 3 qui] om. *F* | ephesios...5 hebreos] om. *P* XXVII.4.1 Probatio...2 ade] om. *F* 14 in...corpus] in aliquo alius tempus *P* 16 Patarenus] om. *F* 20 sed] set *P* 25 Catholicus] om. *F*

XXVII.3.17 prolixitate|fol. 92r *F* XXVII.4.4 probatur|fol. 120vb *P* 32 introire|fol. 121ra *P*

Patarenus: Item magistri romane ecclesia uestre diffiniunt peccatum sic. peccatum est dictum uel factum uel concupitum contra legem dei etcet. sed puer nichil facit contra legem dei. quam illi non dedit deus. ergo sine baptismate saluatur.

Catholicus: Responsio. quod illa diffinitio est de actuali peccato. preterea contra legem dei est non baptizari. dixit enim christus deus. nisi quis renatus fuerit ex aqua et spiritu sancto etcet. alias autem peccatum in genere sic diffinitur. peccatum est priuatio boni.

[**Patarenus:**] Item anima pueri fuit creata pura et bona et corpus eius per se nec bonum nec malum est. nec in ipsius coniunctione peccatum fuit. cum illius solus auctor sit deus. ergo nullum peccatum est in puero. et si multis dicere quod in anima pueri sit peccatum quod non consentimus. siue enim in anima siue in corpore eius fuerit macula originalis peccati. dimissa est propter quod dixit apostolus. in prima ad corinthios. v. sicut in adam omnes moriuntur ita et in christo omnes uiuificabuntur etcet.

Catholicus: Responsio. quod licet anima pueri cum carne et etiam corporalibus magni sit bona quantum est creatura dei tamen in ea et in carne peccatum est originale donec deletum est per christi baptisma. nec obstat quod dicit de auctoritate apostoli sicut in adam etcet. quia in christo uiuificari dicuntur qui eius seruauerunt doctrinam maxime baptisma.

[**Patarenus:**] Ad hebreos. ii°. decebat enim eum propter quem omnia qui multos filios in gloriam adduxerat auctorem salutis eorum per passionem consummare etcet. ergo christus ante passionem eius multos adduxerat in gloriam.

Catholicus: Respondeo adduxerat eos in gloria per spei firmitatem. simile. mattheus v. beati pauperes spiritus quoniam ipsorum est regnum celorum etcet. uel dicuntur in gloria fuisse quando in limbo fuerunt. quoniam ibi multiplici consolatione fouebantur sicut in exemplo legitur de diuite et lazaro. lucam xvi. ibi. nunc autem hic consolatur etcet. uel appellat gloriam gratiam noue legis. in quam christi multos. adduxerat per suam predicationem et eius miracula. que quidem conseruationem et robur accepit in passione ipsius.

Pat: Also the masters of your Roman Church define sin thusly (Augustine Cont. Faust. xxii, 27) "Sin is a word, deed, or desire against the law of God," but a child does not act against the law of God, since God did not give it to him, therefore he is saved without baptism.

Cath: I reply that your definition is regarding actual sin, further it is contrary to the law of God not to baptize, for Christ God said (Jn 3:5) "unless one be born again of water and the holy spirit." Elsewhere though sin is defined in general as "sin is a privation of a good."

[**Pat:**] The soul of the child was created pure and good and his body is by itself neither good nor bad, neither in their joining there sin, since God is the sole author of that act. Therefore there is no sin in the child, and if many people say that there be sin in the soul of the child, something we do not agree to, or that the stain of original sin will have been found in his soul or his body, it is remitted according to what the Apostle said in 1 Corinthians 5 (15:22) "And as in Adam all die, so also in Christ all will be made alive."

Cath: I reply that although the soul of the child with the flesh, and in all bodies whatsoever, is of the greatest good insofar as it a creation of God, yet in it and in the flesh original sin is to be found until it be removed by the baptism of Christ. Nor does what is said by the authority of the Apostle oppose this "as in Adam," because in Christ are made alive those who observe His doctrine, especially in baptism.

[**Pat:**] Hebrews 2 (2:10) "For it was worthy of him, for whom are all things exist, and by whom are all things, who had brought many children into glory, to perfect the author of their salvation, by his passion." So Christ led many into glory before His passion.

Cath: I reply that He led them into glory by a firmness of hope. Like Matthew 5 (5:3) "Blessed are the poor in spirit, for theirs is the kingdom of heaven. Or they are said to have been 'in glory' when they were actually in Limbo, because there they were comforted by many consolations, just as one reads in the example of Lazarus and Dives, Luke 16 (16:25) "but now he is comforted here." Or he calls 'glory' the grace of the New Law, into which Christ led many by His preaching and His miracles, for whom He accepted the consummation and power of His passion.

---

34 peccatum²...35 dei] Augustine, *Con. Faust.* xxii. 27, definition taken from the Stoic tradition, see; Plutarch, *De Rep. Stoic.* 11. 40 nisi...41 sancto] Ioh. 3:5. 52 sicut...53 uiuificabuntur] 1 Cor. 15:22. 61 decebat...64 consummare] Heb. 2:10. 67 beati...68 celorum] Matt. 5:3. 72 nunc...consolatur] Luc. 16:25.

33 Patarenus] om. *F* 35 sed...36 dei] om. *F* 38 Catholicus] om. *F* 54 Catholicus] om. *F* 55 corporalibus magni] cuiuslibet magna *F* 61 decebat] dicebat *F* 66 Catholicus] om. *F*

60 maxime|fol. 121rb *P* 74 eius|fol. 92v *F*

De pauperibus leonistis. quorum sunt iiii^{or} errores proprii

Sequitur de pauperibus leonistis quorum sunt iiii^{or} errores proprii scilicet quod unicuique bono uiro liceat tractare et dare sacramenta ecclesiastica et quod nullus possit saluari cum possessionibus neque temporaliter laborando neque reddendo carnale debitum in matrimonio et in hunc quartum errorem a paucis temporibus inciderunt. Sunt autem fere LX anni quod ista heresis pullulauit que habuit originem a quodam nomine gualdese de ciuitate lugduni supra renum. unde et isti dicti sunt lugdunenses seu leoniste. et isti pauperes leoniste inceperunt sub ecclesia romana. sed postea per superbiam in contumaciam sunt deducti et excommunicati in multos errores sunt prolapsi et postmodum in duas partes sunt diuisi et unius predictus gualdese constitutus est heresiarcha. alterius autem quidam nomine iohannes de runcharolo qui fuit placentinus et primi dicuntur pauperes ultramontani. alii uero lombardi nuncupantur et est diuisio inter eos. ultramontani uero credunt quod multi boni homines sunt in ecclesia romana et quod malus prelatus seu sacerdos suo fungit officio. quibus lombardi contradicunt. lombardi etiam postea in duas partes fuerunt diuisi in quodam concilio in terra mediolanensi habita occasione cuiusdam sciphy magni de uino pleni quem sparserat quedam gallina quod predictus Iohannes more suo sacrificauerat et mulieres istorum sub propriis pedibus calcauerant. quod quidam ipsorum uidentes indignati dixerunt quod nullus poterat sacrificare corpus et sanguinem christi nisi esset sacerdos ab ecclesia romana institutus. et isti uocati sunt illi de prato quorum pars penitus est abolita. horum autem pauperum leonistarum tam ultramontanorum quam lombardorum quidam quodam tempore cum bernardo primo ad fidem catholicam fuerunt conuersi et isti dicti sunt pauperes reconciliati. sed postea admoniti a summo pontifice intrauerunt ordines ecclesie. de quibus aliqui in nostro ordine usque in hodiernum diem religiose perseuerant et aliqui dormierunt in domino. predictorum autem hereticorum sunt etiam alii errores communes. de quibus dicemus inferius in tertio libro. ubi est de ecclesia romana et de iuramento et potestate et huiusmodi. In hoc autem tractatu improbabimus proprios eorum errores scilicet tres quos primo

XXVIII On the Poor of Lyons,[1] whose particular errors are four

Next we treat of the errors of the Poor of Lyons, which are four in particular, namely, it is permitted to any good man to minister and give the sacraments of the Church, and that no one can be saved with possessions, neither those who labor in the world, nor those who render the carnal debt in marriage. This fourth error they have only adopted in recent times. For around sixty years,[2] this heresy has been growing, which had its origin with a certain one by the name of Waldo of the city of Lyons on the Rhone. From this place they are called Lyonists or Leonists. These Poor of Lyons began under the Roman Church, but later were led by pride into contumacy and — being excommunicated — were led into many errors and after a while split into two groups. Of one of these groups the aforementioned Waldes was made the heresiarch but of the other a certain person named John of Runcharolo [of Ronco],[3] who was from Piacenza. The first are called the Ultramontane Poor, and the second are called Lombards. There is division between them. The Ultramontanes believe that there are many good men in the Roman Church and that an evil prelate or priest can fulfill his office, which the Lombards contradict.[4] The Lombards also later were divided into two groups at a certain council held in the neighborhood of Milan,[5] on the occasion of a large goblet full of wine being knocked over by a hen. The aforementioned John had sacrificed it after his fashion, and the women of his group had crushed the wine with their own feet. Some seeing this were indignant, and said that no one was able to sacrifice the body and blood of Christ except a priest ordained by the Roman Church, and this group was called "those of the meadow," but this group has entirely disappeared. But some of the Poor of Lyons, both from the Ultramontanes and the Lombards, converted back to the Catholic faith at the same time with Bernard Prim and these are called the Reconciled Poor. But later, by the advice of the supreme pontiff, they entered into the orders of the Church. Of these some have persevered down to the present time in our order, and others have fallen asleep in the Lord. There are other errors common to these heretics, of which we will speak below in book three, where one can find a discussion of the Roman Church, and of swearing oaths, of temporal power, and similar issues. In this tract we will disprove their particular errors,

---

XXVIII.1.1 De...2 proprii] om. *F* | add. *al. man. marg. sin.* De erroribus leonistis *F* **5** ecclesiastica] om. *P* **9** LX] tribus *P* **11** renum] *sic PF* leg. **Rodanum** **15** sunt] item *F* **20** ultramontani] ultramuntani *P* **21** ultramontani] ultramuntani *P* **24** etiam] et *P* **26** habita] habeto *P* | sciphy] syphi *F* **27** sparserat] sumpserat *P* | quod] que *F* **42** errores] add. scilicet *F*

XXVIII.1.17 heresiarcha|fol. 121va *P* **44** et¹|fol. 121vb *P*

---

1) It is clear that the author is far more familiar with the Italian Waldensians than the French branch. For the Waldensians see Gabriel Audisio, *The Waldensian Dissent* (Cambridge: Cambridge University Press, 1999). | 2) The Waldensians were founded in 1173. | 3) Salvo Burci, a Piacentine layman who wrote an antiheretical summa contemporary with this one, claims to have known John personally, see Wakefield, *Heresies*, 273 and Burci, 238. | 4) For this division see Moneta, 406, 431, 433–434. | 5) This is the only source that informs us of the schism in the Italian Waldensians. Those "of the meadow" were apparently later reconciled to the Church through the efforts of Durand of Huesca. Wakefield, *Heresies*, 735, n. 44.

posuimus. quartus autem scilicet de matrimonio iam improbatus est supra in primo libro.

Quod solus sacerdos tractare ecclesiastica sacramenta

Lucam. xxii. et cum facta esset hora discubuit et duodecim apostoli cum eo etcet. et infra. hoc facite in meam commemorationem etcet. et iohannes. xx. et dixit eis. accipite spiritum sanctum quorum remiseritis peccata remittuntur eis etcet. et i^a ad timotheum. iiii. noli negligere gratiam dei que est in te. que data est tibi per prophetiam cum impositione manuum presbyterii etcet. et v. uidua eligatur non minus. lx annorum et ii^a. ad timotheum. i^o. ut resuscites gratiam dei que est in te. per impositionem manuum mearum etcet. et ad titum. i^o. et constituas per ciuitates presbyteros. etcet. et ad hebreos. v. nec quisquam sumit sibi honorem sed qui uocatur a deo tamquam aaron etcet. et actus. vi^o. hos statuerunt ante conspectum apostolorum et orantes imposuerunt eis manus etcet. et xiii. tunc ieiunantes et orantes imponentesque eis manus dimiserunt illos etcet. et iacobus. ultimo. infirmatur quis in uobis inducat presbyteros ecclesie etcet. ex quibus patet manifeste quod dignitates et ordines dantur a superioribus nec habentur ex sola uita et quod non est datum sacramenta ecclesiastica tractare. nisi solis sacerdotibus. nec possunt dare alii. excepto sacramento baptismi in casu necessitatis. et excepto matrimonio.

Quod eleemosyna de superhabundantia mundat a peccatis

Lucam. xi. uerumptamen quod superest date eleemosynam et ecce omnia munda sunt uobis etcet. audi pauper. uel. quod christus dicit quod eleemosyna facta de superhabundantia mundat a peccatis et loquitur phariseis qui non erant in bono statu. ergo licet habere possessiones. de quibus fiant eleemosyne ad redemptionem peccatorum et dixit dominus quod faciendo eleemosynam de superfluitate mundantur a peccatis. ad hoc quod dicit. marcum xiiii. quid illi molesti estis? bonum opus operata est in me. semper enim pauperes habetis uobiscum et cum uolueritis potestis illis benefacere etcet. ad hoc est dicit apostolus ad romanos. xv. probauerunt enim macedonia et achaia collationem aliquam facere in pauperes sanctorum etcet. usque ibi. obsecro etcet. item i^a. ad corinthios. xi^o. numquid

namely, the first three which we wrote above, but the fourth, on marriage, we have already disproved above in book one.

That only a priest may celebrate the sacraments of the Church

Luke 22 (22:14) "And when the hour was come he sat down, and the twelve apostles with him." And later (22:19) "Do this in commemoration of me." And John 20 (20:22–23) "Receive the Holy Spirit, whose sins you shall forgive, they are forgiven." And 1 Timothy 4 (4:14) "Do not neglect the grace that is in you, which was given to you by prophesy, with imposition of the hands of the priesthood." And 5 (5:9) "Let a widow be chosen of no less than sixty years of age." And 2 Timothy 1 (1:6) "I admonish you, that you stir up the grace of God which is in you by the imposition of my hands." And Titus 1 (1:5) "and you should ordain priests in every city." And Hebrews 5 (5:4) "Neither does any man take the honor for himself, but he who is called by God, like Aaron." And Acts 6 (6:6) "These they set before the apostles; and they praying, imposed hands upon them." And 13 (13:3) "Then they, fasting and praying, and imposing their hands upon them, sent them away." And in the last chapter of James (5:14) "Is any man sick among you? Let him bring in the priests of the church." And from these it is perfectly clear that dignities and orders are given by superiors, nor do they have [authority] solely on account of [uprightness of] life, and that it is not given to them to celebrate the sacraments of the Church, excepting only priests. Neither are others able to confer any [of the sacraments], excepting the sacrament of baptism in the case of necessity, and excepting marriage.

That alms from one's excess wealth cleanses from sin

Luke 11 (11:41) "But yet of that which remains, give alms, and behold, all things are clean to you." Listen, O Poor Man, that Christ said that alms given from one's excess cleanses from sin and He said that to the Pharisees who were not in a good condition. Therefore it is permissible to hold possessions, from which they might give alms for the remission of sins, and the Lord said that by giving alms from one's excess they are cleansed from sin. He speaks to this point in Mark 14 (14:6–7) "why do you bother her? She has accomplished a good work for me. For the poor you have always with you, and whenever you wish, you may do them good." Also to the point, the Apostle says in Romans 15 (15:26) "For it has pleased those of Macedonia and Achaia to make a contribution for the poor of the saints," up to "I beseech." Also 1 Corinthians 11 (11:22) "What, have you not houses to eat and to drink in?" Also

---

XXVIII.2.3 et^1...4 eo] Luc. 22:14. 4 hoc...5 commemorationem] Luc. 22:19. 5 et^2...7 eis] Ioh. 20:22-23. 8 noli...10 presbyterii] 1 Tim. 4:14. 10 uidua...annorum] 1 Tim. 5:9. 11 ut...12 mearum] 2 Tim. 1:6. 13 et...presbyteros] Tit. 1:5. 14 nec...15 aaron] Heb. 5:4. 16 hos...17 manus] Act. 6:6. 18 tunc...19 illos] Act. 13:3. 20 infirmatur...ecclesie] Iac. 5:14.
XXVIII.3.3 uerumptamen...4 uobis] Luc. 11:41. 11 quid...14 bene-facere] Mar. 14:6-7. 15 probauerunt...16 sanctorum] Rom. 15:26. 17 numquid...18 bibendum] 1 Cor. 11:22.

48 supra] om. F XXVIII.2.1 Quod...2 sacramenta] om. F XXVIII.3.1 Quod...2 peccatis] om. F 5 eleemosyna] helemosina F 7 phariseis] pharyseis F 8 eleemosyne] helemosine F 10 eleemosynam] helemosinam F 13 uobiscum] add. m P exp.

XXVIII.2.20 infirmatur|fol. 93r F 24 possunt|fol. 122ra P

domos non habetis ad manducandum et bibendum etcet. item. xvi. de collectis autem que fiunt in sanctis sicut ordinaui ecclesiis gallatie etcet. usque ibi. quod si dignum etcet. item. iiᵃ. viiii. nam de ministerio quod fit in sanctos etcet. per totum et xi. alias ecclesias expoliaui. accipiens stipendium ad ministerium uestrum etcet. Item actus. xx. beatius est magis dare quam accipere etcet. ergo licet habere possessiones et est utile propter redemptionem peccatorum et propter subueniendum egentibus et possunt homines saluari cum illis et mereri et hec etiam perfectis habere et tractare illas. mattheus. xvii. ut autem non scandalizemus eos uade ad mare et mitte amum etcet. et. iohannes. ultimo. dixit eis. mittite in dexteram nauigii rete et inuenietis etcet. Et. iᵃ. ad thesalonenses. iiiiᵒ. ut uestrum negotium agatis et operemini manibus uestris etcet. et secunda. ultimo. audiuimus enim inter uos quosdam ambulare inquiete nihil operantes etcet. et infra. cum silentio operantes panem suum manducent etcet. et in eodem supra. denuntiabimus uobis quoniam siquis non uult operari nec manducet et actus. xx. quoniam ad ea que opus mihi erant et hiis qui mecum sunt ministrauerunt manus iste. omnia ostendi uobis. quoniam sic laborantes oportet suscipere infirmos. ac meminisse uerbi domini ihesu. quoniam dixit beatius est etcet. Ex hiis patet quod bonum est laborare temporaliter etiam perfectus.

Patarenus: Marcum. xiii. in finem. quod autem uobis dico omnibus dico etcet. ergo omnem potestatem quam christus dedit apostolis dedit omnibus bonis hominibus.
Catholicus: Responsio. stulte non loquitur ibi de potestate sed loquitur de uigilia ad quam hortatur omnes supple autem litteram et uidebis ueritatem. littera enim sic stat. quod autem uobis dico omnibus dico. uigilate etcet.
Patarenus: Item Gregorius. omnes boni homines sunt presbyteri. ergo omnis bonus homo est presbyter et potest sacramenta tractare.
[Catholicus:] Presbyter dicitur duobus modis scilicet ratione ordinis et ratione uite et hoc est quod dicit ibi gregorius in illa auctoritate. multi presbyteri et pauci presbyteri. omnes boni homines sunt presbyteri. sed non omnes presbyteri sunt boni homines. etcet. et propter hoc non sequitur quod qui sunt presbyteri ratione uite tantum possint tractare sacramenta fidei quorum potestas tradita est solus presbyteris ordinatis.

16 (16:1) "Now concerning the collections that are made for the saints, as I have ordered the churches of Galatia," up to "and if it be worthy." Also in 2 Corinthians 9 (9:1) "For show to them, in the sight of the saints," and through the rest and chapter 11 (11:8) "I have taken from other churches, receiving wages of them for your ministry." Also Acts 20 (20:35) "It is more blessed to give than to receive." Therefore it is permitted to have possessions and to use them on account of the remission of sins and for succoring the poor and men are able to be saved who have them, and to obtain merit [by them], and it is permitted for those in the life of perfection to possess and use them. Matthew 17 (17:26) "But that we may not scandalize them, go to the sea, and cast in a hook." And at the last chapter of John (21:6) "He said to them, 'Cast the net on the right side of the ship, and you shall find.'" And 1 Thessalonians 4 (4:11) "and that you do your own business, and work with your own hands." And in 2 Thessalonians at the end (3:11) "For we have heard there are some among you who walk disorderly, not working at all." And later (3:12) "working in silence, they would eat their own bread." And in the same, but above (3:10) "this we declared to you: that if any man will not work, neither let him eat." And Acts 20 (20:34–35) "for such things as were necessary for me and those who are with me, these hands have furnished. I have shown you all things, how that so laboring you ought to support the weak, and to remember the word of the Lord Jesus, how he said, 'It is a more blessed thing to give, than to receive.'" From these authorities it is clear that it is a good thing to do daily labor, even for the perfect.
Pat: Mark 13 at the end (13:37) "And what I say to you, I say to all." Therefore the power which Christ gave to the Apostles, He gave to all good men.

Cath: Response. Fool, He is not speaking there of power but of the watchfulness towards which He exhorts all men. Provide the whole text and you will see the truth. For the literal text stands "And what I say to you, I say to all: watch."

Pat: Also Gregory. "All good men are priests." Therefore every good man is a priest and can confect the sacraments.

[Cath:] 'Priest' is said in two ways, namely, by reason of ordination and by reason of life and this is what Gregory means in your quotation. "There are many priests and few priests, all good men are priests, but not all priests are good men." Because of this it does not follow that those who are priests by manner of life are able to confer the sacraments of faith, it is only ordained priests to whom authority is handed on.

---

19 de...20 gallatie] 1 Cor. 16:1 (sanctis) sanctos *Vulg.*) 21 nam...22 sanctos] 2 Cor. 9:1. 22 alias...23 uestrum] 2 Cor. 11:8. 24 beatius...25 accipere] Act. 20:35. 29 ut...30 amum] Matt. 17:26. 31 dixit...inuenietis] Ioh. 21:6. 32 ut...33 uestris] 1 Thes. 4:11. 34 audiuimus...35 operantes] 2 Thes. 3:11. 35 cum...36 manducent] 2 Thes. 3:12. 37 denuntiabimus...38 manducet] 2 Thes. 3:10. 38 quoniam...43 est¹] Act. 20:34-35. 45 quod...46 dico²] Mar. 13:37. 54 omnes...55 presbyteri] non invenitur. Probably taken from a list of mutilated authorities used by Waldensians, described by David of Augsburg.

---

28 hec] licet *P* 45 Patarenus] om. *F* 49 Catholicus] om. *F* 50 hortatur] ortatur *P* 51 supple] suple *P* 54 Patarenus] om. *F* 58 et¹...uite] om. *F* 60 omnes...presbyteri²] om. *F*

XXVIII.3.23 ministerium|fol. 122rb *P* 51 supple|fol. 122va *P* 64 quorum|fol. 93v *F*

[Patarenus:] Mattheus. xviiii. si uis perfectus esse uade uende omnia quod habes et da pauperibus et habebis thesaurum in celo etcet. et infra. omnis qui reliquerit domum uel fratres etcet. sed omnis bonus homo est perfectus. ergo non licet alicui habere possessionem. si uult esse bonus homo.

Catholicus: Responsio. quod duplex est perfectio scilicet substantialiter et habitus. prima uero habet omnis bonus homo. secundam uero non nisi possessiones relinquerit et nudus nudum secutus fuerit. Et de ista est consilium domini nostri ihesu christi. sed non preceptum et quod possit esse aliquis bonus homo et saluari cum possessione sine habitus perfectione ostendit ipse dominus ibi. si autem uis ad uitam ingredi serua mandata etcet.

Patarenus: Item marcus. vi°. et precepit eis ne quid tollerent in uia. nisi uirgam tantum. non peram. neque panem neque in zona uestra es etcet. ergo nihil licet bonis possidere.

Catholicus: Responsio. totum est consilium domini ut predicatores nudi nudum christum citius sequantur et lupum melius insequi ualeant. sed respondete uos mihi. nonne portatis panem per uiam et zucham uini et his similia? et scio quod facitis. ergo non estis boni homines. quod uerum est.

Patarenus: Item actus. iiii°. quotquot possessores agrorum aut domorum erant uendentes adderebant pretia eorum que uendebant et ponebant ante pedes apostolorum etcet. ergo boni homines nichil possidebant.

Catholicus: Responsio. quod uendebant immobilia propter in statem persecutionem et quia nolebant hoc facere alias enim non tendebantur. sicut dixit beatus petrus. infra. v. nonne manens tibi manebat et uenundatum erat in tua potestate etcet. Sed respondete uos mihi. nonne omnes homines tenentur esse boni. ergo omnes tenentur uiuere sine possessionibus. sed hoc faciendo destrueretur mundus et impediretur salus animarum et isti per negligentiam perirent fame. et sic occiderent se ipsos et ita peccarent mortalissime qualis est ergo predicatio uestram?

hereticus: Actus. vi°. non est equum nos relinquere uerbum dei et ministrare mensis etcet. ergo non licet bonis hominibus laborare.

Catholicus: Responsio. non dixit quod non esset bonum. sed quod non esset equum apostolos relinquere uerbum dei propter illud. alias enim elegerit. vii. uiros plenos spiritu sancto. ad illud ut ibi subditur. preterea non loquitur de labore sed de ministratione

[Pat:] Matthew 19 (19:21) "If you will be perfect, go sell what you have, and give to the poor, and you shall have treasure in heaven." And later (19:29) "And every one that has left house, or brothers." But every good man is perfect, therefore it is not permitted to anyone to have possessions, if he wants to be a good man.

Cath: I reply that perfection is twofold, namely, essentially and habitually. The first every good man has, the second one does not have unless one leaves possessions and (Jerome, *Ep.* 52.5) "nude follows the nude Christ." This was a counsel of our Lord Jesus Christ, but not a command, and that one can be a good man and to be saved with possessions, even without the habit of perfection is shown by the Lord himself there (19:17) "if you wish to enter into life keep the commandments."

Pat: Also Mark 6 (6:8) "And he commanded them that they should take nothing for the way, but a staff only, no scrip, no bread, nor money in their purse." So it is absolutely forbidden for the good to have possessions.

Cath: The whole counsel of the Lord is that preachers "nude, follow the nude Christ" more readily, and that they might be able to pursue the wolf better. But tell me this, why do you carry bread for the journey and flasks of wine and the like? I know that you do this, so you are not good men, and this is true.

Pat: So, Acts 4 (4:34–35) "For as many as were owners of lands or houses, they sold them, and brought the price of the things they sold, and laid it down at the feet of the apostles." Therefore good men possessed nothing at all.

Cath: I reply that they sold their estates on account of the state of persecution, and because they did not want to do this they did not in fact do this at other times, as Blessed Peter says later in 5 (5:4) "While it remained, did it not remain for you? And after it was sold, was it not in your power?" But tell me, are not all men bound to be good? Therefore all men should embrace living without possessions. But by doing so the world would be destroyed and the salvation of souls would be impeded, and by negligence they would perish in hunger, and so they would be killing themselves and thereby sin mortally. What kind of message is yours?

Heretic: Acts 6 (6:2) "It is not right that we should leave the word of God, and serve at tables." So it is not permitted for good men to work.

Cath: Reply. He did not say that it was not good, but that it was not right for apostles to leave the word of God on account of that. For he had called (6:3) "seven men full of the Holy Spirit," for that task, as is added in the same passage. Further he does not speak of work but of ministry

---

65 si...67 celo] Matt. 19:21 (omnia) om. *Vulg.*) 67 omnis...68 fratres] Matt. 19:29. 74 nudus...fuerit] Jerome, *Ep.* 52.5. 78 si...79 mandata] Matt. 19:17. 80 et...82 es] Mar. 6:8. 90 quotquot...93 apostolorum] Act. 4:34-35. 98 nonne...99 potestate] Act. 5:4. 106 non...107 mensis] Act. 6:2. 111 alias...112 sancto] Act. 6:3.

71 Catholicus] om. *F* 78 dominus] add. superius *F* 80 Patarenus] om. *F* 82 es] om. *P* 84 Catholicus] om. *F* 85 predicatores] add. multi *F* | citius] cuius *F* 87 zucham] zuccam *F* (*the vernacular word for "flask", cp. "zòcca" still in use in Bolognese dialect, from 'a gourd' out of which such flasks are made.*) 88 his] hiis *F* 90 Patarenus] om. *F* 95 Catholicus] om. *F* 102 destrueretur] dextrueretur *F* 106 hereticus] om. *F* 109 Catholicus] om. *F* 110 sed...equum] om. *P*

83 possidere]fol. 122vb *P* 109 esset]fol. 123ra *P*

que fit ad mensas egentium quod si malum est. ergo maledicti sunt qui uobis aliquid ministrant et in ueritate sunt. propter hoc quia fouent uos in erroribus uestris.

at the tables of the poor, which if it were evil, then they are cursed who minister anything to you and they are in truth about this because they help you along you in your errors.

De rebapticatis. quorum proprius est error bis baptizare

sequitur de rebapticatis quorum proprius est error bis baptiçare. Orta est autem heresis eorum simul cum leonistis. quod autem sanctum baptisma non reiteretur patet quia dominus dixit. mattheo ultimo. baptizantes eos etcet. non dicit rebaptizantes et in iohannem. iii°. amen amen dico uobis nisi quis renatus fuerit denuo etcet. et infra nisi quis renatus fuerit ex aqua etcet. quod sonat bis debere nasci hominem ad perfectam salutem scilicet semel secundum carnem et semel secundum spiritum et uocat spiritualem natiuitatem baptismum et hoc est quod subdit. quod natum est ex carne. caro est. et quod natum est ex spiritu spiritus est. etcet. igitur non sunt nisi due natiuitates hominis. quarum una est carnalis. et altera spiritualis. et quod spiritualis non debeat esse nisi una baptizatio specificat cum subinfert. sic est omnes qui natus est ex spiritu etcet. non dixit qui renatus sed qui natus. item paulus ad ephesios. iiii°. unum baptisma etcet. non ergo duo. preterea numquam legitur quod christus dixerit quod baptisma eius deberet reiterari. nec aliquis apostolorum eius. nec umquam legimus in diuina scriptura. aliquid fuisse rebaptizatus. quare o uos rebaptizati non est uestra catholica doctrina sed diabolica.

XXIX On the Rebaptizers,[1] whose particular error is to baptize twice

Now to treat of the Rebaptizers whose particular error is to baptize twice. This heresy arose at the same time as the Leonists. That holy baptism is not to be repeated is clear since the Lord said in the last chapter of Matthew (28:19) "baptizing them," and not saying "rebaptizing." And in John 3 (3:3) "Amen I say to you, unless you are born anew." And later (3:5) "unless you are born again of water." What He declares is that man ought to be born twice for perfect salvation, namely, once according to the flesh and once according to the spirit, and it is called the spiritual birth of baptism, and here is what follows (3:6) "that which is born of flesh is of the flesh, and that which is born of the Spirit." Therefore there are none but the two births of man, of which one is carnal and the other spiritual, and that the spiritual one should be none other than the one baptism He specifies when adding (3:8) "so is every one who is born of the Spirit." He did not say "who is reborn" but "who is born." Also Paul to the Ephesians 4 (4:5) "one baptism." Therefore not two. Further it is never read that Christ said that His baptism ought to be repeated, neither did any of His apostles, nor do we ever read in the divine scriptures that anyone has been rebaptized. Hence, O you Repabtizers, your doctrine is not Catholic teaching, but that of the devil.

De errore illorum qui dicunt baptismum posse reiterare

[**Hereticus:**] Actus. xix. Ille uero ait. in qui ergo baptizati estis. qui dixerunt in iohannis baptismate. etcet. et infra. hiis auditis. baptizati sunt in nomine domini ihesu. etcet. ergo bis sunt homines baptizandi. si saluari uolunt.

Catholicus: Responsio. baptizauerant primo baptismate scilicet iohannes. in qui non dabatur spiritus sanctus. sicut dicit ibi apostolus et tale baptisma pro non baptismate reputatur et ideo postea baptizati uero baptismate christi. non dicuntur rebaptizati. sed modo respondete mihi de hac uestra doctrina. aut enim spiritus sanctus datur in prima baptizatione. et non in secunda et tunc secunda est superflua. aut datur in

2 On the error of those who say that baptism can be repeated

[**Heretic:**] Acts 19 (19:3) "And he said, 'In what then were you baptized?' They said, 'In John's baptism.'" And later (19:5) "Having heard these things, they were baptized in the name of the Lord Jesus." Therefore men should be baptized twice if they want to be saved.

Cath: Response. They were baptized in the first baptism, that of John, in which the Holy Spirit was not given, just as the Apostle said here, that such a baptism was not reputed as true baptism, and so later they were baptized in the baptism of Christ. It is not said that they were rebaptized. But just tell me this about your doctrine, for either the Holy Spirit is given in the first baptism, and not in the second, and so then the second is superfluous, or it is given

---

XXIX.1.6 baptizantes...7 eos] Matt. 28:19.   8 amen¹...denuo] Ioh. 3:3 (uobis] tibi *Vulg.*)   9 nisi...aqua] Ioh. 3:5.   13 quod²...15 est] Ioh. 3:6.   18 sic...spiritu] Ioh. 3:8.   20 unum baptisma] Eph. 4:5.   XXIX.2.3 Ille...4 baptismate] Act. 19:3.   5 hiis...6 ihesu] Act. 19:5.

XXIX.1.1 De...2 baptizare] om. *F* | proprius] primus *P*   7 rebaptizantes] baptizantes *F*   8 renatus] natus *P*   13 quod²...15 etcet] om. *F*   24 rebaptizati] baptizati *P*   XXIX.2.1 De...2 reiterare] om. *F*   3 xix] xviiii *P*   8 Catholicus] om. *F*

XXIX.1.20 ephesios|fol. 94r *F*   21 legitur|fol. 123rb *P*

---

1) A minor group, perhaps the offshoots of Waldensianism, found in both France and Milan, Käppeli, 334, n. 92.

secunda et non in prima. et nunc prima est otiosa. et hoc ipsum etiam requiro a uobis quam scriptura dicatis. quod magis prima uite detur quam in secunda et econtrario. ut si non habetis ex scriptura sicut uerum est quod non habetis. eadem facilitate reprobetur. quod sine scripture uigore profertis. item aut in utraque uice datur. spiritus sanctus. tunc aut secundo superflue datur. aut ad alium usum datur quam in prima et si alium usum datur. probate per scripturam si potestis. ad quid uidelicet usum detur quod facere numquam potest. Et nota quod isti rebaptiçati habent etiam alius errores proprios scilicet quod non sit ieiunandum in tota uita hominis nisi per unam quadragesimam et huiusmodi similes de quibus hic inserere non curaui. fuerunt autem quam plures alie hereses simul exorte cum predictis scilicet arnaldones. corruçani. milui. leuantes. cappelleti et huiusmodi. de quibus quia iam temporibus nostris sunt penitus delete. non curaui cartam inultiliter occupare.

in the second and not in the first, and now the first is emptied of power. This also I ask of you, that you point out in scripture what greater life could be given in the first than the second, and vice versa. So if you do not have it from scripture as true, then you do not have it at all. With the same facility is rejected that which you advance with the backing of scripture. Also, either the Holy Spirit is in turn given both times, for then the second would be given without effect, or it is given for another purpose than in the first, and if is given for another purpose, prove that by scripture if you can. For what purpose is it given which you could not achieve before? And note that these Rebaptizers have other particular errors, namely that one need not fast except for one Lent in one's life, and others like it of which I did not care to include here. Yet there are many other heresies which arose at the same time as those above, namely, the Arnaldones,[1] the Corrucani,[2] the Milui,[3] the Levantes, the Cappelleti,[4] and the like. Since they are nearly already extinct in our day, I have not bothered to waste paper on them.

LIBER III

De communibus erroribus in quibus hereses omnes uel plures errare uidentur

Tractatum est superius de propriis erroribus hereticorum. Nunc autem uidendum est. de communibus in quibus omnes hereses uel plures errare uidentur et primo de articulo illo fidei scilicet credo in sanctam ecclesiam catholicam. in quo communiter errant heretici uniuersi. negantes sanctam ecclesiam romanam esse christi sponsam et ueram ipsius ecclesiam inficiantes etiam potestatem suam. illi esse collatam diuinitus proponentes. singuli et diuersimode illi hereses suas impudenter affirmans uniusquisque suam sectam esse dei et christi eius ecclesiam. quod autem ipsa sit uera ecclesia dei et quod potestas qua utitur sit a deo et quod omnes qui pertinaciter ei contra dicunt. sint heretici et quod ipsorum opiniones seu secte. sint hereses condempnate a spiritu sancto multis et uariis rationibus. In hoc titulo declarabimus in nomine ihesu christi.

Prima est quia credit ac tenet et predicat fidem in omnibus et per omnia quam deus docuit. pro ista

Book III

XXX On the common errors in which all heresies, or many of them, seem to err

The previous section was concerned with the particular errors of the heretics. But now we are concerned with the errors which all or many heresies have in common. It seems they err first on that article of faith "I believe in the Holy Catholic Church." The heretics err universally on this, denying that the Holy Roman Church is the spouse of Christ and His true Church and refusing to acknowledge her power. Each of these heresies in different ways impudently affirm their own sects to be the church of God and of Christ. That she is the true church of God and that the power which she uses is from God and that all those who pertinaciously speak against her are heretics and that their opinions or sects are heresies condemned by the Holy Spirit with many and varied reasons: in this section we declare these things in the name of Jesus Christ.

The first is because they believe and hold and preach the faith in all things and through all which God taught for

---

17 a uobis] om. *P* **23** quam] om. *P* **32** corruçani] correzani *F* | milui] unsui *P* | cappelleti] cappellen *P* **35** LIBER…XXX.1.2 uidentur] om. *F* **XXX.1.2** omnes] om. *P* **6** illo] om. *P* **12** uniusquisque] add. de *P* exp. **14** ipsa sit] ipsi sint *P* **16** opiniones] oppiniones *P* **17** condempnate] condemnare *F*

XXIX.2.26 rebaptiçati|fol. 123va *P* **XXX.1.20** predicat|fol. 123vb *P*

---

[1] The followers of Arnold of Brescia, see Lambert, 52-55. See also Vacarius, 44–52. | [2] Käppeli, 335, suggests this may be a corruption of "Runcarii" which may be a German sect of Waldensians. Frederick II uses a similar term, "Roncaroli", in his anti-heretical laws, see Mansi, *Concilia*. xxii, 590. | [3] Käppeli, 335, suggests this may be a corruption of Slavic word for "Have mercy" "Pomilui", occasionally used as a term for Bogomil heretics. | [4] Wakefield, *Heresies*, 735, n. 47, suggests that this might be the *Capuciati*, a group of French peasant vigilantes that had been denounced as heretics by 1184.

ratione facit quod legitur. mattheus. xiii°. ait illis. ideo omnis scriba doctus in regno celorum similis est homini patrifamilias. qui profert de thesauro sui noua et uetera etcet. et xxiii°. et reliquistis que grauiora sunt legis. iudicium et misericordiam et fidem etcet. et lucam ultimum. et ipse dixit ad eos. O stulti et tarde corde ad credendum in omnibus que locuti sunt prophete etcet. et iohannes. xviiii. et qui uidit testimonium perhibuit et uerum est testimonium eius et ille scit quia uera dicit ut uos credatis etcet. et ii^a. ad corinthios. iiii°. quod si etiam opertum est euangelium nostrum in his qui pereunt opertum est. in quibus deus huius seculi excecauit mentes infidelium ut fulgeat illis illuminatio euangelii glorie christi et i^a ad timotheum. i°. et si quid aliud sane doctrine aduersatur que est secundum euangelium glorie beati dei quod creditum est mihi etcet. et actus. xxiii. sic deseruio deo meo patri credens omnibus que in lege et prophetis scripta sunt. spem habens in deum quam et hii ipsi expectant resurrectionem futuram iustorum et iniquorum etcet. ex hiis ergo habes quod ecclesia dei debet credere omnia que deus docuit in ueteri et in nouo testamento ergo ecclesia romana est ecclesia dei et constat quod heretici isti uel illi negant omnia uel aliquia que in ueteri uel nouo testamento sunt scripta. ergo ipsi errant a tramite ueritatis.

Secundus articulus

Secunda est quia in ecclesia dei debet esse unitas sicut scriptum est ad ephesios. iiii°. unus dominus. una fides. unum baptisma. unus deus et pater omnium etcet. Item ad phylippenses. iii°. idem sapiamus. et in eadem permaneamus regula. item. i^a. petri. iii°. in fide autem omnes unanimes. etcet. et constat quod in ecclesia romana est unitas fidei. at contra omnes heretici ut patareni et leoniste cum ceteris in plures sectas sunt diuisi contrarias in fidei articulis siue capitulis. uere ergo ecclesia romana est illa columba de quam dominus dicit in cantica. vi. una est columba mea etcet. et una quem heresis cum suis fautoribus est illud regnum desolandus de quo saluator ait. lucam. xi. omne regnum in seipsum diuisum desolabitur et domus supra domum cadet etcet. et maxime de patarenis qui multas sectas constituerunt per uanas fidei diuisiones. dicit beatus petrus. ii^a. ii°. in uobis erunt magistri mendaces qui introducent sectas perdicionis et eum qui emit eos dominum uel dominum negant etcet.

[**Hereticus:**] Nonne et ecclesia romana diuisa est in fide? numquid augustinus et ambrosius et ceteri doctores eius nam contradicunt sibi ad inuicem in pluribus fidei questionibus. item nonne greci contrariantur latinis de processione spiritus sancti a filio et in pluribus aliis fidei capitulis. ergo et ecclesia romana diuisa est in fide.

Catholicus: Doctores nostri non sunt contrarii in questionibus fide que sunt expressim terminate per uetus et nouum testamentum. uel alias per ecclesiam sanctam dei. preterea que dicunt ad inuicem contrariando non dicunt asserendo neque contumaciter in suo sensu persistendo. sed loquuntur humiliter opinando. salua sunt per ueritatem quod relinquiit spiritu sancto et ecclesie reuelandam dei. et ideo opiniones eorum non sunt diuisiones in fide quamquam diuerse. quod autem de grecis opposuistis falsum est. quia sancti et doctores grecorum et uniuersaliter populus eorum in nullo discrepant a fide ecclesie romane. licet aliqui ex illis nuper errare uideantur in quibus dixistis. preterea greci non sunt de ecclesia romana neque secundum nomen neque secundum ritus. unde nulla est oppositio uestra. et esto quod ipsi sint de romana ecclesia et quod ipsi uniuersaliter discesserint a fide. est illud completum in eis quod circa finem mundi dicit apostolus debere compleri. de quo dicit. ii^a. ad thesalonicenses. ii°. quonium nisi discessio peruenerit etcet.

Tertia est quia fides uera cum ratione debet habere concordiam. quia ut de beatus petrus in libro clementis ueritas ratione non caret. unde et beatus paulus dicit ad romanos. ii^a. inuisibilia enim ipsius a creatura mundi per ea que facta sunt intellecta conspiciuntur etcet. et constat quod ratio fidei romane ecclesie deseruit prout patet in articulo de uno principio et in omnibus aliis idem reperies si bene inuestigaueris. sed econtrario hereses sunt ratione contrarie nichil ueritatis amplectentes. ut legitur ii^a. petri. ii°. hi uero ueluð irrationabilia pecora naturaliter in corruptionem et in perniciem in his que ignorant blasphemantes in corruptione sua peribunt etcet.

Quarta est quia in ipsa deprehenditur esse sapientia scripturarum plenissime que in ecclesia dei legitur esse debere. adeo ut per eam uincat omnes aduersa sibi dicentes. unde dominus dicit lucam. xxi. ego enim dabo uobis os et sapientiam cui non poterunt resistere et contradicere omnes aduersarii uestri etcet. et iohannes. v. scrutamini scripturas etcet. ad hoc est ad

[**Heretic:**] Is not also the Roman Church divided in faith? Is it possible that Augustine and Ambrose and the rest of her doctors contradicted each other in many questions of faith? Also are not the Greeks contrary to the Latins on the procession of the Holy Spirit from the Son and in many other matters of faith? Therefore even the Roman Church is divided in faith.

Cath: Our doctors are not opposed to one another in the questions of faith which are expressly settled by the Old and New Testaments, or others through the holy Church of God. Moreover when they disagree with one another they do not do so by assertion nor by asserting obstinately in their own interpretations, but they speak by humbly advancing their opinion. Those things are safe that through the truth of God's revelation were left by the Holy Spirit to the Church and to be revealed by God. And so their opinions were not divisions in faith, however different they might have been. That which you assert about the Greeks is false, since the Greek saints and doctors and the whole of their people do not differ from the faith of the Roman Church, although a few of them have recently erred in those things of which you spoke. Further the Greeks are not of the Roman Church, either in name or in rite, so your objection does not hold. But even conceding that [the Greeks] were from the Roman Church and that they have universally departed from the faith, it is done in them that the number at the end of the world might be considered complete as the Apostle says. Regarding this he speaks in 2 Thessalonians 2 (2:3) "for unless a revolt comes first."

3 The third is that the true faith ought to be in concord with reason, just as Blessed Peter says in the Clementine Books (41:28) "Truth is not without reason." Wherefore also Blessed Paul says to the Romans 2 (1:20) "For the invisible things of him, from the creatures of the world, are clearly seen, being understood by the things that are made." And it is clear that the resonableness of the faith of the Roman Church served well, as is evident in the article on the One Principle, as you will discover in all the others if you bother to look well, but on the contrary heresies are contrary to reason for they embrace no truth, as is read in 2 Peter 2 (2:12) "But these men, like irrational beasts, naturally tending to the snare and to destruction, blaspheming those things which they do not know, will perish in their corruption."

4 The fourth is because in her the wisdom of the scriptures is most fully discovered, in which it is read that it ought to be in the Church of God to the extent that through them she conquers all who speak against her. Whence the Lord says in Luke 21 (21:15) "For I will give you a mouth and wisdom, which all your adversaries shall not be able to resist and gainsay." And John 5 (5:39) "search the

---

48 quonium...49 peruenerit] 2 Thes. 2:3.   **XXX.3.3** ueritas...caret] *Pseudo-Clementine Recognitions*, II. 69.   **4** inuisibilia...5 conspiciuntur] Rom. 1:20.   **10** hi...13 peribunt] 2 Pet. 2:12 (corruptionem] captionem *Vulg.*)   **XXX.4.4** ego...6 uestri] Luc. 21:15.   **7** scrutamini scripturas] Ioh. 5:39.

---

25 nonne] om. F   **29** Catholicus] om. F | sunt] om. P   **34** loquuntur] locuntur P   **35** opinando] oppinando P | sunt...quod] semper ueritate quam F   **37** opiniones] oppiniones P   **38** de] om. F   **39** et] om. F   **47** mundi] om. P   **XXX.3.1** est] om. P   **7** principio] om. P   **8** reperies] experies P   **XXX.4.3** adeo] ad eo F   **4** dominus] om. P

31 alias|fol. 124rb P   **39** grecorum|fol. 95r F   **XXX.3.11** in¹|fol. 124va P

romanos. ultimo. uolo uos esse sapientes in bono etcet. item i^a. corinthios xiiii. nolite pueri effici sensibus etcet. et infra. siquis autem ignorat ignorabitur etcet. et ad ephesios. i°. in omni sapientia et prudentia etcet. et v. non quasi insipientes sed ut sapientes. item ad colosenses. i°. in omni sapientia et intellectu spirituali et infra. crescentes in scientia dei etcet. et infra. docentes omnem hominem in omni sapientia etcet. et ii°. ut consolentur corda ipsorum instructi in caritate et in omnes diuitias plenitudinis intellectus. et iii°. uerbum christi habitabat in uobis habundanter in omni sapientia docentes etcet. et infra. in sapientia ambulate ad eos qui foris sunt. tempus redimentes. sermo uester semper in gratia sit sale conditus ut sciatis quomodo oporteat respondere unicuique etcet. item. i^a ad timotheum. iiii°. dum uenio actende lectioni exortationi et doctrine. item ii^a. ad timotheum. 3°. quia ab infantia sacras litteras nosti etcet. item. ad titum i°. ut potens sit exortari in doctrina sana etcet. et ii°. loquere que decet sanam doctrinam etcet. et infra. uerbum sanum irreprehensibile etcet. et actus. vi. et non poterant resistere sapientie et spiritui qui loquebatur etcet. Ex hiis apparet quod maxima sapientia debet esse in ecclesia dei maxime scripturarum diuinarum econtrario heretici debet esse et sunt ydiote de quibus dicit dominus. mattheus. xxii°. erratis nescientes scripturas etcet. item. marcum. xii. nonne ideo erratis non scientes scripturas etcet. ad hoc est. i^a. ad corinthios. xv. ignorantiam enim dei quidam habent et ad ephesios. iiii°. habentes intellectum alienatum a uita dei per ignoratiam que est in illis etcet. et i^a ad timotheum. i°. a quibus quidem aberrantes conuersi sunt in uaniloquium uolentes legis esse doctores non intelligentes neque qui locuuntur neque de quibus affirmant etcet. et ii^a. ad timotheum. iii°. numquam ad scientiam ueritatis peruenientes etcet. et infra. insipientia enim eorum manifesta erit omnibus etcet. et ii^a. petri. ultimo. sicut et karissimus frater noster paulus secundum datam sibi sapientiam scripsit uobis sicut et omnibus epistolis loquens in eis de hiis in quibus sunt quedam difficilia intellectu que indocti et instabiles deprauant sicut et ceteras scripturas etcet. et infra. ne insipientium errore traducti excidatis a propria firmitate etcet.

scriptures." Related to this is the last chapter of Romans (16:19) "But I want you to be wise in the good." Also 1 Corinthians 14 (14:20) "do not become children in the senses." And later (14:38) "But if any man does not know, he will not be known." And Ephesians 1 (1:8) "in all wisdom and prudence." And 5 (5:15–16) "not as fools, but as wise men." Also Colossians 1 (1:9) "in all wisdom, and spiritual understanding," and later (1:10) "growing in the knowledge of God," and 2 (2:2) "That their hearts may be comforted, being instructed in charity," and 3 (3:16) "Let the word of Christ dwell in you abundantly, in all wisdom, teaching," and below (4:5–6) "Walk with wisdom towards those who are outside, redeeming the time. Let your speech be always in grace seasoned with salt, that you may know how you ought to answer every man." Also 1 Timothy 4 (4:13) "Until I come, attend to reading, to exhortation, and to doctrine." Also 2 Timothy 3 (3:15) "And because from your infancy you have known the holy scriptures." Also Titus 1 (1:9) "that he may be able to exhort in sound doctrine," and 2 (2:1) "But speak the things that become sound doctrine," and later (2:8) "The sound word that cannot be blamed." And Acts 6 (6:10) "And they were not able to resist the wisdom and the spirit that spoke." From these it is clear that the greatest wisdom ought to be in the Church of God, especially of the Divine Scriptures, on the contrary the heretics ought to be and are fools, of which the Lord says in Matthew 22 (22:29) "You err, not knowing the Scriptures." Also Mark 12 (12:24) "Do you not therefore err, because you do not know the scriptures." To this point is 1 Corinthians 15 (15:34) "For some do not have the knowledge of God." And Ephesians 4 (4:18) "having their understanding darkened, being alienated from the life of God through the ignorance that is in them." And 1 Timothy 1 (1:6–7) "From which things some going astray are turned aside to vain babbling, desiring to be teachers of the law, understanding neither the things they say, nor of what they affirm." And 2 Timothy 3 (3:7) "never attaining to the knowledge of the truth." And later (3:9) "for their folly will be manifest to all men." And 2 Peter at the end (3:15) "as also our most dear brother Paul, according to the wisdom given him, has written to you as also in all his epistles, speaking in them of these things in which are certain things hard to understand, which the unlearned and unstable wrest, as they do also the other scriptures." And later (3:17) "lest being led aside by the error of the unwise, you fall from your own steadfastness."

---

8 uolo…bono] Rom. 16:19.   9 nolite…sensibus] 1 Cor. 14:20.   10 siquis…ignorabitur] 1 Cor. 14:38.   11 in…prudentia] Eph. 1:8.   12 non…sapientes] Eph. 5:15-16.   13 in…spirituali] Col. 1:9.   14 crescentes…dei] Col. 1:10.   15 docentes…sapientia] Col. 1:28.   16 ut…17 intellectus] Col. 2:2.   18 uerbum…19 docentes] Col. 3:16 (habitabat] habitet *Vulg.*)   19 in…22 unicuique] Col. 4:5-6.   23 dum…24 doctrine] 1 Tim. 4:13.   25 quia…nosti] 2 Tim. 3:15.   26 ut…sana] Tit. 1:9.   27 loquere…28 irreprehensibile] Tit. 2:1.   28 uerbum…irreprehensibile] Tit. 2:8. | et^2…30 loquebatur] Act. 6:10.   33 erratis…34 scripturas] Matt. 22:29.   34 nonne…35 scripturas] Mar. 12:24.   36 ignorantiam…37 habent] 1 Cor. 15:34.   37 habentes…38 illis] Eph. 4:18 (alienatum] alienati *Vulg.*)   39 a…42 affirmant] 1 Tim. 1:6-7.   43 numquam…peruenientes] 2 Tim. 3:7.   44 insipientia…45 omnibus] 2 Tim. 3:9.   45 sicut…50 scriptu-ras] 2 Pet. 3:15.   50 ne…51 firmitate] 2 Pet. 3:17.

---

9 ia] add. ro *P* exp.   11 et^1] add. doctrina *P* exp.   16 consolentur] consulentur *P* | caritate] karitate *P*   18 habitabat] habitat *F*   26 titum i°] timotheum. i°. *P*

XXX.4.27 sanam|fol. 124vb *P*   37 habentes|fol. 95v *F*

Patarenus: Sed uidetur quod ecclesia dei debet habere paruam scientiam maxime de litteratura unde legitur ad romanos. xi. noli altum sapere. etcet. et xii. non plus sapere quam oportet sapere etcet. et prima ad corinthios. i°. non in sapientia uerbi ut non euacuetur crux christi etcet. et infra. perdam sapientiam sapientium etcet. per totum et maxime ibi. placuit deo per stultitiam predicationis saluos facere credentes etcet. et ibi non multi sapientes secundum carnem etcet. et ii°. predicatio mea non in persuasibilibus humane sapientie uerbis sed in ostensione spiritus et uirtutis ut fides uestra non sit in sapientia hominum etcet. et iii°. sapientia huius mundi stultitia est apud deum. etcet. et infra. deus nouit cogitationes sapientium quoniam uane sunt. et ii^a. ad corinthios. i°. non in sapientia carnali etcet. et iiii°. non ambulantes in astutia etcet. et ad colosenses. ii^a. uidete ne quis uos decipiat per philosophiam et inanem fallaciam secundum traditionem hominum etcet. item. actus. iiii°. uidentes autem petri constantiam et iohannis comperto quod homines esset sine litteris et ydiote admirabantur etcet.

Catholicus: Respondeo quod illa sapientia est uitanda que est contra fidem christi. et hoc est quod dicit apostolus. i^a. ad corinthios. i°. nos autem predicamus christum crucifixum iudeis quidem scandalum gentibus autem stultitiam etcet. et iii°. sapientiam autem loquimur inter perfectos. sapientiam uero non huius seculi qui destruuntur sed loquimur dei sapientiam in misterio etcet. et ad colosenses. ii°. ubi dixit de phylosophia et inani fallacia ibi enim subdit. secundum elementa mundi et non secundum christum etcet. nec obstat quod legitur in actibus. apostolorum quod iudei comperissent apostolos esse sine litteris. quia non uiderant eos didicisse litteras in scholis eorum. simile est quod legitur de christo in iohannes. vii°. et mirabantur iudei dicentes. quomodo hic litteras scit cum non didicerit etcet. Sed Respondete mihi apostolus enim dicit. ad romanos. xv. quecumque enim scripta sunt etcet. et ii^a ad timotheum. iii°. omnis enim scriptura diuinitus inspirata utilis est ad docendum etcet. ergo fideles debent scire omnem scripturam diuinam et probatus est supra. quod debent scire omnem scientiam et patet quod uos heretici estis omnes ydiote maxime in scripturis. quod declaratur. quia neque sententiam earum scitis neque saltem illarum uerba proferre nostis quod aliter de apostolis apparet si bene aduertis in eorum epistolis.

Pat: But it seems the church of God ought to have little knowledge, especially of letters, as is read in Romans 11 (11:20) "be not mindful of lofty things." And 12 (12:3) "not to be more wise than it befits to be wise." And 1 Corinthians 1 (1:17) "not in wisdom of speech, lest the cross of Christ should be made void," and later (1:19) "I will destroy the wisdom of the wise," through the rest and especially there (1:21) "it pleased God, by the foolishness of our preaching, to save those who believe," and there (1:26) "there are not many wise according to the flesh." And 2 (2:4-5) "my preaching was not in the persuasive words of human wisdom, but in the showing of the Spirit and power that your faith might not stand on the wisdom of men." And 3 (3:19) "the wisdom of this world is foolishness before God," and later (3:20) "The Lord knows that the thoughts of the wise are vain." And 2 Corinthians 1 (1:12) "and not in carnal wisdom." And 4 (4:2) "not walking in craftiness." And Colossians 2 (2:8) "Beware lest any man cheat you by philosophy and vain deceit according to the tradition of men." Also Acts 4 (4:13) "Now seeing the constancy of Peter and of John, understanding that they were illiterate and ignorant men, they marveled."

Cath: I reply that the wisdom that is to be shunned is that which is contrary to the faith of Christ, and this is what the Apostle says in 1 Corinthians 1 (1:23) "for we preach Christ crucified, a scandal to the Jews and a folly to the Gentiles." And 3 (2:6-7) "But we speak wisdom among the perfect, yet not the wisdom of this world, neither of the princes of this world who are destroyed, but we speak the wisdom of God in a mystery." And to Colossians 2 where he speaks of philosophy and empty fallacies he adds (2:8) "according to the elements of the world, and not according to Christ." Nor does what is read in the Acts of the Apostles make any difference, that the Jews discovered the apostles not to have learned reading, since they did not seem to them to have learned letters in their schools. It is similar to that which is read of Christ in John 7 (7:15) "And the Jews wondered, saying, 'How does this man know letters, having never learned?'" But answer me this, for the Apostle says in Romans 15 (15:4) "For whatever things were written," and 2 Timothy (3:16) "for all scripture is inspired by God and useful for teaching," and it was proven above that they ought to know all knowledge and it is clear that you heretics are all the greatest fools, especially as regards the scriptures, since it is proven that you neither know their teachings nor do you even know how to quote

---

54 noli...sapere] Rom. 11:20. | non...55 sapere²] Rom. 12:3. 56 non¹...57 christi] 1 Cor. 1:17. 57 perdam...58 sapientium] 1 Cor. 1:19. 58 placuit...59 credentes] 1 Cor. 1:21. 60 non...carnem] 1 Cor. 1:26. 61 predicatio...63 hominum] 1 Cor. 2:4-5. 64 sapientia...65 deum] 1 Cor. 3:19. 65 deus...66 sunt] 1 Cor. 3:20. 66 non...67 carnali] 2 Cor. 1:12. 67 non...68 astutia] 2 Cor. 4:2. 68 uidete...70 hominum] Col. 2:8. 71 uidentes...73 admirabantur] Act. 4:13. 76 nos...78 stultitiam] 1 Cor. 1:23. 78 sapientiam...81 misterio] 1 Cor. 2:6-7. 83 secundum¹...christum] 1 Cor. 2:8. 88 et...89 didicerit] Ioh. 7:15. 90 quecumque... 91 sunt] Rom. 15:4. 91 omnis...93 docendum] 2 Tim. 3:16.

---

52 Patarenus] om. *F* 53 scientiam] sapientiam *F* 74 Catholicus] om. *F* 85 comperissent] compensent *F* 86 scholis] scolis *F* 89 mihi] michi *F* 98 apostolis] appostolis *P* 99 aduertis] ad votis *F*

54 sapere|fol. 125ra *P* 86 litteras|fol. 125rb *P* 96 omnes|fol. 96r *F*

Quinta quia ueritas absque uelamine demonstratur. falsitas autem et turpitudo uelamine cooperitur. De ueritatis autem manifestatione dicit dominus mattheum. v. uos estis lux mundi. Non potest ciuitas abscondi supra montem posita neque accendunt lucernam et ponunt eam sub modio sed super candelabrum etcet. et x. quod dico uobis in tenebris dicite in lumine et quod in aure auditis predicate super tecta etcet. item paulus ad colosenses. ultimo. ut sciatis quomodo uos oporteat unicuique respondere etcet. et petrus. in prima. iii°. parati semper ad satisfactionem omni poscenti uos rationem de ea que in uobis est spe etcet. sed constat quod ecclesia romana publice predicat fidem suam et aperte absque uelamine et euidenter satisfacit omnibus de illa quare noster aperte quod eius fides sit uera et sancta. at heretici semper suos errores palliant et cum timore et uerecundia illos notificant. quare uidetur quod falsa sit eorum moneta et quod mala sit illorum merces. et quod sint latrones pessimi iuxta quod ueritas dicit. iohannes. iii°. omnis enim qui male agit et non uenit ad lucem ut non arguantur opera eius qui autem facit ueritatem uenit ad lucem etcet. et ad ephesios. v. omnia autem que arguuntur a lumine manifestantur etcet. et prima ad timotheus. iiii°. in ypocrisi loquentium mendacium etcet.

Sexta est quia ecclesia debet esse catholica id est uniuersale. quia debet esse diffusa per uniuersum orbem terrarum. unde dominus dicit mattheus viii. dico autem uobis quod multi ab oriente et occidente et recumbent cum abraham etcet. et xxvi. amen dico uobis ubicumque predicatum fuerit hoc euangelio in toto mundo dicetur etcet. et ultimo. euntes ergo docete omnes gentes etcet. et marcum. xiii. et in omnes gentes primum oportet predicari euangelium etcet. et ultimo. euntes in mundum uniuersum predicate euangelium omni creature etcet. et dauid dicit de apostolis et ceteris predicatoribus ecclesie dei. in omnem terram exiuit sonus eorum etcet. Sed constat quod sola fides ecclesie romane diffusa est per mundum uniuersum sicut et apostolus dicit ad romanos. i°. Gratias ago deo meo per ihesum christum pro omnibus uobis quia fides uestra annuntiatur in uniuerso mundo etcet. quare patet quod ipsa sola est uera fides christi et est ratio quare si debet fides christi per totum mundum predicari et apparere scilicet ne

5 The fifth is that truth is revealed without a veil, while falsity and shame are covered by one. Regarding the revelation of the truth the Lord says in Matthew 5 (5:14) "you are the light of the world," and 10 (10:27) "That which I say to you in the dark, preach in the light." Also Paul to the Colossians at the end (4:6) "that you may know how you ought to answer every man," and 1 Peter 3 (3:15) "always be ready with a reason for the hope that is in you." But it happens that the Roman Church publicly preaches its faith openly, without a veil, and evidently satisfies all that our preaching is open because her faith is true and holy, but the heretics always disguise their errors and preach them with fear and shame, hence it seems that their money is fake and that their recompense is evil, and that they are the worst of all thieves, among whom the Truth says in John 3 (3:20) "For every one who does evil hates the light, and does not come to the light, so that his works may not be reproved. But he that does truth, comes to the light." Ephesians 5 (5:13) "But all things that are blameworthy are made manifest by the light." And 1 Timothy 4 (4:2) "Speaking lies in hypocrisy."

6 The Sixth is that the Church ought to be catholic, that is, universal, since it ought to be diffused throughout the whole world, for the Lord says in Matthew 8 (8:11) "And I say to you that many shall come from the east and the west, and shall sit down with Abraham," and 26 (26:13) "Amen I say to you, wherever this gospel shall be preached in the whole world." And Mark 13 (13:10) "And the gospel must first be preached to all nations." And at the end (16:15) "go into the whole world, preaching the gospel to every creature." And David spoke of the Apostles and certain other preachers of the Church of God (Ps 18:5) "their sound went out to all the earth." But it happens that only the faith of the Roman Church is spread throughout the whole world, as the Apostles said in Romans 1 (1:8) "First I give thanks to my God, through Jesus Christ, for you all, because your faith is spoken of in the whole world." Hence it is clear that it alone is the true faith of Christ and this is the reason the faith of Christ ought to be preached and spread through the whole world, lest one might be able to excuse himself if he might not have heard

---

XXX.5.4 uos...7 candelabrum] Matt. 5:14-15. 7 quod...9 tecta] Matt. 10:27. 9 ut...10 respondere] Col. 4:6. 11 parati...12 spe] 1 Pet. 3:15. 20 omnis...23 lucem] Ioh. 3:20. 23 omnia...24 manifestantur] Eph. 5:13. 25 in...mendacium] 1 Tim. 4:2. XXX.6.4 dico...5 abraham] Matt. 8:11. 5 amen...7 dicetur] Matt. 26:13. 7 euntes...8 gentes] Matt. 28:19. 8 et²...9 euangelium] Mar. 13:10. 10 euntes...11 creature] Mar. 16:15. 13 in...eorum] Ps. 18:5. 16 Gratias...18 mundo] Rom. 1:8.

XXX.5.2 falsitas] fluas F 4 Non...7 candelabrum] om. P 8 et...9 tecta] om. P 12 omni...spe] om. P 17 palliant] om. P 18 notificant] notificent notificare P 21 et...23 lucem] om. P XXX.6.4 et¹...5 abraham] om. P 6 in...7 dicetur] om. P 11 euangelium...creature] om. P 17 uestra...18 mundo] om. P 18 quare] quare quod F 19 si...fides²] sic debet P

XXX.5.23 et|fol. 125va P

quis possit se excusare ne audiuerit uerba uite. ait apostolus ad romanos. x. quomodo audient sine predicante etcet. et infra. ergo fides ex auditu auditus autem per uerbum christi etcet. at hereses omnes sunt particulares aliquam certam mundi particulam tenentes et ideo sunt omnes a tramite ueritatis deuiantes.

VIIa

Septima est. quia ecclesia dei debet in se omnes status continere salutis. ne quis merito se possit excusare. et ut summe bonus deus appareat qui omnium deus est et creator. unde deus per prophetam de ipso dicitur. circumdata uarietate etcet. ut etiam significatum est per archam noe. in qua diuersa genera animalium sunt saluata. dominus etiam demonstrat istud aperte. tam in illa parabolam de prandio. mattheus. xxii. quam illa de cena. lucam xiiii. et expressim habemus de singulorum statibus. de pueris enim supra in primo libro. titulus. de sacramento baptismatis. in rubricella quod pueri baptizati saluantur de magnis planum est. et de utrisque dicit. psalmus. iuuenes et uirgines senes cum iunioribus laudent nomen domini etcet. de prelatis uero et continentibus et coniugatis significatum est in ezechiel. xiiii. et si fuerunt heres isti in medio eius. noe. daniel. et iob. ipsi iustitia sua liberabunt animas suas etcet. ad hoc est. mattheus. xiii. alii autem ceciderunt in terram bonam et dederunt fructum aliud centesimum. aliud sexagesimum. aliud tregesimum etcet. et de coniugatis dictum est spiritualiter supra. in primo libro. titulus de matrimonio. de uirginibus autem et de prelatis et subditis planum est nec indiget probatione. de laborantibus autem temporaliter dicit ut supra in secundo libro titulus de pauperibus leonistis. de laborantibus autem spiritualiter non est contrarietas. de nolentibus autem aliud cum non possunt. dic ut supra in primo libro titulus de penitentia. de uolentibus uero et operantibus non est questio. de sapientibus enim dic ut supra in hoc tractatu in quarta ratione. de simplicibus non est contrarium. de militibus uero et de his qui in sublimitate sunt positi ut infra de potestate et iudicio seculari. de ceteris uero planum est et propter istos status omnes dicit dominus in iohannes. xiiii. in domo patris mei mansiones multe sunt id est diuersa premia secundum merita uniuscuiusque status. sed ecclesia romana continet sola status istos uniuersos. ergo est sola dei ecclesia. hereses autem omnes aliquos predictorum statuum a salute repellunt in suo singulari sensu ambulantes inflati. quare manifestum est illas extra dei ecclesia esse.

the word of life. The Apostle says in Romans 10 (10:14) "how shall they hear without a preacher" and later (10:17) "Faith then comes by hearing; and hearing by the word of Christ." But all heresies are local, holding only to a particular area of the world, and so they are all on the path deviating from the truth.

Seventh

The Seventh is that the church ought to contain in itself all the conditions of salvation, lest anyone might be able to excuse themselves justly, and that God, who is God and creator of all things, might be seen as good in the highest degree. As God says through his prophet (Ps 44:10) "surrounded with variety." Also that is signified by the Ark of Noah, in which different types of animals were saved. The Lord showed this clearly as in the parable about the marriage feast, Matthew 22 (22:4) as well as on that supper in Luke 14 (14:16), and we have it explicitly about each single state [of life]; for we spoke about children above in the first book, in the section on the sacrament of baptism, in the subsection that baptized children are saved equally with adults is plain, and of both types the Psalm speaks (148:12) "Young men and maidens, let the old with the young praise the name of the Lord." And also regarding prelates and the celibate and the married it is symbolized in Ezekiel 14 (14:14) "And if these three men, Noah, Daniel, and Job, shall be in it, they shall deliver their own souls by their justice." To this is also Matthew 13 (13:8) "And others fell upon good ground and they brought forth fruit, some a hundredfold, some sixtyfold, and some thirtyfold." And of spouses it was said above in a spiritual sense in the first book, in the section on matrimony. Regarding virgins and prelates and their subjects it is plain and needs no proof. Earthly laborers are spoken about above in the second book, under the section about the Poor Leonists. Regarding spiritual laborers there is no disagreement. But concerning those who refuse to do anything because they are unable, speak as above, in the section in the first book on penitence. Yet of the willing and the working there is also no dispute. Regarding the wise it was spoken about above in this section, on the fourth reason, regarding the simple there is no disagreement. Regarding soldiers and those who are placed in positions of power see below on power and secular judgment. Regarding others it is clear and on account of all those conditions the Lord says in John 14 (14:5) "in my Father's house there are many mansions," that is, different rewards according to the condition of each person. But only the Roman Church bears those universal marks, therefore it alone is the Church of God. But heresies all having only some of the marks, drive away salvation,

---

22 quomodo...23 predicante] Rom. 10:14.   23 ergo...24 christi] Rom. 10:17.   **XXX.7.6** circumdata uarietate] Ps. 44:10.   9 quam... 10 cena] Matt. 22:4.   14 iuuenes...15 domini] Ps. 148:12.   17 et...19 suas] Ez. 14:14 (heres] om. tres uiri *Vulg.*)   20 alii...22 tregesimum] Matt. 13:8 (dederunt] dabant *Vulg.*)   37 in²...38 sunt] Ioh. 14:2.

21 audiuerit] aut numerus F *(unclear word)*   **XXX.7.1** VIIa] om. F   7 noe] om. P   26 dicit] dic F   29 de...30 penitentia] om. P   34 his] hiis F   36 status] om. F

XXX.7.3 possit|fol. 96v F   6 significatum|fol. 125vb P   39 sed|fol. 126ra P

Octaua est laus dei que debet in eius ecclesia fieri deo. multis et uariis modis. sicut ipse sua beneficia multimode impetitur hominibus. de quibus declarabitur iam in rubricella de potestate ecclesie romane et constat quod ecclesia romana laudat deum omnibus illis modis de quibus legitur in sacra scriptura. at hereses omnes non nisi uno modo licet paucis more suo laudant deum. quare patet quod sola romana est ecclesia dei.

Nona est quia talia sunt que credit ecclesia romana que etiam si non essent uera. dum tamen uera esse credat sicut credit non deberet a deo puniri. quia sunt omnia ad honorem dei. sicut est de omnipotentia et passione et huiusmodi. non est enim aliquis. ita crudelis dominus. quia seruo suo det tormenta. si bona fide laudat ipsum plusquam forte sit laudandus. illa uero que credunt heretici. planum est quod sunt ad detractionem et uituperium dei. et ideo non solum quod falsissima sunt. sed etiam si uera essent debent ab ipso in eternum cruciari. tamquam cham filius noe. qui uerenda patris non cooperuit.

Decima est quia ecclesia dei debet esse constans et firma ac perseuerans inconcussa sicut dominus dicit. mattheus. xvi. super hanc petram hedificabo ecclesiam meam etcet. et apostolus. ii^a. ad timotheus. ii^o. sed firmum fundamentum stat. habens signaculum hoc et hereses debent cito deficere et mutari. de quibus dicitur. actus. v. ante hos enim dies estitit theodas dicens se esse aliquem magnum cui consensit numerus uirorum circiter. cccc. qui occisus est. et omnes qui credebant ei dissipati sunt et redacti ad nichilium. post hunc estitit iudas galileus in diebus professionis et aduertit populum post se. et ipse perit et quotquot consenserunt ei dispersi sunt etcet. et infra. quoniam si est ex hominibus consilium hoc aut opus dissoluetur. si uero ex deo est non poteritis dissouere illud etcet. et constat quod hereses non diu durat sed cito dissiparetur. sicut patet de illi de quibus dixit gamaliel et de phariseis et saduceis et nicholaitis et manicheis et arianis et sabellianis et monothitis et ualentinis et huiusmodi heresibus antiquis que dextructe ad nichilum deuenerunt. et iam etiam noue fere dissipate sunt. sicut patet de circumcisis et speronistis et arnaldistis et leonistis et huiusmodi et patareni translati sunt in alias hereses quia suos errores mutauerunt et miscuerunt. fides uero ecclesie romane in nullo penitus

walking in their own particular inflated opinions, hence it is clear that these are outside of the Church of God.

8 The eighth is the praise of God which one ought to find in the Church towards God, in many and various ways as His beneficence is beseeched in diverse manners by men, of which is outlined in the subsection on the power of the Roman Church, and it happens that the Roman Church praises God in all these ways of which it is read in the holy scriptures, but on the other hand in all heresies there is only one way, although a few praise God in the normal way. Hence it is clear that only the Roman Church is the Church of God.

9 The ninth is that there are such things which the Roman Church believes, which even if they were not true, yet provided that She believed them to be true, just as She believes, She would not be bound to be punished by God, since all these things are for the honor of God, just as is the case concerning omnipotence and the Passion and the like. For there is no lord so cruel, that he would inflict torments on his own servant, if he should praise him in good faith more perhaps than he ought to be praised. But those things which the heretics believe, it is clear, are for the detraction and disparagement of God, and therefore not only are they most false, but also if they were true, they ought to be tormented by Him forever. Just like Ham, the son of Noah, who did not cover up his father's nakedness (Gen 9:2027).

10 The tenth is that the Church of God ought to be constant, firm, persevering, and unshaken as the Lord says in Matthew 16 (16:18) "On this rock I will build my Church." And the Apostles in 2 Timothy 2 (2:19) "But the sure foundation of God stands firm, having this seal," while heresies quickly change and fail. Concerning this it is said in Acts 5 (5:36–27) "For before these days Theodas rose up, affirming himself to be someone, to whom a number of men, about four hundred, joined themselves: who was slain; and all who believed him were scattered, and brought to nothing. After this man, rose up Judas of Galilee, in the days of the census, and drew the people away after him. He also perished, and all, even as many as followed him, were dispersed," and later (5:38–39) "for if this council or this work be of men, it will come to nothing, but if it be of God, you cannot overthrow it." And so it happens that heresies do not endure long, but are quickly scattered, as it is clear of those of which Gamaliel spoke, like the Pharisees, the Sadducees, the Nicolaitans, the Manichees, the Arians, the Sabellians, the Monothelites, the Valentinians and similar heresies of old which were destroyed and came to nothing, and of the new ones which nearly all have recently disappeared, like the Circumcisers, the Speronists, the Arnaldists, the Leonists and the like, and the Patarenes have transformed into other heresies since they have changed and mixed their errors.

XXX.9.11 tamquam...12 cooperuit] Gen. 9:20-27. XXX.10.3 super...4 meam] Matt. 16:18. 4 sed...5 signaculum] 2 Tim. 2:19. 7 ante...13 sunt] Act. 5:36-37. 13 quoniam...15 illud] Act. 5:38-39.

XXX.9.1 talia] et sua F 6 quia] *sic* PF leg. qui 10 quod] quia F XXX.10.2 perseuerans] add. sicut P exp. 16 sed] si P 19 monothitis] monochitis F 21 fere] om. P 25 uero] om. P

XXX.9.10 debent|fol. 97r F XXX.10.3 hanc|fol. 126rb P

est mutata neque alterata. sed firma et immobile perseuerat.

Vndecima est quia fideles uere fidei debet esse firmi in ipsa non dubitantes neque hesitantes. unde apostolus ad ephesios. iiii. ut iam non simus paruuli fluctantes et circumferamur omni uento doctrine etcet. et ad colosenses. secundo. Et firmamentum eius que est in christo fidei uestre etcet. et infra. confirmate in fide etcet. sed tales sunt fideles ecclesie romane. quia firmiter et indubitater credunt et tenent sibi fidem traditam a christo et sanctis eius. econtrario. heretici debent dubitare et habere conscians remordentes de suis erroribus. sicut dicit apostolus. i^a. ad timotheus. iiii^o. cauteriatam habentium conscientiam etcet. et ad titum. ultimo. hereticum hominem post unam et secundam correptionem deuita etcet. et constant quod heretici omnes dubitant de suis erroribus sicut didici a multis eorum conuersis ad fidem catholicam et quod dubitent probabiliter possumus conuincere propter superiores et inferiores causas tractatus huius.

Duodecima est quia ecclesia dei debet habere quosdam per sanctos in se. quibus appropinquantes per familiaritatem de malis efficiantur boni. de bonis meliores sicut qui appropinquant luci uident. et qui appropinquant apoteche odorem sentiunt. sicut qui tangant odorifera redolent. unde mattheus. v. uos estis lux mundi etcet. et infra. sic luceat lux uestra coram hominibus ut uideat opera uestra bona etcet. ad phylippenses ii^o. inter quos lucetis tamquam luminaria etcet. actus. iiii^o. quotquot possessores agrorum aut domorum erant uendentes afferebant pretia eorum que uendebant etcet. et constat quod ecclesia romana habet in se quosdam uiros perfectos in sciencia et uita quibus per familiaritatem appropinquantes peccata deserunt et si boni sunt ad meliora proueniunt econtrario ecclesia malignantium debet habere quosdam perfidos qui debent esse sicut tenebre sicut feces quibus appropinquantes ad deteriorem statum peruerniunt. de quibus dominus dicit. mattheus. xvi. cauete a fermento phariseorum et sadduceorum etcet. et xxiii. ue uobis scribe et pharisei qui circuitis mare et aridam ut faciatis unum proselitum et cum fuerit factus facitis eum filium gehenne duplo quam uos etcet. et constat quod familiares et credentes hereticorum super omnes homines de mundo sunt peccatores ueluti blasphemi. per uiri sodomite. usurarii proditores raptores et huiusmodi. unde filius dei docet nos hoc modo illos cognoscere dicens. mattheus. vii. actendite a falsis

Yet the faith of the Roman Church has changed in no way whatsoever, neither has it been altered, but has endured firm and unshakeable.

11 The eleventh is that the faithful of the true faith ought to be firm in her, neither doubting nor hesitating. Whence the Apostle says to the Ephesians 4 (4:14) "That henceforth we be no more like children tossed to and fro, and carried about with every wind of doctrine." And Colossians 2 (2:5) "and the steadfastness of your faith which is in Christ," and later (2:7) "and confirmed in the faith." But such are the faithful of the Roman Church, since they believe firmly and unquestionably and they hold for themselves the faith handed over by Christ and His saints. On the contrary, the heretics ought to doubt and to have pangs of conscience about their errors, as the Apostle says in 1 Timothy 4 (4:2) "having their conscience seared," and at the end of Titus (3:10) "After the first and second admonition, avoid a man who is a heretic." And it happens that all heretics have doubts about their errors just as I have learned from many of them converted to the Catholic faith. And that they should probably doubt, we are able to demonstrate on account of the reasons above and below in this work.

12 The twelfth is that the Church of God ought to have some saints in it, which evil ones may approach with familiarity so that they might be made good, and the good so as to become better, just like those who might come closer see the light, and that those who approach the apothecary might sense the smell, just as those who might touch fragrant things may be made sweet-smelling. Hence Matthew 5 (5:14) "you are the light of the world," and (5:16) "let your light shine before men, that they may see your good works." And Philippians 2 (2:15) "among whom you shine as lights in the world." Acts 4 (4:34) "For as many as were owners of lands or houses sold them, and brought the price of the things they sold." And it happens that the Roman Church has some of those men, perfected in knowledge and life, within her, by whom those who draw near in familiarity might withdraw from sin, and if they are good, they might progress into becoming better. On the contrary the church of the wicked ought to have faithless ones who ought to be like the darkness, just like the dregs which lead those who approach it to a worse condition, of these the Lord says in Matthew 16 (16:6) "beware the leaven of the Pharisees and Sadducees," and 23 (23:15) "Woe to you scribes and Pharisees, hypocrites, because you go round about the sea and the land to make one proselyte and when he is made, you make him the child of hell twice more than yourselves." And it happens that the servants and believers of the heretics are of all men the greatest sinners in the world, just like blasphemers, sodomites, usurers, traitors, robbers, and the like, whence the son of

---

XXX.11.3 ut...4 doctrine] Eph. 4:14.   5 Et...6 uestre] Col. 2:5.   6 confirmate...fide] Col. 2:7.   12 cauteriatam...conscientiam] 1 Tim. 4:2.   13 hereticum...14 deuita] Tit. 3:10.   XXX.12.6 uos...7 mundi] Matt. 5:14.   7 sic...8 bona] Matt. 5:16.   9 inter... luminaria] Php. 2:15.   10 quotquot...12 uendebant] Act. 4:34.   19 cauete...20 sadduceorum] Matt. 16:6.   20 ue...23 uos] Matt. 23:15.   28 actendite...31 eos] Matt. 7:15.

XXX.11.8 sibi fidem] transp. F   XXX.12.16 perfidos] om. P   21 qui...23 uos] om. P   26 proditores raptores] transp. F

XXX.11.3 non|fol. 126va P   XXX.12.9 phylippenses|fol. 97v F   15 proueniunt|fol. 126vb P

prophetis qui ueniunt ad uos in uestimentis ouium. intrinsecus autem sunt lupi rapaces a fructibus eorum congnoscetis eos etcet. fructus enim sunt predicati quasi dicat a predicatis suis. et sibi adherentibus cognoscetis illos. quia quales erunt discipuli tales erunt et eorum doctores.

Tertia decima est quia bonus spiritus seu bona intentio siue bonus cordis motus ducit ad bonum. et econtrario malus spiritus siue mala intentio. uel malus cordis motus ducit ad malum. unde dominus dicit. mattheus vi. si fuerit oculus tuus fuerit simplex totum corpus tuum lucidum erit. si autem oculus tuus fuerit nequam totum corpus tuum tenebrosum erit etcet. vii°. non potest arbor bona fructus malos facere. neque arbor mala fructus bonos etcet. et constat quod illi qui ueniunt ad fidem ecclesie romane uel ad eius opera que docet mouentur ex bono corde id est ex timore seu dolore peccatorum suorum seu ex amore dei et premiorum uite eterne. quare patet quod bona est fides et sancta sunt opera ad que bona intentio uel bonus motus cordis ducit illos. sed omnes heretici mouentur mala intentione et tortuoso corde ducuntur ab ecclesia romana et eius doctrina separari et heresibus adherere ut puta desperatio. uel auaritia. uel superbia. quia noluerunt audire uel interrogare de ueritate a doctoribus et predicatoribus ecclesie et inobedientia et curiositas uel luxuria et immunditia. uel indignatio et huiusmodi. unde ad ephesios. iiii°. qui desperantes semetipsos tradiderunt etcet. et ii^a. ad timotheus. ii°. ut milites in illis bonam militiam etcet. et vi°. radix enim omnium malorum est cupiditas etcet. et secunda ad thesalonicenses. ii°. ideo mittet illis deus operationem erroris ut credant mendacio ut iudicentur omnes qui non crediderunt ueritati etcet. et iii°. denuntiamus autem uobis fratres in nomine domini nostri ihesu christi ut subtrahatis uos ab omni fratre ambulante inordinate etcet. et infra. audiuimus enim inter uos quosdam ambulare inquiete nichil operantes sed suriose agentes etcet. et ii^a. petri. ii°. libertatem illis promittentes etcet. et secunda ad timotheos. iii°. ex hiis enim sunt qui penetrant domos et captiuas ducunt mulierculas honeratas peccatis que ducuntur uariis desideriis etcet. et secunda petri. secundo. in conuiuiis suis luxuriantes uobiscum oculos plenos adulterium et incessabilis delicti. pellicientes animas instabiles. cor exercitatum auaritie habentes. maledictionis filii. derelinquentes. uiam rectam errauerunt etcet. et iude. iii°. hi sunt murmuratores querulosi. secundum

God teaches us to know in this manner, saying in Matthew 7 (7:15–16) "Beware of false prophets, who come to you in sheep's clothing, but inwardly they are ravening wolves, by their fruits you shall know them." For their fruits are proclaimed, as if to say, by their preaching. And you shall know by their adherents, since if the disciples are in a certain way, so will be their doctors.

13 The thirteenth is that a good spirit, or a good intention, or a good heart stirs a movement to the good. And on the contrary a bad spirit or a bad intention or an evil heart leads one to evil. Whence the Lord says in Matthew 6 (6:22) "The light of your body is your eye. If your eye is single, your whole body shall be light, but if your eye is evil your whole body shall be dark." And 7 (7:18) "A good tree cannot bring forth evil fruit, neither can an evil tree bring forth good fruit." And it is evident that those who come to the faith of the Roman Church or to the works which it teaches act from a good heart, that is, through fear or through a sorrow for sins or from love of God and the reward of eternal life. Hence it is clear that faith is good and holy whose works are toward a good intention or are led by a good movement of the heart. But all heretics are moved by an evil intention and are led by a twisted heart to be separated from the Roman Church and her doctrine, and to cleave to heresy, for example, by desperation, or by avarice, or on account of pride, since they do not wish to hear or ask about the truth from the doctors and preachers of the Church regarding disobedience and curiosity or extravagance and impurity and anger and the like. So Ephesians 4 (4:19) "Who ,despairing, have given themselves up." And 2 Timothy 2 (1:18) "that you fight with them a good warfare," and 6 (6:10) "for the root of all evil is the love of money." And 2 Thessalonians 2 (2:11) "Therefore God shall send them the operation of error, to believe by lying, that all may be judged who have not believed the truth, but have consented to iniquity," and 3 (3:6) "And we charge you, brethren, in the name of our Lord Jesus Christ, that you withdraw yourselves from every brother walking disorderly," and later (3:11) "For we have heard there are some among you who walk disorderly, working not at all, but curiously meddling." And 2 Peter 2 (2:19) "Promising them liberty." And 2 Timothy 3 (3:6) "For of these sort are they who creep into houses, and lead captive silly women laden with sins, who are led away with various desires." And 2 Peter 2 (2:13–15) "rioting in their feasts with you, having eyes full of adultery and of sin that has not end, alluring unstable souls, having their heart exercised with covetousness, children of malediction, leaving the right way, they have gone astray." And Jude 3 (1:16) "These are murmurers, full of complaints, walking

---

XXX.13.5 si...7 erit] Matt. 6:22. 7 non...9 bonos] Matt. 7:18. 22 qui...23 tradiderunt] Eph. 4:19. 23 ut...24 militiam] 2 Tim. 1:18. 24 radix...25 cupiditas] 2 Tim. 6:10. 26 ideo...28 ueritati] 2 Thes. 2:11. 28 denuntiamus...31 inordinate] 2 Thes. 3:6. 31 audiuimus...33 agentes] 2 Thes. 3:11. 33 libertatem...34 promittentes] 2 Pet. 2:19. 34 ex...37 desideriis] 2 Tim. 3:6. 37 in... 41 errauerunt] 2 Pet. 2:13. 42 hi...44 causa] Iud. 1:16.

---

29 ad...31 eos] om. P XXX.13.2 et...4 ducit] om. P 5 totum...7 erit] om. P 7 etcet] add. etcet vi F exp. 8 malos...9 bonos] om. P 10 ueniunt] add. in P exp. 12 amore] amare F 16 ducuntur] dicuntur F 20 doctoribus] add. et docti F exp. 27 ut^1...28 ueritati] om. P 30 ut...31 inordinate] om. P 32 nichil...33 agentes] om. P 38 plenos] add. habentes P | et...41 errauerunt] om. P 42 secundum...44 etcet] om. P

XXX.13.18 puta|fol. 127ra P 29 in|fol. 98r F

desideria sua ambulantes et os eorum loquitur superbia mirantes personas questus causa etcet. et hanc rationem reddit dominus. mattheus. xii. bonus homo de bono thesauro cordis profert bona et malus homo de malo thesauro profert malum etcet.

xiiii^a

Quarta decima est cordis. et anima deuotio que debet esse in ecclesia dei. unde dominus dicit. in iohanne. iiii°. sed uenit hora et nunc est quando ueri adoratores adorabunt patrem in spiritu et ueritate etcet. et hoc est in ecclesia romana. quare patet quod ipsa est ecclesia dei. at heretici debent esse sine deuotione mentis. unde apostolus. ii^a. ad timotheum. iii°. ingrati scelesti. sine affectione. etcet. et infra. homines corrupti mente reprobi circa fidem etcet. et tales sunt heretici omnes. quia nullam habet deuotionem cordis sicut ego didici a quibusdam de illis conuersis et satis est probabile. quia nec credunt in corde. nec seruant aut faciunt exterius que illos excitent ad deuotionem se potius ad contraria.

xv^a

Quinta decimum est priuilegium miraculorum quod est in ecclesia romana quod ihesus tradidit sponse sue in spirituale prerogatiuam. unde dixit in iohanne. xiiii. amen amen dico uobis qui credit in me opera que ego facio et ipse faciet et maiora horum faciet etcet. et marcum ultimo. signa autem eos qui crediderint hec sequenter in nomine meo demonia eiicient etcet. et hoc est manifestum signum quod dei uirtus est in romana ecclesia. sicut et saluator noster de se allegauit. iohannes. x. opera que ego facio in nomine patris mei hec testimonium perhibent de me et infra si non facio opera patris mei nolite credere michi. si autem facio et si mihi non uultis credere operibus credite etcet. et de fidelibus suis scriptum est. marcum. ultimo. illi autem profecti predicauerunt ubique domino cooperante. et sermonem confirmate sequentibus signis etcet. et actus. v. per manus apostolorum autem fiebant signa et prodigia multa in plebe etcet. Et constat quod per fideles ecclesie romane facte sunt et fiunt cotidie miracula illa que fecit dominus ihesus christus cum apostolis suis et discipulis. de quibus totum nouum testamentum plenum est. et que debent facere fideles eius.

Patarenus: Sed nonne dominus noster ihesus christus dicit. mattheus. vii°. multi dicent mihi in illa die

Fourteenth

The fourteenth is the devoted heart and soul which ought to be in the Church of God, whence the Lord says in John 4 (4:23) "But the hour comes, and now is here, when the true adorers shall adore the Father in spirit and in truth." And this is in the Roman Church, hence it is clear that she is the Church of God, while the heretics ought to be without devotion of the mind, whence the Apostle in 2 Timothy 3 (3:2) "ungrateful, wicked, without affection," and later (3:8) "men corrupted in mind, reprobate concerning the faith." And such are all heretics, since none of them have devotion of heart, as I have learned from some of their converts, and this is quite probable since they neither believe in their hearts nor observe or do anything exteriorly which would excite themselves to devotion, rather more the contrary.[1]

Fifteenth

The fifteenth is the privilege of miracles which is in the Roman Church, since Jesus handed over this spiritual prerogative to His spouse, as He said in John 14 (14:12) "Amen, amen I say to you, he who believes in me, the works that I do, he also shall do, and greater than these shall he do." And Mark at the end (16:17) "And these signs shall follow those who believe, in my name they will cast out devils." And this is the clear sign that the power of God is in the Roman Church, just as our Savior alleged about Himself in John (10:25) "the works that I do in the name of my Father, they give testimony of me," and later (10:37-38) "If I do not the works of my Father, do not believe me, but if I do, though you will not believe me, believe the works." And of his faithful it is written at the end of Mark (16:20) "But they going forth preached everywhere, the Lord working with them, and confirming the word with signs that followed." And Acts 5 (5:12) "And many signs and wonders were wrought among the people by the hands of the apostles." And it is obvious that there are many deeds wrought by the faithful of the Roman Church and those miracles happen daily, which the Lord Jesus Christ did with His apostles and disciples, of which the New Testament is full, and which ought to be accomplished by his faithful.

Pat: But does not our Lord Jesus Christ say in Matthew 7 (7:22) "Many will say to me in that day, 'Lord, Lord, have

---

45 bonus...47 malum] Matt. 12:35 (cordis) om. *Vulg.*) XXX.14.4 sed...5 ueritate] Ioh. 4:23. 8 ingrati...9 affectione] 1 Tim. 3:2-3. 9 homines...10 fidem] 1 Tim. 3:8. XXX.15.5 amen¹...6 faciet²] Ioh. 14:12. 7 signa...8 eiicient] Mar. 16:17. 11 opera...12 me] Ioh. 10:25. 12 si...14 credite] Ioh. 10:37-38. 15 illi...17 signis] Mar. 16:20. 18 per...19 plebe] Act. 5:12. 26 multi...31 iniquitatem] Matt. 7:22-23.

46 et...47 malum] om. P XXX.14.1 xiiiia] om. F 12 de...conuersis] conuersis de illis F XXX.15.1 xva] om. F 7 hec...8 eiicient] om. P 11 in...12 me] om. P 16 ubique...17 signis] om. P 18 et...19 plebe] om. P 25 Patarenus] om. F

XXX.14.10 sunt|fol. 127rb P

---

1) Very similar to Sacconi's sentiments, for which see Sacconi, c. 6.

domine domine nonne in nomine tuo prophetauimus. et in nomine tuo demonia eicimus. et in nomine tuo uirtutes multas fecimus. et tunc confitebor illis. quia numquam noui uos. Discedite a me omnes qui operamini iniquitatem et paulus dicit. secunda. ad thesalonicenses. ii⁰. eum cuius est aduentus secundum operationem sathane in omni uirtute et signis et prodigiis etcet. et apocalypsis. xvi. et uidi de ore draconis et de ore bestie et de ore pseudoprophete spiritus immundos in modum ranarum exisse. sunt enim spiritus demoniorum facientes signa etcet. et in hunc modum inuenies multas scripturas que dicunt miracula mala esse et a diabolo peruenire. ergo malum signum est facere miracula.

Catholicus: Respondeo quod dominus ihesus christus loquitur in marcum. de illis qui fecerunt miracula in eius uirtute. unde dicit. in nomine meo etcet. sed postea preuaricati sunt. uel non destruerunt a prauis operibus. paulus autem et iohannes et ceteri sancti qui loquuntur de malis miraculis. Intelligunt de miraculis antichristi et pseudo eius et magorum. que miracula non erunt in ueritate. Tria enim mala erunt in eis scilicet quia non erunt facta in dei inuocatione et quia non erunt de ueram utilitatem animarum uel corporum et quia falsa erunt sicut ostendit apostolus in predicta auctoritate ad thesalonicenses. ibi. secundum operationem sathane etcet. et ibi. prodigiis mendacibus. etcet. et iohannes in prima allegata auctoritate. apocalypsis. ubi et procedent ad reges totius terre congregare illos in prelium etcet. et xiii. et seducet habitantes in terra propter signa que data sunt illi in conspectu bestie etcet. Sed respondete uos mihi. Constat quod ecclesia dei debet facere uera miracula. de quibus nulla facitis et ecclesia romana facit illa. ergo ipsa est ecclesia dei et uos estis heretici.

xvi^a

Sextadecima est. quia legitur quod heretici debent separari a fide ecclesie dei. ut dicit apostolus. i^a. ad timotheus. i⁰. quam quidam repellentes circa fidem naufragauerunt etcet. et iiii. spiritus autem manifeste dicit quia in nouissimis temporibus discedent quidam a fide etcet. et ii^a. ad timotheus. i⁰. scis enim quod aduersi sunt a me omnes qui in asia sunt. ex quibus est phyletus et hermogenes etcet. et ii^a. petri. ii⁰. fuerunt uero et pseudo prophete in populo sicut et in uobis etcet. et infra. derelinquentes rectam uiam etcet. et i^a. iohannes. ii⁰. ex nobis prodierunt etcet. et iude. ii⁰. sidera errantia etcet. et infra. hii sunt qui segregant

not we prophesied in your name, and cast out devils in your name, and done many miracles in your name?'" And Paul says in 2 Thessalonians 2 (2:9) "Whose coming is according to the working of Satan, in all power, and signs, and lying wonders." And Apocalypse 16 (16:13) "And I saw from the mouth of the dragon, and from the mouth of the beast, and from the mouth of the false prophet, three unclean spirits like frogs, for they are the spirits of devils working signs." And in this way you find many scriptures that speak of evil miracles, coming from the devil, therefore it is a bad mark to do miracles.

Cath: I reply that our Lord Jesus Christ speaks in Mark of those who do miracles by His power, when He says (16:17) "in my name" but later they are liars, or not destroyed by their depraved works. Yet Paul and John and certain saints who spoke of evil miracles understood that they were the miracles of antichrist and his imitators and magicians, which were not, in truth, actual miracles. For there are three evils in them, namely, because they are not done by the invocation of God and that they are not of true use to souls or bodies, and that they are false just as is shown by the Apostle in the foregoing example to the Thessalonians where (2 Thes 2:9) "according to the working of Satan," and there "and lying wonders." And John in your first alleged authority, Apocalypse where (16:14) "and they go forth unto the kings of the whole earth," and 13 (13:14) "And he seduced them who dwell on the earth, for the signs which were given him to do in the sight of the beast." But answer me this, it is obvious that the Church of God ought to do true miracles, of which you do none, and the Roman Church does, therefore she is the Church of God and you are heretics.

Sixteenth

The sixteenth is that it is read that heretics ought to be separated from the faith of the Church of God, as the Apostle says in 1 Timothy 1 (1:19) "which some rejecting have made shipwreck concerning the faith," and 4 (4:1) "Now the Spirit clearly says, that in the last times some shall depart from the faith." And 2 Timothy 1 (1:15) "You know this, that all they who are in Asia are turned away from me, of whom are Phygellus and Hermogenes." And 2 Peter 2 (2:1) "But there were also false prophets among the people, even as there shall be among you." And 1 John 2 (2:19) "They went out from us," and Jude 2 (1:13) "wandering stars," and later (1:19) "These are those, who

---

32 eum...34 prodigiis] 2 Thes. 2:9.   34 et²...37 signa] Act. 16:13.   43 in...meo] Mar. 16:17.   52 secundum...53 sathane] 2 Thes. 2:9.   55 et...56 prelium] Apoc. 16:14 (procedent) procedunt *Vulg.*)   56 et²...58 bestie] Apoc. 13:14 (seducet) seduxit *Vulg.*)   XXX.16.4 quidam...5 naufragauerunt] 1 Tim. 1:19 (quidam) quidem *Vulg.*)   5 spiritus...7 fide] 1 Tim. 4:1.   7 scis...9 hermogenes] 2 Tim. 1:15.   9 fuerunt...10 uobis] 2 Pet. 2:1.   11 derelinquentes...12 prodierunt] 2 Pet. 2:15.   12 ex...prodierunt] 1 Ioh. 2:19.   13 sidera errantia] Iud. 1:13. | hii...14 semetipsos] Iud. 1:19.

27 nonne...31 iniquitatem] om. *P*   33 in...34 prodigiis] om. *P*   35 et¹...37 signa] om. *P*   41 Catholicus] om. *F*   42 qui] add. dixerunt *F* exp.   45 autem] om. *P*   46 malis] add. operibus *F* exp.   50 erunt] om. *P*   55 ubi] add. subdit *F*   **XXX.16.1** xvia] om. *F*

XXX.15.29 tunc|fol. 98v *F*   45 operibus|fol. 127va *P*

semetipsos etcet. Et constat quod omnes heretici fuerunt de ecclesia romana et nos numquam de illis fuimus separati a fide ipsius. igitur ipsi sunt heretici et nos sumus ecclesia christi qui numquam fuimus separati a fide ipsius.

Patarenus: Dicimus quod predicte auctoritates loquuntur de ecclesia romana que fuit separata a nobis tempore constantini et siluestri. uel loquuntur de quibusdam ex nostris qui quandoque separatur a nobis.

Catholicus: Sed probo quod uterque huiusmodi intellectus falsus est. dicit enim beatus iohannes. ex nobis prodierunt etcet. et iudas. dicit hii sunt qui segregant semetipsos etcet. Sed ecclesia romana non erat tempore eorum secundum uos. ergo minime de illa loquuntur et apostolus dicit. in nouissimis temporibus discedunt quidam a fide etcet. sed siluester et constantinus non fuerunt in nouissimus temporibus sed fuerunt iuxta tempus apostolorum. preterea fideles ecclesie romane non sunt quidam immo sunt pro longe plures quam omnes heretici. item dicit apostolus quod illi qui discedent a fide prohibent nubere et abstinere a cibis quos deus creabit. quod non facit ecclesia romana uel illi qui de uobis exeunt. ergo uos heretici estis illi de quibus dicunt predicte scripture. tum quia pauci estis tum quia de nobis existis. tum quia illos habetis errores quos illi debent habere.

xvii^a

Septimadecima est. quia sicut de christo quasi totus mundus bene sentit licet imperfectione. sicut de sponsa ipsius quasi uniuersis bene debet opinari. et patet quod non solum fideles sed etiam infideles et heretici quodam modo bene opinantur de ecclesia romana licet minus debito. nam iudei dicunt et saraceni et patareni et pauperes leoniste et ceteri status deuiantes ab ecclesia romana. quod si non ipsi saluantur. quia fideles ecclesie saluantur et non alii que opinio boni numquam est de aliquo statu fidelitatis uel hereticis. itaque ista est sponsa dei de qua bonus odor emanat ubique.

Octaua decima est. quia legitur quod in ecclesia dei sunt boni et mali quam diu in hoc mundo peregrinantur prout probabitur infra titulus. quod boni et mali sunt in ecclesia dei et constat quod ecclesia romana bonos et malos in se continet. ergo ipsa est ecclesia dei et hereses omnes mendacitur gloriantur se non nisi bonos habere. ergo non sunt de ecclesia dei.

separate themselves." It is obvious that all heretics were [separated] from the Roman Church and we will never be separated from Him and from His faith, therefore those are heretics and we are the Church of Christ who were never separated from His faith.

Pat: We say that the foregoing authorities are speaking of the Roman Church which was separated from us at the time of Constantine (r. 312–337) and Sylvester (r. 314–335), or speak of certain of us who were at some time separated from us.

Cath: But I prove that both of these are false opinions, for Blessed John says (2:19) "they went out from us." And Jude says (1:19) "These are those, who separate themselves." But the Roman Church did not exist at that time according to you, therefore could not be speaking of it, and the Apostle says (4:1) "In the last times some shall depart from the faith." But Sylvester and Constantine were not in the last days but were nearer to time of the Apostles, further the faithful of the Roman Church are not they, for they have existed for much longer than all heretics. For the Apostle says those "who depart from the faith." (1 Tm 4:3) "Forbidding to marry, to abstain from meats, which God has created," which the Roman Church does not do or those who go forth from you, therefore you heretics are those which are spoken of by the foregoing scriptures, as much as because you are so few, as because you have left us, and because you have those errors which they ought to have.

Seventeenth

The seventeenth is that just as nearly the whole world has heard of Christ, although imperfectly, so one ought to suppose well of His spouse nearly universally, and it is clear that not only the faithful, but also the infidels and heretics think well of the Roman Church, although less than is appropriate. For the Jews and Saracens and Patarenes and Poor Leonists and the others in the condition of straying from the Roman Church say that if they themselves are not saved, why are the faithful of the Church saved, and not others whose perception of the good does not relate to some level of disbelief or to the heretics. Therefore she is the spouse of God, from whom a good scent spreads everywhere.

The eighteenth is that it is read that in the Church of God there are good men and evil men, as long as she journeys in this world, just as was proven in the section, that there are good men and evil men in the Church of God, and it is obvious that the Roman Church contains within herself both the good and the evil, therefore she is the Church of God and all heresies lie, boasting that there is none within

---

24 ex...25 prodierunt] 1 Ioh. 2:19.   25 hii...26 semetipsos] Iud. 1:19.   28 in...29 fide] 1 Tim. 4:1.   34 prohibent...35 creabit] 1 Tim. 4:3 (paraphrase).

16 igitur...18 ipsius] om. *P*   19 Patarenus] om. *F*   23 Catholicus] om. *F*   28 loquuntur] locuntur *P*   30 et] om. *P*   31 tempus] om. *P*   34 prohibent] prohibebunt *F*   38 quia²...existis] om. *F*   XXX.17.1 xviia] om. *F*   3 sicut] sic *F*   8 pauperes] add. et *P*   10 ecclesie] add. romane *F*   11 opinio] oppinio *P*   12 ista] ita *F* | de] om. *P*

XXX.16.14 semetipsos|fol. 127vb *P*   26 semetipsos|fol. 99r *F*   XXX.17.7 nam|fol. 128ra *P*

xix

Nonadecima est quia ecclesia dei debet assimilari filio dei. in prosequendo inimicos dei propter zelum iustitie sicut legitur de ipso. iohannes. ii°. et cum fecisset quasi flagellum de funiculis omnes eiecit de templo etcet. et infra. recordati sunt uero discipuli eius quia scriptum est. zelus domus tue comedit me etcet. et de zelo ecclesie dei legitur. ii^a. ad corinthios. x. redigentes omnem intellectum in obsequium christi et in promptu habentes ulcisci omnem inobedientiam etcet. et constat quod ecclesia romana ex zelo iustitie persequitur inimicos dei et maxime blasphemos hereticos. ergo ipsa est filia. et sponsa christi. at heretici excusant omnes iniqua agentes et pro uiribus suis adiuuant illos ergo ipsi ostendunt se maleficos esse et diuine maiestatis inimicos.

xx

uicesima est. quia in fidelibus dei quedam ylaritas debet esse in uultu que procedit ex lumine fidei quod in eis est. unde. i^a. ad corinthios. viiii. illarem datorem diligit deus et i^a. ad thesalonicenses. ultimo. semper gaudete etcet. et hic est in fidelibus ecclesie romane. at infideles et heretici debent habere uultum tristitie et obscurum. sicut dominus dicit. mattheus. vi. cum autem ieiunatis nolite fieri sicut ypocrite tristes etcet. et hic est karacter bestie. de quo dicit beatus iohannes. apocalypsis. xiii°. et si bene aduertas omnes infideles et heretici habent uultus palidos et tristes et obscuros atque oculos reuolutos et intercisos seu obtenebratos. quia sunt priuati uultuositate dei lucida. que est fides orthodoxa.

uicesima prima est. que ecclesia dei debet habere unum pastorem seu uicarium pro christo qui debet esse super omnes ut habetur mattheo. xvi. et ego dico tibi quia tu es petrus et super hanc petram hedificabo ecclesiam meam etcet. et iohannes. ultimo. dixit symoni petro ihesus. Simon iohannis diligis me plus his etcet. et postea dixit ei. pasce oues meas et constat quod hunc habet ecclesia romana et nulla heresis habet. ergo sola ecclesia est ecclesia dei.

xxii^a

Vicesima secunda est. quia omnia bona que predicantur de ecclesia romana. sunt in ecclesia romana que non reperiuntur per singula in aliqua heresi etiam secundum hereticos. ergo ecclesia romana est sola sponsa christi et ecclesia dei.

Nineteen

The nineteenth is that the Church of God ought to become like the son of God in persecuting the enemies of God on account of zeal for justice, as is read of Him in John 2 (2:15) "And when he had made, as it were, a scourge of little cords, he drove them all out of the temple," and later (2:17) "And his disciples remembered that it was written, 'zeal for your house has consumed me.'" And zeal for the Church of God is read about in 2 Corinthians 10 (10:5–6) "and bringing into captivity every understanding to the obedience of Christ and having in readiness to revenge all disobedience." And it is obvious that the Roman Church, on account of zeal for justice, persecutes the enemies of God, and especially blaspheming heretics, therefore she is the daughter and spouse of Christ, while the heretics excuse all evildoers and help them by their efforts, so they show themselves to be evildoers and enemies of the divine majesty.

Twentieth

The twentieth is that there should be a certain cheerfulness in the face of the faithful that proceeds from the light of faith which is in them, whence 1 Corinthians 9 (2 Cor 9:7) "for God loves a cheerful giver." And 1 Thessalonians at the end (5:16) "rejoice always," and this is in the faithful of the Roman Church, while the infidels and heretics ought to have sad and gloomy faces, just as the Lord says in Matthew 6 (6:16) "And when you fast, do not be sad like the hypocrites." And this is the character of the beast as Blessed John says in Apocalypse 13. And you well notice that all infidels and heretics have pallid, sad, and gloomy faces, and remote, darkened or wandering eyes, since they are deprived of the shining face of God, which is the orthodox faith.

The twenty-first is that the Church of God ought to have one shepherd or vicar of Christ, who ought to be over all, as one has it in Matthew 16 (16:18) "and I say to you that you are Peter and on this rock I will build my church," and at the end of John (21:15) "Jesus said to Simon Peter, 'Simon, son of John, do you love me more than these?'" And later He said to him "feed my sheep," and it is obvious that the Roman Church has this, and no heresy has it, therefore the Church alone is the Church of God.

Twenty-Second

That all the good things that are preached by the Church of Rome are found in the Roman Church, but they are not all found in any heresy even according to the heretics.

XXX.19.4 et...5 templo] Ioh. 2:15.   6 recordati...7 me] Ioh. 2:17.   8 redigentes...10 inobedientiam] 2 Cor. 10:5-6. XXX.20.4 illarem...5 deus] 2 Cor. 9:7.   5 semper...6 gaudete] 1 Thes. 5:16.   8 cum...9 tristes] Matt. 6:16.   XXX.21.3 et...5 meam] Matt. 16:18.   5 dixit...6 his] Ioh. 21:15.

XXX.19.1 xix] om. F   XXX.20.1 xx] om. F   2 ylaritas] claritas P   9 nolite...tristes] om. P   13 atque...obtenebratos] om. F XXX.22.1 xxiia] om. F

XXX.19.16 diuine|fol. 128rb P   XXX.20.14 sunt|fol. 99v F

Therefore the Roman Church alone is the spouse of Christ and the Church of God.

Omnis potestas est a deo   XXXI   All power is from God

Dicimus et uerum est quod omnis potestas qua utitur ecclesia romana est a christo et ab apostolis eius ut patet primo ex illis uerbis generalibus que dixit dominus petro mattheus. xvi. tibi dabo claues regni celorum et quodcumque ligaueris super terram erit ligatum et in celis et quodcumque solueris super terram erit solutum in celis etcet. et possumus probare de singulis et primo de septem ordinibus quos ecclesia romana dat. quia legimus quod christus qui est caput ecclesie exercuit eos de ostiariatu legitur in iohannes. ii°. et cum fecisset quasi flagellum de funiculis omnes eiecit de templo. De lectoria legitur lucam. iii°. et intrauit secundum consuetudinem suam die sabbati in synagoga et surrexit legere et traditus est illi liber ysaie prophete etcet. De exorcitatu habetur in euangeliis ubi percipiens expellebat demones de hominibus. de accolitatu uero legitur. iohannes. xii°. ego lux in mundum ueni etcet. De subdiaconatu habetur. iohannes. xiiii°. precinxit se linteo et lauare pedes discipulorum etcet. Diaconatum uero exercuit cum predicauit euangelium. sacerdotium autem cum in cena sacrificauit corpus et sanguinem suum. Et uirtutem huius ordinis tradidit apostolis cum dixit eis in cena. hoc facite in meam commemorationem et cum post resurrectionem suam dedit eis spiritum sanctum et dixit quorum remiseritis peccata remittuntur eis etcet. et de subdiaconatu spiritualiter quod ecclesia romana potuerit eum facere sacrum ordinem probatur. tum quia dominus dixit mattheus. xviii. dico uobis quia si duo ex uobis consenserint super terram de omni re quamcumque petierint fiet illis a patre meo qui in celis est. ubi enim sunt duo uel tres congregati in nomine meo etcet. ergo uniuersalis ecclesia potuit obtinere ut subdiaconatus esset ordo sacer. tum quia legitur in actibus apostolorum quod apostoli ordinauerunt. septem. diacones et fecerunt eis manus impositionem. in qua dabatur spiritus sanctus et sicut apostoli potuerunt diaconatum facere ordinem sacrum ita et ecclesia uniuersalis potuit subdiaconatum ordinare ordinem sacrum esse.

We say, and it is true, that all power used by the Roman Church is from Christ and from His Apostles, as is first shown in those general words which the Lord spoke to Peter in Matthew 16 (16:19) "I give you the keys of the kingdom of heaven, and whatsoever you shall bind upon earth shall be held bound in heaven and whatsoever you shall loose upon earth shall be loosed in heaven." And we are able to prove each and every one of the seven orders which the Roman Church gives since we read that Christ, who is the head of the Church, carried them out. Regarding the office of porter, it is read in John 2 (2:5) "And when he had made, as it were, a scourge of little cords, he drove them all out of the temple." Regarding lectors it is read in Luke 3 (4:16) "and he went into the synagogue, according to his custom, on the Sabbath day and he rose up to read." Regarding exorcists you have in the gospels where one can learn of the expulsion of demons from men. Regarding acolytes it is certainly read in John 12 (12:46) "I am coming as a light into the world." Concerning the subdiaconate, one has John 14 (13:4–5) "and he girded himself and washed the feet of the disciples." And He executed the [office of the] diaconate when He preached the gospel. Moreover the priesthood when He sacrificed His body and blood at the supper. And this power of orders He handed on to his disciples when He said at the supper (Lk 22:19) "do this in memory of me," and when, after His resurrection, He gave the Holy Spirit to them and said (Jn 20:23) "Whose sins you forgive, they are forgiven them." And of the subdiaconate, spiritually, that the Roman Church was able to institute it as a sacred order is proven when the Lord said, in Matthew 18 (18:19) "Again I say to you, that if two of you agree on earth concerning anything whatsoever they will ask, it shall be done for them by my Father who is in heaven. For where there are two or three gathered together in my name." So the universal Church could make the subdiaconate a sacred order, since it is read in the Acts of the Apostles that the Apostles ordained seven deacons and laid their hands on them during which the Holy Spirit was given and just as the Apostles were able to make the diaconate a sacred order so also is the universal Church able to create the subdiaconate as a sacred order.

De dignitatibus   2   On ranks

De dignitatibus habemus et primo de papatu in predictis auctoribus. tu es petrus et pasce oues meas. De patriarchis habemus. mattheus x conuocatis duodecim discipulis suis dedit eis potestatem etcet. De cardinalibus autem legitur. lucam x. post hec autem

About ranks we have first the papacy, in the aforementioned authorities, (Mt 16:18) "you are Peter" and (Jn 21:17) "feed my sheep." As regards patriarchs we have Matthew 10 (10:1) "And having called his twelve disciples together, he gave them power." Moreover of

---

XXXI.1.5 tibi...8 celis] Matt. 16:19.   12 et...13 templo] Ioh. 2:15.   13 et...16 prophete] Luc. 4:16.   18 ego...19 ueni] Ioh. 12:46.   20 precinxit...21 discipulorum] Ioh. 13:4-5.   25 hoc...commemorationem] Luc. 22:19.   27 quorum...28 eis] Ioh. 20:23.   30 dico...34 meo] Matt. 18:19.   XXXI.2.4 conuocatis...5 potestatem] Matt. 10:1.   6 post...7 lxxii] Luc. 10:1.

XXXI.1.1 Omnis...deo] om. *F*   6 et...8 celis] om. *P*   9 singulis] add. spiritualiter *F*   11 ostiariatu] hostiariatu *P*   15 et¹...16 prophete] om. *P*   16 exorcitatu] exorcita *P*   32 de...34 meo] om. *P*   35 obtinere] optinere *F*   37 septem] vii *F*   XXXI.2.1 De dignitatibus] om. *F*   2 dignitatibus] add. autem *F*

XXXI.1.1 deo|fol. 128va *P*   37 eis|fol. 128vb *P*

designauit dominus et alios lxxii etcet. de archiepiscopis legitur ad titum. iᵒ. et constituas per ciuitates presbiteros id est episcopos genere titus erat archiepiscopus si constituebat episcopos et idem fuit de timotheo. de episcopis uero habetur actus. xx. in quo uos spiritus sanctus posuit episcopos regere ecclesiam dei etcet. et ad phylippenses cum episcopis et diaconibus etcet. et multis aliis locis. de clericis uero legitur communiter iᵃ. petri. ultimo. neque ut dominantes in cleris etcet. de legatis legitur. iiᵃ. ad corinthios. viii. ordinatus est ab ecclesiis comes peregrinationis nostre etcet. et in multis aliis locis diuine scripture. De ecclesiis uero materialibus habundis et de munditia earum et de oratoribus et predicatoribus in eis faciendis habetur. in euangeliis ubi legitur quod dominus ihesus intrauit in templum dei et eiecit omnes uendentes et ementes de templo et numulariorum et cathedras uendentium columbas euertit. et dixit eis. scriptum est. domus mea domus orationis est etcet. et actus. iiᵒ. in finem. cotidie quoque perdurantes unanimiter in templo etcet. et iiiiᵒ. in finem. omni autem die non cessabant in templo etcet. de horis autem canonicis in templo faciendis publice et in sono eundo ad illas inuenitur. actus. 3. petrus autem et iohannes ascedebant in templum ad horam orationis nonam etcet. de lectoribus et huiusmodi legendis in ministerio ecclesiastico sollempniter et alte coram populo habemus exemplo deum qui surgens legit prophetiam coram populo. in officio sabbati ut dictum est superius de uestibus sacerdotalibus habendis in officio diuino et de mutatione illarum habemus. iohannes. xiii. surgit a cena et ponit uestimenta sua. de thurificatione uero. lucam. iᵒ. ut incensum poneret etcet. et apocalypsis. viii. et alius angelus uenit et stetit ante altare habens thuribulum aureum et data sunt illi incensa multa etcet. de processionibus habemus exemplo deum qui recepit eam cum uenerit a monte oliueti de muneribus offerendis sacerdotibus habemus mattheus iiᵒ. et apertis thesauris suis obtulerunt ei munera etcet. et in pluribus locis habemus in euangelio quod dominus precepit munera offereri sacerdotibus. de gratiarum actione deo facienda pro beneficiis habetur. mattheus xv. gratias agens fregit et dedit discipulis suis etcet. et ad colosenses. iiiiᵒ. in gratiarum actione etcet. de hymnis et psalmis et de canticis publice faciendis habetur. mattheus. xxviᵒ. et hymno dicto exierunt in montem oliueti. et iᵃ. ad corinthios. xiiii. cum conuenitis unusquisque uestrum psalmum habet etcet.

Cardinals it is read in Luke 10 (10:1) "And after these things the Lord appointed also another seventy-two." Concerning archbishops it is read in Titus 1 (1:5) "you should ordain priests in every city," that is, bishops like Titus who was archbishop if he was creating bishops, and the same was [can be said of] Timothy. Regarding bishops one has Acts 20 (20:28) "in which the Holy Spirit has placed you as bishops, to rule the church of God." And to the Philippians (1:1) "with the bishops and deacons," and in many other places. Regarding clerics it is ordinarily read in 1 Peter, at the end (5:3) "Neither as lording it over the clergy." Concerning legates it is read in 2 Corinthians 8 (8:19) "but he was also ordained by the churches, companion of our travel," and in many other places in divine scripture. Regarding having many physical churches and regarding their purity, and of the prayers and preaching that should be done in them, one has the passage in the gospels where it is read that the Lord Jesus entered into the Temple of God and ejected all the buyers and sellers from the temple and overturned the benches of the money changers and the dove sellers, and he said to them (Lk 19:46) "It is written that my house shall be a house of prayer." And Acts 2 at the end (2:46) "And continuing daily with one accord in the temple." And at the end of 4 (5:42) "And every day they did not cease in the temple." In regards to the canonical hours publicly performed in the temple and in going to them at the sound [of a bell] one finds Acts 3 (3:1) "Now Peter and John went up into the temple at the ninth hour of prayer." On lectors and the like who read in solemn ecclesiastical ministry in the sight of the people we have the example of God (Lk 4) who, rising, read the prophecy in the sight of the people. On the Sabbath office you have what was said above. Regarding priestly vestments worn in the divine office and of their changes we have John 13 (13:4) "He arose from supper, and laid aside his garments." Regarding incensing in truth is Luke 1 (1:9) "that he might impose incense," and Apocalypse 8 (8:3) "And another angel came, and stood before the altar, having a golden censer, and much incense was given to him." Regarding processions we have the example of God who received those when He came from Mount Olivet with the offerings presented by the priests, we have Matthew 2 (2:11) "and opening their treasures, they offered him gifts." And in many places in the gospel we have it that the Lord commanded gifts to be offered to the priests, making thanksgiving to God for the benefits that had been granted, Matthew 15 (15:36) "giving thanks, he broke and gave it to his disciples." And Colossians 4 (4:2) "in thanksgiving." (Col 3:16) Concerning hymns and psalms and spiritual canticles publicly performed one has

---

8 et...9 presbiteros] Tit. 1:5.   11 in...13 dei] Act. 20:28.   13 cum...14 diaconibus] Php. 1:1.   15 neque...16 cleris] 1 Pet. 5:3.   17 ordinatus...18 nostre] 2 Cor. 8:19.   25 scriptum...26 est] Luc. 19:46.   26 in...27 templo] Act. 2:46.   28 omni...29 templo¹] Act. 5:42.   31 petrus...32 nonam] Act. 3:1.   38 surgit...39 sua] Ioh. 13:4.   40 ut...poneret] Luc. 1:9.   41 et¹...42 multa] Apoc. 8:3.   45 et...46 munera] Matt. 2:11.   50 gratias...suis] Matt. 15:36.   51 in...actione] Col. 4:2. | de...52 canticis] Col. 3:16 (paraphrase).   53 et...54 oliueti] Matt. 26:30.   54 cum...55 habet] 1 Cor. 14:26.

9 genere...10 episcopos] om. P   19 ecclesiis] clericis F   31 3] ɜ iii F   35 deum] add. al. man. sup. lucam. iiii. P   42 et...multa] om. P   49 beneficiis] beneficium P   54 oliueti] olivarum F

XXXI.2.9 titus|fol. 100r F   27 perdurantes|fol. 129ra P

et ad ephesios. v. implemini spiritu sancto loquentes uosmetipsis in psalmis et hymnis et canticis spiritualibus cantantes et psallentes etcet. et ad colosenses. iii°. commonentes uos metipsos in psalmis et hymnis et canticis spiritualibus in gratia cantantes etcet. et apocalypsis. xviiii. dicentium alleluia etcet. et infra. dicentium alleluia. De tonsura uero habetur. actus. xviii. ibi. qui totum dederant in carceris capit etcet. De solempnitate uero dierum habetur. mattheus. xxvi. tempus meum prope est apud te facio pascha etcet. et iohannes. v. Erat dies festus iudeorum et ascendit ihesus ierosolimam etcet. et actus. xviii. oportet me solempnem diem aduenientem facere ierosolymis etcet. et apocalypsis. i°. fui in spiritu in dominica die etcet. De solempnitate uero sepulturarum fidelium habemus in euangeliis ubi legitur de corpore domini nostri ihesu christi que de sepultum est in monumento nouo cum aromatibus et actus. viii. curauerunt autem stephanum uiri timorati et fecerunt planctum magnum super eum. de glosis autem sanctorum habes. lucam x. ubi legitur de samaritano qui traditis duobus denarios stabulario id est doctrina ueteris et noui testamenti. dixit ei. quodcumque supererogaueris ego etcet. supererogatum enim intelliguntur glose et expositiones sanctorum. de potestate uero seculari constituenda quod ecclesia se habeat intromittere. habes. iª. ad corinthios. vi. an nescitis quoniam sancti de hoc mundo iudicabunt? etcet. de excommunicatione autem ecclesie legitur. mattheus xviii. amen dico uobis quodcumque ligaueris super terram etcet. et iª. ad corinthios. v. iam iudicaui qui sic operatus est. in nomine domini nostri ihesu christi. tradere huiusmodi sathane etcet. et ultimo. siquis non amat dominum nostrum ihesum christum sit anathema. et iª. ad timotheus. i°. quos tradidi sathane ut discant non blasphemare. De plenaria uero potestate ecclesie quam habet tam in constituendis religionibus in ordinandis statibus hominem quam in faciendo iura. ut puta decretales et huiusmodi. in dando indulgentias et in ordinandis ieiuniis et huiusmodi. in absoluendo a uotis. et in faciendo et in ordinando omnia que non sint expressim contra precepta dei et apostolorum eius habemus. ex istis. iiii°ʳ. auctoritatibus. mattheus. vi. tu es petrus etcet. et xviii. quodcumque ligaueris etcet. et lucam. xxii. qui non habet gladium uendat etcet. et infra. at illi dixerunt. ecce duo gladii hic. at ille dixit eis. accipite.

Matthew 26 (26:30) "And they sang a hymn and went to Mount Olivet." And 1 Corinthians 14 (14:26) "When you come together, every one of you has a psalm." And Ephesians 5 (5:18–19) "but be filled with the Holy Spirit, speaking to yourselves in psalms, and hymns, and spiritual canticles, singing." And Colossians 3 (3:16) "admonishing one another with psalms, hymns, and spiritual canticles singing in grace." And Apocalypse 19 (19:1) "saying 'Alleluia,'" and later (19:6) "saying 'Alleluia.'" On the tonsure you have Acts 16 (16:26–38) there, where he was seized and they were taken to prison. Regarding solemn days one has Matthew 26 (26:18) "My time is near at hand, with you I take the pasch with my disciples." And John 5 (5:1) "It was a festival day for the Jews, and Jesus went up to Jerusalem." And Acts 18 (18:21 in some Vulgates) "it was fitting for me to take a solemn feast at Jerusalem." And Apocalypse 1 (1:10) "I was in the spirit on the Lord's day." Regarding the solemn burial of the faithful we have in the gospels were it is read that the body of the Lord Jesus Christ, which had been laid in a new tomb, was preserved with spices, and Acts 8 (8:2) "And devout men took care for Stephen's funeral, and made great mourning over him." Concerning the interpretations of the saints you have Luke 10 (10:35) where it is read of the Samaritan who left two denarii for the innkeeper, that is, the teaching of the Old and New Testaments, saying to him "and whatsoever you spend over and above." That which is "over and above" is understood to be the explanations of the saints. Of the constitution of secular power that the Church has permitted to herself you have 1 Corinthians 6 (6:2) "Do you not know that the saints will judge this world?" Regarding ecclesiastical excommunication it is read in Matthew 18 (16:19) "Amen I say to you, whatever you bind on earth." And 1 Corinthians 5 (5:3) "I have already judged, as though I were present, in the name of our Lord Jesus Christ, to deliver such a one to Satan." And at the end (16:22) "If any man does not love our Lord Jesus Christ, let him be anathema." And 1 Timothy 1 (1:20) "whom I have delivered up to Satan, that they may learn not to blaspheme." On the plenary power of the Church which it has in erecting religious orders and in ordaining states of life and in making laws like the decretals and suchlike, in granting indulgences, and in ordering fasts and the like, and in absolving vows and in doing and ordering all those things which are not expressly contrary to the commands of God and his Apostles, we have four authorities for these. Matthew 6 (16:18) "You are Peter," and 18 (16:19) "whatsoever you bind." And Luke 22 (22:36) "Let him who has no sword buy one," and later (22:38) "But they said, 'Lord, behold here are two swords.'

---

56 implemini...58 psallentes] Eph. 5:18-19.   59 commonentes...60 cantantes] Col. 3:16.   61 dicentium alleluia] Act. 19:1.   62 dicentium alleluia] Act. 19:6.   63 ibi...capit] Act. 16:26-38.   65 tempus...pascha] Matt. 26:18.   66 Erat...67 ierosolimam] Ioh. 5:1.   67 oportet...68 ierosolymis] Act. 18:21 addition present in some Greek and Latin mss.   69 fui...die] Apoc. 1:10.   73 curauerunt...74 eum] Act. 8:2.   75 ubi...76 stabulario] Luc. 10:35.   81 an...82 iudicabunt] 1 Cor. 6:2.   84 amen...85 terram] Matt. 16:19.   85 iam...87 sathane] 1 Cor. 5:3-5.   88 siquis...89 anathema] 1 Cor. 16:22.   89 quos...90 blasphemare] 1 Tim. 1:20.   98 tu...petrus] Matt. 16:18.   99 quodcumque ligaueris] Matt. 16:19. | qui...100 uendat] Luc. 22:36.   100 at...102 est] Luc. 22:38.

57 et¹...58 psallentes] om. P   98 vi] sic PF leg. xvi

59 metipsos|fol. 129rb P   69 in²|fol. 100v F   91 potestate|fol. 129va P

satis est scilicet. et ioannes xx spiritum sanctum quorum remiseritis peccata remittuntur eis etcet.

And he said to them, 'take it up. It is enough'" And John 20 (20:22–23) "Receive the Holy Spirit, whose sins you shall forgive, they are forgiven them."

Quod secundum patarenum ecclesia romana dicitur babillonia siue meretrix

Quod secundum patarenum ecclesia romana dicitur babillonia siue mulier meretrix. de que legitur in apocalypsis. patet multis inditiis. primum est quia sedet super bestia coccineam. bestia enim coccinea. papa est. qui totus est rubricatus a deo ut etiam birretum habeat rubeum et super hanc bestia sedet id est requiescit ecclesia romana.

Secundum est quia sedet super vii montes id est super romam ubi sunt septem montes naturales ad litteram. patet enim quod sedes ecclesie romane. est in urbe romana. unde et nomen accepit.

Tertium est. quia ipsa accepit potestate suam a dracone id est a constantino. a quo ecclesia romana totam suam habuit potestatem.

Quartum est quia portat caracterem bestie id est signum crucis et precipit illum portari.

Quintum est. quia mater est fornicationum. et omnium turpitudinum et peccatorum.

Sextum est. quia plena est deliciis

Septimum est quia multis habundat diuitiis

Octauum est. quia ipsa ambulat in mirabilibus honorum et dignitatum seculi huius.

Nonum est quia fouet malos et nutrit.

Decimum est quia malum habet caput et corpus eius est infirmum et aplanta pedis usque ad uerticem non est in eo sanitas.

undecimum est. quia de ipsa exeunt locuste id est illi qui dicuntur religiosi ad percutiendum et occidendum homines.

Duocecimum est. quia ipsa blasphemat sub spem excommunicationis faciende.

Tertium decimum est quia compellit homines transgredi mandata christi. ut puta iurare et occidere et huiusmodi.

Quartum decimum est. quia persequitur et occidit sanctos.

Quintum decimum est. quia est ydolatria.

De primo legitur. apocalypsis. xvii. Vidi mulier sedentem super bestiam coccineam etcet. de secundo in eodem. habentem capita septem etcet. et infra. septem capita septem montes sunt super quos mulier sedet etcet. De tertio habetur. xiiiº. et dedit illi draco uirtutem suam et potestatem suam magnam etcet. de quarto in eodem et faciet ut quicumque non

XXXII That according to the Patarenes the Roman Church is called 'Babylon' or 'Whore'

That according to the Patarenes the Roman Church is called 'Babylon' or 'Whore' about which it is read in Apocalypse, is clear by many indications. The first is that she is seated on a scarlet beast, for the scarlet beast is the Pope, who is totally reddened by God that he should even have a red biretta, and upon the beast, sits, that is, sleeps, the Roman Church.

The second is that she is seated on seven hills, that is, in Rome where there are literally seven natural hills, for it is obvious that the seat of the Roman Church is in the city of Rome, whence the name.

The third is that she has accepted power from the dragon, that is, Constantine, from whom the Roman Church has received all her power.

The fourth is that she carries the mark of the beast that is, the sign of the cross and commands that it be carried.

The fifth is that she is the mother of fornications, and of all vileness and sin.

The sixth is that she is full of luxuries.

The seventh is that she has copious riches.

The eighth is that she walks in the marvelous honors and dignities of this world.

The ninth is that she cherishes and nourishes evildoers.

The tenth is that she has an evil head and her body is weak and from her head to her feet there is in her nothing of health.

The eleventh is that locusts come out of her, that is, those who are called 'religious' for the persecution and murder of men.

The twelfth is that she blasphemes by making the promise of excommunication.

The thirteenth is that she compels men to transgress the commands of Christ, for example to swear and kill and the like.

The fourteenth is that she persecutes and kills saints.

The fifteenth is that she is an idolater.

Concerning the first it is read in Apocalypse 17 (17:3) "I saw a woman seated upon a scarlet beast." The second in the same place (17:3) "Having seven heads," and later (17:9) "the seven heads are the seven hills upon which the woman sits." On the third one has 13 (13:2) "And the dragon gave him his own strength, and great power." Regarding the fourth, in the same and (13:14) "and should

---

102 spiritum...103 eis] Ioh. 20:22-23. XXXII.1.40 Vidi...41 coccineam] Apoc. 17:3. 42 habentem...septem] Apoc. 17:3. 43 septem¹...44 sedet] Apoc. 17:9. 44 et...45 magnam] Apoc. 13:2. 46 faciet...49 manu] Apoc. 13:14.

102 satis est] om. P | et...sanctum] om. P XXXII.1.1 Quod...2 meretrix] om. F 3 secundum patarenum] om. F | dicitur] sit F 17 caracterem] karacterem P 21 deliciis] delitiis P 22 Septimum...diuitiis] om. F 34 homines] hominem F 40 xvii] vii F

XXXII.1.17 bestie|fol. 129vb P 26 habet|fol. 101r F 46 ut|fol. 130ra P

adorauerunt ymaginem bestie occidatur et faciet omnes pusillos et magnos et diuites et pauperes et liberos et seruos habere caracterem in dextera manu etcet. ecce quomodo compellit omnes portantes caracterem bestie id est corone que dicitur esse bestie id est siluestri. quia ipse primo ordinauit hoc signum portari et fecit marca fieri preceptum per constantinum imperatorem.

De quinto habetur. xiiii. cecidit babillon illa magna que a uino ire fornicationis sue potauit omnes gentes etcet. et xvii. babillon magna mater fornicationum et abhominationum terre etcet. et infra. hii odient fornicariam etcet. xviii. plangent super illam reges terre qui cum illa fornicati sunt etcet. De sexto legitur. xviii. et in deliciis uixerunt etcet. et infra. porna tua et desiderii anime tue discesserunt a te et omnia pinguia et preclara perierunt a te etcet. et xvii. habens poculum aureum in manu sua. de septimo uero legitur et xvii°. et mulier circumdata erat purpura et coccino et inaurata auro et lapide pretioso et margaritis etcet. et xviii. et lugebunt super illam. quoniam merces eorum nemo emet amplius. merces auri et argenti etcet. et infra. ue. ue. ciuitas illa magna que amicta erat purpura et cocco et deaurata auro et lapide pretioso et margaritis. quoniam una hora destitute sunt tante diuitie etcet. et supra eodem et mercatores terre de uirtute delitiarum eius diuites facti sunt etcet.

De octauo legitur. xvii. hii unum et consilium habent et uirtutem et potestatem suam bestie tradent etcet. et xviii. quia in corde suo dicit sedeo regina etcet. De ix legitur. xviii. et facta est demoniorum habitatio et custodia omnia spiritus immundi etcet. de decimo. patet quod papa qui est caput eius est bestia coccinea et ideo malus et alios manifesta sunt opera eius et quales sunt cardinales et ceteri prelati eius. patet lupis et tonsoribus et ipsa tota in uoluta est in peccatis eorum. unde de ipsa dicit ysaias. iª. omne caput languidum et omne cor morens a plant pedis usque ad uerticem etcet. et apocalypsis. xviii. de meretrice magna que corrupit terram in prostitutione sua etcet. ed undecimo habetur. viiii°. et data est ei clauis putei abyssi etcet. et infra. et de fumo putei exierunt locuste in terram. etcet.

cause, that whosoever will not adore the image of the beast, should be slain, and he shall make all, both little and great, rich and poor, freemen and bondmen, to have a mark in their right hand." Behold how he compels all carrying the mark of the beast, that is, of the crown which is said to be from the beast, that is, Sylvester, who first ordered that sign to be carried and commanded the sign to be made through Constantine the emperor.

Regarding the fifth one has 14 (Apoc 14:8) "That great Babylon is fallen which made all nations drink of the wine of the wrath of her fornication," and 17 (17:5) "A mystery, Babylon the great, the mother of the fornications and abominations of the earth," and later (17:16) "these shall hate the harlot," and (18:9) "and the kings of the earth shall weep over her who had fornicated with her." On the sixth it is read in 18 (18:9) "and they lived with her in luxuries," and later (18:14) "And the fruits of the desire of your soul are departed from you, and all fat and goodly things are perished from you," and later 17 (17:4) "having a golden cup in her hand, full of the abomination and filthiness of her fornication." Concerning the seventh it is truly read in 17 (17:4) "And the woman was clothed round about with purple and scarlet, and gilt with gold, and precious stones and pearls," and 18 (18:11-12) "and mourn over her, for no man shall buy their merchandise any more, merchandise of gold and silver," and later (18:16-17) "Woe! Woe! That great city, which was clothed with purple, and scarlet, and was gilt with gold, and precious stones, and pearls, for in one hour are so great riches come to nought." And regarding the same thing (18:3) "the merchants of the earth have been made rich by the power of her luxuries."

Regarding the eighth it is read in 17 (17:13) "These have one design, and their strength and power they shall deliver to the beast," and 18 (18:7) "because she says in her heart, 'I sit a queen.'" Of the ninth it is read in 18 (18:2) "and it has become the habitation of devils, and the hold of every unclean spirit." On the tenth, it is obvious that the pope who is her head and is the scarlet beast, and so he is evil and his works have been manifested to others, which are the cardinals and certain of his bishops. It is clear that she is herself wrapped in the sins of the wolves and debasers [of money], and of such Isaiah says (1:5) "the whole head is sick, and the whole heart is sad, from the sole of the foot to the top of the head." And Apocalypse 19 (19:2) "the great harlot which corrupted the earth with her fornication." And concerning the eleventh one has 9 (9:1) "and there was given to him the key of the bottomless pit," and later (9:3) "And from the smoke of the pit there came out locusts upon the earth."

---

55 cecidit...56 gentes] Apoc. 14:8.   57 babillon...58 terre] Apoc. 17:5.   58 hii...59 fornicariam] Apoc. 17:16.   59 plangent...60 sunt] Apoc. 18:9.   61 et¹...uixerunt] Apoc. 18:9. | porna...63 te] Apoc. 18:14.   63 habens...64 sua] Apoc. 17:4.   65 et¹...66 margaritis] Apoc. 17:4.   67 et...68 argenti] Apoc. 18:11-12.   69 ue¹...72 diuitie] Apoc. 18:16-17.   72 et²...73 sunt] Apoc. 18:3.   74 hii...75 tradent] Apoc. 17:13.   76 quia...regina] Apoc. 18:7.   77 et¹...78 immundi] Apoc. 18:2.   83 omne...85 uerticem] Is. 1:5.   85 de...86 sua] Apoc. 19:2.   87 et...88 abyssi] Apoc. 9:1.   88 et²...89 terram] Apoc. 9:3.

50 portantes] portare F   51 caracterem] karacterem F   52 primo] om. P   64 manu] add. tua P exp.   74 consilium] solium P   76 ix] ix octavo P   79 est²] om. P   80 malus] aliis F

71 margaritis|fol. 130rb P   85 meretrice|fol. 101v F

Iste locuste sunt religiosi qui habent caudas capuciorum et habent coronas aureas quia propter coronas capillorum suorum inter homines multum honorantur et iste percutiunt homines in ore scorpionum maxime qui dicuntur fratres predicatores. De duodecimo habetur. xvii. plena nominibus blasphemie etcet. De tertiodecimo manifestum est. De xiiii°. legitur. xvii°. et uidi mulierem ebriam de sanguine sanctorum et de sanguine martyrum ihesu etcet. et xix. uindicauit sanguinem seruorum suorum de manibus eius etcet. De quintodecimo uero habetur. viiii. neque penitentiam egerunt de operibus manuum suarum ut non adorarent demonia et simulacra aurea et argentea et erea et lapide et lignea que neque ambulare etcet. et xiii. et faciat ut quicumque non adorauerint ymaginem bestie occidantur etcet. Ex hiis patet quod ecclesia romana est ecclesia perditionis et confusionis.

Catholicus: Reponsio. quod ea que loquitur beatus iohannis. in apocalypsis. numquam de ecclesia romana possunt intelligi scilicet quando loquitur de muliere meretrice siue babillonia quod probo multis rationibus et primo quia dicit quod illa sedet super bestiam coccineam est. quia dicit beatus iohannes. xvii°. quod illa bestia coccinea est. quomodo enim siluester uel alius papa dicitur octauus? preterea dicit ibi quod illa bestia fuit et non est quod numquam de papa potest intelligi nec ad litteram nec spiritualiter. ad litteram planum est. spiritualiter autem in quantum bestia esset numquam fuisset. nec obstat quod dicis papa rubricatus est. ut per hoc necessarium sit eum intelligi per bestiam coccineam quia eodem modo imperator constantinopolitanus et potestas uenetorum qui est constantinopolis semper induuntur de scarleto rubeo. quod faciunt plures alii principes mundi. ergo iam non una bestia coccinea sed plures esse dicerentur. quod falsum est. preterea uos dicitis quod papa. est caput ecclesie romane et ex alia parte dicitis quod est equus eius. secundum hoc est impossibile quod aliquis sedeat super caput suum. ad secundam dico quod falsum est quod ecclesia romana sedeat super illos. vii. montes materiales qui sunt rome. nec in eis aliquo modo confidit. nec quicquam habet in illis. ad tertium. Respondeo quod numquam potest intelligi quod draco ille fuerit constantinus. nec quod illa bestia que accepit potestatem a dracone. sit ecclesia romana. quia dicitur in duodecimo expressim. quia draco ille fuit diabolys

These locusts are the religious men who have hoodlike tails and gold crowns, since on account of their hair crowns [tonsures] they are honored among men and they strike men with their scorpion mouths, especially those who are called Friars Preachers. Regarding the twelfth, one has 17 (17:3) "full of names of blasphemy." On the thirteenth it is plain. Concerning the fourteenth one reads in 17 (17:6) "and I saw the woman drunk on the blood of the saints and of the martyrs of Jesus Christ," and 19 (19:2) "and he has revenged the blood of his servants, at her hands." Regarding the fifteenth, one has 9 (9:20) "they did not do penance from the works of their hands, that they should not adore devils, and idols of gold, and silver, and brass, and stone, and wood, which neither can see, nor hear, nor walk," and 13 (13:15) "and should cause that whoever will not adore the image of the beast, should be slain." From these it is clear that the Roman Church is the church of ruin and confusion.

Cath: Reply. That which blessed John speaks of in Apocalypse can in no way apply to the Roman Church, namely, when he speaks of the harlotwoman or Babylon. I prove this by numerous reasons, and first because he says that she is seated on a scarlet beast, which blessed John says in 17 (17:3) that the beast is scarlet. For how was Sylvester or another pope called the eighth?[1] Further he says there that the beast 'was,' and not 'is,' so that one could never understand this about the pope, neither literally nor spiritually. Literally is plain enough, yet spiritually insofar as the beast never would have existed. Neither does it matter that you say that the pope wears red, so that it might be necessary to understand him as the scarlet beast, since in the same manner the Emperor of Constantinople and the Podestà of Venice, who is at Constantinople, always wear scarlet red, as also many other worldly princes do. Therefore one might say there is not only one but many scarlet beasts, which is false. Further you say that the pope is the head of the Roman Church and on the other hand you say that he is equal to her, accordingly it is impossible that another might sit over his head. To the second I say that it is false that the Roman Church sits over those seven physical hills which are in Rome, neither does it trust them in any manner, nor have anything in them. To the third. I reply that it is impossible to interpret that the dragon was Constantine, nor that the beast which received power from the dragon be the Roman Church, since it is clearly stated in the twelfth chapter that the dragon was the devil and Satan who seduced the whole world who was ejected from heaven with his angels.

---

90 Iste locuste] Apoc. 9:3.   95 plena...96 blasphemie] Apoc. 17:3.   97 et...98 ihesu] Apoc. 17:6.   99 uindicauit...100 eius] Apoc. 19:2.   101 neque...104 ambulare] Apoc. 9:20.   104 et²...105 occidantur] Apoc. 13:15.   113 quod...114 est] Apoc. 17:3 paraphrase.

90 Iste] add. sunt *P* exp. | capu-ciorum] caputiorum *P*   92 inter...honorantur] multum honorantur inter homines *F*   93 iste] sic *PF* trans.pl.   95 De] om. *P*   99 xix] xviiii *P*   103 neque] add. audire *F*   106 perditionis] perdicionis *P*   108 Catholicus] om. *F*   113 est] om. *F*   114 coccinea] om. *F*   124 principes] add. forte *P*   126 uos...papa] vos quod papa dicitis *P* | caput] capud *P*   128 aliquis] alias *P*   131 eis] *sic PF* leg. eos

100 uero|fol. 130va *P*   131 in|fol. 130vb *P*

---

[1] The "eighth" in reference to the seven heads of the scarlet beast upon which the woman sits.

et sathanas qui seducit uniuersum orbem qui proiectus fuit de celo cum angelis suis. ergo non fuit constantinus. illam autem que accepit potestatem a dracone appellat beatus iohannes bestiam in tertio decimo et hic ubi agri de babillonia dicitur quod mulier sedebat super bestiam coccineam. ergo alia est bestia que ascendit de mari et alia est bestia coccinea et aliud est bestia et aliud est mulier que dicitur babylonia. ergo numquam potest intelligi de ecclesia romana illud quod dicitur de potestate quam accepit bestia ascendens de mari a dracone. etiam si per babiloniam ecclesia romana significaretur. ad iiii^{um} dicimus quod non appelat karacterem cruce. crux enim appelatur signum filii hominis. sicut dominus dicit. mattheum. xxiiii. et tunc apparebit signum filii hominis in celo etcet. de quo dicemus iam inferius in rubricella. preterea ibi legitur quod babylonia occidit sanctos. sed ecclesia romana nutrit et fouet illos. ad alia omnia dico quod non possunt intelligi de ecclesia romana. quia tota babylonia facit illa. sed non omnes de ecclesia romana faciunt hoc. immo sunt multi in ipsa casti. parce uiuentes et pauperes. et despecti. nec sunt aliqui in ipsa ydolatrie. prout ostendemus inferius nec ipsa mittit locustas immo persequitur et comburit illas. uos enim heretici estis ille locuste et non religiosi quod patet quod capillos hereticis longos ut ille et estis multi et diuersi. ad modum locustarum. nec obstat quod dicitis de caudis earum ut per illas intelligatis caputia religiosorum quia fatuissimus apparet intelligis iste caude enim numquam in capitibus sunt sed in parte inferiori. nec obstat quod dicitis de coronis aureis. quia propter tonsuras religiosi non honorantur a stultis et reprobis immo propter hoc sunt apud eos in derisum et in comtemptum. preterea si religiosi sint locuste et preceptum est illis ne lederent nisi tantum homines qui non habent signum dei in frontibus suis. igitur cum ipse uos ledant non habetis signum dei in frontibus uestris igitur estis reprobi. tamen uos ille locuste estis qui non leditis nisi uestros credentes qui carent signaculum sancte crucis et qui sunt pleni omni nequitia et turpitudine.

Hec sunt dicta falsorum hereticorum

Ecclesia uero dei non debet sedere super bestiam coccineam. sicut nos non sedemus. nec debet esse eius confidentia super ciuitatem romanam. sicut nec natura est. nec debet habere potestatem ab aliquo principe seculari sed a solo christo. sicut ipse dicit. lucam. x. ecce dedi uobis potestatem calcandi supra serpentes et scorpiones et super omnem uirtutem inimici et nos habemus potestatem a principibus secularibus immo

Therefore it was not Constantine. Yet that which received power from the dragon blessed John called the beast in the thirteenth chapter and here where 'the fields of Babylon,' it is said that the woman sat upon a scarlet beast. Therefore one beast is that which arose from the sea and another is the scarlet beast and one is the beast and another is the woman which is called Babylon. Therefore one can never interpret as referring to the Roman Church that which is said regarding the power that the scarlet beast accepted, arising from the sea to the dragon, even if by 'Babylon' the Roman Church were signified. To the fourth we say that it does not apply to the sign of the Cross. For the cross is called the sign of the Son of man, just as the Lord says in Matthew 24 (24:30) "And then shall appear the sign of the Son of man in heaven," of which we spoke already in the subsection. Further there is read that Babylon killed the saints, but the Roman Church fosters and cherishes them, to all other things I say that one cannot interpret them as the Roman Church, since all of Babylon does these things, but not all of the Roman Church does this, yet there are many in her who are chaste, living simply and poorly and insignificantly, neither are there any in that idolatry, just as we will show below, neither indeed does she send locusts to persecute and burn them. For you heretics are the locusts and not the religious since it is clear that heretics have long hair like this one, and you are many and diverse, in the manner of locusts. Nor does it matter what you say about their "tails" so that by those you understand the hoods of the religious since they appear extremely vain, understand these hoods are never on the heads but always on the back. Neither does it matter that you speak of gold crowns, since on account of the religious tonsure they are not honored by fools and knaves, rather on account of this they are held in derision and contempt. Further, if religious were locusts and they are commanded not to do harm except only to men who do not have the sign of God on their foreheads, so when they strike you it means that you do not have the sign of God on your foreheads, therefore you are reprobate. Yet you are those locusts because you do not harm except your own believers who lack the sign of the holy cross and who are full of every wickedness and scandal.

These are the sayings of the false heretics

The Church of God ought not sit upon a scarlet beast, just as we do not sit upon it, neither ought it to place its trust in the city of Rome, for such it not its nature. Neither ought it hold power from any secular prince, but only from Christ, as he said in Luke 10 (10:19) "Behold, I have given you power to tread upon serpents and scorpions, and upon all the power of the enemy," and we have power from secular princes yet we do not oppress and kill, as it is

---

151 et…celo] Matt. 24:30. **XXXII.2.7** ecce…8 inimici] Luc. 10:19.

140 bestiam] om. *P* | tertio decimo] tertia decima *F* 144 babylonia] babillonia *P* 145 illud…148 romana] om. *P* 149 karacterem…enim] om. *P* | enim] add. non *P* 153 babylonia] babillonia *P* 156 babylonia] babillonia *P* | facit illa] faciunt illos *F* | illa] illos *F* 158 despecti] despati *P* 165 fatuissimus apparet] *sic* PF **leg. fatuissima apparent** 166 caude] add. sunt *P* exp. enim] add. non *P* 168 stultis] stulti *F* 172 suis] uestris *P* **XXXII.2.1** Hec…hereticorum] om. *F*

146 quam|fol. 102r *F* 162 et|fol. 131ra *P*

ipsum nos opprimunt et occidunt. sicut legitur quod debent facere de fidelibus christi. unde beatus iacobus. dicit. ii°. nonne diuites per potentiam opprimunt uos et ipsi trahunt uos ad iuditia etcet. et dominus dicit in iohannes. xv. sed quia elegi uos de mundo propterea odit uos mundus etcet. item ecclesia dei non debet portare caracterem bestie immo debet occidi. quia non portabit illum et ecce quia nos non portamus karacterem crucis. immo frangimus et contempnimus illum et sub pedibus nostris calcamus et deicimur et laceramur quia nolumus adorare ipsum. item ecclesia dei debet esse sancta et immaculata et sine aliquo peccato. sicut ostendemus inferius in suo tractatu sicut nos sumus. item debet esse in artitudine uite. sicut dominus dixit. mattheus. v. beati qui lugent etcet. et vii°. quam angusta est uia et arcta que ducit ad uitam et pauci sunt qui inueniunt eam etcet.

Catholicus: et apostolus qui autem sunt christi carnem suam crucifixerunt cum etcet. et iacobum. iiii. miseri estote et lugete etcet. et in multis aliis locis diuine scripture reperitur et nos sumus in multa uite artitudine positi. item debet esse in pauperitate. sicut dominus dixit. mattheus. v. beati pauperes etcet. marcus. x. facilius est camelum per foramen acus transire quam diuitem intrare in regnum dei etcet. et nos sumus sine diuitiis huius mundi in pauperitate ambulantes. ipsa debet ambulare in humilitate et contemptu et sine honoribus uite huius et supple et prosequere de hac materia pro et contra ut infra in libro IIII°. de practicationibus hereticorum notatum inuenies. et titulo de portis mortis hereticorum suplebitur de babylonia. quod hic diximus minus.

Catholicus: Mattheus. iii°. et permundabit aream suam et congregabit triticum suum in horream suum. paleas autem comburet igni inextinguibili etcet. sed arca christi est ecclesia. in quam est palea mixta cum tritico donec ponat triticum in horreum et paleas comburat igni inextinguibli. ergo boni et mali sunt in ecclesia dei usque ad finem mundi. idem. viiii. ecce multi publicani et peccatores ueniebant discumbebant cum ihesu et discipulis eius etcet. et infra. at ihesus audiens ait. non est opus ualentibus medicus male habentibus. etcet. ergo male habentibus etcet. ergo in ecclesia christi erant peccatores et ipse participabat cum illis. idem. xiii. simile factum est regnum celorum homini qui seminauit bonum semen in agro suo etcet. et infra. serui autem dixerunt ei. uis imus et colligimus ea etcet. et ait non etcet. et infra. sicut ergo zizania

read, that they ought to do to the faithful of Christ, whence Blessed James says in 2 (2:6) "Do not the rich oppress you by power and do not they haul you before the judgment seats?" And the Lord says in John 15 (15:19) "but I have chosen you out of the world, since the world hates you." Further the Church of God should not carry the mark of the beast, on the contrary, it ought to be killed, since it will not bear it and behold because we do not bear the mark of the cross. On the contrary we break and spurn it and crush it under our feet and we throw it down and destroy it, since we do not want to adore it. Further the Church of God ought to be holy and immaculate, and without any sin. Just as we showed below in your section, just as we are. Further it ought to be strict in life, as the Lord said in Matthew 5 (5:5) "Blessed are those who mourn," and 7 (7:13) "How narrow is the gate, and straight is the way that leads to life and few there are who find it!"

Cath: And the Apostle, (Gal 5:24) "And they are Christ's, who have crucified their flesh." And James 4 (4:9) "be afflicted, and mourn," and it is repeated in many other places in divine scripture, and we are placed in the hard straits of life, further one ought to be in poverty, as the Lord said in Matthew 5 (5:3) "Blessed are the poor," and Mark 10 (10:25) "It is easier for a camel to pass through the eye of a needle, than for a rich man to enter into the kingdom of God." And we are without the riches of this world, walking in poverty. The Church ought to walk in humility and contempt and without the honors of this life, and we shall supply and pursue these matters, for and against, below in book four, where you will find noted the known practices of the heretics, and in the section "on the gates of death" is added about the heretics from Babylon, which we speak less of here.

Cath: Matthew 3 (3:12) "and he will thoroughly cleanse his floor and gather his wheat into the barn, but the chaff he will burn with unquenchable fire." But the ark of Christ is the Church, in which the chaff is mixed with the wheat until the wheat is put into the barn, and the chaff is burnt with inextinguishable fire. Therefore the good and evil are mixed in the Church of God until the end of the world. The same in 9 (9:10) "Behold many publicans and sinners came and reclined with Jesus and his disciples," and later (9:12) "But Jesus hearing it, said, 'Those who are healthy do not need a physician, but those who are ill.'" Therefore those who are ill, so in the Church of Christ there were sinners and He partook [of food] with them. The same in 13 (13:24) "the kingdom of heaven is like a man who sowed good seed in his field," and later (13:28–29) "And the servants said to him, 'Do you wish that we go and

---

12 nonne…13 iuditia] Iac. 2:6.   14 sed…15 mundus] Ioh. 15:19.   24 beati…lugent] Matt. 5:5.   25 quam…26 eam] Matt. 7:14.
27 qui…28 cum] Gal. 5:24.   28 miseri…29 lugete] Iac. 4:9.   32 beati pauperes] Matt. 5:3.   33 facilius…34 dei] Mar. 10:25.
42 et…44 inextinguibili] Matt. 3:12.   48 ecce…50 eius] Matt. 9:10 (ueniebant] uenientes *Vulg.*)   50 at…52 habentibus¹] Matt. 9:12.
54 simile…55 suo] Matt. 13:24.   56 serui…57 non] Matt. 13:28-29.   57 sicut…60 scandala] Matt. 13:40.

16 caracterem] karacterem *P*   26 etcet] add. et apostolus *PF*   27 Catholicus] om. *F* | et apostolus] om. et apostolus *PF* | sunt christi] transp. *F*   29 aliis] add. vestris *P* exp.   30 reperitur] repperitur *F*   33 acus…34 dei] om. *P*   36 ambulantes] add. item *F* | ipsa] ipse *P* | et] om. *P*   41 babylonia] babillonia *P* | diximus minus] transp. *F*   42 Catholicus] om. *F*   46 horreum] orreum *F*   55 in…suo] om. *P*

XXXII.2.13 etcet|fol. 131rb *P*   29 diuine|fol. 102v *F*   44 paleas|fol. 131va *P*

colliguntur et igni comburuntur. sic erit in consummatione seculi. mittet angelos suos et colligent de regno eius omnia scandala etcet. et sicut in agro mundi sunt scandala mixta tritico usque ad consummationem seculi. sic et in ecclesia dei erunt mixti mali cum bonis. quia dominus uocat hic regnum celorum. nec potes dicere quod regnum suum uocet mundum. quia dicit quod symile est regnum celorum homini qui seminauit bonum semen in agro suo scilicet in mundo. ergo aliud est regnum celorum et aliud est mundus. nec etiam potes exponere de regno celorum id est patria eterna. quia ibi non sunt scandala.

Patarenus: Ergo nec de mundo nec de ecclesia dei sunt extirpandi mali. et facitis uos in utroque contrarium.
Catholicus: Nos tam de ecclesia quam de mundo dicimus illos extirpandos esse qui possunt ibi esse sine scandalo bonorum et de quibus legitur et constat quod sint zizania. et ab illis qui habent ex officio debito. alias enim neque de ecclesia. neque de mundo sint extirpandi sed usque ad seculi consummationem reliquandi.

Item idem in eodem

Item idem in eodem. simile est regnum celorum sagene misse in mare et ex omni genere piscium congreganti quam cum impleta esset educentes elegerunt bonis in uasa sua. malos autem foras miserunt. sic erit in consummatione seculi etcet. ergo usque ad consummationem seculi celorum id est in ecclesia dei mixti sunt mali cum bonis et sunt omnis de sagena id est de ecclesia christi.
Patarenus: Dicimus quod ista est parabola. et ideo non est ad litteram. quod sonare uidetur.
Catholicus: Et ego non curo quod sit ad litteram sagena missa in mare sed similitudo eius est que est regnum celorum congregatis bonis et malos et tenens utrosque usque ad seculi consummationem. sicut dominus ipsemet exponit que non potest esse nisi ecclesia dei. sed modo respondete mihi bruta animalia. numquid intelligitis quod ea que in parabolis dicit ueritas non sint seruanda et credenda. ergo male nobis obicitis de parabola zizanorum contra potestates. Discite namque homines nequaquam quod in parabolis duo sunt scilicet similitudo et simulatum. primum uero non tenemur credere quia figura est et potest enim esse et forte non est. secundum uero et credere et seruare debemus. quia figurata ueritas est.

gather it up?' And he said, 'No,'" and later (13:40) "Even as cockle is gathered up and burnt with fire, so shall it be at the end of the world. [The Son of man] will send his angels, and they will gather out of his kingdom all scandals." And so it is in the field of the world where there are scandals mixed in the grain until the end of the age. So also in the Church of God there will be evil men mixed with good, because the Lord has called this the kingdom of Heaven, neither are you able to say that He called the world His kingdom, since He said that the kingdom of heaven is like a man who sowed good seed in his field, that is, in the world. So the kingdom of heaven is one thing, and the world is another. Nor even can you explain about the kingdom of heaven that it is the eternal fatherland, since there are no scandals there.
Pat: So then evildoers are not to be rooted up either in the world or in the Church of God, and you act contrariwise in both.
Cath: All the same, we say that those are to be rooted up as much in the Church as in the world who are able to be removed from there without scandal to the good, and of which it is read, and it is obvious that they are cockles, and by those who have the appropriate office. Else they are not to be extirpated, neither from the Church nor the world, but are to be left until the consummation of the world.

Also regarding the same topic.

Also regarding the same topic (13:47) "The kingdom of heaven is like a net cast into the sea, gathering together all kind of fishes. Which, when it was filled, they drew out and ... they selected out the good and put them in storage, but the bad they cast forth." For so it will be until the consummation of the world, that is, in the Church of God the evil are mixed with the good and they are all in the net, that is, in the Church of Christ.
Pat: We say that is a parable, and it should not be taken literally, as what it seems to sound like.
Cath: And I do not care if there was a literal net put into the sea, but its analogy is that it is the kingdom of heaven where good and evil are gathered together, holding them both until the consummation of the world, just as the Lord himself explained that it cannot be anything save the Church of God. But only answer me, you brutish animals, how you can ever understand that those things which He, truth itself, speaks in parables are not to be observed and believed? Therefore you make a poor objection to us of the parable of the cockles against the powerful. For learn, evil men, that there are two things in the parables, namely, the likeness and the thing likened [to another]. The first we are not bound to believe since it is a figure, for it can both be and perhaps not be. But the second we ought to believe and to observe, since truth is figured in it.

XXXII.3.2 simile...6 seculi] Matt. 13:47.

60 in agro] om. *P* | mundi] add. erit *P* exp.   61 sunt...62 dei] om .*P*   64 uocet] uocetur *P*   70 Patarenus] om. *F*   71 sunt] sunt *F* facitis uos] transp. *F*   73 Catholicus] om. *F*   74 qui] **leg. add. non**   XXXII.3.1 Item...eodem] om. *F*   4 congreganti...6 seculi] om. *P*   10 Patarenus] om. *F*   12 Catholicus] om. *F*   21 nequaquam] leg. nequam.   22 sunt] signat *F*

76 zizania|fol. 131vb *P*   XXXII.3.11 uidetur|fol. 103r *F*

Patarenus: Item si autem peccauerit in te frater tuus etcet. ergo est frater quis etiam cum peccat. nec est reiciendus ab ecclesia dei quamdiu legitime amonitus et conuictus non fuerit inuentus contumax et rebellis ipsi ecclesie. ergo peccatores sunt de ecclesia dei quam diu sustinentur ab illa et non uult christius eos expelli. de illa atque uitari. nisi propter rebellionem et contumacionem. idem. xxii. simile est regnum celorum homini regi qui fecit nuptias filio suo etcet. et infra. et egressi serui eius in uias congregauerunt omnes quos inuenerunt etcet. ergo in nuptias fidei ecclesiae dei que dicitur regnum celorum. sunt simul mali cum bonis.

Patarenus: Dicimus quod sunt in uita eterna boni et mali id est qui fuerunt boni et qui fuerunt mali anima.
Catholicus: Sed omnes qui sunt ibi fuerunt quandoque male ut dicit apostolus ad ephesios. ii°. nos omnes aliquando conuersati sumus in desideriis carnis nostre. facientes uolunatem carnis et cogitationum et eramus natura filii ire sicut et ceteri etcet. item omnes fuerunt boni qui infuerunt in eam. quia aliter non intrassent sicut dicitur apocalypsis. ultimo. foris autem canes etcet. et penultimum. non intrabit in eam aliquos coinquinatum etcet. et sic essent idem boni et mali. quod falsum est quia dicit inuenerunt bonos et malos etcet. ergo alii sunt boni et alii mali qui sunt in regno celorum. quod non nisi de militante ecclesia potest intelligi quod probat apertius cum subiungit. intrauit autem rex ut uideret discumbentes et uidit ibi hominem non uestitum ueste nuptiali etcet. quod non nisi dei ecclesia que per fidem regnat in terra potest intelligi.
Catholicus: Item lucam. xxii. intrauit autem sathanas in iudam qui cognominabatur scarioth unum de duodecim etcet. et infra. et cum facta esset hora discubuit et duodecim apostoli cum eo et postea et accepit pane gratias egit et dedit eis dicens. hoc est corpus meum etcet. et infra. uerumptamen ecce manus tradentis me mecum est in mensa etcet. ecce habes quod postquam iudas scarioth ordinauit traditionem christi qui et fur erat et loculos habens etcet. uocatus est apostolus et dominus cum eo celebrauit pascha et tradidit ei corpus suum et neque eiecit illum de congregatione sua quam diu ille sponte se ipsum non eiecit et sic habemus expresse quod qui malus erat. fuit de christi ecclesia dignitate et familiaritate ac sacramenti participatione. nec est eiectus de illa nec

Pat: Further (18:15) "But if your brother should offend against you." Therefore he is still a brother even when he sins, neither is he to be expelled from the Church of God so long as he be legitimately warned and convicted, he will have not been found contumacious and rebellious against the Church itself. Therefore there are sinners in the Church of God which are sustained by her for howsoever long, and Christ does not want them to be cast out from her and to be shunned, excepting on account of rebellion and contumacy. It is the same in 22 (22:2) "the kingdom of heaven is like a king who held a marriage feast for his son," and later (22:10) "And his servants went forth into the streets, gathered together all that they found." So in the marriage feast of faith, the Church of God which is called the kingdom of heaven, contains evil ones together with the good.
Pat: We say that in eternal life there are the good and the evil, that is, who were good souls and who were evil souls.
Cath: But all who are here were evil at some time, as the Apostle says to the Ephesians 2 (2:3) "also we all conversed in time past, in the desires of our flesh, fulfilling the will of the flesh and of our thoughts, and were by nature children of wrath, even as the rest." Also all were good who were in her [eternal life], since otherwise they could not have entered as the Apostle said at the end of Apocalypse (22: 15) "the dogs are outside," and in the next to last (21:27) "nothing defiled shall enter into it," and so there were the same good and evil, which is false since he says they will find good and evil. Therefore some are good and others evil who are in the kingdom of heaven, which one cannot understand if not the Church militant, which is patently clear when he adds (Mt 22:11) "And the king went in to see the guests and he saw there a man who did not have on a wedding garment." So one cannot interpret it in any other way than the Church of God which reigns through faith on earth.
Cath: Also Luke 22 (22:3) "and Satan entered into Judas, who is called Iscariot, one of the twelve," and later (22:14) "and when the hour had come he reclined at table, and the twelve apostles were with him," and after (22:17) "and he took bread, gave thanks, and gave it to them, saying, 'This is my body.'" See you have it that after Judas Iscariot was ordained after the manner of Christ, and who (Jn 12:6) "was a thief, holding the purse," and was called Apostle, and the Lord celebrated the Pasch with him and gave him His body and did not expel him from the assembly, as long as he freely did not absent himself and thus we have it expressly demonstrated that [though] he was evil, he was of the Church of Christ, worthy, and befriended, and admitted to sacramental participation. Neither was he expelled from her, nor shunned by the Lord and by the

---

26 si...tuus] Matt. 18:15. 33 simile...34 suo] Matt. 22:2. 35 et...36 etcet] Matt. 22:10. 42 nos...45 ceteri] Eph. 2:3. 47 foris... 48 canes] Apoc. 22:15. 48 non...49 coinquinatum] Apoc. 21:27. 54 intrauit...55 nuptiali] Matt. 22:11. 58 intrauit...60 duodecim] Luc. 22:3. 60 et²...61 eo] Luc. 22:14. 61 et³...63 meum] Luc. 22:17. 63 uerumptamen...64 mensa] Luc. 22:21. 66 fur...habens] Ioh. 12:6.

---

26 Patarenus] om. *F* 27 etiam] om. *P* 28 legitime] legittime *P* 29 non...inuentus] om. *F* 31 et...32 illa] om. *P* 39 Patarenus] om. *F* 40 mali²] om. *F* 41 Catholicus] om. *F* 44 uolunatem] uoluntates *P* 49 boni] add. qui *F* 54 ut...55 nuptiali] om. *P* 58 Catholicus] om. *F* 67 pascha] pasca *P* 70 habemus] om. *P*

28 reiciendus|fol. 132ra *P* 58 Catholicus|fol. 132rb *P* 71 familiaritate|fol. 103v *F*

uitatus a domino et ab ecclesia apostolorum eius. donec ipse laqueo se ipsum suspendit. item ad romanos. i°. omnibus qui sunt rome dilectis dei uocatis sanctis etcet. et postea inferius multos ex illis reprehendit de peccatis mortalibus. item iª. ad corinthios. i°. ecclesie dei que est corinthi sanctificatis in christo uocatis sanctis etcet. et postea in eodem dicit eisdem. significatum est idem mihi de uobis fratres mei ab his qui sunt cloes quia contentiones sunt inter uos etcet. sed peccata et contemptiones et gloriatio et alia de quibus ibidem repredendit illos sunt peccata et facientes ea uocat carnales. infra. tertio. dicens cum enim sit inter uos zelus et contentio nonne carnales estis etcet. igitur contentiosi et gloriantes inaniter et carnales sunt fratres in ecclesia dei. idem. v. omnino auditur inter uos fornicatio etcet. sed hoc scribit ecclesie illi quam prius sanctam dixerat et postea illum fornicationem anathematizat et iubet illum expelli de ipsa. ergo fornicarii possunt esse in ecclesia dei quam diu canonice non eiiciuntur de illa. idem. vi. contemptibiles qui sunt in ecclesia etcet. ibi. sed frater cum fratre iudicio contendit et hoc apud infideles etcet. et infra. an nescitis quia iniqui etcet. ergo fratris et de ecclesia dei fideles qui sunt mali per praua opera. idem. xi. conuenientibus uobis in ecclesiam audio scissuras etcet. infra. unusquisque enim suam cenam presumit ad manducandum et alius quidem esurit et alius autem ebrius etcet. et infra. aut ecclesiam dei contempnitis eos qui non habent etcet. et infra. ideo inter uos multi infirmi et imbecilles et dormiunt multi etcet. ergo in ecclesia dei sunt etiam mali. item ad phylippenses. i°. plures e fratribus in domino confidentes uinculis meis habundantius audirent sine timore uerbum dei loqui quidam quidem et propter inuidiam et contentionem quidam autem et propter bonum uoluntatem etcet. et infra. quidam autem ex contentione christum predicant non sincere. existimantes pressuram se suscitare uinculis meis. etcet. audi quia fratres uocat apostolus qui erant inuidi et contentiosi et qui pressuram suscitabant uinculis eius et hii omnes erant mali. ergo et mali sunt de ecclesia dei. idem. ii°. neminem enim habeo tam unanimem qui sicera affectione pro uobis sollicitus sit. omnes enim que sua sunt querunt non que sunt ihesu christi etcet. et hoc dicit de fidelibus. igitur mali sunt in ecclesia dei. item. jacobum. iiii°. unde bella et lites in uobis etcet. sed hos sepe uocauerat fratres. ergo bellatores et litigiosi et concupiscentes et homicide et çelatores et adulteri et seculi amatores sicut ibi de conuenerat sunt in ecclesia dei. item actus. iiii°. multitudinis autem credentium

Church of his Apostles, until he hung himself from the noose. Also Romans 1 (1:7) "To all who are at Rome, beloved and called saints," and later below he upbraids many of them for mortal sins. Also 1 Corinthians 1 (1:2) "To the church of God that is at Corinth, to those who are sanctified in Christ Jesus, called to be saints." And later in the same letter he says to them (1:11) "For I have been told, my brethren, of you, by those who are of the house of Chloe, that there are contentions among you." But sins and contentions and boasting and others of which he condemns those here as sins, and he calls those who do them carnal. Later in the third chapter, he says (3:3) "For, since there is envying and contention among you, are you not carnal." Therefore contentious people and empty boasters and the carnal are brethren in the Church of God. Also 5 (5:1) "It is absolutely heard that there is fornication among you." But he is writing this to the Church that before he had called 'saints,' and later he anathematizes them as fornicators and orders them to be expelled from her, therefore fornicators are able to be in the Church of God as long as they are not canonically expelled from her. Also 6 (6:4) "who are the most despised in the church," there (6:6) "But brother goes to law with brother, and that before unbelievers," and later (6:9) "do you not know that the unjust." Therefore the faithful who are evildoers on account of their bad works are brothers and members of the Church of God. The same in 11 (11:18) "For first of all I hear that when you come together in the church, there are schisms among you," and later (11:21) "For every one takes before his own supper to eat. And one indeed is hungry and another is drunk," and later (11:22) "Or do you despise the church of God, and put them to shame who have not?," and later (11:30) "Therefore are there many infirm and weak among you, and many sleep." Therefore in the Church of God there are many evildoers. Also in Philippians 1 (1:14-15) "And many of the brethren in the Lord, growing confident by my chains, are much more bold to speak the word of God without fear. Some indeed, even out of envy and contention, but some also for good will preach Christ," and later (1:17) "And some out of contention do not preach Christ sincerely: supposing that they raise affliction to my chains." Hear that the Apostle calls them brothers who err in envy and contention and who raise affliction to his chains and these all are evil. Therefore the evil are members of the Church of God. The same in 2 (2:20-21) "For I have no man so of the same mind, who with sincere affection is solicitous for you, for all seek the things that are their own, not the things that are Jesus Christ's," and this is said of the faithful, therefore there are evildoers in the Church of God. Also James 4 (4:1) "From where are wars and contentions among you," But those are often called brothers, therefore

erat cor unum etcet. et infra. v⁰. uir autem quidam nomine ananias cum saphyra uxore sua etcet. ergo inter credentes et fideles ecclesie computantur fradatores pretii agri uenditi.

De ecclesia militante

Item. ii^a. ad timotheum. ii⁰. in magna autem domo non solum sunt uasa aurea et argentea sed et lignea et fictilia et quedam quidam in honorem quedam autem in contumeliam etcet. ergo in magna domo id est in ecclesia militante sunt quidam boni qui sunt uas aurea et argentea in honorem. et quidam mali qui sunt uasa lignea et fictilia in contumeliam. hoc autem de diaboli ecclesia non possunt intelligi quia non sunt aliqui boni in ea. nec possunt etiam intelligi de triumphante ecclesia. quia ibi nulli sunt mali.

Patarenus: Dicimus quia intelliguntur de mundo ubi sunt multi mali et aliqui boni.

Catholicus: Sed nullam mentionem fecerat apostolus de mundo sed de ecclesia. unde dixerat superius in principio capituli. hoc comenda fidelibus etcet. et supra proxime. Et subuerterunt quorumdam fidem. sed firmum fundamentum dei stat. habens signaculum hoc. cognouit dominus qui sunt eius et discedat ab iniquitate omnis qui nominat nomen domini etcet. Ex hiis ergo patet euidenter quod in ecclesia dei et de ecclesia dei sunt etiam mali et quod non sunt uitanda quamdiu non sunt ab illa canonice precisi.

Patarenus: Dauid. cum peruerso peruerteris etcet. et idem. non mortui laudabunt te domine et ecclesiasticus iii⁰. filii sapientie ecclesia iustorum et natio illorum obedientia et dilectio et iohannes. xiiii. dicit ei ihesus. ego sum ueritas et uita et xv. si quis in me non manserit mittetur foras etcet. item ad romanos. viii. qui autem in carne sunt deo placere. non possunt. etcet. et ultimo. rogo autem uos fratres ut obseruetis eos etcet. item i^a. ad corinthios. i⁰. ut tollatur de medio uestrum qui hoc opus fecit etcet. et infra. modicum fermentum totam massam corrumpit. expurgate uetus fermentum etcet. et vi⁰. auferte malum ex uobis ipsis etcet. et infra. iniqui regnum dei non possidebunt etcet. idem. x. nolo autem uos sotios fieri demoniorum etcet. idem. ultimo. si quis non amat dominum nos-trum ihesum christum sit anathema etcet. item ii^a. corinthios. vi⁰.

the warlike and litigious and sensual and killers and the envious and adulterers and lovers of the world, just as here, are gathered together in the Church of God. The same in Acts 4 (4:32) "And the multitude of believers had but one heart," and later (5:1) "But a certain man named Ananias, with Sapphira his wife." Therefore among the believers and the faithful of the Church was counted embezzlers of the price of a sold field.

On the Church Militant

Also 2 Timothy 2 (2:20) "But in a great house there are not only vessels of gold and of silver, but also of wood and earth, and some indeed unto honor, but some unto dishonor," that is, in the Church militant there are certain ones who are good and who are the vessels of gold and silver, unto honor, and certain evil ones who are the vessels of wood and earth, unto dishonor. Yet one cannot interpret this as the Church of the devil, since there are no good men in it, neither is one able to interpret it as the Church Triumphant for in that place none are evil.

Pat: We say that it is to be understood of the world where there are many evil men and some good ones.

Cath: But the Apostle makes no mention of the world, but of the Church, whence he said above in the first chapter (2:2) "the same commend to faithful men," and next above (2:18–19) "and they have subverted the faith of some, but the sure foundation of God stands firm, having this seal, the Lord knows who are his, and let everyone depart from iniquity who calls the name of the Lord." From these therefore it is evidently clear that in the Church of God and from the Church of God there are also evil men and that they are not to be shunned as long as they are not cut off from her canonically.

Pat: David (Ps 17:27) "and with the perverse you will be perverted." And the same (113:25) "The dead shall not praise you, O Lord," and Ecclesiasticus 3 (3:1) "The sons of wisdom are the church of the just and their generation, obedience and love." And John 14 (14:6) "Jesus said to him, 'I am the truth and the life,'" and 15 (15:6) "If any one does not abide in me, he shall be cast out." Also Romans 8 (8:8) "And those who are in the flesh, cannot please God." And at the end (16:17) "Now I beseech you, brethren, to mark those." And 1 Corinthians 1 (5:2) "that he might be taken away from among you, who has done this deed," and later (5:6–7) "Don't you know that a little leaven corrupts the whole lump? Purge out the old leaven," and 6 (5:13) "put out the evil from among yourselves," and later (6:9) "Do you not know that the unjust will not possess the kingdom of God." The same in 10 (10:20) "And I do not want that you should be made partakers with devils," also at the end (16:22) "If any man does not

---

123 uir…124 sua] Apoc. 5:1 (sua) suo *Vulg*.)   XXXII.4.2 in…5 contumeliam] 2 Tim. 2:20.   16 hoc…fidelibus] 2 Tim. 2:2.   17 Et…20 domini] 2 Tim. 2:18-19.   24 cum…peruerteris] Ps. 17:27.   25 non…domine] Ps. 113:25.   26 filii…27 dilectio] Ecclesiastic. 3:1.   27 dicit…28 uita] Ioh. 14:6.   28 si…29 foras] Ioh. 15:6.   29 qui…30 possunt] Rom. 8:8.   31 rogo…eos] Rom. 16:17.   32 ut…33 fecit] 1 Cor. 5:2.   33 modicum…34 fermentum] 1 Cor. 5:6-7.   35 auferte…ipsis] 1 Cor. 5:13.   36 iniqui…possidebunt] 1 Cor. 6:9.   37 nolo…demoniorum] 1 Cor. 10:20.   38 si…39 anathema] 1 Cor. 16:22.

XXXII.4.1 De…militante] om. *F*   6 boni] add. et quidam mali *F*   12 Patarenus] om. *F*   14 Catholicus] om. *F*   22 uitanda] uitandi *F*   24 Patarenus] om. *F*

XXXII.4.5 contumeliam|fol. 104r *F*   15 mundo|fol. 133ra *P*

nolite igitur ducere cum infidelibus que enim participatio etcet. et infra. uos enim estis templum dei uiui sicut dicit deus. etcet. et infra. exite de medio eorum et separamini dicit dominus etcet. et apocaly-psis. ultimo. Nec intrabit in illa aliquod coinquinatum etcet. et quibus patet quod in ecclesia dei non debent esse nisi boni et quod omnes mali sunt uitandi.

Catholicus: Omnes auctoritates quas induxisti in hac parte loquuntur de peccatoribus uitandis in quantum sunt peccatores circa fidem uel circa opera quia sunt excomunicati ab ecclesia et hoc quantum ad uitationem. secundum primum intelliguntur ille auctoritates scilicet dauid cum peuerso etcet. et i^a. ad corinthios. x. nolo autem uos sotios fieri etcet. et ii^a. ad corinthios. vi^o. nolite igitur ducere cum infidelibus etcet. nec obstat quod legitur i^a. ad corinthios x. non potestis mense dei esse participes etcet. quia sic intelliguntur scilicet digne. secundum uero secundum intelliguntur ille scilicet i^a. ad corinthios. v. ut tollatur etcet. et illud. modicum fermentum etcet. et vi. auferte malum etcet. et ad romanos. ultimo. rogo autem uos fratres etcet. et ii^a ad thessalonicenses. iii^o. denuntiamus etcet. item auctoritates alie quas induxistis quod mali non sint in ecclesia dei intelliguntur uel de ecclesia triumphante sicut ille. iohannes. xv. si quis in me non manserit etcet. i^a. ad corinthios. vi^o. iniqui regnum dei non possidebunt etcet. et ultimo si quis non amat etcet. et apocalypsis. ultimo. Nec intrabit in illam etcet. uel intelliguntur de excomunicatis uel de peccatoribus qui non sunt de ecclesia dei. merito uel perfectione. et sic intelliguntur cetere auctoritates a uobis introducte.

Patarenus: Sed audi quod dicit apostolus. ephesios. v. ut ipse exiberet sibi ecclesia non habentem maculam aut rugam aut aliquid huiusmodi sed ut sit sancta et immaculata. ergo peccatores nullo modo sunt de ecclesia dei.

Catholicus: Responsio. non dicit quod ecclesia dei sit macula et sine ruga et huiusmodi. sed dicit quod christus semetipsum tradidit ut talem exiberet illam. unde dicit supra diligite uxores uestras sicut et christus dilexit ecclesiam et semetipsum tradidit pro ea ut etcet. nec propter hoc sequitur. ergo est sine macula et sine ruga. quia dicit idem. prima ad timotheus. ii^o. hoc enim bonum est et acceptum coram deo saluatore

love our Lord Jesus Christ, let him be anathema." The same in 2 Corinthians 6 (6:14) "Do not bear the yoke with unbelievers, for what association," and later (6:16) "For you are the temple of the living God, as God says," and later (6:17) "So go out from among them, and be separate, says the Lord." And at the end of Apocalypse (21:27) "Nothing unclean shall enter into it," and by which it is obvious that in the Church of God there ought to be nothing other than good men and that evil men are to be shunned.

Cath: All the authorities you have adduced in this part speak of sinners to be shunned insofar as they are sinners regarding the faith, or regarding works that are excommunicable from the Church and as to that, to shun. According to the first, the passages are to be interpreted, namely David, "with the perverse," and 1 Corinthians 10 (10:20) "and I do not want that you should be made partakers," and 2 Corinthians 6 (6:14) "Do not bear the yoke with unbelievers." Nor does what is read in 1 Corinthians 10 oppose this interpretation (10:21) "you cannot be partakers of the table of the Lord," since they are to be understood thus, "worthy," yet the next are to be interpreted according to the second, namely, 1 Corinthians 5 "that he might be taken," and that (5:6–7) "a little leaven." And 6 (5:13) "Put away the evil one from among yourselves," and to the Romans at the end (16:7) "I beseech you brethren." And 2 Thessalonians 3 (3:6) "we proclaim." Again the other authorities that you adduce that evil men are not in the Church of God, they are to be understood, either of the Church Triumphant as that in John 15 (15:6) "if any one does not abide in me," and 1 Corinthians 6 (6:9) "the unjust shall not possess the kingdom of God," and at the end (16:22) "if anyone does not love," and Apocalypse at the end (21:27) "Nothing unclean shall enter into it." Or they are to be interpreted as referring to the excommunicated or of sinners who are not of the Church of God by merit or by perfection, and this is how the other authorities adduced by you are to be interpreted.

Pat: But hear what the Apostle says in Ephesians 5 (5:27) "That he might present it to himself a glorious church, not having spot or wrinkle, or any such thing; but that it should be holy, and without blemish." Therefore in no way are sinners from the Church of God.

Cath: Reply. He did not say that the Church of God would be without spot or wrinkle and any such thing, but he said that Christ handed Himself over that she might be showed forth in such a way. Whence He said above (5:25) "Love your wives just as Christ loved the Church, and handed himself over for her," nor on account of what follows, (5:27) "therefore it is without spot or any wrinkle," since he said the same in 1 Timothy 2 (2:3–4) "For this is good

---

40 nolite...partici-patio] 2 Cor. 6:14.   41 uos...42 deus] 2 Cor. 6:16.   42 exite...43 dominus] 2 Cor. 6:17.   44 Nec...coinquinatum] Apoc. 21:27.   53 nolo...fieri] 1 Cor. 10:20.   54 nolite...infidelibus] 2 Cor. 6:14.   55 non...56 participes] 1 Cor. 10:21.   58 ut tollatur] 1 Cor. 5:2.   59 modicum fermentum] 1 Cor. 5:6-7. | auferte malum] 1 Cor. 5:13.   60 rogo...fratres] Rom. 16:7. 61 denuntiamus] 2 Thes. 3:6.   64 si...manserit] Ioh. 15:6.   65 iniqui...66 possidebunt] 1 Cor. 6:9.   66 si...amat] 1 Cor. 16:22. 67 Nec...illam] Apoc. 21:27.   72 ut...74 immaculata] Eph. 5:27.   79 diligite...80 ut] Eph. 5:25.   81 sine^1...82 ruga] Eph. 5:27. 82 hoc...84 fieri] 1 Tim. 2:3-4.

47 Catholicus] om. F   48 loquuntur] add. uel F   51 ille] om. P   56 sic] sicut P   71 Patarenus] om. F   76 Catholicus] om. F

45 in|fol. 133rb P   59 auferte|fol. 104v F   79 dicit|fol. 133va P

nostro. qui omnes homines uult saluos fieri etcet. et tamen non omnes saluantur. uel loquitur de ecclesia electorum seu triumphante quam exhibet sine macula mortale peccati et sine ruga uenialis et sine eiusmodi id est sine postea pro peccatis. quia in patria eterna neque peccatum erit aliquod neque pena ulla. notandum est ergo quod ecclesia dicitur duobus modis scilicet secundum statum militie et secundum statum triumphi. secundum uero primum statum dicitur dupliciter scilicet ratione numeri et ratione meriti. ratione autem numeri maculata est id est amixta malis ut probatum est supra. in allegatione nostra. et de hac dicitur actus. ix. ecclesia per totam iudeam et galileam et samariam habebat pacem etcet. ibi enim comprehendit omnes christianos bonos et malos nomine ecclesia. ad idem est in eodem. vii. hic est qui fuit in ecclesia in solitudine angelo etcet. ratione uero meriti habet maculam uenialis peccati sed non mortale. sicut dominus dicit. iohannes. xiii. qui lotus est non indiget nisi ut pedes lauet sed est mundus totus etcet. et sic intelligitur illud. iiª. ad corinthios. viiº. in omnibus exibuistis uos incontaminatos esse negotio etcet. secundum uero statum triumphy. erit absque ulla macula tam mortalis peccati quam uenialis ut dicit hic apostolus. ut exibet etcet. et sic intelligitur illud. Canticum canticorum. iiiiº. tota pulcra es amica mea et macula non est in te etcet.

Patarenus: Dicit apostolus ad hebreos. xii. quod si extra disciplinam estis. cuius participes facti sunt omnes filii dei. ergo adulteri et non filii dei estis etcet. ergo qui sunt extra disciplinam correctiones dei. sunt adulteri et non sunt filii. igitur non filii ecclesie dei. sed dicitis quod sunt ecclesie romane filii. ergo ecclesia romana non est sponsa christi. de qua suos habet filios. sed est adultera.

Catholicus: Responsio. quod non dicit apostolus quod non sint filii ecclesie christi. sed dicit quod non sunt filii scilicet dei de quod dixerat supra. quid enim filius quem non corripit pater etcet. et supra. tamquam filius offert se uobis deus etcet. Et quod dico malos non esse filios dei intellige scilicet per imitationem. de qua filiatione dicit. ad ephesios. v. estote ergo imitatores dei etcet. sed modo respondete mihi de hac blasphemia qua dicitis romanam ecclesiam esse adulteram. adultera enim dicitur que miscuit se uiro alieno. aut que uiro suo contempto miscuit se alteri non suo. In primo casu aut ille est diabolus et tunc non est sponsa diaboli. sed mater uestra o heretici. Si nam est deus. tunc aut male fecit aut bene. si male ergo deus est adulterus qui secum mechatus est quod absit. si autem bene ergo

and acceptable in the sight of God our Savior, who wishes all men to be saved." And yet not all are saved. Or it speaks of the Church of the elect or Triumphant which shows itself without the stain of mortal sins and without the wrinkle of venial sins and without anything of the sort, that is, without later sins. For in the eternal fatherland there is neither any sin nor further penalties. Therefore one should note that the Church is so-called in two ways, namely, according to the state of journeying and according to the state of triumphing. Yet according to the first state it can also be distinguished in two ways, namely according to numbers and according to merit, but according to numbers she is stained, that is, by mixture with evil people as was proven above in our contentions. And of this Acts 9 says (9:31) "The Church through all of Judea and Galilee and Samaria had peace," for this comprises here all Christians, good and evil, in the name of the Church. To the same is also there in 7 (7:38) "This is he that was in the church in the wilderness, with the angel." Yet according to merit it has the stain of venial sin, but not mortal, as the Lord says in John 13 (13:10) "He that is washed, needs only but to wash his feet, but is clean wholly." And so it has been interpreted as that 2 Corinthians 7 (7:11) "in all things you have shown yourselves to be undefiled in the matter." But according to the state of triumph, it is without any stain, whether mortal or venial, as the Apostle says here, "that he might show," and it is to be interpreted by that in Song of Songs 4 (4:7) "you are wholly fair, O my love, and there is not a spot in you."

Pat: The Apostle says to the Hebrews in 12 (12:8) "But if you be without chastisement, of which all are made sons of God, then are you bastards, and not sons." Therefore those who are outside the discipline of the correction of God are bastards and not sons, therefore they are not sons of the Church of God. But you say that they are sons of the Roman Church, therefore the Roman Church is not the spouse of Christ, by which she has sons, but she is an adulteress.

Cath: I reply that the Apostle did not say that they are not sons of the Church of Christ, but he said that they are not sons, namely, of God of which he spoke above (12:7) "for what son is there, whom the father does not correct?" And before "God deals with you as with his sons." And that I say evil men are not to be sons of God, understand, namely, by imitation, of which sonship he says in Ephesians 5 (5:1) "Be you therefore imitators of God," but how can you reply to me with this blasphemy by which you say the Roman Church is an adulteress. For an adulteress is said to be she who embroils herself with another man, or in contempt of her husband mingles herself with another not hers. In the first case either it is the devil and then she is not the spouse of the devil, but your mother, O heretic. But if it is God, then she either does badly or well. If badly,

non est adultera. si uero dicis quod est adultera quia
uiro suo contempto adhesit alieno. tunc uir suus est
deus. et tunc est sponsa dei. mater autem uostra sponsa
est diaboli. aut est diabolus eius uir. et tunc non male
fecit. sed diabolo contempto adhesit deo. uel si male
fecit peius fecit deus. obmutescite igitur blasphematores pessimi. item Respondete mihi de hac uestra
opinione qua dicitis malos non esse de ecclesia dei et
esse uitandos. aut enim peccatores non sunt de ecclesia
dei et sunt uitandi quia peccatores sunt. uel quod
notorii. siquidem quia peccatores. igitur non est
ecclesia dei aliquis peccator occultus cum ille sit
peccator. sed cum nemo possit scire de statu occulto
alterius semper status ecclesie erit incertus. si uero non
est de ecclesia dei quia notorius est. tunc aut licebit
uncuique secundum iudicium sequastrare illum ab
ecclesia dei. et tunc multa indicia falsa inuenientur et
sepe iustus sequastrabitur iniuste. et multe alie sequuntur inconuenientie. aut uero auctoritate fiet ecclesie et
hoc est quod fides tenet orthodoxa.

then God is an adulterer who commits adultery with you, God forbid. But if well then she is not an adulteress. Yet you say that she is an adulteress since, in contempt of her husband, she cleaves to another, her husband is God, and she is then the spouse of God. But your spouse is the mother of the devil, or the devil is her husband, and then she does not do evil, but she cleaves to God in contempt of the devil, or if she does badly, God does worse. Be silent, therefore, O worst of blasphemers. Also respond to me regarding your opinion by which you say that evil men are not from the Church of God and ought to be shunned. For either sinners are not of the Church of God, and ought to be shunned, because they are sinners, or because they are notorious. If because they are sinners, then there is no sinner hidden in the the Church of God while he is a sinner. But since no one can know the secret condition of another, the condition of the Church will always be uncertain. But if truly he is not of the Church of God because he is notorious, then either it will be permitted to each person according to judgment to separate him from the Church of God, and then many false proofs would be put forth, and often a just man would be unjustly separated, and many other difficulties will follow, rather this should be done by the authority of the Church and this is what the orthodox faith holds.

Quod malus prelatus seu sacerdos uel predicator potest fungi suo officio

Quod malus prelatus seu sacerdos uel predicator potest fungi suo officio. nec noceat in bono obedientibus illi. quamquam fere omnes inficientur heretici. tam per rationes quam per scripturas potest manifeste probari.

Catholicus: Eodem modo quo aliquid constituitur uel colligatur eodem dextruitur et soluitur sed prelatus uel sacerdos constituitur per ecclesiasticam solempnitatem. ut habetur ad hebreos. v. nec quisquam sibi sumit honorem etcet. et supra. de hac materia ut supra in libro ii°. titulus. de pauperibus leonistis. eodem ergo modo per solempnitatem ecclesiasticam debet absolui igitur interea erit prelatus uel sacerdos.

Catholicus: Item nemo nouit quis sit bonus et absque mortali peccato nisi deus. ergo incertum esset semper quis esset prelatus uel sacerdos. si ratione uite bone uel male fieret. aut non esset et sic nesciretur utrum essent prelati uel sacerdotes in ecclesia dei. sed certum est quia sunt. ergo uita non facit illos aut deponit. sed ecclesiastica solempnitas.

Catholicus: Item si sola mala uita absoluit prelatum uel sacerdotem seu predicatorem ab officio suo ergo

XXXIII That an evil prelate, priest, or preacher can exercise his office

That an evil prelate or priest or preacher can exercise his office, nor might one be harmed by obeying him in good things, even though nearly all the heretics have denied it. This can be clearly proven both by reason and by the scriptures.

Cath: In the same manner in which some are appointed or gathered together, some are destroyed and dissolved. But a prelate or priest is appointed by a solemn ecclesiastical ceremony, as one has it in Hebrews 5 (5:4) "nor does any man take the honor for himself," and above, regarding these things, in book two in the section on the Poor of Lyons. So in the same way, therefore, one ought to be absolved by a solemn ecclesial rite, therefore in these circumstances, it will be a prelate or a priest.

Cath: Further no one knows who might be good and without mortal sin, save God. Therefore there would always be uncertainty in who should be a prelate or a priest, if one was made so by reason of a good or unmade by an evil life. One would never know whether there could be prelates or priests in the Church of God. But it is certain that thre are. And so therefore their moral life does not make them so, nor does it depose them, but only the solemn rites [of the Church].

Cath: Also if an evil life alone released a prelate or priest or preacher from his office, therefore how much more would

---

XXXIII.1.10 nec...11 honorem] Heb. 5:4.

134 quia] quod *F* 136 mater] add. i *P* exp. | autem] enim *F* 138 sed] si *F* 141 opinione] oppinione *P* | non esse] transp. *P* 143 quod] quia *F* 144 non] add. sunt *P* exp. 145 ecclesia om. *P* 146 scire] om. *P* 147 incertus] modus *P* 148 notorius] notarius *F* 150 dei] om. *P* | indicia falsa] iudicia *P* XXXIII.1.1 Quod...2 officio] om. *F* | sacerdos uel] om. *P* 3 sacerdos uel] om. *P* potest...4 suo] possint suo fungi *F* 5 quamquam] add. hoc *P* 7 Catholicus] om. *F* | uel] ut *P* 15 Catholicus] om. *F* 19 est] om. *P* 22 Catholicus] om. *F*

137 et|fol. 134ra *P* XXXIII.1.12 libro|fol. 134rb *P*

multo fortius bona restituit eum. quia plus potest sanita quam malitia. ergo septies in die uel centies erit quis et desinet esse et uerum fiet prelatus uel sacerdos seu predicator et semper incertitudine quod nichil est.

Catholicus: Item probatum est superius in primo tractatu et uerum est quod aliquis in mortali peccato existens potest recipere corpus christi. licet indigne recipiat illud. ergo eodem modo malus prelatus uel sacerdos seu predicator. potest suum tractare officium licet indigne hoc faciat.

Catholicus: Item si solum peccatum non absoluit prelatum et sacerdotem et predicatorum ab officio sed notitia eius. ergo si non est notum non amittet officium suum licet in ueritate sit malus. preterea que notitia ipsum absoluet? numquid uniuscuiusque? si ita est. cum sepe humanum fallitur iudicium. sepe iustus iniuste absolutus erit. item uidebitur uerum. quod de ipso dicetur malum et alter falsum et hoc secundum centies in die simul et semel deponetur et absoluetur quod est impossibile. preterea secundum hoc omnes uos heretici peccatis mortalissime cum iudicatis prelatos et sacerdotes ecclesie romane ammisisse eorum officia propter peccata eorum quorum notitiam non habetis.

Catholicus: Mattheus. x. et conuocatis xii discipulis suis dedit eis potestatem spirituum immundorum et curarent eos. et curarent omnem languorem et omnem infirmitatem. xii discipulorum nomina sunt hec etcet. ibi et iudas iscarioth etcet. et infra. hos xii misit ihesus etcet. et infra. euntes autem predicate dicentes. quia appropinquauit regnum celorum. infirmos curate. etcet. et marcum. vi. conuocauit xii. et cepit eos mittere binos etcet. et infra. et exeuntes predicabant ut penitentiam agerent et demonia multa eiciebant et ungebant oleo multos egros et sanabantur etcet. et iohannes. iiii°. quamquam ipse ihesus non baptizaret sed discipuli eius etcet. et vi. in finem. nonne ego uos xiicim. elegi et ex uobis unus diabolus est. dicebat enim de iuda symonis scarioth etcet. et xiiii°. uos mundi estis sed non omnes etcet. et actus. i°. de iuda qui fuit dux eorum qui comprehenderunt ihesum qui connumeratus erat in nobis et sortitus est sortem ministerii huius etcet. et infra. et episcopatum eius accipiat alter etcet. et infra. accipere locum ministerii huius et apostolatus de quo preuaricatus est iudas ut abiret in locum suum etcet. Ecce ex his patet manifeste quod iudas scarioth fuit electus a domino nostro ihesu christo. ad discipulatum et a apostolatum eius. et quod ipse fuit apostolus et episcopus et predicator et fecit miracula et tractauit sacramenta ecclesiastica usque ad

a good life restore him, since holiness is much more powerful than wickedness. Therefore seven times in a day or a hundred times will he cease to be and truly become a prelate or priest or preacher, and so it will always be uncertain, and there is no reason for this.

Cath: Further it was proven above in the first section, and it is true, that one living in mortal sin can receive the body of Christ, although he receives it unworthily. Therefore in the same way an evil prelate or priest or preacher can undertake his office, even though he should do this unworthily.

Cath: Also if sin alone does not release a prelate, priest, or preacher from office, but only the [public] knowledge of it, then if it is not known he will not lose his office, although he in truth is evil. Further what knowledge will absolve him [of office]? Will any one's? If it is so, since human judgment often errs, the just man will be unjustly deprived of office. Also it will seem true that if one might speak ill of him, and another falsely, and this one hundred times a day, together at the same time he is deposed and absolved, and that is impossible. Furthermore according to this, all you heretics sin most mortally when you judge that the prelates and priests of the Roman Church have lost their offices on account of their sins, of which you have no knowledge.

Cath: Matthew 10 (10:1–2) "And having called his twelve disciples together, he gave them power over unclean spirits, to cast them out, and to heal all manner of diseases, and all manner of infirmities. And the names of the twelve apostles are these." And here is Judas Iscariot, and later (10:5) "Jesus sent these twelve," and later (10:7) "And going, preach, saying, 'The kingdom of heaven is at hand.'" And Mark 6 (6:7) "He called together the twelve and sent them two-by-two," and later (6:12–13) "And going forth they preached that men should do penance and they cast out many devils, and anointed with oil many that were sick, and healed them." And John 4 (4:2) "Though Jesus himself did not baptize, but his disciples," and 6 at the end (6:71–72) "Have not I chosen you twelve; and one of you is a devil? Now he meant Judas Iscariot, the son of Simon," and 13 (13:10) "And you are clean, but not all." And Acts 1 (1:16–17) "concerning Judas, who was the leader of those who apprehended Jesus, who was numbered with us, and had obtained part of this ministry," and later (1:20) "and let another take his episcopacy," and later (1:25) "To take the place of this ministry and apostleship, from which Judas has fallen by transgression, that he might go to his own place." See from these it is plainly clear that Judas Iscariot was elected by our Lord Jesus Christ to the office of disciple and Apostle and that he was an Apostle and

---

48 et...**51** hec] Matt. 10:1-2 (eis) illis *Vulg.*)   **52** hos...ihesus] Matt. 10:5.   **53** euntes...**54** curate] Matt. 10:7.   **55** conuocauit...**56** binos] Mar. 6:7.   **56** et²...**58** sanabantur] Mar. 6:12-13.   **59** quamquam...**60** eius] Ioh. 4:2.   **60** nonne...**62** scarioth] Ioh. 6:71-72.   **62** uos...**63** omnes] Ioh. 13:10.   **63** de...**66** huius] Act. 1:16-17.   **66** et²...**67** etcet] Act. 1:20.   **67** accipere...**69** suum] Act. 1:25.

25 sanita] sanitas *P* **Sic leg. sanctitas**   **28** Catholicus] om. *F* | primo] primo proximo *P*   **33** licet] om. *P*   **34** Catholicus] om. *F*   **40** item] add. uni *F*   **48** Catholicus] om. *F*   **59** quamquam] postquam   **69** his] hiis *F*   **70** electus] om. *P*   **73** ecclesiastica] om. *P*

25 septies|fol. 105v *F*   **38** uniuscuiusque|fol. 134va *P*   **66** episcopatum|fol. 134vb *P*

mortem eius maxime unctionis. at baptismatis et eucharistie et tamen secundum patarenos semper fuit malus et secundum alios malus fuit longe ante morte ipsius. quia dudum anima fur erat et nec dominus sequastrauit eum a comunione corporis sui et aliorum misteriorum suorum in cena sua nec ab officio suo priuauit illum. donec ipsemet laqueo se suspendens priuauit se ipsum. igitur malus prelatus uel sacerdos seu predicator suo potest officio fungi. nec peccatum suum priuat eum ab officio sibi a deo et ecclesia commisso. nisi per ecclesiastica sollempnitatem ab ipso absoluatur. idem. mattheus. xxiii. super cathedram moysi sederunt scribe et pharisei omnia ergo quecumque dixerint uobis seruate et facite secundum opera uero eorum nolite facere dicunt enim et non faciunt etcet. si enim malum esset eos audire et ipsi non possent predicare et consulere nequaquam dixisset christus. omnia quecumque etcet. item. iohannes. xi. unus ex ipsis caiafas nomine cum esset pontifex anni illius prophetauit etcet. ergo caifas licet malus esset prophetauit. item. i^a. ad timotheus. v. qui bene presunt prebiteri duplici honore digni habeantur. ergo possunt esse presbiteri. qui non digni nisi uno honore. qui sunt illi qui officium habent et non uitam. si enim mali non possent esse presbiteri dixisset utique apostolus qui bene possunt sunt presbiteri et non alii et sunt honorandi quod non dixit. sed qui bene possunt presbiteri duplici honore etcet. quasi dicat. magis sunt honorandi boni quam mali presbiteri. ergo mali sunt. presbiteri sunt honorandi licet minus quam boni. idem. in eodem. aduersus presbiterum accusationem noli recipere nisi sub duobus uel tribus testibus etcet. ergo presbiter non debet puniri ab ecclesia uel deponi nisi sub maiori fuerit legitime conuictus. Si enim ex solo peccato esset depositus uel puniendus uel ad uoluntatem uniuscuiusque quare cum ordine iudicario mandaret apostolus. primo esse examinandum sub iudice suo? Item. apocalypsis. ii^o. et angelo ephesi etcet. memor esto itaque unde excideris et age penitentiam et prima opera fac sin autem uenio tibi et mouebo candelabrum tuum de loco suo nisi penitentiam egeris etcet. ecce quod iste prelatus exciderit et indigebat penitentia. igitur non erat bonus et tamen non dicit deus eum remotum esse. ipso facto sed dicit eum esse remouende nisi peniteat. item in eodem. et angelo pergami etcet. ibi similiter penitentiam age. si quominus ueniam tibi cito etcet. et iste in eadem conditione ponitur cum alio. idem. iii^o. et angelo ecclesie sardis etcet. ibi. scio opera tua quia nomen habes quod uiuas et mortuus es etcet. et infra. age penitentia. si ergo non

bishop and preacher, and did miracles, and performed the sacraments of the Church until his death, especially anointing, and baptism, and the Eucharist, and yet according to the Patarenes he was always evil and according to others he was evil long before his death, since formerly he had the soul of a thief and neither did the Lord separate him from communion of His body and of His other mysteries in His last supper, neither did He deprive him of his office, until he deprived himself of it, hanging himself by a noose. Therefore an evil prelate or priest or preacher can exercise his office. Neither does his sin deprive him of the office committed to him by God and by the Church, unless he is separated from her by the solemn rite of the Church. The same in Matthew 23 (23:2–3) "The scribes and the Pharisees sit on the chair of Moses. Do all things therefore whatsoever they say, observe and do, but do not do according to their works; for they teach and do not observe." For if it were bad to listen to them and they themselves could not preach and advise, Christ would by no means have said this. Also John 11 (11:49) "But one of them, named Caiaphas, being the high priest that year." Therefore Caiaphas, though evil, prophesied. Also 1 Timothy 5 (5:17) "Let the priests who rule well be esteemed worthy of double honor," therefore they are able to be priests who are not worthy except of one honor, who are those who have the office but not the uprightness of life. For if evil men were not able to be priests, the apostle might certainly say, those who are able to be good are priests, and not others, and they are to be honored, but he does not say that, but those who are able to be good are priests of a double honor, just as if to say, good priests are more to be honored than evil priests, therefore evil priests are to be honored, just less than good priests. It says the same there (5:19) "Do not receive not an accusation against a priest, but only with two or three witnesses." Therefore a priest ought not to be punished by the Church or deposed unless he has been convicted of serious crimes. For if he were deposed or punished for a single sin or at the whim of any one person, why would the Apostle command with the order of judgment that, first, he must be examined under his own judge? Also Apocalypse 2 (2:1) "And to the angel at Ephesus," (2:5) "Be mindful therefore from where you are fallen, and do pen-ance, and do the first works. Or else I come to you and will move your candlestick out of its place, unless you do penance." See that this prelate was cut off and lacked penance, therefore he was not good and yet God did not command him to be removed, but He commanded him to

---

85 super...91 quecumque] Matt. 23:2-3. 92 unus...93 prophetauit] Ioh. 11:49. 94 qui...101 honore] 1 Tim. 5:17. 104 aduersus...105 testibus] 1 Tim. 5:19. 111 et...ephesi] Apoc. 2:1. 112 memor...114 egeris] Apoc. 2:5. 118 et...pergami] Apoc. 2:12. 119 similiter...120 cito] Apoc. 2:16. 121 et...123 es] Apoc. 3:1.

75 patarenos] patharenos F 85 absoluatur] soluatur P 86 omnia...88 faciunt] om. P 92 anni...93 prophetauit] om. P 110 mandaret] non daret F 113 sin...114 egeris] om. P 117 esse^1] add. remotum P 119 quominus] nicholominus P 122 habes... 123 es] om. P 123 non...124 fur] om. P

84 commisso|fol. 106r F 95 possunt|fol. 135ra P

uigilaueris ueniam ad te tamquam fur etcet. iste etiam in eadem condicione ponitur cum aliis duobus. idem in eodem. et angelo laudatie. etcet. scio opera tua quia neque calidus es et nec frigidus utinam frigidus esses aut calidus sed quia tepidus es et nec frigidus nec calidus incipiam te euomere ex ore meo etcet. et infra. emulare ergo et penitentiam age etcet. et hic pessimus erat quia erat tepidus et miser et miserabilis et pauper et cecus et nudus et hii omnes supradicti essent mali fungebantur officiis suis et nec de ipso facto dixit illos esse remotos sed modo eos esse arguit et minatus est imposterum illis.

Patarenus: Dicimus quia predicti non erant episcopi nec prelati.

Catholicus: Qua ratione dicuntur angeli ecclesiarum unusquisque de sua speciali et quare redarguuntur a domino quod malos homines in suis ecclesiis relinquerant? ut habentur de angelo ecclesie pergami cui dixit. habeo aduersus te pauca quia habes illic tenentes doctrinam balaam etcet. et infra. ita habes et tu tenentes doctrinam nicholaitarum etcet. et de angelo tiatile dicit ibi. sed habeo aduersus te pauca quia permittis mulierem iezabel etcet. quare diceret dominus angelo sardis. sed habes pauca nomina in sardis qui non inquinauerunt uestimenta sua etcet. igitur erant prelati ecclesiarum et episcopi. ergo mali possunt fungi officio prelationis in ecclesia dei et possunt sub esse boni homines eis.

Quod malus homo non potest esse sacerdos uel prelatus seu predicator

Dauid. peccatori autem dixit deus. quare tu enarras iustitias meas. et assumis testamentum per os tuum. tu uero odisti disciplinam et proiecisti sermones meos retrorsum. si uidebas furem currebas cum eo et cum adulteris portionem tuam ponebas etcet. et ad romanos ii°. qui ergo alium doces. teipsum non doces? qui predicas non furandum furaris etcet. et mattheus v. uos estis sal terre quod si sal euanuerit in quo salietur? ad nichilum ualet ultra nisi ut mittatur foras etcet. sic luceat lux uestra coram hominibus ut uideant opera uestra bona et glorificent patrem uestrum qui in celis est etcet. idem vii. quid autem uides festucam in oculo fratris tui et trabem in oculo tuo non consideras. aut quomodo dicis fratri tuo etcet. et infra. non potest arbor bona fructus malos facere. nec arbor mala bonos fructus facere etcet. idem. xii. aut facite arborem

be removed unless he did penance. And in the same (3:14) "and to the angel of Laodicea" (3:15–16) "I know your works, that you are neither hot nor cold. I wish that you were hot or cold, but because you are lukewarm, and neither hot nor cold I will vomit you out of my mouth." And later (3:19) "Be zealous therefore, and do penance." And this man was terrible, for he was tepid and wretched and miserable and poor and blind and nude, and all these foregoing were evil, and they exercised their offices and neither did he order these same to be removed, but only that they should be convicted and menaced for their futures.

Pat: We say that the foregoing were neither bishops nor prelates.

Cath: By what rationale can they be called "angels of the churches" each of his own specific one, and why would they be convicted by the Lord as evil men if they might leave their Churches? As one has of the angel of the Church of Pergamum, to whom he says (2:14) "But I have a few things against you, because you have there some that hold the doctrine of Balaam," and later (2:15) "So you also have those that hold the doctrine of the Nicolaitans." And to the angel of Thyatira he says there (2:20) "But I have a few things against you, because you tolerate the woman Jezebel." Why might the Lord say to the angel of Sardis (3:4) "But you have a few names in Sardis that have not defiled their garment." Therefore they were prelates of the Church and bishops. So evil men are able to exercise the office of prelate in the Church of God and good men are able to be subject to them in those churches.

That an evil man cannot be a priest or prelate or preacher

David (Ps 49:16–18) "But to the sinner God has said, 'Why do you proclaim my justices, and take my covenant in your mouth? Seeing you have hated discipline, and have cast my words behind you. If you saw a thief you ran with him, and you have been a partaker with adulterers.'" And Romans 2 (2:21) "You therefore who teach another, why do you not teach yourself. You who preach that men should not steal, and you steal." And Matthew 5 (5:13) "You are the salt of the earth. But if the salt loses its flavor, with what shall it be salted? It is good for nothing any more but to be cast out." (5:16) "So let your light shine before men, that they may see your good works, and glorify your Father who is in heaven." And the same in 7 (7:3) "And why can you see the speck in your brother's eye, and you do not see the beam that is in your own eye?" And later (7:18) "A good tree cannot bring forth evil fruit, neither can an evil tree bring forth good fruit." The same

---

126 et...laudatie] Apoc. 3:14. | scio...129 meo] Apoc. 3:15. 130 emulare...age] Apoc. 3:19. 142 habeo...143 balaam] Apoc. 2:14. 143 ita...144 nicholaitarum] Apoc. 2:15. 145 sed...146 iezabel] Apoc. 2:20. 147 sed...148 sua] Apoc. 3:4. XXXIII.2.3 peccatori...7 ponebas] Ps. 49:16-18. 8 qui¹...9 furaris] Rom. 2:21. 9 uos...11 foras] Matt. 5:13. 11 sic...14 est] Matt. 5:16. 14 quid...16 tuo] Matt. 7:3. 16 non...18 facere] Matt. 7:18. 18 aut...21 cognoscitur] Matt. 12:33.

---

127 calidus...129 meo] om. *P* | frigidus¹] add. nec calidus *F* exp. 133 suis] om. *P* 134 modo...esse²] tamen eos *F* 136 Patarenus] om. *F* 138 Catholicus] om. *F* | Qua] add. ergo *F* | angeli] om. *P* 146 permittis...iezabel] om. *P* 148 qui...sua] om. *P* 151 eis] om. *F* XXXIII.2.1 Quod...2 predicator] om. *F* 6 et...7 ponebas] om. *P* 10 quod...11 foras] om. *P* 12 ut...14 est] om. *P* 15 et...16 tuo] om. *P* 16 non] om. *P*

131 erat²|fol. 135rb *P* 142 quia|fol. 106v *F*

bonam et fructum eius bonum aut facite arborem malam et fructum eius malum. siquidem ex fructu arbor cognoscitur etcet. et postea quomodo potestis bona loqui cum sitis mali etcet. et infra. bonus homo de bono cordis thesauro profert malum bonum et malus homo de malo thesauro profert malum etcet. idem. xv. sinite illos ceci sunt et duces cecorum. cecus autem si ceco ducatum prestet ambo in foueam cadunt etcet. Item. iohannes x. amen amen dico uobis qui non intrat per ostium in ouile ouium sed ascendit aliunde ille fur est et latro. Item. iª. ad corinthios. iiiº. templum enim dei sanctum est quod estis uos etcet. Item. iiª. ad corinthios. vi. que autem conuentio christi ad belial etcet. item. iacobum. ultimo. infirmatur quis in uobis inducat presbiteros ecclesie etcet. et postea multum enim ualet deprecatio iusti assidua etcet. item iude. iiº. hii sunt in epulis suis macule conuiuantes etcet. Ex his patet quod malus homo non potest esse sacerdos uel prelatus seu predicator.

Catholicus: Responsio. quod predicta auctoritates sic intelliguntur quod predicta non possunt officia huiusmodi exercere digne ad suam salutem uel perfectione ad proximorum utilitatem et sic intelliguntur ille auctoritates scilicet de dauid. peccatori autem dixit deus. etcet. et ad romanos. qui ergo alium doces. et de euangelio. mattheum. uos estis sal terre etcet. et sic luceat etcet. quid autem uides etcet. non potest arbor bona etcet. et aut facite etcet. et quomodo potestis etcet. et bonus homo etcet. et ad corinthios templum enim dei et que autem conuentio etcet. et iacobus. infirmatur aliquis etcet. et quedam intelliguntur de illis qui carent scientia et uita. ut illa sinite illos etcet. et huius quod patet quia dominus loquitur de cecis. cecus enim proprie dicitur qui utriusque oculi lumine caret scilicet scientia et uita secus est de monoculis. quia possunt alios ducere licet non ita comode. sicut si utroque uiderent oculo. Item. quidam intelliguntur de hereticis. uel de symoniacis. ut illa Iohannes. qui non intrat per hostium etcet. ut illa. iude hii sunt in epulis suis macule etcet.

Patarenus: Sed audite quid dicit christus. iohannes. xx accipite spiritum sanctum quorum remiseritis peccata remittuntur eis etcet. ergo illi soli sacerdotes habent potestatem ligandi atque soluendi qui spiritum sanctum habent. alias enim si ligati sunt uinculis peccatorum quomodo possunt ligatos soluere.

Catholicus: Responsio. Non dixit hic christus quod daret potestatem ligandi et soluendi solis illis qui spiritum sanctum habent. Sed spiritum sanctum dedit apostolis quam non dat successiue. potestatem uero ligandi et soluendi dedit illis quam succesiue dat prelatis et sacerdotibus omnibus. nec obstat quod dicitis quia ligati ligatos non possunt soluere quia inquantum ligati mali sacerdotes non soluerunt sed ex uirtute clauium quam a christo et ab ecclesia eius recipiunt secundum quam non ligati.

Patarenus: Sed audi quid dicit apostolus. iᵃ. ad timotheus. iiiᵒ. oportet ergo episcopum irreprehensibilem esse. etcet. et ad titum iᵒ. constituens per ciuitates presbiteros, sicut et ego disposui tibi si quis sine crimine est etcet. et infra. oportet enim episcopum sine crimine esse. etcet.

Catholicus: Respondeo quod apostolus non diffinit in his uerbis dignitates. sed tantum qualites ordinandorum id est ad qualia debent se preparare ut sint utiles sibi et aliis. et hoc est quod dicit in principio predicti capituli ad timotheum. si quis episcopatum desiderat bonum opus desiderat etcet. non dixit bonam dignitatem. sed bonum opus. ergo non diffinitatem dignitatem. preterea beatus petrus fuit reprehensibilis sicut dicit apostolus ad Galathas. iiᵒ. cum autem uenisset cephas antiochiam in faciem eius restiti quia reprehensibilis erat. et tamen episcopus erat. preterea si diffiniret apostolus dignitates his uerbis. ergo omnis bonus homo esset episcopus et diaconus et omnis bona mulier esset prelata. qui ergo essent subditi si omnes essent prelati. ad quid diceret apostolus tito. constituas per ciuitates presbiteros. si bonitas sua faceret illos presbiteros.

Item inducunt contra nos in hac parte quasdam auctores doctorum maxime gregorii quas sub silentio studiose pertransiui ne daret eis occasionem malignandi propter prauitatem ipsorum intellectus et ne furiosis porrigere arma quibus se ipsos perimerent. quas duobus modis inducunt uel quia uidentur dicere quod boni debent esse predicatores uel prelati et sacerdotes uel quia uidentur sonare quod non ualet oratio. absolutio uel prelatio oratio ualet ad solutio seu prelatio. uel predicatio. mali sacerdotis et praui prelati uel perversi predicatores. ad quorum primus Respondemus. quod boni debent esse et oportet quod tales sint propter tria. iᵒ. ut deo placeat in officio suo ut eis

Spirit. For others if they are bound by the chains of sins, in what way are they able to dissolve those so bound?

Cath: Reply. Christ did not say here that He might have given the power of binding and loosing only to those Apostles to whom He gave the Holy Spirit. But He gave the Holy Spirit to the Apostles which He did not give in stages, yet He gave to them the power of binding and loosing which they successively gave to all prelates and priests. Nor does it matter that you say that bound men are unable to unbind on account of the bounded thing, evil priests are not able to absolve save by the power of the keys which they have received from Christ and from the Church whereby they are not bound.

Pat: But hear what the Apostle says in 1 Timothy 3 (3:2) "It is fitting therefore for a bishop to be blameless." And Titus 1 (1:56) "establishing priests in every city, as I also appointed you, if any be without crime." And below (1:7) "For a bishop must be without crime."

Cath: I reply that the Apostle does not restrict dignities by these words, but only the qualities of the ordinands, that is, as to what sorts of things they ought to do to prepare themselves so that they might be useful to themselves and to others, and this is what he says at the beginning of the foregoing chapter to Timothy (3:1) "if a man desires the office of a bishop, he desires a good work." He did not say a good dignity, but a good work, therefore he did not define it a dignity. Further Blessed Peter was reprehensible just as the Apostle said in Galatians 2 (2:11) "But when Cephas came to Antioch, I withstood him to the face, because he was to be blamed." And yet he was still a bishop. Further if the Apostle had defined dignity in these words, then every good man would be a bishop and deacon and every good woman a prelate, who therefore were under authority if they were all prelates, to which the Apostle says to Titus (1:5) "and you should ordain priests in every city," if your goodness makes them priests.

Also they adduce against us in this part certain authorities and doctors, especially Gregory (Regula Pastoralis 1.2) which in silence I have carefully passed over lest it might give them an opportunity to malign, on account of the depravity of their intellects and lest they brandish weapons with fury, with which they might slay themselves. These they indicate in two ways, either they seem to say that the good ought to be preachers, or prelates, and priests, or that they seem to imply that neither prayer or absolution, prelacy or preaching is valid in bad priests or corrupt prelates or evil preachers. Regarding which we will reply to the first that they indeed ought to be good and it is appropriate that they should be for three reasons: first that God might be pleased with their ministry so that He

---

76 oportet...77 esse] 1 Tim. 3:2.   77 constituens...79 est] Tit. 1:5-6 (constituens] constituas *Vulg.*)   79 oportet...80 esse] Tit. 1:7.   85 si...86 desiderat²] 1 Tim. 3:1.   89 cum...91 erat²] Gal. 2:11.   96 constituas...97 presbiteros] Tit. 1:5.   99 gregorii] Gregory, *Regula Pastoralis*, 1.2.

64 quomodo] add. pat *P* exp.   65 Catholicus] om. *F*   66 illis] istis *P*   71 dicitis] diciti *F* | quia²] propter *P*   75 Patarenus] om. *F*   77 titum] timotheum *P*   81 Catholicus] om. *F*   87 ergo...88 dignitatem] om. *F*   90 cephas] kephas *P*   92 preterea] add. disti *P* exp. his] hiis *F*   94 bona] add. e *P* exp.   98 quasdam] add. dignitates *F* exp.   100 ne] ut *P*   101 ipsorum intellectus] transp. *F*   106 oratio...prelatio²] om. *F*   110 iᵒ] scilicet *F*

82 dignitates|fol. 136ra *P*

prosit eorum officium et ut magis expediat subditorum saluti. si autem argumentatur. ergo si non sunt tales non habent officium uel clauem non sequitur. quia in diuina pagina et maxime in auctoritatibus doctorum quas contra nos allegant dicitur mali sacerdotes aut praui prelati seu peruersi predicatores. ergo sunt sacerdotes aut prelati seu predicatores uel inperfecti. et dantur instantie contra suam argumentationem in hunc modum. iste est malus miles. ergo non est miles. uel ille est malus scolaris ergo non est scolaris. uel hic est malus homo ergo non est homo. et huius non sequitur. sin autem argumentarentur sic. ipse sacerdos siue prelatus. uel predicator non habet scientiam uel bonam uitam. ergo est inutilis. uel parum utilis sed dampnosus plenumque concedenda esset argumentatio quia uera esset. ad secundum modum dicimus quia intelliguntur de precisis ab ecclesia per errorem uel per excommunicationem. uel quia non habent officium in ueritate. uel quando populus uadit ad sacerdotem contra interdictum ecclesie. secundo dicimus quod non ualet oratio uel absolutio seu prelato sacerdotis et predicatoris et prelati praui quantum ad eius utilitatem. et sic intelligitur quod dominus dicit. malachias. ii°. maledicam benedictionibus uestris etcet. uel intelligitur illa auctoritas secundum primum modum. tertio intelligimus quod sacerdos et prelatus exercet officium suum duobus modis scilicet ratione sue perfectione et ratione ordinis uel officii ratione uero primi non ualet uel parum ualet uel quando nocet cum malus est. et sic potest etiam intelligi predictum malachie. ratione autem ordinis uel officialis non tantum sit efficax sicut si iuuaretur a uita sancta et intentione pura et quod sacerdos uel prelatus habeat duplicem potestatem scilicet ratione ordinis uel dignitatis et ratione uite bone cum illam habeat. ostendit dominus. mattheus. xvii. et quodcumque ligaueris super terram erunt ligata et in celis etcet. et ecce de prima et infra. si duo ex uobis consenserint super terram de omni re quamcumque petierint. fiet eis a patre meo qui in celis est. ubi enim sunt deo uel tres congregati in nomine meo etcet. ecce de secunda. caue tibi catholice ab auctoritatibus doctorum repro-batis quos heretici contra nos allegare conuenerunt in isto capitulo uel in aliis. sicuti de quibusdam quas beatus augustinus cum esset neophytus dixit. quas postea prouectus correxit in libro retractionum. et sicuti de quadam cipriam que talis est. quomodo autem sacrificare potest qui immundus ipse est etcet. quia ipse hoc dicente errauit sed quia ex simplicitate fecit et non contumaciter crederit quod deus dederit illi de hoc cogitationem in eius morte

might be a benefit to them in their work and that it might conduce better to the salvation of his subordinates. But even if one argues so, it does not follow that therefore when they are not [good] they do not hold the office or the key. Because in the Sacred Page and especially among the doctors which they allege against us, it speaks of evil priests, or corrupt prelates, or twisted preachers. Therefore they are priests or prelates or preachers, though imperfect ones. An example against their argument is given in this way. This is an evil soldier, therefore he is no soldier. Or this is a bad student, therefore he is no student. Or this is an evil man, and therefore he is not a man, and these do not follow. Yet on the contrary they might be proven thusly: that a priest or prelate or preacher who has himself no knowledge or uprightness of life, is useless, or of little use, but rather full of damnation. This argument should be conceded because it is true. To the second way we say that it is to be understood of those cut off from the Church by error or by excommunication, either because they do not hold office in truth, or when the people go to a priest in spite of the interdict of the Church. To the second we say that it does no benefit by prayer or absolution or the elevation of priests and preachers and evil prelates insofar as to their utility, and this is what is to be understood when the Lord says in Malachi 2 (2:2) "and I will curse your blessings." Or that passage is to be interpreted according to the first way. The third is that we understand that the priest and the prelate execute their office in two ways, namely, by reason of their perfection and by reason of their ordination. The first is of no benefit, or of little benefit, or when it harms because it is evil. And thus also one can interpret the aforementioned passage of Malachi, but by reason of his order or office he is not efficacious as much as if he were helped by a holy life and a pure intention and because a priest or prelate might have a double power, namely, by reason of order or dignity, and by reason of uprightness of life when he has it. The Lord showed that in Matthew 17 "and whatsoever you shall bind on earth shall be held bound in heaven," and see about the first, also later (18:19) "that if two of you shall consent upon earth concerning anything whatever they shall ask, it shall be done for them by my Father who is in heaven, for where there are two or three gathered together in my name." See of the second. Beware Catholic if you are reproved by the authorities of the doctors that those heretics have alleged against us. They are collected together in this chapter or in others, for example, those about which Blessed Augustine spoke of when he was a neophyte, which as an old man he later cast out and corrected in his book of Retractions, and the authority of Cyprian which goes like this, (Ep. 70.1) "yet how can he be able to sacrifice, who was himself unclean." Since he

---

134 maledicam...uestris] Mal. 2:2.   147 si...150 meo] Matt. 18:19.   157 quomodo...158 est] Cyprian, *Ep.* 70.1. "Quomodo autem mundare et sanctificare aquam potest, qui ipse immundus est."

112 sunt] add. n *P* exp.   114 auctoritatibus] add. sanctorum *F* exp.   135 tertio] om. *P*   138 uel] add. illis *P* | ratione²] add. ualet licet non tantum sit efficax sicut si iuraretur *F* exp.   141 officialis] officii valet licet *F*   145 illam] illa *P*   146 super...147 celis] om. *P*   148 de...150 meo] om. *P*   153 sicuti] sicut *F*   154 neo-phytus] neophitus *P*   156 cipriam] cypriani *F*   157 qui] que *F*   158 est] *ante corr.* esse *F*

112 argumentatur|fol. 136rb *P*   118 suam|fol. 107v *F*   142 intentione|fol. 136va *F*

propter priuilegium martyrii quod pro fide sustinuit et sic dicit beatus augustinus et quia plerumque dolosi heretici contra nos allegant auctoritates doctorum nostrorum falso uel correpte aut correctas ideo uerum esse credo ut cum illas allegauerint. exigatur ab eis probatio earumdem scilicet utrum ita sit quod dicunt et ubi sit ostendant euidenter quod alias tamquam falsi testes et criminosi calumpniatores repellantur. Sed respondete mihi parum. quo sensu dicitis o uos ydiote et heretici turpissimi quod prelati et sacerdotes et predicatores non possunt eorum fungi officiis licet sint mali cum ipsi sint ordinati a superioribus licet missi presbiteri cum scientiam habeant. propter hoc enim quod non sint ordinati uel missi a superioribus potestis dicere uel quia scientiam habeant non sint autem uultis dicere quod ideo sit quod uita bona careant. hoc a uobis requiro ut mihi ostenditis quod uita bona faciat prelatum uel quod eius defactus illum deponat. item secundum hoc omnes boni homines essent episcopi uel quacumque dignitate uellent fungerentur et sic non esset discretio dignitatum et ordinum et graduum in ecclesia dei quod est contra apostolum qui ait. iª. ad corinthios. xii. unicuique autem datur manifestatio spiritus ad utilitatem. alii quidem posuit deus in ecclesia primum apostolos secundo prophetas tertio doctores. deinde uirtutes. exinde gratias curationum. opitulationes. gubernatores genera linguarum inter-pretationes sermonum. numquid omnes apostoli. numquid omnes prophete. numquid omnes doctores. numquid omnes uirtutes. numquid omnes gratiam habent curationum. numquid omnes linguis loquuntur. numquid omnes interpretantur etcet. et ad ephesios. iiiiº. et ipse dedit quosdam quidem apostolos. quosdam autem prophetas. alios uero euangelistas. alios autem pastores. et doctores. etcet.

said this he erred but he did this out of simplicity and not because he believed it contumaciously, since God gave to him this understanding at his death on account of the privilege of martyrdom which he suffered for the faith, and thus blessed Augustine says, and since most the cunning heretics adduce these against us by misattribution or corrupted or emended texts, but I believe that when they adduce these, the same proof is thoroughly required by them of the same [authorities], that is, whether they are really as they say [they are] and that they should show where they are clearly, for otherwise they have to be rejected as false witnesses and unlawful slanderers. But answer me a little, you fools and shameful heretics, in what sense you declare that prelates and priests and preachers cannot exercise their offices although they may be evil, since they are ordained by superiors, namely commissioned priests because they have learning. You may say about this that they are not ordained or commissioned by superiors or you wish to say that because they have learning [that they are not ordained and sent] which is the same as to say that they lack a good life. I require this of you, that you show me what kind of upright life makes a prelate, and what he has to do to undo it in order to be deposed. Also according to this all good men will be bishops, or they would exercise whatever office they wish and thus there would not be any difference of dignity or order in the Church of God, which is against the Apostle who says in 1 Corinthians 12 (12:7) "And the manifestation of the Spirit is given to every man for a purpose." (12:28–30) "But these are different whom God placed in the church; first apostles, secondly prophets, thirdly doctors; after that workers of miracles for their powers; then the graces of healings, helps, governments, kinds of tongues, interpretations of speeches. Are all apostles? Are all prophets? Are all doctors? Are all workers of miracles? Have all the grace of healing? Do all speak with tongues? Do all interpret?" And Ephesians 4 (4:11) "And he gave some as apostles, and some as prophets, and others as evangelists, and others as pastors and doctors."

De iuramento

De iuramento contra hereticos procedendum est tribus modis. et primo questionando hoc modo dic mihi heretice quid est iuramentum.

De iuramento

Iuramentum est alicuius assertio cum attestatione diuina. ergo apostolus multotiens iurauit. quia multotiens asserint cum actestatione diuina. ut ad romanos. iº. testis enim mihi est deus cui seruio in spiritu meo in

On oath taking

On taking oaths we follow three paths against the heretics. The first is by questioning, tell me heretic, what is swearing.

On oath taking

Swearing is a particular assertion with divine attestation. Therefore the Apostle swore on many occasions, since many times he asserted with divine attestation. See Romans 1 (1:9) "For God is my witness, whom I serve in

---

183 unicuique...184 utilitatem] 1 Cor. 12:7.   184 alii...192 interpretantur] 1 Cor. 12:28-30.   193 et...195 doctores] Eph. 4:11.
XXXIV.2.5 testis...7 meis] Rom. 1:9.

164 uerum] tutum F   165 ab eis] om. P   174 missi...superioribus] om. F   194 alios...195 doctores] om. P   XXXIV.1.1 De iuramento] om. F   3 mihi] michi F   XXXIV.2.1 De iuramento] om. F   2 attestatione] actestatione P   3 ergo...4 diuina] om. F   5 seruio...7 meis] om. P

174 sint|fol. 136vb P   182 in|fol. 108r F

euangelio filii eius. quod sine intermissione memoriam uestri facio. semper in orationibus meis etcet. idem. ix. ueritatem dico in Christo non mentior testimonium mihi perhibente mihi conscientia mea in spiritu sancto. quoniam tristitia mihi magna est et continuus dolor cordi meo etcet. item. ii^a. ad corinthios. ii^o. non enim sumus sicut plurimi adulterantes uerbum dei sed ex sinceritate sed sicut ex deo coram dei in christo loquimur etcet. idem. xii. circa finem. olim putatis quod excusemus nos apud uos coram deo in christo loquimur etcet. idem. ad Galathas. i^o. circa finem. que autem scribo uobis ecce coram deo quia non mentior etcet. item ad ephesios. iiii^o. hoc igitur dico et testificor in domino etcet. Item ad phylippenses. i^o. testis enim mihi est deus quomodo cupiam uos omnes in uisceribus christi ihesu etcet. item ii^a. ad timotheus. iiii^o. testificor coram deo et christo ihesu qui iudicaturus est uiuos et mortuos etcet.

Item de eodem

[**Patarenus:**] Uel iuramentum est coniuratio dei. Et hoc fecit apostolus. i^a. ad thesalonicenses. ultimo in finem. adiuro uos per dominum ut legatur epistola hec etcet. Dicamus ergo quod iuramentum est. quicquid aliud dicitur in assertione quam est illud quod precepit nobis christus scilicet est est uel non non.
Catholicus: Sed quero a te utrum illa uerba tantum debeant dici et non alia. an sententia uerborum illorum. primum enim non potest dicere quia nec christum nec apostolos inuenimus umquam illis uerbis usos fuisse in assertionibus suis. si uero dicis quod sententia illorum uerborum sit dicenda quero que nam sit illa.
[**Patarenus:**] Dico quod sententia uerborum illorum est tenenda. que hoc est scilicet aliquid asserere uel negare per duas dictiones tantum.
Catholicus: Dico quod tam christus quam eius apostoli per plures asseruerunt uel negauerunt quam sepius de christo enim legitur. iohannes. iii. amen amen dico tibi nisi quis renatus fuerit etcet. bis enim dixit amen. amen. quod representat duo est est. et postea addidit assertionem suam per illud uerbum non potest. quod representat. tertium est et sepe enim legitur christum taliter locutum fuisse. de apostolo uero paulo multotiens habetur et de aliis apostolis quod per tres uel iiii^{or} docens affirmitiuas uel negatiuas asseruerunt uel negauerunt maxime de paulo legitur. ad romanos. viiii. ubi dixit. ueritatem dico ecce una

my spirit in the gospel of his Son, that without ceasing I make a commemoration of you, always making request in my prayers." And the same in 9 (9:1) "I speak the truth in Christ, I do not lie, my conscience bears witness to me in the Holy Spirit that I have great sadness, and continual sorrow in my heart." Also 2 Corinthians 2 (2:17) "For we are not peddlers of God's word like so many, but in Christ we speak as persons of sincerity, as persons sent from God and standing in his presence." The same in 12 near the end (12:19) "Of old, do you think that we excuse ourselves to you? We speak before God in Christ." The same in Galatians 1 near the end (1:20) "Now the things which I write to you, behold, before God, I do not lie." Also Ephesians 4 (4:17) "this then I say and testify in the Lord." Also Philippians (1:8) "For God is my witness, how I long after you all in the affection of Jesus Christ." Also 2 Timothy 4 (4:1) "I bear witness before God and Jesus Christ, who shall judge the living and the dead."

More on the same

[**Pat:**] Or swearing is a conjuring of God. And the Apostle does this in 1 Thessalonians at the end (5:27) "I adjure you by the Lord, that this epistle be read to all the holy brethren." Therefore let us say that is what swearing is. Whatsoever else is said as an assertion, which is that which Christ commanded us, namely (Mt 5:37) "yes, yes, or no, no."
Cath: Yet I ask you, whether those words only might be said and not others, or rather the meaning of these words. For the first one cannot say because we find neither Christ nor the Apostles ever using those words in their assertions. If yet you say that the meaning of those words should be pronounced, I ask what that might be in fact.

[**Pat:**] I say that the meaning of those words is to be held thusly, that one should assert or deny something through two manners of speaking only.
Cath: I say that both Christ and his Apostles many times asserted and denied, which is read more often about Christ in John 3 (3:5) "Amen, Amen, I say to you, unless a man be born again." For twice did He say "Amen, Amen," that represents two "Yes, Yes." And later is appended his assertion in those words "one is not able," which represents the third "yes" and for often one reads that Christ is speaking in such a manner. Truly of the Apostle Paul one has many occasions and of the other Apostles teaching in [groups of] three or four asserted positive or negative things or they denied them. as it is especially read of Paul, in Romans 9, when he said (9:1–2) "I speak the truth,"

dictio affirmatiua in christo ihesu ecce secundo. non mentior. ecce tertia. testimonium mihi perhibente conscientia mea in spiritu sancto. ecce quarta. quoniam tristitia mihi magna. ecce quinta et continuus dolor corde meo subintelligitur est. ecce sexta. Dico ergo quod sententia uerborum illorum est assertio uel negatio per nuda uerba sicut sunt ista uerba uel est. uel. non. et secundum hoc tantum ualet est est uel non non. quam unum est et unum non. uel tria est uel tria non. quotienscumque enim uelit dicere est uel non. dum tamen non utatur uerbis adiurationis in quibus deus uel aliqua substantia inducitur in testem uel iudicem.

Sed christus usus est uerbis adiurationis scilicet amen. amen. quod sonat in ueritate. in ueritate. que quidem ipse est ut ipse dicit in iohannes. xiiii ego sum uia ueritas etcet. et ipse est deus. ergo dicebat in deo in deo. et apostolus paulus usus est pluries uerbis iurantis attestando de deo uel coniurando ut supra ostensum est.

De iuramento

Dicam ergo aliter quod iuramentum est dicere si deus me adiuuet.

De eodem

Sed hoc iuramentum numquam legitur prohibitum. presertim cum tempore christi et apostolorum non fieret huiusmodi uerbis iuramentum. sed aliis ut puta uiuit dominus. uel hoc faciat mihi dominus et hoc addat. uel testis est deus. uel in deo et huiusmodi.

De Juramento

[**Patarenus:**] Dico ergo quod iuramentum est. iurare per euangelia sicut facit ecclesia romana.

De iuramento

Sed eadem restat oppositio de isto que et de proximo. preterea. si istud tantum est iuramentum. ergo non est iuramentum alio modo iurare scilicet per crucem uel per reliquias sanctorum et huiusmodi. quod tu inficiaris. preterea. qua ratione quo sensu ista sunt iuramenta. et inueniam quod tu pones aliquam de supradictis causis.
Patarenus: Sed dic tu quid est iuramentum
Catholicus: Iuramentum est iuris constitutio in consciencia alicui cum attestatione religionis diuine. iuris constitutio ponit. quia ius constituitur id est iuris probatio in iurante deficientibus aliis probationibus. sicut dicit apostolus ad hebreos. vi. Omnis controuersie finis ad confirmationem est iuramentum. in consciencia uero additur propter ueritatem cordis que

behold one positive utterance, "in Christ Jesus," behold the second, "I do not lie," behold the third, "my conscience bearing me witness in the Holy Spirit," behold the fourth, "That I have great sadness," behold the fifth, "and continual sorrow in my heart," is added, behold the sixth. So I say that the meaning of these words is assertion or negation by clear words just as these words are either yes or no and according to the value of "yes, yes, or no, no," one yes and one no, or three yes or three no, for as often as one wishes to say yes or no, provided that one does not use words of adjuration, in which God or another substance is introduced in witness or judgment.

But Christ used words of adjuration, namely "amen, amen," which means "in truth, in truth", which indeed He is Himself, as He says in John 14 (14:6) "I am the way, the truth," and He Himself is God, therefore He was saying "in God, in God." And the Apostle Paul used words of swearing, calling God as [his] witness or taking oaths as was shown above.

About swearing

So I could say that another way of swearing is to say "God help me,"

On the same topic

But this swearing is nowhere read to be prohibited, particularly in the time of Christ and of the Apostles they would not make oaths with words of this kind, but with others, for example, "the Lord lives" or "May the Lord do this for me," and "May He add this," or "God is the witness" or "in God" and the like.

About swearing

[**Pat:**] I say that swearing is to swear by the gospels just as the Roman Church does.

About swearing

But the objection remains the same about this and of the next. Moreover, if this alone is swearing, then it is not swearing; to swear in a different manner, namely, by the cross or by the relics of the saints, and the like, which you refuse to acknowledge. Further, by what reason, in what sense are these oaths? And I might find that you propose some in the foregoing cases.
Pat: But you tell me what swearing is.
Cath: Swearing is a legal statement in conscience to someone with the attestation of divine religion. "Legal statement" supposes that a law is enacted, that is, by legal proof in swearing, in the absence of other proofs, as the Apostle says in Hebrews 6 (6:16) "and an oath for confirmation is the end of all their controversy." "In conscience," it is added on account of truth in the heart

---

45 ego…46 ueritas] Ioh. 14:6. XXXIV.7.14 Omnis…15 iuramentum] Heb. 6:16.

36 uel] om. *F* 41 inducitur] om. *F (with space left for word)* 45 xiiii] iii° *P* 48 attestando] actestando *P* XXXIV.4.1 De iuramento] om. *F* 2 Dicam] dico *P* XXXIV.5.1 De eodem] om. *F* XXXIV.6.1 De Juramento] om. *F* XXXIV.7.1 De iuramento] om. *F* 9 Patarenus] Catholicus *P* | om. *F* leg. **Patarenus** 10 Catholicus] om. *P* 11 attestatione] actestatione *P*

32 mea|fol. 108v *F* XXXIV.6.3 euangelia|fol. 137va *P*

debet in eo esse. alias enim non est iuramentum sed periuriam cum attestatione autem diuine religionis ponit propter creaturas per quas non licet iurare propter duas rationes. una est propter ydolatriam remouendam a cordibus hominum. si enim iurarent per creaturas putarent forte plerumque quod ipsa pura creatura non habito respectu ad deum. haberet quamdam diuinam potentiam et sic essent ydolatre. alia est ne tamquam per rem uilem et quam non timerent iurantes non crederent se seruari iuramenta et sic haberent occasionem plerumque deierandi et ideo positum est in forma iuramenti ut iuretur per deum. cuius timore falsitas taceatur et cuius amore dicatur ueritas. unde apostolus dicit in predicto loco homines enim per maiorem sui iurant. secundus modus est quia paulus apostolus iurauit et angelis atque deus. de iuramento apostoli habetur. ii^a. ad corinthios. i^o. in finem. ego autem testem deum inuoco in animam meam quod parcens uobis non ueni ultra corinthum etcet. de iuramento angeli legitur. apocalypsis. x. et angelus quem uidi stantem super mare et super terra. leuauit manum suam ad celum et iurauit per uiuentem in secula seculorum qui creauit celum et omnia que in illo sunt etcet. de iuramento autem dei dicit apostolus ad hebreos. iiii^o. quibus iuraui in ira mea si introibo in requiem meam etcet. et vi^o. abrahe namque promittens deus quoniam neminem habuit per quem iuraret maiorem. iurauit per semetipsum dicens nisi benedicens te benedicam te etcet. et vii. et quantum est non sine iureiurando sacerdotes facti sunt. hic autem cum iureiurando per eum qui dixit ad illum. iurauit dominus et non penitebit eum tu es sacerdos in eternum. secundum ordinem melchisedech etcet. si ergo iurauit apostolis et angelis et deus. secure uos heretici iurare potestis siquidem iurare dedignandum. proponentes uos non solum apostolis et angelo. sed ipsi deo. superbiores estis ipso principe superbie qui non dixit ero melior altissimo sed similis. unde merito postquam ipse cruciari debetis. sicut dicit beatus petrus. ii^a. ii^o. ubi angeli fortitudine et uirtute cum sint maiores non portant aduersus se execrabile iudicium etcet.

Patarenus: Responsio. quod apostolus non iurauit licet inuocare deum testem. angelus potuit iurare quia non erat ei prohibitum. deus uero fecit sicut dominus. multa namque licent domino que non licent seruo eius nec potest facere homo que facit deus.

Catholicus: Quod apostolus iurauerit probo. dicit enim in animam meam id est contra animam. est igitur dictum si mentior deus fecit testimonium contra

which one ought to possess, for otherwise it is no oath but a perjury, yet with "the attestation of divine religion," he inserts on account of creatures, by which it is not permitted to swear for two reasons. One is on account of having to remove idolatry from the hearts of men, for if they swore by creatures, they might consider perhaps generally that the creature — through not having respect towards God — that they might have certain divine powers and thus they would be idolatrous. Another is lest by swearing by something insignificant which they do not fear, they should not consider themselves blamed [for breaking it] and so they might have ample occasion to perjure themselves, and so the form of the oath is established so that one should swear by God, fear of whom silences falsehood and love of whom speaks the truth. Whence the Apostle says in the aforementioned place, "for men swear by a thing greater than themselves." The second manner is what Paul the Apostle swore, and the angel too, and God. Of swearing one has the Apostle in 2 Corinthians 1 at the end (1:23) "But I call God to witness upon my soul, that to spare you, I came not any more to Corinth," Of the oath by the angel it is read in Apocalypse 10 (10:5–6) "And the angel, whom I saw standing upon the sea and upon the earth, lifted up his hand to heaven, and he swore by him who lives for ever and ever, who created heaven, and the things which are in it." And of the oaths of God, the Apostle says in Hebrews 4 (4:3) "As I have sworn in my wrath, if they shall enter into my rest." And 6 (6:13–14) "For God making promise to Abraham, because he had no one greater by whom he might swear, swore by himself saying: 'Unless blessing I shall bless you.'" And 7 (7:20) "And inasmuch as it is not without an oath who were made priests, but this with an oath, by him that said to him: The Lord has sworn, and he will not repent, you are a priest forever according to the order of Melchizedek." So if the Apostles and Angels and God swore, you can be sure that you heretics can swear even though you disdain it, since it is not only the Apostles and the angel who propose it but God Himself. You are more prideful than the prince of Pride who did not say, 'I will be better than the most high,' but something similar, thus you ought deservedly to suffer for following after him, just as Blessed Peter says in 2 Peter 2 (2:11) "Whereas angels who are greater in strength and power bring not against themselves a railing judgment."

Pat: I reply that the Apostles did not swear, but invoked the witness of God. The angels were able to swear because it was not prohibited to them. Truly God did it, just like the Lord, for many things are permitted to the Lord which are not permitted to His servant, neither is man able to do what God does.

Cath: That the Apostle swore I prove, for he said (2 Cor 1:23) "upon my soul," that is, against my soul, therefore if I lie may God give testimony against my soul, or may God

---

34 ego...35 corinthum] 2 Cor. 1:23.   36 et...40 sunt] Apoc. 10:5-6.   41 quibus...42 meam] Heb. 4:3.   42 abrahe...45 te^2] Heb. 6:13-14.   45 et^2...49 melchisedech] Heb. 7:20.   56 ubi...57 iudicium] 2 Pet. 2:11.   65 in...meam] 2 Cor. 1:23.

17 sed] set F   18 attestatione] actestatione P   22 per creaturas] om. P   31 sui iurant] transp. P   48 penitebit...49 melchisedech] om. P   53 superbiores] superiores P   54 unde] tam P   59 Patarenus] om. F   64 Catholicus] om. F   66 mentior] cantior P

XXXIV.7.31 maiorem|fol. 137vb P   38 uiuentem|fol. 109r F   60 inuocare|fol. 138ra P

animam meam uel cumque testimonium et iudicium dei idem sit. idem ergo iuramentum fuit apostoli cum nostro qui dicimus. si deus me adiuuet. immo etiam fortius. quia nos ponimus priuationem diuini auxilii nobis si mentiretur. sic enim sonant uerba eius. inuoco deum testem etcet. id est si uerum dico ferat deus testimonium suum pro me. sin autem mentior noceat michi cum illo. ergo iuramentum fuit quod fecit apostolus. preterea dico tibi o heretice. dicas tu hoc uerba et sufficit michi et scio quod non uis facere. igitur reputas uerba hoc iuramentum. de hoc autem quod dixisti nos non debere imitari angeli in exemplum iurandi eo quod dicas nobis iuramentum esse prohibitum. et non illi. exigo a te rationem quare potius homini quam angelo dicas esse prohibitum iuramentum et quare beatus iohannes. scribat angeli iuramentum. si peccatum est nobis imitari illud. quod autem dicis quod non debemus nec possumus omnia facere que deus facit. que scilicet possumus uel saltem non est nobis peccatum si facimus illa cum apostolus dicat ad ephesios. v. estote imitatores dei sicut filii karissimi etcet. et dominus mattheus. v. in finem. estote ergo uos perfecti sicut et pater uester celestis perfectus est. scilicet in quantum possimus iurare. igitur nobis licet iurare postquam deus iurauit. quia quod non dedecet regem. nec dedecet militem. et quod dedecet militem multo fortius dedeceret regem sicut est exemplum in fornicatione et mendatio et huiusmodi que deus non potest facere quia peccata sunt. ergo nec iurare posset si peccatum esset. et quia iurauit peccatum non est iuramentum. et nota catholice quod eadem ratione unum peccatum est. eadem ratione dicunt heretici et alia esse peccata. omnia enim peccata dicunt una eademque ratione esse.
Patarenus: Dicam ergo quod deus non iurauit sicut uos facitis. sed simpliciter per nuda uerba promisit et promissio dicitur iuramentum in deo propter firmitatem ueritatis que in eo est.
Catholicus: Immo ultra nudam pollicitationem adiecit iuratoriam promissionem promittens et iurans per diuinitatem suam sicut et nos facimus. ut dicit apostolus ad hebreos. vi. iurauit per semetipsum etcet. et infra. in quo habundantius uolens deus ostendere pollicitationis heredibus immobilitatem consilii sui interposuit iusiurandum ut per suas res immobiles quibus impossibile est mentiri deum fortissimum solatium habeamus etcet. ergo deus duas promissiones pro eadem re fecit scilicet nudam et iuratoriam. Tertius modus est. quia cuius rei partes bone sunt. ipsa quos bona est res ut exemplum de equo de qui si probo quod bonum habeat caput et pedes et sic ceteras partes.

take witness and judgment against it at the same time. But our oath is the same as the Apostle's when we say, "may God help me," but more strongly, when we propose a privation of the divine help for ourselves if we might lie. Thus his words mean "I call God as witness," that is, if I say the truth, may God bear His witness for me, but if I lie instead may it be a harm to me. Therefore the Apostle made an oath. Further I say to you, O Heretic, you say these words and it suffices for me, and I know why you do not want to [swear]. Therefore you consider these words as an oath, but because you said that we ought not to imitate the angels in their example of swearing, for whom you say that swearing is forbidden to us and not to them, I require a reason from you why you say that men more than angels are to be forbidden from swearing and why Blessed John wrote about angels taking oaths, if it would be a sin for us to imitate this. Since also you say that we ought not, nor are we able to do anything that God does, which, actually, we are able or at least it is not a sin if we do these, as the Apostle says in Ephesians 5 (5:1) "Be imitators of God, just as beloved sons," and the Lord in Matthew 5 (5:48) "therefore be perfect, as your heavenly Father is perfect," namely insofar as we are able to swear. Therefore it is permitted for us to swear after God swore, since what is not unbecoming for a king, neither is it for a soldier, and if unbefitting for a soldier, how much more unbefitting would it be for a king, just as in the examples of fornication, and lying, and the like, which God cannot do since they are sins, likewise neither could He swear, if it were a sin, and since He did swear, then swearing is not a sin. And note, Catholic, that by the same reason one is a sin, the heretics declare others to be sins. For they say that all sins are identical by one and the same reason.

Pat: I might say therefore that God did not swear as you would do, but simply by the plain sense of the words He promised, and in God a promise is called an oath on account of the firmness of truth that is in Him.

Cath: On the contrary beyond the plain promising He is promising a binding promise and swearing by His divinity, just as we also do. As the Apostle says in Hebrews 6 (6:13) "He swore by himself," and later (6:17–19) "Wherein God, meaning more abundantly to show to the heirs of the promise the immutability of his counsel, interposed an oath that by two immutable things, in which it is impossible for God to lie, we may have the strongest comfort, who have fled for refuge to hold fast the hope set before us, which we have as an anchor of the soul." Then God made two promises about the same thing, namely, plainly and in an oath. The third way is because the parts of a thing are good the whole is good, just as the example of a horse, of which if I prove that it has a good head and

---

87 estote...88 karissimi] Eph. 5:1.   89 estote...90 est] Matt. 5:48.   108 iurauit...semetipsum] Heb. 6:13.   109 in...113 habeamus] Heb. 6:17-19.

---

68 dei...sit] om. idem sit dei *P*   75 o] om. *F*   80 et...82 iuramentum] om. *P*   87 sicut...88 karissimi] om. *P*   89 sicut...90 iurare] om. *P*   93 dedecet] decet *F* | dedeceret] deceret *F*   95 huiusmodi] huius *P*   97 peccatum...est] non est ergo peccatum *F*   98 unum... 99 ratione] om. *P*   101 Patarenus] om. *F*   105 Catholicus] om. *F*

92 dedecet²|fol. 138rb *P*   98 ratione|fol. 109v *F*

restat quod ipse totus bonus sit. sed constat quod iuramento uero et necessario per deum facta. sunt tria tantum partes et ille omnes bone sunt. igitur enim sunt tria tamen scilicet ueritas. necessitas iurandi ueritatem et diuini auxilii inuocatio. sed ista omnia bona sunt. uel nichil illorum malum est. ergo iuramentum taliter factum totum bonum est. uel saltem non est malum et attende catholice quod quicumque garriant heretici quod ipsi habent in consciencciis suis quod apostolus iurauerunt pluries et quod deus et angelis iurauerunt similiter.

Quod iurare sit peccatum. secundam patarenum

Patarenus: Zacharias. v. omnis fur sicut scriptum est iudicabitur et omnis iurans ex hoc similiter iudicabitur etcet. ergo iuramentum est peccatum. sicut furtum etiamsi fit in nomine dei.

Catholicus: Responsio. quod loquitur de iuramento mendaciter facto. unde subdit. educam illud dicit dominus exercituum et ueniet ad domum furis et ad domum iurantis in nomine meo mendaciter etcet.

Patarenus: Item. mattheus. v. dictum est antiquis non periurabis. reddes autem domino iuramenta tua. Ego autem dico uobis non iurare omnino. neque per celum quia thronus dei est neque per terram. quia scabellum est pedum eius. neque per Ierosolymam quia ciuitas est magni regis neque per caput tuum iuraueris quia non potes unum capillum album facere aut nigrum. sit autem sermo uester. est. est. non. non. quod autem abundantius est. a malo est etcet. ergo preceptum christi est non iurare.

Catholicus: Responsio. quinque modis possunt ista uerba domini intelligi primo sic. Non iurare omnino id est in uanum. quasi dicat. quocumque modo iuretis etiam si per creaturas ut puta per celum et terram et huius. uolo ut fidem seruetis. unde subdit. sit autem sermo uester. est. est. non. non. id est concordet os cum corde. siue in affirmatione siue in negatione et quod ista uerba est. est. non. non id est concordet os cum corde. sic debeat intelligi ostendit apostolus. ii^a. ad corinthios. i^o. fidelis autem deus quia sermo noster qui fuit apud uos non est in illo est et non sed est in illo est etcet. et quod iste sit sanus intellectus patet ex duobus uerbis que superius dixerat in hoc capitulo scilicet. non ueni soluere legem sed adimplere etcet. et non habundauerit iustitia uestra plusquam scribarum et phariseorum. etcet. si enim christus non tollit legem et si iustitia nostra plus debet habundare quasi scribarum et phariseorum que erat docere homines reddere iuramentum deo secundum legis preceptum.

relinquitur quod ipse non tollit iuramentum sed supplet autem legem quantum ad priuam doctrinam scribarum et phariseorum et supplet illorum iustitiam quia deficiebat. docebant autem predicti et obseruabant quod siquis iuraret per creaturas eo quod male iuraret. non deberet seruare iuramentum et sic docebant fieri periuria. excipiebant tamen quasdam creaturas scilicet munera que offerebantur illi. ut inducerent semplices ad offerenda munera illi. dominus uero quia ueritas est ueritatem iubet seruari etiam si per creaturas iuretur quia in creaturis creator intelligit. presertim in illi de quibus scribe et pharisei uilipendebant iuramentum factum et hoc est quod subdit. neque per celum quia thronus dei est etcet. quasi dicat. thronus dei est celum et ideo qui iurant in throno dei iurare utique et per deum intelligitur et sic de ceteris et probantur hoc infra xxiii. ue uobis duces ceci. qui dicitis quicumque iurauerit per templum nichil est. qui autem iurauerit in aula templi debet etcet. et infra. qui iurat in celo iurat in throno dei. et in eo qui sedet super eum. etcet. et nota catholice quod dominus cum dicit de iuramento reddendo per creaturas facto et reddit rationem quod in creaturis creator intelligitur. loquitur fidelibus qui intelligebant in creaturis creatorem. et qui erant docti a phariseis. quod iuramentum non debebat seruari nisi esset factum per deum. qui etiam ipsi intelligebant in creaturis creatorem intelligi tamen excipiebant quosdam digniores de quibus etiam magis uidetur et contra illorum stultitiam dominus inuehitur. uerumptamen scire debes quod etiam si per ydolum factum sit iuramentum debet seruari ne fides frangitur promissa et hoc est quod dominus claudit in illis uerbis. est. est. non. non. quia quidcumque modo fiat iuramentum. uult quod iuramentum seruetur nisi esset pernitiosum. secundo modo intelliguntur uerba domini sic quod in his uerbis. tria facit scilicet prohibet precipit et indulget. prohibet scilicet non iurare omnino neque per celum etcet. precipit uero dicere ueritatem ibi. sit autem sermo uester est. est. etcet. indulget uero ex necessitate uerum iurare ibi. quod autem his habundantius est a malo etcet. Omnia enim que in hic capitulo dominus addit legi. sunt consilia maioris perfectionis et occasionis uitandi peccata. Tertio modo exponuntur sic ut dominus prohibeat his uerbis tantum iuramentum factum per creaturas presertim cum habeatur respectus ad ipsas puras creaturas et tunc non sit preuaricatio ab illo uerbo non iurare usque ad illud sit autem sermo uester etcet. quasi dicat. non iuretis per celum. quia non est deus sed est thronus eius. igitur creatura. neque per terram eandem eadem ratione. ne per ciuitatem ierusalem eadem de causa per capud uestrum quia capud uestrum nullam habet potentiam propter quod timeatis mentiri. quia uos toti non potestis facere capillum nigrum aut album quod autem sequitur. sit autem sermo uester etcet. preceptum est uitandi periurium. Quarto modo exponitur sic. ut christus prohibeat duos modos iurandi. primo scilicet non iurare omnino id est passim. hoc est semper uel ex quacumque causa. non dicit omnino non iurare. quia si hoc diceret tunc esset dictum nullo iures. cum autem dicit non iurare omnino est dictum non iurare passim uel semper. quia negatio quando proponitur signo uniuersali affirmatiuo conuertitur in particulare affirmationem et negationem. ut non omnis homo cur id est quidam non cur. et quidam non non cur. id est sic ponitur hic. non iurare omnino id est aliquo modo iures et aliquo modo non. si autem posponitur reddit uniuersalem negationem. ut omnis homo non cur. id est nullus homo cur. et sic esset si dixisset omnino non iurare quod sonaret nullo iuris quod non fecit. secundo prohibet iurare per creaturas cum dicit neque per celum etcet. quod patet etiam ex illo uerbo neque. si enim esset dictum non iurare omnino id est nullo modo iures. quare postea dixisset neque per celum etcet. ergo aliud est non iurare omnino et aliud est non iurare per celum etcet. quinto uero modo intelliguntur uerba hoc ut sit consilium domini datum perfectis. si bene aduertas in hoc capitulo. sunt tantum consilia que perfectis dedit christus.

Patarenus: Item. iacobus. ultimo. ante omnia autem fratres mei nolite iurare neque per celum neque per terram neque per aliud quodcumque iuramentum etcet. ergo nullo modo licet iurare.

Catholicus: Et hinc. v. modis respondeo primo sic. ante omnia id est ante omnes res. hoc est ex quacumque re. quia adiectum in neutro genere resoluitur in hoc substantiuum res et in suum adiectum feminini generis. et secundum hoc cetera plana sunt. et nota quod iiii^{or} sunt iuramenta. quorum tria sunt prohibita primum est periuriam. de quo dicit dominus. mattheus. v. dictum est antiquis non periurabis. secundum est quod sit sine causa uel sine necessitate. de quo dicit beatus iacobus. et dominus in mattheus. ibi. non iurare omnino secundam unam lecturam. et ecclesiasticus. xxiii. iurationi non assuescat os tuum multi enim casus in illa nominatio uero dei non sit assidua in ore tuo etcet. Tertium est quod sit per creaturas ut in mattheus. neque per celum etcet. et hic neque per celum etcet. secundum aliam lecturam. quartum uero est quod sit in ueritate et per deum et in necessitate quod concessum est. sicut probatum est superius in parte catholicorum et aliter non potest exponi istud uerbum ante omnia. non enim potest dici ante omni

---

121 ante...**123** iuramentum] Iac. 5:12. **132** dictum...periurabis] Matt. 5:33. **134** non...**135** omnino] Matt. 5:24. **136** iurationi... **137** tuo] Ecclesiastic. 23:9. **139** neque^1...celum] Matt. 5:33.

93 quod] quam F **105** id est] et F **106** non^1] homo P **107** et] uel F **110** sic] cur P **121** Patarenus] om. F **122** neque^2...**123** iuramentum] om. P **125** Catholicus] om. F **128** suum] add. uel P **136** multi...**137** tuo] om. P

103 signo|fol. 110v F **129** sunt|fol. 139va P

id est primo. quia quasi ultimo dicit hoc. nec etiam potest dici ante omnia precipue uel principaliter quia ante et post. maiora et utiliora saluti dicit. ante enim dicit in primo. siquis autem uestrum indiget sapientia postulet a deo etcet. et illud. estote factores uerbi et non auditores tantum etcet. et ii^a. superexaltat autem misericordia iudicium etcet. et iii^o. nolite glorari et mendaces esse aduersus ueritatem etcet. et iiii^o. subditi estote deo etcet. et postea dicit. siquis ex uobis errauerit a ueritate et conuertit quis eum etcet. et ista omnia et multa alia que dicit in epistoli beatus iacobus maiora et utiliora sunt saluti animarum quam sit non iurare. secundo modo Respondeo. exponendo uerba hic sic. Nolite iurare id est non uelitis iurare quia licet iurare ex necessitate non sit peccatum. non est tamen bonum uelle et appetere iurare etcet. tertio uero modo sic. nolite iurare neque per celum etcet. id est per creaturas. nec obstat quod subdit neque per aliud quodcumque iuramentum. quia sic intelligitur de prohibitis et recitatis a magistro christo ihesu. hoc est neque per ciuitatem ierusolymam neque per capud tuum. iiii^o. autem modo sic. nolite iurare scilicet in uanum et ideo dicit ne sub iudicio decidatis. quia quodcumque iuramentum iuretis debetis seruare illud. quinto. uero modo respondeo sic. quia dico quod beatus iacobus consulit in uerbis istis perfectis cauete a iuramento. eo quod per iuramentum sepe uenitur ad periuriam et si bene aduertas omnia fere que dicit in hac epistola. sunt consilia maioris securitatis et perfectionis uite. maxime. ubi dixit nolite. istarum autem. v. expositionum prime due securiores esse uidentur. pro prima uero facit quod subdit. ne sub iudicio decidatis etcet. et auctoritas ecclesiastica supradictam. et ysaias. viii. omnia enim quecumque loquitur populus iste coniuratio est. etcet. et secunda uero confirmat. quod sequitur. est. est. non. non. etcet.

Patarenus: Item augustinus. propter reatum false iurationis Dominus prohibuit omnem iurationem etcet. item alia glosa eius. iuramentum non est bona etcet. ergo augustinus intellexit peccatum esse iuramentum prohibitum esse a deo.

Catholicus: Respondeo qualiter augustinus intelligat iuramentum prohibitum esse a deo exponit cum dixit. non penitus iurare prohibuit sed occasionem periurii tollens. quod perfectius est euitare docuit. ostendens quod ulterius est a malo esse. apostolus iurat. ut fidem

that saying "above all things." For in fact it cannot be said before all, that is, the first, because He says this as if it were last, or above all, since before and after, He says greater and more useful things for salvation. For above He said in the first chapter (1:5) "But if any of you lack wisdom, let him ask of God," and that one (1:22) "be doers of the word, and not hearers only," and 2 (2:13) "And mercy exalts itself above judgment." And 3 (3:14) "do not glory, and do not be liars against the truth." And 4 (4:7) "Be subject therefore to God," and later he says (5:19) "if any of you err from the truth, and one convert him." And all these, and many others, which Blessed James speaks of in the epistle, are greater and more useful things for the salvation of souls than not swearing. To the second I reply, by explaining the saying here thusly, "do not swear," that is, you should not wish to swear since it is permitted to swear from necessity, and though it is not a sin, it is nevertheless not good to wish or desire to swear. To the third point is this (5:12) "do not swear by heaven," that is, by creatures. Nor does what is added oppose this "neither by any other oath," since it is to be understood of forbidden oaths and read by the Master Jesus Christ, "neither by the city of Jerusalem, nor by your head." Yet the fourth way is this, "do not swear" namely, in vain, and so He says, "that you do not fall under judgment." Since whatever oath you might swear you ought to keep it. The fifth way I reply thus, since I say that Blessed James counsels in these passages for the perfect to beware of oaths, for the reason that those who swear often come to perjury, and if you pay attention to nearly all those things which he says in this epistle, they are counsels to greater security and perfection of life, especially when he said "do not." Yet of these five expositions the first two seem to be the more secure, for the first he makes that which comes next (5:12) "that you do not fall under judgment," and by the ecclesiastical authorities mentioned above, and Isaiah 8 (8:12) "for all that this people speak is a conspiracy," and the second readily confirms what follows "yes, yes, no, no."

Pat: Also Augustine (Sermon 307 on John the Baptist) "on account of the crime of false swearing the Lord prohibited all oaths," also another of his glosses "Swearing is not good."[1] Therefore Augustine understood swearing to be a sin prohibited by God.

Cath: I reply how Augustine might have understood swearing to be prohibited by God he explains when he says, (Gregory on Mt 3, Ordinary Gloss on Mt 5:33-37) "He did not completely prohibit swearing but removing the occasion for perjury, by which he taught it is more

---

148 siquis...149 deo] Iac. 1:5.   149 estote...150 tantum] Iac. 1:22.   150 superexaltat...151 iudicium] Iac. 2:13.   151 nolite...152 ueritatem] Iac. 3:14.   152 subditi...153 deo] Iac. 4:7.   153 siquis...154 eum] Iac. 5:19.   161 nolite...celum] Iac. 5:12.   176 ne... 177 decidatis] Iac. 5:12.   178 omnia...179 est] Is. 8:12.   181 propter...182 iurationem] Augustine, Sermon 307, on John the Baptist. 183 iuramentum...bona] Perhaps Augustine, on the Sermon on the Mount.   188 non...189 docuit] Gregory (Paschasius Radbertus) on Mt. 3, cf. Ordinary Gloss, Matt. 5:33-37.   189 ostendens...194 resecauit] Ordinary Gloss, on Mt. 5:37.

149 et^2...150 tantum] om. *P*   152 aduersus ueritatem] om. *P*   158 iurare^1] om. *P*   172 fere] fecit *P*   181 Patarenus] om. *F*   186 Catholicus] om. *F*   187 exponit] om. *P*

166 nolite|fol. 139vb *P*   172 periuriam|fol. 111r *F*

---

1) Possibly taken from his commentary on the Sermon on the Mount.

persuadeat ecclesia etiam pro federe pacis et fidei iurare suos concedit. sed christus quod perfectius est docuit quod infirmitas est indulsit quod superstitiosum est resecauit etcet. et ibi super illo uerbo. quod autem hiis habundantius est a malo est ait. non dicit malum est. sed a malo est. a malo scilicet incredulitatis. iuramentum exigentis que utique incredulitas quandoque culpa est quandoque postea tamen etcet. Qualiter autem intelligat quod iuratio non sit bona exponit glosa. unde hoc uerbum fuisti furatus sic dicens. iuratio non est bona. iuratio non est bona non tamen mala cum necessaria id est non est appetenda sicut bona. nec tam fugienda tamquam mala cum est necessaria. non est enim contra preceptum dei iuratio etcet. item alia glosa. super mattheus. qui non iurat periurare non potest. etcet. glosa intelligit non esse iurandus.

Catholicus: Responsio. super. glosam. ubi sequitur. qui non loquitur mentiri non potest et intelliges quod non dicit quod omne iuramentum sit malum. sicut non dicit quod omnis locutio mala sit. sed dicit de utroque quod qui non iurat periurare non potest. et qui non loquitur mentiri non potest. sic econtrario qui numquam iurat numquam uerum iurat. et qui numquam loquitur. numquam uerum dicit. bonum est enim non iurare ut non periuretur et bonum est non loqui ut mendatium taceatur sic et bonum est iurare ut ueritas cognoscatur. bonum est loqui ut ueritas dicatur. sed responde tu mihi nullum est enim malum nisi in bono. quia malum est corruptio boni seu priuatio. ideo enim homicidium malum est quia indebite corrumpit creaturam dei. et sic de adulterio quia matrimonium uiolat. sic de futro quia iustum dominium turbat. sic de periurio quia iuramentum uitiat. ergo uerum iuramentum cui oppositum est periurum non est malum.

Patarenus: Sed quare non recipitis nos ad fidem et obedientiam ecclesie romane sine iuramento. siquidem ad illam uenire uolumus. cum etiam secundum nos perfectius sit iurare non quam iurare.

Catholicus: Respondeo quia nolumus uos recipere lupos secundum agnos nec uos agnos esse cognoscimus quamdiu lupiam pellem non depositis. nolumus enim recipere uos hereticos sed catholicos et uos catholicos esse non uidemus quamdiu amplecti non uultis quod errando blasphematis et in hoc causa utique melius est iurare quam non iurare. immo hoc bonum est et illud malum.

perfect to avoid, showing it is further removed from evil. The Apostle swears that some might be convinced of the faith. Even the Church permits swearing by its faithful for a peace treaty. But Christ taught more perfectly, that He would indulge the weak and that He might remove superstition." And here, regarding that word (Mt 5:37) "and that which is over and above these, is of evil." He does not say it is evil, but it is from evil. Namely, of the evil of unbelief, in exacting an oath, which unbelief certainly is sometimes a fault and sometimes even a sin. In what way He understands that swearing is not good is explained by the gloss. Whence you have stolen the sense thus, by saying swearing is not good, (Augustine, Sermon on the Mount, 1.17) "swearing is to be reckoned not among things that are good, but among things that are necessary," that is "it is not to be desired as if it were a good, nor is it to be fled from like an evil, since it is necessary," (Augustine on Galatians) "for it is not contrary to the command of God to swear." Also another gloss, on Matthew (Augustine, Sermon on the Mount) "He who does not swear, is unable to perjure himself," the Gloss understands that one should not swear.

Cath: Reply about the gloss. When it adds, "he who does not speak is unable to lie," and understand that it does not say that all swearing is evil, just as it does not say that all speech is evil, but it does say of both that he who does not swear is unable to perjure himself and that he who does not speak cannot lie. Thus on the contrary he who never swears, never swears the truth, and he who never speaks never speaks the truth. For it is good not to swear that one might not perjure himself, and it is good not to speak that one might not lie thus, and it is good to swear for one who might know the truth. It is good to speak that the truth be spoken. But answer me this, for there is no evil except in the good, since evil is the corruption of the good or its privation. For so is a killing evil, because it unduly destroys a creature of God. Likewise adultery, since it violates a marriage. Likewise about theft, since upsets rightful ownership. So also of perjury since it corrupts an oath. Therefore swearing in truth, which is opposed to acts of perjury, is not an evil.

Pat: But why will you not receive us to the faith and to the obedience of the Roman Church without swearing, even supposing we wish to come to her, also since according to us it is more perfect not to swear than to swear.

Cath: I reply that we do not want to receive you wolves like lambs, neither do we know you to be lambs, so long as you have not put off your skins of wolves. For we do not wish to receive you as heretics, but Catholics, and we do not see you as Catholics until you no longer wish to embrace that by which you blasphemously err, and regarding this especially, that it is better to swear than not to swear, in fact the first is good, and the second evil.

---

201 iuratio...**202** necessaria] Augustine, *De Serm. Dom. in Mont.*, I. 17. 51. **203** non...**204** iuratio] Augustine, *Expos. Epis. ad Galat.* cf. Peter Lombard, III. d. 39, c. 4. **205** qui...**206** potest] Augustine, *De Serm. Dom. in Mont.*, I. 17. 51.

198 postea] sic *PF* **leg. peccata.** **207** Catholicus] om. *F* | super] supple *F* **208** intelliges] intelligit *F* **216** ut² ...**217** cognoscatur] ueritas cognoscatur *P* **218** mihi] add. et *F* **222** iustum] iusto *F* **225** Patarenus] om. *F* **229** Catholicus] om. *F*

195 est¹|fol. 140ra *P* **224** periurum|fol. 140rb *P*

Patarenus: Sed quid si uolimus non iurare. numquid uotum debemus frangere.
Catholicus: utique quia erroneum sit et fraudulenter factum. maxime autem solui potest auctoritate ecclesie cui christus dixit. quecumque solueritis super terram. etcet.

Pat: But what if we wish not to swear, because we can never break our vow?
Cath: Yes, because it is false and fraudulently made, especially it can be released by the authority of the Church, to whom Christ said (Mt 18:18) "whatsoever you shall loose upon earth."

Quod iustitia temporalis sit bona et a deo ordinata

XXXV That earthly justice is good and ordained by God

De potestate et iudicio seu iustitia temporali quod sint bona et a deo. proceditur contra hereticos. vii. modis. primo sic. Constat quod per potestatem et iustitiam temporalem mala dimittuntur fieri et bona fiunt et conseruantur igitur cum eius effectus bonus sit. igitur bona est et ipsa causa. Si enim potestates non essent in terra et iudicia non fierent de malefactoribus. malis omnibus plenus esset uniuersus orbis et nulla possent esse bona uel fieri. cum nec humana natura consisteret. hanc argumentationem inducat apostolus ad romanos. xiii. principes non sunt timori boni operis sed mali. uis autem non timere potestatem. bonum fac et habebis laudem ex illa. dei enim minister est tibi in bonum. si autem malum feceris time. non enim sine causa gladium portat. dei tamen minister est uindex in iuram ei qui malum agit. ideo necessitati subditi estote. non solum propter iram sed etiam propter conscientiam. ideo enim et tributa prestatis. ministri enim dei sunt in hoc ipsum seruientes etcet. Item i^a. ad timotheum. ii^o. obsecro igitur primum omnium fieri obsecrationes orationes postulationes gratiarum actiones pro omnibus hominibus. pro regibus. et omnibus qui in sublimitate sunt constitui. ut quietam et tranquillam uitam agamus in omni pietate et castitate etcet. Eandem enim rationem allegat beatus petrus. i^o. ii^o. subiecti igitur estote omni humane creature propter deum. siue regi quasi precellenti siue ducibus tamquam ab eo missis ad uindictam malefactorum laudem uero bonorum.

Catholicus: Secundo uero sic. omnia sunt a deo concessa nisi prohibita inueniantur per ipsum ut innuit apostolus. ad Romanos. iiii^o. ubi dicit ubi enim non est lex nec preuaricatio. sed deus non prohibet fieri iustitiam per potestates. igitur concedit et si hereticus dicat contrarium oportebat ipsum probare quod non poterit. quia nulla scriptura hoc dicit.

Tertio uero sic. in opere enim relucet magister. sed in deo duo sunt propria scilicet misericordia et iustitia. ergo in homine qui est precipuum opus dei debet

On power and judgment, or earthly justice, which are good and ordained by God. We shall proceed against the heretics in seven ways. The first is this. It is obvious that through power and earthly justice, evil comes to be diminished and good things are promoted and conserved, so since through them good is effected, therefore the cause itself is also good. For if there were no powers on earth and sentence was not passed on malefactors, the whole earth would be filled with all evils and no one would be able to be good or to become good, since not even human nature would stand. The Apostle uses this argument in Romans 13 (13:3–6) "For princes are not a terror to the good, but to the evil. Will you then not be afraid of the power? Do that which is good, and you will have praise from the same, for he is God's minister for you, for good. But if you do that which is evil, fear, for he does not bear the sword in vain. For even as God's minister, he is an avenger to execute wrath upon him who does evil. So be subject of necessity, not only for wrath, but also for conscience's sake, for therefore you also pay tax, for they are the ministers of God, serving for this purpose." Also 1 Timothy 2 (2:1) "I desire therefore, first of all, that supplications, prayers, intercessions, and thanksgivings be made for all men, for kings, and for all that are in high station, that we may lead a quiet and a peaceable life in all piety and chastity." For the same reason, Blessed Peter pleads in 1 Peter 2 (2:13–14) "Be subject therefore to every human creature for God's sake, whether it be to the king as excelling or to governors as sent by him for the punishment of evildoers, and for the praise of the good."

Cath: To the second is thus, all things are conceded by God unless they are found to be prohibited by Him, as the Apostle notes in Romans 4, where he says (4:15) "For where there is no law, neither is there transgression." But God does not prohibit justice being done by those in power, therefore He conceded it, and if a heretic says the contrary, it is fitting to put them to the test, since he is unable to defend it, because no passage in scripture says this.

The third is this. In his works the teacher shines forth, but in God there are two proper things, namely, mercy and justice. Therefore in man who is above all the work of

---

241 quecumque...terram] Matt. 18:18.   **XXXV.1.13** principes...21 seruientes] Rom. 13:3-6.   22 obsecro...26 castitate] 1 Tim. 2:1.   28 subiecti...31 bonorum] 1 Pet. 2:13-14.   34 ubi^2...35 preuaricatio] Rom. 4:15.

237 Patarenus] om. *F*   239 Catholicus] om. *F*   **XXXV.1.1** Quod...2 ordinata] om. *F*   11 esse...fieri] fieri bona *F* | consisteret] consistent *F*   23 orationes...26 castitate] om. *P*   25 sublimitate] add. positi *F* exp.   28 omni...31 bonorum] om. *P*   32 Catholicus] om. *F* | omnia] add. enim *F* exp.   36 fieri iustitiam] transp. *F*

237 numquid|fol. 111v *F*   **XXXV.1.13** sunt|fol. 140va *P*

relucere misericordia et iustitia. ergo iustita debet uelle et facere de malefactoribus. ergo debent esse aliqui homines quorum proprium sit iustitie officium exequi. hanc argumentationem facit apostolus. ii^a. ad corinthios. x. in promptu habentes ulcisci omnem inobedientiam.

Catholicus: Quarto autem sic. Constat quod deus uult quod omnes uirtutes sint in homine. sicut declaratur per totam scripturam diuinam. sed iustitia est uirtus. sed eius effectus summus est corrigere ac punire delinquentes. ergo uult deus quod aliqui sint qui puniant et corrigant malefactores. Quinto autem sic. bonum est quod malum dextruit et resistere bono malum est. per consequentiam ergo uelle et operari bonum bonum est. sed iustitia temporalis dextruit mala ut dictum est in prima ratione. et ideo bona est. ergo qui resistunt ei male faciunt. et qui uolunt et faciunt illam bene. sicut exemplum tibi pono. latrones enim odiunt furcas et funes et contra potestates irascuntur. quia per illas a malis suis exequendis prohibentur et de perpetratis cruciantur. et mercatores ac peregrini super illas gaudent et congratulantur quia per eas uitam recipiunt securam et tranquillam. ergo latrones se ostendunt heretici esse. quia huius odiunt et infamant et bene faciunt qui hoc diligunt et exerceret ad hoc est. iohannes. iii°. omnis enim qui male agit odit lucem etcet. sexto autem sic. constat quod in ueteri testamento deus ordinauit potestates et per illas iustitia precepit fieri temporalem. quod numquam postea retractauit. igitur bona est et licita iustitia temporalis et si uelit dicere patarenus uetus testamentum et eius deum esse malum proba contrarium ut supra in libro primo. titulo. de deo. ueteris testamenti. et titulo. de ueteri testamento.

Catholicus: Septimo modo uero proceditur per auctoritates noui testamenti. ut ecce. mattheus. xv. nam deus dixit. honora patrem et matrem tuam et qui maledixerit patri uel matri morte moriatur etcet. ergo deus uult iustitiam fieri de malefactoribus per mortem temporalem. Nec potest dicere hereticus quod christus correxerit hoc per illud scilicet non resistere malo etcet. quia longe post illud dixit istud. Nec etiam potest intelligere de morte eterna dictum hoc. quoniam introducit mandatum dei quod de morte temporali fuit ad litteram. idem. xxii. et misit exercitibus suis perdidit homicidias illos et ciuitatem illorum succendit. ergo deus mittit exercitus ad perdendos homicidas. ergo placet deo ut homicide occidantur per potestates. nec dicat hereticus non sit ad litteram. seruandus istud propter hoc quod est parabola. et ego dicam quod illa fuit parabola de agro zizanorum per quam uult argumentari quod mali non sint occidendi ab aliquibus. idem in eodem. Reddite ergo que sunt cesaris cesari et que sunt dei deo etcet. sed ea que sunt cesaris. sunt honores et tributa et obedientia in penis ad eo sustinendis pro maleficiis. sed christus uult illa sibi reddi et dicit ea illius esse. ergo iusta est potestas cesaris. et deo placet. item marcum. xii. quid ergo faciet dominus uinee. ueniet et perdet colonos et dabit uineam aliis etcet. sed hoc factum est de iudeis per titum et uespatianum imperatores romanorum. ergo cum imperatores perdunt malos deus hoc facere dicitur. ergo deo placet temporalis iustitia. nec potest dicere hereticus quod hoc intelligatur de perditione impiorum que fiet in die iudicii. quia statim dicitur infra. cognouerunt enim quoniam ad eos parabolam hanc dixerit. et in Mattheum. xxi. ubi est hoc parabola. dicitur. ideo dico uobis quia auferetur a uobis regnum dei et dabitur genti facienti fructus eius etcet. et infra. Cum audissent principes sacerdotum et pharisei parabolas eius cognouerunt quod de ipsis diceret etcet. ergo de temporali uindicta intelligitur que facta est iudeis a tito et uespasiano de passione christi qui amiserunt regnum dei id est gratiam dei per quam facti regnauit cum deo et datum est gentibus post passionem christi. sicut dicit paulus et barnabas. actus. xiii. uobis opportebat primum loqui uerbum dei. sed quoniam repellitis illud et indignos uos iudicatis eterne uite. ecce conuertimur ad gentes etcet. dominus ipsemet dicit expressim. lucam. xviiii. et ut appropinquauit uidens ciuitatem fleuit super eam dicens. quia si cognouisses et tu etcet. et infra. quia uenient dies in te. et coangustabant te undique inimici tui uallo et circumdabunt te et coangustabunt te undique et ad terram prosternent te et filios tuos qui in te sunt. et non relinquent in te lapidem super lapidem eo quod non cognoueris tempus uisitationis tue etcet. et xxi. cum autem audieritis circumdari ab exercitu ierusalem. tunc scitote quia appropinquauit desolatio eius tunc qui in iudea sunt fugient in montes. et qui in medio eis discedent. et qui in regionibus non intrent in eam quia dies ultionis hii sunt etcet. et infra. et captiui ducentur in omnes gentes et ierusalem calcabitur a gentibus donec impleantur tempora nationum etcet. et xxiii. filii ierusalem nolite flere super me sed super uos ipsas flere. et super filios uestros. quoniam ecce dies uenient in quibus dicent beate steriles etcet.

anyone. The same there (22:21) "Render to Caesar the things that are Caesar's, and to God what are God's." But those things which are due to Caesar are honor and taxes and obedience to punishments meted out by him for evil acts. But Christ wants these to be rendered to him and He says that they are his, therefore the power of Caesar is just and pleasing to God. Also Mark 12 (12:9) "What therefore will the lord of the vineyard do? He will come and destroy those husbandmen and will give the vineyard to others." But this was done to the Jews by the Roman emperors Titus and Vespasian, therefore when the emperors destroyed the evildoers, God is said to do it, so God is pleased by earthly justice. Nor is a heretic able to say that it might be understood of the perdition of the impious which will be accomplished on the day of judgment, since it immediately follows (Mk 12:12) "For they knew that he spoke this parable to them." And in Matthew 21 where His parable is, (21:43) "therefore I say to you that the kingdom of God will be taken from you, and will be given to a nation that will yield fruit." And below (21:45) "And when the chief priests and Pharisees had heard his parables, they knew that he spoke of them." So earthly vengeance is what is understood by that which was done to the Jews by Titus and Vespasian for the passion of Christ, and who lost the kingdom of God, that is, the grace of God by which he reigned with God and was given to the gentiles after the passion of Christ, as Paul and Barnabas say in Acts 13 (13:46) "To you it was fitting first to speak the word of God: but because you reject it, and judge yourselves unworthy of eternal life, behold we turn to the Gentiles." The Lord says the same thing expressly in Luke 19 (19:41) "And when he drew near, seeing the city, he wept over it, saying, 'If you also had known.'" And later (19:43–44) "For the days shall come upon you, and your enemies will dig a trench about you, and compass you around, and straiten you on every side, and will beat you flat to the ground, and your children who are in you, and they will not leave in you one stone upon another, because you did not know the time of your visitation." And 21 (21:20–22) "And when you shall see Jerusalem surrounded by an army, then know that the desolation thereof is at hand. Then let those who are in Judea flee to the mountains, and those who are in the midst thereof, depart out, and those who are in the countries not enter into it. For these are the days of vengeance." And later (21:24) "And they shall fall by the edge of the sword, and shall be led away captives into all nations, and Jerusalem shall be trodden down by the Gentiles, till the time of the nations be fulfilled." And 23 (23:28) "Daughters of Jerusalem, weep not over me, but weep for yourselves, and for your children. For behold, the

---

94 Reddite...95 deo] Matt. 22:21. 99 quid...101 aliis] Mar. 12:9. 107 cognouerunt...108 dixerit] Mar. 12:12. 108 ubi...110 eius] Matt. 21:43. 111 Cum...112 diceret] Matt. 21:45. 117 uobis...120 gentes] Act. 13:46. 121 et...123 tu] Luc. 19:41. 123 quia... 128 tue] Luc. 19:43. 129 cum...133 sunt] Luc. 21:20 (audieritis] uideritis *Vulg.*) 133 et²...135 nationum] Luc. 21:24. 136 filii... 138 steriles] Luc. 23:28.

95 et...deo] om. *P* 100 ueniet...101 aliis] om. *P* 109 a...110 eius] om. *P* 111 et...112 diceret] om. *P* 114 amiserunt] admiserunt *F* 119 eterne...120 gentes] om. *P* 122 fleuit...123 tu] om. *P* 124 undique...128 tue] om. *P* 130 tunc²...133 sunt] om. *P* 135 donec...nationum] om. *P* 136 sed...138 steriles] om. *P*

113 facta|fol. 141rb *P* 130 appropinquauit|fol. 112v *F*

Catholicus: Item. lucam. xviiii. uerumptamen inimicos meos illos qui noluerunt me regnare super se. adducite huc et interficite ante me etcet. Constat quod hoc dicit christus de iudeis occidendis per titum et uespasianum imperatores romanorum. quia negauerunt ipsum ut ostendit infra. quia uenient dies etcet. ergo de uoluntate christi occisi fuerunt iudei et per consequentiam uult quod occidantur omnes heretici quia negant fidem quam sibi promiserunt. idem. xx. quid ergo faciet illis dominus uinee ueniet et perdet colonos istos et dabit uineam aliis etcet. ad idem. idem. xxii°. sed nunc qui habet sacculum tollat similiter et peram et qui non habet gladium uendat tunicam suam et emat gladium etcet. et infra. at illi dixerunt domino gladii duo hic at ille dixit eis. satis est. ergo in ecclesia dei duo sunt gladii. spiritualis et materialis significati per illos. et si dicit hereticus quod signit duo testamenta. dicam quod secundum hoc peccant omnes heretici quia recusant aliquod testamentorum uel partem alicuius. et sic non sunt ecclesia dei que debet habere duos gladios integros non dimidios nec truncatos. Item iohannes vii. nolite iudicare secundum faciem sed iustum iudicium iudicare etcet. ergo uult christus quod iudicia fiant dum tamen iusta. idem. viii. qui sine peccato est uestrum primus in eam lapidem mittat etcet. ergo dominus uoluit fieri iudicium mortis ab illis siquid essent sine peccato scilicet consimili quod possibile erat. alias enim otiose et pro nichilo dixisset hic uerba. idem. xviii. hec autem cum dixisset unus assistens ministerorum dedit alapam ihesu dicens. sic respondes pontifici. respondit ei ihesus. si male locutus sum testimonium perhibe de malo. si autem bene quid me cedis etcet. ergo christus uult quod potestas iudicialis exerceatur contra male loquentes. licet nolit illam exercere contra bene loquentes et innocentes.

Catholicus: Item. ad Romanos. i°. in finem. quoniam qui talia agunt digni sunt morte etcet. ergo malefactores digni sunt morte. ergo bonum est ut occidantur. idem. ii. quicumque in lege peccauerunt per legem iudicabuntur etcet. ergo lex punit delinquentes. igitur iuste puniantur. item ad titum. ii°. seruos dominis suis subditos esse etcet. idem. ultimo. admone illos principibus et potestatibus subditos esse.

days shall come, in which they will say, 'Blessed are the barren.'"
Cath: Also Luke 19 (19:27) "But as for those my enemies, who would not have me reign over them, bring them here, and kill them before me." It is obvious that Christ speaks this of the Jews killed by the Roman Emperors Titus and Vespasian, since they denied Him, as was shown later (19:43) "for the days will come." So the will of Christ was that the Jews be killed and, consequently, He willed that all heretics be killed, since they deny the faith which they promised to Him. The same in 20 (20:15–16) "What therefore will the lord of the vineyard do to them? He will come, and will destroy these husbandmen, and will give the vineyard to others." The same in 22 (22:36) "But now he who has a purse, let him take it, and likewise a satchel, and he that does not have one, let him sell his coat, and buy a sword." And later (22:38) "But they said, 'Lord, behold here are two swords.' And he said to them, 'It is enough.'" Therefore there are two swords in the Church of God, by which are signified the material and spiritual power, and if the heretic might say that this signifies the two testaments, I would say that according to this understanding all heretics sin since they refuse some Testament, or some part of it, and thus they are not of the Church of God since she ought to have two whole swords, neither incomplete nor mutilated. Also John 7 (7:24) "Do not judge according to the appearance, but judge with right judgment." So Christ wills that justice be done provided that it is just. The same in 8 (8:7) "Let he who is without sin cast the first stone." Therefore the Lord wished for the judgment of death to be executed by those, if indeed they were without sin, namely, insofar as it was possible, otherwise these words would be empty of meaning, and He would have spoken for nothing. The same in 18 (18:22–23) "And when he had said these things, one of the servants standing by gave Jesus a blow, saying, 'Is this how you answer the High Priest?' Jesus answered him, 'If I have spoken evil, give testimony of the evil, but if well, why do you strike me?'" Therefore Christ wills that the judicial authority might proceed against those who speak wickedly, although He does not want them to proceed against those who speak well and innocently.

Cath: Also Romans 1 at the end (1:32) "they who do such things are worthy of death." So evildoers are worthy of death, therefore it is good to kill them. Also 2 (2:12) "and whoever has sinned in the law, will be judged by the law." Therefore the law punishes offenders, therefore they are justly punished. Also Titus 2 (2:9) "Exhort servants to be obedient to their masters," (3:1) "admonish them to be subject to princes and powers." Therefore they are

---

139 uerumptamen...141 me] Luc. 19:27. 148 quid...149 aliis] Luc. 20:15-16. 150 sed...152 etcet] Luc. 22:36. 152 at...153 est] Luc. 22:38. 160 nolite...161 iudicare] Ioh. 7:24. 163 qui...164 mittat] Ioh. 8:7. 167 hec...171 cedis] Luc. 18:22-23. 175 quoniam...176 morte] Rom. 1:32. 178 quicumque...179 iudicabuntur] Rom. 2:12. 181 seruos...esse] Tit. 2:9. 182 admone...esse] Tit. 3:1.

139 Catholicus] om. F 140 regnare...141 me] om. P 142 dicit] dixit P 148 ueniet...149 aliis] om. P 151 et...152 gladium] om. P 154 duo sunt] transp F 156 quod] om. P 157 uel] per F 173 licet] nulla P 175 Catholicus] om. F 177 malefactores] add. igitur P | digni] om. P 182 admone] amone P

158 alicuius|fol. 141va P

ergo domini et principes et potestates et illorum regimina sunt a deo. si de uoluntate apostoli debent admoneri homines ut sint illi subditi quam doctrinam minime habent heretici. item iacobi. ii°. similiter raab meretrix nonne ex operibus iustificata est suscipiens nuntios et per aliam uiam eiiciens etcet. sed raab. meretrix. iustificata fuit sola de ierico occisis omnibus ciuibus a iosue et populo israel ergo de occisis placuit deo. quia sicut beatus iacobus laudat salutem raab. quia de iustitia fuit. sic uituperasset aliorum occisionem si de iustitia fuisset. item. i^a. petri. ii°. deum timete regem honorificate etcet. ergo post dei timorem uult beatus petrus ut regem honoremus. ergo a deo est rex cum omni potestate. idem in eodem. serui subditi estote in omni timore dominis non tantum bonis et modestis sed etiam discolis etcet. ergo dominia secularia sunt a deo. item iiii°. nemo autem uestrum patiatur ut homicida aut fur. aut maledictus aut alenorum appetior. si autem ut christianus non erubescat etcet. ergo malefactores iuste puniuntur a potestatibus. item. secunda. petri. ii°. dominationem-que contemnunt audaces etcet. et iudas. i°. dominationem autem spernunt etcet. ergo dominatio a deo est. et bene si non debet contempni. et dicuntur et sunt heretici qui contempnunt illam. item actus. iii°. uos autem sanctum et iustum negastis et petistis uirum homicidam donari uobis etcet. quasi dicat duo peccata magna fecistis et quia condempnastis innocentem et quia dimisistis maleficum. ergo bonum est iudicare malefectores. idem. vii. et cum uidisset quemdam iniuriam patientem uindicauit illum et fecit ultionem ei qui iniuriam substinebat percusso egyptio existimabat autem intelligere fratres quoniam deus per manus ipsius daret salutem illis etcet. ergo bona est iustitia que fit de malefactoribus quia ponit beatus stephanus in laudem moysi. quia iustitiam fecit de predicto egyptio homicida. idem. xvi. paulus autem dixit. cesos nos publice indempnatos homines romanos etcet. allegauit ergo apostolus quod illi offendebant. quia innocentes ledebant et homines priuilegiatos. ergo alias non offendissent. ad hoc est. xxiii. quod cum audisset filius sororis pauli insidias uenit et intrauit in castra nuntiauitque paulo. uocans autem paulus ad se unum ex centurionibus ait. adolescentem hunc perduc ad tribunum etcet. Ecce hic habetur manifeste quod beatus paulus petiit per nepotem suum per principis potestatem armatam et usus est tali auxilio. ubi et uerissime potuit credere propter bellum quod accidere poterat. aliquos occidi. quod quidem non fecisset si mortale peccatum esset uti talibus auxiliis et tale

established by God, if by the will of the Apostle men ought to be admonished that they are to be submissive to them, rather than the foolish teaching of the heretics. Also James 2 (2:25) "And in like manner also Rahab the harlot, was not she justified by works, receiving the messengers and sending them out another way?" But Rahab the harlot alone was justified among all the citizens of Jericho who were killed by Joshua and the people of Israel, therefore the killing pleased God, because just as Blessed James praised the salvation of Rahab, because it was in justice, so he would have found fault with the killing of the others, if it had [not] been in justice. Also 1 Peter 2 (2:17) "Fear God, honor the king." Therefore, after the fear of God, Blessed Peter wants that the king be held in honor, therefore the king is from God, and likewise everyone in authority. Also in the same (2:18) "Servants, be subject to your masters with all fear, not only to the good and gentle, but also to the harsh." So secular dominion is from God. Also 4 (4:15–16) "But let none of you suffer as a murderer, or a thief, or a criminal, or a coveter of other men's things. But if as a Christian, let him not be ashamed." So evildoers are justly punished by secular powers. Also 2 Peter 2 (2:10) "those who despise government are audacious." And Jude 1 (1:8) "these men despise dominion." Therefore dominion is from God and, if good, it ought not to be held in contempt, and those are called heretics who hold it in contempt. Also Acts 3 (3:14) "But you denied the Holy and Just One, and desired a murderer to be granted unto you." Therefore it is good to judge evildoers. Also 7 (7:24–25) "And when he had seen one of them suffer wrong, he defended him and, striking the Egyptian, he avenged him who suffered the injury. And he thought that his brethren understood that God would save them by his hand." Therefore justice is good which is done unto evildoers, which Blessed Stephen asserted in praise of Moses, that justice was done of the aforementioned Egyptian homicide. Also 16 (Acts 16:37) "But Paul said to them, 'They have beaten us publicly, uncondemned, men that are Romans.'" So the Apostle accused that they offended since they beat innocent and privileged men, otherwise they would not have offended, to this is 23 (23:16) "Which when Paul's sister's son had heard of their lying in wait, he came and entered into the camp and told Paul, and Paul, calling one of the centurions to him, said, 'Bring this young man to the tribune.'" Behold, here one has it plainly that Blessed Paul asked for his child, through the authority armed by the prince, and used the aid of such a one. Perfectly and correctly was he able to believe on account of the war that could happen that some would be killed, which in fact he would not have done if to use such aid would have been a mortal sin, and the help of such a murderer would have been damnable on the part of the

---

186 similiter...188 eiiciens] Iac. 2:25. 193 deum...194 honorificate] 1 Pet. 2:17. 196 serui...198 discolis] 1 Pet. 2:18. 199 nemo...202 erubescat] 1 Pet. 4:15-16. 203 dominationem-que...204 audaces] 2 Pet. 2:10. 204 dominatio-nem...205 spernunt] Iud. 1:8. 207 uos...209 uobis] Act. 3:14. 212 et...216 illis] Act. 7:24-25. 219 paulus...220 romanos] Act. 16:37. 223 quod...227 tribunum] Act. 23:16.

185 admoneri] amoneri P   191 salutem] add. de P exp.   193 iustitia] sic PF (I have added a negation as a means of making more sense)   197 non...198 discolis] om. P   208 et^2...209 uobis] om. P   218 iustitiam] iustitia P   229 potestatem armatam] transp. F

187 suscipiens|fol. 141vb P   192 uituperasset|fol. 113r F   214 substinebat|fol. 142ra P

homicidium esset dampnosum ex parte iuuantium eum. idem. xxv. paulo in omnibus rationem reddente. quoniam neque in legem iudeorum neque in templum neque in cesarem quidquam peccaui etcet. et infra dixit autem paulus ad tribunal cesaris. sto ubi oportet iudicari. iudeis non nocui sicut melius nosti. si enim nocui aut dignum morte aliquid feci non recuso mori. si uero nihil est eorum que hii accusant me nemo potest me illis donare cesare appello etcet. ergo aliqui faciunt dignum morte et iuste a potestatibus occiduntur et auxilium iuris ciuilis bonum est quod apostolus implorauit.

Catholicus: Item ad romanos xiii. omnis anima potestatibus sublimioris subdita sit. non est enim potestas nisi a deo. que aut sunt deo ordinata sunt. itaque qui resistit potestati dei ordinationi resistit. qui autem resistunt ipsi sibi damnationem acquirunt etcet. hic non uideo quod apostolus apertius potuisset ostendere quod potestates seculares et eorum iudicia sunt a deo quam per huiusmodi uerba. loquitur de potestatibus spiritualibus id est de prelatis ecclesie.
Catholicus: Qua ratione uis hoc intelligere de prelatis ecclesie. non enim debet aliquis litteram maxime noui testamenti aliter exponere quam sonare uideatur nisi per textum probet. aliter intelligi non posse. alioquin si ad libitum unuscuiusque aliter litteram exponere. quam sonet pro nichilo facta est. preterea. si uis exponere scripturas que loquuntur de potestatibus et regibus et principibus et eorum iustitia. spiritualiter et ego exponam omnes illas quas introducis in contrarium. similiter spiritualiter ut prohibeant homicidia spiritualia et huiusmodi uel de spiritualibus hominis. item. ubi habes o miser ydiota quod prelati ecclesie uocentur potestates et reges et duces seu principes et quod illorum correctio uocetur gladius et quod tributa debeant illis prestari.

Patarenus: Dicam ego quod apostolus commendat hic potestates secundum laudem humanam tantum.
Catholicus: Quomodo ergo dicit apostolus. qui resistunt potestati dei ordinationi resistit. qui resistunt sibi ipsi dampnationem acquirunt etcet. et illud ideo necessitate subditi estote non solum propter iram sed etiam propter conscientiam etcet.
Patarenus: Sed nonne loquitur de potestatibus gentilium. uidetur quod sic. quia tunc temporis christiani non habebant seculares potestates. et secundum fidem tuam o romane non est gladius materialis concessus a deo nisi in ecclesia dei. ergo non commendat potestatem hic secundum deum.

youth. Also 25 (25:8) "Paul making answer for himself, 'Neither against the law of the Jews, nor against the temple, nor against Caesar, have I offended in anything,'" and later (25:10–11) "Then Paul said, 'I stand at Caesar's judgment seat, where I ought to be judged. To the Jews I have done no injury, as you know very well. For if I have injured them, or have committed anything worthy of death, I do not refuse to die. But if there be nothing in these things of which they accuse me, no man may deliver me to them. I appeal to Caesar.'" Therefore some are made worthy of death and are justly killed by authorities and the authority of the civil law, to which the Apostle appealed, is good.

Cath: Also Romans 13 (13:1–2) "Let every soul be subject to higher powers, for there is no power except from God, and those in authority are ordained by God. Therefore he who resists [those in] power, resists the ordinance of God. And they who resist purchase damnation for themselves."
Here I do not see that the Apostle clearly might have showed that secular power and its judgments are from God by words of this sort. He was speaking of spiritual powers, that is, of the prelates of the Church.
Cath: By what reason do you wish to interpret this as referring to the prelates of the Church, for one ought not to read otherwise than literally, especially in the New Testament, or to construe otherwise than what the passage seems to say, unless one can prove it from the text, otherwise it could not be understood, for if it were left to the liberty of each reader to explain differently than what the literal meaning means, it would reduce it to meaninglessness. Furthermore, if you wish to construe the scriptures which speak about authorities, and about kings and princes and their justice spiritually, I too will construe all those which you adduce in a contrary manner. Similarly spiritually as if they might prohibit spiritual homicide and the like, or of spiritual men, also, where do you have it, O wretched fool, that the prelates of the Church are called authorities and kings, and dukes, or princes, and that their correction is called "sword" and that taxes ought to be paid to them.
Pat: I might say that the Apostle commends here authorities according to human praise alone.
Cath: How therefore does the Apostle say (13:1) "Therefore he who resists the power, resists the ordinance of God. And they who resist, purchase to themselves damnation," and that (13:5) "Wherefore be subject of necessity, not only for wrath, but also for conscience's sake."
Pat: But is he not speaking of the gentile authorities? It seems so, since at that time Christians had no secular authority, and according to your faith, O Roman, the material sword is not conceded by God except through the Church of God. Therefore he does not commend authority here according to God.

---

234 paulo…236 peccaui] Act. 25:8. 237 dixit…241 appello] Act. 25:10-11. 245 omnis…249 acquirunt] Rom. 13:1-2. 271 qui…273 acquirunt] Rom. 13:1. 273 ideo…275 conscientiam] Rom. 13:5.

245 Catholicus] om. *F* actually Patarene 251 seculares] add. est *F* exp. 254 Catholicus] om. *F* 260 loquuntur] locuntur *P* 266 et²] uel *F* 269 Patarenus] om. *F* 271 Catholicus] om. *F* 272 potestati] peccant *P* 276 Patarenus] om. *F* 277 temporis] om. *F*

238 nosti|fol. 142rb *P* 252 uerba|fol. 113v *F* 267 correctio|fol. 142va *P*

Catholicus: Responsio. quod falsum loqueris cum dicis christianos non habere temporales potestates tunc temporis ut statim probabitur. habebant iam namque quam plures et in proximio habituri erant multas et maiores et dico quod etiam apud infideles est gladius temporalis potestatis. cum dicat hic apostolus. non est potestas nisi a deo. etcet. et maxime fuit apud eos ante fidei christiane dilatationem et pacem.

Patarenus: Dicam ergo aliter quod potestates debent esse in ecclesia dei que faciant iustitiam de malefactoribus sine morte tamen uel huiusmodi generi pena.

Catholicus: Si apostolus non determinat earum iurisdictionem. igitur non tibi licet determinare illam. uel dico quod expressim dicit de illarum iurisdicionem per mortem uel per aliam generem penam. cum subdit. non enim sine causa gladium portat etcet. cum gladio enim capita et alia membra corporis inciduntur et amputantur.

Patarenus: Item. iª. ad corinthios. vi. audet aliquis uestrum habens negotium aduersus iudicari apud iniquos et non apud sanctos. an nescitis quoniam sancti de hoc mundo iudicabunt. et si in uobis iudicabitur mundus indigni estis qui de minimis iudicetis. nescitis quoniam angelos iudicabimus quanto magis secularia etcet. Ecce quam manifeste paulus exprimit. quod secularia iudicia debent fieri a fidelibus et sanctis. ergo bona sunt.

Catholicus: Responsio. loquitur hic derisiue et yronice et ideo dicit ad uerecundiam uestram dico etcet. iudicia namque non debent esse infidelibus in quibus non debent esse litigia. unde subdit. iam quidem delictum est in uobis quod iudicia habetis inter uos. sed uos iniuriam facitis et fraudatis et hoc fratribus etcet.

Catholicus: Stulte non dixit apostolus illud uerbum scilicet ad uerecundiam uestram etcet. propter hoc quod ipse prohibat iudicia. cum iam dixerat illa fieri. sic enim esset sibi contrarius. sed ideo dicit quia apud infideles litigabant relictis iudicibus fidelibus et ideo subdit. sic non est inter uos quisquam qui possit iudicare inter fratrem suum etcet. nec propter illud uerbum scilicet omnino delictum est in uobis etcet. reprehendit iudicia id est sententias dari inter litigantes. sed reprehendit causas iudiciorum quas appelleat iudicia que sunt superbia et fraus et alia peccata eorum. unde subdit. sed uos iniuriam facitis et frauda-tis etcet. Nec propter hoc sequitur si male faciunt quia litigant quam malum sit inter eos sententiam ferre. uel illos pro meritis peruenire. immo sequitur contrarium. sicut

Cath: I reply that you speak falsely when you say Christians did not have temporal authority at that time, as immediately will be proved. They had it already, in fact, as much as possible and in the near future they were to have more and greater, and I say also that among the infidels secular power was also exercised, since the Apostle said (13:1) "there is no power except from God." And especially it was among them before the expansion of the Christian Faith and its peace.

Pat: Therefore I may say that the authorities should be in the Church of God, since they do justice on evildoers without resorting to the death penalty, and of penalties of this type.

Cath: If the Apostle did not determine their jurisdiction, then it is not permitted for you to determine it, or I say that he expressly said of their jurisdiction over death or for any general punishment when he adds (13:4) "for they do not bear the sword without cause." For by the sword the head and other members are cut off and separated.

Pat: Also 1 Corinthians 6 (6:1–3) "Dare any of you, having a matter against another, go to be judged before the unjust, and not before the saints? Do you not know that the saints shall judge this world? And if the world shall be judged by you, are you unworthy to judge the smallest matters? Do you not know that we shall judge angels? How much more things of this world?" See how clearly Paul expresses himself, that secular judgments ought to be done by the faithful and the saints, therefore they are good.

Cath: Response. Here he speaks derisively and ironically and so says (6:5) "I speak to your shame." Judgment in fact ought not to be for infidels among whom they ought not to litigate, so he adds (6:7–8) "Already indeed there is plainly a fault among you, that you have lawsuits one with another ... But you do wrong and defraud, and that to your brethren."

Cath: Fool, the Apostle did not say that phrase, namely (6:5) "I speak to your shame," that he might forbid lawsuits, otherwise he would be contradicting himself because he had already said these should happen, but he says that because they litigated before infidels, when they should have been left to the judgments to the faithful, and so he adds, (6:5) "Is it so that there is not among you any one wise man, who is able to judge between his brethren?" Neither on account of that word, namely, (6:7) "Already indeed there is plainly a fault among you," he reproves judgments, that is, to give sentence between litigants, but he reproves the cause of judgment which he might call "judgment," which are pride and fraud, and any other of their sins, whence he adds (6:8) "But you do wrong and defraud." Nor for this reason does it follow that if they do evil since they litigate, how evil might it be to render a sentence between them, or that they should attain [a judgment] in accordance with what they deserve. Indeed

---

287 non...288 deo] Rom. 13:1.   297 non...portat] Rom. 13:4.   300 audet...306 secularia] 1 Cor. 6:1-3.   310 ad...dico] 1 Cor. 6:5.   312 iam...314 fratribus] 1 Cor. 6:7-8.   320 sic...321 suum] 1 Cor. 6:5.   326 sed...frauda-tis] 1 Cor. 6:8.

282 Catholicus] om. F   284 iam namque] transp. F   289 christiane] om. P   290 Patarenus] om. F   293 Catholicus] om. F   300 Patarenus] om. F   301 aduersus] add. alterum F   309 Catholicus] om. F   315 Catholicus] om. F   329 sicut] si F

300 Patarenus|fol. 142vb P   320 est|fol. 114r F   325 fraus|fol. 143ra P

de penitentia que datur propter peccata refrenanda et corrigenda et ideo bona est.

Patarenus: Dicam ergo quod loquitur rerum et non de iudiciis corporam et ideo subdit. indigni estis qui de minimis iudicetis etcet.

Catholicus: Sed apostolus non distinguit de quibus iudiciis loquatur realibus uel personalibus. unde de omnibus est intelligendum. quia quod profertur indistincte accipere et possem dicere quod maxime de personalibus loquitur. cum dicit. audet aliquis uestrum habens negotium aduersus alterum iudicari etcet. nec obstat illud uerbum scilicet de minimis etcet. quia illud dicit ratione uniuersalis iudicii quod totum mundum iudicabimus unde dicit. et si in uobis iudicabitur mundis indigni estis qui de minimis iudicetis.

Catholicus: Item. i^a. ad timotheum. i^o. iusto non est lex posita sed iniustis et non subditis etcet. Ecce quod de lege moysi loquitur apostolus quam dicit esse bonam et contra peccatores positam et loquitur de lege iudiciaria et punit maleficos maxime per mortem corporis prout de singulis hic ab apostolo ponitis sunt capitula in lege moysi spiritualia. ut ecce de iniustis et non subditis. etcet. Exodi. xxii. maleficos non patieris uiuere etcet. uel per iniustos intelliguntur qui contra legem nature faciunt ut qui coeunt cum iumentis uel cum masculis more femineo. de quibus legitur exodi. qui coierit cum iumento morte moriatur. et leuitici. xx. qui coierunt cum masculo femineo uterque operati sunt nefas morte moriantur etcet. et infra. qui cum iumento et pecore coierit morte moriatur etcet. non subditi uero dicuntur qui contempnunt parentes. unde debent mori. deuteronimi. xxi. si genuerit homo filium contumacem et proteruum etcet. ibi lapidibus obseruet eum ciuitatis et morietur. uel non subditi dicuntur qui contra principem suum per contumaciam et rebellionem incitant scisma. de quibus habemus. numeri ecce autem chore etcet. impii uero sunt qui peccant in deum principaliter ut ydolatrie. de quibus dicitur. exodi. xxii. Qui immolat diis occidetur preterquam deo soli etcet. peccatores autem proprie dicuntur qui se et proximum ledunt et deum offendunt ut falsi prophete et doctores peruerse doctrine de quibus deuteronimi. xiii. si surrexerit in medio tui prophetes etcet. et infra. propheta autem ille aut fictor sompniorum interficietur etcet. scelerati uero sunt qui enormia penetrant sunt sicut illa de quibus legitur. leuitici. xx. si quis dederit de semino suo ydolo moloch morte moriatur etcet. per totum de patricidis legitur exodi. xxi. qui percusserit patrem suum aut matrem morte moriatur etcet. et leuitici. xx. qui maledixerit patri suo aut matri morte moriatur. patri matrique maledixit sanguis eius sit super eum etcet. De homicidis habetur. exodus. xxi. si quis per industriam occiderit proximum suum et per insidias ab altari meo euelles illum ut moriatur. Fornicarii uero dicuntur hic adulteri. de quibus leuitici. xx. si mechatus fuerit quis cum uxore alterius et adulterium perpetrauit cum coniuge proximi sui morte moriantur et mechus et adultera etcet. De masculorum concubitoribus dictum est supra. plagiarii sunt qui liberum hominem uendunt pro seruo. de quibus habetur. deuteronimi. xxiiii. si deprehensus homo sollicitans fratrem suum de filiis israel. et uendito eo acceperit pretium occidetur etcet. uel alia littera plagiariis qui sunt qui plagas inferunt proximo uolentes eum occidere de quibus legitur. exodus. xxi. si quis percusserit hominem uolens occidere morte moriatur etcet. quid autem subdit apostolus mendacibus et periuris. pro eodem ponitur id est mendacibus cum periurio. uel ponit lex mendaces in doctrina. deuteronomi. xviii. propheta autem qui arrogantia deprauatus uoluerit loqui nomine meo que ego non precepi illi ut diceret aut ex nomine alienorum deorum interficietur etcet. et leuitici. xx. in finem. uir siue mulier in quibus pythonicus uel diuinationis fuierit spiritus morte moriantur etcet. uel mendaces puniuntur a lege. qui per mendatium calumpniam faciunt proximo sicut fuerit putati calumpniatores susanne per danielem prophetam. per uim uero puniuntur per legem cum falsum testimonium peierando dicunt deut. xix. si steterit testis mendax etcet. et infra. non misereberis eius sed animam pro anima. oculum pro oculo etcet. in omnibus istis causibus et in aliis multis puniuntur malefactores corporaliter per legem moysi et ideo subdit. uerbum generale scilicet et si quid aliud sane doctrine aduersatur quod est secundum euangelium id est secundum legem nature. cui concordat euangelii et dixit apostolus quod hoc lex bona est que punit malefactores. nec de alia lege potest intelligi quam de lege moysi. cum dicat superius. ut denuntiares quibusdam ne aliter docerent neque intenderent fabulis et genealogiis interminatis etcet. et postea a quibus quidam aberrantes conuersi sunt in uaniloquium uolentes legis esse doctores non intelligentes. neque que loquuntur. neque de quibus affirmat scimus autem etcet. nec potest hereticus dicere quod apostolus commendet legem moysi secundum laudem mundi. quia ponit manifeste. scimus autem quia bona est lex.

someone gives of his seed to the idol Moloch, let him die the death." Above all of parricides it is read in Exodus 21 (21:15) "he who strikes father or mother, let him die the death," and Leviticus 20 (20:9) "He who curses his father or mother, let him die the death, he has cursed his father and mother, let his blood be upon him." Regarding murderers one has Exodus 21 (21:14) "If a man kills his neighbor on purpose and by lying in wait for him, you will take him away from my altar, that he may die." Fornicators are called adulterers here, of which Leviticus 20 has it (20:10) "If any man commits adultery with the wife of another, and defiles his neighbor's wife, let them be put to death, both the adulterer and the adulteress." Homosexuals were spoken about above. Kidnappers are those who sell free men as slaves, of which one has Deuteronomy 24 (24:7) "If any man be found soliciting his brother of the children of Israel, and selling him shall take a price, he shall be put to death." Or in another passage, kidnappers are those who strike their neighbor, wishing to kill them, of which it is read in Exodus 21 (21:12) "He who strikes a man with a will to kill him, let him die the death." Moreover what the Apostle adds regarding liars and perjurers, is appointed for the same, that is, to liars with perjury, as the law proposes for liars in doctrine, Deuteronomy 18 (18:20) "But the prophet, who being corrupted with pride, shall speak in my name things that I did not command him to say, or in the name of strange gods, shall be slain." And Leviticus 20 at the end (20:27) "A man, or woman, in whom there is a pythonical or divining spirit, let them die the death." Or liars let them be punished by the law, who, by calumnious lying injure their neighbor, just as the putative calumniators of Susanna were punished by force through the prophet Daniel, through the law by perjuring themselves through false witness. Deuteronomy 19 (19:6) "If a lying witness stand against a man," and later (19:21) "you will not pity him, but shall require life for life, eye for eye." In all these cases and in many others evildoers are punished bodily by the law of Moses and so is added that general saying, namely, (1 Tm 1:10) "and whatever other thing is contrary to sound doctrine," that is, according to the natural law, to which the gospels agree and the Apostle said that this law is good which punishes evildoers. Nor is one able to interpret that another law is meant here, other than the law of Moses, since he said above (1 Tm 1:3-4) "that you may charge some not to teach otherwise, not to give heed to fables and endless genealogies," and after (1:6-7) "are turned aside unto vain babbling, desiring to be teachers of the law, understanding neither the things they say, nor what they affirm, but we know." Nor is the heretic able to say that the Apostle commended the law of Moses according to worldly praise, since he clearly mentions (1:8) "But we

---

378 qui...379 moriatur] Ex. 21:15.   379 qui...381 eum] Lev. 20:9.   382 si...384 moriatur] Ex. 21:14.   385 si...388 adultera] Lev. 20:10.   390 si...392 occidetur] Deut. 24:7.   395 si...396 moriatur] Ex. 21:12.   399 propheta...402 interficietur] Deut. 18:20.   403 uir...405 moriantur] Lev. 20:27.   409 si...410 mendax] Deut. 19:16.   410 non...411 oculo] Deut. 19:21.   419 ut...421 interminatis] 1 Tim. 1:3-4.   421 a...424 autem] 1 Tim. 1:6.   427 scimus...428 utatur] 1 Tim. 1:8.

384 hic] sed *P*   402 deorum] om. *F*   408 uim] tim *P*   422 conuersi...424 autem] om. *P*

379 et|fol. 143va *P*   380 patri¹|fol. 114v *F*   406 proximo|fol. 143vb *P*

si quis ea legitme utatur etcet. et potest quis legitime uti ea.

Catholicus: Item multi facientes iudicia temporalia commendatur in ueteri et nouo testamento sicut moyses et dauid et huiusmodi. igitur sine peccato possunt hoc fieri.

Catholicus: Mattheus. xviii. si autem ecclesiam non audierit sit tibi sicut ethnicus et publicanus. amen dico uobis. quicumque alligaueritis super terram erunt ligata et in celo. et ii^a. ad. timotheo. ii^o. et hos deuita. etcet. et ii^a. iohannes. si quis uenit ad uos et hanc doctrinam non affert nolite recipere eum in domo. nec aue ei dixeritis. comunicat operibus eius malignis etcet. Item Paulus ad titum ultimo. hereticum hominem post primam et secundam correptionem deuita etcet. et ii^a. ad timotheo. ultimo. alexander erarius multa mala ostendit mihi reddet illi dominus secundum opera eius. quem et tu deuita etcet. et i^a. ad corinthios. v. si quis frater nominatur etcet. Cum huiusmodi nec cibum sumere etcet. Ecce qualiter iubemur uitare hereticos et scismaticos.

Catholicus: Mattheus. xxi. et intrauit ihesus in templum dei et eieciebat omnes uendentes et ementes de templo etcet. et iohannes. ii^o. et cum fecisset quasi flagellum de funiculis omnes ieicit de templo etcet. item. i^a. ad corinthios. v. ut tollatur de medio uestro uestrum qui hoc opus fecit etcet. et vi. auferte malum ex uobis ipsis etcet. item ad Galathas. iiii. sed quid dicit scriptura. eice ancillam et filium eius etcet. et v. utinam et abscindantur qui uos conturbant etcet. Item apocalypsis. ii^o. angelo ephesi etcet. ibi. sed hoc habes bonum quia odisti facta nicholaitarum etcet. et infra. angelo pergami etcet. et ibi. sed habeo aduersus te pauca quia habes illic tenentes doctrinam balaam etcet. et infra. ita habes et tu tenentes doctrinam nicholai-tarum etcet. et infra. et tiatira. etcet. sed habeo aduersus te pauca et ibi. quia permittis mulierem gezabel que seducit prophetam docere et seducere seruos meos etcet. ergo expellendi sunt localiter de populo dei heretici et scismatici.

Catholicus: Lucam. xix. uerumptamen et inimicos meos etcet. ergo heretici sunt occidendi quia non uere confitentur christum esse regem. item. iohannes. iii. qui autem non credit iam iudicatus est. ergo heretici quia non credunt iudicati sunt. igitur iuste comburuntur quia se ipsos iudicauerunt. item. i^a. ad

know that the law is good, if a man use it lawfully." And one can legitimately use it.

Cath: Further, many making earthly judgments are commended in the Old and New Testaments, like Moses and David and the like. Therefore one can make them without sin.

Cath: Matthew 18 (18:17–18) "And if he will not hear the church, let him be to you as the heathen and publican. Amen I say to you, whatsoever you shall bind upon earth, shall be bound also in heaven." And 2 Timothy (3:5) "now avoid these," and 2 John (1:10–11) "If any man comes to you, and does not bring this doctrine, do not receive him into the house nor say to him, 'hail.' For he who says to him, 'hail,' communicates with his wicked works." Also Paul to Titus at the end (3:10) "Avoid a man who is a heretic, after the first and second admonition." And 2 Timothy at the end (4:14) "Alexander the coppersmith has done me much evil, the Lord will reward him according to his works." And 1 Corinthians 5 (5:11) "if any man that is named a brother ... with such a one do not so much as eat." See how we are ordered to shun heretics and schismatics?

Cath: Matthew 21 (21:12) "And Jesus went into the temple of God, and cast out all them that sold and bought in the temple." And John 2 (2:15) "And when he had made, as it were, a scourge of little cords, he drove them all out of the temple." Also 1 Corinthians 5 (5:2) "that he might be taken away from among you," and 6 (5:13) "Put away the evil one from among yourselves." Also Galatians 4 (4:30) "But what does the scripture say? 'Cast out the bondwoman and her son'" And 5 (5:12) "I wish they were even cut off, who trouble you." Also Apocalypse 2 (2:1) "To the angel of Ephesus," there (2:6) "But you have this for good, that you hate the deeds of the Nicolaitans," and later (2:12) "to the angel of Pergamum," and there (2:14) "But I have a few things against you, because you have there those who hold the doctrine of Balaam," and later (2:15) "You also have some who hold the doctrine of the Nicolaitans," and later (2:18) "to Thyatira," (2:20) "But I have a few things against you, because you suffer the woman Jezebel, who calls herself a prophetess, to teach, and to seduce my servants." Then heretics and schismatics are to be expelled locally from among the people of God.

Cath: Luke 19 (19:47) "But as for those my enemies," Therefore those heretics are to be killed since they do not truly confess Christ to be king. Also John 3 (3:18) "But he who does not believe, is already judged," then heretics are judged, because they do not believe, so they are justly burned, for they brought judgment upon themselves. Also

---

434 si...437 ligata] Matt. 18:17-18. 437 et^3...deuita] 2 Tim. 3:5. 438 si...440 malignis] 2 Ioh. 1:10-11. 441 hereticum...442 deuita] Tit. 3:10. 443 alexander...445 deuita] 2 Tim. 4:14. 445 si...447 sumere] 1 Cor. 5:11. 449 et...451 templo] Matt. 21:12. 451 et^2...452 templo] Ioh. 2:15. 453 ut...454 fecit] 1 Cor. 5:2. 454 auferte...455 ipsis] 1 Cor. 5;13. 455 sed...456 eius] Gal. 4:30. 457 utinam...conturbant] Gal. 5:12. 458 angelo ephesi] Apoc. 2:1. | sed...459 nicholaitarum] Apoc. 2:6. 460 angelo pergami] Apoc. 2:12. | sed...461 balaam] Apoc. 2:14. 462 ita...nicholai-tarum] Apoc. 2:15. 463 et tiatira] Apoc. 2:18. 464 quia...466 meos] Apoc. 2:20. 468 uerumptamen...469 meos] Luc. 19:27. 471 qui...est] Ioh. 3:18.

428 si...utatur] om. P 430 Catholicus] om. F 434 Catholicus] om. F 441 titum] timotheo P 444 reddet...445 deuita] om. P 448 et] add. non F | scismaticos] sismaticos P 449 Catholicus] om. F 452 omnes...templo] om. P 454 uestrum...fecit] om. P 461 quia...balaam] om. P 465 gezabel...466 meos] om. P 467 scismatici] sismatici P 468 Catholicus] om. F 472 sunt] om. P

437 ad|fol. 144ra P 440 operibus|fol. 115r F 469 etcet|fol. 144rb P

timotheum. i°. si quid aliud sane doctrine aduersatur que est secundum euangelium beati dei etcet. ergo lex mortis et penalis iudicii de qua loquebatur apostolus posita est contra hereticos quia ipsi aduersantur doctrine sane. que est in euangelio et hec est bona ergo bonum est ut occidantur. preterea probatum est supra quod malefactores debent occidi. sed cum heretici siue blasphematores patris uel matris scilicet dei uel prelati ecclesie et sint adulteri diuine scripture et fures et homicide aliarum et falsi testes contra deum insuper et pleni sint omni peccato tam spirituali quam etiam carnali. constat quod ipsi debent ad mortem dampnari. item in nouo testamento commendantur et laudantur moysis et helyas et huiusmodi. qui occidetur ydolatrias et falsos prophetas ut habes supra. in libro primo. de ueteri testamento et rubricella de principibus et prophetis ueteris testamenti. ergo commendabile et sanctum est ut heretici et huiusmodi occidantur. preterea. cum occidantur heretici non occiduntur anime ab occidentibus sed corpora tantum. et secundum patarenos ipsa sunt opera diaboli. ergo bonum est occidere illos. quia qui hoc faciunt imitantur dei filium. de quo scribit beatus iohannes. in iª. iiiº. in hoc apparuit filius dei ut dissoluat opera diaboli etcet. iª. ad corinthios. v. tradere huiusmodi sathane in interitum carnis etcet. et iiª. corinthios. et in promptu habentes ulcisci omnem inobedientiam etcet. Item iª. ad Timotheo. iº. in finem. circa fidem naufragauerunt ex quibus est hymeneus et alexander errarius et quos tradidi sathane ergo heretici et scismatici a prelatis spiritualibus traduntur sathane in interitum. multo fortius ergo tradidi ab eis potestatibus secularibus in carnis penas. item. iude. et hos quid arguite iudicatos etcet. ergo heretici sunt iudicandi ab ecclesia. item actus. v. uir autem quidam nomine ananias cum saphyra uxore sua etcet. ergo ministerio petri occisi sunt eo iudicante illos per uerbum suum. ergo heretici et scismatici reliquendi sunt per prelatos ecclesie iudicio mortis.

Patarenus: Responsio. quod ex uerbo petri non sunt mortui. sed deus occidit eos et petrus prouidens hoc tantum per spiritum sanctum dixit eis quod futurum erat.

Catholicus: Sed probo quod ad uerbum petri mortui sunt. dixit enim hic lucas. audiens autem ananias hec

1 Timothy 1 (1:10) "and whatever other thing is contrary to sound doctrine, which is according to the gospel of the glory of the blessed God." So the death penalty and judicial punishments, of which the Apostle was speaking, are applied against heretics since they have turned against sound teaching, which is in the Gospel and this is good, because it is good that they be killed. Further it was proven above that evildoers deserve to be killed, but with heretics and blasphemers of fathers and mothers, namely, of God or the prelates of the Church, and that be they adulterers of divine Scripture and thieves and killers, and false witnesses against God, and on top of all are full of every sin, be it spiritual or carnal. It is evident that such ought to be condemned to death. Also in the New Testament Moses is commended and praised, along with Elijah and the like, and they killed idolaters and false prophets, as you see above in the first book on the Old Testament, and in the section on princes and prophets of the Old Testament. Therefore it is commendable and holy that heretics and the like be killed. Further, since in killing heretics one does not kill the soul, but only the body, and according to the Patarenes these are works of the devil, therefore it is good to kill them, since those who do this imitate the Son of God, of which Blessed John writes in his first letter (3:8) "For this purpose, the Son of God appeared, that he might destroy the works of the devil." And 1 Corinthians 5 (5:5) "To deliver such a one to Satan for the destruction of the flesh," and 2 Corinthians (10:6) "And being ready to revenge all disobedience." Also 1 Timothy 1 at the end (1:19-20) "which some rejecting have made shipwreck concerning the faith of whom is Hymenaeus and Alexander," — therefore heretics and schismatics by spiritual prelates — "whom I have delivered up to Satan." How much more then have I handed them over for bodily punishments to the secular powers.[1] Also Jude (1:22) "And some indeed reprove, being judged." Therefore heretics are to be judged by the Church. Also Acts 5 (5:1) "Yet there was a certain one named Ananias and his wife Sapphira." So by the ministry of Peter they were killed, being judged by him through his word, therefore heretics and schismatics are to be released by the prelates of the Church for the sentence of death.

Pat:[2] I reply that they were not killed by the words of Peter, but God killed them and Peter, foreseeing this, only said what was to happen in the future, by the Holy Spirit.

Cath: But I prove that they are killed by the words of Peter, for Luke says here (5:5) "but upon hearing these

---

474 si...475 dei] 1 Tim. 1:10.   496 in²...497 diaboli] 1 Ioh. 3:8.   498 tradere...499 carnis] 1 Cor. 5:5.   499 et²...500 inobedientiam] 2 Cor. 10:6.   501 circa...504 interitum] 1 Tim. 1:19-20.   506 et...iudicatos] Iud. 1:22.   508 uir...509 sua] Act. 5:1.   518 audiens...519 expirauit] Act. 5:5.

475 que...dei] om. P   476 loquebatur] add. b F exp.   478 doctrine sane] transp. F   492 occidantur] occiduntur F   503 ergo...504 sathane] om. F   505 tradidi] gradendi sunt F   506 arguite] add. iudicantes uel F | iudicatos] iudicantes P   511 scismatici] sismatici P   513 **Patarenus**] om. F | **Catholicus** P, leg. **Patarenus**   517 **Catholicus**] om. F | **Patarenus** P leg. **Catholicus**

500 etcet|fol. 144va P   505 secularibus|fol. 115v F

---

[1] A clear indication that the writer was an inquisitor. See also above, II.5,69–71, and below, XXIV.2,200–202. | [2] I have corrected the following several speakers from P.

uerba cecidit et expirauit etcet. et infra. confestim cecidit ante pedes eius etcet. ergo per uerba petri mortui sunt.

Patarenus: Non dixit quod per uerba petri sint mortui sed quod statim post uerba petri.

Catholicus: Sed modo respondeas parum. legitur in iohannes. xviii. unde ergo dixit eis. ego sum. abierunt retrorsum et ceciderunt in terra etcet. ergo uerbum christi fecit illos cadere in terram. quare ergo non credis quod et uerba petri occiderint istos. cum legatur quod statim in eis uerbis sint mortui maxime cum alius modus eorum mortis non ponatur.

Patarenus: Quia christus maior fuit petro et plus est occidere quam in terram pro sustinere.

Catholicus: hec nulla ratio est. quia christus dicit. iohannes. xiiii. qui credit in me opera que ego facio et ipse faciet et maiora horum faciet. preterea quomodo probabis quod quis occidat alium.

Patarenus: Probabo sic quia uidi aliquam euaginare gladium et eum eicere uersus illum et post eiectionem ille cecidit mortuus. ergo iste occidit eum.

Catholicus: Et idem. de istis est. quia petrus eduxit uerbum de uagina cordis et eiecit eum contra illos et post hoc illi statim ceciderunt mortui. ergo petrus cum uerbo occidit eos. preterea. deus per subiectas creaturas cotidie occidit aliquos ut puta per angelos per tonitura. per infirmitates et huiusmodi et ille creature non peccant obediendo diuine uoluntati. quare non eodem modo per uerbum petri et per potestates non potuit et non potest deus occidere maleficos.

[**Patarenus:**] Credisne in ueritate quod petrus occiderit ananiam et saphyram cum uerbo suo?

[**Catholicus:**] Credo.

[**Patarenus:**] Quare et tu eodem modo non occidis quos hereticos credis.

Catholicus: Et hoc facio. uerbum dico tantum et moriuntur. Dico namque. reliquo istos hereticos iudicio seculari. et statim comburuntur.

Patarenus: Hoc non est tantum propter uerbum tuum sed quia potestas te adiuuat.

Catholicus: Et aliqua uirtus dei ut puta angelis. uel alia sicut deus uoluit. iuuit petrum sicut et uermes inuertur angelum in morte herodis. ut habes. actus. xii. in finem. confestim autem percussit eum angelus domini etcet. et superius et consumptus a uermibus expirauit etcet. et sic angelis iuuit danielem in morte

words, Ananias fell to the ground and died," and later (5:10) "immediately she fell at his feet." Therefore they were killed by the words of Peter.

Pat: He did not say, through the words of Peter they were killed, but that immediately after the words of Peter.

Cath: But now you respond insufficiently. It is read in John 18 (18:6) "As soon therefore as he had said to them, 'I am he,' they went backward, and fell to the ground." Why then do you not believe that they might have been killed at the word of Peter, since it is read that immediately by these words, they died, especially since another manner of death is not proposed.

Pat: Because Christ was greater than Peter, and it was a greater thing to kill than to be cast to the ground.

Cath: That is nonsense, since Christ said in John 14 (14:12) "he who believes in me, and the works that I do, he also shall do, and greater than these shall he do." Further, how will you prove that he who killed is another?

Pat: I will prove it thus, since I saw another one unsheathe a sword and thrust it towards him, and after the thrust he fell dead, therefore he killed him.

Cath: And the same is of this because Peter drew the word from the scabbard of his heart and thrust it against them and after this they immediately fell dead. So Peter killed them with his word. Further, God daily kills some by means of lesser creatures, for example, through angels, through thunder, through sickness, and the like, and those creatures do not sin by obeying the divine will. For this reason God in the same way, through the word of Peter and that of authorities, as He can now, kill evildoers.

[**Pat:**] Do not you believe in truth that Peter killed Ananias and Saphira by his word?

[**Cath:**] I believe it.

[**Pat:**] Why then, in the same manner, do you not kill those you believe to be heretics?

Cath: And I do this, I only say the word, and they are killed. For instance I say, I release these heretics to secular judgment, and they are immediately burned.[1]

Pat: This is not only because of your sentence, but because the secular power assists you.

Cath: And by some power of God, for example, the angels, or another that God wills, just as he commanded Peter and worms were inflicted by an angel in the death of Herod, as one has in Acts 12 at the end (12:23) "And immediately an angel of the Lord struck him. . . and being eaten up by worms, he died." And so the angels ordered Daniel to kill

---

519 confestim...520 eius] Act. 5:10.   525 unde...526 terra] Ioh. 18:6.   534 qui...535 faciet²] Ioh. 14:12.   562 confestim...563 domini] Act. 12:23.   563 et²...564 expirauit] Act. 12:23.

---

521 sunt] om. *P*   522 Patarenus] **om.** *F* | Catholicus *P*, leg. Patarenus   523 petri] om. *P*   524 Catholicus] **om.** *F* | Patarenus *P* leg. Catholicus   528 occiderint] occiderint ceciderint *F* | cum] om. *P*   531 Patarenus] om. *F*   533 Catholicus] om. *F*   537 Patarenus] om. *F*   540 Catholicus] **om.** *F* | Patarenus *P* leg. Catholicus   549 Patarenus] om. *F* | Credisne] credis *F*   551 Catholicus] om. *F*   552 Patarenus] om. *F* | occidis] credis *F*   554 Catholicus] om. *F*   557 Patarenus] om. *F*   559 Catholicus] om. *F*   563 et¹...564 etcet] om. *P*

531 fuit|fol. 144vb *P*   559 Catholicus|fol. 145ra *P*

---

[1] Another clear indication that the author was an inquisitor.

duorum senum ut legitur. danielem. xiii. et ecce angelus dei etcet.
Patarenus: Non est hoc scriptum quod angelis iuuerit petrum.
Catholicus: Nec est scriptum quod petrus non occiderit illos et quod deum tantum occiderit eos. sed quod petrus occiderit uerbo suo illos. propter rationem supra dictam patet quod subditur ibi post hoc miraculum immediate per manus apostolorum fiebant signa et prodigia multa in plebe etcet. et idem xiii. saulus autem qui et paulus repletus spiritu sancto intuens in eum dixit. o plene omni dolo et omni fallacia filii diaboli inimice omnis iustitie. cur non desinis subuertere manus domini rectas et nunc ecce manus domini super te. et eris cecus non uidens solem usque ad tempus et confestim cecidit in eum caligo et tenebre etcet. ergo paulus excecauit illum uerbo suo. igitur huiusmodi sunt corporali iudicio tradendi per sententiam prelatorum.

Quod nullum iudicium seculare possit exerceri in corpus humanum

Quod nullum iudicium seculare debeat exerceri maxime in corpus humanum. probatur pluribus modis et primo exemplo saluatoris. in quo fuit omnis perfectio qui nullum iudicium temporale exercuit reale uel personale. pro aliis uel pro se. de reali uero quod non exercuit illud pro aliis legitur. lucam. xii. ait autem ei quidam de turba. magister dic fratri meo ut mecum diuidat hereditatem. at ille dixit ei. homo qui me constituit iudicem aut diuisorem super uos etcet. De corporali uero habetur. iohannes. viii. dixit ei ihesus. nec ego te condempnabo uade et amplius noli peccare. etcet. Quod autem non exercuit pro se. habes. mattheus. xxvi. ubi prohibuit petrum ne prestaret ei auxilium gladii materiale et prestantem redarguit dicens. conuertas gladium tuum in locum suum. omnes enim qui acceperint gladium gladio peribunt. an putas quia non possum rogare patrem meum et exhibebit mihi modo plusquam duodecim legiones angelorum etcet. idem etiam et in aliis euangeliis legitur. ad hoc est quod dicit beatus petrus. in prima. ii°. qui cum malediceretur non maledicebat. cum pateretur non comminabatur. tradebat autem iudicanti se iniuste etcet. et quod nullum dominus iudicauerit. ipsemet dicit in iohannes. viii. ego non iudico quemquam etcet. ergo nec nobis licet iudicare.
Catholicus: Solutio. dicimus quod christus non iudicauit alios triplici de causa. una fuit quia iudei non habebant eum iudicem. sicut ipse dixit in predicto capitulo. lucam. ad illum qui petebat ut diuideret

the two old men, as is read in Daniel 13 (13:55) "and behold the angel of the Lord."
Pat: It is not written that angels assisted Peter.
Cath: Neither is it written that Peter didn't kill them or that only God might have killed them, but that Peter killed them by his words. On account of the foregoing, it is obvious by what follows there immediately after the miracle (5:12) "And many signs and wonders were wrought by the hands of the apostles among the people." And the same in 13 (13:9–11) "Then Saul, otherwise Paul, filled with the Holy Spirit, looking upon him said, 'O full of all guile, and of all deceit, child of the devil, enemy of all justice, you never cease to pervert the right ways of the Lord and now behold, the hand of the Lord is upon you, and you will be blind, not seeing the sun for a time.' And immediately there fell a mist and darkness upon him." Therefore Paul blinded him by his word, and in a similar manner are those handed over to bodily punishment through the verdicts of the prelates [i.e. the inquisitors].

That no earthly justice is to be executed on the human body

That no earthly justice ought to be done, especially on the human body. This is proven in many ways, and the first is the example of the Savior, in whom was every perfection, and who never executed earthly justice, either in property or in personal matters, for others or for Himself in connection with goods of property yet this He did not exercise for others, as is read in Luke 12 (12:13–14) "And one of the crowd said to him, 'Master, speak to my brother so that he divides the inheritance with me.' But he said to him, 'Man, who has appointed me judge, or arbiter, over you?'" Concerning corporeal judgment one has John 8 (8:11) "Jesus said to her, 'Neither will I condemn you, go and sin no longer.'" But that He does not exercise it on His own behalf, you have Matthew 26, where he prohibits Peter lest he take the aid of the material sword, and He rebukes the attempt, saying (Mt 26:52) "Put up again your sword into its place, for all who take the sword shall perish by the sword. Do you think that I cannot ask my Father, and he will now give me more than twelve legions of angels?" Also the same, and in other gospels it is read. To this point is what Blessed Peter says in 1 Peter 2 (2:23) "Who, when he was reviled, did not revile, when he suffered, he did not threaten, but delivered himself to him who judged him unjustly." And that the Lord never judged, as He himself says in John 8 (8:15) "I do not judge any man." Therefore neither is it permitted for us to judge.
Cath: Solution. We say that Christ did not judge others for three reasons. One was because the Jews did not [legally] appoint Him as a judge as He said in the previous chapter of Luke, to him who asked that Christ might

---

565 et...566 dei] Dan. 13:55.   573 per...574 plebe] Act. 5:12.   575 saulus...581 tenebre] Act. 13:9-11.   **XXXV.2.8** ait...11 uos] Luc. 12:13-14.   **12** dixit...13 peccare] Ioh. 8:11.   **17** conuertas...21 angelorum] Luc. 26:52.   **23** qui...25 iniuste] 1 Pet. 2:23.   **26** ego...quem-quam] Ioh. 8:15.

567 Patarenus] om. F   569 Catholicus] om. F   577 inimice...581 tenebre] om. P   **XXXV.2.1** Quod...2 humanum] om. F   **11** aut... uos] om. P   **19** et...21 angelorum] om. P   **23** qui] add. mal P exp. | cum²...25 iniuste] om. P   **28** Catholicus] om. F

573 apostolorum|fol. 116r F   **XXXV.2.11** etcet|fol. 145rb P

hereditatem inter ipsum et fratrem suum. ibi. homo qui me constituit etcet. secunda fuit quia non occurit ei casus in quo posset iudicare secundum ordinem iudiciorum quia mulierem deprehensam in adulterio non debuit iudicare quia deficiebat ordo iudiciorum quia fugiunt accusatores eius et sine accusatore nemo debet puniri. unde dixit ibi. mulier ubi sunt qui te accusabant. nemo te condempnat. que dixit. nemo domine etcet. nec etiam iudei dixerant illam tamquam ad iudicem sed tamquam temptantes eum etcet. nec obstat de predicto in lucam. qui petebat diuisionem hereditatis. quia non legitur quod frater eius peteret illam. Tertia causa fuit potentissimam quia christus dominus non debuit per se iudicare de minimis ad modum strenui imperatoris et elegantis principis qui de huiusmodi per se non iudicatur sed per inferiores uicarios suos. sic et dominus noster iudicauit uel iudicat. de secularibus causis tamquam de minimis per ministrum suum potestatem seculare. sicut apostolus dicit apostolus ad romanos. xiii. minister enim dei est etcet. unde et ipse dominus in iohannes. ubi dixerat. ego non iudico quemquam. statim subdit. et si iudico ego iudicium meum uerum est. uel possumus dicere quod ipse iudicauit tam realiter quam corporaliter. de reali dicitur in predicto loco. lucam. dixitque ad illos. uidete et cauete ab omni auaritia etcet. ubi remouit auaritiam que erat causa litigii ipsorum. de iudicio uero corporali legitur de muliere deprehensa in adulterio quam iudicauit iudicio absolutionis sicut debuit propter defectum accusatorum et quod raro iudicauit dominus fuit propter hoc. quia principaliter uenerat ad misericordiam faciendam et non ad iudicium exercendum. quod autem oppositis quod ipse non se defendit uel non permisit se defendere fuit propter duas rationes. una ne daret nobis exemplum proprias iniurias iudicandi. non enim secundum humanum cursum poterat se defendere a tanta multitudine armatorum nisi super excellenti uirtute sua et tunc uisa fuisset uindicta simplicibus. secunda fuit ut cursus passionis eius impediretur quam uoluntarie sumebat. unde et dixit petro se defendenti. quomodo implebuntur scripture prophetarum quia sic oportet fieri etcet. nec obstat quod dixistis quod teneamur facere et implere perfectionem christi. quia non est uerum usquam. quia nec ad uirginitatem tenemur nec uoluntarie. nos ingerere ad passiones et ad multa alia que impleuit ipse.

Patarenus: Item apostoli non iudicauerunt. nec etiam se defenderunt per arma bellica nec ergo nobis licet huiusmodi facere.
Catholicus: Respondeo quod falsum est hoc quia et petrus iudicauit ananias et saphyram et paulus elimam

---

32 homo...33 constituit] Luc. 12:14.   38 mulier...40 domine] Ioh. 8:10.   51 minister...est] Rom. 13:4.   53 ego...quemquam] Ioh. 8:15. | et...54 est] Ioh. 8:16.   56 dixitque...57 auaritia] Luc. 12:15.   73 quomodo...74 fieri] Matt. 26:54.

66 ne] add. sic *F*   69 uirtute] add. n *P* exp.   72 sumebat] sumebat summebat *P*   79 Patarenus] om. *F*   82 Catholicus] om. *F*

45 iudicare|fol. 145va *P*   51 dei|fol. 116v *F*   75 teneamur|fol. 145vb *P*

magum. ut ostensum est supra. et paulus armatorum impetrauit defensionem. licet per manus proprias non exercuerint gladium materialem. sicut nec ecclesia romana exercet. quoniam usus eius concessus est laicis tamquam contemptibilibus personis in ecclesia sicut dicit apostolus. iª. ad corinthios. vi. contemptibiles qui sunt in ecclesia illos constitute ad iudicandum etcet. sicut non defenderant se apostoli per arma bellica subaudi percutiendo quod nec religiosi nec alii qui in sacris ordinibus sunt constituti de ecclesia romana hoc faciunt. quia non licet huiusmodi personis percutere aut omnino scandalo se defendere.

Patarenus: Item christus et apostolis eius prohibent hoc fieri. ut ecce. mattheus. v. audistis quia dictum est antiquis. non occides etcet. ergo nemini licet occidere.

Catholicus: Solutio aut tu es patarenus qui mihi hoc opponis aut pauper leonista uel huiusmodi. siquidem si patarenus es. dic mihi. quis hoc preceptum dederit christus enim in nouo testamento non dedit illud. sed tam antiquis datum recitat illud. ergo ante nouum testamentum datum est quod si dedit deus bonus in celo. nichil ergo ad nos qui sumus in terra. ubi enim datum est illic teneatur. siquidem si bonus deus dedit eum in ueteri testamento. ergo deus ueteris testamenti bonus deus fuit quod tu inficiaris. siquidem si malus fuit non teneor eius seruare preceptum. nec potes dicere quod deus bonus dedit hoc preceptum moysi et alia moralia et deus malus dederit iudicia mortis quia christus dicit quod deus bonus dedit morale preceptum et mortis iudicium. mattheus xv. nam deus dixit. honora patrem et matrem tuam et qui maledixerit patri uel matri morte moriatur etcet. siquidem si pauper leonista es et huiusmodi qui uetus testamentum confitearis. audi quod deus ueteris testamenti dedit hoc preceptum. exodi. xx. in eadem carta. xxii. maleficos non patieris uiuere etcet. ergo licet ipse fuit contrarius sibi ipsi. licet istud scilicet non occides intelligebatur secundum determinationem quam facit. xxiii. insomptem et iustum non occides quia aduersor impium etcet. uel intelligitur esse predictum personis priuatis uel qui non ad uindictam occidatur. nec obstat quod christus hic subdit. ego autem dico uobis. quia omnis qui irascitur etcet. quia sic intelligitur quod scribe et pharisei docebant quod homo poterat irasci fratri suo et dicere ei improperia sine peccato propter hoc quod non uidebatur esse prohibita iniuria proximi. nisi per homicidium fieret. unde dominus supplendo primum intellectum eorum dicit quod ubi non licebat occidere secundum legem moysi. ibi non licet irasci et improperia dicere et secundum hoc. non occides. non fuit prohibito omnium homicidiorum quod et uerum est.

Patarenus: Idem in eodem. audistis quia dictum est. oculum pro oculo dentem pro dente. ego autem dico uobis non resistere malo etcet. sed istud scilicet oculum pro oculo dictum erat in lege iudiciaria. exodi. xxi. sin autem mors eius fuerit subsecuta reddet animam pro anima. oculum pro oculo dentem pro dente etcet. et deuteronimi. xviii. in finem. oculum pro oculo et christus dicit. ego autem dico uobis non resistere malo etcet. ergo tollit prius dictum a fidelibus suis quibus precepit ut non resistant malo neque contempnant in iudicio.

Catholicus: Respondeo quod oculum pro oculo etcet. dictum erat non solum iudici. sed etiam dictum erat cuilibet ut in iudicio posset petere penam tallionis a suo aduersario et ipsemet poterat eam dare uel exigere iudicis auctoritate. tamen nec iudici nec alicui licebat. hoc facere libidine iudicandi. ut legitur. leuitici. xix. non queras ultionem nec memor eris iniurie ciuium tuorum etcet. et tamen scribe et pharisei docebant contrarium. unde dominus supplet legem interpretando uel exponendo quantum ad scribarum et pharyseorum prauum intellectum dicens. non resistere malo id est iniurie nobis facte non queratis ultionem. cum enim quis uindictam querit ipse malo resistit. si uero iustitiam petit tunc non ipse sed lex resistit malo et sic intelliguntur sequentia si quis te percusserit uel possumus dicere quod dominus tollit in uerbis istis legem tallionis tantum quia non uult quod secundum eam procedatur in iudiciis. uel aliter dicimus quod hoc sunt consilia maioris perfectionis que dominus dat in sermone isto. quod autem non sint precepta patet quia ipse dominus ostendit iram ut legitur. marci. iii. et circumspiciens eos cum ira etcet. et uocauit duos discipulos suos euntes in emaus stultos ut legitur. lucam. ultimi. O stulti et tardi corde etcet. et paulus et alii apostoli plerumque irati sunt contra fratres suos et multotiens dixerunt eis uerba huiuscemodi et deus danti sibi alapam non prebuit sibi aliam maxillam. sed dixit ei. quid me cedis? etcet. ut habetur iohannes xviii. et paulus se percutienti dixit. actus. xxiii. percutiet te deus paries dealbate etcet. item paulus apostolus concedit iudicio contendere. ut legitur. iᵃ. ad corinthios. v. audet aliquis etcet. ergo sunt tamen hoc uerba consilii ad maioris uite securitatem. uel aliter intelliguntur ista uerba domini sic. quod non debemus resistere malo cum hodio cordis aut in iudicio

Pat: In the same (5:38) "You have heard that it has been said, 'An eye for an eye, and a tooth for a tooth.' But I say to you not to resist evil." But that, namely, the saying "eye for eye" was in the law of judgment in Exodus 21 (21:23) "But if her death immediately follows, he will render life for life. Eye for eye, tooth for tooth." And in Deuteronomy 18 at the end (19:21) "eye for eye." And Christ says (5:38) "But I say to you not to resist evil." Therefore He removed the binding force of the first saying for His faithful, by which He commanded that they not resist evil, neither do they condemn in judgment.

Cath: I reply that "an eye for an eye" was said not only for judgment, but was also said for whomever so that he can seek the punishment of retaliation from his adversary and he himself could give it or [have it] be examined by the authority of the judge, yet this was permitted neither to the judge nor to any other, to do this with a lust for judgment, as is read in Leviticus 19 (19:18) "Do not seek revenge, and be mindful of the injury of your citizens." And nevertheless the scribes and Pharisees were teaching the contrary, so the Lord amended the law by interpreting or by laying bare the wicked interpretations of the scribes and Pharisees, saying "do not resist evil," that is, do not seek vengeance for injuries done to us, for when one seeks vengeance, he resists evil. If however he seeks justice then he does not resist evil, the law does. And this is how the following are to be understood (5:39) "if someone strikes you," or we might be able to say that the Lord removes the law of retaliation with these words, as much as He does not wish that one might proceed in judgment according to it. Or we might otherwise say that this is a counsel of greater perfection which the Lord gives in this passage. That these are not commands is clear because the Lord Himself shows anger, as is read in Mark 3 (3:5) "And looking around about them with anger," and he called two of his disciples going to Emmaus fools, as is read in the last chapter of Luke (24:25) "O fools, and slow of heart." And Paul and the other Apostles were angry many times against their brethren and repeatedly said to them angry words and, God, having been struck, did not turn the other cheek, but said to him (Jn 18:23) "why do you strike me?" As one has in John 18 and Paul, to the one striking him, said (23:3) "God shall strike you, you whitewashed wall." Also Paul the Apostle conceded the right to contend in judgments, as is read in 1 Corinthians 5 (6:1) "Dare any of you." Therefore these words are counsels to greater security of life, or these words of the Lord can otherwise be understood thusly, that we ought not to resist evil with

---

136 audistis...138 malo] Matt. 5:38. 140 sin...142 dente] Ex. 21:23. 142 oculum...143 oculo] Deut. 19:21. 143 ego...144 malo] Matt. 5:38. 153 non...154 tuorum] Lev. 19:18. 161 si...percusserit] Matt. 5:39. 167 et...168 ira] Mar. 3:5. 170 O...corde] Luc. 24:25. 174 quid...cedis] Ioh. 18:23. 175 percutiet...176 dealbate] Act. 23:3. 178 audet aliquis] 1 Cor. 6:1.

136 Patarenus] om. F 137 dico...138 malo] om. P 141 dentem...142 dente] om. P 142 et...143 oculo] om. F 144 etcet...145 resistant] om. F | add. non resistere F 147 Catholicus] om. F 151 tamen] causam P 156 uel exponendo] om. P 158 cum...160 petit] om. F 176 dealbate] dealbata P

134 occides|fol. 146rb P 164 iudiciis|fol. 146va P 175 percutienti|fol. 117v F

contempnere. sed potius debemus patientem ferre plura mala qua nobis fiant. uel alio modo loquitur hic dominus perfectionis qui cum scandalo non debent resistere malo. uel iudicio contendere cum aliquo sed potius plus debent dimittere quam sit illud ad quod coguntur sed et illud sine scandalo habere non possunt. Sed dicite michi ypocrite heretici. nonne resistitis nobis uolentibus introire ad uos et uiolenter eicitis nos cum multis opprobriis et percussionibus quam pluribus multoties. ergo resistis in malo immo bono quod peius est. item siquis percutit uos in una maxilla. numquid prebetis et alteram. et siquis aufert a uobis duo paria subtellarium numquid prebetis illi et tertium. an potius de duobus non murmuratis et ploratis cum lacrimis non paucis? Item. nonne contenditis de causis ciuilibus apud iudices nostros quandoque et si per uos non audetis facitis tamen per interpositas personas? ergo trangressores estis preceptorum christi.

[Patarenus:] Idem in eodem audisti quod dictum est. Diliges proximum tuum et hodio habebis inimicum tuum ego autem dico uobis diligite inimicos uestros etcet. ergo ecclesia romana male facit quia persequitur et occidit quos inimicos reputat.

Catholicus: Responsio. quod inimicos diligere est. id diligere in eis quod facit illos ueros amicos id est orationem correctionem. reprehensionem. punitiorem. per que a suis erroribus et peccatis conuertantur. sicut econtrario odire amicos est illud odire in eis quod facit inimicos. de quod habetur in lucam. xiiii. si quis uenit ad me et non odit patrem suum et matrem et uxorem et filios et fratres et sorores etcet. et hoc nos facimus quia diligimus in uobis hereticis omnia ista ad correctionem et ad salutem animarum uestrarum ea enim ratione qua medicus diligit infirmos quando eis cerebrum incidit propter furiam sanandam et qua pater filium furiosum diligit quando ipsum ligat et uerberat ne se in precipitium mortis tradat qua et paulus dilexit corinthum incestuosum. quando illum in carnis interitum sathane tradidit. qua etiam et deus omnes quos uerberat et flagellat. diligit inmensum et discite stulti quod non omnis qui parcit amicus est. nec omnisque uerberat inimicus. iuxta illud. meliora sunt uulnera diligentis quam fraudulentia obscula inimici etcet. et illud. qui parcit uirge odit filium suum etcet. sed dicite mihi uos qualiter compleatis istud dominicum. quia neque affectum dilectionis habetis ad nos. neque pro nobis oratis neque elemosinas facitis pauperibus nostris.

---

201 audisti…203 uestros] Matt. 5:43. 211 si…213 sorores] Luc. 14:26. 224 meliora…226 inimici] Pr. 27:6 (om. inimici] add. odientis *Vulg.*) 226 qui…suum] Pr. 13:24.

183 qua] quam *P* 197 contenditis] actenditis *P* | nostros] add. etiam apud nostros quandoque *F* 203 ego…uestros] om. *P* 206 Catholicus] om. *F* 211 habetur] habemus *F* 212 et²…213 sorores] om. *P* 219 et] om. *P* 225 sunt] add. obscula *P* exp. 226 suum] om. *P* 227 qualiter] add. uos *F*

192 una|fol. 146vb *P* 222 uerberat|fol. 147ra *P*

Patarenus: Idem. xviii. si autem peccauerit in te frater tuus uade et corripe eum inter te et ipsum solum etcet. non dixit occide eum.

Catholicus: Quia prelatus spiritualis erat. nec tamen auferet potestatem cesari.

De eodem

Patarenus: Idem in eodem. tunc accendens petrus ad eum dixit. domine quoties peccauit in me frater meus etcet. ad idem.

Catholicus: Non agebatur nisi de dimissione proprie iniurie et quoties ad penitentiam debet recipi peccator.

Patarenus: item. xxvi. tunc ait illi ihesus. omnes enim qui acceperint gladium gladium peribunt etcet. ergo nulli licet exercere gladium materialem.

Catholicus: Non dixit qui exercuerint gladium sed qui acceperint gladium scilicet sua auctore sicut petrus qui non habebat auctoritatem percutiendi in gladio triplici de causa. tum quia episcopus erat cui non licet percutere sicut dicit apostolus. i^a. ad timotheo. iii^o. non percussorem etcet. tum quia impediebat passionem domini contra uoluntatem eius. unde et dominus dixit. iohannes. xviii. calicem quem dedit mihi pater non bibam illum etcet. et quia sine licencia domini percutiebat cuius subditus erat. a quo nondum acceperat potestatem etiam exercendi gladium spiritualem. ut patet iohannes. xxi. ubi dixit ei dominus. pasce oues meas etcet. quod fuit tantum post resurrectionem eius. ante uero passionem ipsius dixit illi. de futuro. tibi dabo claues regni celorum etcet. item ad romanos. xii. benedicite persequentibus uos etcet. et infra. nulli malum pro malo reddentes etcet. oppositio et responsio ut supra. mattheus. v. audistis quia dictum est diliges proximum tuum etcet.

Patarenus: Idem in eodem. non uos defendentes karissimi sed date locum ire etcet.

Catholicus: Responsio. quod illud dictum est tamen perfectis. quibus non licet se defendere cum scandalo. uel est consilium maioris perfectionis. uel aliter locum habet istud pauli quando comode quis per alium modum post uitare pugnam. sed ex calore indignationis. uel ex motu odii seu ex humana laude caduca magis uult se ostentare cum minimo. quod quidem peccatum est. unde sapienter dixit. non uos defendentes karissimi sed date locum ire. alioquin si laicus est potest defendere non solum se sed etiam proximum ad instar moysi qui occidit egyptium percutientem hebreum. sin autem de perfectionis est potest aliorum auxilium impetrare. exemplo pauli. uel melius. non uos defendentes id est non uos uindicantes. et quod iste fuerit intellectus apostoli patet per auctoritatem per quam probat que de uindicta loquitur. unde subdit. scriptum est enim mihi uindicta et ego retribuam etcet. defensionem uero que est ex iustitia statim concedit in sequenti capitulo. cum dixit. omnia anima potestatibus sublimioribus etcet. Ex hiis modis soluuntur omnes auctoritates que defensionem prohibere uidentur.

Patarenus: Item. xiii. qui enim diligit proximum legem implebit etcet. ibi. non occides. oppositio et responsio ut supra. mattheo. v. audistis quia dictum est antiquis. non occides etcet.

Patarenus: Item i^a. ad corinthios x. in finem. sine offensione estote iudeis et gentibus et ecclesie dei. etcet.

Catholicus: Responsio. loquitur de esu ydolatiti. uel responde. ut supra. mattheo. v. audistis quia dictum est diliges proximum tuum etcet. preterea. uos heretici non estis iudei neque gentes neque ecclesia dei.

Patarenus: Item. ii^a. ad corinthios. vi^o. nemini dantes ullam offensionem etcet. et vii. neminem lesimus etcet. ergo male facit ecclesia romana. quia ledit quos hereticos putat.

Catholicus: Non ledit sed a lesione retrahit.

Patarenus: Item. x. nam arma militie nostre non sunt carnalia sed potentia deo etcet. ergo peccatum est exercere arma temporalia.

Catholicus: loquitur de iuris spiritualibus qui non debet exercere arma carnalia. uel uocat arma carnalia confidentias peccatorum. uel dicit quod arma carnalia non sunt nobis principaliter. uel ad hoc que ibi conumerat secundum potentia deo id est a deo hoc est spirituale uirtus.

Patarenus: Item. ii^a. thesalonicenses. iii^o. in fine. nolite quasi inimicum existimare illum. sed corripite ut fratrem etcet. ergo male facit ecclesia romana que iubet occidi inobedientes sibi.

Catholicus: Respondeo quia loquitur ibi de fratre curiose ambulante. preterea quod ecclesia romana facit ex dilectione agit quam habet ad delinquentes ut corrigantur.

[**Patarenus:**] Item. mattheus. vii. nolite iudicare ut non iudicemini etcet. et lucam. v. nolite iudicare etcet. et ad romanos. ii^o. propter quod inexcusabilis es o homo omnis qui iudicas etcet. ergo potestates peccant mortaliter iudicando.

[the state of] perfection one can request the help of others, as in the example of Paul, or better, "do not revenge yourselves," that is, do not avenge. And that this was the understanding of the Apostle is obvious through the passage by which one proves that he is speaking of avenging, whence he adds, (12:19) "for it is written, 'revenge is mine, I will repay.'" Yet vengeance which is done in justice is immediately conceded in the following chapter when he said (13:1) "Let every soul be subject to higher powers." From these the way is clear to a solution for all the authorities which seem to prohibit vengeance.

Pat: Also 13 (13:8) "For he who loves his neighbor, has fulfilled the law," there, "do not kill," in opposition and response to the above Matthew 5 (5:21) "you have heard it said of old, you shall not kill."

Pat: Also 1 Corinthians 10 at the end (10:32) "Be without offence to the Jews, and to the Gentiles, and to the church of God."

Cath: I reply that this is regarding eating things sacrificed to idols, or in responding as above in Matthew 5 (5:43) "you have heard it said of old, you shall love your neighbor," further, you heretics are neither Jews, nor gentiles, nor the Church of God.

Pat: Also 1 Corinthians 6 (6:3) "Giving no offence to any man," and 7 (7:2) "We have injured no man," therefore the Roman Church does evil since it injures those whom it considers to be heretics.

Cath: She does not injure, but draws them back from injury.

Pat: Also 10 (10:4) "For the weapons of our warfare are not carnal, but in the power of God," therefore it is a sin to bear temporal arms.

Cath: He is speaking of spiritual laws, which ought not bring carnal arms to bear, or he terms carnal arms as the impudence of sinners, or he says that carnal arms are not principally for us, or to this which here he reckons according to the power of God, that is, from God this is spiritual power.

Pat: Also in 2 Thessalonians 3 (3:15) "Yet do not consider him as an enemy, but admonish him as a brother." Therefore the Roman Church does evil, since it orders the disobedient to be killed.

Cath: I reply that he is speaking there of brethren walking like busybodies, further what the Roman Church does, it acts through love when it holds up delinquents for correction.

[**Pat:**] Also Matthew 7 (7:1) "do not judge, lest you be judged," and Luke 5 (6:37) "do not judge," and Romans 2 (2:1) "So you are inexcusable, o man, all you who judge." Therefore authorities sin mortally in judging.

---

47 scriptum...48 retribuam] Rom. 12:19.   50 omnia...etcet] Rom. 13:1.   53 qui...54 implebit] Rom. 13:8.   55 audistis...56 occides] Matt. 5:21.   57 sine...58 dei] 1 Cor. 10:32.   60 audistis...61 tuum] Matt. 5:43.   63 nemini...64 etcet^1] 2 Cor. 6:3.   64 neminem lesimus] 2 Cor. 7:2.   68 nam...69 deo] 2 Cor. 10:4.   77 nolite...79 fratrem] 2 Thes. 3:15.   85 nolite...86 iudicemini] Matt. 7:1.   86 nolite iudicare] Luc. 6:37.   87 propter...88 iudicas] Rom. 2:1.

53 Patarenus] om. *F*   54 implebit] implevit *F*   57 Patarenus] om. *F*   59 Catholicus] om. *F*   61 tuum] om. *P*   63 Patarenus] om. *F*   67 Catholicus] om. *F*   68 Patarenus] om. *F*   71 Catholicus] om. *F*   77 Patarenus] om. *F*   81 Catholicus] om. *F*

53 Patarenus|fol. 147va *P*   66 putat|fol. 118v *F*   85 mattheus|fol. 147vb *P*

Catholicus: Responsio. quia dominus et apostolus loquitur in predictis auctoritatibus de iudicio quod est secundum faciem sed iustum iudicium iudicate etcet. uel loquuntur de iudicio occultorum quod soli deo relinquendus est ut dicit apostolus iª ad corinthios. iiii. nichil enim mihi conscius sum. sed non in hoc iustificatus sum qui autem iudicat me deus est. itaque nolite ante tempus iudicare. quoadusque ueniat dominus uenias qui illuminabit abscondita tenebrarum et manifestabit consilia cordium et tunc laus erit unicuique a deo etcet. Sed dic mihi o heretice. credisne in ueritate quod christus loquatur hic de iudicio manifestorum et scio quod non credis. uel si hoc est. propter hoc aufert potestatem cesari. quia perfectis tantum loquitur.

Patarenus: Item. xiii. simile factum est regnum celorum homini qui seminauit bonum semen in agro suo etcet. et ideo dominus parabolam istam exponit quod sator est filius hominis. ager mundus. bonum semen filii regni. zizania filii nequam. super seminator diabolus. messis consumatio seculi et messores sunt angeli. ergo per aliquos homines non sunt tollendi de mundo aliqui mali.

Catholicus: Responsio. quod christus prohibet in hoc loco seruis zizania extirpare secundum enim qui seruilem statum gerunt sunt persone priuate. quibus non licet sua auctoritate occidere peccatores. principibus autem et potestatibus qui non pro se sed pro iustitia ex officio suo comisso sibi faciunt non prohibet de quibus habetur. tam in ueteri testamento quam in nouo testamento copiose dispositum et ista solutio probatur ex principio capituli. ubi dicitur. in illa die exiens ihesus de domo sedebat secus mare et congregate sunt ad eum turbe multe. ex quo patet non principibus sed priuatis personis loquebatur. uel aliter per seruos intelliguntur uiri spirituales. qui formam seruilem habent quorum officium est materiam potestate peccatoribus. et non complere zelum iustitie quem habent contra illos. simile. lucam. viiii. cum uidissent autem discipuli eius iacobus et ioannes dixerunt. domine uis dic ut descendat ignis de celo et consumat illos et conuersus increpauit illos etcet. potest hic locus et aliter et planius intelligi scilicet ut dominus loquatur de peccatoribus in fide uel opere qui non sunt manifesti in forma iudicii. licet sint presumpti. ad instar enim zizanorum tres sunt species peccatorum scilicet eorum qui sunt occulti. de quibus peccatum est suspicari de illis dicit dominus. nolite iudicare etcet. et eorum qui sunt presumpti et de istis dicit hic. quod patet per similitudinem zizanorum que non dum habebant fructum maturum que quamdiu non sunt matura. non possunt a tritico descerni. licet a diligenter inspicientibus propter folii et spice subtilitatem et patet etiam quia dicit. ne forte quod est aduerbium euentus. quasi dicat. presumptiones sepe decipiunt per scrutantes et ideo per eas non iudicandus est de facto. tamen seruos iudicantes huiusmodi de cordis iudicio. et inde ore loquentes. non reprehendit dominus et sunt peccatores manifesti. qui iam sunt segregati a tritico quos uult christus eradicari de agro per principes et potestates ut probatum est supra in nostra parte et de istis etiam insinuat in hoc euangelio cum dicit. sicut ergo colliguntur zizania et igni comburuntur etcet. non dixit. colligentur et comburentur, sed dixit colliguntur et comburentur in presenti. potest et aliter intelligi locus iste ut prohibebat dominus eradicari zizania que non possunt eradicari nisi tritico et ideo dicit. ne forte colligentes zizania eradicetis simul et triticum cum eis etcet. tutius est enim malos cum bonis tolerare. quam bonis cum malis eradicare.

Hereticus: Sed audi quid dicit augustinus. super hunc locum. hic datur locus penitentie et monemur non cito amputare. quoniam qui hodie errat. forsitan cras defendet ueritatem. si ergo modo euelleretur. triticum quod futurum erat eradicaretur etcet. ergo non uult augustinus quod heretici occidantur.

Catholicus: Responsio. quod augustinus intelligit loqui hoc euangelium de hereticis dubiis et non examinatus et ideo dicit hic datur locus penitentie et monemur non cito amputare. et in alia glosa dicit. inter triticum et lolium quamdiu herba est parum distat. ita monet dominus ne de ambiguo iudicemus quod dominius in die iudicii non suspitiose sed manifeste dampnabit etcet. quod autem augustinus intelligit hereticos et alios peccatores manifestos esse iudicandos per potestates patet ex glosa sua quam hic facit scilicet non aufert hic christus potestate cesari et quod uelit spiritualiter hereticos comburi declaratur. ex epistola de correctione donatistarum quam misit bonifatio comiti. que incipit laudo etcet. ibi quod agit ergo fraterna dilectio. utrum dum paucis transitorios ignes metuit caminorum dimittit omnis eternis ignibus gehennarum et tamen multos uel iam nolentes uel postea non ualentes per catholicam pacem ad uitam uenire perpetuam. reliquit in interitum uenire perpetuum cauendo ne quidam uoluntario moriantur

did not yet have mature fruit, and as long as they are not mature and are unable to be distinguished from the wheat, though [one may distinguish them] by diligently inspecting them by their leaves and the thinness of their seeds. And it is obvious also because He says, "lest perhaps," which is an adverb of chance/possibility, as if to say, presumptions often escape notice by those who examine closely, and so one should not judge by them on the basis of fact, rather the Lord does not upbraid the servants judging in this way by a judgement of the heart, and thence speaking with their mouths. And they are clearly sinners, who are already separated from the wheat, those whom Christ wills to be eliminated from the field by princes and authorities, as is proven above in our section on those, and also is intimated in this gospel when He says (13:40) "Even as cockle therefore is gathered up, and burnt with fire," He did not say "shall be gathered up and shall be burned," but He said "are gathered up and burned" in the present tense. One is able otherwise to understand this passage as the Lord prohibiting the tares to be eliminated, which it is not possible to do unless the wheat also be eliminated, so He says (13:29) "lest perhaps gathering up the cockle, you root up the wheat also together with it." It is safer then for the evil to be tolerated along with the good, than for the good to be eliminated along with the evil.

Heretic: But hear what Augustine says about this passage (Ordinary Gloss) "here is given a space for penitence, and we are warned not to be quick to amputate, since those who err today may perhaps be defenders of truth tomorrow. But if it were extirpated so, what might become wheat in the future would be eliminated." So Augustine does not wish heretics to be killed.

Cath: I reply that Augustine understands this gospel to speak of presumed heretics and not those who have been examined, and so he says here that a space for penitence is given, and we are advised not quickly to amputate, and another gloss says (Gloss from Jerome) "between grain and cockle, as long as the plant is not far, so the Lord warns, lest from ambiguity we might judge, because the Lord on the day of judgment will condemn not based on suspicion, but plainly." That Augustine understands heretics and other public sinners to be judged by authorities is clear from his gloss which one finds here, namely, Christ does not here remove the power of Caesar, and that He wishes heretics to be burned spiritually, he pronounces on his letter on the correction of the Donatists which he sent to Count Boniface, which begins 'laudo' (Ep. 185) "What then is the function of brotherly love? Does it, because it fears the short-lived fires of the furnace for a few, therefore abandon all to the eternal fires of hell? And does it leave so many, who are either already desirous, or hereafter are not strong enough to pass to life eternal, to perish everlastingly,

---

152 sicut...com-buruntur] Matt. 13:40. 157 ne...158 eis] Matt. 13:29. 161 hic...164 eradicaretur] Augustine, Ordinary gloss of Matt. 13. 170 inter...173 dampnabit] Jerome, Ordinary Gloss of Matt. 13 (lolium] zizania). 179 ibi...190 festinare] Augustine, Ep. 185.

144 aduerbium] ad uerbum F 145 iudicandus...146 est] transp. F 154 potest] om. P 160 Hereticus] om. F 166 Catholicus] om. F 174 intelligit] intelligat F 179 quod] quid F 184 perpetuam] add. ca P exp.

148 manifesti|fol. 148rb P 178 correctione|fol. 148va P

interitum qui uiuunt ad impedimentum salutis aliorum quos non permittunt secundum christi doctrinam uiuere. ut eos doceant quocumque secundum consuetudinem doctrine diabolice ad eas que in illis modi timentur mortes uoluntarias festinare. sed modo Respondete mihi uos omnes heretici que sunt isti servi quibus christus prohibet extirpare zizaniam. siquid si uos estis. ergo uobis datum est tantum istud preceptum sin autem nos sumus. ergo uos estis zizania nos sumus serui dei. preterea non estis vos illi qui dicitis euangelia in quibus continetur de maleficis occidendis parabolas esse et ideo non debere seruari quod in eis ad litteram. sonare uidetur et ego ex ore uestro uos iudicans dico quod ista est parabola similiter et ideo falsa contra nos allegatis de malis non occidendis in hac uita. Erubescite igitur filii perditionis et oppone hic contra patarenos pro ut notatum est supra in primo libro. primo titulum rubricella quod mundus est a deo. mattheo. xiii. simile factum est etcet.

while taking precautions that some few should not perish by their own hand, who are only living to be a hindrance in the way of the salvation of others, whom they will not permit to live in accordance with the doctrines of Christ, in the hopes that some day or other they may teach them too to hasten their death by their own hand, in the manner which now causes them themselves to be a terror to their neighbors, in accordance with the custom inculcated by their devilish tenets? Or does it rather save all whom it can, even though those whom it cannot save should perish in their own infatuation?" But how will you reply to me, heretics, who are those servants which Christ prohibits one to eliminate in the cockle? Even if you are they, then to you is given only this command, but if also we are they, therefore you are cockle and we are the servants of God. Further are you not those who say the Gospels — in which are contained parables on the killing of evildoers — ought not to be observed in what they literally seem to say. And I judging you from your own mouth say that this sounds like a parable, and therefore you bring false accusations against us concerning not killing evildoers in this life. Blush then, sons of perdition, and oppose this against the Patarenes as was noted above in the first book, in the first section about the world being made by God, Matthew 13 "The kingdom of heaven is like."

---

194 istud preceptum] transp. *F*   195 estis²] ~~estis~~ *P*   199 iudicans] iudicas *P*   201 perditionis] perdicionis *P*   202 contra] om. *P*   203 supra] om. *P*

188 doctrinam|fol. 119v *F*

Quod confessio debet fieri sacerdotibus

Quod confessio peccatorum sit facienda sacerdotibus siquid si fieri potest tam per rationes quam per scripturas declaratur.

Idem de eodem

Iustitia dei exigit ut per que peccant homo. per hoc in penitentia torqueatur sicut dicit. per que peccant homines per hec et torquatur etcet. et constat quod homo tribus modis peccat scilicet corde. ore. et opere. ergo puniendus est in corde per dolorem contritionis in ore per uerecundiam confessionis. in opere per laborem satifactionis. uel aliter peccant homines per uoluntatem et per impudentiam. et per consumationem peccati sic ergo iustum est ut contra uoluntatis peccatum torquatur per cordis dolorem contra impudentiam per oris confessionem et contra peccati consumationem per bonorum operum perfectionem. ergo secundum iustitiam dei tentur peccator homini confiteri peccata sua. homini dico qui habet potestatem ipsum absoluendi id est sacerdoti.

Catholicus: Item duo sunt socii in absoluendo peccatorem scilicet deus et sacerdos. deus enim absoluat a culpa. sacerdos a pena. sicut patet in multis scripturis. sed constat quod deus non absoluit peccatorem nisi peccator reuelet ei peccat per corde dolorem. ergo eodem modo et sacerdos non absoluit eum nisi reuelet illa sibi per uerba aut per alia signa manifesta. preterea. sacerdos absoluit peccatorem a penis peccatorum. sed quomodo absoluet a quibus nesciet. ergo propter hoc scire debet peccata peccatoris et propter satisfactionem iniungendam illi quam debet iniungere secundum quantitatem et qualitatem peccatorum et secundum statum peccatum quod facere non potest nisi sciat peccata. mattheus. iii. tunc exibat ad eum ierosolyma et omnis iudea et omnis regio circa iordanem et baptizabantur ab eo in iordane confitentes peccata sua etcet. marci. i°. et baptizabantur ab illo in iordanis flumine confitentes peccata sua etcet. ergo confessio peccatorum facienda est sacerdoti. item. mattheo. xviii. si autem peccauerit in te frater tuus uade et corripe eum inter te et ipsum solum etcet. et lucam. xvii. actendite uobis. si peccauerit in te frater tuus increpa illum et si penitentiam egerit dimitte illi etcet. ergo peccator debet manifestare peccatum suum sacerdoti de quo redarguat illum et de quo penitentiam faciat et sic sacerdos peccatum ipsum absoluat. alioquin quomodo redargueret eum si nesciret peccatum ipsius quomodo staret istud si penitentiam egerit dimitte illi. ergo non dimittit sacerdos peccatum

That confession ought to be made to priests

That confession of sins is to be made to priests if one is able to do so, is as plain from natural reason as from the scriptures.

Also regarding the same

The justice of God demands that those things through which men sin must be atoned for in penitence, just as it says (Wis 11:17) "a man is punished by the very things through which he sins." And it is obvious that man sins in three ways, namely, in his heart, in his mouth, and in his works. Therefore he is to be punished in his heart by the sorrow of contrition, in his mouth by the shame of confession, and in works by efforts of satisfaction. Or men sin either through will and through shamelessness, and through the commission of sin, so then it is just that there be punishment of sorrow of heart with respect to sin of the will against shamelessness by oral confession, and against sins committed by the perfection of good works. Therefore according to the justice of God, the sinner is bound to confess his sins to a man. I say to a man who himself has the power of absolution, that is, to a priest.

Cath: Also there are two associates in absolving sinners, namely, God and the priest. For God absolves from guilt and the priest from penalties, as is clear in many passages of scripture, but it is obvious that God does not absolve the sinner, except that the sinner might reveal to Him that he sins through sorrow of heart, therefore in the same way the priest does not absolve him unless he reveals these to him through words or through other clear signs. Further, the priest absolves the sinner from the penalties of sins, but how can he absolve in those things that he does not know, so on account of this he ought to know the sins of the sinner, and for satisfaction enjoins those things which ought to be enjoined according to the number and type of sins, and according to the state in life of the sinner, which he cannot do unless he knows the sins. Matthew 3 (3:5–6) "Then Jerusalem and all Judea, and all the country about the Jordan went out to him, and they were baptized by him in the Jordan, confessing their sins." Mark 1 (1:5) "and were baptized by him in the river of Jordan, confessing their sins." Therefore confession of sins must be made to a priest. Also Matthew 18 (18:15) "But if your brother shall offend against you, go, and rebuke him between you and him alone." And Luke 17 (17:3) "Take heed for yourselves. If your brother sins against you, reprove him, and if he does penance, forgive him." So a sinner ought to make known his sins to a priest, for which the priest might rebuke him and about which he should do penance and thusly the priest might absolve him from his sin. Because how otherwise might he might rebuke him if he does not know his sins, for how could this be if he does penance, and forgives him. Therefore the priest does not

---

XXXVI.2.3 per...4 torquatur] Sap. 11:17.   30 tunc...33 sua] Matt. 3:5-6.   33 et...34 sua] Mar. 1:5.   36 si...37 solum] Matt. 18:15.
38 actendite...39 illi] Luc. 17:3.

XXXVI.1.1 Quod...sacerdotibus] om. *F*   XXXVI.2.1 Idem...eodem] om. *F*   17 Catholicus] om. *F*   18 deus² ...19 sacerdos] om. *P*
20 scripturis] om. *P*   21 corde] cordis *P*   22 ergo eodem] transp. *F*   37 uade...solum] om. *P*   39 et...illi] om. *P*

XXXVI.1.2 sacerdotibus|fol. 148vb *P*   XXXVI.2.32 iordanem|fol. 149ra *P*   39 illi|fol. 120r *F*

peccanti nisi prius ille penitentiam agat id est se ostendit paratum ad illa agendam et sic oportet quod prius sacerdos sciat eius peccatum. item. infra. lucam. xvii. quos ut uidit dixit. ite ostendite uos sacerdotibus et factum est dum irent mundati sunt etcet. ergo peccatores debent ostendere peccata sua sacerdotibus. item ad romanos. x. corde enim creditur ad iustitiam ore autem confessio sit ad salutem etcet. item iacobo. ultimo. confitemini ergo alterutrum peccata uestra et orate pro inuicem ut saluemini etcet. ergo confessio omnis facienda est sacerdotibus de peccatis. ut sit salus quia illi soli sunt qui habent potestatem absoluendi a peccatis id est a penis. peccatorum et quod de sacerdotibus loquatur patet ex superioribus ubi dicit infirmatur quis in uobis inducat presbyteros ecclesie etcet. ergo subdit confitemini alterutrum peccata uestra etcet. quare patet quod de confessione peccatorum facienda sacerdotibus loquitur.

item. iª. iohannes. iº. si confiteamur peccata nostra fidelis et iustus est ut remittat nobis peccata nostra et emundet nobis ab omni iniquitate nostra etcet. sed confiteri idem est quod cum alio fateri ergo debemus peccata reuelare aliis id est sacerdotibus quibus solis licet sacramenta ecclesiastica tractare excepto baptisme quod quibus tractare potest in necessitate cum sacerdotes inueniri non possunt. preterea propter confessionem faciendam sacerdotibus a multis cauent sibi homines. igitur facta est eius confessio. que sit sacerdotibus et patet ex supradictis quod ipsa est necessaria ad salutem scilicet siquidem fieri potest.

Patarenus: Dauid. dixi confitebor domino et tu remisisti impietatem peccati mei etcet. ergo soli deo facienda est confessio peccatorum.
Catholicus: Respondeo non dixit hoc dauid. sed dixit quod ex confessione quam fecit deo remissum est peccatum eius. quia ex contritione principaliter remittuntur peccatum cum uoluntate confitendi. sacerdoti. ut patet in illo uerbo luce. dum irent mundati sunt. uel per dominum intelligitur deus et sacerdos.

Patarenus: preterea. numquam legitur quod christus audiuerit confessiones peccatorum quos mundabat.
Catholicus: Responsio. quia nulla erat indigentia audiendi. tum quia ipse sciebat peccata eorum. tum quia non latebat peccatoribus hoc. et ideo ita erubescant coram eo ac si primo ore dicerent illa. sed modo respondete mihi. nonne uos miserrimi facitis cum fratres uestros accusare se de peccatis comissis post uestri status susceptionem coram uobis. ergo ut incidatis in foueam quam parastis uos confitemini

remit the sin to the sinner unless first he does penance, that is, he shows himself ready to do it, and thus it is fitting that before [this moment] the priest should know his sins. Also later in Luke 17 (17:14) "Whom when he saw him, said, 'Go, show yourselves to the priests.' And it came to pass, as they went, they were made clean." Therefore sinners ought to show their sins to priests. Also Romans 10 (10:10) "For, with the heart, we believe unto justice, but with the mouth confession is made unto salvation." Also James at the end (5:16) "Confess therefore your sins to one another, and pray one for another, that you may be saved." Therefore all confession of sins is to be made to priests that one might be saved, since they alone are those who have the power of absolving from sins, that is, from punishment of sins, and that he is speaking of priests is clear from the foregoing words, where he says (5:15) "Is any man sick among you? Let him bring in the priests of the church." Therefore he subjoins "Confess therefore your sins to one another." Hence it is obvious that he is saying that confession of sins is to be made to priests.

Also 1 John 1 (1:9) "If we confess our sins, he is faithful and just, to forgive us our sins, and to cleanse us from all iniquity." But to confess is the same as to disclose it to another, therefore we ought to reveal our sins to others, that is, to priests, to whom alone it is permitted to celebrate the sacraments of the Church, with the exception of baptism, which anyone can celebrate in case of necessity when priests are unable to be found. Further, on account of making confession to priests men are on guard against many things for themselves. Therefore one must make his confession, which is to priests, and it is obvious from the foregoing that this is necessary for salvation, namely, insofar as one is able.

Pat: David (Ps 31:5) "I said I will confess . . . to the Lord, and you have forgiven the wickedness of my sin." Therefore confession of sins is to be made only to God.
Cath: I reply that David did not say this, but that his sin was remitted through confession which he made to God, since it is principally by contrition that sins are forgiven, with the resolve to confess them to a priest, as is clear in that passage in Luke (17:14) "as they went, they were made clean." Or through the [word] 'Lord,' God and the priest are to be understood.

Pat: Further it is never read that Christ heard confessions of sinners whom He then made clean.
Cath: I reply that there was never any need to hear them, since He knew their sins. This knowledge did not escape sinners, and so they would blush before Him even as they uttered the first word to Him. But answer me, are you not made most miserable since your brethren accuse themselves of sins committed after their reception of your rank in your presence? Therefore lest you fall into the pit which you prepared for yourselves, profess that sins are to

peccata esse confitenda hominibus. nec potestis dicere quod aliqua sint confitenda et aliqua non. quia eadem est ratio de uno que et de alio. et ubi eadem est ratio. eadem est iuris censura.

be confessed to men. Neither are you able to say that some sins are to be confessed and others not, since the same reason applies to one as to the other, and where the reason is the same, there is the same censure of the law.

De purgatorio XXXVII

Quod autem sit purgatorium probari potest tam rationabiliter quam per scriptura.
Catholicus: Deus iustus est et reddit uniuscuisque secundum opera sua. sed esto quod duo peccauerunt unus parum et alter longe plus. ambo simul penitent et equaliter conteruntur et statim moriuntur. sed aut sufficit eis ista contritio ad salutem. et tunc peccantes pro equalia satisfactione consequitur ad salutem quod non est iustum aut requiritur penitentia exterior. sed non potest amplius fieri ab eis in hoc mundo. quia mortui sunt. nec in paradiso potest fieri. quia ibi nulla datur pena. nec in inferno quia illuc non uadunt contriti. ergo restat locus medius qui purgatorius dicitur ubi plus et minus punitatur pro meritis uniuscuiusque secundum quod dei iustitia requirit.
Catholicus: Item ponatur quod aliquis sine mortali existat et comittat ueniale et comittendo ueniale moriatur. iste simul non potest commitere et purgari et non est dignum ut intret in paradisum nisi purgatus. nec in infernum cum non habet mortale. et si dicis quod nullum est peccatum ueniale contradicit tibi scriptura diuina. aboret etiam ratio quia non est deus tam crudelis reputandus ut pro qualibet peccato modico dampnaret hominem in inferno.

preterea. phylosophy. etiam cesserunt hoc. unde augustinus. in libro de ciuitate dei dicit. quod platonici dicebant. nullas penas nisi que purgant animas esse post mortem.

Quod purgatorium sit iterum probatur

Mattheus. xii. omne peccatum et blasphemia remittetur hominibus etcet. et infra. qui autem dixerit contra spiritum sanctum uerbi non remittetur ei neque in hoc seculo neque in futuro. ergo est aliquod genus peccata remiscibile in futuro. sed hoc non potest esse in paradiso uel in inferno ut supra dictum est. ergo in purgatorio erit. item. i^a. ad corinthios. iii^o. si quis autem superhedificat super fundamentum hoc. aurum. argentum. lapides. pretiosos. ligna. fenum. stipulam. uniuscuiusque opus manifestum erit dies enim domini declarabit. si cuius opus manserit. quod superhedificauit mercedem accipiat. si cuius opus asserit detrimentum patietur. ipse autem saluus erit. sic tamen

On Purgatory

That also there is a purgatory can be proven both rationally and from scripture.
Cath: God is just and renders to each person according to their works, but suppose that two men sin, one a little bit, and the other more seriously. But both suddenly repent and are shriven and immediately die. But either that contrition is sufficient for them for salvation, and then sinning with equal satisfaction results in salvation, which is not just, or external penance is required. But unable to do any more in this world, because they are dead, neither can it be done in paradise, since there no penance is given, nor in hell, since the contrite do not go there. So it remains that there is a middle place which is called purgatory, where one is punished more or less according to each one's deserts, as the justice of God requires.

Cath: Further one may suppose that one could live without mortal sin, and yet commit venial sins, and in committing venial sins one might die. This person cannot commit and purge at the same time, and is unworthy to enter into paradise unless he be purged. Neither is he sent to hell since he does not have mortal sin. Yet if you say that there is no such thing as venial sin the divine scripture contradicts you, reason abhors that there should be a God regarded as so cruel that for any little sin He would condemn a man to hell.

Further the philosophers also draw back from this, whence Augustine in his book the City of God says (21.13) "The Platonists, indeed, maintain that no sins exist after death except those that expiate the soul."

That Purgatory exists again be proven

Matthew 12 (12:31) "Therefore I say to you, Every sin and blasphemy shall be forgiven men," and later (12:32) "but he who shall speak against the Holy Spirit, it shall not be forgiven him, neither in this world, nor in the world to come." Therefore there is a kind of sin that can be remitted in the future, but this cannot be in paradise or in hell, as was said above, therefore it will be in purgatory. Also 1 Corinthians 3 (3:12) "Now if any man build upon this foundation, gold, silver, precious stones, wood, hay, straw. Every man's work shall be manifest, for the day of the Lord shall declare it, because it shall be revealed in fire and the fire shall try every man's work, of what kind it is. If any man's work abide, which he has built thereupon, he

---

XXXVII.1.27 quod...29 mortem] Augustine, *De. Civ. Dei*, 21.13.   XXXVII.2.2 omne...3 hominibus] Matt. 12:31.   3 qui...5 futuro] Matt. 12:32.   8 si...15 ignem] 1 Cor. 3:12-15.

98 est] ratio et *P*   XXXVII.1.1 De purgatorio] om. *F*   4 Catholicus] om. *F*   13 pena] om. *P*   17 Catholicus] om. *F*   20 in] om. *F*   21 et...22 ueniale] om. *P*   25 inferno] add. Patarenus *P*   XXXVII.2.1 Quod...probatur] om. *F*   5 ergo...6 futuro] om. *P*

98 censura|fol. 120v *F*   XXXVII.1.21 non|fol. 149vb *P*

quasi per ignem etcet. hoc non potest intelligi de presenti tempore quia dies domini non declarat modo opus uniuscuiusque. preterea. tam ille qui hedificat aurum et argentum et lapides pretiosos quam ille qui hedificat lignum. fenum et stipulam mercedem recipiet uite eterne in alia uita. et utroque hic patitur detrimentum pene temporalis. nec potest hoc intelligi de hoc igne infernali quia per illum nullus saluatur. nec potest intelligi de paradiso. quia ibi non est ignis ardens et detrimentum faciens. ergo necessario intelligitur de igne purgatorii per quem transeuntes. qui hedificauerunt aurum. argentum et lapides pretiosos id est qui habuerunt opera pura uel purificata recipient mercedem id est inmmunitate a pena et alii qui hedificauertur ligna. fenum. stipulari id est opera contaminata de quibus plenarie non satisfecerunt. detrimentientur patientur quasi per ignem id est uere per ignem. leuitici. xxiii. ubi loquitur lex de festo quod erat. x. die. vii. mensis. quod uocabatur tribus nominibus scilicet dies propitiationis. quia ea die sanguine uitule russe expiabatur tabernaculum et altare. et ipsi a peccatis anni illius expiabant per emissionem yrci. dies afflictionis quia ea die ieiunabant homines et iumenta a uespera usque ad uesperam pro memoria mortuorum. inutile autem esset pro illis qui sunt in paradiso uel in inferno hoc facere. ergo secundum legem erat alius locus ubi positi erat quibus hoc prosunt ergo suffragia prosunt defunctis. item ii^a. mach. in fine. facta collatione xii millia dragmas argenti misit ierosolymam offerri pro peccatis mortuorum sacrificium etcet. obsequia prosunt defunctis. item. i^a. ad corinthios. xv. si omnino mortui non resurgunt ut quid et baptizantur pro illis etcet. ergo secundum paulum non est ibi utile baptizari pro mortuis quod non intelligit de baptismo sacramenti. quia in illo baptizari pro mortuis penitus esset inutile. ergo loquitur de alio baptismo scilicet de illa purgatione que sit per elemosinas et ieiunia et huius. ergo talia non fuerit inutiliter pro mortuis. item. i^a. iohannes. ultimo. est peccatum ad mortem non pro illo dico ut roget quis etcet. sed hoc non intellexit de peccato uiuentis. quia pro illo possumus orare quandoque exemplo domini qui etiam pro persecutoribus suis exorauit. si autem de peccato mortui intellexit. ergo dat intelligere a contrariis. quod aliquid est genus peccati non mortuis pro quo potest orari. ergo oratio prodest defunctis. preterea. in euangelio et in actibus apostolorum legitur quod orationes quorumdam profuerunt defunctis quia per illas fuerunt a morte suscitati multo fortius debent sibi prodesse ad pene temporalis dimissionem. item qui sunt in purgatorio aut sunt de ecclesia triumphante. de triumphante non sunt. quia non sunt in triumpho. ergo sunt de corpore

shall receive a reward. If any man's work burn, he shall suffer loss, but he himself shall be saved, yet so as by fire." One cannot interpret this according to the present age, since the day of the Lord does not declare the works of each, further both he who builds in gold, and silver and precious stones, and he who builds with wood, hay, and straw will receive eternal life in the next life, and both shall suffer here the defeat of earthly pain. Neither is one able to understand this of hellfire, since through it no one is saved. Neither is one able to interpret paradise here, since there is no burning fire there, nor is any defeat suffered. Therefore it is necessary to interpret it as purgatorial fire through which they pass. Regarding those who built in gold, silver, and precious stones, that is, who have pure works or they have received the purification of mercy, that is, of immunity to punishment, and others who have built in wood, hay, and straw, that is, contaminated works of which they have not fully atoned for, they shall be defeated by suffering as if through fire, that is, truly through fire. Leviticus 23 (23:27) where the law speaks of the feast on the tenth day of the seventh month, which was called by three titles, namely, "the day of atonement," since on that day the altar and tabernacle were cleansed by the blood of the red calf, and they were cleansed from their sins for the year by the releasing of the goat. "The day of affliction" since on that day men and beasts fasted from evening until the next evening for the memory of the dead, but this would have been useless to do for those who were in paradise or in hell, therefore according to the law, there was another place where some were found in which they were able to benefit from suffrages for the dead. Also in 2 Maccabees at the end (12:43) "And making a collection he sent twelve thousand drachmas of silver to Jerusalem for sacrifice to be offered for the sins of the dead." Therefore offerings can benefit the dead. Also 1 Corinthians 15 (15:29) "if the dead do not rise again at all, why are they then baptized for them?" Therefore according to Paul here it is not fruitful to be baptized for the dead, but he does not mean sacramental baptism, since in that baptism to be baptized for the dead is thoroughly useless. Therefore he is speaking of another baptism, namely, of that purgation whereby offerings and fastings and the like are done. Therefore such things are not done vainly for the dead. Further 1 John at the end (5:17, 16) "And there is a sin unto death, for that I do not say that any man asks." But he does not understand it as a sin of a living man, since we are able to pray for him anytime, following the example of the Lord who even pleaded for his persecutors. But if he understood it as a sin of a dead man, then one should understand the contrary, that there is a type of sin not for the dead, for which we are able to pray, therefore prayer benefits the dead. Further one reads in the gospel and in the Acts of the Apostles that the prayers of some people benefitted the dead, since through them some were raised from the dead, how much more ought they to be a benefit

---

32 ubi...33 mensis] Lev. 23:27.   43 facta...45 sacrificium] 2 Macc. 12:43.   46 si...47 illis] 1 Cor. 15:29.   54 est...55 quis] 1 Ioh. 5:17, 16.

22 hoc] om. *F*   38 ad] add. mane *F* exp.   42 hoc] add. su *P* exp.

XXXVII.2.20 uite|fol. 150ra *P*   29 est|fol. 121r *F*   43 collatione|fol. 150rb *P*

militantis ecclesie et cibus corporis omnibus membris prodest. ergo bona que facit ecclesia militans prosunt illis.

Item De purgatorio

Hereticus: Mattheus xxiiii. orate autem ut non fiat fuga uestra in hyeme uel sabbato etcet. sed per sabbatum intelligit aliam uitam. etiam secundam glosas uestras. ergo non est purgatorius locus in quo possit aliquis fugere et cui prosint aliqua obsequia.

Catholicus: Responsio. loquitur de illis qui non habent hic contritionem. simile est illud. quicumque potest manus tua instanter operare quia non sciam nec opus apud inferos qui tu properas. uel aliter. non est fugiendus in alia uita per opera meritoria.

Hereticus: Item ii^a. ad corinthios. v. scimus enim quoniam si terrestris domus nostra huius habitationis dissoluatur. quod hedeficationem a deo habemus. domum non manufactam. eternam in celis etcet. ergo statim post dissolutionem corporis boni uadunt in celum et sic non est purgatorium et inutilia sint suffragia pro defunctis.

Catholicus: Responsio. non dicit hic paulus. sed dicit quod post dissolutionem corporis id est non ante habemus uitam eternam ut innuit ex subsequentibus.

[**Hereticus:**] Item ad Galathas. ultimo. unusquisque enim onus suum portabit etcet. et infra. que enim seminauerit homo hec et metet etcet. ergo tantum opera que fecit hic homo nocebunt uel proderunt ei in alia uita.

[**Catholicus:**] Non dicit apostolus tantum. preterea loquitur de operibus meritoriis. et de meritoriis que quis per se facit et in hunc modum introducunt multa que ad rem non faciunt. sed dicite mihi uos heretici nonne oratis pro defunctis uestris. et scio quod facitis. ergo innuitis esse locum purgatorium. ubi sunt suffragia prosunt defunctis uel alias uos stultos et fatuos esse ostenditis.

to those for the remission of temporal punishment. Also those who are in purgatory are either in the Church Triumphant but they are not in triumph therefore they are of the body of the Church Militant, and bodily food is of benefit to all members. Therefore the good things that the Church Militant does are is useful to them.

Also on Purgatory

Heretic: Matthew 24 (24:20) "But pray that your flight may not be in the winter, or on the Sabbath." But by the Sabbath is understood another life, also according to your glosses. Therefore there is not a place of purgation in which anyone can flee and to which offerings are able to be of benefit.

Cath: Response. It is speaking of these who do not have contrition here. This is similar (Eccl 9:10) "Whatsoever your hand is able to do, do it earnestly, for neither work, nor reason, nor wisdom, nor knowledge shall be in hell, where you are hastening." Or to put it another way, there is no flight in the next life through meritorious works.

Heretic: Also 2 Corinthians 5 (5:1) "For we know, if our earthly house of this habitation be dissolved, that we have a building of God, a house not made with hands, eternal in heaven." Therefore immediately after the dissolution of the body, the good go to heaven, and so there is no purgatory, and suffrages for the dead are in vain.

Cath: Response. Paul does not say "here," but he says after the dissolution of the body, that is, not before we have eternal life, as one can infer from the following.

[**Heretic:**] Also at the end of Galatians (6:5) "For everyone shall bear his own burden," and later (6:8) "For what things a man shall sow, those also shall he reap." Therefore only the works which a man does here shall either harm or profit him in the next life.

[**Cath:**] The Apostle does not only say this of meritorious works. He is speaking also of meritorious works which one does for oneself and in this way they introduce many things not to the point. But tell me, do you heretics not pray for your dead? I know you do, therefore you tacitly agree there to be a place of purgation where suffrages are beneficial for the dead, or otherwise you are fools and show yourselves to be stupid.

XXXVII.3.2 orate…3 sabbato] Matt. 24:20.   8 quicumque…10 properas] Eccl. 9:10.   12 scimus…15 celis] 2 Cor. 5:1.   22 unusquisque…23 portabit] Gal. 6:5.   23 que…24 metet] Gal. 6:8.

XXXVII.3.1 Item…purgatorio] om. *F*   7 Catholicus] om. *F*   12 Hereticus] om. *F*   19 Catholicus] om. *F*   28 de meritoriis] om. *P*   30 que] add. re *P* exp.

XXXVII.3.5 est|fol. 150va *P*   17 celum|fol. 121v *F*   34 ostenditis|fol. 150vb *P*

INDEX BIBLICVM

Gen. 1	1-2.	86			21.	343
	1.	59			23.	109
	2.	59	Deut. 23		19.	222, 224
	3.	59	Deut. 24		7.	343
	22.	86-87	Deut. 32		29.	88
	25-26.	59-60			39.	21
	26.	89	Iudic. 20		2.	91
	27.	170			22.	92
	28.	87			23.	92
Gen. 2	17.	90			28.	92
	21.	182	1 Reg. 15		29.	92
Gen. 3	5.	59			30.	92
	15.	87	1 Reg. 18		10.	93
	17.	87	2 Reg. 24		1.	93
	18.	87			17.	93
	19.	222	3 Reg. 22		20.	93
	22.	87-88, 90	Neh. 5		7.	222
Gen. 4	11.	87			9.	222
Gen. 6	5.	89			13.	222
	6.	89	Tob. 8		5.	48
	7.	150	Iob 7		20.	42
Gen. 9	20-27.	296	Iob 19		25-27.	178
Gen. 17	8.	90	Iob 34		24-25.	44
	14.	88	Iob 40		10.	22
Gen. 18	2-3.	59			14.	22
	9.	59	Ps. 1		5.	187
	10.	59	Ps. 8		8.	54
Gen. 19	17.	38	Ps. 14		1.	222
Gen. 32	28.	90, 91			5.	222
Ex. 7	1.	42	Ps. 17		27.	314
Ex. 20	2.	60	Ps. 18		5.	295
	21.	110	Ps. 21		3.	72
Ex. 21	12.	343	Ps. 24		10.	36
	14.	343	Ps. 31		5.	357
	15.	343	Ps. 32		6.	60
	23.	349			7.	60
Ex. 22	18.	343, 349			15.	169
	19.	343	Ps. 44		10.	296
	20.	343	Ps. 49		16-18.	320-22
	28.	42			16.	97
Ex. 23	7.	349	Ps. 50		7.	42
Ex. 37	5-6.	178			9.	42
Lev. 19	18.	350	Ps. 54		12.	222
Lev. 20	2.	343	Ps. 57		11.	188
	9.	343	Ps. 65		12.	174
	10.	343	Ps. 66		7-8.	60
	13.	343			8.	60
	15.	343	Ps. 73		23.	153
	27.	343	Ps. 76		4.	223
Lev. 23	27.	360	Ps. 77		39.	44
Num. 16	1.	343			49.	94
Deut. 5	16.	117	Ps. 80		10.	39
Deut. 6	4.	63	Ps. 81		6.	42
Deut. 13	1.	343	Ps. 84		2.	87
	5.	343	Ps. 86		5.	64-65
	13.	48	Ps. 95		5.	39-40, 42
Deut. 18	20.	343	Ps. 101		26.	21-22
Deut. 19	16.	343	Ps. 103		26.	22
	21.	343, 349	Ps. 109		3.	65
Deut. 21	18.	343			7.	65

Ps. 113	12.	40		21-22.	161
	25.	315	Is. 25	8.	37
Ps. 119	5.	161	Is. 27	1.	162
Ps. 136	1.	174	Is. 29	11-12.	231
Ps. 138	22.	111	Is. 34	10.	37
Ps. 141	8.	47	Is. 40	3.	127
Ps. 148	12.	296	Is. 42	5.	22, 170
Pr. 13	24.	351	Is. 43	12-13.	21
Pr. 27	6.	351		25.	197
Eccl. 1	4.	48, 172, 187	Is. 44	6.	21
	9.	172		10.	39
	10.	52, 172		24-25.	22
	14.	42-43	Is. 45	6.	21
Eccl. 3	19.	275		9.	22
Eccl. 9	10.	360		12.	22
Eccl. 12	13-14.	276		23.	21
Cant. 4	7.	316	Is. 48	13.	22
Cant. 6	8.	291	Is. 52	6.	65
Sap 2	25.	51	Is. 53	8.	67
Sap. 1	13.	52	Is. 54	16.	22
	16.	52	Is. 63	12.	37
Sap. 2	1.	276	Is. 66	4.	110
	24.	51, 132	Ier. 2	11.	40
Sap. 5	1.	188		32.	162
Sap. 7	22.	82	Ier. 3	1.	162
Sap. 9	15.	47	Ier. 10	10.	22
Sap. 11	17.	356		12-13.	22
Sap. 12	8.	43-44		16.	22
	10.	43, 44, 49	Ier. 13	11.	44
	11.	43, 44		32.	44
	20.	44	Ier. 17	1.	44
Ecclesiastic. 42	24.	187		5.	195, 197
Ecclesiastic. 3	1.	315		20.	45
Ecclesiastic. 10	2.	53		22.	45
Ecclesiastic. 11	14.	44	Ier. 23	16.	118
Ecclesiastic. 14	18-19.	173	Ier. 27	5.	22
Ecclesiastic. 18	1.	172		14-15.	118
Ecclesiastic. 23	9.	333	Ier. 29	7.	111
Ecclesiastic. 24	5.	65, 72	Ier. 31	35.	22
	6.	65	Lam. Ier. 4	2.	162
	13.	65	Bar. 3	10.	162
	14.	71-72		14.	162
Ecclesiastic. 33	15.	44		19.	162
Ecclesiastic. 39	30.	38		36-37.	65
	33.	50		36.	21
	35-36.	50	Ez. 3	18.	260
Ecclesiastic. 40	9-10.	50		20.	260
Ecclesiastic. 42	23.	187	Ez. 14	14.	296
	25	44	Ez. 18	20.	210
Ecclesiastic. 47	15.	37	Ez. 20	25-26.	110
Ecclesiastic. 48	27.	37	Ez. 22	12.	222
Is. 1	5.	308	Ez. 23	4.	95
Is. 5	20.	76	Ez. 28	3.	159
Is. 6	3.	60		11.	159
Is. 7	14.	65		14.	159
Is. 8	12.	333		16.	159
Is. 9	3.	129		18.	159
	6.	65, 76		19.	159
Is. 11	2-3.	82	Ez. 35	3.	37
Is. 14	4.	158		4.	37
	11.	158		5.	37
	12.	158		11.	37
	13.	158	Ez. 37	1.	178
	14.	158		12.	178
	19.	158	Dan. 12	2.	162
Is. 24	5.	37		2.	178

INDEX BIBLICVM

Dan. 13	55.	346		43.	111, 280, 350, 352
Amos 3	6.	94		44.	111
Ion. 1	12.	132		45.	26
Mic. 5	2.	65		48.	74, 247, 328
	13.	97	Matt. 6	16.	302
Zac. 5	3.	329		22.	299
	4.	329		24.	52
Mal. 2	2.	325		25.	26, 27
	11.	40		26.	26, 27
Mal. 3	1.	75-76		28.	27
	1.	127		30.	27
2 Macc. 12	43-44.	178		32.	27
	43.	360		33.	27
Matt. 1	1.	134-36	Matt. 7	1-2.	219
	1.	65, 123, 145		1.	353
	16.	122-23, 136-37, 234-35		3.	321-22
	18.	67, 122, 235		5.	248
	20.	235		6.	88
	22-23.	97		12.	221, 280
	25.	137		14.	310
Matt. 2	9.	38		15.	298
	10.	137		18.	45, 299, 321-22
	11.	306		22-23.	300
	14.	102	Matt. 8	1.	103-04
	17-18.	97		4.	101
	19.	102		8-9.	67
	23.	97		10.	69
Matt. 3	3.	127		11.	295
	4.	127		13.	205-06
	5-6.	357		20.	136
	6-7.	127		24.	139
	11.	127, 206		26.	69
	12.	27, 187, 310-11		29.	19, 53, 149, 162
	13.	127		31.	19, 29
	14.	127	Matt. 9	2.	206
	17.	127		6.	67
Matt. 4	2.	137, 144		10.	137, 139, 311
	3.	69		11.	137
	4.	97, 148		12.	311
	7.	97		16.	116, 117
	8.	53		17.	32
	9.	53, 69	Matt. 10	1.	306, 318
	10.	97		2.	319
	17.	217-19, 221		5.	163, 320
Matt. 5	3.	223, 284, 310		6.	163
	5.	310		7.	320
	13.	197, 321-22		14-15.	210
	14.	197-98, 270, 294, 298		20.	198
	15.	294		27.	294
	16.	298, 321-22		34.	87
	17.	86, 102, 243, 279-80,		37.	244
331			Matt. 11	2-3.	127-28
	18.	189		4.	128
	20.	243, 331		6.	128
	21.	280, 348, 352		7.	128
	22.	349		9.	127
	23-24.	219-21		10.	127, 130
	24.	333		11.	127
	27.	243, 280		13.	86, 116
	28.	242-43		19.	137
	32.	237, 243		22.	189-90
	33-37.	329		23.	260
	33.	280, 333		27.	32, 70, 72
	37.	325		28.	194, 211-13, 260
	38.	88, 349		30.	213
	39.	88, 337, 350	Matt. 12	3.	97

	4.	83		10.	206
	7.	215		15.	312, 351, 357
	8.	67		17-18.	343
	9.	139		18.	334
	10.	43		19.	304, 325
	17.	352		21.	351
	25.	69		23.	30
	31.	78, 358-60		25.	213
	32.	200, 360		26-27.	213
	33.	321-22		28.	255
	34.	265, 321-22		34.	94
	35.	299, 321-22	Matt. 19	3-6.	235
	36-37.	219		3.	242
	41.	190		4.	30-31, 38, 83
	42.	190		6.	83, 236
	43.	29-30		7.	236
	47.	137		8.	236, 246
	48.	144		9.	235
Matt. 13	1-2.	354		10.	244
	1.	139		11.	244
	8.	190-91, 296		12.	243-44
	15.	260		16.	101
	17.	108-09		17.	23, 40, 63, 86, 101, 117, 213, 244, 287
	24.	24-25, 67, 311, 353			
	28.	311		18.	86, 221
	29.	311, 354		19.	221-22
	37.	67		21.	244, 287
	40-41.	142-43		23.	219
	40.	311, 354, 142-43		26.	33
	41.	25, 142-43, 189, 186, 219		28.	191, 192
				29.	192, 244, 287
	42.	187, 219		30.	192
	47.	311	Matt. 20	1.	25
	52.	86, 97, 109, 290		6.	38, 219, 222
Matt. 14	3.	127		7.	222
	10-11.	127		10.	192
	26-27.	136		11.	192
Matt. 15	2.	110-11		16.	117, 168-69
	3.	83, 101, 244, 252, 337, 349		18-19.	140
				23.	265
	4.	83, 244, 337, 349	Matt. 21	12.	343-44
	8-9.	208		13.	219
	11.	252		19.	87
	13.	45, 265		32.	127
	14.	321-22		33.	30, 85
	19.	253		37.	90
	20.	242		41.	85
	24.	163		42.	97
	26.	173		43.	337
	28.	206		45.	337
	36.	306	Matt. 22	2.	312
Matt. 16	6.	298		4.	296
	18.	235, 297, 303, 306		7.	188, 337
	19.	304, 306, 352		10.	312
	21.	139-40		11.	312
	27.	28, 67, 219		13.	187
Matt. 17	1-2.	144		21.	221, 337
	3.	107		23.	178-80
	12.	130, 140		29-30.	180
	13.	130, 140		29.	293
	26.	87, 221, 286		30.	122, 184
Matt. 18	2-3.	206		31-32.	180
	4.	191		43.	97
	5.	206	Matt. 23	2-3.	320
	6.	206, 221		3.	219
	7.	221		13.	190

INDEX BIBLICVM

	15.	190, 298		5.	94, 134, 350
	16.	331		20.	139
	22.	331		26.	38
	23.	101, 290		27.	33
	24.	221, 248		28-29.	190
	25.	221, 242	Mar. 6	7.	249, 320
	35.	102, 107-08		8.	287
	37.	108		12.	219, 320
Matt. 24	15.	97		13.	249, 320
	20.	200, 360	Mar. 7	21.	221
	22.	91	Mar. 9	21-22.	206
	27.	143		22.	63
	30-31	143		35-36.	206
	30.	143, 310	Mar. 10	6.	31, 38
	31.	143		18.	23, 41
	35.	189		19.	101
	44.	143		24.	221
Matt. 25	12.	72		25.	310
	14.	30	Mar. 11	25.	219
	22.	192-93	Mar. 12	9.	337
	23.	193		12.	337
	27.	225		24.	293
	31-32.	143, 185-86		32.	23
	34.	87, 185		34.	23
	35.	186.	Mar. 13	10.	295
	41.	27, 52, 87, 153-55, 187		32.	72
Matt. 26	12.	140		37.	286
	12.	136	Mar. 14	6-7.	286
	13.	295		21-24.	227
	18.	306		25.	137
	20.	137		33-34.	134
	23.	137		36.	33
	24.	173	Mar. 15	15.	136
	26-28.	227		44.	140
	30.	306	Mar. 16	7.	123
	38	133		9.	223
	38.	89		15.	205, 210, 281, 295
	38.	223		16.	205, 209, 282, 224
	39.	73, 133-34, 266		17.	211, 300
	52.	351		18.	211
	54.	348		19.	142
	56.	97		20.	300
	64.	143	Luc. 1	6-7.	236-37
Matt. 27	28.	139		6.	127
	31.	139		9.	306
	35.	139-40		13.	127
	46.	72, 134		13.	127
	47.	140		14.	127
	50.	134		15.	127
	52-53.	180		16.	127
	58-60.	136, 140		17.	127, 130
Matt. 28	5-6.	140		18.	127
	9.	69		19-20.	28
	18.	33		19.	127
	19-20.	202-05		26.	123, 127
	19.	60, 81, 163, 207, 283,		28.	122
289, 295				31.	137
	20.	199		32.	53
Mar. 1	2.	97		33.	52, 75
	5.	357		36.	122
	7.	127, 139		38.	122
	9.	127, 136		41.	127
Mar. 2	7.	67		42.	122, 127
	16.	137		43.	67, 127, 137
	27.	26		44.	127, 169
Mar. 3	1.	139		46.	122

	48.	122		14.	348
	58.	127, 169		15.	221, 348
	63-64.	127		25.	31
	65.	127		47-48	190
	67-68.	127	Luc. 13	2-3.	219
	70.	108		6.	30
Luc. 2	1.	162		24.	266
	4-5.	122		28.	104, 108, 192
	7.	137		29.	192
	16.	169		30.	192
	21.	102, 136, 279		48.	268
	22.	101, 102, 279	Luc. 14	1.	137, 139
	23.	101, 279		20.	244
	29.	152		26.	244, 351
	34.	140	Luc. 15	2.	137
	42.	101-02, 169		3.	164
	48.	137		4.	163
	49.	67		6-7.	164
Luc. 3	7.	127		8.	163
	16.	127		11.	48
	19-20.	127	Luc. 16	1.	159
	21.	127, 205		8.	48, 160, 225
	23.	136, 144, 169		9.	52, 160, 224-25
	27-29	129		14.	224
	38.	31, 136		19.	219
Luc. 4	6.	53		22.	187, 219
	16.	304		23.	186
	26.	101		24.	19
	27.	101, 107		25.	284
Luc. 5	29.	137		26.	19
	36.	280		29.	101
Luc. 6	20.	55	Luc. 17	1.	266
	35.	222		3.	357
	36.	74		10.	130
	37.	353		14.	279, 357
	38.	191		24.	143
Luc. 7	19.	129		29-30.	186
	23.	129	Luc. 18	6.	225
	24.	129		7.	28, 225
	25.	127, 129		8.	28
	28.	128-29		19.	17, 22
	34.	137		22-23.	338
	36.	139	Luc. 19	5.	139
	47.	191		8.	221
	50.	223		9.	221
Luc. 7-4-5.		139		23.	225
Luc. 8	23.	139		27.	28, 337-38, 344-45
	44.	138		41.	337
Luc. 9	54.	354		43.	337
	55-56.	219		46.	306
	55.	223	Luc. 20	15-16.	28, 338
	56.	155, 223		41.	145
Luc. 10	1.	306		47.	190
	7.	252	Luc. 21	15.	293
	8.	252		20.	337
	18.	30		22.	28
	19.	310		24.	337
	22.	53		27.	143
	35.	306	Luc. 22	1.	101
Luc. 11	17.	291		3.	312-14
	27.	122, 137		7	137-38, 279
	28.	122		8.	138, 279
	39-40.	31		11.	101, 138
	41.	224, 285-86		13.	138
Luc. 12	4-5.	28		14.	285, 314
	13-14.	347		15-16.	138

	17.	314		18.	69, 187-88, 345
	18.	230		20.	294, 336
	19.	231-32, 227, 285, 304		22.	205
	20.	227		25.	129
	21.	230, 314		27.	127, 266
	25-26.	87		29.	127
	29.	161		31.	69
	36.	306, 338	Ioh. 4	1-2.	205
	38.	306, 338		2.	320
	43.	134, 139		6.	139
	44.	139		12.	22
	53.	55		23.	299
Luc. 23	11.	139		24.	79, 223
	28.	337		32.	148
	43-44.	148		34.	148
	43.	213		36.	108
	46.	134		38.	108
Luc. 24	25.	101, 141, 290, 350	Ioh. 5	1.	306
	26.	141		17.	70, 169
	38.	140		18.	70, 169
	39.	136, 140		19.	70, 169
	41-43.	138		22.	143
	44.	148		27.	143
	46.	148		28.	143, 162, 180
	49.	195		29.	180
	51.	142		33.	127
Luc. 26	52.	347		35.	127, 129
Ioh. 1	1.	38, 70		39.	98, 293
	3.	23, 67		43.	118
	4.	45		44.	23
	6-7.	127		45.	98
	8.	129		46.	101, 105
	10.	25, 51, 54	Ioh. 6	4.	101
	11.	30		19.	146
	12-13.	45		31.	117, 230
	12.	46		37.	266
	13.	47-48		39.	180
	14.	147		41.	146
	17.	111		44.	266
	18.	67		45.	97
	20.	127		50.	230
	21.	129		54-56.	230
	22-23.	127		56.	146, 232
	27.	127		64.	232-33
	29.	127		71.	173, 270, 320
	33.	195-97		72.	320
	34-36.	127	Ioh. 7	15.	294
	38-39.	139		19.	98
	42.	91		24.	338, 353
Ioh. 2	1.	235		38.	206
	3.	145		39.	117-18, 206
	4.	145	Ioh. 8	7.	338
	5.	145		10.	348
	15.	302, 304, 344		11.	88, 224, 347
	17.	97, 302		12.	270
	19.	136		15.	347-48
	21.	136		16.	348
	25.	69		19.	67
Ioh. 3	3.	170, 289		23.	46
	5.	171, 205, 282, 283, 289,		24.	46
326				25.	69
	6.	46, 174, 289		27.	70
	7.	46, 174		34.	51
	8.	79, 171, 174, 289		37.	104
	13.	67, 145, 153-54, 282		39.	104
	14.	101		44.	30, 37-38, 46, 48, 158

	52.	130	Ioh. 17	3.	23, 69
	54.	83		5.	32, 69
	56.	104		6.	266
	58.	104		10.	57, 72
Ioh. 9	3.	28		16.	46
	6.	136		22-23.	74
	39.	41		24.	32
Ioh. 10	1.	321, 322	Ioh. 18	6.	345
	8.	118		11.	352
	11.	134		23.	136, 350
	15.	223		36.	54
	17.	134, 219	Ioh. 19	2.	139
	18.	266		3.	280
	25.	300		11.	29, 190
	30.	71		13.	30
	32.	219		22.	30
	33.	73		23.	139
	34.	73, 86		26.	122, 137
	35-38.	73		28.	137
	37-38.	300		30.	116, 134, 219
	38.	70		33.	136
Ioh. 11	4.	28-29		34.	136
	9.	269		35.	290
	23.	180		37.	136
	33.	134	Ioh. 20	40.	136, 140
	35.	136		17.	75
	49.	320		21.	74, 118
Ioh. 12	3.	139		22.	81, 198, 285, 306, 322
	6.	314		23.	199, 285, 304, 306
	25.	223, 270		27.	136
	27.	219		28.	136
	31.	54		29.	144
	40.	41	Ioh. 21	6.	87, 286
	43.	30		15.	191, 303
	46.	30, 304		17.	352
Ioh. 13	3.	72		18.	221
	4-5.	304		20.	69
	4.	139, 306	Ioh. 22	17.	69
	10.	316, 320	Act. 1	4.	138
	12.	139		5.	207
Ioh. 14	2.	296		9.	142
	6.	315, 326		11.	142-43
	7.	70		14.	122
	8-10.	70		16.	101, 107, 320
	12.	300, 345		17.	320
	13.	197		20.	320
	16.	81		25.	320
	27.	74, 87	Act. 2	1.	198
	28.	73, 74		2.	133
	30.	53-54, 205		14.	205
Ioh. 15	2.	30		16.	97
	3.	198		19.	91
	5.	44		22.	219
	6.	315		23.	139
	8.	34		24.	140, 142
	9.	74, 198		25.	107
	13.	132, 154		27.	142
	18	46		29-31.	107
	18.	51		31.	142, 147
	19.	198, 310		38.	205
	22.	110, 112		38.	195, 207, 219, 222
	26.	60, 82		46.	306
Ioh. 16	8.	82	Act. 3	1.	306
	15.	57, 70, 72		12.	197
	23.	30		13.	83, 197
	33.	54		14.	339

INDEX BIBLICVM

	15.	219		47-48.	205
	18	79, 108	Act. 11	17.	197
	19.	219		18.	108
	24.	106, 108	Act. 12	23.	29, 94, 346
	25.	108	Act. 13	2.	216
Act. 4	12.	197		3.	216, 285
	13.	293		9-11.	346
	25.	101, 107		16-17.	83-84
	31.	197, 213		16.	101
	32.	314		17.	88
	34.	287, 298		20.	106
	35.	287		21.	101
Act. 5	1.	345		22.	84, 101, 107, 141
	4.	288		23.	84, 107, 141
	5.	345		24.	84
	10.	345		27.	108
	12.	300, 346		40-41.	97
	36-37.	297		42.	101
	38-39.	297		46.	163, 337
	38.	45	Act. 14	13.	197
	39.	268		14.	24, 197
	42.	306		16.	26
Act. 6	2.	288	Act. 15	5.	277
	3.	288		10-11.	108
	5.	214		10.	277
	6.	285		10.	115
	10.	293		20.	254
Act. 7	2.	83, 88, 101	Act. 16	5-6.	108
	5.	90		13.	300
	20.	105		26-38.	306
	24-25.	339		31.	213
	24.	105		33.	205
	26.	105		37.	339
	29-31	105	Act. 17	23.	25, 170
	36.	105		26.	26, 31, 170, 174
	37.	105		28.	17
	38.	105, 316	Act. 18	21	306
	42.	97		24.	108
	43.	40	Act. 19	1.	306
	45.	101, 105-06, 107		2-3.	205
	46.	107		2.	211
	47.	101		3.	289
	51.	101		5.	205, 211, 213, 289
	54.	83		6.	211, 213, 306
Act. 8	1.	214	Act. 20	28.	67, 306
	2.	306		34.	286
	12.	205, 213-14		35.	286
	12.	205	Act. 22	16.	205
	14.	214	Act. 23	3.	350
	15-17.	214		6.	180
	17-19.	199		16.	339
	17.	214	Act. 24	14.	86, 101, 290
	20.	200		15.	181, 290
	36.	205	Act. 25	8.	339
	38.	205		10-11.	339
Act. 9	4.	149	Act. 26	8.	180
	8.	216		13.	69
	9.	216		23.	136
	17.	205, 215	Act. 28	27.	41
	18.	205, 216	Rom. 1	1.	83
	31.	316		2.	83, 101, 108
Act. 10	11-13	252		3.	67, 83, 136
	34-35	260		7.	314
	36.	69		8.	295
	41	138		9.	79, 325
	44.	213		18.	22, 29, 94, 219

	20.	24, 37, 60, 292		10.	42
	23.	27		11.	181
	24.	41		12.	245
	24.	29		20.	170
	25.	27		21.	170
	28.	29, 41		29.	266-67
	32.	208, 219, 338-39		30.	267
Rom. 2	1.	353	Rom. 9	1.	79, 325, 326
	2.	29		2.	326
	4.	219		5.	67
	5.	29, 98, 186		8.	47
	6.	28, 186		11.	169
	8.	29		12.	267
	9.	29		13.	267
	11.	213		14.	83, 215
	12.	339		15.	83, 267
	14-15.	213		16.	267
	21.	321-22		18.	41
	23.	83		20-21.	31
	25.	279-80		22.	48
	28-29.	280	Rom. 10	4.	116
Rom. 3	1-2.	101		6-7.	142
	5-7.	263		10.	213, 357
	9.	118		12.	23, 33, 213, 260
	20.	112, 116		13.	213, 260
	22-23.	191		14.	165, 295
	22.	213		17.	165, 295
	24.	213	Rom. 11	2.	97
	27.	116		6.	197
	28.	280		11.	174-75
	29.	48		12.	175
	30.	23, 279-80		16.	109
	31.	98		17.	175
Rom. 4	1.	48, 104		20.	175, 293
	5.	213		21.	30, 175
	15	283		22-23.	198
	15.	112, 253, 335		22.	29
	18.	162		23.	175
	22.	104		24.	175-76
Rom. 5	1.	213		32.	41, 94, 164
	12.	43, 47, 173, 210		33.	272
	13.	112		36.	24, 60-61
	14.	101, 174, 210	Rom. 12	2.	50
	15.	215		3.	293
	17.	210, 282		14.	352
	20.	112-13, 132		19.	29, 352
Rom. 6	3.	205	Rom. 13	1.	88, 339, 340, 352
	7.	141-42		2.	339
	9.	140, 147		3.	335
	13.	31		4.	335, 340, 348
	19.	31, 219		5.	335, 340
	21.	219		6.	335
Rom. 7	1.	278-79		7.	221
	6.	112, 113, 279		8.	352
	7.	101, 113		9.	221
	11.	113	Rom. 14	3.	252
	12.	101, 113		10-11.	69
	14.	98		11.	33
	16.	101		12.	69, 210
	18.	46-47, 49		17.	54
	21.	101		21.	254
	22.	101	Rom. 15	4.	86, 294
	23.	47		8.	102, 280
	24.	47		26.	286
Rom. 8	3.	136, 144	Rom. 16	7.	315
	8.	245, 315		17.	315

INDEX BIBLICVM

	19.	293		6.	245
	20.	29		7.	246
	26.	32		8.	246
1 Cor. 1	2.	314		10-11.	238
	11.	314		12-14.	238
	12-13.	197		27.	238-39
	14.	205		28.	239, 241
	17.	205, 293		29.	246
	18.	141		31.	247
	19.	293		32.	247
	21.	293		33.	247
	23-24.	67, 141		34.	247
	23.	294		35.	247
	25.	45, 148		36.	239
	26.	293		37.	241
1 Cor. 2	4-5.	293		38.	241
	6.	294		39.	239
	7.	32, 249		40.	238, 239
	8.	69, 294	1 Cor. 8	4.	23, 40
	10.	164, 223		5.	40
	14.	223, 231		6.	24, 40
	15.	231		8.	252
1 Cor. 3	3.	197, 314	1 Cor. 9	9.	171, 253
	4.	197		10.	253
	6.	45, 197, 205		24.	260
	7.	197	1 Cor. 10	1.	85, 109
	8.	191, 260		3.	109
	9.	260		4.	85, 109, 228
	12-15.	360		5.	109
	16.	31, 79, 198		6.	109
	17.	321-22		9.	29, 85
	19.	293		10.	94
	20.	293		11.	101, 109, 230
	21.	197		16.	230
	22.	24		18.	230
1 Cor. 4	1.	197		20.	40, 315
	4-5.	353		21.	230, 315
	8.	90		25-28.	252
1 Cor. 5	1.	198, 219, 314		32.	352
	2.	198, 219, 315, 344	1 Cor. 11	7.	31
	3.	306		12.	31
	5.	306, 345		13-14.	31
	6-7.	315		18.	314
	11.	343		20.	233
	13.	315		21.	233, 314
1 Cor. 6	1.	340, 350, 341		22.	286, 314
	2.	306, 340, 341		23.	230
	3.	340		24.	232
	4.	314, 348		26.	232
	5.	341		27.	230
	6.	314		28-29.	230
	7.	341		30.	233, 314
	8.	221, 341	1 Cor. 12		
	9.	314-15		4.	80, 82
	10.	221		4-8.	195
	13.	31		7.	325
	14.	180		11.	79, 80, 197
	15.	31		13.	80
	16.	245		22-23.	31
	18.	31, 245		24-25.	31
	19.	31, 79		28-30.	325
	20.	31		31.	195
1 Cor. 7	1.	237, 245	1 Cor. 14	20.	293
	2.	237		26.	306
	3-4.	237		38.	293
	5.	237-38		40.	282-83

1 Cor. 15	10.	197		8.	26
	12-13.	180		10.	26
	21.	132-33	2 Cor. 10	4-5.	231
	22.	283		4.	353
	24.	74		5-6.	302
	29.	180, 360		6.	335, 345
	32.	180	2 Cor. 11	3.	101
	34.	293		4.	118
	35-38.	182-83		8.	286
	38.	183	2 Cor. 12	6.	246
	40.	183		7.	48
	41-42.	191		19.	325
	42-43.	184		21.	198
	44.	184	2 Cor. 13	13.	61
	46.	184	Gal. 1	4.	48
	47.	133, 146, 184		6.	198, 279
	48.	184		20.	325
	49.	49, 184	Gal. 2	3-4.	277
	50.	184		6.	260
	51.	181, 184, 187		9.	278
	53.	181		11.	322
	54-57.	183		16.	116, 213
1 Cor. 16	1.	286		18-19.	113
	13.	38		21.	114
	22.	306, 315	Gal. 3	1.	198
2 Cor. 1	12.	293		5.	198
	18.	331		6.	104
	23.	328		10.	118, 279
2 Cor. 2	16.	113		13.	110, 136
2 Cor. 3	5.	197		16.	91, 104
	6.	279		18.	104, 116
	7.	113		19.	86
	9.	113		20.	23
	18.	109		21.	98, 114
2 Cor. 4	2.	293		22.	114
	3-4.	290		24.	86, 101, 279
	4.	41		25.	279
	6.	24, 86		26.	46
	10-11.	181	Gal. 4	4.	116, 122, 137, 147
	13.	79		5.	116
	18.	48		8.	40
2 Cor. 5	1.	360		9-10.	116
	4.	180		22.	85, 97, 228
	4.	47		24.	85, 97
	10.	143, 180		30.	344
	16-17.	280	Gal. 5	2.	88, 277-78
	16.	146-47		4.	279
	17	173		6.	277
	17.	116, 147, 169		9.	279
	18.	24		12.	344
2 Cor. 6	1-2.	260		14.	116
	3.	352		17.	49
	10.	260		19.	219, 239, 254
	14-15.	20		21.	219
	14.	208, 315		24.	29, 310
	15.	321-22	Gal. 6	1.	198
	16.	315		5.	210, 282, 360
	17.	101, 315		8.	191, 360
2 Cor. 7	1.	219		16.	162
	2.	352	Eph 4	22-24.	49
	8-9.	198	Eph 5	15.	24
	11.	316	Eph. 1	4.	32
2 Cor. 8	19.	306		5.	267
2 Cor. 9	1.	286		7.	136
	6.	191		8.	293
	7.	302	Eph. 2	2.	53

	3.	43, 49, 282, 312		21-22.	252
	4.	282	Col. 3	1.	176
	5.	197, 282		4.	176
	6.	282		5.	49
	8-9.	197		6.	219, 260
	10.	49		9.	49, 282
	15.	116		16.	293, 306
	18.	80	Col. 4	2.	306
Eph. 3	10.	24		5-6.	293
Eph. 4	3-4.	80		6.	294
	5.	23, 205, 289, 291	1 Thes. 1	7-8.	29
	6.	33, 291	1 Thes. 4	3.	219
	7.	191		11.	286
	8.	171-72, 282		12-13.	180
	11.	325		14.	176
	14.	297		16.	176
	17.	325	1 Thes. 5	16.	302
	18.	293		19.	98, 198
	19.	299		20.	98
Eph. 5	1.	48, 317, 328		23.	180, 222-23
	5.	219		27.	325
	13.	294	2 Thes. 1	7-8.	94
	15-16.	293	2 Thes. 2	3.	291
	18-19.	306		9.	300
	18.	242		11.	41, 93, 299
	22.	239-40		12.	93, 219
	25.	205, 240, 247, 316	2 Thes. 3	6.	299, 315
	26.	205		10.	286
	27.	316		11.	286, 299
	28-29.	240		12.	286
	31-32.	240		14.	198
Eph. 6	8.	191		15.	198, 353
	24.	147	1 Tim. 1	3-4.	343
Php. 1	1.	306		6.	293, 343
	8.	325		7.	293
	14-15.	314		8.	101, 343
	17.	314		9.	98, 341-43
Php. 2	6.	70		10-11.	290
	7.	136, 143		10.	345
	10.	69, 143		17.	23, 33, 197
	11.	69		19.	301, 345
	13.	197		20.	306, 345
	15.	298	1 Tim. 2	1.	335
	20-21.	314		3.	260, 316
Php. 3	2-3.	277		4.	36, 260, 316
	16.	291		5.	23, 133
	18.	141, 219		13.	170
	19.	42, 219		14.	101, 240
	20.	69, 180, 182		15.	240
	21.	33, 69, 180,		16-18.	180
Col. 1	9.	293	1 Tim. 3	1.	322
	10.	293		2.	299, 322
	15.	69, 75		3.	299, 352
	16.	17, 24, 32, 69		8.	299
	17.	32	1 Tim. 4	1-3.	240
	18.	32		1.	26, 168, 219, 240, 252,
	20.	136			301
	28.	293		2.	240, 294, 297
Col. 2	2.	293		3.	26, 240, 301
	5.	297		4.	49-50, 252
	7.	297		5.	252-53
	8.	293		13.	293
	9.	69		14.	211, 285
	11-12.	278	1 Tim. 5	9.	285
	16.	252, 253, 279		11.	240
	17.	253		14.	240

INDEX BIBLICVM

	17.	191, 320		8.	69, 85, 282
	19.	320		9.	282
1 Tim. 6	10.	221		9-11.	172
	15.	33		15.	136
2 Tim. 1	6.	211, 285	Heb. 5	4.	105, 285, 318
	9.	267		7.	136
	15.	301		20.	69
	18.	299	Heb. 6	1.	116, 206
2 Tim. 2	2.	314		4-6.	157
	4.	219		4.	200
	8.	141		6.	158, 200
	12-13.	267		13.	328, 329
	18-19.	314		14.	328
	19.	267, 297		16.	328
	20.	314		17-19.	329
2 Tim. 3	5.	343		20.	39
	6.	299	Heb. 7	1.	39, 103
	7.	293		2.	39
	9.	293		3.	38-39
	15.	101, 293		5.	174
	16.	101, 294		6.	39
2 Tim. 4	1.	143, 325		7.	39
	14.	201, 343		10.	174
2 Tim. 6	10.	299		12.	279
Tit. 1	2.	32, 267		14.	136
	5.	285, 306, 322		18.	116
	6.	322		19.	116
	7.	322		20.	328
	9.	293		22.	116
	10-11.	277		28.	116
	16.	219	Heb. 8	7.	114
Tit. 2	1.	293		8.	85, 118
	4.	240-41		9.	85, 97
	8.	293		10.	114
	9.	339		13.	97, 116
	11.	67	Heb. 9	1.	116
	13.	67		2.	101
Tit. 3	1.	339		8.	86, 101
	4.	147		10.	116
	9.	115		11.	142
	10.	297, 343		12.	136, 142
Heb. 1	1.	79		13.	98, 101
	2.	26		14.	136
	3.	69		18.	98
	5.	69		25-26.	142
	6.	69		27.	171, 142, 234
	7.	223		28.	142, 234
	8.	69	Heb. 10	1.	86, 116
	10.	25, 187		4.	116
	11.	25, 187		5.	86, 136, 233
	12.	187		6.	86
Heb. 2	5.	69		8.	233
	8.	24		14.	142, 233
	9.	129		22.	205
	10.	24, 69, 172, 283		26.	200, 233
	14-16.	153	Heb. 11	1.	231
	16.	69		2.	108
Heb. 3	4.	24		3.	24, 26
	5-6.	105		4.	102
	7.	69, 85		5.	102
	11.	69		6.	210
	12.	69		7.	102-03
	16.	105, 109		8.	104
	19-20.	103		9.	91, 104
Heb. 4	3.	328		11.	104, 237
	4.	97, 101		12.	162

	17.	104		23.	347
	20.	104	1 Pet. 3	5.	104, 237
	23.	104-05		6.	46, 104, 237
	24-26.	105		7.	48
	27.	105		8.	291
	28.	105		15.	294
	29.	101, 105		17.	246
	30-31.	101		20.	205
	32.	106		21.	205, 207
	32.	106		22.	207
	33.	109	1 Pet. 4	1.	136
	39-40.	109, 282		5.	29
Heb. 12	5.	260		15-16.	339
	6.	29		19.	50
	7.	267, 317	1 Pet. 5	3.	306
	8.	316	2 Pet. 1	19.	108
	9.	170		21.	101, 108
	15.	202, 260	2 Pet. 2	1.	67, 291, 301
	20.	115		3.	221
	24.	119		4.	29, 85, 155, 157, 162, 186
	29.	91			
Heb. 13	4.	219, 241, 247		5.	103
	14.	161		7-9.	103
Iac. 1	5.	333		9.	186, 190
	6-8.	202		10.	33, 190, 192, 219, 339
	17.	20		11.	192, 328
	22.	333		12.	19, 50, 292
Iac. 2	6.	310		13.	299
	10.	191, 208		14.	221
	13.	215, 333		15.	301
	21.	104		19.	299
	23.	104	2 Pet. 3	3.	276
	24.	260		7.	25, 186
	25.	339		9.	260
Iac. 3	2.	43, 210		10.	189
	8.	43		15.	293
	9.	34		17.	293
	11.	34	1 Ioh. 1	5.	86
	14.	333		9.	357
	15.	50	1 Ioh. 2	7.	38
Iac. 4	1.	219		11.	219
	1.	219, 314		15.	50
	7.	333		16.	50
	9.	221, 310		19.	201, 301
Iac. 5	10.	108		27.	165
	11.	103	1 Ioh. 3	8.	27, 38, 205, 345
	12.	331, 333		9.	51, 202
	14.	211, 249, 285, 321, 322, 357		11.	102
				12.	51, 102
	15.	249		16.	51, 67
	16.	107, 321, 357		19.	201
	17.	29	1 Ioh. 4	1-2.	81
	19.	198, 333		1.	81
1 Pet. 1	2.	136		2.	81, 136, 147
	9-11.	101		3.	136
	17.	260		7.	51
	18-19.	67		8.	79
	19.	67, 136, 150	1 Ioh. 5	1.	46
	20.	32, 150		7.	61
	21.	79		16.	200-01, 360
1 Pet. 2	9.	86		17.	360
	11.	254		18.	51, 201
	13-14.	335		19.	54
	17.	339	2 Ioh. 1	7.	136
	18.	339		10-11.	343
	22.	147	Iud. 1	4.	69, 268

INDEX BIBLICVM

	5.	29, 69, 85, 155	Apoc. 10.6.		24
	6.	69, 85, 155, 157	Apoc. 10	1.	76
	7.	155		5-6.	328
	8.	33, 155, 339		7.	108
	9.	180	Apoc. 11	6.	29
	12.	198, 321-22		9.	180
	13.	301		10.	29
	14.	102, 186, 219		11.	180
	15.	186, 219		15.	26, 75, 189
	16.	299	Apoc. 12	7.	157, 160
	19.	301		8.	157
	22.	345		9.	19
	25.	23		11.	161
Apoc 5	3.	154		12.	53
Apoc. 1	1.	161	Apoc. 13	2.	54, 307
	4.	69, 82		8.	149
	5.	69, 136, 180		11.	29
	7.	140, 180, 188		14.	300, 307
	8.	38, 69		15.	55, 308
	10.	306	Apoc. 14	1.	172
	13.	144		3-4.	172, 206
	17.	89, 140		5.	172
	18.	29, 89, 140		7.	24, 69, 197
Apoc. 2	1.	320, 344		8.	307
	5.	198, 320		13.	172, 186
	6.	344		19.	161
	7.	88		20.	160-61
	10.	164	Apoc. 16	14.	300
	12.	320, 344	Apoc. 17	3.	310
	14.	136, 320, 344		3.	307-08
	15.	320, 344		4.	307
	16.	320		5.	307
	18.	344		6.	308
	20.	320, 344		9.	307
Apoc. 3	1.	320		13.	307-08
	4.	320		16.	307
	7.	29	Apoc. 18	2.	308
	11.	198		3.	307
	14.	320		6.	190
	15.	320		7.	190, 308
	19.	320		9.	307
Apoc. 4	11.	24		11-12.	307
Apoc. 5	1.	314		14.	307
	3.	132		16-17.	307
	4.	231		20.	188
	5.	94, 132, 136, 231	Apoc. 19	2.	308
	6.	82, 148-49		6.	33
	8.	69, 94		15.	33, 143
	9.	67		16.	69
	10.	54	Apoc. 20	2.	33
	13.	24		11.	186
Apoc. 6	11.	172, 268		12.	186
Apoc. 7	4.	172, 206		13.	180, 186
	9-11.	172	Apoc. 21	1.	189
	14-15.	172		5.	150, 280
Apoc. 8	3.	306		10.	146
	10.	54		27.	268, 312, 315
Apoc. 9	1.	29, 55, 308	Apoc. 22	6.	85-86
	3.	308		8.	69
	11.	94		12.	143, 210
	20.	308		13.	67
	21.	219		15.	312

www.ingramcontent.com/pod-product-compliance
Lightning Source LLC
Chambersburg PA
CBHW060303010526
44108CB00042B/2616